Lecture Notes in Computer Science 4199

Commenced Publication in 1973
Founding and Former Series Editors:
Gerhard Goos, Juris Hartmanis, and Jan van Leeuwen

Oscar Nierstrasz   Jon Whittle
David Harel   Gianna Reggio (Eds.)

Model Driven Engineering Languages and Systems

9th International Conference, MoDELS 2006
Genova, Italy, October 1-6, 2006
Proceedings

Volume Editors

Oscar Nierstrasz
University of Bern, Institute of Computer Science and Applied Mathematics
Neubrückstr. 10, 3012 Bern, Switzerland
E-mail: oscar.nierstrasz@acm.org

Jon Whittle
George Mason University, Department of Information and Software Engineering
Science & Tech II, 4400 University Drive, Fairfax, VA 22030-4444, USA
E-mail: jwhittle@ise.gmu.edu

David Harel
The Weizmann Institute of Science
Department of Computer Science and Applied Mathematics
Rehovot 76100, Israel
E-mail: dharel@weizmann.ac.il

Gianna Reggio
University of Genova, DISI, Department of Computer Science
Via Dodecaneso 35, 16146 Genova, Italy
E-mail: gianna.reggio@disi.unige.it

Library of Congress Control Number: 2006932843

CR Subject Classification (1998): D.2, D.3, K.6, I.6

LNCS Sublibrary: SL 2 – Programming and Software Engineering

ISSN 0302-9743
ISBN-10 3-540-45772-0 Springer Berlin Heidelberg New York
ISBN-13 978-3-540-45772-5 Springer Berlin Heidelberg New York

Springer is a part of Springer Science+Business Media

springer.com

Printed in Germany

Typesetting: Camera-ready by author, data conversion by Scientific Publishing Services, Chennai, India
Printed on acid-free paper SPIN: 11880240 06/3142 5 4 3 2 1 0

Preface

MoDELS/UML 2006 was the ninth incarnation of this series of conferences on Model Driven Engineering Languages and Systems. The conference was held in Genoa, Italy during the week of October 1-6, 2006. The local arrangements were provided by DISI, the Department of Computer and Information Science at the University of Genoa.

This volume contains the final versions of the papers accepted for presentation at the conference, as well as two invited papers by the keynote speakers, Hassan Gomaa (George Mason University, USA) and Irun Cohen (The Weizmann Institute of Science, Israel).

We received 178 full paper submissions for review from 34 different countries. Of these, 24 papers were submitted with authors from more than one country. The top three countries submitting papers were Germany (25), USA (23) and France (20). A total of 51 papers were accepted for inclusion in the proceedings, including six experience papers. This reflects an acceptance rate of 29%, a rate comparable to those of previous MoDELS/UML conferences.

Each paper was reviewed by at least three Program Committee members. Reviewing was thorough, and authors received, in most cases, detailed comments on their submissions. Conflicts of interest were taken very seriously. No one participated in any way in the decision process of any paper where a conflict of interest was identified. In particular, PC members who submitted papers did not have access to any information concerning the reviewing of their papers. (The acceptance rate for PC papers was similar to the overall acceptance rate.)

We would like to thank everyone who submitted papers as well as proposals for workshops and tutorials. We would also like to thank the large number of volunteers who contributed to the success of the conference, including the PC members, the additional reviewers who supported the review process, the members of the local Organizing Committee, the volunteers who helped with the local organization, and the two invited speakers. We would also like to thank Richard van de Stadt for his prompt and gracious service in supporting special requests for CyberChairPRO, the conference management system used to manage papers submissions and the virtual PC meeting. Finally, we would like to thank our sponsors, ACM, IEEE Computer Society and DISI, for their support of the MoDELS/UML 2006 conference.

October 2006

Oscar Nierstrasz
Jon Whittle
David Harel
Gianna Reggio

Organization

Organizing Committee

General Chair	David Harel (Weizmann Institute of Science, Israel)
Conference Chair	Gianna Reggio (U. of Genoa, Italy)
Program Chair	Oscar Nierstrasz (U. of Bern, Switzerland)
Experience Track Chair	Jon Whittle (George Mason U., USA)
Workshop Chair	Thomas Kühne (Darmstadt U. of Tech., Germany)
Tutorial Chair	Egidio Astesiano (U. of Genoa, Italy)
Panel Chair	Douglas C. Schmidt (Vanderbilt U., USA)
Doctoral Symposium Chair	Robert G. Pettit (The Aerospace Corporation, USA)
Educators Symposium Chair	Ludwik Kuzniarz (Bleking Inst. of Tech., Sweden)
Poster Chair	Eda Marchetti (ISTI-CNR, Italy)
Local Arrangements Chair	Maura Cerioli (U. of Genoa, Italy)
Tool Exhibition Chair	Walter Cazzola (U. of Milan, Italy)
Web Chairs	Andrea Baresi (U. of Genoa, Italy) Emanuele Crivello (U. of Genoa, Italy)
Publicity Chairs	Emanuel Grant (U. of North Dakota, USA) Laurence Tratt (King's College, London, UK)

Program Committee

Gabriela Beatriz Arévalo (Argentina)
Colin Atkinson (Germany)
Thomas Baar (Switzerland)
Paul Baker (UK)
Antonia Bertolino (Italy)
Jean Bézivin (France)
Francis Bordeleau (Canada)
Lionel Briand (Norway)
Shigeru Chiba (Japan)
Siobhán Clarke (Ireland)
Pascal Costanza (Belgium)
Krzysztof Czarnecki (Canada)
Serge Demeyer (Belgium)
Christophe Dony (France)
Stéphane Ducasse (France)
Gregor Engels (Germany)
Jean-Marie Favre (France)
Harald Gall (Switzerland)
Geri Georg (USA)
Sudipto Ghosh (USA)
Martin Gogolla (Germany)
Hassan Gomaa (USA)
Susanne Graf (France)
Øystein Haugen (Norway)
Robert Hirschfeld (Germany)
Seongsoo Hong (Korea)
Paola Inverardi (Italy)
Jean-Marc Jézéquel (France)

Jörg Kienzle (Canada)
Thomas Kühne (Germany)
Michele Lanza (Switzerland)
Timothy C. Lethbridge (Canada)
Radu Marinescu (Romania)
Tom Mens (Belgium)
Hafedh Mili (Canada)
Dragan Milicev (Serbia)
Pierre-Alain Muller (France)
Robert G. Pettit IV (USA)
Alexander Pretschner (Switzerland)
Bernhard Rumpe (Germany)
Douglas C. Schmidt (USA)
Jean-Guy Schneider (Australia)
Bran Selic (Canada)
Juha-Pekka Tolvanen (Finland)
Ellen Van Paesschen (Belgium)
Alain Wegmann (Switzerland)
Thomas Weigert (USA)
Claudia Maria Lima Werner (Brazil)
Jon Whittle (USA)
Clay E. Williams (USA)
Alan Cameron Wills (UK)

Steering Committee

Thomas Baar (Switzerland)
Jean Bézivin (France)
Lionel Briand (Norway)
Steve Cook (UK)
Andy Evans (UK)
Robert France (USA)
Geri Georg (USA)
Martin Gogolla (Germany)
Heinrich Hussmann (Germany)
Jean-Marc Jézéquel (France)
Stuart Kent (UK)
Cris Kobryn (USA)
Ana Moreira (Portugal)
Pierre-Alain Muller (France)
Oscar Nierstrasz (Switzerland)
Gianna Reggio (Italy)
David Rosenblum (UK)
Bernhard Rumpe (Germany)
Bran Selic (Canada)
Perdita Stevens (UK)
Jon Whittle (USA)

Sponsors

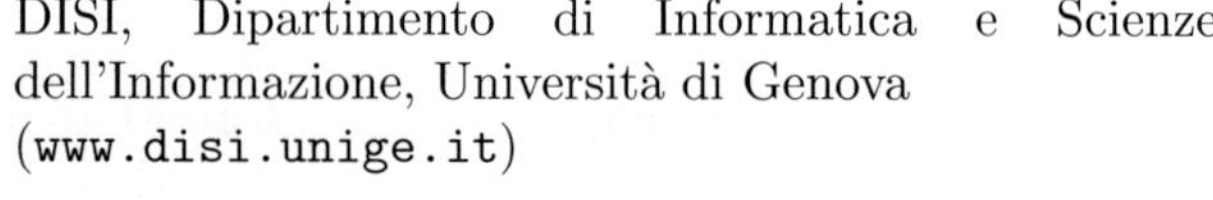

DISI, Dipartimento di Informatica e Scienze dell'Informazione, Università di Genova (www.disi.unige.it)

ACM Special Interest Group on Software Engineering (www.sigsoft.org)

IEEE Computer Society (www.computer.org)

CyberChairPRO Operation and Support

Richard van de Stadt, Borbala Online Conference Services

Additional Referees

Ilham Alloui
Carsten Amelunxen
Paul Ammann
Dave Arnold
Marco Autili
Olivier Barais
Benoit Baudry
Hanna Bauerdick
Alexandre Bergel
Christian Berger
Kirsten Berkenkötter
Ana Paula Terra Bacelo Blois
Conrad Bock
Elisa Gonzalez Boix
Antonio Bucchiarone
Fabian Büttner
Thomas Cleenewerck
Olivier Constant
Steve Cook
Alexandre Luis Correa
Jean-Pierre Corriveau
Guglielmo De Angelis
Jose Diego de la Cruz
Maja D'Hondt
Alexandre Ribeiro Dantas
Jessie Dedecker
Marcus Denker
Wolfgang De Meuter
Coen De Roover
Dirk Deridder
Brecht Desmet
Antinisca Di Marco
Jürgen Doser
Cédric Dumoulin
Peter Ebraert
Ghizlaine El-Boussaidi
Maged Elaasar
Taewook Eom
Johan Fabry
Micheal Fischer
Franck Fleurey
Beat Fluri
Lars Frantzen
Vahid Garousi
Sofie Goderis
Vincenzo Grassi
Hans Groenniger
Yann-Gaël Guéhéneuc
Kris Gybels
Baris Gühldali
Jun Han
Ulrich Hannemann
Michel Hassenforder
Michael Haupt
Jan Hendrik Hausmann
Berthold Hoffmann
Eckhardt Holz
Duwon Hong
Marianne Huchard
Marc-Philippe Huget
Karsten Hölscher
Andrew Jackson
Eshref Januzaj
Andy Kellens
Stuart Kent
Ismail Khriss
Dae-Kyoo Kim
Soyeon Kim
Anneke Kleppe
Holger Krahn
Jochen Kuester
Adrian Kuhn
Thomas Lambolais
Lam-Son Le
Jaesoo Lee
Eric Lefebvre
Lingling Liao
Jonas Lindholm
Arne Lindow
Marc Lohmann
Marco Alexandre Lopes
Marco Aurélio Mangan
Eda Marchetti
Slaviša Marković
Isabel Michiels
Raffaela Mirandola

Stijn Mostinckx
Henry Muccini
Olaf Muliawan
Leonardo Gresta Paulino Murta
Sadaf Mustafiz
Clémentine Nebut
Johann Oberleitner
Erika Olimpiew
Francesco Parisi-Presicce
Jiyong Park
Patrizio Pelliccione
Jean-Marc Perronne
Jean-François Perrot
Paulo Pires
Andrea Polini
Damien Pollet
Claudia Pons
Juha Pärssinen
Gil Regev
Gerald Reif
Matthias Rieger
Dirk Riehle
Romain Robbes
Irina Rychkova
Antonino Sabetta
Murat Sahingöz
Stefan Sauer
Tim Schattkowsky
Martin Schindler
Hans Schippers
Andy Schürr
Karsten Sohr
Mike Sowka
Jim Steel
Julie A. Street
Bernard Thirion
Laurent Thiry
Yves Le Traon
Guy Tremblay
Christelle Urtado
Jorge Vallejos
Tom Van Cutsem
Ragnhild Van Der Straeten
Niels Van Eetvelde
Pieter Van Gorp
Bart Van Rompaey
Filip Van Rysselberghe
Hans Vangheluwe
Sylvain Vauttier
German Vega
Herve Verjus
Steven Voelkel
Hendrik Voigt
Didier Vojtisek
Dennis Wagelaar
Seungmin We
Duminda Wijesekera
Jonghun Yoo
Wooseok Yoo
Sergio Yovine
Tao Yue
Tewfik Ziadi

Table of Contents

Keynote 1

A Software Modeling Odyssey: Designing Evolutionary Architecture-Centric Real-Time Systems and Product Lines 1
Hassan Gomaa

Evaluating UML

Uses and Abuses of the Stereotype Mechanism in UML 1.x and 2.0 16
Brian Henderson-Sellers, Cesar Gonzalez-Perez

An Experimental Investigation of UML Modeling Conventions 27
Christian F.J. Lange, Bart Du Bois, Michel R.V. Chaudron, Serge Demeyer

Improving the Definition of UML 42
Greg O'Keefe

MDA in Software Development

Adopting Model Driven Software Development in Industry – A Case Study at Two Companies 57
Miroslaw Staron

Use Case Driven Iterative Development: Hurdles and Solutions 73
Santiago Ceria, Juan José Cukier

Model-Driven Development with SDL – Process, Tools, and Experiences 83
Thomas Kuhn, Reinhard Gotzhein, Christian Webel

Concrete Syntax

Model-Driven Analysis and Synthesis of Concrete Syntax 98
Pierre-Alain Muller, Franck Fleurey, Frédéric Fondement, Michel Hassenforder, Rémi Schneckenburger, Sébastien Gérard, Jean-Marc Jézéquel

Correctly Defined Concrete Syntax for Visual Modeling Languages 111

Thomas Baar

Applying UML to Interaction and Coordination

Compositional MDA 126
Louis van Gool, Teade Punter, Marc Hamilton, Remco van Engelen

CUP 2.0: High-Level Modeling of Context-Sensitive Interactive Applications 140
Jan Van den Bergh, Karin Coninx

Aspects

Domain Models Are NOT Aspect Free 155
Awais Rashid, Ana Moreira

A Slice of MDE with AOP: Transforming High-Level Business Rules to Aspects 170
María Agustina Cibrán, Maja D'Hondt

Model Intergration

Package Merge in UML 2: Practice vs. Theory? 185
Alanna Zito, Zinovy Diskin, Juergen Dingel

Detecting and Resolving Model Inconsistencies Using Transformation Dependency Analysis 200
Tom Mens, Ragnhild Van Der Straeten, Maja D'Hondt

Merging Models with the Epsilon Merging Language (EML) 215
Dimitrios S. Kolovos, Richard F. Paige, Fiona A.C. Polack

Formal Semantics of UML

Mappings, Maps and Tables: Towards Formal Semantics for Associations in UML2 230
Zinovy Diskin, Juergen Dingel

Semantic Variations Among UML StateMachines 245
Ali Taleghani, Joanne M. Atlee

Facilitating the Definition of General Constraints in UML 260

Dolors Costal, Cristina Gómez, Anna Queralt, Ruth Raventós, Ernest Teniente

Security

Towards a MOF/QVT-Based Domain Architecture for Model Driven Security ... 275
Michael Hafner, Muhammad Alam, Ruth Breu

MDA-Based Re-engineering with Object-Z ... 291
Jörn Guy Süß, Tim McComb, Soon-Kyeong Kim, Luke Wildman, Geoffrey Watson

A Model Transformation Semantics and Analysis Methodology for SecureUML ... 306
Achim D. Brucker, Jürgen Doser, Burkhart Wolff

Model Transformation Tools and Implementation

Incremental Model Transformation for the Evolution of Model-Driven Systems ... 321
David Hearnden, Michael Lawley, Kerry Raymond

A Plugin-Based Language to Experiment with Model Transformation ... 336
Jesús Sánchez Cuadrado, Jesús García Molina

SiTra: Simple Transformations in Java ... 351
David H. Akehurst, Behzad Bordbar, Michael J. Evans, W. Gareth J. Howells, Klaus D. McDonald-Maier

Analyzing Dynamic Models

Analysis and Visualization of Behavioral Dependencies Among Distributed Objects Based on UML Models ... 365
Vahid Garousi, Lionel C. Briand, Yvan Labiche

Model Extraction Using Context Information ... 380
Lucio Mauro Duarte, Jeff Kramer, Sebastian Uchitel

Dynamic and Generic Manipulation of Models: From Introspection to Scripting ... 395
Christophe Tombelle, Gilles Vanwormhoudt

Specifying Transformations

Model Transformation by Example 410
Dániel Varró

Graphical Definition of In-Place Transformations in the Eclipse Modeling Framework 425
Enrico Biermann, Karsten Ehrig, Christian Köhler, Günter Kuhns, Gabriele Taentzer, Eduard Weiss

Model Transformations? Transformation Models! 440
Jean Bézivin, Fabian Büttner, Martin Gogolla, Frédéric Jouault, Ivan Kurtev, Arne Lindow

MOF

A Mapping Language from Models to DI Diagrams 454
Marcus Alanen, Torbjörn Lundkvist, Ivan Porres

Basic Operations over Models Containing Subset and Union Properties 469
Marcus Alanen, Ivan Porres

A Metamodeling Approach to Pattern Specification 484
Maged Elaasar, Lionel C. Briand, Yvan Labiche

Keynote 2

Immune System Computation and the Immunological Homunculus 499
Irun R. Cohen

Bridging Models

Building Abstractions in Class Models: Formal Concept Analysis in a Model-Driven Approach 513
Gabriela Arévalo, Jean-Rémi Falleri, Marianne Huchard, Clémentine Nebut

Lifting Metamodels to Ontologies: A Step to the Semantic Integration of Modeling Languages 528
Gerti Kappel, Elisabeth Kapsammer, Horst Kargl, Gerhard Kramler, Thomas Reiter, Werner Retschitzegger, Wieland Schwinger, Manuel Wimmer

Incremental Model Synchronization with Triple Graph Grammars 543
Holger Giese, Robert Wagner

Risk, Trust and Dependability

Model-Driven Assessment of Use Cases for Dependable Systems 558
Sadaf Mustafiz, Ximeng Sun, Jörg Kienzle, Hans Vangheluwe

A Graphical Approach to Risk Identification, Motivated by Empirical Investigations 574
Ida Hogganvik, Ketil Stølen

Reusable MDA Components: A Testing-for-Trust Approach 589
Jean-Marie Mottu, Benoit Baudry, Yves Le Traon

Tool Environments

Using Smalltalk as a Reflective Executable Meta-language.............. 604
Stéphane Ducasse, Tudor Gîrba

UML Model Interchange in Heterogeneous Tool Environments: An Analysis of Adoptions of XMI 2 619
Björn Lundell, Brian Lings, Anna Persson, Anders Mattsson

Applying Model Fragment Copy-Restore to Build an Open and Distributed MDA Environment 631
Prawee Sriplakich, Xavier Blanc, Marie-Pierre Gervais

OCL

An OCL-Based Technique for Specifying and Verifying Refinement-Oriented Transformations in MDE 646
Claudia Pons, Diego Garcia

An OCL Semantics Specified with QVT 661
Slaviša Marković, Thomas Baar

Specification of Invariability in OCL........ 676
Piotr Kosiuczenko

Roundtrip Engineering

Framework-Specific Modeling Languages with Round-Trip Engineering 692
Michał Antkiewicz, Krzysztof Czarnecki

A Visualization Framework for the Modeling and Formal Analysis of High Assurance Systems 707
Heather Goldsby, Betty H.C. Cheng, Sascha Konrad, Stephane Kamdoum

Layered Class Diagrams: Supporting the Design Process 722
Scott Hendrickson, Bryan Jett, André van der Hoek

Real Time and Embedded Systems

Using UML Activities for System-on-Chip Design and Synthesis 737
Tim Schattkowsky, Jan Hendrik Hausmann, Gregor Engels

Modeling and Early Performance Estimation for Network Processor Applications 753
Antonia Bertolino, Alvise Bonivento, Guglielmo De Angelis, Alberto Sangiovanni-Vincentelli

A Formal Semantics of UML-RT 768
Michael von der Beeck

Workshops, Tutorials and Panels

Workshops and Symposia at MoDELS 2006 783
Thomas Kühne

Tutorials at MoDELS 2006 791
Egidio Astesiano

Panels at MoDELS 2006 795
Douglas C. Schmidt

Author Index 797

A Software Modeling Odyssey: Designing Evolutionary Architecture-Centric Real-Time Systems and Product Lines

Hassan Gomaa

Department of Information and Software Engineering
George Mason University
Fairfax, Virginia 22030, USA
hgomaa@gmu.edu

Abstract. According to OMG, "modeling is the designing of software applications before coding." This paper describes a modeling approach to software design. The paper describes the key elements of design methods for component based software product lines, which promote reuse, variability management, and evolution. Approaches for executable models and performance analysis of concurrent and real-time design are discussed. Finally, some outstanding challenges are outlined, in particular the design of evolutionary and dynamically reconfigurable software architectures.

Keywords: software modeling, software design, real-time systems, software product lines, software architecture.

1 Introduction

Modeling is used in many walks of life, going back to early civilizations, where it was used to provide small scale plans in art and architecture. Modeling is widely used in science and engineering to provide abstractions of a system at some level of precision and detail. The model is then analyzed in order to obtain a better understanding of the system being developed. According to OMG, "modeling is the designing of software applications before coding." This paper describes a modeling approach to software design, in particular the design of real-time systems and software product lines.

Real-time systems are reactive systems, so that control decisions are often state dependent, hence the importance of finite state machines in the design of these systems. Real-time systems typically need to process concurrent inputs from many sources, hence the importance of concurrent software design. They have real-time throughput and/or response time requirements, so there is a need to analyze the performance of real-time designs. Furthermore, there is a need to integrate real-time technology with modern software engineering concepts and methods.

A software product line (SPL) consists of a family of software systems that have some common functionality and some variable functionality [Parnas79, Clements02, Weiss99]. Software product line engineering involves developing the requirements, architecture, and component implementations for a family of systems, from which products (family members) are derived and configured. The problems of developing

O. Nierstrasz et al. (Eds.): MoDELS 2006, LNCS 4199, pp. 1 – 15, 2006.

individual software systems are scaled upwards when developing software product lines because of the increased complexity due to variability management.

In model-based software design and development, software modeling is used as an essential part of the software development process. Models are built and analyzed prior to the implementation of the system, and are used to direct the subsequent implementation. The different versions of a system as it evolves can be considered a product line, with each version of the system a member of the product line. In order to keep track of the evolution of the system, it is necessary to explicitly model the different features of the system as it evolves, and use the feature model to differentiate among the different versions of the system.

A better understanding of a system or product line can be obtained by considering the multiple views [Gomaa98, GomaaShin04], such as requirements models, static models, and dynamic models of the system or product line. A graphical modeling language such as UML helps in developing, understanding and communicating the different views. A key view in the multiple views of a software product line is the feature modeling view [Kang90]. The feature model is crucial for managing variability and product derivation as it describes the product line requirements in terms of commonality and variability, as well as defining the product line dependencies [Gomaa06]. Furthermore, it is necessary to have a development approach that promotes software evolution, such that original development and subsequent maintenance are both treated using feature-driven evolution.

This paper describes an architecture-centric evolutionary modeling and development approach for real-time systems and software product lines. After presenting an overview of the evolutionary software product line engineering approach in Section 2, this paper describes how the different modeling views provide a better insight into and understanding of the software product line architecture, in particular through requirements (use case and feature) modeling in Section 3, analysis (static and dynamic) modeling in Section 4, design modeling (modeling component-based software architectures and software architectural patterns) in Section 5, tool support for SPL engineering in Section 6, performance models and executable models of software designs in Section 7, and dynamic software reconfiguration in Section 8.

2 Evolutionary Software Product Line Engineering

The Software Process Model for SPL Engineering [Gomaa05] is a highly iterative software process that eliminates the traditional distinction between software development and maintenance. Furthermore, because new software systems are outgrowths of existing ones, the process takes a software product line perspective; it consists of two main processes (see Fig. 1):

a) Product line Engineering. A product line multiple-view model, which addresses the multiple views of a software product line, is developed. The product line multiple-view model, product line architecture, and reusable components (referred to as core assets in [Clements02]) are developed and stored in the product line reuse library.

b) Software Application Engineering. A software application multiple-view model is an individual product line member derived from the software product line multiple-view model. The user selects the required features for the individual product line member. Given the features, the product line model and architecture are adapted and

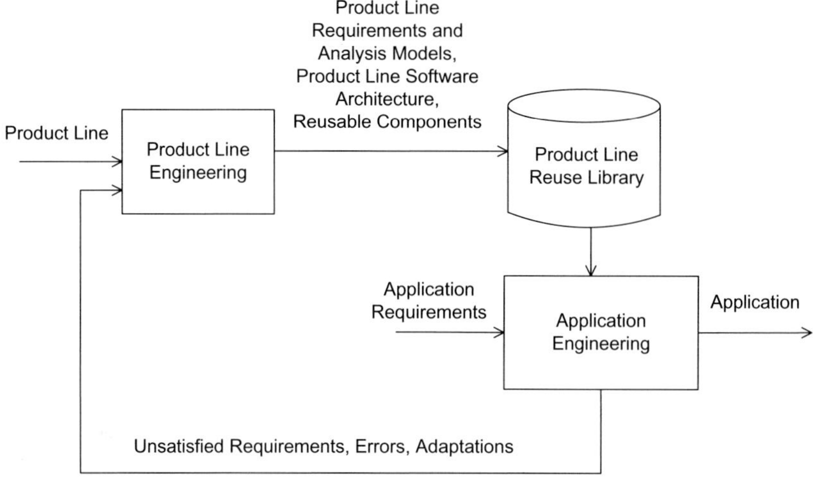

Fig. 1. Evolutionary Process Model for Software Product Lines

tailored to derive the application architecture. The architecture determines which of the reusable components are needed for configuring the executable application.

The architecture centric evolution approach described in this paper follows the model driven architecture concept in which UML models of the software architecture are developed prior to implementation. With this approach, the models can later evolve after original deployment. The kernel software architecture represents the commonality of the product line. Evolution is built into the software development approach because the variability in the software architecture is developed by considering the impact of each variable feature on the software architecture and evolving the architecture to address the feature. The development approach is a feature-driven evolutionary approach, meaning that it addresses both the original development and subsequent post-deployment evolution. Being feature based, the approach closely relates the software architecture evolution to the evolution of software requirements.

3 Requirements Modeling

3.1 Use Case Modeling

The functional requirements of a system are defined in terms of use cases and actors [Rumbaugh05]. For a single system, all use cases are required. In a software product line, only some of the use cases, which are referred to as kernel use cases, are required by all members of the family. Other use cases are optional, in that they are required by some but not all members of the family. Some use cases may be alternative, that is different versions of the use case are required by different members of the family. In UML, the use cases are labeled with the stereotype «kernel», «optional» or «alternative» [Gomaa05]. In addition, variability can be inserted into a use case through variation points, which specify locations in the use case where variability can be introduced [Jacobson97, WebberGomaa04, Gomaa05]. Examples of kernel and optional product line use cases for a microwave oven SPL are given in Fig. 2.

Fig. 2. Product Line Use Cases

3.2 Feature Modeling

Feature modeling is an important aspect of product line engineering [Kang90]. Features are analyzed and categorized as common features (must be supported in all product line members), optional features (only required in some product line members), alternative features (a choice of feature is available) and prerequisite features (dependent upon other features). There may also be dependencies among features, such as mutually exclusive features. The emphasis in feature modeling is capturing the product line variability, as given by optional and alternative features, since these features differentiate one member of the family from the others.

Features are used widely in product line engineering but are not used in UML. In order to effectively model product lines, it is necessary to incorporate feature modeling concepts into UML. Features can be incorporated into UML using the meta-class concept, in which features are modeled using the UML static modeling notation and given stereotypes to differentiate between «common feature», «optional feature» and «alternative feature» [Gomaa05]. Furthermore, feature groups, which place a constraint on how certain features can be selected for a product line member, such as mutually exclusive features, are also modeled using meta-classes and given stereotypes, e.g., «zero-or-one-of feature group» or «exactly-one-of feature group» [Gomaa05]. Examples of an optional feature and a feature group consisting of a default feature and an alternative feature (microwave oven SPL) are given in Fig. 3.

In single systems, use cases are used to determine the functional requirements of a system; they can also serve this purpose in product families. Griss [Griss98] has pointed out that the goal of the use case analysis is to get a good understanding of the functional requirements whereas the goal of feature analysis is to enable reuse. Use cases and features complement each other. Thus optional and alternative use cases (Section 3) are mapped to optional and alternative features respectively, while use cases variation points are also mapped to features [Gomaa05]. In Fig. 3, the Light variation point is mapped to an optional feature (light is present or not) and the Display Unit variation point is mapped to a feature group with a default one-line display or alternative multi-line display.

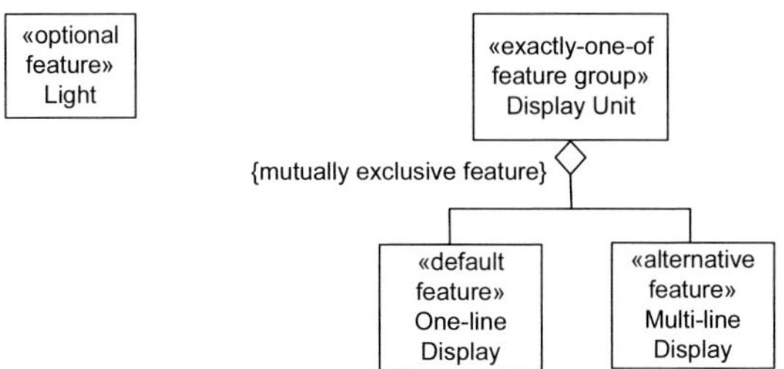

Fig. 3. Features and feature groups in UML

4 Analysis Modeling

4.1 Static Modeling

In single systems, a class is categorized by the role it plays. Application classes are classified according to their role in the application using stereotypes, such as «entity class», «control class», or «interface class». In modeling software product lines, each class can be categorized according to its reuse characteristic using the stereotypes «kernel», «optional», and «variant». In UML 2.0, a modeling element can be described with more than one stereotype. Thus one stereotype can be used to represent the reuse characteristic while a different stereotype is used to represent the role played by the modeling element [Gomaa05]. The role a class plays in the application and the reuse characteristic are orthogonal. Examples of a kernel state dependent control class and an optional output class are given in Fig. 4. The optional Lamp Interface class (Fig. 4) supports the optional Light feature (Fig. 3).

Fig. 4. Role and Reuse Stereotypes in Product Line Classes

4.2 Evolutionary Dynamic Analysis

Evolutionary dynamic analysis is an iterative strategy to help determine the dynamic impact of each feature on the software architecture. This results in new components being added or existing components having to be adapted. The **kernel system** is a minimal member of the product line. In some product lines the kernel system consists of only the kernel objects. For other product lines, some default objects may be needed in addition to the kernel objects. The kernel system is developed by considering the kernel use cases, which are required by every member for the product line. For each kernel use case, an interaction diagram is developed depicting the objects needed to realize the use case. The kernel system consists of the integration of all these objects and the classes from which they are instantiated.

The **software product line evolution approach** starts with the kernel system and considers the impact of optional and/or alternative features [Gomaa05]. This results in the addition of optional or variant components to the product line architecture. This analysis is done by considering the variable (optional and alternative) use cases, as well as any variation points in the kernel or variable use cases. For each optional or alternative use case, an interaction diagram is developed consisting of new optional or variant objects – the variant objects are kernel or optional objects that are impacted by the variable scenarios, and therefore need to be adapted.

4.3 Managing Variability in Statecharts

When components are adapted for evolution, there are two main approaches to consider, specialization or parameterization. Specialization is effective when there are a relatively small number of changes to be made, so that the number of specialized classes is manageable. However, in product line evolution, there can be a large degree of variability. Consider the issue of variability in control classes, which are modeling using statecharts [Harel96], which can be handled either by using parameterized statecharts or specialized statecharts. Depending on whether the product line uses a centralized or decentralized approach, it is likely that there will be several different state dependent control components, each modeled by its own statechart. The following discussion relates to the evolution within a given state dependent component.

To capture product line variability and evolution, it is necessary to specify optional states, events and transitions, and actions. A further decision that needs to be made when using state machines to model variability is whether to use state machine inheritance or parameterization. The problem with using inheritance is that a different state machine is needed to model each alternative or optional feature, or feature combination, which rapidly leads to a combinatorial explosion of inherited state machines. For example, with only three features that could impact the statechart, there would be eight possible feature and feature combinations, resulting in eight variant statecharts. With 10 features, there would be over 1000 variant statecharts. However, 10 features can be easily modeled on a parameterized statechart as 10 feature dependent transitions, states, or transitions.

It is often more effective to design a parameterized state machine, in which there are feature-dependent states, events, and transitions. Optional transitions are specified by having an event qualified by a feature condition, which guards entry into the state. Thus Minute Pressed is a feature dependent transition guarded by the feature condition minuteplus in Fig. 5. Similarly, there can be feature-dependent actions, such as Switch On and Switch Off in Fig. 5, which are only enabled if the light feature (Fig. 3) condition is True. Thus the feature condition is True if the optional feature is selected for a given product line member, and false if the feature is not selected. The impact of feature interactions can be modeled very precisely using state machines through the introduction of alternative states or transitions. Designing parameterized statecharts is often more manageable than designing specialized statecharts.

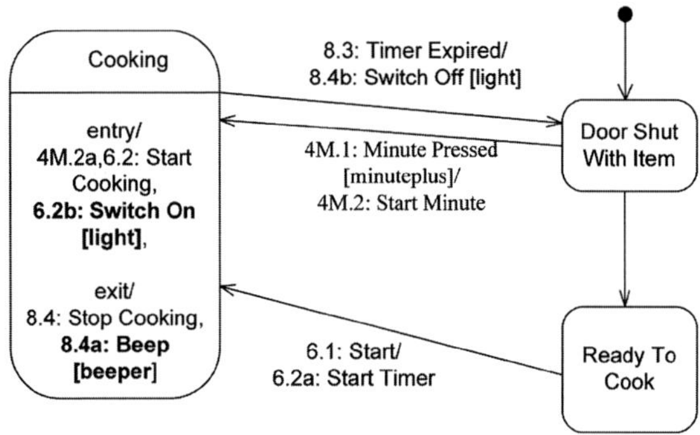

Fig. 5. Feature Dependent Transitions and Actions

5 Design Modeling

5.1 Modeling Component-Based Software Architectures

A software component's interface is specified separately from its implementation and, unlike a class, the component's required interface is designed explicitly in addition to the provided interface. This is particularly important for architecture-centric evolution, since it is necessary to know the impact of the change to a component on all components that interface to it.

Software components can be effectively modeled in UML 2.0 with structured classes and depicted on composite structure diagrams [Rumbaugh05]. Structured classes have ports with provided and required interfaces. Structured classes can be interconnected via connectors that join the ports of communicating classes.

To provide a complete definition of the component-based software architecture for a software product line, it is necessary to specify the interface(s) provided by each component and the interface(s) required by each component. A **provided interface** is a collection of operations that specify the services that a component must fulfill. A **required interface** describes the services that other components provide for this component to operate properly in a particular environment.

This capability for modeling component-based software architectures is particularly valuable in product line engineering, to allow the development of kernel, optional and variant components, "plug-compatible" components, and component interface inheritance. There are various ways to design components. It is highly desirable, where possible, to design components that are **plug-compatible**, so that the required port of one component is compatible with the provided ports of other components to which it needs to connect [Gomaa05]. Consider the case in which a producer component needs to be able to connect to different alternative consumer components in different product line members, as shown in Fig. 6. The most desirable approach, if possible, is to design all the consumer components with the same provided interface, so that the producer can be connected to any consumer without changing its required interface. In Fig. 6, Microwave Control can be connected to either version of the Microwave Display component (which correspond to the default

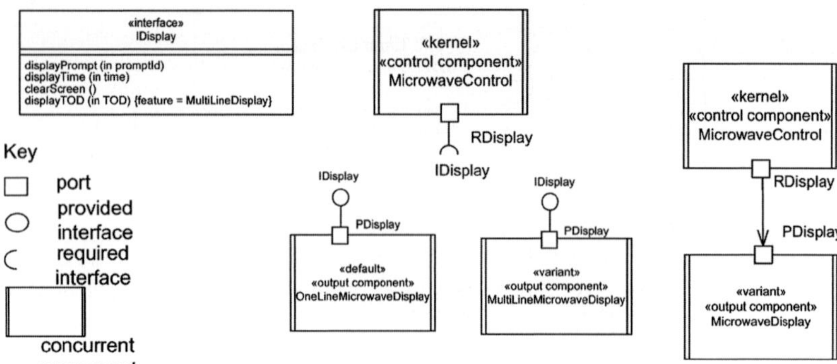

Fig. 6. Design of Plug-compatible Components

and alternative features in Fig 3). As the product line evolves new producers can communicate with the consumer.

It is possible for a component to connect to different components and have different interconnections such that in one case it communicates with one component and in a different case it communicates with two different components. This flexibility helps in evolving the software architecture. When plug-compatible components are not practical, an alternative component design approach is **component interface inheritance**. Consider a component architecture that evolves in such a way that the interface through which the two components communicate needs to be specialized to allow for additional functionality. In this case, both the component that provides the interface and the component that requires the interface have to be modified—the former to realize the new functionality, and the latter to request it. The above approaches can be used to complement compositional approaches for developing component-based software architectures.

5.2 Software Architectural Patterns

Software architectural patterns [Buschmann96, Gomaa01] provide the skeleton or template for the overall software architecture or high-level design of an application. These include such widely used architectures [Bass03] as client/server and layered architectures. Basing the software architecture of a product line on one or more software architectural patterns helps in designing the original architecture as well as evolving the architecture. This is because the evolutionary properties of architectural patterns can also be studied.

There are two main categories of software architectural patterns [Gomaa05]. Architectural structure patterns address the static structure of the software architecture. Architectural communication patterns address the message communication among distributed components of the software architecture.

Most software systems and product lines can be based on well understood overall software architectures. For example, the client/server software architecture is prevalent in many software applications. There is the basic client/server architecture, with one server and many clients. However, there are also many variations on this theme, such as multiple client / multiple server architectures and brokered client/server architectures. Furthermore, with a client/server pattern, the server can evolve by adding new services, which are discovered and invoked by clients. New clients can be added that discover services provided by one or more servers.

Many real-time systems [Gomaa00] provide overall control of the environment by providing either centralized control, decentralized control, or hierarchical control. Each of these control approaches can be modeled using a software architectural pattern. In a centralized control pattern, there is one control component, which executes a statechart. It receives sensor input from input components and controls the external environment via output components, as shown in Fig. 7. In a centralized control pattern, evolution takes the form of adding or modifying input and/or output components that interact with the control component, which executes a statechart that can evolve as described in Section 4.3. Another architectural pattern that is worth considering because of its desirable properties is the layered architecture. A layered architectural pattern allows for ease of extension and contraction [Parnas79] because components can be added to or removed from higher layers, which use the services provided by components at lower layers of the architecture.

In addition to the above architectural structure patterns, certain architectural communication patterns also encourage evolution. In software product lines, it is often desirable to decouple components. The Broker, Discovery, and Subscription/Notification patterns encourage such decoupling. With the broker patterns, servers register with brokers, and clients can then discover new servers. Thus a product line can evolve with the addition of new clients and servers. A new version of a server can replace an older version and register itself with the broker. Clients communicating via the broker would

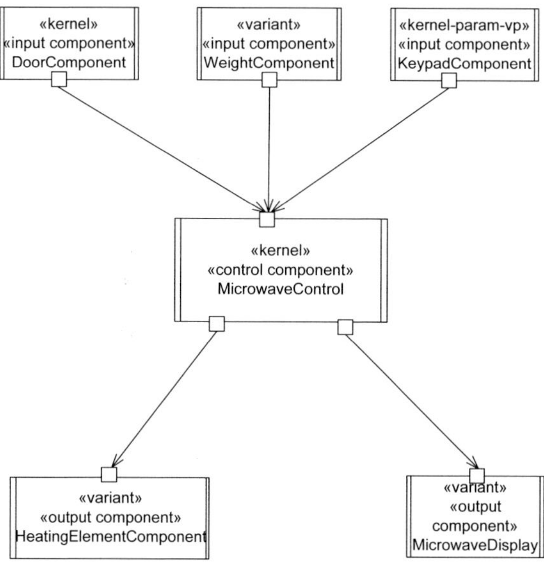

Fig. 7. Example of Centralized Control Pattern

automatically be connected to the new version of the server. The Subscription/ Notification pattern also decouples the original sender of the message from the recipients of the message.

A very important decision is to determine which architectural patterns—in particular, which structure and communication patterns—are required. Architectural structure patterns can initially be identified during dynamic modeling because patterns can be recognized during development of the communication diagrams. For example, client/server and any of the control patterns can first be used during dynamic modeling. Unlike other software architectural patterns, which can be recognized earlier in the application design, the architecture of the software application can be molded to the layered architecture. However in many applications, other patterns, such as the client/server and control patterns, can be integrated with the layered pattern. Although architectural structure patterns can be identified during dynamic modeling, the real decisions are made during software architectural design. It is necessary to decide the architectural structure patterns first and then the architectural communication patterns.

6 Tool Support for Software Product Line Engineering

Automated tool support is highly desirable for managing the complexity and variability inherent in software product lines. At George Mason University, we have been investigating methods and tools for software product lines over several years [Gomaa96, Gomaa99, GomaaShin04]. To provide tool support for representing the multiple graphical views of a product line, we have used various CASE tools, including Rose, to capture the multiple views. Using the open architecture provided by some CASE tools, we then developed our own tools to extract the underlying representation of each view and store this information in a product line repository, which consists of an integrated set of data base relations. We then developed a multiple view consistency checking tool to check for consistency among the multiple views and report any inconsistencies to the user [GomaaShin04]. We also provided automated support for product derivation from the product line repository. This was achieved by developing a knowledge based requirements elicitation and product derivation tool, which interacts with the user to ensure selection of a consistent set of product features and then derives a product (member of SPL) from the product line repository [Gomaa96, Gomaa06]. All the tools developed are product line independent, as they treat all product line specific information as data and facts to be manipulated by the product line independent tools. We also integrated our product line tools with Imperial College's Darwin/Regis distributed programming and configuration environment [Magee94] to allow component-based distributed applications to be configured from product line features, architectures and components [Gomaa99], which were previously developed and stored in the SPL repository.

7 Performance Models and Executable Models of Software Designs

Performance modeling of a system at design time is important to determine whether the system will meet its performance goals, such as throughput and response times.

Performance modeling methods include queuing modeling [GomaaMenasce01, [MenasceGomaa00] and simulation modeling. Performance modeling is particularly important in real-time systems, in which failing to meet a deadline could be catastrophic. Real-time scheduling in conjunction with event sequence modeling is an approach for modeling real-time designs executing on given hardware configurations.

In COMET, performance analysis of software designs is achieved by applying **real-time scheduling** theory. **Real-time scheduling** is an approach that is particularly appropriate for hard real time systems that have deadlines that must be met [Gomaa00]. With this approach, the real time design is analyzed to determine whether it can meet its deadlines. A second approach for analyzing the performance of a design is to use **event sequence analysis** and to integrate this with the **real-time scheduling** theory. Event sequence analysis is used analyze scenarios of communicating tasks and annotate them with the timing parameters for each of the participating tasks, in addition to considering system overhead for inter-object communication and context switching [Gomaa00].

Executable models of software designs allow the logic of the design to be simulated and tested before the design is implemented. Existing modeling tools such as Rose Real-Time and Rhapsody frequently use statecharts as the key underlying mechanism for dynamic model execution.

An alternative approach for developing executable models for concurrent and distributed designs is to model concurrent object behavior in the form of concurrent behavioral design patterns (BDP), which are then mapped to Colored Petri Net (CPN) templates [PettitGomaa06]. Each BDP represents the behavior of concurrent objects together with associated message communication constructs, and is depicted on a UML concurrent communication diagram. The software architecture is organized using the concept of components and connectors, in which concurrent objects are designed as components that can be connected through passive message communication objects and entity objects. Each concurrent object has a behavioral role (such as I/O, control, algorithm) which is given by the COMET concurrent object structuring criteria and depicted by a UML stereotype. An example of a behavioral design pattern for an asynchronous device input concurrent object is given in Fig. 8a.

For each BDP, a self-contained CPN template is designed, which by means of its places, transitions, and tokens, models a given concurrent behavioral pattern. Figure 8b depicts the CPN template for an asynchronous device input concurrent object. Each template is generic in the sense that it provides a basic behavioral pattern and component connections for the concurrent object but does not contain any application-specific information. Furthermore, concurrent component templates are designed such that they can be interconnected via connector templates.

Using this approach, a concurrent software architecture is described in terms of interconnected concurrent behavioral design patterns, which are then mapped to a CPN model by interconnecting the corresponding CPN templates. The CPN templates are elaborated to provide application specific behavior. The CPN model is then executed using a CPN tool, thereby allowing the designer to analyze both the dynamic behavior and performance of a simulation of the concurrent design, with a given external workload applied to it.

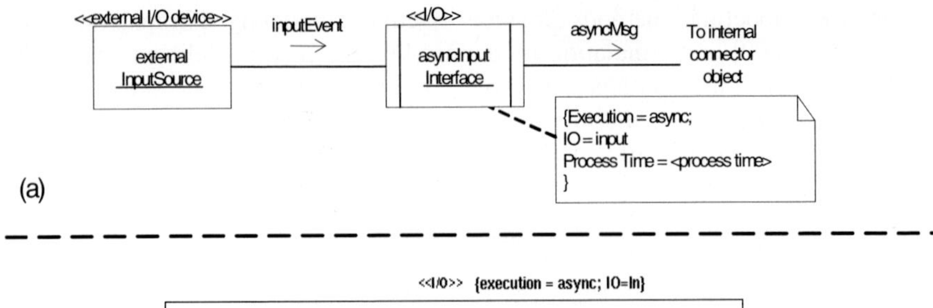

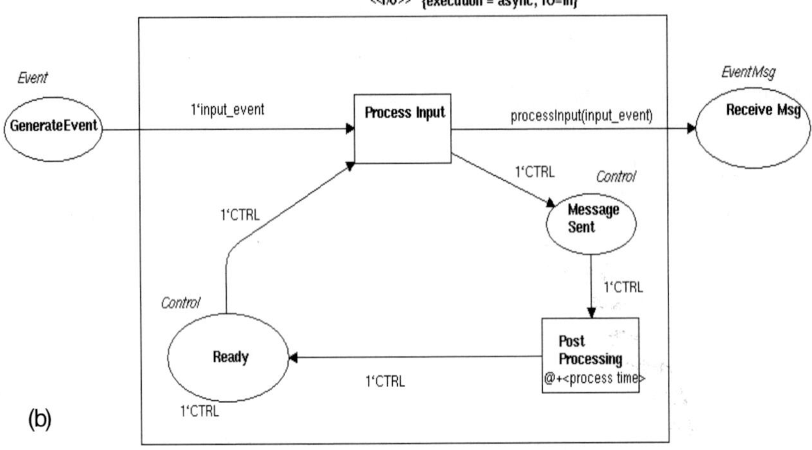

Fig. 8. Asynchronous Input Concurrent Object: (a) Behavioral Design Pattern (b) CPN Template

8 Software Evolution and Dynamic Software Reconfiguration

A more challenging situation is when a software system has to evolve after deployment while the system is operational. The different versions of the software system together constitute a software product line. Software configuration is the process of adapting the architecture of a SPL to create a specific product line member in terms of components and their interconnections. Dynamic software reconfiguration is concerned with changing the application configuration at runtime after it has been deployed and is needed for systems that have to evolve after original deployment.

In order to support dynamic software reconfiguration in software product lines, the Evolutionary Process Model for SPLs (Fig. 1) needs to be extended, as depicted in Fig. 9, to support dynamic software reconfiguration [Gomaa04]. During Target System Reconfiguration, users specify runtime configuration changes so that the executable target system is dynamically changed from the target system run-time configuration for one product line member to a new target system run-time configuration for a different product line member.

The product line design is composed of distributed software architectural patterns, such as client/server, master/slave, and distributed control patterns, which describe the software components that constitute the pattern and their interconnections. For each of these architectural patterns, there is a corresponding software reconfiguration

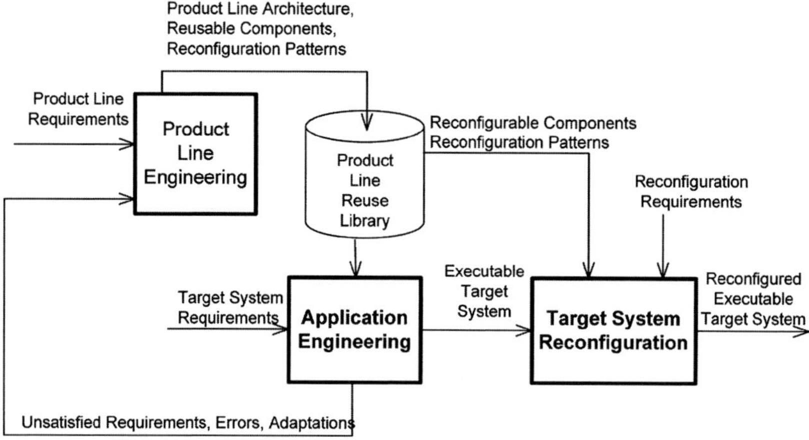

Fig. 9. Reconfigurable Evolutionary Process Model for Software Product Lines

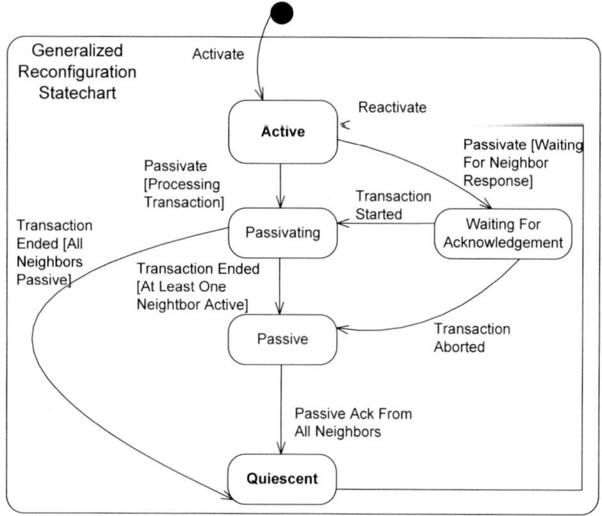

Fig. 10. Reconfiguration State Machine Model

pattern [Gomaa04], which models how the software components and interconnections can be changed under predefined circumstances, such as replacing one client with another in a client/server pattern, inserting a control component between two other control components in a distributed control pattern, etc. A change management model defines the precise steps involved in dynamic reconfiguration to transition from the current software run-time configuration to the new run-time configuration. Thus, a component that needs to be replaced has to stop being active and become quiescent, the components that it communicates with need to stop communicating with it; the component then needs to be unlinked, removed and replaced by the new component, after which the configuration needs to be relinked and restarted. A dynamic software reconfiguration framework is designed and implemented to initiate and control the steps of the change management model for automatic reconfiguration of the product line system from one run-time configuration to another.

A software reconfiguration pattern defines how a set of components that make up an architecture or design pattern dynamically cooperate to change the software configuration to a new configuration given a set of reconfiguration commands. A reconfiguration pattern requires state- and scenario-based reconfiguration behavior models to provide for a systematic design approach. The reconfiguration patterns are described in UML with reconfiguration communication models and reconfiguration statechart models (such as Fig. 10). A reconfiguration statechart defines the sequence of states a component goes through during reconfiguration from a normal operational state to a quiescent state. Once quiescent, the component is idle and can be removed from the configuration, so that it can be replaced with a different version of the component.

9 Conclusions

This paper has described an architecture-centric evolutionary modeling and design approach for software product lines. Models are built and analyzed prior to implementation of the system, and direct the subsequent implementation. The different versions of an evolutionary system are considered a product line, with each version of the system a product line member. After implementation, the model should co-exist with the system and evolve with the system. Just as model development precedes and directs the implementation of the system, so should evolution of the model precede and direct evolution of the system. This paper has discussed several key factors for consideration in the modeling and design of real-time systems and product lines, which assist in developing the software architecture before implementation and evolving the software architecture after original deployment.

Acknowledgments. The author gratefully acknowledges the contributions of R. Pettit, M. Hussein, M.E Shin, M. Saleh, and E. Olimpiew to this research.

References

[Bass03] L. Bass, P. Clements, R. Kazman, "Software Architecture in Practice", Addison Wesley, Reading MA, Second edition, 2003.

[Buschmann96] F. Buschmann, R. Meunier, H. Rohnert, P. Sommerlad, "Pattern Oriented Software Architecture: A System of Patterns", John Wiley & Sons, 1996.

[Clements02] P. Clements and L. Northrop, Software Product Lines: Practices and Patterns, Addison Wesley, 2002.

[Gomaa96] H. Gomaa, L. Kerschberg, V. Sugumaran, C. Bosch, I Tavakoli, "A Knowledge-Based Software Engineering Environment for Reusable Software Requirements and Architectures", Journal of Automated Software Engineering, Vol. 3, 285-307, 1996.

[Gomaa98] H. Gomaa and E. O'Hara, "Dynamic Navigation in Multiple View Software Specifications and Designs", Journal of Systems and Software, Vol. 41, 93-103, 1998.

[Gomaa99] H. Gomaa and G.A. Farrukh, "Methods and Tools for the Automated Configuration of Distributed Applications from Reusable Software Architectures and Components", IEE Proceedings – Software, Vol. 146, No. 6, December 1999.

[Gomaa00] H. Gomaa, "Designing Concurrent, Distributed, and Real-Time Applications with UML", Addison-Wesley Object Technology Series, 2000.

[Gomaa01] H. Gomaa, D. Menasce, E. Shin, "Reusable Component Interconnection Patterns for Distributed Software Architectures," Proceedings ACM Symposium on Software Reusability, ACM Press, Pages 69-77, Toronto, Canada, May 2001

[Gomaa04] H. Gomaa and M. Hussein, "Software Reconfiguration Patterns for Dynamic Evolution of Software Architectures", Proc. Fourth Working IEEE/IFIP Conference on Software Architecture, Oslo, Norway, June, 2004.

[Gomaa05] Gomaa, H., "Designing Software Product Lines with UML: From Use Cases to Pattern-based Software Architectures", Addison-Wesley Object Technology Series, 2005.

[Gomaa06] H. Gomaa and M. Saleh, "Feature Driven Dynamic Customization of Software Product Lines", Proc. Intl. Conf. on Software Reuse, Torino, Italy, Springer LNCS 4039, June 2006.

[GomaaMenasce01] H. Gomaa and D. Menasce, "Performance Engineering of Component-Based Distributed Software Systems". In "Performance Engineering", Eds. R. Dumke, C. Rautenstrauch, A. Schmietendorf, A. Scholz, Springer Verlag LNCS 2047, 2001.

[GomaaShin04] H. Gomaa and M.E. Shin, "A Multiple-View Meta-Modeling Approach for Variability Management in Software Product Lines", Proc. International Conference on Software Reuse, Madrid, Spain, Springer LNCS 3107, July 2004.

[Griss 98] Griss, M., J. Favaro, and M. d'Alessandro, "Integrating Feature Modeling with the RSEB." In *Fifth Intl. Conf. on Software Reuse: Proc: June 1998, Victoria, BC, Canada*, P. Devanbu and J. Poulin (eds.), pp. 1–10. Los Alamitos, CA: IEEE Computer Soc. Press.

[Harel96] Harel, D. and E. Gary, "Executable Object Modeling with Statecharts", Proc. 18th International Conference on Software Engineering, Berlin, March 1996.

[Jacobson97] Jacobson, I., M. Griss, and P. Jonsson. 1997. *Software Reuse: Architecture, Process and Organization for Business Success*. Reading, MA: Addison-Wesley.

[Kang90] Kang K. C. et. al., "Feature-Oriented Domain Analysis," Technical Report No. CMU/SEI-90-TR-21, Software Engineering Institute, November 1990.

[Magee94] J. Magee, N. Dulay and J. Kramer, "Regis: A Constructive Development Environment for Parallel and Distributed Programs", *Journal of Distributed Systems Engineering*, 1994, pp. 304-312.

[MenasceGomaa00] D. Menasce and H. Gomaa, "A Method for Design and Performance Modeling of Client/Server Systems," IEEE Transactions on Software Engineering, Vol. 26, No.11, Pages 1066-1085, November 2000.

[Parnas79] Parnas D., "Designing Software for Ease of Extension and Contraction", IEEE Transactions on Software Engineering, March 1979.

[PettitGomaa06] R. Pettit and H. Gomaa, "Modeling Behavioral Design Patterns of Concurrent Objects", Proc. International Conf. on Software Engineering, Shanghai, China, May 2006.

[Rumbaugh05] J. Rumbaugh, G. Booch, I. Jacobson, "The Unified Modeling Language Reference Manual," Second Edition, Addison Wesley, Reading MA, 2005.

[WebberGomaa04] D. Webber and H. Gomaa, "Modeling Variability in Software Product Lines with the Variation Point Model", Journal of Science of Computer Programming, Volume 53, Issue 3, Pages 305-331, Elsevier, December 2004.

[Weiss99] D M Weiss and C T R Lai, "Software Product-Line Engineering: A Family-Based Software Development Process," Addison Wesley, 1999.

Uses and Abuses of the Stereotype Mechanism in UML 1.x and 2.0

B. Henderson-Sellers and C. Gonzalez-Perez

Faculty of Information Technology
University of Technology, Sydney
PO Box 123, Broadway, NSW 2007, Australia
brian@it.uts.edu.au,
cesargon@verdewek.com

Abstract. Stereotypes were introduced into the UML in order to offer extensibility to the basic metamodel structure *by the user and without actually modifying the metamodel*. In UML version 1.x, this was accomplished by means of permitting virtual subtyping in the metamodel. However, this facility led many to misuse stereotypes, particularly in places where regular domain-level modelling would be more appropriate. In version 2.0 of the UML, the portion of the metamodel pertaining to stereotypes was drastically revised. The resulting mechanism is reviewed here and compared with that of version 1.x. From a set theory point of view, the new (2.0) metamodel is unfortunately untenable and the examples used in the OMG documentation unconvincing. This paper outlines the issues and suggests some possible steps to improve the UML 2.0 stereotype theory and practice.

1 The Idea Behind Stereotypes – The Need for Extensibility

Before the UML was mooted, each individual methodologist had their own notation, based on (often ill-defined) concepts. Such modelling languages often passed through several versions, each extending, refining and moderating the previous version. Thus extensibility was easy but the product itself essentially unstable.

Suggestions that a standard modelling language for object-oriented systems might be sought were mooted (actually for the second time) in the early 1990s [1]. Although a single standard (finally created under the auspices of the OMG) was envisaged, there was also an idea that this would be some sort of core language which would form the basis for tailored extensions [2]. At that time, the form of such an extension was unclear.

When the UML began to coalesce ideas from many sources, the extension mechanism we know today as stereotypes began to emerge (see e.g. [3]). This was catalysed by a discussion on the secondary badging of *objects* made in [4]. They suggested that a secondary classification might, in some specific circumstances, be useful – by attributing a prescribed responsibility for each so-labelled object. The categories of these responsibilities were intentionally implementation-focussed with names such as "coordinator object" and "interface object". UML took this idea originally espoused for *object* classification as a secondary classification mechanism for *classes*. The

O. Nierstrasz et al. (Eds.): MoDELS 2006, LNCS 4199, pp. 16–26, 2006.

main aim was to avoid the obvious way of extending the UML (by means of direct extensions to the metamodel – known as a UML variant, see e.g. example of the use of this variant approach in [5]) and replace it with an artificial means of *apparently* extending the metamodel without actually so doing.

In this paper, we first review the material available on the stereotype mechanism in UML version 1.x and then introduce a novel analysis of the new stereotype mechanism introduced recently in UML version 2.0 and identify its similarities and differences with version 1.x, critically examining whether these new features improve or degrade the previous model.

2 Stereotypes in UML Version 1.x

Based on the need for language extensibility but without extending the metamodel itself, UML version 1.x introduced a mechanism known as a stereotype, which can be defined as a “user-defined virtual sub-metatype”. Although this went through a variety of incarnations [6], the basic idea is as depicted here in Figure 1. Although there is much confusion regarding the definition of stereotypes [7] and, particularly, their correct usage (e.g. [3]), the basic idea is that the user can effectively define a new metaclass that exists only in the context of the stereotype definition and is *not* actually added to the UML metamodel. Atkinson and Kühne [7] suggest that this “represents an alternative way of expressing the instantiation relationship[1] without offering any additional modelling power”. In Figure 1, the user wishes to enhance the standard UML metamodel by a new concept called ControlClass that he/she envisages as a subclass of the pre-existing metaclass called Class. Once “imagined”, then this new

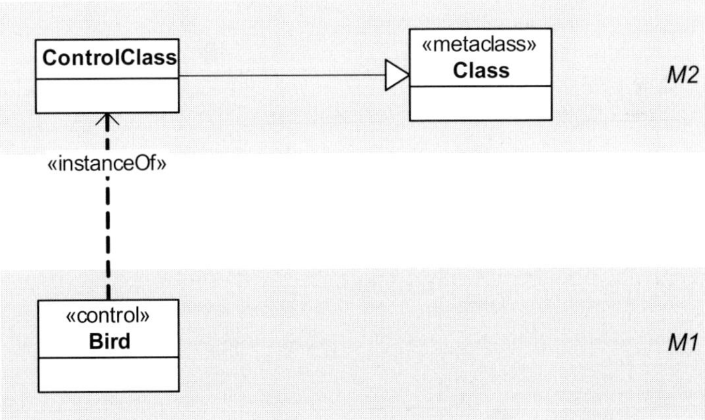

Fig. 1. Schematic example of how a stereotype works. The stereotype here is ControlClass which is not part of the UML metamodel but “invented” by the developer and imagined (virtual) as being part of the M_2 model as depicted here.

[1] The kernel of strict metamodelling [8], as used in all versions of UML.

ControlClass metaclass can be used to create instances at the model or M_1 level in exactly the same way as instantiating any other class from the metamodel. Thus, in this example, an instance of the metaclass ControlClass is depicted as the (stereotyped) class Bird. The Bird class is an instance of ControlClass and also of Class. Thus, it remains a regular class as well as carrying its stereotype or "branding" [9].

The actual definition (metamodel fragment) of the stereotype mechanism of UML version 1.4 is shown in Figure 2. A stereotype can be applied to an instance of a metaclass defined by the baseClass attribute of Stereotype. A stereotype then may have a tag definition (which gives the additional tagged values supported by the addition of the stereotype) and one or more constraints. Gogolla and Henderson-Sellers [6] stress the need to incorporate OCL [10] not only for constraint definition but also in other parts of the stereotype definition in order that the mechanism can work effectively and efficiently. In addition, tagged values of stereotypes play the same role as attributes of classes: they implement properties of the type that take values for each instance. The duality of tagged values *vs.* attributes is puzzling for many, because both constructs (attributes and tagged values) seem to attempt to solve the same problem, namely, add scalar properties to a type; if that is the case, why not a single, unified mechanism?. Finally, another problem is that the UML 1.x specification indicates that a model element can be marked with multiple stereotypes; although this may make sense from an intuitive perspective, it would mean that the model element in question is a direct instance of multiple user-defined virtual sub-metatypes. This contradicts the widespread understanding that an object is a *direct* instance of one and only one type [11-14] – although it can of course be an *indirect* instance of several types through single and multiple inheritance.

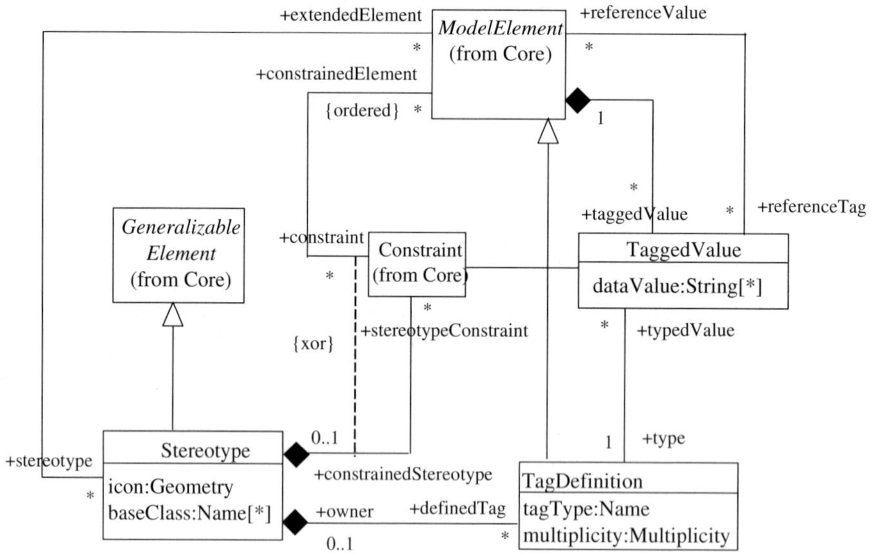

Fig. 2. Metamodel fragment for the stereotype mechanism in UML version 1.x

A key (yet often ignored) part of the version 1.x stereotype definition is the meta-attribute of baseClass. This has to be defined and represents the ModelElements to which it is allowable to add the particular stereotype being defined (Figure 3). Here, the base class is shown graphically by the definitional arrow to the metaclass called Class. In this example, then, the stereotype label «persistent» can only be placed on to a (M_1 level) class (i.e. any instance of the metaclass called Class) – as shown in Figure 4.

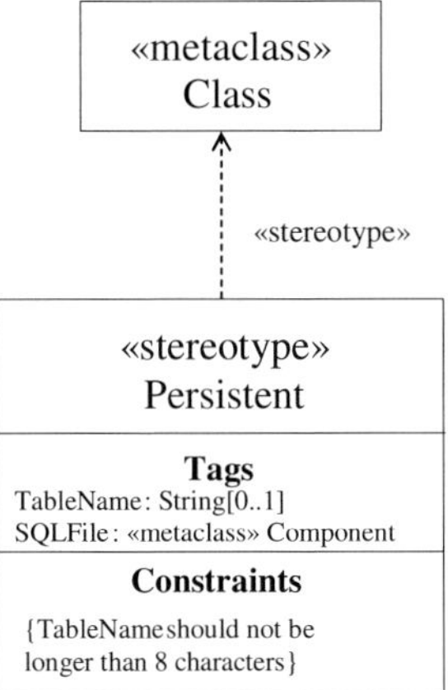

Fig. 3. Graphical definition of a stereotype «persistent»

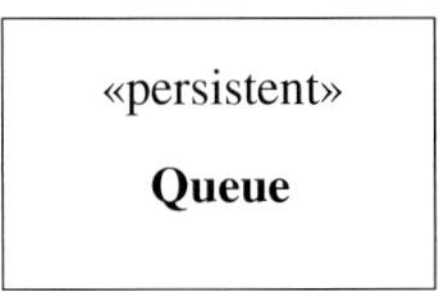

Fig. 4. Application of the stereotype «persistent», as defined in Figure 3, to a (M_1 level) class Queue

In practice, however, there were many abuses of this stereotype mechanism. Users chose to employ a mixture of branding at the class level (as specified in the standard) and branding at the instance level (not part of the standard). This led Atkinson *et al.* [15] to identify three kinds of stereotype use/misuse. The first two focus on the notion of object stereotypes and class stereotypes whereas the third identified kind of usage simultaneously brands a class and all its objects (again strictly outside the UML standard).

A typical good example (conformant with the UML standard) would be the branding of a class as a "commentedClass" (Figure 5) or a "controlClass" (as in Figure 1). More dubious examples are those in which the stereotype seems to be an excuse or replacement for a model that should be entirely at the M_1 level using a generalization relationship rather than the instantiation relationship of the version 1 stereotype mechanism. These are readily identifiable because they typically use problem domain concepts as labels to classifiers (less so to relationships) rather than conceptual modifiers at the M_2 level (Figure 6).

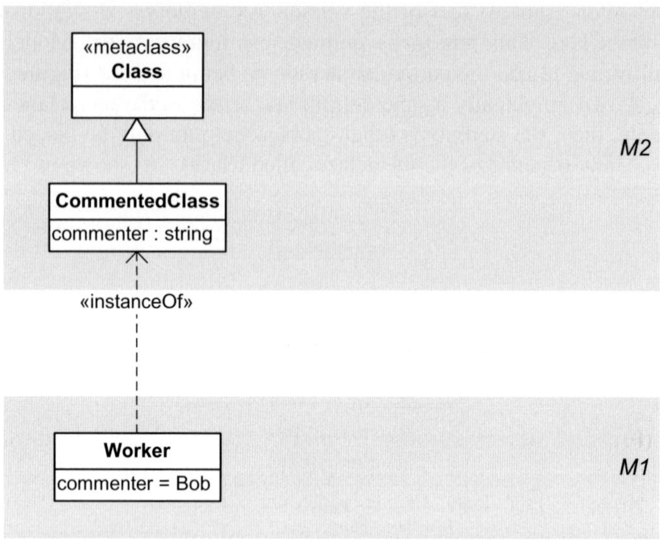

Fig. 5. Effect of stereotype on metamodel (after [15])

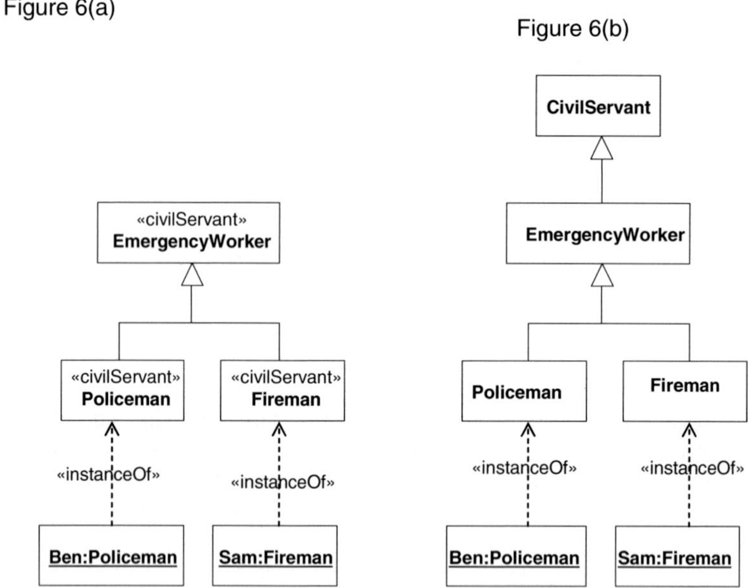

Fig. 6. Instance classification using (a) stereotypes and (b) superclasses (modified from [15])

Subsequent to these concerns being raised, both through the publications cited above and through formal submissions to the OMG in their deliberations towards UML version 2.0, there was optimism that a clear cut definition of a mechanism to support extensibility would be introduced. This might take the existing mechanism (as a user-defined virtual sub-metatype) and enforce it more strongly, perhaps explicitly forbidding what Atkinson *et al.* have described as "unofficial" usage or, conversely, accepting the common practice and supplying a new mechanism to support and make this unofficial usage into the "official" usage, abandoning the complicated extensions through virtual subtyping. In the event, as is shown in the next section, the committee did neither but introduced a new extension mechanism (though still called stereotype) that parallels 1.x in the sense that its definition is at the metalevel but its examples are counter to this at the object branding level.

3 Stereotypes in UML Version 2.0

The standard for the UML 2.0 Superstructure was finalized in late 2005 [16]. Its metamodel (Figure 7) shows that the TaggedValue and TaggedDefinition have been replaced by making Stereotype a (meta)class inheriting directly from Class. Since Class has Properties that are instantiated to values, then the new 2.0 Stereotype automatically inherits Properties that can be aliased to TaggedDefinition and TaggedValue. What appears to be missing is the association to Constraint (Figure 2) and the important baseClass. The baseClass concept is replaced by the newly introduced concept of Extension (and ExtensionEnds) that permits the connexion of two classes (but, surprisingly, only instances of metaclass Class and no other metaclass). Extension is a kind of Association (i.e. a relationship) and may or may not be required (meta-attribute of isRequired). Since an association has ends, there is a parallel here for Extension to have ends, appropriately named ExtensionEnds. However, although version

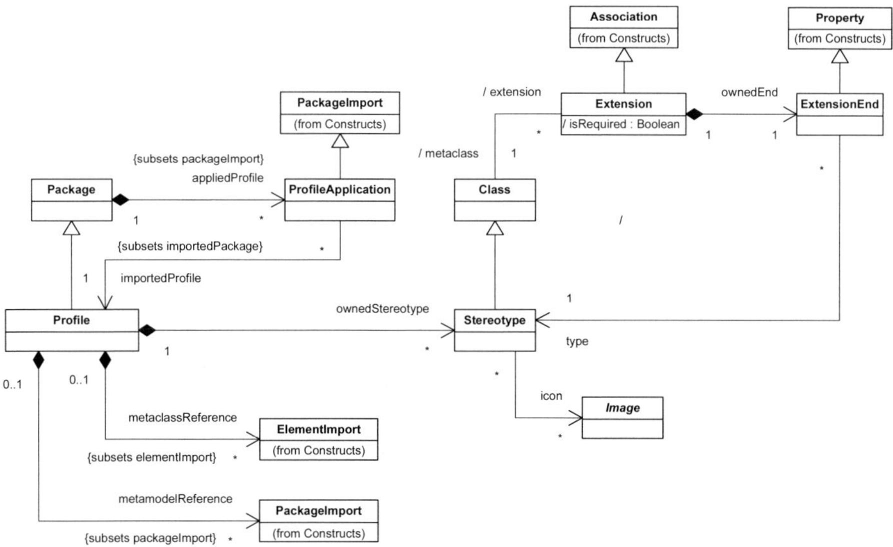

Fig. 7. UML version 2.0 metamodel fragment for the metaclass Stereotype and related metaclasses (after [16])

1.x had an AssociationEnd metaclass, this is no longer the case. The place of association ends is taken by the Property. Classes have Properties that provide the linkages between pairs of classes via an association. However, as can be seen in Figure 7, Extension inherits from Association (so that it links Properties not Classes) but this seems to be negated for Extension which directly links together Classes (not their Properties as does the Association parent class).

It is the newly introduced metaclass of Extension that we examine here first in some detail since it is the prime mechanism for stereotypical definitions and usage. The definition states that "An extension is used to indicate that the properties of a metaclass are extended through a stereotype, and gives the ability to flexibly add (and later remove) stereotypes to classes". The intention appears to be a good one – to enhance the existing properties of classes by those defined via the stereotype. But an instance of Extension is a relationship, a kind of "super" association that links the class in question to a set of additional properties. These additional properties must be part of the instance of the Stereotype metaclass. The immediate problems are that the merging of two disparate classes cannot be supported directly when one views classes using set theory (see e.g. [17]). Merging instances of class A with instances of class B (here the stereotype) results in a single set with mixed instances as members. It does not and cannot amalgamate pairs of values – the one from the stereotype and the one from the class in question – since there is no way to create and enforce a one-to-one mapping between elements of the two sets. So perhaps the extension mechanism is intended not to conform to set theory but to be a newly defined set operation that takes a *single* set of values as defined by the instance of Stereotype and concatenate these with the list of Property values in the class in question.

Finally, since only classes are now allowed to have stereotypes rather than a range of classifiers as in version 1.x, then it appears that there are no longer any legal stereotypes on, for instance, associations. This is very different from version 1.x and violated in many places in the version 2.0 documentation.

Fig. 8. An example of using an Extension (after [16])

In Figure 8 is shown an example from the OMG documentation of the use of the 2.0 stereotype mechanism. The associated text states "An instance of the stereotype *Home* can be added to and deleted from an instance of the class *Interface* at all". Our understanding from this sentence would support the above analysis since it is clear that the addition and deletion is not a set theoretic possibility but that the stereotype instance can only contain a list of property values to be concatenated with those of the class, here class *Interface*. If this is correct, then the stereotyped class (here *Home*) must always be a singleton.

Secondly, it is later stated, in discussion of "Changes from previous UML" [16, page 639] that an occurrence of the baseClass attribute of the 1.4 Stereotype metaclass "is mapped to an instance of Extension" [in 2.0]. The base class in version 1.x is the metaclass, which states to which instances (M_1 entities) the stereotype may be legally applied. If the baseClass is Class, then only M_1 classes may carry the stereotype; if the baseClass is given as Association, then only an (M_1) association can be thus branded. The baseClass name is thus the name of a M_2 class in UML version 1.x. Mapping this to an instance of Extension would appear to be incorrect on two counts. Firstly, the baseClass name in version 1.x is the name of an M_2 class whereas an instance of an Extension must be at the M_1 level. Secondly, the baseClass may be the M_2 classes of, say, Class, Association, UseCase whereas the Extension is only affiliated with the Association metaclass and not with Class, UseCase etc.

On Page 649 of the UML 2.0 Superstructure specification [16], we read that:

> An instance "S" of Stereotype is a kind of (meta)class. Relating it to a metaclass "C" from the reference metamodel (typically UML) using an "Extension" (which is a specific kind of association), signifies that model elements of type C can be extended by an instance of "S" ... At the model level... instances of "S" are related to "C" model elements (instances of "C") by links (occurrences of the association/extension from "S" to "C")

In our analysis of this paragraph, firstly, an instance of a metaclass is a (M_1) class and *cannot* be a kind of metaclass. Secondly, at the M_1 level, it is not instances of association/extension (a.k.a. links) that exist but the association or extension itself. Links occur at the M_0 level in standard UML modelling.

The examples that follow are very much of the same kind as those labelled as "unofficial" by [15] in 2003. Indeed, based on the above analysis, if an instance of Stereotype is a class with a set of fixed property values, and the merging/concatenation mechanism is accepted as valid, then these additional values will be able to be added to the stated instance of metaclass Class. However, since the stereotype instance is just a bunch of structural properties (i.e. no behaviour is possible), then the stereotype can be regarded as a data type rather than as a class/object. The example shown in [16] on page 651 is thus perturbing since the stereotype example shown is Clock – an M_1 concept that clearly has behaviour (or at least any modeller using it would presume so). Clock, after all, is an instance of (M_2) class Class in regular OO modelling. The notation (Figure 9) is further confusing since the name in guillemets on the right hand side is the name of a metaclass called Stereotype whereas the name in guillemets on the left hand side is a generic name (metaclass) that could be any entity in the M_2 metamodel. Similarly, the name Clock refers to the instance of the stereotype (the M_1 class) but the name Class on the left hand side, according to the text, is the name of the appropriate metaclass (here the metaclass named Class) – a similar confusion of levels as noted by [7] in version 1. This is supported by the instance notation shown in figure 18.14 of the OMG documentation (here as Figure 10). Figure 9 is said to be "defining a stereotype" which presumably occurs at the user level (i.e. M_1). One would thus assume that the name of the target of the extension should be something meaningful in the domain being modelled (not just "class") and similarly the (old version 1.x) base class should be indicated by a specific name in guillemets above the class name (not metaclass as in Figure 9). Although figure 18.12 (Figure 9) of [16] is confusing, the presentation options given suggest a more reasonable notation with an actual (M_1) class name and an actual (M_1) stereotype name (Figure 11).

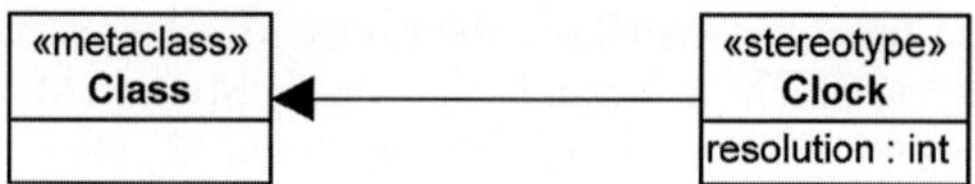

Fig. 9. Stereotype definition (after [16])

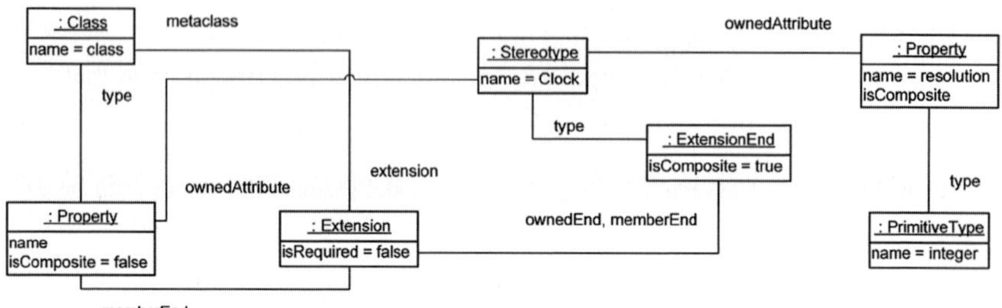

Fig. 10. Instance specification (after [16])

Fig. 11. Notation for a stereotype (modified from [16])

Finally, it is worth noting that in the accepted changes to create UML version 2.1 [18], there are a number of modifications to this part of the standard (the term "stereotype" occurs 208 times in the document!). Comments range from the need to describe what happens when an extending stereotype has subclasses through to the proposal for extensive changes in order to support SysML that requires that stereotypes can reference UML metaclasses (this requires changes to those figures shown here as Figure 9 and Figure 10).

4 Conclusions

In this paper we have presented some problems related to the concept of *stereotype* in UML 1.x and 2.0. From a theoretical perspective, stereotypes in UML 1.x are defined as virtual metatypes that pretend to be part of the metamodel (M_2) without really being there. Also, stereotypes make use of tagged values, which duplicate the concept of attributes without a good reason, and it is supposedly possible to apply multiple stereotypes to a single class, making the class, in fact, a direct instance of multiple classes, which is not allowed in UML 1.x. From the practical side, stereotypes are often misused, being applied for class and object branding indiscriminately, and very often to model application-domain concepts that should be modelled using conventional classes and subtyping rather than by using stereotypes.

In UML 2.0, a new approach is used for stereotypes. Unfortunately, this approach introduces new issues. First of all, the new Extension metaclass makes stereotyping incompatible with set theory, since an extension, when associated to a class, is supposed to change the properties of instances of such class; from a set theory viewpoint, the resulting product would be rather a mixed collection of instances of the class being extended and Extension. Secondly, the Stereotype metaclass in UML 2.0 is a subtype of Class, so only classes can be stereotyped. The inability of stereotypes to express behaviour (in addition to structure) and some notation issues pertaining to the usage of guillemets make stereotypes in UML 2.0 as puzzling as in UML 1.x.

Although it seems that UML 2.1 will make some changes in relation to stereotypes, the problems identified in this paper are hard to solve, especially since, as we have shown, the model used for stereotypes in UML 2.x appears to be flawed from a theoretical viewpoint. This suggests that any further improvement will need to utilize a different (meta)modelling approach for representing UML language extensions, such as stereotypes.

References

1. Monarchi, D., Booch, G., Henderson-Sellers, B., Jacobson, I., Mellor, S., Rumbaugh, J., Wirfs-Brock, R.: Methodology standards: help or hindrance? Procs. Ninth Annual OOPSLA Conference, ACM SIGPLAN, 29(10) (1994) 223-228
2. Henderson-Sellers, B.: Methodologies - frameworks for OO success, *American Programmer,* 7(10) (1994) 2-11
3. Atkinson, C., Kühne, T.: Rearchitecting the UML infrastructure, ACM Trans. Modeling and Computer Simulation, 12(4) (2002) 290-321
4. Wirfs-Brock, R., Wilkerson, B., Wiener, L., Responsibility-driven design: adding to your conceptual toolkit, ROAD, 1(2) (1994) 27-34
5. Henderson-Sellers, B., Atkinson, C., Firesmith, D.G.: Viewing the OML as a variant of the UML, «UML»'99 - The Unified Modeling Language. Beyond the Standard (eds. R. France and B. Rumpe), Lecture Notes in Computer Science 1723, Springer-Verlag, Berlin (1999) 49-66
6. Gogolla, M., Henderson-Sellers, B.: Analysis of UML stereotypes within the UML metamodel, «UML»2002, Dresden, Germany, 30 September - 4 October 2002, in UML 2002 - The Unified Modeling Language (eds. J.-M. Jezequel, H. Hussman and S. Cook), LNCS Volume 2460, Springer-Verlag, Berlin (2002) 84-99
7. Atkinson, C., Kühne, T.: Meta-level independent modelling. In *International Workshop on Model Engineering at 14th European Conference on Object-Oriented Programming* (2000)
8. Atkinson, C.: Metamodelling for distributed object environments, *Procs. First International Enterprise Distributed Object Computing Workshop (EDOC'97)*, Brisbane, Australia (1997)
9. Atkinson, C., Kühne, T., Henderson-Sellers, B. Stereotypical encounters of the third kind, **in** *UML 2002 - The Unified Modeling Language* (eds. J.-M. Jezequel, H. Hussman and S. Cook), LNCS Volume 2460, Springer-Verlag, Berlin (2002) 100-114
10. Warmer, J.M. Kleppe, A.: *The Object Constraint Language: Precise Modeling with UML*, Addison-Wesley (1998)
11. Feinberg, N., Keene, S.E., Mathews, R.O. and Withington, P.T., 1997, *Dylan™ Programming,* Addison-Wesley Longman, Section 3.2.1
12. Description of *Eiffel object model* accessed on 14 June 2006 at http://www.objs.com/x3h7/eiffel.htm

13. Evans, A. and Kent. S., 1999, Core meta-modelling semantics of UML: the pUML approach, *Procs. UML'99 – Beyond the Standard* (eds. R. France and B. Rumpe), LNCS 1793, Springer-Verlag, Berlin, 141-155
14. Soley, R.M. and Stone, C.M., 1995, Object Management Architecture Guide, Object Management Group document 97-05-05
15. Atkinson, C., Kühne, T., Henderson-Sellers, B.: Systematic stereotype usage, *Software and System Modelling,* 2(3) (2003) 153-163
16. OMG: Unified Modeling Language: Superstructure, Version 2.0, formal/05-07-04, 709pp (2005)
17. Steimann, F., Kühne, T.: A radical reduction of UML's core semantics, **in** *UML 2002 - The Unified Modeling Language* (eds. J.-M. Jezequel, H. Hussman and S. Cook), LNCS Volume 2460, Springer-Verlag, Berlin (2002) 34-48
18. OMG: RTF/FTF Report of the UML 2 Revision Task Force (Revision 2.1), document ptc/2006-01-01 (January 20, 2006), 802 pp. (2006)

An Experimental Investigation of UML Modeling Conventions

Christian F.J. Lange[1], Bart DuBois[2], Michel R.V. Chaudron[1], and Serge Demeyer[2]

[1] Department of Mathematics and Computer Science, Technische Universiteit Eindhoven, P.O. Box 513, 5600 MB Eindhoven, The Netherlands
C.F.J.Lange@tue.nl, M.R.V.Chaudron@tue.nl
[2] Lab On REengineering (LORE), University of Antwerp, Belgium
Bart.Dubois@ua.ac.be, Serge.Demeyer@ua.ac.be

Abstract. Modelers tend to exploit the various degrees of freedom provided by the UML. The lack of uniformity and the large amount of defects contained in UML models result in miscommunication between different readers. To prevent these problems we propose modeling conventions, analogue to coding conventions for programming. This work reports on a controlled experiment to explore the effect of modeling conventions on defect density and modeling effort. 106 masters' students participated over a six-weeks period. Our results indicate that decreased defect density is attainable at the cost of increased effort when using modeling conventions, and moreover, that this trade-off is increased if tool-support is provided. Additionally we report observations on the subjects' adherence to and attitude towards modeling conventions. Our observations indicate that efficient integration of convention support in the modeling process, e.g. through training and seamless tool integration, forms a promising direction towards preventing defects.

1 Introduction

The Unified Modeling Language (UML [19]) is used in different phases during software development such as requirements analysis, architecture, detailed design and maintenance. In these phases it serves various purposes such as communication between project stakeholders, prediction of quality properties and test case generation. The UML is designed as a visual multi-purpose language to serve all these needs. It allows to choose from 13 diagram types, it offers powerful extension mechanisms, but it lacks a formal semantics. Due to these characteristics the user has the freedom to choose the language features that fit his purpose of modeling. However, the UML does not provide guidelines on how to use the language features for a specific purpose. For example, there is no guidance that describes when it is useful to use multiplicities or when a class' behavior should be described by a state diagram. As a result, the UML user is confronted with a large degree of freedom.

The UML possesses the risk for quality problems due to its multi-diagram nature, its lack of a formal semantics and the large degree of freedom in using

O. Nierstrasz et al. (Eds.): MoDELS 2006, LNCS 4199, pp. 27–41, 2006.

it. The large degree of freedom and the lack of guidelines results in the fact that the UML is used in several different ways leading to differences in rigor, level of detail, style of modeling and amount of defects. Industrial case studies [16] and surveys give empirical evidence that individuals use the UML in many different ways (even within the same project team) and that the number of defects is large in practice. Moreover, experiments have shown that defects in UML models are often not detected and cause misinterpretations by the reader [15].

The effort for quality assurance is typically distinguished between *prevention* effort and *appraisal* effort [22]. Prevention effort aims at preventing for deviations from quality norms and appraisal effort is associated with evaluating an artifact to identify and correct deviations from these quality norms. There are techniques in software development to detect and correct the deviations from quality norms. Reviews, inspections and automated detection techniques are used in practice to detect weak spots. They are associated with appraisal effort. In programming preventive techniques to assure a uniform style and comprehensibility of the source code are established as coding conventions or coding standards [20]. As an analogy for UML modeling we propose *modeling conventions* to prevent modelers to deviate from quality norms. We define modeling conventions as: ***Conventions to ensure a uniform manner of modeling and to prevent for defects.***

The main purpose of this paper is to explore experimentally the effectiveness of modeling conventions for UML models with respect to prevention of defects.

An additional purpose of this study is to explore subjects' attitude towards modeling conventions and how modeling conventions are used. The observations can be used to improve the future use of modeling conventions.

This paper is structured as follows: Section 2 describes modeling conventions and related work. Section 3 describes the design of the experiment. Section 4 presents and discusses the results. Section 5 discusses the threats to the validity of the experiment and Section 6 discusses conclusions and future work.

2 Modeling Conventions

2.1 Related Work

There is a large variety of coding conventions (also known as guidelines, rules, standards, style) for almost all programming languages. The amount of research addressing coding conventions is rather limited though. Omam and Cook [20] present a taxonomy for coding conventions which is based on an extensive review of existing coding conventions. They identify four main categories of coding conventions: general programming practice, typographic style, control structure style and information style. They found that there are several conflicting coding conventions and that there is only little work on theoretical or empirical validation of coding conventions.

Our review of literature related to modeling conventions for the UML revealed the following categories: design conventions, syntax conventions, diagram conventions and application-domain specific conventions.

Design conventions address the design of the software system in general, i.e. they are not specific for UML. Design conventions such as those by Coad and Yourdon[6] aim at the maintainability of OO-systems. The conventions that include for example high cohesion and low coupling are empirically validated by Briand et al. [5]. The results of their experiment show that these conventions have a beneficial effect on the maintainability of object-oriented systems.

Syntax conventions deal with the correct use of the language. Ambler [3] presents a collection of 308 conventions for the style of UML. His conventions aim at understandability and consistency and address syntactical issues, naming issues, layout issues and the simplicity of design. Object-oriented reading techniques (OORT) are used in inspections to detect defects in software artefacts. OORT's for UML are related to modeling conventions in the sense that the rules they prescribe for UML models can be used in a forward-oriented way during the development of UML models to prevent for defects. Conradi et al. [7] conducted an industrial experiment where OORT's were applied for defect detection (i.e. an appraisal effort). The results show defect detection rates between 68% and 98% in UML models.

Diagram conventions deal with issues related to the visual representation of UML models in diagrams. Purchase et al. [21] present diagram conventions for the layout of UML class diagrams and collaboration diagrams based on experiments. Eichelberger [9] proposes 14 layout conventions for class diagrams aiming at algorithms for automatic layout of class diagrams.

Application-domain specific conventions. A purpose of UML profiles is to support modeling in a particular application domain. Hence, profiles are in fact application-domain specific conventions. Kuzniarz et al. [12] conducted an experiment on the effect of using stereotypes to improve the understandability of UML models. Their results show that stereotypes improve the correctness of understanding UML class diagrams by 25%.

2.2 Model Quality

In this experiment we investigate the effectiveness of modeling conventions on model quality, in particular we are interested in:

- Syntactic quality: The degree to which the model contains flaws.

Here we define *flaws* as: lack of coverage of the model's structural parts by behavioral parts, presence of defects, non-conformamce to commonly accepted design rules, and absence of uniformity in modeling.

Syntactic quality is one of the three notions of model quality according to Lindland's framework for conceptual models [17]. The two other notions according to Lindland are:

- Semantic quality: The degree to which the model correctly represents the problem domain.
- Pragmatic quality: The degree to which the model is correctly understood by its audience.

Evaluation of semantic and pragmatic quality involves participation of several people, and, hence, is an experiment itself. This would be beyond the scope of this experiment. We will investigate the effect of modeling conventions on semantic and pragmatic quality in a follow-up experiment.

2.3 Modeling Conventions in This Experiment

Based on the literature review and the experience from our case studies, we selected a set of modeling conventions. To keep the set of modeling conventions manageable and comprehensible we decided that it should fit on one A4 page. This led to 23 modeling conventions after applying these selection criteria:

- Relevance. The modeling convention should be relevant to improve the quality of the UML model by preventing for frequent defects [16].
- Comprehensibility. The modeling convention should be easy to comprehend (e.g. it relates to well-known model elements).
- Measurability. The effect of the modeling convention should be measurable.
- Didactic value. Applying the modeling convention should improve the subjects' UML modeling skills.

Examples of modeling conventions used in this experiment are given in Table 1. The entire set of modeling conventions can be found in [13]. In this experiment we focus on assessing syntactic quality, but we deliberately don't limit the collection of modeling conventions to syntactic conventions only. As described by Omam and Cook [20] there can be interaction between several conventions. To obtain realistic results it is necessary to use a representative set of modeling conventions. Therefore we chose conventions of all categories presented in Section 2.1.

Table 1. Examples of Modeling Conventions used in this Experiment

ID	Name	Description
4	Homogenity of Accessor Usage	When you specify getters/setters/constructors for a class, specify them for all classes
9	Model Class Interaction	All classes that interact with other classes should be described in a sequence diagram
10	Use Case Instantiation	Each Use Case must be described by at least one Sequence Diagram
14	Specify Message Types	Each message must correspond to a method (operation)
15	No Abstract Leafs	Abstract classes should not be leafs (i.e. child classes should inherit from abstract classes)
19	Low Coupling	Your classes should have low coupling. (The number of relations between each class and other classes should be small)

3 Experiment Design

3.1 Purpose and Hypotheses

We formulate the goal of this experiment according to the Goal-Question-Metric paradigm by Basili et al. [4]:

Analyze modeling conventions for UML
for the purpose of investigating their effectiveness
with respect to model quality and effort
from the perspective of the researcher
in the context of masters students at the TU Eindhoven.

Modeling conventions require model developers to adhere to specific rules. Therefore we expect the quality of models to be better, i.e. there are fewer defects in a model that is created using modeling conventions. When additionally using a tool to check for adherence to the modeling conventions, we expect the model quality to be even better than without tool-support. In other words, we formulate in the null hypothesis that there is no difference between the treatments:

- $H1_0$: There is no difference between the syntactic quality of UML models that are created without modeling conventions, with modeling conventions and with tool-supported modeling conventions.

Adherence to modeling conventions requires special diligence. We expect that this leads to higher effort for modeling. When additionally using the tool, the expected effort is even higher. Therefore we formulate the second hypothesis of this experiment as follows:

- $H2_0$: There is no difference between the effort for modeling UML models that are created without modeling conventions, with modeling conventions and with tool-supported modeling conventions.

3.2 Design

The purpose of this experiment is to investigate the effect of modeling conventions. Therefore the treatment is to apply modeling conventions with and without tool-support during modeling. We define three treatment levels:

NoMC: no modeling conventions. The subjects use no modeling conventions. This is the *control group.*
MC: modeling conventions. The subjects use the modeling conventions that are described in Section 2.3.
MC+T: tool-supported modeling conventions. The subjects use the modeling conventions and the analysis tool to support adherence.

The experimental task was carried out in teams of three subjects. We have randomly assigned subjects to teams and teams to treatments. According to [10] this allows us to assume independence between the treatment groups. Each team performed the task for one treatment level. Hence we have an unrelated between-subjects design with twelve teams for each treatment level.

3.3 Objects and Task

The task of the subjects was to develop a UML model of the architecture of an information system for an insurance company. The required functionality of the system is described in a document of four pages [13]. The system involves multiple user roles, administration and processing of several data types. The complexity of the required system was chosen such that on the one hand the subjects were challenged but on the other hand there was enough spare time for possible overhead effort due to the experimental treatment. The subjects used the Poseidon [2] UML tool to create the UML models. This tool does not assist in adhering to the modeling conventions and preventing model flaws.

The task of the teams with treatment MC and MC+T was to apply modeling conventions during development of the UML model. The modeling conventions description contains for each convention a unique identifier, a brief descriptive name, a textual description of the convention, and the name of the metric or rule in the analysis tool, that it relates to.

The subjects of treatment MC+T used the SDMetrics [24] UML analysis tool to assure their adherence to the modeling conventions. SDMetrics calculates metrics and performs rule-checking on UML models. We have customized [13] the set of metrics and rules to allow checking adherence to the modeling conventions used in this experiment.

3.4 Subjects

In total 106 MSc students participated in the experiment, which was conducted within the course "Software Architecting" in the fall term of 2005 at the Eindhoven University of Technology (TU/e). All subjects hold a bachelor degree or equivalent. Most students have some experience in using the UML and object oriented programming through university courses and industrial internships. We analyzed the results of the students' self-assessment from the post-test questionnaire and found no statistically significant differences.

The students were motivated to perform well in the task, because it was part of an assignment which was mandatory to pass the course (see Section 4.4).

The students were not familiar with the goal and the underlying research question of the experiment to avoid biased behavior.

3.5 Operation

Prior to the experiment we conducted a pilot run to evaluate and improve the comprehensibility of the experiment materials. The subjects of the pilot experiment did not participate in the actual experiment.

In addition to prior UML knowledge of the students we presented and explained UML during the course before the experiment. The assignment started with an instruction session to explain the task and the tooling to all students. Additionally the subjects were provided with the assignment material [13] including a detailed task description, the description of the insurance company system, and instructions of the tools. The modeling conventions and the SDMetrics tool were only provided to the teams which had to use them. The teams of treatment MC and MC+T were explicitly instructed to apply the treatment regularly and to contact the instructors in case of questions about the treatment. The experiment was executed over a period of six weeks.

3.6 Data Collection

We collected the defect data of the delivered UML models using the SDMetrics, because the majority of the applied modeling conventions is related to rules and metrics that we defined for SDMetrics.

The subjects were provided with an Excel Logbook template to record the time spent during the assignment in a uniform manner. They recorded their time for the three activities related to the development of the UML model: modeling itself, reviewing the model and meetings related to the model.

We used a post-test questionnaire to collect data about the subjects' educational background, experience, how the task was executed and subjects' attitude towards the task. The 17 questions of the questionnaire were distributed through the university's internal survey system.

3.7 Analysis Techniques

For quality and effort we have to analyze number of defects and time in minutes, respectively. These metrics are measured on a ratio scale. We use descriptive statistics to summarize the data. For hypothesis testing we compare the means using a one-way ANOVA test. We have analyzed the data with respect to the assumptions of the ANOVA test and have found no severe violations. The analysis is conducted using the SPSS [1] tool, version 12.0. As this is an exploratory study we reject the null hypothesis at the significance level of 0.10 ($p<0.10$).

The data from the post-test questionnaire, which was designed as a multiple-choice questionnaire, were answers on a five-point Likert-scale. Hence, they are measured on an ordinal scale. We summarize the data by presenting the frequencies as percentages for each answer option and providing additional descriptive statistics where appropriate. The answer distributions between different treatment groups are compared using the χ^2-test [18]. Microsoft Excel was used for this test. We apply the threshold of $p<0.10$ for statistical significance. When comparing three distributions (NoMC, MC and MC+T) a χ^2 value greater than 13.36 implies that $p<0.10$. In cases of comparing only two distributions the threshold is $\chi^2 = 7.78$.

4 Results

4.1 Outlier Analysis

During the duration of the experiment eight subjects dropped out (7.5%). The affected teams were distributed evenly over all treatments, therefore we do not exclude their data. One team in group MC+T completely dropped out, therefore we exclude its data.

To check whether the data is reasonable and to identify invalid data sets we analyze the outliers. Figure 1 shows the boxplots for the size of the obtained models (number of classes, on the left) and the total amount of time needed by the teams to complete the task (on the right). According to Wohlin [23] the

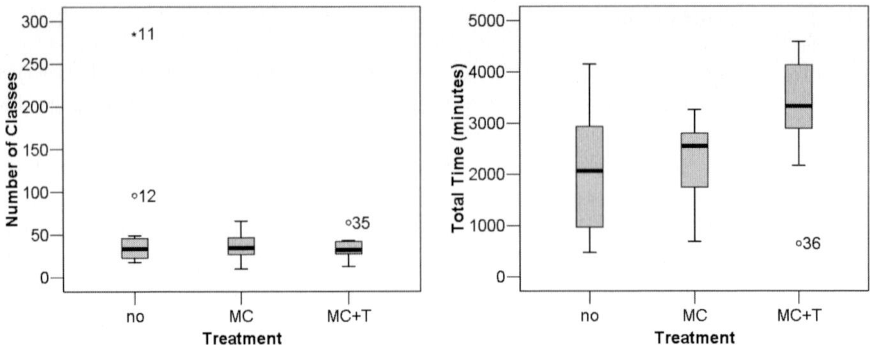

Fig. 1. Boxplots for Number of Classes and Total Time

reasons for an outlier should be analyzed in order to decide whether to include or to exclude the data point in the analysis. We scrutinized the outliers and came to the conclusion that they are not due to a rare event that can never happen again. As these outliers can happen in other situations as well, we decided to include them in the analysis.

4.2 H1: Presence of Defects

Total Number of Defects. We assess the quality of the UML model in terms of number of defects as described in Section 3.2. Figure 2 shows the boxplot for the total number of defects (on the left) and the number of defects normalized by the size of the model (on the right). Table 2 shows the descriptive statistics. The percentages in Table 2 are relative to the treatment level NoMC. The descriptive statistics for the normalized number of defects show that modeling conventions (MC) reduce the mean and the median. Tool-supported modeling conventions (MC+T) result in a larger reduction of defects. However, according to the ANOVA test (see Table 3) the results are not statistically significant and we cannot reject the null hypothesis $H1_0$.

Detailed Results. In addition to the total number of defects which is discussed above, we have conducted a detailed analysis of 19 metrics and rules that are related to the modeling conventions applied in this experiment. For nine of these metrics the results for both MC and MC+T are better than for the control group. An example is the metric *Number of Sequence Diagrams per Use Case* which indicates how well the functionality defined in use cases is specified by the sequence diagrams. Compared to the control group this metric is 30.8% greater for MC and 80.5% greater for MC+T (these results are statistically significant). Three metrics show an improvement for MC+T but a decrease for MC. An example is the metric *Number of Objects*. The metric *Coupling between Objects (CBO)* is the only one that has worse results for both MC and MC+T than for the control group. A possible explanation could be, that the subjects applying

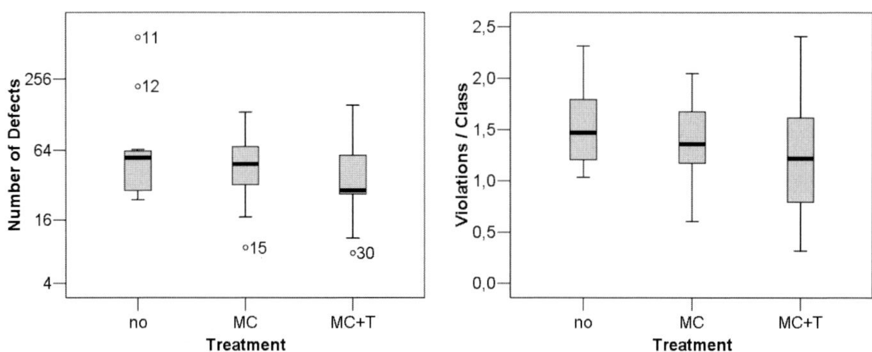

Fig. 2. Boxplots for absolute Number of Defects and Defect Density

modeling conventions model associations between classes more explicitly, resulting in a higher CBO. The results of six metrics are inconclusive because of the small number of occurrences of the rule-violations. Due to space limitations we cannot provide the entire detailed results here. They can be found in [14].

4.3 H2: Effort

We measure the effort to develop the UML model in minutes using logbooks. Table 2 shows the descriptive statistics for modeling, reviewing and team meetings. The columns showing percentages are relative to the treatment level NoMC. The descriptive statistics show that both the mean and the median increase for MC are higher for MC+T. Additionally we performed an ANOVA-test for hypothesis testing. The results of the ANOVA-test are shown in Table 3. The results for the total effort are statistically significant. Hence, we reject the null-hypothesis $H2_0$. However, when we analyze at the level of activities, we see that only the results of modeling are statistically significant.

4.4 Attitude

To fully investigate the usefulness of modeling conventions it is necessary to assess the subject's attitude towards modeling conventions. We investigated the subjects's attitude using the post-test questionnaire. The questions are multiple-choice questions with answers on a Likert scale ranging from 1 (very low agreement) to 5 (very high agreement). The results are summarized in Table 4.

The subjects perceived the difficulty of the task as medium. The difficulty of performing the task with tool-supported modeling conventions is about 10% higher than for MC.

There is a statistically significant difference in the degree to which the subjects enjoyed the task. The mean for control group (NoMC) is almost one point higher than for the other two treatment groups. The lower enjoyment might be caused by the extra effort (see Section 4.3).

Table 2. Descriptive Statistics for Defects and Modeling Effort (in Minutes)

	Treatment	Mean	Perc.	Median	Perc.	StDev	Max	Min
Defects (total)	NoMC	102.42	100.0%	55.5	100.0%	157.280	572	42
	MC	53.67	52.4%	49.0	88.3%	34.102	135	9
	MC+T	46.91	45.8%	29.0	52.3%	40.990	154	8
Defects (normalized)	NoMC	1.5181	100.0%	1.4720	100.0%	0.3964	2.312	1.032
	MC	1.3740	90.5%	1.3564	92.1%	0.4121	2.045	0.607
	MC+T	1.2443	82.0%	1.2195	82.8%	0.6671	2.406	0.320
Effort (Modeling)	NoMC	1069.17	100.0%	910	100.0%	670.22	2125	120
	MC	1157.92	108.3%	982.5	108.0%	718.225	2280	105
	MC+T	1885	176.3%	2010	220.9%	834.554	3130	540
Effort (Reviewing)	NoMC	367.5	100.0%	300	100.0%	329.224	1155	0
	MC	385.83	105.0%	272.5	90.8%	299.4	900	75
	MC+T	524.55	142.7%	600	200.0%	379.727	1250	0
Effort (Meeting)	NoMC	555.42	100.0%	375	100.0%	499.297	1710	0
	MC	720	129.6%	640	170.7%	632.488	1770	0
	MC+T	862.73	155.3%	690	184.0%	839.069	3060	0
Effort (Total)	NoMC	1992.08	100.0%	2062.5	100.0%	1187.498	4150	480
	MC	2245.42	112.7%	2545	123.4%	852.471	3265	690
	MC+T	3272.27	164.3%	3330	161.5%	1151.838	4590	650

The results show that the subjects of all treatment groups slightly indicate that they have confidence in the quality of their models. There is no significant difference between the treatment groups.

The results show that the task and the treatment were well understood and that the subjects were well motivated. This is necessary to be able to draw valid conclusions from the experiment. The χ^2-test did not show significant differences between the treatments groups.

4.5 Adherence to the Treatment

We used the answers to the post-test questionnaire to investigate the subjects' adherence to treatment MC and MC+T. The answers are summarized in Table 5. The table shows the percentages for the points '1' (very low adherence) to '5' (very high adherence). On average both treatment groups adhere better than neutral to the modeling conventions (the mean is greater than 3). The χ^2-test shows that the difference between MC and MC+T is not statistically significant.

The reported average adherence to the analysis tool is below the neutral point (3). We conducted a χ^2-test to find out whether the adherence differs significantly from the adherence to the modeling conventions of the same treatment group. The difference is statistically significant at the 10% significance level.

Furthermore we asked the subjects how they applied the treatment. For both treatment groups that applied modeling conventions, more than 80% of the subjects indicate that they read the modeling conventions several times during the project. The tool was used up to ten times during the project at an average of 3.32 times. The two authors who were instructors of the course report that

Table 3. Results of the ANOVA test for Defects and Effort

		$\sum$ Squares	df	Mean Squr.	F	Sig.	Hypothesis
Defects (total)	Betw. Groups	21570.1	2	10785.09	1.144	.331	$H1_0$ failed to reject
	With. Groups	301708.5	32	9428.39			
	Total	323278.7	34				
Defects (normalized)	Betw. Groups	.432	2	.216	.858	.433	$H1_0$ failed to reject
	With. Groups	8.048	32	.251			
	Total	8.479	34				
Effort (Modeling)	Betw. Groups	453675.4	2	2268187.708	4.129	.025	rejected
	With. Groups	17580265	32	549383.268			
	Total	22116640	34				
Effort (Reviewing)	Betw. Groups	166964.89	2	83482.446	.738	.486	failed to reject
	With. Groups	3620239.4	32	113132.481			
	Total	3787204.3	34				
Effort (Meeting)	Betw. Groups	544447.47	2	272223.736	.614	.547	failed to reject
	With. Groups	14183091	32	443221.597			
	Total	14727839	34				
Effort (Total)	Betw. Groups	10421703	2	5210851.564	4.535	.018	$H2_0$ rejected
	With. Groups	36772764	32	1149148.875			
	Total	47194467	34				

Table 4. Subjects' Attitudes towards the Task

	Treatment	N	χ^2	Mean	1	2	3	4	5
Difficulty	NoMC	34	11.860	2.94	0.00%	23.53%	61.76%	11.76%	2.94%
	MC	36		3.00	2.78%	19.44%	52.78%	25.00%	0.00%
	MC+T	33		2.61	6.06%	42.42%	36.36%	15.15%	0.00%
Enjoy	NoMC	34	18.886	3.47	0.00%	14.71%	32.35%	44.12%	8.82%
	MC	36		2.58	16.67%	27.78%	36.11%	19.44%	0.00%
	MC+T	33		2.58	21.21%	21.21%	36.36%	21.21%	0.00%
Confidence in Quality	NoMC	34	5.526	3.18	2.94%	17.65%	41.18%	35.29%	2.94%
	MC	36		3.31	0.00%	11.11%	47.22%	41.67%	0.00%
	MC+T	33		3.24	3.03%	21.21%	27.27%	45.45%	3.03%
Understanding Task	NoMC	34	4.089	3.18	8.82%	14.71%	35.29%	32.35%	8.82%
	MC	36		3.08	2.78%	27.78%	33.33%	30.56%	5.56%
	MC+T	33		2.91	9.09%	27.27%	30.30%	30.30%	3.03%
Motivation	NoMC	34	3.862	3.56	5.88%	8.82%	23.53%	47.06%	14.71%
	MC	36		3.44	5.56%	5.56%	36.11%	44.44%	8.33%
	MC+T	33		3.67	3.03%	3.03%	30.30%	51.52%	12.12%

Table 5. Adherence to the treatment

Adherence to	Treatment	N	χ^2	Mean	1	2	3	4	5
Modeling Conventions	MC	36	5.027	3.638	0.00%	5.56%	33.33%	52.78%	8.33%
	MC+T	33		3.303	3.03%	6.06%	54.55%	30.30%	6.06%
Analysis Tool	MC+T	33	9.326	2.727	12.12%	27.27%	42.42%	12.12%	6.06%

they received questions about both the modeling conventions and the analysis tool starting from the second week of the experiment.

5 Threats to Validity

Internal Validity. Threats to internal validity can affect the independent variables of an experiment. A possible threat to internal validity is that the treatment groups behave differently because of a confounding factor such as difference in skills, experience or motivation. Our analysis results show no significant differences between the treatment groups for these factors.

A risk is that subjects apply a treatment they should not apply, because they are eager to learn about new technology. We minimized this risk by (i) not telling the subjects the goal of the experiment, (ii) by informing the subjects that their grade is not influenced by the treatment group that they were in, (iii) by making modeling conventions and tool available only to the appropriate teams, and (iv) by informing the subjects that all technology would be made available to all subjects after completion of the task. In the case that subjects would have received a different treatment despite these precautions, it would only decrease the effect between the treatment groups. Hence, in case this happened, the effect would be larger in reality.

External Validity. Threats to external validity reduce the generalizability of the results to industrial practice. As described in Section 3 the experiment is designed to render a realistic situation. Hence, the experimental environment is designed to maximize generalizability (at the cost of statistical significance). We use students as subjects, which might be a threat to external validity. However, all students in this experiment hold a BSc degree in computer science and have relevant experience.

Due to curricular constraints the amount of training and, hence, experience with modeling conventions and the analysis tool is limited. This renders the situation in the introduction phase of the technology. We assume that more experience results in a reduction of extra effort and possibly a larger effect on model quality.

Construct Validity. Construct validity is the degree to which the variables measure the concepts they are to measure. The concept of quality is difficult to measure and it consists of several dimensions[11]. It is not feasible to cover all dimensions in a single experiment. We limit the scope of this experiment to defect containment. Using well-established tooling to measure the defect containment we are confident to measure this dimension of model quality correctly.

Conclusion Validity. Conclusion validity is concerned with the relation between the treatment and the outcome. The statistical analysis of the results is reliable, as we used robust statistical methods.

We minimized possible understanding problems by testing the experiment material in a pilot experiment and improving it according to the observed issues. The course instructors were available to the students for clarification questions.

The results of the post-test questionnaire show that the task was well understood. Hence, we conclude that there were no understanding problems threatening the validity of the reported experiment.

The metrics of the UML models (defects, size...) were collected using an analysis tool and are therefore repeatable and reliable. A possible threat to the conclusion validity is the reliability of the measured time and the data from the post-test questionnaire. For time collection a logbook template was used to assure uniformity. The authors analyzed the data for validity and no obvious problems were found.

6 Conclusions

The UML consists of different diagram types, has no formal semantics and does not provide guidelines on how to use the language features. Inherent to these characteristics is the risk for quality problems such as defects and non-uniform use of the language. In this study we propose modeling conventions as a forward-oriented means to reduce these quality problems. Our literature review shows that existing work focusses on particular categories of conventions for UML modeling and that there is lack of empirical validation of conventions for UML modeling.

Our main contribution is an experiment that provides empirical data about the application of modeling conventions in a realistic environment. Our results show that the defect density in UML models is reduced through the use of modeling conventions. However, the improvement is not statistically significant. Additionally, we provide data about the additional effort needed to apply modeling conventions with and without tool-support. The presented data quantifies the trade-off between improved model quality by using modeling conventions and the cost of extra effort. Additional observations describe the developers' attitude towards modeling conventions and how the modeling conventions were applied within the development teams. We observed that the adherence to modeling conventions, especially for tool-supported modeling conventions, bears potential for improvement. Furthermore the subjects using modeling conventions enjoyed their task less than the subjects who did not use modeling conventions, indicating that the commitment in using modeling conventions can be improved.

Due to the time constraints of the experiment, we provided the subjects with a set of modeling conventions, instead of letting them select the conventions themselves. However, the subjects had no experience whether the modeling conventions were useful for their task, and the subjects received no reward for delivering a better quality model (the typical reward would be less effort during use of the UML models in a later phase). In practice it would be desirable if the developers who must eventually use the conventions participate in establishing the set of modeling conventions. This would increase their knowledge about and trust in the conventions and we expect they would have more commitment in using modeling conventions. We expect that the commitment will also be improved in a practical situation because the models will be used after they have been developed, resulting in rewarding the models' quality. The subjects in this experiment were not experienced using modeling conventions or the analysis tool. Therefore the experiment resembles the introduction of modeling conventions to a project. We expect that for more experienced developers the quality improvement is larger and the amount of extra effort will be reduced.

The tool-support for adherence to the modeling conventions was given by a stand-alone tool. We expect that integrating adherence checks into UML development tools will decrease the extra effort and result in higher adherence, because of a shorter feedback loop. Egyed's instant consistency checking [8] is a promising technique for short feedback loops.

The observations made in this experiment potentially lead to the following guidelines for applying UML modeling conventions:

- Attention must be paid to control the adherence to the modeling conventions.
- Commitment of the developers increases the adherence to the modeling conventions.
- Modeling conventions should be tailored for a specific purpose of modeling.
- Tool support to enforce adherence to the modeling conventions increases the quality improvement. A short feedback loop is required to minimize the amount of necessary rework.

In future work the effect of adherence and experience on the effectiveness and efficiency of modeling conventions should be investigated in more detail. External replications of the reported experiment should be conducted to further confirm our findings. We focussed at syntactical quality of UML models in this experiment. We are conducting a follow-up experiment where we investigate semantic and pragmatic quality.

References

1. SPSS, version 12.0. http://www.spss.com.
2. Gentleware AG. Poseidon for UML, community edition, version 3.1. http://www.gentleware.com.
3. Scott W. Ambler. *The Elements of UML 2.0 Style.* Cambridge University Press, 2005.
4. Victor R. Basili, G. Caldiera, and H. Dieter Rombach. The goal question metric paradigm. In *Encyclopedia of Software Engineering*, pages 528–532, 1994.
5. Lionel C. Briand, Christian Bunse, and John William Daly. A controlled experiment for evaluating quality guidelines on the maintainability of object-oriented designs. *IEEE Transactions on Software Engineering*, 27(6):513–530, June 2001.
6. Peter Coad and Edward Yourdon. *Object Oriented Design.* Prentice-Hall, first edition, 1991.
7. Reidar Conradi, Parastoo Mohagheghi, Tayyaba Arif, Lars Christian Hedge, Geir Arne Bunde, and Anders Pedersen. Object-oriented reading techniques for inspection of UML models – an industrial experiment. In *Proceedings of the European Conference on Object-Oriented Programming ECOOP'03*, volume 2749 of *LNCS*, pages 483–501. Springer, July 2003.
8. Alexander Egyed. Instant consistency checking for the UML. In *Proceedings of the 28th International Conference on Software Engineering (ICSE'06)*, pages 381–390. ACM, May 2006.

9. Holger Eichelberger. Aesthetics of class diagrams. In *Proceedings of the First IEEE International Workshop on Visualizing Software for Understanding and Analysis (VISSOFT 2002)*, pages 23–31. IEEE CS Press, 2002.
10. Norman E. Fenton and Shari Lawrence Pfleeger. *Software Metrics, A Rigorous and Practical Approach.* Thomson Computer Press, second edition, 1996.
11. Barbara Kitchenham and Shari Lawrence Pfleeger. Software quality: The elusive target. *IEEE Software*, 13(1):12–21, Januari 1996.
12. Ludwik Kuzniarz, Miroslaw Staron, and Claes Wohlin. An empirical study on using stereotypes to improve understanding of UML models. In *Proceedings of the 12th IEEE International Workshop on Program Comprehension (IWPC'04)*, pages 14–23. IEEE CS Press, 2004.
13. Christian F. J. Lange. Material of the modeling conventions experiment. http://www.win.tue.nl/~clange.
14. Christian F. J. Lange, , Bart DuBois, Michel R. V. Chaudron, and Serge Demeyer. Experimentally investigating the effectiveness and effort of modeling conventions for the UML. CS-Report 06-14, Technische Universiteit Eindhoven, 2006.
15. Christian F. J. Lange and Michel R. V. Chaudron. Effects of defects in UML models - an experimental investigation. In *Proceedings of the 28th International Conference on Software Engineering (ICSE'06)*, pages 401–411. ACM, May 2006.
16. Christian F. J. Lange, Michel R. V. Chaudron, and Johan Muskens. In practice: UML software architecture and design description. *IEEE Software*, 23(2):40–46, March 2006.
17. Odd Ivar Lindland, Guttorm Sindre, and Arne Sølvberg. Understanding quality in conceptual modeling. *IEEE Software*, 11(2):42–49, March 1994.
18. Meerling. *Methoden en technieken van psychologisch onderzoek*, volume 2. Boom, Meppel, The Netherlands, 4th edition, 1989.
19. Object Management Group. *Unified Modeling Language, Adopted Final Specification, Version 2.0*, ptc/03-09-15 edition, December 2003.
20. Paul W. Omam and Curtis R. Cook. A taxonomy for programming style. In *Proceedings of the 18th ACM Computer Science Conference*, pages 244–250, 1990.
21. Helen C. Purchase, Jo-Anne Allder, and David Carrington. Graph layout aesthetics in UML diagrams: User preferences. *Journal of Graph Algoritms and Applications*, 6(3):255–279, 2002.
22. Sandra A. Slaughter, Donald E. Harter, and Mayuram S. Krishnan. Evaluating the cost of software quality. *Communications of the ACM*, 41(8):67–73, August 1998.
23. Claes Wohlin, Per Runeson, Martin Höst, Magnus C. Ohlesson, Björn Regnell, and Anders Wesslen. *Experimentation in Software Engineering - An Introduction.* Kluwer Academic Publishers, 2000.
24. Jürgen Wüst. The software design metrics tool for the UML, version 1.3. http://www.sdmetrics.com.

Improving the Definition of UML

Greg O'Keefe

Research School of Information Science and Engineering, Australian National University, Canberra, ACT 0200, Australia
greg.okeefe@anu.edu.au

Abstract. The literature on formal semantics for UML is huge and growing rapidly. Most contributions open with a brief remark motivating the work, then quickly move on to the technical detail. How do we decide whether more rigorous semantics are needed? Do we currently have an adequate definition of the syntax? How do we evaluate proposals to improve the definition? We provide criteria by which these and other questions can be answered. The growing role of UML is examined. We compare formal language definition techniques with those currently used in the definition of UML. We study this definition for both its content and form, and conclude that improvements are required. Finally, we briefly survey the UML formalisation literature, applying our criteria to determine which of the existing approaches show the most potential.

Many would argue that UML has no semantics [HR04, HS05], despite the numerous subheadings with that title in the documents which define the language [Obj06, Obj03, Obj05c, Obj05a]. Bran Selic [Sel04] counters these claims by collecting and summarising the scattered material on semantics from the main official document [Obj05c]. He also encourages theoreticians to study ways of making the semantics more precise.

The only real disagreement here is over the usage of the word "semantics." This is the topic of Harel and Rumpe's excellent article [HR04], and their position is that "semantics" is a mathematical term:

> Regardless of the exposition's degree of formality, the semantic mapping $M : L \longrightarrow S$ must be a rigorously defined function from the language's syntax L to its semantic domain S. Needless to say, an adequate semantic mapping for the full UML does not exist.

Selic, we believe, takes "semantics" to be an ordinary English word. Calling the prose from the official UML documents "semantics," is just saying that it describes the intended meaning of the models. The official UML documents exhibit an appreciation of the distinction between ordinary and technical usages:

> It is important to note that the current description is not a completely formal specification of the language because to do so would have added significant complexity without clear benefit.
>
> The structure of the language is nevertheless given a precise specification, which is required for tool interoperability. The detailed semantics

O. Nierstrasz et al. (Eds.): MoDELS 2006, LNCS 4199, pp. 42–56, 2006.

> are described using natural language, although in a precise way so they can easily be understood. Currently, the semantics are not considered essential for the development of tools; however, this will probably change in the future. [Obj03, §8]

This quote sets the scene for our investigation. It notes that some degree of precision is required to fulfil UML's mission. It claims, with a little hesitation, that this has been achieved without the use of rigorous mathematics. We will argue that there is a need for improvements, which we will identify.

The task is not to invent a new language, but to improve the definition of an existing one. The building industry has analogous situations. Sometimes a building of cultural significance is found to be structurally lacking. The builders will often suggest bulldozing it, and starting afresh, or making insensitive modifications like replacing a timber floor with concrete.

Too much of the UML formalisation literature takes the ham-fisted builder's approach to the problem, largely ignoring the existing definition, omitting large parts of the language or suggesting significant changes to it. We propose instead a minimal and sensitive adaptation of the existing definition to make it strong and stable enough, and more suitable to its new usage in model driven development. Like a good restoration architect, we should carefully consider the option of leaving things as they are.

Throughout this paper, we state criteria by which UML definitions ought to be evaluated. The first overarching criterion captures the conclusion just reached.

Criterion 0. *An improved definition of UML should not change the language or the definition any more than is needed to enable UML to fulfil its role.*

In our first section we consider the task of defining a language, and in the second, we show why the semantic part of the definition is important. The third section examines the purpose of UML, and in the fourth we study two of the more difficult aspects of the current UML definition. The fifth section evaluates the existing definition of UML and the sixth briefly surveys the literature to identify the most promising efforts to improve that definition. We conclude by saying how we hope the future of UML semantics research will differ from its past.

1 Defining Languages

Diagrams do not need to conform to some defined language in order to help us communicate. People find it quite natural to express their ideas by drawing pictures, as any survey of publications, presentation slides or white-boards will verify. Most of these diagrams do not conform to any specified diagram type. If they are part of a language, it is a *natural* language, like English[1].

A description of a natural language is a scientific theory, which must be judged by how well it predicts actual usage. Artificial languages on the other hand, are *defined.* Usage which does not conform to the definition is incorrect.

[1] We will speak of "English" when we mean any arbitrary natural language such as English, Occitan or Brazilian Portuguese.

Sometimes the primary purpose of creating diagrams is not to communicate ideas, but rather to generate or organise them. The "mind maps" technique [Buz95] is one example. UML can be used in this way too. Building a UML model can drive the collection of information about a problem domain, and provide a convenient structure for organising that information. This role does not, however, conflict with its status as a defined language.

The mind-map book provides guidelines for creating and reading these mind-maps, which we might, very charitably, regard as a language definition. It is certainly not a precise definition, nor is it intended to be, because precision simply is not required. In a commentary attached to the amusing article "Death by UML Fever" [Bel04], Philippe Kruchten implies that UML does not need to be precisely defined.

> UML is a notation that should be used in most cases simply to illustrate your design and to serve as as a general road-map for the corresponding implementation.

UML can be used as documentation of code, but it is also intended as a means of *specifying* a system. Model Driven Architecture (MDA) [MM03] calls for complete systems to be generated automatically from UML models. If the language is not precisely defined, the generated system may not be what the model creators intended.

Computer programs are usually written as linear text, but compilers and interpreters parse this text into a tree-like structure which is easier to process. These structures are called the abstract syntax. Similarly, UML has an abstract syntax which is processed by model transformation and code generation. The relation in UML between concrete diagrammatic syntax and the abstract syntax it represents, is complicated enough to be a potential source of error. Precisely defining this relationship could simplify the creation of graphical model editors, and facilitate animations [EHHS00, §6] and reverse engineering. The definition should clearly delineate concrete syntax, abstract syntax and semantics, and it should also specify the relationships between these parts. We therefore require that

Criterion 1. *A UML definition should unambiguously define*

concrete syntax *the diagrams and other notation*
abstract syntax *the UML models*
notational conventions *a unique model for each diagram collection*
semantic domain *the abstract systems which models "talk about"*
semantics *whether a given model is true of a given system*

2 Applied Semantics

Avoiding possible disagreements about whether or not a given system satisfies a model is enough to motivate the semantic parts of Criterion 1. Model driven development raises other questions whose answer depends on well defined semantics.

Since the abstract syntax of UML is defined by a UML metamodel, we actually require a subset of the semantics to even know whether an alleged model actually is a well-formed model.

We need it to be clear whether or not a given model is consistent. That is, can some system satisfy this model? When we have separately modelled distinct aspects of an envisaged system, we need a system which satisfies all of the aspect models. Model consistency includes: preservation of association multiplicities and other invariants; satisfaction of pre-post-condition contracts by object behaviours; satisfaction of use-case contracts by a model; safety properties (bad things can not happen) and liveness properties (system does not get stuck).

If a model is made more concrete as a project progresses, we may wish to determine whether the more concrete model is a refinement of the more abstract one. Indeed, we may wish to establish once and for all that a certain model transformation always produces a refinement of its input model. We tentatively call such a model transformation *sound*. Refinement and soundness have various mathematical definitions, but this is not the place to make these choices. Note however that it is not enough to say that one model is a refinement when it adds some detail, because we probably want to consider non-trivial model transformations like the famous class to database schema example [BRST05] to be a kind of refinement.

We not only want these questions to have definite answers, but we would also appreciate any tool support in finding these answers.

Criterion 2. *A UML definition should settle the following questions:*

- **model consistency** *is there a system which satisfies all these models?*
- **model refinement** *is this model a refinement of that one?*
- **transformation soundness** *does output model always refine input?*

The definition should also support maximally automatic tools to help determine the answers to these questions.

3 Working with Ideas

Bran Selic has wisely observed that "software development consists primarily of expressing ideas" [Sel03]. A project attempts to improve some situation by introducing or modifying a system[2]. Ideas describing the situation must be expressed, absorbed, discussed, analysed, tested, revised and agreed on. The system itself must also be described, both at a high level, in terms of the ideas about the situation, and at the low level, using ideas about specific technologies. The high and low levels must agree, and all the ideas must be clear and free from confusion and contradiction. Indeed, the part of software development that is not about expressing ideas is mostly about generating, negotiating and translating them.

High level languages have contributed enormously to development productivity [Bro87], but ideas expressed in Fortran or Java are still far from the requirements level ideas of the human beings for whom a system is built. It is

[2] I am indebted to Shayne Flint for this view of engineering.

well known that requirements are not fully known, understood or agreed on at the beginning of a project, and that they will change before project completion. Hence effective software development requires the most direct possible coupling between the thoughts of the stakeholders and their expression in implementation languages.

When a skilled programmer writes code for her own purposes, this coupling is perfect. The jewels of computer programming are usually formed in this way. Extreme programming and other agile processes seek to couple high and low level ideas by constant face-to-face communication between stakeholders and programmers, and frequent delivery of useful code to stimulate feedback. These forms of idea coupling depend heavily on individuals. For large projects and organisations, it is desirable for the coupling of ideas to be systemic. This can be achieved by establishing model transformation and code generation chains.

We agree with Steve Cook that "... for a language to be usable to drive an automated development process, it is essential for the meaning of the language to be precise" [HS05]. Without an agreed precise meaning, an automatic translators interpretation of a model might differ from that of the stakeholders. Then the delivered system might be unsatisfactory, even dangerous. The definition of UML should therefore provide a reference for those who build model translators.

Criterion 3. *UML and friends should enable people to reach agreement on, and to directly express ideas about:*

problem domains *telecommunications, finance, logistics, ...*
implementation platforms *linux cluster, enterprise Java, ...*
translation *between these representations*

The definition should enable tools to agree with people about what these expressions mean.

We prefer to speak of "direct expression" rather than "raising the level of abstraction." A highly abstract expression of ideas might still be far from the stakeholders understanding, and thus not particularly useful.

A widespread agreement between users and toolmakers about the meaning of UML would enable trade in models and transformations. This would in turn greatly reduce the cost of developing systems. Brooks [Bro87] notes that the ability to buy software rather than build it has contributed greatly to reducing software cost. Organisations whose needs can not be met by direct purchase of software might one day be able to purchase models and transformations which can be assembled to satisfy those requirements much more cheaply than "ground up" development.

4 The Definition of UML 2.0

UML 2.0, we have observed, is not defined in the way artificial language experts normally do business. How then is it defined? In this section we will take a brief look at the small mountain of documentation [Obj06, Obj03, Obj05c, Obj05a] which defines UML. These documents will be collectively referred to from here on as *the definition*.

4.1 Metamodelling, Metacircularity and Reflection

The long and complicated story that is UML's definition begins with the "Infrastructure Specification" [Obj03]. This gives a UML model called the "Infrastructure Library," which "contains all the metaclasses required to define itself" [Obj03, §7.2.8]. The Meta Object Facility (MOF) [Obj06] builds on the infrastructure library to create a metamodelling language used to define UML [Obj05c]. This definition of UML proper begins by including the infrastructure library.

This technique, of using a modelling language to define a modelling language is called *metamodelling*.

Metamodelling need not be circular. A metamodelling language with an independent definition can properly define the abstract syntax of a modelling language. The UML definition describes its usage of metamodelling as metacircular [Obj03, §8.1], because it uses a UML subset to define UML. Without an independent definition of the metamodelling language though, the "meta" seems like an unwarranted euphemism.

Because the metamodelling language used to define the abstract syntax of UML is a subset of UML, that abstract syntax inhabits the semantic domain of the language. Having the syntax inside the semantics is also required in order to make sense of one of UML's notions of instantiation. Consider a model with a class C and an instance specification $: C$. Although it would be redundant in this situation, we join the instance specification to the class with an ≪`instanceOf`≫ arrow. Fix a semantic mapping i (interpretation) which takes the instance specification to an instance, and the class to a set of instances. The situation then can be depicted as shown in Figure 1.

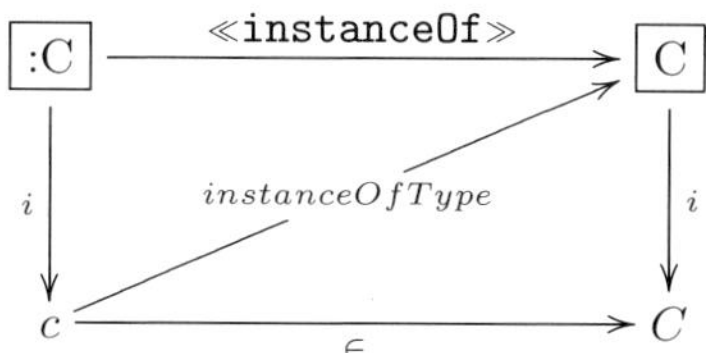

Fig. 1. Semantics of Instantiation

Ignoring the $instanceOfType$ arrow for a moment, we have a neat separation between syntax on the top line, and semantics on the bottom. So we see that the ≪`instanceOf`≫ notation in a UML diagram corresponds to "element of" ($\in$) in the system state.

The operation $instanceOfType$, defined in MOF for the metaclass Element, "returns true if this element is an instance of the specified Class..." [Obj06, §13.3]. The arrow in Figure 1 marked with this name, indicates an Element, Class pair where the operation returns true. The operation crosses the syntax/semantics divide. To make sense of such reflective notions, we not only require the syntax to be in the semantic domain, we actually need each syntactic model to be present in every system state which satisfies it.

Element is a superclass of everything in UML, and of most things in MOF. However this *instanceOfType* operation is only present in the MOF version. The superstructure explicitly disowns such reflective ideas: "The [action] semantics are also left undefined in situations that require classes as values at runtime" [Obj05c, §11.1]. A distinction is sometimes drawn between "runtime semantics" and "repository semantics" [Obj05c, §6.3]. We do not consider it necessary or desirable to support two distinct semantic definitions for what is essentially the one language. It would add work, and potentially lose the benefits of tool reuse between metamodel and model levels. The differences arise because the metamodels, as we have just seen, are slightly different. We therefore require semantics that can account for reflective operations, even though the current definition chooses to ignore them at runtime.

We summarise our findings in the following criterion. Although the last two points entail their predecessors, we list them to provide a range of "compliance levels" (in the style of [Obj05c, §2.2]).

Criterion 4. *The definition of UML should satisfy*

unity *common semantics for repository and runtime*
self-containment *semantic domain contains abstract syntax*
reflection *model contained in each of its instances*

4.2 Varieties of Variation

The UML definition contains a great number of "semantic variation points." These are places where the semantics are explicitly undefined, or where a range of possibilities are allowed. Chapter 18 of [Obj05c] describes the profiles mechanism of UML, which allows subsets and extensions of UML to be defined. Model driven development may also call for domain specific languages which can interoperate with UML models. Finally, UML 2.0 is only the latest of many revisions of the language, and will not be the last. For all these reasons, we require semantics which are *flexible.*

Criterion 5. *The definition of UML must enable the language to be adapted and extended. In particular, it requires a "semantic envelope" [Sel04] which enables precise treatment of:*

semantic variation points
profiles
domain specific languages *interoperable with UML*
later versions *of UML*

5 The UML Definition Evaluated

Having established the properties that a definition of UML ought to have, we turn now to the existing definition and ask, is it any good? We begin with a perfect score on Criterion 0, since no definition can be more faithful to the current definition than the current definition.

Criterion 1 can be summarised by saying that any proposed "definition" of UML should actually define it. Debates on whether or not a given diagram is a correct UML diagram, whether a system satisfies a given model and so on, should be easily resolved by referring to the definition. Indeed, if the definition was clear and understandable, these debates would seldom occur. That is to say, satisfying Criterion 3 on enabling agreement, is probably our best indication of whether Criterion 1 has been met. We therefore consider Criterion 3 before returning to Criteria 1 and 2.

UML does not fulfil Criterion 3 so well as we could hope, because users are not currently able to easily reach agreement about the meaning of a model.

> ... many people are confused about what these [UML] concepts ... really mean and how to understand and use them [HR04]

> Developers can waste considerable time resolving disputes over usage and interpretation of notation. [BF98]

We have had similar experiences when attempting to extract the precise meaning of a diagram from groups of experienced UML practitioners: diverse interpretations each received vigorous support. Debate continues at the OMG over fundamental matters such as the semantics of associations and their ends [Obj, Issue #5977][Mil06]. It seems fair to conclude that there is not widespread agreement about the meaning of UML models.

It is not valid to infer from this that the definition lacks precision, because the lack of agreement could be the result of the definition being difficult to understand. This would be unfortunate, since it explicitly strives for understandability, even at the cost of some precision [Obj03, §8] (quoted on Page 42). To us, it seems more plausible that the definition is neither precise nor understandable.

The quote from the UML definition argues that a mathematical approach involves too much work, and is not necessary to get the job done. Whether or not Greek letters and other fancy symbols are employed, precise definitions of abstract ideas *are mathematical*. If we choose to ignore the accumulated wisdom of the mathematical discipline, and define things our own way, we commit the same error as "hackers" who refuse to follow established software engineering practice. Like the hackers, we are likely to get ourselves into the kind of trouble that the experts know how to avoid. One simply does not find disagreements about the meaning of definitions in mathematics, but after almost 10 years even the basics of UML are still in dispute.

Turning to Criterion 2, one could hardly hope to settle questions of model consistency, refinement and transformation soundness without true definitions of the relevant concepts. It should not surprise us then that Stephen Mellor finds a lack of support for model consistency testing in the current definition [HS05]. He claims that the definition fails to detect the apparent inconsistency of his small example model. We conclude then that the definition rates poorly on Criteria 1, 2 and 3.

Criterion 4, on reflection, is really a detail of Criterion 0, since it records what is entailed by the definition. Criterion 5 on flexibility, is only challenging for a rigorous definition. "Semantic variation points" offer perfect flexibility. Interpretation of the metamodel diagrams by object-oriented folk-law is sufficient for current tools, which only manipulate the syntax. Without adequate support for the other criteria though, these benefits are of little use.

To achieve a definition which satisfies our criteria then, we may have to tolerate a little mathematics. The next section surveys some of the work applicable to this task.

6 The UML Formalisation Literature

Since the current definition does not satisfy the requirements, we would like an improved definition for UML. The new definition should agree with the current one, including its reflective metamodelling approach, it should define the semantics sufficiently to enable automated checking of consistency, refinement and soundness, and it should be flexible and understandable. We now take a brief look at some work related to improving the definition of UML, in the light of our criteria.

Kim, Carrington and Burger [KC00, KBC05] give explicit translations between Object-Z and class diagrams. In the earlier work, the syntax of both languages is expressed in Object-Z, and the translation is also defined there. A metamodel of Object-Z is provided for the benefit of modellers unfamiliar with this formal language. In the later work, the metamodels define the syntax, and the translation is defined using a dedicated model transformation language. Unfortunately, even this recent work only addresses a subset of the class diagram fragment of UML. The work aims to enable formal verification of UML models, but as yet we have no demonstration nor descriptions of specific techniques.

Model Driven Architecture [MM03] aims to enable the simultaneous use of many languages, each with syntax defined in MOF, by using model transformations between these languages. The real contribution of [KBC05] is in recognising that formal languages can also participate in this way. Definitive formal semantics could be provided by a Z (or Object-Z or dynamic logic or ...) metamodel and UML to Z model transformation. This would enable tool integration, and provide insight into the formalism for the more advanced modellers. Attempts to directly translate diagrams into formal languages usually ignore the metamodel definition of the language, and thus violate Criterion 0.

Bruel and France [BF98] advocate an integration of UML and formal methods, in which a UML class diagram is translated into the formal specification language Z. The Z specification is then manually refined, adding details not expressible using class diagrams. The rules and guidelines for semi-automatic translation, they hope, will give insights for developing a more precise semantics for UML.

Rasch and Wehrheim [RW03] also advocate integration of a formal language, in this case Object-Z, into the development process. The Object-Z specification manually derived from the class diagram also specifies the class operations. The class is further constrained by a protocol state-machine, which together with the Object-Z schema, is translated into CSP. The choice of CSP, which is even less readable than Z, seems to be motivated mostly by the availability of a model checker[3] which they aim to use for consistency testing. They consider several notions of consistency and study which of these are preserved under CSP notions of refinement. We are not convinced that the intended semantics of the UML fragment are captured by this translation. It is also not clear that the CSP notions of refinement are applicable. We see little hope that modellers and transformation authors will become familiar with both Object-Z and CSP.

The association end annotation {`unique`} is the subject of a recent controversy [Obj, Issue #5977]. Dragan Milicev [Mil06] proposes semantics which reconcile the apparently conflicting parts of the UML definition. These semantics concern associations, their ends and the read, create, and destroy link actions. In an appendix to the report, Milicev gives an example model to illustrate the controversy, and expresses his semantics for it in Z. This is intended merely as a precise statement of the proposal explained in the body of the paper. However, this is the most convincing example we have seen of using Z to express dynamic aspects of UML. It is also a good example of why Z will never be widely used by developers: it is not easy to read.

Algebraic specification extended with "generalised labelled transition systems" is used by Gianna Reggio, Maura Cerioli and Egidio Astesiano to formalise parts of UML in [RCA01] and earlier papers by the same authors. They do this by translating UML diagrams into the language Casl-LTL, though they emphasise that the particular language is immaterial. This work explicitly aims for a way of giving useful formal semantics to the whole of UML, and as the title suggests, they take seriously the idea that the different diagrams combine to specify a single system. However they ignore the fact that the official definition already interprets the variety of diagrams into a single abstract syntactic entity, the model. The authors note the expressive demands made by UML's dynamic diagrams.

> It is worth noting that to state the behavioural axioms we need some temporal logic combinators available in Casl-Ltl that we have no space to illustrate here. The expressive power of such temporal logic will also be crucial for the translation of sequence diagrams...

Indeed, Z and its derivatives would face similar difficulties. A later paper [AR02] by Astesiano and Reggio studies UML consistency from their algebraic point of view, and also uses a metamodel to describe the formal language being used.

The Object Constraint Language (OCL) [Obj05a] is very much like the languages of traditional symbolic logic, and at least two groups have attempted to make it precise by translating it into well understood systems of logic, intending to enable theorem proving about models. Brucker and Wolff [BW02] use higher order logic (HOL) as implemented in the generic interactive theorem prover Isabelle. Beckert, Keller and Schmitt [BKS02] use first order logic. OCL 2.0 has a third truth value "undefined" and allows collections of collections, so first order logic will probably not suffice to formally define it. Neither group make use of

[3] Note that this is not a tool intended for checking UML models. "Model" here is a technical term from symbolic logic, meaning interpretation.

the OCL metamodel in their translations. Beckert's group offer different, equivalent translations optimised for readability or for automated theorem proving respectively. With a foundation as suggested in these works, OCL itself could be the target formal language for a model transformation defining the semantics of UML. This would probably require additions to the current limited temporal operators of OCL though.

The OCL formalisation of Beckert and Schmitt [BKS02] is used in their the KeY project [ABB+05]. This is a tool for the deductive verification of Java-Card programs using a specialised dynamic logic [Bec01]. This logic is implemented in a generic theorem prover integrated with the Together modelling tool, and thus provides a practical platform integrating UML modelling and formal methods. Although this work is not aimed at improving the definition of UML, it is instructive. The deductive rules symbolically execute the Java-Card program, and thus give a clear and precise account of the language semantics. The rules could even provide educational interactive animations of the language.

Unlike Java-Card, UML is non-deterministic and has no `main` procedure, but it is conceivable that one could develop such a dynamic logic for UML. The logic would have rules for each of the UML actions. This would define model dynamics, and the meaning of each of the diagrams could be expressed by translation into the dynamic logic language. It would also enable deductive verification of UML models. In its traditional form, dynamic logic is even less readable than Z. But a UML specific logic could use OCL notation for its static parts, whilst the program parts would be written using the yet to be fixed standard UML action language.

Wieringa and Broerson [WB97] use a formal language derived from dynamic logic to give formal semantics for parts of UML class and state machine diagrams. As in earlier work by Wieringa, a "methodological analysis" leads the authors to diverge radically from the official definition: a system is a black box, which responds instantly to external stimuli. It is not possible for example to make sense of a sequence diagrams in such a system. This might be a useful interpretation of UML for requirements engineering, as these authors see it, but from our perspective, it is inventing a new language rather than providing a better definition of the existing one.

We take this opportunity to mention our own work [O'K06], which uses standard dynamic logic to give precise semantics to a UML subset with class, state machine and sequence diagrams, and send and receive actions. Tableau theorem proving techniques are employed to test model consistency. Other work on sequence diagrams require every occurrence to be made explicit in the diagram, whereas our formalisation allows hidden occurrences in between the explicit ones. This raises the level of abstraction, appropriately ignoring details that the sequence diagram author does not care about. This work makes no attempt to handle visibility and polymorphism issues. Standard dynamic logic is probably not suitable for a full UML fomalisation, as it lacks higher order expressions and parallel composition.

The first plausible demonstration of deductive verification of UML models is given by Arons, Hooman, Kugler, Pnueli and van der Zwaag, in [TAKP+04]. The semantics are not described in this paper, but are derived from those of [DJPV03]. That paper gives formal semantics to a small executable subset of UML intended for real-time applications, using Pnueli's "symbolic transition systems." Much of the considerable complexity of that work comes from the need to model hard real-time systems, which makes us wonder whether the general modelling community might get by with something simpler. The abstract syntax of the official definition is ignored, and a traditional formal syntax is given for the selected UML subset. The later deductive verification work uses a temporal logic embedded into the higher order logic of the PVS interactive theorem prover. A model given by a class diagram and state machine diagrams with some actions, is automatically translated from `.xmi` form into PVS sources. Issues of consistency are deliberately avoided, since deductive verification of liveness properties and safety properties are challenging enough at this stage. Several strong assumptions are made about the execution semantics, which are not present in the official definition. Deductive verification is not required for most applications of UML, but supporting formal proof demonstrates that a definition is precise and unambiguous, which we have demanded in Criterion 1. This formalisation uses a language with both temporal and higher order features, so it is not subject to many of the limitations we have identified for other approaches. Most of our criteria are not addressed by this work however. Most urgently, we need techniques to check consistency, and we need the meaning of models to be understood by non-technical modellers and end users.

Several workers [ZHG05, EHHS00] employ graphs and graph transformations [BH02] to give formal semantics to UML. In this way, a system state can literally be an object diagram, which is clearly much easier to understand than the usual logico-mathematical offerings. The graph transformation rules, which define the system dynamics, can be given using UML collaboration diagrams [EHHS00]. Metamodels are usually static, consisting of only class diagrams. If we included collaboration diagrams in the metamodelling language, we could view metamodels as specifications of graph transformation systems. Thus we can define semantics for a modelling language by providing a model transformation from the modelling language to the metamodelling language! This would be a significant change to MOF, but seems well motivated and could win support. Unfortunately the specific metamodel proposed in [EHHS00] depends on the Object metaclass in 1.x UML metamodels. This is widely accepted to have been confused, and has been removed in UML 2.0. Model consistency from a graphical point of view is considered in [EHHS02]. Graph transformation offers the attractive prospect of a common language for practical software engineers and academic theoreticians. This combination of rigour and understandability, we believe, is the key to satisfying all our Criteria. The present author will be reading more about graph transformation.

All the work we have discussed takes part of UML and translates it into another language with formal semantics. An alternative would be to use English and elementary mathematics to define the semantics[4]. This approach would allow us to use specific formalisms for specific tasks, whilst avoiding their expressive limitations when defining the semantics. It is easy to adapt an English/mathematical text, but this does not automatically integrate the new interpretation with existing tools. An alternative is to directly define semantics for a core of UML, then translate the remainder of the language into this by model transformation. This seems to be the intention of the OMG's current request for proposal on an executable UML foundation [Obj05b].

Model transformation from UML to a language with precise semantics seems the most promising method for improving the definition of UML. The formal language must be able to express temporal and higher order concepts, handle scoping and polymorphism, and admit automated consistency checking. Perhaps the most challenging requirement though, is that it should enable people to better understand UML models.

7 Conclusion

Too much of the work on UML semantics looks like a technical answer which is glad to have found a good practical question. We have asked what that question actually is, and refined it in the form of criteria for an improved definition. It is our hope that future work will explicitly address the larger task of improving the definition of UML. Our criteria might serve as goalposts for formalisation work, or as targets for demolition by more worthy replacements. Either way, it is a step towards the more desirable situation where a practical question seeks a technical answer.

References

ABB+05. Wolfgang Ahrendt, Thomas Baar, Bernhard Beckert, Richard Bubel, Martin Giese, Reiner Hähnle, Wolfram Menzel, Wojciech Mostowski, Andreas Roth, Steffen Schlager, and Peter H. Schmitt. The KeY tool. *Software and System Modeling*, 4(1):32–54, 2005.

AR02. Egidio Astesiano and Gianna Reggio. An attempt at analysing the consistency problems in the UML from a classical algebraic viewpoint. In *WADT*, pages 56–81, 2002.

Bec01. Bernhard Beckert. A dynamic logic for the formal verification of java card programs. In *Java on Smart Cards: Programming and Security*, number 2041 in LNCS, pages 6–24. Springer, 2001.

Bel04. Alex E. Bell. Death by UML fever. *Queue*, 2(1):72–80, 2004.

BF98. Jean-Michel Bruel and Robert B. France. Transforming UML models to formal specifications. In *Proceedings of the OOPSLA'98 Workshop on Formalising UML*, 1998.

[4] This apparently obvious idea had not occurred to us before it was pointed out by Peter Schmitt.

BH02. Luciano Baresi and Reiko Heckel. Tutorial introduction to graph transformation: A software engineering perspective. In *Proceedings of the first International Workshop on Theory and Application of Graph Transformation*, pages 402–429, 2002.

BKS02. Bernhard Beckert, Uwe Keller, and Peter H. Schmitt. Translating the object constraint language into first-order predicate logic. In *Proceedings of VERIFY, Workshop at Federated Logic conferences (FLoC)*, 2002.

Bro87. Frederick P. Brooks, Jr. No silver bullet: Essence and accidents of software engineering. *Computer*, May 1987.

BRST05. Jean Bézivin, Bernhard Rumpe, Andy Schür, and Laurence Tratt. Model transformations in practice workshop, call for papers. web, July 2005. `http://sosym.dcs.kcl.ac.uk/events/mtip05/long_cfp.pdf`.

Buz95. Tony Buzan. *The Mind-Map Book*. BBC Books, 2nd edition, 1995.

BW02. Achim D. Brucker and Burkhart Wolff. A proposal for a formal OCL semantics in Isabelle/HOL. In V.A Carren no, C. Mu noz, and S. Tahar, editors, *TPHOLS 2002*, volume 2410 of *LNCS*, pages 99–114. Springer-Verlag, 2002.

DJPV03. Werner Damm, Bernhard Josko, Amir Pnueli, and Angelika Votintseva. Understanding UML: A formal semantics of concurrency and communication in real-time UML. In *Formal Methods for Components and Objects, Proceedings 2002*, volume 2852 of *LNCS*. Springer, 2003.

EHHS00. Gregor Engels, Jan Hendrik Hausmann, Reiko Heckel, and Stefan Sauer. Dynamic meta modeling: A graphical approach to the operational semantics of behavioural diagrams in UML. In *Proceedings of UML*, volume 1939. LNCS, 2000.

EHHS02. Gregor Engels, Jan Hendrik Hausmann, Reiko Heckel, and Stefan Sauer. Testing the consistency of dynamic uml diagrams. *Integrated Design and Process Technology*, 2002.

HR04. David Harel and Bernhard Rumpe. Meaningful modeling: What's the semantics of "semantics"? *Computer*, pages 64–72, October 2004.

HS05. Brian Henderson-Sellers. UML - the good, the bad or the ugly? perspectives from a panel of experts. *Software and System Modeling*, 4(1):4–13, 2005.

KBC05. Soon-Kyeong Kim, Damian Burger, and David A. Carrington. An MDA approach towards integrating formal and informal modeling languages. In *FM*, pages 448–464, 2005.

KC00. Soon-Kyeong Kim and David A. Carrington. A formal mapping between UML models and object-Z specifications. In *Proceedings of the First International Conference of B and Z Users on Formal Specification and Development in Z and B*, pages 2–21, 2000.

Mil06. D. Milicev. On the semantics of associations and association ends in UML. Technical report, University of Belgrade, School of Electrical Engineering, February 2006.

MM03. Joaquin Miller and Jishnu Mukerji. MDA guide. Technical report, Object Management Group, 2003. `http://www.omg.org/mda`.

Obj. Object Management Group. Issues for the UML 2 revision task force. web. `http://www.omg.org/issues/uml2-rtf.html`.

Obj03. Object Management Group. UML 2.0 infrastructure specification. Technical report, Object Management Group, 2003. `http://www.omg.org/docs/ptc/03-09-15.pdf`.

Obj05a. Object Management Group. OCL 2.0 specification. Technical report, Object Management Group, 2005. `http://www.omg.org/docs/ptc/05-06-06.pdf`.

Obj05b. Object Management Group. Request for proposals: Semantics of a foundational subset for executable UML models, 2005. `http://www.omg.org/docs/ad/05-04-02.pdf`.

Obj05c. Object Management Group. Unified modeling language: Superstructure. Technical report, Object Management Group, 2005. `http://www.omg.org/docs/formal/05-07-04.pdf`.

Obj06. Object Management Group. Meta object facility (MOF) 2.0 core specification. Technical report, Object Management Group, 2006. `http://www.omg.org/docs/formal/06-01-01.pdf`.

O'K06. Greg O'Keefe. Dynamic logic for UML consistency. In *ECMDA-FA, European Conference on Model Driven Architecture*, number 4066 in Lecture Notes in Computer Science, pages 113–127. Springer, 2006. `http://rsise.anu.edu.au/~okeefe/dl4uml.pdf`.

RCA01. Gianna Reggio, Maura Cerioli, and Egidio Astesiano. Towards a rigourous semantics of UML supporting its multiview approach. In H. Hussmann, editor, *FASE 2001*, volume 2029 of *LNCS*, pages 171–186. Springer, 2001.

RW03. Holger Rasch and Heike Wehrheim. Checking consistency in uml diagramms: Classes and state machines. In *FMOODS*, pages 229–243, 2003.

Sel03. Bran Selic. The pragmatics of model-driven development. *IEEE Software*, 2003.

Sel04. Bran V. Selic. On the semantic foundations of standard UML 2.0. In Marco Bernardo and Flavio Corradini, editors, *Formal Methods for the Design of Real-Time Systems: International School on Formal Methods for the Design of Computer, Communication, and Software Systems*, number 3185 in LNCS, 2004.

TAKP+04. J. Hooman T. Arons, H. Kugler, A. Pnueli, , and M. van der Zwaag. Deductive verification of UML models in tlpvs. In *Proceedings UML*, 2004.

WB97. Roel Wieringa and Jan Broerson. Minimal transition system semantics for lightweight class and behaviour diagrams. In Manfred Broy, Derek Coleman, Tom S. E. Maibaum, and Bernhard Rumpe, editors, *Proceedings PSMT'98 Workshop on Precise Semantics for Modeling Techniques*. Technische Universitaet Muenchen, TUM-I9803, April 1997.

ZHG05. Paul Ziemann, Karsten Hölscher, and Martin Gogolla. From UML models to graph transformation systems. *Electr. Notes Theor. Comput. Sci.*, 127(4):17–33, 2005.

Adopting Model Driven Software Development in Industry – A Case Study at Two Companies

Miroslaw Staron

Software Engineering and Management
Department of Applied IT
IT University in Göteborg, Box 8718
SE-402 75 Göteborg, Sweden
miroslaw.staron@ituniv.se

Abstract. Model Driven Software Development (MDD) is a vision of software development where models play a core role as primary development artifacts. Its industrial adoption depends on several factors, including possibilities of increasing productivity and quality by using models. In this paper we present a case study of two companies willing to adopt the principles of MDD. One of the companies is in the process of adopting MDD while the other withdrew from its initial intentions. The results provide insights into the differences in requirements for MDD in these organizations, factors determining the decision upon adoption and the potentially suitable modeling notation for the purpose of each of the companies. The analysis of the results from this case study, supported by the conclusions from a previous case study of a successful MDD adoption, show also which conditions should be fulfilled in order to increase the chances of succeeding in adopting MDD.

1 Introduction

Model Driven Software Development (MDD, [2, 3]) is a new trend in utilizing models in software development. The models are used as primary artifacts in constructing software; in practice it often means that the code is generated from models and thus the models need to be used efficiently and effectively. The vision of MDD requires shifting the focus of estimations, analyses, or evaluations from code to models. For example, the initial complexity analyses should be done based on models or test planning and development should be done based on models.

In this paper we present an exploratory study at two companies on the adoption of MDD in their organizations: ABB Robotics in Västerås, Sweden and Ericsson, Sweden. The main goal of this study is to provide evidence on how industry approaches the issues related to adopting MDD. The results are related to the findings from other studies on MDD or software process improvement adoption in industry (described in the related work section). Combining these results allows choosing the most cost efficient realization of MDD in industry given the current state-of-the-art in modeling methods and tools. Together with another experience report [4] on MDD realization, this paper outlines the requirements for making the introduction of MDD smoother in large industrial organizations. In this paper we address the main research question in

O. Nierstrasz et al. (Eds.): MoDELS 2006, LNCS 4199, pp. 57–72, 2006.

the study: *Which elements are important in adopting MDD in companies developing software for embedded systems with a large knowledge base and legacy code?* It was our main intention to investigate the companies with large legacy code and proprietary processes as the introduction of new technologies is significantly more difficult than in small and medium size companies. The main research question was then divided into three sub-questions:

RQ1: *What are requirements for adopting MDD in the company?*
RQ2: *Which factors determine whether MDD should be adopted in the company?*
RQ3: *Which scenario of using models in software development is the most suitable for the company?*

Our previous case studies on the adoption of a particular instance of MDD, the Model Driven Architecture (MDA, [2]), resulted in setting up the background for the studies presented in this paper [5, 6]. These are evaluated in another context in the two companies in this study.

The findings from the two companies presented in this paper show that high demands of quality, and measurements based on models lead to the decision that the current state of the art in MDD and technology maturity do not provide enough support for cost efficient adoption of MDD. This was in the case of a company which had a large base of legacy code to be integrated with the new code developed in the MDD-compatible way. In the case of the company which was not so much dependent on the legacy code (although the integration issues were still crucial, these were based on interfaces and protocols, not static linking) it is possible to adopt MDD in a cost efficient way.

This paper is structured as follows. The related work is presented in Section 2. The main principles of MDD are presented in Section 3. The design of the case study is presented in Section 4 and the results of the case study are analyzed in Section 5. Threats to validity of the study are presented in Section 6, and are followed by identification of conditions that should be fulfilled for successful adoption are presented in Section 7 and conclusions are drawn in Section 8.

2 Related Work

MacDonald et al. [4] present an experience report from a case study, performed partially at a company and partially at academia, on model driven development of embedded software. The context of the company is similar to the context of ABB as there was a substantial amount of legacy code involved. The results of that case study show that currently MDD does not lead to increase in efficiency, effectiveness, or productivity in the context of software development with a large amount of legacy code. Although their results are in line with the conclusions from ABB (part of our study) their case study lacked the analysis of the decision on whether MDD should be adopted or not. The results of that case study, nevertheless, are used to complement the factors investigated in RQ2: Which factors determine whether MDD should be adopted in the company?

An experiment performed in an industrial context by Middleware company [7] showed that using MDA in projects increases productivity significantly. The results seem to be contradictory to the results from the case study by MacDonald et al. The difference might be caused by the fact that the domains and development methods differ. These differences indicate also that at this stage of MDD maturity it is impossible to draw conclusions about MDD adoption in general and more empirical evidence is needed to establish the conditions that determine the success or failure of introducing MDD. This paper contributes with such evidence.

Modeling notations play a central role in MDD and thus building them is an important issue for MDD adopters. Evans et al. [8] provide a set of theoretical considerations on the differences between various ways of building modeling languages in MDD. The experiences reported in their paper were included as a basis for the study in this paper. Their results, however, suffer from two deficiencies – they are done theoretically and seem to overlook software engineering aspects of creating and using modeling languages. Therefore we complement their results with a study by Atkinson and Kühne [9] which showed various ways building the modeling tools that influence ways of defining modeling languages and creating models. In particular the combined results were used in the workshops conducted at Ericsson (due to the time of publishing their paper, it was not possible to use it in the study at ABB). As an addition to the study of Atkinson and Kühne, we need to consider the ideas of software factories, an alternative approach presented by Greenfield and Short [10]. The scenarios of using models in their approach were taken into consideration while designing the case study presented in this paper.

As UML is a core element in MDA, its adoption in industry has a significant influence on the adoption of MDA and MDD in general. A survey of the adoption of UML by Grossman et al. [11] addressed this question. His conclusions and results are used in the discussion while addressing RQ3 (Which scenario of using models in software development is the most suitable for the company?*)*. The results presented by Grossman et al. indicated that UML is widely adopted in industry, although the sample in their survey consisted of companies that use UML for communicating requirements and not during designing.

3 MDD Principles

The way in which the companies can adopt MDD is presented in Figure 1 which shows an adaptation of the modeling spectrum by Brown [1]. In this paper we perceive this spectrum as a basis for describing how models are used in software development. The left hand side of the spectrum represents the traditional development without graphical modeling – the code is the main artifact. The right hand side of the spectrum represents the opposite of it, the code playing a secondary role and the development is done solely using models (e.g. utilizing executable modeling techniques). The model centric approach is an ambitious goal of MDD as it still is based on code while the models are the main artifacts. Most (or all, if possible) of the code is generated from models; the developers, however, are given a possibility to add the code and synchronize it with models. The fact that the code can be altered after it is generated and it can be synchronized is close to the idea of roundtrip engineering, where the code and the model coexist and one is synchronized once the other is updated. Such a usage scenario can be seen as an advanced usage of models which is the

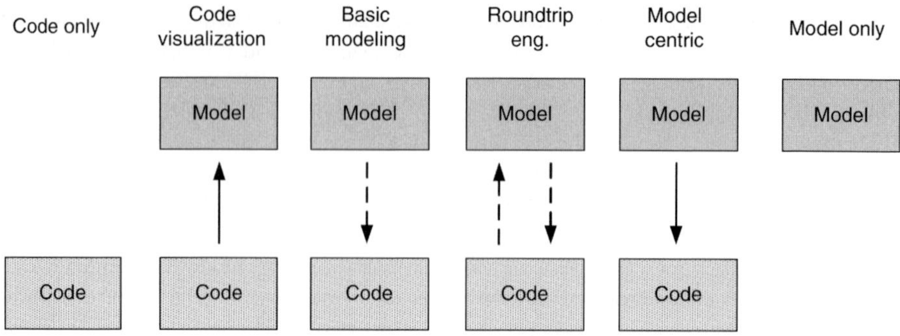

Fig. 1. MDD adoption spectrum, adapted from [1]

extension of the idea of basic modeling. The basic modeling represents a situation when models are used as a documentation and as basic (usually architectural only) sketches of the software to be built. The models and the code coexist but the code is the main artifact which is used in the course of software development. In the code visualization scenario the code is the main artifact; models are generated automatically and are not used to develop software, but to provide means of understanding the code. There is no sharp borderline which of the usage scenarios (except for "code only") can be seen as a realization of MDD; all of them are included in RQ3.

4 Case Study Design

This case study was based on the experiences from a previous case study conducted at a company which successfully adopted MDD [6]. In this case study we adopted the principles of fixed research design as advocated by Robson [12] in order to increase the comparability of results between the two companies in the study. As the two companies are essentially different, the interviews were quite open albeit customized for each company.

4.1 Context and Subjects

The first studied company is ABB Robotics (further abbreviated to ABB). The core business area of the company is development of mechatronic systems with embedded software. The studied development unit was responsible for developing the embedded software for the robots built in cooperation between several units at the company. The overall intention behind the company's interest in MDD was improving such quality attributes of their software as portability, correctness and early assessment. The development environment in the company consists of several development units specializing in development and lifecycle management of specialized components. The components have been (and still are) developed for a number of years, which resulted in a large amount of legacy code to be constantly maintained and extended. Components are developed using various programming languages and paradigms – ranging from assembler to C#. The company has good control over their process and their development practices, although they could see potential for improvements. This company was studied as it had precise goals for adopting modeling with the long term aim of using models as core development artifacts. There were no pilot projects related to MDD adoption in the organization prior to the case study, although the company did study the applicability of MDD in their context prior to our visit.

The other company included in this case study is a unit of Ericsson in Sweden. The overall business of Ericsson is mobile telecommunication technology and the studied organization was responsible for development of new services for mobile platforms. The overall intention of this organization in adopting MDD was to increase the competitiveness of the company by increasing the productivity of its developers. The productivity increase could be achieved by increasing the portability and reuse of the software developed in the organization. In the study of this company we used the same materials as for ABB after verifying their applicability.

The subjects in the case study were staff of two teams (one at each company) consisting of people deciding upon the adoption; staff well into the domain of the company although admitting that they are not so much into MDD (at least at the time of the study). They, nevertheless, had experience in modeling using UML and their intention was to increase the use of models to increase productivity. This staff could be seen as frontier development people or early adopters of the technology. Their roles in the organizations were:

- at ABB: three designers/developers and a manager
- at Ericsson: two managers, a technical coordinator, and an architect.

All subjects are working for the companies for a significant period of time and participated in projects similar to the projects for which they considered adopting MDD practices. At the time of the study their knowledge in modeling was sufficient since the focus of the case study is put more on the issues related to adopting MDD in industry and not evaluating MDD or its applicability. However, we also evaluated the other approach – Software Factories, but it was not applicable, due to the fact that the technology was not mature enough at the current stage. The project needed stable and reliable technology, thus going for the UML-based tools.

4.1.1 Context Differences

Despite the fact that the companies operate in a similar domain, their contexts are different. The direct difference is the fact that Ericsson had conducted a pilot project prior to making the decision, which was not the case of ABB. It seems that the pilot project influenced the decision at Ericsson in the following way:

- it showed that the technology considered in the company is usable,
- it provided estimates on the required amount of changes in processes, methods, and tools used in software development

The above bullets are feasible and we see them as highly probable, but no formal evaluation of the pilot project was conducted at the company due to the lack of sufficient data. In our interviews, however, we asked whether the success of the pilot project was one of the major adoption factors; we found that the pilot project was mainly done as a feasibility study to estimate the amount of effort needed to adopt MDD. As we started our preparations for the case study, the pilot project was still on-going so it was at a similar point of time (with respect to making the decision) as at ABB.

Although the studied organization within Ericsson has already a lot of expertise in the domain, they are in the process of adopting Java-based technologies together with MDD principles in this particular part of the organization. The company is also adopting the MDD and, as a part of that, the factors identified in the previous case study at Volvo IT [6]. Ericsson's ability to access experiences (simply due to the time difference) from other adopters might have been one of the factors influencing the decision. This seemed not to be the factor as the studied unit at ABB did not change their decision over the course of time.

Another notable difference between the companies is the strong need for integration of diverse programming languages and paradigms at ABB. This need, together with the need to incorporate a large legacy code-base made it impossible to introduce MDD in a cost-effective way with risk minimization strategies – e.g. introducing MDD in stages. These strategies are being implemented at Ericsson.

4.2 Data Collection and Analysis Methods

The instruments in the case study were questionnaires in which had several alternatives to evaluate. We also used unstructured interviews as a complement to the questionnaires. At the beginning we used a workshop (with a focus group) at ABB to elaborate the initial set of requirements, factors and modeling scenarios that should be included in the later evaluation.

The questionnaires contained a set of questions to be valued using the 5 point Likert scale. We deliberately chose the Likert scale since it does not force the respondents to directly prioritize alternatives, but evaluate each of them independently. Naturally, for each question there were empty spaces left for adding new alternatives and evaluating them. The questions to be evaluated consist of three questions (corresponding to research questions RQ1 – RQ3) with several alternatives to be evaluated separately using the Likert scale.

The questions in the interviews regarded such aspects as: the purpose of adopting MDD, the role of MDD in software development, and their intentions and hopes for introducing MDD. In order to analyze the quantitative data from questionnaires we used descriptive statistics (mean, median, and standard deviation). Due to a small number of data points caused by a sample size (four persons in each organization) no inferential statistics were used. The data obtained during the interviews was analyzed in a qualitative way in order to obtain a more in-depth understanding of the organizations' needs and requirements for MDD. Using qualitative approach minimized the threat of combining the data biased by their context as advocated by Miller [13].

4.3 Operation

The case study at two companies was done in two distinct periods of time. The study at ABB was conducted in between March and October 2004 and the study at Ericsson was conducted between March and December 2005. At each company the study was done in the following steps:

1. Focus group workshop and interviews
2. Questionnaires

During the interviews and focus group meeting the context of the company we elicited and exploited their intentions and views on MDD. The list of requirements, factors and potential modeling scenarios were defined as a result of step 1 at ABB. They were later on used in the questionnaires at ABB and Ericsson. Step 1 at Ericsson was dedicated to verifying the applicability of the study for Ericsson.

5 Results and Analysis

The results are analyzed based on the research questions posed in the introduction. They are preceded with the presentation of the results of workshops with the focus group at ABB which were the basis for further evaluation – i.e. the basis for creating the questionnaires.

5.1 Aspects Important in Adopting MDD

During the workshops with both companies the aspects important in the adoption of MDD were identified. The issues of organizational change were not considered since the sample was not appropriate to evaluate them. The particular aspects, presented as questions in the questionnaire were:

Question 1: If you use (would use) models how important it is to …?

a) Automatically generate code from models
b) Be able to estimate (based on models) the cost of software to be built
c) Verify correctness of software before it is built by verifying models
d) Improve quality of the created software by using models to improve understanding
e) Measure designs and to identify potential problems (e.g. fault-prone classes)
f) Use models to improve communication with customers
g) Use models to improve communication within your development team
h) Enable traceability throughout software development by using models
i) Automate software development process by providing means of automated generation of various artifacts from models (e.g. initial versions of design models from analysis models)

Question 2: If you were to decide upon choosing what kind of models to build, which would be the factors that you would consider?

a) Availability of modeling tools
b) Knowledge of staff involved in modeling
c) Cost of introducing the modeling technique to the process
d) Cost of creating models while developing software
e) Possibility to quality assessment of model and then predict (and improve) the quality of code
f) Ability of the model to be executed (the model itself can be executed before the code is generated)
g) Number of changes required to use models in your current software development practices

Question 3: What kind of modeling language(s) do you think would be the most suitable for your purposes?
a) standard UML used only for documentation
b) standard UML used for code generation
c) UML + one specific UML profile for your needs (e.g. RT profile)
d) UML + several specific UML profiles
e) UML + another modeling language (e.g. BetterState)
f) Other modeling languages
g) None, the intention is to invent our own notation and use it informally

The answers to these questions provided us with the data to analyze the issues related to adoption of MDD.

5.2 Requirements for MDD (RQ1)

Table 1 contains the descriptive statistics for answers to question 1. It should be noted that no additional requirements were added by any of the respondents. The averages which are ranked as important and very important are in boldface.

Table 1. Results for requirements

Alternative	ABB			Ericsson		
	Mean	Median	Std. dev	Mean	Median	Std. dev
a: automatically generate code	2	1.5	1.41	3.25	3	0.50
b: estimate cost	3.75	3.5	0.96	**4.25**	4	0.50
c: verify correctness	3.5	3.5	0.58	3.5	3.5	0.58
d: improve quality / understanding	**4.75**	5	0.50	**4.25**	4	0.50
e: measure des. / identify problems	**4.25**	4	0.50	3.75	3.5	0.96
f: improve com. w/customer	2	2	0.82	2.75	3	0.50
g: improve com. w/dev. team	**4.75**	5	0.50	**4.25**	4	0.50
h: enable traceability	3.25	3.5	0.96	**4.25**	4.5	0.96
i: automate generation of artifacts	2.5	2.5	1.29	3.5	4	1.00

Table 1 shows that for the adopters of MDD, the main requirements for MDD are:

b) the ability to estimate costs based on models
d) improving quality by increasing understanding
g) improving communication within development team
h) traceability throughout software development artifacts (models)

These requirements are equally important and two of them (d and g) overlap with the most important requirements as stated by the other company which did not decide to adopt MDD. This indicates that companies see MDD as a solution to similar problems. The third of the most important requirements for that company is the ability to measure designs and identify problem areas based on the measurements (requirement e). On the other hand, the non-adopting company (*non-adopter*) did not consider the requirements b and h as important to the same extent as the adopting company (*adopter*). Furthermore, the small values of the standard deviations indicate that the respondents were consistent with their views, which could indicate their maturity in opinions.

5.3 Factors Determining Adoption (RQ2)

Table 2 contains the evaluation of the factors that are considered during the decision whether MDD should be adopted. Neither of the respondents added any alternatives for this question.

Table 2. Results for factors

Alternative	ABB			Ericsson		
	Mean	Median	Std. dev	Mean	Median	Std. dev.
a: availability of tools	**4.25**	4.5	0.96	**4**	4	0.00
b: staff knowledge	**4.5**	5	1.00	3.33	3	0.58
c: introduction costs	3.75	3.5	0.96	**4**	4	1.00
d: modeling costs	3.75	3.5	0.96	**4**	4	1.00
e: quality assessment	**4.5**	4.5	0.58	3.67	4	0.58
f: model execution	2.5	3	1.00	2.67	3	0.58
g: process adaptation	3.75	3.5	0.96	3.67	4	1.53

The MDD adopters value three factors as the most important ones:
 a) availability of modeling tools
 c) cost of introducing the modeling technique to the process
 d) cost of creating modeling during software development
In addition to factor a, the most important factors for the non-adopters were:
 b) knowledge of staff involved in modeling
 e) possibility to control quality using models
What seems to be interesting is that the adopters did not consider the knowledge of the staff to be an important factor, while the availability of tools was rated as an important issue. This indicates that the company is willing to adopt the solutions provided by tool vendors rather than to pose requirements for their own MDD framework and tools. This seems to be a solution that is cheaper since the company is willing to adopt the tools that are on the market. Such an approach was also considered as one of the crucial ones in another industrial case study [6] on MDD adoption.

In the case study by MacDonald et al [4] a set of requirements for tools supporting MDD was drawn. These requirements contained such desired features as:

- Full support for the modeling language (i.e. the ability to use all language constructs in the tool – e.g. not a subset of UML)
- Rich platform independent libraries, and a possibility to map these libraries to platform specific constructs
- Intermediate language for "text diagrams" (e.g. textual representation of UML models) in order to increase the possibilities of using different languages that map to the intermediate language – e.g. separate languages for PIMs and PSMs
- Sophisticated analysis which provides such possibilities as measuring models, building prediction models and analyzing various aspects of software already at the model level.

The last requirement seems to be one of the critical ones as it was also identified while addressing RQ1 (requirement b – cost estimation based on models; requirement e – identifying potential problem areas). Although these issues might be caused by the specific domain in which all three companies operate – embedded software it seems that these issues are more general.

5.4 Modeling Scenarios (RQ3)

The modeling scenarios evaluated in the companies are presented in Table 3. As in the previous questions, no alternatives were added for this question either.

Table 3. Results for modeling scenarios

Alternative	ABB			Ericsson		
	Mean	Median	Std. dev	Mean	Median	Std. dev.
a: standard UML for doc.	3.75	4	1.26	3.5	3.5	0.71
b: standard UML for code gen.	2.25	2	1.26	**4**	4	0.00
c: UML + one profile	3.25	3.5	0.96	**4**	4	0.00
d: UML + several profiles	2.5	2.5	0.58	**4.5**	4.5	0.71
e: UML + an existing DSL	2.5	2.5	1.29	2	2	1.41
f: existing DSLs	1.5	1.5	0.58	1.5	1.5	0.71
g: new DSLs	1.5	1.5	0.58	1	1	0.00

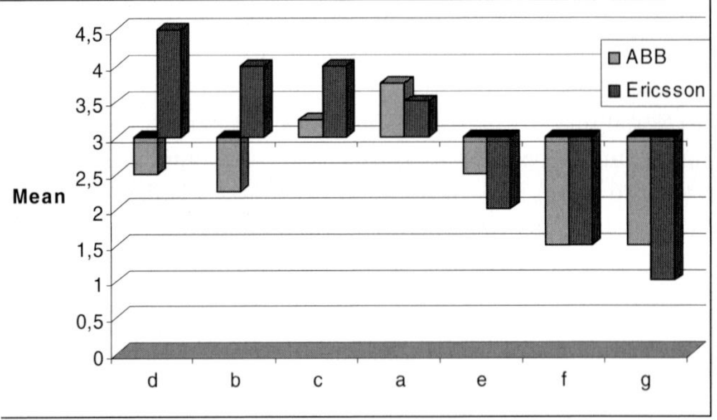

Fig. 2. Evaluation of modeling scenarios

As it is shown in the table, the non-adopters found that none of the scenarios is very suitable for them. This stems from their intentions (improving the quality control and measurements of models) and it is supported by the decision not to adopt MDD in the organization. On the other hand the adopters showed that the most suitable would be to use UML with a set of profiles dedicated for their purposes (alternative d). Another two alternatives were also considered as suitable, although to a lesser extent than the alternative d: b) using standard UML for code generation; c) using UML and a single specific profile. The results from evaluating the modeling scenarios are presented in the chart in Figure 2. The results presented in Table 3 indicate that even though adopting MDD seems to require advanced modeling techniques and notations, the simple notation is preferred. It is UML which is the notation which seems to be the most suitable one as perceived by the adopters of MDD. Such a situation could be explained by investigating the state-of-practice in industrial usage of UML. The survey of 150 companies by Grossman et al. [11] shows that UML is used in industry and is perceived to be moderately suited for its needs. Despite some deficiencies with the standard UML notation it seems that it fulfills the needs posed by industry. This is indicated by the average value of 3.17 (on the 5 points Likert scale where 5 denoted the positive value) when asking about whether UML is able to represent the right information for the companies.

5.5 Results from Interviews

We complemented the questionnaires with interviews and by observations of the work done in the companies. As a result of these it could be observed that there are two levels of modeling (users of modeling notations and the creators of these) at the organizations, as shown in Figure 3.

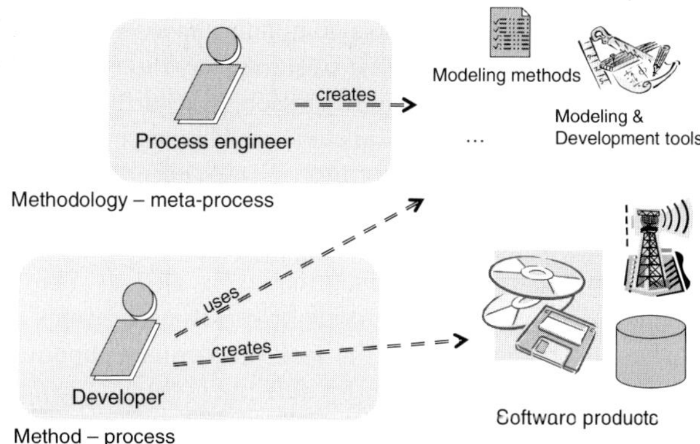

Fig. 3. Two levels of modeling in companies realizing MDD

It was also identified that creation of a specific notation should be done by engineers in the companies, not by language engineers or tool vendors. In the case of Ericsson, the level of framework creators is mainly choosing which elements should be modeled and which should only be coded in each iteration of the development, thus customizing their modeling requirements and needs.

A set of issues related to adopting MDD in particular projects was identified. The following questions need to be addressed:

- How much modeling is needed in the project?
- When to stop modeling and start coding?
- How to identify domain specific rules for the domains in the project?
- How many domains are there in the project?
- How to integrate the domains?
- How much reusability should the project aim for?
- How much will it cost to use only models and no code?

Some of these issues could be addressed by utilizing the evidence-based software engineering approach [14] and analyzing experiences from generative programming. The others, however, need to be researched and further empirical studies on these issues should be conducted.

It was found that the right end of the spectrum in Figure 1 is an utopia and that coding is necessary in all projects – even if everything can be modeled, then "someone" has to build the generators (c.f. [15]). The intentions of the companies are to gradually adopt the ideas of MDD and introduce modeling practices in stages – from architectural modeling to using models as the main artifacts. In the end, the intention is to use models instead of code for measurements, predictions and estimations.

It was found that the investments in adopting MDD in the case of a large base of legacy code to be reused cannot be done in a single step – it requires the effort which needs to be distributed across several phases. These phases should be planned and a lot of effort needs to be put, which in turn would require high return on investment after adopting MDD. This return on investment, however, seems to be too slow at this stage of technology maturity; this mainly applies to MDD tools.

We have observed that there is a very high maturity (with respect to the awareness of the potential costs and benefits of these new technologies) in organizations willing to adopt MDD. In particular these companies have precisely defined needs and indications which are supported by their own interpretations of certain aspects of MDD. The perception of MDD at ABB and Ericsson were different although they have several commonalities and the same expectations. The perception of MDD at Ericsson and at Volvo IT (c.f. [6]) show that industry is moving in the same direction regardless of their domain – i.e. using domain specific languages (sometimes simulated by UML profiles) instead of shoe-horning domain specific constructs into standard UML modeling elements. However, we found that at the current stage of technology using software factories and Microsoft's domain-specific languages was not feasible in these cases. The reason for that was the lack of adequate support at that time (both in the technology and the knowledge) for full integration of separate domain-specific languages. Without this support, the way of working at the company would have to be adjusted to the extent exceeding the possibilities of changing the software processes in the company.

6 Conditions for Adopting MDD

Based on the observations and the results from the questionnaires it is possible to provide a set of conditions that should be fulfilled by companies in order for the MDD adoption to be successful in their organizations. Although several requirements that should be fulfilled from different perspectives have already been identified in the literature (e.g. [4, 7, 16-18]), we have focused on software engineering aspects in the conditions. If the conditions are fulfilled by MDD adopters, then the risks of not succeeding in their adoption endeavors are minimized. The conditions that were identified in the case study are as follows (prioritizing according to importance):

1. **Maturity of modeling technology:** The technology used in the company should:
   - provide advanced features for developing and executing model transformations (c.f. requirements posed in [19]),
   - developing and executing model analysis methods (e.g. model measurements, test case generation, and identification of problem areas), and
   - developing and introducing domain-specific modeling (e.g. using UML profiles if the base language is UML).

   This condition has been identified in other studies as well.
2. **Maturity of modeling related methods:** In addition to the modeling tools, the methods for using models should be mature. These methods include activities like:

- early model-based verification and validation,
- model-based quality assurance,
- model-based project planning and management (development efforts are different when using modeling, thus project managers need to know how to structure their projects taking that into consideration), etc.

MDD should be the next step in using models based on evolution of software development processes (c.f. [6]).
3. **Process compatibility:** The process used in the company should be "compatible" with MDD principles. The compatibility means that
   - it should be possible to use models effectively in the process without a complete redefinition of the process
   - there should be a room in the process to actually use models as primary artifacts in the process – i.e. quality assessment should be done on models, estimations should be done on models, testing should be done on models.

   This condition is especially important for large companies as in such companies software process improvement activities require heavy efforts.
4. **Core language-engineering expertise:** Since the advanced model usage scenarios require either customizing a modeling language or engineering (at least to some extent) a new language, there should be staff available in the company with the required expertise (c.f. [20]). The required expertise is a combination of: domain knowledge (to the most extent), tool building/extending methods, and language engineering (to some extent, related to the expertise in tool building/extending).
5. **Goal-driven adoption process:** A set of precisely defined goals for introducing MDD should be in place in the company – e.g. to improve quality of data modeling or improve productivity of development of a given part of software. The scope and the methods for introducing MDD should be defined before the adoption in order to decrease the risk of changing scope of the MDD framework and thus providing better control of the costs in the projects.

The above fundamental conditions stem from the findings presented in the paper, although they could be supplemented with additional ones by close investigation of MDD related research papers and experience reports (e.g. [7, 16]).

7 Validity Analysis

There exists an internal validity threat regarding the completeness of the questionnaires as they were identified in the course of the part of the case study conducted at ABB. The requirements, factors and modeling scenarios identified seem to be complete as none of the respondents identified additional elements. In addition to that, the modeling scenarios were discussed and evaluated during meetings at ABB.

There is a construct validity threat in this case study, which is the fact that the adopters have already conducted a pilot project, which was discussed in section 4. There exists a conclusion validity threat, namely the lack of statistical inference testing. This is caused by the small number of data points. It was our choice to choose a small sample of people that were very much into the issues related to adopting MDD in their organization instead of performing a survey on a larger population without the control of their appropriateness for the purpose. Because of the variability in subjects' background we refrained from using statistics as advocated by [13]. Using a large, yet uninformed, sample would diminish the credibility of the results.

There exists an external validity threat that only two companies were investigated. Although this threat cannot be minimized at the current stage we believe that the results are generalizable to more than only two companies because the studied companies were an adopter and non-adopter of MDD. Furthermore, the staffs at these companies know the domain and have precisely specified requirements for MDD. The fact that one of the companies did not decide to introduce MDD at this point of time means that they are not blindly introducing innovations and software process improvements.

8 Conclusions

Despite the promised advantages of MDD (c.f. [2, 22, 23]), the state-of-practice in adopting it in large industrial projects shows that the technologies behind MDD are not yet mature enough for the industry to fully adopt the ideas of using models as the only artifacts in software development (e.g. [4, 16, 24]). The goal of the case study presented in this paper was to investigate the issues related to adopting MDD in industry. The study was conducted at two companies – a company adopting MDD and a company considering the adoption and later deciding to refrain from it. The results from interviews in the companies indicated that at the current state-of-practice in MDD, it seems to be unrealistic to use only models in the course of software development. There are two reasons for that: (i) the software development methods are not fitted to use models as the main artifacts in, for example estimations, and (ii) the software development environments are not mature enough to support the companies to a sufficient extent. In particular, there exist a large number of modeling tools and methods, but the integration of these is not a straightforward task. There are also several open issues in the definition of MDD (or MDA) which cause confusion among development teams (e.g. the meaning of the notion of "platform" is not clear for the adopters who need to identify one in their domain). Even in the case of adopting the new technology for new projects does not involve advanced technologies like the dedicated domain specific modeling languages. The companies seem to rely on well investigated UML-based technologies as they provide a large competence base (c.f. [11]). Although it limits the possibilities of productivity increase, in comparison to advanced technologies, they do not require that much initial investments with non-customized notation and software processes (c.f. a study on initial productivity bottlenecks after adopting a new development platform in a very similar organization [25]). The interviews also indicated that the most sensible roadmap towards advanced adoption of MDD is to go through stages – from introducing modeling at specific points in the process through increasing the use of models to using models as main artifacts in software development. It seems that the company is at the stage of experimental adoption as defined by Grady and Van Slack [26]. This stage is characterized by steep learning curve and initial failures; the failures which lead to optimizing and fine-tuning methods for local needs.

The high initial investments and unsure benefits of MDD were one of the issues which influenced the decision of non-adopters to refrain from introducing MDD at the current state of it. The case study presented in this paper provides empirical evidence on the requirements from the vision of MDD and the possible scenarios of how to achieve MDD in large companies. These issues seem to be important for the software engineering community in order to direct the research into the directions that would ease the transition to MDD for such companies.

Acknowledgments

The author would like to thank the companies for their commitment during the study and for the possibility to cooperate.

References

1. Brown, A.: An introduction to Model Driven Architecture - Part I: MDA and today's systems. The Rational Edge (2004)
2. Miller, J., Mukerji, J.: MDA Guide. Vol. 2004. Object Management Group (2003)
3. Kent, S.: Model Driven Engineering. In: Butler, M., Petre, L., Sere, K. (eds.): The Third International Conference on Integrated Formal Methods, Vol. 2335. Springer-Verlag, Turku, Finland (2002) 286-299
4. MacDonald, A., Russell, D., Atchison, B.: Model-Driven Development within a Legacy System: An Industry Experience Report. Australian Software Engineering Conference (2005) 14-22
5. Staron, M., Wohlin, C.: An Industrial Case Study on the Choice between Language Customization Mechanisms. PROFES. Springer-Verlag, Amsterdam, The Netherlands (2006).
6. Staron, M., Kuzniarz, L., Wallin, L.: A Case Study on Industrial MDA Realization - Determinants of Effectiveness. Nordic Journal of Computing **11** (2004) 254-278
7. The Middleware Company: Model Driven Development for J2EE Utilizing a Model Driven Architecture (MDA) Approach. Vol. 2004 (2003)
8. Evans, A., Maskeri, G., Sammut, P., Willians, J.S.: Building Families of Languages for Model-Driven System Development. Workshop in Software Model Engineering, San Francisco, CA (2003) Np
9. Atkinson, C., Kühne, T.: Concepts for Comparing Modeling Tool Architectures (2005)
10. Greenfield, J., Short, K.: Software factories: assembling applications with patterns, models, frameworks, and tools. Wiley Pub., Indianapolis, IN (2004)
11. Grossman, M., Aronson, J.E., McCarthy, R.V.: Does UML make the grade? Insights from the software development community. Information and Software Technology **47** (2005) 383-397
12. Robson, C.: Real World Research. Blackwell Publishing, Oxford (2002)
13. Miller, J.: Statistical significance testing--a panacea for software technology experiments? Journal of Systems and Software **73** (2004) 183-192
14. Dyba, T., Kitchenham, B.A., Jorgensen, M.: Evidence-Based Software Engineering for Practitioners. IEEE Software, **22** (2005) 58-65
15. Czarnecki, K., Eisenecker, U.: Generative programming. Addison Wesley, Boston (2000)

16. De Miguel, M., Jourdan, J., Salicki, S.: Practical Experiences in the Application of MDA. In: Stevens, P., Whittle, J., Booch, G. (eds.): The 6th Int. Conf. on UML, Vol. 2460. Springer-Verlag (2002) 128-139
17. Staron, M., Kuzniarz, L., Wallin, L.: Factors Determining Effective Realization of MDA in Industry. In: Koskimies, K., Kuzniarz , L., Lilius, J., Porres, I. (eds.): 2nd Nordic Workshop on the Unified Modeling Language, Vol. 35. Åbo Akademi, Turku, Finland (2004) 79-91
18. Knodel, J., Anastasopolous, M., Forster, T., Muthig, D.: An Efficient Migration to Model-driven Development (MDD). Electronic Notes in Theoretical Computer Science **137** (2005) 17-27
19. Porres, I.: A toolkit for model manipulation. Software and Systems Modeling **2** (2003) 262 - 277
20. Staron, M.: Improving Modeling with UML by Stereotype-based Language Customization. Doctoral thesis. Blekinge Institute of Technology, Ronneby (2005) 270
21. Wohlin, C., Runeson, P., Höst, M., Ohlsson, M.C., Regnell, B., Wesslèn, A.: Experimentation in Software Engineering: An Introduction. Kluwer Academic Publisher, Boston MA (2000)
22. Mellor, S.J.: MDA distilled : principles of model-driven architecture. Addison-Wesley, Boston (2004)
23. Kleppe, A.G., Warmer, J.B., Bast, W.: MDA explained, Addison-Wesley, Boston (2003)
24. Thomas, D.: MDA: Revenge of the Modelers or UML Utopia? IEEE Software **21** (2004) 15-18
25. Tomaszewski, P., Lundberg, L.: Software development productivity on a new platform: an industrial case study. Information and Software Technology **47** (2005) 257-269
26. Grady, R.B., Slack, T.V.: Key lessons in achieving widespread inspection use. IEEE Software **11** (1994) 46-57

Use Case Driven Iterative Development: Hurdles and Solutions

Santiago Ceria[1] and Juan José Cukier[2]

[1] Hexacta SA, Arguibel 2860, Buenos Aires, Argentina
santiago@hexacta.com
[2] Pragma Consultores, San Martín 575, Buenos Aires, Argentina
jcukier@pragmaconsultores.com

Abstract. Theory says that typical construction iterations in an iterative software development project consist of taking some use cases previously identified and then developing and testing them. However, reality says that use cases are revisited in several iterations, creating a challenging problem in terms of how to specify these "deltas" of functionality in a practical manner, and manage these deltas as their number increase and "deltas of deltas" spawn. The longer the project, the more probable is that this will happen. This paper elaborates on the experience of a use case driven software development project and explains how to deal with this issue.

1 Introduction

Literature on use cases and iterative development methods usually describe a series of best practices that can be grouped in the realm of "develop your use cases iteratively" [1].

In a recent development project we faced some of the hidden challenges of this idea. We used RUP as our methodological framework, and therefore use case descriptions contained the project's functional requirements. The system was built along several construction iterations.

Usually the first iterations do not present a problem. For example, during the first construction iteration the team had a list of identified use cases, and applying the criteria proposed by RUP we chose some of them to get started –for simplification purposes we will ignore development done during the architecture definition iterations-. Then we specified them and built them. In the second iteration we chose some other use cases to develop, but we also wanted to enhance the ones we had previously built. After 6 construction iterations, we had no new use cases: all development was a series of small changes and enhancements to functionalities that had already been implemented. And the obvious question is: how do you specify a change to a use case? Do you manage "deltas" or do you specify them completely again, highlighting the changes in some way? The problem may be easy to understand, but unfortunately, solving it is not as easy as it seems.

The answer to that question has strong implications for the Development, Analysis and Testing teams, and the Key Users (users representative of a vested-interest group) in general. On one side of the spectrum, re-specifying again all use cases that will be

O. Nierstrasz et al. (Eds.): MoDELS 2006, LNCS 4199, pp. 73–82, 2006.

changed during an iteration renders a full specification per iteration and determines the current scope, but it can produce large volumes of information due to the repetitiveness of specifications. On the other side of the spectrum, a purely use case delta-based approach reduces verboseness to a minimum and clarifies to the Development and Testing teams where the focus should be, but makes documentation harder to read for key users, and demands regrouping and consolidation efforts to keep the number of deltas under control for practical use.

Another issue to consider is that Use Cases play a central role in iterative projects, as many other deliverables are based on them, such as design documentation and test cases. Also, they act as the main documentation for end users for validation purposes. Therefore, maintaining a consistent and updated use case document is key for ensuring requirements traceability and a smooth communication between the development team and the end users.

In this paper we present the characteristics of our solution, a tradeoff between studied options and a series of recommendations based on our experience, both in this and past projects. The objective is to provide the community with possible solutions to a problem that, we believe, is pervasive but usually underestimated.

The structure of the paper is as follows: background project information is provided as for the type of project, its size, technology and methodology. Then the concept of and motivation for deltas is introduced, together with a proposed segmentation and notation. Problems related to delta management are accounted for, followed by a proposal on delta management, tool aids and conclusions.

2 Background

2.1 Project Information

The project encompassed the development of a corporate core system for an international company, which included, at high level, the reception of client orders, its processing and delivery, and all interfaces with ERP's and extranets. The system was built with generality as a critical design principle, so it could be extended to adapt to the company's local branches around the globe.

The project was structured in three main groups: a development group, also in charge of analysis and design, a Project Management Office (PMO), in charge of Quality Assurance, both of processes and products and a third group of key users that represented our customer.

The development efforts extended for 18 months, since January 2004 until June 2005. The complete team averaged 25 people.

Iterations averaged 5 weeks long. Each of the iterations included, either fully or partially, around 10 new or modified use cases. The complete application had a total of 35 use cases and 15 iterations.

2.2 Technology and Methodology Used

The application was developed using J2EE under the Oracle Suite. The Rational Unified Process® was chosen as the methodological framework, and hence use cases were the requirements' specification technique. The main rationale for choosing RUP was twofold: on the one hand, this was an unprecedented endeavor for the company, so requirements had to be discovered more than elicited; in that way, the use of iterations was thought to be particularly beneficial. On the other hand, since the system was to be deployed in a number of branches around the globe, a standard notation and syntax were of prime importance, and RUP provided for this.

No particular requirements management tool was used. Requirements were specified in a word processor, and the system's scope was managed, due to changes throughout the lifecycle, with a spreadsheet. Users reported requirement changes either in a change management tool, that generated a unique change identification for tracking purposes, or informally to the members of the functional team in requirements gathering meetings or user acceptance testing sessions.

All the processes used complied with the requirements of levels 2 and 3 of the Capability Maturity Model for Software from the Software Engineering Institute, as the development organization had been assessed at Level 3 of this model shortly before the project stated.

3 Deltas: Need, Use and Consequences

In this section we present the case for use case deltas (from now on simply deltas), and explain the need for this specification method. We elaborate on the different deltas and how to write them, and how to determine whether a full use case rewrite should be implemented. We conclude by explaining the problems that arise with the proliferations of deltas if these are not managed properly.

3.1 The Need for Deltas

RUP's approach of choice for segregating use cases is to identify the major risk factors, and prioritize the most architecturally significant ones. A choice should be made on whether to select time-box segregation (fix the iteration duration and select enough use case functionality to fit into that time frame) or scenario segregation (fix the use case functionality and determine the time needed to carry that functionality to code). In either, partitioning of use cases (that is, use cases that spread out though multiple iterations) is mostly inevitable.

Following RUP's framework, use cases with higher risk and architectural significance were selected for specification and development in the early iterations. Once the architecture was stable, the second line of use cases dealt with the core business processes. These were developed early, and as consequence, suffered multiple revisits. Reasons for these include: a dynamic business environment, changes in the project focus due to strategy shifts in the corporation, and a powerful group of key users that were hard to contain and represented a never-ending source of requirement changes. Though we understand this is not a desirable situation in a project, it is the case in many development undertakings, no matter how mature the requirements management processes used.

As a consequence of this, use cases had to be revisited in more than one iteration. The extent to which the use cases suffered modifications, enhancements or changes in general revealed the size of the delta.

A case could be made for better use case granularity. It is common sense to think that finer-grained use cases should lead to a better fit of these within one iteration, eliminating the need for increments. This was not our experience with this particular project and, according to our understanding, it is not what the literature recommends. First, some core use cases were clearly not candidates for development into a single iteration since they represented a main flow for the user, and further decomposition proved discouraging for them, as they saw these flows as indivisible. Second, even with some finer grained use cases, change requests resulting from user acceptance tests forced to revisit many of them in later iterations. After all, this is what iterative development is all about.

Screen prototyping was implemented and helped users think more thoroughly about the functionality, reducing changes during the acceptance phase. Still this only worked partially, and changes remained.

3.2 Delta Spectrum

There were cases when a shift in the business processes rendered a use case inadequate. An example of this was the following: during the development, our Client switched providers for the delivery of its product, effectively altering the business flow and the distribution of responsibilities.

In other cases, changes to use cases were very minor. There are numerous examples of this, including the addition of new fields in a screen or changes to the validations performed after data entry.

Cleary, these minor changes do not justify the full rewrite of a use case. And a change in logic and business flow would make the treatment of deltas cumbersome, and would probably justify a rewrite of the use case altogether.

Therefore, when planning for the scenario of use case revisiting, we came across a whole shade of gray for deltas. And we had to define a cost-effective threshold to define when a use case should be handled with deltas, or be rewritten completely.

3.3 Writing Deltas

As we mentioned above, a delta is any change in a use case description that has already been implemented. This can be produced by the addition, change or deletion of functionality described in a use case.

Table 1 describes a possible way to specify a delta. The table, that has an example, includes the critical information that needs to be specified.

Table 1. Delta Specification

Module	**MED – Media Management**
Use Case / Step	Changing delivery state – Step III
Delta Spec	Instead of entering a single parcel number for changing the delivery state, the system shall accept a range of parcel numbers. All the parcels in that range will be changed by the system to the new state indicated by the user.
Source	Meeting Minute – 05 / 04 / 2005

The other options for specifying such a change, both tried by the team with no success are:

- Use the "Track Changes" feature of the word processor. This will produce many pages of useless documentation, and is not efficient when different persons are making many changes to the same document, as your use case will end up resembling a color palette.
- Manually highlighting changes to the document. This also has the problem of generating useless documentation, and additionally includes the risk of a use case writer forgetting to highlight a change.

After trying the later options, we concluded that use case deltas were the best way to go.

3.4 Delta Threshold

During the process of revisiting a use case, it should be clear that the work involved in the rewriting is somewhat proportional to the percentage of change in the use case, this considering that no changes are radical. To cope with this later case, and to maintain a favorable "redo vs. rewrite" effort ratio, we defined a threshold. If changes to the use case fell below the threshold, it was to be added a delta. If the threshold was exceeded, the use case was to be rewritten.

The largest determinant of this threshold was the type of change to the use case. On the one hand, cosmetic changes were candidates to be treated as deltas, while information flow or business changes favored the use case to be rewritten.

It should be clear though that, unless a full rewrite approach is taken (that is, a use case is rewritten irrespective to the impact of the change), even with a low threshold, deltas are bound to exist and proliferate.

3.5 Early Deltas, Later Nightmares

This revisiting process of early use cases generated a large number of deltas. And in cases where the change belonged to a delta, a delta's delta had to be created. This, as can be seen in Figure 1, generated a chain of deltas that dismembered the functional specification.

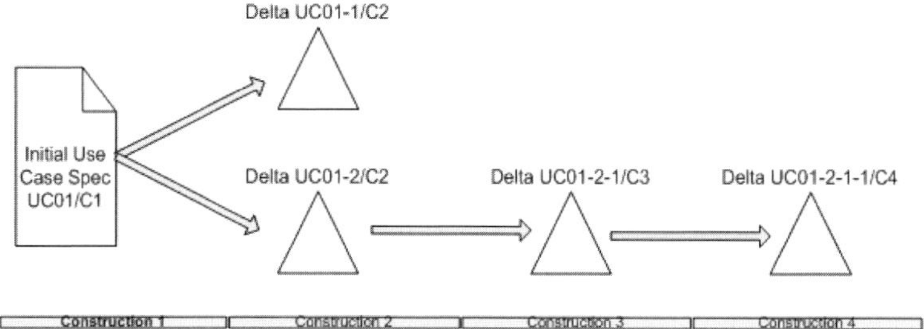

Fig. 1. Delta Tree - Evolution of higher order deltas for a use case

In this example, a use case specified initially in the first construction iteration (C1), suffers two deltas on C2. We call these first-order deltas (that is, a delta that modifies a use case specification directly). The second delta is again revisited in C3 and then on C4. We call these "higher order" deltas (that is, a delta that modifies another delta). Like this, the most updated version of the use case is given by walking the delta tree, and replacing the original text by the update expressed in the delta.

The delta technique was useful and rendered satisfactory results for first-order deltas. Among others:

- It reduced the verboseness of the iteration's specification to a minimum, speeding up the specification time.
- It pointed the Development team exactly to what should be modified, increasing focus and avoiding distractions.
- It instructed the Testing team on the specific test cases (or part of a test case) that had to be modified.
- It helped with the specification validation from the Key Users by focusing them on their latest change request, instead of functionality that was already reviewed and approved.

However, once higher order deltas came into play, these advantages promptly turned into drawbacks. In general, the proliferation of higher order deltas had strong consequences for the project:

- The time needed to comprehend a use case increased, sometimes two- or three-fold.
- This specification technique was hard to master for the Key Users.
- Newcomers for the project had to invest a long time in reading and understanding parts of the specification that, at the current time, was useless, with the sole purpose of understanding the evolution of the deltas.
- The system's scope (that is, the sum of approved functionality) was harder to maintain and administer against changes during the lifecycle, since the same use cases extended in more than one document.
- There was a load of administration tasks to make sure that the delta tree was tidy and understood equally by all team members.

4 Delta Management

4.1 Project and Iteration Use Cases

While designing a practical strategy to deal with the proliferation of deltas, it was useful to create a classification of use cases in project versus iteration use cases.

Project use cases are persistent, represent the functional repository, and hold the true project scope. They embody the latest version of the use case, no matter the modification, or when this was made.

Iteration use cases, on the other hand, are temporary. They act as working documents for refining the specification of specific use cases which are dealt with in a particular iteration. All refinement put forth and represented in an iteration use case will eventually have to be merged with the project use cases to be incorporated into the project's functional repository. This situation is represented in Figure 2.

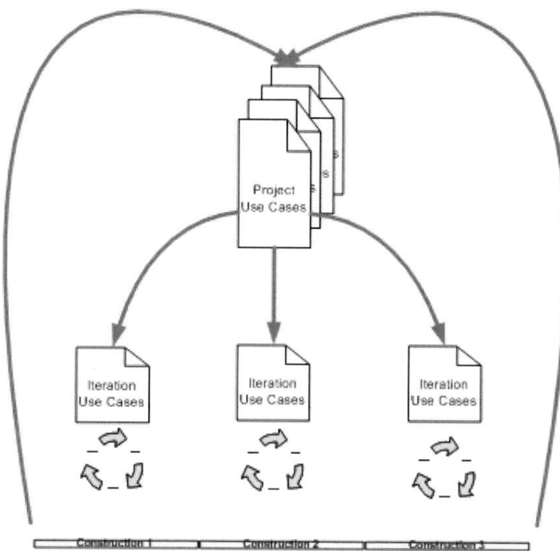

Fig. 2. Relationship between Project and Iteration Use Cases

The merging activity includes not only the iteration use cases, but also the deltas. They key point here is how, and when, this merging should be carried out.

4.2 Merging Alternatives

As with the deltas themselves, here we find a spectrum of possible milestones to proceed with the merging. On one side, merging could be done after each of the iterations. On the other, merging could be done solely at the end of the construction.

Merging at the end of the construction minimizes overhead, but offers little help in solving the proliferation of deltas.

Merging at the end of every iteration seems to be the reasonable approach, and a good mitigation for the proliferation of deltas. All changes to a use case are merged back to the project's use case, which will then always represent the most updated functional specification. Still, this approach has two main disadvantages:

- It can produce large works of overhead.
- The merge can potentially operate on deltas that will be rendered useless due to new changes.

As for the first drawback, it was our experience that the extra workload was largely compensated by a more orderly specification. As for the second, it should diminish as the functional specification stabilizes, and as the project progresses.

Another alternative was studied and implemented with greater success, which consists on performing periodical merges after a definite number of iterations. This number is dependent on:

- Total number of iterations within the project: if only two construction iterations are planned, this scenario derives into the merge-at-the-end strategy; on the other hand, as the number of iterations increase, more frequent merges will be needed.

- Project milestones: if the project is expected to deliver intermediate releases for production, for instance, these might be natural moments for the merge.
- Number of the use cases: the number of deltas and the complexity of delta management is somewhat proportional to the number of use cases per iteration; therefore, project with only a handful of use cases per construction iteration might consider a larger number of iterations before the merge.
- Level of the threshold: it should be clear that a low threshold would produce less deltas, and therefore, less higher order deltas.

An alternative trigger for the merge can also be the number of higher order deltas. If these start to proliferate, a merge will likely be needed.

It should also be observed also that the effort needed for the merge increases as the deltas live longer. This is due to the fact that the existence of living first order deltas favors the creation of higher order ones. In this way, the case for merging at the end of each iteration is strengthened.

4.3 The Project Use Case Repository

In the light of these approaches, what constitutes the project use case repository? If merging is done at the end of construction, it should detail the delta tree path that leads to the complete specification, indicating the correct sequencing of deltas. If merging is done at each construction iteration, it is a document itself with the latest version of the use case. The only changes not reflected in the project use cases will be the ones under construction in the current iteration, which, after all, have not been validated yet.

In this way, the Project Use Case Repository, supplemented by the merging process, is an effective tool for obtaining, and managing, the most current and complete requirements specification. The following section gives details of a practical example on obtaining a current specification.

4.4 Aids: Use Case Map

A good help for delta management was a mapping tool we called "use case map". The tool, developed in Excel by the Functional Team and the PMO, represented a description of the delta tree paths and detailed the following:

- The originating use case document (that is, the baseline), the document's name and location.
- Any rewrites for the use cases that replaced the original baseline.
- The reading order for any successive deltas and the iteration use case document these belong to.
- New uses cases, and the iteration these belong to.

A real project use case map is represented in Figure 3. In this example, no merge has been carried out yet.

Module	Use Case	Version 1.0	Delta [D] / New Use Case [N] / Rewritten [R]				Reading Order
			C1	C2	C3	C4	
ABC	Inputting addresses	CP_ABC_UseCases.doc	D	D			CP_ABC_UseCases.doc + C1 + C2
ABC	Managing agreements with affiliates	CP_ABC_UseCases.doc			R	D	C3 + C4
ABC	Managing agreements with customers	CP_ABC_UseCases.doc			R	D	C3 + C4
ABC	Managing companies	CP_ABC_UseCases.doc			R	D	C3 + C4
ABC	Administrando datos de contacto					N	C4
ABC	Administrando facturación de clientes y					N	C4

Fig. 3. Use case map

In this example, the use case "Inputting addresses" departs from an initial document (CP_ABC_UseCases.doc) and suffers two deltas in construction iterations C1 and C2. Therefore, three documents should be reviewed for the complete use case specification: the originating use case document and iterations use documents for C1 and C2. The case for "Managing agreements with affiliates" is somewhat different. Since there was a rewrite in iteration C3, reading should start there, and continue with deltas specified in iteration use case document C4.

The tool proved to be extremely useful for navigating the use cases and managing, at least in part, the complexity of delta proliferation. Its implementation is simple and cost effective, and its use highly recommended.

4.5 Use of Deltas in Maintenance

Use case deltas can also be used for maintenance. How useful this technique can be depends on several factors, such as the size of the changes (the smaller the changes, the more useful it will be to use deltas), and the value assigned to maintaining the use cases of the application updated. If the system's use cases document is used frequently, for example for training purposes, the deltas can be incorporated into the use case documents with a predefined frequency (once every one or two months).

5 Conclusions and Further Work

We can draw the following conclusions from our experience:

- Although it presents some difficulties, use case deltas are probably the best way to minimize problems caused by changes to use cases in different iterations.
- It is useful to conceptually differentiate project use cases from iteration use cases, and employ some merging mechanism to update the former.
- The project team will need some guidance on when to write a delta vs. when to re-specify the complete use case. We have presented in this paper a few recommendations about this issue including periodical merges after a definite number of iterations, dependent on total number of iterations within the project, project milestones and total number of use cases.
- On long projects, make sure you update your project use cases after a small number of iterations. Otherwise, the "rebuild" task will become a nightmare.

In terms of further work, we think there is a need for tools that address this issue. Use cases are centric to iterative development, and their management will become more important as this technique makes it way to becoming the de-facto standard for functional specifications. Still, this also applies to other artifacts that may fulfill the role of a use case in specifying what a requirement should do.

Also, the reader is invited to consider that this problem is not restricted to use cases. Activity diagrams and all other UML diagrams are subject to this change process during iterations. Separation between project documentation and iteration documentation, and their periodic merge is a difficult issue for any large development project.

Acknowledgments

We would like to thank our customer, SodexhoPass International, for letting us share the experiences of the project. Also, we want to thank our companies, Hexacta and Pragma Consultores that encourage this type of activities. We are also grateful to many of the team members of the project team, from the functional, technical, QA and testing teams, who had many of the creative ideas that are presented in this paper.

References

[1] Ivar Jacobson, Grady Booch, James Rumbaugh, *The Unified Sotware Development Process*. Addison Wesley, 1998.
[2] Ellen Gottesdiener, *Use Cases: Best Practices*. IBM Technical Paper, 2003.
[3] Kurt Bittner, Ian Spence, *Use Case Modeling*. Addison-Wesley, 2003.
[4] Gary Evans, Getting from use cases to code Part 1: Use-Case Analysis. IBM Technical Paper, 2004.
[5] Alistair Cockburn, *Writing effective use cases*. Addison Wesley, 2001.

Model-Driven Development with SDL – Process, Tools, and Experiences

T. Kuhn, R. Gotzhein, and C. Webel

{kuhn, gotzhein, webel}@informatik.uni-kl.de

Abstract. Model-Driven Development is a challenge and a promising methodology for creating next-generation software systems. In this paper, we present SDL-MDD, a model-driven development process that is based on the ITU-T design language SDL. We present a semantically integrated tool suite, especially supporting model-driven code generation and model-driven simulation. Both production and simulation code are entirely generated from SDL models and automatically instrumented to interface with different operating systems and communication technologies. The use of SDL-MDD and of the tool suite is illustrated by an extensive case study from the ubiquitous computing domain.

1 Introduction

Model-Driven Development (MDD) [1] is a software engineering approach that places the abstract, formal system model in the center of the development activity. The objective is that models guide and direct all development activities, ranging from system design over code generation and deployment to system maintenance, resulting both in quality improvements and productivity increases.

One of the main benefits of MDD is the ability to specify the structure and the behavior of a software system in a more platform-independent way than with traditional programming approaches. This is especially relevant for software systems within the ubiquitous computing domain, which consist of dynamic, distributed applications and heterogeneous hardware platforms. Since ubiquitous computing systems aim at creating an invisible, unobtrusive environment, there is a need of supporting various hardware platforms with different resource constraints. These platforms range from micro controllers with scarce computational and energy resources to pc-style hardware. While some software components will be tailored to a specific hardware platform, most components of these systems – in particular, the communication middleware – must be able to run on multiple platforms.

In this paper, we present SDL-MDD, a domain-specific, model-driven development process for communication systems that is based on SDL [2], the ITU-T Specification and Description Language, and a semantically integrated tool suite for SDL-MDD. This tool suite consists of several commercial tools, including a graphical SDL editor, an SDL model debugger, and an SDL-to-C compiler. To entirely avoid manual coding, we have added a tool and a library to automatically instrument the generated C-code to interface with different operating systems and communication technologies. Furthermore, we have extended an existing network simulator in order

O. Nierstrasz et al. (Eds.): MoDELS 2006, LNCS 4199, pp. 83 – 97, 2006.

to enable performance simulation of SDL models. We demonstrate the applicability of SDL-MDD and the tool suite by an extensive case study from the ubiquitous computing domain.

The remaining part of this paper is structured as follows: Section 2 gives an overview of SDL-MDD. In Section 3, the Assisted Bicycle Trainer (ABT), which will be used to illustrate the use of SDL-MDD, is briefly described. Section 4 elaborates on the design stage of SDL-MDD. In Section 5, the tool suite of SDL-MDD is presented. In Section 6, we survey related work, and conclude in Section 7.

2 The SDL-MDD Process

SDL-MDD is a model-centric, domain-specific, development process, whose main focus is the development of distributed systems and communication systems in the area of ubiquitous computing. It is supported by a tool suite, and uses a generic system structure to obtain clear separation and reusability of platform-dependent and platform-independent models.

SDL-MDD is based on SDL [2], ITU's Specification and Description Language, which is widely used throughout the telecommunication industry. SDL has a formal semantics and enables developers to specify system structure and behavior in a platform-independent manner. Additionally, it is possible to integrate native, platform-specific code into SDL models. These features turn SDL into a valuable candidate for model-driven development.

SDL-MDD decomposes the development of a software system into a number of stages. Since it is an iterative process, the development of a software system may go through some stages repeatedly, while certain stages may be skipped in the early cycles. The following stages are distinguished (see Fig. 1):

- In the *requirements stage* (*REQ*), the requirements are elicited and described in an informal way.
- In the *formalize requirements stage* (*FRQ*), the requirements document is partially formalized, yielding a computation-independent model (CIM). Similar to the MDA [3], the CIM is a system specification from the viewpoint of the domain expert. Since SDL-MDD is directed towards the ubiquitous computing domain, we specify message scenarios with MSC [5] on different levels of granularity. This specification can be traced throughout all models of subsequent development stages, and be validated against scenarios that are generated by the SDL model debugger.
- In the *platform-independent design* (*PID*) stage, the platform-independent model[1] (PIM) is specified, using SDL as design language. It contains both the platform-independent structure of the software system, and the platform-independent behavior. The result of this stage is a functionally complete, closed SDL design model, which can be analyzed using existing tools for debugging and validation of the functional system behavior.

[1] Actually, the concept of platform-independence is somewhat misleading. In fact, the PIM is a model suitable for use with a number of different platforms of similar type, i.e., a generic platform. For instance, a basic communication service consisting of send and receive primitives could be assumed, which is later replaced by a communication platform with specific encodings as well as specialized and additional service primitives.

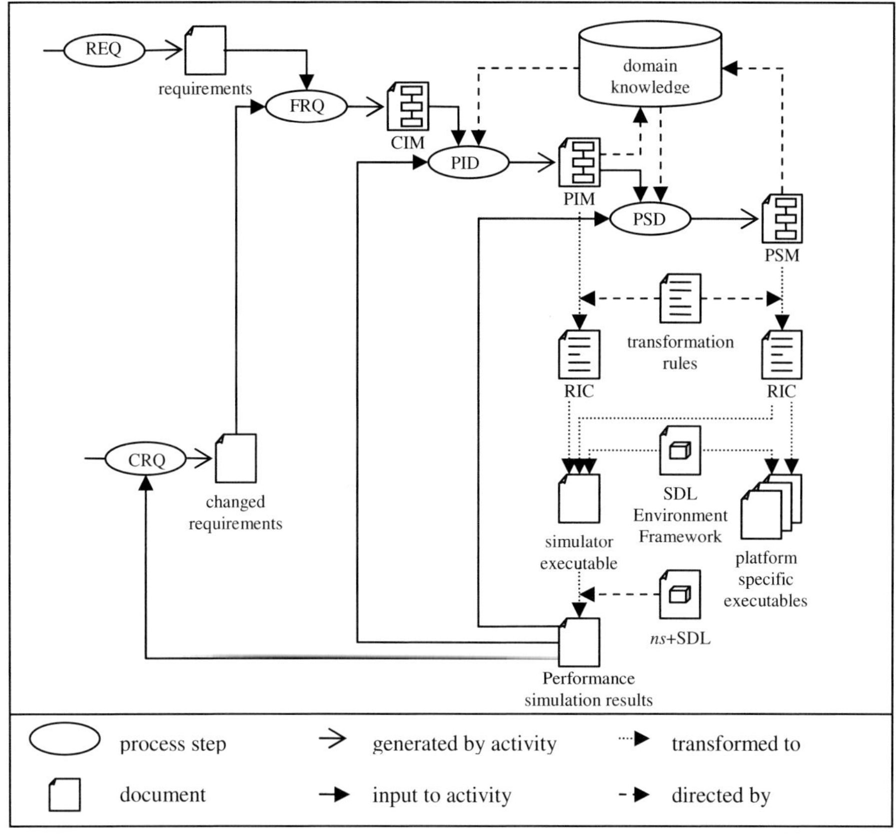

Fig. 1. SDL-MDD process

- In the *platform-specific design* (*PSD*) stage, the platform-specific model (PSM) is specified, again using SDL as design language. The fact that the PSM incorporates the PIM, and that the same design language as for the PIM is used, make transformations between PIM and corresponding parts of the PSM obsolete. However, design decisions leading to platform-specific PSM components are to be made. The resulting SDL design model can be analyzed using existing tools for debugging and validation of the functional system behavior. In addition, the design model forms the basis for model-driven performance simulations (see Section 5).
- In the *changed requirements* (*CRQ*) stage, the initial requirements may be modified, based on feedback from the performance assessment.

It should be noted that the SDL-MDD process does not contain an explicit implementation stage. The reason is that implementations including code for interfacing with system environments are entirely generated from SDL models (see Section 5). This includes the runtime-independent code (RIC), which is used for performance simulations and part of the production code. By using customized transformation rules and a tailored runtime environment, we are able to generate efficient code even for small, embedded devices.

3 The Assisted Bicycle Trainer

To illustrate the use of SDL-MDD, we will show excerpts from the development of the Assisted Bicycle Trainer (ABT), a distributed system for the training of a group of cyclists. In a typical training scenario, a group of up to 30 cyclists covers a distance of up to 200 km, with a varying road profile. For best training effects, each cyclist should ride with an individual target and maximum pulse rate. The pulse rate depends on various parameters, in particular on speed, head wind, road incline, and physical condition of the cyclist.

The objective of the ABT is to improve the training effects such that each cyclist is as close to his individual target pulse rate profile as possible, without exceeding his maximum pulse rate. To achieve this objective, the ABT dynamically collects status data of each cyclist, and displays a summary of these data to the trainer accompanying the group of cyclists by car. Based on this information, the trainer may adjust training parameters, for instance, by ordering the group to change speed, or by ordering a particular cyclist to take the lead, exposing him to the headwind, while all others can exploit the slipstream and thus need less pedal power. Orders of the trainer are shown on small displays attached to each bicycle. The ABT is a self-organizing system, supporting, in particular, dynamic group formation and mobility. Communication among cyclists and human trainer is via wireless ad-hoc network. The software system for this demonstrator consists of four main parts:

- Application software for cyclists and trainer.
- Graphical user interfaces for cyclists and trainer.
- Software for preprocessing the sensor data, running on sensor nodes (few lines of code).
- Communication middleware to collect local sensor data, to exchange sensor data among bicycles and with the trainer.

Both the application software and the communication middleware have been developed with SDL-MDD.

4 Model-Driven Design with SDL-MDD

In this section, the generic structure of PIMs and PSMs for systems in the ubiquitous computing domain is presented. This structure is instantiated and refined when specific models are specified, as illustrated for the Assisted Bicycle Trainer.

4.1 Platform-Independent Model

The *platform-independent model* (*PIM*) is structured into two major units, containing, for each logical node, application-specific and platform-independent functionalities, respectively (see Fig. 2). This is a general design decision for all PIMs in the ubiquitous computing domain developed with SDL-MDD. The application viewpoint supports the developer in focusing on high-level design decisions. For the interaction of distributed application components, tailored platform-independent functionalities, such as high-level communication protocols, are identified and combined, yielding the device middleware.

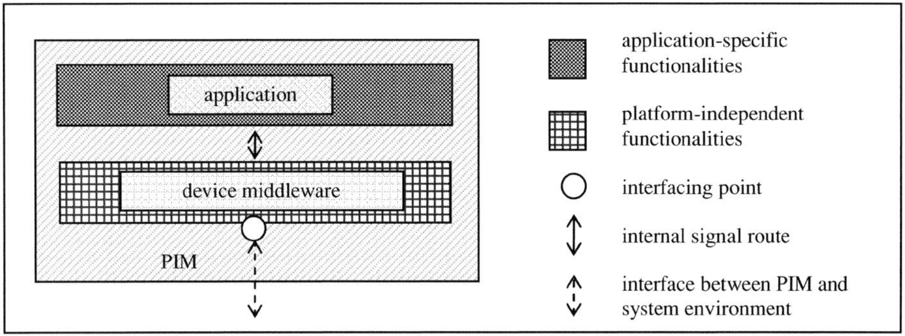

Fig. 2. Generic high-level architecture of platform-independent models

In the ubiquitous computing domain, system functionalities strongly depend on the resource situation. For instance, in the ABT system, cyclist nodes have to be lightweight and mobile, which calls for micro processors operating with scarce resources. In a distributed environment, this requires specialized communication protocols that are tailored to the resource situation. For this reason, we have decided to incorporate the device middleware into the PIM, which therefore is domain specific. Note that at this point, no specific decision about devices, e.g., particular communication technology classes such as serial communication or broadcast is made. This decision is postponed until the platform-specific design (see Section 4.2). Also, no decisions about operating system or compilers to generate production code are made. Therefore, we argue that the SDL model so far is largely platform-independent.

The high-level architecture of the platform-independent model of the ABT is derived from the generic architecture in Fig. 2. Fig. 3 shows an SDL block *cyclistApplication* that incorporates all application-specific functionality that is to be placed on bicycle nodes. In addition, a trainer application has been specified. The SDL block *cyclistCommunicationMiddleware* provides a platform-independent view of the communication functionalities, which are tailored towards the application. Both SDL blocks are refined into further SDL blocks and finally into SDL processes (not

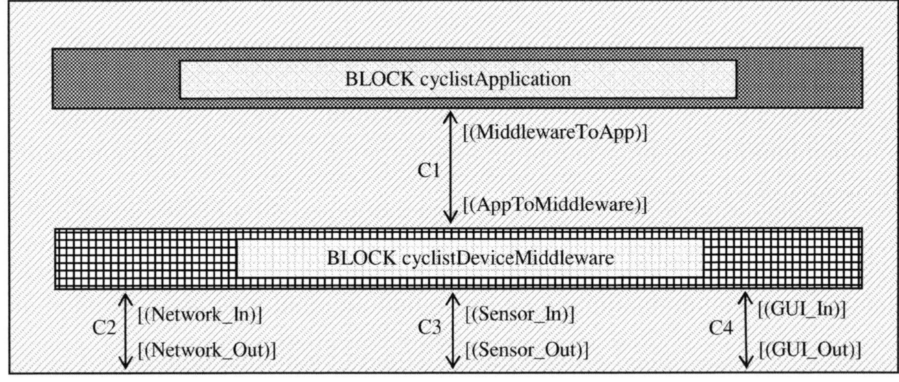

Fig. 3. Assisted Bicycle Trainer – PIM (abstract SDL model)

shown here). These processes form a hierarchically structured system of extended finite state machines interacting through signal exchange. Signals are sent along typed SDL channels and signal routes, connecting blocks and processes. For instance, the bidirectional channel *C1* in Fig. 3 is typed with lists of signals exchanged between the two blocks. The size of the PIM for the ABT is 68 pages of SDL specification.

4.2 Platform-Specific Model

The *platform-specific model* (*PSM*) contains both platform-independent and platform-specific parts of a system. A platform encapsulates the operational environment of a system, consisting of hardware devices, operating system, and code generators. In SDL-MDD, the PSM is obtained by adding platform-specific functionalities and device interfaces to the PIM (see Fig. 4). These extensions are specified with SDL, which means that the same design language as for the PIM is used, providing a smooth transition between models.

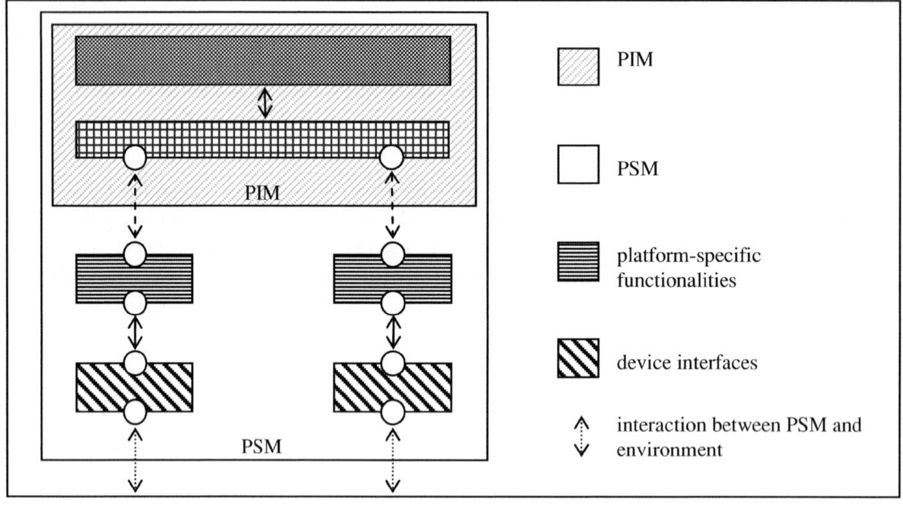

Fig. 4. Generic architecture of platform-specific models

When moving from PIM to PSM, the device classes of the platform are determined. Platform-specific functionalities depend on these device classes, for instance, sensor types or types of communication technologies. Additionally, the actual interface to interact with concrete devices is added. For instance, the device class of serial communication may be mapped to Bluetooth, USB, or RS232. Note that on model level, device interfaces may still be abstract in the sense that procedure calls to device drivers are represented by SDL signal exchanges. However, the interface is platform-specific in the sense that the procedure calls can later be generated automatically (see Section 5).

The architecture of the platform-specific model of the ABT is derived from the generic architecture in Fig. 4 and the PIM (see Fig. 3). In Fig. 5, the PSM for an

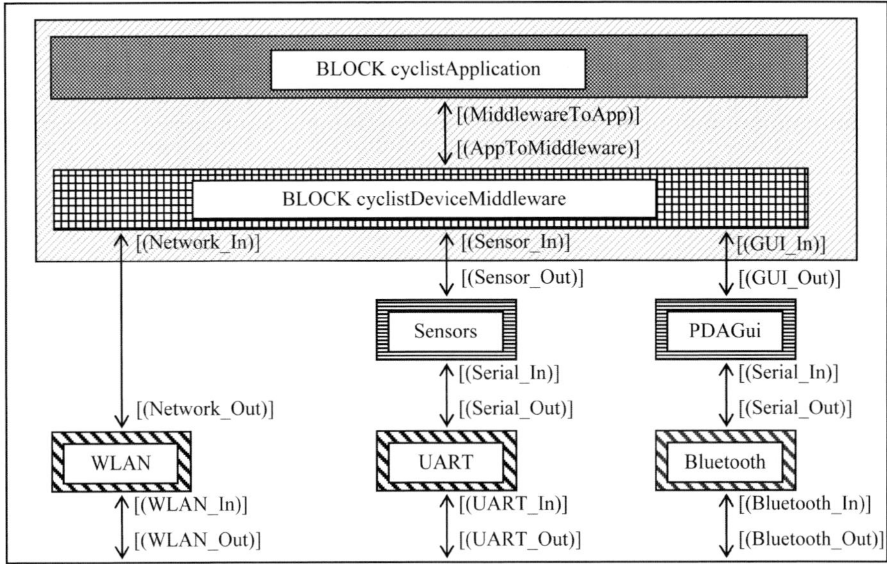

Fig. 5. Assisted Bicycle Trainer – PSM (abstract SDL model)

embedded PC platform is shown. Here, SDL blocks encapsulating platform-specific functionalities to support sensor classes – pulse rate, speed – and PDAs serving as graphical cyclist interfaces are added. Furthermore, abstract interfaces to three different communication technologies are specified. Interaction with local sensors is via UART, communication with the PDA is via Bluetooth, and message exchange among bicycles and trainer is via WLAN. This covers all platform-specific design decisions that have to be made at this point of the development. Further platform-specific decisions can be postponed until code generation, which is fully automated, taking the PSM as starting point (see Section 5). The size of the PSM for the ABT is 103 pages of SDL specification, which includes 68 pages of the PIM.

We have specified another PSM for a micro controller platform, which is very similar to the PSM in Fig. 5. The main difference is that communication among bicycles and trainer is via CC2420, a ZigBee controller. To incorporate this into the PSM, the WLAN interface of Fig. 5 is replaced by a CC2420 interface, and an SDL block encapsulating platform-specific functionality for ZigBee is added.

At this point, we observe that the same PIM is used for both types of platforms. This provides some evidence that the PIM is indeed platform-independent. Also, the changes to the PSM when changing parts of the platform are straightforward and systematical, even in the above case of very heterogeneous platforms.

4.3 Transitions Between PIM and PSM

SDL-MDD supports transitions between PIM and PSM in both directions (see Fig. 6). From PIM to PSM, detailed developer guidelines are provided. Since the PSM requires major design decisions on platform-specific functionalities, this transition is not an automatic one. However, it is simplified by the fact that in SDL-MDD, the

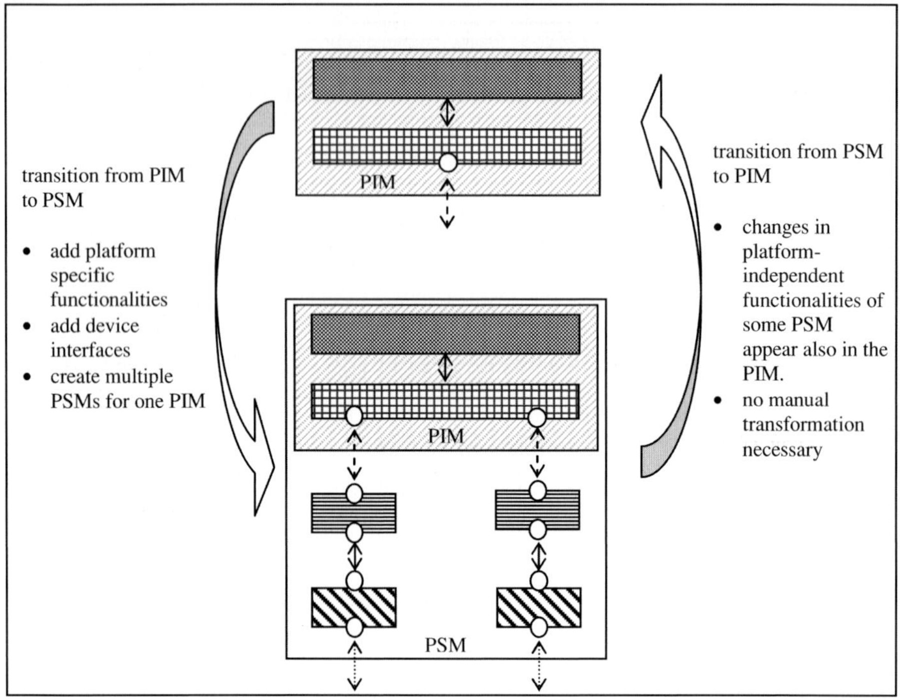

Fig. 6. Transitions between PIM and PSM

PIM is part of the PSM, without any modifications[2]. This makes the backward transition from PSM to PIM, which is desirable in iterative processes such as SDL-MDD, straightforward.

Given a PIM, we take the following steps to obtain a PSM:

1. Select one or multiple native platforms for subsequent code generation.
   Multiple native platforms may be selected as long as they only differ in their operating system and hardware platform – the offered environmental interfaces must be identical. This information is used subsequently to select platform-specific transformation rules when generating native code from the PSM. When selecting a platform, the size and accuracy of data types in the final code are determined, too.
2. Incorporate the PIM into the PSM.
   The PIM can be either incorporated as an SDL reference or as a copy into the PSM. Using an SDL reference has two advantages. First, a clean separation of PIM and platform-specific parts is enforced, since only the latter can be modified when the PSM is specified. Second, all changes applied to the PIM immediately apply to all related PSMs, which is important in case of iterative design.

[2] One may argue that using the PIM without any modifications may lead to suboptimal realizations of the PSM. In Section 5, we will show that the code generated from the PSM (including the PIM) is a set of macros, which leaves much room for code optimizations. Also, modifying the PIM would lead to different system behaviour.

3. Add platform-specific functionalities.
   Platform-specific functionalities model device classes that are only available on selected target platforms, or that depend on special, platform-dependent devices. These functionalities are either specified from scratch or are selected from a repository. Typical examples of platform-specific functionalities are MAC layers or sensor data processing.
4. Add platform-specific device interfaces.
   Platform-specific device interfaces abstract concrete devices from device classes, e.g. devices for serial communication. They are used to connect the abstract interfaces that are exposed to the other modeled components to real devices. These device interfaces are semantically integrated within the runtime environment, which detects the presence of device interfaces and reconfigures itself to include the interfacing code into the generated code (see Section 5).

For a given platform and a platform-specific repository, it is possible to automate steps 2 to 4. The reason is that the platform-specific functionalities are usually not application-specific, so the degree of reusability is substantial. Also, platform-specific device interfaces are stable. This gives rise to a tool that, for a given platform and PIM, generates a PSM.

5 The SDL-MDD Tool Suite

A particular strength of SDL-MDD is the availability of a semantically integrated tool suite, i.e. a tool suite that covers all aspects of model-driven development with SDL. This tool suite is based on Telelogic TAU SDT [11], a commercial tool suite that comes with a graphical SDL editor, an SDL debugger (called SDT simulator), an SDL validator to detect defects such as deadlocks and unspecified receptions, and two SDL-to-C compilers. However, SDT has two major shortcomings. First, SDT does not support performance simulations of SDL models. Second, the interface for the interaction of an open SDL system with its environment (e.g. a WLAN driver) must be hand-coded. These restrictions are similar for the PragmaDev tool suite [12]. In this section, we present tools that we have developed to remove these restrictions.

5.1 Model-Driven Performance Simulation with *ns*+SDL

To support performance simulations of SDL models, we have developed *ns*+SDL [4], the network simulator for SDL specifications. *ns*+SDL is an extension to the well-known network simulator *ns*-2 [6], adding the capability of loading SDL models as nodes into a simulated network. Thus, it is possible to directly simulate SDL models without having to re-implement them as *ns*-2 classes in C++. *ns*+SDL supports both platform-independent and platform-specific interfaces between SDL models and their environment. Since it is capable of simulating platform-independent devices and networks as well as platform-specific devices, the performance of PIMs and PSMs can be assessed.

ns+SDL is capable of simulating hardware components that form part of the system platform, in particular, communication hardware and processors. This way, simulation studies for selecting a particular communication technology that is best suited for the current application scenario can be performed already during system design. These early simulation studies prevent bad design decisions that would result in costly iterations at a later development stage.

During the development of the Assisted Bicycle Trainer, we have conducted a number of performance simulations, based on the PSM (see Section 4.2). In the simulated scenario, a group of 20 cyclists and one trainer are communicating via a simulated wireless LAN (IEEE 802.11b) with a range of about 200m. The cyclists are riding one behind the other, accompanied by the trainer. According to the mobility model of the scenario, positions and distances of cyclists change during the ride. While this has no consequences on connectivity between nodes in most cases, due to the wide range of WLAN, there are two situations where the field and the network are partitioned. At simulation times t1 = 100 sec and t2 = 530 sec, there is a gap of 200m between two groups of nodes.

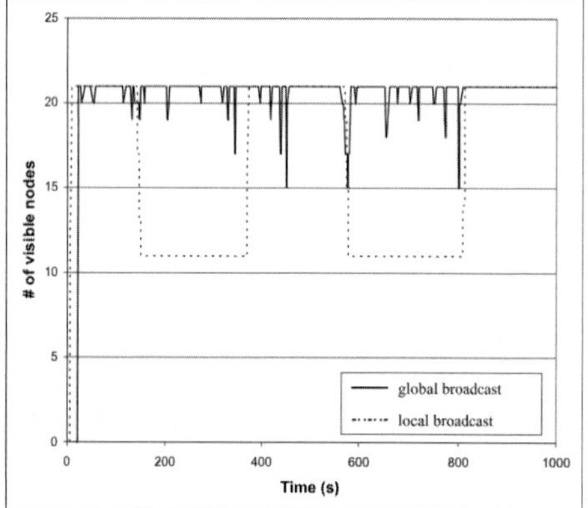

Fig. 7. Comparison of global and local broadcast

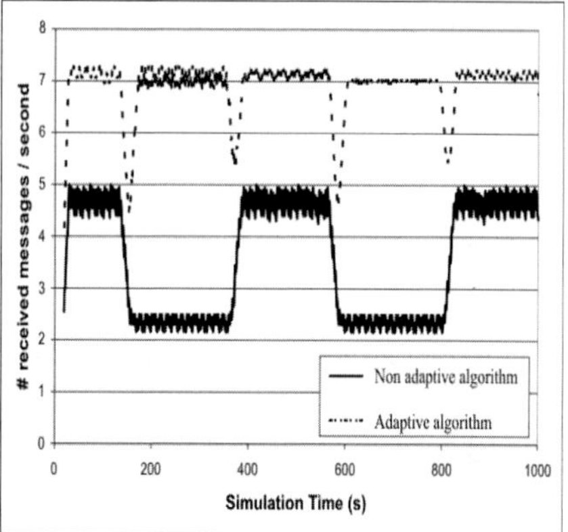

Fig. 8. Benefits of status message rateadaptation

In the simulated scenario, we have examined two aspects. First, we have compared the connectivity for local and global broadcast (see Fig. 7). When using local broadcast, the connectivity decreases to about 50%, when the field is partitioned. The selective flooding protocol NXP/MPR [7] improves this situation substantially, providing for almost full connectivity during the entire simulation. Reduced connectivity only occurs for short periods of time, and is due to frame collisions that prevent neighbors to receive the updated network status.

The second aspect concerns the benefits of the algorithm to adapt the status message rate to the current number of cyclists in the group, and the available network bandwidth. Simulation results are shown in Fig. 8 for local broadcast communication. In the non-adaptive case, the maximum number of cyclists in the group, i.e. 30 (see Section 3), is used to statically determine the status message rate as supported by the network and observed by the trainer, which is 7 per second. Since the actual group size is only 20, this leads to an actual status message rate of 5 per second when all members of the group are within reach of the trainer. This rate drops to 2 per second during periods of network partitioning.

In the adaptive case, the actual number of cyclists is determined and updated dynamically. In the simulation, the actual number of cyclists in the group allows for 7 status messages per second at the beginning. When the group is split, there is a short drop down to 5 status messages per second before the updated number of cyclists leads to a reduced status message interval of the cyclists within range of the trainer, and therefore to the maximum rate of 7 per second. Interestingly, there is another drop when the field of cyclists fuses. This can be explained by the fact that the previous field members reduce their message rate immediately (due to the larger group size), but the new field members start their status message transmission only after their status interval has expired for the first time.

5.2 Model-Driven Code Generation with TAU SDT and SEnF

The transformation of a model to a native implementation is a crucial step in model-driven development processes. Code generation from SDL models is highly customizable. The Cadvanced code generator of TAU SDT [11] creates files that mainly consist of macros, each macro associated with a specific language construct of SDL. A transformation provides concrete, platform dependent code for all of these constructs. In Fig. 9, this principle is illustrated for an SDL action.

We have extended the code generation of TAU SDT by defining special transformations and an advanced macro processor. In addition to simple substitutions, the macro processor can perform loops, iterations and decisions based on previously processed macros. This way, more complex transformations are possible. So far, we have defined two kinds of transformations. First, there is a transformation to traceable, readable code that is used for documentation purposes. Second, optimized code for a micro controller platform is produced, which is closely integrated with the SDL Environment Framework (SEnF).

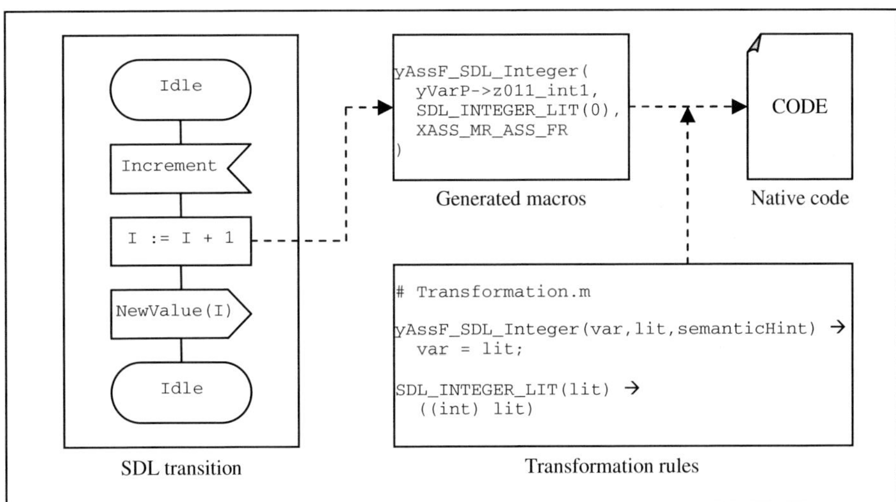

Fig. 9. Transformation of an SDL transition to native code

The SEnF is a library of interfacing routines for the interaction of an open SDL system with its environment (e.g. a WLAN driver). Currently, these interfacing routines cover the communication technologies IEEE 802.11a/b/g (WLAN), IEEE 802.15.1 (Bluetooth), RS-232 (UART), the input/output devices web cam, joy stick, LEDs, several sensors/actuators, and are available for the operating systems Windows NT/2000/XP, Linux, and for bare micro controller hardware. From the device interfaces of the PSM and additional configuration information, the required library routines are determined and added to the generated code. Thus, hand-coding of interfacing routines is made obsolete.

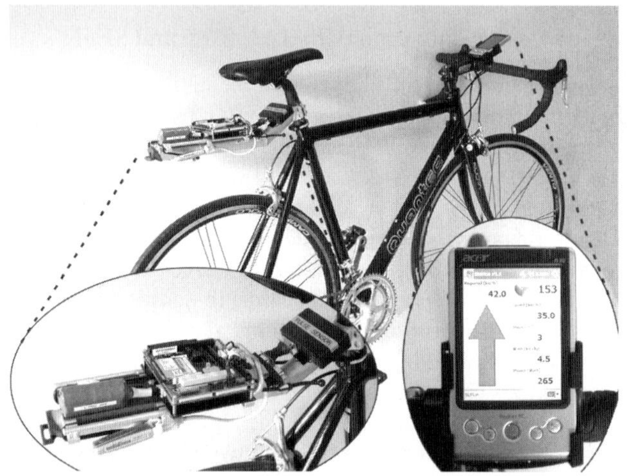

Fig. 10. The Assisted Bicycle Trainer (embedded PC configuration)

We have used the Telelogic SDL-to-C code generators and SEnF in order to automatically generate code for the Assisted Bicycle Trainer (ABT) from the PSM. The hardware platform of the ABT is mounted on a bicycle, as shown in Fig. 10. On the carrier, the embedded PC *Arbor Technology Em104Pi6023* (with WLAN stick Netgear MA-111, Bluetooth adapter D-Link DBT-120, and UART interface), pulse rate receiver, and batteries (Lithium-Polymer, 1500 mAh) are mounted. A PDA (Acer n-30) showing the current driver status (e.g., pulse rate, actual speed) and the trainer orders (e.g., required speed, required position changes) is attached to the handlebar. Communication between embedded PC and PDA is via Bluetooth. The cyclist carries a pulse rate transmitter. The trainer system (not shown here) is installed on a laptop, with a sophisticated graphical interface to monitor and direct the training. So far, we have equipped 3 bicycles with the cyclist system, and have successfully run several training sessions.

Due to restrictions of size and weight, we have also implemented the ABT system on a MicaZ platform, an ultra low power wireless sensor mote manufactured by Crossbow Industries. The MicaZ mote consists of an embedded microcontroller with 128 KB of Flash Rom and 4 KB of Ram. It is equipped with a ZigBee-Ready transceiver chip and with two UART ports. As already mentioned, the PSM for the

MicaZ platform is very similar to the PSM of the embedded PC solution. While the PIM is identical for both platforms, the WLAN driver interface has been replaced by a CC2420 interface. In addition, a tailored MAC layer called MacZ has been added. Also, different SDL-to-C compilers and different SEnF interface routines have been used to generate the production code for the two platforms, which is due to resource constraints.

6 Related Work

Model-driven software development has been standardized by the OMG with MDA [3], the Model Driven Architecture. Although not being fully MDA compliant, SDL-MDD has many similarities with the MDA.

As in the MDA, the models are separated into CIM, PIM and PSM. Models are stepwise refined, and platform dependent functionalities are added during the development process. Changeable and adaptable transformation rules are used for transforming the PSM into code that can be compiled for a specific platform. Since the PIM is incorporated into the PSM without any modifications, the transition from a PSM back to a PIM is straightforward.

SDL-MDD aims at generating complete implementations – the platform-specific code that is created out of the PSM should not have to be edited manually by developers. If this becomes necessary for some reason, either the transformation should be changed, or platform-dependent specification should be added to the PSM.

The MDA could be extended with SDL-MDD by using SDL as a domain-specific language for developing distributed systems and communication systems. Domain specific languages are encouraged by the MDA – by creating an UML2 profile for SDL, SDL could be integrated into MDA as a domain specific language for specifying embedded communication systems. There is ongoing work to define such a profile for the UML [8] that is also capable to transform activity charts to SDL.

SDL-MDD encourages simulations. In the domain of communication systems, it is not possible to predict the behavior and the performance of a system in operation effectively by static analysis techniques, especially when developing in the domain of wireless ad-hoc networks. As a result of this, SDL-MDD and its tool-chain provide developers the ability to simulate their models throughout the development process, starting in the early development stages.

There are also different approaches of adding semantics to UML. Executable UML (xUML) [9] is a UML profile that defines the semantics for the UML based on the idea of every object having a communicating state machine. As SDL, xUML can also be mapped to any programming language when the model is transformed to code.

7 Conclusions and Future Work

In this paper, we have presented SDL-MDD, a model-driven development process based on the ITU-T design language SDL. SDL-MDD is an iterative development process targeted towards distributed systems and communication systems in the ubiquitous computing domain. For this domain, SDL-MDD provides a specific methodology to define PIMs and PSMs, keeping the balance between platform-independent and platform-specific detail. We have also presented the SDL-MDD tool suite, consisting of commercial tools that we have extended in two directions. First, we have developed *ns*+SDL, a tool for the performance simulation of SDL models. Second, we have provided the SDL Environment Framework SEnF, a library of interfacing routines to entirely avoid manual coding steps during the implementation of open SDL systems. To illustrate the use of SDL-MDD, we have shown excerpts of the model-driven development of the Assisted Bicycle Trainer, a demonstrator developed in our lab. The size of the SDL specification for PIM and PSM is 68 pages and 103 pages, respectively.

We aim at further integrating SDL-MDD with MDA and also with UML2 [10], for instance, by modeling the inner structure and behavior of UML2 components with SDL. This way, SDL could be integrated into UML models as a domain-specific language for modeling protocols and other communication-related components.

Future work should include research on generating code for further platforms, for example, embedded Java or .NET frameworks. Also, the field of dynamic system reconfiguration at runtime is still widely unexplored, as well as the entirely automatic transformation from PIM to PSM with SDL-MDD.

Acknowledgements

The work presented in this paper was carried out in the µPros project (funded by DFG under the project number Go503/5-1), the research center Ambient Intelligence at the University of Kaiserslautern (supported by Ministry for Science, Education, Research, and Culture (MWWFK) of Rheinland-Pfalz), and the BelAmI project (funded by BMBF, Fraunhofer-Gesellschaft, and MWWFK of Rheinland-Pfalz).

References

[1] M. Book, S. Beydeda, and V. Gruhn. *Model-driven Software Development.* Springer, 2005

[2] International Telecommunications Union. *Specification and Description Language (SDL).* ITU-T Recommendation Z.100, August 2002

[3] J. Miller and J. Mukerji (Eds.). *MDA Guide Version 1.0.1.* OMG, 2003

[4] T. Kuhn, A. Geraldy, R. Gotzhein, and F. Rothländer. *ns+SDL - The Network Simulator for SDL System*, in: A. Prinz, R. Reed, and J. Reed (Eds.), SDL 2005, Lecture Notes in Computer Science (LNCS) 3530, pages 103-116. Springer, 2005.

[5] International Telecommunications Union. *Message sequence chart (MSC).* ITU-T Recommendation Z.120, April 1996

[6] *The Network Simulator ns-2.* `http://www.isi.edu/nsnam/ns.` Information Sciences Institute, University of Southern California

[7] I. Fliege, A. Geraldy. *NXP/MPR - An Optimized Ad-Hoc Flooding Algorithm.* Technical Report 343/05, Computer Science Department, University of Kaiserslautern, Germany, 2005

[8] D. Hogrefe, C. Werner: UML Profile for Communicating Systems, Technical Report No. IFI–TB–2006–03, Institute for Informatics, University of Göttingen, Germany, ISSN 1611–1044, March 2006
[9] S. J. Mellor, M. J. Balcer: Executable UML: A Foundation for Model Driven Architecture, Addison-Wesley, 2002, ISBN: 0-201-74804-5
[10] Object Management Group. *Unified Modeling Language 2.0 Infrastucture. Final Adopted Specification.* `http://www.omg.org/cgi-bin/doc?ptc/2003-09-15`, 2004
[11] Telelogic AB: *TAU SDT*, http://www.telelogic.com/products/tau/index.cfm
[12] PragmaDev: RTDS V3.1, http://www.pragmadev.com/

Model-Driven Analysis and Synthesis of Concrete Syntax

Pierre-Alain Muller[1], Franck Fleurey[1], Frédéric Fondement[2], Michel Hassenforder[3], Rémi Schneckenburger[4], Sébastien Gérard[4], and Jean-Marc Jézéquel[1]

[1] IRISA / INRIA Rennes
Rennes, France
{pierre-alain.muller, franck.fleurey}@irisa.fr
[2] Ecole Polytechnique Fédérale de Lausanne (EPFL)
Lausanne, Switzerland
frederic.fondement@epfl.ch
[3] MIPS, Université de Haute-Alsace
Mulhouse, France
michel.hassenforder@uha.fr
[4] Laboratoire d'Intégration des Systèmes et des Technologies (LIST)
Commissariat à l'Energie Atomique (CEA)
Saclay, France
{remi.schneckenburger, sebastien.gerard}@cea.fr

Abstract. Metamodeling is raising more and more interest in the field of language engineering. While this approach is now well understood for defining abstract syntaxes, formally defining concrete syntaxes with metamodels is still a challenge. Concrete syntaxes are traditionally expressed with rules, conforming to EBNF-like grammars, which can be processed by compiler compilers to generate parsers. Unfortunately, these generated parsers produce concrete syntax trees, leaving a gap with the abstract syntax defined by metamodels, and further ad-hoc hand-coding is required. In this paper we propose a new kind of specification for concrete syntaxes, which takes advantage of metamodels to generate fully operational tools (such as parsers or text generators). The principle is to map abstract syntaxes to concrete syntaxes via bidirectional mapping-models with support for both model-to-text, and text-to-model transformations.

1 Introduction

Meta-languages such as MOF [1], Ecore [2], Emfatic [3], KM3 [4] or Kermeta [5], model interchange facilities such as XMI [6] and tools such as Netbeans MDR [7] or Eclipse EMF [8] can be used for a wide range of purposes, including language engineering. While metamodeling is now well understood for the definition of abstract syntax, formal definition of concrete syntax is still a challenge, even though concrete syntax definition is considered as an important part of metamodeling [9].

Being able to parse a text and transform it into a model, or being able to generate text from a model are concerns that are being paid more and more attention in industry. For instance Microsoft with the DSL Tools [10] or Xactium with XMF Mosaic [11] in the domain-specific language engineering community, are two industrial solutions for language engineering that involve specifications used for the generation of tools such as parsers and editors. A new OMG standard, MOF2Text

O. Nierstrasz et al. (Eds.): MoDELS 2006, LNCS 4199, pp. 98 – 110, 2006.

[12], is also being developed regarding concrete-to-abstract mapping. Although this paper focuses on textual concrete syntaxes, it is worth noticing that there are also ongoing researches about modeling graphical concrete syntax [13,14].

Many of the concepts behind our work take their roots in the seminal work conducted in the late sixties on grammars and graphs and in the early eighties in the field of generic environment generators (such as Centaur [15]) that, when given the formal specification of a programming language (syntax and semantics), produce a language-specific environment.

There is currently a lot of interest in the modelware community about establishing bridges between so-called technological spaces [16]. For instance M. Wimmer and G. Krammler have presented a bridge from grammarware to modelware [17], whereas M. Alanen and I. Porres discuss the opposite bridge from modelware to grammarware, in the context of mapping MOF metamodels to context-free Grammars [18]. A. Kunert goes one step further and generates a model parser once the annotated grammar has been converted to a metamodel [19].

While a grammar could be considered as a metamodel, the inverse is not necessarily true, and an arbitrary metamodel cannot be transformed into a grammar [20]. Even metamodels dedicated to the modeling of a given concrete syntax (such as HUTN [21]) may require non-trivial transformations to target existing grammarware tools. We discuss some of these issues in a previous work, where we have experimented how to target existing compiler compilers to generate a parser for the HUTN language. A similar experience, turning an OMG specification (OCL) into a grammar acceptable by a parser generator [22] has been described by D. Akehurst and O. Patrascoiu.

As we have seen, the issue of transforming models into texts, and texts into models has been addressed as two different topics. At this time, we are not aware of a model-based specification of concrete syntax that would allow both concrete-to-abstract and abstract-to-concrete mappings.

In this paper, we explore such a bidirectional mapping by defining a metamodel for the specification of textual concrete syntax in a context where abstract syntax is also represented by metamodels. The transformations described in this paper (from model-to-code, and from code-to-model) are symmetric, and their effect can be reversed by each other. In the context of this paper, we call analysis the process of transforming texts into models, and synthesis the process of transforming models into texts.

The major difference with related works is that we do not try to bridge existing tools from modelware and grammarware. Actually, we are rather experimenting a new way of building tools for programming languages (such as compilers or IDEs) by using metamodels which embed results from the language theory directly in the modelware space. Our work is close to HUTN also, but in a more general context, as we support arbitrary concrete.

This work takes place in the context of the Kermeta project [3]. Kermeta is an executable DSL (Domain Specific Language) for meta-modeling, which can be used to specify both abstract syntax and operational semantics of a language.

This paper is organized as follows: the introduction examines some related works and motivates our proposal; section 2 presents our metamodel for concrete syntax, and explains the mechanics which are behind. Section 3 presents two examples which illustrate the way concrete syntax can be modeled and associated to models of the abstract syntax. Finally section 4 draws some general conclusions, and outlines future works.

2 Modeling Concrete Syntax

Let's consider the following metamodel of a language which defines models as collection of types where types have attributes, which in turn have a type.

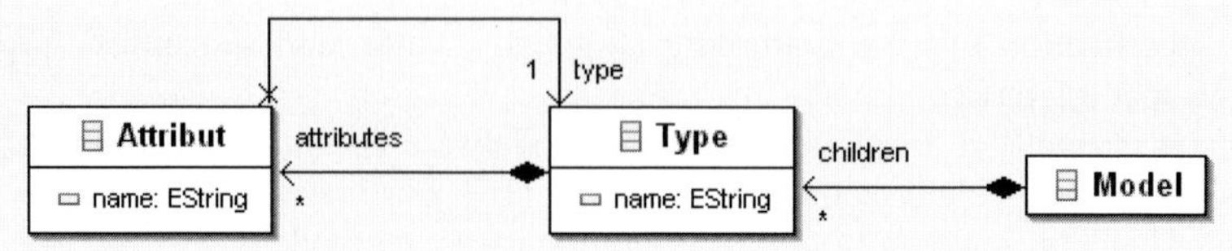

Fig. 1. Metamodel of abstract syntax for a simple language

A typical concrete syntax may be:

```
Type Mail {
   From : User
   To : User
}

Type User {
   Name : String
}

Type String;
```

Fig. 2. Example of concrete syntax

The metamodel on figure 1 defines the abstract syntax (the concepts of the language), but nothing is said about concrete syntax. We have to find some way of specifying how a construction of the language is rendered in text. In the next subsections we will examine how a metamodel could be used for that purpose.

2.1 Overview of Our Metamodel for Concrete Syntax

As seen in the previous example, when defining a language, the metamodel of the abstract syntax has to be complemented with concrete syntax information. In our case, this information will be defined in terms of another metamodel, which has to be used as a companion of the metamodel already used for defining the abstract syntax of the language under specification. This work is an evolution of our previous work which was limited to concrete syntax synthesis [23].

Figure 3 summarizes the approach. At runtime, both for analysis or synthesis, the models of abstract and concrete syntax are interpreted by a generic machine (written in terms of both metamodels) which performs the bidirectional transformation between texts and models

The metamodel for concrete syntax is displayed on figure 4. A concrete syntax has a top-level entry point, materialized by the root class which owns top-level rule fragments and meta-classes. A model of concrete syntax is built as a set of rules (the

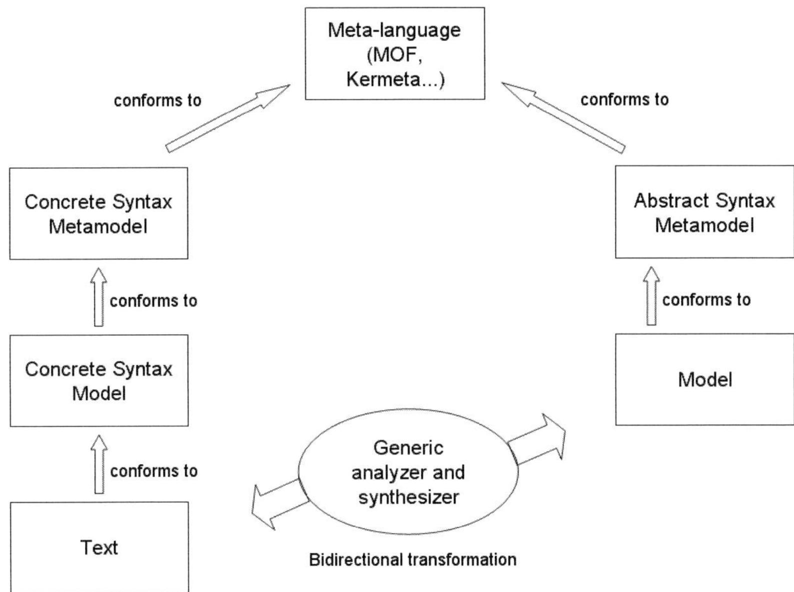

Fig. 3. A model driven generic machine performs the bidirectional transformation

sub-classes of abstract class *Rule*). The bridge between the metamodel of a language and the model of its concrete syntax is based on two meta-classes: *Class* and *Feature* respectively referencing the class of the abstract syntax metamodel and their properties. Class *Template* makes the connection between a class of the metamodel and its corresponding rules. Class *Value* (and its sub-classes) and class *Iteration* make the connection between the properties of a class and their values. Class Value is used for properties whose multiplicity is greater than 1. The remaining classes of the metamodel provide the usual constructions for the specification of concrete syntax such as terminals, sequences and alternatives.

During analysis, the input stream is tokenized, and parsed by a generic parser which operates by model-driven recursive descent. By model-driven recursive descent, we designate a recursive top-down parsing process which is taking advantage of the knowledge captured in the models of abstract and concrete syntaxes. While the parser recognizes valid sequences of tokens, it instantiates the abstract syntax, and builds an abstract representation (actually a model) corresponding to the input text.

During synthesis, text is generated by a generic synthesizer which operates like a model-driven template engine. The synthesizer visits the model (conform to the abstract syntax metamodel) and uses the presentation information available in the concrete syntax model (conform to the concrete syntax metamodel) to feed text to the output stream.

Interestingly, both processes of analysis and synthesis are highly symmetric, and since they share the same description, they are reversible. Indeed, a good validation

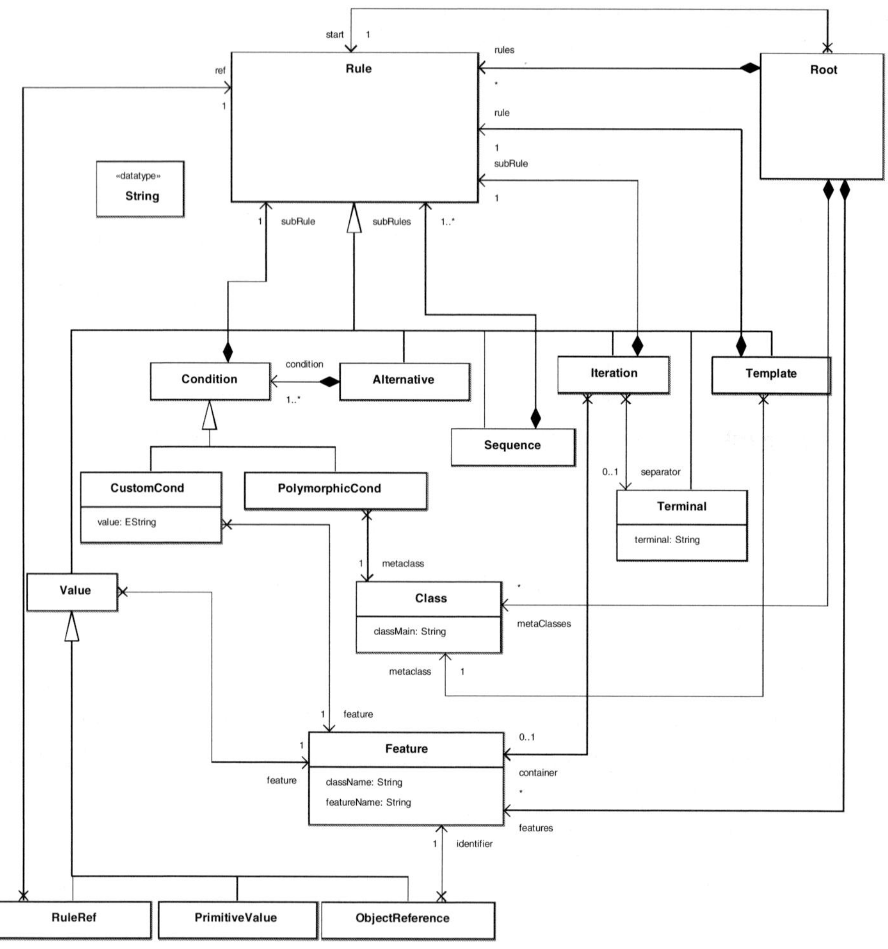

Fig. 4. Overview of the metamodel for concrete syntax

exercise is to perform two synthesis-parse sequences, and observe that there are no significant differences in both generated texts.

The following sub-sections detail the semantics associated to each elements of our concrete syntax metamodel, from both analysis and synthesis prospectives.

2.2 Template Rule

A Template rule makes the connection between a class of the metamodel (property *metaClass*) and a sub-rule.

Analysis semantics: The template specifies that an object should be created. The metaclass is instantiated and the object is set as the current object. The sub-rule is invoked and the current object is initialized. If an error occurs the current object is dismissed.

Synthesis semantics: The template specifies which object to serialize. The sub-rule is invoked to generate the corresponding text.

2.3 Terminal Rule

A terminal rule represents a text whose value is constant and known at modeling time. The text value is stored in the property *terminal* of type *String* in class *Terminal.*

Analysis semantics: The text in the input stream must be equal to the terminal value. The text is simply consumed. If the text does not correspond an exception is thrown.
Synthesis semantics: The terminal value is appended to the output stream along with formatting information, such as white spaces.

2.4 Sequence Rule

A sequence rule specifies an ordered collection of sub-rules. A sequence has at least one sub-rule.

Analysis semantics: The sub-rules are invoked successively. If any sub-rule fails the whole sequence is dismissed.
Synthesis semantics: The sub-rules are invoked successively.

2.5 Iteration Rule

Iterations specify the repetition of a sub-rule an arbitrary number of times. An iteration uses a collection (property *container* of type *Feature*), and may have a terminal to be used as a separator between elements (property *separator* of type *Terminal*).

Analysis semantics: The sub-rule (and separator, if specified) is invoked repetitively, until the sub-rule fails. For each successful invocation the collection specified by the container feature is updated.
Synthesis semantics: The sub-rule is applied to each object in the referenced collection, and the optional separator (if specified) is inserted between the texts which are synthesized for two consecutive elements.

2.6 Alternative Rule

Alternatives capture variations in the concrete syntax. An alternative has an ordered set of conditions which refer each to a given sub-rule. We have defined two kinds of conditions. Custom conditions are built over the features of a given class (may be a derived property, if the condition has to involve more than one class), while polymorphic conditions are built over the sub-classes of a given class.

Analysis semantics: This is the most complex operation. Often there is no clue in the input stream to determine the condition (in the sense defined in the metamodel for concrete syntax) which held when the text was created. It is therefore necessary to infer this condition while parsing the input stream. The simplest solution (but also the most time consuming) is to try each branch of the alternative until there is a match. We have chosen to implement such backtracking algorithm in our prototype

implementation. It is worth noticing that the ordered collection of conditions can also be used to handle priorities between conflicting sub-rules.
Synthesis semantics: The conditions are evaluated in the order defined in the collection, and the first one which evaluates to true, triggers the associated rule.

2.7 Primitive Value Rule

The rule *PrimitiveValue* specifies that the value of a feature is a literal. The type of the referenced feature should be a primitive type such as Boolean, Integer or String.

Analysis semantics: The literal value corresponding to the type of the feature is parsed in the input stream. The result is assigned to the corresponding feature of the current object unless the type conversion failed.
Synthesis semantics: The value of the feature in the current object is converted to a string and appended to the output stream.

2.8 Object Reference Rule

This rule implements the de-referentiation of textual identifiers to objects. Identifiers (such as names or numbers) are used in texts to reference objects which bear an attribute whose value contains such identifiers.

Analysis semantics: The reference which is extracted from the input stream is used as a key to query the model so as to find a matching element. If there is a match, the parser updates the element under construction. If there is no match, the parser assumes that the referenced item does not yet exist (because it might be defined later in the text) and creates a ghost to be referenced in place, and finally updates the element under construction with a reference to that ghost. By the end of the parsing process, all ghosts have to be resolved unless there is a parsing error.
Synthesis semantics: The identifier is printed to the output stream.

2.9 Rule Reference Rule

The rule *RuleReference* references a top-level template, stored under the root of the concrete syntax model.

Analysis semantics: The *ref* rule is triggered and the result is assigned to the feature of the current object.
Synthesis semantics: The *ref* rule is triggered.

The following section shows how the concrete syntax metamodel is used for specifying concrete syntax.

3 Examples

The following examples illustrate our approach.

3.1 A Very Simple Example of Concrete Syntax Specification

Going back to our small language example, we may use the reflexive editor of EMF (see Figure 5 below) to create a model directly as instances of the classes of the abstract syntax. This model defines three types (Mail, User and String).

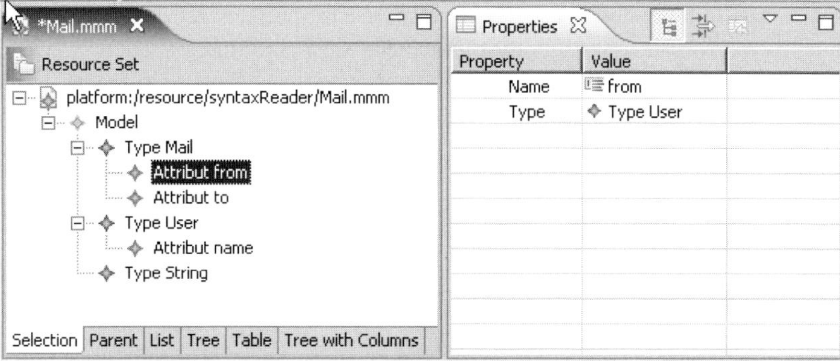

Fig. 5. Use of the reflexive editor of EMF to create a model

We will now use our metamodel of concrete syntax to specify the textual representation. In the example of concrete syntax given earlier (see Figure 2), there is no specific materialization of the model in the text. A type is declared by a keyword followed by a name and an optional collection of attributes. A collection is denoted by curly braces; an empty collection is specified by a semi-column. Notice that the notation allows forward references to *User* and *String*.

Again, we may use the reflexive editor of EMF to instantiate the classes of the metamodel for concrete syntax. A straightforward model of this concrete syntax might be:

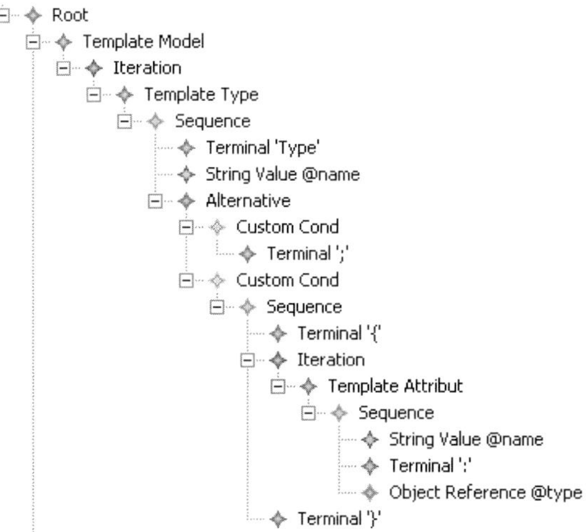

Fig. 6. Use of a reflexive editor to model concrete syntax

In this model, there is only one top-level rule which describes the concrete syntax of the language. The model is built as a cascade of rules. The model starts with an iteration over types. The sequence explains that types start with the keyword “Type”, followed by a name, and then an alternative because types may have a collection of attributes. Attributes when present are delimited by curly braces. The collection of attributes is expressed by an iteration, which in turn contains a sequence made of a name, followed by a separator (terminal ':') and finally a reference to a type.

Often, it is desirable to share some part of the concrete syntax. Therefore templates do not have to be nested, and can be defined individually at the top level of the model of the concrete syntax. The following picture represents such variation, for the same concrete syntax. Links between independently defined templates are realized with rule references (*RuleRef*).

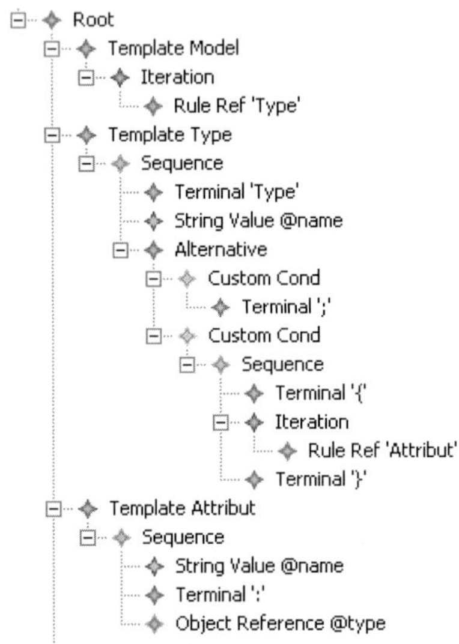

Fig. 7. Variation with top-level reusable templates

Both representations are totally equivalent. The parsed models or the generated texts are identical.

3.2 Modeling Simple Arithmetic Expressions

This second example is based on the traditional example of arithmetic expressions as found in many textbooks about compilation such as [24]. The following picture represents the metamodel (the abstract syntax) for simple arithmetic expressions.

The abstract syntax contains the following elements:

- **Model.** Represents the root of any arithmetic expression.
- **NumberInteger.** Represents an integer.
- **MultiplicativeOp.** Represents a binary multiplication operator.
- **AdditiveOp.** Represents a binary addition operator.

Let's first examine a prefixed concrete syntax for expression. The operator is always located in front of the operands, and the priorities are implicitly expressed at the invocation of each operator. The following concrete syntax model addresses such prefixed notation.

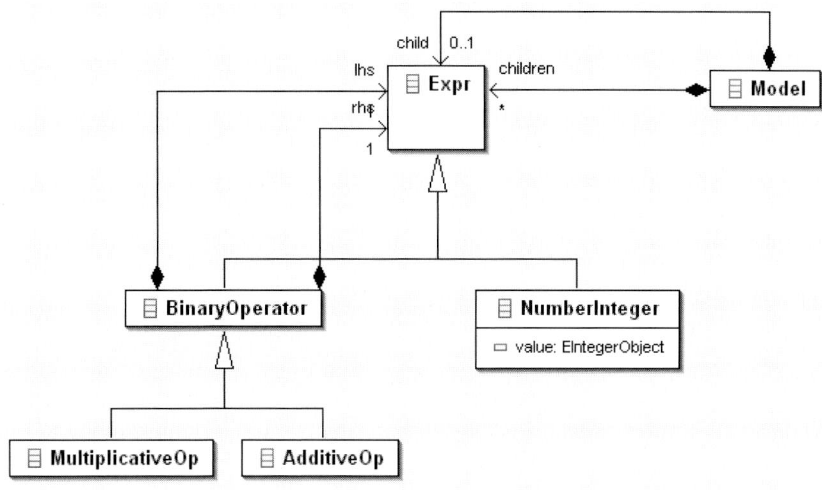

Fig. 8. Metamodel for simple arithmetic expressions

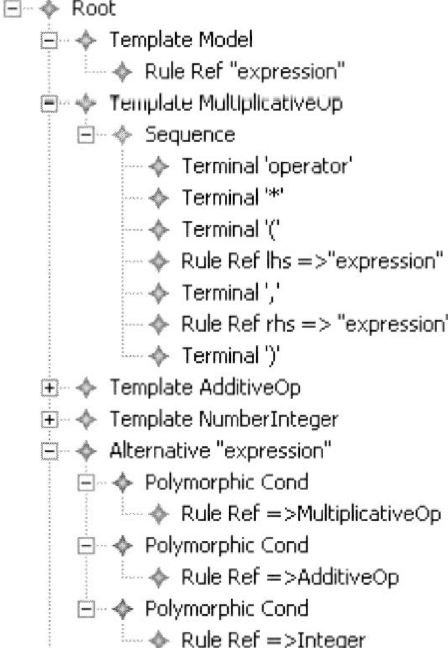

Fig. 9. Concrete syntax for prefixed expressions

Notice that we have here several independent top-level templates. The first template is the entry point. The second template (`MultiplicativeOp`) is in charge of multiplication operators. It is built as a sequence made of the keyword "operator" followed by a star sign and (between parentheses) two consecutive invocations of the expression rule, to handle respectively the left-hand-sign (lhs) and right-hand-side (rhs) of the expression (separated by a comma). The third template (`AdditiveOp`) is built on the same scheme as the precedent template. The (`NumberInteger`) models simple integer values. The last template (the expression alternative) states which branch to take based on the actual class of the parsed element. The order of these alternatives is not meaningful for prefixed expressions.

Non-factorized alternatives are a typical issue for parsers which operates by recursive descent. With our approach, a non-factorized grammar (such as the repetition of "`operator`" in both multiplicative and additive operators) is not really an issue, because the strategy used to analyze an alternative is based on backtracking. Branches are tried in a row, until there is no parsing error, which means that the correct branch has been found. Practically speaking, this process remains reasonably quick, as it is possible to validate (or not) the current branch as soon as the symbol of the operator is encountered in the input stream.

A typical concrete syntax example might be:

```
operator + ( operator * ( 3 , 2 ) , 1 )
```

While such prefixed notation is easy to parse by machines, humans tend to prefer an infixed representation, closer to the way computation is done manually. The same expression represented in infix notation is:

```
3*2+1
```

Now it is not possible anymore to ignore the operator precedence, as it was the case with the non-ambiguous prefixed notation. The usual approach consists in encoding the priority of operators by introducing new intermediate symbols such as `Term` and `Factor`.

In line with parsers which operate by recursive descent, our prototype implementation requires also converting rules with left-recursivity into rules with right-recursivity. In the end, the grammar (expressed in BNF) becomes:

```
<Expression>::= <AdditiveOP> | <Term>
<Term> ::= <MultiplicativeOp> | <Factor>
<Factor> ::=<NumberInteger>
<AdditiveOp> ::=<Term> '+' <Expr>
<MultiplicativeOp> ::= <Factor> '*' <Term>
<NumberInteger> ::= [0-9]+
```

Such rewriting may be a little bit tedious, but is only required for languages which support infix notation for arithmetic expressions. The following picture shows how this reformulation is presented in a model conform to our concrete syntax metamodel.

The template `AdditiveOp` defines a sequence which starts by invoking the `term` rule, follows by a plus sign and finishes by a call to the `expression` rule. The `MultiplicativeOp` is built on the same scheme, while the `NumberInteger` template handles Integer values. As described earlier in BNF, the expression alternative is made of either a call to the `AdditiveOp` rule or a call to the `term` rule.

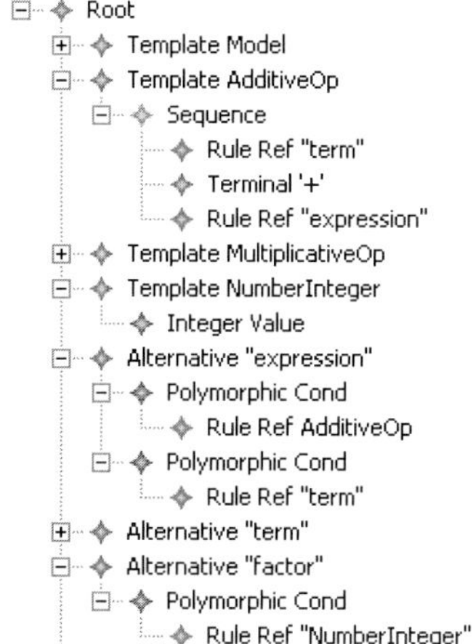

Fig. 10. Concrete syntax for infixed expressions

4 Conclusion

This work may be viewed as an experimentation for the specification of concrete syntax in the context of meta-modeling applied to language engineering.

We have proposed a new approach, based on metamodels, which supports a formal bi-directional mapping of both concrete-to-abstract, and abstract-to-concrete syntax.

A prototype, based on recursive descent, which realizes both analysis and synthesis of concrete syntax has been implemented on top of EMF in Eclipse. This prototype has been used to parse and pretty-print several DSLs, as well as the examples presented in this paper.

Our work is obviously far from bringing definitive answers to the complex problems of applying metamodels to language engineering but, along with the capabilities of executable meta-languages such as Kermeta, it suggests that languages can be fully specified in terms of metamodels, and that tools can be automatically derived from these metamodels to support these languages.

In the short future, we will be investigating how to avoid rewriting rules, potentially by using mechanisms similar to those behind LL* engines such as found in ANTLR v3 [25]. We are also working on a graphical editor (based on templates), to make the specification of the concrete syntax even more intuitive for non-specialists.

A lot of work is still beyond us to make tools based on this approach as robust and efficient as the one in the grammarware space. However, the presented material may contribute, with many other ongoing research works to a better understanding of metamodeling applied to language engineering.

References

[1] OMG, *Meta-Object Facility (MOF) 1.4*, OMG Document formal/02-04-03 (2002).

[2] Budinsky F., Steinberg D., Merks E., Ellersick R., Grose T. J., *Eclipse Modeling Framework, Chapter 5 Ecore Modeling Concepts*, Addison-Wesley, 2003.

[3] IBM, *Emfatic*, http://www.alphaworks.ibm.com/tech/emfatic

[4] Jouault F., Bézivin J., *KM3: A DSL for Metamodel Specification*, FMOODS 2006: 171-185

[5] Muller, P.-A., F. Fleurey and J.-M. Jézéquel, *Weaving executability into object-oriented meta-languages*, in: International Conference on Model Driven Engineering Languages and Systems (MoDELS), LNCS 3713 (2005), pp. 264–278.

[6] OMG, *Xml Metadata Interchange (XMI 2.1)*, OMG Document formal/05-09-01 (2005).

[7] Sun Microsystems, *Metadata repository (MDR),* (2005), http://mdr.netbeans.org/

[8] Eclipse, *Eclipse Modeling Framework (EMF),* (2005) http://www.eclipse.org/emf/

[9] Atkinson, C. and Kuehne T., *The role of meta-modeling in MDA*, in: Workshop in Software Model Engineering (WISME@UML), Dresden, Germany, 2002.

[10] Greenfield, J., Short K., Cook S. and Kent S., *Software Factories: Assembling Applications with Patterns, Models, Frameworks, and Tools*, Wiley, 2004.

[11] Clark, T., Evans A., Sammut P. and Willans J., *Applied metamodelling: A foundation for language-driven development* (2005). URL http://albini.xactium.com

[12] OMG, *MOF Model to Text Transformation Language* (Request For Proposal), OMG Document ad/2004-04-07 (2004).

[13] de Lara, J. and Vangheluwe H., *Using AToM3 as a meta-case tool*, in: Proceedings of the 4th International Conference on Enterprise Information Systems (ICEIS), 2002, pp. 642–649.

[14] Fondement, F. and Baar T., *Making Metamodels Aware of Concrete Syntax*, in: European Conference on Model Driven Architecture (ECMDA), LNCS 3748 (2005), pp. 190–204.

[15] Borras, P., Clement, D., Despeyroux, T., Incerpi, J., Kahn, G., Lang, B. and Pascual, V. Centaur: the system. *Proceedings of the ACM SIGSOFT/SIGPLAN software engineering symposium on practical software development environments*, *13* (5). 14-24.

[16] Kurtev, I., Aksit, M., and Bezivin, J., *Technical Spaces: An Initial Appraisal*. CoopIS, DOA´2002 Federated Conferences, Industrial track, Irvine, 2002.

[17] Wimmer, M., Kramler, G., *Bridging Grammarware and Modelware*, WISME Workshop, MODELS / UML'2005, Ocotober 2005, Montego Bay, Jamaica.

[18] Alanen, M., and Porres, I., *A Relation Between Context-Free Grammars and Meta Object Facility Metamodels*. Technical report, Turku Centre for Computer Science, 2003.

[19] Kunert A., *Semi-Automatic Generation of Metamodels and Models from Grammars and Programs*, in Proceedings of the Fifth International Workshop on Graph Transformation and Visual Modeling Techniques at ETAPS 2006, april 2006.

[20] Klint P., Lämmel R., and Verhoef C., *Towards an engineering discipline for grammarware*. ACM TOSEM, Vol. 14, N. 3, PP 331-380, May 2005.

[21] Muller, P.-A., Hassenforder M., *HUTN as a Bridge between ModelWare and GrammarWare – An Experience Report*, WISME Workshop, MODELS / UML'2005, Ocotober 2005, Montego Bay, Jamaica.

[22] OMG. UML2.0 Object Constraint Language (OCL) Final Adopted specification, Object Management Group, http://www.omg.org/cgi-bin/doc?ptc/2003-10-14, 2003

[23] Muller, P.-A., P. Studer and J.-M. Jézéquel, *Model-driven generative approach for concrete syntax composition*, in: Workshop in Best Practices for Model Driven Software Development, Vancouver, Canada, 2004.

[24] Aho A.V., Sethi R., Ullman J.D., *Compilers, Techniques and Tools*, Addison Wesley, 1986.

[25] Parr, T., *Another Tool for Language Recognition* (ANTLR) (2005), http://www.antlr.org/

Correctly Defined Concrete Syntax for Visual Modeling Languages

Thomas Baar

École Polytechnique Fédérale de Lausanne (EPFL)
School of Computer and Communication Sciences
CH-1015 Lausanne, Switzerland
thomas.baar@epfl.ch

Abstract. The syntax of modeling languages is usually defined in two steps. The abstract syntax identifies modeling concepts whereas the concrete syntax clarifies how these modeling concepts are rendered by visual and/or textual elements. While the abstract syntax is often defined in form of a metamodel there is no such standard format yet for concrete syntax definitions; at least as long as the concrete syntax is not purely text-based and classical grammar-based approaches are not applicable. In a previous paper, we proposed to extend the metamodeling approach also to concrete syntax definitions. In this paper, we present an analysis technique for our concrete syntax definitions that detects inconsistencies between the abstract and the concrete syntax of a modeling language. We have implemented our approach on top of the automatic decision procedure SIMPLIFY.

1 Introduction

The trend to model-driven development is facing the question how modeling languages can be defined precisely in a standardized format. Metamodeling is today the prevailing technique in order to define the abstract syntax of modeling languages in a precise, non-ambiguous way: metaclasses represent all modeling concepts, metaattributes their variations, metaassociations their relationships. Well-formedness rules written as OCL invariants insure that certain conditions are satisfied in all syntactically correct sentences of the modeling language. The abstract syntax definition is the most basic block when defining a modeling language but, at the same time, it is the only block for which a commonly agreed format exists. All other blocks of a modeling language definition, e.g. the definition of concrete syntax and the definition of semantics, are given in many cases only informally. A prominent example for an informal language definition is UML, see [1]. The most important disadvantage of informal definitions is the lack of tool support for checking the consistency of the definition.

This paper is about formal *concrete syntax* definitions for modeling languages having a visual, i.e. not purely textual, notation. In the first part (Sect. 2 and Sect. 3), we briefly describe a metamodeling approach to define not only the abstract syntax but also the concrete syntax of a modeling language formally

O. Nierstrasz et al. (Eds.): MoDELS 2006, LNCS 4199, pp. 111–125, 2006.

(this approach has been already presented with more details in [2]). As an illustration, we use UML class diagrams, mainly, because class diagrams have a well-known visual concrete syntax. In the paper's main part (Sect. 4), we show how concrete syntax definitions can be analyzed rigorously and automatically checked. Intuitively, the concrete syntax is ill-defined if two different models (i.e. instances of the abstract syntax metamodel) can be rendered by the same diagram. As a tiny example, one can take UML class diagrams whose classes can be abstract and non-abstract according to the abstract syntax. Suppose, the concrete syntax would only stipulate to render each class by a rectangle and to label the rectangle with the name of the class. Then, one could not infer from a given diagram whether a rectangle represents an abstract or a non-abstract class and this ambiguity is an error of the concrete syntax definition.

Such errors can be automatically detected by using deductive tools. More precisely, we generate out of a formal concrete syntax definition a proof obligation that is valid if and only if the syntax definition does not contain any error. Then, this proof obligation is passed to the deductive tool SIMPLIFY [3], which was able to automatically discharge all of them for the examples given in this paper.

2 Visual Languages

Modeling languages having a visual concrete syntax use for the representation of models graphical elements such as rectangles, circles, lines, stickmen, etc. Graphical elements are also called *visual objects* since they can easily be described as objects whose state is given by the value for certain attributes such as *shape*, *lineColor*, *backgroundColor*, *attachRegion*, etc. A set of visual objects is a syntactically correct *sentence of a visual language* when all well-formedness rules of the visual language are met. A typical example for a well-formedness rule is that a visual object of shape *Line* always connects two other visual objects, more technically, that the start- and endpoint of the line coincide with the attach regions of the connected visual objects. We call a syntactically correct sentence of a visual language also *diagram*.

The definition of a visual language is done in two steps: (1) identification of all attributes for visual objects, and (2) formulation of well-formedness rules. For non-trivial visual languages, it is worthwhile to distinguish classes of visual objects because not all possible attributes are relevant for each object, e.g. a visual object of shape *Line* does not need a value for an attribute *backgroundColor*. Once the classes of visual objects together with their attributes are identified, many well-formedness rules of the visual language can easily be expressed by associations between classes. For example, the above given restriction for a line to connect two other visual objects is best expressed by two associations from class `Line` to a class, let's say, `ConnectableObject` (which represents the connected visual objects) with multiplicity 1 at the latter class.

Having said this, it is obvious that a metamodel is a very appropriate format to define a visual language formally. A diagram is then just an instance of the metamodel of the visual language.

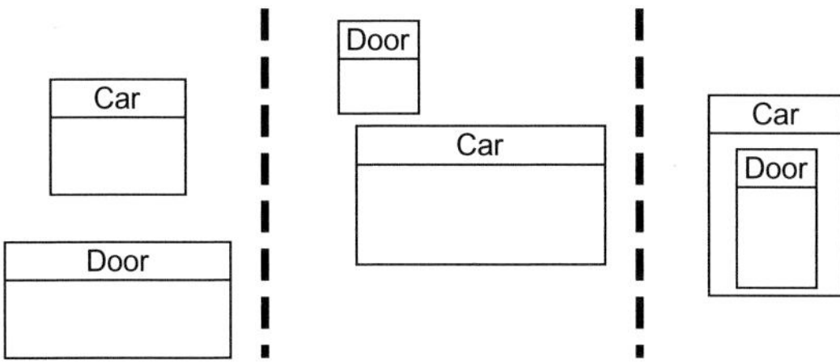

Fig. 1. Three diagrams – when read as representations of class diagrams, the first two diagrams should not be distinguishable

As an example, we discuss the three diagrams given in Fig. 1. What we see – at a first glance – are two labeled rectangles, which have in all three diagrams different dimensions and different positions. An initial version of the metamodel could consist of one class `Rectangle` with attributes for (1) the label, (2) the x and y coordinates of the position, and (3) the dimension (width, height). According to this metamodel, all three diagrams are different. This initial metamodel is very suitable if the layout information of the diagrams have to be captured; for instance, when diagramming tools have to exchange diagrams. Actually, the initial metamodel can be seen as a drastically simplified version of the upcoming OMG standard for Diagram Interchange [4]. However, the initial metamodel is less useful as a basis for a concrete syntax definition for class diagrams. When read as class diagrams, the left and middle diagram should coincide, despite the fact, that the dimensions and positions of the two rectangles are different. While the right diagram also shows the same classes as the first two, just the position and the dimension were changed again, it is nevertheless semantically different from the others.[1]

What this tiny example already shows is the fact, that layout information in form of coordinates and dimensions are not necessary for the definition of a concrete syntax. It is better to choose such attributes for visual objects that reflect differences of rendered models. For example, we cannot fully ignore layout information because this would make all three diagrams in Fig. 1 non-distinguishable.

Figure 2 shows a more suitable metamodel for the visual language used in Fig. 1. The class `Rectangle` has again one attribute for label but none for position and dimension. In order to distinguish the last diagram from the two others, a self-association on `Rectangle` has been introduced that encodes graphical nesting of rectangles. In the lower part of Fig. 2, the three diagrams from Fig. 1 are given as instances of the visual language metamodel and the first two diagrams coincide indeed.

The definition and efficient processing of visual languages is a current research area, which we cannot develop further here due to space limit. A warmly recommended introduction is [5] where a classification of visual languages is presented and formats for elegant language definitions are derived. A core technique, which

[1] When read as a UML class diagram, the graphical containment of class `Door` in class `Car` means that `Car` is composed of `Door`.

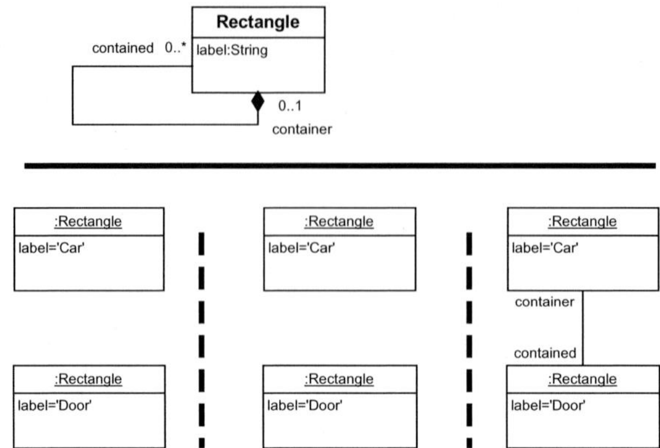

Fig. 2. Visual language definition and representation of diagrams given in Fig. 1

has been also applied in the above example, is to substitute absolute layout information (such as position, dimension) by relative ones, called *spatial relationships*. When defining a metamodel for a visual language, one has to identify – in a first step – all relevant spatial relationships. For example, the rendering of UML models requires graphical nesting as one spatial relationship but there are other spatial relationships needed as well.

3 Concrete Syntax Definition

In the previous section, we have outlined how a visual language can be formalized in form of a metamodel; we will now answer the question how sentences of a modeling language, which are given as instances of the abstract syntax metamodel, can be rendered in this visual language. The missing part is, informally speaking, the bridge from the abstract syntax metamodel to the metamodel of the visual language. In the following, we describe briefly our approach to define the concrete syntax and illustrate it on a fragment of UML class diagrams. The approach of *defining* the concrete syntax has been already described in one of our previous papers [2] and was recently implemented based on SVG technology [6]. The core idea for bridging both metamodels is to introduce new classes in between. This technique is well-known from Triple-Graph-Grammars [7] and is also applied in the OMG standard for Diagram Interchange [4].

Figure 3 gives an overview on the structure of concrete syntax definitions. In the left part, a metamodel for the abstract syntax is shown: each instance of `Class` is connected to a sequence of `Attribute` instances and instances of `Association` have two `AssociationEnd`s which refer to exactly one `Class`. The metamodel of the visual language is shown in the right part and describes graphical elements like rectangles, lines and text fields.

The two classes `ClassDM` and `AssociationDM` are so-called *display manager classes* (the name of these classes has, by convention, always the suffix `DM`) and realize the bridge from the abstract syntax to the visual language. Strictly speaking,

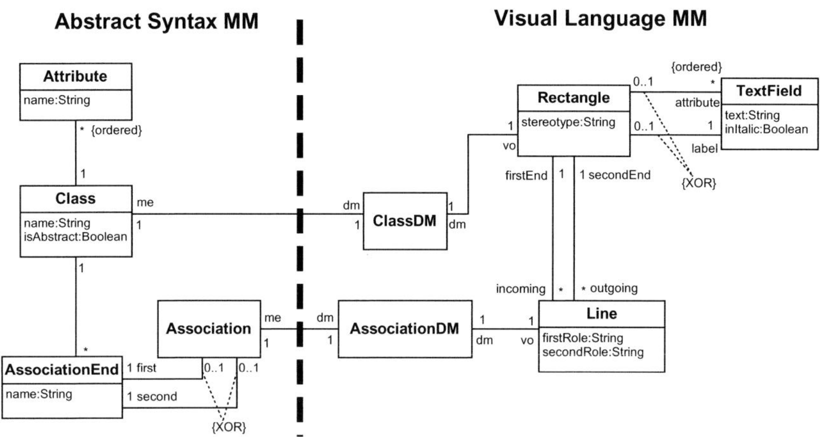

Fig. 3. Bridging the metamodels describing abstract syntax and visual language

display manager classes belong neither to the metamodel of the abstract syntax nor to that of the visual language since they are added later on, when the concrete syntax is defined. For our argumentation, however, it has advantages if they are seen as part of the metamodel of the visual language. A display manager class is always connected via an association with multiplicity 1-1 to a class from the abstract syntax metamodel. The display manager class manages the rendering of the referenced class. By convention, we always use `me` (for **m**odel **e**lement) and `dm` (for **d**isplay **m**anager) as role names on this association. Display manager classes have also an association to a class in the visual language metamodel. Usually, this association has multiplicity 1-1 as well and role names `dm` and `vo` (for **v**isual **o**bject).

The bridge from the abstract syntax to the visual language is realized by invariants that are attached to the display manager classes. These invariants formalize synchronization conditions on the states of modeling elements and the corresponding visual objects (which realize the rendering of the modeling elements). For our example, the invariants are:

```
context AssociationDM inv:
      self.me.first.name=self.vo.firstRole
  and self.me.second.name=self.vo.secondRole
  and self.vo.firstEnd=self.me.first.class.dm.vo
  and self.vo.secondEnd=self.me.second.class.dm.vo

context ClassDM inv:
      self.me.name=self.vo.label.text
  and (self.me.isAbstract implies
        (self.vo.stereotype='abstract' or
         self.vo.label.inItalic))
  and (not(self.me.isAbstract) implies
        (self.vo.stereotype='' and
```

```
        not(self.vo.label.inItalic)))
and self.me.attribute->size()=self.vo.attribute->size()
and Set{1..self.me.attribute->size()}->forAll(i|
      self.me.attribute->at(i).name=
        self.vo.attribute->at(i).text)
```

Based on Fig. 3 and the invariant for AssociationDM one can conclude, that each instance of Association is rendered by a Line, whose annotations firstRole and secondRole correspond to the names of the two association ends. Furthermore, the line connects the two rectangles which render the classes the two association ends are referring to. The invariant for ClassDM is slightly more complicated since it allows for *presentation options* when rendering a class. An abstract class can be marked by a stereotype 'abstract' attached to the corresponding rectangle or the label of the rectangle is displayed in an italic font. The attributes of a class are presented in the same order as textfields in the rectangle. For the rendering of the attributes it does not matter whether they are set in italic or not, they just represent attributes that are given by their names.

To summarize, our approach to define concrete syntax

- describes in a declarative way all possible representations of models (instances of the abstract syntax metamodel) by diagrams (instances of the visual language metamodel). Note that our technique allows to define presentation options, i.e. one model can be rendered by different, i.e. non-isomorphic, diagrams. But – since the concrete syntax definition is symmetric – the opposite case that one diagram renders different, i.e. non-isomorphic, models is possible as well. Such a concrete syntax definition would be incorrect (a diagram should always represent only one model) and in Sect. 4 we will discuss an approach to detect such incorrect concrete syntax definitions.
- does not require to define a display manager class for all classes of the abstract syntax metamodel. In our example, display manager classes are defined only for Class and Association whereas for Attribute, AssociationEnd this was not necessary, since the rendering of these classes are captured by ClassDM, AssociationDM as well. We will give in Sect. 4.2 a detailed analysis, under which circumstances a class from the abstract syntax metamodel does not need its own display manager class.

4 Analysis of Concrete Syntax Definitions

As already mentioned in the introduction and at the end of the last section, concrete syntax definitions can be incorrect. Correctness basically[2] means in our context that each diagram must correspond to only one model. As a tiny example for an incorrect concrete syntax definition we refer to the upper part

[2] There is another criterium on the completeness of the concrete syntax definition saying that for each model there is at least one diagram. However, this is not discussed in this paper.

of Fig. 4. Suppose, that the display manager class `ClassDM` has attached the following invariant:

```
context ClassDM inv:
    self.me.name=self.vo.text
```

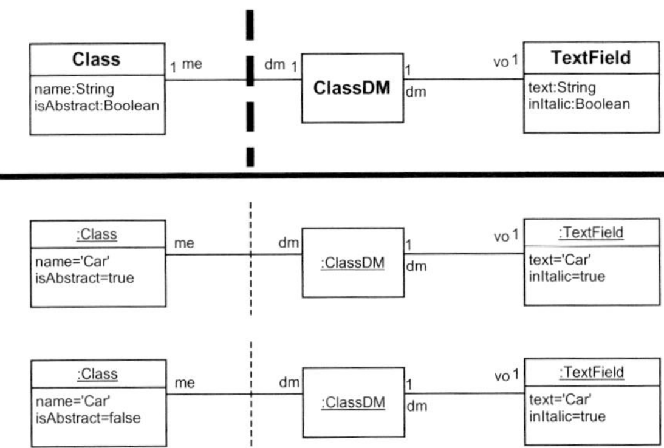

Fig. 4. Incorrect syntax definition and counterexample

The lower part of Fig. 4 shows two instantiations that conform to all multiplicity constraints and to the invariant for `ClassDM`. These instantiations witness an error in the concrete syntax definition since they show how two isomorphic diagrams refer to two non-isomorphic models. If the user of an editor would draw one of the diagrams, he could not be sure which of the two possible models this diagram actually represents. The instantiations are possible because the invariant attached to `ClassDM` only stipulates how attribute `name` of the model element is related to attribute `text` of its visual representation but ignores the value of attribute `isAbstract`.

The correctness criterion for concrete syntax definitions is given with mathematical rigor by the following definition:

Definition 1 (Correctness of Concrete Syntax Definitions). *Let CSMM be a concrete syntax definition given in form of a metamodel (cmp. Fig. 3). Since CSMM is divided into two parts describing abstract syntax and visual language, this division can also be applied to instances of CSMM. Let cs1, cs2 be two instances of CSMM. We denote the part of cs1/cs2 belonging to the abstract syntax part of CSMM as as1/as2 and the part belonging to the visual language part as vl1/vl2.*

We call the concrete syntax definition CS correct *(or* well-defined*) if and only if the following holds:*

Whenever vl1 is isomorphic to vl2 then as1 must also be isomorphic to as2.

In the sequel, we show how this correctness criterion can be encoded into first-order logic so that the decision procedure SIMPLIFY can prove or disprove the generated proof obligation. SIMPLIFY was originally developed to decide the validity of a given formula in the theory of *Pressburger Arithmetik* [8], a set of axioms defining the arithmetic operators for natural numbers except multiplication. SIMPLIFY is also applicable to prove validity in any other first-order theory, but then, due to the undecidability of first-order logic, SIMPLIFY is not able to prove all valid theorems. For the proof obligations that has been generated as the encoding of our correctness criterion, however, SIMPLIFY was impressively powerful and could prove or disprove every proof obligation for all examples we discuss in this paper. A very useful feature of SIMPLIFY is, that it gives back a counterexample if the proof goal has been disproven. This happens when the concrete syntax definition is erroneous and the generated proof obligations are not valid.

4.1 Encoding of Proof Obligations into First-Order Logic

In this subsection, we justify our encoding of the proof obligations for the most simple kind of syntax definitions, in which the metamodel of the abstract syntax consist of one class only (the definition given in Fig. 4 will serve as an illustrating example). The goal of our argumentation is to justify, that an encoding of the above given correctness criterion into first-order logic is possible. Note that the criterion given in Def. 1 refers to the isomorphism of graphs, a property that can usually not be expressed using first-order logic. Fortunately, in our case, the graphs have a unique structure, which simplifies the encoding of graph isomorphism so that first-order logic has sufficient expressive power. In the next subsection we will present a heuristic on how a concrete syntax definition with more than one class in the abstract syntax part can be reduced to the case we discuss now, where the abstract syntax part has merely one class.

For the rest of this subsection, we assume a concrete syntax definition as illustrated by Fig. 4: The abstract syntax part has only one class (`Class`) that is connected by an 1-1 association with a display manager class (`ClassDM`) that in turn is connected to other classes in the visual language part, in our example we have a 1-1 association to class `TextField`.

The correctness criterion given in Def. 1 requires to check that two isomorphic instances $vl1$, $vl2$ of the visual language part are always connected to isomorphic instances $as1$, $as2$ of the abstract syntax part. The situation is sketched in Fig. 5.

We can assume that $vl1$ is isomorphic to $vl2$, that is, it exists a bijection $mapVL$ that maps in particular each display manager object, i.e. each instance of display manager class `ClassDM`, in $vl1$ to an isomorphic instance in $vl2$. For the display manager objects in $vl1$ and $vl2$ we further know that there is an isomorphism to the objects in $as1$ and $as2$ (because the display manager class `ClassDM` and the abstract syntax class `Class` are connected by an association with multiplicity 1-1). We call this mapping $vl2as$. Based on $mapVL$ and vl2as we can now define a function $mapAS$ as follows (variable cdm represents all instances of `ClassDM` in $vl1$):

$mapAS(vl2as(cdm)) = vl2as(mapVL(cdm))$

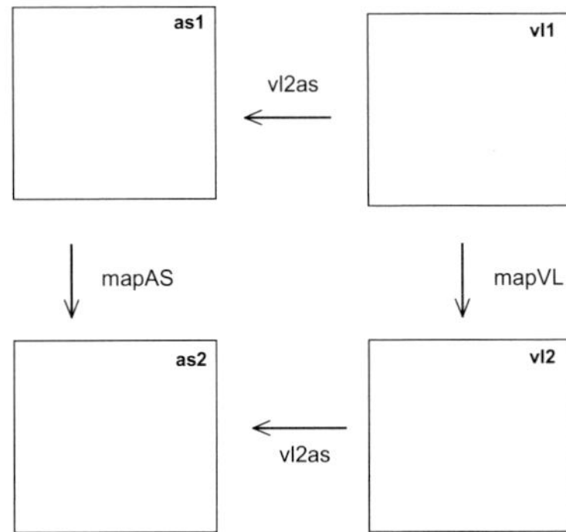

Fig. 5. Bijections that justify correctness criterion

Please note that *mapAS* is defined as a total function from $as1$ into $as2$, because each object in $as1$ has a corresponding display manager object in $vl1$.

If we could show now that *mapAS* maps the objects from $as1$ to *isomorphic* objects in $as2$ then this would prove that $as1$ and $as2$ themselves (both are sets of objects) are isomorphic what in turn would complete the proof on the correctness of the concrete syntax definition.

It remains to show for each isomorphism *mapVL* between $vl1$ and $vl2$ that the derived function *mapAS* is an isomorphism too (*cdm* is again a variable of type `ClassDM`):

$$isIsomorphicClassDM(cdm, mapVL(cdm)) \rightarrow isIsomorphClass(vl2as(cdm), mapAS(vl2as(cdm)))$$

According to the above given definition of *mapAS*, this can be simplified to:

$$isIsomorphicClassDM(cdm, mapVL(cdm)) \rightarrow isIsomorphClass(vl2as(cdm), vl2as(mapVL(cdm)))$$

Fortunately, this proof obligation does not require anymore to formulate the isomorphism of the whole graph but just to specify the isomorphism of two objects, a property for which first-order logic is expressive enough. For instance, two objects of `ClassDM` are isomorphic if their attributes have the same values and the connected `TextField` objects are isomorphic. Since `ClassDM` and `TextField` are connected by a 1-1 association, the latter means that two isomorphic instances of `ClassDM` are always linked to two instances of `TextField` whose attributes have also the same value. Formulated in first-order logic, the criteria for isomorphic `ClassDM` instances looks like:

$$isIsomorphicClassDM(cdm1, cdm2) \leftrightarrow (text(vo(cdm1)) = text(vo(cdm2)) \wedge (inItalic(vo(cdm1)) \leftrightarrow inItalic(vo(cdm2))))$$

Figure 6 shows the full encoding of the correctness criterion for the example given in Fig. 4. We do not show here the final input file for SIMPLIFY, because such input files have to be written in a low level notation, which is hard to read for humans. What is shown here is an input file for the KeY system [9], which

```
\sorts {
    class;
    classdm;
    textfield;
    string;
}
\functions{
  // associations
  class me(classdm);
  classdm dm(class);
  textfield vo(classdm);
  // attributes
  string name(class);
  string text(textfield);
}
\predicates{
  // attributes
  isAbstract(class);
  inItalic(textfield);
  // predicates to encode isomorphism
  isIsomorphicClass(class, class);
  isIsomorphicClassDM(classdm, classdm);
}
\problem {
// invariant on ClassDM (core of syntax definition)
(\forall classdm cdm; name(me(cdm)) = text(vo(cdm))) &
// isomorphism of instances of Class
(\forall class c1;\forall class c2; (isIsomorphicClass(c1,c2)
           <-> name(c1) = name(c2) &
                (isAbstract(c1) <-> isAbstract(c2)))) &
// isomorphism of instances of ClassDM
(\forall classdm cdm1; \forall classdm cdm2;
            (isIsomorphicClassDM(cdm1,cdm2)
           <-> text(vo(cdm1)) = text(vo(cdm2)) &
                (inItalic(vo(cdm1)) <-> inItalic(vo(cdm2)))))
->
// conclusio
\forall classdm cdm1;\forall classdm cdm2;
  (isIsomorphicClassDM(cdm1,cdm2) -> isIsomorphicClass(me(cdm1), me(cdm2)))
}
```

Fig. 6. Encoding of correctness criterion for SIMPLIFY in KeY format

can be used as a front-end for SIMPLIFY since the KeY system is able to generate automatically equivalent input files for SIMPLIFY.

The KeY syntax requires to declare at the beginning of the file all types, functions and predicates. There are standard techniques how an UML class diagram is represented by such declarations, mainly, the classes are represented by types, associations by functions and attributes by functions or predicates (see [9] for details). The clause 'problem' contains the proof obligation and has always the form of an implication *premise* `->` *conclusio*. In KeY syntax, the logical connectors 'not', 'and', 'or', 'if-then', 'if-and-only-if' are denoted by '`!`', '`&`', '`|`', '`->`', '`<->`', respectively, and the two quantifiers are written as '`forall`', '`exists`'. The premise of the proof obligation contains the encoding of the invariant of the display manager class `ClassDM` and the isomorphism criteria for instances of `ClassDM` and `Class`. The conclusio has exactly the form as analyzed above.

When invoked for this input file, SIMPLIFY cannot find a proof because the syntax definition, for which the input file encodes the correctness criterion, is not correct. Nevertheless, SIMPLIFY gives very useful feedback in form of a counterexample. The found counterexample is exactly the same counterexample as we have already presented in the lower part of Fig. 4. Such counterexamples are extremely useful for the developer of the concrete syntax to find and to resolve errors in the concrete syntax definition.

There are (theoretically) two possibilities to fix errors in a syntax definition. As the first possibility, one could refine the visual language or change the constraints attached to the display manager classes. In our example, it would be sufficient to rewrite the invariant of `ClassDM` to

```
context ClassDM inv:
  self.me.name=self.vo.text and
  self.me.isAbstract = self.vo.inItalic
```

A second possibility is to add to the abstract syntax metamodel a new well-formedness rule but this of course changes the original abstract syntax definition. The idea behind is to avoid the occurrence of all those models that could be cause ambiguous interpretations of the diagrams. An example for such a well-formedness rule is

```
context Class inv:
  self.isAbstract = true
```

In both cases, SIMPLIFY is now able to prove the proof obligation fully automatically what certifies the correctness of the concrete syntax definition.

4.2 Analysis of Complex Syntax Definitions

The encoding presented in the last section covers only the case where the abstract syntax metamodel consists of merely one class. Fortunately, the same encoding also works for abstract syntax metamodels having more than one class, as long as all classes are not connected by any association and each class has its own display manager class in the visual language metamodel.

We discuss now, under which circumstances our encoding is also applicable to more complex abstract syntax metamodels, where classes are connected by associations and not every class has its own display manager class. The basic idea, however, remains the same as in the above case where the abstract syntax metamodel consists only of isolated classes: We strive to find a cluster of classes, i.e. a set of class groups, that induce a partition of the metamodel. Then, we apply our encoding for each of these class groups separately. We illustrate our analysis with the syntax definition for simplified class diagrams as shown in Fig. 3.

In order to find a useful cluster of classes we mark all classes that have a direct connection to a display manager class. The display manager class does not manage only the rendering of the directly connected class, but sometimes also the rendering of the neighboring classes, e.g. `ClassDM` manages the rendering for the instances of both `Class` and `Attribute`. The relevant neighboring classes together with the class directly connected to a display manager form one *class group* in the cluster. At the end of this cluster analysis, we get a situation as shown in the left part of Fig. 7. The cluster consists of two class groups (`Class`, `Attribute`) and (`Association`, `AssociationEnd`) and each class group corresponds to exactly one display manager class (`ClassDM`, `AssociationDM`).

The cluster will be the basis for the formal proof that the concrete syntax definition is correct. The formal proof, however, can only be successful if the cluster satisfies two properties, *completeness* and *unique ownership*. Basically, these two properties ensure that all instances of abstract syntax classes can

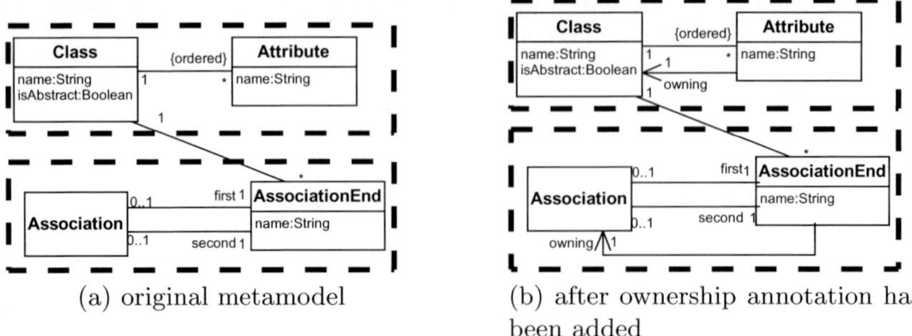

(a) original metamodel (b) after ownership annotation has been added

Fig. 7. Cluster analysis for abstract syntax classes

be uniquely mapped to display manager objects which are responsible for the rendering of these instances.

Completeness. The found cluster must cover all non-abstract classes, i.e. each non-abstract class must be a member of (at least) one class group. If a class is not a member of any group then the instances of this class do not have any connection to any display manager object.

Unique ownership. The completeness criterion is a necessary but not a sufficient condition for the cluster. Sometimes, even instances of classes covered by the cluster miss a corresponding display manager object. Suppose, in our running example the association between `Class` and `Attribute` had on the side of `Attribute` not the multiplicity 1 but '0..1'. That would allow, that some instances of `Attribute` had no connection to any `Class` instance and thus also the connection to a display manager object would be missing. In this case, the current concrete syntax definition would be incorrect, just for structural reasons.[3]

In order to prevent the case, in which an object of any abstract syntax class has no connection to a display manager object, we change the abstract syntax metamodel as follows. In each class group there is exactly one class, called *anchor class*, that has a direct connection to a display manager class (in our example, anchor classes are `Class` and `Association`). We add from each non-anchor class an association with role name 'owning' and multiplicity 1 to the anchor class of the same class group. Furthermore, this association must be derived and the referenced object has to be determined by a constraint.

In our running example, we have added associations from `Attribute` to `Class` and from `AssociationEnd` to `Association` (see right part of Fig. 7). The constraints are

```
context Attribute inv: self.owning=self.class

context AssociationEnd inv: self.owning=
  Association.allInstances()->select(as|
    as.first=self or as.second=self)->any()
```

[3] However, one could easily solve this problem by adding a new display manager class `AttributeDM` to the concrete syntax definition.

After the properties *Completeness* and *UniqueOwnership* have been verified for the cluster, we know that each instantiation of the abstract syntax metamodel can be partitioned with respect to the class groups identified by the cluster. What remains to do, is to define predicates for the isomorphism between instances of the same class group.

```
// isomorphism of instances of Class
(\forall class c1;\forall class c2; (isIsomorphicClass(c1,c2)
        <-> name(c1) = name(c2) &
            (isAbstract(c1) <-> isAbstract(c2)) &
            \forall int i; (attributeDefined(c1,i) <-> attributeDefined(c2,i)) &
            \forall int i; (attributeDefined(c1,i)
                -> name(attribute(c1,i)) = name(attribute(c2,i)))))
```

Fig. 8. Encoding of isomorphism for a whole class group

Figure 8 shows (in KeY syntax) the definition of the isomorphism-predicate for the class group containing class `Class`. Two instances of `Class` are isomorphic if their attributes have the same value and if the sequence of linked attributes are isomorphic. The sequence of linked attributes is encoded for SIMPLIFY by a function `attribute` with two arguments, the second argument encodes the position within the sequence. Two sequences of attributes are isomorphic, if they contain on the same position always isomorphic elements.

The final step is the generation of a proof obligation for each class group; the proof obligations have the same structure as the one discussed in Sect. 4.1. For our example, SIMPLIFY was again successful in discharging all proof obligations fully automatically.

5 Related Work

Our approach of defining the concrete syntax presented in Sect. 3 has many similarities with Triple-Graph-Grammars, already invented by Schürr in 1994 [7] (see also [10] for a more recent survey and a case study). The most important difference between our approach and TGGs is that our goal is merely to describe valid instances of the concrete syntax metamodel, but we are not interested in how such instances are constructed. While the main idea of defining the concrete syntax is quite similar to TGG, we are not aware of any work in the TGG area, that aims at analyzing TGG definitions as we do.

Xia and Glinz present in [11] an approach to describe the concrete syntax of their own graphical modeling language ADORA [12]. The main idea is to map the graphical representation of a language construct to a textual representation and to define the syntax finally in EBNF style. One restriction of this approach is that each graphical element must correspond to exactly one model element, and vice versa. On the other hand, Xia/Glinz were able to handle advanced features like graphical nesting in an elegant way, the constraints they give are much more concise than the corresponding invariants we could give as OCL invariants in display manager classes.

6 Conclusion and Future Work

In this paper, we have described an approach to formally define the concrete syntax of a modeling language. The formalization we propose is directly based on the primary language definition, i.e. the metamodel that encodes the abstract syntax. The big advantage of having a formalized version of the concrete syntax definition is, compared to informal syntax definitions, the possibility to analyze automatically correctness properties (cmp. Sect. 4). If the syntax definition is incorrect, our rigorous analysis is able to report an erroneous situation. For correct definitions, our approach is able to certify that erroneous situations never occur.

So far, we have encoded all proof obligations manually but we plan to automatize this step in a tool dedicated to formal concrete syntax definition. This tool should also provide a visualization of the counterexamples found by SIMPLIFY, so that the user of the tool gets feedback in the same format in which the concrete syntax is defined. Another direction of future activities is the development of an OCL axiom library that codifies the knowledge on OCL's predefined data structures. For example, the fact that for all sets `s` and elements `x` the term `s->including(x)->excluding(x)` is semantically equivalent to `s` is sometimes needed. Such axiom libraries have been developed extensively for other specification languages, e.g. Z, but – to our knowledge – not for OCL, yet. It is very likely, that SIMPLIFY will show some weaknesses in proving proof obligations, once the proof requires certain types of axioms, e.g. axioms describing sophisticated properties of sets. For this case, we plan to integrate other decision procedures or model checkers into our tool.

References

1. James Rumbaugh, Ivar Jacobson, and Grady Booch. *The Unified Modeling Language Reference Manual.* Object Technology Series. Addison-Wesley, second edition, 2005.
2. Frédéric Fondement and Thomas Baar. Making metamodels aware of concrete syntax. In Alan Hartman and David Kreische, editors, *Proc. European Conference on Model Driven Architecture (ECMDA-FA)*, volume 3748 of *LNCS*, pages 190–204. Springer, 2005.
3. D. L. Detlefs, G. Nelson, and J. Saxe. Simplify: the ESC theorem prover. Technical report, DEC, 1996.
4. OMG. Unified Modeling Language: Diagram interchange version 2.0. Convenience Document ptc/05-06-04, June 2005.
5. Gennaro Costagliola, Andrea De Lucia, Sergio Orefice, and Giuseppe Polese. A classification framework to support the design of visual languages. *Journal of Visual Languages and Computing*, 13(6):573–600, 2002.
6. Fabien Rohrer and François Helg. Synchronization between display objects and representation templates in graphical language construction. Minor thesis at Software Engineering Laboratory of EPFL, 2006. Available from http://lglpc35.epfl.ch/lgl/members/fondement/projects/probxs/HelgRohrer.pdf.

7. Andy Schürr. Specification of graph translators with triple graph grammars. In *Proceedings of 20th International Workshop on Graph-Theoretic Concepts in Computer Science (WG'94)*, volume 903 of *LNCS*, pages 151–163. Springer, 1995.
8. M. Pressburger. Über de vollständigkeit eines gewissen systems der arithmetik ganzer zahlen, in welchen, die addition als einzige operation hervortritt. *Sprawozdanie z I Kongresu Matematikow Krajow Slowcanskich Warszawa*, pages 92–101, 1929.
9. Bernhard Beckert, Reiner Hähnle, and Peter H. Schmitt, editors. *The KeY Book – The Road to Verified Software*. Springer, 2006. To appear.
10. A. Königs and A. Schürr. Tool Integration with Triple Graph Grammars - A Survey. In R. Heckel, editor, *Proceedings of the SegraVis School on Foundations of Visual Modelling Techniques*, volume 148 of *Electronic Notes in Theoretical Computer Science*, pages 113–150, Amsterdam, 2006. Elsevier Science Publ.
11. Yong Xia and Martin Glinz. Rigorous EBNF-based definition for a graphic modeling language. In *Proceedings of 10th Asia-Pacific Software Engineering Conference (APSEC 2003)*, pages 186–196. IEEE Computer Society Press, 2003.
12. Martin Glinz, Stefan Berner, and Stefan Joos. Object-oriented modeling with ADORA. *Information Systems*, 27(6):425–444, 2002.

Compositional MDA

Louis van Gool[1], Teade Punter[1], Marc Hamilton[2], and Remco van Engelen[2]

[1] Technische Universiteit Eindhoven
Den Dolech 2, P.O. box 513, 5600 MB Eindhoven, The Netherlands
l.v.gool@tue.nl, t.punter@tue.nl
[2] ASML
De Run 6501, 5504 DR Veldhoven, The Netherlands
marc.hamilton@asml.com, remco.van.engelen@asml.com

Abstract. In this paper we present a language that models an important aspect of ASML waferscanners, called coordination. The language is a compositional subset of UML2.0 activity diagrams which by themselves are not compositional in our sense of the word. We show how we transform models in this language into models for the ASML platform that implements coordination. The fact that the language is compositional enables us to define the transformation in a simple and compact manner.

1 Introduction

ASML[1] is a world-leading manufacturer of lithography systems (called waferscanners) for the semiconductor industry. Important requirements of ASML waferscanners are high performance and accurate timing. Because off-the-shelf solutions do not suffice, ASML uses a proprietary *coordination* platform for controlling the machine parts of their waferscanners. Input for this coordination platform is a definition of high-level services (*abstract behaviours*) in terms of low-level services (*resource behaviours*) and the machine parts (*resources*) that execute them.

Currently the input for the coordination platform is written in plain C-code and documented in Word documents. Technische Universiteit Eindhoven (TU/e) is investigating how ASML can benefit from model-driven architecture (MDA) as defined by the Object Management Group[2] (OMG). We developed a language for the design of abstract behaviours and constructed a model transformation that enables automatic transformation into models for the ASML coordination platform. In MDA terms, we are transforming platform-independent models (PIMs) into (semantically equivalent) platform-specific models (PSMs).

For the description of PIMs, we developed a *compositional* language that is based on the activity diagrams[3] of the Unified Modeling Language (UML), version 2.0. By "compositional" we mean that the language is built up from a few

[1] www.asml.com
[2] www.omg.org
[3] This paper focuses on the behavioural part of coordination. The behavioural part is complemented with a structural part that is not described in this paper.

O. Nierstrasz et al. (Eds.): MoDELS 2006, LNCS 4199, pp. 126–139, 2006.

simple patterns that can have subparts that are again built with these patterns. This is the key idea behind the well-established principle of structured programming [1], where a language consists for example only of assignment statements, sequentially composed statements, guarded statements and looped statements.

In section 2 we present a short overview of MDA and its potential benefits for ASML. Section 3 discusses the compositionality principle and explains what is gained by applying this principle. In section 4 we explain the basic principles of the coordination aspect of ASML waferscanners and define the compositional language that we developed for it, illustrating it by means of an example PIM. Section 5 describes a simplified version of the ASML coordination platform and shows parts of the PSM that is the result of applying the model transformation to the example PIM. The definition of the model transformation is given in section 6. Section 7 concludes the paper.

2 MDA

Model-driven development (MDD) is considered to be the next step in software engineering's strive to construct systems at a higher level of abstraction [6]. Development in MDD is based on assemblies of domain-specific abstractions, called models. The added value of MDD over traditional object-oriented development (OOD) is the concept of model transformation, in particular the ability to (semi)-automatically transform high-level models (PIMs) into (semantically equivalent) models that fit a specific platform (PSMs), possibly enabling generation of executable code. MDA is the term used for the specific way the OMG defines MDD.

An important ingredient in MDA is the explicit definition (standardization) of the domain-specific languages (DSLs) that are used to describe models. ASML expects that the use of standardized languages for concepts in their machine domain will increase quality of designs and improve communication within and between development teams.

MDA distinguishes two approaches for defining DSLs. In the approach called *metamodeling*, DSLs (metamodels) are designed from scratch for a specific goal. In MDA, a metamodel is described by means of the meta-object facility (MOF). The other approach, called *profiling*, is based on the reuse of existing MOF-based languages, like UML, that are customized to one's specific needs by means of profiles. The customization is performed by means of stereotypes, tagged values and OCL-constraints [2].

For our case we have chosen the profiling approach. The main reason is the expectation that (re)using standardized languages as much as possible improves communication within the organisation. Furthermore, tools specifically designed for a standardized language like UML can already offer advanced support for a DSL that is based on this language. Profiling looses its benefits over metamodeling if one only uses a few basic elements of the existing language to represent the elements of the profiled language. In principle one could only use the classes and associations of UML to model any of the elements and connections of the profiled language. However, more is gained in terms of standardization and tool support if one reuses other UML elements as much as possible.

As mentioned at the beginning of this section, model transformation is a key concept in MDA. An important element of our case study was the implementation of an (automated) model transformation. Automated model transformation of PIMs into PSMs reduces coding effort because the mental gap between PSMs and code is much smaller than the gap between PIMs and code. Furthermore, automated construction of PSMs is only a small step away from automatic code generation. We also created a version of the transformation that produces code (via a code metamodel) instead of the model presented in this paper.

Apart from the UML, MOF and profile standards, OMG is also working on the Query/View/Transformation (QVT) standard. Like UML has become the standard for modeling, OMG's intention is that QVT becomes the standard for describing model transformations. The main reason for ASML to comply to standards like UML and QVT is better alignment of multiple modeling initiatives that exist within and outside of ASML. To investigate feasiblity of automated transformation when complying to QVT, the model transformation has been implemented in the (QVT-compliant) model-transformation language of Borland[4] Together Architect 2006.

3 Compositionality

As pointed out in the introduction, we have chosen to develop a language that is compositional. Many graphical general-purpose languages, like Petri nets or the activity diagrams of UML, are not compositional in our sense of the word. In principle, arbitrary complex networks of elements and connections can be created in these languages, as illustrated by the activity diagram in Fig. 1. There are no clear identifiable patterns in such a model which makes it difficult to understand how the activity behaves.

Besides the fact that unrestrained use of a language like activity diagrams can easily lead to incomprehensible models, transformation of these kind of models into models for a specific target platform, is also not feasible in general. This would require the target platform to support the behaviour of arbitrary complex activity-diagrams, which cannot and should not be expected from a dedicated platform.

In the context of profiling, the remedy is to confine oneself to a sublanguage that *is* compositional, like for example structured workflow languages [3]. The constructs of a compositional sublanguage of a general-purpose language are built using simple patterns of elements of the general-purpose language (in our case patterns of activity-diagram elements). Figures 2 and 3 illustrate this notion of compositionality. Figure 2 defines the patterns that are used to build the activity that is presented in Fig. 3. The clouds in Fig. 2 represent an arbitrary construct that is built using only the right three patterns.

[4] www.borland.com

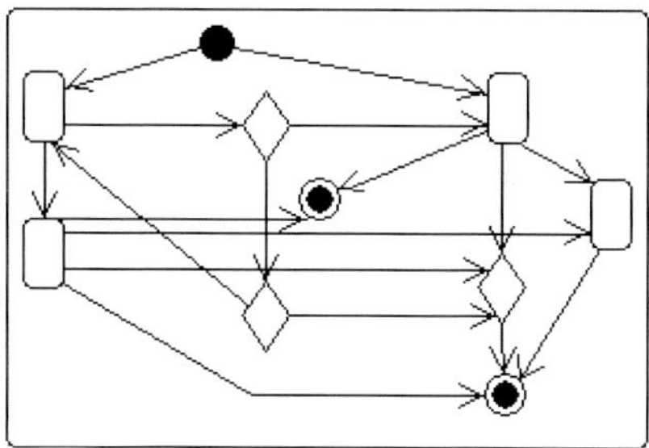

Fig. 1. Non-compositional activity

Fig. 2. Compositional patterns

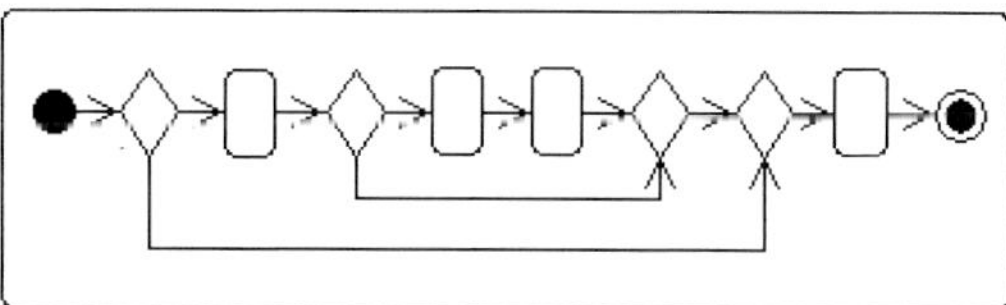

Fig. 3. Compositional activity

The use of a language that is compositional helps in the construction of specifications that are easy to understand. This principle holds under the assumption that the language's constructs are rich enough for a designer to express his or her thoughts in a clear and concise manner. The development of our language was therefore performed hand-in-hand with the reconstruction from ASML documentation and C-code of several abstract behaviours, one of which (CLBS) was considered the most complex instance.

The PIM of CLBS was presented to ASML architects to review its correctness, completeness and understandability. The fact that the architects were immediately able to understand the model and use it to discuss details about CLBS, gave a clear indication of the strength of the language.

Besides understandability of specifications, another important advantage of using a compositional language is that it makes automated model transformation feasible because one only needs to be able to transform a few simple patterns. The clear structure of the transformation is also expected to make it easy to adapt the transformation to other platforms, which is crucial for a company like ASML that develops and has to maintain many different versions of their machines.

Next to a PIM, we also reconstructed a PSM of CLBS. The reconstruction went hand in hand with the design of the transformation of which a simplified version is described in this paper. As already mentioned, we also created an adapted version of the transformation that can generate code. Because of the clear structure of the transformation, this turned out to be a straightforward task.

4 PIM

In this section we define our language for the coordination aspect of ASML waferscanners (from now on simply called "coordination") and illustrate it by means of an example PIM. As mentioned in the introduction, coordination is about the definition of *abstract behaviours*. An abstract behaviour consists of algorithmically combined *resource behaviours* which are behaviours of parallel executing parts (of an ASML waferscanner), called *resources*.

An abstract behaviour is not as straightforward as a simple sequence of resource behaviours, but can contain decisions that are based on the results of resource behaviours. Loops and parallellism are also part of abstract behaviours, but are outside the scope of this paper.

An important aspect of coordination is that abstract behaviours are not executed in isolation. Abstract behaviours may execute concurrently if they do not need a certain resource at the same moment. Sometimes one wants to prevent that a resource is affected by another abstract behaviour, although one does not need the resource to perform any resource behaviour. This can be guaranteed by performing so-called *passive behaviour* on that resource.

We now define our language for coordination. It consists of any activity that can be built with the patterns proc, seq, assign, guard, if and call, presented in Fig. 4. A cloud represents an arbitrary construct that is built using the last five patterns. We only show a specific case of the call pattern. In general there is one active resource and several passive ones. Furthermore, the number of input pins and output pins on the ≪active≫ action can be arbitrary (including zero).

We illustrate the language by means of a simple fictional example PIM, shown in Fig. 5. The example describes the testing of a lamp. Two resources are involved in this example: a lamp that can be turned on and off and a sensor that can check if the lamp produces light. The test starts with resource behaviour CHECK_LIGHT on the sensor. The result of this resource behaviour is stored in variable LGT. Next, it is checked if variable LGT is equal to OFF (the %s are explained below). If this is the case, variable LMP is set to ON and used as input for resource behaviour SET_LAMP on the lamp. In other words, the lamp is turned on in that case. It is then checked again if the sensor receives light. The ≪passive≫ action for the lamp ensures that no other abstract behaviour can use the lamp during this check. If the sensor reports that it does not receive any light, we know for sure that something is wrong and return with return value BROKEN, aborting all further execution. If in the end variable LGT is equal to ON, the test terminates, returning the (default) return value OK.

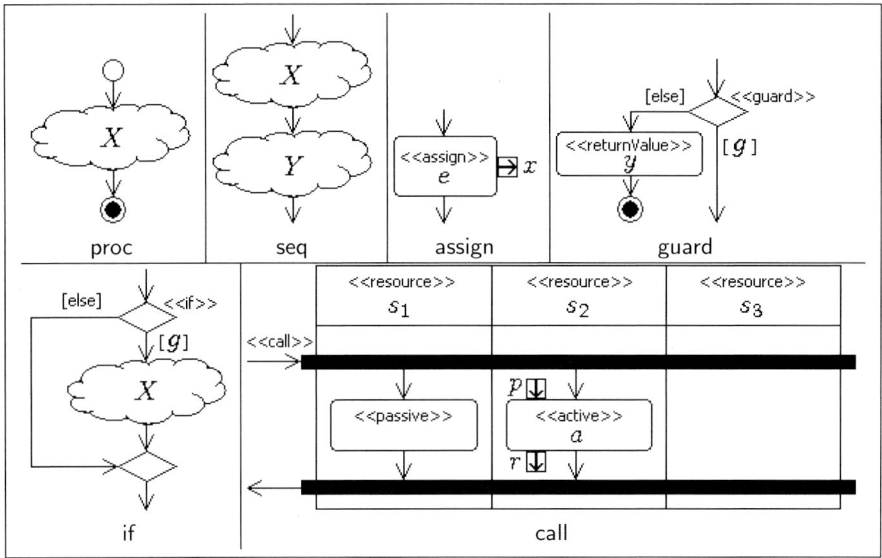

Fig. 4. PIM Patterns

We now explain some peculiar details of the example. In the version of Borland Together Architect 2006 that is available to us, expressions are strings without any structure. For the transformation we have to be able to identify the variable names in an expression however. We put %s around the variable names in an expression to make it easier to recognize them. Parameter passing has been simplified by only allowing the use of variable names instead of arbitrary expressions for the specification of inputs for a resource behaviour. The variable name that specifies an input or output also determines (by name) the resource behaviour's parameter that is associated with this input or output. A consequence is that a parameter of a resource behaviour can only be associated with the variable that has the same name as the parameter. These simplifications have no serious influence on the expressiveness of the language and allow us to implement the transformation with the available version of the tool.

5 PSM

We now describe the ASML platform that implements coordination and show parts of the PSM that is obtained by transforming the lamp-test PIM. For presentation and confidentiality reasons, we present a simplified version of the platform.

Within the platform, an abstract behaviour is described by a sequence of *concrete behaviours* and separate definitions of these concrete behaviours. During the execution of a sequence of concrete behaviours, the platform offers a means to skip all concrete behaviours in the sequence until a certain one. This enables the implementation of conditional execution.

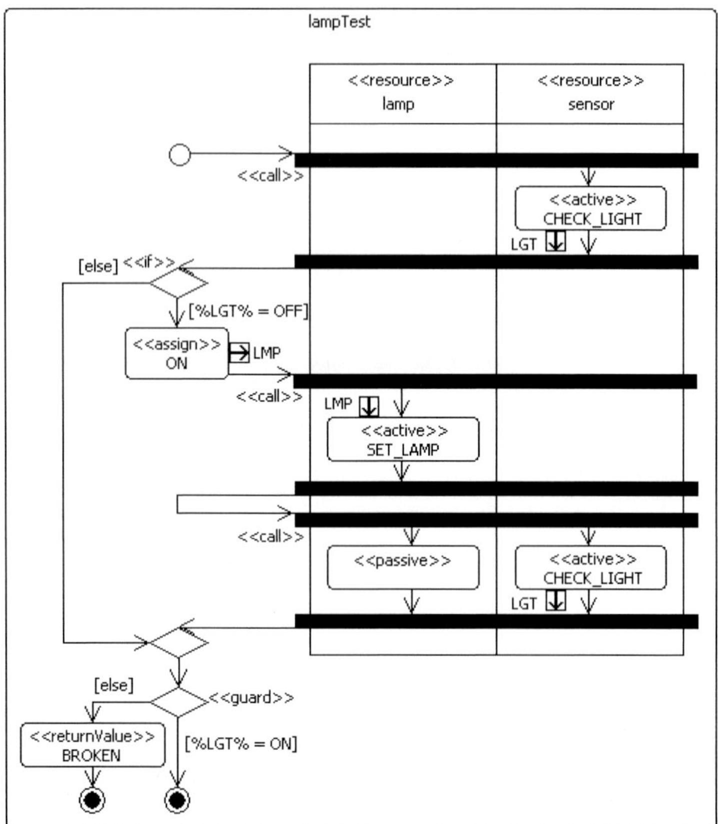

Fig. 5. PIM of lamp test

Abstract behaviours are (in their platform-specific form) offered to a scheduling component that tries to execute them in an optimal manner. For each abstract behaviour, the scheduling component determines the set of resources that are needed for its execution and when they are needed. This defines a kind of Tetris brick for each abstract behaviour that is used to determine optimal execution of abstract behaviours in a manner that resembles a game of Tetris [4]. Figure 6 illustrates this Tetris game. The + combines two Tetris bricks into the schedule on the right-hand side of the =. Notice that the shape of the Tetris bricks is fixed and does not change under the influence of 'gravity'. As mentioned in the previous section, passive behaviour can be used to prevent unwanted interference of abstract behaviours. In terms of the Tetris game, passive behaviour can be used to extend Tetris bricks. The white Tetris brick in Fig. 6 contains passive regions, indicated by a grey color.

Transforming algorithmic coordination of resource behaviours (PIM) into a sequence of concrete behaviours (PSM) is a first step in determining when resource

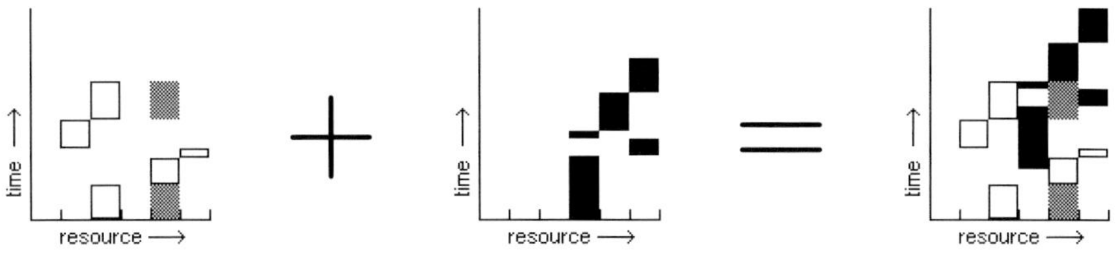

Fig. 6. Scheduling, seen as a game of Tetris

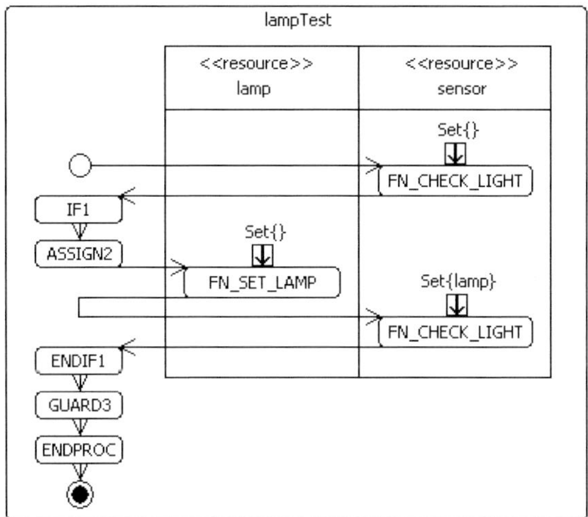

Fig. 7. Sequencing part of the lamp-test PSM

behaviours are executed. In terms of the Tetris game, this step corresponds to the definition of the overall structure of the Tetris bricks.

We distinguish two kinds of concrete behaviours: *functional behaviours* and *control behaviours*. A functional behaviour corresponds to a ≪call≫ of a PIM. It determines which resource behaviour is executed and which resources are passive during this execution. Control behaviours are used to implement coordination constructs like ≪if≫ and ≪assign≫.

Figure 7 shows an activity diagram that describes the sequencing of concrete behaviours for the lamp-test example. The behaviours IF1, ASSIGN2, ENDIF1, GUARD3 and ENDPROC are control behaviours. The integer labels on control behaviours are necessary to distinguish control behaviours of the same kind[5,6]. The behaviours FN_CHECK_LIGHT and FN_SET_LAMP are functional behaviours. A functional behaviour has the set of resources that should be passive as input.

[5] Labeling is actually not necessary for our lamp-test example as each kind of control behaviour occurs only once.

[6] For simplicity we ignore the fact that an extra label should be added in order to distinguish control behaviours of different abstract behaviours.

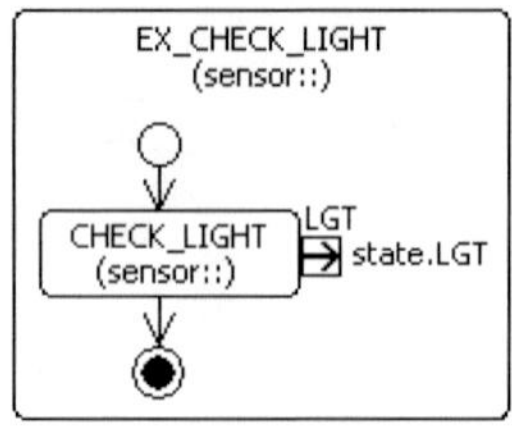

Fig. 8. Definition of EX_CHECK_LIGHT

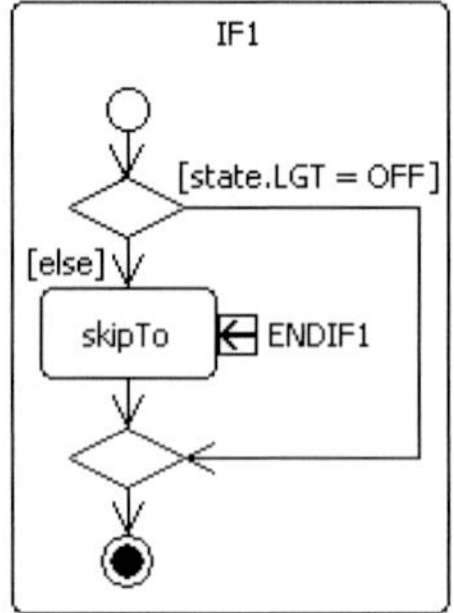

Fig. 9. Definition of IF1

The definitions of concrete behaviours are specified separately from the sequencing of concrete behaviours. We omitted the definitions of the functional behaviours as this requires a level of detail that would only distract from the core issues. What is important to know, is that each functional behaviour FN_X is associated with a behaviour EX_X that executes resource behaviour X with the appropriate parameter values[7].

Figure 8 shows the definition of EX_CHECK_LIGHT. A special variable state contains a record of the variables that occur in the PIM (LGT and LMP in the lamp-test example). These variables are used to provide resource behaviours with parameter values, store resource-behaviour results and steer control behaviours. During execution of EX_CHECK_LIGHT, the result of resource behaviour CHECK_LIGHT is stored in variable LGT.

Figure 9 shows the definition of control behaviour IF1. If the value of variable LGT is not equal to OFF when control behaviour IF1 is executed, all concrete behaviours until ENDIF1 are skipped.

Figures 7, 8 and 9 only specify part of the lamp-test PSM. How a complete PSM is obtained from a PIM, is defined by the transformation that is described in the next section.

Notice that although both PIM and PSM are represented by activity diagrams, they are written in *different* languages. Due to space limitations, the language for the PSMs is not explicitly described in this paper.

[7] The definitions of the resource behaviours are outside the PSM's scope.

6 Transformation

We now describe the model transformation that transforms PIMs like the lamp test of Fig. 5 into PSMs. A schematic description of the transformation is presented in Figs. 10, 11, 12, 13, 14 and 15. The fact that our language is compositional and the fact that the target platform has sufficient expressive power, together make it possible to define the transformation in a compositional manner. We now explain the notation that we used to describe the transformation, without going into the specifics of the transformation itself.

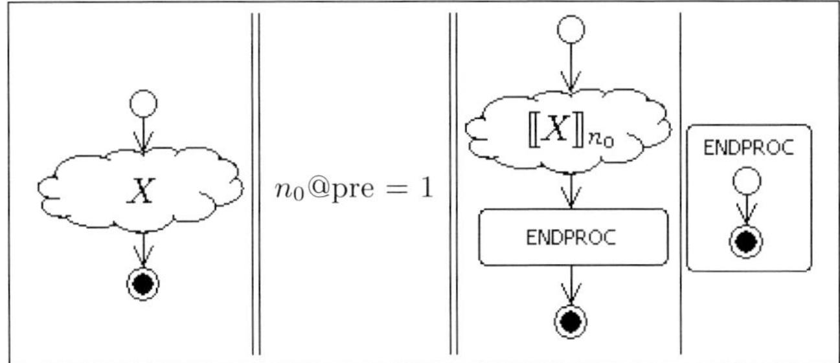

Fig. 10. Transformation rule for proc

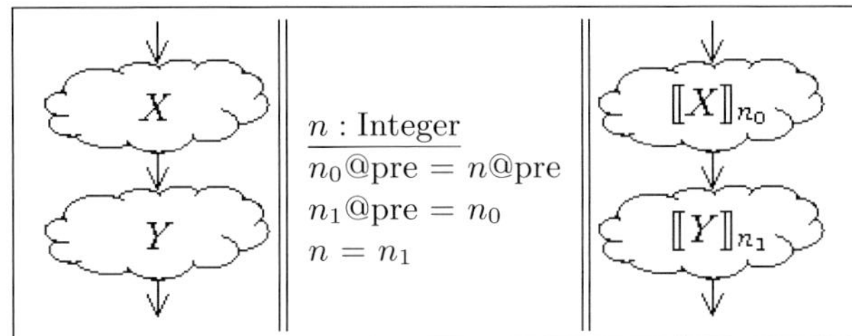

Fig. 11. Transformation rule for seq

Each figure shows the *transformation rule* for a certain pattern. A transformation rule consists of three sections, separated by double lines. The left[8] section is called the *source section*, the middle section the *variable section* and the right section the *target section*.

The source section contains a *source pattern*, describing a pattern that can be used in the construction of a PIM. In the source pattern, *source pattern variables* may be used to abstract from specific parts. In Fig. 14 for example, X and g are source pattern variables. Source pattern variable X is an arbitrary construct that is inductively built with the patterns seq, assign, guard, if and call and source pattern variable g is a string. We left these types implicit.

[8] For layout-technical reasons, the transformation rule for the call (Fig. 15) is presented top-down. For this rule "left" is "top" and "right" is "bottom".

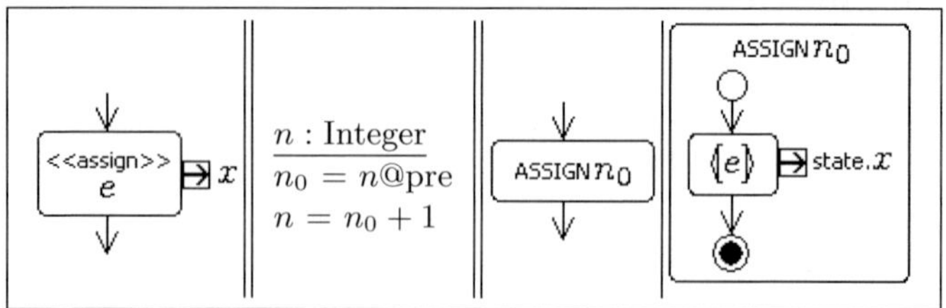

Fig. 12. Transformation rule for assign

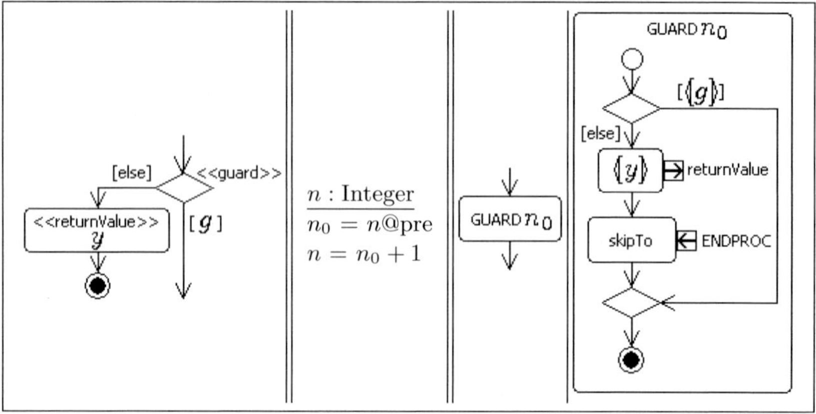

Fig. 13. Transformation rule for guard

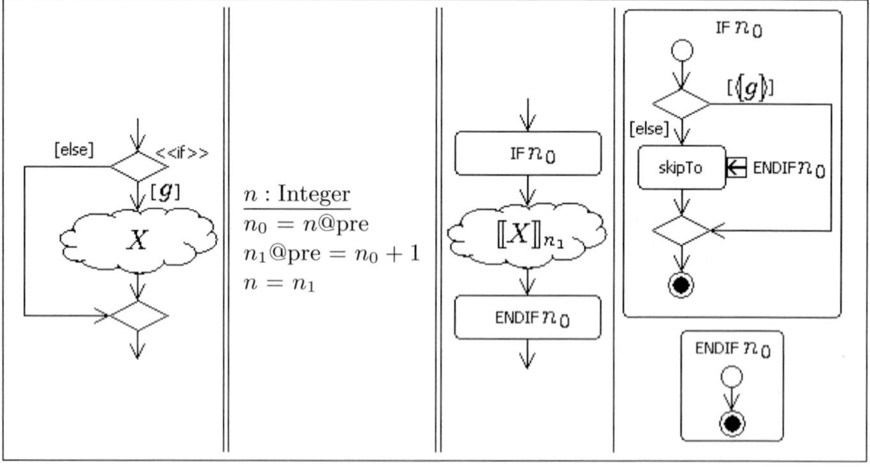

Fig. 14. Transformation rule for if

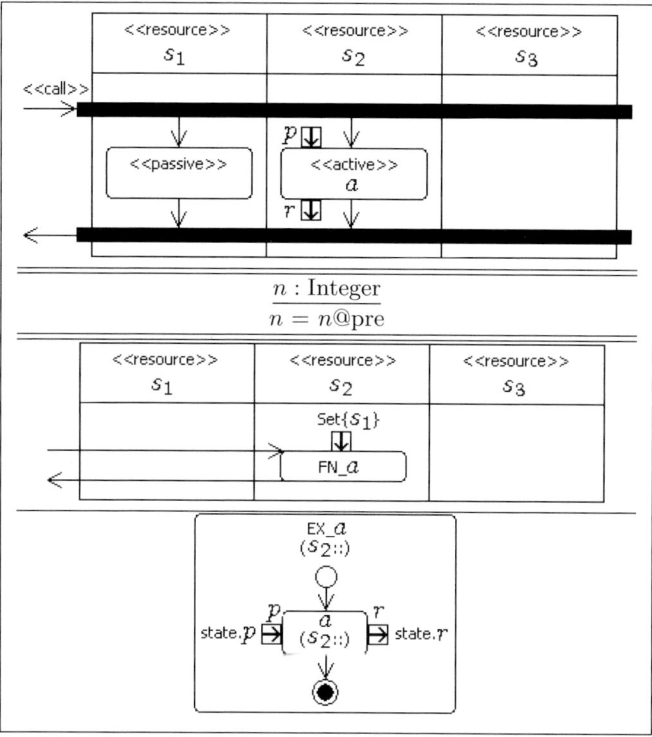

Fig. 15. Transformation rule for call

The target section contains a *target pattern* that describes how the source pattern is implemented in the PSM. In Fig. 14 for example, the target pattern is divided into two parts, separated by a single line. The left part describes the sequencing of concrete behaviours and the right part describes their definition. The cloud with $[\![X]\!]_{n_1}$ in it represents the sequencing part of the result of transformation of X. The n_1 is an integer input/output parameter for the transformation rule that is used to transform X. This parameter is used to label control behaviours. As mentioned in the previous section, labeling of control behaviours is necessary to distinguish control behaviours of the same kind.

The variable section consists of a list of typed parameters for the transformation (above the line) and constraints on the variables that occur in the transformation rule (below the line). The transformation rule for proc has no parameters and the transformation rules for seq, assign, guard, if and call each have an integer parameter n ("n : Integer"). In the specification of a constraint, the value that a variable x has when a transformation is initiated (its *pre* value), is represented by "x@pre" and the value that a variable has when a transformation is completed (its *post* value), is represented by "x". Equation $n_1\text{@pre} = n_0 + 1$ in the transformation rule for if (Fig. 14) for example defines that the pre value of variable n_1 equals the post value of variable n_0 plus 1.

Like source pattern variables represent parts of a source pattern, *target pattern variables* represent parts of a target pattern. The post value of a target pattern variable determines how it is instantiated. If the transformation rule for if (Fig. 14) is initiated with n equal to 1, then (equation $n_0 = n$@pre defines the post value of n_0 equal to the pre value of n) each occurrence of IFn_0 and ENDIFn_0 in the target pattern is instantiated as IF1 and ENDIF1 respectively. In other words, in this particular execution of the if transformation rule, the IFs and ENDIFs are labeled with 1 (notice the implicit conversion of the integer 1 to the string 1).

The function $\langle\!\vert \_ \vert\!\rangle$ that occurs in the target section of the transformation rules for assign, guard and if transforms an expression (string) such that each variable name "x" (indicated by %s) is replaced by the expression "state.x" that represents the value of variable x in the target platform. If a source pattern variable g equals for example the string "%LGT% = OFF", then $\langle\!\vert g \vert\!\rangle$ is equal to "state.LGT = OFF".

7 Conclusion

In this paper we presented a language that models the concept of coordination as it occurs in ASML waferscanners. The language is a compositional subset of UML2.0 activity diagrams, meaning that it is built up from a few simple patterns of UML2.0 activity-diagram elements, where the patterns can have subparts that are again built with these patterns. We defined a model transformation that transforms models in the language (PIMs) into models for a proprietary ASML platform that implements coordination (PSMs).

The approach to use a compositional subset of a standardized language turned out beneficial. ASML architects were quickly able to understand the language and discuss details of a coordination instance that was considered very complex. Furthermore, the language's compositionality guided the definition of the model transformation. Feasibility has been shown by a working implementation of the model transformation.

We think that the compositional approach that we took can be beneficial for companies who, like ASML, cannot use off-the-shelf solutions because of high demands on their platforms, but still want to use well-supported easy-to-learn design languages with a feasible approach to generation of code for all kinds of different platforms that are used in different versions of their products.

Acknowledgements

The research presented in this paper was conducted within the IDEALS research project, under the responsibility of the Embedded Systems Institute (ESI). This project is partially sponsored by the Dutch Ministry of Economic Affairs under the Senter program. We like to thank Tanja Gurzhiy from TU/e (OOTI) who implemented the model transformation, Wilbert Alberts and Stefan Slootjes from ASML for reviewing our models and Michel Reniers for discussing a draft version of the paper. We also thank the anonymous referees for their helpful comments.

References

1. E.W. Dijkstra. *Notes on Structured Programming.* In Structured Programming (1972) 1–82.
2. L. Fuentes, A. Vallecillo. *An Introduction to UML Profiles.* In UPGRADE, The European Journal for the Informatics Professional (2004) 5–13.
3. B. Kiepuszewski, A.H.M. ter Hofstede, C. Bussler. *On Structured Workflow Modelling.* In Conference on Advanced Information Systems Engineering (2000) 431–445.
4. N.J.M. van den Nieuwelaar. *Supervisory Machine Control by Predictive-Reactive Scheduling.* Ph.D. thesis. Technische Universiteit Eindhoven (2004).
5. D.A.C. Quartel, R.M. Dijkman, M. van Sinderen. *Extending Profiles with Stereotypes for Composite Concepts.* In MoDELS, Proceedings of the 8th ACM/IEEE International Conference on Model Driven Engineering Languages and Systems (2005) 232–247.
6. S. Sendall, W. Kozaczynski. *Model Transformation – the Heart and Soul of Model-Driven Software Development.* In IEEE Software, Special Issue on Model Driven Software Development (2003) 42–53.

CUP 2.0: High-Level Modeling of Context-Sensitive Interactive Applications

Jan Van den Bergh and Karin Coninx

Hasselt University – transnationale Universiteit Limburg
Expertise Centre for Digital Media – Institute for BroadBand Technology
Wetenschapspark 2
3590 Diepenbeek
Belgium
{jan.vandenbergh, karin.coninx}@uhasselt.be

Abstract. The Unified Modeling Language is mainly being used to communicate about the design of a software system. In recent years, the language is increasingly being used to specify models that can be used for partial code generation. These efforts are mainly focussed on the generation of the application structure. It has been used to a lesser extend to model the interaction with the user and the user interface. In this paper, we introduce CUP 2.0, a Unified Modeling Language profile for high-level modeling of context-sensitive interactive applications. The profile was created to ease communication about the design of these applications between human-computer interaction specialists and software engineers. We further argue that the data provided by the models, suffices to (semi-) automatically create interactive low-fidelity prototypes that can be used for evaluation.

1 Introduction

With the advent of mobile computing, the interest in development support for context-sensitive interactive applications has also increased. Indeed, the usage of applications while the users are moving makes that the context in which interactive applications is no longer a static given. The small form-factor of most of these mobile devices makes that one should make optimal use of the features of such a device and the context it is being used in. For example, in a museum a digital mobile guide can automatically display information about the art works closest to the user. Another factor is that users no longer use a single computing device but they still want to use the same applications or services on these different devices. Such applications can range from websites to word processors or even games.

The design of such context-sensitive interactive applications is a complex task that can benefit from the use of models at different levels of abstraction. The abstraction can be useful to reduce the complexity when designing the overall interactive application and reduce the chance to get lost in low-level features, such as the detailed layout of the user interface of the application on a certain target platform.

O. Nierstrasz et al. (Eds.): MoDELS 2006, LNCS 4199, pp. 140–154, 2006.

In this work, we present CUP 2.0, a profile for the Unified Modeling Language (UML) for modeling context-sensitive user interfaces that improves on an earlier version [19]. The profile provides a set of stereotypes and the accompanying tagged values that can be used to construct high-level models for these context-sensitive applications. The models are based on the models that are used in the model-based user interface design but are expressed using the UML. They document the interaction of the user with the system, the data structures accessible through the user interface, the high-level structure of the user interface and the deployment of a user interface to a certain platform.

The rest of this paper is structured as follows: after a short discussion of some related work, we will give an overview of the models that are supported by the introduced profile, followed by detailed discussions of each of the models. Finally, we will provide a discussion of the profile and conclusions.

2 Related Work

The UML has already been used by several approaches to model the user interfaces of interactive applications. Wisdom [13] is a UML profile for modeling interactive applications that is targeted towards small organizations. It supports modeling of interactive applications using eight different models that are expressed using the UML use case, class, activity and state diagrams. The diagrams are extended using a set of stereotypes. All models are also on a fairly abstract level and the generation process to an abstract user interface description language (AUIML) from those models is provided. CanonSketch [1] is a tool that supports the presentation model, one of the models of the Wisdom-notation, and combines it with the Canonical Abstract Prototypes [3] (CAP)[1] to provide multilevel modeling and HTML for prototyping on a concrete level.

UMLi [5] extends the UML using the MOF-constructs to model user interfaces. The authors introduce two new diagram types. The presentation diagram, specifying the user interface structure, is represented using a notation similar to that of the deployment diagram (for the presentation model). An enhanced version of the activity diagram is used to represent the behaviour. They extended an open-source UML-modeling tool to support their notation.

Elkoutbi et al. [8] use annotated collaboration diagrams and class diagrams to model form-based user interfaces. From these diagrams, they can generate statechart diagrams. Based on these statecharts, complete functional prototypes are generated. The approach is concentrating on form-based user interfaces for a single user. The specifications that are used as input, however, have to be rigorously defined to support the generation process.

MML [16] is a UML profile to model interactive multimedia applications. They use the notation we proposed in earlier work [19] to define the abstract user interface and link it with a multimedia specification, and state and activity

[1] The CAP notation uses nested rectangles and a set of icons to identify the type of interaction objects contained in user interface.

diagrams. A skeleton of the interactive multimedia application using SVG and JavaScript can be generated from these models.

None of the above approaches, however, have dedicated support for modeling context-sensitive user interfaces. Some model-based approaches that do not use UML, however, have some support for modeling context-sensitive user interfaces. Clerckx et al. [2] propose a method that starts from a hierarchical task model from which they can generate a dialog model. This model can be annotated with high-level user interface descriptions. These models are combined with a context model to generate some concrete prototypes that can use simulated or real context input. All models can be manipulated graphically and are serialized to XML.

UsiXML [11] is a modeling language expressed using XML. It features support for the specification of task models, abstract and concrete user interface models, context models and model transformations. Tool support for various models is provided, however there is no published tool support for context-sensitive user interfaces.

3 Model Overview

The Context-Sensitive User interface Profile (CUP 2.0) is a UML 2.0 [14] profile that provides stereotypes and corresponding tagged values to increase support for the expression of the models, relevant to the high-level modeling of context-sensitive user interfaces, in a limited number of diagrams. Figure 1 gives an overview of the models that can be specified using the CUP 2.0 profile.

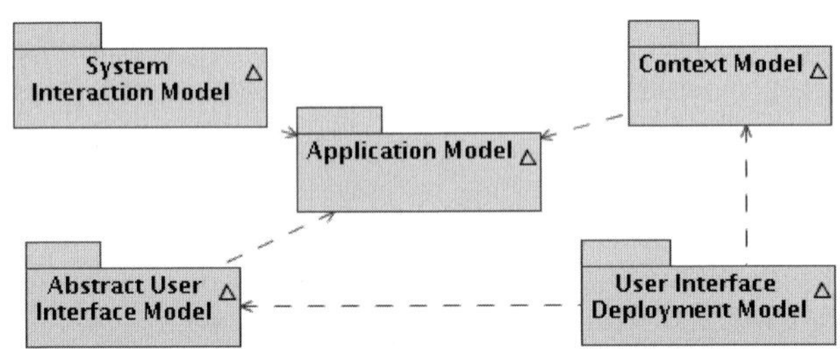

Fig. 1. Overview of the models supported by the UML profile CUP 2.0

The *application model* specifies the data structures and functionality that can be accessed through the user interface. This includes the data structures and functionality that is not part of the modeled application but that is used to provide relevant information (context) to the application. The model is used by both the system interaction model and the abstract user interface model to provide details of the data structures which are respectively used in the interaction with the modeled application and in the user interface structure. The model is discussed in more detail in section 4.

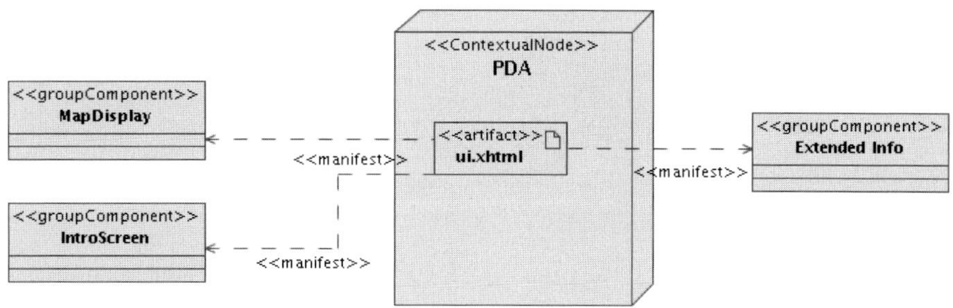

Fig. 2. Example of user interface deployment model: A context-sensitive mobile museum guide

A second model is the *system interaction model*. This model corresponds to the user task model, which is the core model in many model-based user interface design approaches. It is an hierarchical specification of the user's tasks and user-observed tasks. In contrast to the most-used task model notation, the ConcurTaskTrees notation [15], it does not use a tree-based notation but uses the flow-based notation of the activity diagram. It does however support all temporal operators that are supported by the ConcurTaskTrees notation and is enhanced with support for context sensitiveness. More details about this model can be found in section 6.

The structure of the context-sensitive user interface is specified in the *abstract user interface model*. A single model represents a user interface structure that is shared in multiple contexts and on multiple platforms (see section 7). The deployment of an abstract user interface to a certain platform or to a set of platforms for distributed user interfaces can be specified in the *user interface deployment model*. To accomplish this, the stereotype ≪`contextualNode`≫ can be applied to a `Node` to specify the relation with a certain context of use as specified in the context model. Figure 2 shows an example of a deployment of the user interface to a PDA. Specific contexts of use can be specified in the *context model*, which uses the classes defined in the application model. More details of the context model are found in section 5.

4 Application Model

The application model is specified using a class diagram. The model contains all classes of the application logic that are relevant for the user interface. In addition to those classes, also the context information and the interfaces of the relevant applications or services to get the relevant context information are included in the model. The latter classes are respectively identified using the stereotypes ≪`context`≫ and ≪`contextCollector`≫. The definition of a seperate stereotype for the entities that gather context information is motivated by the fact that frameworks and toolkits built to support the development of context-sensitive applications use similar abstractions. Examples of such abstractions are context

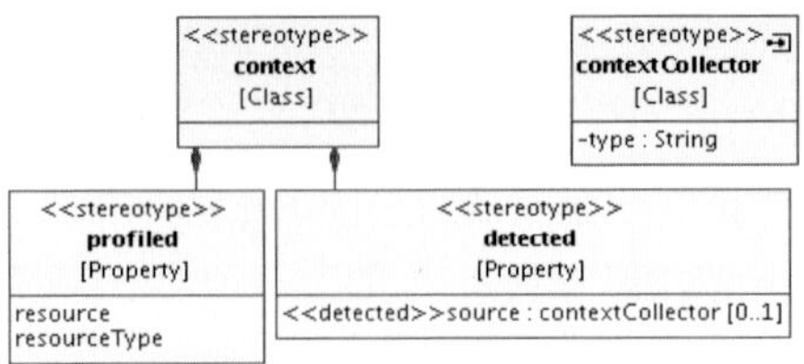

Fig. 3. Stereotypes of the UML profile CUP 2.0 relevant for the application model

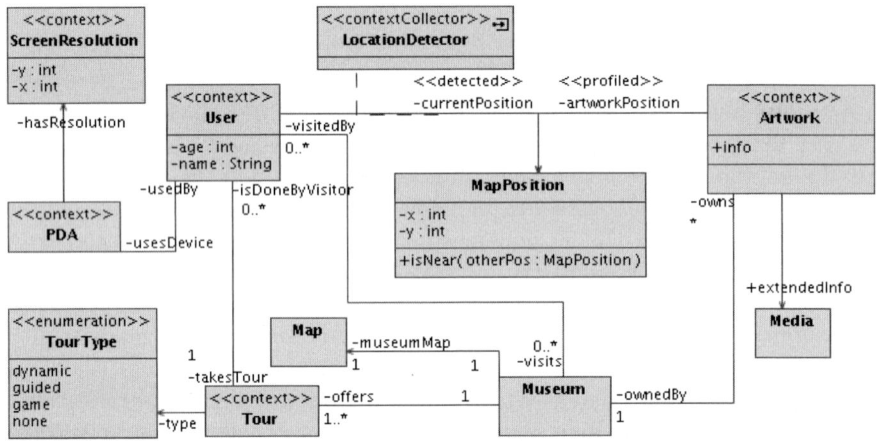

Fig. 4. Example of application model: A context-sensitive mobile museum guide

widgets in the Context Toolkit [6], contextors [4] and information spaces in ConFab [10]. A different name was chosen to be independent of the final implementation.

Each `Property` of classes with the stereotype ≪`context`≫, can have a stereotype indicating how the modeled information is gathered since this information can be important for the further design or eventual code generation. The two stereotypes that are supported are ≪`detected`≫ for context information that is delivered to the application directly from sensors or from any source after being manipulated, merged or derived by some service or application. Profiled context information is provided by an application or entered by a user and is indicated by the stereotype ≪`profiled`≫. The difference is also clear from the tagged values of these stereotypes. While the values of profiled context information can be gathered from a resource of a certain type (e.g. a URI referencing a file), the detected context information is gathered from a context collector. The choice to categorize context in profiled and detected was motivated by the implications this difference has on the design of the application; an appropriate user interface has to be defined to modify profiled context information, while detected information requires mechanisms to detect the information and possibly

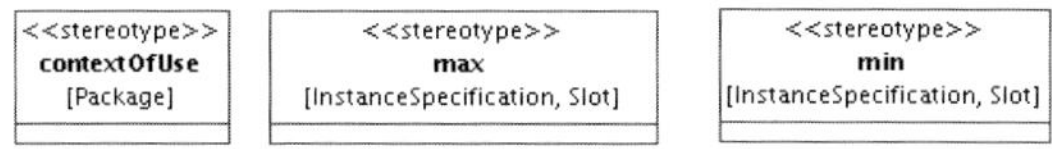

Fig. 5. Stereotypes of the UML profile CUP 2.0 relevant for the context model

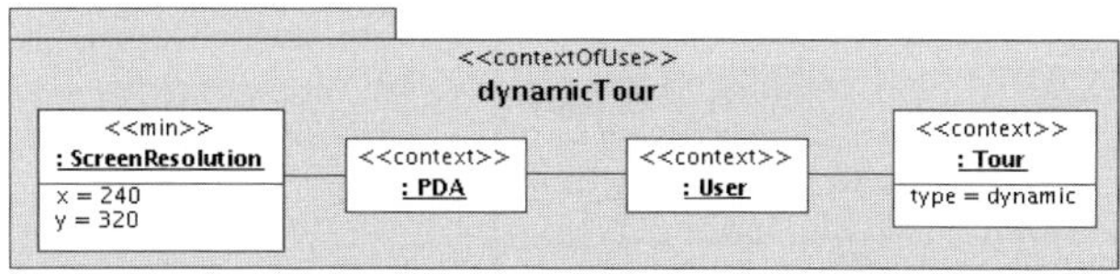

Fig. 6. Example of context model: A context-sensitive mobile museum guide

appropriate feedback to the user when problems are encountered. This categorisation of context is more extensively motivated in [19].

The stereotypes that can be applied in the application model are shown in Figure 3, while Figure 4 shows an example application model. The example shows a particial application model of a museum guide. It clearly shows that the information that many relations exist between parts of the model that are part of the context and those that are not. It also shows that the location of a user is detected by a LocationDetector, while the location of the museum artifacts is profiled.

5 Context Model

The context model specifies the different situations in which an application can be used. For each context of use the context model contains a package with the stereotype ≪`contextOfUse`≫. Such a package can only contain instances of classes that have the stereotype ≪`context`≫ as specified in the application model. As such the context model is more open than the context model used in UsiXML [11], which uses instances of predefined classes to specify the contexts of use.

Each instance specifies one value to which a parameter of the context of use has to adhere. Ranges of values can be specified by specifying a minimum and a maximum (using the corresponding stereotypes), or by listing the possible values; when multiple instances of the same class are specified they represent alternatives. To avoid ambiguity, when both a minimum and a maximum value is provided, the involved instances should be linked. Figure 5 shows the stereotypes that can be applied to the model elements, while Figure 6 shows a small example model, demonstrating the usage of the different stereotypes. The specified context of use is relevant for users that follow a dynamic tour through the museum and have a PDA with a certain minimal resolution.

6 System Interaction Model

The system interaction model describes the interactions of the system with the user and the environment in which it is executed. It can be used to describe the

Table 1. Icons of task categories in ConcurTaskTrees, Contextual ConcurTaskTrees and CUP 2.0

Task Category	ConcurTaskTrees	Contextual ConcurTaskTrees	CUP
Abstract task			/
User task			
Contextual User Task	/		
Application task			
Contextual Application task	/		
Interaction task			
Contextual Interaction task	/		
Environment task	/		

tasks of both the users and the application as well as the relevant interaction with the environment in more detail. The basis for the system interaction model is the UML 2.0 activity diagram. In this model, all actions have to have the stereotype ≪`task`≫ or a derived stereotype applied to them.

A task corresponds to an UML Action. The task goal can be expressed using a local postcondition, if desired. Basic tasks – tasks that are not refined within the model – belong to four different categories. These categories are based on the categories of the Contextual ConcurTaskTrees [18] notation, an extension of the earlier mentioned ConcurTaskTrees notation that allows for specification of context influences. We defined four stereotypes with the appropriate tagged values, that cover all task categories present in the Contextual ConcurTaskTrees as can be seen in Table 1.

One notable difference is the elimination of the task category type *abstract task*, which is a task that can be refined into tasks that belong to different categories. Since there are a great number of ConcurTaskTrees models that do not follow this definition and a change in semantics would only be confusing, we decided to remove this task category and to use a generic stereotype `task` instead. In practise, this has the consequence that CallBehaviourActions and StructuredActivityNodes have to have the stereotype `task` and not one of the derived stereotypes.

The four stereotypes that correspond to the remaining task categories are:

≪`userTask`≫ A user task is a task that is performed by the user without direct interaction with the application. A user task can however have indirect impact on an application. E.g. A museum visitor might carry an electronic mobile guide while strolling, performing no direct interaction. The electronic guide can however get updates about the position of the user through the use of a positioning system in the museum. This can be modeled by applying the stereotype to an AcceptEventAction and specifying an interface to the positioning system in the tagged value *contextSource*. User tasks that are applied to other types of Actions are optional and will not be used during further specification of the system.

≪`applicationTask`≫ An application task is a task performed entirely by the application without user interaction. Examples of such tasks are showing

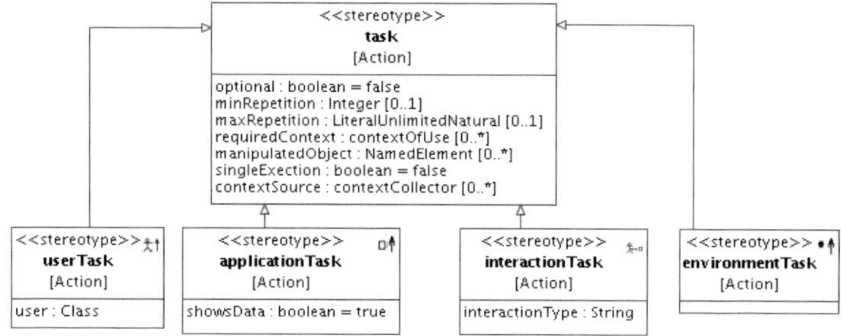

Fig. 7. Stereotypes of the UML profile CUP 2.0 relevant for the system interaction model

information to a user or performing a computation. When an application task has influence on the platform or the environment, the affected data structures or systems can be indicated through the tagged value *manipulatedObject*. Examples of such influences are putting information in the system paste buffer and triggering an external logger that has an influence on future application execution.

≪`interactionTask`≫ Direct user interaction with an application is modeled with an interaction task. Like the previously mentioned tasks, an interaction task can have effects on the environment which are indicated with tagged values. The type of user interaction is indicated through the tagged value *interactionType*.

≪`environmentTask`≫ An environment task covers all actions that have an influence on the execution of the interactive application but are performed by an entity other than the user and the application. An example of an environment task is a car accident that happens on the route calculated by a car navigation system. Similar to the user task, an environment task will be modelled through an AcceptEventAction when it has an immediate effect on the execution of the application, such as in the example of the car accident, which triggers a recalculation of the route.

All stereotypes indicating task categories are derived from the stereotype ≪`task`≫, which defines some tagged values that are shared by all task categories. These tagged values are important to reduce the complexity of the diagrams: the tagged value *optional* indicates whether or not a certain task is required or not, while the tagged value *repetition* indicates the number of times a task should be executed. The tagged values *manipulatedObject* and *requiredContext* are only applicable to basic tasks and thus are required to be empty sets for the stereotype ≪`task`≫. Figure 7 gives an overview of the stereotypes and their tagged values.

If the tagged value *singleExecution* is set to true for a certain task, that task interrupts all other tasks that are running in parallel until it is completed. This has as consequence that when all actions following a `ForkNode` have this tagged value set to true, they have to be carried out one after the other. This makes

Table 2. Temporal operators in ConcurTaskTrees and corresponding activity diagram notation

Temporal operator	Symbol	Activity diagram constructs
Enabling	>> and [] >>	control and object flow Task E1 Task E2 Task E1 Task E2
Disabling	[>	InterruptableActivityRegion with InterruptionEdge Task D1 Task E2
Concurrency	||| and |[]|	ForkNode and JoinNode with control or object flows Task P1 Task P2 Task P1 Task P2
Choice	[]	Decision and MergeNodes with control flows Task C1 Task C2
OrderIndependent	|=|	same as concurrency but all tasks have tagged value singleExecution set to true
Interruption	|>	concurrency with tagged value singleExecution set to true for the interrupting task

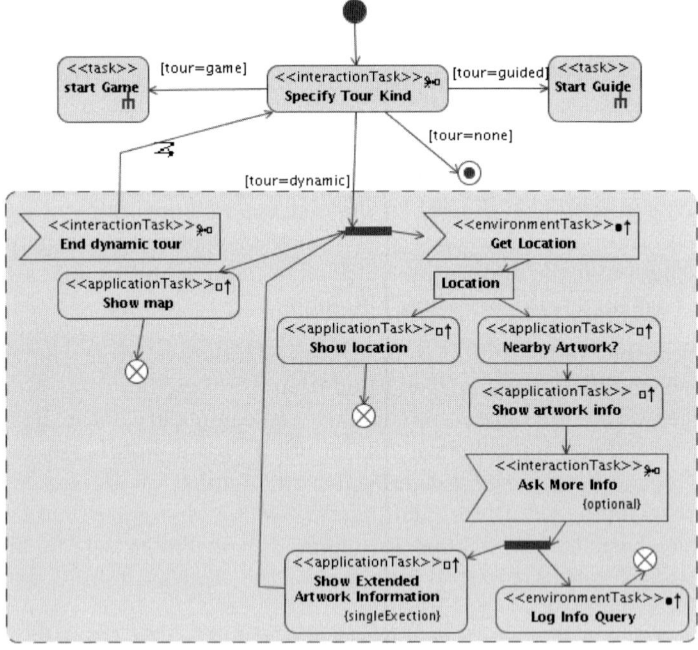

Fig. 8. Example of system interaction model: A context-sensitive mobile museum guide

that all temporal operators supported by the ConcurTaskTrees notation can be expressed using the UML activity diagram when the stereotypes in Figure 7 are applied as can be seen in Table 2.

An example of a system interaction model can be seen in Figure 8. The example shows a partial specification of a mobile museum guide that offers different types of tours. The diagram gives only details about one type of tour: the dynamic tour. This type of tour does not offer a specified trajectory to the user, but shows the user's position in the museum as well as information about a nearby artwork if one is available. A user can ask more information about an artifact. This additional information temporarily blocks all other information. Note that this example is simplified for brevity and as such will not really result in a user-friendly application.

7 Abstract User Interface Model

The abstract user interface model provides information about the structure of the user interface independent of the platform it will ultimately be deployed on. This means that we abstract from the concrete components and drastically reduce the number of components, coming to a minimal set of kinds of user interface components. The components are differentiated according to the functionality they offer to the user. We identified four types of abstract user interface components: *input components*, which allow users to enter or manipulate data, *output components*, which provide data from the application to the user, *action components*, which allow a user to trigger some functionality, and *group components*, which group components into a hierarchical structure.

In the UML, we represent the abstract user interface model (AUIM) using a class diagram. All classes in a AUIM need to have a stereotype identifying a type of abstract user interface component. There are also restrictions on the

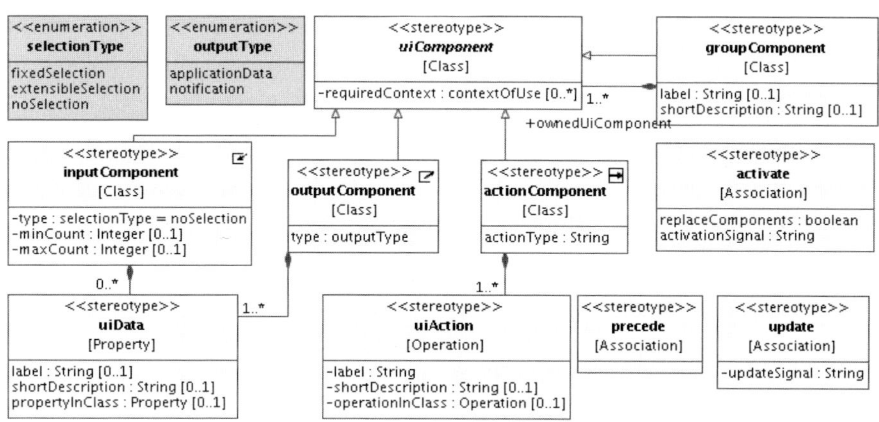

Fig. 9. Stereotypes of the UML profile CUP 2.0 relevant for the abstract user interface model

associations that can be specified between the classes, they need to indicate containment or have one of the stereotypes discussed later in this section applied to them. The definition of the stereotypes is shown in Figure 9. Only one of these stereotypes can be applied to one class. There is one exception to this rule: a group component can also be an input component, but in this case the input component must be a selection over the contained user interface components.

One should note that the classes with the stereotypes ≪`inputComponent`≫ or ≪`outputComponent`≫ can each have multiple attributes that would each be represented using a separate user interface component in a notation such as the Canonical Abstract Prototypes [3]. Each of the attributes has the stereotype ≪`uiData`≫. The tagged value *propertyInClass* can be used in case there is a reference to a property of a class. Additional meta-information, such as a label or more detailed information can be provided using the remaining tagged values. All `Operations` related to an action component must have the stereotype ≪`uiAction`≫ that allows to specify information similar to the stereotype ≪`uiData`≫ for each `Property` of an input component or output component.

The visibility specification for each `Property` and `Operation` with the stereotype ≪`uiData`≫ or ≪`uiAction`≫ is adapted to be more relevant to their meaning in the model, but remains consistent with the UML specification:

public Public visibility means that the associated part of the user interface is visible to not only the user of the application, but also other persons that might see the user interface. This visibility is, for example, appropriate for the part of a presentation application that shows slides.

protected Protected visibility means that the associated part of the user interface is only visible to the user of the user interface. This might mean that the value of an input component with protected visibility is hidden when shown on a public display. An example of user interface components for which this visibility is appropriate are the controls for moving through slides in a presentation application.

package Parts of the user interface that have package visibility are only accessible to other parts of the user interface, but are not shown to the users of the user interface. This visibility should be avoided in the abstract user interface model.

private Private visibility is used for parts of the user interface whose contents may not be seen by a user without being masked. An example of a user interface component with private visibility is a password field.

We also defined some stereotypes for associations between abstract user interface components to express relationships other than containment. These relationships indicate constraints on the structure of the user interface which are implied by the system interaction diagram and thus reduce the number of *hidden dependencies* within the abstract user interface model. These relationships can also be used to specify relationships between user interface components within the model that are specified in different diagrams. At the same time they also increase *visibility*. The reduction of hidden dependencies is important to

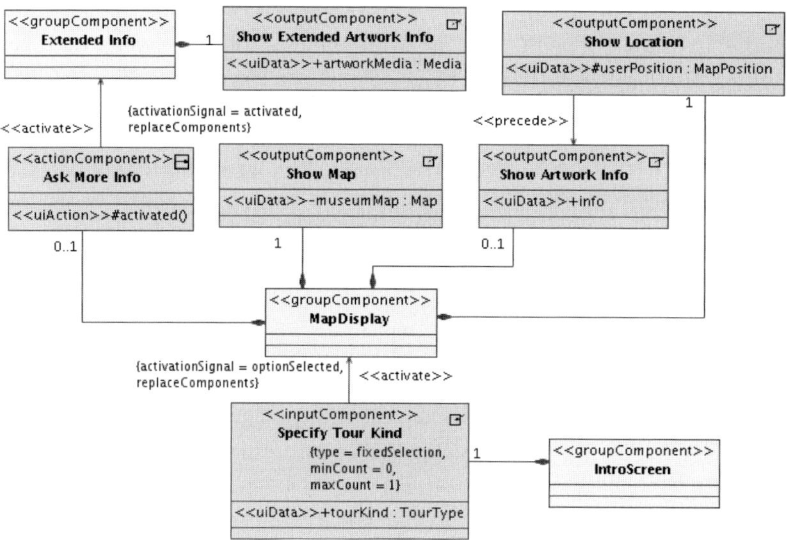

Fig. 10. Example of abstract user interface model: A context-sensitive mobile museum guide

effectively support *modification*, a good visibility is also important for *exploratory design* [9].

The first stereotype is ≪precede≫, which indicates that one user interface component should be presented to a user before another user interface component. The precedence can be spacial, temporal or both. The usage of this stereotype is limited to user interface components that are contained by the same group component and can be used to establish an order in which the user interface components are presented to the user. A second stereotype, ≪activate≫, can be applied to an association to indicate that a user interface component activates another component. The activated components can be added to the currently active components or can replace them. A third stereotype for associations is ≪update≫. Application of this stereotype to an association indicates that the contents of the target user interface component is updated by the source user interface component.

An example of an abstract user interface model is shown in Figure 10. The depicted model corresponds to the part of the system interaction model that shows the functionality offered in the case of a *dynamic* tour. The figure shows three group components that the user can interact with. The first group component contains one interaction component that allows the selection of a type of tour. When the user selects a type of tour, a second group component is activated and replaces the one that contains the interaction component, as can be seen from the tagged values on the association. This group shows a map, the current user position and, optionally[2] some information about a nearby artwork

[2] This can be derived from the multiplicity specified for the containment relations.

and, also optional, an option to show more information about the artwork. This information is shown within a group component *Extended Info*, which replaces the group component *MapDisplay*.

The abstract user interface description we use assigns one type of user interaction to a component, similar to the approach taken for XForms [7], UMLi [5] and Wisdom [13]. TERESA XML [12] also uses this approach but defines a deeper hierarchy that contains special components for inputs of simple datatypes and selections based on the number of options. UsiXML [11] only has one type of user interface components having facets that are based on the type of interaction.

8 Discussion

The profile can be useful for designers to have rather unambiguous and relatively compact models of a context-sensitive interactive application. Nevertheless, the ability to generate some parts of the models and ultimately generate code templates, can help the designer to be more productive. Therefore we explored the possibilities for automation.

We have identified two main areas where transformations as specified in the model-driven architecture [17] can be applied. The first is a model-to-model transformation from the system interaction model to the abstract user interface model. The second is the generation of high-level user interface descriptions from the abstract user interface model. The user interface deployment model can be used to add style to the different user interface skeletons and add some design guidelines specifically for the target platform.

To test the feasability of the prototype generation, we choose XHTML + XForms [7] as a target language and investigated how the prototype generation could be established. The mapping of the elements in the abstract user interface model to XForms tags is shown in Table 3. A ≪`uiAction`≫ is translated into a submission if a value is specified for the tagged value *operationInClass*, and into a trigger otherwise. In XForms each component can make references to separately defined object structure in instances. This object structure as well as its XML-Schema can be derived from the tagged value *propertyInClass* of the attributes with a ≪`uiData`≫ stereotype. The fully-qualified name of its class can be used

Table 3. CUP 2.0 stereotyped Elements and XForms counterparts

CUP-profile	XForms tags
groupComponent	group
- contained number of elements of same type > 1	repeat
uiData in inputComponent,	
- selectionType is none	input
- max. selectionCount = 1	select1
- max. selectionCount > 1	select
uiData in outputComponent	output
uiAction in actionComponent	trigger or submission

to generate a meaningful hierarchy of xml-tags, while the datatype itself can be used to define the types in XMLSchema.

The effects of the activation of components can be converted to bind tags with the right `relevant` settings. Precedence relations between user interface components are reflected in the order of the corresponding XForms controls in the document. The update relationships can also be translated into bind-tags with the right nodeset and optionally calculate attributes. Conversion of application or context-driven updates to the user interface are more difficult since they cannot be described declaratively in XForms.

9 Conclusion

Despite the fact that there is no dedicated support for multimedia applications, as is offered by the MML (see section 2) and that tool support for the proposed transformations is ongoing or planned as future work, we can conclude that the revised UML profile, CUP 2.0, presented in this paper offers some benefits over related approaches. The profile allows a detailed description of both the behavior and structure of the user interface of *context-sensitive* interactive applications using a limited amount of constructs of the UML using regular UML modeling tools that allow metamodel extension through profiles.

The profile also allows a clear specification of all datatypes that are involved, allowing to make optimal use of specifically designed user interface components for complex datatypes on platforms where they are available. Finally, the fact that all information is expressed in UML makes it easier to integrate the user interface specification with the specification of the application core.

Acknowledgements. This research was partly performed within the IWT project Participate of Alcatel Bell. Part of the research at the Expertise Centre for Digital Media is funded by the European Regional Development Fund (ERDF), the Flemish Government and the Flemish Interdisciplinary institute for Broadband Technology (IBBT).

References

1. Pedro F. Campos and Nuno J. Nunes. CanonSketch: a User-Centered Tool for Canonical Abstract Prototyping. In *Proceedings of EHCI-DSVIS 2004*, volume 3425 of *LNCS*, pages 146–163. Springer, 2005.
2. Tim Clerckx, Frederik Winters, and Karin Coninx. Tool support for designing context-sensitive user interfaces using a model-based approach. In *Proceedings TaMoDia 2005*, pages 11–18, Gdansk, Poland, September 26–27 2005.
3. Larry L. Constantine. Canonical Abstract Prototypes for Abstract Visual and Interaction Design. In *Proceedings of DSV-IS 2003*, number 2844 in LNCS, pages 1 – 15, Funchal, Madeira Island, Portugal, June 11-13 2003. Springer.
4. J. Coutaz and G. Rey. Foundations for a Theory of Contextors. In *CADUI*, pages 13–34. Kluwer Academic Publishers, 2002.

5. Paulo Pinheiro da Silva and Norman W. Paton. User Interface Modelling in UMLi. *IEEE Software*, 20(4):62–69, July–August 2003.
6. Anind K. Dey, Daniel Salber, and Gregory D. Abowd. A Conceptual Framework and a Toolkit for Supporting the Rapid Prototyping of Context-Aware Applications. *Human-Computer Interaction (HCI) Journal*, 16(2-4):97–166, 2001.
7. Micah Dubinko, Leigh L. Klotz, Roland Merrick, and T. V. Raman. XForms 1.0. W3C, `http://www.w3.org/TR/2003/REC-xforms-20031014/`, 2003.
8. Mohammed Elkoutbi, Ismaïl Khriss, and Rudolf Keller. Automated Prototyping of User Interfaces Based on UML Scenarios. *Automated Software Engineering*, 13(1):5–40, January 2006.
9. Thomas Green and Alan Blackwell. *Cognitive Dimensions of Information Artifacts: a Tutorial*, 1.2 edition, October 1998.
10. Jason I. Hong and James A. Landay. An architecture for privacy-sensitive ubiquitous computing. In *Proceedings of MobiSYS'04*, pages 177 – 189. ACM Press, 2004.
11. Quentin Limbourg and Jean Vanderdonckt. *Engineering Advanced Web Applications*, chapter UsiXML: A User Interface Description Language Supporting Multiple Levels of Independence. Rinton Press, December 2004.
12. Giulio Mori, Fabio Paternò, and Carmen Santoro. Design and Development of Multidevice User Interfaces through Multiple Logical Descriptions. *IEEE Transactions on Sofware Engineering*, 30(8):507–520, August 2004.
13. Nuno Jardim Nunes. *Object Modeling for User-Centered Development and User Interface Design: The Wisdom Approach*. PhD thesis, Univ. da Madeira, 2001.
14. Object Management Group. *UML 2.0 Superstructure Specification*, October 8 2004.
15. Fabio Paternò. *Model-Based Design and Evaluation of Interactive Applications*. Springer, 2000.
16. Andreas Pleuss. MML: A Language for Modeling Interactive Multimedia Applications. In *Proceedings of Symposium on Multimedia*, pages 465–473, December12–14 2005.
17. Joaquin Miller and Jishnu Mukerji. *MDA Guide Version 1.0.1*. World Wide Web, `http://www.omg.org/ docs/omg/03-06-01.pdf`, 2003.
18. Jan Van den Bergh and Karin Coninx. Contextual ConcurTaskTrees: Integrating Dynamic Contexts in Task Based Design. In *Second IEEE Conference on Pervasive Computing and Communications WORKSHOPS*, pages 13–17, Orlando, FL, USA, March 14–17 2004. IEEE Press.
19. Jan Van den Bergh and Karin Coninx. Towards Modeling Context-Sensitive Interactive Applications: the Context-Sensitive User Interface Profile (CUP). In *Proceedings of SoftVis '05*, pages 87–94, New York, NY, USA, 2005. ACM Press.

Domain Models Are NOT Aspect Free

Awais Rashid and Ana Moreira

Computing Department, Lancaster University, Lancaster LA1 4WA, UK
awais@comp.lancs.ac.uk
Departamento de Informática, Universidade Nova de Lisboa, 2829-516 Lisboa, Portugal
amm@di.fct.unl.pt

Abstract. In proceedings of MoDELS/UML 2005, Steimann argues that domain models are aspect free. Steimann's hypothesis is that the notion of aspect in aspect-oriented software development (AOSD) is a meta-level concept. He concludes that aspects are technical concepts, i.e., a property of programming and not a means to reason about domain concepts in a modular fashion. In this paper we argue otherwise. We highlight that, by ignoring the body of work on Early Aspects, Steimann in fact ignores the problem domain itself. Early Aspects techniques support improved modular and compositional reasoning about the problem domain. Using concrete examples we argue that domain models do indeed have aspects which need first-class support for such reasoning. Steimann's argument is based on treating quantification and obliviousness as fundamental properties of AOSD. Using concrete application studies we challenge this basis and argue that abstraction, modularity and composability are much more fundamental.

1 Introduction

As new software development paradigms appear on the horizon, it is normal that debates rage over their merits and demerits. Aspect-oriented software development (AOSD) [13] is no stranger to this situation. Since Kiczales et al's invited paper at ECOOP'97 [22], several points and counterpoints have been made in literature arguing about the merits and demerits of modularising crosscutting concerns in separate abstractions. Over the years the focus of aspect-orientation has significantly expanded beyond programming. A number of aspect-oriented analysis and design approaches, e.g., [2, 6, 17, 26, 27, 34, 39], aimed at disentangling requirements, architecture and design descriptions have appeared. These approaches provide explicit support for identification, modular representation, composition and analysis of broadly-scoped properties of both a functional and non-functional nature. In fact, several approaches, e.g., [8, 27, 38], take a multi-dimensional perspective on the problem and remove the strong distinction between aspects and the concerns they crosscut. Thus they also remove any distinction about whether a concern is functional or non-functional hence facilitating uniform modelling of concerns and their crosscutting influences (amidst other dependencies and interactions).

In his MoDELS/UML 2005 paper [35], Friedrich Steimann, however, argues that AOSD approaches in general, and aspect-oriented analysis and design approaches in particular, are merely useful for representing meta-level concepts. His hypothesis is

O. Nierstrasz et al. (Eds.): MoDELS 2006, LNCS 4199, pp. 155 – 169, 2006.

that aspects are second order entities that only require meta-modelling support and that domain models are in fact aspect free. His overall conclusion is that aspects are technical concepts, i.e., a property of *programming*, and not a means to reason about domain concepts in a modular fashion. In other words: there are no *functional* aspects and non-functional aspects are properties of the solution domain that do not require first-order representation. In his discussion, Steimann disregards the work on Early Aspects indicating that just because a functional requirement crosscuts other requirements does not mean that it should be treated as an aspect. Steimann's notion of an aspect is rooted in the properties of *quantification* and *obliviousness* as proposed by Filman and Friedman [14]. He treats these as fundamental properties of any aspect-oriented approach and, on this basis, argues about the second-ordered nature of aspects – to paraphrase Steimann: aspects are meta-level concepts that manipulate base-level (or first-order) elements.

In this paper we argue otherwise. We contend that if one is to discuss whether a domain model has crosscutting concerns, one cannot disregard the problem descriptions themselves. Therefore, we base our argument on Early Aspects techniques which support improved modular and compositional reasoning about the problem domain. Using concrete examples rooted in these techniques we argue that domain models do indeed have aspects which need to be modularised effectively to enable us to reason about them in a modular fashion. Similarly, using concrete application studies we challenge the fundamental basis of Steimann's argument, i.e., the notion of quantification and obliviousness. We demonstrate that *abstraction*, *modularity* and *composability* are much more fundamental to AOSD than quantification and obliviousness (which, though desirable are not necessary defining characteristics of an *aspect*). We conclude by discussing that, even if quantification and obliviousness were to be considered fundamental, firstly, early aspects techniques meet these characteristics and, secondly, the notion of aspects in the problem domain, as demonstrated by Early Aspects techniques, flows into the solution space, requiring first-class modelling of functional and non-functional aspects.

The rest of the paper is structured as follows. Section 2 lists Steimann's main four perspectives that give body to his argument. Section 3 debates each of these four arguments, showing counter examples. Section 4 explains why quantification and obliviousness cannot be understood as necessary defining properties of an aspect, discussing other equally valid views not aligned with Filman and Friedman's perspective. We argue that, just like with other separation of concerns approaches, abstraction, modularity and composability are the fundamental characteristics of AOSD. In Section 5 we discuss how first-class aspects, both functional and non-functional, in the problem domain flow into the solution space hence requiring their first class representation in the solution domain. Finally, Section 6 concludes the paper by discussing how our argument invalidates Steimann's hypothesis while still satisfying several constraints set by him.

2 Steimann's Argument

Steimann's argument about domain models being aspect free is based on four different perspectives:

1. Relationship between the notion of an aspect and a role;
2. The lack of any observed examples of arbitrary functional aspects in the current literature;
3. Aspects being strictly non-functional properties that are in fact aspects of the solution rather than the problem domain;
4. The second-order nature of aspects, i.e., aspects must always manipulate entities in a first-order separation.

From the above four perspectives, Steimann argues that for functional aspects to exist, and hence the need for them to be modelled, they must be at the same level of abstraction as other elements in the domain. Using a semi-formal proof based on *quantification* and *obliviousness* [14] he argues that aspects are always second-order statements that manipulate first-order elements thus concluding that they are meta-level concepts. From this semi-formal proof he also draws his conclusion that no functional (or domain) aspects exist.

We discuss quantification and obliviousness in detail in Section 4. Before that, in section 3, we debate each of the above four perspectives underpinning Steimann's argument. As mentioned above, Steimann disregards the work on Early Aspects stating that natural language descriptions are too imprecise to be aspectised. However, stakeholders, who are the primary descriptors of a problem domain, tend to specify their problems using natural language. These natural language descriptions are where aspects first manifest themselves as broadly-scoped properties leading to tangled representations in requirements models and subsequently in architecture, design and implementation. If we are to look for the existence of functional aspects in domain models we must start at the requirements analysis stage. Thus, this is where we start our search for aspects in domain models.

3 Aspects in Domain Models

When discussing the existence of aspects in domain models, we first examine Steimann's perspective on aspects and roles. In subsection 3.1, we demonstrate that his perspective is just one observation on the relationship between the two concepts and other equally valid arguments exist that demonstrate the synergy between the two concepts and their mutual complementarity. Then, in subsection 3.2, we show evidence, by means of practical examples drawn from the body of work on Early Aspects, that functional aspects do exist and can be found in everyday problems. In subsection 3.3, we discuss that non-functional requirements are not just properties of the solution but in fact properties of the problem that, too, require first-class modelling support. Finally, in subsection 3.4, we provide additional arguments as to why aspects require a first-order representation.

3.1 On the Relation Between Aspects and Roles

Steimann *equates* an aspect to a role. He argues that for roles to be appropriately realised, each object must explicitly implement all the roles it intends to play. In his view, since most role implementations tend to be specific to the particular class of objects, it is not reasonable to assume that role implementations can indeed be aspectised. This is, however, not the case. Several roles can be very generic. Most design patterns utilise the notion of roles to decouple the pattern implementation from its concrete usage in a specific application. For instance, the Observer pattern uses the Subject and Observer roles for this purpose. A number of design modelling approaches, e.g., Theme/UML [8] have shown how aspect-oriented techniques can be employed to improve the modular representation of design patterns such as the Observer pattern. Similarly, Hannemann and Kiczales [16] have demonstrated how design pattern implementations can benefit from the use of aspect-oriented programming (AOP) in terms of code locality, reusability, composability and pluggability. Garcia et al. have used these implementations as a basis of their quantitative evaluation of the benefits and scalability of AOP [5, 15]. Their studies show significant improvements in the case of 13 out of 23 design patterns with regards to metrics such as separation of concerns, coupling, cohesion and size. These studies mostly represent roles as interfaces with the glue code, between their abstract representation in the modularised pattern implementation and its concrete application instantiation, being provided through aspect-oriented composition mechanisms. This relationship between roles and aspects is entirely different from what is perceived by Steimann. Roles remain completely polymorphic as they are realised through interfaces while aspects provide the modularity and composition support essential to modularise the pattern implementation in a separate *aspectual component*.

Kendall's work [20] demonstrates a similar yet orthogonal relationship. She utilises AOP as a means to improve the implementation of role models. Through re-engineering of an existing role-based framework to an AspectJ implementation, she demonstrates that an aspect-oriented implementation is more cohesive than an object-oriented one.

Hannemann and Kiczales as well as Kendall utilize AOP as a means to improve the modularity of role-based implementations. Another different, yet equally valid, perspective arises from the ability of roles to help us realise multi-faceted objects. Roles can apply (often dynamically) across the system and hence, role-based systems tend to be less prescriptive about how objects interact. This ability makes it possible for role-models to facilitate aspect composition as is the case in CaesarJ [28]. In this case the *provided* and *required* interfaces specify the roles an aspect can play in a composition and those it expects of other modules in the system.

Steimann further argues that roles are polymorphic by nature and aspects are not. This is not true. Firstly, most aspect-oriented approaches facilitate aspect inheritance hence respecting the substitutability semantics that are normal in object-oriented hierarchies. Though approaches such as AspectJ [1] restrict the programmer to implicit aspect instantiation through the language framework, other techniques, e.g., CaesarJ [28], Composition Filters [4], JBoss [18] and Vejal [33], facilitate explicit aspect instantiation hence supporting substitutability of an aspect instance of a sub-aspect-type whenever an instance of a super-aspect-type is required. Since most of these approaches reify aspects as first-class objects (or use Java classes to specify aspect behaviour with XML descriptors specifying the aspect compositions), any role realisation using such AOP mechanisms can have the same polymorphic nature as a pure OO role realisation. It is perfectly conceivable that using an approach such as Composition Filters one can have a core object with a set of attached filters, each of which realises a specific role the object has to play (cf. Figure 1 – note only incoming message filters are shown but similar logic applies to outgoing messages). The per instance attachment ability of Composition Filters further facilitates an object-specific (unlike class-specific implementation in most standard OO techniques) configuration of roles that an object may participate in – this has been realised in the context of implementing roles at each edge of association and aggregation relationships using the SADES implementation of composition filter concepts [31]. Since such filters are implemented as first-class elements, polymorphic properties of roles are fully preserved.

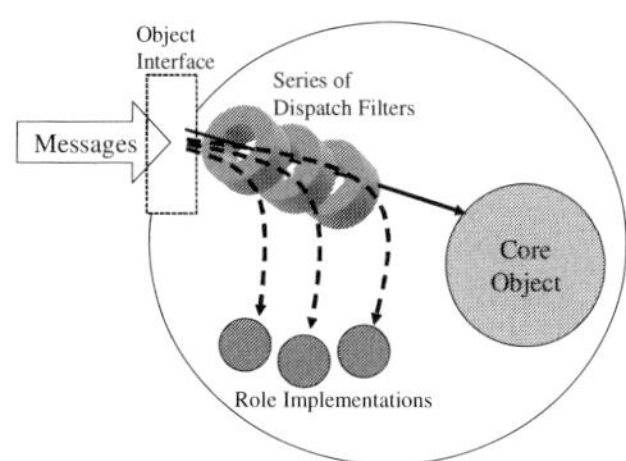

Fig. 1. Polymorphic Role Implementations with AOP using Composition Filters

Having established the complementary nature of roles and aspects, we can also say that aspects do exist in domain models. Roles are a domain concept. Different objects in different domains play different (perhaps sometimes overlapping) sets of roles. Since roles have a broadly-scoped nature and aspects can be used to realise role models in a fashion that supports role modularity without compromising role polymorphism, aspects do exist in domain models. However, one might argue that roles naturally form good candidates for aspects. In a system not following a role model design principle, are there indeed crosscutting functional and non-functional properties that are first-order domain elements? We discuss this next.

3.2 Observed Examples of Arbitrary Functional Aspects

For such observed examples, we turn to the extensive body of work on Early Aspects [2, 6, 8, 17, 26, 27, 34, 39]. Steimann disregards the work in this space by stating that the language of requirements is informal and that aspect-oriented requirements engineering approaches do not satisfy the quantification and obliviousness properties. Requirements engineering is mainly concerned with reasoning about the problem domain and formulating an effective understanding of the stakeholders' needs. Such an understanding leads to the emergence of a requirements specification that forms a bridge between the problem domain and the solution domain, the latter being the system architecture, design and implementation. So if one is to argue about the existence of aspects in domain models, one must examine the body of work in Early Aspects and specifically that on aspect-oriented requirements engineering. Though we argue in Section 4 that quantification and obliviousness are desirable, not fundamental, properties of AOSD approaches, Steimann's assertion that Early Aspects techniques do not satisfy these properties is incorrect. In fact, several approaches, e.g., [2, 6, 27, 34, 39], do not require any specific hooks within the base decomposition hence satisfying the obliviousness property. Furthermore, they have powerful composition mechanisms based on high-level declarative queries and semantics-based join point models that certainly do satisfy the quantification property. Figure 2 shows simplified viewpoint and aspect definitions as well as an example composition specification in the viewpoint-based aspect-oriented requirements engineering approach we presented in [34] – note we omit the XML notation for simplification. The problem domain in question is that of online auction systems. We can observe that the base concerns, i.e., the viewpoints Seller and Buyer are oblivious of the aspect Bidding whose associated composition specification quantifies over a set of viewpoint requirements to which it applies. Incidentally, note that the aspect Bidding is a core functional property of the system and not a non-functional one.

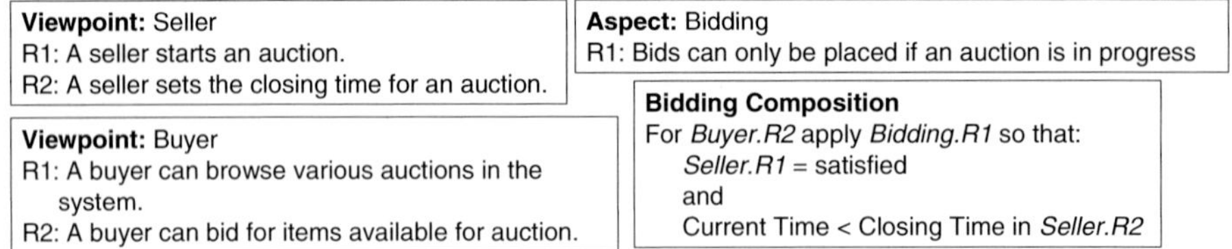

Fig. 2. Obliviousness in viewpoint-based aspect-oriented requirements engineering

Reasoning about the problem domain with early aspects

Let us look at the specific problem description of an online auction system and analyse what are the various crosscutting functional and non-functional concerns. We use a viewpoint-based requirements specification mechanism. Aspects in the specification crosscut the viewpoints, each of which represents requirements from a specific stakeholders' perspective. The viewpoints in this specific problem description are also analogous to roles as they capture the requirements about specific user roles, i.e. the System Administrator, Customer, Seller, Buyer, System Owner and Webmaster. As shown in Figure 3, such a system has a number of concerns that crosscut the requirements of these various viewpoints (or roles). For instance, the *bidding* aspect affects the customer viewpoint because customers are interested in bidding for the items being auctioned. It also affects sellers as they are the primary stakeholders interested in the bids. At the same time, the system administrator is interested in ensuring that bids are only received until the specified auction closing time, and so on. The same is true of the *selling* aspect which affects these multiple viewpoints. Another aspect of significance is the *bid solvency* concern which dictates that all placed bids must be solvent, i.e. a customer must have more credit than the sum total of all the bids s/he has in progress. This is of key concern to the system administrator and owner as they wish to ensure that sellers recover their due payments. At the same time, this is a key factor in the seller choosing the specific auction system for the security and trust the bid solvency aspect offers. All the aspects, i.e. bidding, selling, bid solvency, etc. are functional properties of the domain hence requiring first-class modelling support. They are not *properties of the program* to be developed to satisfy the auction system requirements. Nor are they second order entities as the various viewpoints have strong dependencies on the semantics of these aspects and are at the same level of abstraction as the aspects themselves.

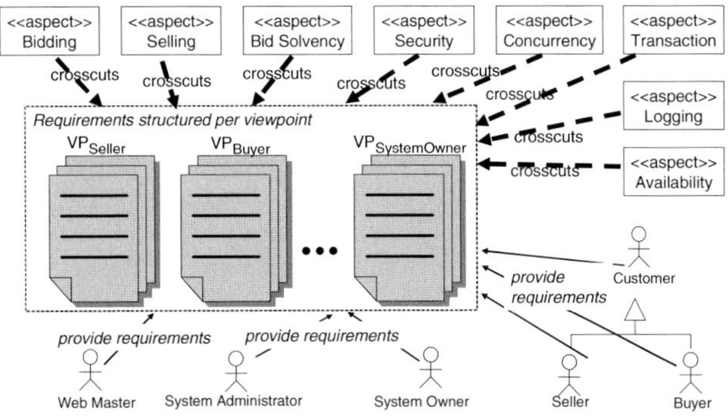

Fig. 3. Aspects in a viewpoint-oriented model of the auction system

Other evidence in existing literature

Jacobson and Ng [17] offer an aspect-oriented use case approach to handle stakeholder concerns from requirements analysis through to low-level design. Their proposal is based on the observation that use cases reflect stakeholders' concerns and are crosscutting by nature. Therefore, each use case is encapsulated in a use-case module which typically contains one non-use-case specific slice (that only adds classes to the module) and one or more use-case slices which contain classes and aspects specific to the realisation of the use case. It is worth observing that use-case slices (and, therefore, aspects) identified in this work are typical functional aspects and may represent extensions, inclusions and certain secondary flows used in classical object-oriented modelling, which makes use case slices abundant for each new problem. In their hotel reservation system example, Jacobson and Ng have identified a number of functional aspects, such as *handle waiting list*, *checking in customer* and *handle no room*.

In the Theme approach by Clarke and Baniassad [8], a *theme* encapsulates a piece of functionality or aspect or concern that is of interest to a developer. At the requirements analysis level, themes are classified sets of requirements (taken directly from the requirements description document). Aspect themes are those that might be triggered in multiple different situations. They identify several examples of theme aspects, many of them being functional, e.g., functional crosscutting themes in a crystal collection game, namely, *Track-Energy*, *Challenge*, *Drop*.

In [26], Moreira et al use aspects to modularise and compose volatile concerns. Many of these volatile concerns are functional, such as *card solvency* and *calculate fares* in a subway system and *bidding*, *order handling*, *payment* and *monitoring* in a transport system.

D'Hondt and Jonckers [10] provide an approach for representing business rules as aspects. Business rules are highly domain- and application-dependent and crosscut other domain elements. Examples of such business rules include: *loyal customers are entitled to a 5% discount; all customers who have a charge card are loyal,* and so on.

3.3 On the Notion of Non-functional Requirements Being Solution Domain Properties

Steimann argues that non-functional requirements are not elements of the problem domain and are, instead, technical properties and therefore only appear at the solution domain level. This is not so, however. Several other well-established approaches (goal- and agent-oriented [7, 11], for example) have demonstrated the need for putting non-functional requirements at the forefront of developers' thinking. In fact, many of these properties reflect real stakeholder concerns, even at the strategic organisational level, and their existence can be noticed explicitly and implicitly in the requirements descriptions. Therefore, we should not put those concerns on hold until the implementation phase is reached. And, as mentioned earlier, if we are to prove that aspects exist at the modelling analysis level, we cannot ignore a significant part of what constitutes one of the primary bases for our work: the requirements descriptions.

Our auction system model in Figure 3 also shows a number of non-functional aspects, i.e., *security*, *concurrency, transaction, logging* and *availability*. Again, though these non-functional aspects will be present in other domains, the requirements pertaining to these will nevertheless be domain specific and dictate different types of needs. For instance, in the auction system, the security needs are mainly concerned with ensuring that all users accessing the system are authorised, the communication between the client and server uses a secure connection and so on. On the other hand, security requirements for a home security monitoring system will include ensuring that all doors and windows have locks, alarms are wired to those locks, motion detectors fitted, etc. Security requirements for a transportation system might be related to special arrangements necessary when transporting military assets or sensitive documents. Though the non-functional property *security* appears in all these domains, the specific requirements differ and so will the solutions to satisfy those requirements. Also note that the *transaction* aspect is also a property of the domain as it relates to customers completing their transactions and obtaining their goods. Just because it may map on to a concrete transaction processing aspect in the implementation does not imply that it is a property of the programming (as stated by Steimann). When analysing the problem domain, the concept of a transaction will have specific properties, e.g., a long transaction in an auction system where a customer places several bids on the same item in response to increasing bids from other users. This is in contrast to a transaction in a banking system where the general nature of a transaction is typically short: users go to the ATM or bank clerk to withdraw cash and the transactions do not last for days or weeks as is the case for an auction system. At the domain analysis level we are interested in modelling the semantics of a transaction from a user/stakeholder perspective and not from the perspective of specific locking or concurrency protocols that may be employed during implementation.

3.4 On the First-Order Nature of Aspects

The discussion in Sections 3.1-3 clearly demonstrates that functional and non-functional aspects are properties of the domain and therefore must be modelled at the same level of abstraction as other domain concepts being analysed. Here we offer further evidence of the first-order nature of aspects.

In his paper, Steimann offers a semi-formal proof regarding the second-order nature of aspects. This proof is founded on the presence of a base decomposition, i.e. he envisages that there will always be a dominant decomposition paradigm employed for modelling domain concepts and that aspects will crosscut concerns in this dominant decomposition. However, a number of approaches in AOSD remove the strong distinction between base concerns and aspects. Instead they take a multi-dimensional perspective on separation of concerns and their subsequent modelling. This means that there is no dominant decomposition. All concerns, whether they are functional or non-functional, classes or aspects, are at the same level of abstraction. This has significant advantages for domain analysis and modelling. One can *fold* or *project* one set of concerns on another set of concerns, as needed, to understand their mutual dependencies and influences, including crosscutting ones. This provides a powerful composition mechanism as all concerns are composable in a uniform fashion. Concerns can be incrementally composed to build composite concerns which can in turn be composed together to form more coarse-grained concerns. Such multi-dimensional approaches have been proposed for requirements analysis [8, 27, 37, 38], design [3, 8, 19] and implementation [3, 38]. Models in such approaches invalidate Steimann's proof as all concerns in a multi-dimensional model are first-order entities.

4 Quantification and Obliviousness

In [14] Filman and Friedman proposed a simple classification of the relationship between aspects and classes based on the notions of *quantification* and *obliviousness*. Quantification is defined as the ability of an AOP pointcut language to specify a predicate which can match a variety of join points in the static class definitions and dynamic object interaction graphs. Obliviousness, on the other hand, is the ability of a class to be *aspectised* without having to specially provide any hooks to expose the various join points that aspects might want to quantify over. The statement in [14] is, however, a position statement and the authors do not imply that their classification is the only classification of fundamental properties of AOP. Nor is the classification intended as a definition of the fundamentals of AOP. There are other classifications that focus on other facets of the relationship between aspects and classes. For instance, Kersten and Murphy [21] have proposed a classification based on their experience in developing the ATLAS web-based learning system. They categorise aspect-class relationships into:

- *class directional:* the aspects know about the classes but not vice versa. This is analogous to Filman and Friedman's obliviousness.
- *aspect directional:* the classes know about the aspects but not vice versa. This means that classes are no longer oblivious of the aspects. Classes may need to be annotated to specify the intention of fields and methods, e.g., as in meta-data-based pointcut expressions [25], instead of relying on lexical matching in existing pointcut expression mechanisms.
- *open:* this is a union of aspect directional and class directional – both aspects and classes know about each other.
- *closed:* neither the aspects nor the classes know about each other. This applies to systems with strong encapsulation, e.g., [30].

Kersten and Murphy's classification demonstrates that there are several *non-oblivious* modalities of the aspect-class relationship. In fact, a number of application studies have shown that, in a variety of cases, obliviousness is neither achievable nor desirable. Kienzle and Guerraoui [24] and Fabry [12] argue that when modularising transaction management concerns only *syntactic obliviousness* is achievable, i.e. syntactic representation of aspects and class models may not contain direct references to each other. However, *semantic obliviousness* is not desirable as objects need to be aware of their transactional nature. Similarly, Rashid and Chitchyan [32] demonstrate that, in the context of a database application, persistence can be effectively aspectised. However, only partial obliviousness is desirable. This is because persistence has to be accounted for as an architectural decision during the design of data-consumer components – GUI components, for instance, need to be aware of large volumes of data so that they may be presented to users in manageable chunks. Furthermore, designers of such components also need to consider the declarative nature of retrieval mechanisms supported by most database systems. Similarly, deletion requires explicit attention during application design as mostly applications trigger such an operation.

Quantification too is only a desirable property of any AOSD technique. No doubt predicate-like pointcut expressions, e.g., [29, 36] provide a means to match a range of join points in design or code models. However, in several situations that Colyer et al. [9] refer to as *heterogeneous aspects*, a pointcut expression may only select a single join point (i.e. no pattern-matching a la AspectJ is employed). The encapsulation of a number of such pointcuts and their associated advice in an aspect still modularises a crosscutting concern, though pointcuts do not employ any quantification mechanism.

There are, of course, alternative aspect composition models that do not rely on predicate-like pointcut expressions. We discussed role-based composition in Section 2.1. Such role-based composition models are often found in aspect-oriented architecture design approaches where connectors and associated roles manage aspect composition [2, 30]. Similarly, the increasing drive towards semantics-based pointcut expressions in AOSD means that at first glance a pointcut may not be explicitly quantifying over multiple join points. However, the semantics to be matched by the pointcut expression will inevitably be implicitly quantifying over other system elements. One such semantics-based pointcut expression mechanism has been developed in the requirements description language from AOSD-Europe [6]. The language enriches existing requirements descriptions with additional semantics derived from the semantics of the natural language itself. Therefore, as shown in Figure 4, the constraint specification (analogous to a pointcut expression) can match all the aspect requirements where the subject of the sentence (in a grammatical sense) is a *seller* and the object (again in a grammatical sense) an *auction* with an *end* relationship between the subject and object. Similar semantics-based matching is done in the *base* and *outcome* expressions. Instead of using a syntactical match as in Figure 2 (bidding composition), we are instead matching elements based on the semantics derived from the requirements descriptions, i.e. the subject, object and nature of relationship between the subject and object. Such semantics-based join point models have also been proposed for aspect-oriented design [36] and programming [29, 33].

```
<Composition name="CancelAuction">
  <Constraint operator="begin/end">subject="seller" and relationship="end" and object="auction"</Constraint>
  <Base operator="ifNot">subject="auction" and relationship="begin"</Base>
  <Outcome operator="satisfy">all requirements where subject="start date“ or object=“start date”</Outcome>
</Composition>
```

Fig. 4. Semantics-based composition in the AOSD-Europe RDL

So if *quantification* and *obliviousness* are not fundamental characteristics of an AOSD approach, what is fundamental for aspects? In our view, the same characteristics that hold for other separation of concerns mechanisms are also fundamental for aspects, i.e. *abstraction*, *modularity* and *composability*. It is not quantification and obliviousness but the *systematic* support for abstraction, modularity and composability of *crosscutting* concerns [34] that distinguishes AOSD techniques from other separation of concerns mechanisms.

4.1 Aspects Are About Abstraction

Abstraction is a means to hide away the details of how a specific concept or feature may be implemented in a system. Abstract types provide us a means to reason about relevant properties of a problem domain without getting bogged down in implementation details. So the first question we need to address is whether aspects provide any benefits in terms of abstraction. In fact, abstraction is as fundamental to AOSD as it is to any other separation of concerns mechanism. The notion of an aspect allows us to abstract away from the details of how that aspect might be scattered and tangled with the functionality of other modules in the system. At the modelling level, aspects help us abstract away from implementation details, for instance, the examples of security and transactions in Section 3.3. At the same time, we can refine aspects at a higher-level of abstraction, e.g., aspects in requirements models, to more concrete aspects hence gaining invaluable knowledge about how crosscutting properties in requirements map to architecture-, design- and implementation-level aspects (this is discussed further in Section 5). This is analogous to refining objects in requirements models to their corresponding designs and implementations. The key difference is that, as abstractions, aspects facilitate tracing the impact and influence of crosscutting relationships through the various refinements.

4.2 Aspects Are About Modularity

Abstraction and modularity are closely related. When we abstract away from specific details that may not be of interest at a certain level of abstraction, we also want to modularise details that are of interest so that we may reason about them in isolation. This is termed *modular reasoning* [23]. When modelling domain concepts, modular reasoning is fundamental to understand the main concerns of a problem and to reason about the individual properties of the domain concerns. The modularisation of crosscutting requirements in aspects greatly facilitates such modular reasoning. Returning to our example from Section 3.2, the modularisation of bidding, selling and bid solvency requirements allows us to reason about the needs they impose on the system as well as about their completeness regardless of how they affect or influence various viewpoints in the system. The same applies to the non-functional aspects we discussed. Without modularisation of such crosscutting properties, we would need to reason about them by looking at their tangled representations in the various viewpoint requirements, which would be an arduous and time consuming task. Because these crosscutting concerns would be tangled with the viewpoints in the absence of aspect modularity, this is further evidence that they are properties of the domain and not of the programming solution.

4.3 Aspects Are About Composability

Modularity must be complemented by composability. The various modules need to relate to each other in a systematic and coherent fashion so that one may reason about the global or emergent properties of the system – using the modular reasoning outcomes as a basis. We refer to this global reasoning as *compositional reasoning*. Aspects facilitate such compositional reasoning about the problem domain as well as the corresponding solution. For instance, when composing the various aspects and viewpoints in our auction system example, we can understand the trade-offs between the aspects even before the architecture is derived. For example, we can observe that the bidding and bid solvency concerns may be at odds at times: we wish to allow people to place bids yet the solvency requirements must prohibit this at times. This allows us to reason about the overall bidding process and its administration. In addition to reasoning about inter-aspect interactions, we can also reason about how aspects influence the requirements of the various viewpoints. For instance, the various viewpoints are constrained by the security requirements which may require customers to register, login and use secure transmissions before participating in any auctions. How this compositional reasoning is carried out is beside the point. Quantification in pointcut expressions is just one way of doing this. That does not mean that one is manipulating first-order elements in second-order expressions. The goal is to compose the various domain elements, i.e. the aspects, classes, etc. to be able to reason about the global properties of the system.

5 From Early Domain Aspects to Design and Implementation Aspects

Capturing aspects early in the life-cycle has several advantages. In particular, this can help to guarantee that all stakeholders' concerns are identified and captured properly, reducing the possibility of either losing significant requirements during development or else keeping them in a separate list that needs to accompany the developer through to the solution domain. Such an approach increases the consistency between requirements, architecture, design and implementation, providing, at the same time, improved support for traceability of all types of concerns across the development lifecycle activities. Moreover, a systematic means to identify and manage crosscutting concerns at the problem domain level contributes to completeness of requirements specifications and their corresponding architecture, design and implementation. An evident consequence is that the requirements specification can truly function as a bridge to narrow the classic gap between the problem and the solution domains.

In [27] and [34] we observed that analysis of requirements-level aspects provides us with an improved understanding of their mutual trade-offs and, consequently, with the ability to make improved architectural choices. Each functional or non-functional aspect leads to a number of architecture choices that would serve its needs with varying levels of stakeholder satisfaction. These architectural choices are unlikely to be the same and could even be conflicting (which is often the case). All these, often conflicting architectural choices *pull* the final architecture choice in various directions. Our requirements-level trade-off analysis gives us some early insights into such a pull and helps us resolve some of the conflicts. This arms us with a better understanding of the diverse and conflicting needs of aspectual concerns hence facilitating the choice of an optimal architecture that balances these conflicting needs.

However, requirements-level aspects are more than just identifying architectural choices and trade-offs. A requirements-level aspect can be stepwise refined into one or more architectural aspects, and, subsequently, design and implementation aspects. For instance, in our auction system example, the bid solvency aspect would be refined into an aspect implementing specific algorithms for ensuring solvency across multiple, concurrent bids by the same customer. At the same time, such an aspect would require an awareness that customers could be selling items at the same time, and hence receiving top-ups on their accounts. The availability aspect, on the other hand, would map onto a decision for an architectural choice, i.e. involving backup servers, high stability network connections and so on. At the same time, it will also refine into concrete solution domain aspects realising replication, session management, etc.

Similar mappings have been proposed by others. Jacobson and Ng [17], for instance, handle each use case module, and in particular each use case slice, separately through architecture to code, by refining the analysis elements into design structures (classes and components) and, when necessary, adding new solution structures. In their examples, all the use case slices identified during the requirements analysis are kept during architecture and low level design. During architecture design, new aspects appear to keep platform specific elements separate from the platform independent ones. Similarly, in Theme [8], requirements analysis themes are carried forward to the design level – each analysis-level theme is designed separately from all the others and contains all the necessary solution domain structures to implement it.

6 Conclusion

In his conclusion Steimann encourages others to challenge and disprove his hypothesis and sets three conditions [35]:

1. *"The aspect must be an aspect in the aspect-oriented sense (in particular, it must not be a subroutine or a role);*
2. *It must not be an artefact of the (technical) solution, but must be seen as representative of an element of the underlying problem domain;*
3. *Its choice must have a certain arbitrariness about it so that the example provides evidence that there are more aspects of the same kind, be it in the same or in other domains."*

In this paper, we have shown several examples where aspects are not mere sub-routines or roles – i.e. they are first-class problem domain concepts that crosscut other problem domain concepts (satisfying condition 1). Modelling of such concerns as sub-routines would require them to be triggered by viewpoints in different situations, hence tangling these concerns with the core descriptions of the viewpoints. We have also shown that quantification and obliviousness, though desirable, are not fundamental properties of AOSD. However, even if these were to be considered fundamental, aspect-oriented requirements engineering approaches offer strong modularisation and composition mechanisms satisfying both obliviousness and quantification (in contrast to what Steimann affirms). We have demonstrated that functional and non-functional aspects represent important stakeholders concerns at the domain-level and therefore need a first-order representation (satisfying condition 2). Finally, we have pointed out a considerable number of arbitrary functional aspects that can be found in the existing Early Aspects body of work, therefore satisfying condition 3.

We hope to have convinced the reader that aspects are not about obliviousness and quantification, and that they represent important stakeholder concerns present in the requirements descriptions which cannot be ignored and left to be treated during the implementation phase. Aspects are about more fundamental software engineering principles. Aspects are about abstraction, modularity and composability. These are the lemmas that should guide our decisions throughout the development lifecycle.

Acknowledgements. This work is supported by the projects: AOSD-Europe (IST-2-004349), MULDRE (EPSRC EP/C003330/1) and SOFTAS (POSC/EIA/60189/2004). The authors wish to thank Ruzanna Chitchyan for helpful comments and discussions.

References

[1] AspectJ Project, http://www.eclipse.org/aspectj/, 2006.
[2] E. Baniassad, et al., "Discovering Early Aspects", IEEE Software, 23(1), pp. 61-69, 2006.
[3] D. Batory, et al., "Scaling Stepwise-Refinement", IEEE Trans. on Soft. Engg., 30(6), 2004.
[4] L. Bergmans, M. Aksit, "Composing Crosscutting Concerns using Composition Filters", CACM, 44(10), pp. 51-57, 2001.
[5] N. Cacho, et al., "Composing Design Patterns: A Scalability Study of Aspect-Oriented Programming", Proc. AOSD Conf., 2006, ACM, pp. 109-121.
[6] R. Chitchyan, et al., "Initial Version of Aspect-Oriented Requirements Engineering Model", AOSD-Europe Report D36 (AOSD-Europe-ULANC-17) http://www.aosd-europe.net 2006.
[7] L. Chung, et al., Non-Functional Requirements in Software Engineering: Kluwer, 2000.
[8] S. Clarke, E. Baniassad, Aspect-Oriented Analysis and Design: The Theme Approach: Addison-Wesley, 2005.
[9] A. Colyer, et al., "On the Separation of Concerns in Program Families", Lancaster University Tech. Report COMP-001-2004 (http://www.comp.lancs.ac.uk/computing/aose).
[10] M. D'Hondt, V. Jonckers, "Hybrid Aspects for Weaving Object-Oriented Functionality and Rule-based Knowledge", Proc. AOSD Conf., 2004, ACM, pp. 132-140.
[11] A. Dardenne, et al., "Goal-directed Requirements Acquisition", Science of Computer Programming, 20, pp. 3-50, 1993.

[12] J. Fabry, "Modularizing Advanced Transaction Management - Tackling Tangled Aspect Code": PhD Thesis, Vrije Universiteit Brussel, Belgium, 2005.
[13] R. Filman, et al. (eds.), "Aspect-Oriented Software Development": Addison-Wesley, 2004.
[14] R. Filman, D. Friedman, "Aspect-Oriented Programming is Quantification and Obliviousness", OOPSLA WS on Advanced Separation of Concerns, 2000.
[15] A. Garcia, et al., "Modularizing Design Patterns with Aspects: A Quantitative Study", Proc. AOSD Conf., 2005, ACM, pp. 3-14.
[16] J. Hannemann, G. Kiczales, "Design Pattern Implementation in Java and AspectJ", Proc. OOPSLA, 2002, ACM, pp. 161-173.
[17] I. Jacobson, P.-W. Ng, Aspect-Oriented Software Development with Use Cases: Addison-Wesley, 2004.
[18] JBoss Aspect Oriented Programming Webpage, http://www.jboss.org/products/aop, 2006.
[19] M. Kande, "A Concern-Oriented Approach to Software Architecture": PhD, EPFL, 2003.
[20] E. A. Kendall, "Role Model Designs and Implementations with Aspect-Oriented Programming", Proc. OOPSLA, 1999, ACM, pp. 353-369.
[21] M. A. Kersten, G. C. Murphy, "Atlas: A Case Study in Building a Web-based Learning Environment using Aspect-oriented Programming", Proc. OOPSLA, 1999, ACM, 340-352.
[22] G. Kiczales, et al., "Aspect-Oriented Programming", ECOOP 1997, Springer, pp. 220-242.
[23] G. Kiczales, M. Mezini, "Aspect-Oriented Programming and Modular Reasoning", Proc. ICSE, 2005, ACM, pp. 49-58.
[24] J. Kienzle, R. Guerraoui, "AOP: Does It Make Sense? The Case of Concurrency and Failures", Proc. ECOOP, 2002, Springer, pp. 37-61.
[25] R. Laddad, "AOP with Metadata: Principles and Patterns", Industry Talk at AOSD 2005.
[26] A. Moreira, et al., "Modeling Volatile Concerns as Aspects", Proc. CAiSE, 2006, Springer.
[27] A. Moreira, et al., "Multi-Dimensional Separation of Concerns in Requirements Engineering", Proc. Requirements Engineering Conf., 2005, IEEE CS, pp. 285-296.
[28] K. Ostermann, "CaesarJ", http://caesarj.org/, 2006.
[29] K. Ostermann, et al., "Expressive Pointcuts for Increased Modularity", Proc. ECOOP, 2005, Springer, pp. 214-240.
[30] M. Pinto, et al., "DAOP-ADL: An Architecture Description Language for Dynamic Component and Aspect-Based Development", Proc. GPCE, 2003, Springer, pp. 118-137.
[31] A. Rashid, Aspect-Oriented Database Systems: Springer-Verlag, 2003.
[32] A. Rashid, R. Chitchyan, "Persistence as an Aspect", Proc. AOSD, 2003, ACM, 120-129.
[33] A. Rashid, N. Leidenfrost, "VEJAL: An Aspect Language for Versioned Type Evolution in Object Databases", AOSD 2006 Workshop on Linking Aspect Technology and Evolution.
[34] A. Rashid, et al., "Modularisation and Composition of Aspectual Requirements", Proc. AOSD Conf., 2003, ACM, pp. 11-20.
[35] F. Steimann, "Domain Models are Aspect Free", Proc. MODELS 2005, Springer, 171-185.
[36] D. Stein, et al., "Expressing Different Conceptual Models of Join Point Selections in Aspect-Oriented Design", Proc. AOSD Conf., 2006, ACM, pp. 15-26.
[37] S. M. Sutton, I. Rouvellou, "Modeling of Software Concerns in Cosmos", Proc. AOSD Conf., 2002, ACM, pp. 127-133.
[38] P. L. Tarr, et al., "N Degrees of Separation: Multi-Dimensional Separation of Concerns", Proc. ICSE, 1999, ACM, pp. 107-119.
[39] J. Whittle, J. Araujo, "Scenario Modelling with Aspects", IEE Proceedings - Software, 151(4), pp. 157-172, 2004.

A Slice of MDE with AOP: Transforming High-Level Business Rules to Aspects

María Agustina Cibrán[1] and Maja D'Hondt[2]

[1] System and Software Engineering Lab
Vrije Universiteit Brussel
Pleinlaan 2, 1050 Brussel, Belgium
mcibran@vub.ac.be

[2] INRIA Jacquard - Laboratoire d'Informatique Fondamentale de Lille
Université des Sciences et Technologies de Lille
59655 Villeneuve d'Ascq, Cédex, France
dhondt@lifl.fr

Abstract. We propose an approach that combines MDE and AOSD to automatically translate high-level business rules to aspects and integrate them with existing object-oriented applications. The separation of rule-based knowledge from the core application as explicit business rules has been the focus of existing approaches. However, they fail at supporting rules that are both high-level, i.e. defined in domain terms, and operational, i.e. automatically executable from the core application. In this paper we propose high-level languages for expressing business rules at the domain level as well as their connections to the core application. We provide support for automatically translating high-level rules to object-oriented programs and their connections to aspects, since these crosscut the core application. Separation of concerns is preserved at the domain and implementation levels, facilitating traceability, reusability and adaptability. A prototype implementation and a discussion on trade-offs are presented.

1 Introduction

Explicit business rules are a widely accepted approach to decoupling implicit rule-based knowledge, such as regulations, policies, recommendations and preferences, from a software application in a certain domain or business. This decoupling is pursued in all phases of the software development process [11, 17]. Ultimately, business rules are implemented either using standard software engineering approaches, such as object-oriented programming languages or XML, or dedicated approaches, such as rule-based languages.

We have observed in different industrial applications, in domains as diverse as finance and healthcare, that once the initial application is developed, unanticipated business rules need to be incorporated to accommodate the change of regulations, policies, etc. As such, we consider as the context of this paper existing applications that are developed and maintained with traditional software

O. Nierstrasz et al. (Eds.): MoDELS 2006, LNCS 4199, pp. 170–184, 2006.

engineering techniques, in which possibly unanticipated business rules have to be integrated.

Although existing approaches support the separation of business rules from the core application, they fail to satisfy two requirements. First of all, as business rules are driven by the domain, they need to be defined and understood by domain experts, who are typically not adept at programming. Therefore, it is required that business rules are expressed in high-level domain terms, hiding technical concerns, but are also executable. Moreover, it is more likely that business rules expressed in terms of the domain can be more easily reused among a variety of similar applications in the same domain. Secondly, the *connection* of the business rules — i.e. applying the rules at certain events and gathering the necessary information for their application — crosscuts the core application. We have used *Aspect-Oriented Programming* (AOP) for encapsulating the connection code in earlier work [2, 4, 5, 8]. At the same time, we identified that the connection code consists of several recurring issues, which we abstracted in aspect patterns. However, these patterns are again entirely expressed at the programming level and are hence not understandable by domain experts. Therefore, we also want to express the aspect patterns in terms of the domain, as we do the business rules.

Our approach consists of defining business rules and their connections to the existing application in dedicated, high-level languages and expressing them in terms of the domain. In order to make these rules executable and integrate them with the existing application according to the connections, we follow a *Model-Driven Engineering* (MDE) approach: the rules and connections are automatically translated to object-oriented and aspect-oriented programs, respectively. The transformations use a mapping from the domain entities, used in the high-level rules and connections, to implementation elements in the existing application. Our approach maintains separation of concerns from the domain level to the implementation level, thus facilitating traceability of the business rules and their connections. Moreover, the automatically generated code pertaining to rules and connections remains separated from the existing application code and therefore does not interfere with the development and maintenance of the application.

This paper is organized as follows: section 2 presents the high-level rule and connection languages, expressed in terms of the domain entities of a domain model. The transformations from high-level specifications in those languages to implementation are described in section 3. A prototype implementation of our approach is described in section 4. Related work is presented in section 5. Finally, section 6 discusses several issues as well as the advantages and limitations of our approach and conclusions are presented in section 7.

2 A Domain Model for Business Rules

We propose a *high-level domain model* consisting of: domain entities, business rules about domain entities, and connections of business rules to the core application in terms of domain entities. The domain entities represent the domain vocabulary of interest and are based on the typical modeling elements that all data modeling approaches have in common: class, attribute, method and association. In this paper we present examples in the domain of e-commerce in which we identify some typical domain entities used in the rest of this paper: *Shop*, *ShoppingBasket*, *Customer* and *ShopAccount* are domain classes; *ShopAccount* defines the *amountSpent* domain attribute, *ShoppingBasket* defines the *applyDiscount(discount)* domain method and associations exist relating *Customer* with *ShopAccount* and *ShoppingBasket*.

2.1 High-Level Business Rules

Our aim is to explicitly represent business rules at the domain level. Thus, a high-level business rule language that allows defining rules in terms of domain entities is proposed. Below we present the features of our high-level rule language and argue their need:

High-level rules: As proposed by other current high-level rule languages [13, 16, 19, 10], we define a high-level rule as an *IF condition THEN action* statement, meaning that the action of the rule is only triggered when its condition is met. The condition and action parts only involve domain entities of a domain model. Therefore, the business rule metamodel is related to the domain entities metamodel.

Generic rules: A rule typically defines a comparison between some domain entity and a hardcoded value, or analogously, a certain action involving a hard-coded value. In order to avoid the repetition of the same logic in many rules that only vary these hard-coded values, rules are parameterized with rule properties. In our language this is done using the *PROPS ⟨domainClassName⟩ AS ⟨propertyName⟩* clause.

Connection-aware rules: Rules are parameterized with values from the context in which they are going to be executed. In our language, this is done by means of the *USING ⟨domainClassName⟩ AS ⟨domainObjectName⟩* clause. The details on how a rule is connected to the core application are presented in section 2.2.

An example high-level rule, *BRDiscount*, is shown below. It applies a discount on a customer's shopping basket if the customer has already spent more than a certain amount of money. This rule involves the identified domain entities of the e-commerce domain.

```
BR  BRDiscount
PROPS  int amount, float discount
USING  ShoppingBasket AS basket
IF  basket.customer.account.amountSpent >= amount
THEN  basket.applyDiscount(discount)
```

2.2 High-Level Business Rule Connections

When looking at current approaches that advocate the separation of business rules, we observe that they fail at decoupling the *connection* of the business rules, i.e. applying the rules at certain events and gathering the necessary information for their application. At the implementation level, rule connections crosscut the core application and therefore AOP is a good technique for encapsulating it, as identified and addressed in previous work [2, 4, 5, 8]. This work has shown that the aspects that encapsulate the rule connections are built up of the same elements, that vary with certain situations: rule application time, contextual information and activation time. As such, we identified several aspect patterns for implementing different kinds of business rule connections. Although these aspect patterns achieve the decoupling of rule connections, they are entirely expressed at the programming level, and thus cannot be understood by the domain expert. Moreover, as many different issues need to be taken into account as part of the connection aspects, it becomes hard for the application engineer to write these aspects. Thus, as the same issues recur in every connection aspect, we propose abstracting them in high-level features of a high-level rule connection language. This language allows expressing rule connections as separate and explicit entities at the domain level. Separating rules from their connections (also at the domain level) allows reusing both parts independently. Moreover, we do not only propose new high-level abstractions but also provide a set of variations for each different issue involved in the definition of the rule connections:

Dynamic rule application time: A rule typically needs to be applied at a well-defined point in the execution of the core application. In our domain model this well-defined point corresponds to the execution of a domain method and is expressed by an *event*. Applying a rule at an event implies the following steps: 1) the core application is interrupted at that point, 2) the rule's condition is checked, 3) when the condition is met, the rule's action is triggered, 4) the core application's execution is resumed, taking into account the eventual changes introduced by the rule. Steps 1) and 2) occur as an atomic unit. In what follows we refer to the execution of the domain method captured by the event as *event execution*. We identify three ways in which a rule can be connected at an event:

a) *before* an event, meaning that the rule's condition is checked just before the execution of the event, which is then immediately followed by (in case the condition is met) the execution of the rule's action. For example, a rule can be connected *before a customer is checking out*, meaning the point in time just before the domain method *checkout(shoppingBasket)* defined in the domain class *Shop* is executed.
b) *after* an event, meaning that the rule's condition is checked just after the execution of the event, which is then immediately followed by (in case the condition is met) the execution of the rule's action. For example, a rule can be connected *after a customer logs in*, which maps to the point in time just after the domain method *logIn()* is executed on a customer.

   A rule that is applied *before* or *after* an event and whose condition is satisfied executes the new behavior (defined in its action part) in addition to the original functionality of the core application, possibly modifying it in two ways: 1) by invoking domain methods that modify the state of the core application (e.g. the domain method *increaseStock(product1, 100)* on a *shop* domain object, having as a result an increase on the amount of product1 in stock), 2) by using the IS operator to assign new values to information passed to the rule in the USING clause. As an example of the latter, imagine a product price being provided to a rule at connection time and it being assigned a new value (e.g., the rule specifies 'price IS price - 10'). The connection language ensures that the new value is considered (instead of the old one) in the connection context where the rule was applied.

c) *instead of* an event, meaning that the core application is interrupted just before the execution of the event, the rule's condition is checked and if met, its action is triggered, completely replacing the original behavior captured by the event. For instance, a payment rule encapsulating a new payment policy can be connected instead of *the payment process*, which means in replacement of the execution of the domain method *proceedPayment()* in *Shop*.

In our proposed high-level connection language, a rule connection is specified as follows: *CONNECT* ⟨*brname*⟩ *[BEFORE|AFTER|INSTEAD OF]* ⟨*eventname*⟩, where *brname* is the name of the rule to be connected and *eventname* is the name of the event at which to connect the rule. If *brname* corresponds to a rule template, then the *PROPS* ⟨*value1*⟩, ..., ⟨*valueN*⟩ clause is used to instantiate the rule template to an actual rule.

Contextual rule activation: The application of a given rule can be restricted to certain contexts. For instance, a discount rule — which would typically be applied when the product price is retrieved — can be restricted only to those price retrievals that occur *while the customer is checking out*, or within the period of time *between the moment the customer logs in and the moment he/she adds a product to the shopping cart*, or *not while the customer is browsing the products.* In our connection language, the applicability context of a rule is referred to as *activation time.* The activation time is defined in terms of one or more events in one of the following ways: a) *ACTIVATE WHILE* ⟨*event*⟩, meaning that the rule is active during the period of time denoted by the execution of *event*, b) *ACTIVATE NOT WHILE* ⟨*event*⟩ meaning that the rule is active not while *event* is executing, and c) *ACTIVATE BETWEEN* ⟨*event1*⟩ *AND* ⟨*event2*⟩ meaning that the rule is active during the period of time initiated by the execution of *event1* and terminated by the execution of *event2.* The specification of the activation time is optional and when not specified it is assumed that the rule is always active.

Connection-specific information: A rule expects to receive the information declared in the USING clause at rule connection time. At the moment the rule is connected at an event, two situations can occur: 1) the required information is available in the context of the connection event and thus it can be directly passed to the rule. The kind of information that can be passed to the rule depends on whether the rule is connected before, after or instead of an event: in case of a connection *before* or *instead of* an event, the parameters and the receiver of the domain method are exposed by the event and thus can be passed to the rule, whereas if the rule is connected *after* an event, the parameters, the receiver *and* the result of invoking the domain method are available. 2) the rule requires information that is not available in the context of the connection event: in order to capture this unavailable information, *capture points* are defined as an extra component of the connection specification, as follows: *CAPTURE AT* ⟨*event1*⟩, ..., ⟨*eventN*⟩, where *event1*, ..., *eventN* are names of events that capture the moment when the required information is reachable, and expose it. Moreover, the rule connection language allows specifying how the available or captured information needs to be mapped to the information required by the rule by linking the two in *mapping* specifications of the form: *MAPPING* ⟨*event*⟩.⟨*infoExposed*⟩ *TO* ⟨*infoRequired*⟩.

The example below specifies that the *BRDiscount* rule should only be considered in the context of an express checkout (a special kind of checkout which uses payment information already stored in the shop and that does not require validation by the client). *CheckoutExpress* is a high-level event capturing the invocation of a domain method mapped to the *checkoutExpress(Customer)* method defined in the class *Shop*.

```
CONNECT  BRDiscount PROPS 100
BEFORE  Checkout
MAPPING Checkout.basket TO basket
ACTIVATE WHILE CheckoutExpress
```

3 Transforming the High-Level Domain Model

We propose the automatic translation of high-level rules and their connections to executable implementations in OOP and AOP, as explained in sections 3.2 and 3.3 respectively. As a required initial step, a mapping must exist which links the domain entities involved in the high-level definitions to a concrete implementation, as explained in the following section.

3.1 Initial Step: Mapping Domain Entities

In the previous section we described how high-level rules are defined in terms of high-level domain entities of a domain model. Our approach aims at generating executable rules from those high-level specifications. Thus, in order to generate an implementation for the rules which is ready to be integrated with an existing core application, the high-level entities involved in the rule definition, need to be mapped to the implementation. We briefly describe this mapping, although it is not the focus of this paper. Given a domain entity, defining this mapping requires pointing out which entity or entities in the existing application implement that domain concept. If this is the case, a *one-to-one* mapping exists between the domain entity and the concrete implementation entities. These one-to-one mappings are the only ones supported in current high-level languages [13,16,19,10]. However, the definition of the mapping can become more sophisticated when it is not possible to identify existing implementation entities realizing the desired domain concept. In this case we say that the mapping is *unanticipated* or that we are in the presence of an *unanticipated* domain entity. In our approach, sophisticated unanticipated mappings are supported using AOP. More details on these mappings can be found in [3].

3.2 Transforming High-Level Business Rules

Following the rule object pattern [1], a high-level rule is transformed into a class which defines methods implementing its condition and action, with return types boolean and void respectively. For each property — defined in the *PROPS* clause — a local variable is created which is assigned to a concrete object in the constructor of the class. For each object expected at connection time — defined in the *USING* clause — a local variable and a getter and setter are generated. The bodies of the condition and action methods include the concrete implementations that result from obtaining the mappings of the domain entities referred to in the *IF* and *THEN* clauses respectively. This translation is done fully automatically. The code below illustrates the transformation from the *BRDiscount* business rule to a Java class.

```
public class BRDiscount {
  int amount; float discount; ShoppingBasket basket;

  public BRDiscount(int amount, float discount) {
    this.amount = amount;
    this.discount = discount;
  }
 ...//getter and setter for basket variable

  public boolean condition() {
    return basket.getCustomer().getShopAccount().getTotalSpent() >= amount;
  }
  public void action() {
    basket.setDiscountRate(this.discount);
  }
}
```

3.3 Transforming High-Level Business Rule Connections

The connection of business rules crosscuts the core application, as observed in [2, 4, 5]. In this work we identified the suitability of AOP for implementing the connection of rules and propose aspect patterns for implementing rule connections. The goal of AOP is to achieve the separation of crosscutting concerns, not possible when using standard object-oriented software engineering methodologies. AOP claims that some concerns of an application cannot be cleanly modularized as they are scattered amongst or tangled with different modules of the system [14]: the code implementing a concern is either repeated in different modules or split amongst different parts of the system. As a consequence, it becomes difficult to add, edit or remove such a crosscutting concern in the system. AOP proposes to capture such a crosscutting concern in a new kind of module construct, called an *aspect*. An aspect typically consists of a set of points in the base program where the aspect is applicable (called *joinpoints*) and the concrete behaviour that needs to be executed at those points (called *advice*).

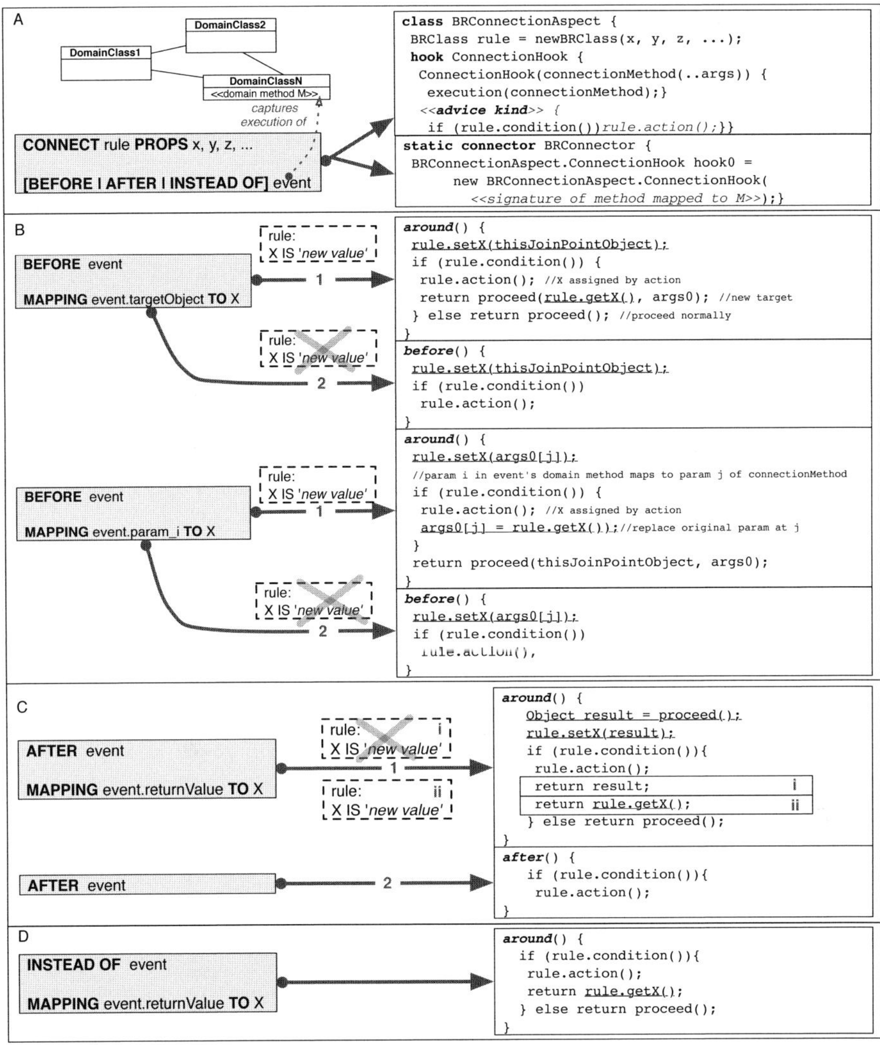

Fig. 1. A: Transformations (1) and (2); B, C and D: Transformations (2) and (3)

Aspect *weaving* consists of merging the aspects with the base implementation of the system.

In this section we present the automatic transformation from high-level rule connections to aspects (based on the patterns identified in previous work). The use of AOP in this transformation is completely transparent for the domain expert, as the AOP peculiarities are not exposed in the high-level rule connection language (as described in Section 2.2). We illustrate this transformation using JAsCo [18], a dynamic AOP language that introduces two concepts: an *aspect bean* which is able to specify crosscutting behavior in a reusable way by means of one or more logically related *hooks*, and a *connector* responsible for deploying the reusable crosscutting behavior in a specific context and declaring how several of these aspects collaborate.

Table 1 gives an overview of the proposed transformations in our approach: each high-level feature is translated into an AOP implementation. However, we observe and show that these transformations cannot be analyzed independently of each other, as dependences exist between them. Due to the lack of space, we illustrate this situation only describing transformations (1), (2) and (3) in detail. Note however that all of the listed transformations have been implemented.

Table 1. Transformations from high-level rule connection constructs to AOP

High-level rule connection construct	transformation output
(1) CONNECT	- aspect bean defining connection hook
(2) BEFORE/AFTER/INSTEAD OF	- advice in charge of applying the rule - checks on whether the mapped information is assigned in the rule
(3) MAPPING	- code managing in/out information to and from the rule respectively - code injecting the information assigned by the rule back into the application (if any)
(4) CAPTURE AT	- hook capturing the required information - variables keeping the captured information
(5) ACTIVATE WHILE/NOT WHILE	- cflow and !cflow joinpoint respectively
(6) ACTIVATE BETWEEN AND	- stateful hook intercepting the application at two defined events that mark the start and end of the activation period

Transformation (1) takes as input a CONNECT specification and produces an aspect bean in charge of creating a new instance of the class implementing the rule that is being connected and, if the instantiated rule is a template, it assigns concrete values to the rule properties by means of the *PROPS* clause. The aspect bean defines a *hook* capturing the execution of the connection method (in JAsCo, aspect beans are reusable and thus the hooks are defined in terms of abstract methods, which are deployed on concrete methods in connectors). Transformation (2) takes as input a BEFORE/AFTER/INSTEAD OF ⟨event⟩ specification and translates it into an advice in charge of first checking the rule's condition — by invoking the corresponding method on the rule — and then triggering the rule's action (if the rule's condition is satisfied).

Any connection specification must include at least elements (1) and (2) and optionally elements (3) and (4) and either (5) or (6). Although the translation of each feature is rather straightforward, it is their combination that becomes complex: the advice (result of transformation (2)) is defined on the connection hook (output of transformation (1)). Moreover, as a result of this combination, a JAsCo connector is generated in charge of deploying the connection hook on a concrete method. This concrete method is only known when a concrete event is specified and thus when the construct (2) comes into place. Part A of Figure 1 depicts the combination of transformations (1) and (2).

As mentioned before, transformation (2) generates an advice in charge of applying the rule. However, depending on the case of a BEFORE, AFTER or INSTEAD OF connection, a different kind of advice has to be generated. Moreover, determining the kind of advice also depends on whether the contextual information — passed to the rule using the MAPPING clause — is assigned to a new value in the rule. This implies the existence of dependencies between transformations (2) and (3) as their outputs cannot be analyzed independently of each other. The following three cases are considered, as depicted in parts B, C and D of Figure 1 (underlined lines correspond to transformation (3) whereas the rest corresponds to transformation (2)):

B) If the rule is connected *before* the connection event, then two cases are possible:

1) the information available in the context of the connection event is passed to the rule where it is assigned to a new value: we need to be able to access the contextual domain objects and make them available for the rule, trigger the rule's action where the domain objects are assigned to new values, and retrieve the modified information from the rule to be taken into account in the invocation of the original behavior captured by the connection event. Thus, an *around advice* is created for this purpose, since it allows intercepting the application at a certain point, adding some extra business logic and proceeding with the original execution, eventually considering a different target object and parameters.
2) the contextual information is passed to the rule and *not* assigned by the rule: in this case, a *before advice* suffices to trigger the rule's action, as the original event execution does not need to be modified.

C) If the rule is connected *after* an event, then two cases are possible:

1) the result of invoking the event is passed to the rule: in this case, an *around advice* is created which first invokes the original behavior captured by the event and passes the result of that execution to the rule. Two cases are possible regarding the return value of the around advice: i) if in the rule the passed value is assigned to a new value, then the around advice returns that new value; ii) otherwise, the original result is returned.
2) no result is passed to the rule: an *after advice* suffices to trigger the rule's action, after the execution of the connection event.

D) If a rule is connected *instead of* the execution of the connection event: the original execution has to be replaced by the rule's action. This is achieved in an *around* advice which invokes the rule's action and does not proceed with the original execution.

Figure 2 illustrates the translation of the high-level connection of BRDiscount introduced in Section 2.2.

```
class BRDiscountConnection {                                   aspect bean
 BRDiscount rule = new BRDiscount(100);
 hook ConnectionHook {
  ConnectionHook(connectionMethod(..args0), contextMethod(..args1)) {
   execution(connectionMethod) && cflow(contextMethod); }
  before() {
   global.rule.setBasket(args0[0]);
   if(global.rule.condition())
    global.rule.action(); }
 }
}
```

```
static connector BRDiscountConnector {                          connector
 BRDiscountConnection.ConnectionHook hook0 =
    new BRDiscountConnection.ConnectionHook(
       float Customer.checkoutBasket(ShoppingBasket),
       float Shop.checkoutExpress(Customer)); }
```

Fig. 2. Transformation from the high-level connection of BRDiscount to JAsCo

4 Implementation

The entire domain model has been implemented supporting the definition of domain entities, high-level rules and their connections, as explained in section 2. Parsers for the presented rule and connection languages have been implemented using JavaCC. Following the transformations described in 3.2 and 3.3, high-level rules are automatically translated into Java classes and high-level rule connections are automatically translated into JAsCo aspect beans and connectors. During this implementation, the following challenges were tackled:

- *dependencies between transformations to AOP:* The transformation of a high-level specification that combines many high-level rule connection features is not as simple as concatenating the outputs of the individual transformations for the involved features. On the contrary, the different outputs have to be combined in a non-trivial way in order to obtain a running aspect. This makes the transformation process more complex as dependences between the individual transformations need to be taken into account.
- *consistency checking*: At transformation time, the models involved in the high-level definitions need to be consulted in order to ensure consistency. Dependences between the models exist as the rule and connection models refer to elements in the domain entities model. Thus, the domain entities model needs to be consulted to check for the existence of the domain entities referred to in the rules and connections.
- *nested mappings*: During the transformations, the mappings of the involved domain entities are obtained in order to get an expression only in terms of implementation entities which is included in the generated code. This process can become very complex in the case of nested mappings.
- *optimized implementations*: The generated AOP implementations only involve the AOP constructs that are most adequate for each connection case.

5 Related Work

High-level rule languages are proposed in some existing approaches [13, 16, 19, 10]. However, in these approaches rules are expressed in terms of high-level domain concepts that are simply aliases for implementation entities and thus anticipated one-to-one mappings are required. This is a problem since a high-level specification of business rules can be discrepant from the implementation of the core application as they are not always anticipated in the original application. Thus, one-to-one mappings are not enough to realize unanticipated business rules. Moreover, connections are crosscutting in the core application and cannot be expressed at the high level. Some of these approaches translate the high-level rules to an intermediate language which is understood by a rule engine. For instance, in [13] high-level rules are mapped to low-level executable rules expressed in IRL (ILOG Rule Language). However, there is a certain kind of business rules that do not require the power of a full-fledge rule engine [7]. As our approach focusses on this last kind of business rules, high-level rules are directly translated into OOP and AOP implementations, without relying on a rule engine.

Most of the work that attempts at combining ideas from MDE and AOSD, focuses on extending a general purpose modeling language (e.g. UML) with explicit support for aspects. Within this research area, approaches can be classified as (1) model-to-code (our approach clearly fits in this category) and (2) model-to-model: (1) Clarke et. al. extend UML to specify composition patterns [6] that explicitly capture crosscutting concerns, which are translated into aspect code. Similarly to our anticipated mappings, bindings are used to point to the concrete implementation elements used to instantiate the patterns. The typical AOP constructs are not directly exposed at the design level. (2) In [12] standard UML stereotypes are used to model aspects whereas in [15] extensions of UML are proposed. They both differ from our approach in that they do not raise the level of abstraction of AOP constructs and that transformations occur at the model level. Also in category (2), Gray et al. propose the ECL transformation language to model aspects that quantify the modeling elements that need to be transformed and apply the desired changes upon them [9]. Besides the fact that transformations occur at the model level, this approach differs from ours in that the modeler is in charge of specifying the desired modeling aspects, writing and varying the set of rules considered by the transformation engine. In our approach the modeler is unaware of the use of aspects. The set of transformations is part of the proposed framework, encapsulating expert knowledge on how rule connections are translated into aspect code.

6 Discussion

A first issue in our approach is the importance of maintained modularity in generated code and, related to that, the overhead of using AO technology in order to achieve this modularity. One could argue that in MDE, the generated code does not have to be modular since it is typically not regarded by humans. However, in our particular context, the generated code is integrated with existing code, which *is* most likely regarded by developers. Therefore, it is of utmost importance that the generated code that pertains to rules and their connections does not affect the existing source code in numerous places. However, we all know that aspects ultimately affect the existing application at run time even if this is not visible in the source code. The more mature AO approaches provide excellent tool support for showing the impact of aspects in a base application. The same mature AO approaches have an acceptable performance overhead, especially if one knows which are the costly features to avoid.

A second important issue is the scalability of our approach, in particular when the number of rules grows. As always, scalability depends largely on the quality of the tool support. Since this paper identifies, argues and presents the fundamental concepts of our approach, we feel that tool support and a quantitative evaluation is outside its scope. Note, however, such an evaluation of our approach is currently undertaken using an industrial application in the healthcare domain, where a huge amount of business rules on healthcare regulations, medications and so on is present. One of the concerns with respect to scalability is the size of the domain model in terms of the number of rules. We have found that a set of business rules typically considers the same domain entities, even if the reference to some attributes or methods on these entities may vary between the rules. Therefore, an initial effort is required for building the domain model, whereas a much smaller effort is required for adapting the domain model as new rules are added. In [3], a paper that focusses on the domain model and how it is mapped to the implementation, we discuss possible tools that automate the construction of the initial domain model.

Another issue related to the scalability of our approach with numerous rules, is rule interference. In previous work we investigated current AO approaches and their support for combining rule connection aspects at the implementation level [4,2,5]. As such, we could extend our high-level languages with explicit constructs for specifying rule precedence and so on. However, with large amounts of rules, manually detecting and resolving dependencies is not scalable. Therefore, we are currently investigating alternative techniques such as critical pair analysis for automatically, exhaustively and statically determining dependencies between rules. Since our high-level languages have a limited number of constructs and use elements from the domain model, such an analysis technique is feasible.

Although in this paper we opted for illustrating the proposed transformations using JAsCo, their implementation is not bound to the specific features of this particular technology. We build on the common AOP concepts (i.e. aspect, advice and joinpoint) and therefore, any other AOP approach that supports the pointcut-advice model can be used as well. As with JAsCo, in case the chosen AOP technology is dynamic (i.e. aspects can be added or removed at run-time), the hot deployment of rules is achieved. Otherwise, in the case of a static AOP technology, explicit support must exist in the high-level connection language to be able to dynamically deploy and undeploy rules.

The choice of constructs of our high-level languages is the result of extensive previous work [2,4,5]. As such we are able to express the business rules that we find in the applications of our industrial partners as well as the ones presented in books on business rules [11,17]. However, special business rules, for example that have time-dependent conditions, cannot be expressed and this is subject of future work. Moreover, some applications have knowledge-intensive subtasks, such as (semi-)automatic scheduling, intelligent help desks and advanced support for configuring products and services, which require not only the specification of rule-based knowledge in an *if...then...* format, but also a rule engine that supports chaining of rules. This category of rule-based knowledge is considered in [7], but not at the domain level.

7 Conclusion

In this paper we proposed an approach that combines MDE and AOSD in order to automatically translate high-level business rules to OOP programs and their connections to aspects in charge of integrating them with existing object-oriented applications. Moving to a higher level of abstraction improves understandability as it becomes possible to easily reason about the rule and connection concerns in terms of the domain. Moreover, it is possible for the domain expert to add, modify and remove rules. Furthermore, the use of AOP in the transformations allows us to keep the implementation of the rules and their connections well modularized and localized, without invasively changing the existing core application. Moreover, as the mapping from high-level entities to their implementation is made explicit, rule traceability becomes possible. This work also contributes to raising the level of abstraction of common AOP constructs, at the same time keeping domain experts oblivious to the use of AOP. Finally, the use of a dynamic AOP approach enhances run-time adaptability and variability, as it becomes possible to dynamically adapt the behavior of the core application by simply plugging in different sets of business rules, creating different versions of the same application. A prototype implementation of our approach as well as a discussion on its advantages and limitations were presented.

Acknowledgements. This work was carried out during the tenure of Maja D'Hondt's ERCIM fellowship.

References

1. A. Arsanjani. Rule object 2001: A Pattern Language for Adaptive and Scalable Business Rule Construction. 2001.
2. M. A. Cibrán, M. D'Hondt, and V. Jonckers. Aspect-Oriented Programming for Connecting Business Rules. In *Proceedings of BIS International Conference*, Colorado Springs, USA, June 2003.
3. M. A. Cibrán, M. D'Hondt, and V. Jonckers. Mapping high-level business rules to and through aspects. *L'Objet*, 12(2-3), Sept. 2006 (to appear).
4. M. A. Cibrán, M. D'Hondt, D. Suvée, W. Vanderperren, and V. Jonckers. JAsCo for Linking Business Rules to Object-Oriented Software. In *Proceedings of CSITeA International Conference*, Rio de Janeiro, Brazil, June 2003.
5. M. A. Cibrán, D. Suvée, M. D'Hondt, W. Vanderperren, and V. Jonckers. Integrating Rules with Object-Oriented Software Applications using Aspect-Oriented Programming. In *Proceedings of ASSE'04, Argentine Conference on Computer Science and Operational Research*, Córdoba, Argentina, 2004.

6. S. Clarke and R. J. Walker. Composition patterns: An approach to designing reusable aspects. In *International Conference on Software Engineering*, pages 5–14, 2001.
7. M. D'Hondt. *Hybrid Aspects for Integrating Rule-Based Knowledge and Object-Oriented Functionality.* PhD thesis, Vrije Universiteit Brussel, Belgium, 2004.
8. M. D'Hondt and V. Jonckers. Hybrid Aspects for Weaving Object-Oriented Functionality and Rule-Based Knowledge. In *Proceedings of the 3th International Conference on AOSD*, Lancaster, UK, 2004.
9. J. Gray, Y. Lin, and J. Zhang. Automating change evolution in model-driven engineering. *Computer*, 39(2):51, 2006.
10. HaleyRules. http://www.haley.com/products/HaleyRules.html.
11. B. V. Halle. *Business Rules Applied: Building Better Systems Using the Business Rules Approach.* John Wiley & Sons, Inc., New York, NY, USA, 2001.
12. W.-M. Ho, J.-M. Jézéquel, F. Pennaneac'h, and N. Plouzeau. A toolkit for weaving aspect oriented UML designs. In *Proceedings of the 1st International Conference on AOSD*, pages 99–105, New York, NY, USA, 2002. ACM Press.
13. JRules. http://www.ilog.com/products/jrules/.
14. G. Kiczales, J. Lamping, A. Mendhekar, C. Maeda, C. V. Lopes, J.-M. Loingtier, and J. Irwin. Aspect-oriented programming. In *ECOOP*, pages 220–242, 1997.
15. R. Pawlak, L. Seinturier, L. Duchien, G. Florin, L. Martelli, and F. Legond-Aubry. A uml notation for aspect-oriented software design. First AOSD Workshop on Aspect-Oriented Modelling with UML, April 2002.
16. QuickRules. http://www.yasutech.com/.
17. R. G. Ross. *Principles of the Business Rule Approach.* Addison-Wesley Publishing Company, 2003.
18. D. Suvée, W. Vanderperren, and V. Jonckers. JAsCo: an Aspect-Oriented approach tailored for Component Based Software Development. In *Proceedings of the 2nd International Conference on AOSD*, Boston, USA, 2003.
19. Visual Rules. http://www.visual-rules.de.

Package Merge in UML 2: Practice vs. Theory?*

Alanna Zito, Zinovy Diskin, and Juergen Dingel

School of Computing, Queen's University
Kingston, Ontario, Canada
{zito, zdiskin, dingel}@cs.queensu.ca

Abstract. The notion of compliance is meant to facilitate tool interoperability. UML 2 offers 4 compliance levels. Level L_{i+1} is obtained from Level L_i through an operation called *package merge*. Package merge is intended to allow modeling concepts defined at one level to be extended with new features. To ensure interoperability, package merge has to ensure *compatibility*: the XMI representation of the result of the merge has to be compatible with that of the original package. UML 2 lacks a precise and comprehensive definition of package merge. This paper reports on our work to understand and formalize package merge. Its main result is that package merge as defined in UML 2.1 does not ensure compatibility. To expose the problem and possible remedies more clearly, we present this result in terms of a very general classification of model extension mechanisms.

1 Introduction

Since UML is intended to support systems engineering in general, its scope is extremely broad. Potential application domains include not only software and hardware engineering, but also data and business process engineering. Particular domains may only require certain features of UML, while others may be completely irrelevant. To support its use in different domains, UML was designed in a modular fashion: Modeling features are defined in separate, and, as much as possible, independent units, called *packages*.

To support exchange of models and interoperability between UML tools, UML 2 partitions the set of all its modeling features into 4 horizontal layers called *compliance levels*. Level L_0 only contains the features necessary for modeling the kind of class-based structures typically encountered in object-oriented languages. Level L_3, on the other hand, encompasses all of UML. It extends level L_2 with features that allow the modeling of information flows, templates, and model packaging. According to the UML 2.1 specification, a tool *compliant at level* L_i must have "the ability to output diagrams and to read in diagrams based on the XMI schema corresponding to that compliance level" [13, Section 2.3]. Moreover, to achieve interoperability, the tool must be *compatible* with tools at

* Research supported by IBM CAS Ottawa and OCE Centre of Communications and Information Technology.

O. Nierstrasz et al. (Eds.): MoDELS 2006, LNCS 4199, pp. 185–199, 2006.

lower compliance levels; that is, it must be able to load all models from tools that are compliant at lower levels, without loss of information.

The precise definition of the compliance levels in UML 2.1 rests on a novel operation called *package merge*. Informally, package merge is intended to allow concepts defined in one package to be extended with features defined in another. The package defining level L_{i+1} is obtained from L_i by merging new features into the package describing L_i. For instance, the level L_1 package is created by merging 11 packages (e.g., *Classes::Kernel*, *Actions::BasicActions*, *Interactions::BasicInteractions*, and *UseCases*) into the level L_0 package. In the UML 2.1 specification, package merge is described by a set of transformations and constraints grouped by metamodel types [13, Section 7.3.40]. The constraints define pre-conditions for the merge, such as when two package elements "match", while the post-conditions are given by the transformations. The merge of two packages proceeds by merging their contents as follows: Two matching elements are merged recursively. Elements that do not have a matching counterpart in the other package are deep-copied. The specification describes the general principle behind package merge as follows [13, Section 7.3.40, page 116]:

> "a resulting element will not be any less capable than it was prior to the merge. This means, for instance, that the resulting navigability, multiplicity, visibility, etc. of a receiving model element will not be reduced as a result of a package merge."

In the same paragraph, the specification states that package merge must ensure compatibility in the sense that the XMI representation of the resulting package must be compatible with that of the original package. This "compatibility property" of package merge is crucial. It guarantees that a tool T compliant at some level is compatible with all tools compliant at lower levels, because it allows T to load models created with lower level tools without loss of information.

Theoretically at least, package merge may be useful not only for the definition of the UML metamodel, but also for users of UML in general. However, a more thorough evaluation of package merge, not to mention a more general adoption, is not straight-forward:

- The detailed semantics of package merge is currently only discussed for certain types found mostly in metamodels (e.g., classes, associations, and properties). It is not clear how to extend package merge to other types such as interactions and state machines.
- The semantics of package merge is perceived as complicated. For instance, the UML manual describes it as "complex and tricky" and recommends the use of package merge only for "metamodel builders forced to reuse the same model for several different, divergent purposes" [14, p. 508]. One reason for this perception may be that the general intent of package merge is not clear. The general principle in the specification cited above is too imprecise.

The long-term goal of our work is to study the general principles underlying package merge. The goal of this paper is to report on the first results of our work. In particular, we will present a general classification of package extension mechnisms based on some mathematical theory, and elaborate a convenient notational and terminological framework. Moreover, the application of this classification to package merge in UML 2 will allow us to conclude that:

1. Package merge as *defined* in the UML 2.1 specification does not ensure compatibility; that is, the XMI representation of the result of the merge is not necessarily compatible with the XMI representation of the original package.
2. It appears that package merge as *used* for the definition of the compliance levels of UML 2.1 does ensure the compatibility property.

After providing the necessary background and briefly reviewing related work in the next section, Section 3 will present the general classification. Section 4 will describe its application to package merge. Section 5 will conclude and outline further work.

2 Background

2.1 Package Merge

To illustrate package merge, consider a simple class model of employees as shown in package *BasicEmployees* on the left of Figure 1.

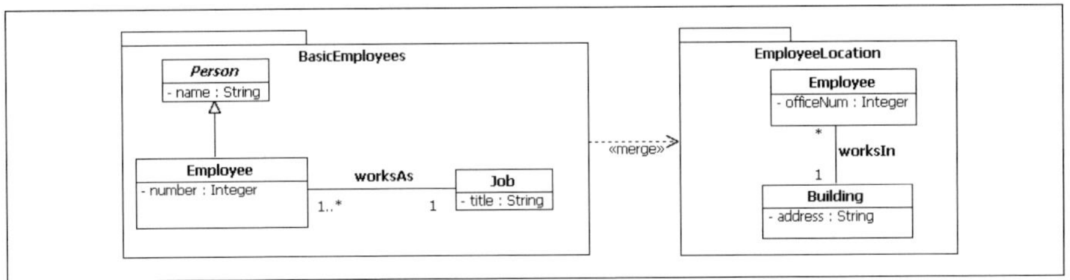

Fig. 1. A package merge example

Suppose we want to extend this model with the information an office manager might have as shown in package *EmployeeLocation*. To this end, package *EmployeeLocation* is merged into package *BasicEmployees*, as indicated by the arrow in between the two packages in Figure 1. We say that *BasicEmployees* is the *receiving package*. Its elements (classes *Person*, *Employee*, and *Job* and the association *worksAs*) are called *receiving elements*. *EmployeeLocation* is the *merged package*. Its elements (classes *Employee* and *Building* and association *worksIn*) are called the *merged elements*. The *resulting package* is shown in Figure 2. It is obtained by merging the merged elements into the receiving package. Since the class *Employee* in *EmployeeLocation* matches the class of the same name in *BasicEmployee*, the two are merged recursively by adding the property *officeNum* to the receiving class. The class *Building* and the association *worksIn*, however, do not match any elements in the receiving package and are simply copied. Note that the ≪*merge*≫ arrow merely implies these transformations and that the resulting package is actually not shown in Figure 1.

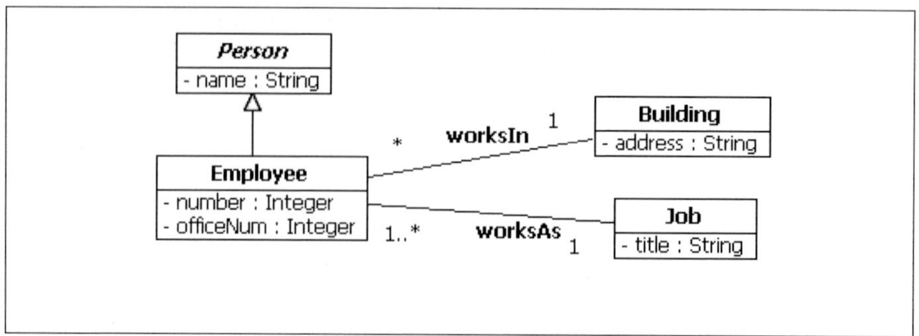

Fig. 2. The result of the merge in Figure 1

2.2 Compatibility

The UML specification clearly states that all model extension mechanisms used to define compliance levels such as package merge must have the "compatibility property" mentioned above. This property asserts the compatibility of the XMI representation of the resulting package with that of the receiving package and thus ensures that a tool is compatible with all tools compliant at lower levels. We refine the definition of the "compatibility property" as follows. We say that *package A is compatible with package B*, if every document allowed by the XML Schema of *B* is also allowed by the XML Schema of *A*. We refer to the constraints expressable in XML Schema (e.g., the elements and attributes that can appear in a document, and the order and number of child elements) as *compatibility constraints*. Additional constraints that a package may contain such as OCL constraints are referred to as *validity constraints*.

2.3 Related Work

According to [15], package merge was partially inspired by two specification combination mechanisms offered in Catalysis: "and" and "join". However, while related on first glance, both differ substantially from package merge. The "and" operation is for use with subtyping, while the "join" operation allows a specification to "impose additional preconditions to those defined in another view" [10, p. 697].

Speaking in more precise terms, two issues are to be distinguished in package merge. The first is the merge procedure as such. In this context, package merge is a particular case of a known problem in databases and, more recently, the Semantic Web. About twenty years ago this problem was referred to as *view/schema integration* [3]; its more recent name is *model merge* [6]. Package merge is a typical example of the schema integration problem when schema matching is easy (because schemas to be merged were designed by the same team) and based on name coincidence. It also shares many similarities with the operation of *composition* in aspect-oriented modeling (AOM) [11, 4], where primary models describing functional requirements are merged with aspect models.

The second issue is an evaluation of the merge result: whether it is good or bad w.r.t. the goals of package merge. The primary criterion here is level compliance; that is, in more detail, compatibility of the legal instances of the receiving package with the resulting package (as a metadata schema). It follows then that we need to evaluate the relationship between the resulting P' and receiving P packages in terms of sets of their instances. This issue is well-studied in mathematical logic and model theory under the name of *theory extension* (and yes, *theory* is one more synonym for our term *package*; definition and basic results can be found in any textbook on mathematical logic, see e.g., [2]). This observation is essential for package merge, since it is a well-known fact that extensions can be *non-conservative*; that is, new data/structure added to the theory can influence the "old" part of the theory in such a way that not all old instances can be augmented with new structure (be compatible with the new structure). It shows that package merge mechanism as such does not guarantee, in general, compatibility between the packages and a more thorough investigation is needed.

The notion of theory as it is formulated in mathematical logic is heavily based on a specific syntax (logical connectives and quantifiers) and is not suited for package merge studies. The same dependance on syntax also prevents the use of many results obtained in schema/model integration for package merge. We need a more abstract framework, and here the so-called *institutions*, introduced in [12] and now well known in the algebraic specifications community, provide the necessary instrumentary. Our theoretical considerations in Section 3 are inspired by institutions and, in fact, just adjust the definitions to the package merge context (see also [7, 1] for a similar elaboration in other contexts).

The issues of package merge and extension can be seen in a even wider context as particular problems in *generic model management*, a prominent program that has recently appeared in databases [5] and is rapidly broadening its agenda towards a general theory of model manipulation and transformation (see [9] for a survey).

3 Theoretical Foundations Via Examples

In this section we describe a general framework for package merge and extension. Here we use the term package as a generic term meaning either a data model/schema, or XML Schema, or metadata model, or, in general, any object P having an associated set of instances, $inst(P)$.

Our plan is as follows. We will begin with considering a series of generic examples of package merge, presented in Tables 1 and 2, to outline the scope of the issue. While discussing these examples, we offer a convenient terminology and notation to encode them. Particularly, we show that relations between the (sets of) instances of the receiving and the resulting packages constitute the essence of the compatibility issues in package merge. Moreover, we will develop a taxonomy of these relationships and demonstrate how it works. Then we elaborate the notation in more precise terms and, in fact, make it ready for formalization. The latter is omitted due to space limitations.

3.1 Basic Terminology, Definitions and Taxonomy of Package Extensions

In formal terms, *package merge* (PM) is an operation that takes two packages, P_1, called the *receiving* package, and $P2$, the *merged* package, then integrates their contents in a certain way, and assigns the name P_1 to the result. In the usual programming language notation, it can be written as $P_1 := P_1 + P_2$. The intuition of incremental increase of the content of the receiving package suggests another notation, $P' = P + \Delta$, which we will follow further.

Consider Table 1. The top row presents a (piece of some) receiving package P, and the second row is the merged package Δ; the resulting package is shown in the third row. The contents of each package participating in the table are separated into three parts: the structural base (graph of classes and associations), multiplicities (left and right) for the participating associations and correspondences (constraints) between associations (columns 2..4). The merged package Δ is parameterized by the left, L, and right, R, multiplicities of the association *drives*. Since there is no association *drives* in the receiving package, this association together with its multiplicities L, R will be copied to the resulting package;

Table 1. Generic examples of package extensions

1	2	3				4	5
Package	Pure structural base of the package	Multiplicities for associations				Correspondences between associations	Compatibility of old instances and, if not, their fixability
		owns		*drives*			
		left	right	left	right		
P	Person —*owns*→ Car	1..*	1..3	N/A		N/A	N/A
Δ(L,R)	Person —*owns*→ Car; Person —*drives*→ Car	2..4	2..4	L	R	Context *P:Person*: *P.drives* ⊆ *P.owns*	N/A
P'(L,R)= P+Δ(L,R)	Person —*owns*→ Car; Person —*drives*→ Car	1..*	1..4	same		same	Depends on (L,R)
	A few versions of merge with different values of parameters (L,R)						
P'$_1$	same	same		1..2	0..3	same	***Optional*** extension: **all** old instances are compatible
P'$_{21}$	same	same		same	1..*	same	***Mandatory*** extension: **none** of old instances is compatible. Yet there is an option to fix ...: (i) all of them
P'$_{22}$	same	same		same	2..*	same	(ii) some of them
P'$_{23}$	same	same		same	5..*	same	(iii) none of them (as extension is inconsistent)
P'$_3$	same	*	same	*	same	same	(iv) none of them but the extension is consistent
P'	Structure/Schema, *S*	Compatibility constraints, C_C				Validity constraint, C_V	Type of extension: Conservative, non-conservative, inconsistent, totally non-conservative

hence, the latter is also parameterized by L, R. As for multiplicities for association *owns*, according to the PM-rules, the resulting multiplicity has the lowest lower bound and greatest upper bound of the receiving and merged multiplicities.. This explains the $P'(L, R)$ row in the table. Thus, the PM-procedure as defined in UML unambiguously determines the resulting package P'(L,R) for any values of parameters L and R. Our goal is to analyze the relationship between packages P and P' in terms of their sets of instances.

The next five rows present five samples of merge differing only in the values of parameters, mainly in the right multiplicity for *drives*. These quantitative changes, however, cause all five cases to be qualitatively different w.r.t. relations between the sets of package instances, $inst(P)$ and $inst(P')$ respectively. We will call the elements of the former *old* instances and those of the latter *new*. In the 1st example (package P'_1), since the right end of association *drives* has the optional multiplicity, all old instances can be well considered as new instances and we have inclusion $inst(P) \subset inst(P')$. In such cases, we will say that all old instances are *compatible* with the new package structure, and that package P' is an *optional extension* of package P.

The next four rows present cases when none of the old instances can be loaded into the new package structure; in other words, sets $inst(P)$ and $inst(P')$ are disjoint. We will say that package P' is a *mandatory* extension of P.

If an instance I of package P is incompatible, we may try to fix it by adding missing items, in our case, missing *drives*-links. As examples $P'_{21}, P'_{22}, P'_{23}$ show, we can encounter situations when (i) *all*, (ii) *some* or (iii) *none* of the old instances are fixable in this sense. Note that package P'_{23} is totally *inconsistent* (has no instances), because the merged package was already inconsistent, which of course implies that none of the old instances can be loaded into it. The case (iv) in the P'_3-row is more interesting. There, the left multiplicity of the *owns*-association for the merged package $\Delta(L, R)$ is changed from 2..4 to *. This multiplicity will go to the result (by the same PM- rule described above), and then package P'_3 – in contrast to package P'_{23} – is consistent: it does have instances consisting of *Car*-objects only. However, none of the old instances (of package P) can be fixed to become one of these P_3-instances. Correspondingly, we call the three subtypes (i,ii,iv) of *consistent* mandatory extensions *conservative, non-conservative and totally non-conservative* while in case (iii) the extension is itself *inconsistent*.

Among these three, the case of non-conservative extension (P'_{22}) is the most interesting. In general, the new constraints in package P' are statements about new items in the structure. Often, they relate these new items with the old ones (those in package P) like, for example, the correspondence statement in Table 1. The question is whether such statements can somehow constrain the old structure embedded in the new structure. In other words, let us take an instance $I' \in inst(P')$ of the resulting package, and forget about its additional structure, thus coming to a instance $I = \overleftarrow{\ } I' \in inst(P)$ of the receiving package. Let $inst_{\Delta}^{\leftarrow}(P)$ (where Δ refers to the package extension in question) denote the set of all such reduct-instances. At first glance, it may seem that the equality

$inst^{\leftarrow}_{\Delta}(P) = inst(P)$ should hold but, in general, this is not the case. The point is that the new structure together with new constraints may be such a strong imposition over its old structure subset that not every old instance can be a reduct of some new instance. This phenomenon is well studied in mathematical logic and model theory under the name of non-conservative extension of theories (see, e.g., [2]). In the package merge context (where packages are, in fact, theories in a special graph-based logic [8]), it means that (for a mandatory package extension), not every old instance can be fixed to become compatible with the new structure (and hence be loaded into it).

Table 2 presents a simple example of non-conservative package extension (in the bottom row); some details for the extension P'_{22} in Table 1. It clearly shows that while every new instance can be mapped to an old instance by forgetting about its new extra structure (move from the right to the left in every row of the table), the inverse mapping is only partially defined (and, of course, is multivalued). In more formal terms, for any mandatory package extension $P' = P + \Delta$, a *forgetful* or *reduct* mapping $\mathsf{red}_{\Delta} : inst(P') \rightarrow inst(P)$ (to be read "forget Δ") is always defined but is not surjective. The inverse multi-valued mapping $\mathsf{ext}_{\Delta} : inst(P) \rightarrow inst(P')$ (read "fix it by extending with Δ") is only partially defined. Note that in general we need to consider two versions of extending mappings: one is the (incomplete) extension of old instances towards compatibility into new package, the other is their complete extension to *valid* instances of P'. The example in the $I_2 - J_2$ row of Table 2 shows that these two mappings can be fundamentally different.

3.2 Unification and Notation

All the examples above can be considered in some unified way and conveniently specified as follows. Let us consider a package as a triple $P = (S, C_C, C_V)$ where:

– S is some *structure* or *schema* having a certain set of instances, $inst(S)$. A typical example of a schema is a graph underlying a UML class diagram (nodes are class names and edges are associations), whose instances are specified by object diagrams over this schema. Another example is the tree structure of an XML document declared in its DTD, where its instances are all possible XML documents with this structure.

– C_C is a set of constraints regulating *compatibility* (hence the subscript ^{C}) of instances with the structure (think of UML multiplicities for associations or DTD constraints specifying optionality of elements in the XML document).

– C_V is an additional set of constraints specifying (in, say, OCL) *valid* instances among the compatible ones.

Since constraints narrow the set of instances, a package has three sets of instances associated with it:

$$inst_V(P) \subset inst_C(P) \subset inst_B(P) \stackrel{\text{def}}{=} inst(S)$$

which we will call, respectively, *valid, compatible and basic* instances of P. For example, instance J_2 in Table 2 is a compatible but not valid instance of package P', while instance J_3 is valid (and hence compatible).

Correspondingly, package extension is described by the expression $P' = P + \Delta$ with the increment $\Delta = (\Delta_S, \Delta_C, \Delta_V)$ consisting of three component increments: in pure structure, Δ_S, in compatibility constraints to it, Δ_C, and in validity constraints to compatible instances, Δ_V.

There is a delicate and important issue in specifying increments for constraints. The example in the top three rows of Table 1 shows that the merged package Δ can (i) change the compatibility of items in the (old) structure in the receiving package (multiplicities for association *owns*) and, of course, (ii) specify compatibility of new items added to the structure in the resulting package (multiplicities for *drives*). Thus, in general, $\Delta_C := \Delta_C + \Delta^*_C$, and similarly for Δ_V, where the $*$-index near Δ refers to constraints talking about the new items

Table 2. Example of non-conservative package extension (some details for the row P'_{22} in Table 1). The table is to be read from bottom to top.

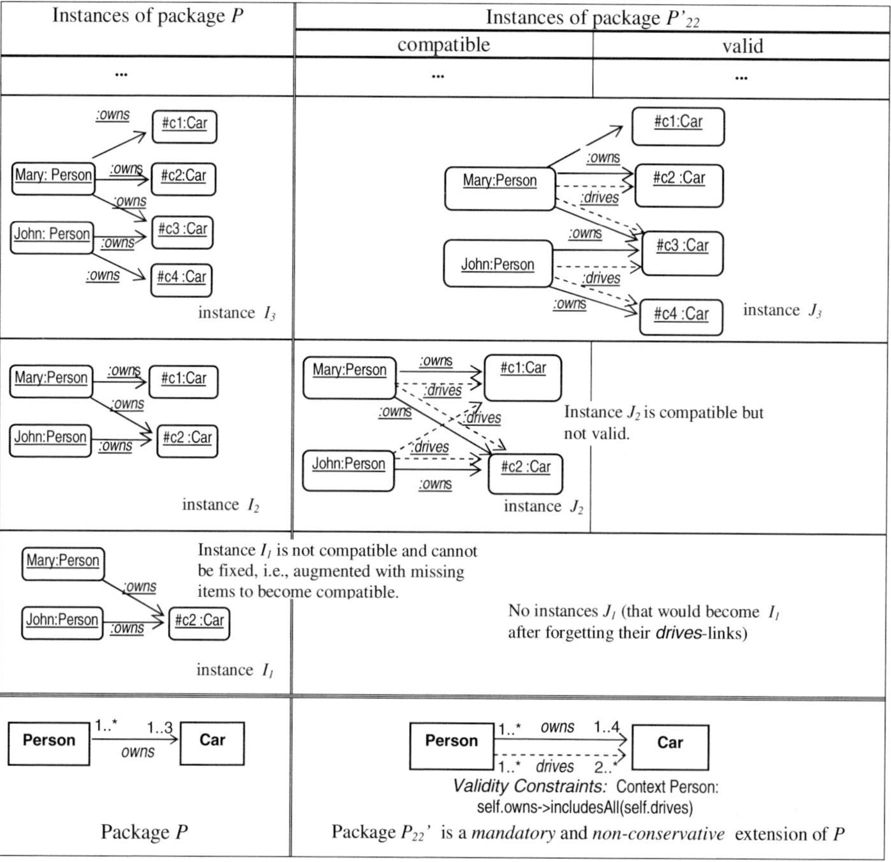

in the new structure while Δ without this index refers to changes in constraints for old items in the new structure.

We will also assume that our Δ's are always positive increments (addition), and to specify a decrement we write $(-\Delta)$. In more formal terms, it means that the sets of structures and constraints are partially ordered and, for example, $S' = S + \Delta$ means that $S \subset S'$ while $S' = S - \Delta$ means that $S' \subset S$ in that partial order on structures (normally, an ordinary sub-structure relation). Similarly, $C' = C + \Delta$ means that we strengthened the set of constraints by either adding new constraints to it or, maybe, by strengthening some of the constraints in C. In this notation, for example, the relation between packages P and P'_{22} in Table 2 can be specified by the following equalities: $S' = S + \Delta_S$, $C'_C = C_C - \Delta_C + \Delta^*_C$, $C'_V = C_V + \Delta^*_V$.

4 Applications to UML 2.1 Compliance Levels

Having described and classified the general forms that package extension can take, we can now consider in more detail how the theory applies to package merge and the definition of UML compliance levels. The resulting package of a package merge can extend the receiving package in different ways, depending on the contents of the merged package. Some of these ensure compliance level compatibility, while others do not. We present here several examples of how package merge is used to define the compliance levels of UML 2.1, and show how each fits into the taxonomy of package extensions introduced in the Section 3. The taxonomy can be briefly summarized in pseudo-code as

```
if (extension is optional) then
  all instances are compatible
else //extension is mandatory
  if (extension is conservative) then
    all instances are not compatible, but can be fixed
  else if (extension is non-conservative) then
    if (extension is totally non-conservative) then
      no instances are compatible or fixable
    else
      no instances are compatible, but some are fixable
```

4.1 Examples of Optional Extension

The top row of Table 3 shows an example of a package merge taken from the definition of UML compliance levels in [13]. The *Level 2* package shows the relationship between the metaclasses *Classifier* and *Generalization* at level 2 compliance. One of the packages merged in to form level 3 compliance is the *PowerTypes* package, which contains additional structure for *Classifiers* and *Generalizations*. These additional elements (one class and two associations) are copied into the resulting package (which is also shown in Table 3), since they do not have matching elements in the receiving package. According to the definitions introduced

Table 3. Examples of package merge resulting in optional extension

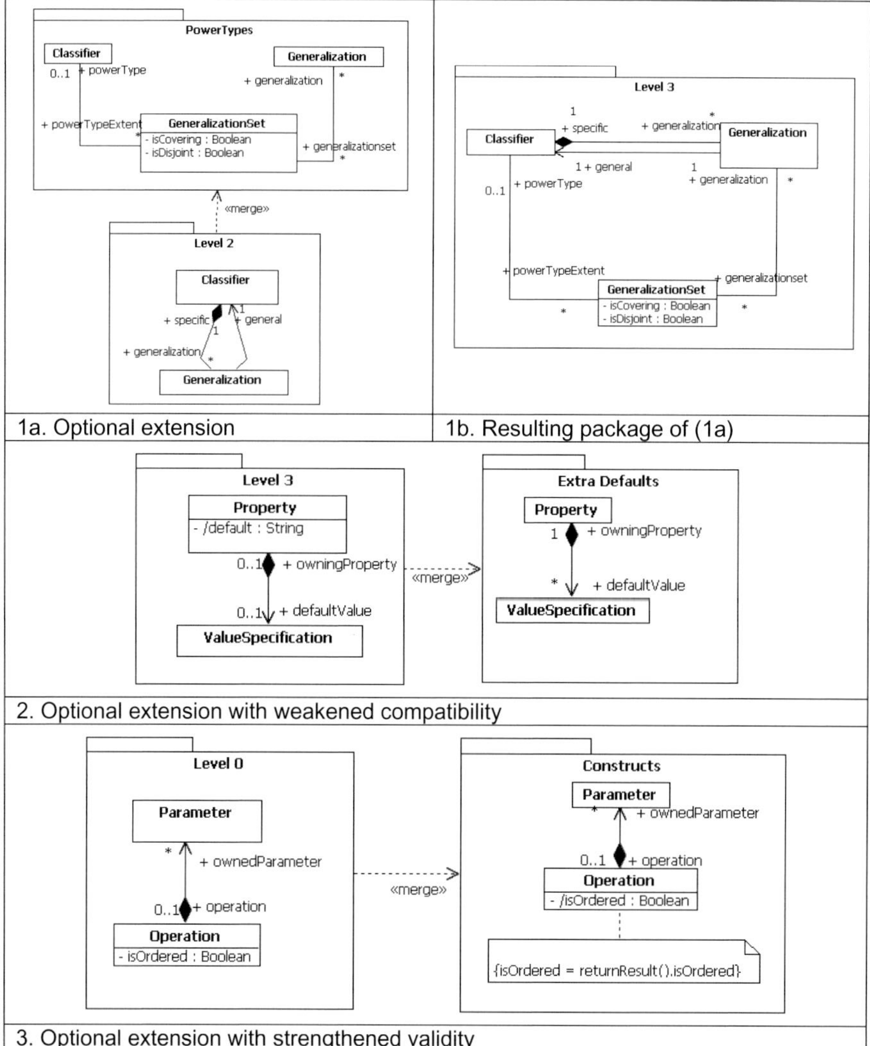

in the previous section, the resulting package is an *optional* extension of the receiving package, meaning that it ensures that level 2 models are compatible with level 3-compliant tools.

The resulting package does not always add extra structure to the receiving package; it may only change the compatibility or validity constraints of the existing structure. This is a special case of optional extension. The second row of Table 3 shows two examples; since the resulting packages for both have the same structure as the receiving, they are not shown. The rules for package merge are such that existing compatibility constraints are always made less strict (weakened).

For example, imagine that we want to add more features to UML with a fourth level of compliance. In Table 3, the *Level 3* package contains part of the definition of the metaclass *Property* at level 3 compliance. The (imaginary) *Extra Defaults* package defines that a *Property* may have more than one default value. According to package merge rules, the associations *owningProperty:Property* → *defaultValue:ValueSpecification* in the merged and receiving package will match, and their matching association ends will be recursively merged. The resulting *defaultValue* end has a multiplicity of 0..*, which is calculated by taking the lowest lower bound and the highest upper bound from the merged and receiving ends. A level 3-compliant model will thus never lose information when being imported into a level-4 compliant tool, since the resulting multiplicity is wider (weaker) than that of the receiving. It is interesting to note that, while the rules for merging multiplicities ensure the compatibility of the receiving and resulting packages, they also allow for previously illegal instances to be legal in the resulting package. For example, consider merging multiplicities 1..2 and 5..7. The resulting multiplicity will be 1..7, which includes values (i.e., 3..4) that were not allowed in either of the two original multiplicities. This is a consequence of the fact that, as defined in UML 2.1, multiplicities must be a single, continuous interval.

Validity constraints, on the other hand, can be strengthened as the result of a merge. Section 3 introduced the notion of valid instances of a package as those instances which are compatible and which satisfy any additional semantic constraints on the model. The rules for package merge do not guarantee that instances of lower compliance levels will remain valid at higher levels. For example, Table 3 shows a package *Level 0*, which contains a part of the definition of operations at compliance level 0. One of the packages merged in to form level 1 compliance is the *Infrastructure::Constructs* package, which contains an identical definition of *Operation*, but with the additional constraint that the orderedness of an operation is derived from its return value. According to the rules for package merge, the constraint on the merged element *Operation* is added to the constraints on the receiving element Operation. The resulting package has the same structure as the receiving package, but its validity constraints have been added to (strengthened). If a model created at compliance level 0 does not derive the *isOrdered* property of its operations from their return parameters, it could be imported into a level 1-compliant tool, but would not fulfill all semantic constraints of that level.

4.2 Examples of Mandatory Extension

The resulting package of a package merge can also be a mandatory extension of the receiving. Figure 3 shows an example from [13]. The *Level 1* package contains a part of the definition of an *ActivityEdge* at that compliance level. The *IntermediateActivities* package, which is merged in to form level 2 compliance, contains an association *ActivityEdge* → *guard:ValueSpecification*, which has a non-optional (i.e., non-zero) multiplicity. A model created at level 1 compliance would not be compatible with a level 2-compliant tool, since its activity edges do not have a corresponding guard; it could not be imported "as-is" into the tool. However, since the extension in this case is conservative, it is possible to fix a non-compatible instance. The UML 2.1 specification explicitly states [13, Section 12.3.5], that the default value for the guard is "true", so a non-compatible model can be fixed by simply adding the default value as a guard on all *ActivityEdges* which do not have one.

It is also possible for a package merge to result in a *non-conservative* mandatory extension of the receiving package. Although we do not present an example of this situation in terms of UML compliance levels, it is illustrated in examples P'_{21}, P'_{22} and P'_{23} of Table 1.

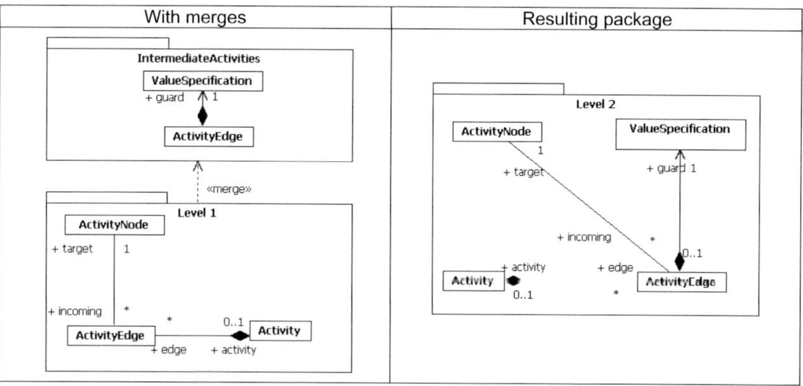

Fig. 3. Example of package merge resulting in mandatory extension

4.3 Summary

In terms of the notation introduced in Section 3, the UML rules for package merge ensure the following properties:

1. $S' = S + \Delta_S$, structure is never removed;
2. $C'_C = C_C - \Delta_C + \Delta^*_C$, compatibility constraints to the old structure are always weakened,
3. $C'_V = C_V + \Delta_V + \Delta^*_V$, validity constraints to the old structure can be strengthened.

Based on these rules, the relation of the receiving package to the resulting can range over our entire taxonomy of package extension. To the best of our knowledge, most of the uses of package merge for defining compliance levels of UML 2.1 result in optional extensions, and are thus compatible. The few instances of mandatory extension are conservative with fixes explicitly defined. However, in general, using package merge to define compliance levels for MOF-based models does not guarantee that successive levels will be compatible.

5 Conclusion and Future Work

UML 2.1 introduced the operation of package merge to faciliate the definition of compatible compliance levels. In order to better understand package merge, we have developed a theory of package extension, which is based on viewing an extension to a package as being made up of a pure structural increment, a compatibility constraint increment, and a validity constraint increment. This theory leads us to a taxonomy of the possible relationships between the original and extended package. The taxonomy distinguishes between optional extensions, which ensure compatibility, and mandatory extensions which do not. Mandatory extensions can be further subdivided into conservative, non-conservative and totally non-conservative extension, based on whether all, some or none of the original instances can be fixed to become compatible. This theory is influenced by concepts in model theory and mathematical logic, where theory extension has been well-studied. Our classification of package extension types allowed us to look at the relationship between the receiving and resulting package of a package merge in a more formal way. We have discovered that the rules for package merge do not prevent mandatory extension, and thus, it cannot guarantee compatibility when used to define compliance levels. However, in the definition of the compliance levels of UML 2.1, it appears that package merge is used in such a way as to ensure compatibility.

Future work on this topic includes completing a full formalization of our theory of package extension, as well as a formal definition of package merge. We are also interested in examining the notion of "fixability" in more depth to determine some sort of general guidelines or canonical way to fix incompatible models (where possible). Finally, another potential area of study is the impact of this work on UML modeling tools - for example, the ideal tool would have to assess the compatibility and validity of models imported from tools of a lower compliance level, as well as suggest possible ways of fixing incompatible models.

Acknowledgements. We would like to thank Bran Selic and Jim Amsden for taking the time to answer our questions about packge merge.

References

[1] S. Alagic and P. Berstein. A model theory for generic schema management. In *Eighth International Workshop on Databases and Programming Languages*, pages 228–246, 2001.

[2] J. Barwise, editor. *Handbook of Mathematical Logic*, volume 90 of *Studies in Logic and the Foundations of Mathematics*. North-Holland Publishing Company, 1977.

[3] C. Batini, M. Lenzerini, and S. Navathe. A comparative analysis of methodologies for database schema integration. *ACM Computing Surveys*, 18(4):323–364, 1986.

[4] Robert France Benoit Baudry, Franck Fleurey and Raghu Reddy. Exploring the relationship between model composition and model transformation. In *Proc. of Aspect Oriented Modeling Workshop, in conjunction with MoDELS'05*, 2005.

[5] P. Bernstein, A. Halevy, and R. Pottinger. A vision for management of complex models. *SIGMOD Record*, 29(4):55–63, 2000.

[6] P. Bernstein and R.Pottinger. Merging models based on given correspondences. In *Proc. Very large databases, VLDB'2003*, 2003.
[7] Z. Diskin. Abstract metamodeling, I: How to reason about meta-metamodeling in a formal way. In K. Baclawski, H. Kilov, A. Thalassinidis, and K. Tyson, editors, *8th OOPSLA Workshop on Behavioral Specifications, OOPSLA99*. Northeastern University, College of Computer Science, 1999.
[8] Z. Diskin, B. Kadish, F. Piessens, and M. Johnson. Universal arrow foundations for visual modeling. In *Diagrams'2000: 1st Int. Conf. on the Theory and Applications of Diagrams*, Springer LNAI#1889, pages 345–360, 2000.
[9] Zinovy Diskin and Boris Kadish. Generic model management. In Doorn, Rivero, and Ferraggine, editors, *Encyclopedia of Database Technologies and Applications*, pages 258–265. Idea Group, 2005.
[10] D.F. D'Souza and A.C. Wills. *Objects, Components, and Frameworks with UML*. Addison Wesley, 1999.
[11] Robert France Geri Georg and Indrakshi Ray. Composing aspect models. In *The 4th Aspect Oriented Software Development Modeling With UML Workshop*, 2003.
[12] J.A. Goguen and R.M. Burstall. Institutions: Abstract model theory for specification and programming. *Journal of ACM*, 39(1):95–146, 1992.
[13] Object Management Group. *Unified Modeling Language: Superstructure (version 2.1, ptc/06-01-02)*, January 2006.
[14] I. Jacobson J. Rumbaugh and G. Booch. *The Unified Modeling Language Reference Manual*. Addison Wesley, 2 edition, 2004.
[15] B. Selic, January 2006. Personal communication.

Detecting and Resolving Model Inconsistencies Using Transformation Dependency Analysis

Tom Mens[1], Ragnhild Van Der Straeten[2,⋆], and Maja D'Hondt[3,⋆⋆]

[1] Software Engineering Lab, Université de Mons-Hainaut
Av. du champ de Mars 6, 7000 Mons, Belgium
tom.mens@umh.ac.be

[2] Systems and Software Engineering Lab, Vrije Universiteit Brussel
Pleinlaan 2, 1050 Brussel, Belgium
rvdstrae@vub.ac.be

[3] Jacquard INRIA project, Laboratoire d'Informatique Fondamentale de Lille
59655 Villeneuve dAscq Cedex, France
dhondt@lifl.fr

Abstract. Model inconsistency management is a crucial aspect of model-driven software engineering. It is therefore important to provide automated support for this activity. The problem is, however, that the resolution of inconsistencies may give rise to new inconsistencies. To address this problem, we propose to express inconsistency detection and resolutions as graph transformation rules, and to apply the theory of critical pair analysis to analyse potential dependencies between the detection and resolution of model inconsistencies. As a proof-of-concept, we report on an experiment that we have carried out along these lines using the critical pair analysis algorithm implemented in the state-of-the-art graph transformation tool *AGG*. The results show that both anticipated and unexpected dependencies between inconsistency detection and resolution rules are found by AGG. We discuss how the integration of the proposed approach into contemporary modelling tools may improve inconsistency management in various ways.

1 Introduction

One of the important challenges in current-day model-driven software engineering is the ability to manage model inconsistencies. When designing models in a collaborative and distributed setting, it is very likely that inconsistencies in and between the models will arise because: (i) different models may be developed in parallel by different persons; (ii) the interdependencies between models may be poorly understood; (iii) the requirements may be unclear or ambiguous at an early design stage; (iv) the models may be incomplete because some essential information may still be unknown. In a model evolution context, the ability to deal with inconsistent models becomes even more crucial, as models are continuously subject to changes.

⋆ Financial support provided through the European Community's Human Potential Programme under contract HPRN-CT-2002-00275, SegraVis.

⋆⋆ This work was carried out during the tenure of an ERCIM fellowship.

O. Nierstrasz et al. (Eds.): MoDELS 2006, LNCS 4199, pp. 200–214, 2006.

Nowadays, the UML is the de-facto general-purpose modelling language [1]. Current UML tools, unfortunately, provide poor support for inconsistency management and, if they do, it is usually ad-hoc. We believe that, in the process of managing inconsistencies, support should be provided to detect and resolve inconsistencies at any time the modeller wishes to do so. One way to approach this is to express inconsistency detection and resolutions as transformation rules [2]. In previous work, we explored the use of description logics as an alternative formalism for expressing inconsistency detection and resolutions as transformation rules [3, 4]. However, these transformation rules are typically not independent of one another: applying one rule might inhibit the application of another rule or, the opposite, it might trigger another rule, which suggests that an optimal ordering of rules has to be inferred, if possible. To be able to reason about such parallel and sequential dependencies between rules, we rely on the underlying theory of graph transformation, that allows us to exploit theoretical results about critical pair analyis [5].

As a proof of concept, we carry out an experiment with *AGG*[1] (version 1.4), a state-of-the-art graph transformation tool that implements a critical pair analysis algorithm [6]. We express model inconsistency detection and resolutions as graph transformation rules in this tool, and show how the transformation dependency analysis allows us to detect opportunities for ordering, refactoring and generally fine-tuning the inconsistency resolution rules. The experiment reported on in this article is carried out in four consecutive steps: *(a) Identification*. What are the model inconsistencies of interest for the subset of the UML metamodel that will be considered? *(b) Specification*. How can we formally express the model inconsistencies and their resolutions as graph transformation rules? *(c) Dependency analysis*. How can we detect parallel conflicts and sequential dependencies between the rules specified in the previous step, using the technique of critical pair analysis? *(d) Interpretation of results*. What can we learn from this dependency analysis? How can we exploit this information to automate the inconsistency management process?

While our intitial results look very promising, it needs to be said that this research is still in the exploratory phase. Fully automated support of our ideas, as well as an empirical validation on industrial case studies, remains to be done.

2 Experimental Setup

For illustration purposes, we restrict ourselves to model inconsistencies in UML models consisting of a simplified subset of UML 2.0 class diagrams and protocol state machine diagrams only. It is, however, straightforward to relax this restriction and to apply our approach to other types of UML diagrams as well. For example, we are currently extending our experiment to take sequence diagrams into account.

Rather than specifying the model inconsistencies and resolutions in some dedicated modelling tool we decided, for reasons of genericity, to represent UML models in a graph-based format in the general-purpose graph transformation tool *AGG*. The *metamodel* for the considered UML subset is expressed as a so-called *type graph* as shown in Fig. 1. The UML *models* themselves will be represented as *graphs* that are constrained

[1] See `http://tfs.cs.tu-berlin.de/agg/`

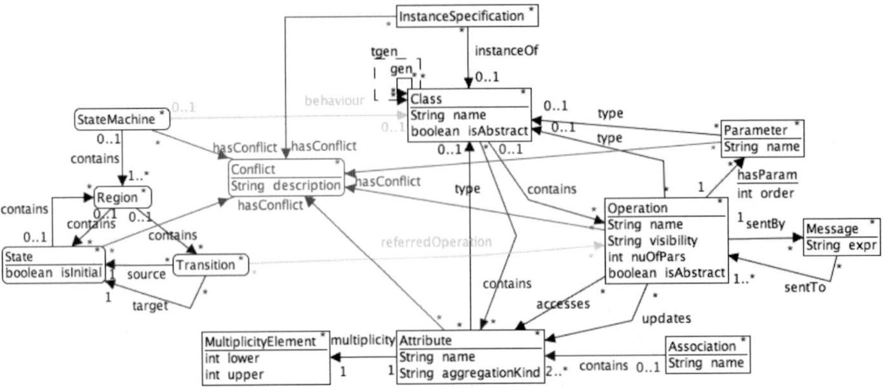

Fig. 1. Simplified metamodel for UML class diagrams and state machine diagrams, expressed as a type graph with edge multiplicities in AGG. In addition, a node type `Conflict` is introduced to represent model inconsistencies.

by this type graph. These graphs can be generated automatically from the corresponding UML models by exporting them from a modelling tool in XMI format, converting them into GXL format, and importing them into *AGG*. An experiment along these lines has been carried out by Laurent Scolas as a student project. Note that there need not be any loss of information when generating graphs from UML models, provided that the type graph is sufficiently close to the UML metamodel. Given an explicit description of this metamodel, it would even be possible to generate the corresponding type graph automatically.

2.1 Identification of Model Inconsistencies and Their Resolutions

The set of inconsistencies we restrict ourselves to is based on the model elements occurring in the chosen subset of the UML. In [3], a classification of inconsistencies and its motivation has been presented. In the current article, we only take into account *structural inconsistencies*. For example, the constraint that a concrete class should not contain abstract operations yields a structural inconsistency that can be resolved in various ways.[2] Structural model inconsistencies can be found by detecting the presence or absence of certain patterns in the graph representing the model. In the example above, this would be the presence of a concrete class node, and the presence of abstract operation nodes contained in this class.

The specification of behaviour (especially in presence of inheritance) can also introduce *behavioural inconsistencies*. Because structural patterns do not suffice to express such inconsistencies, we used the formalism of description logics in earlier work [3]. As such, we do not consider this type of inconsistencies in the current article.

For each inconsistency we describe a set of resolutions using the following template:

[2] Alternatively, this inconsistency could be avoided by imposing a graph invariant that prevents this situation, but this would impose to many restrictions on the modeler.

NameOfModelInconsistency. Description of model inconsistency.

1. First possible resolution to resolve the model inconsistency
2. Second inconsistency resolution, and so on ...

The resolutions proposed for each inconsistency boil down to the addition, deletion or modification of relevant model elements. Below we provide a representative, yet incomplete, list of structural model inconsistencies and several alternative ways to resolve them.

DanglingTypeReference. An *operation* has one or more *parameters* whose *types* are not specified. It can be resolved in 3 different ways:

1. Remove the *parameter* whose *type* is undefined.
2. Assign an existing class as the *type* of the previously undefined *parameter*.
3. Assign a new class as the *type* of the previously undefined *parameter*.

ClasslessInstance. A model contains an *instance specification* without a corresponding *class*. Possible resolutions are:

1. Remove the *instance specification*.
2. Link the *instance specification* to an **existing** *class*.
3. Link the *instance specification* to a **new** *class*.

AbstractObject. A model contains an *instance specification* of an *abstract class* that does not have any concrete subclasses. (This is an inconsistency since abstract classes cannot be instantiated.)

1. Change the *abstract class* into a concrete one.
2. Redirect the target of the *instance of* relation to a **new** concrete descendant class of the *abstract class*.
3. Remove the *instance specification*.

AbstractOperation. An *abstract operation* is defined in a *concrete class*. (This is an inconsistency since a concrete class is not supposed to have abstract operations.)

1. Change the *abstract operation* into a concrete one.
2. Remove the *abstract operation*.
3. Change the *concrete class* containing the *abstract operation* into an abstract class.
4. Move **up** the *abstract operation* to an **existing** abstract ancestor class of the *concrete class*.
5. Move **up** the *abstract operation* to a **new** abstract ancestor class of the *concrete class*.
6. Move **down** the *abstract operation* to an **existing** abstract descendant class of the *concrete class*.
7. Move **down** the *abstract operation* to a **new** abstract descendant class of the *concrete class*.

AbstractStateMachine. A *state machine* expresses the behaviour of an *abstract class* that does not have any concrete subclasses.

1. Remove the *state machine*.
2. Connect the *state machine* to an existing concrete class.
3. Change the *abstract class* into a concrete one.

DanglingOperationReference. A *state machine* contains a *transition* that refers to an *operation* that does not belong to any *class*.

1. Add the *operation* to the *class* whose behaviour is described by the *state machine*.
2. Let the *transition* refer to an existing *operation* belonging to the *class* whose behaviour is described by the *state machine*.
3. Remove the reference from the *transition* to the *operation*.
4. Remove the *transition*.

2.2 Specification of Inconsistency Detection and Resolution Rules in AGG

In this section we explain how to specify inconsistency detection and resolutions as graph transformation rules in *AGG*.

To detect occurrences of model inconsistencies, we specify them as graph transformation rules. Their left-hand side contains the graph structure corresponding to a model inconsistency. This structure can be composed of a positive condition (presence of certain combinations of nodes and edges) and a set of negative conditions (absence of certain combinations of nodes and edges). On the right-hand side of the transformation rule a new node of type *Conflict* is introduced. It always points to one of the nodes that characterise the model inconsistency. To avoid detecting the same occurrence of a model inconsistency more than once, we attach a default negative application condition (NAC) to each rule, specifying that a *Conflict* node should be absent in the graph structure determining the model inconsistency. Figure 2 gives some examples of model inconsistencies specified as transformation rules. The default NACs are not shown.

In the remainder of this article, "resolution rules" denote the graph transformation rules expressing an inconsistency resolution. To specify such resolution rules, we assume that a model inconsistency occurrence has been detected before. Hence, the graph

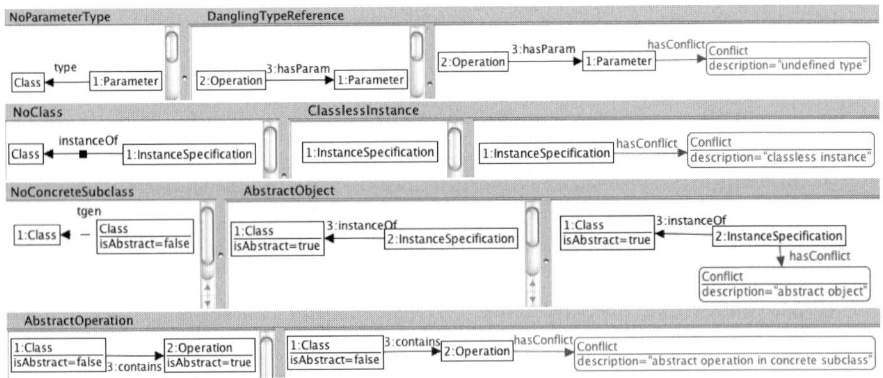

Fig. 2. Detecting model inconsistency occurrences as graph transformation rules with optional NACs in AGG. If a rule contains more than two panes, the leftmost pane represents a NAC, which should be seen as a forbidden structure. The next pane represents the positive part of the rule's left-hand side. The rightmost pane represents the right-hand side of the rule. For the rule **AbstractOperation**, no NAC has been specified.

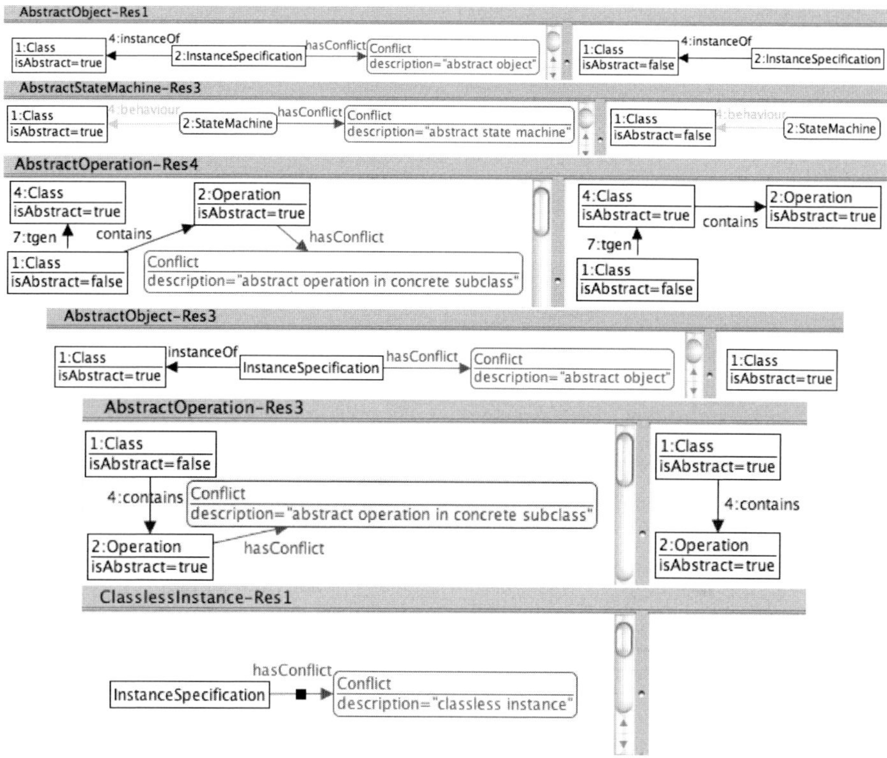

Fig. 3. Specification of inconsistency resolutions as graph transformation rules. The left-hand side always contains a *Conflict*-node, which is removed in the right-hand side.

will already contain at least one *Conflict*-node indicating an inconsistency that needs to be resolved. After applying the resolution rule, the model inconsistency is no longer present, and the corresponding *Conflict*-node is removed from the graph structure.

Figure 3 shows some examples of inconsistency resolutions specified as graph transformation rules. For the names of the resolution rules, we use the numbering scheme introduced in Sect. 2.1. For example, rule **AbstractObject-Res3** corresponds to the third resolution for the **AbstractObject** model inconsistency. Our resolution rules typically do not require negative application conditions since they always check for the presence of a *Conflict* node, introduced previously by the corresponding detection rule.

3 Transformation Dependency Analysis in AGG

In this section, we explain how to use *static analysis* on graph transformation rules to detect mutual exclusions and causal dependencies between the transformation rules introduced before. The analysis is based on the formal notion of *independence* of graph transformations. It expresses the idea that, in a given situation, two transformations are neither causally dependent nor mutually exclusive. A distinction can be made between

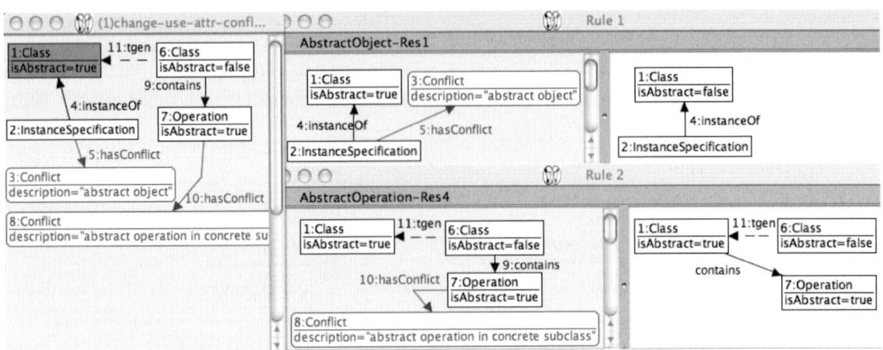

Fig. 4. Example of a critical pair illustrating a mutual exclusion between resolution rules **Abstract Object-Res1** and **AbstractOperation-Res4**

the notions of *parallel independence* (absence of mutual exclusions) and *sequential independence* (absence of causal dependencies). A formal treatment of these concepts is given in [7].

Based on this notion of independence, a potential *parallel* or *sequential dependency* is defined as a pair of transformation rules for which a counter example to parallel or sequential independency can be found. More precisely, two rules are mutually exclusive if application of the first rule prevents application of the second one or vice versa. They are *sequentially dependent* if application of the second rule requires prior application of the first rule.

The goal of critical pair analysis [5] is then to compute all potential mutual exclusions and sequential dependencies for a given set of transformation rules by pairwise comparison. A critical pair formalises the idea of a minimal example of a conflicting situation. To achieve such critical pair analysis, we use the tool *AGG*, since it is the only available graph transformation tool that implements this technique.

Fig. 4 illustrates a critical pair that identifies a mutual exclusion between the resolution rules **AbstractObject-Res1** and **AbstractOperation-Res4**. It is computed by

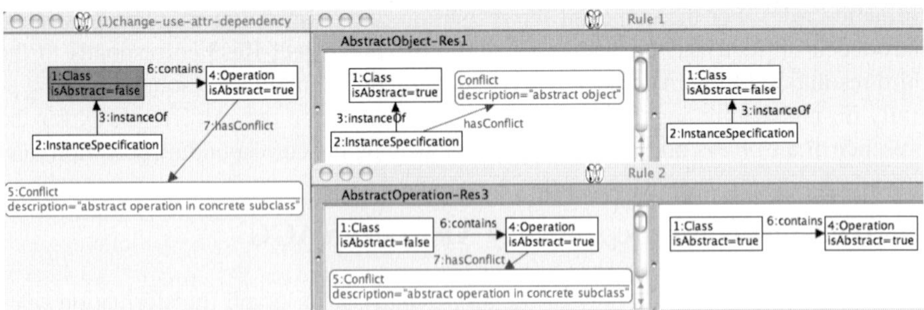

Fig. 5. Example of a critical pair illustrating a sequential (causal) dependency of resolution rule **AbstractOperation-Res3** on resolution rule **AbstractObject-Res1**.

Table 1. Classification of mutual exclusions and sequential dependencies. The numbers between parentheses correspond to the explanation that can be found in the numbered lists in the text. The top table summarises the results of the mutual exclusion analysis of Section 4.1, whereas the bottom table summarises the results of the sequential dependency analysis of Section 4.2.

mutual exclusion analysis	for the same kind of inconsistency	between different kinds of inconsistencies
detection rule conflicts with detection rule	Always (1)	Never (2)
detection rule conflicts with resolution rule	Always (3)	Sometimes (4)
resolution rule conflicts with resolution rule	Always (5)	Sometimes (6)

sequential dependency analysis	for the same kind of inconsistency	between different kinds of inconsistencies
detection rule depends on detection rule	Never (1)	Never (2)
resolution rule depends on resolution rule	Sometimes (3)	Sometimes (4)
resolution rule depends on detection rule	Always (5)	Never (6)
detection rule depends on resolution rule	Sometimes (7)	Sometimes (8)

comparing the left-hand sides of both rules, that partially overlap in the coloured class with label 1. This corresponds to a mutually conflicting situation (of type "change-use-attr-conflict"), since the first resolution rule will make the class concrete, whereas the second resolution rule requires for its application that the class remains abstract.

Figure 5 illustrates a critical pair that identifies a *sequential dependency* between two resolution rules. The rules **AbstractObject-Res1** and **AbstractOperation-Res3** are clearly sequentially dependent, if applied to the same class, since the first rule makes an abstract class concrete, whereas the second rule requires the class to be concrete for its application. As such, the application of the first rule enables the application of the second rule. This causal dependency is detected as an overlap (the coloured class with label 1) between the right-hand side of the first rule and the left-hand side of the second rule.

4 Interpretation of Results

The main contribution of the proposed technique is that it allows for the static analysis (i.e., independent of any concrete UML model) of mutual exclusions and sequential dependencies between different resolution rules for structural model inconsistencies. This section provides a detailed analysis of the results of the transformation dependency analysis that we performed on the inconsistency detection and resolution rules presented in Sect. 2.1.

4.1 Mutual Exclusion Analysis

When we apply the critical pair analysis algorithm to identify all mutual exclusions between inconsistency detection and resolution rules, we get the following results, which are also summarised in the top part of Table 1:

1. Each inconsistency detection rule is mutually exclusive to itself, in order to avoid the same occurrence of a model inconsistency being detected more than once.

2. No mutual exclusions are found between pairs of distinct detection rules. This corresponds to our intuition, since each rule detects a different kind of model inconsistency. As a result, all detection rules are parallel independent of one another.
3. By construction, every detection rule is mutually exclusive to each of the resolution rules for a particular kind of inconsistency. This is because, for any particular inconsistency, each of the resolution rules disables the detection rule.
4. Some detection rules are also mutually exclusive to a resolution rule for another kind of model inconsistency, or vice versa. These situations indicate that the different kinds of model inconsistencies and their resolutions are not completely orthogonal. Such information may be exploited to refactor the detection and resolution rules to make them less redundant (see Sect. 6).
5. Alternative resolution rules for the same model inconsistency are always mutually exclusive, because they represent alternative resolutions. One needs to select a single resolution in order to resolve the inconsistency and thus disable the other resolutions.
6. The most interesting result concerns the mutual exclusions between resolution rules for distinct inconsistencies. In Fig. 6, we see many such examples. They imply that the application of a particular resolution for a particular model inconsistency may prohibit the application of a certain resolution for another model inconsistency. An example of such a situation was explained in the previous section, and visualised in Fig. 4. If we have a *class* that causes an **AbstractObject** inconsistency and an **AbstractOperation** inconsistency at the same time, certain pairs of resolutions for both inconsistencies will be mutually exclusive. This is for example the case between **AbstractObject-Res1** and **AbstractOperation-Res4**.

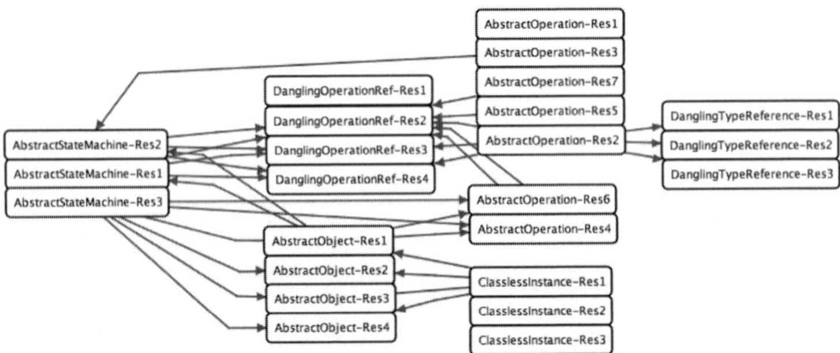

Fig. 6. Graph depicting mutual exclusions between resolution rules of distinct model inconsistencies. Except for some layout issues, this graph has been generated automatically by AGG. In order not to clutter the figure, mutual exclusions between different resolution rules of the same model inconsistency have been omitted.

4.2 Sequential Dependency Analysis

We also used AGG to compute all critical pairs that identify *sequential dependencies* between the inconsistency detection and resolution rules. This leads to the following results, which are summarised in the bottom part of Table 1:

1. By construction, a detection rule never causally depends on itself.
2. In a similar vein, distinct detection rules are not causally dependent because they do not essentially modify the graph structure. The only thing they do is adding a new *Conflict*-node.
3. Alternative resolution rules for the same model inconsistency are sometimes sequentially dependent. This may be a sign of redundancy between the resolution rules, and it may indicate an opportunity for refactoring the resolutions in order to make them more orthogonal. For example, we noticed a dependency from the second to the third resolution rule of **DanglingTypeReference**, from the second to the third resolution of **ClasslessInstance**, from the fourth to the fifth resolution of **AbstractOperation**, and from the sixth to the seventh resolution of **AbstractOperation**. These four dependencies all boil down to the same underlying problem. For each resolution rule that adds some link to an *existing* class, there is a similar resolution rule that first introduces a *new* class before adding a link to it. Such redundancies can easily be avoided by restructuring the resolution rules.
4. As shown in Fig. 7, there are many sequential dependencies between resolution rules for distinct model inconsistencies. This has two important implications. First, it shows that the resolution of a particular model inconsistency may introduce new and different opportunities for resolving other model inconsistencies. As such, the order of resolution of model inconsistencies may be important. Second, some of the identified sequential dependencies indicate a lack of orthogonality between the various resolutions. This can be seen clearly in the mutual dependency between **AbstractObject-Res1** and **AbstractStateMachine-Res3**, and between **ClasslessInstance-Res1** and **AbstractObject-Res3**. In both cases, the resolutions are exactly the same, even though they are used to solve different kinds of model inconsistencies. Again, our analysis helps us to detect such redundancies.
5. Every resolution rule for a given model inconsistency sequentially depends on the detection rule of the same inconsistency, since the detection rule produces a *Conflict*-node that is required for the application of the resolution rule.
6. In our current setup, resolution rules for a certain inconsistency never depend on detection rules for another kind of inconsistency, because the *Conflict*-node contains a *description* specifying the kind of inconsistency being detected or resolved.
7. Sometimes, the detection of a model inconsistency is triggered by the resolution of another occurrence of the same model inconsistency. This is a degenerate case of the more general situation that is discussed below.
8. In general, the resolution of a model inconsistency may give rise to the introduction of new model inconsistencies. The left part of Fig. 8 shows many such cases of model inconsistencies that are caused by application of a resolution rule. For example, there is a sequential dependency from **AbstractObject-Res1** to **AbstractOperation**. Indeed, by applying the resolution rule **AbstractObject-Res1** (see Fig. 3), a previously abstract class will become concrete. If this abstract class happened to have one or more abstract operations (a situation that is completely acceptable), after the resolution all of these operations will lead to an **AbstractOperation** inconsistency because a concrete class is not allowed to have abstract operations.

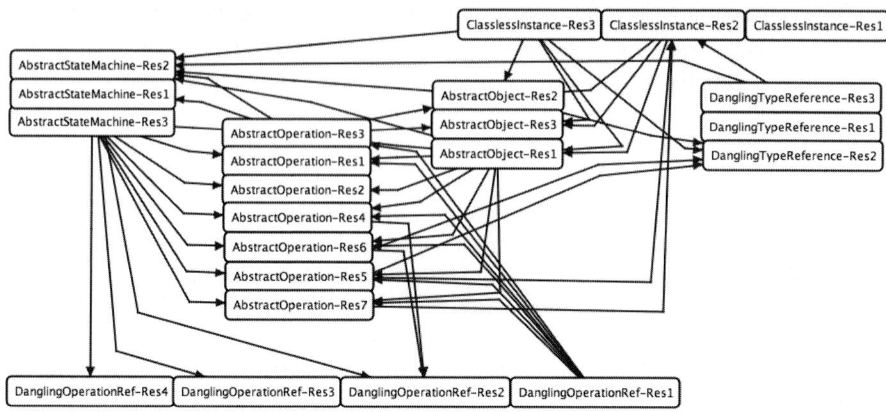

Fig. 7. Graphs depicting all sequential dependencies between distinct resolution rules

5 Discussion

The ultimate goal of the mutual exclusion analysis and sequential dependency analysis carried out in the previous subsections is to improve the inconsistency resolution process. Mutual exclusion relationships can be used to identify situations where resolution rules for seemingly different model inconsistencies may interfere in unexpected ways. Sequential dependencies allow us to assess the propagation of model inconsistencies during the resolution process.

The fact that the resolution of one model inconsistency may introduce other inconsistencies is a clear sign of the fact that inconsistency resolution is a truly iterative process, similar in spirit to bug fixing: when fixing one bug, new bugs may appear that need to be fixed as well. One of the challenges is to find out whether the resolution process will ever terminate. Situations that may lead to infinite application of resolution rules can easily be recognised as cycles in the rule dependency graph. As an example of a cycle of length two, we can repeatedly apply resolution rules **AbstractObject-Res1** and **AbstractOperation-Res3** ad infinitum, without ever reaching a solution. On the right of Fig. 8, another example of a cycle of three resolution rules is presented, that was detected by analysing the dependency graph. In general, the more inconsistencies and resolution rules there are, the more likely it becomes that longer cycles occur, and the more difficult it becomes to detect these cycles. Therefore, automatic detection of such cycles is essential to improve the resolution process.

Based on the analysis of all mutual exclusion relationships and causal dependencies between resolution rules, we realised that these rules are not truly orthogonal, and can be refactored in order to remove redundancy. For example, we observed that some resolution rules for certain inconsistencies disable detection rules of other inconsistencies. These resolution rules can be made more orthogonal so that they only affect the inconsistency that they are meant to resolve. Another refactoring possibility becomes apparent by comparing the dependencies detected by different resolution rules of the same inconsistency. In both cases, investigating the overlap graph that is constructed in

Fig. 8. The left graph depicts which model inconsistencies sequentially depend on which resolution rules. The right graph shows how these dependencies can give rise to cycles in the conflict resolution process.

the critical pair analysis may be used in a semi-automatic way to suggest refactoring opportunities.

With respect to tool support, the results of the analysis can be exploited in various ways. If we target semi-automated tool support, we can easily imagine a user interface (integrated into a UML modelling tool) where, for a given UML model, all model inconsistencies are identified in an automated way, and the user is presented a list of resolution actions. Upon selection of such an action, all mutually exclusive actions will be disabled, and all sequentially dependent actions will become enabled. As such, at any point in time, the user knows exactly which rules can be applied and which not. Currently, different student projects are underway to integrate this kind of support into current-day modelling environments. Once this is achieved, we will perform concrete experiments with the evolution of UML models, which will allow us to refine and extend the incomplete list of model inconsistencies and resolution rules presented in this paper.

A more automated kind of support would offer the user a set of different resolution strategies and, upon selection of one of these strategies, a path of resolution rules is computed to resolve all model inconsistencies. Since there can be many such paths, it remains an open question on what would be the most optimal resolution strategy. In order to find an answer to this question, practical case studies are needed in order to determine the typical ways in which model inconsistencies are resolved in practice.

6 Limitations and Future Work

A limitation of the current approach that we are well aware of, is the fact that not all kinds of model inconsistencies and resolution rules can be expressed easily as graph transformation rules. For some complex model inconsistencies and resolution rules, *pro-*

grammed graph transformations are required, which allow for expressing sequences, loops and branches of transformation rules. For example, to detect the presence of unreachable states in a state machine, we need to apply a sequence of two rules. The first rule should be applied as long as possible to infer all transitively reachable states, starting from the initial state. The second rule is needed to identify all remaining states, which are by construction those that are unreachable.

Behavioural inconsistencies are also difficult to express in a graph-based way. Because of this, in earlier work we have explored the formalism of description logics for this purpose [3, 4]. How this formalism can be combined with the formalism of graph transformation, so that we can still benefit from the technique of critical pair analysis, remains a topic of future work.

Another limitation of our current work is that we restricted ourselves to a subset of class diagrams and state machine diagrams only. Our work should be extended to cover the full version of these diagrams, as well as other UML diagrams such as sequence diagrams, component diagrams, activity diagrams, and so on.

AGG's current implementation of critical pair analysis suffers from performance problems. It took several hours to compute all results. This is not an immediate concern to us since, for any given set of model inconsistency detection and resolution rules, the computation of mutual exclusion relationships and sequential dependencies needs to be carried out only once, and the results can be stored for future reference. Moreover, a comparison of AGG with another tool, *Condor*, seems to suggest that performance of the transformation dependency analysis algorithm may be improved without loss of expressiveness [8].

7 Related Work

In [4, 2], another logic rule-based inconsistency resolution approach similar in spirit to the one presented here was proposed. The main novelty of the current paper, however, is the use of dependency analysis between the different resolution rules. The same remark holds when comparing our work to other attempts to use graph transformation in the context of inconsistency management. In [9], distributed graph transformation is used to deal with inconsistencies in requirements engineering. In [10], graph transformations are used to specify inconsistency detection rules. In [11] repair actions are also specified as graph transformation rules.

There are other approaches to inconsistency management that define resolution actions and the way the user can select these actions [12, 13, 14, 15]. Again, in contrast to our current work, these approaches do not rely on a formal analysis of the relationships between the various resolution actions.

In order to analyse dependencies between transformation rules, we relied on the technique of critical pair analysis of graph transformations. [16] also used this technique to detect conflicting functional requirements in UML models composed of use case diagrams, activity diagrams and collaboration diagrams. In [17], critical pair analysis was used to detect conflicts and dependencies between software refactorings. Other work on critical pair analysis is reported by [18].

8 Conclusion

This article focused on the problem of model inconsistency management, and the ability to provide more disciplined support for iteratively and incrementally detecting and resolving model inconsistencies. For this purpose we explored the use of graph transformation dependency analysis, and critical pair analysis in particular. The main contribution of the proposed approach is that it enables a formal and static analysis of mutual exclusion relationships and causal dependencies between different alternative resolutions for model inconsistencies that can be expressed in a graph-based way. This analysis can be exploited to improve the inconsistency resolution process, for example, by facilitating the choice between mutually incompatible resolution strategies, by detecting possible cycles in the resolution process, by proposing a preferred order in which to apply certain resolution rules, and so on. In the future, we intend to integrate our ideas into a modelling environment in order to provide more disciplined semi-automated tool support for model inconsistency management.

References

1. Object Management Group: Unified Modeling Language 2.0 Superstructure Specification. http://www.omg.org/cgi-bin/apps/doc?formal/05-07-04.pdf (2005)
2. Van Der Straeten, R., D'Hondt, M.: Model refactorings through rule-based inconsistency resolution. In: ACM SAC 2006 - Track on Model Transformation. (2006) To appear.
3. Van Der Straeten, R., Mens, T., Simmonds, J., Jonckers, V.: Using description logics to maintain consistency between UML models. In: UML 2003 - The Unified Modeling Language. Volume 2863 of Lecture Notes in Computer Science., Springer-Verlag (2003) 326–340
4. Van Der Straeten, R.: Inconsistency Management in Model-driven Engineering. An Approach using Description Logics. PhD thesis, Department of Computer Science, Vrije Universiteit Brussel, Belgium (2005)
5. Plump, D.: Hypergraph rewriting: Critical pairs and undecidability of confluence. In: Term Graph Rewriting. Wiley (1993) 201–214
6. Taentzer, G.: AGG: A graph transformation environment for modeling and validation of software. In: Proc. AGTIVE 2003. Volume 3062 of Lecture Notes in Computer Science., Springer-Verlag (2004) 446–453
7. Ehrig, H., Prange, U., Taentzer, G.: Fundamental theory for typed attributed graph transformation. In: Proc. Int'l Conf. Graph Transformation. Volume 3256 of Lecture Notes in Computer Science., Springer-Verlag (2004) 161–177
8. Mens, T., Kniesel, G., Runge, O.: Transformation dependency analysis - a comparison of two approaches. Série L'objet - logiciel, base de données, réseaux (2006)
9. Goedicke, M., Meyer, T., , Taentzer, G.: Viewpoint-oriented software development by distributed graph transformation: Towards a basis for living with inconsistencies. In: Proc. Requirements Engineering 1999, IEEE Computer Society (1999) 92–99
10. Ehrig, H., Tsioalikis, A.: Consistency analysis of UML class and sequence diagrams using attributed graph grammars. In: ETAPS 2000 workshop on graph transformation systems. (2000) 77–86
11. Hausmann, J.H., Heckel, R., Sauer, S.: Extended model relations with graphical consistency conditions. In: Proc. UML 2002 Workshop on Consistency Problems in UML-Based Software Development. (2002) 61–74

12. Easterbrook, S.: Handling conflict between domain descriptions with computer-supported negotiation. Knowledge Acquisition **3** (1991) 255–289
13. Nentwich, C., Emmerich, W., Finkelstein, A.: Consistency management with repair actions. In: Proc. 25th Int'l Conf. Software Engineering, IEEE Computer Society (2003) 455–464
14. Spanoudakis, G., Finkelstein, A.: Reconciling requirements: a method for managing interference, inconsistency and conflict. Ann. Softw. Eng. **3** (1997) 433–457
15. Kozlenkov, A., Zisman, A.: Discovering, recording, and handling inconsistencies in software specifications. Int'l Journal of Computer and Information Science **5** (2004)
16. Hausmann, J.H., Heckel, R., Taentzer, G.: Detection of conflicting functional requirements in a use case-driven approach. In: Proc. Int'l Conf. Software Engineering, ACM Press (2002)
17. Mens, T., Taentzer, G., Runge, O.: Analyzing refactoring dependencies using graph transformation. Software and Systems Modeling (2006) To appear.
18. Bottoni, P., Taentzer, G., Schürr, A.: Efficient parsing of visual languages based on critical pair analysis and contextual layered graph transformation. In: Proc. IEEE Symp. Visual Languages. (2000)

Merging Models with the Epsilon Merging Language (EML)

Dimitrios S. Kolovos, Richard F. Paige, and Fiona A.C. Polack

Department of Computer Science, The University of York, UK, York, YO10 5DD
{dkolovos, paige, fiona}@cs.york.ac.uk

Abstract. In the context of Model Engineering, work has focused on operations such as model validation and model transformation. By contrast, other model management operations of significant importance remain underdeveloped. One of the least elaborated operations is *model merging*. In this paper we discuss the special requirements of model merging and introduce the Epsilon Merging Language (EML), a rule-based language, with tool support, for merging models of diverse metamodels and technologies. Moreover, we identify special cases of model merging that are of particular interest and provide a working example through which we demonstrate the practicality and usefulness of the proposed language.

1 Introduction

As models are promoted to primary software development artefacts, demand for model management facilities is growing. Currently, management operations such as model validation and transformation have been extensively studied while other aspects of Model Engineering, perhaps of equivalent importance, remain significantly underdeveloped. One of the least elaborated management operations is *model merging*.

Today, there are many existing and upcoming standards for Model Engineering, most of which are managed by the Object Management Group (OMG) [1]. The Object Constraint Language (OCL) [2] is the standard language for expressing constraints on models and metamodels. The Queries-Views-Transformations (QVT)[3] standard targets model-to-model transformations and relations. Regarding model to text transformations (code generation), proposals for a suitable language have been requested [4] by the OMG. Finally, for text to model transformations (reverse engineering), the Abstract Syntax Tree Metamodel (ASTM) [5] and Knowledge Discovery Metamodel (KDM) [6] have been proposed and are currently under standardisation.

Despite the wealth of standards, there are none that address model merging. By contrast, the need for a generic model merging mechanism has been identified in both research publications [7, 8, 9] and OMG documents [10]. For instance, in the MDA Guide [10] a scenario of merging *Platform Independent Models (PIM)* with *Platform Definition Models (PDM)* to produce *Platform Specific Models (PSM)* is illustrated.

O. Nierstrasz et al. (Eds.): MoDELS 2006, LNCS 4199, pp. 215–229, 2006.

The paper is organized as follows: In Section 2 we discuss proposed approaches to model merging. In Section 3, we introduce the *Epsilon Merging Language (EML)*, a language for merging models of diverse metamodels and technologies. We discuss the abstract syntax, the execution semantics and tool-support of the language. In Section 4, we present a case study through which we discuss the concrete syntax of the language and demonstrate its practicality and usefulness. Finally, in Section 5 we conclude and outline our future plans for the evolution of EML.

2 Background

In this paper we refer to model merging as the process of merging two source models, M_A and M_B, instances of the metamodels MM_A and MM_B, into a target model M_C, which is an instance of the MM_C metamodel. We represent this process as $MERGE_{M_A,M_B \rightarrow M_C}$. In this section, we review proposed approaches to model merging and discuss their strong and weak points. The purpose of this review is to elaborate a set of guidelines for a generic model merging facility.

2.1 Phases of Model Merging

Existing research [8, 11] has demonstrated that model merging can be decomposed into four distinct phases: comparison, conformance checking, merging and reconciliation (or restructuring).

Comparison Phase. In the comparison phase, correspondences between equivalent elements of the source models are identified, so that such elements are not propagated in duplicate in the merged model. Several approaches to comparison, ranging from manual to fully automatic, have been proposed.

In [12] the ModelWeaver, a generic framework for capturing different types of relationships, such as match relationships, between elements of different models is illustrated. Matching pairs of elements can be defined graphically through a tree-based user interface and declared relationships can be stored in a separate *weaving model*. Weaving models can be used later by other tools such as model transformation or model merging tools. While this is a flexible approach that promotes reuse, it does not scale well since manual definition of each matching pair is a labour intensive process.

In [13], matching is performed using persistent model-element identifiers (i.e. using the *xmi.id* identifier). However, this only applies to comparison of models that are versions of a common ancestor. In [14], matching is performed by comparing the *names* of the elements of the two models. Nevertheless, there are model elements that do not have a name (e.g. instances of the $Multiplicity$ UML metaclass) to compare.

Conformance Checking Phase. In this phase, elements that have been identified as matching in the previous phase are examined for conformance with each other. The purpose of this phase is to identify potential conflicts that would render merging infeasible. The majority of proposed approaches, such as [15], address conformance checking of models complying with the same metamodel.

Merging Phase. Several approaches have been proposed for the merging phase. In [8,9], graph-based algorithms for merging models of the same metamodel are proposed. In [15], an interactive process for merging of UML 2.0 models is presented. There are at least two weaknesses in the methods proposed so far. First, they only address the issue of merging models of the same metamodel, and some of them address a specific metamodel indeed. Second, they use an inflexible merging algorithm and do not provide means for extending or customizing its logic.

Reconciliation and Restructuring Phase. After the merging phase, the target model may contain inconsistencies that need fixing. In the final step of the process, such inconsistencies are removed and the model is *polished* to acquire its final form. Although the need for a reconciliation phase is discussed in [11,9], in the related literature the subject is not explicitly targeted.

2.2 Relationship Between Model Merging and Model Transformation

A merging operation is a transformation in a general sense, since it transforms some input (source models) into some output (target models). However, as discussed throughout this section, a model merging facility has special requirements (support for comparison, conformance checking and merging pairs of input elements) that are not required for typical *one-to-one* or *one-to-many* transformations [16] and are therefore not supported by contemporary model transformation languages.

3 The Epsilon Merging Language (EML)

The Epsilon Merging Language (EML) is a rule-based language for merging models of diverse metamodels and technologies. In this section we discuss the infrastructure on which EML is built as well as the abstract syntax, the execution semantics and tool support for the language. The concrete syntax is presented in the case study that follows.

3.1 The Epsilon Platform

EML is built atop the *Extensible Platform for Specification of Integrated Languages for mOdel maNagement* (Epsilon) [17]. Epsilon is a platform that provides essential infrastructure for implementing task-specific model management languages (e.g. model transformation, model merging, model validation languages).

The foundation of Epsilon is a generic model management language, the Epsilon Object Language (EOL) [18]. EOL builds on the navigation facilities of the Object Constraint Language (OCL) [2] but also provides essential model management facilities such as model modification, statement sequencing, error reporting and multiple model access that OCL currently lacks.

Epsilon is intended to be a global model management platform. It provides an abstraction layer that hides the implementation details of specific modelling technologies, thus providing uniform access to different types of models. So far, Epsilon provides stable support for management of MOF-based models, using MDR [19], EMF [20] models, and experimental support for XML documents. Currently, we are developing support for models of the Microsoft Domain Specific Languages Toolkit (MSDSL) [21].

The main advantages of building task-specific languages, such as EML, on a common foundation are orthogonality, reusability and uniformity. All task-specific languages reuse the EOL for declaring model management logic instead of implementing a custom language each. Thus, evolution of EOL (e.g. to enhance performance or syntax brevity) and integration of support for new modelling technologies (e.g. MSDSL or GME [22]) enhances all the languages that build atop it. In terms of tool support, Epsilon provides a set of reusable components for implementing support for new task-specific languages (editors, launch configurations) in the Eclipse [23] platform.

Apart from the merging language we are presenting in this paper, we have implemented a model comparison language (ECL) discussed in [24], a model to model transformation language (ETL) and a prototype of a model to text transformation language (EGL).

3.2 Abstract Syntax of EML

As discussed in Section 2, a model merging process can be divided into four distinct phases. In this section, we structure our discussion on the elements of the EML abstract syntax, displayed in Figure 1, based on the phase in which they participate. In addition to the abstract syntax, Figure 2 provides an insight to the internals of the EML engine to facilitate better understanding of *strategies* and the execution process of EML.

Comparison and Conformance Phase. In EML, matching is performed with *match-rules*. Each match-rule can compare pairs of instances of two specific meta-classes and decide if they match and conform with each other. Those decisions are made in the boolean-returning *compare* and *conform* blocks of the rule respectively.

Merging Phase. In the merging phase, there are two activities that produce elements in the target model; The elements that have been identified as matching are *merged* into a sequence of model elements in the target model and a selection of the elements for which a match has not been found in the opposite model are *transformed* into elements of the target model. Therefore, EML provides two different types of rules; *merge-rules* and *transform-rules*.

Each merge-rule defines the types of elements it can merge, as well as a list of the elements it produces in the target model. In its body, the merge-rule defines the exact way in which source elements are related to the newly created elements in the target model. Similarly, each transform-rule defines the type of instances it can transform, a list of model elements that it produces in the target model and a body that implements the actual transformation.

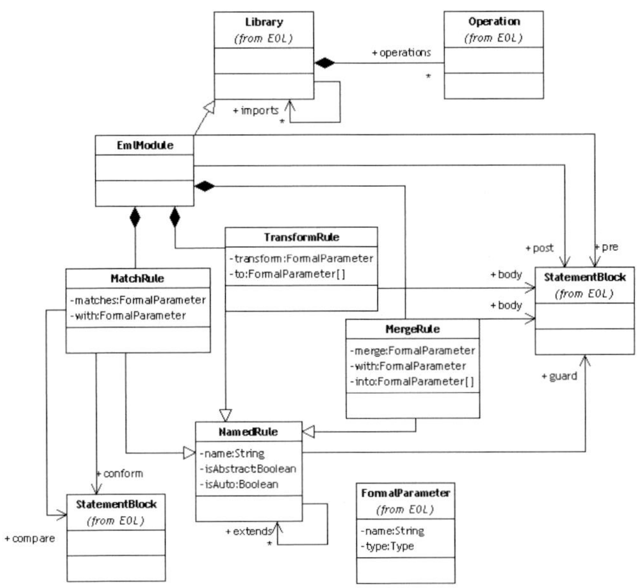

Fig. 1. EML Abstract Syntax

Common characteristics of EML rules. All types of EML rules share some common characteristics which we discuss here to avoid repetition.

Each rule can inherit the functionality of one or more rules of the same type by *extending* them. A rule can be also declared as *abstract* which means that it cannot be invoked directly, but can be extended by other rules. The effect of inheritance on the execution semantics of the rule is discussed in the sequel.

Each rule can optionally define a *guard* block that enforces additional constraints on its applicability. For example, the *guard* part of a transform-rule may define that the rule does not apply to all instances of the *UML!Class* but only to those that have a certain stereotype attached.

The guard and body of each rule, as well as the compare and conform part of match-rules, are blocks (sequences) of EOL statements. From a technical perspective, each rule actually prepares the context by putting the specific instances on which it is invoked in the current *scope* so that the EOL body can query or modify them to implement the desired functionality of the rule.

Strategies. There are certain cases where definition of match, merge and transform rules is trivial but lengthy. For example, the UML 1.4 metamodel consists of 120 meta-classes and consequently, a specification for merging two UML 1.4 models would consist of $3 * 120 = 360$ rules (for matching, merging and transforming). While the length of each rule can be significantly reduced using rule inheritance, the number of rules is still large and difficult to manage.

Through case studies on merging different types of models, we have identified cases where this complexity can be managed in a much more elegant man-

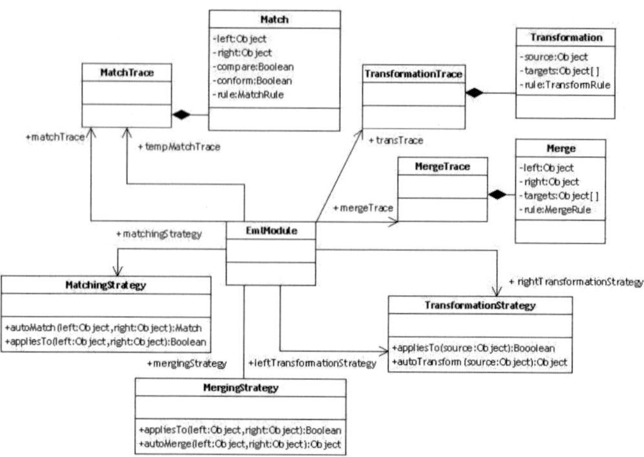

Fig. 2. EML Engine Internals

ner. This is particularly true when the merging process involves more than one model of the same metamodel. For instance, when merging models of the same metamodel, the merging logic can be largely inferred from the structure of the metamodel and there should be no need to define it manually. To confront such issues in a generic way, in EML we have introduced the concept of *strategies*. Strategies are pluggable (exogenous) algorithms that can be attached to an EML specification to implement functionality that would otherwise require extensive rule hand-writing. There are three types of strategies in EML, one for each type of rule.

Matching Strategy. A matching strategy compares two arbitrary model elements and returns an *Match* instance containing information about whether the two instances match and conform with each other.

Practical matching strategies we have identified and implemented include the *MofIdMatchingStrategy* and *EmfIdMatchingStrategy* that compare elements of MOF and EMF-based models respectively by examining their persistent XMI identity. These concrete strategies are particularly useful in the case where the models under comparison are versions of a common ancestor model. In this case, the vast majority of their elements are expected to have selfsame persistent identities, a clue strong enough to characterize elements as matching.

Merging Strategy. A merging strategy has two methods. The *appliesTo(left Element : Object, rightElement : Object) : Boolean* decides if the strategy applies to a specific pair of instances by returning a *Boolean* value. The *autoMerge(leftElement: Object, rightElement: Object)* specifies the logic that merges the two instances.

Practical merging strategies we have developed include the *CommonMofMetamodelMergingStrategy* and the *CommonEmfMetamodelMergingStrategy* strategies for merging elements of the same type originating from MOF or EMF-based models of a common metamodel. The merging algorithm they follow is quite straightforward; for single-valued features they choose the value of the element from left model while for multi-valued features they perform a union of the left and right values and assign them to the feature of the target element.

Transformation Strategy. Similarly to the previous two types of strategies, a transformation strategy can transform a source element into an equivalent element in the target metamodel. An EML module has two associated transformation strategies; the *leftTransformationStrategy* and the *rightTransformationStrategy* that can transform elements from M_A or M_B respectively. As an example, a useful concrete transformation strategy is the *CommonMofMetamodelTransformationStrategy* that creates a deep copy of the source element on which it is applied in the target model.

Extending the behaviour of Strategies. Strategies can relieve developers from defining rules of trivial functionality. On the other hand, for some types of model elements a strategy may not have the exact behaviour that the user needs. In this case, the user can define a rule that applies to specific types of elements thus overriding the strategy. While this makes overriding feasible it is not the most efficient way since, for example, the strategy may implement a large proportion of the desired functionality and the user may need to tweak some minor details, thus making rewriting the rule from scratch unnecessarily heavyweight. To resolve this issue, in EML a rule can be characterized as *auto*. In this case, the respective strategy is executed and following that the body of the rule.

In *merge* and *transform* rules, this affects the contents of the elements in the target list (which would otherwise be empty). In the case of the *match* rules, the *autoCompare* and *autoConform* variables are placed in the *scope* so that the bodies of the *compare* and *conform* parts of the rule can combine them with other criteria to finally decide if the two elements constitute or not a match.

Many of the strategies discussed in this section implement algorithms (e.g. persistent identifier-based matching, metamodel-driven merging) also discussed in Section 2. The difference is that there, they are described as standalone algorithms that cannot be extended or customized by users. By contrast, in EML they are pluggable components of a more complex architecture that allows the user to dynamically attach them to merging specifications and customize their behaviour.

Restructuring and Reconciliation Phase. After the merging phase, the target model can possibly require some restructuring. Restructuring can be performed in the *post* block of the specification. The *post* block is a pure EOL block that has access to the models as well as the internal traces of the EML engine. There, users can specify the desired restructuring functionality in an imperative manner.

3.3 Execution Semantics

In this section we discuss the execution semantics of EML. As with the previous section, we provide a separate paragraph for each phase.

Comparison and Conformance Phase. For each pair of elements in M_A, M_B, the non-abstract match-rules are iterated to find one that applies to the pair. In case two or more rules are found to apply to a pair, this is reported to the user and execution stops. The reason we have chosen this approach instead of invoking all applicable rules is to reduce complexity since reuse can be still implemented via rule extension. For a match-rule to apply, the elements of the pair must be instances of the types the rule declares and the guard of the rule must also return *true*. If no applicable match-rule is found, the attached *matchingStrategy* compares the elements, and the results are stored in the *matchTrace*.

If an applicable rule is found, the *compare* parts of the rule it extends as well as the rule's own *compare* part are executed. In the *compare* part of a rule, the built-in *matches(element)* operation may be invoked on any element to check (by consulting the *matchTrace* or invoking an appropriate match-rule) whether it matches with the element set as parameter. The *matches(element)* operation will be further discussed through a concrete example in the case study. If any *compare* part returns *false*, the elements are stored in the *matchTrace* as non-matching.

If all the *compare* parts return *true*, the *conform* parts are executed. If any of them returns *false*, the elements are stored in the *matchTrace* as non-conforming, else they are stored as conforming. In the end of the matching phase, the *matchTrace* contains information about all pairs of elements in the source models. Then, if there are elements that match with elements of the opposite model but do not conform to them, they are reported to the user and the execution is terminated since it is not desirable to attempt to merge models that contain conflicting elements.

Merging Phase. After the matching phase, by examining the *matchTrace*, the elements of the source models are separated into two main groups. Those that have one or more matching elements in the opposite model and those that have not.

For each element with one or more matching opposites, for each match the non-abstract merge-rules are iterated to find one that applies to the pair. As with match rules, a rule applies to a pair if the elements are instances of the rule-defined parameters and the guard part of the rule returns true. If no rule is applicable, the pair is merged using the defined *mergingStrategy* and the results are stored in the *mergeTrace*.

For each element with no matching opposites, the non-abstract transform-rules are iterated to find one that applies to the element. Applicability for transform-rules is decided similarly to the match and merge-rules. If no transform-rule is found, the element is transformed using the *leftTransformationStrategy* or the *rightTransformationStrategy* depending on whether it originates from M_A or M_B respectively, and the results are stored in the *transTrace*.

Breaking the Default Rule Execution Order. There are cases when it is desirable to break the default execution order. For example, for a match-rule that compares two UML attributes, a commonly accepted definition is that for two attributes to match, apart from their names, their owning classes must also match. To check this, the rule should invoke another rule capable of comparing the owning classes or examine the *matchTrace* to discover if the owning classes have been already matched. Since this is a usual requirement in comparison rules, in EML we provide the built-in *matches(element)* operation that can be invoked on any element with any other element (it can also compare collections of elements) as argument to inspect the *matchTrace* or invoke any applicable rule if necessary.

Similarly, in merge and transform-rules, it is often needed to determine the equivalent of an element (or a collection of elements) from M_A or M_B in M_C. To avoid iteration of *mergeTrace* and *transTrace* and explicit invocation of rules, EML provides the *equivalent(element)* and *equivalents(elements)* operations, which inspect the traces and invoke any necessary rules automatically to return the equivalent element(s), in M_C, of the elements on which they are applied. Another advantage of the *matches(element)* and *equivalent(element)* operations is that they are guaranteed to terminate, in contrast with explicit rule invocation that can result to infinite circular rule invocation.

3.4 Tool Support

In the context of tool support, we have implemented an EML execution engine built atop the EOL engine. Moreover, to enhance usability, we have developed a set of plug-ins for Eclipse (editor, syntax validator, outline viewer, wizards and launcher) for editing, inspecting, configuring (e.g. models, strategies) and executing EML specifications.

4 Case Study

In this section, we demonstrate two scenarios of using EML. In the first we merge a Platform Independent Model (in UML) with different Platform Definition Models (PDMs) to acquire different Platform Specific Models (PSMs). In the second we merge two complementary UML 1.4 models. The main reason we use UML models for our examples is that the UML metamodel is well understood and thus we do not need to explain it here. Moreover, UML has a standard graphical notation that readers should be familiar with. Although discussed before, we should state again that EML (and Epsilon in general) is agnostic of UML and treats UML models like any other MOF-based models.

4.1 Merging a PIM with Different PDMs

In this scenario, we need to merge a Platform Independent Model expressed in UML with different Platform Description Models, expressed in a simple MOF-based language, in order to acquire different Platform Specific Models. The simple Platform Description Metamodel contains only a PrimitiveTypeMapping metaclass with two attributes (*independent* and *specific*) that is used to define

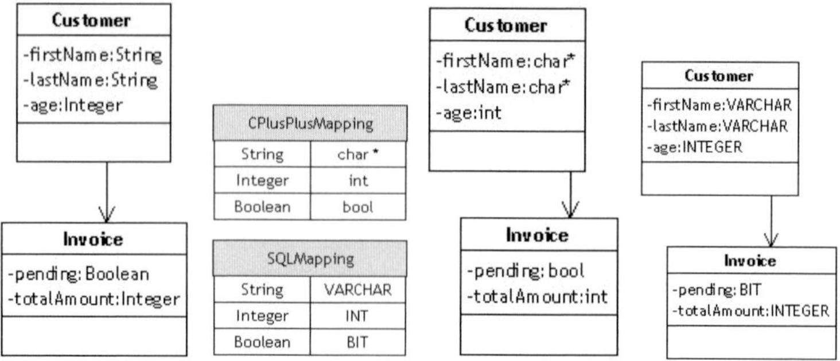

Fig. 3. PIM, PDM and PSM Instances

mappings between platform independent and platform specific types. An exemplar PIM, instances of the PDMs for two different platforms (SQL and C++), as well as the result of merging are displayed in Figure 3.

The merging is achieved with the EML specification displayed in Listing 1.1. Since the left and the target model are of the same metamodel, we set the merging strategy to *LeftAndMergedCommonMetamodelStrategy* and the left transformation strategy to *CommonMofMetamodelStrategy* while we leave the right transformation strategy to *None*.

In the *PimTypeMapping* match-rule, a PIM primitive type is declared to be matching with a mapping (PrimitiveTypeMapping) if the *name* of the primitive type is equal to the value of the *independent* attribute of the mapping. The *guard* part of the rule defines that a PIM primitive type is a normal UML class with a `<<primitive>>` stereotype attached.

In the *PimTypeToPsmType* merge-rule, matching pairs of primitive types from PIM and mappings from PDM are merged to create the platform specific types in the PSM (which is in all other aspects an exact copy of the PIM).

Listing 1.1. PIM with PDM merging specification

```
rule PimTypeMapping
  match pimType : PIM!Class
  with mapping : PDM!PrimitiveTypeMapping {

  guard {
    return pimType.stereotype.exists(s|s.name = 'primitive');
  }

  compare {
    return pimType.name = mapping.independent;
  }

}

auto rule PimTypeToPsmType
  merge pimType : PIM!Class
  with mapping : PDM!PrimitiveTypeMapping
  into psmType : PSM!Class {

  psmType.name := mapping.specific;
}
```

4.2 Merging Two UML Models

In this scenario, we merge two UML 1.4 models that have been developed independently of each other[1]. An extra requirement is to add appropriate stereotypes to the classes of the merged model so that users can trace back which classes originated only from the left or right model and which existed in both of them.

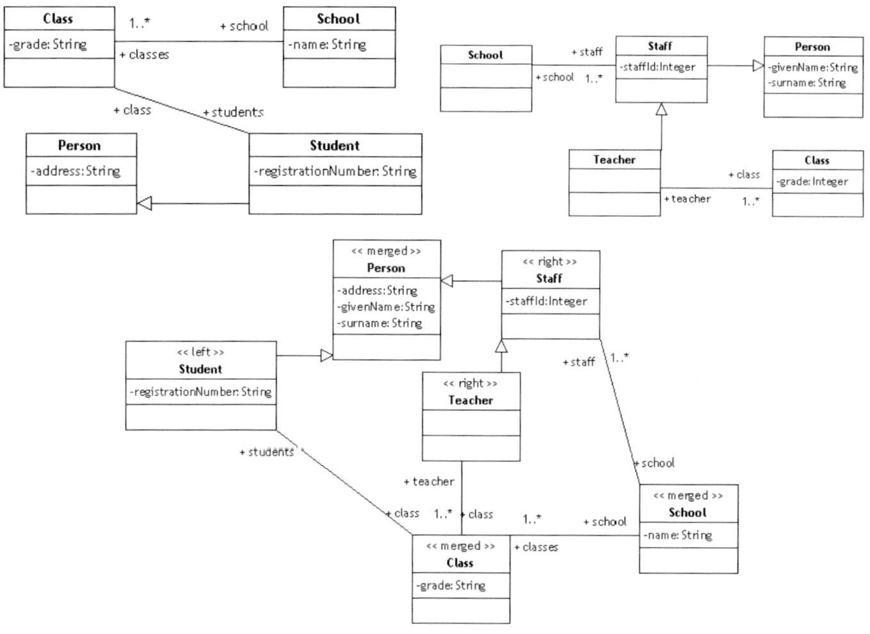

Fig. 4. Source and Merged Models

We achieve this through the specification presented in Listing 1.2. Since the source models are of the same metamodel (UML 1.4) with the target model, we also set the merging strategy to *AllCommonMofMetamodelStrategy* so that matching elements of the same metaclass may be merged automatically, and the left and right transformation strategies to *CommonMofMetamodelTransformationStrategy* so that elements of the source models that do not have matching elements in the opposite model may be deeply copied in the target model. Due to space restrictions, we discuss only rules of particular interest.

Rule *ModelElements* is declared as *abstract* which means that it can be invoked only through the rules that extend it (e.g. *Classes, Packages*). The body of the rule defines that for two model elements to match, their names should be equal and their namespaces should also match (using the *matches()* built-in operation). Invocation of the *matches()* operation in this context will result in the invocation of either the *Packages* or *Models* rule depending on whether the model element is contained in a Package or in the Model itself.

[1] Therefore we can not rely on persistent identities for comparison.

Listing 1.2. Partial UML merging

```
pre {
  def mergedStereotype : new Merged!Stereotype;
  mergedStereotype.name := 'merged';

  def leftStereotype : new Merged!Stereotype;
  leftStereotype.name := 'left';

  def rightStereotype : new Merged!Stereotype;
  rightStereotype.name := 'right';
}

rule Models
  match left:Left!Model
  with right:Right!Model {

  compare {
    return true;
  }
}

abstract rule ModelElements
  match left:Left!ModelElement
  with right:Right!ModelElement {

  compare {
    return (left.name = right.name and
      left.namespace.
        matches(right.namespace));
  }
}

rule Packages
  match left:Left!Package
  with right:Right!Package
  extends ModelElements {}

rule Classes
  match left:Left!Class
  with right:Right!Class
  extends ModelElements {}

rule Attributes
 match left:Left!Attribute
 with right:Right!Attribute
 extends ModelElements {

 compare{
   return left.owner.matches(right.owner);
 }
 conform {
   return left.type.matches(right.type);
 }
}

rule DataTypes
 match left:Left!DataType
 with right:Right!DataType
 extends ModelElements {}

rule Generalizations
 match left:Left!Generalization
 with right:Right!Generalization{

 compare {
  return (
    left.parent.matches(right.parent) and
    left.child.matches(right.child));
 }
}

rule Association
 match left:Left!Association
 with right:Right!Association
 extends ModelElements {

 compare {
  return (
    left.connection.matches(right.connection));
 }
}

rule AssociationEnds
 match left:Left!AssociationEnd
 with right:Right!AssociationEnd
 extends ModelElements {

 compare {
  return (
    left.participant.matches(right.participant) and
    left.otherEnd().matches(right.otherEnd()) and
    left.association.name = right.association.name);
 }
}

auto rule ModelWithModel
 merge left : Left!Model
 with right : Right!Model
 into merged : Merged!Model {

 merged.name := left.name + ' and ' + right.name;
}

auto rule ClassWithClass
 merge left : Left!Class
 with right : Right!Class
 into merged : Merged!Class {

 merged.stereotype.add(mergedStereotype);
}

auto rule ClassToClass
 transform source:UML!Class
 to target:Merged!Class {

 if (Left.owns(source)){
  target.stereotype.add(leftStereotype);
 } else {
  target.stereotype.add(rightStereotype);
 }
}

operation UML!AssociationEnd
 otherEnd() : UML!AssociationEnd {
  return self.association.connection.
   reject(ae|ae=self).first();
}

post {
 def mergedModel : Merged!Model;
 mergedModel := Merged!Model.allInstances().first();
 leftStereotype.namespace := mergedModel;
 rightStereotype.namespace := mergedModel;
 mergedStereotype.namespace := mergedModel;
}
```

Rule *ModelWithModel* is declared as *auto* which means that before the invocation of its body, the strategy merging behaviour is invoked. In its body the rule defines that instead of the name of the left model[2], the merged model should have a name equal to the concatenation of the names of both models separated with the string 'and'.

In the *pre* section of the specification, three stereotypes are created in the target model imperatively. In the *ClassToClass* and *ClassWithClass* *auto*-rules, those stereotypes are attached to classes in the merged model to implement the traceability requirement discussed above. Finally, in the *post* section, restructuring is performed. In the *pre* section, the three stereotypes were created but they were not assigned to a namespace since at that time, the merged model was empty. This renders the merged model invalid since all model elements (except for instances of the Model metaclass) should be contained in a namespace. In this section, the stereotypes' namespace is assigned to the only instance of Model in the merged model. The result of merging two exemplar UML source models is displayed in Figure 4.

5 Conclusions and Further Work

In this paper we have presented the Epsilon Merging Language (EML), a rule-based language for merging models of diverse metamodels and technologies. EML is a novel effort to provide a solution to the underdeveloped field of model merging. Through the case study, we have demonstrated its practicality and usefulness in different merging scenarios.

Currently, we are in the final stages of the process of separating the transformation (transform-rules) and comparison (match-rules) parts of EML so that they can be used as standalone languages. Moreover, we are working on loosening the coupling between the comparison and the merging phase. Our plan is to allow exporting the results of the matching phase in a *weaving model* compatible with ModelWeaver, so that it can be refined manually. The *weaving model* would then be imported back to EML to support the merging phase.

Finally, another interesting direction for future research is the three-way merging task in which the models under merge are descendants of a common ancestor [8]. Although experiments have demonstrated that EML can support this special type of merging, this is not achieved in the most efficient and elegant way. Therefore, we plan to study and evaluate the possibility of integrating new constructs in EML or even that of defining a new language, specific to the task, atop EML (since the architecture of Epsilon renders this possible).

Acknowledgements

The work in this paper is partially supported by the European Commission via the MODELWARE project, co-funded under the "Information Society Tech-

[2] This is the default behaviour of the *CommonMofMetamodelMergingStrategy* as discussed in Section 3.2.

nologies" Sixth Framework Programme (2002-2006). Information included in this document reflects only the authors views. The European Commission is not liable for any use that may be made of the information contained herein.

References

1. Object Management Group, official web-site. http://www.omg.org.
2. Object Management Group. UML 2.0 OCL Specification. http://www.omg.org/docs/ptc/03-10-14.pdf.
3. Object Management Group. MOF QVT Final Adopted Specification. http://www.omg.org/cgi-bin/doc?ptc/05-11-01.pdf.
4. Object Management Group. MOF Model to Text Transformation Language Request For Proposals (RFP). http://www.omg.org/cgi-bin/doc?ad/04-04-07.pdf.
5. Object Management Group. Abstract Syntax Tree Metamodel, Request For Proposals (RFP). http://www.omg.org/cgi-bin/doc?admtf/05-02-02.pdf.
6. Object Management Group. Knowledge Discovery Metamodel, Request For Proposals (RFP). http://www.omg.org/cgi-bin/doc?lt/03-11-04.pdf.
7. Stephane Bonnet and Raphael Marvie and Jean-Marc Geib. Putting Concern-Oriented Modeling into Practice. In *2nd Nordic Workshop on UML, Modeling, Methods and Tools*, 2004.
8. Rachel A. Pottinger and Philip A. Bernstein. Merging Models Based on Given Correspondences. Technical Report UW-CSE-03-02-03, University of Washington, 2003.
9. S. Melnik, E. Rahm and P. A. Bernstein. Rondo: A Programming Platform for Generic Model Management. In *Proc. SIGMOD*, pages 193–204, 2003.
10. Object Management Group, Jishnu Mukerji, Joaquin Miller. MDA Guide version 1.0.1, 2001. http://www.omg.org/cgi-bin/doc?omg/03-06-01.pdf.
11. C. Batini, M. Lenzerini, S.B. Navathe. A Comparative Analysis of Methodologies for Database Schema Integration. *ACM Computing Surveys*, 18(4):323–364, December 1986.
12. Marcos Didonet Del Fabro, Jean Bezivin, Frederic Jouault, Erwan Breton, Guillaume Gueltas. AMW: A Generic Model Weaver. *Proceedings of IDM05*, 2005.
13. Marcus Alanen and Ivan Porres. Difference and Union of Models. Technical Report 527, TUCS, April 2003.
14. Yuehua Lin, Jing Zhang, and Jeff Gray. A Testing Framework for Model Transformations. In Sami Beydeda, Matthias Book, and Volker Gruhn, editor, *Model-driven Software Development*, pages 219–236. Springer, 2005. http://www.gray-area.org/Pubs/transformation-testing.pdf.
15. Kim Letkeman. Comparing and merging UML models in IBM Rational Software Architect. IBM Developerworks, July 2005. http://www-128.ibm.com/developerworks/rational/library/05/712_comp.
16. Krzysztof Czarnecki and Simon Helsen. Classification of Model Transformation Approaches. In *OOPSLA?03 Workshop on Generative Techniques in the Context of Model-Driven Architecture*, 2003.
17. Dimitrios S. Kolovos. Extensible Platform for Specification of Integrated Languages for mOdel maNagement (Epsilon), Official Web-Site. http://www.cs.york.ac.uk/~dkolovos/epsilon.

18. Dimitrios S. Kolovos, Richard F. Paige and Fiona A.C. Polack. The Epsilon Object Language (EOL). In *Proc. Model Driven Architecture Foundations and Applications: Second European Conference, ECMDA-FA*, volume 4066 of *LNCS*, pages 128 – 142, Bilbao, Spain, June 2006.
19. Sun Microsystems. Meta Data Repository. http://mdr.netbeans.org.
20. Eclipse.org. Eclipse Modelling Framework. http://www.eclipse.org/emf.
21. Microsoft Domain Specific Languages Framework, Official Web-Site. http://msdn.microsoft.com/vstudio/teamsystem/workshop/DSLTools/ default.aspx.
22. Generic Modeling Environment. http://www.isis.vanderbilt.edu/Projects/gme.
23. Eclipse Foundation, Official Web-Site. http://www.eclipse.org.
24. Dimitrios S. Kolovos, Richard F. Paige, and Fiona A.C. Polack. Model comparison: a foundation for model composition and model transformation testing. In *Proc. International workshop on Global integrated model management, GaMMa, ICSE*, pages 13–20, Shanghai, China, 2006.

Mappings, Maps and Tables: Towards Formal Semantics for Associations in UML2*

Zinovy Diskin and Juergen Dingel

School of Computing, Queen's University,
Kingston, Ontario, Canada
{zdiskin, dingel}@cs.queensu.ca

Abstract. In fact, UML2 offers two related yet different definitions of associations. One is implicit in several *Description* and *Semantics* sections of the specification and belongs to the UML folklore. It simply says that an association is a set of links. The other – official and formal – definition is explicitly fixed by the UML metamodel and shows that there is much more to associations than just being sets of links. Particularly, association ends can be owned by either participating classes or by the very association (with a striking difference between binary and multiary associations), be navigable or not, and have some constraints on combining ownership and navigability.

The paper presents a formal framework, based on sets and mappings, where all notions involved in the both definitions can be accurately explained and formally explicated. Our formal definitions allow us to reconcile the two views of associations, unify ownership for binary and multiary associations and, finally, detect a few flaws in the association part of the UML2 metamodel.

1 Introduction

Associations are amongst the most important modeling constructs. A clear and accurate formal semantics for them would provide a guidance for a convenient and precise syntax, and greatly facilitate their adequate usage. Moreover, in the context of model-driven software development, semantics must be crystal clear and syntax has to specify it in an unambiguous and suggestive way. An additional demand for clarifying the meaning of associations comes from UML2 metamodel that is based on binary associations.

Unfortunately, the UML2 specification [8], further referred to as the Spec, does not satisfy these requirements. While complaints about informality of semantics are common for many parts of UML, for associations even their (abstract) syntax seems to be complicated and obscure in some parts. For example, the meaning of the (meta)associations *ownedEnd* and *navigableOwnedEnd* of the Association (meta)class in the metamodel is not entirely clear. More accurately, it is not

* Research supported by OCE Centre for Communications and Information Technology and IBM CAS Ottawa.

O. Nierstrasz et al. (Eds.): MoDELS 2006, LNCS 4199, pp. 230–244, 2006.

easy to comprehend their meaning in a way equally suitable for both binary and multiary (arity $n \geq 3$) associations. The infamous multiplicity problem for multiary associations is another point where the cases of binary and multiary associations are qualitatively different in UML (see, e.g., [3]). Even the very definition of association, in fact, bifurcates for the binary and multiary cases, though this fact is hidden in the excessively fragmented presentation of the UML metamodel via packages. A sign of distortion of the association part of the metamodel is that many modeling tools do not implement multiary associations (not to mention qualified associations - a rarity among the implemented modeling elements).

We will show in the paper that all these problems grow from the same root, and can be readily fixed as soon as the root problem is fixed. The point is that UML mixes up three conceptually and technically different sides of the association construct. In the most popular view, an association is just a collection of tuples or a table. For example, a ternary association between classes X_1, X_2, X_3 is a three-column table $T = (R, p_1, p_2, p_3)$ with R the set of rows or tuples of the association and p_1, p_2, p_3 the columns, that is, mappings $p_i \colon R \to X_i$,$i = 1, 2, 3$, called association ends. This is a purely extensional view and the roles of the classes are entirely symmetric.

A more navigation-oriented view of the same association is to consider it as a triple of binary mappings

$$f_1 \colon X_2 \times X_3 \to X_1,\ f_2 \colon X_1 \times X_3 \to X_2,\ \text{and}\ f_3 \colon X_1 \times X_2 \to X_3 \qquad (1)$$

which we call *structural* (Table 1 on p.240 presents it in visual form). Note that each of the structural mappings is asymmetric and has a designated target, or *goal*, class. Yet the set of three mappings $M_S = (f_1, f_2, f_3)$ retains the symmetry of the tabular view. We will call such sets *structural maps* of associations.

When we think about implementation of structural maps, we need to decide, first of all, which of the possible navigation directions should be most effective and which of the classes will implement it. For example, the mapping f_1 can be implemented as either a retrieval operation in class X_2 with a formal parameter of type X_3, $f_{12}(x{:}X_3) \colon X_2 \to X_1$,[1] or as a retrieval operation in class X_3 with a formal parameter of type X_2, $f_{13}(x{:}X_2) \colon X_3 \to X_1$. We will call such mappings *operational* or *qualified*, since UML calls formal parameters *qualifiers*. Thus, the same association can be viewed as a six-tuple M_Q of qualified mappings f_{ij} (see Table 1 where only three of them shown). Note that each of the qualified mappings brings more asymmetry/navigational details to its structural counterpart yet their full set M_Q retains the symmetry of the entire association; we will call such sets *operational* or *qualified maps*.

Thus, in general an association is a triple $A = (T, M_S, M_Q)$ of mutually derivable components, with T, M_S and M_Q also consisting of multiple member mappings. Unfortunately, for specifying this rich instrumentary of extensional and navigational objects, the UML metamodel offers just one concept of the

[1] Which might be written as $f_{12} \colon X_2 \to [X_3 \to X_1]$ in the functional programming style.

association *memberEnd*. For example, a ternary association consists of the total of twelve mappings while the UML metamodel states only the existence of its three ends. Not surprisingly, that in different parts of the Spec the same notion of *memberEnd* is interpreted as either a projection mapping (column), or a structural mapping, or a qualified mapping (operation). Inevitably, it leads to ambiguities and misconceptions, only part of which was mentioned above.[2]

In the paper we build a formal framework, where the notions outlined above together with their relationships can be accurately defined and analyzed. In a sense, we disassemble the rich intuition of the association construct into elementary building blocks and then join them together in various ways to model different views of associations. Particularly, if association is a triple $A = (T, M_S, M_Q)$ as above, we can consider the pair $A_S = (T, M_S)$ as its *structural view* and the pair $A_O = (T, M_Q)$ as its *operational view*. The metamodel in Fig. 3 on p.243 presents our building blocks and their relationships in a concise way. It shows a few remarkable symmetries between the components and views of associations, which is interesting to discuss (see Section 4.3). On the other hand, it forms a useful frame of reference for analyzing the UML metamodel (Section 4.4).

Formalities as such can be boring or interesting to play with. When they are intended to model engineering artifacts, the first and crucial requirements to them is to be an adequate and careful formalization of the intuitions behind the artifacts to be modeled. We have paid a close attention to deducing our formalization from the Spec rather than from our own perception of what the association should be. To achieve this goal, we have read the Spec as carefully as possible, and discussed possible interpretations with the experts [10, 7]. Sections 2 and 3 present the results together with an outline of some preliminary framework of main constructs. Section 4 presents an accurate formal model and sets the stage for our discussion of what is association in UML2; the culmination is in Sections 4.3 and 4.4.

Remark: What is *not* in the paper. Semantics for the concepts of association/relationship and particularly, of aggregation and role is a well-known research issue that can be traced back to the pioneering works on data semantics by Abrial, Brodie, Chen, Mylopoulos, Tsichritzis and Lochovsky in seventies-early eighties. Since then a vast body of work on the subject was done and reported in the literature, see [5] for an early survey. Certainly, UML's concept of association is built on top of this work, and it might be an interesting research issue to study the evolution of ideas and their realization in the standard (see [2] for some results). Moreover, we believe that a real understanding of such a software phenomenon as UML does need evolutionary studies, particularly, for association and related concepts, and for many other parts of UML as well. However, such a discussion would go far beyond our goals in the paper. The latter are purely technical: take the standard as the only source of information about the association construct and provide an accurate formal semantics for it.

[2] Even the much more formally precise OCL confuses operational and projection mappings when it borrows UML's notation (abstract syntax) for association classes.

2 What Is a Property? The *Structural* View of Associations

According to UML metamodel ([8, Fig.7.12], see our Fig. 1) an association A between classifiers $X_1...X_n$, $n \geq 2$, is an n-tuple of properties $(f_1, ..., f_n)$ called A's *memberEnds* or just *ends.*

Each of the properties has its *type* [8, Figures 7.5 and 7.10], and explanations in Sect. 7.3.3 and 7.3.44 allow us to set the correspondence $f_i.type = X_i$ for all $i = 1..n$. The main question is *what is the semantic meaning of* property *in this definition?* The Spec says [8, Sect.7.3.44, p.121]:

> when instantiated, a property represents a value or collection of values associated with an instance of one (or, in the case of a ternary or higher-order association, more than one) type. This set of classifiers is called the *context* for the property; in the case of an attribute the context is the owning classifier, and in the case of an association end the context is the set of types at the other end or ends of the association.[3]

A natural way to interpret this definition is to consider a property in general as a mapping from some source set called the *context* (and whose elements play the role of instances "owning" the property), to a target set called the *type* of the property (whose elements play the role of values that the property takes). In particular, if the properties in question are the ends of some association, then the quote above says that each f_i is a mapping

$$f_i \colon X_{j_1} \times ... \times X_{j_{n-1}} \twoheadrightarrow X_i, i \notin \{j_1...j_{n-1}\} \subset \{1...n\}, \tag{2}$$

where the Cartesian product is the context, and the double-arrow head means that the actual target of the mapping is the set $\mathsf{coll}_{f_i}(X_i)$ of collections of specified (with f_i) type (sets, bags or lists) built from elements of X_i. A special case, when the value is a single element of the target class, will be denoted by the single-arrow head, and such mappings will be called *functional* or *functions.*

The left column of Table 1 on p.240 shows examples of mappings of this form for association arities $n = 2$ and $n = 3$. The term *multiary,* will be used generically to refer to the cases $n \geq 3$. Thus, an n-ary association is an n-element set of $(n-1)$-ary mappings called Properties. This definition still lacks a crucial condition. Namely, we need to require that all mappings $f_1, .., f_n$ are just different parts of the same association, or, as we will say, are *mutually inverse,* meaning that they all are mutually derivable by inverting/ permuting sources and targets (this condition is well known for the binary case).

Formally, this can be captured as follows. Given an n-ary mapping $f \colon X_1 \times .. \times X_n \twoheadrightarrow Y$, its *extension* $\mathsf{ext}(f)$ is the collection of tuples

$$\text{((extension))} \quad [(x_1, \ldots, x_n, y) : x_1 \in X_1, ..., x_n \in X_n, y \in f(x_1...x_n) \in \mathsf{coll}_f(Y)],$$

[3] In this piece, the terms "type" and "classifier" are used interchangeably and, hopefully, can be considered synonyms here.

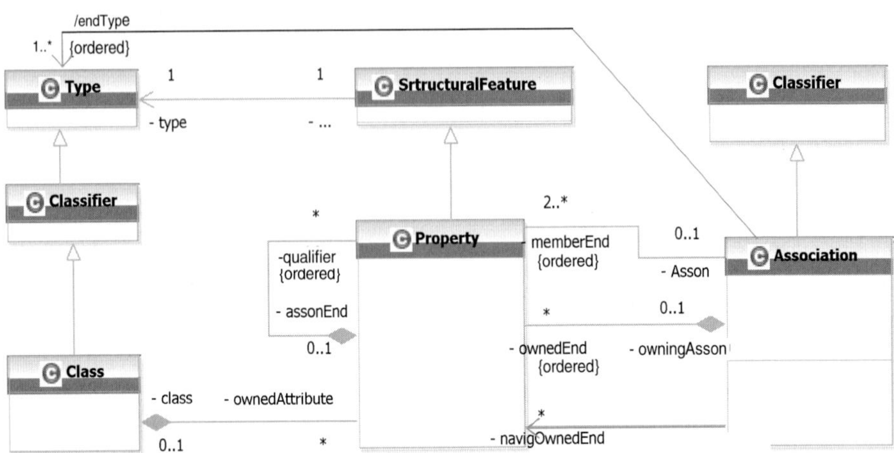

Constraints for Association context in OCL
(to shorten expressions we write end for memberEnd):

(2) self.end->includesAll(self.ownedEnd) ->includesAll(navigOwnedEnd)

(3) def: self.endType = self.end->collect(type)

(4) if self.end->size() > 2 then self.ownedEnd = self.end[a]

[a] this is the Constraint 5 in [8, p.37],

Fig. 1. A piece of UML metamodel extracted from [8, Fig. 7.12] with additions from [8, Fig. 7.5, 7.10, 7.17]

which is a bag if f is bag-valued.[4]The most natural way of presenting such a collection is to store it in a table. In fact, we have a mapping ext: Mapping $\rightarrow$ Table sending any n-ary mapping to a (n+1)-column table recording its extension.

Now we can formulate the condition in the following way.

2.1 Definition: Let $\mathbf{X} = (X_1 ... X_n)$ be a family of classes.
(i) Any $(n-1)$-ary mapping of the form (2) is called a *structural mapping* over $\mathbf{X}$. Its source tuple of classes is called the *context*, and the target class the *type* of the mapping.
(ii) Two or more structural mappings $f_1 ... f_k$ over $\mathbf{X}$ are called *mutually inverse* if they have the same extension (up to renaming of the tables' columns)

$$\text{((inverse))} \qquad \mathsf{ext}(f_1) = \mathsf{ext}(f_2) = ... = \mathsf{ext}(f_k).$$

(iii) An n-element set $M_S = \{f_1 ... f_n\}$ of mutually inverse structural mappings over $\mathbf{X}$ is called a *structural map* over $\mathbf{X}$. In other words, a structural map is a maximal set of mutually-inverse structural mappings.

Thus, the Spec defines associations as nothing but structural maps.

[4] If f is list-valued, we can either disregard the ordering information by considering the underlying bag, or consider the extensional set to be partially-ordered.

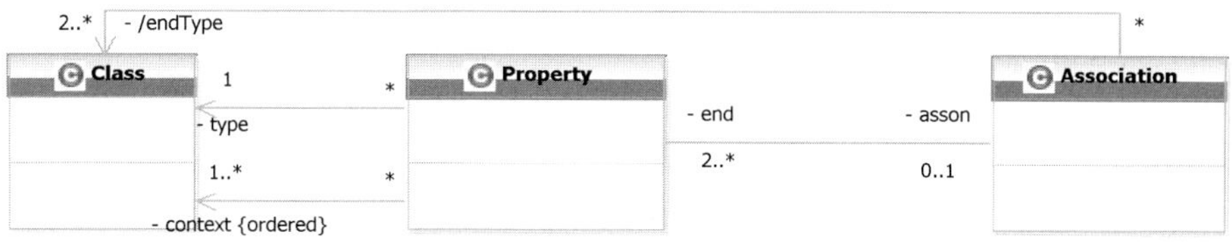

Constraints for Association:

(6) def: self.endType = self.end->collect(type)

(7) self1≠ self2 implies disjoint(self1.end, self2.end)=true

(8) self.end satisfies the constraint (inverse) in Definition 2.1(ii) [a]

Constraints for Property:

(9) self.asson.endType->includesAll(self.context)

(10) self.context->size() +1 = self.asson.end->size() [b]

[a] constraints (7) and (8) are missed in the Spec

[b] constraints (9) and (10) cannot be declared in the Spec because the meta-association *context* is not there

Fig. 2. Metamodel for the *structural* view of associations

2.2 Definition: Structural view of association. An n-ary association, *structurally*, is an n-element set of mutually inverse $(n-1)$-ary mappings (called properties in UML).

Precise details and terminology associated with this definition are presented in Fig. 2. This (formal) metamodel accurately describes the corresponding part of the Spec, and it is instructive to compare it with the UML metamodel in Fig. 1 (disregarding there, for a while, the ownership aspect).

2.3 UML metamodel of associations in the light of formalization, I.

We note that the Spec misses two important constraints on associations: disjointness, (7), and being inverse, (8), in Fig. 2 (though, of course, implicitly they are assumed). Note also that our formal metamodel does not require the set of ends to be ordered. Indeed, ends are analogous to labels in labeled records: ordering is needed when there are no labels for record fields (and means, in fact, using natural numbers as labels). Thus, ordering of meta-association *memberEnd* required in the UML metamodel is redundant.

Finally, the most serious (and even striking) distinction is that the meta-association *context* is absent in the UML metamodel. As we have seen, the Spec does talk about this fundamental component of the association constructs, yet formally it is not entered into the metamodel. Is it hidden or lost in the long package merge chains in which the UML metamodel is separated? Note that even if the (meta)association *context* can be derived from other parts of the metamodel, its explicit presence in Figure 7.12 of the Spec, the main part of the UML association metamodel, is essential. Indeed, without this association we cannot formulate important structural constraints (9,10) in Fig. 2 and, which maybe even more important, without *context* the understandability of the metamodel is essentially lessened.

3 A Battle of Ownerships: The *Operational* View of Associations

In this section we consider that part of the UML association metamodel, which specifies ownership relations between Classes, Properties and Associations. The Spec considers two specific subsets of the set $A.memberEnd = \{f_1..f_m\}$ of association ends: the set of ends *owned* by the association, $A.ownedEnd \subseteq \{f_1..f_m\}$, and the set of *navigable owned ends*, $A.navOwnedEnd \subseteq A.ownedEnd$. Unfortunately, there is no direct explanation of the meaning of these two notions and we need to extract it from semi-formal considerations in Sect. 7.3.3 and 7.3.44.

Since for multiary association (when $n \geq 3$), the notions of *memberEnd* and *ownedEnd* coincide due to the constraint (4) in Fig. 1, we have to consider binary associations to understand the difference.

It appears that the Spec assumes (though does not state it explicitly) that if an end, say, f_1, is not owned by the association, $f_1 \notin A.ownedEnd$, then it is owned by its source classifier X_2, $f_1 \in X_2.ownedAttribute$. In this case, f_1 is considered to be an X_2's attribute [8, p.121]. What is, however, the meaning of the other end, f_2, owned by A?

We have two subcases:
(+), when f_2 is a navigable end, $f_2 \in A.navOwnedEnd$, and (–), when it is not.

In case (+), the association is navigable from X_1 to X_2 (Sect.7.3.3, p.36) and hence we have a mapping $f_2 \colon X_1 \twoheadrightarrow X_2$ yet f_2 is not an attribute of X_1 (otherwise it would be owned by X_1 rather than A). The only reasonable explanation that we could find for this situation is that mapping f_2 is not supposed to be stored in the instantiations of X_1 yet it can be derived from other data. Namely, we assume that mapping f_1 is actually stored (with the instantiations of classifier X_2 as its attribute) while f_2 can be derived from (the extension of) f_1 by taking the inverse. Strictly speaking, in case (+) association A consists of only one end f_1 (stored and owned by X_2!) but can be augmented with the other end, f_2, by a suitable derivation procedure (of inverting a mapping).

Case (–): the end f_2 is owned by A and is *not* navigable. The Spec says that in this case A is *not* navigable from X_1 to X_2 (Sect.7.3.3, p.36) and, hence, f_2 cannot be considered as a mapping. Then the only visible role of f_2 is to serve as a place-holder for the respective multiplicity constraint, m_2. We can consider this situation as that semantically association A consists of the only end/mapping $f_1 \colon X_2 \twoheadrightarrow X_1$, whose extension (graph, table) is constrained by a pair of multiplicity expressions $C = (m_1, m_2)$. In this treatment, the second end f_2 appears only in the *concrete* syntax as a way to visualize the second component of a single constraint $C = (m_1, m_2)$ rather than have any semantic meaning.

We can reformulate this situation by saying that some constraint to mapping f_1 is specified by setting a constraint m_2 to a mapping f_2 derived from f_1.In such a formulation case (–) becomes close to case (+). In both cases, association A consists, in fact, from the only end f_1 (owned by X_2) while the second end is derivable rather than storable and serves for (i) specifying the m_2-half of the multiplicity constraint to A and, (ii, optionally) for navigation from X_1 to X_2.

Thus, with help of implementation concepts, we were able to explain the mixed ownership cases (+) and (–). To be consistent, now we need to reconsider the case when both ends are owned by the association. Thinking along the lines we have just used, we conclude that in this case we deal with a situation when information about the association is stored somewhere but not in the participating classifiers (otherwise the ends were attributes owned by the classifiers). Hence, to make the ends derivable mappings we need to have a source of storable data for deriving the mappings, and the classifiers X_1, X_2 cannot be used for that.

A reasonable idea is to introduce onto the stage a new set, say, R, immediately storing links between instances of X_1, X_2, that is, pairs (x_1, x_2) with $x_1 \in X_1, x_2 \in X_2$, together with two projection mappings $p_i \colon R \to X_i$. In other words, we store the links in a table $T = (R, p_1, p_2)$ with R the set of rows and p_1, p_2 the columns so that if for a row r we have $r.p_1 = o_1 \in X_1$ and $r.p_2 = o_2 \in X_2$, it means that the row stores the link (o_1, o_2) (see Table 1). We can advance this interpretation even further and identify R with A and projection mappings p_i with A's ends f_i, $i = 1, 2$. This new view of associations (though may look somewhat unusual for the UML style) possesses a few essential advantages:

1. It perfectly fits in with the UML idea that an association is a classifier whose extension consists of links.
2. It is generalized for n-ary associations in a quite straitforward way: just consider R with a family of n projections $p_i \colon R \to X_i$, $i = 1..n$, which automatically makes R a collection of n-ary tuples/links.
3. A *property* is again a mapping and, moreover,
   3.1 the classifier owning the property is again the source of the mapping,
   3.2 the type of the property is the target of the mapping as before.

This interpretation brings an essential unification to the metamodel, and possesses a clear sets-and-mappings semantics. It also shows that the "ownership-navigability" part of the UML metamodel implicitly switches the focus from the analysis/structural view of association (Definition 2.2) to more technical (closer to design) view, where the modeler begins to care about which parts of the association will be stored, and which will be derived (with an eye on how to implement that later). We will call this latter view of associations *operational.*

The UML metamodel attributes the operational view to binary associations only (see Constraint (4) in Fig. 1). It appears to be an irrelevant restriction as in the next section we show that the operational view, including all nuances of ownership relations, can be developed for the general case of n-ary associations as well.

4 Formal Model for UML Associations: Separation and Integration of Concerns

In this section we build a formal framework for an accurate definition of the concepts that appeared above. We also introduce a new, and important, actor on the stage: qualified or operational mappings, which are an analog of attributes for multiary associations. It is this actor whose improper treatment in the UML metamodel leads to a striking difference between binary and multiary associations.

4.1 Basic Definitions and Conventions

Our first concern is to set a proper framework for working with names/labels in labeling records and similar constructs.

4.1.1 Definition: Roles and contexts. Let $\mathcal{L} = \{\ell_1 ... \ell_n\}$ be a *base* set of n different labels/symbols called *role names.*

(i) A *role* is a pair $\ell{:}X$ with $\ell \in \mathcal{L}$ a role name and X a class. A(n *association*) *context* is a set of roles $\mathbf{X} = \{\ell_1{:}X_1, \ldots, \ell_n{:}X_n\}$ such that all role names are distinct (while the same class may appear with different roles). We write X_ℓ for the class X in the pair $(\ell{:}X)$. Cardinality of the base set is called the *arity* of the context. For example, the set $\{$*course:Subject, student:Person, professor:Person*$\}$ is a ternary context.
(ii) We use the term class and set interchangeably. For our goals in this section, classes are just sets of elements (called objects). We write $\bigcup \mathbf{X}$ for $\bigcup \{X_\ell \mid \ell \in \mathcal{L}\}$. We also remind the reader our convention about distinguishing general and functional mappings (presented in Section 2 immediately below formula (2)).
(iii) All our definitions will be parameterized by some context $\mathbf{X}$. We will say that the notions are defined *over the context* $\boldsymbol{X}$.

4.1.2 Definition: Links, products, relations.
(i) A *link* over $\mathbf{X}$ is a functional mapping $r\colon \mathcal{L} \to \bigcup \mathbf{X}$ s.t. $r(\ell) \in X_\ell$. The set of all links over $\mathbf{X}$ will be denoted by $\prod_{\ell \in \mathcal{L}} X_\ell$ or $\prod_{\mathcal{L}} \mathbf{X}$ or just $\prod \mathbf{X}$. If $\{(\ell : X) \mid \ell \in \mathcal{K}\}$ is a sub-context of $\mathbf{X}$ for some $\mathcal{K} \subset \mathcal{L}$, we will write $\prod_{\mathcal{K}} \mathbf{X}$ for the set of the corresponding sub-links.
(ii) A *(multi)relation* over $\mathbf{X}$ is a (multi)set of links over $\mathbf{X}$. If R is a multirelation, $R!$ will denote R with duplicates eliminated, thus, $R! \subset \prod \mathbf{X}$. Note that R can be written down as a table whose column names are role names from the base set and rows are links occurring in R. Since each column name must be assigned with its domain, actually column names are pairs $\ell{:}X$, that is, roles.

4.1.3 Construction: Tables vs. relations. In the relational data model a table is viewed as a collection of rows (links). However, it is possible to switch the focus from rows-links to columns-roles and consider the same table as a collection of columns. Each column $\ell{:}X$ gives rise to a functional mapping $[\![\ell]\!]\colon R \to X$, $[\![\ell]\!](r) \stackrel{\text{def}}{=} r(\ell)$. Note that R is always a set but it may happen that two different rows $r \neq r'$ store the same link if $[\![\ell_i]\!](r) = [\![\ell_i]\!](r')$ for all $\ell_i \in \mathcal{L}$.

(i) A *table* over $\mathbf{X}$ is an n-tuple $T = (p_1...p_n)$ of functions $p_i: R \to X_i$, $i = 1..n$ with a common source R called the *head*. Elements of R will be also called *rows*, and functions p_i *columns* or, else, *projections*, of the table. We will often make the head explicit and write a table as an $(n+1)$-tuple $T = (R, p_1...p_n)$.
(ii) We can identify projections p_i with semantics of the roles in the context, and set $p_i = [\![\ell_i]\!]$.

4.1.4 Definition: Mappings and maps over a context.
(i) A *structural* mapping over $\mathbf{X}$ is a mapping of the form $f: \prod_{\mathcal{K}} \mathbf{X} \twoheadrightarrow X_\ell$, where $(\mathcal{K}, \{\ell\})$ is a partition of $\mathcal{L}$ (with the second member being a singleton). The sub-context $\{\ell{:}X_\ell \mid \ell \in \mathcal{K}\}$ is called the *source context* of f.
(ii) A *qualified* or *operational* mapping over $\mathbf{X}$ is a mapping of the form $g: X_{\ell'} \to [\prod_{\mathcal{P}} \twoheadrightarrow X_{\ell''}]$, where $(\{\ell'\}, \mathcal{P}, \{\ell''\})$ is a partition of $\mathcal{L}$. The square brackets denote the set of all structural mappings of the form inside the brackets.

The set $X_{\ell'}$ is the source, the roles in $\mathcal{P}$ are parameters and $X_{\ell''}$ is the target (goal) set. If $\mathcal{P} = \{j_1..j_k\}$, in a standard programming notation the mapping could be written as $g(\ell_{j1}{:}X_{j1}, \ldots, \ell_{j_k}{:}X_{j_k}\ ): X_{\ell'} \twoheadrightarrow X_{\ell''}$. We will call the sub-context $\mathbf{P} = \{X_\ell | \ell \in \mathcal{P}\}$ the *parameter context* or *qualifier*.
(iii) Given a structural and operational mappings f and g as above, we say that g *implements* f if $\ell'' = \ell$ (and hence $\mathcal{K} = \mathcal{P} \cup \{\ell'\}$). This is nothing but a well-known Curry construction (see, e.g., [4]), and we will also call the passages from f to g and back *Currying* of f and *unCurrying* of g. Note that they do not change the extension of mappings.

The left and middle columns of Table 1 show how it works for the cases of n=2 and n=3. For the case $n = 2$, Currying is trivial. For $n = 3$, Currying will produce six operational mappings: two for each of the structural mappings. We show only three of them. It is easy to see that any n-ary structural mapping has n operational/qualified implementations.
(iv) An *operational/qualified map* over $\mathbf{X}$ is a set M_O of $n(n-1)$ qualified mappings with the same extension. In other words, such a map is the set of all qualified mappings generated by some structural map.
(v) To ease comparison of our formal constructs with those defined in UML and avoid terminological clash, we will call the members of a qualified map *legs* while members of a structural map (Definition 2.1) will be called *arms*.

Let $f: \prod_{\mathcal{K}} \mathbf{X} \twoheadrightarrow Y = X_j$, $\mathcal{K} = \mathcal{L} \setminus \{j\}$, be a structural mapping as above. Its extension can be presented as a table $T = \mathsf{ext}(f)$. However, during this passage the information about which of the columns of the table corresponds to f's target is lost. Any other mapping with the same extension will result in the same table, and conversely, by looking table T up in different "directions", we will obtain n different structural mappings including f. We remind the reader that we have called such sets of structural mappings *structural maps* (Definition 2.1(iii)). Thus, a table is an exact extensional representation of maps rather than mappings.

4.1.5 Construction: Adding navigation to tables. We can enrich tables with "navigational" information about the mapping generated the table if the

Table 1. Three views of associations

	Structural: maps of (structural) mappings	Operational: maps of operations (parameterized mappings)	Extensional: tables (i.e., maps of projection mappings)
$n{=}2$	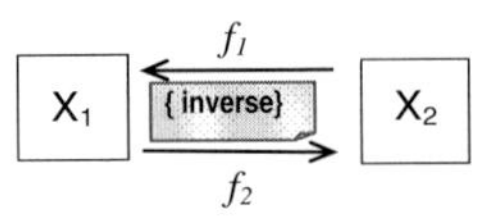 X_1 f_1 {inverse} f_2 X_2		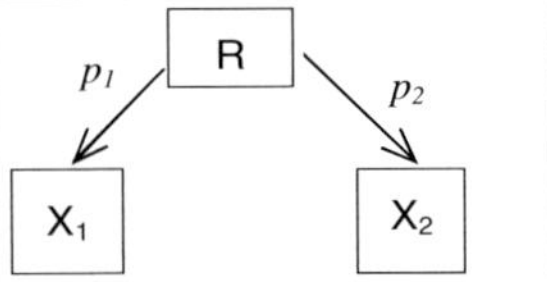 R p_1 p_2 X_1 X_2
$n{=}3$	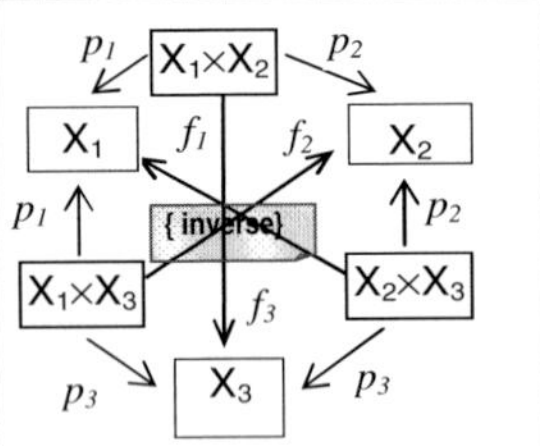 p_1 $X_1{\times}X_2$ p_2 X_1 f_1 f_2 X_2 p_1 {inverse} p_2 $X_1{\times}X_3$ f_3 $X_2{\times}X_3$ p_3 X_3 p_3	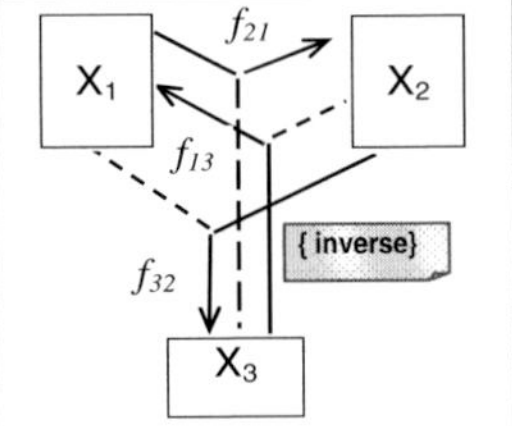 X_1 f_{21} X_2 f_{13} f_{32} {inverse} X_3	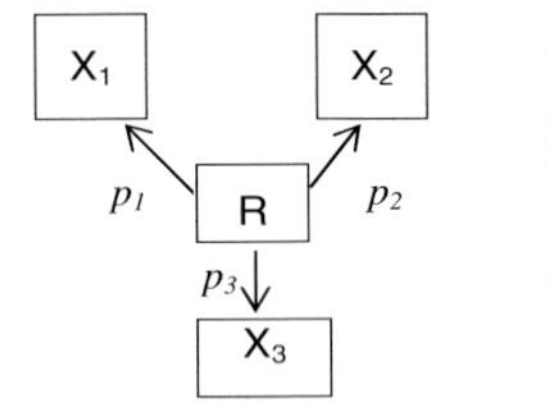 X_1 X_2 p_1 R p_2 p_3 X_3
$n{=}4$	...	...	...

corresponding column name will be marked (say, by a star). Similarly, if a table stores the extension of a qualified mapping, we can keep this information by marking the two corresponding columns. In this way we come to the notions of (i) *star-table*, a table with one column specially designated and called the *goal*, and (ii) *double-star table*, a star-table with one more column designated/marked as the *source* or, in programming terms, *self*.

4.2 Formalization of *Ownership* in the UML Metamodel of Associations

As it was noticed in sect.3, the ownership meta-associations in the UML metamodel are related to possible implementations of structural associations. The latter can be implemented either by a table, or/and by a number of qualified mappings between the participating classes. Which implementation is most suitable depends on which navigation directions need to be implemented efficiently.

4.2.1 Definition: Operational view of associations. *Operationally*, an association over $\mathbf{X}$ is an triple $A = (M_O, T, B)$ with M_O an operational map of qualified mappings over $\mathbf{X}$, T their common extension table, and B a non-empty subset of the set $M_O \cup \{T\}$, whose elements are called *basic* while other elements of $M_O \cup \{T\}$ are called *derived.* The intuition is that the elements of the set $M_O \cap B$ are to be implemented as retrieval operations of the corresponding classes (their attributes in the binary case); the classes then own these elements. If also $T \in B$, then the extension is to be really stored in some table T. The elements formally called "derived" can be indeed derived from the basic elements (by say looking up the extension table in the required direction, and the extension table can be derived by recording the input-output pairs).

The rightmost part of Fig. 3 present the metamodel of this definition.

4.2.2 Remark: uniqueness constraints. It was proposed in [6], that even if the extension table contains duplicates and hence all qualified mappings from M_O are bag-valued, it may be useful for navigational purposes to choose for some of them their versions with eliminated duplicates. Then, operationally, an association over **X** is defined to be a quadruple $A = (M_O, T, B, U)$ with the triple (M_O, T, B) as above and $U \subset M_O$ is the set (perhaps, empty) of those members that we have chosen to consider with eliminated duplicates. Details and a thorough discussion can be found in [6].

4.3 The Metamodel: Playing LEGO Blocks with Associations

Figure 3 on p.243 presents the metamodel of the notions and transformations we have defined above. All meta-classes in the model are parameterized by the association's arity n. It allows us to capture numerous important size constraints (like constraint (10) in Fig. 2) by stating the corresponding multiplicities. We believe that this presentation would be also useful for the UML metamodel.

In the vertical direction, the metamodel consists of two parts: the upper half presents the extensional, or tabular, view of associations, the lower half shows the procedural, or map-based, view. Each of the parts is based on the corresponding structural foundation: the role context for the maps, and the column context for the tables. These two context are in one-one correspondence via the *semantics-name* meta-association, see Construction 4.1.3(ii), and it is our conjecture that in a deeper formal setting they could be unified into a single notion.

There is also a nice parallelism between the two parts in their treatment of navigability as the consecutive augmentation of the respective constructs with additional "navigational" information (what is declared to be the source and the target of the corresponding mapping). To underline this parallelism, we have denoted the (meta) associations "source context" for structural mappings, and "parameter context" for operational mappings, by *context** and *context*** respectively. This "addition of navigability" is governed by one-to-many associations in both parts. One n-column Table generates n starTables, and each starTable generates $(n-1)$ doubleStarTables, and similarly for Maps, structuralMappings and operationalMapppings. The two parts are tightly connected by vertical meta-associations *ext-lookUp* and diagonal meta-associations (shown in dashed line) derived by the respective compositions of horizontal and vertical meta-association ends.

In the horizontal direction, the metamodel also consists of two parts: the structural view of associations (the left half) and the operational view of associations (the right half). These two views are also tightly connected by horizontal meta-associations of *Currying-unCurrying* and (*set* self-*column*) – (*forget* self-*column*).

In fact, our metamodel presents a toolbox of blocks for building different views/notions of associations. For example, structurally an association is a pair $A_S = (M_S, T)$ with M_S a map of mutually inverse structural mappings and T the table representing their common extension (A_S's collections of links). Operationally, an association is a triple $A_O = (M_O, T, B)$ with M_O a map of mutually inverse operational/qualified mappings, T the extension table and B sorting the elements of $M_O \cup \{T\}$ into basic-derived. We say that A_O *implements* A_S if they have the same extension T (and hence, mappings in M_O are Currying versions of mappings in M_S). Extensionally, an association is a table T, and procedurally, it is a pair of maps (M_S, M_O). We can consider an integrated notion of association by defining it as a quadruple $A = (M_S, T, M_O, B)$. Then all the views mentioned above are indeed views, that is, different projections/parts of the whole construct.

4.4 UML Metamodel in the Light of Formalization, II

It is instructive to compare our formal model of associations specified in Fig. 3 with the UML model (Fig. 1). Our formalization clearly shows three components of the association concept: extensional, structural and operational (Table 1). They all have the same underlying structure: a host object (a table/ structural map/ qualified map) holds a number of member mappings (columns/ arms/ legs respectively). Though these components are closely related and, in fact, mutually derivable, they consist of *different* elements: a simple calculation shows that an n-ary association $A = (T, M_S, M_O)$ consists of the total of $m(A) = n + n + n(n-1) = n(n+1)$ mappings (columns, arms and legs) plus one set of links (the head). Note that all these association's elements appear in one or another way in different *Semantics* and *Description* sections of the Spec, and are used for defining associations' (meta)properties like ownerships, navigability, multiplicity. However, as formally defined by the UML metamodel, an n-ary association A consists of only $m_{UML}(A) = n$ elements, its *memberEnd* Properties (UML's analog of mappings). Thus, UML metamodel offers only n-elements to name and manipulate $n(n+1)$ constructs. In Fig. 3, we have pointed out UML counterparts of our formal constructs by their names in square brackets, which makes the shortage of constructs in the UML metamodel explicit. Not surprisingly, this shortage leads to ambiguities in practical usage of associations reported by experts [7].

The comparison also reveals two more flaws in the UML metamodel. First is the absence of meta-association *context* for meta-class Property. In fact, it means that the fundamental notion of *property* is not completely defined in UML. We consider this as one of the most serious problem of the entire UML metamodel (see [2] on the value of the property construct in semantics of OO visual modeling).

The second problem is less fundamental yet is important for practical modeling: the meta-association *qualifier* is improperly defined in the metamodel. Our formalization clearly shows that the target of this meta-association is the meta-class of Roles rather than that of Properties. This mistake in the metamodel can lead to mistakes in practical modeling with qualified associations. Space limitations do not allow us to demonstrate the issue with a few remarkable examples we have in our archive (see [1] for one of them).

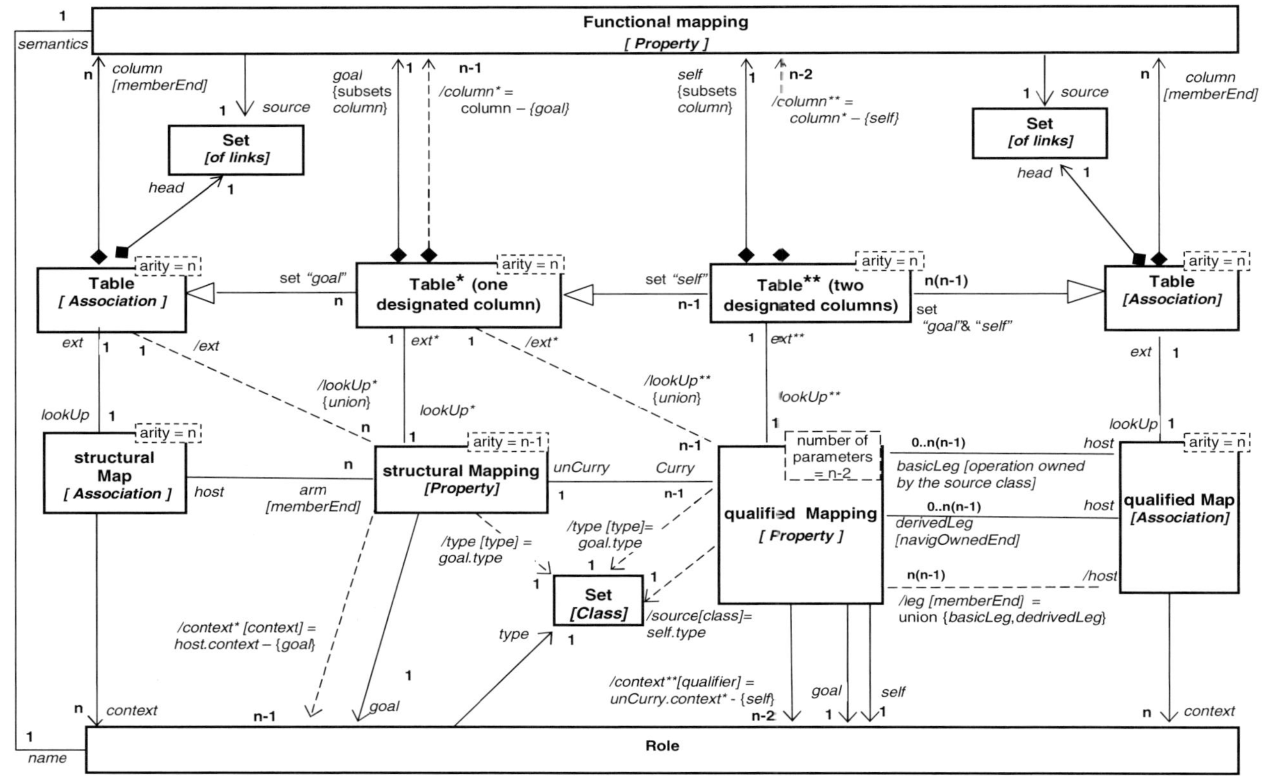

Fig. 3. Metamodel of our formal model for associations. Italic terms in square brackets refer to UML counterparts of our formal constructs. *Warning:* The node Table with its meta-associations is repeated twice to avoid clutter!

5 Conclusion

We have developed a formal framework where the complex notion of association can be disassembled into a few basic blocks. We then built from these blocks a few constructs that formally model different aspects of associations as described and used in UML2. We have found that semantics of the association construct can be uncovered in a few *Semantics* and *Description* sections of the specification, and is presented there in a sufficiently consistent way. However, the part of this semantics formally captured in the UML2 metamodel is much poorer, which makes the latter incomplete and ambiguous.

Our formal model allowed us to explain a few known problems with associations and to detect several omissions in the metamodel, which have been unnoticed so far (see sections 2.3 and 4.4). We have also proposed a few general suggestions on augmenting and restructuring the metamodel for associations to capture their semantics in a precise and unambiguous way.

Acknowledgements. We are grateful to Bran Selic and Dragan Milicev for a few stimulating discussions. Special thanks go to Bran for showing us many delicate issues in the subject.

References

[1] Z. Diskin. Visualization vs. specification in diagrammatic notations: A case study with the UML. In *Diagrams'2002: 2nd Int. Conf. on the Theory and Applications of Diagrams*, Springer LNAI#2317, pages 112–115, 2002.
[2] Z. Diskin and B. Kadish. Variable set semantics for keyed generalized sketches: Formal semantics for object identity and abstract syntax for conceptual modeling. *Data & Knowledge Engineering*, 47:1–59, 2003.
[3] G. Génova, J. Llorens, and P. Martínez. Semantics of the minimum multiplicity in ternary associations in UML. In M. Gogolla and C. Kobryn, editors, *UML'2001, 4th Int.Conference*, volume 2185 of *LNCS*, pages 329–341. Springer, 2001.
[4] C. Gunter. *Semantics of programming languages.* MIT Pres, 1992.
[5] R. Hull and R. King. Semantic database modeling: Survey, applications and research issues. *ACM Computing Surveys*, 19(3):201–260, 1987.
[6] D. Milicev. On the semantics of associations and association ends in UML. Submitted for publication.
[7] Dragan Milicev, Bran Selic, and the Authors. Joint E-mail Discussion, Fall 2005.
[8] Object Management Group, `http://www.uml.org`. *Unified Modeling Language: Superstructure. version 2.0. Formal/05-07-04*, 2005.
[9] J. Rumbaugh, I. Jacobson, and G. Booch. *The Unified Modeling Language Reference Manual. Second Edition.* Addison-Wesley, 2004.
[10] Bran Selic. Personal Communication, Fall 2005.
[11] P. Stevens. On the interpretation of binary associations in the unified modeling language. *Software and Systems Modeling*, (1), 2002.

Semantic Variations Among UML StateMachines

Ali Taleghani and Joanne M. Atlee

David R. Cheriton School of Computer Science
University of Waterloo, Canada

Abstract. In this paper, we use *template-semantics* to express the execution semantics of UML 2.0 StateMachines, resulting in a precise description that not only highlights the semantics decisions that have been documented but also explicates the semantics choices that have been left unspecified. We provide also the template semantics for StateMachines as implemented in three UML CASE tools: Rational Rose RT, Rhapsody, and Bridgepoint. The result succinctly explicates (1) how each of the tools refines the standard's semantics and (2) which tools' semantics deviate from the standard.

1 Introduction

Unified Modeling Language (UML) Behavioral State Machines (hereafter called StateMachines) are an object-based variant of Harel statecharts [6] that are used primarily to describe the behaviour of class instances (objects) in a UML model. Their semantics, as defined by the Object Management Group (OMG), is described in a multi-hundred-page natural-language document [19] that is not easy to use as a quick reference for precise queries about semantics. Moreover, the OMG standard leaves unspecifed a number of details about the execution semantics of UML 2.0 StateMachines. This underspecification means that users can create a UML semantic variant that suits their modelling needs and yet still complies with the OMG standard.

Template semantics [17] is a template-based approach for structuring the operational semantics of a family of notations, such that semantic concepts that are common among family members (e.g., enabled transitions) are expressed as parameterized mathematical definitions. As a result, the task of specifying a notation's semantics is reduced to providing a collection of parameter values that instantiate the template. And the task of comparing notations' semantics is reduced to comparing their respective template-parameter values.

In this paper, we extend the template-semantics templates and composition operators to support notations that allow queue-based message passing among concurrent objects. We then use the extended template semantics to document concisely the semantics of UML 2.0 StateMachines, as defined in the OMG standard [19]. Related efforts [7, 13, 12, 24] to provide a precise semantics for UML StateMachines refine the standard's semantics, so as to produce a complete, formal semantics that is suitable for automated analysis. In contrast, our template-semantics representation retains the semantics variation points that are documented in the standard.

O. Nierstrasz et al. (Eds.): MoDELS 2006, LNCS 4199, pp. 245–259, 2006.

We also express the template semantics for StateMachines as implemented in three UML CASE tools: Rational Rose RT [8], Rhapsody [5, 11], and Bridgepoint [1]. Related efforts [2] to compare UML StateMachine variants mention some semantic distinctions, but they focus more on the differences in syntax and in the language constructs supported. In contrast, our work formally compares the variants' execution semantics. As a side effect, the template-semantic description of a UML model can be used in configurable analysis tools, where the template parameters provide the configurability.

The rest of the paper is organized as follows. Section 2 is a review of template semantics, as used in this paper. Sections 3 and 4 provide the template semantics for the OMG standard for UML 2.0 StateMachines. Section 5 compares this semantics with the template semantics for StateMachines as implemented in three UML CASE tools. The paper concludes with related work and conclusions.

2 Template Semantics

In this section, we review the template semantics and the template parameters that we use to represent UML StateMachine semantics. A more comprehensive description of template semantics can be found in [17, 18].

2.1 Computation Model

Template semantics are defined in terms of a computation model called a *hierarchical transition system (HTS)*. An HTS is an extended StateMachine, adapted from statecharts [6], that includes control states and state hierarchy, state transitions, events, and typed variables, but not concurrency. Concurrency is achieved by composing multiple HTSs. Transitions have the following form:

src —— trig, [cond], ^gen, /asn, #prty ——► dest

whose elements are defined in Table 1. Each transition may have one or more source states, may be triggered by zero or more events, and may have a guard condition (a predicate on variable values). If a transition executes, it may lead to one or more destination states, may generate events, and may assign new values to variables. A transition may also have an explicitly defined priority *prty*, which is an integer value. An HTS includes designation of initial states, of default substates for hierarchical states, and of initial variable values.

Table 1. HTS accessor functions from state s or transition τ

Function	Signature	Description
$src(\tau)$	$T \rightarrow 2^S$	set of source states of τ
$dest(\tau)$	$T \rightarrow 2^S$	set of destination states of τ
$trig(\tau)$	$T \rightarrow 2^E$	events that trigger τ
$cond(\tau)$	$T \rightarrow exp$	τ's guard condition, where exp is a (predicate) expression over V

Function	Signature	Description
$prty(\tau)$	$T \rightarrow \mathbb{N}$	τ's priority value
$ancest(s)$	$S \rightarrow 2^S$	ancestor states of s
$gen(\tau)$	$T \rightarrow [E]^*$	sequence of events generated by τ
$asn(\tau)$	$T \rightarrow [V \times exp]^*$	sequence of variable assignments made by τ

We use helper functions to access static information about an HTS. The functions used in this paper appear in Table 1. In the definitions, S is the HTS's set of control states, T is the set of state transitions, V is the set of variables, and E is the set of events. The notation 2^X refers to the powerset of X; thus, *src* maps a transition τ to its set of source states. The notation $[X]^*$ refers to a sequence of zero or more elements of X.

2.2 Parameterized Execution Semantics

The execution of an HTS is defined in terms of sequences of snapshots. A *snapshot* is data that reflects the current status of the HTS's execution. The basic snapshot elements are

- CS - the set of current states
- IE - the set of current internally generated events
- AV - the current variable-value assignments
- O - the set of generated events to be communicated to other HTSs

In addition, the snapshot includes auxiliary elements that store history information about the HTS's execution:

- CS_a - data about states, like enabling states or history states
- IE_a - data about internal events, like enabling or nonenabling events
- I_a - data about inputs I from the StateMachine's environment
- AV_a - data about variable values, like old values

The types of information stored in the auxillary elements differ among modelling notations. The expression $ss.X$ (e.g. $ss.CS$) refers to element X in snapshot ss.

An execution of an HTS is a sequence of snapshots, starting from an initial snapshot of initial states and variable values. Template semantics defines a notation's execution semantics in terms of functions and relations on snapshots:

ENABLED_TRANS$(ss, T) \subset T$ returns the subset of transitions in T that are enabled in snapshot ss.

APPLY(ss,τ,ss') : *bool* holds if applying the effects of transition τ (e.g., variable assignments, generated events) to snapshot ss results in next snapshot ss'.

$N_{MICRO}(ss,\tau,ss')$: *bool* is a *micro* execution step (a *micro-step*) representing the execution of transition τ, such that τ is enabled in snapshot ss and its execution results in next snapshot ss'.

RESET(ss,I) : ss^r resets snapshot ss with inputs I, producing snapshot ss^r.

$N_{MACRO}(ss,I,ss')$: *bool* is a *macro* execution step (a *macro-step*) comprising a sequence of zero or more micro-steps taken in response to inputs I. The macro-step starts in snapshot RESET(ss,I) and ends in snapshot ss', in which the next inputs are sensed.

We provide the definitions of ENABLED_TRANS and APPLY below, as examples of our template definitions. The other definitions can be found in [17].

$$\begin{aligned}
&\text{APPLY}(ss,\tau,ss') \equiv \\
&\quad \text{let } \langle CS', IE', AV', O', CS'_a, IE'_a, AV'_a, I'_a\rangle \equiv ss' \text{ in} \\
&\qquad \mathbf{next_CS}(ss,\tau,CS') \wedge \mathbf{next_CS}_a(ss,\tau,CS'_a) \wedge \mathbf{next_IE}(ss,\tau,IE') \wedge \mathbf{next_IE}_a(ss,\tau,IE'_a) \wedge \\
&\qquad \mathbf{next_AV}(ss,\tau,AV') \wedge \mathbf{next_AV}_a(ss,\tau,AV'_a) \wedge \mathbf{next_O}(ss,\tau,O') \wedge \mathbf{next_I}_a(ss,\tau,I'_a)
\end{aligned}$$

$$\begin{aligned}
&\text{ENABLED_TRANS}(ss,T) \equiv \\
&\quad \{\tau \in T \mid \mathbf{en_states}(ss,\tau) \wedge \mathbf{en_events}(ss,\tau) \wedge \mathbf{en_cond}(ss,\tau)\}
\end{aligned}$$

Table 2. Template parameters provided by users

	States	Events	Variables	Outputs
Beginning of Macro-step	**reset_CS**(ss, I): CS^r **reset_CS**$_a(ss, I)$: CS^r_a	**reset_IE**(ss, I):IE^r **reset_IE**$_a(ss, I)$:IE^r_a **reset_I**$_a(ss, I)$:I^r_a	**reset_AV**$(ss, I) : AV^r$ **reset_AV**$_a(ss, I) : AV^r_a$	**reset_O**(ss, I): O^r
Micro-Step	**next_CS**(ss, τ, CS') **next_CS**$_a(ss, \tau, CS'_a)$	**next_IE**(ss, τ, IE') **next_IE**$_a(ss, \tau, IE'_a)$ **next_I**$_a(ss, \tau, I'_a)$	**next_AV**(ss, τ, AV') **next_AV**$_a(ss, \tau, AV'_a)$	**next_O**(ss, τ, O')
Enabledness	**en_states**(ss, τ)	**en_events**(ss, τ)	**en_cond**(ss, τ)	
Others	**macro_semantics** **pri**$(T) : 2^T$			

The SMALL-CAPS FONT denotes a template definition, and **bold font** denotes a template parameter. Thus, definition APPLY uses template parameters **next_X**, each of which specifies how a single snapshot element, X, is updated to reflect the effects of executing transition τ. And definition ENABLE_TRANS uses template parameters to determine whether a transition's source states, triggering events, and guard conditions are enabled in snapshot ss.

The template parameters are listed in Table 2. Functions **reset_X**(ss, I) specify how inputs I are incorporated into each snapshot element $ss.X$ at the start of a macro-step, returning new value X'. Predicates **next_X**(ss, τ, X') specify how the contents of each snapshot element $ss.X$ is updated to new value X', due to the execution of transition τ. Parameters **en_states, en_events,** and **en_cond** specify how the state-, event-, and variable-related snapshot elements are used to determine the set of enabled transitions. Parameter **macro_semantics** specifies the type of HTS-level macro-step semantics (e.g., when new inputs are sensed). Parameter **pri** specifies a priority scheme over a set of transitions. Each of the 21 parameters[1] represents a distinct semantics decision, although the parameters associated with the same construct are often related.

2.3 Composition Operators

So far, we have discussed the execution of a single HTS. Composition operators specify how multiple HTSs execute concurrently, in terms of how the HTSs' snapshots are collectively updated.

A *Composed HTS (CHTS)* is the composition of two or more operands via some composition operator *op*. The operands may be HTSs or may themselves be composed HTSs. The snapshot of a CHTS is the collection of its HTSs' snapshots, and is denoted using vector notation, $\overrightarrow{ss}$. Template definitions and access functions are generalized to apply to collections of snapshots. Thus, ENABLED_TRANS$(\overrightarrow{ss}, T)$ returns all transitions in T that are enabled in any snapshot in $\overrightarrow{ss}$.

A micro-step for a CHTS that composes operands N_1 and N_2 via operation *op* has the general form

$$N^{\text{OP}}_{\text{MICRO}}((\overrightarrow{ss_1}, \overrightarrow{ss_2}), (\overrightarrow{\tau_1}, \overrightarrow{\tau_2}), (\overrightarrow{ss_1}', \overrightarrow{ss_2}'))$$

[1] Template semantics has a 22nd parameter, **resolve**, that specifies how to resolve concurrent assignments to shared variables. This parameter is not used in this paper.

$$
\begin{array}{l}
\mathrm{N}^{\mathrm{INTERR}}_{\mathrm{MICRO}}((\overrightarrow{ss_1}, \overrightarrow{ss_2}),\ (\overrightarrow{\tau_1}, \overrightarrow{\tau_2}),\ (\overrightarrow{ss_1}', \overrightarrow{ss_2}'))\ T_{interr} \equiv \\
\quad \left[\begin{array}{l} \overrightarrow{\tau_1} \subset \overrightarrow{T_1} \ \wedge\ \overrightarrow{\tau_1} \subset \mathbf{pri}(\text{ENABLED\_TRANS}(\overrightarrow{ss_1}, \overrightarrow{T_1} \cup T_{interr})) \\ \wedge\ \mathrm{N}^{1}_{\mathrm{MICRO}}(\overrightarrow{ss_1}, \overrightarrow{\tau_1}, \overrightarrow{ss_1}') \ \wedge\ \overrightarrow{ss_2}' = \overrightarrow{ss_2}|^{AV}_{assign(\overrightarrow{ss_2}.AV,\, \overrightarrow{ss_1}'.AV)} \end{array}\right] \quad \text{(* component 1 takes a step *)} \\
\vee \\
\quad \exists \overrightarrow{iss}. \left[\begin{array}{l} \overrightarrow{\tau_1} \in T_{interr} \ \wedge\ \overrightarrow{\tau_1} \in \mathbf{pri}(\text{ENABLED\_TRANS}(\overrightarrow{ss_1},\ \overrightarrow{T_1} \cup T_{interr})) \\ \wedge\ \text{APPLY}(\overrightarrow{ss_2}, \overrightarrow{\tau_1}, \overrightarrow{iss}) \ \wedge\ \overrightarrow{ss_2}' = \overrightarrow{iss}|^{CS}_{ent\_comp(\overrightarrow{ss_2}, \overrightarrow{\tau_1})} \\ \wedge\ \overrightarrow{ss_1}' = \overrightarrow{ss_1}|^{CS}_{\emptyset}|^{AV}_{assign(\overrightarrow{ss_1}.AV,\, \overrightarrow{ss_2}'.AV)} \end{array}\right] \quad \text{(* transition to component 2 *)} \\
\vee \\
\quad \text{(* symmetric cases of the above two cases, replacing 1 with 2 and 2 with 1 *)}
\end{array}
$$

Fig. 1. Micro-step for CHTS with interrupt operator

where operand N_1 starts the micro-step in snapshots $\overrightarrow{ss_1}$, executes transitions $\overrightarrow{\tau_1}$ (at most one transition per HTS), and ends the micro-step in snapshots $\overrightarrow{ss_1}'$. Operand N_2 executes in a similar manner, in the same micro-step.

What differentiates one composition operator from another are the conditions under which it allows, or forces, its two operands to take a step. For example, a composition operator may force its two operands to execute concurrently in lock step, may allow its operands to execute nondeterministically, or may coordinate the transfer of a single thread of control from one operand to the other. Operators also differ in the assignments they make to their components' snapshots. For example, a composition operator may affect message passing by inserting each operand's set of generated events into the other operand's event pool.

We use substitution notation to specify an operator-imposed override on snapshot contents. Expression $ss|^x_v$ is equal to snapshot ss, except for element x, which has value v. Substitution over a collection of snapshots denotes substitutions to all of the snapshots. For example, substitution $\overrightarrow{ss}\,|^{CS}_{\emptyset}$ is equal to snapshots $\overrightarrow{ss}$, except that all of the snapshots' CS elements are empty.

Interleaving. Composition operator *interleaving*, defined by template $\mathrm{N}^{\mathrm{INTL}}_{\mathrm{MICRO}}$, specifies that one but not both of its operands executes in a micro-step:

$$
\begin{array}{l}
\mathrm{N}^{\mathrm{INTL}}_{\mathrm{MICRO}}((\overrightarrow{ss_1}, \overrightarrow{ss_2}),\ (\overrightarrow{\tau_1}, \overrightarrow{\tau_2}),\ (\overrightarrow{ss_1}', \overrightarrow{ss_2}')) \equiv \\
\quad N^1_{micro}(\overrightarrow{ss_1}, \overrightarrow{\tau_1}, \overrightarrow{ss_1}') \ \wedge\ \overrightarrow{ss_2}' = \overrightarrow{ss_2}|^{AV}_{assign(\overrightarrow{ss_2}.AV,\, \overrightarrow{ss_1}'.AV)} \\
\vee\ N^2_{micro}(\overrightarrow{ss_2}, \overrightarrow{\tau_2}, \overrightarrow{ss_2}') \ \wedge\ \overrightarrow{ss_1}' = \overrightarrow{ss_1}|^{AV}_{assign(\overrightarrow{ss_1}.AV,\, \overrightarrow{ss_2}'.AV)}
\end{array}
$$

In each micro-step, exactly one of the CHTS's operands takes a micro-step. The snapshot of the non-executing operand is overridden, to update its variable values to reflect the executing transitions' assignments to shared variables. (The macro $assign(X, Y)$ updates variable-value mappings in X with variable-value mappings in Y, ignoring mappings for variables in Y that are not in X.)

Interrupt. *Interrupt* composition, shown in Figure 1, specifies how control is passed between an CHTS's two operands, via a provided set of *interrupt transitions*, T_{interr}. In each micro-step, the operand that has control either takes a micro-step or transfers control to the other operand. The first bracketed clause in Figure 1 shows operand N_1 taking a micro-step:

Table 3. Mapping UML syntax to HTS syntax

UML	Template Semantics
simple state	$s \in S$
event	$e \in E$
simple attribute	$v \in V$
state variable	$v \in V$
pseudostate (except fork and join)	$s \in S$
simple transition	$\tau \in T$

UML	Template Semantics
transition segment (except fork and join)	$\tau \in T$
maximal composite state with no orthogonal substate	HTS
orthogonal composite state	CHTS (interleaving)
nonorthogonal composite state with orthogonal substates	CHTS (interrupt)
fork, join transitions	interrupt transitions

- Transitions $\overrightarrow{\tau_1}$ in operand N_1 have the highest priority (according to template parameter **pri**) among enabled transitions, including interrupt transitions.
- Operand N_1 takes a micro-step.
- The snapshot of N_2 is updated to reflect assignments to shared variables.

The second bracketed clause shows a transition from operand N_1 to operand N_2:

- Interrupt transition $\overrightarrow{\tau_1}$ has the highest priority among all enabled transitions.
- N_2's snapshots $\overrightarrow{ss_2}$ are updated by (1) applying the effects of the interrupt transition $\overrightarrow{\tau_1}$ and (2) overriding their CS elements with the sets of states entered by the interrupt transition (as determined by macro *ent_comp*).
- N_1's snapshots $\overrightarrow{ss_1}$ are updated by (1) emptying their CS elements (since this operand no longer has control) and (2) updating their variable-value elements AV to reflect $\overrightarrow{\tau_1}$'s assignments to shared variables.

The cases in which operand N_2 has control are symmetric.

3 Syntactic Mapping from UML to HTS

The first step in defining a template semantics for UML is to map UML modelling constructs to our computational model, the HTS. This is essentially a mapping from UML syntax to HTS syntax, and is summarized in Table 3. Most of the mappings are straightforward: Simple states, events, variables, and simple transitions in UML have corresponding constructs in HTS syntax. Pseudostates in UML (except for fork and join) are mapped to simple states in HTS syntax, and the pseudostates' transition segments are mapped to transitions in HTS syntax. As will be seen in the next section, a UML compound transition maps to a sequence of HTS transitions that executes over several micro-steps.

Recall that an HTS is a state machine with no internal concurrency, and that concurrency is introduced by composition operators. Thus, each highest-level (maximal) nonorthogonal composite state that contains no orthogonal descendant states is mapped to an HTS. A UML orthogonal state is mapped to a CHTS whose operands are the orthogonal regions and whose operator is *interleaving* composition. And a nonorthogonal composite state that has one or more orthogonal descendant states is mapped to a CHTS, whose operands are the state's child substates, whose composition operator is *interrupt*, and whose interrupt transitions transfer control between the operands. Fork and join transitions in UML, which enter or exit multiple regions of an orthogonal state, map to interrupt transitions that enter or exit interleaved CHTSs (see Section 4.2).

We treat state entry/exit actions and submachines as *syntactic macros* that are expanded by a preprocessor into transition actions and complete StateMachines, respectively. Entry and exit pseudostates can be treated similarly if the action language evaluates actions sequentially. To simplify our presentation, we do not consider history states in this paper, but they can be handled [17]. State activities and operations can be supported if their effects can be represented as generated events and variable assignments. We have not attempted a template semantics for object creation and termination and do not describe TimeEvents in the current work.

4 Semantics of OMG UML

In this section, we describe the execution semantics of a UML StateMachine, in terms of its corresponding HTS's template parameters and composition operators. In what follows, we use OMG-UML to refer to the semantics of UML as defined by the OMG [19]. In addition, we assume that a StateMachine describes the behaviour of a UML object, and we use these two terms interchangeably.

4.1 Template Parameters

The template-parameter values for OMG-UML are listed in the second column of Table 4. To the right of each entry (i.e., the corresponding entry in the third column) are the page numbers in the OML-UML documentation [19] that contain the textual description of semantics that we used in formulating that entry's value. Unused parameters, IE and IE_a are omitted from the table.

State-Related Parameters. Rows 1-5 in Table 4 pertain to the semantics of states. We use snapshot element CS to record the set of current states. This set does not change at the start of a macro-step (i.e., **reset_CS** does not modify CS). When a transition τ executes, element CS is updated by template parameter **next_CS** to hold the states that are current, or that become current, whenever τ's destination state is entered, including the destination state's ancestors and all relevant descendants' default states.

We use snapshot element CS_a to record the states that can enable transitions ($en\_states = (src(\tau) \subseteq CS_a)$). In OMG-UML, only one compound transition can execute per macro-step. To model this semantics, CS_a is set to $dest(\tau)$ if the destination state is a pseudostate, so that only the rest of the compound transition may continue executing; otherwise, CS_a is set to $\emptyset$, thereby ending the macro-step.

Event-Related Parameters. Rows 6-10 in Table 4 pertain to event semantics. We use snapshot element I_a to hold the event that an HTS is currently processing. At the start of a macro-step, an event I from the event pool is input to the

Table 4. Template Parameter Values for Multiple UML Notations

	Parameter	OMG-UML	[19] Page#	RRT-UML	[9] Page#	RH-UML	[5] Page#	BP-UML	[23] Page#	
States	$reset\_CS(ss, I) =$	$ss.CS$	-	$ss.CS$	-	$ss.CS$	-	$ss.CS$	-	1
	$next\_CS(ss, \tau, CS')$	$CS' = active(dest(\tau))$	531	$CS' = active(dest(\tau))$	52	$CS' = active(dest(\tau))$	25	$CS' = dest(\tau)$	50, 101	2
	$reset\_CS_a(ss, I) =$	$ss.CS$	-	$ss.CS$	-	$ss.CS$	-	$ss.CS$	-	3
	$next\_CS_a(ss, \tau, CS'_a)$	**if** $pseudo(dest(\tau))$ **then** $CS'_a = dest(\tau)$ **else** $CS'_a = \emptyset$	523, 535, 547	**if** $pseudo(dest(\tau))$ **then** $CS'_a = dest(\tau)$ **else** $CS'_a = \emptyset$	52, 60	$CS'_a = active(dest(\tau))$	3, 5, 26	$\emptyset$	50	4
	$en\_states(ss, \tau)$	$src(\tau) \subseteq ss.CS_a$	556	$src(\tau) \subseteq ss.CS_a$	52	$src(\tau) \subseteq ss.CS_a$	25	$src(\tau) \subseteq ss.CS_a$	50	5
Events	$reset\_I_a(ss, I) =$	I	546	I	54	I	25	I	103	6
	$next\_I_a(ss, \tau, I'_a)$	$I'_a = \emptyset$	546	$I'_a = \emptyset$	54, 49	$I'_a = \emptyset$	26	$I'_a = \emptyset$	47, 107	7
	$en\_events(ss, \tau)$	$ss.I_a \subseteq trig(\tau)$	556	$ss.I_a \subseteq trig(\tau)$	52	$trig(\tau) = ss.I_a$	3, 25	$trig(\tau) = ss.I_a$	50	8
	$reset\_O(ss, I) =$	$\emptyset$	-	$\emptyset$	-	$\emptyset$	-	$\emptyset$	-	9
	$next\_O(ss, \tau, O')$	$O' = gen(\tau)$	557	$O' = gen(\tau)$	48, 49	$O' = gen(\tau)$	6	$O' = gen(\tau)$	47, 107	10
Variables	$reset\_AV(ss, I) =$	$ss.AV$	-	$ss.AV$	-	$ss.AV$	-	$ss.AV$	-	11
	$next\_AV(ss, \tau, AV')$	$AV' = ss.AV \oplus_? asn(\tau)$	557	$AV' = assign(ss.AV, seq\_eval(ss.AV, asn(\tau)))$	47	$AV' = assign(ss.AV, seq\_eval(ss.AV, asn(\tau)))$	7, 25	$AV' = assign(ss.AV, seq\_eval(ss.AV, asn(\tau)))$	45, 111	12
	$reset\_AV_a =$	$ss.AV$	-	$ss.AV$	-	$ss.AV$	-	N/A	-	13
	$next\_AV_a(ss, \tau, AV'_a)$	**if** $choice(dest(\tau))$ **then** $AV'_a = (ss.AV \oplus_? asn(\tau))$ **else** $AV'_a = ss.AV_a$	523	**if** $choice(dest(\tau))$ **then** $AV'_a = assign(ss.AV, seq\_eval(ss.AV, asn(\tau)))$ **else** $AV'_a = ss.AV_a$	47, 60	$AV'_a = ss.AV_a$	25	N/A	-	14
	$en\_cond(ss, \tau)$	$ss.AV_a \models cond(\tau)$	556	$ss.AV_a \models cond(\tau)$	52	$ss.AV_a \models cond(\tau)$	25	$TRUE$	-	15
	$macro\_semantics$	stable	546	stable	54, 57	stable	24	simple	50, 103	16
	pri	$pri(\Gamma) \equiv \{\tau \in \Gamma \mid \forall t \in \Gamma. rank(src(\tau)) \geq rank(src(t))\}$	547	$pri(\Gamma) \equiv \{\tau \in \Gamma \mid \forall t \in \Gamma. rank(src(\tau)) \geq rank(src(t))\}$	62	$pri(\Gamma) \equiv \{\tau \in \Gamma \mid \forall t \in \Gamma. rank(src(\tau)) \geq rank(src(t))\}$	22	N/A	-	17
	Composition	INTERR, INTL, OBJECT, MULTI-OBJECT	523, 535, 547, 555	OBJECT, MULTI-OBJECT	50, 82 83	INTERR, INTL, OBJECT, MULTI-OBJECT	14, 24 26	OBJECT, MULTI-OBJECT	104, 107	18

Key

(light shading)	Semantics that refine a semantic variation point in the OMG standard
(dark shading)	Semantics that deviate from the OMG standard
$active(s)$	States that are active when state s becomes active, including s's ancestors and relevant descendants' default states
$pseudo(s)$	Returns true if state s is a choice, junction or initial pseudostate
$choice(s)$	Returns true if state s is a choice point.
$assign(X, Y)$	Updates assignments X with the assignments Y, and ignores assignments in Y to variables that are not in X
$seq\_eval(X, A)$	*Sequentially* evaluates assignment expressions in A, starting with variable values in X and updating these as assignments are processed; returns updated variable-value assignments.
$pri(\Gamma)$	Returns the subset of transitions Γ that have highest priority.
$rank(s)$	Distance of state s from the root state. $rank(root) = 0$. $rank(S)$ returns the rank of the state with the highest rank within set S.

HTS and saved in I_a. A transition is enabled only if one of its triggers matches this event ($ss.I_a \subseteq trig(\tau)$). I_a is set to $\emptyset$ after the first transition executes; but subsequent segments of a compound transitions may still be enabled, since they have no triggers.

We use snapshot element O to hold an HTS's outputs, which are the events generated by the HTS's executing transition. These events are output in the same micro-step in which they are generated. Thus, element O need only record the events generated by the most recent transition.

Variable-Related Parameters. Rows 11-15 in Table 4 pertain to the semantics of variables. We use snapshot element AV to record the current values of variables. A transition may perform multiple variable assignments, and may even perform multiple assignments to the same variable. OMG-UML [19] does not pin down the action language, so the semantics of variable assignments, especially with respect to evaluation order or execution subset, is a semantic variation point. We use the symbol $\oplus_?$ to indicate that some of the assignments in τ's actions have an overriding effect on the variable values in AV, but that the exact semantics of this effect is left open.

We use auxiliary snapshot element AV_a to record the variable values that are used when evaluating transition guards ($ss.AV_a \models cond(\tau)$) and assignment expressions. In OMG-UML semantics, transition guards are evaluted with respect to variables' values at the start of a macro-step – unless the transition is exiting a choice pseudostate. Thus, AV_a records the variables' current values at the start of a macro-step, and is not updated during the macro-step unless an executing transition enters a choice pseudostate.

Macro-Semantics and Priority Parameters. OMG-UML has *stable* macro-step semantics, meaning that an HTS processes an event to completion before inputing the next event. With respect to priority among transitions, transitions whose source states have the highest rank (i.e., are deepest in the state hierarchy) have highest priority. Thus, substate behaviour overrides super-state behaviour. The priority of a join transition is the priority of its highest-ranked segment.

4.2 Composition Operators

We use composition operators to compose HTSs into CHTSs that represent UML StateMachines and collections of communicating StateMachines. We use *interleaving* and *interrupt* operators for intra-object composition, to create orthogonal and composite states, respectively. We also introduce two inter-object composition operators that define the behaviour of object-level composition: *object composition* defines how a single object takes a micro-step with respect to UML's run-to-completion step semantics, and *multi-object composition* defines how multiple objects execute concurrently and communicate via directed events.

Interleaving Composition. We use *interleaving composition*, defined in Section 2.3, to model orthogonal composite states. According to OMG-UML semantics [19], each orthogonal region executes at most one compound transition per run-to-completion step, and the order in which the regions' transitions, or transition segments, execute is not defined. This behaviour is captured by the micro-step interleaving operator, which allows fine-grained interleaving of HTSs and their transitions. The order in which the interleaved transitions' generated events or variable assignments occur is nondeterministic.

Interrupt Composition. We use *interrupt composition*, defined in Figure 1, to model nonorthogonal composite states that contain orthogonal substates. The semantics of execution is as described in Section 2.3: Only one of the composite state's direct substates is ever active; and in each micro-step, either the active substate executes internal transitions, or one of the interrupt transitions executes and transfers control from the active substate to another substate.

In a typical case, interrupt composition models fork and join transitions that enter or exit, respectively, an orthogonal composite state. We model forks and joins as single HTS transitions that have multiple destination states (forks) or multiple source states (joins). If a fork does not specify a destination state in one of the orthogonal regions, the macro *ent_comp* in the interrupt operator determines the region's implicit (default) destination states.

Object Composition. In OMG-UML, each active object is modelled as a StateMachine with its own event pool and thread of control[2]. An object executes by performing *run-to-completion steps*, defined as follows:

1. An event is removed from the object's event pool for the object to process.
2. A maximal set of non-conflicting enabled transitions are executed. Conflicts are resolved using priorities (reflected in template parameter **pri**)
3. The events generated by these transitions are sent to the targeted objects.
4. Steps 2 and 3 are repeated, until no more transitions are enabled.

The *object composition* operator, shown in Figure 2, defines an allowable micro-step taken by an object. Macro $stable(\overrightarrow{ss})$ determines whether a run-to-completion step has ended, meaning that no transitions are enabled. If so, then a new event e is selected from the object's event pool and is incorporated into the object's snapshots ($\text{RESET}(\overrightarrow{ss}, e)$). To effect a micro-step, the operator invokes the micro-step operator for the object's top-most hierarchical state: $\text{N}^{\text{HTS}}_{\text{MICRO}}$, if the state represents an HTS; $\text{N}^{\text{INTL}}_{\text{MICRO}}$, if the state is an interleaved CHTS; or $\text{N}^{\text{INTERR}}_{\text{MICRO}}$, if the state is an interrupt CHTS.

In OMG-UML, the order in which events are removed or added to an event pool is purposely left undefined. To model this semantics variation, we introduce new template parameters **reset_Q** and **next_Q** to specify how an event pool Q is updated with inputs from the environment or with events sent by other objects, respectively; parameter **pick** specifies how an event is selected from an event pool. The second column of Table 5 presents the parameter values for OMG-UML. We use symbols $+_?$ and $-_?$, to represent OMG-UML's undefined semantics for adding and removing events from an event pool. In addition, we

[2] UML also has the notion of a *passive object*, which contains data only and which executes only when an active object invokes one of its methods.

$$
\begin{array}{l}
\mathrm{N}^{\text{OBJECT}}_{\text{MICRO}}(\overline{\overrightarrow{ss}}, \overrightarrow{\mathcal{T}}, \overline{\overrightarrow{ss}}')(Q, Q') \equiv \\
\quad \text{if } stable(\overline{\overrightarrow{ss}}) \text{ then} \\
\qquad \exists\, \overline{\overrightarrow{ss}}^{\,r}, e \,.\, \left[\begin{array}{l} \mathbf{pick}(\overline{\overrightarrow{ss}}, Q, e, Q') \ \wedge \ \overline{\overrightarrow{ss}}^{\,r} = \text{RESET}(\overline{\overrightarrow{ss}}, e) \ \wedge \\ (\mathrm{N}_{\text{MICRO}}(\overline{\overrightarrow{ss}}^{\,r}, \overrightarrow{\mathcal{T}}, \overline{\overrightarrow{ss}}') \ \vee \ (stable(\overline{\overrightarrow{ss}}^{\,r}) \wedge \overline{\overrightarrow{ss}}^{\,r} = \overline{\overrightarrow{ss}}')) \end{array} \right] \\
\quad \text{else} \\
\qquad \mathrm{N}_{\text{MICRO}}(\overline{\overrightarrow{ss}}, \overrightarrow{\mathcal{T}}, \overline{\overrightarrow{ss}}') \wedge Q = Q'
\end{array}
$$

$$
\begin{array}{l}
\mathrm{N}^{\text{MULTI-OBJECT}}_{\text{MACRO}}((\overline{\overrightarrow{ss}}_1, ..., \overline{\overrightarrow{ss}}_n), I, (\overline{\overrightarrow{ss}}'_1, ..., \overline{\overrightarrow{ss}}'_n))(Q_1 ... Q_n, Q'_1 ... Q'_n) \equiv \\
\quad \exists\, k,\ \overrightarrow{\mathcal{T}},\ Q''_k,\ Q^r_1, ..., Q^r_n \,. \\
\qquad \left[\begin{array}{l} \forall i \,.\, 1 \leq i \leq n \,.\, Q^r_i = \mathbf{reset\_}Q(Q_i, directed\_events(I, i)) \ \wedge \\ 1 \leq k \leq n \ \wedge \ \mathrm{N}^{\text{OBJECT}}_{\text{MICRO}}(\overline{\overrightarrow{ss}}_k, \overrightarrow{\mathcal{T}}, \overline{\overrightarrow{ss}}'_k)(Q^r_k, Q''_k) \ \wedge \\ \forall i \,.\, 1 \leq i \leq n \,.\, ((i = k \rightarrow \mathbf{next\_Q}(Q''_k, directed\_events(\overline{\overrightarrow{ss}}'_k.O, k), Q'_k) \ \wedge \\ \qquad\qquad\qquad (i \neq k \rightarrow \mathbf{next\_Q}(Q^r_i, directed\_events(\overline{\overrightarrow{ss}}'_k.O, i), Q'_i)) \end{array} \right]
\end{array}
$$

Fig. 2. Multi-object and object composition

Table 5. Event-Pool Related Template-Parameter Values

	OMG-UML [19] pg. 546	RRT-UML [10] pg. 79	RH-UML [5] pg. 25	BP-UML [23] pg. 107
$pick(\overline{\overrightarrow{ss}}, Q, e, Q')$	$ready\_ev(\overline{\overrightarrow{ss}}, Q, e) \wedge$ $Q' = Q -_? e$	$e = top(Q) \wedge$ $Q' = pop(Q)$	$e = top(Q) \wedge$ $Q' = pop(Q)$	$e = top(Q) \wedge$ $Q' = pop(Q)$
$reset\_Q(Q, I) =$	$Q +_? I$	$append(Q, I)$	$append(Q, I)$	$append(Q, I)$
$next\_Q(Q, I, Q')$	$Q' = Q +_? I$	$Q' = append(Q, I)$	$Q' = append(Q, I)$	$Q' = append(Q, I)$

Key

(light shading)	Semantics that refine a semantic variation point in the OMG standard
(dark shading)	Semantics that deviate from the OMG standard
$ready\_ev(\overline{\overrightarrow{ss}}, Q, e)$	Select e such that $deferred(e, \overline{\overrightarrow{ss}}.CS) = \emptyset \vee$ $(rank(deferred(e, \overline{\overrightarrow{ss}}.CS)) \leq rank(src(\text{EN\_TRANS}(\text{RESET}(\overline{\overrightarrow{ss}}, e), \overrightarrow{\mathcal{T}}))))$
$deferred(e, S)$	Returns the subset of the states S in which event e is deferred
$X +_? Y$	Undefined operator for adding element Y to container X
$X -_? Y$	Undefined operator for removing element Y from container X
$append(Q, I)$	Appends the event sequence I to the end of Q, and returns the resulting queue
$top(Q)$	Returns the front element of queue Q
$pop(Q)$	Removes the front element from Q, and returns the resulting queue

use macro $ready\_ev(\overline{\overrightarrow{ss}}, Q, e)$ to help represent deferred events: it returns an event e that either (1) is not deferred in any current state or (2) triggers a transition whose source state has higher priority than the state(s) that defer e.

Multi-object Composition. *Multi-object composition*, shown in Figure 2, models the concurrent execution of n objects. It is a UML model's top-most composition operator, and thus defines how input events I (e.g., user inputs) and inter-object messages are handled. In each macro-step, (1) the inputs I are added to the appropriate objects' event pools, (2) some object is nondeterministically chosen to execute a micro-step, and (3) the events generated in that micro-step are added to the target objects' event pools. Macro *directed_events* filters events by their target object, returning only the events destined for that object.

5 Semantics of UML Tools

In this section, we present template-semantics descriptions for StateMachines as implemented in three UML CASE tools: Rational Rose RealTime [8]

(RRT-UML), Rhapsody [5, 11](RH-UML) and BridgePoint [1, 23](BP-UML). We then evaluate how well each tool complies with UML 2.0 semantics by comparing how well its template-parameter values match those for OMG-UML 2.0, which were presented in the last section.

The template-parameter values for the three UML CASE tools are given in Table 4, in columns 4, 6, and 8. The reference that we used in determining each parameter value is given in the table entry to the right of the parameter value.

State-Related Parameters. RRT-UML's state semantics match exactly those of OMG-UML. In RH-UML, the set of enabling states, CS_a, is always equal to the current set of states, CS. Thus, an HTS may execute multiple transitions in a macro-step, but only the first transition can have a trigger. An HTS can even get into an infinite loop if the states and variable values always enable a next transition. In BP-UML, an HTS never executes more than one transition in a macro-step, so CS_a is always empty after the first transition executes.

Event-Related Parameters. All three UML variants have similar event semantics: an input event can trigger only the first transition of a macro-step, and generated events are output (to the target objects' event pools). The only difference is that, in OMG-UML and RRT-UML, a transition may have multiple triggers ($ss.I_a \subseteq trig(\tau)$), whereas in RH-UML and BP-UML, a transition may have only one trigger ($trig(\tau) = ss.I_a$).

Variable-Related Parameters. OMG-UML does not specify how variable values are updated due to transitions' assignments. RRT-UML, RH-UML, and BP-UML all refine OMG-UML's semantics in the same way: variable values are updated in the order, left to right, in which they appear in the transition label.

In RRT-UML and RH-UML, (non-choice-point) transition guards and assignment expressions are always evaluated with respect to variable values from the start of the macro-step ($ss.AV_a \models cond$). In contrast, RH-UML does not support dynamic choice points, so its $\mathbf{next\_AV_a}$ variable values are never updated in the middle of a macro-step. BP-UML does not support guard conditions, so its predicate *en_cond* is always *true*.

Macro-Semantics and Priority Parameters. RRT-UML and RH-UML have *stable* macro-semantics, to support compound transitions (in RRT-UML) or to allow an HTS to execute multiple transitions in a macro-step (in RH-UML). In contrast, BP-UML does not support compound transitions, and its semantics allow an HTS to execute at most one transition per macro-step, so BP-UML has *simple* macro-semantics. RRT-UML and RH-UML use the same transition priority scheme as OMG-UML uses. BP-UML has no priority scheme.

Composition Operators. Neither RRT-UML nor BP-UML support orthogonal composite states. Thus, a StateMachine in these notations maps to an HTS and no intra-object composition is needed. RH-UML supports orthogonal composite states, as well as join and fork pseudostates. Moreover, the order in which orthogonal regions execute, and thus the order in which their transitions' actions take effect, is nondeterministic [5]. As a result, the *interleaving* and *interrupt* composition operators defined in Sections 2.3 apply also to RH-UML.

All three UML variants use the *object* and *multi-object* composition operators; their template-parameter values for these operators appear in columns 3-5 of Table 5. All three variants implement event pools as FIFO queues to ensure that the order of events, as generated by a transition or as sensed by the environment, is preserved during message passing. And they all deviate from OMG-UML semantics by not supporting deferred events. In RRT-UML and RH-UML, several objects may share a thread of control and an event pool for efficiency reasons [4, 15, 21], but this has no effect on the semantics of execution.

6 Evaluation

Our template-semantics description of UML 2.0 is based on OMG documents [19], supplemented by questions sent to the "Ask an Expert" facility on the OMG Website. For RRT-UML, we used the Modeling Language Guide [9], our experiences with Rational Rose RT [8], and e-mail correspondence with Bran Selic [21]. For RH-UML, we used conference papers [5], our experiences with Rhapsody [11], and e-mail correspondence with David Harel [4]. For BP-UML, we used Shlaer and Mellor's text [23], our experiences with Nucleus Bridgepoint [1], and e-mail correspondence with Campbell McCausland [15].

Because these sources are written in a combination of natural language, pseudocode, and examples, it is impossible for us to formally prove that our template-semantics descriptions accurately represent the documented semantics. Instead, we trace each of our template-semantics' parameter values to statements in these sources. We include this traceability information in Tables 4 and 5.

7 Related Work

There has been extensive work to formalize the semantics of statecharts [6, 20, 16] and to compare different semantics [22, 14]. Shankar et al. [22] describe a two-dimensional temporal logic that could be used to describe semantic variations of statecharts. Maggiolo-Schettini et al. [14] use structural operational semantics and labeled transition systems to describe the semantics of two statechart variants. In both cases, it could be argued that it would be somewhat harder to use their logics to compare statecharts variants, because it would mean comparing collections of free-form axioms rather than collections of specific template parameters.

There have been several attempts at making the semantics of UML StateMachines more precise [7, 12, 13, 24], usually to enable automated analysis. Fecher et al. [3] outline 29 new unclarities in the semantics of UML 2.0 and provide informal pointers as how to eliminate those ambiguities. To our knowledge, there has not been any other attempt to formally define and compare the semantics of different UML StateMachine variants.

Crane and Dingel [2] informally compare Rhapsody StateMachines against the UML standard. Most of their results relate to syntax, language constructs, and well-formedness constraints rather than the semantics of execution. In particular, little discussion is devoted to crucial aspects of the semantics, such as orthogonal composite states, composition operators, and event pools. Also, the differences are described using natural language, which makes an exact definition and comparison very difficult. In contrast, our work focuses on execution semantics; we use a formalism that highlights semantics variation points; and our work takes into consideration composition, concurrency, and event pools.

8 Conclusions

The contributions of this work are threefold. First, we add event-pool-related template parameters to template semantics, to model message passing between components. Second, we provide a template-semantics representation of the execution semantics of UML StateMachines, as defined by the OMG. Unlike similar work, our approach does not result in a more precise semantics of UML, but rather it results in a formal and concise description of UML semantics that highlights the semantics variation points in the standard. Third, we provide template-semantics representations for StateMachines as implemented in three UML CASE tools, showing precisely how these tools address unspecified semantics in the standard and how they deviate from specified semantics in the standard.

One of our future goals is a more comprehensive comparison of UML StateMachine variants and traditional statecharts variants, in the form of a formal version of von der Beeck's informal comparison of statechart variants [25]. In addition, we are investigating the potential of automatically analyzing UML models using tools that are semantically configured by template-parameter values.

Acknowledgments

We thank Bran Selic from IBM, David Harel from the Weizman Institute, and Campbell McCausland and Stephen Mellor from Accelerated Technology for helping us to understand the semantics details of UML StateMachines and of their respective tools.

References

1. Accelerated Technology. Bridgepoint. www.acceleratedtechnology.com/, 2005.
2. M. Crane and J. Dingel. UML vs. Classical vs. Rhapsody State machines: Not All Models are Created Equal. In *Proc. 8th Int. Conf. on Model Driven Eng. Lang. and Sys. (MoDELS/UML 2005)*, Montego Bay, Jamaica, Oct. 2005.
3. H. Fecher, J. Schönborn, M. Kyas, and W. P. de Roever. 29 New Unclarities in the Semantics of UML 2.0 State Machines. In *ICFEM 2005*, volume 3785, pages 52–65. Springer-Verlag, 2005.
4. D. Harel. Email disucssion. Email, July 2005.

5. D. Harel and H. Kugler. The RHAPSODY Semantics of Statecharts (or, On the Executable Core of the UML). In *Integration of Software Specification Techniques for Appl. in Eng.*, volume 3147 of *LNCS*, pages 325–354. Springer-Verlag, 2004.
6. D. Harel, A. Pnueli, J. P. Schmidt, and R. Sherman. On the Formal Semantics of State machines. In *Logic in Comp. Sci.*, pages 54–64. IEEE Press, 1987.
7. Z. Hu and S. M. Shatz. Explicit Modeling of Semantics Associated with Composite States in UML State machines. *Intl. Jour. of Auto. Soft. Eng.*, 2005.
8. IBM Rational. Rational Rose RealTime. http://www.ibm.com/rational, 2002.
9. IBM Rational. Rational Rose RealTime - Modeling Language Guide, Version 2003.06.00. http://www.ibm.com/rational, 2002.
10. IBM Rational. Rational Rose RealTime - UML Services Library, Version 2003.06.00. http://www.ibm.com/rational, 2002.
11. ilogix, Inc. Rhapsody. http://www.ilogix.com, 2005.
12. Y. Jin, R. Esser, and J. W. Janneck. Describing the Syntax and Semantics of UML State machines in a Heterogeneous Modelling Environment. In *Proc. 2nd Int. Conf. on Diag. Repr. and Infer. (DIAGRAMS '02)*, pages 320–334, London, UK, 2002. Springer-Verlag.
13. J. Jürjens. A UML State Machines Semantics with Message-passing. In *Proc. ACM Symp. on App. Comp.(SAC '02)*, pages 1009–1013, 2002.
14. A. Maggiolo-Schettini, A. Peron, and S. Tini. A comparison of statecharts step semantics. *Theor. Comput. Sci.*, 290:465–498, 2003.
15. C. McCausland. Email disucssion. Email, July 2005.
16. E. Mikk, Y. Lakhnech, C. Petersohn, and M. Siegel. On Formal Semantics of Statecharts as Supported by STATEMATE. In *2nd BCS-FACS Northern Formal Methods Workshop*. Springer-Verlag, 1997.
17. J. Niu, J. M. Atlee, and N. Day. Template Semantics for Model-Based Notations. *IEEE Trans. on Soft. Eng.*, 29(10):866–882, October 2003.
18. J. Niu, J. M. Atlee, and N. A. Day. Understanding and Comparing Model-Based Specification Notations. In *Proc. IEEE Intl. Req. Eng. Conf.*, pages 188–199, 2003.
19. OMG. Unified Modelling Language Specification: Version 2.0, Formal/05-07-04. http://www.omg.org, 2003.
20. A. Pnueli and M. Shalev. What is a Step: On the Semantics of Statecharts. In *Proc. TACS*, volume 526, pages 244–264. Springer-Verlag, 1991.
21. B. Selic. Email disucssion. Email, July 2005.
22. S. Shankar, S. Asa, V. Sipos, and X. Xu. Reasoning about Real-Time State machines in the Presence of Semantic Variations. In *ASE*, pages 243–252, 2005.
23. S. Shlaer and S. J. Mellor. *Object Lifecycles: Modeling the World in States.* Yourdon Press, Upper Saddle River, NJ, USA, 1992.
24. A. Simons. On the Compositional Properties of UML State machine Diagrams. In *Proc. of Rigorous Object-Oriented Methods (ROOM2000)*, York, UK, 2000.
25. M. von der Beeck. A Comparison of State machines Variants. In *Formal Techniques in Real Time and Fault-Tolerant Systems*, volume 863 of *LNCS*, pages 128–148. Springer-Verlag, 1994.

Facilitating the Definition of General Constraints in UML

Dolors Costal, Cristina Gómez, Anna Queralt, Ruth Raventós, and Ernest Teniente

Dept. Llenguatges i Sistemes Informàtics, Universitat Politècnica de Catalunya
{dolors, cristina, aqueralt, raventos, teniente}@lsi.upc.edu

Abstract. One important aspect in the specification of conceptual schemas is the definition of general constraints that cannot be expressed by the predefined constructs provided by conceptual modeling languages. In general this is done by means of general-purpose languages, like OCL. In this paper we propose a new approach to facilitate the definition of such general constraints in UML. More precisely, we define a profile that extends the set of UML predefined constraints with some types of constraints that are used very frequently in conceptual schemas. We also study the application of our ideas to the specification of two real-life applications and we show how results in constraint-related problems may be easily incorporated to our proposal.

1 Introduction

An information system maintains a representation of the state of a domain in its information base (IB). The conceptual schema of an information system must include all relevant knowledge about the domain. Hence, the structural conceptual schema defines the structure of the IB while the behavioral conceptual schema defines how the IB changes when events occur. In UML, structural conceptual schemas are represented by means of class diagrams [14].

A complete conceptual schema must include the definition of all relevant integrity constraints [6]. The form of the definition of such constraints depends on the conceptual modeling language used [10]. Some constraints are inherent in the model in which the language is based. This is the case, for example, of referential constraints in UML class diagrams. Nevertheless, almost all constraints require an explicit definition. Most conceptual modeling languages offer a number of special constructs for defining some of them. In particular, UML offers graphical constructs for constraints such as multiplicity and also provides a set of predefined constraints which includes, for instance, association "xor" constraints and "disjoint" constraints.

However, there are many types of constraints that cannot be expressed using predefined constructs. These are general constraints whose definition requires the use of a general-purpose sublanguage. With this objective, UML provides OCL [12, 15]. The use of OCL is not mandatory and the UML designer may use other languages for writing general constraints such as Java or C++ or even natural language.

There are some problems associated to the definition of general constraints through general-purpose languages. Constraints defined in natural language are often imprecise and ambiguous. Editing OCL constraints manually, although providing the means to write constraints with a precise semantics, is time-consuming and error-prone and

O. Nierstrasz et al. (Eds.): MoDELS 2006, LNCS 4199, pp. 260–274, 2006.

OCL expressions may be difficult to understand for non-technical readers. Moreover, an automatic treatment of those constraints (either for reasoning or for automatic code generation) may be difficult to achieve.

For these reasons, it becomes necessary to reduce the extent of cases in which constraints must be defined through general-purpose languages. In this sense, we propose to extend the set of UML predefined constraints with some types of constraints that are used very frequently in conceptual schemas. We make the extension by defining a UML profile, the standard mechanism that UML establishes to incorporate new constructs to the language. The application of this profile has been studied in the specification of two real-life applications: the EU-Rent Car Rentals system [4] and a conceptual schema for e-marketplaces [13].

Our proposal facilitates the definition of general constraints in UML since it decreases significantly the number of constraints that must be defined and, consequently, it reduces the scope of the problems associated to their use.

Our approach provides also important advantages regarding the automatic treatment of constraints. In particular, our profile easily allows incorporating previous results on reasoning about constraint-related problems (such as satisfiability or redundancy) and facilitates obtaining an automatic implementation of the constraints. In this way, another contribution of our work is to show the significant advantages provided by the use of constraint stereotypes in conceptual modeling.

The rest of the paper is organised as follows. Next section illustrates the problems regarding the definition of general constraints. Section 3 presents our profile, whose application to two case studies is discussed in Section 4. Section 5 shows how to reason about the constraints specified in our profile. Section 6 reviews related work while, finally, Section 7 presents our conclusions and points out future work.

2 Problems in the Definition of General Constraints

There are some problems associated to the definition of general constraints. We will illustrate them according to the example in Figure 1 which refers to a fragment of a system that supports teaching activities of a University. The structural schema shows the definition of courses and their sections. It also contains information on teachers, their course of expertise and their assignment to sections. The structural schema includes eight general constraints, whose specification as OCL invariants is given in Figure 1: 1) Courses are identified by their name; 2) Courses are identified by their code; 3) Teachers are identified by the union of their name and last name; 4) Each section is identified by its number within each course; 5) A course cannot be directly or indirectly prerequisite of itself; 6) Teachers assigned to sections of a course must be experts in that course; 7) The size of sections cannot be greater than 80; 8) Courses must have at least a lecturer or a professor.

If general constraints are defined in natural language, they are often imprecise and ambiguous and their interpretation and treatment remain as a human responsibility. In our example, the previous descriptions of the constraints may be subject to wrong interpretations because they do not establish unambiguously their precise meaning.

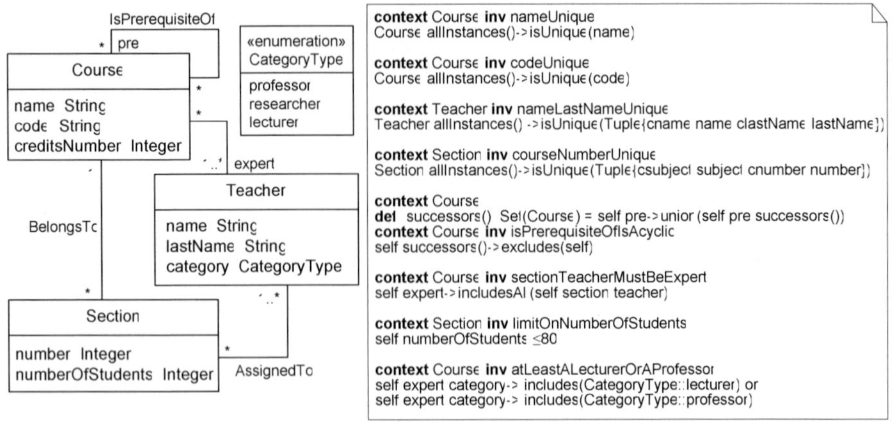

Fig. 1. Fragment of the class diagram for the example application

This problem may be avoided by using formal general-purpose languages such as OCL. Formal languages provide the means to write constraints with precise semantics. Nevertheless, we can also identify some disadvantages of using them:

- Difficulty of understanding for non-technical readers. For example, previous constraints would not be easy for readers not familiar with OCL.
- Time-consuming definition: the designer must define explicitly the underlying semantics of each particular constraint. Additionally, in the frequent case in which there are groups of constraints that share common semantic aspects, the complete semantics of all these constraints must be defined for each individual constraint. This happens, for example, in the definition of textual constraints *nameUnique*, *codeUnique*, *nameLastNameUnique* and *courseNumberUnique* of Figure 1.
- Error-prone definition: formal languages are sometimes difficult to use for the designers inducing the possibility of mistakes. For instance, the constraint *isPrerequisitOfIsAcyclic* is not easily defined in OCL. Moreover, the designer could use '`includes`' instead of '`includesAll`' in constraint *sectionTeacher-MustBeExpert* and then the expression would be wrong.
- Difficulty of automatic treatment: constraints expressed by means of general-purpose languages are very difficult to interpret automatically since they do not have a pre-established interpretation that can be easily incorporated to CASE tools. The lack of easy automatic interpretation has the following consequences on the automatic treatments that may be performed:
  - Some well-studied rules that allow reasoning about the constraints cannot be automatically applied.
  - Constraint semantics are difficult to incorporate to subsequent models generated automatically and, in particular, to code generation. This is a drawback towards obtaining one of the goals of the MDA, i.e., making the transformation from platform-independent models (PIMs) to platform-specific models (PSMs) as automatic as possible [11].

From the above listed difficulties, we can conclude that it is interesting to reduce the extent of cases in which UML constraints must be defined using general-purpose languages. Next section presents our proposal in this direction.

3 Predefining Constraints

A constraint is a condition expressed in natural language or in a machine readable language to add some semantics to an element. UML offers a number of graphical constructs to define some common constraints, such as multiplicity. In addition, certain kinds of constraints, such as a disjoint constraint, are predefined in UML, but there are many others that cannot be expressed using these constructs and their definition requires the use of a specific language, such as OCL.

There are, however, some kinds of user-defined constraints that occur very frequently in conceptual schemas. For instance, a very prominent kind of constraint is the *identifier constraint* [5, 8], which may have several realizations such as *nameUnique* or *codeUnique* for a given class, i.e., either the attribute *name* or the attribute *code* uniquely identify instances of said class.

In this section we present our proposal to extend the set of predefined constraints offered by UML. We use the standard extension mechanism provided by UML, the definition of a profile [12, 14, 15], to achieve this goal. In particular, we define a set of stereotypes that provide some additional semantics to UML constraints that play the role of invariants.

We have defined stereotypes for some of the most frequent generic kinds of constraint, namely uniqueness, recursive association, path comparison and value comparison constraints. The use of these stereotypes allows the designer to avoid defining explicit expressions to specify the corresponding constraints every time they appear. Instead, these constraints can be graphically represented in the class diagram, and, optionally, can be generated automatically in OCL.

Once applied our stereotypes to the example in Figure 1, seven out of the eight textual constraints (all except the last one) could be expressed graphically in the class diagram, making unnecessary their definition in natural language or in OCL.

Since one of the main goals of our paper is to illustrate the advantages provided by the use of constraint stereotypes in conceptual modeling, we have not intended to be exhaustive as far as the extent of constraints we are able to predefine. Instead, we have selected here the most representative ones to stress our contribution. The representation of other constraints in our approach as well as the complete details of the profile may be found in [2].

3.1 UML Profile for Predefined Constraints

Our profile contains a set of stereotypes that extend the semantics of a constraint. Thus, the metaclass *Constraint* of the UML metamodel is extended by means of several stereotypes representing generic kinds of constraints, divided in four groups according to their semantics. The metaclass *Constraint* refers to a set of *constrainedElement*, i.e. those elements required to evaluate the constraint. The *context* of *Constraint* may be used as a *namespace* for interpreting names used in the expression. Each constraint has an associated *OpaqueExpression* that includes the constraint expression and the language used to define it. Each instance of *Constraint* represents a user-defined constraint, which may play the role of invariant, precondition, postcondition or body condition of an operation.

Figure 2 shows the abstract stereotype *PredefinedConstraint,* with four subtypes: *Uniqueness, RecursiveAssociation, PathComparison* and *ValueComparison* stereotypes. *PredefinedConstraint* defines those features shared by all constraints that are instances of this stereotype. In particular, the constraint cannot be a precondition, postcondition or body condition of an operation (since we only deal here with class diagram constraints), and the language of the associated *OpaqueExpression* may be either OCL (if the designer chooses to represent the constraint also in this language) or it is left empty (if only the graphical representation is selected). This profile has been defined in such a way that additional stereotypes can be easily extended by defining additional subtypes of *PredefinedConstraint.*

Also, we provide a UML-compliant notation that allows using these stereotypes in a class diagram. Each instance of a stereotype is represented by means of a stereotyped constraint tied to the corresponding model elements. For those stereotypes requiring additional information from the designer, values can be indicated in a comment attached to the stereotyped constraint.

3.1.1 Uniqueness Constraints

A uniqueness constraint defines a uniqueness condition over the population of a class. We distinguish two types of uniqueness constraints: the *identifier constraint* and the *weak identifier constraint.*

Identifier constraint. Let *A* be a class with a set of attributes *{a1,...,an}*. An *identifier constraint* specifies that a subset *{ai,...,aj}* of those attributes uniquely identifies the instances of *A*. This constraint may be expressed in OCL as follows, where *cai,...,caj* are the named parts of the tuple:

context A **inv:** A.allInstances()->isUnique(Tuple{cai=ai,...,caj=aj})

Weak identifier constraint. Let *A* be a class with a set of attributes *{a1,...,an}* and associated, via the member end *b*, to a class *B*. A w*eak identifier constraint* specifies that a subset *{ai,...,aj}* of those attributes, combined with *B*, uniquely identifies the instances of *A*. This constraint may be formally expressed in OCL as follows:

context A **inv:** A.allInstances()->isUnique(Tuple{cb=b,cai=ai,...,caj=aj})

To specify these constraints we define the abstract stereotype *Uniqueness,* with two concrete subtypes *Identifier* and *WeakIdentifier,* shown in Figure 2. Since these stereotypes define uniqueness conditions over a set of attributes of a class, their *constrainedElement* must be of type *Property.* Additionally, this stereotype has a constraint that guarantees that none of those attributes has the lower bound of their multiplicity equal to zero, otherwise this identifier would not be valid.

An example of the *identifier constraint* is *nameLastNameUnique,* shown in Figure 1. It states that instances of *Teacher* are identified by the union of their *name* and *lastName*. The constraint *courseNumberUnique* corresponds to the *weak identifier constraint*, since it states that each instance of *Section* is identified by its *number* within each instance of *Course*.

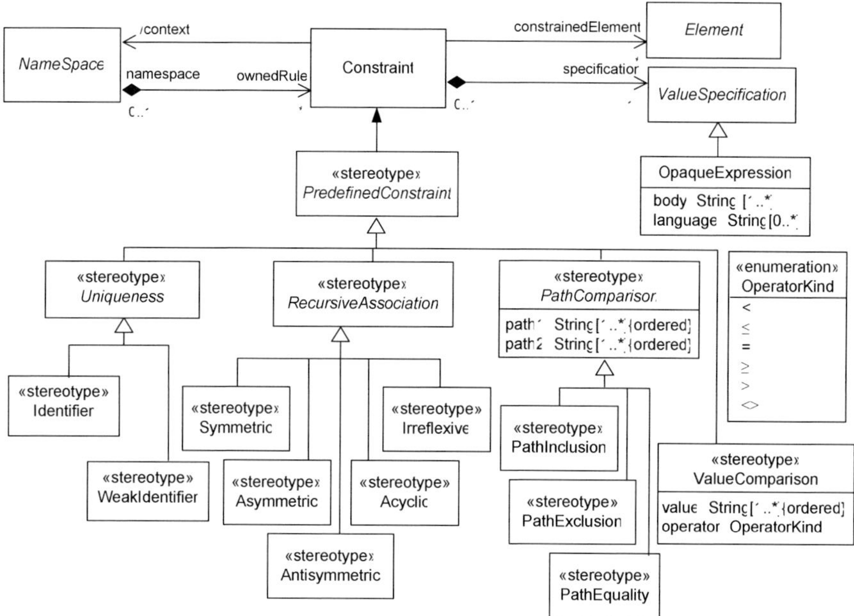

Fig. 2. UML Profile for Predefined Constraints

Figure 3 shows the use of the corresponding *Uniqueness* stereotypes to represent the constraints *nameLastNameUnique* and *courseNumberUnique* stated above. There is a dashed line between the constraint with the corresponding stereotype and its constrained elements.

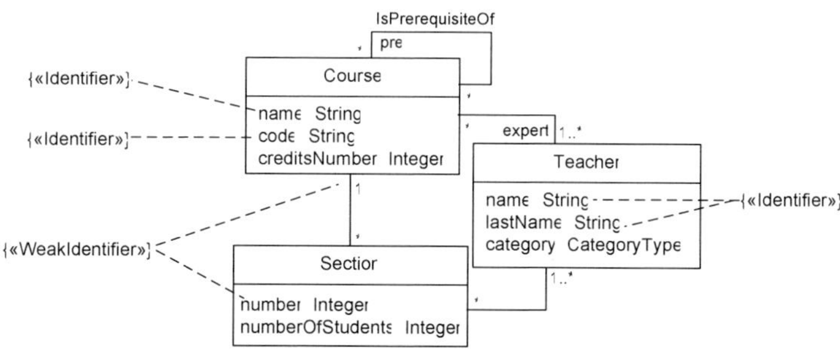

Fig. 3. Example of the use of *Identifier* and *WeakIdentifier* stereotypes

3.1.2 Recursive Association Constraints

Recursive association constraints, called ring constraints in [5], are a type of constraints that apply over a recursive binary association, guaranteeing that the association fulfills a certain property. We consider five types of those constraints: *irreflexive*, *symmetric*, *antisymmetric*, *asymmetric* and *acyclic* constraints.

Irreflexive constraint. Let *A* be a class and *R* a recursive association over *A*, with *r1* a member end. An irreflexive constraint over *R* guarantees that if *a* is instance of *A* then *a* is never R-related (i.e. directly linked by R) to itself. This constraint may be formally expressed in OCL as follows:

context A **inv:** self.r1->excludes(self)

Symmetric constraint. Let *A* be a class and *R* a recursive association over *A*, with *r1* a member end. A symmetric constraint over *R* guarantees that if *a* and *b* are instances of *A* and *a* is R-related to *b* then *b* is R-related to *a*. Formally, in OCL:

context A **inv:** self.r1.r1->includes(self)

Antisymmetric constraint. Let *A* be a class and *R* a recursive association over *A*, with *r1* a member end. An antisymmetric constraint over *R* guarantees that if *a* and *b* are instances of *A*, *a* is R-related to *b* and *b* is R-related to *a*, then *a* and *b* are the same instance. In OCL:

context A **inv:** self.r1->excludes(self) implies self.r1.r1->excludes(self)

Asymmetric constraint. Let *A* be a class and *R* a recursive association over *A*, with *r1* a member end. An asymmetric constraint guarantees that if *a* and *b* are instances of *A* and *a* is R-related to *b* then *b* is not R-related to *a*. Observe that this constraint is equivalent to the union of antisymmetric an irreflexive constraints. It may be expressed in OCL as follows:

context A **inv:** self.r1.r1->excludes(self)

Acyclic constraint. Let *A* be a class and *R* a recursive association over *A*, with *r1* a member end. An acyclic constraint guarantees that if *a* and *b* are instances of *A* and *a* is R-related to *b* then *b* or instances R-related directly or indirectly to *b* are not R-related to *a*. Formally, in OCL:

context A
def: successors(): Set(A) = self.r1->union(self.r1.successors())

context A
inv: self.successors()->excludes(self)

We have grouped these constraints in an abstract constraint stereotype *RecursiveAssociation,* which constrains recursive binary associations. As can be seen in Figure 2, it has a concrete subtype for each one of the five kinds of recursive association constraint.

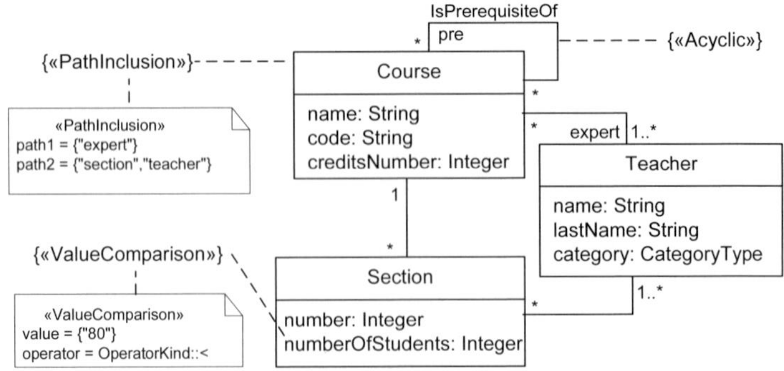

Fig. 4. Applying Acyclic, PathInclusion and ValueComparison stereotypes

In the example of Figure 1, *isPrerequisiteOfIsAcyclic* is a constraint of this type that applies to the recursive association *isPrerequisiteOf*. Figure 4 shows the definition of this constraint as an instance of the *Acyclic* stereotype.

3.1.3 Path Comparison Constraints

Path comparison constraints restrict the way the population of one role or role sequence (path for short) relates to the population of another [5]. Constraints belonging to this type are *path inclusion, path exclusion* and *path equality*. They all apply to a class *A* related to a class *B* via two different paths *r1...ri*, *rj...rn*.

Path inclusion constraint. A path inclusion constraint guarantees that if *a* is an instance of *A*, the set of instances of *B* related to *a* via *r1...ri* includes the set of instances of *B* related to *a* via *rj...rn*. It can be expressed in OCL as follows:

context A **inv:** self.r1...ri->includesAll(self.rj...rn)

Path exclusion constraint. A path exclusion constraint guarantees that if *a* is an instance of *A*, the set of instances of *B* related to *a* via *r1...ri* does not contain any of the instances of *B* related to *a* via *rj...rn*. Formally, in OCL:

context A **inv:** self.r1...ri->excludesAll(self.rj...rn)

Path equality constraint. A path equality constraint guarantees that if *a* is an instance of *A*, the set of instances of *B* related to *a* via *r1...ri* coincides with the instances of *B* related to *a* via *rj...rn*. In OCL, this constraint is expressed as follows:

context A **inv:** self.r1...ri = self.rj...rn

We propose to define path comparison constraints as instances of the abstract stereotype *PathComparison*. The *constrainedElement* associated to an instance of *PathComparison* is an element of type *Class,* which is the start of both paths. As shown in Figure 2, the stereotype includes two attributes, *path1* and *path2*, that represent the paths to be compared. A constraint ensures that the classes reached at the end by both paths are the same. *PathComparison* has a subtype for each kind of path comparison constraint.

In the example of Figure 1 *sectionTeacherMustBeExpert* is a path inclusion constraint that applies to a class *Course* related to a class *Teacher* via two different paths: *expert* and *section.teacher*. Figure 4 shows the definition of this constraint as an instance of the stereotype *PathInclusion*.

3.1.4 Value Comparison Constraints

Value comparison constraints restrict the possible values of an attribute, either by comparing it to a constant or to the value of another attribute [1].

Let *A* be a class, let *a1* be an attribute of *A*, let *v* be either a constant or the value of an attribute accessible from *A* and let *op* be an operator of kind <, >, =, <>, ≤, or ≥. A value comparison constraint restricts the possible values of *a1* regarding the value of *v*. This constraint can be formally expressed in OCL as follows:

context A **inv:** self.a1 *op* v

We propose to define value comparison constraints as instances of the stereotype *ValueComparison*, shown in Fig. 2. The *constrainedElement* associated to an instance of *ValueComparison* is an element of type *Property*, not belonging to an association and with multiplicity 1. The stereotype includes two attributes, *operator* and *value*.

The former is an enumeration of the different kinds of operators (*OperatorKind*) that may be used in the comparison and the latter specifies the value to be compared to the attribute, which can be a constant or the value reached by a path. In any case, the type of the value represented in *value* must conform to the type of the constrained attribute.

For instance, in the example of Fig. 1, the constraint *limitOnNumberOfStudents* is a value comparison constraint that applies to the attribute *numberOfStudents*. Fig. 4 shows its definition as an instance of *ValueComparison* stereotype.

3.2 Creating the Instances of an Stereotype

To be able to specify new predefined constraints, for each stereotype we have also defined an operation that allows creating its instances. This operation associates to each new instance its corresponding context, constrained elements and specification. This specification has an empty *body* attribute if the designer only desires a graphical representation. Otherwise, if the designer also requires the definition of the OCL expression, the operation assigns to the *body* attribute the expression automatically generated according to the type of constraint.

As an example, the operation *newIdentifier* allows to create an instance of the *Identifier* stereotype. The parameters needed are a class, the set of attributes that identify each of its instances, the name of the constraint and the way to represent this constraint in the schema which is an enumeration of two values *ocl* and *graphically*. The value *ocl* indicates that the constraint will be represented graphically and textually in OCL and the value *graphically* indicates that the representation will be only graphical. The postconditions guarantee that a new instance of *Identifier* will be created, the constrained elements will be the set of properties and the namespace will be the indicated class. Moreover, depending on the value of the representation parameter the constraint will be represented graphically and textually in OCL or represented only graphically. This operation can be defined in OCL as follows:

```
context Identifier::newIdentifier(c:Class, a:Set(Property), name:String[0..1],
                                  representation:RepresentationType)
 let ident = 'Tuple{'.concat(Sequence{1..a->size()}-> iterate(pn; s: String = '' | s.concat((if
      (pn>1) then ', ' else'' endif).concat ('c').concat(a->at(pn). name).concat (': ').concat
      (a-> at(pn). name)))).concat('}') in
 post: id.oclIsNew() and id.oclIsTypeOf(Identifier) and
      id.constrainedElement -> includesAll(a.name) and
      c.ownedRule->includes(id) and
      id.name=name and
      expr.oclIsNew() and expr.oclIsTypeOf(OpaqueExpression) and
      id.specification = expr and
      representation=RepresentationType::ocl implies
           expr.language = 'OCL' and expr.body = 'context '.concat(id.context.name).
           concat(' inv ').concat(name).concat(': ').concat(c.name).concat('.allInstances()->
           isUnique('). concat(ident).concat(')')
```

The whole set of operations to create instances of our stereotypes may be found in [2]. In a similar way we could define operations to delete instances of our stereotypes which are also necessary to remove integrity constraints.

4 Case Study

This section summarises the results obtained from the application of our profile to the specification of two real-life applications. The analysis of both schemas allows us to stress the advantages of using the profile. In particular, we have analysed a conceptual schema for the well-known EU-Rent Car Rentals system [4] and we have also studied a generic conceptual schema for the e-marketplace domain [13].

EU-Rent is a (fictitious) car rental company with branches in several countries. The company rents cars to its customers who may be individuals or companies. Different models of cars are offered, organized into groups and cars within a group are charged at the same rates. The class diagram we have studied consists of 59 classes, 50 associations and 40 constraints that require an explicit definition. Our profile allows us to avoid specifying in OCL a considerable amount of said constraints. Only 14 out of 40 do not correspond to any of our stereotypes and, thus, a specific OCL expression needs to be constructed to specify them.

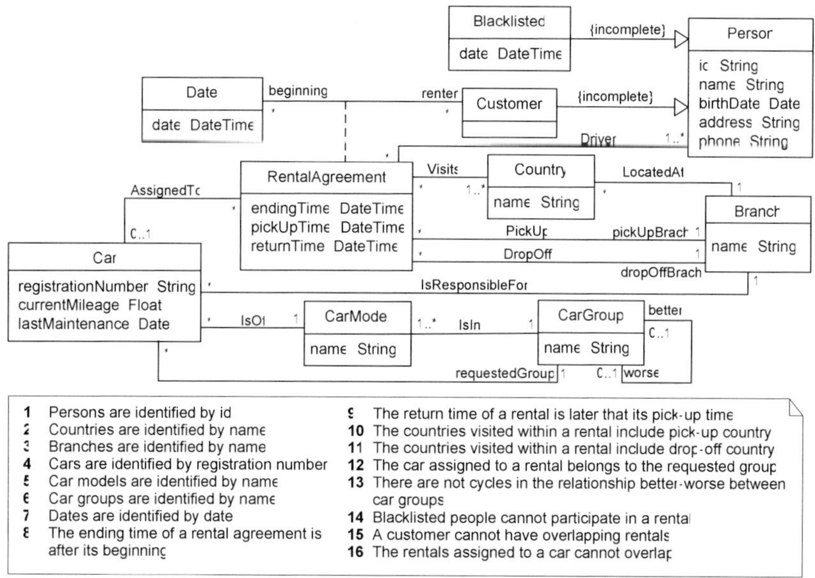

Fig. 5. Fragment of EU-Rent class diagram

Figure 5 shows a small fragment of the EU-Rent class diagram (10 classes and 16 constraints) to further illustrate the conclusions we have drawn from the development of this case study. The first seven constraints may be specified by applying the *Identifier* stereotype since they state the attributes that identify each class. Constraints 8 and 9 may be specified by applying the *ValueComparison* stereotype. Constraints 10 and 11 correspond to the *PathInclusion* stereotype; 12 corresponds to the *PathEquality* stereotype and 13 corresponds to the *Acyclic* stereotype. Finally, constraints 14, 15 and 16 do not match any of our predefined constraints and thus an ad-hoc OCL expression must be built to specify them.

The second case study consists of the specification of a generic conceptual schema for the e-marketplace domain [13] which covers the main functionalities provided by an e-marketplace: determining product offerings, searching for products and price discovery. The whole specification includes 40 classes, 15 associations and 41 constraints that require an explicit definition. After analysing the constraints, the results obtained are quite similar to those obtained with EU-Rent. In this case, the success rate is a bit lower, about 54% instead of 65% as before, but still interesting. This means that we have to specify manually only 19 out of 41 OCL constraints.

From the results of both case studies, we see that it has been possible to use our stereotypes almost in 60% of the constraints, by reducing the number of OCL expressions from 81 to 33.

5 Reasoning and Generating Code

One of the main benefits of the proposed profile is the ability to reason about constraints represented as instances of our stereotypes and their automatic code generation into a given technological platform. In the following we show how our profile facilitates reasoning about constraint satisfiability and constraint redundancy. We outline also how to use the profile to generate code for checking those constraints in a relational database.

5.1 Constraint Satisfiability

A conceptual schema is *satisfiable* if it admits at least one legal instance of the IB. For some constraints it may happen that only the empty or non-finite IBs satisfy them. In conceptual modeling, the IBs of interest are finite and may be populated. We then say that a schema is *strongly satisfiable* if there is at least one fully populated (i.e each class and association has at least one instance) instance of the IB satisfying all the constraints [7]. Otherwise, the schema is incorrect.

Constraint satisfiability has received a lot of attention in conceptual modeling. For instance, [5] presents in the Euler diagram in Figure 6 the relationships between recursive association constraints. Some satisfiability rules can be deduced from the figure. For instance, a recursive association with an acyclic and a symmetric invariant is not strongly satisfiable because there can not exist instances in the IB of the corresponding association that satisfy, at the same time, both invariants.

Unfortunately, and as a consequence of problems associated to the definition of general constraints, known results in constraint satisfiability checking cannot be applied to the definition of constraints by means of general-purpose languages. For example, in Figure 1, the designer could define another constraint that defines the

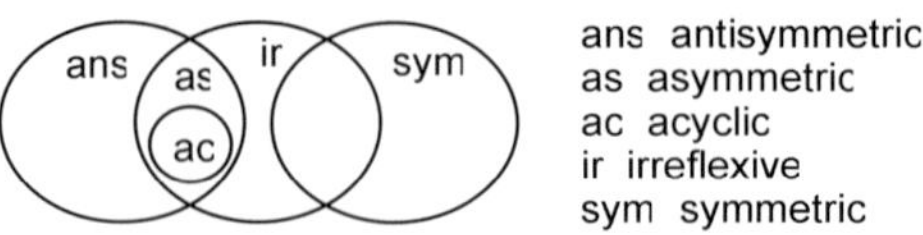

Fig. 6. Relationships between recursive association constraints

association *isPrerequisiteOf* as symmetric. As explained before, this new invariant makes the schema incorrect.

Our proposal allows us incorporating easily some of these results. In fact, the definition of predefined constraints as stereotypes permits to attach new constraints that represent well-studied satisfiability rules that detect if a set of constraints is strongly satisfiable. Table 1 summarizes the stereotypes and the constraints we have attached to them to incorporate the results presented in [5]. Other known results for constraint satisfiability can be incorporated in the same way.

Table 1. Validation of recursive association constraints

Stereotype	Constraint attached to the stereotype
Symmetric	There cannot be another instance of acyclic, asymmetric nor antisymmetric constraint for the same association
Antisymmetric	There cannot be another instance of symmetric constraint for the same association
Asymmetric	There cannot be another instance of symmetric constraint for the same association
Acyclic	There cannot be another instance of symmetric constraint for the same association

5.2 Constraint Redundancy

A conceptual schema is *redundant* if an aspect of the schema is defined more than once [3]. For instance, a constraint is redundant with respect to another constraint if in each state of the IB that violates the second constraint the first one is also violated.

Table 2. Redundancy of recursive association constraints

Stereotype	Constraint attached to the stereotype
Irreflexive	There cannot be another instance of asymmetric nor acyclic constraint for the same association
Antisymmetric	There cannot be another instance of asymmetric nor acyclic constraint for the same association
Asymmetric	There cannot be another instance of antisymmetric nor irreflexive nor acyclic constraint for the same association
Acyclic	There cannot be another instance of asymmetric nor antisymmetric nor irreflexive constraints for the same association

We may also draw from the diagram shown in Figure 6 some rules that permit to detect some redundancies between recursive association constraints. For example, an acyclic constraint is redundant with respect to an asymmetric constraint of the same association because asymmetric associations are always acyclic.

Our proposal also easily allows incorporating results on constraint redundancy. Table 2 summarizes the stereotypes and the constraints we have attached to them to incorporate rules that detect redundancies between recursive association constraints. Other results can be incorporated in a similar way.

5.3 Automatic Code Generation

Many UML CASE tools offer code generation capabilities. However, most of them do not generate the code required to check whether constraints defined in general-purpose languages are violated by the execution of a transaction. We outline in this section how our profile may be used to facilitate such important task.

As we have seen, each stereotype explicitly states a precise semantics for the type of constraints it defines. Semantics may be taken into account during code generation to determine the most adequate translation from the conceptual schema to a particular technology. Thus, assuming an implementation on a relational database, identifier constraints could be translated into primary key or unique constraints; weak identifiers into foreign key plus primary key constraints; value comparisons into check constraints and other constraints by means of triggers or stored procedures. For example, classes Course, Section and their constraints would be translated as follows:

```
CREATE TABLE Course (
  name   char(30)   PRIMARY KEY,
  code   char(30)   UNIQUE,
  creditsNumber int   NOT NULL)
```

```
CREATE TABLE Section (
  nameCourse   char(30),
  number       int,
  numbOfStud   int CHECK (numbOfStud < 80),
  PRIMARY KEY (nameCourse, number),
  CONSTRAINT fkSect  FOREIGN KEY (nameCourse)
                     REFERENCES Course(name) )
```

6 Related Work

In this section, we analyze other works that contribute to facilitating the definition of general constraints in UML.

Executable UML (xUML) is a UML profile that allows defining an information system in sufficient detail that it can be executed [8]. As part of its proposal, xUML extends the set of constraints that can be graphically specified. In particular, it covers our uniqueness constraints and some kinds of path comparison constraints, i.e. path equality and path inclusion. Considering the EU-Rent and the e-marketplace case studies, xUML would cover only 28% of the constraints instead of the 60% covered by our proposal. Moreover, we provide the profile definition in terms of the UML 2.0 metamodel including the definition of the creation operations that permit to add instances to the stereotypes.

Ackermann [1] proposes a set of OCL specification patterns that facilitate the definition of some integrity constraints, namely what we call identifier constraints and a subset of value comparison constraints. When applied to our case studies it covers only 26% of the constraints. This approach is based on the automatic generation of OCL expressions from a set of patterns and, thus, it does not extend the language via a profile definition as we propose. Consequently, it does not extend the set of UML predefined constraints which facilitates their graphical representation. Furthermore, it does not use the established mechanisms to extend the language and, thus, it can not be directly incorporated to UML CASE tools.

In [9] a taxonomy of integrity constraints (which includes constraints that are inherent, graphical and user-defined in UML) is described. However, despite the authors advocate the definition of stereotypes for some of them, the stereotypes are not developed. They only mention that model elements such as associations and attributes should be taken as base class for their definition. We think instead that all the proposed stereotypes should be stereotypes of *Constraint*. The reasons are that the semantics of *Constraint* corresponds to the purpose of the stereotypes, it permits to graphically represent the incorporated constraints similarly to predefined constraints and, finally, it facilitates a uniform treatment of the incorporated constraints together with the rest of constraints of a UML class diagram.

In addition to already stated drawbacks of previous proposals, we must note that none of them deals with the ability to reason about the general constraints they may handle.

7 Conclusions and Future Work

We have proposed a new approach to facilitate the definition of general constraints in UML. Our approach is based on the use of constraint stereotypes in conceptual modeling and it allows specifying as predefined UML constraints some types of general constraints that are frequently used, instead of having to specify them by means of a general-purpose sublanguage such as OCL.

By being able to specify general constraints as predefined constraints we overcome the limitations of having to define them manually which may usually imply a time-consuming and error-prone definition, difficulty of understanding (since the reader may not be familiar with the formal language used to define the general constraint) and difficulty of automatic treatment (since general constraints do not have a pre-established interpretation while predefined ones do).

We have applied our approach to the specification of two real-life applications: the EU-Rent Car Rentals system [4] and a conceptual schema for the e-marketplace domain [13], and we have seen that 60% of the general constraints of those case studies may have been specified as predefined by means of our stereotypes.

Finally, we have also incorporated into our stereotypes previous results regarding constraint satisfiability and constraint redundancy checking. This has been easily done by attaching to our stereotypes well-established rules that detect whether a set of constraints is strongly satisfiable [5] and redundancies between recursive association constraints. We have also outlined how to automate code generation from our profile to check integrity constraints in a relational database.

Since one of the main goals of our paper has been to illustrate the advantages provided by the use of constraint stereotypes, we have not intended to be exhaustive in the extent of predefined constraints considered. Future work may involve the definition of other types of frequent general constraints. We also plan to incorporate into our stereotypes other known results for reasoning about constraints and to further develop the automatic code generation from our stereotypes.

Acknowledgments. We would like to thank Antoni Olivé for suggesting us this work, and Jordi Cabot, Jordi Conesa, and Maria Ribera Sancho for helpful discussions and comments on previous drafts of this paper. This work has been partially supported by the Ministerio de Ciencia y Tecnología under project TIN2005-06053.

References

1. Ackermann, J., Turowski, K.: A Library of OCL Specification Patterns for Behavioral Specification of Software Components. In Proc. CAiSE'06, LNCS 4001 (2006) 255-269
2. Costal, D., Gómez, C., Queralt, A., Raventós, R., Teniente, E.: Facilitating the Definition of General Constraints in UML (extended version). Technical Report LSI-06-14-R, http://www.lsi.upc.edu/dept/techreps (2006)
3. Costal, D., Sancho, M. R., Teniente, E.: Understanding Redundancy in UML Models for Object-Oriented Analysis. In Proc. CAiSE'02, LNCS 2348 (2002) 659-674
4. Frías, L., Queralt, A., Olivé, A.: EU-Rent Car Rentals Specification. Technical Report LSI-03-59-R, http://www.lsi.upc.edu/dept/techreps (2003)
5. Halpin, T.: Information Modeling and Relational Databases: From Conceptual Analysis to Logical Design. Morgan Kaufmann (2001)
6. ISO/TC97/SC5/WG3, J.J. van Griethuysen (Ed.): Concepts and Terminology for the Conceptual Schema and the Information Base (1982)
7. Lenzerini, M., Nobili, P.: On the Satisfiability of Dependency Constraints in Entity-Relationship Schemata. Information Systems 15(4) (1990) 453-461
8. Mellor, S.J; Balcer, M.J.: Executable UML: A Foundation for Model-Driven Architecture. Object Technology Ed. Addison-Wesley (2002)
9. Miliauskaitė, E; Nemuraitė, L.: Representation of Integrity Constraints in Conceptual Models. Information Technology and Control, 34(4) (2005)
10. Olivé, A.: Integrity Constraints Definition in Object-Oriented Conceptual Modeling Languages. In Proc. ER'03, LNCS 2813 (2003) 349-362
11. OMG: MDA Guide Version 1.0.1, omg/2003-06-01 (2003)
12. OMG: UML2.0 OCL Specification, OMG Adopted Specification (2005)
13. Queralt, A., Teniente, E.: A Platform Independent Model for the Electronic Marketplace Domain. Technical Report LSI-05-9-R, http://www.lsi.upc.edu/dept/techreps (2005)
14. Rumbaugh, J., Jacobson, I., Booch, G.: The Unified Modeling Language Reference Manual, Second Edition, Addison-Wesley (2005)
15. Warmer, J., Kleppe, A.: The Object Constraint Language: Getting Your Models Ready for MDA. 2nd edn. Addison-Wesley Professional (2003)

Towards a MOF/QVT-Based Domain Architecture for Model Driven Security

Michael Hafner, Muhammad Alam, and Ruth Breu

Universität Innsbruck, Institut für Informatik, Techniker Straße 21a,
A – 6020 Innsbruck
{m.hafner, muhammad.alam, ruth.breu}@uibk.ac.at

Abstract. The SECTET-framework realizes an extensible domain architecture for the collaborative development and management of security-critical, inter-organizational workflows. Models integrate security requirements at the abstract level and are rendered in a visual language based on UML 2.0. The models form the input for a chain of integrated tools that transform them into artefacts configuring security components of a Web services-based architecture. Based on findings of various projects, this contribution has three objectives. First, we detail the MOF based metamodels defining a domain specific language for the design of inter-organizational workflows. The language supports various categories of security patterns. We then specify model-to-model transformations based on the MDA standard MOF-QVT. The mappings translate platform independent models into platform specific artefacts targeting the reference architecture. Third, we exemplarily show how model-to-code transformation could be implemented with an MDA-framework like OPENARCHITECTUREWARE.

1 Introduction

The SECTET-framework supports business partners during the development and distributed management of a common Global Workflow - a decentralized, security-critical collaboration across domain boundaries. The approach weaves three paradigms - each one pushed by a major standardization initiative - into an extensible framework for Model Driven Security. Based on a methodological standard (Model Driven Architecture [1]), an architectural paradigm (Service Oriented Architecture [2]) and a technical standard (Web services [3]), SECTET realizes a domain architecture aiming at the correct technical implementation of domain-level security patterns. Security requirements are integrated into the specification of a Global Workflow as UML 2.0 model artifacts. The models form the input for a chain of integrated tools that transform the models into artefacts configuring security components of a Web services-based target architecture. The framework consists of three core components.

The ***Modeling Component*** supports the collaborative definition of a Global Workflow and related security requirements at the abstract level in a platform independent context. It implements an intuitive domain specific language (DSL), which is rendered in a visual language and is currently implemented as a UML 2.0 profile for MAGICDRAW [4].

O. Nierstrasz et al. (Eds.): MoDELS 2006, LNCS 4199, pp. 275 – 290, 2006.

The ***Reference Architecture*** represents a Web services based target runtime environment for the Local Workflows and back-end services at the partner node. The workflow and security components implement a set of workflow and security technologies based on XML- and Web services technologies and standards.

The ***Transformation Component*** translates the models into executable configuration artifacts for the Reference Architecture. In a first phase, the component was prototypically implemented with XSLT technology [5]. Models were exported from UML tools as XMI files, parsed by the transformation component and transformed according to rules scripted into templates. The opportunity to apply the approach to different scenarios (e.g., e-government and health-care) gave rise to a set of requirements whose integration into the framework was essential to its usability in a real-life context. Nevertheless, some of them touched the conceptual foundations and questioned some of the early design decisions. Among them was the choice of XSLT for code-generation from respective models. XSLT – a lightweight technology for the transformation of XML documents - perfectly fits the needs of a research project looking for an easy to use technology for the rapid development of a demonstrator tool as a proof-of-concept. Nevertheless, the technology showed its limitations. New requirements in the form of more complex security requirements were constantly emerging. The domain language had to be extended syntactically and the adaptation of XSLT templates to more complex transformation functions took a great deal of time. The handling of XSLT revealed as being too cumbersome. Consequently, the transformation component was redesigned from scratch. Based on OMG's transformation specification MOF Query /View/Transformation (QVT) [6], the prototypical component now supports an intuitive rule-based mapping between platform independent source and platform specific target models. Source and target models can easily be defined or adapted by importing the respective metamodels. This supports domain experts in rapidly developing and adapting a domain specific language in an agile way and visualizes the transformation process.

This contribution has three objectives. First, we detail the metamodels, which integrate a language for modelling inter-organizational workflows and various security patterns to an intuitive domain specific language. We then specify transformations based on QVT. Third, we exemplarily show how model-to-code transformation can be implemented with an MDA-framework like OPENARCHITECTUREWARE.

The paper is organized as follows: section 2 sketches the background and summarizes related work. Section 3 gives an overview of the conceptual foundations of the SECTET-framework in context of a case study from e-government. In Section 4, we present the three parts of the domain architecture: the domain specific language, the QVT-based transformations and extensions and we exemplarily show how models are translated into code for the configuration of a Reference Architecture. Section 5 closes with a conclusion and an outlook on future work.

2 Background

2.1 Standards and Technology

The term **Web services** commonly refers to a set of technologies for platform neutral interaction. It specifies a software interface definong a collection of operations that can be accessed over a network through standardized XML messaging. XML-based protocols describe an operation to execute or data to exchange with another service. Currently, a comprehensive set of Web services security standards is emerging. OASIS has proposed a security extension built on top of the SOAP Protocol [7]. The extension uses the XML encryption and signature mechanism to add security features. Besides transport level security extensions, a variety of standards provides means to manage and exchange security policies. The eXtensible Access Control Markup Language (XACML) [8] is an OASIS standard supporting the specification of authorization policies to access (Web) services. The Role Based Access Control profile of XACML 2.0 extends the standard for expressing policies that use role based access control with a scope confined to core and hierarchical RBAC [9].

Service Oriented Architectures (SOA) and Web services are often referenced to as interchangeable concepts, but they represent two distinct concepts. Web services specifications define the technical detail for services implementation and their interaction. The concept of SOA represents an associated architectural paradigm and expands the focus towards the realization of distributed systems that deliver application functionality. It supports end-to-end integration of services across domain boundaries. SOA may be realized using other technologies as well (e.g., CORBA).

The growing popularity of standards related to Web services, workflows and security fosters the implementation of powerful infrastructures supporting interoperability for inter-organizational workflows. The paradigm of **Model Driven Architecture** (MDA) [10] makes it possible to realize their full potential. The OMG is promoting the approach as a means for the reduction of development costs and the improvement of application quality. The main idea is the switch of focus from technical detail to more abstract concepts, that are principally more stable, change less, and more intuitive. A concept is captured through a model at different levels of abstraction. In the context of software engineering, a model is an abstract representation of some system structure, function, or behaviour. MDA specifies three levels of abstraction. The Platform Independent Model captures the domain level knowledge and abstracts from implementation details of the target architecture. The Platform Specific Model (PSM) describes the system on its intended platform by integrating platform specific syntax and semantics. The Implementation Specific Model (ISM) represents the target architecture that acts as the runtime environment at local partner nodes. Applying the MDA approach means capturing abstract domain-level specification in a PIM, transforming the PIM into a PSM through model-to-model Transformation and / or transforming either the PIM directly or the PSM into an ISM through model-to-code Transformation.

Model Driven Security (MDS) extends the MDA approach in the sense that security requirements are integrated at the abstract level into the PIM. The PIM is mapped onto the PSM and translated into artefacts configuring security components of the runtime environment.

2.2 Related Work

Workflow Security. Security extensions for workflow management systems are treated in [11], [12], [13] and [14] although at a quite technical level. [15] proposes an approach for integrating security at different levels of abstraction in the system development cycle, but the full potential of a model driven approach, linking abstract domain-level models to their technical implementation, is not yet exploited. With our contribution, we claim to fill exactly this gap.

(Model Driven) Security Engineering. We identified three major areas of work related to ours. In [16] the author presents an approach for the application of pattern-based software development to recurring problems in the domain of security. The basic idea is to capture expert-knowledge in the security domain and make it available to developers as a security pattern during software development. The approach provides an in-depth view of security patterns, the development-process through an ontology based knowledge base, and describes the relationship between various security patterns. Although the author uses patterns to systematically capture knowledge about security issues at the model level, the semantics remain close to the technical level. The author does not address transformation in any way. Our approach raises the level of abstraction and also provides a methodology to systematically transform abstracts models into runtime artefacts. In [17], the authors introduce the concept of Model Driven Security for a software development process that supports the integration of security requirements into system models. The models form the input for the generation of security infrastructures. However, the approach focuses exclusively on access control in the context of application logic and targets object oriented platform (.Net and J2EE). Our approach differs in many ways. First, we consider various categories of secrutiy requirements, access control being alone one of them. Second, we raise the level of abstraction and consider security from the perspective of domain experts realizing inter-organizational workflows. And third, we define security patterns in terms of their language. [18] presents a verification framework for UML models enriched with security properties through a UML profile called UMLSec. The framework stores models using XMI format in a Meta Data Repository, which is then queried using Java Metadata Interfaces by different analyzers. These analyzers perform static as well dynamic analysis on the UMLSec models for security properties like confidentiality and integrity. This approach is orthogonal to ours and the abstraction is close to the technical level, whereas our framework is domain specific and focuses on the systematic generation of (standard) security artefacts specified during the early phases of software development. Our objective is to develop abstract languages for the realization of security requirements in distributed systems.

Tools and Frameworks. In [19] the author describes an implementation, where a local workflow is modelled in a case-tool, exported via XMI-files to a development environment and automatically translated into executable code for a BPEL-Engine based on web services. Nevertheless, the approach does not provide any facilities for the integration of security requirements at the modelling level nor does it support the specification of global workflows by means of peer-to-peer interactions as suggested by the concept of abstract processes in [20].

MDA-frameworks provide the plumbing technology for the implementation of domain architectures. They provide the means to define metamodels, to specify model transformations and templates for code generation. ANDROMDA [21] is an open source MDA-framework that provides metadata-handling facilities through the Apache Velocity template language. The framework uses the NETBEANS metadata repository (MDR) [22] for storing metadata and a set of cartridges for access to the MDR. A major drawback of the framework is the complexity involved in defining extensions. OPENARCHITECTUREWARE (OAW) is another framework that provides a more generic solution for domain specific engineering [23]. The reason is that it is open to other modelling frameworks like Eclipse Modelling Framework [24] or tools like MAGICDRAW [4]. Its template language XPAND provides an intuitive way to generate any kind of data from specified models.

3 Conceptual Foundation

In this section, we give an overview of the conceptual foundations by introducing a motivating example, which is drawn from a case that was elaborated within the project SECTINO [25]. The project's vision was defined as the development of a framework supporting the systematic realization of e-government related workflows. After a clarification of the concept Model Driven Security, we present the main definitions of the problem domain and give an exemplary overview of the framework's two orthogonal model views.

3.1 Model Driven Security

Model Driven Security (MDS) is based on ***Model Driven Software Engineering*** and OMG's related standardization initiative ***Model Driven Architecture*** (MDA) in so far as ***Security Requirements*** are realized according to specifications at the model level by model transformation and partial or complete code generation. A framework for MDS realizes a ***Domain Architecture*** (DA) aiming at the correct technical implementation of security patterns. A DA consists of a ***Domain Specific Language*** (DSL), a ***Reference Architecture*** (RA) and ***Model Transformations***. A DSL corresponds to a modelling language that captures key-aspects of a problem domain in a formal way based on the domain's metamodels. The SECTET framework caters to the needs of a specific domain. In our case, the domain is defined as the area of "Security-critical, Inter-organizational and Distributed Workflow Scenarios". Transformations take models from a problem domain and translate them into solutions for a RA. In this way, the RA represents the means to realize the domain. We differentiate between ***Model-to-Model Transformations***, which take a source model and translate it into a target model, and ***Model-to-Code Transformations***, which take the source model and directly generate code for the RA.

3.2 Definitions of the Problem Domain

A ***Global Workflow*** (GWf) specifies the message flow between partners in a distributed environment with no central control. A GWf emerges through the interaction of instances of ***Local Workflows*** executed on a ***Workflow Management System*** (WFMS) hosted in the ***Domains*** of ***Partners***. Our approach is based on two orthogonal views: the ***Interface View*** and the ***Workflow View***. The latter is further divided into the ***Global Workflow Model*** (GWfM) specifying the message exchange between cooperating partners, and the ***Local Workflow Model*** (LWfM), that describes the application and the workflow logic, which is local to each partner. The

Interface View represents the contractual agreement between the parties to provide a set of services. It specifies the minimum set of technical and domain level constraints and thereby links the GWfM to the LWfM. It describes the interface of every partner's services independently of their usage scenario and consists of four sub-models: the Document Model, the Interface (Sub-) Model, the Access Model and the Role Model.

3.3 Model Views

3.3.1 The Workflow View

The example GWf `AnnualStatement` in Figure 1 captures an inter-organizational process in an e-government case study. The workflow describes a Web services based collaboration between three `Partner_Roles` in terms of the interactions in which the participating parties engage: a taxpayer (`Company`), a business agent (`TaxAdvisor`) and a public service provider (`Municipality`).

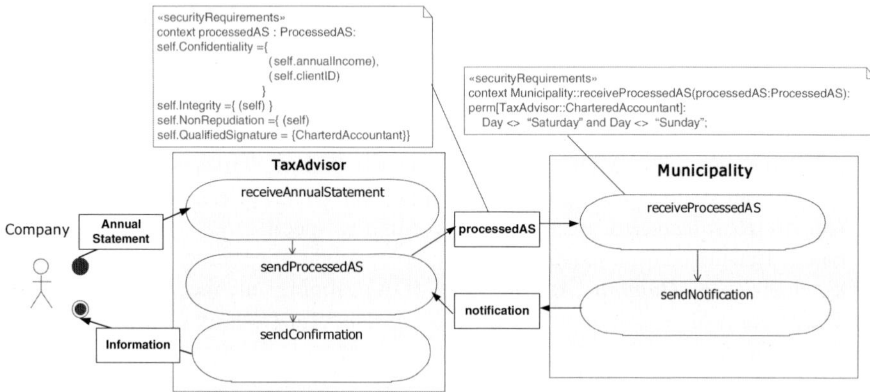

Fig. 1. Global Workflow Model as UML 2.0 Activity Diagram

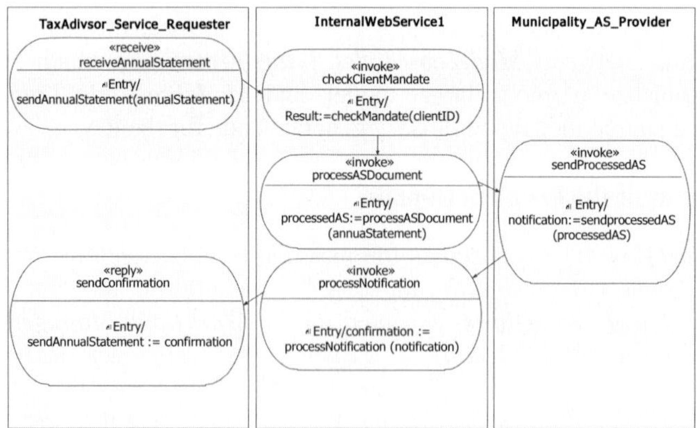

Fig. 2. Local Workflow Model for the `Partner_role TaxAdvisor`

Model information is confined to "observable behavior", corresponding to the message flow between the participants, the interaction logic and the control flow between the elementary actions. End-to-end message security requirements are specified by associating a constraint box to document nodes, whereas dynamic constraints are associated to interfaces.

Figure 2 shows an activity diagram capturing some aspects of the LWfM to be implemented by the `Partner_role TaxAdvisor`. The parts where the local workflow interacts with other partners' workflows are generated from the GWfM (`receiveAnnualStatement sendConfirmation`, and `sendProcessedAS`).

Every actor will have to complement the part accessing his local logic (corresponding to the port `InternalWebService1`). With these additions every user holding a `Partner_role` can then generate WS-BPEL and WSDL files for his execution environment (e.g., using MDA tools like UML2BPEL [19]).

3.3.2 The Interface View

The *Interface View* links the GWfM to the LWfM. It describes the interface of every partner independently of its usage scenario and represents a contractual agreement between the parties to provide a set of services based on the minimum set of technical (operation signatures, invocation style (e.g., synchronous), formats etc.) and domain level constraints, thereby guaranteeing a considerable level of local design autonomy. The Interface View consists of four sub-models:

The *Role Model*, modelled as a UML class diagram specifies the roles accessing the services in the global application scenario and the relationship between them. The *Interface Model* describes a collection of abstract operations. They represent services the component offers to its clients, accessible over some network. The parameters are either basic type or classes in the Document Model. Pre- and post-conditions in OCL-style may put constraints on service behaviour. The *Document Model* specifies the application-level information and the structure of the documents that are exchanged by the partners in the workflow or the application scenario. We model it as a UML class diagram representing the data type view of those partners participating in the interaction. The GWFM and the four models of the Interface View carry all information needed by the workflow and security components of the reference architecture to implement the secure distributed workflow. The application of orthogonal perspectives allows us to combine the design of the components that provide the services that may be part of various global workflows, each one realizing a particular usage scenario. In our scenario, partners have already implemented the application logic and made it available as a Web service.

3.3.3 Workflow Security

Security Objectives provide a generic categorization of security needs of assets that need to be taken care of in order to reach a specific state of security. Literature commonly identifies four basic security objectives [26]. Confidentiality is the goal that data should be readable to actors with appropriate permission. Integrity is the goal that data and information should not be altered if not explicitly allowed. Accountability is the goal that actions should be traceable to the actor who performed it. Availability is the goal that assets will be available as intended when needed. Composite security objectives can be derived from one or more of the four basic security properties (e.g., privacy and authorization are forms of confidentiality). We introduce the term ***Security Requirements*** to underscore the use of the concept of security objectives in the context of security engineering. Secure solutions are realized through the framework with the help of ***Security Patterns***, thereby capitalizing on trusted technology and best practices in the area of security. Summarizing, security requirements are elaborated during requirements analysis and integrated into the models of the Workflow and the Interface View in the design phase and realized with the help of security patterns integrated into the framework. They are then translated into executable configuration artefacts for target architectures. Our framework currently supports the following categories of security requirements:

Basic Workflow Security Requirements. (Module SECTINO) allow the specification of a secure document exchange satisfying End-to-End Security, which means that the requirements are satisfied even in case of being routed via intermediaries. Documents or parts of them can be qualified with the basic security requirements of Confidentiality, Integrity, Non-repudiation of Sending/Reception. The integration into the framework was extensively covered in [27], [28] and [29].

Advanced Workflow Security Requirements. (Module SECTET-Extensions). Many scenarios have to integrate security patterns that satisfy complex legal or business-driven requirements. In most cases, they are based on the basic requirements of confidentiality, integrity, or non-repudiation. The Qualified Signature – covered in [27] - is an e-government specific requirement that extends the concept of the system signature, which is used to guarantee integrity to a legal entity (e.g., a citizen).

Authorization Constraints (Module Authorization)**.** Static Constraints support modelling User-Role and Permission-Role Assignment according to Role Based Access Control. Dynamic Constraints, which are the focus of this contribution, specify conditions under which a role has the right to access services in the Access Model with the help of an extended OCL-style predicate logic [30]. The right to call an operation of a specific Web service may depend either on the caller's role or on parameters that may depend on the system's environment or sent together with the service call.

Referring back to Figure 1 in Section 3.3.1, the document `processedAS` flowing from the `TaxAdvisor` to the `Muncipality` is required to comply to requirements of integrity, non-repudiation and confidentiality (two parts of the document `annualIncome` and `clientId` are encrypted with recipient's key). The constraint associated to the action `receiveProcessedAS` specifies that only a qualified accountant – defined as the role `CharteredAccountant` of the internal role hierarchy of the `Partner_Role TaxAdvisor` - be permitted to submit a statement and this only on working days. The constraint specifies that the `CharteredAccountant` has to refer to an internal role assigned to a natural person. The actor holding the role `TaxAdvisor` has to assign the `Domain_Role CharteredAccountant` to a corresponding internal role. Through this specification, the partner commits himself to assign only qualified persons to the role.

For a detailed account on the conceptual foundation of Basic and Advanced Workflow Security Requirements within the SECTET framework and their application in the context of an e-government case study, please refer to a series of accompanying papers (e.g., [25], [30]and [31]).

4 Domain Architecture

In this section, we present the three parts of the domain architecture. First, we introduce the domain specific language, which is defined through MOF-based metamodels. Second, we specify the transformations of platform independent models of the DSL into platform specific models based on MOF-QVT and third, we exemplarily show, how PSMs are translated into code.

4.1 Metamodels

We differentiate between metamodels for defining the GWfM, the LWfM, the models of the Interface View (Role, Interface and Document Model) and the metamodels specifying the categories of security requirements. Figure 3 shows the core classes of the security metamodel. Each one of the three classes of security requirements references elements of models of the Workflow and / or the Interface View and is implemented as a single Module within the SECTET framework.

The class `WorkflowSecurityRequirements` allows the modelling of basic workflow security requirements, `DocumentSecurityRequirements` supports the modelling of advanced workflow security requirements and `AuthorizationConstraints` provides the means to specify static and dynamic constraints on interfaces. The class `StaticConstraintExpression` supports modelling User-Role and Permission-Role Assignment according to Role Based Access Control. In this contribution, we focus on the class `DynamicConstraintExpression` and its dependency on model elements of the Interface View and its references to elements of the GWfM.

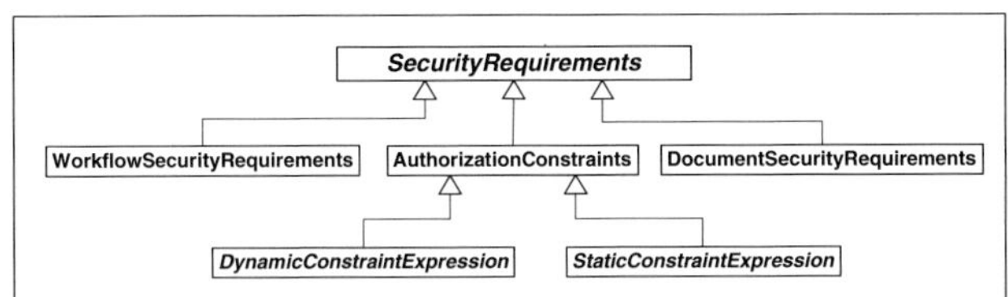

Fig. 3. Overview of Security Metamodel

4.1.1 Platform Independent Models

Figure 4 shows the three metamodels of the Interface View, which are relevant for the modelling of authorization constraints.

Figure 5 shows the metamodel for security requirements of the category `AuthorizationConstraints` (grey shaded box). Four of the model's classes reference elements of other models, which is done by association to elements representing proxy classes (e.g., `ResourceRef`, `ActorAttributeRef`): 1.) a `ResourceRef` references the resource to be protected, 2.) an `ActorAttributeRef` defines attributes of a specific Actor assigned to a Role, 3.) a `RoleRef` references the role, and 4.) an `AssociationEndRef`

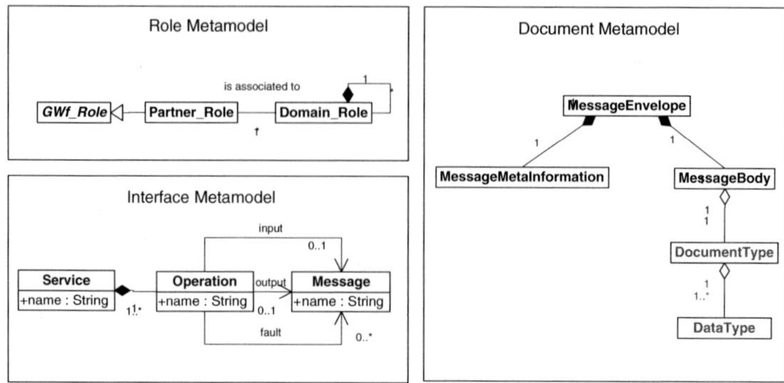

Fig. 4. Metamodels of Models of the Interface View

is a construct specific to the constraint language SECTET-PL, referencing any association end in the metamodels. A `Permission` contains a `ResourceRef` - either a `Service`, an `Operation` in the Interface Model or a `Message` or a `DocumentType` in the Document Model – a `RoleRef` and a `SECTETPLExp`. According to the constraint in our example (Figure 1 in Sect. 3.3.1), we show `ResourceRef` referencing an `Operation`.

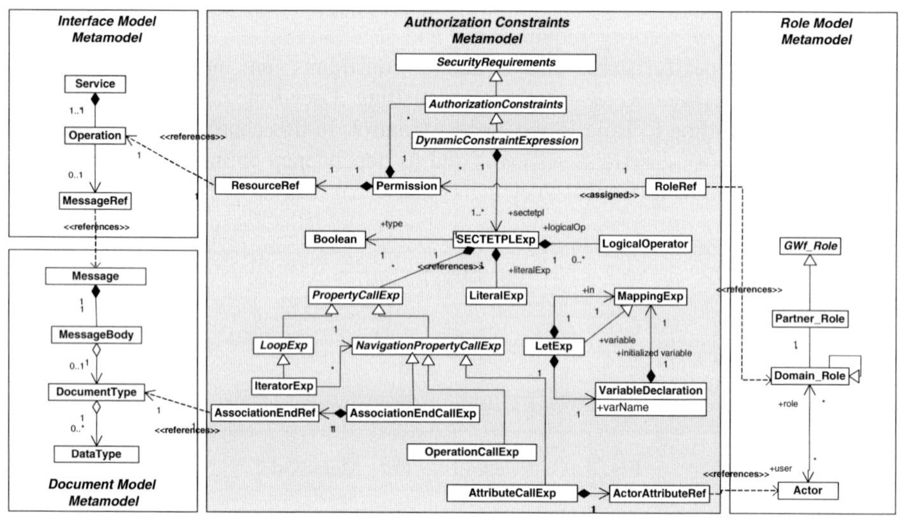

Fig. 5. Metamodel for Authorization Constraints and References to Other Models

The abstract syntax of language SECTET-PL is defined through the element `Permi-ssion`, which is composed of one or more `SECTETPLExp` elements. The `SECTETPlExp` defines the structure of constraint expressions. It is the super class of all other expressions in the metamodel. The return type of this expression class is a `Boolean`. Other expression classes like `PropertyCallExp` define navigation expressions to actor attributes (`ActorAttributeRef`), associations (`AssociationsEndRef`) and operations, services or messages (`ResourceRef`). `LiteralExp` defines string or integer values and the `MappingExp` defines a function that maps the caller of an operation to a model element (`subject.map()` not used here). The class `IteratorExp` extends the class `LoopExp` and implements a loop evaluating its body over a collection of elements. The result of an `IteratorExp` can be a either a single value, set of values or a Boolean value depending on the collection operation used (e.g., `select`, `selectOne`, `forAll`). For a detailed description of the SECTET-PL language, please refer to [30].

4.1.2 Platform Specific Model

Figure 6 shows the extended metamodel of the target model. In our case, it is the abstract syntax of XACML. The grey shaded box defines the syntax for specifying conditions according to a specific syntax pattern. In a further step, the instance of the platform specific model will be transformed into code.

Figure 7 shows an Instance of the Source Model for a Permission Policy Set for the Role `TaxAdvisor`, according to which he is permitted to access the `Municipality`'s interface on working days (see Fig. 1, Sect. 3.3.1).

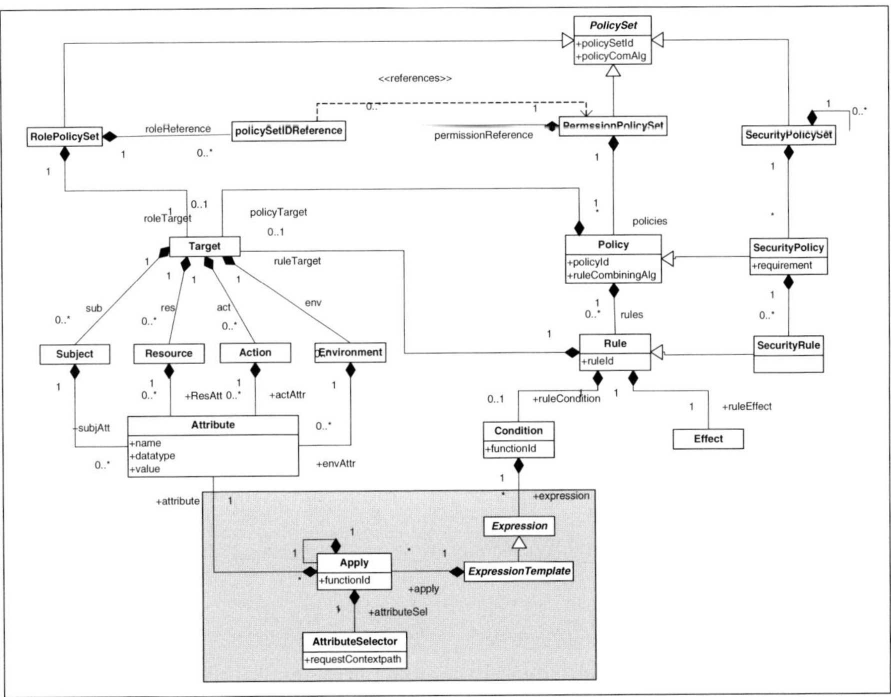

Fig. 6. Abstract Syntax of XACML as Target Model

Figure 8 shows the corresponding instance of the target model. Every source model is translated into a Role Policy Set and a Permission Policy Set. The latter is referenced through its `policyId`.

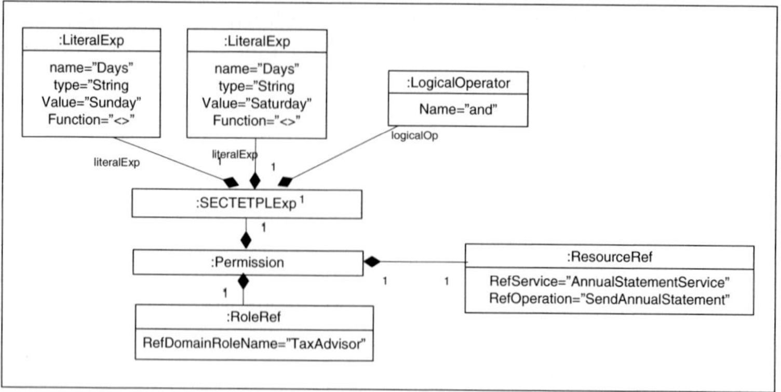

Fig. 7. Instance of Source Model for Constraint "`Access on Working Days only`"

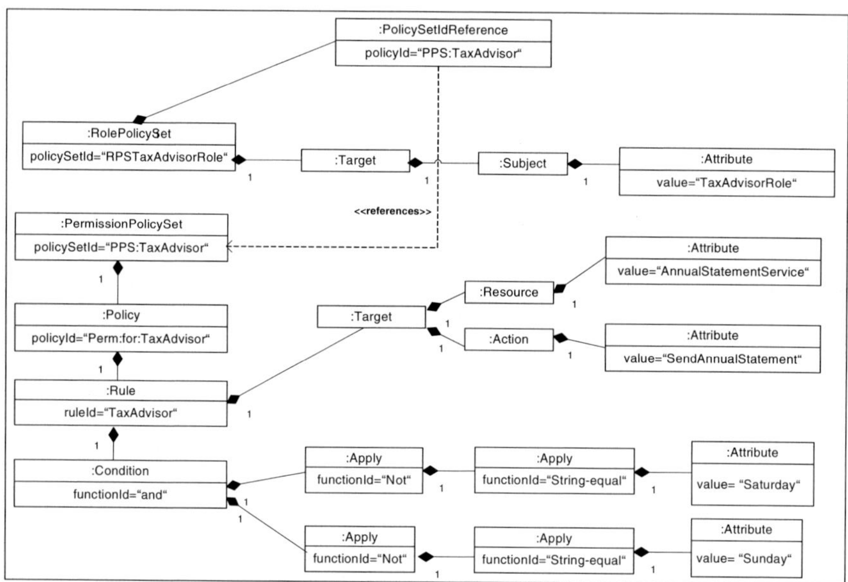

Fig. 8. Instances of Target Model (Role and Permission Policy Set)

4.2 Model Transformation

For the sake of brevity, we subsequently confine ourselves to a partial presentation of the mapping from source to target models. For a comprehensive mapping, please refer to technical reports in [33].

Figure 9 shows an excerpt from the scripts used to transform the domain model to the XACML policy metamodel. The transformation (line 1) defines two typed candidate models: `dm` of type `DomainModel` and `xacml` of type `XACML`. For a successful transformation from `dm` to `xacml`, the set of relations defined within the transformation must hold. Here, the transformation `DomainModelToXACML` contains a relation

```
1 transformation DomainModelToXACML(dm:DomainModel,xacml:XACML)
2 {
3    top relation RoleRefToRolePolicySet
4    {
5         rn:String;
6         domain dm r:RoleRef {
7                             name = rn,
8                             } // end of Domain RoleRef
9         domain xacml rps:RolePolicySet {
10        policySetid = "RPS:" + rn,
11        . . . .
12        . . . .
13   }//top relation RoleRefToRolePolicySet
14   top relation PermissionToPermissionPolicySet
15   {
16        rn:String;
17             domain dm p:Permission {
18             roleref = r:RoleRef {
19                         name = rn,
20             } //RoleRef
21             sectetpl = sec:SECTETPLEXP{
22             logicalOp = logop:LogicalOperator{
23                         name=opName;
24             } //LogicalOperator
25        . . . .
26        . . . .
27        . . . .
28        domain xacml pps:PermissionPolicySet {
29        policySetid = "PPS:for" + rn,
30        . . . .
31        . . . .
32   }//top relation PermissionToPermissionPolicySet
```

Fig. 9. Excerpt of QVT Transformation Functions

RoleRefToRolePolicySet (line 3) which defines two domains RoleRef from the domain dm (line 6) and RolePolicySet from the domain xacml (line 9). According to the QVT specification, these domains define distinguished typed variables that are used to match a model of a given type and related patterns. The domain RoleRef (line 6) contains a pattern, which matches to the model element RoleRef within the domain dm. The name attribute in RoleRef is bound to the variable rn (line 7). These variables are used to exchange information between metamodels e.g. the variable rn is used in the domain RolePolicySet (line 10) to make a pattern of the form policySetId = "RPS"+rn. This pattern implies that the relation RoleRefToRolePolicySet will only hold if RoleRef has the same name as rn and RolePolicySet has the same policySetid as "RPS" + rn (+ means concatenation). Domains can contain nested patterns as well.:e.g. SECTETPLExp (line 21) contains a pattern LogicalOperator which binds the value of the attribute name from the model element LogicalOperator to opName.

4.3 Implementation

Figure 10 shows an excerpt of the XPAND-language script used to transform the XACML RolePolicySet instance model to XACML policy files. The script starts with an IMPORT statement (line 1) that imports the instance model package data. The DEFINE (line 2) statement defines a link to the metamodel class for which this template is defined. Within this definition, the EXPAND statement (line 3) defines another definition block with different variable context (rps in this case) and works as a subroutine.

Line 6 defines the corresponding definition block for the EXPAND statement (line 3). This definition block starts with a FILE statement (line 7) and is used to redirect the output from its body statements to the specified target. The attribute policySetid of the RolePolicySet instance is used as the filename (<<policySetid>>+".xml") within the FILE statement. The Subject of the Target is populated with the name attribute of the corresponding RolePolicySet instance (line 13). The <PolicySetIdReference> element is populated with the PermissionPolicySet (PPS) id of the RolePolicySet (line 21). Figure 11 shows an example RolePolicySet (RPS) generated for the XACML metamodel instance TaxAdvisor (namespaces are omitted for brevity).

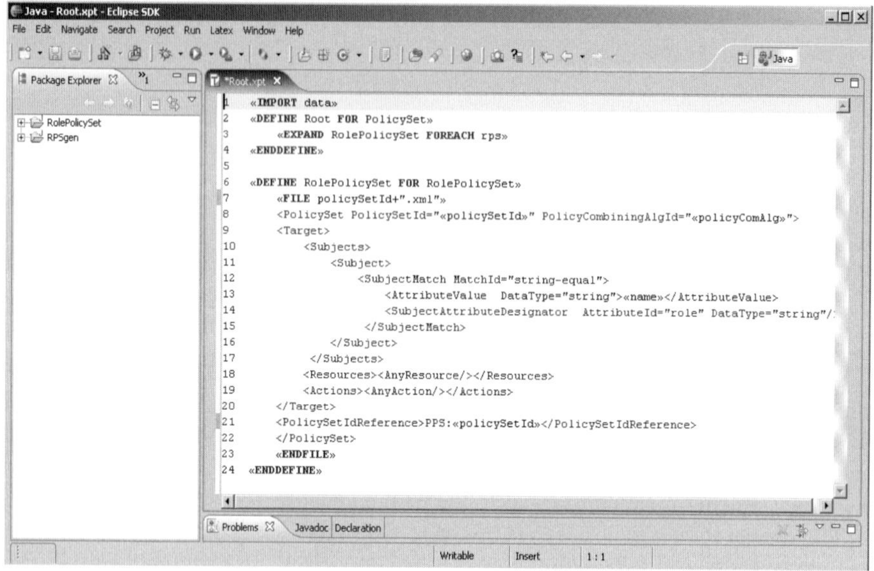

Fig. 10. XPAND Language Script

```
<PolicySet PolicySetId="RPSTaxAdvisor" PolicyCombiningAlgId="Permit-Overrides">
     <Target>
          <Subjects>
               <Subject>
                    <SubjectMatch MatchId="string-equal">
                         <AttributeValue DataType="string">RPSTaxAdvisor</AttributeValue>
                         <SubjectAttributeDesignator AttributeId="role" DataType="string"/>
                    </SubjectMatch>
               </Subject>
          </Subjects>
          <Resources><AnyResource/></Resources>
          <Actions><AnyAction/></Actions>
     </Target>
          <PolicySetIdReference>PPS:RPSTaxAdvisor</PolicySetIdReference>
</PolicySet>
```

Fig. 11. Generated Role Policy Set

5 Conclusion and Outlook

SECTET defines an extensible domain architecture for a broad set of domain-level security patterns. The framework targets the supports of domain experts during the design and the management of security-critical workflows with no central control. Our research efforts heavily draw on input from real-life projects and we are constantly extending our catalogue of security requirements towards more complex patterns, like the four-eyes-principle, transactional security and binding of duties. Conceptually based on OMG standards like MDA, MOF and MOF-QVT, the framework can be implemented with any of the MDA frameworks. In this respect, we are working along two lines. We are pushing an implementation of a model transformation engine based on MOF-QVT with the ECLIPSE MODELLING

FRAMEWORK [25] for research purposes. However, the SECTET approach is also being implemented as a cartridge for the commercial tool ARCSTYLER [32].

References

[1] I. Mukerji and J. Miller, "Overview and guide to OMG's architecture," 2003.

[2] E. Newcomer and G. Lomow, *Understanding Service-Oriented Architecture (SOA) with Web Services.*: Addison Wesley, 2005.

[3] S. Weerawarana, et al., *Web Services Platform Architecture: SOAP, WSDL, WS-Policy, WS-Addressing, WS-BPEL, WS-Reliable Messaging, and More*: Prentice Hall PTR, 2005.

[4] W. M. P. v. d. Aalst, "Formalization and Verification of Event-driven Process Chains," *Information and Software Technology*, vol. 41, pp. 639-650, 1999.

[5] J. Clark, "XSL Transformations (XSLT) Version 1.0," World Wide Web Consortium, W3C Recommendation 16 November 1999.

[6] OMG, "MOF QVT Final Adopted Specification," 2005.

[7] A. X12, "ASC X12 Reference Model for XML Design," ANSI ASC X12C Communications and Controls Subcommittee, Technical Report Type II - ASC X12C/TG3/2002- July 2002.

[8] S. Godik and T. Moses, "eXtensible Access Control Markup Language (XACML) Version 1.0 3," 2003.

[9] A. Anderson, "XACML Profile for Role Based Access Control (RBAC)," OASIS, 2004.

[10] P. Harmon, "The OMG's Model Driven Architecture and BPM," Business Process Trends, http://www.bptrends.com/publicationfiles/05-04 NL MDA and BPM.pdf, Newsletter May 2004.

[11] V. Atluri and W. K. Huang, "Enforcing Mandatory and Discretionary Security in Workflow Management Systems," *Proceedings of the 5th European Symposium on Research in Computer Security*, 1996.

[12] E. Gudes, M. Olivier, and R. v. d. Riet, "Modelling, Specifying and Implementing Workflow Security in Cyberspace. Journal of Computer Security 7 (1999) 4, pp. 287-315," *Journal of Computer Security 7 (1999) 4, pp. 287-315*, 1999.

[13] W. K. Huang and V. Atluri, "SecureFlow: A secure Web-enabled Workflow Management System," *ACM Workshop on Role-Based Access Control 1999, p. 83-94*, 1999.

[14] J. Wainer, P. Barthelmess, and A. Kumar, "W-RBAC A Workflow Security Model Incorporating Controlled Overriding of Constraints," *In: International Journal of Cooperative Information Systems 12 (2003) 4, pp. 455-485.*, 2003.

[15] A. Hall and R. Chapman, "Correctness by Construction: Developing a Commercial Secure System," *IEEE Software*, vol. 19, 2002.

[16] M. Schumacher, *Security Engineering with Patterns. Origins, Theoretical Models, and New Applications.* Berlin: Springer, 2003.

[17] T. Lodderstedt, D. Basin, and J. Doser, "SecureUML: A UML-Based Modeling Language for Model-Driven Security," presented at 5th International Conference on the Unified Modeling Language, 2002.

[18] J. Jürjens, *Secure Systems Development with UML.* Hardcover: Springer Academic Publishers, 2004.

[19] K. Mantell, "From UML to BPEL," IBM-developerWorks 2003.

[20] IBM, "Business Process Execution Language for Web Services JavaTM Run Time (BPWS4J)," IBM, http://www.alphaworks.ibm.com/tech/bpws4j 2002.

[21] S. Jablonski and C. Bussler, *Workflow Management: Concepts, Architecture and Implementation*: Int. Thompson Publishers, 1996.

[22] D. Edmond and A. H. M. t. Hofstede, "A Reflective Infrastructure for Workflow Adaptability," *Data and Knowledge Engineering*, vol. 34, pp. 271-304, 2000.

[23] J. Eder and W. Gruber, "A Meta Model for Structured Workflows Supporting Workflow Transformations," presented at Proc. Int'l Conf. on Advances in Databases and Information Systems (ADBIS'02), 2002.

[24] R. M\"uller, "Event-Oriented Dynamic Adaptation of Workflows.," University of Leipzig, Germany, 2002.

[25] M. Hafner, B. Weber, and R. Breu, "Model Driven Security for Inter-Organizational Workflows in E-Government.," in *Secure E-Government Web Services*, A. Mitrakas, P. Hengeveld, D. Polemi, and J. Gamper, Eds.: Idea Group Inc., 2006.

[26] M. Schumacher, E. Fernandez-Buglioni, D. Hybertson, F. Buschmann, and P. Sommerlad, *Security Patterns. Integrating Security and Systems Engineering*. Chichester: John Wiley and Sons Ltd, 2006.

[27] M. Hafner, R. Breu, B. Agreiter, and A. Nowak, "Sectet – An Extensible Framework for the Realization of Secure Inter-Organizational Workflows" presented at Fourth International Workshop on Security in Information System (WOSIS 2006), Paphos, Cyprus, 2006.

[28] M. Hafner, R. Breu, and b. Weber, *To Appear in: Model Driven Security for Inter-Organizational Workflows in E-Governement*: Idea Group, Inc., 2006.

[29] M. Hafner, R. Breu, M. Breu, and A. Nowak, "Modeling Inter-organizational Workflow Security in a Peer-to-Peer Environment," presented at Proceedings of ICWS, 2005.

[30] M. Alam, R. Breu, and M. Hafner, "Modeling permissions in a (U/X)ML world," in *Accepted for ARES*, 2006.

[31] M. Alam, R. Breu, and M. Breu, "Model Driven Security for Web Services (MDS4WS)." in *INMIC 2004 IEEE 8th International Multi topic Conference. Digital Object Identifier 10.1109/INMIC.2004.1492930 pp 498 - 505.*, 2004.

[32] M. Dumas and A. H. M. t. Hofstede, "UML Activity Diagrams as a Workflow Specification Language.," Proc. UML '01, Toronto, Canada, 2001.

MDA-Based Re-engineering with Object-Z

Jörn Guy Süß, Tim McComb, Soon-Kyeong Kim,
Luke Wildman, and Geoffrey Watson

Information Technology and Electrical Engineering
The University of Queensland, St. Lucia, 4072, Australia
{jgsuess, tjm, soon, luke, gwat}@itee.uq.edu.au

Abstract. This paper describes a practical application of MDA and reverse engineering based on a domain-specific modelling language. A well defined metamodel of a domain-specific language is useful for verification and validation of associated tools. We apply this approach to SIFA, a security analysis tool. SIFA has evolved as requirements have changed, and it has no metamodel. Hence, testing SIFA's correctness is difficult. We introduce a formal metamodelling approach to develop a well-defined metamodel of the domain. Initially, we develop a domain model in EMF by reverse engineering the SIFA implementation. Then we transform EMF to Object-Z using model transformation. Finally, we complete the Object-Z model by specifying system behavior. The outcome is a well defined metamodel that precisely describes the domain and the security properties that it analyses. It also provides a reliable basis for testing the current SIFA implementation and forward engineering its successor.

1 Introduction

The common notion of Model-Driven Architecture [16] is one of gradual refinement of models from a platform-independent to a platform-specific model. The starting point of the process is an abstract specification of the system; the destination is an executable system. This paper describes an experience which runs contrary to that received notion: an existing application is gradually turned into a formal specification: A process of reverse-MDA.

As part of an information security project, one of our research groups developed the "Security Information Flow Analyser" (SIFA) [12,19]. SIFA is an analysis tool with a graphical user interface and is used to predict the impact of faults in electronic circuits on security properties. For example, it can show whether malicious tampering will give an attacker an opportunity to listen to classified information passing through a device. SIFA models components, ports and connections, and its analysis strategy is based on the calculation of paths over the connections. Figure 1 shows a screen-shot of a typical SIFA diagram.

SIFA is a successful research tool that has evolved over time. It was originally constructed as an experimental tool which only considered an adjacency matrix describing global connectivity. It was then extended to include a layer of connected components on a circuit board, linking the different components

O. Nierstrasz et al. (Eds.): MoDELS 2006, LNCS 4199, pp. 291–305, 2006.

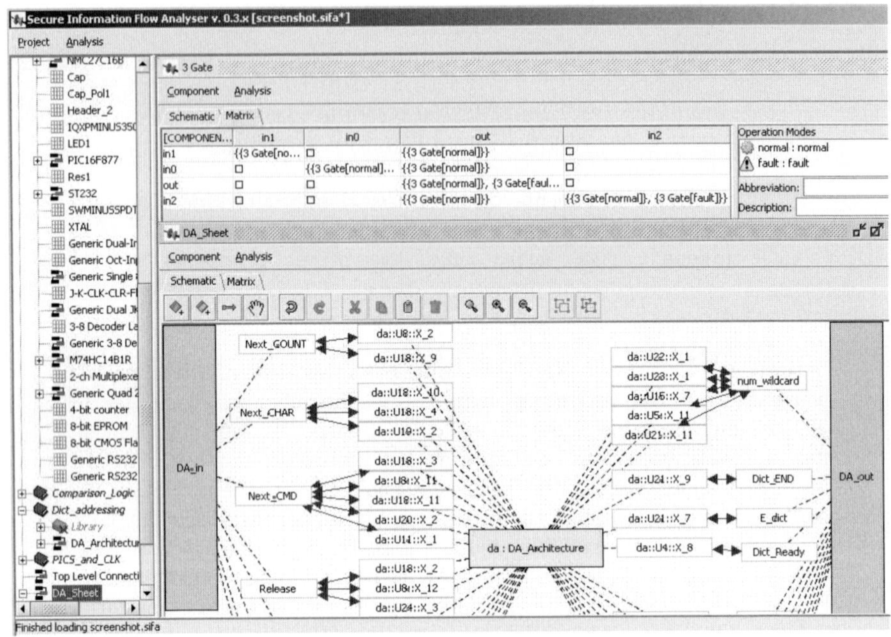

Fig. 1. SIFA user interface

externally. This was further extended to include recursive composition for modelling hierarchical circuits. Finally, usability refinements such as libraries and the reuse of existing definitions (called 'instances') were added. During all these changes, the underlying algorithm for calculation remained largely stable.

As SIFA is a graphical modelling tool, the Java Swing framework components used to construct it provided a default model of the data. As a result, the data for the three major semantic portions—port adjacency matrix, external wiring graph, and component containment tree—were all located in different parts of the source code of the interactive program. Although test cases had been written, they only checked some parts of the functionality.

SIFA was recently tested in a production context and it immediately found security weaknesses under fault conditions for prototype security devices. SIFA's usefulness meant that it is being considered as a serious application in the security context, which means it needs to be well-specified, well-tested and well-organized regarding its data model. We were thus faced with the following tasks:

- To derive a meta-model for SIFA in an accessible format.
- To provide a means to specify SIFA's behavior in a sufficiently formal way to reason about and test it.

In the course of this paper, we describe how we used MDA concepts and the Object-Z specification language [21,5] to deal with these requirements. There are additional benefits to this approach, as it yields

- A coherent metamodel supported by a MOF framework, as the basis for efficient re-implementation, and
- A specification serving as a bridge to automated testing frameworks and standard model-checking packages

The work presented in this paper is based on a set of models, metamodels and services, of which we present an essential part. All resources addressed in this paper are publicly available via an accompanying webpage located at

`http://itee.uq.edu.au/~mdavv/MDA-based%20Re-Engineering_with%20Object-Z/.`

In the text we will refer to this companion page for more detail. The rest of the paper is structured as follows: The following section describes tools and activities involved in the process, Section 3 describes the tool chain architecture and reuse aspects, Section 4 describes the SIFA metamodel and Section 5 shows the application of our approach in more detail. Section 6 describes related work and Section 7 draws conclusions and discusses future work.

2 From Code to Object-Z: Reverse-MDA

In MDA the structure of a metamodel is expressed using class constructs (usually visualized in UML class diagrams) while extended static constraints are expressed using OCL. Initially we defined our SIFA metamodel using this standard approach. However we soon found that OCL is insufficient to express the complex behavioral constraints needed for operations (an example can be found in Section 5). We have previously used Object-Z to formalize the UML metamodel [8], which convinced us that Object-Z would be better suited to the task.

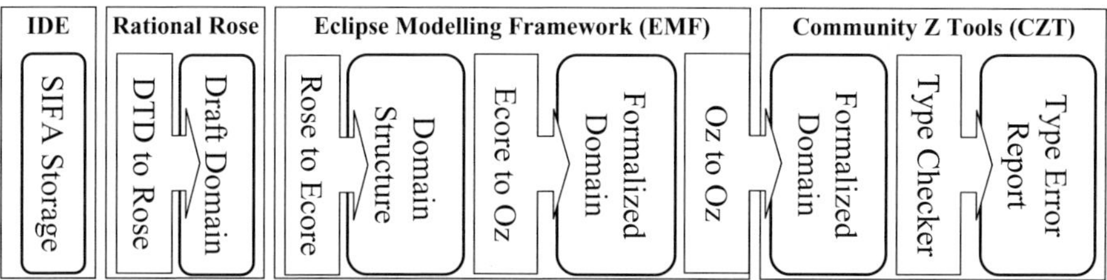

Fig. 2. Toolchain

Object-Z [5] is an extension to the ISO-standardized mathematically-based specification language Z [1] that adds support for object-oriented constructs: classes, attributes, operations, object relationships, and inheritance. In this paper, we use Object-Z to formalize the structural aspects of the SIFA metamodel, initially expressed using the UML class diagram, and to specify behavioral aspects of the metamodel. This enabled integration of structural and behavioral aspects of the metamodel within Object-Z classes, as a single modelling construct. The rest of this section describes the MDA process and tool chain used to define the SIFA metamodel.

Figure 2 shows an overview of our toolchain. In the top row from left to right it shows the four tool spaces involved in the chain. It involves Rational Rose and its XML-DTD importer, Eclipse EMF [3] and its Rational Rose importer, the Tefkat QVT transformation engine [10], a text-storage module, and the Community Z Tools (CZT) suite [11]. While the chain may look complex, it does not have more phases than a standard C^{++} compiler with make, pre-processor, compiler and linker tools. We will now look at the stages of processing in more detail.

We needed to build an initial version of the metamodel quickly. As a source of information, we had both the source code of SIFA and the DTD of its XML-based storage format available to us. Since our primary aim in this step was to recover *structure*, rather than *behavior*, we chose the XML DTD as the basis of our model, because it would be both complete and minimal, and would not contain clutter introduced by the Java graphics framework. We reverse-engineered the data structures into a UML class diagram, using a DTD-to-UML converter, which generated a model based on an XML DTD Profile. We then removed the profile to turn the DTD model into a general UML model.

This model was visualized in several diagrams and reworked and refined with the aid of SIFA's author to yield a first draft metamodel. This metamodel was imported into the Eclipse Metamodelling Framework (EMF). To validate the soundness of the metamodel we created some exemplary model instances using editors generated as part of the import process. We were able to stabilize the model within five rework cycles. Figure 3 shows the EMF Core Metamodel (Ecore) for SIFA, drawn using the conventions of the MOF profile for UML [14].

We then used model transformation to convert the EMF representation of SIFA into an instance of a metamodel of the Object-Z language . We believe the semantics and correctness of this metamodel to be reliable, because these have been demonstrated both mathematically and by example. Both Ecore and Object-Z are object-oriented modelling languages and share the common concepts of object-orientation: classes, attributes, operations, object relationships and inheritance. Thus, transformation between the languages is straightforward.

The transformation system used is DSTC's Tefkat, which has proved reliable in practice. Tefkat uses a declarative language which is expressive and backed by a prolog-based solver. Hence its formalism is well-suited to directly encode the formal correspondences between UML static structure models and Object-Z static structure models, as laid out in [9]. Tefkat's expressive concrete syntax in comparison with the adopted QVT standard[18], its high degree of reliability and good integration with the Eclipse environment make it a particularly effective and convenient for building the kind of semantic bridges involved in this aproach.

The specification was completed by enriching it with a behavioral description. SIFA's author, the program documentation, and a previous specification in Z gave the necessary input to add this facet to the Object-Z model. We also needed to visualize instances of the model. Object-Z is a superset of the Z notation, which has a standard LaTeX concrete syntax. We therefore created a converter from an XMI representation of an Object-Z instance to its LaTeX representation. (This used the Eclipse API to XMI.)

With a complete and formal domain metamodel whose instances could be converted to LaTeX we were now able to tap into the resources of the Object-Z community: the Community Z Tools project (CZT) [11]. Among the CZT tools are editors, textual layout tools for HTML and print-media, a type-checker, and connectors for external model-checking tools. We use CZT to type-check the ObjectZ and add more refined constraints and behaviors. We are currently investigating a tool to generate input to the SAL model-checker from our Object-Z [22], within the CZT toolset.

3 Toolchain Architecture

Originally, experiments on SIFA were conducted manually, copying files and clicking buttons in integrated development environments. This was a substantial impediment, as operations were closely tied to researchers personal work environment on individual computers and parallel work was impossible. We found that in order to automate the process in a tool chain, minimally four services had to be developed: A transformation service from Ecore/EMF to Object-Z/EMF which in turn requires a Tefkat transformation service, a transformation from Object-Z/EMF to Object-Z/Latex, and a transformation from Object-Z/Latex to postscript performed by the pdflatex compiler. Additional services were desirable to aggregate certain steps or the complete chain. This situation justified an investment in development effort for a simple tool interoperability architecture, for which we defined four requirements:

Defensive. The architecture should provide well-defined semantic interfaces, which would reject inconsistent artefacts early. A service should not process or pass on an artefact without examining it for correctness first. Otherwise, errors would be hard to trace in the chain.

Light-weight. The architecture should necessitate little or no installation effort, to allow the researchers to use the different services in parallel and immediately profit from any improvements made to them.

Reusable. Service interfaces should be standardized and allow separate reuse, allowing third parties to integrate provided services into their own efforts.

Simple. Implementation effort should be kept to a minimum, to keep project resources available for research.

The following paragraphs shortly introduce interesting elements of the resulting architecture, which resolve the requirements defined above. All our services are available from the paper's companion site.

Validating parsers and serializers process input and output of every service we built. This provide semantic stability. Also, we aim to build services in established technological spaces like XML and MOF, because of their semantic clarity. Except for the rose import and Object-Z type check, all services in our chain are based on EMF. The transition from the Object-Z/EMF to the Object-Z/Latex technological space was implemented using a templating approach due to time constraints. However, DSTC's AntiYacc [7], an improved version of the OMG Human Usable Transfer Notation [15], would have been preferred.

Resource Description Framework (RDF) [17] graphs and the notion of mega-modelling and technological spaces were used to express the interface types of the services. A service *consumes* and *produces* a set of artefacts identified by an Uniform Resource Identifier. Each artefact *conforms* to one or more artefacts on a higher level. For example for the Ecore to Object-Z service, the input parameter conforms to the Object-Z/EMF metamodel, which conforms to the Ecore/EMF metamodel. Type compatibility is calculated using the graph isomorphism check of the Jena RDF framework.

Java Servlets act as containers for our services, making them available to everyone without installation and allowing arbitrary distribution. Type information is exchanged via HTTP `GET`, service invocation is mapped to `POST`. Base classes allow the implementer to concentrate on functionality, rather than integration.

4 The SIFA Metamodel

This section describes the EMF Ecore model derived from the SIFA software, and the approach and process used to develop the model. As briefly described above, SIFA is a software tool for analysing the connectivity of hierarchical collections of interconnected components. The SIFA interface (see Figure 1) is discussed later, but the basic elements of the SIFA model are components and connections between components. The function of the SIFA program is to generate connectivity graphs from instances of this model and then to calculate queries about connectivity over these graphs. The root of the model (see Figure 3) is the abstract class *NamedElement*. This ensures that each class in the model has a *name* attribute – these names are used in the unification process that generates the connectivity graphs from instances of the model.

Connections are mediated by *Ports*. Each component may have many ports each of which may have many connections. Generally each port is anchored

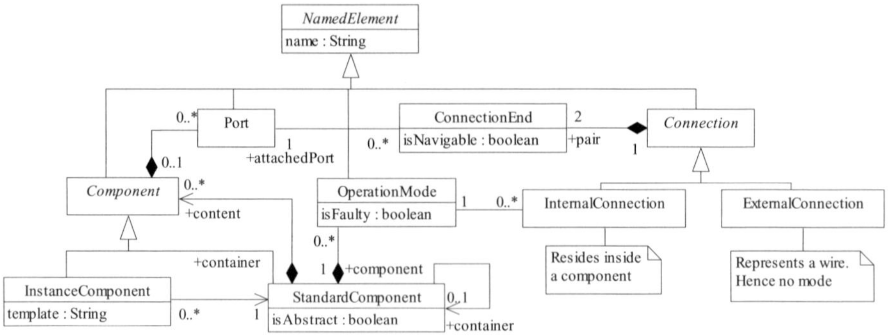

Fig. 3. SIFA Metamodel

to a single component, but it is possible for a port to be disconnected, so the multiplicity of the *Port - Component* association is 0..1. On the other hand each connection has precisely two ports – one at either end. Ports are associated with connections via the *ConnectionEnd* class which models the navigability of connections. This is done via the attribute *isNavigable* of *ConnectionEnd.* Each connection has exactly two connection ends, each associated with a single port, while each port may be associated with any number of connection ends.

SIFA has two kinds of connection: *ExternalConnections* connect distinct components together via their ports, while *InternalConnections* connect ports across a single component. These are modelled by separate subclasses because internal connections are associated with operation modes (which are described below) while external connections are not. Note that both ports associated with an internal connection (via its connection ends) must belong to the same component, and we formalize this constraint in Section 5.

Components are of two kinds. Most components are *StandardComponents.* A *StandardComponent* may contain a collection of other components as defined by the association *content* in the model. This relationship, of a component to its *container*, generates the component hierarchy. Each standard component has a boolean attribute *isAbstract*, which controls whether it is included in the analysis or not. This allows libraries of common components to be constructed as part of the description of a network, whereby instances of these components can be used where required but, by marking the library as abstract, the definitions themselves are ignored in any analysis.

There is a second subclass of component - the *InstanceComponent*, which allows reuse of component definitions. Like a *StandardComponent*, an *InstanceComponent* is a child of some *container* component above it in the hierarchy, and it defines a sub-hierarchy below it. However, this sub-hierarchy is identified indirectly via the string attribute *template*. In a model instance this string must match at least one *StandardComponents* name, because it is substituted by components with corresponding names during analysis. Thus an *InstanceComponent's* sub-hierarchy is not represented explicitly since it is context-dependent.

SIFA also defines *modes*, which are modelled by the *OperationMode* class. These modes are defined per component. Each internal connection of a component is associated with an *OperationMode*, and multiple modes between ports of a component are modelled by multiple internal connections. All internal connections are unidirectional. Modes are used in the analysis of behavior in the presence of faults, so the *OperationMode* class has a boolean attribute *isFaulty*, which indicates whether the mode is a fault mode or a normal mode. A *StandardComponent* may have no modes at all, but typically a component will have one (or more) normal modes and in addition may have fault modes.

Instances of the model described above and illustrated in Figure 3 are visualized in the SIFA GUI—an example is shown in Figure 1. The SIFA window is split into two parts. On the left is a tree view of all components in the model, while the pane on the right shows a view of the currently selected component.

In Figure 1 the main part of the viewing pane shows a view of the "DA-Sheet" component, this general view is known as the *schematic* view. There are two standard components in this view, "DA_in" on the left and "DA_out" on the right. These are connected via an instance of the component "DA_Architecture", this instance is named "da". Ports are shown as named boxes (e.g. "Next_COUNT", "da::U8::X_2"). External connections are visualized as solid lines, with arrows indicating navigability. For convenience of layout, ports are shown attached to components by dotted lines.

Internal connections are not shown in the schematic view; instead, they are visualized in the *matrix* view of a component. A matrix view is shown above the schematic in Figure 1—the pane labelled "3 Gate". The operation modes of this component are listed on the right, with an indication of whether they are faulty or normal modes. The internal connections are shown in the form of a matrix. The rows and columns are labelled with the port names and each cell in the matrix represents one possible internal connection (from port to port). Many cells are empty, but others contain a list of the connections between these ports indicated by their modes (each connection is associated with one of the modes of the component). For example, the cell in row "in2" and column "out" connects "in2" to "out" in the normal operation mode.

5 The SIFA Object-Z Specification

In this section we will outline the generated Object-Z classes first, to show their relationship to the Ecore model, and then present our added consistency constraints. Finally, we will show an Object-Z specification of one of the analytical functions that SIFA performs over instances of the metamodel. The complete specification is available at the paper's companion website.

5.1 Structure of the SIFA Metamodel

At the top of the inheritance hierarchy is the class *NamedElement* which requires the introduction of a data type *EString* representing the set of all possible names (this is a *given type* in Object-Z [21,8]).

$[EString]$

Attributes in Object-Z class definitions correspond to those in the Ecore model. The Object-Z definition of *NamedElement* (see below) includes a declaration *name* of type *EString*, as well as a constraint over the class type *NamedElement* itself.

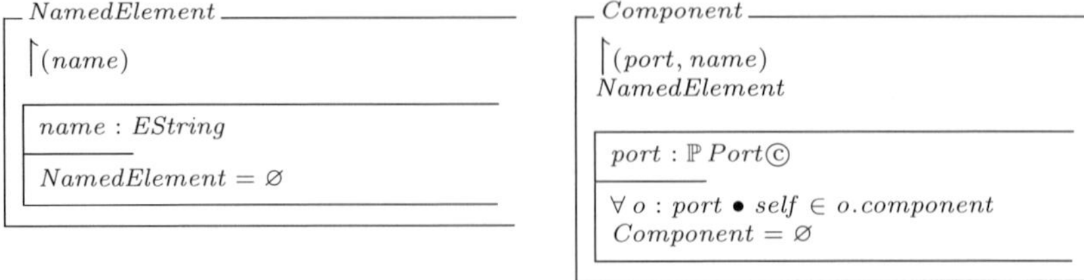

In Object-Z class types are interpreted as disjoint sets of object identities, where such identities represent possible unique instantiations. By default there are an infinite (although countable) number of possible instantiations of classes because these sets are unbounded, but above *NamedElement* is constrained to be empty($\varnothing$ is the empty set). This ensures that *NamedElement* cannot be instantiated, as it is *abstract* in the domain metamodel's specification.

Another abstract class in the metamodel is *Component* (next to *NamedElement* above). The *Component* class inherits from *NamedElement*, which in Object-Z amounts to *class inclusion* [21]—the state and operations of a class are conjoined with any inherited classes. As a result, the state of *Component* includes both *port* and *name*.

The visibility list, denoted by the $\upharpoonright$ symbol, contains the features of the class that are considered public; that is to say, the features which can be externally referenced by other classes. These features may be operations, which will be seen later, or state variables like *name* above. Inheritance of features is not affected by the visibility list, but the visibility list does determine which inherited features are externally visible.

The declaration of *port* signifies that the *port* attribute is a set of *Port* instances, where that set is *contained* [5] (the © symbol stands for object containment in Object-Z). Containment means that the object identities appearing in the set are distinct with respect to other instances of *Component*, i.e. components cannot share ports.

The Object-Z definition of *Port* is as follows.

```
Port
  ↾(connectionEnd, component, kind, name)
  NamedElement

  connectionEnd : ℙ ConnectionEnd
  component : ℙ ↓Component
  ─────────────────────────────
  ∀ o : connectionEnd • self = o.attachedPort
  ∀ o : component • self ∈ o.port
  #component ≤ 1
```

The attribute *component* is defined to be a set of *Component* instances, or instances of any subclass of *Component*, that 'own' this port (the subclasses are included via the $\downarrow$ operator). Technically, $\downarrow$*Component* may be understood as:

$$\downarrow Component == Component \cup StandardComponent \cup InstanceComponent$$

Since the multiplicity relationship from ports to components is specified to be $0\,..\,1$ in the domain model, the Tefkat translation ensures that the size of the *component* set is at most one by adding the predicate "$\#component \leq 1$" [8].

The attribute *component* in the *Port* class corresponds to an attribute *port* in the *Component* class, indicating a bi-directional relationship between a port and the component with which it is associated. The consistency of the bi-directional relationship is ensured via the predicate

$$\forall\, o : port \bullet self \in o.component$$

in *Component* and the predicate

$$\forall\, o : component \bullet self \in o.port$$

in *Port*. These predicates (and classes) are characteristic of the constraints that our Tefkat translation generates to maintain the consistency of bi-directional relationships like this one.

All other classes in the SIFA metamodel introduced in Section 4 are generated in a similar fashion to the above classes, with much the same constraining predicates relating to the UML, so we will omit their detail from our discussion. Instead, we will concentrate on the additional consistency constraints that we add to the generated Object-Z specification, and also an example specification of an analysis that SIFA performs.

5.2 Structural Consistency Constraints

In this section we extend the generated Object-Z classes. The extensions to the Object-Z specification either maintain indirect relationships between classes, or introduce derived convenience variables that aggregate substructures of objects associated with a class. Many of the features we add are to assist the specification of the *Search* operation, which is introduced in Section 5.3. For conciseness, we will not present all of the extensions that we made to the specification, but rather we will show a representative sample.

The Object-Z class *Component* is extended with a derived attribute *allPorts* (declarations underneath a Δ in Object-Z indicate that they are derived values [21]) which contains all of the ports that belong directly to the component as well as all of the ports that belong to any of the component's descendants.

Component

$\upharpoonright(\ldots, allPorts)$

$\ldots$
Δ
$allPorts : \mathbb{P}\, Port$

$\ldots$
$allPorts = (\bigcup\{c : content \bullet c.allPorts\}) \cup port$

The above class definition of *Component* is intended to replace the one generated by the Tefkat translation, but with the detail of the generated class substituted for the ellipses. We will follow this convention for all of the extensions listed below.

An attribute *connections* is added to the *Port* class which aggregates all of the connections to which this port (through a *ConnectionEnd*) is attached.

$$connections = \{ce : connectionEnd \bullet ce.connection\}$$

To find the entire set of components inside which a standard component is contained (its ancestors), we introduce the derived variable *allContainers* to the class *StandardComponent*. Additionally, we add a constraint that holds over the indirect relationship between a standard component and its internal connections (which are defined through operating modes).

StandardComponent

$\upharpoonright(\ldots, allContainers)$

$\ldots$

$\ldots$

Δ

$allContainers : \mathbb{P}\, StandardComponent$

$\ldots$

$allContainers = (\bigcup\{c : container \bullet c.allContainers\}) \cup container$

All internal connections (over all operating modes) connect ports of this component.

$(\bigcup\{mode : operationMode \bullet mode.allPorts\}) \subseteq port$

The derived variable *allPorts* in the class *OperationMode* is the set of all ports that are covered by an operating mode's internal connections.

$$allPorts = \bigcup\{c : internalConnection \bullet c.allPorts\}$$

$$relation = \bigcup\{c : internalConnection \bullet c.relation\}$$

We have also assumed the existence of the attribute *allPorts* in *Connection*, so we must extend the definition of *Connection* to accommodate. Additionally, we have added some extra constraints to the *Connection* class to place restrictions over the connection ends and ports associated with it.

Connection

$\upharpoonright(\ldots, allPorts, relation)$

$\ldots$

$\ldots$

Δ

$allPorts : \mathbb{P}\, Port$

$relation : EString \leftrightarrow EString$

$\ldots$

$allPorts = \{c : pair \bullet c.attachedPort\}$

$relation =$
$\quad \{ce1, ce2 : pair \mid ce1.isNavigable \bullet$
$\qquad ce1.attachedPort.name \mapsto ce2.attachedPort.name\}$

Connections are between two distinct ports.

$\#allPorts = 2$

All connections have at least one navigable connection end.

$\exists\, c : pair \bullet c.isNavigable$

In the definitions of *StandardComponent* and *Connection*, the derived attribute *relation* was added which captures, as a relation between *EStrings*, the connectivity of operation modes and connections respectively (the operation mode *relation* is just the union of all of its constituent connection relations). For a unidirectional connection, this relation will have just one mapping, but for a bidirectional connection it will usually have two. The exception in the bidirectional case is when the ports' names on each end are the same—thus only one entry in the relation is necessary. The *relation* attribute is useful for defining the searching operation, which will be introduced in the next section.

5.3 Behavior of the SIFA Metamodel

As discussed in Section 1, SIFA's primary function is to search for pathways through networks of components, a data structure of which we have represented with the domain model.

Prior to any searching operation is the need to interpret instance components by substituting in their template description (which is a standard component) *in situ*. In this paper we shall assume that this operation has already been performed upon the model and concentrate on the searching functionality. That is, we assume that the model we are searching does not contain any *InstanceComponent* objects.

SIFA's search is based upon port connectivity, specifically on the names of ports. By only considering the names of ports, two or more ports with a common name will be considered as the same point in a search performed over the model—the ports are effectively *unified*. This has many advantages, but the most useful reason for doing this is to allow for the composition of different views of connectivity over the same system just by using a common port naming convention.

StandardComponent

$\upharpoonright(\ldots, Search)$

$\ldots$

Search

$source?, sink? : EString$
$state! : StandardComponent \pfun OperationMode$
$fail! : \mathbb{B}$

Every standard component hierarchically underneath this component is represented in the 'state!' if it has an operation mode.

$$\mathrm{dom}\ state! = \{c : StandardComponent \mid self \in c.allContainers \land c.operationMode \neq \varnothing\}$$

In the 'state!', every component is associated with an operation mode that belongs to it.

$$(\forall c : \mathrm{dom}\ state! \bullet c = (state!(c)).component)$$

With the model in state 'state!', find a connection between 'source?' and 'sink?', otherwise 'fail!'.

$$\begin{array}{l}(\mathbf{let}\ portExternal == \lambda\, p : Port \bullet \\ \qquad \bigcup\{c : ExtenalConnection \mid c \in p.connections \bullet c.relation\} \bullet \\ \quad (\mathbf{let}\ allInternal == \bigcup\{m : \mathrm{ran}\ state! \bullet m.relation\}; \\ \qquad allExternal == \bigcup\{p : (allPorts \setminus port) \bullet portExternal(p)\} \bullet \\ \quad \neg\ fail \Leftrightarrow source?\ (allInternal \cup allExternal)^{+}\ sink?))\end{array}$$

We define a *Search* operation in classe *StandardComponent* and declare its inputs to be a *source? EString* and a *sink? EString* (the "?" symbol denotes that the variable should be considered as an input). From these inputs, we expect our operation to return a *state*! (likewise, "!" denotes an output) of the system in which *source?* and *sink?* can be connected. If no such path exists in any state, the operation sets a boolean flag *fail!* to be true. The *Search* operation is added to the *StandardComponent* class, as SIFA allows searches to be rooted at any component in the hierarchy (thus determining the scope of the analysis). However, typically the operation is invoked upon the absolute root component of the entire hierarchy.

The *state!* of the system is expressed as a partial function from standard components to their operation modes, such that every standard component (that has at least one mode) hierarchically underneath the component where the operation is invoked is assigned to be in exactly one mode. There may be many such configurations that allow for connectivity between the *source?* and *sink?* port labels, in which case the *Search* operation chooses one non-deterministically.

It is possible in Object-Z to invoke the operation with added constraints over which states may be chosen, so this operation serves as a base for many others. For example, we may restrict the possible states to those with no fault modes in order to analyze the system under normal operating conditions.

6 Related Work

The current work attempts to re-engineer an existing application applying an MDA methodology. It thus truly represents a case of Architecture Driven Modernisation, as promoted by the Object Management Group [13]. The toolchain represents an approach to realize open model engineering support and to achieve tool interoperability [2]. Its design is based on the conceptualisation of technological spaces [23], and employs the semantic interrelations of artefacts to *mega*model [6] the dependencies in χ-conformance relationships.

7 Conclusions and Discussions

We have developed a formal specification of the SIFA tool by a process of reverse-MDA. That is, we have reverse engineered a domain-specific meta-model of SIFA from the data structure of the input, then we have transformed the meta-model into a skeletal formal specification to which we are able to add complex constraints and dynamic behaviour. Our approach involved some manual massaging of the model along the way. While some of this was to enable the composition of the tool-chain, much of it came about through clarification of the model with the software owner. This clarification also benefited the tool itself as some concepts were simplified.

The resultant formal model can serve as a basis for formal verification and validation, model-based testing, and possible re-engineering. Verification is possible through add-ons to the CZT infrastructure. In particular we plan to translate the Object-Z model to SAL [22]. This would enable us to use the SAL model-checker to check the correctness of our specification of the search, and also to simulate the operation of SIFA for the purpose of validation.

We will now extend our work to generate test-cases and test-oracles for the SIFA implementation based on work of France et al. [4] and extend it with a metamodel of test conditions. In our case, an instance model will then cover both dynamic and static test conditions of SIFA.

MDA offers real benefits to software engineering when a transformation between models can be described simply and flexibly. Our approach relies heavily on TefKat to enable multiple modelling tools to be brought to the problem. In the future we will investigate how our approach may be applied to large scale developments. Here we see potential benefits in reliably re-engineering legacy modelling systems because of our ability to add descriptions of behaviour to the automatically generated models of the structure.

Acknowledgments

This research is funded by an ARC Discovery grant, DP0557972: Enhancing MDA with support for verification and validation. SIFA was developed on ARC linkage grant LP0347620 "Formally-based security evaluation procedures". We acknowledge David Carrington's comment on this paper.

References

1. ISO/IEC 13568:2002. Information technology—Z formal specification notation—syntax, type system and semantics. International Standard.
2. Jean Bezivin, Hugo Brunelière, Frederic Jouault, and Ivan Kurtev. Model engineering support for tool interoperability. WiSME 2005 4th Workshop in Software Model Engineering, 10 2005. `http://www.planetmde.org/wisme-2005`.
3. Frank Budinsky. *The eclipse modeling framework : a developer's guide.* Addison-Wesley, Boston, MA, USA, 2004.
4. Trung T. Dinh-Trong, Nilesh Kawane, Sudipto Ghosh, Robert B. France, and Anneliese Amschler Andrews. A tool-supported approach to testing UML design models. In *ICECCS*, pages 519–528, 2005.
5. R. Duke and G. Rose. *Formal Object-Oriented Specification Using Object-Z.* 2002.
6. Jean-Marie Favre. Megamodelling and etymology. In James R. Cordy, Ralf Lämmel, and Andreas Winter, editors, *Transformation Techniques in Software Engineering*, volume 05161 of *Dagstuhl Seminar Proceedings.* Internationales Begegnungs- und Forschungszentrum (IBFI), Schloss Dagstuhl, Germany, 2005.
7. David Hearnden, Kerry Raymond, and Jim Steel. Anti-yacc: MOF-to-text. In *EDOC*, pages 200–211. IEEE Computer Society, 2002.
8. Soon-Kyeong Kim. *A Metamodel-based Approach to Integrate Object-Oriented Graphical and Formal Specification Techniques.* PhD thesis, ITEE, 2002.
9. Soon-Kyeong Kim, Damian Burger, and David A. Carrington. An MDA approach towards integrating formal and informal modeling languages. In *Formal Methods 2005*, volume 3582 of *LNCS*, pages 448–464. Springer, 2005.
10. Michael Lawley and Jim Steel. Practical declarative model transformation with Tefkat. In Jean-Michel Bruel, editor, *MoDELS Satellite Events*, volume 3844 of *Lecture Notes in Computer Science*, pages 139–150. Springer, 2005.

11. Petra Malik and Mark Utting. CZT: A framework for Z tools. In Treharne et al. [25], pages 65–84.
12. Tim McComb and Luke Wildman. SIFA: A tool for evaluation of high-grade security devices. In Colin Boyd and Juan Manuel González Nieto, editors, *ACISP*, volume 3574 of *Lecture Notes in Computer Science*, pages 230–241. Springer, 2005.
13. Philip Newcomb. Architecture-driven modernization (ADM). In *WCRE*, page 237. IEEE Computer Society, 2005.
14. Object Management Group. *UML Profile for MOF*, 1999.
15. Object Management Group, Needham, Massachusetts. *Human-Usable Textual Notation (HUTN) Specification*, December 2002.
16. Object Management Group, Framingham, Massachusetts. *MDA Guide Version 1.0.1*, June 2003.
17. World Wide Web Consortium Ora Lassila <Ora.Lassila@research.Nokia.Com>, Nokia Research Center Ralph R. Swick <Swick@w3.Org>. Resource description framework (RDF) model and syntax specification. Technical Report W3C Recommendation 22, W3C, February 1999.
18. *QVT-Partners, Revised Submission for MOF 2.0 Query/View/Transformation RFP*, August 2003. `http://www.qvtp.org`.
19. Andrew Rae, Colin Fidge, and Luke Wildman. Fault evaluation for security-critical communications devices. *Computer*, 39(5):61–68, 2006.
20. Michelle Sibilla, André Barros De Sales, Philippe Vidal, Thierry Millan, and François Jocteur-Monrozier. L'approche Modelware : exploitation des modèles au cœur des systèmes - apports et besoins pour la vérification. In *Génie Logiciel*, volume 69, pages 9–16. juin 2004.
21. Graeme Smith. *The Object Z Specification Language*. Kluwer Academic, 1999.
22. Graeme Smith and Luke Wildman. Model checking Z specifications using SAL. In Treharne et al. [25], pages 85–103.
23. Jonathan Sprinkle. Improving CBS tool development with technological spaces. In *ECBS*, pages 218–224. IEEE Computer Society, 2004.
24. Jörn Guy Süß, Andreas Leicher, Herbert Weber, and Ralf-D. Kutsche. Model-centric engineering with the evolution and validation environment. In Perdita Stevens, Jon Whittle, and Grady Booch, editors, *UML 2003 - The Unified Modeling Language. Model Languages and Applications. 6th International Conference, San Francisco, CA, USA, October 2003, Proceedings*, volume 2863 of *LNCS*, pages 31–43. Springer, 2003.
25. Helen Treharne, Steve King, Martin C. Henson, and Steve A. Schneider, editors. *ZB 2005: Formal Specification and Development in Z and B*, volume 3455 of *Lecture Notes in Computer Science*. Springer, 2005.

A Model Transformation Semantics and Analysis Methodology for SecureUML

Achim D. Brucker, Jürgen Doser, and Burkhart Wolff

Information Security, ETH Zurich, 8092 Zurich, Switzerland
{brucker, doserj, bwolff}@inf.ethz.ch

Abstract. SecureUML is a security modeling language for formalizing access control requirements in a declarative way. It is equipped with a UML notation in terms of a UML profile, and can be combined with arbitrary design modeling languages. We present a semantics for SecureUML in terms of a model transformation to standard UML/OCL. The transformation scheme is used as part of an implementation of a tool chain ranging from front-end visual modeling tools over code-generators to the interactive theorem proving environment HOL-OCL. The methodological consequences for an analysis of the generated OCL formulae are discussed.

1 Introduction

Security is a major concern in the development, implementation and maintenance of many distributed software systems like Web services, component-based systems, or database systems. In traditional software engineering practice, the development of a *design model* (business logic) and of a *security model* are treated as completely different tasks; as a consequence, security features are built into an existing system often in an ad-hoc manner during the system administration phase. While the underlying motivation of this practice, a desire for a separation of concerns, is understandable, the conflict between *security requirements* and *availability of services* cannot be systematically analyzed and reasonably balanced in this approach.

An integration of these two aspects into one unified methodology is necessary, ranging from the modeling over the implementation to the deployment and the maintenance phase of a system. To meet this challenge, in [1], a model driven approach has been suggested, which is built upon the SecureUML language. SecureUML is an embedding of a security language for access control into UML class diagrams and statecharts. SecureUML allows for specifying system models and security models within the same visual modeling tool. Subsequent model transformations translate a combined *secured system model* (enriched by a business model implementation) into code including a security infrastructure, e.g., a configuration of policy enforcement points or other access control mechanisms.

While in previous work [1], the semantics of SecureUML has been given in mathematical paper-and-pencil notation for logic and set theory, in this paper,

O. Nierstrasz et al. (Eds.): MoDELS 2006, LNCS 4199, pp. 306–320, 2006.

we present its semantics as a model transformation into a secured system model described in plain UML/OCL. In this approach, we take the semantic features of the OCL logic into account (such as undefinedness and three-valuedness), both on the side of the design as well as the security model. Besides the advantage of a seamless integration of SecureUML into the semantic foundations of UML, the approach is the basis of an *implementation* for a tool-chain for SecureUML ranging from visual modeling tools such as ArgoUML to both code-generators and analysis tools such as the proof environment HOL-OCL [4].

The goal of SecureUML is to provide means for a fine-grained specification of access-control requirements like "principals of role r may never access an object of class A" or "method m may never be called on an object of class A satisfying condition c." These properties are essentially temporal safety properties, in the sense that "never something bad will happen." By stating them as requirements, and enforcing them by suitably configured access-control points in an implementation, they may obviously conflict with liveness properties such as "eventually the user will get a result, provided he has permission to it." We show several proof-obligations that are generated for the secured system model to check if it satisfies such desirable properties. These proof-obligations can then be transferred to HOL-OCL and verified by tactic scripts.

Related Work. With UMLsec [6] we share the conviction that security models should be integrated into the software engineering development process by using UML. However, UMLsec provides a formal semantics, but does not provide any tool support, neither for code-generation nor for (formal) model analysis.

M. Koch and F. Parisi-Presicce [7] presented an approach for specifying and analyzing access control policies in UML diagrams. They define an access control semantics using graph transformations into attributed graphs. However, their analysis methodology only considers conflicts, safety, etc. of the security policy itself. In contrast, one of our main contributions is the possibility to reason about the relationship between the security model and the design model.

The Plan of the Paper. After a general introduction into the technical and theoretical foundations, we present the three main contributions: In Section 3, we describe the translation of SecureUML models into standard UML/OCL models (thus providing a translation semantics for the security aspects of a system), in Section 4 we present details over the system architecture and our implementation in a tool chain, and in Section 5, we present several relevant proof obligations representing desirable properties for the secured system model.

2 Technical Background

2.1 SecureUML

SecureUML is a security modeling language based on RBAC [5, 12] with some generalizations. The abstract syntax of SecureUML is defined by the metamodel shown in Figure 1. In particular, SecureUML supports notions of users, roles

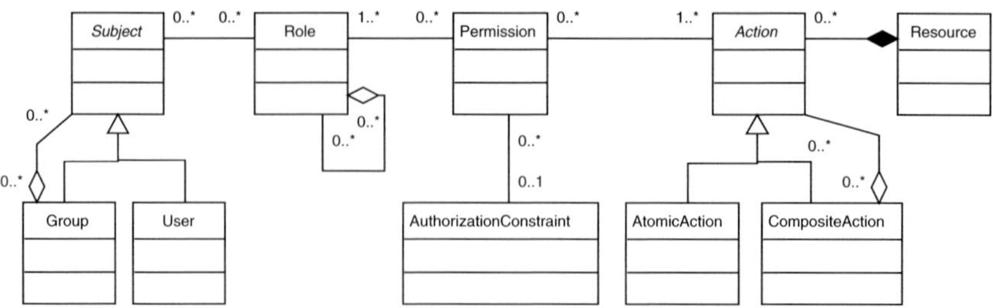

Fig. 1. SecureUML Metamodel

and permissions, as well as assignments between them: Users can be assigned to roles, and roles are assigned to specific permission. Users acquire permissions through the roles they are assigned to. Moreover, users are organized into a hierarchy of groups, and roles are organized into a role hierarchy. In addition to this RBACmodel, permissions can be restricted by *Authorization Constraints*, which are conditions that have to be true (at run-time) to allow access.

Permissions specify which *Role* may perform which *Action* on which *Resource*. SecureUML is generic in that it does not specify the type of actions and resources itself. Instead, these are assumed to be defined in the *design modeling language* which is then "plugged" into SecureUML by specifying (in a SecureUML *dialect*) exactly which elements of the design modeling language are protected resources and what actions are available on them. A dialect may also specify a hierarchy on these actions, so that more abstract actions, like reading a class, can be expressed in terms of lower-level actions, like reading an attribute of the class or executing a side-effect free method. Furthermore, a dialect specifies a *default policy*, i.e., whether access for a particular action is allowed or denied in the case that *no* permission is specified. Usually, and so do we in this paper, one specifies a default policy of *allow* to simplify the security specification.

In previous work, we have presented two dialects: One for a component-based design modeling language, and one for a state-machine based modeling language. Due to limitations of space, we will not address the issue of dialect definitions much further in this paper, and refer to [1] for more details. Instead we will assume as given, without presenting it in detail, a SecureUML dialect definition for UML class diagrams in the spirit of the ComponentUML dialect. This means that the dialect specifies classes, attributes and operations to be resources. The dialect also specifies, among others, the actions *create*, *read*, *update*, and *delete* on classes, *read* and *update* on attributes, and *execute* on operations.

SecureUML features a notation that is based on UML class diagrams, using a UML profile consisting of custom stereotypes. Users, Groups and Roles are represented by classes with stereotypes ≪secureuml.user≫, ≪secureuml.group≫, and ≪secureuml.role≫. Assignments between them are represented by ordinary UML associations, whereas the role hierarchy is represented by a generalization relationship. Permissions are represented as association classes with stereotype ≪secureuml.permission≫ connecting the role and a *permission anchor*. The

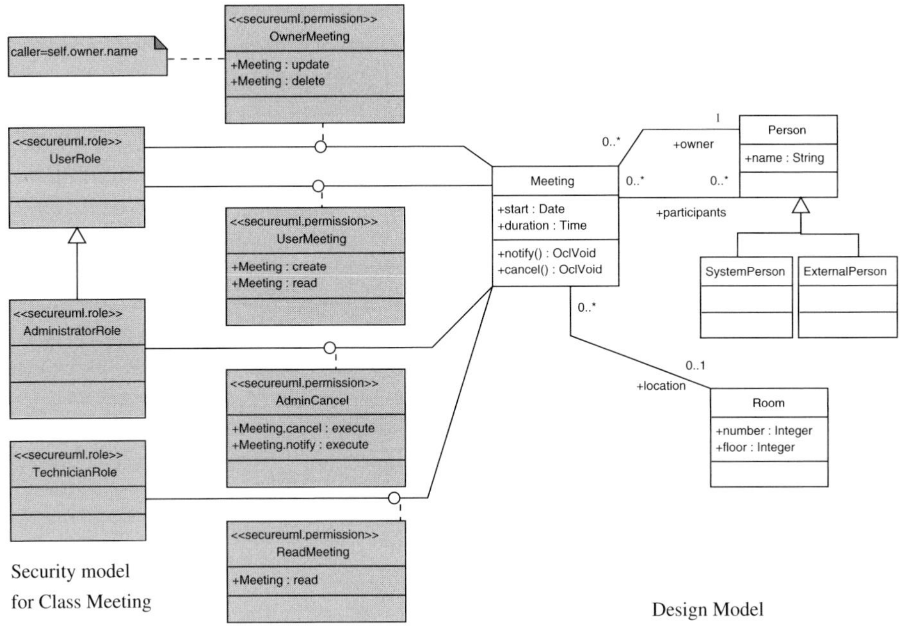

Fig. 2. Access Control Policy for Class Meeting

attributes of the association class specify which action (the attribute's type) on which resource (the attribute's name) is permitted by this permission. Authorization constraints are (OCL) constraints attached to the association class. Note that attributes or operations on roles as well as operations on permission have no semantics in SecureUML and are therefore not allowed in the UML notation.

Figure 2 and 3 show a UML model of a simplified group calendar application together with an exemplary access control policy, which we will use as a running example in this paper.

The left part of Figure 2 shows the access control policy for the class Meeting, whereas the right part shows the design model of the application. The design model consists of *Meetings*, *Rooms*, and *Persons*. Meetings have an owner, participants, and may take place in a particular room. The three association classes specify (from top to bottom) the following access control policy:

1. owners of meetings may delete them, or change the meeting data,
2. ordinary users may read meeting data and create new meetings,
3. administrators may cancel meetings (involves notifying its participants), and
4. technicians may only read meeting data.

For example, the topmost association class (*OwnerMeeting*) has two attributes with type *update* resp. *delete*. This specifies that the associated role (*UserRole*) has the permission to update and to delete meeting objects. According to the policy, however, only *owners* of meetings should be able to do so. The property of being an owner of a meeting cannot be easily specified using a pure RBACmodel. It is therefore specified using the authorization constraint caller = self.owner.name. For this purpose, we introduced a new keyword caller of type String into the OCL language that refers to the name of the authenticated user making the current call. Attaching this authorization constraints to the permission thus restricts the permission to system states where the name of the owner of the meeting matches the name of the user making the request.

The name of the attribute of the association class is used to navigate from the permission anchor, i.e., the classifier associated to the association class, to the actual protected resource. This is necessary because we can only associate classifiers in UML, not operations or attributes. E.g., the permission *AdminCancel* in Figure 2 refers to the operations cancel() and notify() of the class Meeting.

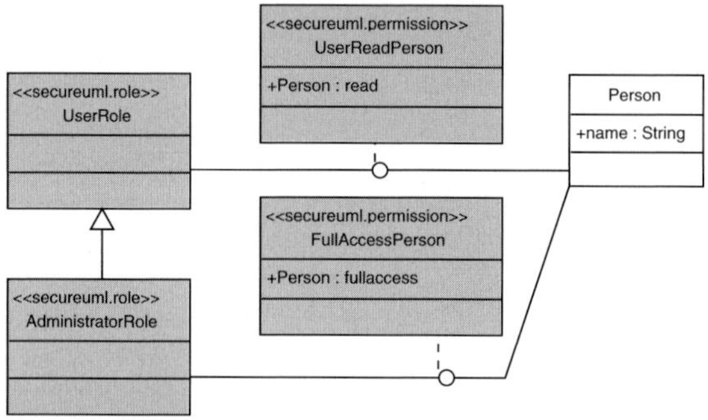

Fig. 3. Access Control Policy for Class Person

In addition to Figure 2, Figure 3 specifies the following access control policy for the class Person: 1. ordinary users may read person data 2. administrators have arbitrary access on person.

Note that technicians have no permissions on person objects. Also note that we left out the specification of users, groups and their role assignments in this example to simplify the presentation.

2.2 HOL-OCL

HOL-OCL [4] is an interactive proof environment for UML/OCL. It defines a machine-checked *formalization of the semantics* as described in the standard for OCL 2.0. This is implemented as a conservative, shallow embedding consisting of OCL into the HOL instance of the interactive theorem prover Isabelle [10]. This includes typed, extensible UML data models supporting inheritance and subtyping inside the typed λ-calculus with parametric polymorphism. As a consequence of conservativity wrt. HOL, we can guarantee the consistency of the semantic model. Moreover, HOL-OCL provides several derived calculi for UML/OCL that allows for formal derivations establishing the validity of UML/OCL formulae. Automated support for such proofs is also provided.

3 Transformation

The transformation is based on the idea of substituting the security model, which is specified with SecureUML, with a model of an explicit enforcement mechanism, which is specified in pure UML/OCL. This enforcement mechanism consists of a constant part, i.e., this part is independent of the design model, and a part that varies with the design model. We call the constant part "authorization environment" and explain it in more detail in Section 3.1.

The basic idea of this enforcement mechanism is to model every action on a protected resource by a UML operation and to transform the access control policy into OCL constraints on these operations. Because there are actions on resources that are not operations in the original design model, for example reading or updating an attribute value, we have to transform the design model accordingly. This design model transformation is described in Section 3.2.

Section 3.3 describes the security model transformation, i.e., how the access control policy specified using SecureUML is transformed into OCL constraints.

3.1 Authorization Environment

The basis for our model transformation is a model of a basic authorization environment, as shown in Figure 4.

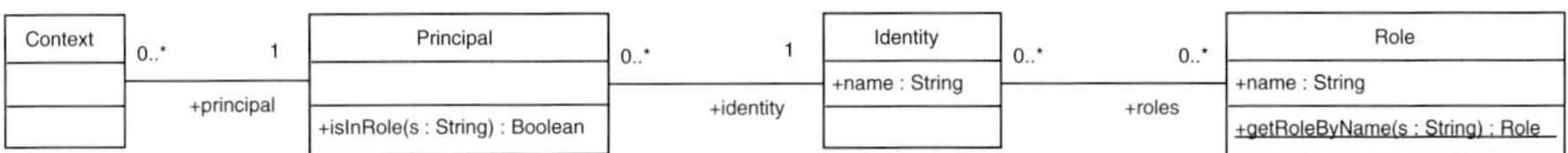

Fig. 4. Basic Authorization Environment

All protected resources get a reference to a Context object, which in turn has a reference to a Principal object. Principal objects represent the authenticated users of the system, i.e., the information of the system user together with authentication information. They are associated with their corresponding identity object, which represent the actual system users. To check role membership and user identities, the principal contains an operation isInRole(s: String): Boolean. The class Identity holds information about the system user(s), which in our case is just its name and its roles. The distinction between Principal and Identity allows a certain flexibility in the treating of authenticated users. For example, they can hold information about the authentication method they used. Also, it allows users to authenticate for a session using only a subset of their assigned roles (which is currently not supported in SecureUML). In the simplified model presented here, the principal object does not hold any extra information, and system users will always have all their assigned roles. This is done by imposing the following constraint:

```
context Principal :: isInRole (s:String) : Boolean
post: result = self. identity . roles .name->includes(s)
```

This environment is minimal on purpose, but sufficient to express authorization requirements. In particular, we do not consider authentication here.

3.2 Design Model Transformation

The model transformation is split into two parts: transforming the design model, and transforming the security model. Transforming the design model is necessary to allow the expression of security policies as OCL constraints. The transformation itself consists of first copying the input design model, adding the authorization environment to it, and adding new (access controlled) operations to the model. In particular, all invariants, preconditions and postconditions of the original design model are preserved, and new constraints are only imposed on generated classes and operations.

For the addition of the authorization environment, we associate each permission anchor with the context class from the authorization environment. Furthermore, all access controlled actions have to be represented as operations in the target model. Table 1 gives an overview over the operations that are generated in this step, and how their semantics is specified using OCL postconditions.

Table 1. Overview of generated operations

model element	generated operation with OCL constraints
Class C	**context** C::new():C
	post: result .oclIsNew() and result −>modifiedOnly()
	context C:: delete (): OclVoid
	post: self . oclIsUndefined () and self@pre −>modifiedOnly()[a]
Attribute att	**context** C::getAtt (): D
	post: result =self. att
	context C:: setAtt (arg: D):OclVoid
	post: self . att=arg and self . att−>modifiedOnly()
Operation op	**context** C::op_sec (...):...
	pre: pre_{op}
	post: $\overline{\text{post}_{op}} = \text{post}_{op}$[f() ↦ f_sec (), att ↦ getAtt ()]

[a] While self@pre is unsupported by the concrete syntax, it is semantically well-defined.

For example, reading and writing an attribute value has to be represented by getter- and setter-methods. This means that for each attribute with public visibility, a public getter and a public setter method has to be generated, and the visibility of the attribute has to be made private. This transformation is similar in spirit to what one has to do when generating executable code or code skeletons from the model, cf. [1] for example. Instead of generating code for these getter and setter methods, we here have to generate OCL constraints to define their semantics. As a consequence, we generate the postconditions shown in Table 1.

Also, for each operation op() in the design model, we generate a second operation op_sec(). The postcondition $\overline{\text{post}_{op}}$ for op_sec() is structurally the same as the postcondition post_{op} for op(), where every occurrence of an attribute call is substituted with the corresponding getter operation call, and every occurrence of an operation call is substituted with the corresponding call of the secured operation. This substitution ensures that the *functional* behavior of the secured operation stays the same, but that it is only "executable" when all security requirements for establishing the postcondition are fulfilled. The reasoning here is that a caller will need (at least) the permission necessary to establish the postcondition for performing an operation call. Furthermore, we make the precondition pre_{op} specified for op() into a precondition for op_sec(), too. For this, we keep the OCL expression unchanged, i.e., no substitutions are necessary this time, and only change the context declaration of the OCL constraint.

In the postcondition of setter methods, i.e., C::setAtt(arg:D):OclVoid, it is not sufficient to specify that the attribute gets the value of the given argument. We also need to specify that "nothing else" happens during this operation call. Using standard OCL this is difficult or even impossible for arbitrary methods: one has to specify that the whole system stays unchanged *except* for this attribute. Therefore, HOL-OCL provides an extension of OCL for specifying frame properties within postconditions: Set(T)::modifiedOnly():Boolean. This allows for specifying explicitly the set of object instances that the system can change during state transition. For example, we can now define C::setAtt(arg:D):OclVoid using the postcondition self.att = arg and self.att->modifiedOnly().

Analogous transformations are done for association ends, i.e., they are handled as they were attributes. Also, operations for constructing and deleting objects are created, with the given constraints specifying their semantics.

Figure 5 shows the generated authorization environment together with the transformed permission anchors of the running example.

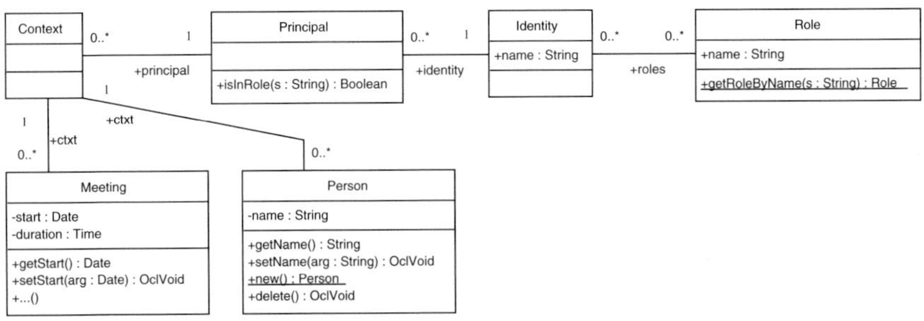

Fig. 5. Authorization Environment with Permission Anchors

3.3 Security Model Transformation

Role Hierarchy First, we transform the role hierarchy of the security model into OCL invariant constraints on the classes of the authorization environment. The total set of roles in the system is specified by enumerating them:

```
context Role inv: Role.allInstances().name=Bag{<List of Role Names>}
```

The inheritance relation between roles is then specified by an OCL invariant constraint on the Identity class:

```
context Identity inv: self . roles .name−>includes('<Role1>') implies
                      self . roles .name−>includes('<Role2>')
```

Given this, role assignments to identities can then be stated by further OCL invariant constraints on the Identity class:

```
context Identity inv: self .name = '<userName>' implies
                      self . roles .name=Bag{<List of Role Names>}
```

We denote by inv_{sec} the conjunction of these invariants. We have to ensure that inv_{sec} is consistent, i.e., that situations like the following do not arise:

```
context Role
inv: Role. allInstances ().name=Bag{'UserRole','AdministratorRole','TechnicianRole'}

context Identity inv: self .name = 'Alice' implies self . roles .name=Bag{'Spy'}
```

Security Constraints The main part, however, of the security model transformation is the generation of the security constraints for the operations generated during the design model transformation. The existing constraints on the generated operations are transformed according to Table 2.

Table 2. Overview of Transformed Constraints

Effect of the Security Model Transformation		
inv_C	$\mapsto$	inv_C
pre_{op}	$\mapsto$	pre_{op}
post_{op}	$\mapsto$	let auth = auth_{op} in if auth then $\overline{\text{post}_{op}}$ else result . oclIsUndefined () and Set{}−>modifiedOnly() endif

Table 2 applies only to operations generated during the design model transformation. As noted above, the pre-existing model elements of the design model are preserved. Only the postconditions are changed during this transformation, i.e., the invariants inv_C for classes C of the design model and the preconditions pre_{op} for access-controlled operations stay the same. The transformation wraps the postcondition generated during the design model transformation with an access control check using the authorization expression auth_{op}, which evaluates to true if access is granted, and false otherwise. If access is granted, the behavior of this operation will not be changed. Otherwise, the transformed postcondition ensures that no result is returned and the system state does not change.

The expression auth_{op} is built in the following way: Let $\text{perm}_1, ..., \text{perm}_n$ be the permissions for this operation call, and let roles_i be the set of roles, constr_i be the authorization constraint associated with permission perm_i, and

$$\overline{\text{constr}_i} = (\text{constr}_i[\text{caller}{\mapsto}\text{ctxt.principal.identity.name}])$$
$$[\text{f()} \mapsto \text{f@pre()},\ \text{att} \mapsto \text{att@pre},\ \text{aend} \mapsto \text{aend@pre}]$$

be the OCL expression where every occurrence of the non-standard keyword caller in constr_i is substituted by the expression ctxt . principal . identity .name, which evaluates the name of the current caller using the authorization environment. Operation, attribute, and association end calls are substituted by their post-state equivalents. auth_{op} is then defined as the following OCL expression:

```
auth_op := let perm1:Boolean = Set{<list of role names r ∈ roles_1>}
                                  ->exists(s|ctxt@pre. principal@pre . isInRole@pre (s))
                                  and constr_1
              -- analogous for perm2 to permn
              perm:Boolean = perm1 or perm2 or ... permn
           in perm.oclIsDefined () and perm
```

We explicitly check the authorization expression for undefinedness, mapping it to false if it is undefined. This is necessary because undefinedness can be caused by user-specified authorization constraints, which form a part of auth_{op}.

For illustration purpose, we show the final postcondition of the setter operation Meeting:: setStart () below:

```
context Meeting:: setStart (arg : Date):OclVoid
post:  let  auth = let perm1:Boolean = Set{'UserRole'}
                                       ->exists(s|ctxt@pre. principal@pre . isInRole@pre (s))
                                       and ctxt@pre. principal@pre . identity@pre .name@pre
                                           = self.owner@pre.name@pre
                       perm2:Boolean = Set{'AdministratorRole'}
                                       ->exists(s|ctxt@pre. principal@pre . isInRole@pre (s))
              in perm_1 or perm_2
       in  if auth. oclIsDefined () and auth then true
           else  result . oclIsUndefined () and Set{}->modifiedOnly() endif
```

4 Implementation

The transformation is part of a tool-chain (see Figure 6) that consists of a UML CASE tool with an OCL type-checker for modeling software systems, a model repository, model analyzers and various code generators.

We use the UML CASE tool ArgoUML (`http://argouml.tigris.org`) and combine it with the Dresden OCL2 Toolkit (`http://dresden-ocl.sf.net/`), which provides a OCL 2.0 compliant [11] parser and type-checker. Both tools use the Netbeans Metadata Repository (MDR), which is a model repository supporting the OMG MOF and the Java JMI standards. Using MDR, one can instantiate arbitrary MOF-compliant metamodels, which results in a *model extent*, a container for models compliant with this metamodel. MDR can automatically generate JMI interfaces from the metamodel so that one can, using these interfaces, access and manipulate the contents of such a model extent.

Our Java-based transformation tool, *su2holocl*, uses different MDR extents, namely: As first step of the transformation we parse the input model using the SecureUML *profile*, into a separate model extent based on the SecureUML *metamodel*. This gives us the ability to deal with the security part of the model on an

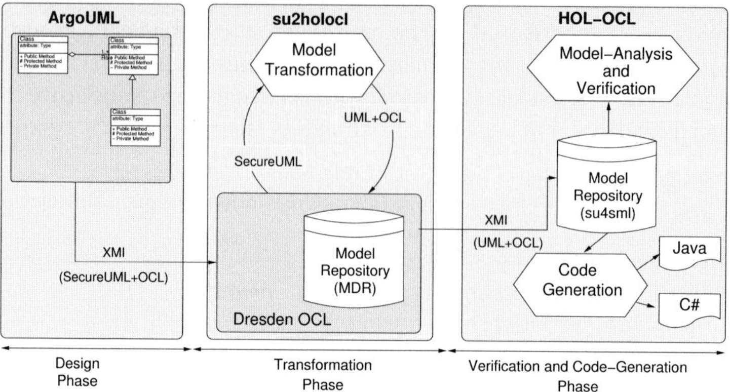

Fig. 6. Tool-chain Overview

abstract level. The Dresden OCL Toolkit uses a specialized metamodel combining the UML 1.5 and the OCL 2.0 metamodel. This results in an upward compatible extension of the UML 1.5 Metamodel: every UML 1.5 model is still a model of the combined metamodel. We use the OCL type-checker for checking user-defined constraints that occur in the design-model and for checking the security constraints that are generated during the transformation. As we currently only typecheck the transformed OCL constraints, not the original authorization constraints, we do not need to extend the Dresden OCL Toolkit, e.g., for supporting "caller" as a new keyword. The toolkit also provides an OCL expression visitor, which we use to implement the substitutions for transformed postconditions.

For interfacing the results of our model transformation with Isabelle and HOL-OCL, which are written in SML, we also developed a data repository: *su4sml*. This repository is also implemented in SML and supports the various metamodels we are using, e.g., UML, OCL, SecureUML. At the moment, su4sml is used for importing UML models into HOL-OCL. We also developed a generic code-generator based on su4sml that generates code from SecureUML models in various SecureUML dialects, that respects the specified access control policy.

5 Methodology

In this section, we discuss three key issues that arise while adding access control specifications to an object-oriented system model. In particular, we define several well-formedness conditions on the security specification: an access control aware variant of Liskov's principle, a data-accessibility condition and a notion of relative consistency.

5.1 Access Control and Inheritance

In an object-oriented system, *inherited methods* inherit the access control policy assigned to the method in the superclass. However, one can assign an access control policy to a subclass which is completely independent from the inherited policy. This leads to the idea of extending Liskov's principle to access control policies, i.e., access rights should be preserved along the class hierarchy. This boils down to the following two well-formedness conditions:

1. all overridden methods must have less or equal role assignments as their counterparts in superclasses and
2. the security constraints for an overridden operation must imply the corresponding security constraints of the original operation.

A secured system model satisfying these requirements is called *overriding-secure*.

Note that the implication required here goes in the opposite direction of Liskov's principle [8]. We want to rule out security problems caused by overridden methods that have more functionality and therefore need a more restrictive access control policy. The overriding-secure property is therefore advisable, although violations may be adequate in certain situations.

5.2 Accessibility of Data

The following problem comparable to "dead-code-detection" in conventional compilers may occur in a secured system model. It is not necessarily implying inconsistency (see next subsection), but indicating bad specification practice potentially resulting from specification errors.

Using potentially inconsistent security constraints may lead to the situation that some operation in a class can be accessed by no principal. We call an operation of this kind *inaccessible*.

Accessibility of an operation op in class C may be defined as follows:

1. if op has no role assignments, it is accessible by all principals (following our default-accessibility rule (c.f. Section 2.1)).
2. if op has role-assignments labeled with security constraints $SC_1, \ldots, SC_n$, then op is accessible iff $SC_1 \vee \ldots \vee SC_n$ holds for all objects of this class.

As a well-formedness condition of a secured system model, we require that all operations are accessible.

5.3 Relative Consistency

Following general practice, we call a system model *consistent* iff the conjunction of all invariants $\mathrm{inv}_{\mathrm{global}}$ is *invariant-consistent* and all operations m are *implementable*. An invariant inv is *invariant-consistent* iff there are satisfying states (i.e., $\exists \sigma . \sigma \models inv$ in the terminology of [11, Appendix A]). An operation m is *implementable* iff for all pre-states σ_{pre} and all input parameter *self*, i_1, ..., i_n there exist a post-state σ_{post} and an output *result* such that the operation specification of m (consisting of pre_{op} and post_{op}) can be satisfied:[1]

[1] We make the implicit binding of the internal free variables $self, i_1, \ldots, i_n$ occurring in the OCL formulae pre_{op} and post_{op} explicit.

$$\forall\, \sigma_{\text{pre}} \in \Sigma, \mathit{self}, i_1, \ldots, i_n.\ \sigma_{\text{pre}} \models \text{pre}_{op}(\mathit{self}, i_1, \ldots, i_n) \longrightarrow$$
$$\exists\, \sigma_{\text{post}} \in \Sigma, \mathit{result}.\ (\sigma_{\text{pre}}, \sigma_{\text{post}}) \models \text{post}_{op}(\mathit{self}, i_1, \ldots, i_n, \mathit{result})$$

where Σ is the set of legal states (i.e., $\Sigma = \{\sigma | \sigma \models \text{inv}_{\text{global}}\}$). Our notion of implementability of an operation is only meaningful for system models where $\text{inv}_{\text{global}}$ is invariant-consistent; otherwise the above definition yields true for the trivial reason that Σ is empty. Being implementable is also called "non-blocking" in the literature and can be viewed as a liveness property.

The question arises what is the "desirable semantic result" of our model transformation on the design model. In particular, we expect that in case of a security violation (i.e., auth_{op} does not hold) an operation preserves the state and reports an error. In the other case (i.e., auth_{op} does hold, meaning that a principal has "enough" permissions), we expect that the model transformation preserves the "functional content" of the operation specification of the system model. These requirements are captured by a *security proof obligation* spo_{op} (which is automatically generated for each operation):

$$\text{spo}_{op} := \text{auth}_{op} \ \ \mathsf{implies}\ \text{post}_{op} \triangleq \overline{\text{post}}_{op}$$

where $x \triangleq y$ is the strong equality yielding true iff $x = y$ (i.e., the strict OCL equality holds) or x and y are both undefined.

The following example illustrates the role of security proof obligations, and what sorts of inconsistencies in secured system models they rule out. Assume that we want to add to the class Meeting the operations:

```
context Meeting::getNames(): Sequence(String)
post:    result = self. participants .name->asSequence()

context Meeting:: getSize (): Integer
post:    result = self. participants ->size()
```

and attempt to give execute permissions for both operations to TechnicianRole. Recall that this role has no read permissions for objects of class Person and therefore is not able to access the names of participants. Following the definitions in Section 3, we have:

$$\overline{\text{post}}_{\text{getNames}} \triangleq \mathsf{result} \ = \mathsf{self.\ getParticipants\ ().\ getName().asSequence()}$$

Since auth_{op} and the strong equality ($\_ \triangleq \_$) never reduce to OclUndefined, the security proof obligation $\text{spo}_{\text{getNames}}$ boils down to:

$$\sigma \models \text{auth}_{op} \longrightarrow (\sigma, \sigma') \models \text{post}_{\text{getNames}} \triangleq \overline{\text{post}}_{\text{getNames}}$$

However, under the assumption $\sigma \models \text{auth}_{op}$ the caller is in the role TechnicianRole, i.e., has execute permission to Meeting::getNames() in the given concrete state σ. Because users in the role TechnicianRole do not necessarily have permission for the accessor Person::getName(), this operation call may yield undefined. In this case, $\overline{\text{post}}_{\text{getNames}}(\mathit{self}, \mathit{result}) =$ OclUndefined. For consistent design models, however, $\text{post}_{\text{getNames}}(self, result)$ is never OclUndefined. Therefore, the conclusion becomes false and the security proof obligation becomes invalid: $\text{spo}_{\text{getNames}} =$ false. This indicates that it does not make sense to give permissions for the operation Meeting::getNames() to the TechnicianRole role, as they cannot execute it anyways. In contrast, we can prove $\text{spo}_{\text{getSize}}$ because read permission for the association end participants is sufficient to satisfy the postcondition. As the TechnicianRole has this permission, we can grant the TechnicianRole role the execute permission for Meeting:: getSize ().

Due to the construction of $\overline{\text{post}}_{op}$ and the accessor functions, the proof or disproof of spo_{op} is fairly easy and can be automatically supported in the most common case: a non-recursive postcondition containing just attribute accesses. For recursive calls induction is needed. An important property of security proof obligations is illustrated by the following theorem:

Theorem 1. *An operation op_sec of the secured system model is implementable provided that the corresponding operation of the design model is implementable and* spo_{op} *holds.*

Proof. The complete proof can be found in the extended version of this paper [2].

Inaccessible operations (as discussed in the previous section) were transformed to totally undefined functions. They are clearly implementable operations, albeit pathological ones.

A class system is called *security consistent* if all spo_{op} hold.

Theorem 2. *A secured system model is consistent provided that the design model is consistent, the class system is security consistent, and the security model is consistent.*

Proof. By definition of the model transformation, we have $\text{inv}_{\text{sec-global}} \equiv \text{inv}_{\text{global}}$ and inv_{sec}. Since the invariant of the security model is consistent, since $\text{inv}_{\text{global}}$ is invariant-consistent by assumption, and since the signature parts of the security model and the design model are disjunct, there must be states that satisfy both invariants. The implementability of all methods follows from Theorem 1. □

These theorems enable modular specifications and reasoning for secure systems, which is important for large-scale applications.

6 Conclusions

We presented a systematic approach to include access control into data models given by UML class diagrams. From an integrated design and security model, a secured system model is generated which can be analyzed for consistency and liveness properties on the one hand and further transformed to code on the other.

Access control is a necessary means to establish security, but not a sufficient one: class invariants or implementation details may allow an attacker to infer implicit secrets of a system. For example, the Name attribute in Person may be correlated via class invariants to other attributes that can be accessed by TechnicianRole. A systematic analysis of this problem on the basis of the secured system model requires data flow analysis (see [9, Sect. 5], for an overview) which is out of the scope of this paper, but clearly an interesting line of future research.

Another line of future research is proving that the generated code—including the code for the methods of the design model—complies to the secured system model, or that a more concrete secured system model represents a *refinement* of a more abstract one. This involves proofs over the correctness of implementation issues of access control points as well as auxiliary data or different data structures which need different internal checks to establish the security behavior specified in the original secured system model. This type of verification problems has already been addressed [3]; however, it remains to show how they can be applied to an object-oriented setting and SecureUML.

References

[1] D. Basin, J. Doser, and T. Lodderstedt. Model driven security: from UML models to access control infrastructures. ACM *Trans. Softw. Eng. Methodol.*, 15(1), 2006.

[2] A. D. Brucker, J. Doser, and B. Wolff. A model transformation semantics and analysis methodology for SecureUML. Tech. Rep. 524, ETH Zürich, 2006.

[3] A. D. Brucker and B. Wolff. A verification approach for applied system security. *Int. Journal on Software Tools for Technology*, 7(3):233–247, 2005.

[4] A. D. Brucker and B. Wolff. The HOL-OCL book. Tech. Rep. 525, ETH Zürich, 2006.

[5] D. F. Ferraiolo, R. Sandhu, S. Gavrila, D. R. Kuhn, and R. Chandramouli. Proposed NIST standard for role-based access control. ACM *Trans. Infor. and System Security*, 4(3):224–274, 2001.

[6] J. Jürjens. *Secure Systems Development with* UML. Springer, 2004.

[7] M. Koch and F. Parisi-Presicce. Access control policy specification in UML. In *Critical Systems Development with* UML, pp. 63–78. 2001. TUM-I0208.

[8] B. H. Liskov and J. M. Wing. A behavioral notion of subtyping. ACM *Trans. Progr. Lang. and Systems*, 16(6):1811–1841, 1994.

[9] H. Mantel. Information flow control and applications – bridging a gap. In J. N. Olivera and P. Zave, eds., FME, LNCS, vol. 2021, pp. 153–172. Springer, 2001.

[10] T. Nipkow, L. C. Paulson, and M. Wenzel. *Isabelle/*HOL *— A Proof Assistant for Higher-Order Logic*, LNCS, vol. 2283. Springer, 2002.

[11] UML 2.0 OCL specification. 2003. Available as ptc/2003-10-14.

[12] R. S. Sandhu, E. J. Coyne, H. L. Feinstein, and C. E. Youman. Role-based access control models. *Computer*, 29(2):38–47, 1996.

Incremental Model Transformation for the Evolution of Model-Driven Systems

David Hearnden[1], Michael Lawley[2], and Kerry Raymond[2]

[1] School of ITEE, University of Queensland, Australia
hearnden@itee.uq.edu.au
[2] Queensland University of Technology, Australia
{m.lawley, k.raymond}@qut.edu.au

Abstract. Model transformations are an integral part of model-driven development. Incremental updates are a key execution scenario for transformations in model-based systems, and are especially important for the evolution of such systems. This paper presents a strategy for the incremental maintenance of declarative, rule-based transformation executions. The strategy involves recording dependencies of the transformation execution on information from source models and from the transformation definition. Changes to the source models or the transformation itself can then be directly mapped to their effects on transformation execution, allowing changes to target models to be computed efficiently. This particular approach has many benefits. It supports changes to both source models and transformation definitions, it can be applied to incomplete transformation executions, and *a priori* knowledge of volatility can be used to further increase the efficiency of change propagation.

1 Introduction

In model-driven systems, the evolution and synchronisation of source and target models often relies on the automated maintenance of transformation relationships. Large models or complex transformation specifications can cause transformation execution time to become quite significant, impeding this process. Live transformation execution is an incremental update technique designed to address these issues.

1.1 Incremental Updates

In broad terms there are two approaches to incremental updates. The first approach involves re-running the entire transformation, producing new output models that must then be *merged* with the previous output models. Updating models *in situ* is a special case of this approach, where the merge is performed implicitly. In this approach the context from the original transformation is lost, which is why a merge strategy is necessary in order to recreate that context. The feasibility of model merging for incremental transformations is heavily dependent on the traceability features of the transformation language.

O. Nierstrasz et al. (Eds.): MoDELS 2006, LNCS 4199, pp. 321–335, 2006.

The second approach involves preserving the transformation context from the original transformation, thus obviating a merge strategy to recreate it. A *live transformation* does not terminate, rather it continuously maintains a transformation context such that the effects of changes to source inputs can be readily identified, and the necessary recomputation performed.

Figure 1 illustrates these two approaches. In Figure 1(a), each successive update to S requires a complete re-transformation t producing new versions of T. If *in-situ* updates are desired, then a merge is required. In Figure 1(b), the transformation t is continuous, starting from an initial transformation from S producing T. Each successive source update ΔS is mapped directly to a target update ΔT. The transformation t does not terminate as such, but rather goes through phases of activity when S is changed.

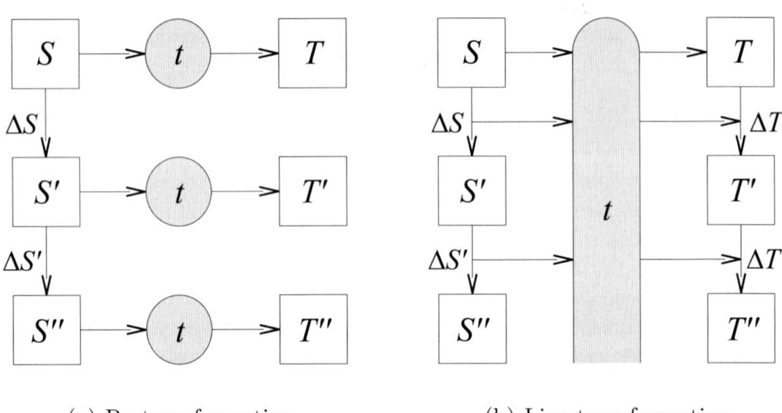

(a) Re-transformation (b) Live transformation

Fig. 1. Incremental Update Strategies

The advantage of the second approach is that it is far more efficient, especially for small changes, and is thus more suitable for the rapid update of transformation outputs. On average, the amount of computation necessary is proportional to the size of the input changes and the output changes. This is particularly important for model-driven tools in an incremental development methodology, where models are constantly evolving and constant synchronisation is necessary for consistency. Another advantage of the second approach is that it is a more direct solution for finding the changes to outputs required in response to changes to inputs, as opposed to finding the actual outputs themselves. For a model evolution tool, this may be an important distinction. Consider the task of selecting, from a set of possible source changes under consideration, the change that produces the *smallest* consequent change on the target models.

The cost of the second approach is that the execution context must be constantly maintained. Unless there are a large number of large transformations being maintained, this is unlikely to be a significant problem, and section 3.1 discusses how the space cost can be scalably traded for computation time should the context become too large.

1.2 Transformation Languages

We restrict our analysis to logic-based transformation languages; these languages turn out to be the most suitable for live transformation.

Of the declarative paradigms, logic languages have an advantage over functional languages because program data has a direct and clear effect on program computation. There is a single inference rule (resolution), that provides sufficient power for computational completeness. With resolution, program data has a direct influence on the evaluation process. One could say that logic languages have *data-driven* evaluation.

While functional languages are also typically classed as declarative, they are less suitable for live transformations than logic languages because the effect of program data is less clear. Reduction operations for functional evaluation are driven by the state of the expression being reduced, so the effect of program data is not direct.

There have been a variety of languages and techniques proposed in response to the MOF 2.0 Query / View / Transformation Request For Proposals [1], the majority of which have emphasised declarative definitions for transformations. The current adopted QVT specification [2] is a hybrid of declarative and imperative languages, with the declarative level being sufficiently powerful to be executable. The DSTC's submission to the QVT RFP [3] presents a transformation language that is completely declarative and can be executed with an open-source tool, Tefkat [4] [5].

The incremental update techniques presented here have been investigated in the context of Tefkat; however because of their foundational nature they should be applicable to any declarative rule-based transformation language, such as the QVT specification.

1.3 Related Work

Incremental update techniques have been extensively researched for deductive databases. The specific problem they address is the maintenance of materialised views in response to changes to base relations. The solution that has been most influential [6] involves transforming the deductive rules that define a view into *delta*-rules that define how additions and deletions to queried data could be transformed to additions and deletions to the view. There have been several variations on this theme (e.g. [7]), however as discussed in [8] they follow the same basic strategy.

The live transformation approach presented in this paper adopts a fundamentally different strategy by addressing the incremental update problem in terms of the execution context of a canonical logic engine. Instead of deriving a new transformation to perform the incremental updates, this approach tries to isolate the effects of updates on the dynamic computation structures used for logical evaluation. This should theoretically enable more efficient update propagation as it is a more direct approach, however the price paid is that an implementation must be tightly integrated with the internal structures of a particular transformation engine rather than only being dependent on language semantics. Recent developments in incremental evaluation of tabled logic programs [9] [10] are also adopting an engine-oriented approach.

1.4 Overview of Paper

Section 2 describes SLD resolution, the theoretical basis for the evaluation of logic languages. Sections 2.3 and 2.4 respectively present the extensions required to preserve dependency information and the algorithms used to respond to changes to input models. Section 3 discusses optimisations that can be performed to further increase update efficiency, as well as how the strategy described in section 2 can be extended to allow incremental updates in response to changes to transformation definitions as well as input models. Finally, section 4 illustrates an example of live transformation execution.

2 Live Propagation

In this section we consider extending a transformation engine based on the standard mechanism for the interpretation of logic languages: SLD resolution. The evaluation of a declarative rule-based transformations is driven by a search for solutions to a *goal*. This search can be conceptualised as a tree, and this tree can be used to represent the trace of a transformation execution. As mentioned previously, because resolution is data-driven, the dependencies of program execution on input models (and also the transformation itself) have a clear manifestation, and can be recorded for later analysis. Our strategy involves recording these dependencies on source model information so that changes to the tree can be made efficiently in response to changes to source models or the transformation definition, as opposed to rebuilding the tree from scratch with a re-transformation. Changes to the search tree can then be readily mapped to consequent changes in target models.

2.1 SLD Resolution

SLD resolution is a deduction rule used for the execution of logic programs. It is a restriction of the general resolution principle [11] (the *S* stands for *Selection*, *L* for *Linear*, and *D* for *Definite* clauses).

Given a goal G consisting of a set of atomic literals and a ruleset R consisting of a set of rules and/or facts, two choices are made. A literal a from G and a rule r from R are *selected* such that a unifies with r (there exists a variable substitution θ such that $a\theta = h\theta$, where h is the head of rule r). The atom a in G is then replaced with the body of rule r, then the most general unifier (mgu) of a and h is applied, giving a new goal G'. The process continues until the goal is empty ($\Box$), and the composition of all the unifiers, Θ, is then a solution for the goal G. In other words, $G\Theta$ is a fact that can be deduced from the ruleset R. SLD resolution is sound and complete, so no wrong solutions are produced and all solutions can be deduced.

$f_1 : class(c_1)$
$f_2 : class(c_2)$
$f_3 : class(c_3)$
$f_4 : super(c_3, c_1)$
$f_5 : owns(c_1, p_1)$
$f_6 : owns(c_3, p_2)$

$r_1 : owns(C, P) \leftarrow$
$\quad super(C, C'), owns(C', P)$

(a) Facts and rules.

$class(C), owns(C, P)$
$\Rightarrow \underline{class(C)}, owns(C, P) \quad [f_3, \{C \mapsto c_3\}]$
$\Rightarrow \underline{owns(c_3, P)} \quad [r_1, \{C \mapsto c_3\}]$
$\Rightarrow \underline{super(c_3, C')}, owns(C', P) \quad [f_4, \{C' \mapsto c_1\}]$
$\Rightarrow \underline{owns(c_1, P)} \quad [f_5, \{P \mapsto p_1\}]$
$\Rightarrow \square$

(b) SLD resolution (one solution).

Fig. 2. Resolving a goal against a rule set

Consider the ruleset in Figure 2(a). Facts f_1 to f_3 describe three classes, c_1, c_2 and c_3, where c_3 is a subtype of c_1 (f_4). c_1 directly owns property p_1 and c_3 directly owns property p_2 (facts f_5 and f_6), and rule r_1 describes the transitive ownership of inherited contents, thus c_3 indirectly owns p_1 too. Figure 2(b) illustrates the resolution of a goal, $class(C), owns(C, P)$, that is a query for classes and their contents. In the first resolution, the selected literal (underlined) is $class(C)$ and the selected fact is f_3. These unify to produce a mgu $\{C \mapsto c_3\}$, and replacing $class(C)$ with the (empty) body of f_3 followed by the application of the mgu results in the new goal $owns(c_3, P)$. Three more resolutions are applied, resulting in an empty goal ($\square$), indicating that a solution has been found. The composition of the unifiers (taking care to distinguish copies of C) results in the unifier $\{C \mapsto c_3, P \mapsto p_1\}$, representing one particular solution to the goal (class c_3 has property p_1). Note that in this example just one solution to the goal is found; there are others. By selecting different facts and rules, resolution can be used to find any solution to a goal.

2.2 SLD Trees

In SLD resolution, there are two non-deterministic choices that must be made at each resolution step: a literal must be selected, and a matching rule found. If we remove the second choice and instead resolve against *every* rule that matches the selected literal, then the resulting structure is an *SLD tree*. SLD trees represent all resolution paths, and therefore contain all solutions to a goal. The leaves of the tree are either success nodes ($\square$) indicating a solution, or failure nodes that have non-empty goals but can not be resolved further ($\times$).

An SLD tree for the previous example is shown in Figure 3. The nodes and edges have been labelled (n_i,e_i) only for future reference. Note that SLD trees are not unique; they depend on the *selection rule* that is used to select a literal from the goal.

The SLD tree forms the basis of an execution environment for logic programs. Often the tree is not explicitly created, but rather exists implicitly via a search strategy. In Tefkat, the SLD trees are explicit. The SLD tree in Prolog, however, exists as a depth-first search.

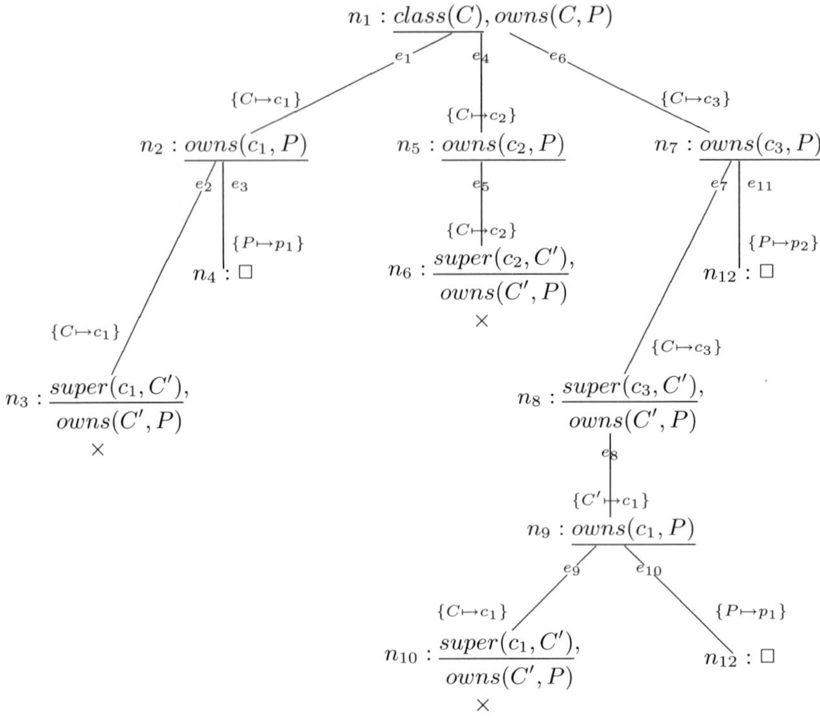

Fig. 3. An SLD tree

2.3 Tagging

Our goal is to provide a live execution environment, where changes to source models can be efficiently mapped to changes to target models. From a logical perspective, source models are manifested as a set of facts, and transformations as a set of rules and facts. As those familiar with logic programming are aware, a fact is simply a special case of a rule, so there is no real need to distinguish the two; however if we are only observing changes to source models then we need only be concerned with facts.

Changes to source models after a transformation has occurred are thus manifested as changes to the fact base used by a logic engine. These facts can influence the SLD tree in precisely one way: by unifying with the selected literal of a node's goal, thus spawning an edge in the tree. Additive changes to source models can therefore cause new branches and subtrees to be computed. Deletive changes can cause branches to be pruned. In order to make these incremental changes as efficient as possible, we tag the facts with references to where they are used in the tree, so that the effects of source changes can be made directly.

Two types of information are recorded while nodes query the fact base: the usage of a fact by an edge, and the failure to find a matching fact for a node. The first requires tagging of facts, the second requires tagging of fact signatures (name and arity). For this purpose it is convenient to group facts with the same

```
RESOLVE(U, R)
1  while U ≠ ∅
2       do n ← choose(U)
3          U ← U − {n}
4          if goal[n] = □
5             then solutions ← solutions ∪ SOLUTION(n)
6             else g ← goal[n]
7                  l ← selectLiteral(g)
8                  matches ← FIND-MATCHES(R, l)
9                  t ← getTable(l)
10                 tableTags[t] ← tableTags[t] ∪ {n}
11                 for each (θ, r) ∈ matches
12                     do e ← CREATE-BRANCH(n)
13                        unifier[e] ← θ
14                        if r is a fact
15                           then factTags[r] ← factTags[r] ∪ {e}
16                                fact[e] ← r
17                        n′ ← childNode[e]
18                        goal[n′] ← ((g − {l}) ∪ body(r))θ
19                        U ← U ∪ {n′}
20 return solutions
```

```
SOLVE(G, R)
1  r ← CREATE-ROOT
2  goal[r] ← G
3  solutions ← ∅
4  return RESOLVE({r}, R)
```

name and arity into *tables*. Algorithms SOLVE and RESOLVE illustrate how such recording can be incorporated into a resolution algorithm (lines 9-10 and 14-16).

While U is non-empty, a node is chosen for expansion and removed from U (line 2). Success nodes are nodes whose goal has been reduced to □ and are a SOLUTION algorithm (elided) is used to compute the composition of all the unifiers used from the root to the success node (line 5). Non-success nodes have a literal selected from their goal (line 7), which is then matched against the rule

Fact	Edges
$class(c_1)$	$\{e_1\}$
$class(c_2)$	$\{e_4\}$
$class(c_3)$	$\{e_6\}$
$super(c_3, c_1)$	$\{e_8\}$
$owns(c_1, p_1)$	$\{e_3, e_{10}\}$
$owns(c_3, p_2)$	$\{e_{11}\}$

(a) Fact tags

Table	Nodes
$class/1$	$\{n_1\}$
$super/2$	$\{n_3, n_6, n_8, n_{10}\}$
$owns/2$	$\{n_2, n_5, n_7, n_9\}$

(b) Table tags

Fig. 4. Dependencies

database to produce a set of matching rules/facts paired with the most general unifier for the match (line 8). The dependency of the node on a table of facts is then recorded (line 10).

A new branch in the tree is created for each of the matching rules/facts (line 12), and the matching rule/fact and unifier are recorded on the edge (line 13). For fact edges, the dependency of the edge on the particular fact that caused its creation is then recorded (lines 14- 16). The selected literal in the goal is replaced with the body of the matching rule/fact, the matching unifier applied, and the result is set as the new node's goal (lines 17-18). The new node is then added to the set of unexpanded nodes, to be expanded on a future iteration. After all the nodes have been expanded, RESOLVE returns the set of unifiers that represent solutions to the goal (line 20). Lines 9, 10 and 14-16 are the only extra work required for the dependency recording.

For brevity, the detail of some used algorithms has been elided. Algorithm CREATE-BRANCH(n) simply creates and returns a branch from node n in the data structure for the resolution tree. FIND-MATCHES(R, l) searches the knowledge base R for rules/facts whose heads unify with l, and returns the set of all such pairs (θ, r).

The SOLVE algorithm builds a tree from scratch by creating a root tree node, setting its goal, and calling RESOLVE. Figures 4(a) and 4(b) show the fact and table tags from the edge and node dependencies for the tree in Figure 3.

2.4 Responding to Change

We consider two types of change to the model and transformation definition: *fact addition* and *fact removal.*

Fact Addition. The algorithms for responding to model or transformation change rely on the existing resolution algorithms. Informally, the response to the addition of new facts is to identify nodes in the tree for which resolution needs to be resumed. Algorithm ADD-FACT describes this procedure.

```
ADD-FACT(f)
nodes ← tableTags[getTable(f)]
U ← ∅
for each n ∈ nodes
      do l ← selectedLiteral[n]
         θ ← UNIFY(l, head(f))
         if θ ≠ NIL
            then e ← CREATE-BRANCH(n)
                 unifier[e] ← θ
                 fact[e] ← f
                 factTags[f] ← factTags[f] ∪ {e}
                 n′ ← childNode[e]
                 goal[n′] ← (goal[n] − {l})θ
                 U ← U ∪ {n′}
return RESOLVE(U)
```

ADD-FACT uses the table tags to identify all the nodes with a selected literal of the same name and arity as the added fact f (line 1). The selected literals of each of these nodes are tested against the added fact, in order to find any nodes with goals that match (more formally, unify) with the head of f (line 5). Any nodes found have branches added from them, and they are added to a set of unexpanded nodes U. Note that lines 7- 13 are equivalent to lines 12- 19 from RESOLVE. Finally, resolution is resumed on all those new nodes (line 14).

ADD-FACT returns the set of unifiers from the new success nodes found in response to the addition of a fact. These unifiers represent valid solutions in the context of the new fact database, however they may not all be *new* solutions since other paths in the tree may have already established some of those solutions prior to the fact addition. Therefore the set of solutions returned by ADD-FACT must be compared with the original solutions in order to identify new solutions.

Fact Removal. In response to the removal of a fact f, all the edges in the tree that were created because of a match with a selected literal must be identified. The subtrees rooted at these edges must then be removed, which involves removing all the dependency information from that subtree as well as identifying solutions that may have been removed. Similarly to ADD-FACT, REMOVE-FACT returns the set of solutions established by success nodes that have now been removed, however other success nodes in the remaining tree may also establish some of those solutions, so again they must be compared with the original solutions in order to identify invalidated solutions.

```
REMOVE-FACT(f)
1  edges ← factTags[f]
2  oldSolutions ← ∅
3  for each e ∈ edges
4          do oldSolutions ← oldSolutions ∪ PRUNE-EDGE(e)
5              DELETE-BRANCH(e)
```

REMOVE-FACT is straightforward. All the edges dependent on the removed fact f are deleted from the tree, however a pruning step occurs (line 4) before the branch removal (line 5). This pruning step removes dependencies recorded for the subtree, as well as accumulating solutions from success nodes in that subtree. Mutually recursive algorithms PRUNE-EDGE and PRUNE-NODE define this procedure.

```
PRUNE-EDGE(e)
f ← fact[e]
if f ≠ NIL
    then factTags[f] ← factTags[f] − {e}
return PRUNE-NODE(childNode[e])
```

```
PRUNE-NODE(n)
1 oldSolutions ← ∅
2 if isSuccess(goal[n])
3     then oldSolutions ← oldSolutions ∪{n}
4 t ← getTable(selectedLiteral[n])
5 tableTags[t] ← tableTags[t] − {n}
6 for each e ∈ childEdges[n]
7         do oldSolutions ← oldSolutions ∪PRUNE-EDGE(e)
8 return oldSolutions
```

PRUNE-EDGE simply removes the edge from the potential fact dependency in which it appears, and then prunes the child node. PRUNE-NODE accumulates a solution if it encounters a success node (line 3), then removes the node from the table dependency in which it appears (line 5), and then recursively prunes its child edges, accumulating their solutions (line 7).

2.5 Negation

So far, we have only analysed SLD resolution, which does not allow *negative* literals to appear in rule bodies. In other words, rules that rely on the *absence* or the *falsity* of facts may not be used. SLD resolution can be extended to *general* clauses, which do allow negative literals in goals and rule bodies; however extra restrictions are required in order to preserve soundness and completeness.

The easiest extension to SLD resolution to allow negative literals is to use the closed-world assumption, where all unprovable facts are considered false. This allows us to treat *negation as failure*, so to prove a literal $\neg p(X)$ it is sufficient to show that there is no proof of $p(X)$. To achieve this, a separate tree is created, and if the tree *finitely fails*, then $p(X)$ is considered false and hence $\neg p(X)$ true. However if a solution is found in this separate tree, then a proof of $p(X)$ has been found, so $\neg p(X)$ is false, and hence the node that spawned the separate tree fails.

This extension is often referred to as SLDNF (SLD with Negation as Failure). SLDNF introduces a fundamental change to the structure of the resolution tree. Instead of a single tree there is now a forest of negation trees plus one positive tree (the root tree). Nodes with a negative selected literal are 'connected' with a negation tree constructed to prove the positive literal. These connections must be maintained as part of the forest.

The algorithms from section 2.4 only apply to SLD resolution and are monotonic: ADD-FACT can only add more solutions and REMOVE-FACT can only invalidate previous solutions. If SLDNF resolution is used instead, then monotonicity is lost, and incremental updates become more complex. The addition of facts may result in the removal of branches (and hence the removal of solutions), and the removal of facts may result in the addition of branches (and hence the addition of solutions). It turns out that the algorithms ADD-FACT and REMOVE-FACT require only minor modifications in order to achieve this behaviour. The update phase then iterates between tree pruning and tree expansion until a fixed point is reached.

3 Discussion

In this section we discuss two ways to further optimise incremental updates, and how the techniques from section 2.3 can be extended to also allow incremental changes to transformation definitions.

3.1 Incomplete Transformation Context

The price for the efficiency of live transformation is the maintenance of the transformation context (the SLDNF trees) and the dependency tables. Previously it was assumed that the context was complete, i.e. the SLDNF trees and dependency tables were completely preserved. This complete context may be costly for large and complex transformations where there may be hundreds of thousands of tree nodes, and hundreds or even thousands of facts and rules.

The live transformation strategy can accommodate an incomplete context with some extensions to the algorithms presented in section 2.4. Arbitrary subtrees can be collapsed into a single 'collapsed' node, with all the dependency information condensed on that node. The space of that subtree is then reclaimed, but the aggregated tags preserve the dependency information. There is a computational cost only if the dependency information identifies that the collapsed node has been potentially affected, and then the entire subtree must be recomputed. However because collapsing can be performed at any point in a tree, it is quite a scalable trade-off.

The trick to making effective choices for node collapsing is to recognise that some facts in a model are more stable than others. For example, a person's name is less likely to change than their height or weight. We use the term *volatility* to describes the likelihood of change for a fact or rule. It is obviously most beneficial to collapse subtrees that are non-volatile. With good estimates of fact volatility (either explicitly provided or obtained via heuristics), an intelligent engine can reduce the size of the transformation context while still providing the efficiency for most incremental changes.

3.2 Ordering of Volatile Literals

The volatility of different facts and rules can be leveraged in an even more fundamental way. The structure of the resolution trees is completely determined by the *selection rule* that chooses which literal in a node's goal is to be resolved. This structure has a significant impact on the efficiency of the initial transformation and also the efficiency of the incremental updates. If volatile facts are used towards the root of a resolution tree, then changes to those facts involve pruning the entire subtree rooted at the usage of those facts and subsequently regrowing the new subtree. If volatile facts are used towards the leaves of a resolution tree, then the impact of changes to those facts is much less, as the subtrees that are pruned and regrown are smaller.

By providing an engine with such volatility estimates, perhaps user specified or even collected from version histories, the selection rule can choose to expand stable literals first, and volatile literals last, reducing the cost of updates to those volatile facts.

3.3 Rule/Fact Equivalence

As mentioned in section 2.3, as far as logic is concerned facts are simply a special type of rule. There is very little in the algorithms of section 2.4 that applies to facts but not rules, and so with some very minor modifications live transformation can be used for rules as well. This is of great importance for the evolution of transformation definitions, since changes to the rules in a transformation can be efficiently propagated to updates on the transformation targets.

4 Live Transformation in Practice

In this section we present some preliminary measurements of the efficiency of incremental model transformation using live resolution trees.

4.1 Sample Transformation

The sample transformation we use to demonstrate live resolution trees is a simplified version of one of the many transformations from an object-oriented class metamodel (such as UML) to a relational database schema metamodel. The complete metamodels have been omitted due to space considerations.

The class metamodel describes classes that own properties which are attributes or references, where attributes are data-valued and references are object-valued. Classes have zero or more superclasses. The relational schema metamodel describes tables that own typed columns, one of which is designated as a primary key.

The transformation maps classes to tables with keys. Properties that are owned directly or indirectly (through inheritance) are mapped to columns of the table corresponding to the property's owning class. For attributes, those columns are typed by the data type corresponding to the attribute's data type. For references, those columns are typed by the data type corresponding to the type of the primary key of the table mapped from the type of the reference. In other words, references are mapped to foreign key columns. Finally, if a class has an attribute marked as an identity attribute, the column mapped from that class-attribute pair becomes the key column for the class's corresponding table. Otherwise, a primary key column called `ID` is inserted. This sample transformation is useful as it is small enough to be easily understood, but complex enough to involve recursion, transitive closure and negation. The main rules for this transformation are described in Tefkat's concrete syntax in Figure 5.

The output of a Tefkat transformation is the unique minimal model (least fixed point) such that all rules are true. A rule is true if and only if, for all variable bindings for its source terms (`FORALL`, `LINKS`, `WHERE`), the target terms (`MAKE`, `LINKING`) are true. *Patterns*, such as `hasProperty/2`, are equivalent to logical predicates. Tefkat also uses *trackings*, which are essentially named relations, and are the only elements that may be both queried/checked (with `LINKS`) and asserted/enforced (with `LINKING`). For example, the `ClassTable` tracking associates a class with a table, and is asserted in the `LINKING` clause of `ClassToTable`, and is queried by the `LINKS` clauses of the other four rules.

4.2 Sample Execution

The transformation was run on the Ecore metamodel [12], followed by three updates. The first update was a simple renaming of an attribute of `ETypedElement`.

```
RULE ClassToTable
FORALL  Class c { name: n; }
MAKE    Table t { name: n; }
LINKING ClassTable WITH class = c, table = t;

PATTERN hasProperty(c, p)
WHERE   c.properties = p OR hasProperty(c.super, p);

RULE AttributeTypes
FORALL  Class c, Attribute a { name: n; }
WHERE   hasProperty(c, a)
AND     TypeType   LINKS ooType = a.type, rdbType = rdbtype
AND     ClassTable LINKS class = c, table = t
MAKE    Column col { name : n; table: t; type: rdbtype; }
LINKING AttributeColumn WITH class = c, attribute = a,
                             column = col, type = rdbtype;

RULE ForeignKeyTypes
FORALL  Class c, Reference r { name: n; type: rc; }
WHERE   hasProperty(c, r)
AND     ClassTable  LINKS class = rc, table = ft
AND     TableKey    LINKS table = ft, key = _, type = fktype
AND     ClassTable  LINKS class = c, table = t
MAKE    Column col { name : n; table: t; type: fktype; };

RULE IdKeyColumn
FORALL  Class c, Attribute a
WHERE   hasProperty(c, a) AND a.id = true
AND     AttributeColumn LINKS class = c, attribute = a,
                              column = col, type = keytype
AND     ClassTable      LINKS class = c, table = t
MAKE    Key k { table: t; column: col; }
LINKING TableKey WITH key = k, table = t, type = keytype;

RULE AutoKeyColumn
FORALL  Class c
WHERE   NOT (hasProperty(c, a) AND a.id = true)
AND     ClassTable LINKS class = c, table = t
MAKE    makeRdbType("Auto", auto),
        Column col { name: "ID"; type: auto; table: t;},
        Key k { table: t; column: col; }
LINKING TableKey WITH key = k, table = t, type = auto;
```

Fig. 5. Sample OO to RDB transformation

The propagated changes involved the renaming of 6 columns, one from each of the tables generated for the 6 subclasses that inherited that attribute. The second update involved the deletion of the `ETypedElement.type` reference. The 6 affected columns were deleted, as were all of their properties. The final change was marking `EClassifier.instanceClassName` as an identity attribute. which caused the most significant structural change. The automatic key columns added to the tables for `EClassifier` and its subclasses were deleted, those tables' keys were set to the columns for the `instanceClassName` attribute, and all columns generated from `EReferences` to `EClassifier` or any of its subclasses (i.e. foreign keys into the `EClassifier` table) had their types changed to `String`, the new type of `EClassifier`'s key column.

Table 1 shows the number of resolution nodes added, removed, and touched in each of the three updates. Node addition and removal are the most significant measurements since those operations involve modifications to the resolution trees and tag structures. Touched nodes are those nodes that were identified by the fact and table tags as being potentially affected, but on closer inspection were not affected.

The number of nodes is correlated with the execution time and space consumption of the incremental transformation. The results clearly show significant performance benefits from live transformation for all three updates.

Table 1. Number of tree nodes used during live transformation

#	Forest Size	Added /Removed	Touched	Total	Changed
-	7026	- / -	-	7026 (100%)	100%
1	7026	78 / 78	176	332 (4.7%)	2.2%
2	6828	0 / 198	0	198 (2.9%)	2.9%
3	6760	198 / 206	349	753 (11.1%)	6.0%

5 Conclusion

Incremental updates for declarative rule-based model transformations can be performed efficiently using live transformations. The dependencies of the transformation execution on its inputs can be recorded by tagging resolution trees. These dependencies can then be used to efficiently propagate source changes to target changes. With minor extensions, the algorithms presented in this paper can be used in the presence of negation and tabling, and also for incremental updates to the transformation definitions. Finally, awareness of model volatility can be leveraged to further increase update efficiency.

References

1. OMG: MOF 2.0 Query / Views / Transformations RFP. OMG document ad/02-04-10 (2002)
2. OMG: Meta Object Facility (MOF) 2.0 Query/View/Transformation Specification. OMG document ptc/2005-11-01 (2005)

3. DSTC, IBM, CBOP: MOF Query / View / Transformation Second revised submission. OMG document ad/2004-01-06 (2004)
4. Lawley, M., Steel, J.: Practical declarative model transformation with Tefkat. In Bruel, J.M., ed.: MoDELS Satellite Events. Volume 3844 of Lecture Notes in Computer Science., Springer (2005) 139–150
5. Tefkat: The EMF transformation engine (2006)
6. Gupta, A., Mumick, I.S., Subrahmanian, V.S.: Maintaining views incrementally. In Buneman, P., Jajodia, S., eds.: Proceedings of the 1993 ACM SIGMOD International Conference on Management of Data, Washington, D.C., May 26-28, 1993, ACM Press (1993) 157–166
7. Ceri, S., Widom, J.: Deriving incremental production rules for deductive data. Information Systems **19** (1994) 467–490
8. Gupta, A., Mumick, I.S.: Maintenance of materialized views: Problems, techniques and applications. IEEE Quarterly Bulletin on Data Engineering; Special Issue on Materialized Views and Data Warehousing **18** (1995) 3–18
9. Saha, D., Ramakrishnan, C.R.: Symbolic support graph: A space efficient data structure for incremental tabled evaluation. In: ICLP. (2005) 235–249
10. Saha, D., Ramakrishnan, C.R.: Incremental evaluation of tabled prolog: Beyond pure logic programs. In: PADL. (2006) 215–229
11. Robinson, J.A.: A machine-oriented logic based on the resolution principle. J. ACM **12** (1965) 23–41
12. Budinsky, F., Brodsky, S.A., Merks, E.: Eclipse Modeling Framework. Pearson Education (2003)

A Plugin-Based Language to Experiment with Model Transformation

Jesús Sánchez Cuadrado and Jesús García Molina

University of Murcia, Spain
{jesusc, jmolina}@um.es

Abstract. Model transformation is a key technology of model driven software development approaches. Several transformation languages have appeared in the last few years, but more research is still needed for an in-depth understanding of the nature of model transformations and to discover desirable features of transformation languages. Research interest is primarily focused on experimentation with languages by writing transformations for real problems.

RubyTL is a hybrid transformation language defined as a Ruby internal domain specific language, and is designed as an extensible language: a plugin mechanism allows new features to be added to core features. In this paper, we describe this plugin mechanism, devised to facilitate the experimentation with possible features of RubyTL. Through an example, we show how to add a new language feature, specifically we will develop a plugin to organize a transformation in several phases. Finally, we discuss the advantages of this extensible language design.

1 Introduction

Model transformation is a key technology for model driven software development (MDD) approaches to succeed. As a result of academic and industrial efforts, several model transformation tools and languages have appeared in the last few years, but more research is still needed for an in-depth understanding of the nature of model transformations and to discover the essential features of transformation languages. Therefore, the research interest of the MDD area is focused on experimentation with existing languages, by writing transformation definitions for real problems. Theoretical frameworks such as the feature model discussed in [1] and the taxonomy of model transformations presented in [2] are very useful to compare and evaluate design choices during experimentation.

A year ago, we started a project for the creation of a tool to experiment with features of hybrid transformation languages whose declarative style is supported by a binding construct, as is the case of the ATL language [3]. The result of this project is RubyTL [4], an extensible transformation language created by the technique of embedding a domain specific language (DSL) in a dynamic programming language such as Ruby [5]. RubyTL supports extensibility through a plugin mechanism: a set of core features can be extended with new features by creating plugins which implement predefined extension points.

O. Nierstrasz et al. (Eds.): MoDELS 2006, LNCS 4199, pp. 336–350, 2006.

In this paper, we present the extensible design of RubyTL, analyzing the extension points identified from the transformation algorithm. In addition, we show how to add a plugin for the needs of a particular problem, concretely a plugin that organizes a transformation in several phases; the extension points involved in this plugin are identified from its requirements.

The paper is organized as follows. The next section presents the core features of the RubyTL language and the transformation algorithm. Section 3 describes how the plugin mechanism is implemented, while Section 4 describes the plugin example. In Section 5 related work is discussed. Finally, conclusions and future work are presented in Section 6.

2 Language and Algorithm

RubyTL is a model transformation language designed to satisfy three main requirements: i) according to the recommendations exposed in [6][7], it should be a hybrid language, because declarative expressiveness may not be appropriate for complex transformation definitions, which may require an imperative style; the declarative style is provided by a binding construct similar to that in the ATL language [3], ii) it should allow easy experimentation with different features of the language, and iii) a rapid implementation should be possible . These requirements have been satisfied through two key design choices: the definition of the language as a Ruby internal DSL and the implementation of a plug-in extension mechanism. RubyTL provides a set of core features, and new features can be added by plugins connected to a set of predefined extension points. In this section we describe the core features and the transformation algorithm, whereas the plugin mechanism will be explained in the following section.

As said in [8] the internal DSL style is much more achievable in dynamic languages like Lisp, Smalltalk or Ruby. We have chosen Ruby, but the approach is language independent. Ruby is a dynamically typed language which provides an expressive power similar to Smalltalk through constructs such as code blocks and metaclasses. Because of these characteristics, Ruby is very suitable for embedding DSLs [8], so that Ruby internal DSLs are being defined in areas such as project automation and electronic engineering [9]. Applying this technique to create RubyTL has allowed us to have a usable language in a short development

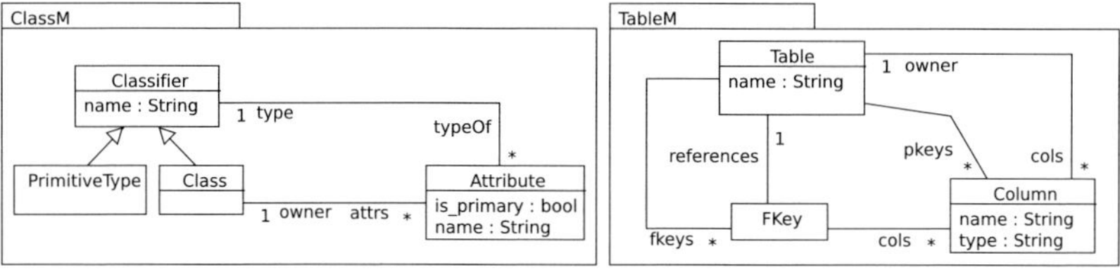

Fig. 1. Class and relational metamodels used in the example

time. Moreover, Ruby code can be integrated in the DSL constructs, so that the hybrid nature can be obtained in a uniform way: everything is Ruby code.

Below we show a simple example of a transformation definition to illustrate the core features of RubyTL, and then explain the basis to understand the language. A more detailed explanation about the core language can be found in [4]. We have considered a classical transformation problem: the class-to-table transformation, whose metamodels are shown in Figure 1.

```
rule 'klass2table' do
  from  ClassM::Class
  to    TableM::Table
  mapping do |klass, table|
    table.name = klass.name
    table.cols = klass.attrs
  end
end

rule 'property2column' do
  from     ClassM::Attribute
  to       TableM::Column
  filter   { |attr| attr.type.kind_of? ClassM::PrimitiveType }
  mapping do |attr, column|
    column.name = attr.name
    column.type = attr.type.name
    column.owner.pkeys << column if attr.is_primary
  end
end

rule 'reference2column' do
  from     ClassM::Attribute
  to       Set(TableM::Column)
  filter   { |attr| attr.type.kind_of? ClassM::Class }
  mapping do |attr, set|
    table = klass2table(attr.type)
    set.values = table.pkeys.map do |col|
      TableM::Column.new(:name => table.name + '_' + col.name,
                         :type => col.type)
    end
    table.fkeys = TableM::FKey.new(:cols => set)
  end
end
```

As can be seen in the example, a transformation definition consists of a set of transformation rules. Each rule has a name and four parts: i) the *from* part, where the source element metaclass is specified, ii) the *to* part, where the target element metaclass (or metaclasses) is specified, iii) the *filter* part, where the condition to be satisfied for the source element is specified, and iv) the *mapping* part, where the relationship between source and target model elements are expressed, either in a declarative style through of a set of bindings or in an imperative style using Ruby constructs. A binding is a special kind of assignment that makes it possible to write what needs to be transformed into what, instead of how the transformation must be performed. A binding has the following form `target_element.property = source_element`, for instance in the `klass2table` rule.

In the example, the first rule (`klass2table`) will be executed once for each element of type `Class`, leading to the creation of an element with type `Table`. In the *mapping* part of this rule, relationships between class features and table features are specified. In particular, it is important to note how the `table.cols = klass.attrs` binding will trigger the execution of the `property2column` rule or `reference2column` rule for it to be resolved.

The `property2column` and `reference2column` rules illustrate how imperative code can be written within a mapping part. In the `property2column` rule, two bindings are followed by a Ruby sentence which checks if an attribute has to be converted into a primary key to add the column to the set of table primary keys. The `reference2column` rule is an example of a one-to-many relationship (one-attribute to many-columns). In this case, all the mapping is written in an imperative way, as the set of columns which take part in the foreign key is explicitly filled.

This example raises an important question about querying the target model. Using the expression `table.pkeys.map`, in the `reference2column` rule, we are relying on the target model to calculate the foreign key columns, which could cause problems because we are navigating on a partially generated model. In this case, if circularity exists in the source model, it may cause the primary keys of a table to be partially calculated when they are used to generate foreign key columns. Of course, this simple example can be solved without relying on the target model but more complex transformations, like the one proposed in [10], could become difficult.

In Section 4 we propose a language extension to address the problem of navigating the target model. With this extension, a transformation would be able to safely navigate the target model.

2.1 Transformation Algorithm

The execution model of RubyTL can be explained through a recursive algorithm. As we will see in the next section, this algorithm is the basis to identify extension points.

Every transformation must have at least one entry point rule in order to start the execution. By default, the first rule of a transformation definition is the entry point rule, for instance the `klass2table` rule in the example. When the transformation starts, each entry point rule is executed, by applying the rule to all existing elements of the metamodel class specified in its *from* part (in the example, to all instances of `ClassM::Class`).

The structure of the main procedure of the transformation algorithm is a loop executing the set of entry point rules. For each entry point rule, target model elements are created for each source model element satisfying the rule filter, and then the rule is applied, i.e. the mapping part is executed.

```
Transformation entry point()
  entry-rules = select entry point rules
  for each rule R in entry-rules
      source-instances = get all instances of source type of rule R
      for each instance S in source-instances
          if S satisfy the rule R filter
              T = create target instances
              apply rule(R, S, T)
```

The `Apply rule` iterates over each binding in the mapping part of a rule, distinguishing two cases: a primitive value must be assigned to the target element property or the binding must be resolved by applying other rules. As said, a binding has the following form: `T.property = S`, therefore `S` and `T` are part of a binding.

```
Apply rule(R : rule to apply,
           S : source element, T : target elements)
  for each binding B in R.bindings
      if B is primitive then assign value to property
                        else resolve binding(B)
```

The `Resolve binding` procedure below shows how the binding resolution mechanism acts in two steps. Firstly, all the rules conforming the binding and satisfying the rule filter are collected. Secondly, for each selected rule, proper target elements are created and linked, and then the rule is applied.

```
Resolve binding(B : binding)
   S = source element of B
   T = target element of B
   P = property of T taken from B
   C = list of conforming rules initially empty

   for each rule R in the set of transformation rules
       if R is conforming with B and R satisfy filter
          add R to C

   for each rule R in C
       T' = create target instances
       link T' with P of T
       apply rule(R, S, T')
```

It is worth noting the recursive nature of the algorithm and how such recursion is implicitly performed by means of bindings. The recursion finishes when a mapping is only composed of primitive value assignments. Another way to finish recursion could be by preventing a rule from transforming the same source element twice. This key feature, which allows the language to deal with metamodels having cycles, has been added by a plugin.

3 Extension Mechanism

RubyTL is an extensible language, that is, the language has been designed as a set of core features with an extension mechanism. In this section we will present the extension mechanism based on plugins. First, we will explain the underlying ideas behind the design of our extensible language, then we illustrate the extension points we have identified.

From the transformation algorithm shown in the previous section, we have identified some parts in the transformation process which are variable, and depending on how they are implemented, the transformation algorithm will behave differently. These variable parts will be extension points. Since the transformation algorithm is general, it can be implemented in any general purpose programming language. What would change from one implementation to another would be: (a) the way extension points are defined and implemented, and (b) the concrete syntax of the language.

A plugin is a piece of code which modifies the runtime behaviour of RubyTL by acting either on the language syntax, the evaluation engine or even the model repository. The language can be considered as a framework providing a set of extension points that plugins can implement to add functionality. According to the language aspect being extended, there are three categories of extension points: (1) related to the algorithm, (2) related to creation of new rules and management of the rule execution cycle, and (3) related to the language syntax. These categories are explained in detail in the following subsections.

Regarding how those extension points are implemented, there are two kinds of extension points: *hooks* and *filters*. *Hooks* are methods which can be overridden to implement a new functionality (similar to the *template method* design pattern [11]), while *filters* follow the same schema as web application filters [12]. Filters allow plugins to collaborate in a certain extension point. In addition, a filter can be seen as an application of the *Observer* pattern [11], as it allows a plugin to register for events occurred in the transformation process.

An extension point always has a corresponding hook, and can also have two filters: a filter which is called just *before* the hook extension point is invoked, and a filter which is called just *after* the hook extension point has been invoked. The reason to use hooks and filters is because if two plugins implement the same hook they could be incompatible, but with filters two or more plugins could share the same extension point. Sometimes, certain extensions can be implemented by a filter without overriding existing extensions.

We will call hook based extension points *hook extension points* and filter based extension points *filter extension points*.

3.1 Algorithm Extensions

Extensions related to the transformation algorithm are directly based on the three procedures explained in Section 2. Each of these procedures is a hook extension point itself. Moreover, some parts of these procedures are also hook extension points, as can be seen in Figure 2, where the execution order of the extension points is shown.

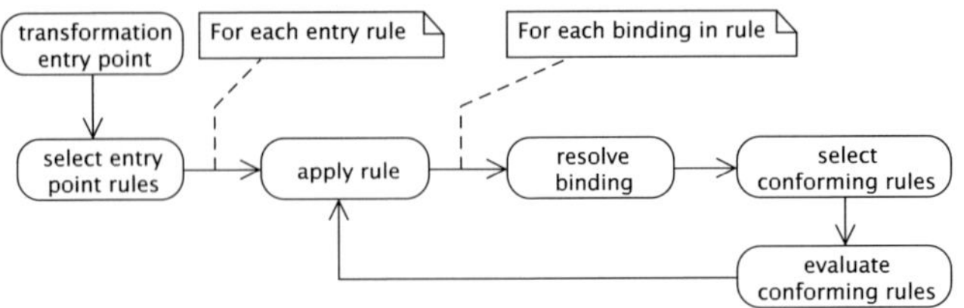

Fig. 2. Execution order of algorithm extension points

Therefore, the available extension points are the following:

- **transformation entry point.** This extension point corresponds to the `Transformation entry point` procedure. It provides a way to apply entry rules in a different manner, as will be shown in the example in Section 4. This extension point has a nested hook extension point, *select entry point rules*.
- **select entry point rules.** The application of entry point rules depends on how they are selected. This extension point allows us to apply different selection strategies, for instance based on a special kind of rule. Usually, it is necessary to declare more than one entry point rule, which can be provided by a plugin implementing this extension point.
- **apply rule.** This extension point, which corresponds to the `Apply rule` procedure, specifies how a rule should be applied (by default executing its mapping part). Since this behaviour could depend on the kind of rule being applied, a similar extension point is included in the rule extension point category, so that the default behaviour of this extension point is delegating to this rule extension point.
- **resolve bindings.** This extension point, which corresponds to the `Resolve binding` procedure, specifies how a binding is resolved by selecting and evaluating conforming rules, so that it delegates in two nested hook extension points: *select conforming rules* and *evaluate conforming rules.*
- **select conforming rules.** It is intended to specify how to select rules conforming a binding. It is useful to change the conformance strategy, as will be shown in the example in Section 4.
- **evaluate conforming rules.** It is intended to specify how conforming rules are evaluated. This evaluation may require creating new target elements. In the plugin example of the next section, this extension point must be implemented because phasing needs an evaluation procedure which is different from the default.

Regarding filter extension points, two filters not related to hook extension points are defined, at the beginning and at the end of the transformation. The first one allows us to set up global information before the transformation starts, for instance, a new model could be created in the model repository to store the transformation trace model. The second one allows us to perform "cleaning" activities after the transformation has finished. In addition, the following filters related to the identified hook extension points are defined: after select entry rules, before/after apply rule, before/after select available rules, before/after evaluate available rules.

3.2 Rule Extensions

Rule extensions points are intended to create new kind of rules, which will have a different behaviour than the default one. These extension points are related to the rule execution cycle (i.e. the set of the states a rule passes through). According to the transformation algorithm, a rule passes through the states shown in Figure 3. Each one of these states (except *waiting to be executed*) is an extension point itself. Actually, these steps are driven by the algorithm (see Figure 2) which is in charge of delegating to the proper rule extension point in each step of its execution.

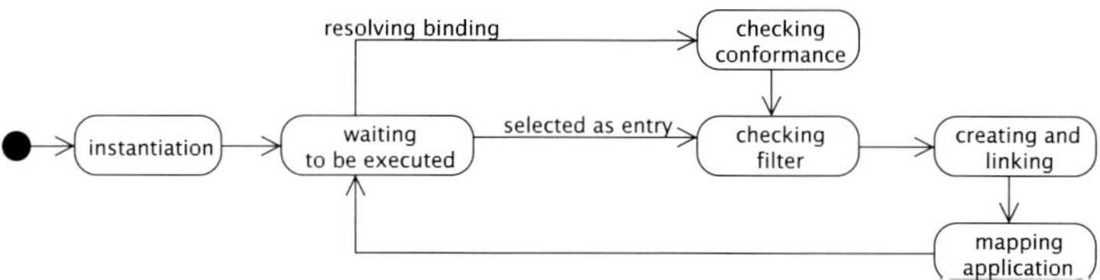

Fig. 3. Rule execution shown as a state machine diagram

When a new kind of rule is created any of the following hook extension points can be implemented to provide the new behaviour. Of course, some algorithm extension points could also be implemented in a plugin in order to complete the rule behaviour.

- **instantiation.** When a rule is encountered in the transformation text its body is evaluated to set up the rule properties This extension point makes it possible to set additional initialization data as if it were the rule constructor.
- **checking conformance.** Resolving a binding involves checking the conformance of the set of rules with that binding. Different kinds of rules could have different conformance strategies.
- **checking filter.** By default the rule filter is checked before applying the rule by evaluating the expression in the *filter* part. However, another kind of rule may establish another way of filtering applicable rules.
- **creating and linking.** Just before a rule is applied, new target elements are created and linked to the corresponding target feature in the binding. This behaviour could be different, for instance, rules which never transform a source element twice, i.e. no new target elements are created if the source element has been already transformed, but the previous result is linked.
- **mapping application.** Rule application normally consists of executing the mapping to assign primitive values and resolve bindings. This extension point allows a rule to modify the rule application strategy, for instance, to have more than one mapping in a rule.

Given the steps shown in Figure 3, the following *filter extension points* makes sense: after definition, before/after check condition, before/after create and link, and before/after rule application.

3.3 Syntax Extensions

Syntax extensions allow a plugin to add new keywords and define nested structures to create new language constructs. In Section 4 we will create a *phase* syntax construct which encloses a set of rules; this construct is a new nested structure defined by a keyword such as *phase*.

There are two kinds of syntax extensions depending on the place the new keyword could appear. If the new construct may appear within a rule, it is said to be rule scoped, while if it can only appear in the transformation body, it is said to be transformation scoped. Transformation scoped syntax is intended to specify configurations that affect the whole transformation, while rule scoped syntax should be used to set rule properties.

Each new keyword is added to an associative table which associates each keyword with a callback to manage it. Such callback provides the new language construct with the proper semantics, and will be called when the keyword appears in the transformation text.

4 Plugin Example

In this section we will show an example of language extension whose main purpose is to allow a transformation to be organized in several phases, and thus facilitate dealing with complex transformations. We will show how this extension is useful in coping with the problem explained in Section 2 related to querying partially built target models. Also, we will show which extension points have been used to implement the phasing mechanism.

When this extension is applied to the language, a transformation is organized into several phases, where each phase consists of a set of rules which can only be invoked in the context of its phase [1], but it can query target elements which have been partially generated in previous phases. It can be considered that each phase has a state defined by the state of all the generated target elements, both in this phase and in previous phases. A transformation progresses by applying

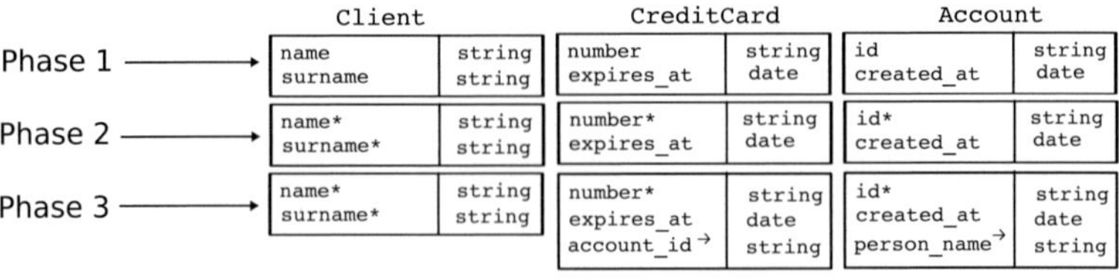

Fig. 4. Use of the phasing mechanism to generate a relational model by refinement

rules which modify the current phase state. Therefore, each phase refines a partial transformation state established by previous phases. This is what we call *rule refinement*. It is worth noting that when a rule navigates on the target model, the query must be consistent with the previous phase state. Figure 4 shows how a relational model is refined in three phases: firstly data columns are created, secondly primary keys are set (marked `*`), and finally, foreign keys are created (marked $^{\rightarrow}$).

We have identified the following requisites, which should be fulfilled by the extension:

- Rules should be enclosed by a higher level syntax structure in order to easily identify which phase a rule belongs to.
- Refinement of transformation state implies a rule can use target elements created by a rule of a previous phase.
- The execution order of phases should be specified.

To satisfy such requisites the following extension points have to be implemented. First, syntax extensions are made in the form of two new keywords in the transformation scope: `ordering` and `phase`. The *ordering keyword* makes it possible to specify the order in which phases will be applied, while the *phase keyword* expects a code block enclosing a set of rules. The example below shows what the syntax looks like.

Now, we must identify which rule and algorithm extension points have to be implemented. Considering the rule execution cycle, it is necessary to know which phase a rule belongs to. Therefore, the `after_instantiation` filter for rules must be implemented to detect when a rule has been read and within which phase.

Next, we must think about how the transformation algorithm is affected by the phasing mechanism, that is, which algorithm extension points have to be implemented. The first difference with the core algorithm is the way entry point rules are applied. Every phase should have its own entry point rules, and these are executed depending on the phase order. All this logic is implemented in the *entry point* extension point (see Figure 2) overriding the previous logic related to the transformation start.

Finally, rule refinement must be addressed. The same rule could be defined in more than one phase but with a different mapping, and new instances are created the first time the rule is applied for a given source element, but when the rule is applied (in another phase) for the same source element, no new target elements are created and the previous ones are used to evaluate the mapping part of the rule. The convention used is that a rule with a name x in a phase A, and a rule with a name x in a phase B are supposed to be the same, with x of B being a refinement of x of A.

In order to do so, we need to redefine how rules are selected and evaluated to resolve bindings. First, rule selection has to take into account that only rules belonging to the current phase can be selected. Since we do not want to override the default behaviour of the `select conforming rules` extension point, but only to remove those rules not belonging to the current phase, the `select` `conforming rules` filter could be used. The use of this filter is a good example of reuse of previous logic (selection of conforming rules), but modifying the result to serve a new purpose. Finally, the `evaluate conforming rules` hook is overridden to keep track of rule refinement, so that new target elements are not created if they have been created by a rule in a previous phase.

Below, the class-to-table example is rewritten, applying the phasing mechanism just explained.

```
ordering :default, :primary_keys, :foreign_keys

phase 'default' do
  rule 'klass2table' do
    from  ClassM::Class
    to    TableM::Table
    mapping do |klass, table|
      table.name = klass.name
      table.cols = klass.attrs.select{ |a| a.type.is_a?(ClassM::PrimitiveType) }
    end
  end

  rule 'property2column' do
    from    ClassM::Attribute
    to      TableM::Column
    mapping do |attr, column|
      column.name = attr.name
      column.type = attr.type.name
    end
  end
end

phase 'primary_keys' do
  rule 'property2column' do
    from    ClassM::Attribute
    to      TableM::Column
    filter  { |attr| attr.is_primary }
    mapping do |attr, column|
      column.owner.pkeys << column
    end
  end
end

phase 'foreign_keys' do
  rule 'klass2table' do
    from  ClassM::Class
    to    TableM::Table
    mapping do |klass, table|
      table.cols = klass.attrs.select{ |a| ! a.type.is_a?(ClassM::PrimitiveType)}
    end
  end

  rule 'reference2column' do
    from    ClassM::Attribute
    to      Set(TableM::Column)
```

```
    mapping do |attr, set|
      table = klass2table(attr.type)
      set.values = table.pkeys.map do |col|
        TableM::Column.new(:name => table.name + "_" + col.name, :type=>col.type)
      end
      table.fkeys = TableM::FKey.new(:cols => set)
    end
  end
end
```

As can be seen in the example, with the phasing approach, the problem of safely navigating the target model explained in Section 2 is solved. As said in Section 2, we should have chosen a more complex transformation example to show the real usefulness of phasing, but use this simpler one for the sake of clarity. The key point of this approach is that, in any phase, it can be known which target element have been already created. In the example, the `reference2column` rule can safely get all primary keys of a table because the previous phase has created them. In addition, the phasing mechanism makes it easy to deal with complex transformations requiring to be organized into more than one pass (it can be thought of as a multi-pass transformation).

5 Related Work

Several classifications of model transformation approaches have been developed [1][6]. According to these classifications, the different model-model approaches can be grouped into three major categories: imperative, declarative and hybrid approaches.

Some of the latest research efforts in model transformation languages are ATL, Tefkat, MTF, MTL and Kermeta. MTL and Kermeta [13] are imperative executable metalanguages not specifically intended to model-model transformation, but they are used because the versatility of their constructs provides high expressive power. However, the verbosity and the imperative style of these languages make writing complex transformations difficult because they abstract less from the transformation details and make transformations very long and not understandable.

ATL is a hybrid language with a very clear syntax [3][14]. It includes several kinds of rules that facilitate writing transformations in a declarative style. However, the complete implementation of the language is not finished yet, and at the moment only one kind of rule can be used. Therefore it may be difficult to write some transformations declaratively. ATL and RubyTL share the same main abstractions, i.e. rule and binding, but ATL is statically typed, while RubyTL uses dynamic typing.

Tefkat is a very expressive relational language which is completely usable [15]. As noted in [2], writing complex transformations in a fully declarative style is not straightforward, and the imperative style may be more appropriate. That is why a hybrid approach is a desirable characteristic for a transformation language to help in writing practical transformation definitions.

MTF [16] is a set of tools including a declarative language based on checking or enforcing consistency between models. MTF provides a extensibility mechanism to extend its syntax by plugging in a new expression language. To our knowledge, RubyTL is the first extensible model transformation language in the sense that it provides a mechanism to extend both its syntax and the transformation algorithm. In any case, the idea of extensible language has been applied in other domains [17][18], and it is widely used in the Lisp language which provides a powerful macro system to extend its syntax.

6 Conclusions and Future Work

MDD approach will succeed only if proper model transformation languages are available. These languages should have good properties, such as being usable and able to provide appropriate expressiveness to deal with complex transformations. In the last few years, several languages have been defined and quality requirements have been identified in proposals such as [2]. Nowadays, experimentation with existing languages is a key activity of the MDD area.

RubyTL [4] is an extensible hybrid language that provides declarative expressiveness through a binding construct. It is a usable language with a clear syntax and a good trade-off between conciseness and verbosity. Moreover, the transformation style is close to the usual background of developers.

In this paper we have described how RubyTL provides a framework to experiment with the features of the language through a plugin mechanism. When a new language feature is going to be added, a new plugin is created. Creating a plugin means identifying which extension points are involved before it is implementation in the Ruby language. An example of transformation organized in phases has illustrated the process of plugin design.

The contribution of this paper is twofold. On the one hand, RubyTL is an extensible model transformation language, which provides some advantages with regard to other non extensible transformation languages: i) the language can be adapted to a particular family of transformation problems, ii) new language constructs can be added without modifying the core and iii) it provides an environment to experiment with language features. Moreover, we have proposed a phasing mechanism to allow a transformation to safely navigate the target model.

However, a limitation of our approach is that extensibility is restricted to a particular family of languages: those which rely on the binding concept. Since we have identified the extension points directly from an algorithm with "holes", only languages following such a scheme can be implemented. Anyway, the same idea can be reused to experiment with other kinds of languages. Another concern is that, since which extensions are going to be developed is not known in advance, the programmatic interface of the language should be as general as possible. At present, we are exploring ways of controlling the scope of plugins changes, so that incompatible extensions cannot be loaded at the same time.

In our experiments with the language, in addition to the phasing mechanism, we have found some language features we believe essential in this kind of transformation languages. We have identified four different types of rules, each one with some properties which help to solve certain transformation problems: *normal rules* like the ones shown in this paper, *top rules* to allow a transformation to have more than one entry point, *copy rules* which can transform a source element more than once, *transient rules* which are able to create elements that are only valid while the transformation is being executed. Moreover, a transformation language should be able to deal with one-to-many and many-to-one transformations. In this paper we have shown an example of one-to-many mappings. We are currently experimenting with different ways of implementing many-to-one mappings, since there are important performance concerns that must be taken into account. Another consideration is that, in a hybrid language, language constructs are needed to call rules explicity from imperative transformation code. Finally, an important property not found in many transformation languages is incremental consistency. We are currently experimenting with different ways to achieve it.

We continue experimenting with RubyTL by writing transformations for real problems, specifically we are applying MDD to portlets development. Also, we are currently working on the integration of our transformation engine inside the Eclipse platform by using RDT.[1] At present, an editor with syntax highlighting, a launcher for transformation definitions, a configuration tool for plugins, and a model-to-code template engine is available.[2]

Acknowledgments

This work has been partially supported by Fundación Seneca (Murcia, Spain), grant 00648/PI/04, and Consejería de Educación y Cultura (CARM, Spain), grant 2I05SU0018. Jesús Sánchez enjoys a doctoral grant from the Spanish Ministry of Education and Science.

References

1. Krzysztof Czarnecki and Simon Helsen. Classification of model transformation approaches. In *Proceedings of the 2nd OOPSLA Workshop on Generative Technique in the Context of the Model Driven Architecture*, Anaheim, October 2003.
2. Tom Mens, Krzysztof Czarnecki, and Pieter Van Gorp. A taxonomy of model transformations, 2005.
3. Jean Bézivin, Grégoire Dupé, Frédéric Jouault, Gilles Pitette, and Jamal Eddine Rougui. First experiments with the ATL model transformation language: Transforming XSLT into XQuery. In *OOPSLA 2003 Workshop*, Anaheim, California, 2003.
4. Jesús Sánchez, Jesús García, and Marcos Menarguez. RubyTL: A Practical, Extensible Transformation Language. In 2nd *European Conference on Model Driven Architecture*, volume 4066, pages 158–172. Lecture Notes in Computer Science, June 2006.

[1] http://rubyeclipse.sourceforge.net/

[2] http://gts.inf.um.es/downloads

5. Dave Thomas. *Programming Ruby. The Pragmatic Programmers' Guide.* Pragmatic Bookshelf, 2004.
6. Shane Sendall and Wojtek Kozaczynski. Model transformation: The heart and soul of model-driven software development. *IEEE Software*, 20(5):42–45, September/October 2003.
7. Tracy Gardner, Catherine Griffin, Jana Koehler, and Rainer Hauser. Review of OMG MOF 2.0 Query/Views/Transformations Submissions and Recommendations towards final Standard, 2003.
8. Martin Fowler. Language Workbenches: The Killer-App for Domain Specific Languages?, June 2005. http://www.martinfowler.com/articles/languageWorkbench.html.
9. Jim Freeze. Creating DSLs with Ruby, March 2006. http://www.artima.com/rubycs/articles/ruby_as_dsl.html.
10. Jean Bézivin, Bernhard Rumpe, Andy Schürr, and Laurence Tratt. Call for Papers of Model Transformations in Practice '05, 2005.
11. Erich Gamma, Richard Helm, Ralph Johnson, and John Vlissides. *Design Patterns: Elements of Reusable Object-Oriented Software.* Addison Wesley, March 1995.
12. Deepak Alur, John Crupi, and Dan Malks. *Core J2EE Patterns: Best Practices and Design Strategies.* 2001.
13. Pierre Alain Muller, Franck Fleurey, Didier Vojtisek, Zoé Drey, Damien Pollet, Frédéric Fondement, Philippe Studer, and Jean-Marc Jézéquel. On executable meta-languages applied to model transformations. In *Model Transformations In Practice*, Jamaica, 2005.
14. Frédric Jouault and Ivan Kurtev. Transforming models with ATL. In *Model Transformations in Practice Workshop*, Montego Bay, Jamaica, 2005.
15. Michael Lawley and Jim Steel. Practical Declarative Model Transformation With Tefkat. In *Model Transformations In Practice Workshop*, Montego Bay, Jamaica, 2005.
16. Sebastien Demathieu, Catherine Griffin, and Shane Sendall. Model Transformation with the IBM Model Transformation Framework, 2005. http://www-128.ibm.com/developerworks/rational/library/05/503_sebas/index.html.
17. Terry A. Winograd. Muir: A Tool for Language Design. Technical report, Stanford, CA, USA, 1987.
18. Macneil Shonle, Karl J. Lieberherr, and Ankit Shah. XAspects: An extensible system for domain-specific aspect languages. In *OOPSLA Companion*, pages 28–37, 2003.

SiTra: Simple Transformations in Java

D.H. Akehurst[1], B. Bordbar[2], M.J. Evans[2], W.G.J. Howells[1], and K.D. McDonald-Maier[3]

[1] University of Kent
{D.H.Akehurst, W.G.J.Howells}@kent.ac.uk
[2] University of Birmingham
B.Bordbar@cs.bham.ac.uk, mje33@cantab.net
[3] University of Essex
kdm@essex.ac.uk

Abstract. A number of different Model Transformation Frameworks (MTF) are being developed, each of them requiring a user to learn a different language and each possessing its own specific language peculiarities, even if they are based on the QVT standard. To write even a simple transformation, these MTFs require a large amount of learning time. We describe in this paper a minimal, Java based, library that can be used to support the implementation of many practical transformations. Use of this library enables simple transformations to be implemented simply, whilst still providing some support for more complex transformations.

1 Introduction

Model Driven Engineering (MDE) or Model Driven Development (MDD) [7] is an approach to software development in which the focus is on *Models* as the primary artefacts in the development process. Central to MDD are *Model Transformations*, which map information from one model to another. In general, we can view MDD as a general principle for software engineering that can be realised in a number of different ways (using different standards) and supported by a variety of tools. One of the most common realisations of MDD is via the set of OMG standards known as Model Driven Architecture (MDA) [25]. MDA, it is claimed, improves the software development process by enhancing productivity, portability, interoperability and ease of maintenance [20]. There are currently a variety of MDD tools that can be used to implement transformations [29].

Specification and definition of a model transformation is a complex task. This involves significant domain knowledge and understanding of both the source and target model domains. Even when you understand both models, defining the mapping between corresponding model elements is no easy task. Recently a variety of model transformation specification languages have been developed e.g. [17, 22, 32]. These languages are very rich and are used in various domains [9, 33, 37]. However, elegant execution of the specifications is still a research issue in many cases and may require significant manual intervention in order to provide an implementation. Implementation of a model transformation requires a different set of skills to those required for specifying a transformation and understanding the domain models.

O. Nierstrasz et al. (Eds.): MoDELS 2006, LNCS 4199, pp. 351 – 364, 2006.

In a large project, it is possible to divide the specification and implementation between two different groups of people who have relevant skills. In the case of smaller groups of developers and newcomers to MDD, the combined effort involved in becoming an expert in the two sets of skills described above is overwhelming. In particular, the steep learning curve associated with current MDD tools is an inhibitive factor in the adoption of MDD by even very experienced programmers.

To address this issue, the current paper describes a simple Java library for supporting a programming approach to writing transformations, based on the following requirements:

- **Use of Java for writing transformations:** This relinquishes the programmer from learning a new language for the specification of transformations
- **Minimal framework:** To avoid the overhead of learning a new Java library, the presented method has a very small and simple API

The presented method is not intended as a replacement for a full Model Transformation Framework or as a model transformation specification language, rather it is intended as a "way in" for experienced programmers to start using the concepts of transformations rules, without the need to learn a new language, or get to grips with a new framework of tools and development environments.

Our library enables transformations rules to be written using Java in a modular fashion and includes the implementation of an algorithm to execute a transformation based on those rules.

The next section of this paper provides some background on MDD. Section 3 introduces an example transformation task which is used in section 4 to aid the description of the use of our simple transformation library. Sections 5 and 6 discuss the Limitations of SiTra and compare it to other model transformations approaches. The paper concludes in section 7.

2 Background

2.1 MDD

A model transformation is a program that takes as input a graph of objects and provides as output another graph of objects. If we consider the development of a program that provides a solution to this problem there are a number of alternative ways to structure it.

A very basic (unstructured) approach would be to write a single function (or method) containing a mix of loops and *if* statements that explore the input model, and create objects for the output model where appropriate. Such an approach would be widely regarded as a bad solution and it would be very difficult to maintain.

A better solution, from a programming perspective, would be to make use of a programming pattern, such as the visitor pattern [14]. This provides a controlled way to traverse a source model, and a sensible means to structure the code for generating an output model. However, this pattern does have a few drawbacks. Firstly, the input model must be implemented in such a way that is supports the visitor pattern (i.e. the objects must implement a certain interface); an input model may well not support the required interfaces. Secondly, the visitor pattern is designed to navigate tree structures rather than graphs.

A Model Transformation approach to structuring a solution would make use of the following two concepts:

1. Transformer – the primary transformation object; it contains a collection of rules, and manages the process of transforming source model objects into target model objects.
2. Rule – a rule deals with specific detail of how to map an object from a source model into an object of the target model. One or more rules may or may be applicable for the same type of object and it is necessary to have a means to determine the applicability of a rule for a specific object, not just its type.

2.2 Model Transformations

Within the context of MDD, model transformation is the primary operation on models that is talked about. However, it is not the only one; operations such as model comparison, model merging etc are also considered, although these could be seen as particular types of model transformation.

The concept of model transformations existed before QVT and even before MDA. The following topics each address some aspect involving the notion of transforming data from one form to another.

- Compiling Techniques [1]
- Graph Grammar/Transformations [11]
- Triple Graph Grammars [30]
- Incremental Parsers [16]
- Viewpoint framework tools [13]
- Databases, Update queries
- Refinement [10]
- XML, XSLT, XQuery [34-36]

To be literal about it, even simple straight forward programming is frequently used as a mechanism for transforming data. This becomes more stylised when programming patterns such as the Visitor pattern [14] are used as a way to visit data in one model and create data in another.

Some techniques [4, 5, 27] base the transformation language on the notion of relations. However, this too is a new application of the old ideas as originally applied (for example) in the fields of databases (e.g. Update Queries) and System Specification (or refinement) using the formal language Z [31] a language which is heavily dependent on the notion of relations and their use for the manipulation of data.

The interesting aspect of the MDD approach to transformation is the focus on:

- Executable specifications; unlike the Z approach.
- Transforming models; models being viewed as higher level concepts than database models and certainly higher level than XML trees.
- Deterministic output; the main problem with Graph Grammars is that they suffer from non-deterministic output, applying the rules in a different order may result in a different output.

Much work on model transformation is being driven by the OMG's call for proposals on Queries, Views and Transformations (commonly known as QVT) [26]. There are a number of submissions to the standard with varying approaches, a good review of which is given by [15] along with some other (independent) approaches such as YATL [28], MOLA[18] etc. and earlier work such as [2].

There are a set of requirements for model transformation approaches given in [15], of which, the multiple approaches it reviews, each address a different subset. As yet there is no approach that addresses all of the requirements.

3 A Simple Transformation Library

Our simple transformation library consists of two interfaces and a class that implements a transformation algorithm. The aim of the library is to facilitate a style of programming that incorporates the concept of transformation rules. One of its purposes is to enable the introduction of the concept of transformation rules to programmers who are, as yet, unfamiliar with MDD; thus enabling the programmer to stay with familiar tools and languages and yet move towards an MDD approach to software engineering.

The two simple interfaces for supporting the implementation of transformation rules in Java are summarised in Table 1. The Rule interfaces should be implemented for each transformation rule written. The Transformer interface is implemented by the transformation algorithm class, and is made available to the rule classes.

Table 1.

```
interface Rule<S,T> {
  boolean check(S source);
  T build(S source, Transformer t);
  void setProperties(T target, S source, Transformer t);
}
interface Transformer {
  Object transform(Object source);
  List<Object> transformAll(List<Object> sourceObjects);
  <S,T> T transform(Class<Rule<S,T>> ruleType, S source);
  <S,T> List<T> transformAll(Class<Rule<S,T>> ruleType,
                             List<S> source);
}
```

Rules

A transformation problem is split up into multiple rules; our SiTra library facilitates this using the *Rule* interface. A class that implements this interface should be written for each of the rules in the transformation. The methods of this interface are described as follows:

1. The implementation of the *check* method should return a value of *true* if the rule is applicable to the source object. This is particularly important if multiple rules are applicable for objects of the same type. This method is used to distinguish which of multiple rules should be applied by the transformer.

2. The *build* method should construct a target object that the source object is to be mapped to. A recursive chain of rules must not be invoked within this method.
3. The *setProperties* method is used for setting properties of the target object (attributes or links to other objects). Setting the properties is split from constructing the target (where possible) so that we can recursively call rules when setting properties.

If it is impossible to distinguish between multiple rules using the *check* method, explicit rule invocation must be used to transform objects for which multiple rules apply. Objects that are derived from properties of the source object should be converted to objects for properties of the target object by calling the transform method on the transformer. It is the job of the transformer algorithm to keep track of already mapped objects, it is not necessary to be concerned about this when writing a rule.

Transformer

In order to use the rules, add the rule classes to an instance of the *Transformer* interface and call the *transform* method with the root object(s) of the source model.

An implementation of the *Transformer* interface is provided with a class *SimpleTransformerImpl*. It implements the simple transformation algorithm shown in Table 2. The full implementation of this algorithm includes additional error handling, not shown here for clarity of reading the algorithm rather than the error handling.

The four methods on the transformer interface are simply different convenience mechanisms for invoking the same algorithm. Two facilitate explicit invocation of a rule, and two facilitate the transformations of a list of source objects into a list of target objects.

Table 2.

```
T transform(Class<Rule<S,T>> ruleType, S source) {
  List<Rule> rules = getRules(ruleType)
  for(Rule r: rules) {
    if ( r.check(source) ) {
      T tgt = getExistingTargetFor(ruleType, source);
      if (tgt==null) {
        tgt = r.build(source, this);
        recordMapping(ruleType, source, tgt);
        r.setProperties(tgt,source,this);
      }
      return tgt;
    }
  }
}
```

The transformation algorithm takes two parameters, the type of the rule to use and the source object to transform. This provides an explicit transformation (i.e. the rule to use is explicitly provided). Alternatively, implicit invocation can be used (an alternative method on the Transformer interface) which passes the Rule interface as the ruleType for this algorithm.

The *getRules* method retrieves (via reflection) a list of rule objects that conform to the type of the passed ruleType. These rules are each checked to see if they are applicable to the source object (using the *check* method of the *Rule* interface). If the rule is applicable, and the source object has not already been mapped using that rule (the *getExistingTargetFor* method), then the build method of the rule is invoked in order to construct the target object. This target is subsequently recorded by the transformer so that future transformations of the same source object by the same rule do not cause duplicate target objects. Finally the *setProperties* method on the rule is invoked; having recorded the mapping between source and target previously, any transformation request within *setProperties* that invokes the same rule on the same source object will simply return the already built object, rather than trying to build a new one and causing a non terminating recursive loop.

4 Case Study

To illustrate the use of our simple transformation library, we define an example transformation problem based on the example addressed at the Model Transformations in Practice workshop of MoDELS 2005 [8]. The next subsection gives an overview of this example, followed by a subsection that discusses the use of our library to provide an implementation.

4.1 Example Problem

This example requires the definition of a transformation from a simple class diagram language into a relational database specification. The models for each of these languages form the source and target models for the transformation. They are illustrated below in Figure 1.

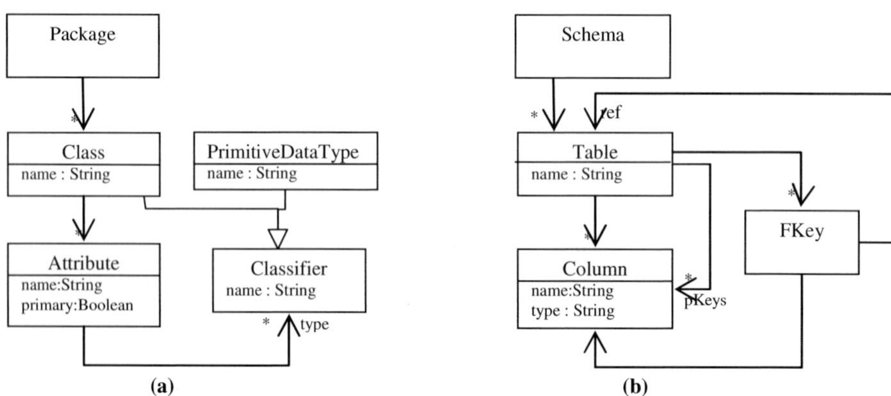

Fig. 1.

The detailed requirements of the transformation are summarised as follows, more details can be read in the call for papers of the workshop [8]:

- Classes are to be mapped to tables
- Attributes are to be mapped to Columns in the table
- An attribute marked as primary forms part of the primary key of the table

- The name of the attribute is the name of the column
- The type of the attribute, if it is a primitive data type, is to be the type of the column
- If the type of the attribute is a class, then the attribute should be mapped to a set of columns that are the primary key columns of the table corresponding to the class. In this case the name of the columns should be formed by combining the name of the attribute being mapped and the existing column name.
- The foreign keys of a table should be defined, in accordance with the columns correspond to an attribute with a class type.

4.2 Using SiTra

We describe here a selection of different rule implementations that help us to illustrate how to write rules of differing complexity. We use the above example as the problem for which the rules are written. The full implementation of the problem can be downloaded from [3].

Simple Rule
A very simple rule to implement is one that maps one object and its attributes directly onto another, i.e. a very simple Class to Table transformation rule. The SiTra implementation for such a rule could be written as indicated in Table 3.

Table 3.

```
class Class2Table implements Rule<Class,Table> {
  ...
  public Table build(Class cls, Transformer t) {
    Table tbl = new Table( cls.getName() );
    return tbl;
  }
  public void setProperties(Table tbl, Class cls, Transformer t) {
    for(Attribute att: cls.getAttribute()) {
      tbl.addColumn( new Column( att.getName(),
                                 att.getType().getName() )
                   );
    }
    return tbl;
  }
}
```

This rule is very simple and does not fully adopt the concepts of transformation rules. The code correctly constructs a corresponding table object for the source class object. The name of the table object has to be set within the build method as the constructor for table objects requires the table name as an argument.

However, the rule explicitly carries out the construction of column objects for each attribute. Using the concept of model transformation rules, this mapping should be carried out by a separate rule.

As a separate rule it could be reused in a different context (e.g. for determining a set of primary keys); as it is currently we would have to repeat the code for mapping attributes to columns if we wished to reuse it.

Facilitating Rule Reuse

To illustrate the reuse of a rule, we extend the Class2Table rule to require it to set the property on the table objects that indicates which columns are primary keys. In the simple class diagram model, there is a property on the Attribute class for indicating which attributes should be considered primary; and in the RDB model there is a property on the Table class which indicates a set of columns that define the primary key.

We split the mapping code into two rules, one for classes to tables and one for attributes to columns. The new Class2Table rule only contains code that concerns constructing a table object and setting its properties. All the code regarding constructing and setting properties of columns is moved to a new Attribute2Column rule. These rules are shown in Table 4.

Table 4.

```
class Class2Table implements Rule<Class, Table> {
  ...
  public Table build(Class cls, Transformer t) {
    Table tbl = new Table( cls.getName() );
    return tbl;
  }
  public void setProperties(Table tbl, Class cls, Transformer t) {
    tbl.setColumn((List<Column>)t.transformAll(cls.getAttribute()) );
    List<Attribute> primAtts;
    ... // select attributes from cls with 'getPrimary()==true'
    tbl.setPKeys( (List<Column>)t.transformAll(primAtts) );
    return tbl;
  }
}
class Attribute2Column implements Rule<Attribute,Column> {
  public Column build(Attribute att, Transformer t) {
    Column col = new Column( att.getName(), att.getType().getName() );
    return col;
  }
  ...
}
```

The transformation of attributes to columns, and thus the invocation of the Attribute2Column rule, is caused by calls to the transformer (shown in bold type), which request the transformation of a list of attributes. The Attribute2Column rule is reused in the Class2Table rule, rather than explicitly constructing columns as in the previous version. In fact, the transformation algorithm will determine whether or not to invoke the Attribute2Column rule, depending on whether or not it has already recorded a mapping for each source attribute object.

Hierarchy of Rules

The ability to write rules and reuse them is sufficient for most simple transformations. However, to support slightly more complex transformation problems, we can introduce a notion of a hierarchy into the rules, thus enabling us to implement situations as follows.

The example requires us to have two mechanisms for mapping attributes onto columns:

1. If an attribute has a type that is a primitive data type, perform the mapping as before.
2. If the type of an attribute is a class, then we map the attribute to a collection of columns, created from the primary key attributes of the class type. The names of the columns must be constructed from the original attribute name, and the names of the primary key attributes of the class type. This mapping process may of course be recursive, and the primary keys may have a type that is a class.

This requirement requires that we alter the Attribute to Column mapping rule, rather than mapping an attribute to a single column, we map an attribute to a set of columns; and we define two separate mapping rules:

- *PrimitiveTypeAttribute2SetColumn*
- *ClassTypeAttribute2SetColumn.*

The Class2Table rule does not need to know which of these rules is being used for a particular attribute; it simply calls the transformer, requesting the transformation of attributes into sets of columns, much as before, but now we must flatten the returned list of sets of columns.

Although a primitive data type attribute always maps to a single column, the transformation is made simpler by treating the two rules the same. We can define a common 'super' rule (a common super type) for the two rules; the intention is to ensure that the target (and source) types of each sub rule are conformant. The common rule and sub rules are defined as shown in Table 5.

Table 5.

```
abstract class Attribute2SetColumn
         implements Rule<Attribute, Set<Column>> {
}
class PrimitiveTypeAttribute2SetColumn extends Attribute2SetColumn {
  public boolean check(Attribute att) {
    return att.getType() instanceof PrimativeDataType;
  }
      ...
}
class ClassAttribute2SetColumn extends Attribute2SetColumn {
  public boolean check(Attribute att) {
    return att.getType() instanceof Class;
  }
    ...
}
```

As you can see in the code, the check method for the two sub rules is different, and this is used by the transformer to determine which rule to invoke for each attribute.

Explicit Rule Invocation

Another more complex feature, useful when defining model transformations, is the ability to explicitly invoke a specific rule (or super rule) for a particular source object.

In fact, based on our experience, we prefer to always invoke rules explicitly wherever possible as this means that the transformation algorithm operates more efficiently, we have a clearer vision of where recursive rule invocation may be occurring, and the Java generics mechanism handles casting the result of the transform method.

In the example, a table may contain many foreign keys, and each foreign key should reference the table for which its set of columns forms a key. Our mapping from class to table must also set the collection of foreign keys for a table, in addition to setting the table's primary keys and columns. The foreign keys for a table can be created by mapping attributes onto FKey objects.

The difficulty here is that attributes are already mapped onto a set of columns (by the Attribute2SetColumn rule). We are now requiring a second rule (Attribute2FKey) that also maps class type attributes, but onto different target objects.

The transformer currently has no way of knowing which of these rules it should use when asked to transform a source object of type Attribute. Both rules are needed, but used at different times. There is no way to distinguish between them using properties of the source object and the check method.

The only solution is to explicitly inform the transformer of which rule we wish to use. (In this specific case there is another way to perform the transformation without specifying the rule, but it is messy.)

Table 6 illustrates a version of the Class2Table rule that make use of explicit rule invocation, by calling the transform method and passing the type of the rule we wish to invoke.

Table 6.

```
class Class2Table implements Rule<Class,Table> {
  ...
  public Table build(Class cls, Transformer t) {
    Table tbl = new Table( cls.getName() );
    return tbl;
  }
  public void setProperties(Table tbl, Class cls, Transformer t) {
    for(Set<Column> cols:
        t.transformAll(Attribute2SetColumn.class,cls.getAttribute()) {
      tbl.getColumn().addAll(cols);
    }
    List<Attribute> primAtts;
    ... // select attributes from cls with 'getPrimary()==true'
    for(Set<Column> cols:
        t.transformAll(Attribute2SetColumn.class, primAtts){
      tbl.getPKeys().addAll(cols);
    }
    tbl.setFKey( t.transformAll( Attribute2FKey.class,
                                 cls.getAttribute())    );
    return tbl;
  }
}
```

The code highlighted in bold type shows the explicit invocation of transformation rules.

5 Limitations of SiTra

The primary purpose of SiTra is to be simple. Some of the limitations can be over come by extending the transformer interface, but we feel that this would violate our primary objective of a "simple" transformation approach. This of course has a cost, specifically that there are limitations in that we cannot tackle some of the more complex transformation problems.

One of the more general limitations regards a situation in which there is more than one rule that should map to the same target object. There is no way to determine, using SiTra, which of the rules should construct the target object. It is necessary for the designer of the transformation to decide which rule should construct the object; the others must retrieve it using that rule.

Another limitation is regarding the recursive invocation of rules. We facilitate this by splitting the construction and setting properties of a target object. However, there is no means to enforce this, and there are potential design issues regarding situations in which some properties may need to be set in the build method and some not.

These limitations are associated to fairly complex transformation problems, and given the main aim of SiTra as a tool to support the implementation of simple transformations, they are not considered to be failings of SiTra, and they are simply acceptable limitations given the primary purpose of the library.

6 Comparison

The example transformation was addressed by a number of different submissions to the MTIP workshop [8]. Using these submissions we can provide a comparison with the approach described in this paper. As stated in the introduction, the library described in this paper is not intended as a replacement for a full Model Transformation Framework or as a model transformation specification language, rather it is intended as a "way in" for experienced programmers to start using the concepts of transformations rules, without the need to learn a new language, or get to grips with a new framework of tools and development environments.

Given this purpose it can be argued that a comparison between SiTra and the existing transformation languages and frameworks is not really appropriate. However, it is interesting to note what can and can't be achieved with SiTra in relation to these other approaches.

The graph transformation approaches [21, 32] have many merits with respect to formalism and a long history of us. However, they require a significant amount of new material to be learnt for novice users and also require significant libraries and development environments in terms of supporting framework. The source and target models are expressed using the notion of graphs, where as with SiTa, the source and target models are simple Java objects. The transformations specification use similar concepts of rules but require a new language to be learnt for writing them, rather than the SiTra approach of using a programming language directly.

The declarative rule based approaches [4, 17, 22] suffer many of the same problems. They all require a specific model transformation specification language to be leant. Tefkat [22] and ATL [17] are both supported by a transformation engine and environment similar in concept to our Transformer implementation class (as the engine) and a Java IDE (as the environment), although in a much more heavyweight manner than SiTra.

Our Java based environment does not of course provide any specific support for debugging transformations; debugging has to be done via Java debugging tools, which are sufficient, however do make debugging a little more complex as one has to debug the rules via the internal workings of the Transformer class.

The imperative approaches [19, 23, 24] are perhaps the most similar to SiTra in terms of the style of writing a transformation rule. However, they too, all expect the transformation writer to learn a new language, and require use of a bespoke environment in which to execute the transformations.

7 Conclusion

The primary conclusion of the paper is that simple transformations can be implemented simply. It is unnecessary to have a huge MTF framework in order to solve a simple problem. Larger MTFs are useful for more complex situation when a full Model Driven Development environment is used; however, for simple transformations a simple framework is sufficient.

Model transformations are a new concept and introducing them to engineers unfamiliar with MDD can be problematic. By using a programming language as the basis for writing transformation rules, we eliminate one of the barriers to learning the concept of software engineering via transformations, namely that of learning a new language.

This paper has illustrated the use of a small code library as the basis to support development of a model transformation. This approach includes mechanisms for rule reuse, sub typing of rules, alternative transformation algorithms, and is not constrained by a specific model repository implementation.

SiTra is obviously not a declarative approach to model transformation; it is definitely an imperative approach, based on the underlying programming language of Java. It supports the explicit or implicit invocation of specific transformation rules; source and target objects can be single objects or collections of objects. It is design to support single direction transformations, with no support for iterative or active transformations. In essence it is designed to support the simplest kinds of transformation, primarily as a means to aid a programmer in learning the concept of writing transformation rules. However, we have found it to be a very useful and effective mechanism for implementing a number of transformations, and made serious use of it as a means to implement transformations as part of other projects.

In addition to the example illustrated in this paper the authors have been making effective use of this library to support other transformation applications such as: OWL-S to BPEL [12]; UML State diagrams to VHDL [6]; diagrams to abstract syntax of State Diagrams; and XML to XMI.

Acknowledgements

This research is supported at the University of Kent though the European Union ERDF Interreg IIIA initiative under the ModEasy grant.

References

1. Aho, A., Sethi, R., Ullman, J.D.: Compilers: Principles, Techniques, and Tools. Addison Wesley. ISBN 0201100886 (1986)
2. Akehurst, D.H.: Model Translation: A UML-based specification technique and active implementation approach. Computing. University of Kent at Canterbury, Canterbury (December 2000)
3. Akehurst, D.H., Bordbar, B.: SiTra. 2006. http://www.cs.bham.ac.uk/~bxb/SiTra.html
4. Akehurst, D.H., Howells, W.G., McDonald-Maier, K.D.: Kent Model Transformation Language. Model Transformations in Practice Workshop, part of MoDELS 2005, Montego Bay,Jamaica (October 2005)
5. Akehurst, D.H., Kent, S., Patrascoiu, O.: A relational approach to defining and implementing transformations between metamodels. Journal on Software and Systems Modeling 2 (November 2003) 215
6. Akehurst, D.H., Uzenkov, O., Howells, W.G., McDonald-Maier, K.D.: Compiling UML State Diagrams into VHDL: An Experiment in Using Model Driven Development. ACM/IEEE 9th International Conference on Model Driven Engineering Languages and Systems (formerly the UML series of conferences), Genova, Italy (submitted)
7. Berre, A., Hahn, A., Akehurst, D.H., Bezivin, J., Tsalgatidou, A., Vermaut, F., Kutvonen, L., Linington, P.F.: State-of-the art for Interoperability architecture approaches. InterOP Network of Excellence - Contract no.: IST-508 011, Deliverable D9.1 (November 2004)
8. Bezivin, J., Rumpe, B., Schurr, A., Tratt, L.: Call for Papers. Model Transformations in Practice Workshop, part of MoDELS 2005, Montego Bay, Jamaica (August 2005)
9. Bordbar, B., Staikopoulos, A.: On Behavioural Model Transformation in Web Services. Conceptual Modelling for Advanced Application Domain. Springer Verlag, Shanghai, China (2004)
10. Derrick, J., Boiten, E.: Refinement in Z and Object-Z: Foundations and Advanced Applications. Springer-Verlag, Berlin, Germany. ISBN 1-85233-245-X (2001)
11. Ehrig, H., Engels, G., Kerowski, H.-J., Rozenberg, G.: editors Handbook Of Graph Grammars And Computing By Graph Transformation Volume 2: Applications, Languages and Tools. World Scientific (1999)
12. Evans, M., Bordbar, B., Akehurst, D.H.: Model tranformation from OWLs to BPEL: a case study. The 9th IEEE International EDOC Conference (EDOC 2005), Hong Kong (submitted)
13. Finkelstein, A., Kramer, J., Nuseibah, B., Finkelstein, L., Goedicke, M.: Viewpoints: A Framework for Integrating Multiple Perspectives in System Development. International Journal of Software Engineering and Knowledge Engineering 2 (March 1992) 31-58
14. Gamma, E., Helm, R., Johnson, R., Vlissides, J.: Design Patterns: Elements of Reusable Object-Oriented Software. Addison-Wesley. ISBN 0201633612 (1995)
15. Gardner, T., Griffin, C., Koehler, J., Hauser, R.: A review of OMG MOF 2.0 Query / Views / Transformations Submissions and Recommendations towards the final Standard. OMG, ad/03-08-02 (2002)
16. Ghezzi, C., Mandrioli, D.: Incremental Parsing. ACM Transactions on Programming Languages and Systems 1 (1979) 564-579
17. Jouault, F., Kurtev, I.: Transforming Models with ATL. Model Transformations in Practice Workshop at MoDELS 2005, Montego Bay, Jamaica (October 2005)
18. Kalnins, A., Barzdins, J., Celms, E.: Basics of Model Transformation Language MOLA. Workshop on Model Driven Development (WMDD 2004), Oslo, Norway (June 2004)

19. Kalnins, A., Celms, E., Sostaks, A.: Model Transformation Approach Based on MOLA. Model Transformations in Practice Workshop at MoDELS 2005, Montego Bay, Jamaica (October 2005)
20. Kleppe, A., Warmer, J., Bast, W.: MDA Explained: The Model Driven Architecture--Practice and Promise. Addison-Wesley. ISBN 032119442X (2003)
21. Konigs, A.: Model Transformations with Tripple Graph Grammars. Model Transformations in Practice Workshop at MoDELS 2005, Montego Bay, Jamaica (October 2005)
22. Lawley, M., Steel, J.: Practical Declarative Model Transformation With Tefkat. Model Transformations in Practice Workshop at MoDELS 2005, Montego Bay, Jamaica (October 2005)
23. Muller, P.-A., Fleurey, F., Vojtisek, D., Drey, Z., Pollet, D., Fondement, F., Studer, P., Jezequel, J.: On Executable Meta-Languages applied to Model Transformations. Model Transformations in Practice Workshop at MoDELS 2005, Montego Bay, Jamaica (October 2005)
24. Murzek, M., Kappel, G., Kramler, G.: Model Transformation in Practice Using the BOC Model Transformer. Model Transformations in Practice Workshop at MoDELS 2005, Montego Bay, Jamaica (October 2005)
25. OMG: Model Driven Architecture (MDA). Object Management Group, ormsc/2001-07-01 (July 2001)
26. OMG: Request for Proposal: MOF 2.0 Query / Views / Transformations RFP. Object Management Group, ad/2002-04-10 (April 2002)
27. OMG: Revised submission for MOF 2.0 Query / Views / Transformations RFP (ad/2002-04-10), QVT-Merge Group, Version 1.0. Object Management Group (April 2004)
28. Patrascoiu, O.: YATL:Yet Another Transformation Language. 1st European MDA Workshop, MDA-IA, University of Twente, the Nederlands (January 2004) 83-90
29. PlanetMDE. http://planetmde.org/
30. Schürr, A.: Specification of Graph Translators with Triple Graph Grammars. In: Tinhofer, G. (ed.): WG'94 20th Int. Workshop on Graph-Theoretic Concepts in Computer Science, Vol. 903. LNCS, Springer Verlag, Herrsching, Germany (June 1994) 151-163
31. Spivey, J.M.: The Z Notation: a reference manual. Prentice Hall (out of print, available at http://spivey.oriel.ox.ac.uk/~mike/zrm/). ISBN 0139785299 (2001)
32. Taentzer, G., Ehrig, K., Guerra, E., Lara, J., Lengyel, L., Levendovszky, T., Prange, U., Varro, D., Varro-Gyapay, S.: Model Transformations by Graph Transformations: A Comparative Study. Model Transformations in Practice Workshop at MoDELS 2005, Montego Bay, Jamaica (October 2005)
33. Vela, B., Acuna, C.J., Marcos, E.: A Model Driven Approach for XML Database Development. ER 2004: 23rd International Conference on Conceptual Modeling. Springer, Shanghai, China (November 2004)
34. W3C: XSL Transformations (XSLT) Version 1.0. Clark, J. (ed.). W3C Recomendation, REC-xslt-19991116 (November 1999)
35. W3C: XML 1.1. Yergeau, F., Cowan, J., Bray, T., Paoli, J., Sperberg-McQueen, C.M., Maler, E. (eds.). W3C Recomendation, REC-xml11-20040204 (April 2004)
36. W3C: XQuery 1.0 and XPath 2.0 Data Model (XDM). Fernandez, M., Malhotra, A., Marsh, J., Nagy, M., Walsh, N. (eds.). W3C Candidate Recomendation, CR-xpath-datamodel-20051103 (November 2005)
37. White, J., Schmidt, D.C., Gokhale, A.: Simplifying Autonomic Enterprise Java Bean Applications Via Model-Driven Development: A Case Study.: MoDELS, Montego Bay, Jamaica (October 2005)

Analysis and Visualization of Behavioral Dependencies Among Distributed Objects Based on UML Models

Vahid Garousi[1], Lionel C. Briand[1,2], and Yvan Labiche[1]

[1] Software Quality Engineering Laboratory (SQUALL)
Department of Systems and Computer Engineering, Carleton University
1125 Colonel By Drive, Ottawa, ON K1S5B6, Canada
{vahid, briand, labiche}@sce.carleton.ca
[2] Simula Research Laboratory, Department of Software Engineering
Martin Linges v 17, Fornebu, P.O. Box 134, 1325 Lysaker, Norway

Abstract. The development of *Behavioral Dependency Analysis (BDA)* techniques and the visualization of such dependencies have been identified as a high priority in industrial Distributed Real-Time Systems (DRTS). BDA determines the extent to which the functionality of one system entity (e.g., an object, a node) is dependent on other entities. Among many uses, a BDA is traditionally used to perform risk analysis and assessment, fault tolerance and redundancy provisions (e.g. multiple instances of a system entity) in DRTS. Traditionally, most BDA techniques are based on source code or execution traces of a system. However, as model driven development is gaining more popularity, there is a need for model-based BDA techniques. To address this need, we propose a set of procedures and measures for the BDA of distributed objects based on behavioral models (UML sequence diagrams). In contrast to the conventional code-based and execution-trace-based BDA techniques, this measure can be used earlier in the software development life cycle, when the UML design model of a system becomes available, to provide engineers with early insights into dependencies among entities in a DRTS (e.g., early risk identification). We also present a dependency visualization model to visualize measured dependencies. Our approach is applied to a case study to show its applicability and potential usefulness in predicting behavioral dependencies based on UML models.

1 Introduction

Distributed Real-Time Systems (DRTS) are becoming more important to our everyday life. Examples include command and control systems, aircraft aviation systems, robotics, and nuclear power plant systems [20]. However, the development and testing of such systems is difficult and takes more time than for systems without real-time constraints or distribution.

Behavioral Dependency Analysis (BDA) determines the extent to which the functionality of one system entity is dependent on other entities. The development of BDA techniques and the visualization of dependencies have been identified as a high priority in industrial DRTS, such as avionics systems [13]. Among many uses, a BDA is used to perform risk analysis and assessment [21], fault tolerance and redundancy

O. Nierstrasz et al. (Eds.): MoDELS 2006, LNCS 4199, pp. 365 – 379, 2006.

provisions (e.g. multiple instances of a system entity) [19], software clustering [23], and complexity measurement [14]. For instance, incorporating fault tolerance and redundancy provisions for all the entities of a DRTS is impossible from cost and resource points of view. When resources are limited, unavailability provisions should be made only for the most critical entities, on which other entities of a system are the most dependent. However, determining the most critical entities of a system is not a trivial task [13]. BDA is a technique which can help developers to achieve such goals.

Furthermore, BDA information can help developers generate a cost-effective test order of entities in unavailability robustness testing of a System Under Analysis (SUA). Unavailability robustness testing is to simulate the unavailability of each entity and verify a system's robustness in such a scenario. If a system consists of thousands of entities and millions of operations among them, the unavailability robustness testing of all of the entities and operations is infeasible. Thus, to be cost-effective, the entities on which other entities are the most dependent on should be tested first. BDA can also be helpful in such applications.

Based on the source of information used to perform a BDA, we can divide the BDA techniques into three groups: *code-based*, *execution-trace-based*, and *model-based*. *Code-Based BDA* (*CBBDA*) (e.g. [17]) and *Execution-trace-Based BDA* (*EBBDA*) (e.g. [5]) are traditional BDA approaches, that rely on the available source code or execution traces of a system. They have been greatly used in the software engineering literature for a variety of purposes (e.g. [12, 14]): program optimization, program comprehension, testing, debugging, maintenance, and evolution.

We define *Model-Based BDA (MBBDA)* to be the derivation of behavioral dependency information from the design model of a software system (for instance defined using UML [18]). There has been a few works [11, 13] on MBBDA and in particular on UML-based BDA. UML provides ways to model the behavior of an OO system using interaction (sequence and collaboration) diagrams, and therefore, performing a BDA from behavioral UML diagrams should be investigated. The motivation of our work is twofold: (1) When and where is MBBDA preferable over CBBDA and EBBDA? and (2) What are open issues in the related MBBDA works that must be addressed by a comprehensive MBBDA technique? Note that the current work is based on UML models but assumes that message exchanges in models are consistent with their implementation so as to provide engineers meaningful BDA information.

To derive behavioral dependency measures between two distributed objects, we perform a systematic analysis of messages exchanged between them in a set of sequence diagrams (SDs). For example, when an object sends a synchronous message to another object and waits for a reply, we define the former object to be behaviorally dependent on the latter. This article provides a precise methodology to perform such analysis, proposes a number of measures, describes a tool developed to automate our technique, and reports on a case study using this tool.

The rest of this article is structured as follows. Related works are presented in Section 0. An overview of the approach is presented in Section 0. Section 0 presents our dependency analysis methodology and an overview of our tool. The application of our methodology to a case study system is presented in Section 0. Finally, Section 0 concludes the article and discusses some of the future research directions.

2 Related Works

Most of the existing model-based dependency analysis techniques analyze *structural* dependency information. This group of works relate to a research area which is referred to as *Impact Analysis* and *Change Management* in UML models by the authors of [2]. However, very few works [11, 13] have been reported on MBBDA. Given size constraints, we focus here on this latter category of works and the reader is referred to [7] for a wider scope discussion.

Hatcliff *et al.* [13] propose a *Component Architecture Development ENvironment for Avionics systems (CADENA)*. Among capabilities provided by CADENA for the development of CORBA component model-based systems, is a dependency analyzer. The technique allows tracing inter/intra-component event and data dependencies by building a *Port Dependence Graph (PDG)*, where each node is a component/port pair and dependencies (i.e., edges) between nodes show *inter/intra-component* dependencies. The dependency heuristics of [13] are the followings: For inter-component dependencies, when there is an event flow from a component/port pair $c_2.p_2$ to another pair $c_1.p_1$ in the component description, it is said that $c_1.p_1$ is *event dependent* on $c_2.p_2$. For intra-component dependencies, a component/port pair $c.p_1$ is defined to be *trigger dependent* on $c.p_2$ if p_2 can trigger p_1.

Gu *et al.* [11] propose a model-based approach to system-level dependency analysis in component-based embedded systems. A tool called *AIRES (Automatic Integration of Reusable Embedded Software)* is the focus of the article. Similar to [13], this work also uses a PDG as dependency analysis model, with two modifications: (1) nodes of a PDG are only ports, instead of being component/port pairs; and (2) an edge has a weight which is equal to the execution rate of the ports that the edge connects multiplied by the size of data transferred at each *execution cycle*. However, [11] does not clearly define what an *execution cycle* is, nor does it further discuss dependency weights. The authors further define a similar graph representation to PDG, referred to as *Component Dependency Graph (CDG),* for analyzing dependencies among components. A CDG captures dependency information at a higher level of abstraction, at the component-level instead of port-level, hiding all the intra-component dependencies. It is claimed a CDG can be derived directly from PDGs. The dependency heuristic between ports and components in [11] is similar to that in [13]. But the authors do not provide a concrete example of a CDG in the paper.

The techniques in [11, 13] are based on structural/architectural models that are not based on UML. As UML is commonly used in the development of non-real-time, non-distributed systems and is gaining popularity in the DRTS community, there is a need for UML-based BDA techniques. Among UML models, behavioral models are interesting to support a MBBDA since they provide information on runtime dependencies.

Furthermore, we need a *hierarchical* representation of dependency information among entities in DRTSs (objects, nodes, and networks). As these entity types are usually deployed hierarchically in DRTSs (i.e., several objects per node, several nodes per network), a hierarchical BDA model seems particularly fit as a visualization mechanism for developers and system analysts. Furthermore, most of the existing BDA works consider binary or enumerated measurement domains for measured dependency weights. The work in [11] seems to be the only MBBDA work which briefly mentions a continuous measurement domain (real values) for dependency weights: "*The weight of an edge is equal to the execution rate of the ports that it connects multiplied by the size of data transferred*". Continuous dependency measurement on ratio scales would greatly facilitate any subsequent, quantitative analysis.

Last, an accurate MBBDA can be performed by defining message weights in SDs (Section 0). No BDA work in the literature has considered message weights when analyzing behavioral dependencies. The work reported in this article aims to address the abovementioned issues. In the remainder of this article, when dependency is mentioned, it implicitly means *behavioral* dependency, unless otherwise mentioned.

3 An Overview of Our Approach

An overview of our approach is depicted using an activity diagram in Fig. 1. The technique takes in the UML model of a system, analyzes the behavioral dependencies among the distributed objects in the model, and then generates, as output, a set of dependency measures (Section 0) and a *Hierarchical Dependency Graph (HDG)* (Section 0) to visualize dependencies. An HDG can be used by different visualization techniques to perform different analyses (Section 0). The input UML model consists of behavioral models (sequence diagrams) and a *Network Deployment Diagram (NDD)* modeling the system topology. If an operational profile of a system is available, a more accurate dependency analysis can be performed (Section 0).

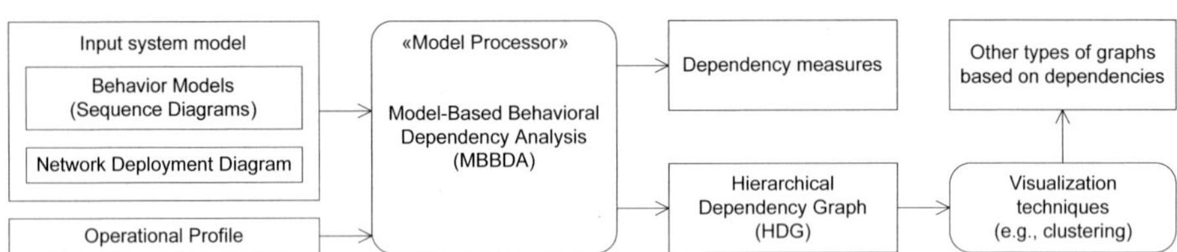

Fig. 1. An Overview of our Approach

Sequence diagrams (SDs) are standard in mainstream UML-based development methodologies. A NDD is our extension to standard UML 2.0 deployment diagram and is needed to describe the distributed architecture of the SUA. This concept is described in Fig. 2-(a) as a metamodel. Such network information is paramount as one of our objectives is to analyze dependencies on different networks and nodes. An example of a distributed architecture appears in Fig. 2-(b) which shows networks in a hierarchical structure (each network can have many subnets and only one supernet), nodes belonging to networks, and objects distributed on nodes, e.g., $node_1$ hosts three objects ($o_{1,1} \ldots o_{1,3}$). Each node is connected to other nodes through several network paths (in general). A path is a sequence of networks. For example, $node_1$ is connected to $node_3$ through the network path <*Network*$_1$, *SystemNetwork*, *Network*$_2$> in Fig. 2-(c).

We want to describe such a distributed architecture using UML 2.0 so as to be able to use it as an input for our dependency analysis in the context of UML-based development. Modeling a hierarchical set of networks and their inter-connectivity is not directly addressed in the UML 2.0 specification [18]. We therefore extend UML 2.0

deployment diagrams by adding two stereotypes to the node notation: *«network»* and *«node»*. We thus identify the type of an entity as a network or a node. Furthermore, association roles *supernet* and *subnet* are used to model the containment relationships between super and sub-networks. As an example, the architecture in Fig. 2-(b) is modeled by the NDD in Fig. 2-(c).

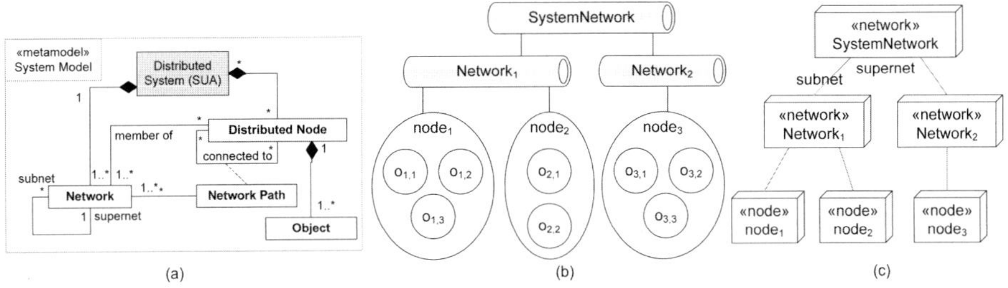

Fig. 2. (a): A metamodel for distributed architectures. (b): An example distributed architecture. (c): The corresponding Networks Deployment Diagram (NDD).

4 Dependency Analysis

Our dependency analysis methodology is presented in this section. Basic definitions are given in Section 0. We then present a set of MBBDA measures: *(Direct) Dependency Index* (Section 0) measures the intensity of a direct dependency from one object to another one, whereas *Transitive Dependency Index* (defined in [7]) measures indirect dependencies among objects via intermediate objects. The above two measures are our simplest measures, and we can be used when no message *weighting* information is available. We then define in Section 0 a set of five more advanced measures (based on five message *weighting mechanisms*). For example, we can assign a higher dependency value between two objects if messages with large sizes of data are exchanged between them. Section 0 presents how measured dependencies can be visualized, how graph visualization techniques can be applied in our context, and the tool we have developed to automate our technique.

4.1 Formalizing SD Messages

In order to determine the dependency between a pair of distributed objects, our technique needs to analyze SD messages. Thus, in order to precisely define how we perform BDA, we formally define SD messages in a way similar to the tabular notation for SDs proposed by UML 2.0 (Appendix D.1 of [18]). Each SD message, in the design model of a distributed system, can be represented as a tuple *message=(sender, receiver, methodOrSignalName, msgSort, parameterList, returnList, msgType)* where:

- *sender* denotes the sender of the message and is itself a tuple of the form *sender=(object, class, node)*, where: *object* is the object name of the sender; *class* is the class name of the sender; and *node* is where the sender is deployed.
- *receiver* denotes the receiver and is itself a tuple of the same form as *sender*.

- *methodOrSignalName* is the name of the method or the signal class name.
- *msgSort* denotes the type of communication reflected by the message, and can be either *synchCall* (synchronous call), *asynchCall* (asynchronous call), or *asynchSignal* (asynchronous signal) [18].
- *parameterList* is the list of parameters for call messages. It is a sequence of the form $<(p_1, C_1, in/out), ..., (p_n, C_n, in/out)>$, where p_i is the i-th parameter name of class type C_i and *in/out* defines the kind of the parameter. If the method call has no parameter, this set is empty.
- *returnList* is the list of return values on reply messages. UML 2.0 assumes that there may be several return values for a reply message. *returnList* is a sequence $<(var_1=val_1,C_1), ..., (var_n=val_n,C_n)>$, where val_i is the return value for variable var_i with type C_i.
- *msgType* distinguishes between signal, call and reply messages. Although *msgSort* can be used to distinguish signal and call messages, the UML metamodel does not provide a built-in way to separate call and reply messages. A discussion of the problem and an approach to distinguish call and reply messages can be found in [8].

4.2 Dependency Index

There can be three types of messages in SDs: synchronous, asynchronous, and reply; and we assume that if an object sends a synchronous message or an asynchronous message with a reply[1] to another object, this indicates that the former (the dependant object) is behaviorally dependent on the latter (the antecedent object). This stems from the fact these are the only two situations where the sender of a message is expecting a reply from the receiver, and thus is dependent on the availability (liveliness) of the receiver. Note that the rationale for choosing message passing as our behavioral dependency (BD) heuristic is consistent with the definition of BD in software engineering: BD exists when a code/model entity requires a service from another entity in order to execute its own function. In asynchronous messages without a reply, the sender sends the message and does not wait for any result or acknowledgment and thus is not dependent on whether the receiver of the message is available (live) or not[2]. Note that although we do not consider such messages in our BDA technique, failures due to the unavailability of the receiver objects of such messages might lead to unpredictable results in a SUA, which have to be further investigated. An approach based on OCL to determine if an asynchronous message has a reply is presented in [7].

We define the *Dependency Index (DI)* measure to quantify the dependency intensity between a dependant and an antecedent entity. Its input domain is *Dependant* × *Antecedent* where *Dependant* = *Nodes* ∪ *Objects* and *Antecedent* = *Nodes* ∪ *Objects* ∪ *Networks; Nodes, Objects* and *Networks* being the set of nodes, objects and networks in the SUA. Networks are not included in the *Dependant* set because they are

---

1 Note that an asynchronous message may or may not have a corresponding reply message. However, every synchronous message must have a reply message.

2 Though two objects may asynchronously communicate through a data structure object (e.g., mailbox), in the design sequence diagrams such level of details is typically not represented. This will usually be represented as asynchronous messages (with replies) from each object to the other. This case is accounted for in our definition.

not active entities (can not initiate an activity), and therefore defining a dependency relationship from a network to a node or object is not relevant in our context. The DI measure captures the ratio of the amount of functionalities an entity needs from another entity, over the overall functionalities it requires. For each given dependant and antecedent entity, the DI measure is thus assigned a value in the [0…1] range, where 0 indicates no dependency and 1 indicates full dependency (i.e., the functionalities required by an object are provided by only one other object). We define in eq. (1) a simple DI measure capturing the dependency of object o_i on object o_j to be the ratio, for all SDs in the SUA, of the number of synchronous or asynchronous (with reply) messages from o_i to o_j over the total number of such type of messages sent from o_i.

$$DI(o_i,o_j)=\frac{\text{\# of synchronous messages or asynchronous (with reply) from } o_i \text{ to } o_j \text{ in all SDs}}{\text{\# of synchronous messages or asynchronous (with reply) from } o_i \text{ in all SDs}} \tag{1}$$

To better explain the DI measure, let us consider the extreme values of DI between two objects. If $DI(o_i, o_j)=1$, this means that all the synchronous or asynchronous messages with reply from o_i are sent to o_j only. We consider this situation as the highest level of dependency of one object on another. In this case, o_i's functionality is highly dependent on the availability of o_j, as all of the services o_i requires are provided by o_j. Conversely, $DI(o_i, o_j)=0$ implies there are no synchronous messages or asynchronous messages with reply from o_i to o_j. Thus whether o_j is available or not (e.g., dead or alive) has no effect on o_i.

Using the definitions in Section 0, eq. (1) can be rewritten in a more formal form: eq. (2). This is useful as it specifies precisely how the measures are computed in our tool based on our formalization of messages. For brevity, *synchRAsynchMsgs* represents the set of synchronous messages and asynchronous messages with reply.

$$DI(o_i,o_j)=\frac{\left|\{msg \mid msg.sender.object=o_i \wedge msg.receiver.object=o_j \wedge msg \in synchRAsynchMsgs\}\right|}{\left|\{msg \mid msg.sender.object=o_i \wedge msg \in synchRAsynchMsgs\}\right|} \tag{2}$$

The definition of the DI measure can be generalized to nodes and networks. When a sender object is dependent on a receiver object, the sender object's node is also dependent on the receiver object and its node. In addition, the sender object and its node are dependent on the network links connecting the two nodes. For example, the dependence of a node on a network, i.e., *DI(node, network)*, can be measured by eq. (3), where *getNetworkPath(senderNode, receiverNode)* is a function which returns a set of networks paths between *senderNode* and *receiverNode*. This function and the rest of our generalized DI measures (for node and networks) are defined in [7].

$$DI(node,network)=\frac{\left|\left\{\begin{array}{l} msg \mid msg.sender.node=node \wedge msg \in synchRAsynchMsgs \wedge \\ network \in getNetworkPath(msg.sender.node, msg.receiver.node) \end{array}\right\}\right|}{\left|\{msg \mid msg.sender.node=node \wedge msg \in synchRAsynchMsgs\}\right|} \tag{3}$$

As an example, we show how some of the DI values for the entities in the system with SDs and the Networks Deployment Diagram (NDD) in Fig. 3 are calculated. For example, $DI(o_{1,3}, o_{2,2})$ and $DI(n_2, network_2)$ are calculated below. Note that the SD messages are referenced with the *SDIndex-messageName* naming convention, e.g., *2-1.1* refers to message numbered *1.1* of SD_2.

$$DI(o_{1,3},o_{2,2}) = \frac{\left|\{msg \mid msg \in synchRAMsgs \wedge msg.sender.object = o_{1,3} \wedge msg.receiver.object = o_{2,2}\}\right|}{\left|\{msg \mid msg \in synchRAMsgs \wedge msg.sender.object = o_{1,3}\}\right|}$$
$$= \frac{\left|\{1-1.1\}\right|}{\left|\{1-1.1, 1-2.1\}\right|} = 0.5$$

$$DI(n_2, network_2) = \frac{\left|\left\{\begin{array}{l} msg \mid msg.sender.node = n_2 \wedge msg \in synchRAMsgs \wedge network_2 \in \\ getNetworkPath(msg.sender.node, msg.receiver.node) \end{array}\right\}\right|}{\left|\{msg \mid msg.sender.node = n_2 \wedge msg \in synchRAMsgs\}\right|}$$
$$= \frac{\left|\{4-1.3\}\right|}{\left|\{1-1.2, 2-1.1, 4-1.3\}\right|} \approx 0.33$$

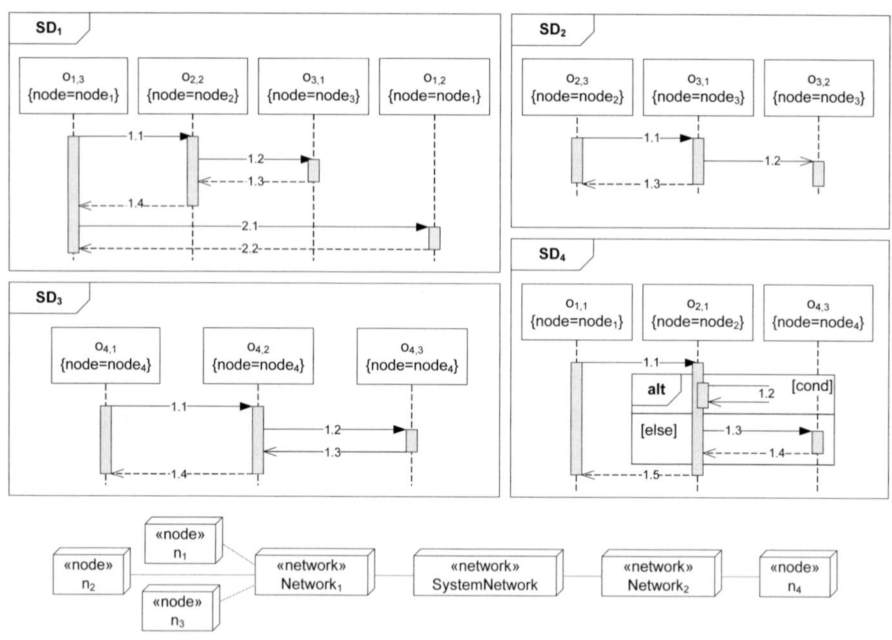

Fig. 3. Four SDs and the NDD of a SUA with distributed messages

We also define two system-wide indices for an entity: (1) *Total Dependency Index (TDI)*, which yields a single value denoting the degree to which an entity (an object or a node) is dependent on other entities; (2) *Service Role Index (SRI)*, which denotes the degree to which an antecedent entity (an object, a node, or a network) provides services to other entities. The range of both indices is [0…1]. The definitions of both indices for all combinations of dependant and antecedent entity types are formalized in [7]. For example *TDI(object)* and *SRI(node)* are shown in eq. (4).

Note that we have excluded the DI values of an object on itself and on its deployment node or of a node on itself. The denominators in the TDI and SRI formulas for nodes and objects are 2 and *2+|Networks|* (i.e., number of networks), because the maximum values of the first two sums and the last sum in the TDI's numerator are 1 and |*Networks*| (due to network hierarchies), respectively. Function *getNodeOf(o)* returns the node name on which object *o* is deployed.

$$TDI(o)=\frac{1}{(2+|Networks|)}\left(\sum_{\substack{\forall o_i\in Objects|\\ o_i\neq o}} DI(o,o_i)+\sum_{\substack{\forall n_i\in Nodes|\\ n_i\neq getNodeOf(o)}} DI(o,n_i)+\sum_{\forall net_i\in Networks} DI(o,net_i)\right)$$
$$SRI(n)=\frac{1}{2}\left(\sum_{\substack{\forall o_i\in Objects|\\ n\neq getNodeOf(o_i)}} DI(o_i,n)+\sum_{\substack{\forall n_i\in Nodes|\\ n_i\neq n}} DI(n_i,n)\right) \tag{4}$$

4.3 Dependency Index Based on Message Weights

In the definition of the DI measure in eq. (2), the messages in the set of SDs are not *differentiated* (*weighted*), i.e., it was assumed that all messages are equivalent in terms of the dependencies they entail. However: (1) Certain messages may be more critical (important), and thus entail more intensive dependency, than other messages; (2) Some messages (call or reply) may carry larger amounts of data; or (3) more parameters (return values) than other messages; (4) The return values from some messages may be used more frequently, or (5) for more critical decisions/calculations in the caller object than other messages; or (6) Some of the messages may be triggered more often than other messages. We thus define six measures based on the above six weighting mechanisms: (i) Dependency Index based on Message Criticality (*DIMC*); (ii) Dependency Index based on Size Of Data (*DISOD*); (iii) Dependency Index based on Number Of Objects (*DINOO*); (iv) Dependency Index based on Number of Return Values Usage (*DINRVU*); (v) Dependency Index based on Criticality of Return Value Usages (*DICRVU*); (vi) Dependency Index based on Operational Profiles (*DIOP*).

A comprehensive discussion of the weighting mechanisms and the five measures, including examples, formulas for the measures, as well as an analysis of how the dependency measurements are affected by changes in the heuristic choices (message weights) is provided in [7]. Due to space constraints, we only describe DISOD next. In data-intensive and data-driven systems, call/reply messages which carry larger amounts of data than others can be considered to involve the respective caller objects in more intense dependency relationships on the called objects. For example, consider a distributed backup system, where a Central Dispatching Server (CDS) receives a large amount of data to backup. It then divides the data into smaller portions to be sent to each of the four Backup Database Servers (BDS): *bds1*... *bds4*. The CDS then sends each portion to the corresponding BDS to be backed up. Each BDS acknowledges back to the CDS upon successful data backup. Suppose in this example that the data partitioning algorithm always assign 40% of data to *bds2*. The rest of the data is divided equally among *bds1*, *bds3*, and *bds4* (20% for each). In such a scenario, we can conclude that CDS's success in backing up 100% of all the given data respectively depends on *bds1*, *bds2*, *bds3*, and *bds4* to an extent captured by the above percentages of data. We define our *DISOD* measure in eq. (5), where *msgSize(msg)* is a function to estimate the data size of a message (presented in [7]). The numerator calculates the total data size of synchronous and asynchronous messages with reply from o_i to o_j, and reply messages from o_j to o_i. The denominator is similar except that it considers all messages from o_i (sync. And async. Messages) and to o_i (reply messages).

$$DISOD(o_i,o_j)=\frac{\sum_{\substack{\forall msg|msg.sender.object=o_i \wedge \\ msg.receiver.object=o_j \wedge msg\in synchRAsynchMsgs}} messageDataSize(msg)+\sum_{\substack{\forall msg|msg.sender.object=o_j \wedge \\ msg.receiver.object=o_i \wedge msg.msgType='reply'}} messageDataSize(msg)}{\sum_{\forall msg|msg.sender.object=o_i \wedge msg\in synchRAsynchMsgs} messageDataSize(msg)+\sum_{\forall msg|msg.receiver.object=o_i \wedge msg.msgType='reply'} messageDataSize(msg)} \quad (5)$$

4.4 Visualizing Measured Dependencies

In order to visualize the results of our dependency analysis technique, we present a graph notation, referred to as *Hierarchical Dependency Graph (HDG)*. HDG is an extension to conventional Dependency Graphs (DG) [11, 13], in which vertices can be *nested*. For example a node can contain several objects in a HDG. A HDG is built based on dependency measurements. Each vertex in a HDG corresponds to an entity (node, network, or object). An edge is made from a vertex corresponding to an entity e_1 to the vertex corresponding to entity e_2 only if $DM(e_1,e_2)>0$, where *DM* can be any of our proposed dependency measures. The edge is labeled with its corresponding DM value. Each edge is directed from a dependant to an antecedent entity. For example, the HDG corresponding to the SUA described in Fig. 3 is shown in Fig. 4. To keep this particular HDG legible, we only retained object dependencies. In general, such filtering mechanisms can enhance the scalability of the visualization and help engineers focus on specific aspects of a SUA when visualizing a HDG corresponding to one if its dependency measures.

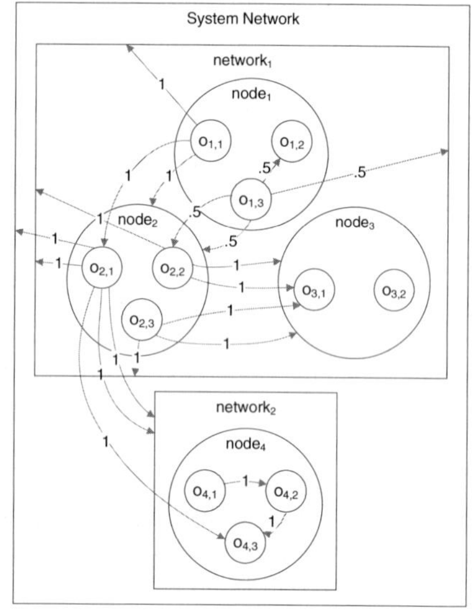

Fig. 4. HDG built from the DI measures of the SUA in Fig. 3

Furthermore, since there is a significant body of work on the visualization of complex graphs, we can use a large range of visualization techniques on a HDG. We have considered three such techniques (e.g., [15]) in our work:

1. Analyzing system architectures by clustering entities based on dependency values: We can cluster entities with dependencies on each other to highlight the set of objects which are most *coupled* to each other. We then follow the popular *low coupling/high cohesion* design paradigm to perform an analysis of system architecture based on such clusters.

2. Visualizing dependency intensities: Based on the DI value between two entities, different line widths can be used to better visualize dependency intensities. A practical scenario where this visualization might be useful is when engineers want to determine the regions of a large DRTS in which there are strong inter-dependencies among objects. Such an analysis is done for a variety of purposes, e.g.: (1) incorporating more reliable/powerful hardware and network components in such regions; (2) performing more rigorous testing (especially testing activities specific to distributed systems) on the software/hardware entities of such regions; and (3) more careful runtime monitoring of distributed communications among nodes in such regions.
3. Visualizing service role (SRI) and total dependency indices (TDI): The values of these two indices can be visualized by a change in the radius of the entity in a HDG. A practical scenario where this visualization would be useful is when engineers want to apply load balancing techniques based on dependencies (e.g. [16]): the less difference among the circle sizes, the more balanced the load in a DRTS.

An example of the first analysis is reported next. The second and third analyses are applied to a SUA in the case study section. More examples can be found in [7]. In a HDG, we can cluster entities with high dependencies on each other to highlight the set of entities which are strongly *coupled*. This can help designers decide whether to perform any architectural reconfiguration (e.g., changing the deployment nodes of objects). However, it requires the identification of a threshold, referred to as *Dependency Cut-Off Threshold (DCOT)*, to define the meaning of strongly connected entities. Only dependencies with a weight higher than the chosen DCOT are then considered when clustering (e.g., using the *max-connected* clustering algorithm [22]). We refer to the resulting graph as a *Clustered HDG (CHDG)*.

For example, assume that our MBBDA technique has generated the HDG in Fig. 5-(a): $o_{i,j}$ denotes object j on node i. The gray-scale color coding has been used to facilitate the visualization of object deployments on nodes. To cluster objects in this HDG, we can consider that any dependency with a weight higher than 0.2 (our chosen DCOT) denotes a strong dependency. We then obtain the CHDG in Fig. 5-(b) where clusters are numbered c_1 to c_5. For example, cluster c_2 includes $o_{1,2}$,. $o_{2,1}$, $o_{2,2}$, $o_{2,3}$, $o_{3,1}$, $o_{3,2}$, $o_{4,1}$ and $o_{4,2}$ and their inter-dependencies.

The architectural reconfiguration advices implied by this cluster are based on the fact that the clustered objects have inter-dependencies on each other and on no other object in the system. Thus, they can potentially be deployed on only one node (minimizing network communications and unnecessary traffic). To perform such a redeployment, however, the designer will need to consider the SUA's design/deployment constraints, such as security/organizational restrictions and software/hardware compatibility issues. Considering such constraints, there might be no choice but to keep the existing deployment architecture. Another important consideration is to take into account the number of objects that will be deployed on one node given specific architectural reconfigurations. Some nodes might not be able to host that many objects running concurrently and using node's resources (e.g., due to excessive memory and CPU usage).

Furthermore, the selected DCOT value has an impact on the number of clusters and thus on reconfiguration advices [7]. Further investigations on heuristics to choose a suitable DCOT are needed.

On a different aspect, providing tool support for the collection and visualization of dependency measures is very important [3]. We designed and implemented a prototype tool, referred to as *BDAnalyzer (Behavioral Dependency Analyzer),* to extract dependency measures from UML design models. The tool was implemented in C++ and the source code is available from the World Wide Web [6]. After reading an input file containing the UML model of a SUA (in a specific format), the tool generates the result of the analysis as a matrix of dependency measurements, refereed to as *Dependency Index Matrix*, and a textual representation for the corresponding HDG. We then use the Graphviz tool [1] to automatically create graphical representations for HDGs. Further details about our tool can be found in [7].

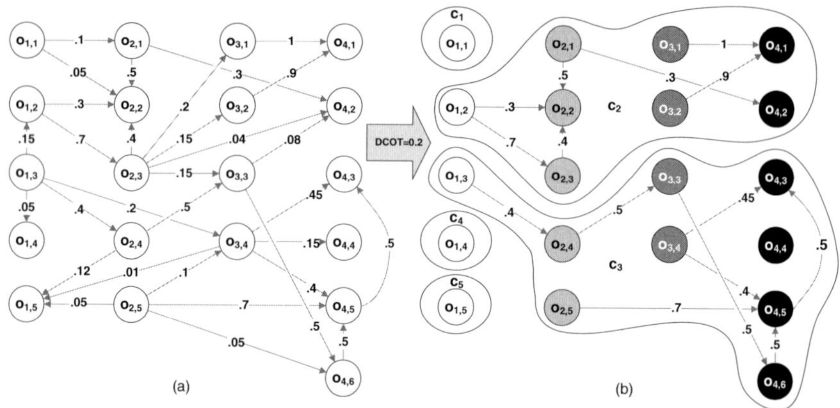

Fig. 5. (a): Example HDG. (b): A CHDG generated from (a) with DCOT=0.2.

5 Case Study

To demonstrate our MBBDA technique's feasibility and to analyze its potential usefulness, we applied it to a distributed system. We report in this section on the results of applying our analysis and deriving DI & DIOP measures (Dependency Index based on Operational Profiles) (Section 0), service role (SRI) and total dependency index (TDI) measures (Section 0) for this particular system.

The case study system we chose is a prototype *SCADA*-based power system (Supervisory Control and Data Acquisition Systems [4]). The system is referred to as *SCAPS (a SCAda-based Power System)* [9]. SCAPS is a system to control the power distribution grid across a nation consisting of several provinces. We designed SCAPS to be used in Canada, and to simplify its design and implementation, we considered only two Canadian provinces in the system: Ontario (ON) and Quebec (QC).

We used our BDAnalyzer tool [6] on the SCAPS model file [10] (transformed to a format specific to our tool) to derive the corresponding HDG. Due to size constraints, only a subset of the results is shown using the partial HDG in Fig. 6 (generated by Graphviz [1]), which, for brevity, is filtered to illustrate only object-to-object dependencies. More detailed results are reported in [7]. Object *asa* deployed in node

SEV_CA1, has significantly higher dependency on itself (self-dependency) than on other objects (*SEV_ON* and *SEV_QC*): DI values of 0.67 and 0.17, respectively. As a practical implication, one might want to consider a more reliable/powerful hardware to the node (SEV_CA1) where *asa* is deployed (*SEV_CA1*).

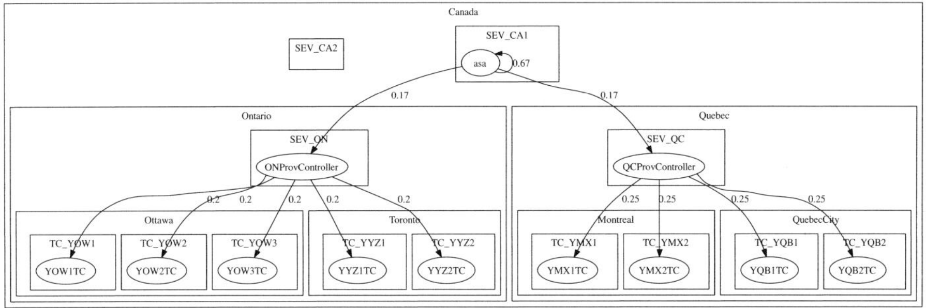

Fig. 6. A partial HDG showing object-to-object dependencies

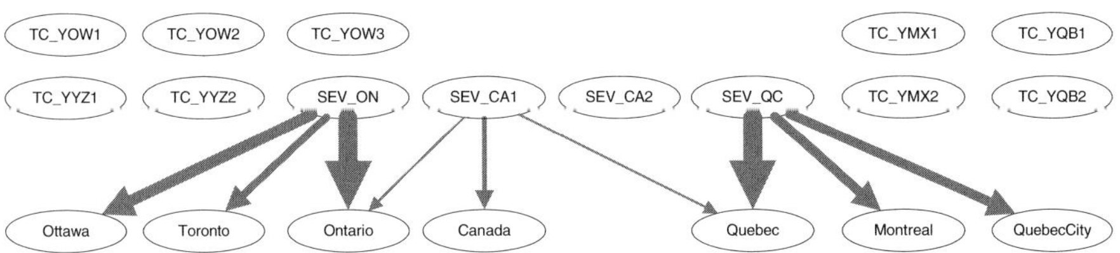

Fig. 7. A graph in which line widths are correlated with a subset of DIOP measures

We furthermore apply the dependency intensities visualization technique based on line widths (Section 0), which yields the graph in Fig. 7. The line widths in this graph are correlated with a subset of the DIOP measures (Section 0), corresponding to object-to-network dependencies only. The measures were generated by our tool based on SCAPS UML model and an operational profile for this system (discussed in detail in [7]). As we can see in Fig. 7, two of the most intense dependencies are: from node *SEV_ON* to network *Ontario*, and from node *SEV_QC* to network *Quebec*. As a practical implication, we might want to increase reliability in those two dependencies by installing more reliable/powerful network interfaces between those nodes and networks (e.g., network cards with extended buffer sizes and higher bandwidths) [7].

We then apply the SRI and TDI visualization techniques to analyze load in SCAPS. Recall that we relate load with objects service role and total dependency in the system (Section 0). The corresponding graphs are shown in Fig. 8.

As it can be easily seen, system load in terms of object service roles are almost balanced throughout the system: circles of approximately the same size in Fig. 8-(a). However the load w.r.t. total dependencies of each object is mostly concentrated on the two provincial controllers (the two large circles in Fig. 8-(b)). Note that such a load imbalance was not clearly visible from simple DI measures in Fig. 6. If needed,

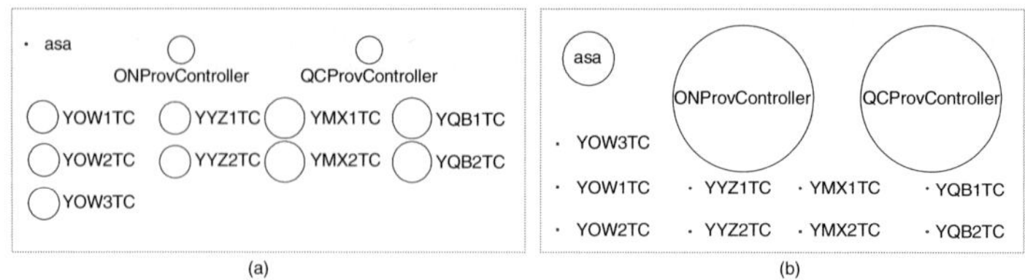

Fig. 8. Visualization of (a): Service Role (SRI) and (b): Total Dependency Indices (TDI)

load balancing practices (e.g., re-architecturing, design changes in message communications) can be performed to normalize load.

6 Conclusions and Future Works

This paper proposes a technique for behavioral dependency analysis of distributed objects based on UML behavioral models. It assigns a dependency index for any pair of system entities (objects, nodes, and networks). Among many uses, the technique can help system analysts and designers to devise appropriate provisions for the most dependable (crucial) entities of a system, and to forecast load level on each system entity before implementation. We also define a behavioral dependency analysis model, referred to as *Hierarchical Dependency Graphs*, to visualize dependencies in distributed systems. The analysis method was applied to a case study to show its applicability and potential usefulness in predicting behavioral dependencies based on UML models: interesting observations could be derived from our dependency analysis and would influence, in practice, practical decisions, which could not have been easily derived without it.

Some of our future works include: (1) generalizing our dependency analysis technique to take into account other dependency attributes such as time, impact, and sensitivity; (2) investigating its usage in component-based and agent-oriented software; (3) assessing its usefulness when applying it to industry-strength distributed real-time systems; (4) applying it to unavailability robustness testing for distributed systems; (5) comparing transitive and weighed DI measures to simple DI measures in practice; (6) applying the visualization techniques discussed in Section 0 to large models and investigating their effectiveness; (7) investigating other clustering algorithms (e.g., k-clustering and self organizing maps) in order to analyze system architectures based on HDGs; (8) investigating the scalability of our BDAnalyzer tool; and (9) investigating whether the dependency information generated by MBBDA is better suited for applications that are usually based on CBBDA and EBBDA (e.g. [12, 14]).

Acknowledgments

This work was in part supported by a CITO grant with IBM Canada, and a Canada research chair grant. The authors would like to thank Michał Sówka for his helpful comments and suggestions.

References

[1] AT&T labs, "Graphviz," www.graphviz.org, last visited: 2006.

[2] L. Briand, Y. Labiche, L. O'Sullivan, and M. Sowka, "Automated Impact Analysis of UML Models," *Journal of Systems and Software*, vol. 79, no. 3, pp. 339-352, 2006.

[3] D. Card and R. Glass, *Measuring Software Design Quality*: Prentice-Hall, Inc., 1990.

[4] A. Daneels and W. Salter, "What is SCADA?," Proc. of Int. Conf. on Accelerator and Large Experimental Physics Control Systems, pp. 39-343, 1999.

[5] T. Eisenbarth, R. Koschke, and D. Simon, "Feature-Driven Program Understanding Using Concept Analysis of Execution Traces," Proc. IWPC, pp. 300-309, 2001.

[6] V. Garousi, "BDAnalyzer," squall.sce.carleton.ca/tools/BDAnalyzer, 2006.

[7] V. Garousi, L. Briand, and Y. Labiche, "Analysis and Visualization of Behavioral Dependencies among Distributed Objects based on UML Models," Technical Report SCE-06-03, Carleton University March 2006.

[8] V. Garousi, L. Briand, and Y. Labiche, "Control Flow Analysis of UML 2.0 Sequence Diagrams," Proc. ECMDA, LNCS 3748, pp. 160-174, 2005.

[9] V. Garousi, L. Briand, and Y. Labiche, "Traffic-aware Stress Testing of Distributed Systems based on UML Models," Proc. ICSE, pp. 391-400, 2006.

[10] V. Garousi, L. Briand, and Y. Labiche, "Traffic-aware Stress Testing of Distributed Systems based on UML Models," Technical Report SCE-05-13, Carleton University 2005.

[11] Z. Gu, S. Kodase, S. Wang, and K. G. Shin, "A Model-Based Approach to System-Level Dependency and Real-Time Analysis of Embedded Software," Proc. of Real-Time and Embedded Technology and Applications Symp., pp. 78-85, 2003.

[12] M. Harrold, G. Rothermel, and S. Sinha, "Computation of Interprocedural Control Dependence," Proc. of Int. Symp. on Soft. Testing and Analysis, pp. 11-20, 1998.

[13] J. Hatcliff, X. Deng, M. B. Dwyer, G. Jung, and V. P. Ranganath, "Cadena: An Integrated Development, Analysis, and Verification Environment for Component-based Systems," Proc. ICSE, pp. 160-173, 2003.

[14] S. Horowitz and T. Reps, "The Use of Program Dependence Graphs in Software Engineering," Proc. ICSE, pp. 392-411, 1992.

[15] M. Kaufmann and D. Wagner, *Drawing Graphs : Methods and Models*: Springer, 2001.

[16] A. Kochut and G. Kar, "Managing Virtual Storage Systems: An Approach using Dependency Analysis," Proc. of Symp. on Integrated Network Management, pp. 593-604, 2003.

[17] B. Li, "Managing Dependencies in Component-based Systems based on Matrix Model," Proc. of Net.ObjectDays Conf., pp. 22-25, 2003.

[18] Object Management Group (OMG), "UML 2.0 Superstructure Specification," 2005.

[19] D. K. Pradhan, *Fault-tolerant Computer System Design*: Prentice-Hall, 1996.

[20] J. Tsai, Y. Bi, S. Yang, and R. Smith, *Distributed Real-Time Systems: Monitoring, Visualization, Debugging, and Analysis*: John Wiley, 1996.

[21] J. K. Vaurio, "Treatment of General Dependencies in System Fault-Tree and Risk Analysis," *IEEE Transactions on Reliability*, vol. 51, no. 3, pp. 278-287, 2002.

[22] X.-H. Vu, D. Sam-Haroud, and B. Faltings, "Clustering for Disconnected Solution Sets of Numerical CSPs," *LNCS*, vol. 3010, pp. 25-43, 2004.

[23] C. Xiao and V. Tzerpos, "Software Clustering based on Dynamic Dependencies," Proc. of European Conf. on Software Maint. and Reeng., pp. 124-133, 2005.

Model Extraction Using Context Information

Lucio Mauro Duarte*, Jeff Kramer, and Sebastian Uchitel

Department of Computing, Imperial College London
180 Queen's Gate, London, SW7 2AZ, UK
{lmd, jk, su2}@doc.ic.ac.uk

Abstract. This work describes a new approach for behaviour model extraction which combines static and dynamic information. We exploit context information as a way of merging these types of information. Contexts are defined by evaluated control predicates and values of attributes. They create a nested structure that can facilitate the extraction of causal relations between system actions. We show how context information can guide the process of constructing LTS models that are good approximations of the actual behaviour of the systems they describe. These models can be used for automated analysis and property verification. Augmentation of the values of attributes recorded in contexts produces further refined models and leads towards correct models. Completeness of the extracted models depends on the coverage achieved by samples of executions. Our approach is partially automated by a tool called LTSE. Results of one of our case studies are presented and discussed.

1 Introduction

A behaviour model is an abstract description of how a system should behave that can be used for model checking [4]. The construction of a behaviour model from an existing system to be used in a model checking tool, known as the *model construction problem* [6], can be difficult, costly and error-prone [5]. Furthermore, it is essential that two basic requirements be attended. Firstly, the construction of the model must be *much simpler and less time-consuming than building the system itself* [12]. Consequently, it is desirable that the model be *constructed (semi-)automatically*. Manual construction of models is usually expensive and likely to introduce errors [6]. Secondly, and most importantly, the model should be a *faithful representation of the system behaviour*. Any analysis based on an incorrect model may bias the understanding of the system behaviour [14].

Model extraction is the process of generating a model for an existing system. Our approach for model extraction follows the idea proposed in [8] of combining static and dynamic information. The use of static information for model extraction [6, 13, 11, 2] has demonstrated to be possible to obtain a view of all possible executions of the system. We use *control flow information* to obtain such a view. As for the dynamic part, we collect *trace information*, which supplies knowledge about real (therefore feasible) executions and has also been applied to construct models [5, 17, 3]. With this combination of information, we can use the traces

* Supported by CAPES (Brazil) under the grant BEX 1680-02/1.

O. Nierstrasz et al. (Eds.): MoDELS 2006, LNCS 4199, pp. 380–394, 2006.

to identify feasible behaviours and, based on them, derive other behaviours not included in - or that could not be easily inferred from - them. Such behaviours represent, for instance, alternative paths, which, though not exercised in any particular trace, can be detected by combining traces and identifying, according to the control flow structure, common subsequences of actions in the code.

In order to carry out this combination, we exploit a concept called context. A *context* is the combination of the execution point in the control flow graph of the system and the system state, represented by values of its attributes. Contexts create a nested structure that can support extracting the causal relation between system actions.

All the information collected is processed by a single tool, called *LTS Extractor* (LTSE), which implements most of the process we describe here. The created model can be analysed using the LTSA tool [16]. Hence, the effort devoted to the model extraction process is reasonable, requiring only basic knowledge of verification. The user does not need to know the programming language nor the modelling language, as the necessary information is collected automatically through code instrumentation and execution of tests, which produce the traces.

Our models have been used to verify safety and progress properties of single- and multi-threaded systems. As expected, though the analyses using our models have demonstrated that they are good approximations of the behaviours of the systems they describe, completeness of our approach (all traces exhibited by the system are described by the extracted model) depends on the coverage of the test suite that generates trace information. In addition, correctness (all traces exhibited by the model are feasible) depends on the selection of attributes on which contexts are built. However, it can be shown that, by augmenting the context attributes, a refined model that is correct can always be built.

This paper is organised as follows. The next section presents the idea of contexts. Section 3 introduces our approach for model extraction in more detail. Section 4 presents some of our experimental results through a case study. In Section 5, we evaluate our approach and discuss related work. Section 6 contains the conclusion and a comment on next steps.

2 Contexts

In this section we define contexts and exemplify how we exploit the combination of control flow information and trace information. We use the code of a simple text editor as a running toy example. The code for the editor is depicted in Fig. 1. The code has two attributes: `isOpen` defines whether a file is open and `isSaved` indicates whether the file's contents have been saved. In addition, a number of operations that modify these attributes and the text file are provided: `open`, `close`, `save`, `edit`, `exit`.

Control flow information. A control flow graph (CFG) [1] is an abstract representation of a program which models the alternative flows of execution that the program allows. A CFG can be extracted automatically by statically analysing the code and can be used to reason about the code behaviour. Fig. 2 illustrates the control flow graph of constructor `Editor()` and method `edit()`.

The diamonds define control flow statements (statements that change the normal, sequential control flow of the system, such as lines 9 and 12 in Fig. 1), whereas ellipses represent all other statements. The arrows indicate the direction of the flow of control from one statement to another.

```
1  public class Editor
2    private boolean isOpen;
3    private boolean isSaved;
4
5    public Editor () {
6      isOpen=false;
7      isSaved=true;
8      int cmd=-1;
9      while(cmd!=4){
10       cmd=readCmd();
11       switch (cmd) {
12         case 0: if(!isOpen)
13                   name=open();
14                 break;
15         case 1: if(isOpen)
16                   edit(name);
17                 break;
18         case 2: if(isOpen)
19                   print(name);
20                 break;
21         case 3: if(!isSaved)
22                   save(name);
23                 break;
24         case 4: exit(name); } }
25     }
26     ....
27     void exit (String n) {
28       if (!isSaved) {
29         int opt=readOpt();
30         if (opt==0)
31           save(n);
32       }
33       if (isOpen) close(n);
34     }
35   }
```

Fig. 1. Example Code

A *control predicate* [20] is a condition associated to a control flow statement. Control predicates can, depending on their evaluation, lead the system to a different path of execution. These alternative paths can be seen in the CFG in Fig. 2 as multiple arrows leaving from the same diamond. The different values of the predicates label the arrows.

The CFG reveals the control predicates that define the system behaviour and which statements and other predicates are dependent on each predicate. However, this static information can include paths that cannot be taken during a real execution. Therefore, some of the paths presented in Fig. 2, though possible according to the CFG, may not be feasible in the code when it is executed.

The use of symbolic execution [15] can, statically, rule out some infeasible paths. However, if the control flow is dependent on the inputs, an analysis of each case may be necessary. The set of input classes may make it impossible to test all possible cases. Furthermore, symbolic execution usually requires the help of a theorem prover, demanding some expertise from the user.

To fully understand the feasibility of a path of execution we need to know the values of the predicates evaluated along that path. As the values of predicates may change over time during the execution (due to inputs or changes in the system state), some paths that were feasible at certain point may become infeasible later on. For example, the path in the CFG in Fig. 2 allowing method `open` to be executed is only feasible while no file has been opened for editing. Once a document is opened, that path can never be taken again due to the fact that the value of the control predicate `!isOpen` becomes false and prevents the call to method `open` from being reached. If these dynamic changes are not considered, path feasibility can be hard to analyse.

Trace information. Trace information usually gives the sequences of actions executed by the system in the form of traces of execution. A *trace* is normally a result of a real execution of the system in response to a set of inputs. For

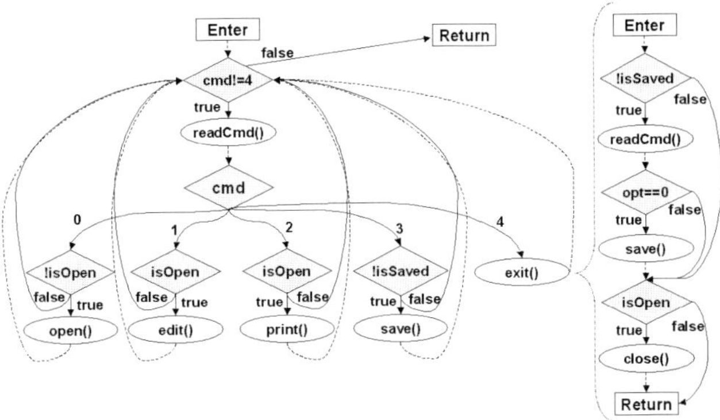

Fig. 2. Control flow graph of the editor code

example, let us consider the following sequence of inputs to the editor in Fig. 1: 0, 1, 3, 2, 1, 1, 2, 3, 2, 1, 4, 0. This generates the following trace (ignoring the calls to method *readCmd*, which does not affect our analysis): `open edit save print edit edit print save print edit exit save close`

Looking at the trace, we can try to infer some relations between the actions and construct a model that approximates the system. In Fig. 3, we show one possible model, where there is one state per label and, for any pair of consecutive events x, y found in a trace, a transition labelled y from the state denoted by x to that denoted by y exists.

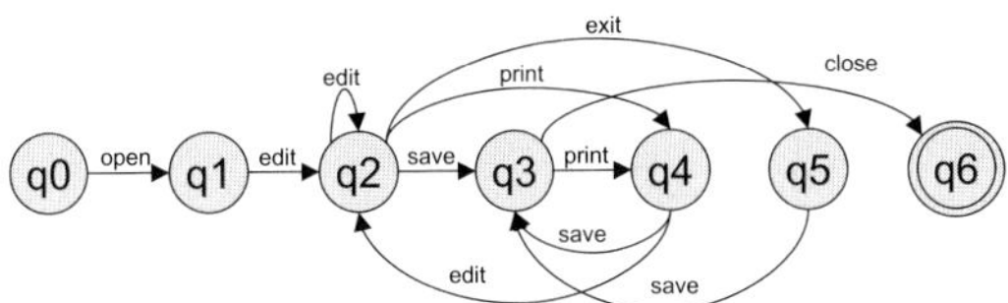

Fig. 3. Inferred model based on trace information

Clearly, this inference is not necessarily correct, and, in particular, the model in Fig. 3 allows the sequence `open`, `edit`, `save`, `print`, `save`,..., which cannot be exhibited by the system because the second `save` would never occur as the file has not been edited since the first `save`.

The procedure we used to construct the model in Fig. 3 is an extremely simplified version of more elaborate approaches to model inference such as [5, 17]. For instance, Cook et al [5] use statistical analysis of patterns in the traces to determine the state space (as opposed to our simplified bijection of events to states). Although these approaches produce models that are good approximations of the system, they suffer from the same problem described above.

Contexts. We now show how, by merging the structural and general knowledge gained from control flow information with the dynamic and specific knowledge obtained from traces, we can ameliorate some of the problems described previously. The basic idea is to use the traces to identify, among all possible paths in the code (represented by its CFG), some feasible paths. Once we know that a path is feasible (i.e., there is a set of inputs and values of predicates that causes the system to exercise it), we can look at the control flow to understand how the trace was generated in the code and possibly infer alternative and recurrent paths based on the control predicates.

Besides sequences of actions, we enrich the trace information including the value of the system state. The *system state*, in this work, comprises the values of a subset of its attributes. In the case of our example in Fig. 1, for instance, it would be composed by the values of attributes `isOpen` and `isSaved`. Attributes are normally used in control predicates, thus affecting the control flow and, consequently, the traces the system can generate.

Based on this, we have created our concept of *contexts*. We define a context as *the combination of the current point in the system control flow, which is determined by the evaluated control predicates, and the current values of the attributes that define the system state.* Therefore, the conjunction of the control flow information and the system state is denominated *context information*. An example of a context $C1$ for our running example would be that the execution is on the while-statement in line 9 of Fig. 1 with values of attributes `isOpen` and `isSaved` being both false.

A *structure of contexts* can be naturally defined based on the nested structure of blocks of code in a program. Each context is associated to a block of code by the point of execution that the context represents. For instance, the context $C1$, mentioned above, can be associated to a block B, representing the code between lines 9 and 24. We say that a context $C2$ is a *subcontext* of $C1$ if the block of code associated to $C2$ is a sub-block of the block of code associated to $C1$. Therefore, in our example, the block between lines 11 and 24 (switch-statement) defines a context $C2$ which is a subcontext of context $C1$.

Because we also consider the evaluation of predicates and the values of attributes, each block of code can generate multiple contexts, one for each possible combination of the evaluation of the associated predicate and the system state. This means that, for example, the block B cited before could generate various contexts other than $C1$ depending on the evaluation of its predicate (`cmd!=4`) and the values of `isOpen` and `isSaved`.

The structure of contexts tells us in which conditions (according to the sequence of evaluated predicates, their values and the system state) a context or action is reachable. This is somewhat similar to the idea of *path condition* [20], which describes the necessary conditions to be satisfied for the system to execute a path in the code between two given statements.

3 Context-Based Model Extraction

Our model extraction approach constructs behaviour models, in the form of Labelled Transition Systems (LTS) [16], from Java source code. LTS has been successfully used to model and reason about the behaviour of complex systems.

We start off the process by instrumenting the code using a source code transformation language and generating traces based on a test suite. Using the collected information, we identify the necessary context information. This information, combined with the sequences of actions in each context, is used to create an FSP description of the system to be used in the LTSA tool to obtain an LTS model. A general view of the process is presented in Fig. 4.

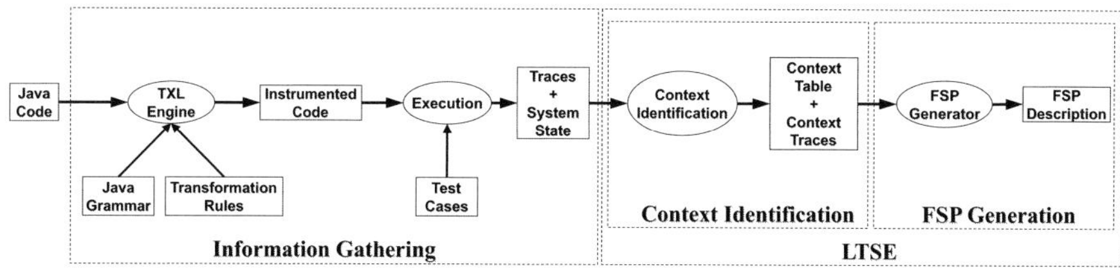

Fig. 4. General view of the model extraction process

Ellipses represent processing phases and boxes represent inputs/outputs of these processes. Horizontal arrows show the sequence of information processing, whereas vertical arrows describe the inclusion of extra inputs needed during the given process execution. The big block on the right-hand side represents the part of the process automated by our tool. The whole process is described in more detail next. We refer to the code in Fig. 1 to exemplify results from each phase.

3.1 Information Gathering

In order to collect the necessary information, we first annotate the Java source codes of some classes of the system and then execute them according to a test suite. The definition of which classes are instrumented depends on the user. They normally involve the classes that produce actions (method calls) included in the properties to be verified. In our example code from Fig. 1, the existent actions are `open`, `edit`, `print`, `save`, `exit` and `close`.

To carry out the instrumentation, we use the TXL engine [7] to apply modifications to the source code according to a set of rules[1]. We apply domain-independent rules to annotate control flow statements, call sites and methods entry and exit points.

Annotations print out predefined labels (`SEL` for selection statements, `REP` for repetition and `MET` for method blocks) to the standard output along with the values of attributes. If the annotation corresponds to a control flow statement, the annotation also prints the predicate tested and the result of its evaluation. Calls to external methods are also annotated at the call site. Part of the instrumented version of the editor code is shown in Fig. 5.

[1] We currently do not supported nested method calls and inheritance.

```
public class Editor {
  ...
  public Editor () {
    ...
    while(cmd!=4){
      System.err.println ("REP_ENTER:(cmd!=4)#"+(cmd!=4)+
      "#{"+isOpen+","+isSaved+"}");
      cmd = readCmd();
      switch (cmd) {
        case 0: System.err.println ("SEL_ENTER:(cmd)#"+cmd+
                "#{"+isOpen+","+isSaved+"}");
                  System.err.println ("SEL_ENTER:(!isOpen)#"+
                  (!isOpen)+"#{"+isOpen+","+isSaved+"}");
                  if(!isOpen)
                    name = open();
                  System.err.println ("SEL_END");
                System.err.println ("SEL_END");
                break;
        ... }
      System.err.println ("REP_END");}
  }

  void exit (String n) {
    System.err.println ("MET_ENTER:exit#{"+isOpen+","+isSaved+"}");
    ...
    System.err.println ("MET_END");
  }
  ...
}
```

Fig. 5. Example of instrumented code

Besides the automatically identified actions, we allow the user to define their own actions. We call these *user-defined actions*, which represent actions other than the execution of a method. This is important in situations where, for example, reaching a given point in the code has some particular meaning, such as the completion of a task, where a task is a set of methods that should be executed in order to realise some specific computation. User-defined actions can be inserted into any part of the code using a predefined format and are automatically converted into the appropriate annotation when the code is instrumented.

The trace generation is done by logging the outputs produced by executing the instrumented code. In order to be able to select the behaviours we want to monitor, we use a test suite. We do not currently use any particular technique for selecting test cases, but all test cases are chosen based on the knowledge we have of the system and to include behaviours we would like to observe. These behaviours are usually related to properties we intend to verify.

The result of executing the instrumented code using the test cases is the creation of a set of logged traces, one for each test case. Part of the log for an execution of the code in Fig. 1 is shown in Fig. 6. It includes the beginning of the log, where the first input was the command to open a file, then the file is edited and saved. We used the same sequence of inputs used to obtain the model in Fig. 3 to generate this log file.

3.2 Contexts Identification

Using the information in the logs, the LTSE tool constructs a table of contexts for each involved class. A *context table* (CT) stores information about the contexts created during execution. It is used to keep track of the contexts found in the logs in order to recognise a previously encountered context and identify new contexts. Each new context found (represented by an annotation in the log describing the

```
REP_ENTER:(cmd!=4)#true#{false,true}
 SEL_ENTER:(cmd)#0#{false,true}
  SEL_ENTER:(!isOpen)#true#{false,true}
   MET_ENTER:open#true#{false,true}
   MET_END
  SEL_END
 SEL_END
REP_END
REP_ENTER:(cmd!=4)#true#{true,true}
 SEL_ENTER:(cmd)#1#{true,true}
  SEL_ENTER:(isOpen)#true#{true,true}
   MET_ENTER:edit#true#{true,true}
   MET_END
  SEL_END
 SEL_END
REP_END
REP_ENTER:(cmd!=4)#true#{true,false}
 SEL_ENTER:(cmd)#3#{true,false}
  SEL_ENTER:(!isSaved)#true#{true,false}
   MET_ENTER:save#true#{true,false}
   MET_END
  SEL_END
 SEL_END
REP_END
```

Fig. 6. Example of log

Context	Predicate	Value	State
0	-	true	{}
0.1	(cmd!=4)	true	{false,true}
0.1.1	(cmd)	0	{false,true}
0.1.1.1	(!isOpen)	true	{false,true}
0.1.1.1.1	open	true	{false,true}
0.2	(cmd!=4)	true	{true,true}
0.2.1	(cmd)	1	{true,true}
0.2.1.1	(isOpen)	true	{true,true}
0.2.1.1.1	edit	true	{true,true}
0.3	(cmd!=4)	true	{true,false}
...	....	...	{...}

Fig. 7. Example of context table

beginning of a control flow statement or method block) is associated to a *context ID*, which uniquely identifies a context.

The result of the context identification phase is the creation of a CT and the generation of a set of *context traces* for each class of the system. These context traces are sequences of contexts IDs and actions, representing the contexts the system went through during the execution and the actions that happened in each one of them. The LTSE analyses each log separately, looking for context information, updating the CT and including the identified contexts and actions in the context traces. Its basic procedure for each class is as follows:

```
Context CurrentContext = INITIAL
ContextTable CT is empty /* Context table */
ContextStack S is empty /* Stack to control current context */
S.push(CurrentContext)
ContextTrace T is empty /* Context trace to be generated */
For each log L containing traces of class C
  While L has more annotations
    Read annotation A from L
    If A.label == REP_ENTER or SEL_ENTER or MET_ENTER
      New Context I
      If (CurrentContext, A) is in CT /* Already in table */
        I = CT.getId(CurrentContext, A) /* Get ID */
      Else I = CT.add(CurrentContext, A) /* Add to table */
      CurrentContext = I
      S.push(I)
      T.write(I) /* Insert context ID in the context trace */
      /* Insert an action name in the context trace */
      If A.type == MET_ENTER
        T.write(A.predicate)
    Else If A.type == REP_END or SEL_END or MET_END
          S.pop()
          CurrentContext = S.top()
```

As an example, Fig. 7 shows part of the CT generated by the LTSE tool based on the log presented in Fig. 6. The first column contains the context IDs. The ID 0 is reserved for the initial context. An ID 0.1 represents the first subcontext of the initial context, 0.2, the second, and so on. The second column describes the predicate evaluated in the context. No predicate is associated to the initial context and the name of the method is used for contexts representing a method execution. The value of the predicate in the context is presented in the third column. The last column contains the system state, with the first value representing the value of attribute `isOpen` and the second showing the value of attribute `isSaved`.

Fig. 8 presents, on its left-hand side, part of the contents of the context trace created by the LTSE tool using this CT and the log in Fig. 6. The context trace is the translation from the annotations in the log to context IDs, in the case of control flow statements, and from annotations to names of actions for methods. Note that, because methods represent the beginning of a new context, they also cause the inclusion of a context ID in the context trace.

3.3 FSP Generation

At this stage, the LTSE tool converts the information contained in the context trace into an FSP process definition. *Finite State Processes* (FSP) [16] is a process algebra for describing LTS models. It allows for local definition (subprocess), action prefix (->), choice (|) and recursion.

In our mapping from context traces to FSP, we create an FSP description to represent the system, where each class for which we have traces is described by a process definition. We create one subprocess definition for each identified context and define the start of a process as the subprocess that represents the initial context. Each subprocess is defined as a number of choices (e.g. of the form $P = (x_1^1 \rightarrow x_2^1 \rightarrow \ldots P^1 | \ldots | x_1^m \rightarrow x_2^m \rightarrow \ldots P^m)$ where each choice describes a sequence of actions $\langle x_1^j \rightarrow x_2^j \rightarrow \ldots \rangle$ found contiguously in a context trace between the contexts denoted by P and P^j.

Implementing this strategy, the LTSE tool constructs the process definition shown on the right-hand side of Fig. 8 for the editor presented in Fig. 1. This process definition was created based on the contents of the context file presented on the left-hand side of Fig. 8.

During the mapping, we apply some reductions in order to create a more compact process definition. These reductions involve the merging of contexts into a single subprocess if the contexts appear consecutively in a context trace, i.e., with no actions between them. These simplifications can be seen in Fig. 8 as the dotted boxes on the left-hand side. Their corresponding subprocesses are pointed by the arrows and the actions added to the subprocesses are presented in bold.

The LTS model derived from the FSP description of the editor is generated automatically by the LTSA tool and is depicted in Fig. 9 (state `E` represents the final state). This model is the result of processing the same trace used to create the inferred model shown in Fig. 3. Note that the model created using contexts does not include invalid behaviours. Moreover, it does not create any restriction not imposed by the code presented in Fig. 1. Hence, though it is not complete, as it does not include some feasible behaviours, it is correct with respect to the alphabet of actions chosen. The use of more traces would eventually lead to a complete representation of the editor's behaviour.

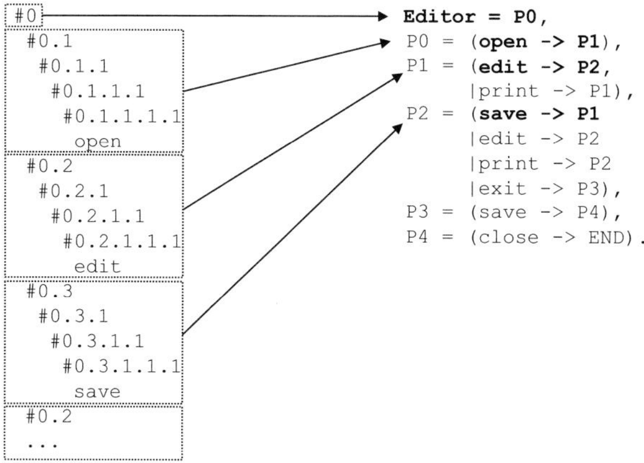

Fig. 8. Mapping from the context trace to the process definition of the editor

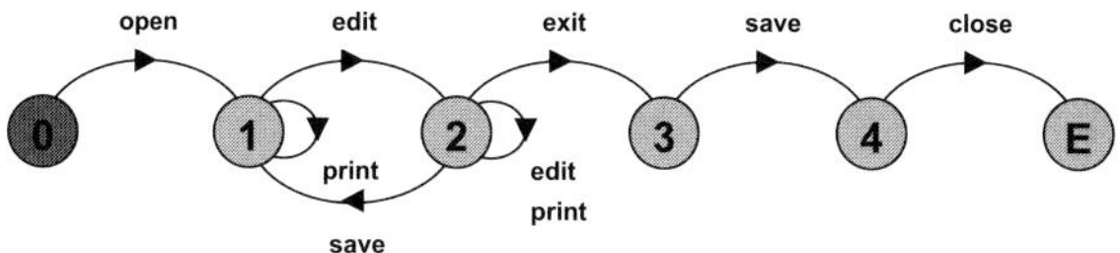

Fig. 9. LTS model for the text editor

It is also important to note that this model includes behaviours that were not described in the trace, such as the possibility of repeating the command `print` on state 1. Actually, the trace did not even include a sequence of two consecutive actions `print`. This additional behaviour could be inferred because the context trace shows that this action happens inside a loop and that it is always enabled after a file has been opened. For this same reason, `print` can also be repeated infinitely on state 2, which represents the context where the file has been edited.

4 Case Study: Cruise Control System

We have validated our approach through a number of case studies involving single- and multi-threaded systems. These case studies include modelling an ATM system, a traffic lights control system and an air conditioner control system. In this paper we report on a cruise control system [16] to demonstrate a practical use of our approach. This case study is a good choice for validation of our approach as both code and model of intended behaviour exist. Hence, we can, compare our automatically generated model to existing ones to evaluate our work. We now present the case study, our analysis results and the discrepancies found between the model we extracted and the existing one.

An automobile cruise control system is controlled by three buttons: `on`, `off` and `resume`. Pressing `on` when the car engine is working causes the system to record the current speed and keep the car at that speed. The same speed is maintained until the car is accelerated or deaccelerated or `off` is pressed. If `resume` is then pressed, the system increases or decreases the speed to set it to the previously recorded speed.

We used the Java implementation of the cruise controller, the `Controller` class, from [16]. In the system, an object of this class is called from the user interface on events `on`, `off`, `resume`, `accelerate`, `brake`, `engineOn` and `engineOff`. The object reacts to these method calls by enabling (`enableControl`), disabling (`disableControl`) and setting the cruise speed (`clearSpeed` and `recordSpeed`) of the speed controller component. The speed controller computes correct throttle values and adjusts throttle according to the desired speed.

Following the approach described in the previous subsection, the code for the `Controller` class was automatically annotated. We selected the attribute `controlState` of the class to compose the context information. Then, traces were generated by executing the instrumented code according to the following test cases:

```
T1 = engineOn,accelerate,on,accelerate,resume,brake,resume,off,resume,
     off,resume,off,engineOff
T2 = engineOn,on,accelerate,on,brake,engineOff,engineOn,accelerate,on,
     off,resume,engineOff
T3 = engineOn,accelerate,on,off,resume,off,on,accelerate,on,brake,
     resume,brake,on,engineOff
T4 = engineOn,accelerate,on,engineOff,engineOn,accelerate,brake,
     accelerate,on,brake,on,off, resume,off,resume,engineOff
```

Each test case includes the sequences of inputs provided via the system interface. In other words, each label represents clicking on a button of the system GUI. However, there is a one-to-one correspondence between these inputs and method calls, hence the test cases can be thought of as actual method calls on the `Controller` object. The test cases were chosen based on a desired safety property *CRUISESAFETY* presented in [16], which states that the `Controller` relinquishes control of the speed as soon as the `brake`, `accelerator` or `off` button is pressed.

The generated logs were used as in the LTSE tool to create the FSP description of the `Controller`. The LTSA tool realised the conversion of the FSP description into its graphical representation as an LTS model, shown in Fig. 10.

This model is very similar to the one presented in [16]. The only difference is that the automatically extracted model describes traces in which the accelerator may be pressed without turning on the cruise control system. This was a detail omitted in the model in [16] even though it can be exhibited by the implementation taken from the same source. Fortunately, this behaviour does not correspond to a behaviour that violates the safety property, otherwise it would have represented undesired behaviour that would have gone undetected.

For the model checking process, we composed our model of the Controller with those of the other components of the system as they were described in [16].

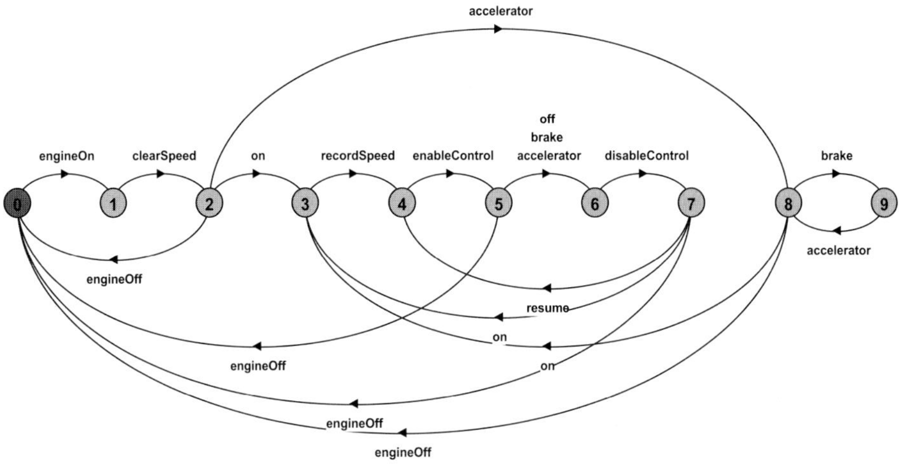

Fig. 10. LTS model of the cruise controller

Even though there was the mentioned difference between our model and the one proposed in [16], we obtained the same results. As expected, the property *CRUISESAFETY* was verified not to be violated when the components of the system were composed. Nevertheless, a progress check provided by the LTSA tool showed the problem described in [16], involving the cruise control system not being disabled when the engine was switched off. Hence, when the car engine was turned back on again, the car would accelerate automatically to the last recorded speed. The error trace obtained with our model in the composition showed exactly the described problem.

In this case, the problem was twofold: firstly, the system allowed this dangerous situation to happen; and secondly, the property specification did not include a check of this possible undesired behaviour. To correct this, we applied the necessary corrections to the implementation, to prevent the system from remaining on once the engine was turned off, and to the property specification, to guarantee that this check was now included. These changes resulted in the creation of a model, which, when composed to the other components models, generated no violations during the verification process.

5 Discussion and Related Work

The completeness of our models depends on the selection of test cases. If sections of the code are never exercised by the test cases, the resulting model will not incorporate all feasible behaviours of the code. An analysis on an incomplete model may generate *false positives*, i.e., fail to identify violations, which occur when the system executes but do not appear in the model. On the other hand, any violation (of safety properties) found in the model corresponds to a real violation. To ameliorate the incompleteness problem and reduce the possibility of false positives, an adequate test coverage must be achieved. This is beyond the scope of this paper.

Correctness, the fact that all behaviours in the model correspond to feasible executions of the code, depends crucially on the selection of attributes for contexts. If the model is correct (all relevant attributes, according to the property, are chosen), the absence of violations means no violations in the system w.r.t. the traces included in the model and the property being verified. However, if key attributes are not selected, then the model may contain spurious behaviours, which may give rise to *false negatives*, i.e., examples of violations of properties that cannot occur when running the code.

Detection of false negatives can be done by replaying counterexamples on the code to check if the counterexample is feasible. Confirming infeasibility of a counterexample triggers an augmentation of the attributes selected as part of a context, which in turn will produce, given the same test cases, a model which is a refinement [18] of the model extracted with the smaller set of attributes (i.e., can be simulated by it). Hence, by identifying false negatives, the extracted model can be refined into a correct model of the system, which rules out the false negatives. The issues described above related to correctness correspond to those also addressed in abstraction in program verification (e.g. [11]). Techniques to support the refinement process are beyond the scope of this paper.

We share the same underlying idea of [19] of putting static and dynamic information together. However, in [19], the focus is on state properties, such as invariants of attributes of a class, rather than the dynamic behaviour of a component in terms of its required and provided services.

Unlike the FeaVer model extractor [13], our mapping from the programming language to the verification language is predefined and automatic. Therefore, the user does not need to know the programming nor the modelling language.

As the Bandera toolset [6], we also direct our model construction by a property to be verified, but the properties we verify do not follow any previously created pattern. Furthermore, we do not use a reduced version of the code to generate models. Rather, we use the complete program to generate the traces and then apply a selective analysis to them according to the actions required to be in the model and the level of abstraction defined by the set of attributes composing the system state.

Verisoft [9] and Java Pathfinder [21] present the possibility of controlling the execution through a custom-made environment to verify all behaviours. Nevertheless, we believe that having a model is useful for a range of purposes other than just verifying properties, such as simulations, animations, performance analysis and model parallel composition to be used, for example, for software evolution.

Whereas modifying the level of abstraction in our work is simple and involves only the selection of additional attributes to be monitored, tools such as SLAM [2] and BLAST [11] use more complex approaches to achieve the appropriate abstraction. They offer techniques for the automatic refinement of abstractions to prove a property. We believe this work is complementary to ours.

Finally, as discussed previously, our work differs from those that take only trace information into account, such as that of Cook & Wolf [5] and Mariani [17].

6 Conclusion and Future Work

We presented a new approach for automatic model extraction based on the identification of contexts, which has been partially implemented by the LTSE tool. We showed how contexts can be used to combine static and dynamic information. We discussed the results of one of our case studies to show some experimental results. These results indicate that our model extraction process can be used for the construction of LTS models which are good approximations of the real systems and can be used for behaviour analysis and property verification. The appropriate selection of the parameters of the process can lead to a compact and faithful partial representation of the behaviour of the system to be analysed.

Future work includes investigating appropriate test coverage criteria for selecting tests to generate system traces and supporting refinement of context information. In addition, we aim to apply our technique to the model extraction of concurrent and distributed systems. Though we have already developed a few case studies on concurrent systems (e.g., a version of the bounded-buffer described in [10] and the single-lane bridge presented in [16]), we still need to gain more experience in using our approach for such systems and introduce some necessary extensions.

We have also developed initial case studies using an incremental version of our approach. In this version, a previously created model can be improved by the addition of new traces without requiring the repetition of the whole process from the beginning. Hence, traces obtained through the execution of new test cases could be added to the model. This will permit us to use our work in other areas, such as conformance and software evolution, and enrich the models we generate and augment their accuracy. This idea has been discussed in [17], but the quantity and quality of the information proved to be insufficient to guarantee good results. In our approach, however, we believe we have enough contextual behavioural information to implement this technique.

References

1. A. Aho, R. Sethi, and J. Ullman. *Compilers: Principles, Techniques and Tools.* Addison-Wesley, 1986.
2. T. Ball and S. K. Rajamani. The SLAM Project: Debugging System Software via Static Analysis. In *POPL'02*, pages 1–3, Portland, OR, USA, 2002.
3. S. Boroday, A. Petrenko, J. Singh, and et al. Dynamic Analysis of Java Applications for Multithreaded Antipatterns. In *WODA'05*, pages 1–7, 2005.
4. E. M. Clarke, O. Grumberg, and D. A. Peled. *Model Checking.* The MIT Press, Cambridge, Massachusetts, USA, 1999.
5. J. E. Cook and A. L. Wolf. Discovering Models of Software Processes from Event-Based Data. *ACM TOSEM*, 7(3):215–249, 1998.

6. J. C. Corbett, M. B. Dwyer, J. Hatcliff, S. Laubach, C. S. Pasareanu, Robby, and H. Zheng. Bandera: Extracting Finite-State Models from Java Source Code. In *ICSE'00*, pages 439–448, Limerick, Ireland, 2000.
7. J. R. Cordy, T. R. Dean, A. J. Malton, and K. A. Schneider. Source Transformation in Software Engineering Using the TXL Transformation System. *Journal of Information and Software Technology, Special Issue on Source Code Analysis and Manipulation*, 44(13):827–837, 2002.
8. M. D. Ernst. Static and Dynamic Analysis: Synergy and Duality. In *WODA'03*, pages 24–27, Portland, OR, USA, 2003.
9. P. Godefroid. Software Model Checking: The Verisoft Approach. Bell Labs Technical Memorandum ITD-03-44189G, Bell Laboratories, August 2003.
10. K. Havelund and T. Pressburguer. Model Checking Java Programs Using Java PathFinder. *Intl. Journal on Software Tools for Technology Transfer*, 2(4):366–381, March 2000.
11. T. A. Henzinger, R. Jahla, R. Majumdar, and et al. Lazy Abstraction. In *POPL'02*, pages 58–70, 2002.
12. G. J. Holzmann. From Code to Models. In *ACSD'01*, pages 3–10, Newcastle upon Tyne, UK, 2001.
13. G. J. Holzmann and M. H. Smith. A Practical Method for Verifying Event-Driven Software. In *ICSE'99*, pages 597–607, Los Angeles, USA, 1999.
14. D. Jackson and M. Rinard. Software Analysis: A Roadmap. In *ICSE'00*, pages 133–145, Limerick, Ireland, 2000.
15. James C. King. Symbolic Execution and Program Testing. *CACM*, 19(7):385–394, July 1976.
16. J. Magee and J. Kramer. *Concurrency: State Models and Java Programs.* Wiley, 1999.
17. L. Mariani. *Behavior Capture and Test: Dynamic Analysis of Component-Based Systems.* Phd, Università degli Studi di Milano Bicocca, 2005.
18. R. Milner. An algebraic definition of simulation between programs. In *IJCAI*, pages 481–489, 1971.
19. J. W. Nimmer and M. D. Ernst. Automatic Generation of Program Specifications. In *ISSTA'02*, pages 232–242, Rome, Italy, 2002.
20. T. Robschink and G. Snelting. Efficient Path Conditions in Dependence Graphs. In *ICSE'02*, pages 478–488, Orlando, Florida, USA, 2002.
21. W. Visser, K. Havelund, G. Brat, S. Park, and F Lerda. Model Checking Programs. *Automated Software Engineering Journal*, 10(2):203–232, 2003.

Dynamic and Generic Manipulation of Models: From Introspection to Scripting

Christophe Tombelle and Gilles Vanwormhoudt

GET / Telecom Lille 1, Laboratoire d'Informatique Fondamentale de Lille
59655 Villeneuve d'Ascq cedex - France
{tombelle, vanwormhout}@enic.fr

Abstract. Model introspection is a powerful feature of existing modeling frameworks like Java Metadata Interface or Eclipse Modeling Framework. It allows a program to work with any model by querying its structure dynamically at runtime. Applications of model introspection are model transformation engines and generic models editor. We show that mechanisms for model introspection are complex to use. To address this problem, we propose the notion of model scripting which uses introspection to automatically and dynamically expose any kind of model to program control through a compact and high-level notation. In this paper, we present several principles for general model scripting. Scripting languages built with these principles can be used for numerous model driven activities, such as interactive model testing and rapid development of scripts to process models and metamodels.

1 Introduction

In model driven approaches such as MDA, transformation languages [6] are not always well-adapted to some kinds of model manipulation (checking, composition, merging, audit, ...). One solution consists in performing these manipulations with classical languages using an API automatically generated from metamodels as specified by standard approaches like MOF [2][11] or proprietary ones like the Eclipse Modeling Framework (EMF) [9].

One interesting and powerful feature of these approaches is that they include reflective interfaces to introspect models. Model introspection allows a program to work with any model by querying its structure, i.e. its metamodel, dynamically at runtime. Model introspection is a key feature of generic modeling environments [13][1] where tools and applications (transformation engines, generic browsers, ...) must be able to manage and process models conforming to different modeling langages, without any prior knowledge of the metamodel.

Despite their benefits for building generic modeling tools and accessing models dynamically, reflective interfaces are complex to use. We identify several sources of complexity : instruction inflations, multilevel knowledge requirement, model and implementation level conflation, model manipulation scattering. To avoid this complexity and help developers building these generic applications, new tools and methodologies must be provided.

O. Nierstrasz et al. (Eds.): MoDELS 2006, LNCS 4199, pp. 395–409, 2006.

In this paper, we propose the notion of model scripting, a new kind of tool for generic modeling environments. The idea of model scripting is the application of scripting techniques, well-known in the field of component-based approaches [7][14], to the model space. It exploits model introspection to automatically and dynamically expose models and their elements to program control through compact and high-level notation. We present the general principles of model scripting mechanisms and show how to integrate them into a programing language. These principles aim to integrate all modeling levels and allow the manipulation of models and metamodels in a uniform, generic way. We illustrate the application of these principles to JavaScript and EMF. The resulting model scripting language can be used for numerous model driven activities such as interactive model testing and the rapid development of generic scripts which process models or metamodels. It is also a simple and powerful tool to investigate model introspection.

Section 2 gives some background about model introspection in existing approaches. Section 3 discusses the pros and cons of reflective interfaces. Section 4 explains the need for model scripting and gives some principles for building a model-oriented scripting mechanism. Section 5 presents their application to EMF and Javascript. Before concluding, we describe related works on model manipulation languages.

2 Model Introspection in Existing Approaches

2.1 Metamodel-Specific and Reflective Interfaces

To write programs that manipulate models, standard specifications like MOF to IDL mapping and JMI (Java Metadata Interfaces) as well as proprietary solutions like EMF have been defined. All these approaches provide two kinds of programing interfaces : metamodel-specific interfaces and reflective interfaces[1].

Metamodel-specific Interfaces. These interfaces are used for the creation and the manipulation of models which conforms to a specific metamodel. Rules for generating these interfaces from the definition of a metamodel are defined by each approach. Figure 1 gives an overview of EMF[2] rules applied to an Ecore[3] metamodel for representing models of a very simple program composed of assignment instructions. To the right of figure 1, we give a subset of the Java interfaces generated for this metamodel[4]. Each class of the metamodel (Program, Assignment) gives rise to a Java interface. Interfaces are also generated for the metamodel package (MiniLangPackage) and an associated factory (MiniLangMMFactory). Thanks to these interfaces, Java programs can create, inspect and modify model elements to obtain a correct model of programs.

[1] This distinction and these terms are the ones used by existing approaches.

[2] In the rest of the paper, we will refer to the EMF approach. However, the discussion and the proposed solution are valid for any approach offering reflective interfaces.

[3] ECore is the metametamodel of EMF. Its specification is similar to Essential MOF.

[4] Unlike JMI, EMF also generates classes implementing these interfaces which we omit for space reasons.

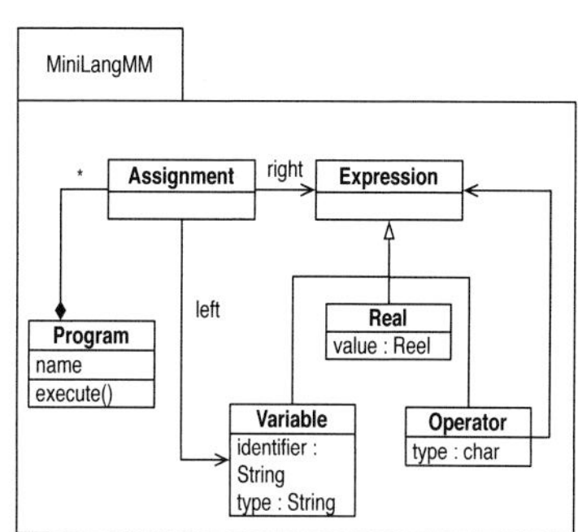

Fig. 1. A mini language metamodel

```
interface Program extends EObject {
        // generated for Program metaclass
         String getName();
         void setName(String n);
         EList getAssignments();
}
interface Assignment extends EObject {
         // generated for Assignment metaclass
         Program getProgram();
         Expression getRight();
         void setRight(Expression e);
         Expression getLeft();
         void setLeft(Expression e);
}
interface MiniLangMMFactory extends EFactory {
          // factory interface
          Program createProgram();
         Assignment createAssignment();
}
interface MiniLangMMPackage extends EPackage {
        // interface generated fo the package
        // factory access
        MiniLangMMFactory getFactory();
        ....
}
```

Reflective Interfaces. These interfaces provide metamodel independant operations to manipulate models of any type. They are systematically inherited by specific interfaces to support generic manipulations. They generally offer operations for two kinds of model introspection[5]: structural and computational introspection.

Structural introspection reifies the description of metamodels and offers reflective operations to access and consult the objects representing the description. Figure 2 illustrates EMF structural introspection for a P1 Program element. The right hand part shows a P1 model element and some elements of its MiniLangMM metamodel. The left hand part shows the Program specific interface inheriting from the reflective EObject interface. At the implementation level, P1 is represented by an instance of this interface while Program is represented by an instance of EClass. The eClass() reflective operation[6] may be invoked on P1 to access the object representing its modeling class, namely Program. Then, one can discover that this class has an attribute named "name" which is contained in the MiniLangMM package. With structural introspection, all relevant informations about the structure of a model can be known.

Computational introspection provides reflective operations to create, inspect and modify model elements from a metamodel description. Once metamodel elements are known thanks to structural introspection, a program can create a model or manipulate its content. In EMF, EObject brings the eGet and eSet reflective operations to read and write a structural feature, i.e. an attribute or link and EFactory includes a reflective operation to create an element from a

[5] Model introspection is similar to introspection in programing language [8] but its goal is to capture metainformation about the structure and properties of models instead of programs.

[6] JMI has a similar interface called RefBaseObject and a similar operation called refMetaObject().

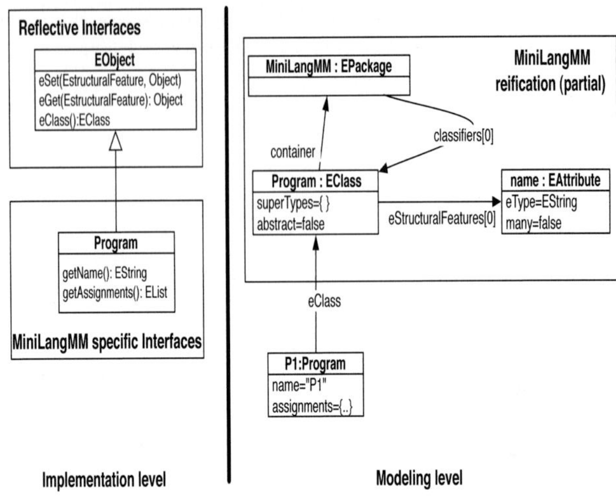

Fig. 2. Reflective interfaces and model introspection

class of the metamodel. With computational introspection, one can read the name attribute of P1 by invoking its eGet operation with the name attribute description (reified by name:EAttribute) as an argument.

2.2 Introspection in Metamodeling Architectures

Existing approaches enable us to represent models and offer introspection facilities to represent, access and use the description of their metamodel. In general, elements composing this description are themselves described logically by a metametamodel and are physically implemented by specific interfaces. This generalised application of principles which are shared by every approach results in a multi-level metamodeling architecture (similar to the OMG architecture from model level (M1) to metametamodel level (M3)) whose implementation is realized by metamodel-specific and reflective interfaces [12]. Figure 3 shows these principles for EMF.

The metamodeling architecture is composed of objects that represent elements of different modeling levels. At the M1 level, objects representing model elements (P1) are described by M2-level objects corresponding to metamodel element (MiniLangMM package, Program class) as seen previously. The latter are themselves described by M3-level objects (EPackage, EClass) which are autodescribed to stop the metalevel ascension (see EClass). This way, each modeling level of the architecture is causally described by objects of the next higher level. These structural principles are similar to the ones adopted for reflective programing language (see Cointe's and Smith's seminal works in [8]).

The implementation architecture consists of specific and reflective interfaces that together implement objects representing elements in the metamodeling architecture. The figure shows the one-to-one correspondance between a modeling level and the specific interfaces that implement this level. Another aspect shown by the figure is that specific interfaces implementing one level serve to create objects of the lower level in the modeling part. Therefore, objects representing model elements have two instanciation links : a modeling one (eClass link) and an implementation one (here the Java instance link).

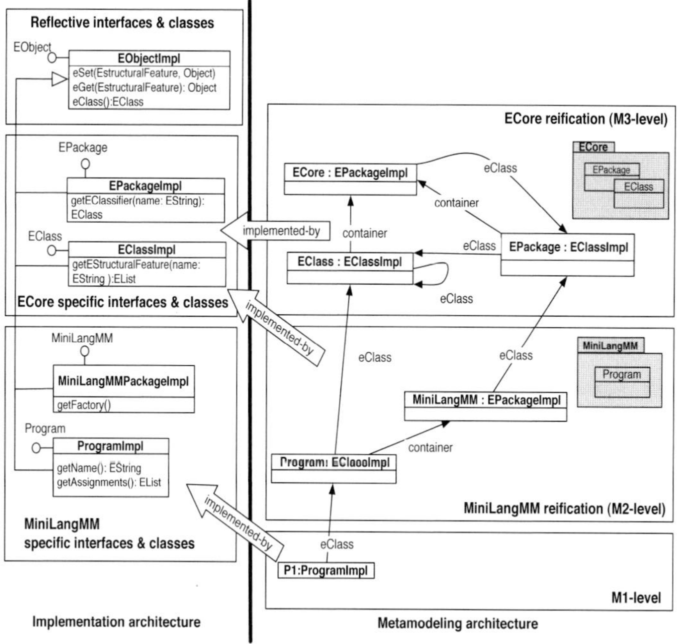

Fig. 3. Metamodeling and implementation architectures

A property highlighted by the previous architecture is the inheritance of reflective interfaces by metamodel and metametamodel-specific interfaces (in the figure, Program, EClass and EPackage inherit from EObject). This property has two consequences. First, it gives a uniform access to every modeling level : elements of each level can be manipulated with the same set of reflective operations. Secondly, structural and computational introspection is generalized for every modeling level and becomes usable to query the description of metamodels and manipulate their content dynamically. In the following sections, we will show how to exploit such a property to provide a simplified access to any kind of model and metamodel. In the next section, we will identify some problems related to reflective interfaces.

3 Pros and Cons of Reflective Interfaces

By using our previous example, we propose to study the use of each kind of interface in the Java programing language. This study will highlight the complexity of reflective interfaces. Reflective interfaces provide all the functionalities that metamodel-specific interfaces support. This property enables us to compare them when building the same model. In order to make this comparison, we give the code related to each interface for building the model of a program including a variable assignment (similar operations are matched by the same number).

```
// Meta-model specific version
1. MiniLangMM pkg = MiniLangMM.eINSTANCE ;          // get the object representing the package
2. MiniLangMMFactory factory = pkg.getEFactory() ; // get the associated factory
3. Program p1 = factory.createProgram() ;           // create a Program element
4. p1.setName( "P1") ;                              // set the Program name
5. Assignment a = factory.createAssignment() ;      // create an Assignment element
6. Variable v1 = factory.createVariable() ;         // create a Variable element
7. v1.setIdentifier("v1") ;                         // set its identifier
8. a.setLeft (v1);                                  // link the Variable to the Assignment
9. p1.getAssignment().add(a) ;                      // link the Assignment to the Program
```

```
// Reflective version
1. EPackage pkg = MiniLangMM.eINSTANCE ;
2. EFactory factory = pkg.getEFactory() ;
3. EClass programClass = (EClass) pkg.getEClassifier("Program") ;
    EObject p1 = factory.create(programClass) ;
4. EStructuralFeature metaatt = programClass.getEStructuralFeature("name") ;
     p1.eSet(metaatt, "P1") ;
5. EClass assignClass = (EClass) pkg.getEClassifier("Assignment") ;
   EObject a = factory.create(assignClass) ;
6. EClass varClass = (EClass) pkg.getEClassifier("Variable") ;
   EObject v1 = factory.create(varClass) ;
7. metaatt = varClass.getEStructuralFeature("identifier") ;
    v1.eSet(metaatt, "v1") ;
8. EStructuralFeature metaref = assignClass.getEStructuralFeature("left") ;
    a.eSet(metaref, v1) ;
9. metaref = programClass.getEStructuralFeature("assignment") ;
   List l = (List) p1.eGet(metaref) ;
   l.add(a) ;
```

The following critiques can be made about the use of reflective interfaces.

Instruction inflations: first, we see that reflective interfaces require more instructions. For each operation, it is necessary to access an object containing a description of a metamodel element and pass this object to the corresponding reflective operation. The example given below is even simplified compared to most situations. Accesses and uses of metamodel elements is often much more complicated requiring complex navigation through the metamodel description and additional type controls.

Multilevel knowledge requirement: a second observation is that reflective interfaces require the handling of several levels of modeling at the same time. For each access at the model level, structural information at the metalevel must be sought. Since this search uses the metametamodel-specific interfaces, knowledge of this last level is also required. As a result, three modeling levels must be known to perform model manipulation with reflective interfaces.

Model and implementation level conflation: reflective interfaces lead to a mix of modeling and implementation concepts in the same program. In the previous code, we can see that classes, attributes and operations from the modeling architecture are tangled with those of the implementation architecture. This mix is confusing for the developer, particularly when using reflective interfaces to access M2 and M3 level.

Model manipulation scattering: finally, we can see that reflective interfaces reduce the readability of the code that manipulates models. In the previous code, elements of the modeling part only appear as parameters of reflective operations that are scattered throughout the code. As a result, the model elements and their features are not highlighted and a precise analysis of code is needed to understand their manipulation.

All these points show that reflective interfaces are less convenient to use than those tailored to the specific metamodel. They are also harder to use, requiring a good understanding of metalevels and a good distinction between the modeling and implementation space.

However, despite these difficulties, reflective interfaces provide interesting capabilities. They allow us to manipulate models dynamically, by discovering their metamodel. More over, they enable us to write generic code, that is code working at any level of modeling (model, metamodel, metametamodel). As an example of this last capability, we give below some code that tests whether a model element has a sub-element of a particular type and if this is not the case, automatically creates such an element and the associated link. This code is generic : it can be applied to model elements of any level. Such a generic code could be useful when writing an algorithm for copying any model as described in [5].

```
void ensureExistance(EObject elt, String linkName, String subEltClassName, EPackage pkg) {
  EClass eltCls = elt.eClass(); // retrieve the class of elt parameter
  // retrieve the link description from its name
  EStructuralFeature metaref =  eltCls.getEStructuralFeature(linkName) ;
  if (metaref instanceof EReference && (EReference) metaref.containment == true &&
  elt.eGet(metaref)) == null) { // test if subcomponent exists at the end of the link
    // subelement creation
    Efactory factory = pkg.getEFactory() ;
    EClass subEltCls= (EClass) pa.getEClassifier(subEltClassName) ;
    EObject subElt = factory.create(subEltCls) ;
    elt.eSet(metaref, subElt); // link the created subelt to its parent via the link
  }
}
```

In this section, we have seen that reflective interfaces offer interesting features to dynamically manipulate models but that they are complex to use. This complexity restricts the use of model introspection and the writing of programs that perform the generic and dynamic manipulations of models. In the next section, we propose our solution to obtain the full benefit from reflective interfaces and facilitate their usage.

4 Scripting for Model Manipulation

4.1 From Model Introspection to Model Scripting

Scripting is a general programing technique which exposes the functionality of existing objects or prepackaged components to program control [7][14]. In general, this exposition is done dynamically to deal with new kinds of components at runtime and is often based on introspection mechanisms to discover the description of these components.

A scripting language is a programing language with an embedded scripting mechanism. Scripting languages are intended primarily to access and connect existing components. They are rarely used for writing applications from scratch or designing complex algorithms and data structures[7]. The main benefits of scripting languages are : 1) simplicity of use since a script is often easier to write and more concise (dynamic typing, high-level instructions) than its equivalent program written in a classical programing language, 2) improved productivity thanks to a faster and more flexible development cycle.

Our aim is to apply a similar technique to the space of models and get the same kind of simplicity and flexibility for model manipulation. We propose to elaborate a mechanism for scripting models and to integrate this mechanism into a programing language. The idea of such a scripting mechanism is to dynamically and automatically expose models and their elements to program control, i.e. to make them scriptable. Moreover, by integrating this mechanism into a language, we want to systematize the scripting process for all models and make it completely transparent thanks to high-level instructions. To build this scripting mechanism, we suggest using model introspection facilities such as the ones described in the previous sections : structural introspection is exploited to discover the structure of any model ; computational introspection is used to dynamically create and manipulate model elements according to their description. By using model introspection, we get a general solution which makes any model scriptable. Such a solution can be used to write scripts that can process models in different modeling languages and process a metamodel instead of a model.

In the context of model-driven development, model scripting languages can be useful for numerous applications [4] and can advantageously replace programs using metamodel-specific interfaces or specific transformation languages. Used interactively via a command prompt, they offer the possibility of directly operating on models and of getting the result immediately. Such an interactive mode can be a time saving tool for tasks such as model or metamodel exploration and testing. Used in batch mode via scripts, a model scripting language can also be used to quickly develop small applications for processing models. Applications can be the transformation of models, the derivation of text-based artefacts from the model such as code or test cases and the checking of models with respect to consistency rules.

4.2 Principles for Model Scripting

In this section, we present our principles for incorporating model scripting inside a programing language. These principles are general and can be applied to any

[7] Features like these are usually provided by components written in foreign and general programing language.

language and any approach supporting model introspection[8]. The set of principles is not intended to be exhaustive but can serve as a starting point for the definition of a more complete set (see also [4] for some other principles).

Scriptable model elements: With existing approaches, every model element is represented by objects. These elements are organised into multiple levels according to a modeling instanciation relationship. To guaranty coherent manipulation, it is important that the scripting language exposes the same set of objects and presents these objects according to the same organisation. Moreover, these objects must appear like other objects of the scripting language. In particular, instructions dedicated to objects should be suitable for model elements. It is important to design complex manipulations by composing such instructions.

Scripting expression: The scripting mechanism for manipulating models must provide the same capacities than the reflective interfaces. However, the complexity must be hidden by the scripting language. It must be possible to accomplish manipulations with simple language expressions. Besides simplicity, these expressions must be chosen so that models of different levels are processed in a uniform way. A metamodel must be manipulated by scripting like a model and with the same ease. Finally, we consider it important that expressions chosen for the scripting reflect the metamodeling architecture and completely hide the implementation one.

Scripting translation: The expressions for scripting models must be translated into invocations of reflective operations. This translation must be transparent for the user and must be performed automatically by the scripting mechanism. It can be specified as a mapping function between scripting expressions and expressions of the language implementing the reflective interfaces. To ensure the generality and uniformity of this translation for multiple modeling levels, it is important that such a function obeys the following principle: for each scripting expression, the description of the model elements available at the metalevel must be retrieved and this description must be used to construct the dynamic invocation of reflective operations that create or modify model elements. To illustrate this principle, we give the definition of such a function for modifying the attributes of a model element. In this example, the function is referred to as Φ and we use an abstract syntax to be language independent. We also consider that the reflective interfaces include the following operations :

- *elt.modelClass()* : return the class of a model element in the metamodeling architecture;
- *class.lookupAtt(name)* : return the attribute of the class with a specific name;
- *elt.setAttValue(meta-attribute, val)* : dynamic assignment of attribute identified by meta-attribute with the val value;

[8] The scripting language need only include a minimal set of object-oriented concepts (object interaction is enough) and some mechanisms to access introspection functionalities.

Here is the definition for translating a scripting expression corresponding to the change of attribute of a model element :

$$\Phi(\text{"}elt.att{=}value\text{"}) \Rightarrow elt.setAttValue((elt.modelClass()).lookupAtt(att),\ value)$$

This translation shows the ascension to the metalevel and the access to the description of the modified attribute. This description is then used with the set operation to dynamically modify the attribute of the model element. Other scripting expressions will be translated following similar principles. We will show a concrete example of translation in section 5.3. It is important to precise that the principles proposed for translating scripting expressions are suitable for any modeling level, thanks to the generality of reflective interfaces.

Scripting validation: There are various errors that can occur in scripting expression: access to inexistant property and incompatibility of type for values are some examples. Thanks to the structural and typing information contained in the metalevel, the validity of a scripting expression can be checked on the fly at execution time, before its translation. This checking consists in accessing dynamically the meta-level description of an element or features referenced by the expression and in verifying that the expression conforms to this description.

In the next section, we describe the application of these principles in order to define a concrete scripting mechanism.

5 Application to Javascript and EMF

Following the principles introduced previously, we have built a concrete scripting mechanism that supports the manipulation of EMF models with the Javascript language [9,10,11]. This mechanism is entirely founded upon the reflective capacities of EMF. It preserves the semantics (well-formedness rules) and the functionalities (XMI support, change notification) provided by the implementation of EMF interfaces.

5.1 Basic Functionalities

With our mechanism, all the model elements which make up the metamodeling architecture are exposed as Javascript objects and can be exploited in interactive or batch mode with simple Javascript instructions that expect objects. The creation and use of model elements (operation call-up, property and link access) are made according to a simplified, uniform object oriented notation which conforms to the modeling part. For instance, elements of a model are directly created by invoking the "create" method of objects representing classes of its metamodel. The following code illustrates the simplified notation. It performs exactly the same set of operations as the example described in section 3.

[9] We chose Javascript because it is a popular object-oriented scripting language and is an instance of the ECMAScript standard.

[10] Available at the url : http://www.enic.fr/people/Vanwormhoudt/modelscripting

[11] A similar approach could be applied for example to construct a scripting mechanism that permits to access MOF-IDL repositories with the IDLScript standard.

```
// Scripting version
miniLang = importModelDef('MiniLangMM') ; // get the object representing the package
p1 = miniLang.$Program.create() ;         // creation of a program element
p1.name = "P1" ;                          //  set the name of the program
assign = miniLang.$Assignment.create() ;  // creation of an assignment element
v1 = miniLang.$Variable.create() ;        // creation of a variable
v1.identifier = "v1" ;                    // set the identifier of the variable
assign.left = v1;                         // link the variable to the assignment
p1.assignments.add(assign) ;              // link the assignment to the program
```

As we can observe, these operations are expressed with the same ease and the same concision as the version using metamodel-specific interfaces. However, they are performed dynamically in the same way as the reflective version, that is by retrieving the description at the metalevel and invoking the reflective operations. Thanks to the scripting mechanism, the use of reflective interfaces is made completely transparent. This transparency eliminates all the drawbacks mentioned in section 3. It is no longer necessary to know the multiple modeling levels since access to the metalevel for retrieving description is not required. Code readability is also improved. Lastly, the mix of modeling and implementation concepts is eliminated because manipulations are directly expressed in conformity with the modeling space. The use of the modeling level for scripting expression has also the effect of giving more natural code than the one based on metamodel-specific interface since references to implementation concepts like factory or accessors have disappeared.

The way of manipulating the model elements is provided uniformly by the scripting mechanism, that is for any level of modeling (model, metamodel, metametamodels). The following script shows how to get structural information about a metamodel. It lists properties of the Program metaclass that are writable. By analyzing the script, we can see that accessing the metamodel and the elements it contains is immediate and is manipulated as easily as for model elements.

```
miniLangMM = importModelDef('MiniLangMM') ; // get the object representing the package
cls = miniLangMM.$Program ;                 // access to the Program class
features = cls.eStructuralFeatures ;        // retrieve its structural properties
for (i in features) {                       // loop over this properties
  f = features[i] ;                         // access a property
  if (f.assignable)                         // if the property is writable
    printf(f.name) ;                        // display its name
}
```

The scripting mechanism also retains the capacity to write generic scripts. The following code corresponds to the scripting version of our generic example introduced in section 3. Like the version written in Java, this code works at any modeling level. However, thanks to the scripting mechanism, the scripting version is more synthetic and is expressed in conformity with the modeling part, which is much more intuitive.

```
function ensureExistance(elt, linkName, subEltClassName, pkg) {
  metaref = elt.eClass()[linkName]; // retrieve the link description
  if (metaref instanceOf ecore.$EReference && metaref.containment &&
    elt[subEltClassName] == null) { //  test if subcomponent exists at link end
    subElt = pkg[subEltClassName].create() ; // create the subcomponent
    subElt[linkName] = e ;          // link the created subelt to its parent
  }
}
```

Finally, the scripting mechanism also uses the structure and typing information available at the metalevel to dynamically check the validity of expressions manipulating models and apply the automatic conversion of values between both environments.

5.2 Specific Functionalities

The basic functionalities described above are general and can be obtained for any scripting mechanism that uses reflective interfaces. It is also possible to introduce some high-level, generic functionalities that exploit features of the scripting langages or compose features of reflective interfaces. In this section, we present two examples of functionalities developed to simplify the manipulation of model elements within scripts[12]

Model Elements as associative arrays: Like the Javascript objects, a model element can be handled like an array, whose elements are properties (attributes, links and operations) and indexes are the name of these properties. Thanks to this mode, a property whose name is not known in advance or is the result of a computation, becomes accessible. Such functionality is interesting to select the properties of model elements that respect a particular pattern or to express generic rules of navigation. It is used on the line 4 of the third example given in the previous section to obtain the end of a link whose name is transmitted as a parameter. Here is another example that uses this facility with the "for" loop to print the value of all properties of a model element whose name satisfies a regular expression.

```
for (prop in elt) { if (prop.regex('ref*' ) then print(elt[prop]) }
```

High-level navigation: Model elements can be reached by expressing navigation paths that are based on specified links. When a link has multiple elements at its end, a particular element can be accessed by using an integer index or its name if it exists. Here is one example that uses the two possibility to access the type of the first attribute of the Variable class contained in a package:

```
typeOfFirstAttribute = package.eClassifiers['Variable'].eAttributes[0].eType;
```

For composition links, some specific mechanisms exists, inspired by DOM (Document Object Model) named-based navigation. Thanks to this mechanism, a sub-element can be accessed by using the $ character and its name. The following expression gives the type of the identifier attribute of Variable class.

```
typeOfIdentifierAttribute = package.$Variable.$identifier.eType;
```

This navigation by name functionality is built by combining several reflective operations. The class of a model element is queried to identify the set of composition links. This set is then used to access the set of subcomponents and to search for the one which has the provided name.

[12] Other high-level functionalities, not presented here for space reasons, are : OCL-like iteration of collections, automatic model-based completion of scripting expressions in interactive mode and dynamic extension of model elements with new properties.

5.3 Implementation

The scripting mechanism described in the previous section was implemented using Rhino, a Javascript interpreter written in Java and extensible thanks to its Scriptable interface. This interface specifies the operations (get, put, ...) used by the interpreter to interact with Java objects. By providing an implementation of this interface, it is possible to integrate new data types into the Javascript language or provide new forms of access to some Java objects. The main idea of our implementation is to extend the EObjectImpl root class inherited by every Java object representing EMF model element so that it implements the Scriptable interface. Our implementation of Scriptable performs a translation function Φ as described in section 4.2. The concrete translation used in the put operation invoked by the interpreter when evaluating an expression that modifies an attribute of a model element is as follows:

$$\Phi(\text{"}elt.att{=}value\text{"}) \Rightarrow elt.eSet(elt.eClass().getEStructuralFeature(att),\ value)$$

This translation retrieves the description of the attribute by querying the class of the element (via eClass() and getEStructuralFeature()) available at the metalevel. The eSet reflective operation is then used to dynamically set the property. The fact that every expression requires an inspection of the meta-level may have a strong impact on performance in the case of compute-intensive manipulations. To optimize performances, our implementation also includes a cache mechanism of metalevel description. This mechanism memorizes objects that describe the metalevel, so that an expression that accesses the same feature as a previous one does not trigger the search at the metalevel and reuses objects from the cache.

6 Related Works

Some commercial UML modeling tools include a scripting language to support model manipulations. These langages are either existing scripting languages (Visual Basic for Rational Rose, Jython for Magic Draw UML) or scripting languages specifically designed for model processing (J for Objecteering). In general, tools integrating these langages are based on a unique metamodel, namely UML. Therefore, manipulations supported by the language are limited to models complying with this metamodel and can not be based on any metamodel like our proposed solution.

Another work that uses an existing scripting language for model processing but is not limited to a unique metamodel is [4]. In this work, the scripting language which is Python, is used to represent and process models. Model representation is done in a similar way to the approach described in section 2.1, by generating Python API from a metamodel specification. Compared to this work, our proposal is different since we do not produce API for a scripting language. In our case, we assume the existence of a powerful API for representing and introspecting multiple modeling levels and our goal is to propose a solution to make any model scriptable and easily accessible to program control.

Several modeling languages specifically designed in the context of model driven development allow to process models. QVT [3] addresses mappings between model structure and is mainly suitable for model-based transformations. MOF-Script is an extension of QVT which provides capabilities for generating text output from MOF models. Two other standard languages can be exploited to process models although this is not their primary usage: OCL and Actions Semantics. Some works [15] have suggested using and extending OCL for model processing with side-effect and imperative constructs similar to the ones included in a programing language. [16] shows it is possible to apply this Action Semantics for model manipulation by using a description of actions at the meta-level.

Apart from standards, other languages dedicated to model manipulation exist. Some examples reviewed in [10] are the Xion platform independant action language, the MTL model transformation language and the Kermeta action language for metamodels These languages are general-purpose, imperative, object-oriented languages with model-navigation and model management capabilities. Our scripting language shares many properties and constructs with them.

The interest of these standard and non standard modeling languages is that they express manipulations with modeling concepts instead of implementation concepts. On the other hand, most of these languages support expressions of manipulation at one level only (for example, QVT works with a specification that maps MOF metamodels, OCL and Action Semantics are tied to the UML metamodel). To our knowledge, none of these language exploits model introspection as our scripting language does. As a result, they require to know metamodels in advance. Moreover, they do not support the writing of metamodel-independant manipulations. We think that some of these modeling language would benefit from adopting an approach similar to the one presented here.

7 Conclusion

In the future, we will face a growing space of diversified models. The management and processing of these models requires the development of generic modeling environments with new tools and methodologies. In this paper, we argue that current mechanisms for introspecting models are of great interest for constructing generic modeling applications but are also complex to use. To facilitate the processing of models in a generic way, we have introduced the notion of model scripting, which is a general approach adding an abstraction level on top of the reflective interfaces. We have presented some general principles to integrate this approach into a language and a concrete application to Javascript and EMF. Our proposal introduces new results to program model manipulations and could serve as a basis for the specification of a model-scripting language which is an important tool in the context of a generic modeling environment[13].

Our scripting language is a simple and powerful tool to investigate the notion of model introspection which has not received a lot of attention. One perspective is to further explore model introspection from a methodological view, to better

[13] Similarly to IDLScript for CORBA or E4X extension of ECMAScript for XML data.

understand its applications, to compare its benefits with those of generative solutions and identify new mechanisms for computational model introspection[14], which is not very developed in existing approaches.

Another perspective is to study the embedding of scripts into models and metamodels. The aim is to promote the scripting language as an action language for specifing operations existing in models. Being able to do this will allow us to specify executable models and metamodels in the way described in [10].

References

1. Modelware Information Society Technologies Project, European Commission.
2. Object Management Group. MOF 2.0 Specification, OMG Document/01-01-06.
3. Object Management Group. MOF QVT Specification, OMG Document/05-11-01.
4. Porres I. A Toolkit for Model Manipulation. In *Journal on Software and Systems Modeling*, volume 2(4). Springer-Verlag, 2003.
5. Porres I. and Alanen M. Generic Deep Copy Algorithm for MOF-Based Models. In *Model Driven Architecture, European MDA Workshops: Foundations and Applications*. University of Twente, Jul 2003.
6. Czarnecki k. and Helsen s. Classification of model transformation approaches. In *In Proceedings of the OOPSLA 2003 Workshop on Generative Techniques in the Context of MDA*, 2003.
7. Ousterhout J. K. Scripting: Higher-level Programming for the 21st Century. *IEEE Computer*, 31(3), 1998.
8. P. Maes and D. Nardi. *Meta-Level Architectures and Reflection*. Elsevier, 1988.
9. Budinsky F.-Steinberg D. Merks E., Ellersick R. and Grose T. *Eclipse Modeling Framework*. Addison Wesley, 2003.
10. D. Studer P.-Vojtisek Z. Drey D. Pollet F. Fondement F. Z. Drey D. Pollet Muller P.A., F.Fleurey and J.M. Jézéquel. On executable meta-languages applied to model transformations. In *Model Transformations In Practice Workshop, Jamaica*, 2005.
11. Java Community Process. Java Metadata Inferface (JMI) Specification.
12. Fraleigh S. Riehle D., Bucka-Lassen D., and Omorogbe N. The Architecture of a UML Virtual Machine. In *Proceedings of OOPSLA '01*. ACM Press, 2001.
13. E. Rahm S. Melnik and P. A. Bernstein. Rondo: A programming platform for generic model management. In *Proceedings of SIGMOD2003*, 2003.
14. J. Schneider and O. Nierstrasz. Components, scripts and glue. In *Software Architectures - Advances and Applications*. Springer-Verlag, 1999.
15. Peltonen J. Siikarla M. and Selonen P. Combining OCL and Programming Languages for UML Model Processing. In *Proceedings of the Workshop, OCL 2.0 – Industry Standard or Scientific Playground*, 2004.
16. Ho W-M. Le Guennec A. Sunye G., Pennaneac'h F. and Jezequel J-M. Using Uml Action Semantics for Executable Modeling and Beyond. In *Proceeding of CAISE 2001*, volume LNCS 2068, Springer-Verlag, June 2001.

[14] Such as generic access mechanisms described in section 5.2 or mechanisms for the introspection of a stack containing all operations performed on a model.

Model Transformation by Example*

Dániel Varró

Budapest University of Technology and Economics
Department of Measurement and Information Systems
H-1117 Budapest, Magyar tudósok körútja 2
varro@mit.bme.hu

Abstract. In advanced XML transformer tools, XSLT rules are generated automatically after relating simple source and target XML documents. In this paper, we generalize this approach for the design of model transformations: transformation rules are derived semi-automatically from an initial prototypical set of interrelated source and target models. These initial model pairs describe critical cases of the model transformation problem in a purely declarative way. The derived transformation rules can be refined later by adding further source-target model pairs. The main advantage of the approach is that transformation designers do not need to learn a new model transformation language, instead they only use the concepts of the source and target modeling languages.

Keywords: model transformation, transformation rule derivation.

1 Introduction

Due to the increasing popularity of model-driven system development techniques, the efficient design of automated model transformations between such languages have become major challenges to software engineering.

The evolution trend of model transformation languages is characterized by gradually increasing the abstraction level of such languages to declarative, rule-based formalisms as promoted by the QVT (Queries, Views and Transformations) [11] standard of the OMG. Since these model transformation languages follow a novel paradigm in software engineering, the role of transformation engineer will soon emerge in a software development process who is skilled in the use of such model transformation languages and tools.

However, the efficient development of a large set of transformation is hindered by the fact that the *solution domain* of a model transformation (i.e., the transformation language) can be largely different from the *problem domain* (i.e., the source and target model languages themselves). To use an analogy of programming, the transformation is not only implemented (designed) in the programming language but also specified there, which is unfortunate.

In the paper, we propose a novel approach for the specification and design of model transformations called as *model transformation by example*. The essence of the approach is that transformation rules are derived semi-automatically from

* This work was partially supported by the Sensoria European IP (IST-3-016004).

O. Nierstrasz et al. (Eds.): MoDELS 2006, LNCS 4199, pp. 410–424, 2006.

an initial prototypical set of interrelated source and target models. These initial model pairs describe critical cases of the model transformation problem in a purely declarative way.

A main advantage of the approach is that the specification (i.e. the prototypical source-target model pairs) and the design (i.e. transformation rules) of a model transformation are kept separated. In this respect, transformation designers use the concepts of the source and target modeling languages for the specification of the transformation, while a large part of the transformation design is generated semi-automatically.

The term "semi-automatic derivation of transformations" refers to the *iterative* and *interactive* nature of the development process. The initial set of transformation rules (generated automatically) can be refined iteratively by regenerating them after interactively refining the specification with additional source-target model pairs. Moreover, the transformation designer can generalize and extend the automatically generated set of transformation rules interactively in order minimize the number of such rules.

While the automated (or semi-automated) synthesis of rules from a data set has been investigated in various research fields (see Sec. 5 for details), the author is not aware of similar results in the field of model transformations. For this reason, both the development process and the technicalities of the "model transformation by example" approach will be presented simultaneously, and consequently, on a relatively high-level of abstraction by using a motivating transformation problem (Sec. 2) for discussing the technicalities of the approach instead of detailed mathematical algorithms and formulae.

2 Motivating Example: Object-Relational Mapping

As the motivating example of the current paper, we map UML class diagrams into relational database tables by using one of the standard solutions. This transformation problem (with several variations) is frequently used as a model transformation benchmark of high practical relevance [2].

The source and target languages (UML and relational databases, respectively) are captured by their corresponding metamodels in Fig. 1. To avoid mixing the notions of UML class diagrams and metamodels, we will refer to the concepts of the metamodel using nodes and edges for classes and associations, respectively.

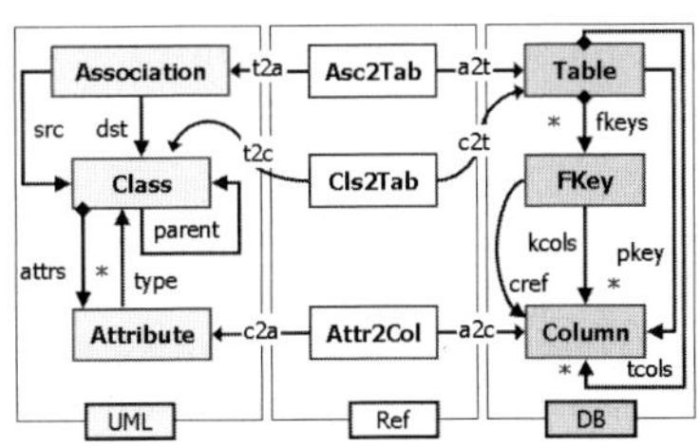

Fig. 1. Metamodels of the example

UML class diagrams consist of class nodes arranged into an inheritance hierarchy (by *parent* edges). Classes contain attribute nodes (*attrs*), which are typed over classes (*type*). Directed edges are leading from a source (*src*) class to a destination (*dst*) class.

Relational databases consist of table nodes, which are composed of column nodes by *tcols* edges. Each table has a single primary key column (*pkey*). Foreign key (*FKey*) constraints can be assigned to tables (*fkeys*). A foreign key refers to one (or more) columns (*cref*) of another table, and it is related to the columns of (local) referencing table by *kcols* edges.

These metamodels (adapted from [2]) are extended with a *reference metamodel* to interconnect the elements of the source and the target language. This way it defines the main guidelines of (this variant of) the object-relational mapping itself, which can be summarized as follows:

- Each top-level UML class (i.e. a top-most class in the inheritance tree) is projected into a database table. Two additional columns are derived automatically for each top-level class: one for storing a unique identifier (primary key), and one for storing the type information of instances.
- Each attribute of a UML class will appear as a column in the table related to the top-level ancestor of the class. For the sake of simplicity, the type of an attribute is restricted to user-defined classes. The structural consistency of storing only valid object instances in columns is maintained by foreign key constraints.
- Each UML association is projected into a table with two columns pointing to the tables related to the source and the target classes of the association by foreign key constraints.

These informal rules provide some guidelines for capturing the transformation rules. In the current paper, we will only rely on a set of interrelated source and target models as the specification when deriving the transformation rules by focusing on prototypical subproblems of the transformation.

3 Model Transformation by Example: An Overview

3.1 Overview of the Approach

This paper presents the foundations of the "model transformations by example" approach. This approach proposes the following iterative process for developing model transformations (illustrated in Fig. 2).

Step 1: Manual set-up of prototype mapping models. The transformation designer assembles an initial set of interrelated source and target model pairs, which are called *prototype mapping models* in the sequel. These prototype mapping models typically capture critical situations of the transformation problem by showing how the source and target model elements should be interrelated by appropriate reference (mapping) constructs.

Step 2: Automated derivation of rules. Based upon the available prototype mapping models, the transformation framework should synthesize the set of model transformation rules, which correctly transform at least the prototypical source models into their target equivalents.

Step 3: Manual refinement of rules. The transformation designer can refine the rules manually at any time by adding attribute conditions or providing generalizations of existing rules.

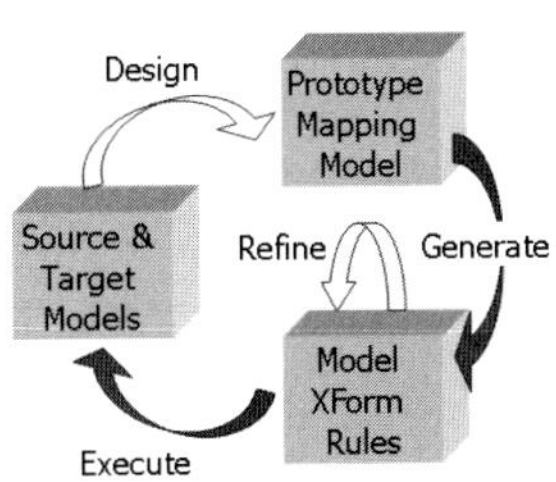

Fig. 2. Process Overview

Step 4: Automated execution of transformation rules. The transformation designer validates the correctness of the synthesized rules by executing them on additional source-target model pairs as test cases. Based upon these new test cases, the transformation designer then comes up with additional prototype mapping models, and the development process is started all over again.

A main benefit of the "model transformations by example" approach is that the transformation designer mainly uses the concepts of the source and target languages as the "transformation language", which is very intuitive.

Moreover, we also emphasize in the paper that the "model transformations by example" approach is a highly iterative and interactive process since it is unlikely that the final set of transformation rules is derived right from the initial set of prototype models. Since the transformation designer can overrule the automatically generated rules at any time, correctness issues are investigated separately where the prototype mapping models may serve as test cases.

3.2 Assumptions

We make the following assumptions on the prototype mapping models (which also comply with the mapping structure between two EMF model instances [1]):

1. *Reference is also a graph.* Reference (mapping) nodes relate source and target nodes (by a pair of edges) while source and target edges are not directly related i.e. we impose a graph structure also on references.
2. *Unique references.* Each reference node uniquely identifies a pair of source and target nodes, i.e. all edges linking reference nodes to a source or target node have exactly one multiplicity.
3. *Existence of unmapped model elements.* On the other hand, there may be source (target) nodes which are not directly mapped to a target (source) node by reference.
4. *No merging transformations.* Each node in the target model is allowed to be mapped via a single reference node from the source model, thus we rule out transformations that merge two source nodes to the same target node by using two separate references.
5. *Aggregation semantics.* Each non-root node in a model is contained by at most one other node (denoted by a corresponding containment edge), which provides traditional containment semantics.
6. *Correctness of prototype models.* Finally, we assume that the prototype mapping models correctly reflect the intentions of the transformation designer, i.e., no edges or nodes are omitted / created unintentionally.

4 Model Transformation by Example: Details by Example

The core of the current paper focuses on the (semi-)automatic generation of model transformation rules, by splitting the generation process into the following phases:

1. *Setting up an initial prototype mapping model.* In the first step, an initial prototype mapping model is set up manually (Sec. 4.1) or from scratch by using existing source and target models.
2. *Creation of mapped target nodes.* Then we derive model transformation rules for each reference node (type) in the reference metamodel in order to derive target nodes from source nodes interconnected by a reference (of some type).
   (a) *Context analysis.* For this purpose, we first examine the contexts of all mapped source and target nodes (Sec. 4.2-4.3).
   (b) *Derivation of transformation rules.* Later, the context of source nodes will identify the precondition of the derived model transformation rules while the context of target nodes will define the postcondition of graph transformation rules (Sec. 4.4).
3. *Interconnection of target nodes.* Afterwards, rules are generated to derive links between target model elements based upon the connectivity of the mapped source and target elements (Sec. 4.5).
4. *Iterative refinement.* The derived rules can be refined at any time by extending the prototype mapping model or manually generalizing the automatically generated rules.

4.1 Initial Prototype Mapping Model

Now we discuss the main concepts of the "model transformation by example" approach on the object-relational mapping introduced in Sec. 2.

Prototype mapping models can be derived by interrelating any existing (real) source and target models. However, prototype mapping models are preferably small, thus they are rather created by hand to incorporate critical situations of the transformation problem. These prototype mapping models can also serve as test cases later on.

Example. A simple class diagram modeling an on-line shop and its corresponding relational database representation is depicted in Fig. 3. The source and target models are related by mapping information based on the reference metamodel of Fig. 1 in order to serve as an initial prototype mapping model.

Note that the target database model has four tables: two for the top-level classes *Customer* and *Product* and two for the associations *orders* and *reviews*. The *favourite* attribute of class *VIPCustomer* is first lifted up to a column in the *Customer* table with a foreign key constraint (referring to the primary key column *ProdId* of table *Product*). Further foreign key constraints (e.g. *FK1*, *FK2*) related to the columns (*RevPid*, *RevCid*) of the association table *tRev* refer to the primary key (*ProdId* and *CustId*) columns of the corresponding tables (*Product* and *Customer*).

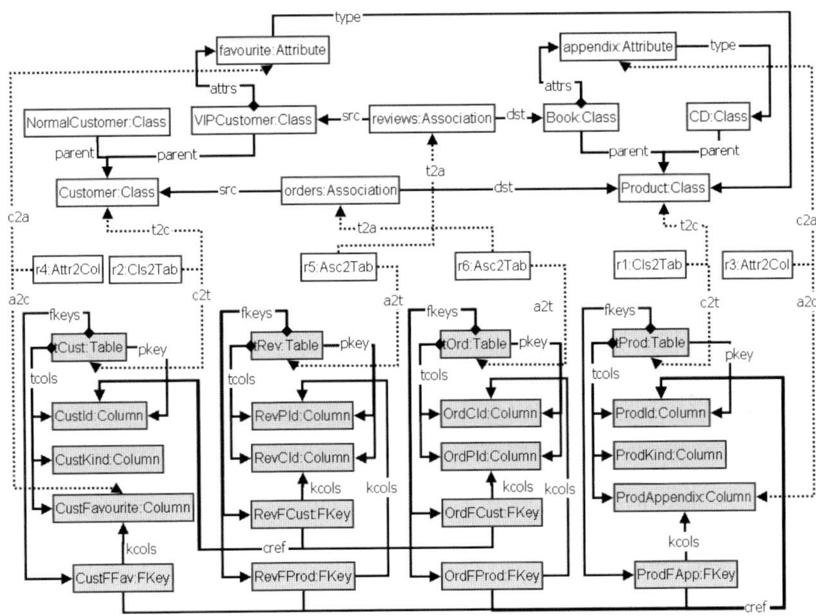

Fig. 3. Initial prototype mapping model

4.2 Context Analysis of the Source Model

As a demonstration of the context analysis of the source model, we will use reference nodes of type *Cls2Tab*, which connect certain (but not all) UML class nodes to database table nodes (e.g. *Product* is mapped while *Book* is unmapped in Fig. 3) to capture the problematic case.

Definition of 1-Context. In order identify which elements in the source model are actually mapped into a corresponding element in the target model, we initially examine one by one all reference nodes of a certain type and determine *the 1-context* of the source element identified by the reference node.

By the 1-context of a source node (of a certain type), we mean the existence or non-existence of incoming and outgoing edges in the prototype mapping model. When calculating the 1-context of a source node, all types of edges allowed by the metamodel (for the type of this source node) are enumerated.

Example. The 1-context of classes *Customer* and *Product* in the prototype mapping model of Fig. 3 is illustrated in Fig. 4.

For instance, class *Customer* has an incoming *src* edge (from association *orders*), an incoming *parent* edge (e.g., from class *VIPCustomer*), but no incoming *dst* edge, no incoming *type* edge, no outgoing *attrs* edge, and no outgoing *parent* edge. According to the metamodel of Fig. 1, there are no other edge types that we need to consider for the 1-context of class *Customer*. The 1-context of class *Product* can be derived in a similar way.

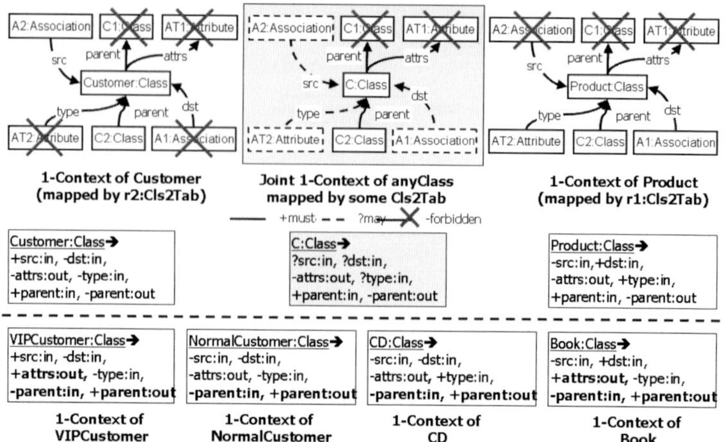

Fig. 4. Context analysis of the source model

For a more compact notation of 1-contexts, we use *+parent:in* to denote that there exists an incoming *parent* edge, and *-parent:out* to denote that there are no outgoing parent edges in the context.

Joint 1-context. The next step is to create a joint 1-context for all mapped source nodes of a certain type calculated as the consistent merging of the individual 1-contexts:

- If an edge of a certain type is present in all individual 1-contexts, then it becomes a *must* edge in the joint 1-context.
- If an edge of a certain type is not present in any of the individual 1-contexts, then it becomes a *forbidden* edge in the joint 1-context.
- if an edge of a certain type is present in some but not all individual 1-contexts then its marked as a *may* (optional) edge in the joint 1-context.

The joint 1-context generalizes our assumption on the existence (or non-existence) of certain edges in the context of a node: if all possible individual contexts are identical then this is assumed to be the general case.

Example. For instance, in the joint 1-context of mapped classes *Customer* and *Product* in Fig. 4, one can deduce that there is an incoming *parent* edge, no outgoing *parent* edge, and no outgoing *attrs* edge, while edges of other types are optional.

Checking the 1-context for unmapped elements. Then we need to show that each 1-context of an *unmapped* source node (of a certain type) differs from the joint 1-context of *mapped* source nodes (of that type).

Example. In our example, we need to check that the joint 1-context of mapped classes (e.g. *Product* and *Customer*) does not match the unmapped classes (like *VIPCustomer* or *Book*). This difference is highlighted by bold-face letters in the 1-context of unmapped class nodes in Fig. 4.

Possible extensions of 1-contexts. It is easy to generalize 1-context of a node to n-contexts etc. by considering all possible pattern graphs (as allowed by the metamodel) with at most n distance from the node itself. Furthermore, we may consider multiple edges of a certain type in the context by considering multiplicities as well (e.g. two parent incoming parent edges instead of one in case of class *Customer*).

However, these extensions are only necessary to be considered if we cannot distinguish between mapped and unmapped model elements of a certain type in the source model based upon their 1-contexts. Our experiments show that this is not a frequent case in typical model transformation problems.

A more common extension of 1-contexts is to identify *attribute conditions* for a node. While the current technique could be easily extended to incorporate attributes of enumeration types by treating attribute values as ordinary graph nodes, the automated categorization of string and numeric attributes definitely requires future investigations. For this paper, we assume that such attribute conditions are attached manually by the transformation designer if required.

4.3 Context Analysis of the Target Model

The context analysis of the target model aims at identifying the postconditions of the transformation rules to be derived. For this purpose, we now investigate the target ends of references.

According to Assumption 2 (of Sec. 3.2), all target nodes are uniquely identified by a reference node. Furthermore, we also collect all the *unmapped nodes that are transitively contained by the target node* in question as the *target context* of the mapped node.

Finally, the joint target context is calculated as the intersection of individual target contexts. This joint target context consists of the mapped target node, all common nodes in the target contexts, and all the edges leading between these nodes.

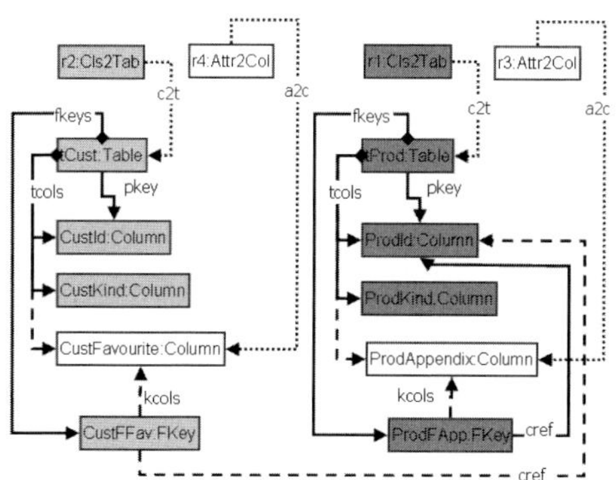

Fig. 5. Context analysis of the target model

The main idea behind this construction is that we need to derive each target node only once. Mapped target nodes are derived according to the appropriate reference types, while unmapped target nodes are created (i) when a mapped target node is created (Sec. 4.4) or (ii) when mapped target nodes are further interconnected (Sec. 4.5).

Example. The context analysis of the target database model is illustrated in Fig. 5 for references of type *Cls2Tab* (which connect classes to tables). Grey nodes denote the derived context of the target model.

The joint target context contains a mapped target node of type *Table*, two unmapped nodes of type *Column*, two unmapped nodes of type *FKey*, and all the edges leading between these nodes of types *tcols*, *pkey*, *fkeys*. Note, however, that while column *CustFavourite* is also contained by table *tCust*, it is not marked since it is mapped by a *Att2Col* reference, thus it belongs to another target context.

4.4 Derivation of Model Transformation Rules

Model transformation rules are derived in the form of graph transformation rules [6] in accordance with the joint source and target contexts. Graph transformation provides a pattern and rule based manipulation of graph models, which is frequently used in various model transformation tools. Each rule application transforms a graph by replacing a part of it by another graph.

Graph transformation rules. A *graph transformation rule* contains a left–hand side graph LHS, a right–hand side graph RHS, and a negative application condition graph NAC. The LHS and the NAC graphs are together called the precondition PRE of the rule.

The *application* of a GT rule to a *host model* M replaces a matching of the LHS in M by an image of the RHS. This is performed by (i) finding a matching of LHS in M (by graph pattern matching), (ii) checking the negative application conditions NAC (which prohibit the presence of certain objects and links) (iii) removing a part of the model M that can be mapped to LHS but not to RHS yielding the context model, and (iv) gluing the context model with an image of the RHS by adding new objects and links (that can be mapped to the RHS but not to the LHS) obtaining the *derived model* M′.

From joint contexts to graph transformation rules. When deriving a GT rule, the joint source context for a reference of a certain type defines the LHS and some NAC graphs, the joint target context defines a NAC for the precondition, while the union of the joint source and target contexts (joined via a reference node) defines the RHS.

Our construction of joint source and target contexts provides a pessimistic approach: in the precondition we prescribe as much as possible, and in the postcondition we generate (guarantee) as little as possible.

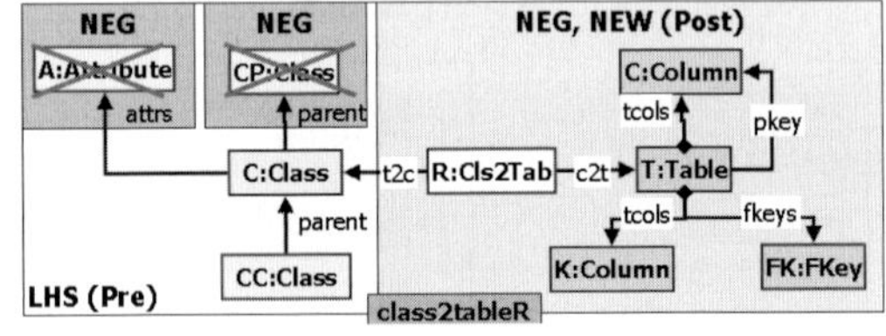

Fig. 6. Initial version of rule *class2tableR*

In the paper, we use a (slightly modified) graphical representation initially introduced in [8] where the union of these graphs is presented. Elements to be deleted are marked by the *del* keyword, elements to be created are labeled by *new*, while elements in the *NAC* graph are denoted by the *neg* keyword.

Example. Figure 6 denotes the graph transformation rule derived for reference *Cls2Tab*. The rule expresses that for each class *C* with a child subclass *CC* but without attributes, a table *T* is generated with two columns *T* and *K* and some foreign key *FK*.

Extending the prototype mapping model. Since the generation of model transformation rules is based entirely on the initial prototype mapping model, and we follow a pessimistic approach for rule generation, usually, the derived rule set does not fully correspond to our expectation. Therefore, the prototype mapping model needs to be extended by the transformation desginer.

Example. Let us take rule *class2tableR* as an example (see Fig. 6), which is derived from the prototype mapping model of Fig. 3. Our intuition says that if a class does not have subclasses, it should be transformed into a database table, but this situation is not allowed by the initial version of rule *class2tableR*. In addition, the rule also prohibits the presence of attributes in the top-level class.

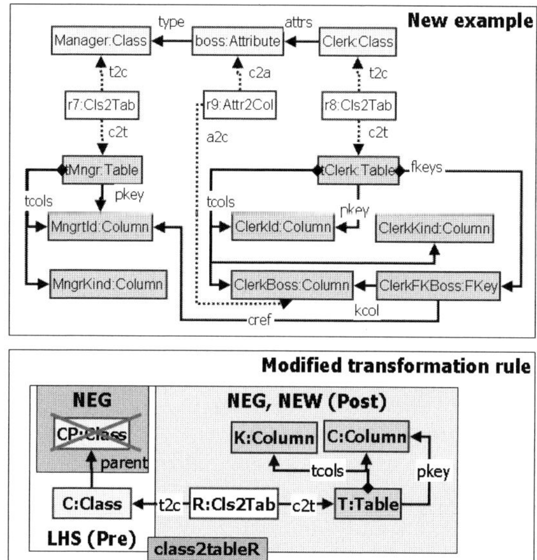

Fig. 7. Refinement of *class2tableR* by providing additional prototype mapping models

Therefore, we extend our prototype mapping model by two top-level classes *Manager* and *Clerk* with a *boss* attribute of the latter to capture these situations (in the upper part of Fig. 7).

Note that this new prototype mapping model is an addition to our initial mapping model (of Fig. 7). After that we re-execute the previous rule generation process, and we obtain a new version of rule *class2tableR* (see the lower part of Fig. 7) instead of the old one (of Fig. 6). This new rule now fully corresponds to our expectations: only top-level classes should be transformed into database tables, but no further restrictions are applicable to classes in the source model. Fortunately, the precondition of this rule distinguishes between mapped and unmapped classes in the source model.

Other model transformation rules. After investigating references of other types (*Attr2Col* and *Asc2Tab*) in the prototype mapping models, two additional rules can be derived to transform attributes into columns (rule *attr2columnR*) and to derive tables for associations (rule *assoc2tableR*, see Fig. 8).

It is worth observing that the target part of rule *assoc2tableR* contains quite a complex structure since not only a class is derived from an association but also two columns and the corresponding foreign keys in the same transformation step. However, these foreign keys are not yet connected to the referenced tables, which will be investigated in the sequel.

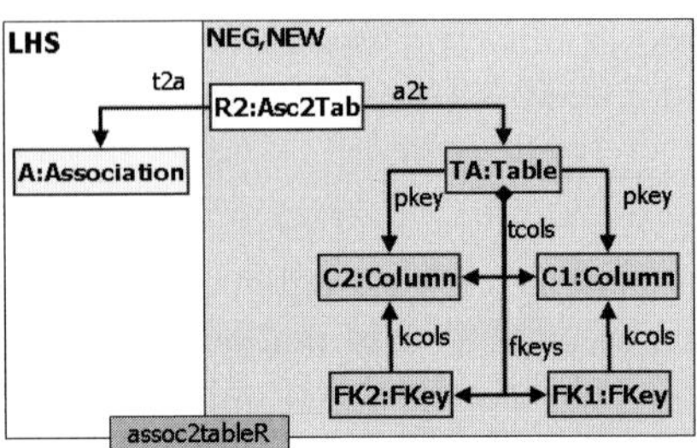

Fig. 8. Rule *assoc2tableR*

As a summary, the model transformation rules generated in this first phase are able to derive (i) the target equivalents of each mapped source node, and (ii) some local context which comprises the unmapped nodes contained by these target nodes, and the interconnecting edges between them. In the next phase, we derive further links between target model elements based upon the connectivity of mapped source nodes.

4.5 Linking Target Model Elements

In the first phase of rule derivation, we only investigated each reference type separately in the prototype mapping model. Now we gradually extend this technique to investigate pairs of reference nodes (and then triples, quadruples, etc.) to derive additional model transformation rules. As the number of reference nodes increases, the derivation of a new transformation rule may become too complex. Fortunately, the transformation designer may interrupt the rule derivation process at any time and continue the creation of transformation rules manually.

The core problem in this step is to identify interconnections (paths) between source nodes mapped by appropriate reference nodes, and then to derive the links between the corresponding target elements created in earlier phases of the transformation. Due to space limitations, we only sketch the essence of our technique on the running example by deriving appropriate target connections between tables generated for mapped associations and classes (see Fig. 9).

Connectivity analysis. Since all individual references of a certain type have been investigated in the previous phase, now we investigate all pairs of reference nodes in the reference metamodel.

If a source node identified by a reference is connected to the another source node identified by the other reference in the prototype mapping model by a *path of edges leading via unmapped source nodes only*, and the corresponding (mapped) target nodes are also connected, then we derive a transformation rule to create the connections between such target nodes.

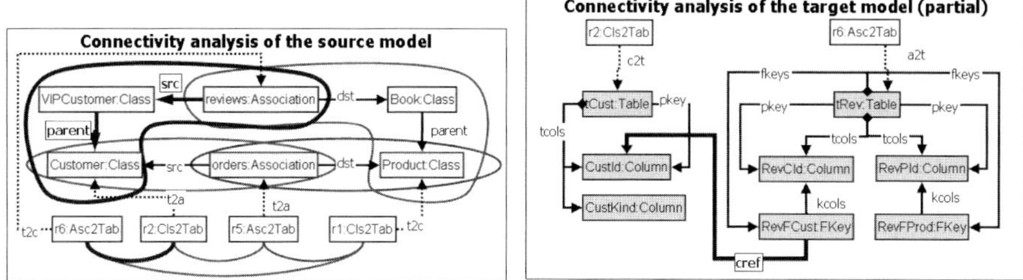

(a) Connectivity analysis of source model (b) Connectivity analysis of target model

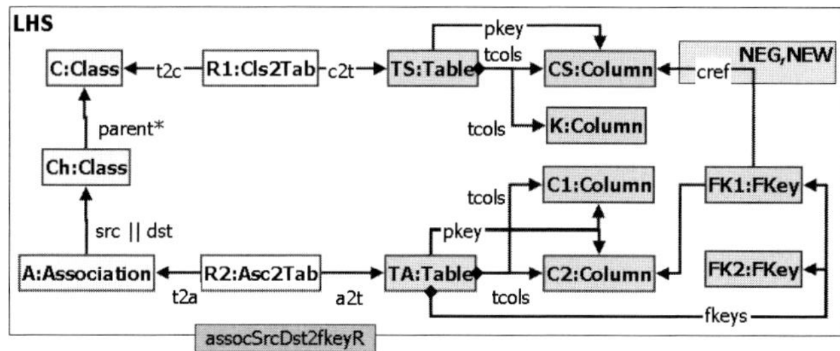

(c) Generalized rule *assocSrcDst2fkeyR*

Fig. 9. Transformation rules derived according to connectivity analysis

If mapped source (or target) nodes are also traversed along the identified source (or target) path, then this path will be investigated later when considering e.g. triples of references. A further restriction is that unmapped target nodes along this path should be contained by a node in the target context (as defined in Sec. 4.3).

Example. As an example, let us select one reference node of type *Cls2Tab* and another node of type *Asc2Tab*[1]. In Fig. 9(a), four different paths can be identified between pairs of reference nodes of these types. For instance, one of them is composed of the *reviews* association linked by a *src* edge to unmapped class *VIPCustomer*, which is connected to class *Customer* by a *parent* edge.

On the target side for this dedicated mapping instance (see Fig. 9(b)), there is a *cref* edge linking the foreign key *RevFCust* belonging to table *tRev* (mapped from association *reviews*) to the primary key column of table *Customer* (mapped from class *Customer*).

Derivation of linking rules. Transformation rules linking target elements in accordance with the connectivity analysis of pairs (triples, etc.) of reference nodes are derived by the following steps:

1. For each reference node the postcondition of transformation rules derived in Sec. 4.4 are copied as preconditions.

[1] Later, we should also investigate *Cls2Tab*-*Cls2Tab* and *Asc2Tab*-*Asc2Tab* pairs.

2. The identified path connecting mapped source nodes is also added to the precondition.
3. The path connecting the mapped target is added as a negative condition to the precondition and it is marked to be created by the postcondition.

Obviously, a rule is only created if for each path of the same kind (i.e. composed of a certain kind of nodes and edges) identified in the source model, there exists a corresponding path in the target model as well. In other terms, when the connectivity of the target nodes is a consequence of the connectivity of the source nodes.

Example. In case of pairs of *Cls2Tab* and *Asc2Tab* reference types, we can derive four transformation rules with different source patterns (corresponding to the four cases in Fig. 9(a)) but identical target pattern (see Fig. 9(b)).

Manual generalization of transformation rules. In order to reduce the number of model transformation rules, the transformation designer should try to generalize the transformation rules by identifying a more general source pattern from which all the different cases can be derived.

Naturally, this generalization step cannot be fully automated in general, but in theory, it is possible to check if a generalized rule (with path expressions) derived by the intuition of the transformation designer really generalizes the automatically derived elementary rules.

Example. Rule *assocSrcDst2fkeyR* (depicted in Fig. 9(c)) is such a generalization which states that (i) the source and target ends of associations are handled identically, and (ii) there may exist a path of *parent* edges between the source (target) of an association (e.g. *VIPCustomer*) and the mapped (top-level) class (e.g. *Customer*).

5 Related work

Up to our best knowledge, the proposed approach is novel in the field of model transformations; but it is not unprecedented in a more general research context.

The name of "model transformation by example" was obviously influenced by the "Programming by Example" paradigm. Programming by Example encompasses a number of approaches to creating programs by giving examples of their behavior or effect, i.e., they emphasize working on concrete examples rather than describing a procedure in the abstract. A more recent approach that has proven quite successful is Programming by Demonstration [5]: the programmer (often the end-user) demonstrates actions on example data, and the computer records and possibly generalizes these actions.

Advanced XSLT tools are also capable of generating XSLT scripts from schema-level (like MapForce from Altova [4]) or document (instance-)level mappings (such as the pioneering XSLerator from IBM Alphaworks, or the more recent StylisStudio [3]). Research in the field of XSLT generation includes interactive approaches like [14] or fully automated ones [7] based on a theory of information-preserving and -approximating XML operations.

Data-driven approaches frequently guide the learning of transformation rules for semantic query optimization (SQO) in the field of databases as proposed e.g. in [12,10]. SQO uses query-transformation rules, e.g. semantic integrity constraints and functional dependencies. The objective of a semantic query optimizer is to find a semantically equivalent query which yields a more efficient execution plan that satisfy the integrity constraints and dependencies.

Finally, the mostly related work in the field of model transformations is identified by interactive model transformation approaches [13] where the composition of certain transformation patterns is driven by the transformation designer. However, these transformation patterns are constructed manually by the transformation designer (and not derived semi-automatically as in our case).

The derivation of executable graph transformation rules from a declarative specification given in the form of triple graph grammars (TGG) is investigated in [9]. While TGG rules are quite close to the source and target modeling languages themselves, they are still created manually by the transformation designer. Anyhow, it is an interesting future work to map the techniques of the current paper into TGGs instead of plain graph transformation rules.

6 Conclusions

The current paper introduced a new approach for the design of model transformations called *model transformation by example*, an iterative and interactive approach which aims at a (semi-)automated derivation of model transformation rules from prototypical pairs of model instances.

This approach uses the fact that the majority of model transformations has a very simple structure, and thus transformation rules can be derived automatically after analyzing the contexts of model elements in related source and target models. As a consequence, this approach can largely assist transformation designers to capture rules for the mechanic, less intuitive parts of a model transformation problem. In the future, transformation designers are planned to be assisted by powerful domain-specific visual languages.

Initial case studies with small and medium size transformation examples (e.g. different versions of the object-relational mapping, and a statechart to Petri net transformation) have been carried out as an initial validation of our approach. The current paper used the most problematic case study to highlight both the strengths and the limitations of the approach (and the importance of user interaction as well). However, it is a future work to assess the scalability of the approach for large, industrial model transformation problems.

Note that a fully automated synthesis of transformation rules has not been addressed in the current paper: the intuition of the transformation designer is still highly required (i) to come up with appropriate pairs of source-target model instances and (ii) to generalize transformation rules (e.g. by path expression) in order to reduce the number of automatically generated rules.

The heuristic techniques introduced in the current paper were derived from the past model transformation experience of the author. However, systematic optimizations in this field introduce immense challenges for the future. Qualitative, unsupervised learning and discovery techniques in the field of artificial intelligence, and data mining techniques provide primary candidates for that.

References

1. Eclipse Modeling Framework. `http://www.eclipse.org/emf`.
2. Model transformations in practice workshop. `http://sosym.dcs.kcl.ac.uk/events/mtip/`.
3. *StylisStudio.* `http://www.stylusstudio.com`.
4. Altova:. *MapForce 2006.* `http://www.altova.com/features_xml2xml_mapforce.html`.
5. A. Cypher (ed.). *Watch What I Do: Programming by Demonstration.* The MIT Press, 1993.
6. H. Ehrig, G. Engels, H.-J. Kreowski, and G. Rozenberg (eds.). *Handbook on Graph Grammars and Computing by Graph Transformation*, vol. 2: Applications, Languages and Tools. World Scientific, 1999.
7. M. Erwig. Toward the automatic derivation of XML transformations. In *1st Int. Workshop on XML Schema and Data Management (XSDM'03)*, vol. 2814 of *LNCS*, pp. 342–354. Springer, 2003.
8. T. Fischer, J. Niere, L. Torunski, and A. Zündorf. Story diagrams: A new graph transformation language based on UML and Java. In H. Ehrig, G. Engels, H.-J. Kreowski, and G. Rozenberg (eds.), *Proc. Theory and Application to Graph Transformations (TAGT'98)*, vol. 1764 of *LNCS*. Springer, 2000.
9. A. Königs and A. Schürr. MDI - a rule-based multi-document and tool integration approach. *Journal of Software and Systems Modelling*, 2006. Special Section on Model-based Tool Integration (In Press).
10. B. G. T. Lowden and J. Robinson. Constructing inter-relational rules for semantic query optimisation. In *Proc. of 13th International Conference of Database and Expert Systems Applications, (DEXA 2002), Aix-en-Provence, France, September 2-6,*, vol. 2453 of *LNCS*, pp. 587–596. Springer, 2002.
11. Object Management Group. *QVT: Request for Proposal for Queries, Views and Transformations.* `http://www.omg.org`.
12. S. Shekhar, B. Hamidzadeh, A. Kohli, and M. Coyle. Learning transformation rules for semantic query optimization: A data-driven approach. *IEEE Trans. Knowl. Data Eng.*, vol. 5(6):pp. 950–964, 1993.
13. M. Siikarla and T. Systä. Transformational pattern system - some assembly required. In *Proc. Intern. Workshop on Graph Transformation and Visual Modelling Techniques (GT-VMT 2006)*, ENTCS, pp. 57–68. Elsevier, 2006. In Press.
14. L. L. Yan, R. J. Miller, L. M. Haas, and R. Fagin. Data-driven understanding and refinement of schema mappings. In *Proc. ACM SIGMOD Conference on Management of Data*. 2001.

Graphical Definition of In-Place Transformations in the Eclipse Modeling Framework

Enrico Biermann[1], Karsten Ehrig[2], Christian Köhler[1], Günter Kuhns[1], Gabriele Taentzer[1], and Eduard Weiss[1]

[1] Department of Computer Science, Technical University of Berlin, Germany
{enrico, jaspo, bunjip, gabi, eduardw}@cs.tu-berlin.de
[2] Department of Computer Science, University of Leicester, UK
karsten@mcs.le.ac.uk

Abstract. The Eclipse Modeling Framework (EMF) provides a modeling and code generation framework for Eclipse applications based on structured data models. Although EMF provides basic operations for modifying EMF based models, a framework for graphical definition of rule-based modification of EMF models is still missing. In this paper we present a framework for in-place EMF model transformation based on graph transformation. Transformations are visually defined by rules on object patterns typed over an EMF core model. Defined transformation systems can be compiled to Java code building up on generated EMF classes. As running example different refactoring methods for Ecore models are considered.

1 Introduction

In the world of model-driven software development the Eclipse Modeling Framework (EMF) [7] is becoming a key reference. It is a framework for describing class models and generating Java code which supports to create, modify, store, and load instances of the model. Moreover, it provides generators to support the editing of EMF models.

EMF unifies three important technologies: Java, XML, and UML. Regardless of which one is used to define a model, an EMF model can be considered as the common representation that subsumes the others. I.e. defining a transformation approach for EMF, it will become also applicable to the other technologies.

In model-driven development, the transformation of models belongs to the essential activities. Different kinds of model transformations [24] are distinguished: endogenous transformations, such as refactoring or optimization in general, modify models within the same language. Exogenous transformation translate models between different languages. A prominent example for exogenous transformations are mappings from Platform Independent Models (PIMs) to Platform Specific Models (PSMs) in the Model-Driven Architecture (MDA) approach [12]. Although different in the intention, exogenous and endogenous transformations can simulate each other in a certain sense. An exogenous transformation with

O. Nierstrasz et al. (Eds.): MoDELS 2006, LNCS 4199, pp. 425–439, 2006.

the same source and target language can be considered as endogenous one. Corresponding transformation engines usually work with two models, the source and the target model, in the exogenous case. This is not adequate for endogenous transformations where mostly in-place model updates are needed. Vice versa, endogenous transformations can emulate exogenous ones by constructing the product of all source and target languages and using it as underlying language.

Furthermore, we can distinguish model-to-model transformation to be used on a higher abstraction level, while model-to-text transformation to be defined by approaches like JET [10], refer to e.g. code generation. In the following, we focus on model-to-model transformations.

It has been shown that source-driven transformation languages such as XSLT being used to transform XML documents, are well suitable for the transformation of documents, but less suited for model transformations [18,27].

In contrast to common model-to-model transformation approaches for EMF, we present an approach for in-place model-to-model transformations. As running example, we will consider model refactorings in EMF. We will introduce a visual notation for transformation rules which differs largely from that of QVT. Relations are a key concept in QVT which does not fit well to endogenous transformations, since relationships between model elements are not of primary interest. In contrast, the transformation approach presented focuses on structure modification and is inspired by graph transformation [19]. Transformation rules contain left and right-hand sides being object structures; moreover, negative object patterns may be defined, restricting the rule application. Since the transformation concepts are close to graph transformation concepts, it is possible to translate the rules to AGG [2], a tool environment for algebraic graph transformation where they might be further analyzed. For efficient execution of model transformations, the rules can be translated to Java code using generated EMF classes.

2 Eclipse Modeling Framework

The Eclipse Modeling Framework (EMF) [7] provides a modeling and code generation framework for Eclipse applications based on structured data models. The modeling approach is similar to that of MOF, actually EMF supports Essential MOF (EMOF) as part of the OMG MOF 2.0 specification [8]. The type information of sets of instance models is defined in a so-called core model corresponding to metamodel in EMOF. The core or metamodel for core models is the Ecore model. It contains the model elements which are available for EMF core models in principle. In Fig. 1, the main part of Ecore is shown. The kernel model contains elements EClass, EDataType, EAttribute and EReference. These model elements are needed to define classes by EClass, their attributes by EAttribute and interrelations by EReference. EClasses can be grouped to EPackages which might be again structured into subpackages. In addition, each model element can be annotated by EAnnotation. Furthermore, there are some abstract classes to better structure the Ecore model, such as ENamedElement, ETypedElement, etc.

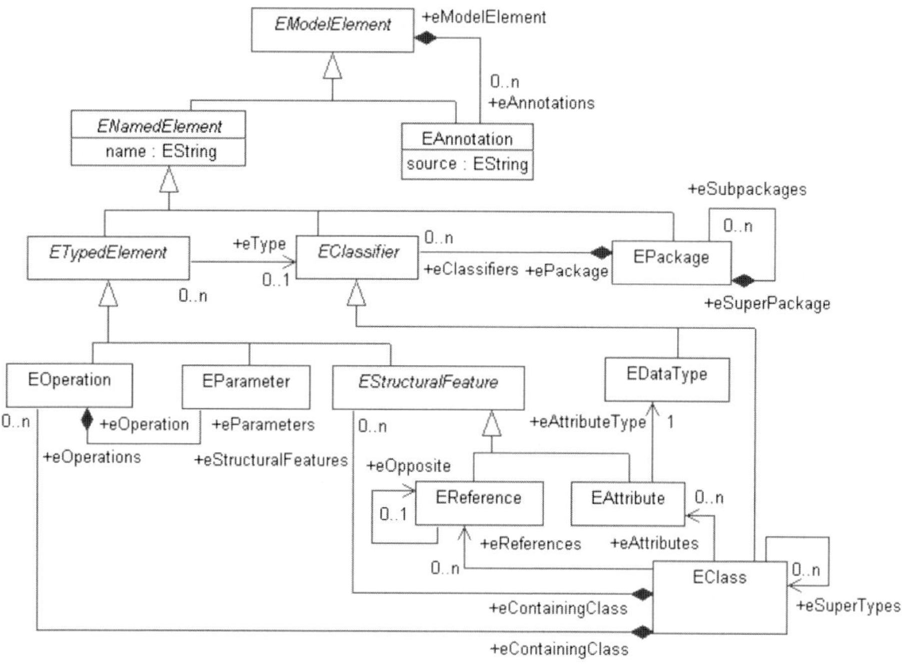

Fig. 1. Kernel of Ecore model

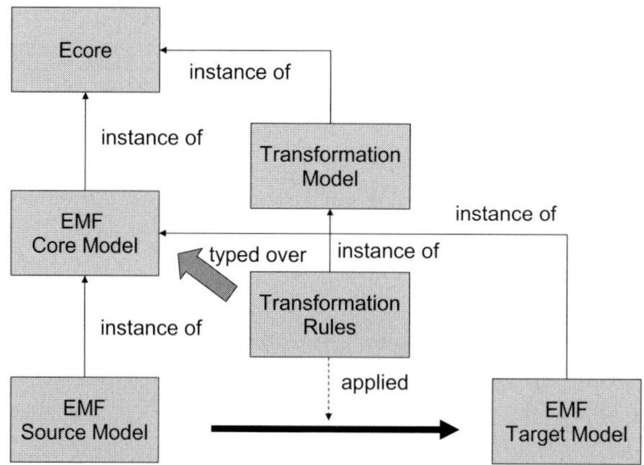

Fig. 2. Transformation Overview

It is important to note that the EMF metamodel (Ecore) again is a core model. That means that the metaclasses EClass, EDatatype, EReference etc. actually cannot just be interpreted as, but in fact *are* classes of an EMF core model. This is of great importance for our approach, since it enables us to use native EMF notions (elements of the metamodel) for the definition of transformation rules and interprete these notions in terms of formal graphs and graph transformations.

From an EMF model, a set of Java classes for the model and a basic, tree based editor can be generated. The generated classes provide basic support for *creating/deleting* model elements and persistency operations like *loading and saving*. Relations between EMF model classes are handled by special EMF lists, extending the Java list classes. Moreover, EMF models can be used as underlying models in new application plugins. But in many cases, the EMF model by its own is not powerful enough to express the complete model behavior. Therefore the generated code can be extended by the developer in order to add new functionalities that are not expressed in the EMF model.

3 Visual Definition of Endogenous Transformations

Basically, an in-place EMF transformation is a rule-based modification of an EMF source model resulting in an EMF target model. Both, the EMF source and target models are typed over the same EMF core model which itself is again typed over Ecore. The transformation rules are typed over the *Transformation Model* shown in Fig. 3 which itself is an instance of Ecore again (see Fig. 2). Since the transformation model is an EMF model, a tree-based editor can be generated automatically. For more convenient editing of the rules we developed an additional visual editor being an Eclipse plug-in based on EMF and GEF [5]. Figs. 4 - 8 show screenshots of this editor.

A *Transformation* consists of a *RuleSet* containing the set of *Rules* for the transformation. Furthermore, it has a link to the core model its instances are typed over. If needed, a start structure can be defined as well to have a fixed starting point for the transformation available. A transformation together with a start structure forms an EMF grammar.

Rules are expressed mainly by two object structures LHS and RHS, the left and right-hand sides of the rule. Furthermore, a rule has mappings between obects and links of the LHS and the RHS indicated by numbers preceding the class names. The left-hand side LHS represents the pre-conditions of the rule, while the right-hand side RHS describes the post-conditions. Those symbols and links of the LHS which are mapped to the RHS, describe a structure part which has to occur in the EMF source model, but which is not changed during the transformation. All objects and links of the LHS not mapped to the RHS define the part which shall be deleted, and all objects and links of the RHS to which nothing is mapped, define the part to be created. Attributes in the LHS have to occur in the EMF source model in addition while they can be reassigned with different values in the RHS of the rule.

The applicability of a rule can be further restricted by additional application conditions. As already mentioned above, the LHS of a rule formulates some kind of positive condition. In certain cases also *negative application conditions* (NACs) which are pre-conditions prohibiting certain object structures, are needed. If several NACs are formulated for one rule, each of them has to be fulfilled. A NAC

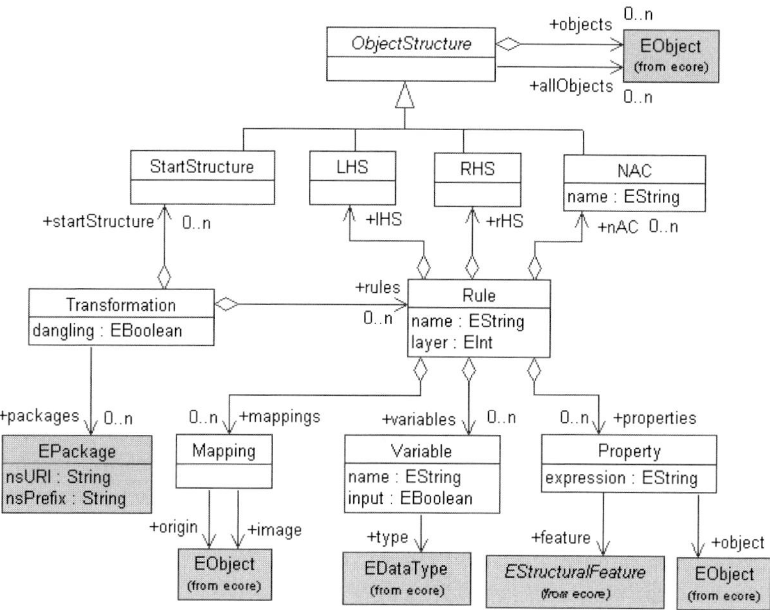

Fig. 3. Transformation Model

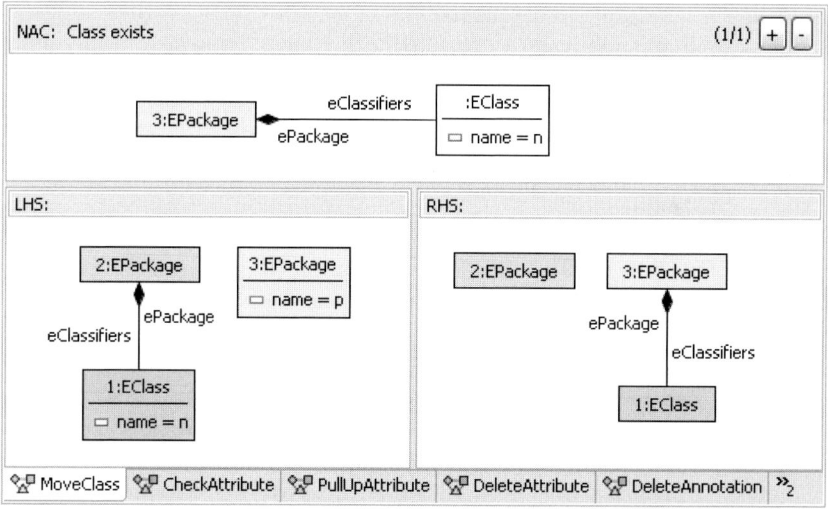

Fig. 4. Rule "MoveClass"

is again an object structure. Moreover, mappings between the LHS and a NAC can be defined. This feature is useful to prohibit structures in relation to the LHS.

The rule's LHS or a NAC may contain constants or variables as attribute values, but no Java expressions, in contrast to a RHS. A NAC may use the variables already used in the LHS or new variables declared as input parameters.

The scope of a variable is its rule, i.e. each variable is globally known in its rule. The Java expressions occurring in the RHS, may contain any variable used within the LHS or declared as input parameter. Multiple usage of the same variable is allowed and can be used to require equality of values.

A rule-based transformation system may show two kinds of non-determinism: (1) for each rule several matches can exist, and (2) several rules can be applicable. There are techniques to restrict both kinds of choices. The choice of matches can be restricted by using input parameters. Moreover, some kind of control flow on rules can be defined by applying them in a certain order. For this purpose, rules are equipped with layers. All rules of one layer are applied as long as possible before going over to the next layer. Later on, we will show how to use Java for controlling rule applications.

Running Example: Refactoring of EMF Models: To illustrate the presented transformation approach for EMF models we show two refactoring methods for EMF models. All transformation rules are typed over the Ecore model, in more detail over the Ecore section shown in Fig. 1. In the following, we define the simple refactoring "move class" where a class is moved from one package to another. Moreover, the complex refactoring "pull up attribute" is shown. If each subclass contains an attribute with the same name, it can be pulled up to their common superclass.

Refactoring rule "MoveClass(EString n, EString p)" in Fig. 4 has two input parameters "n" and "p" to determine the names of the class to be moved and the package it shall be moved to. The LHS describes the pattern to be found for refactoring consisting of the class with name "n", the package it is currently in, and the package with name "p" it shall be moved to. The RHS shows the new pattern after refactoring where the class is contained in the package named "p". In addition, the rule has a NAC which checks if the package named "p" already contains a class named "n".

Refactoring "PullUpAttribute" is more complex, i.e. it cannot be defined by just one rule, but four rules are needed to check the complex pre-condition, to do the kernel refactoring, and to make the model consistent afterwards. For checking the pre-condition, rule "CheckAttribute(EString c, EString a)" in Fig. 5 checks for the class named "c" if there is a subclass not containing an attribute named "a". This rule can be applied at most once, since there are NACs which check if there is already a subclass with this annotation. Thereafter, we try to apply rule "PullUpAttribute(EString c, EString a)" in Fig. 6. If there is no subclass of the class named "c" which has an annotation with source "no attribute" and if the class named "c" has not already an attribute named "a", it looks for a subclass which has an attribute named "a". After the refactoring, the attribute with name "a" is pulled up from one subclass. This rule is applicable at most once. Thereafter, NAC "Attribute already pulled up" will not be satisfied anymore. NAC "Attribute not in all sub-types" checks a necessary pre-condition.

If "PullUpAttribute" was successful, i.e. there is no subclass with a corresponding annotation, all attributes named "a" being still contained in subclasses have to be deleted. This is done by rule "DeleteAttribute(EString c, EString a)"

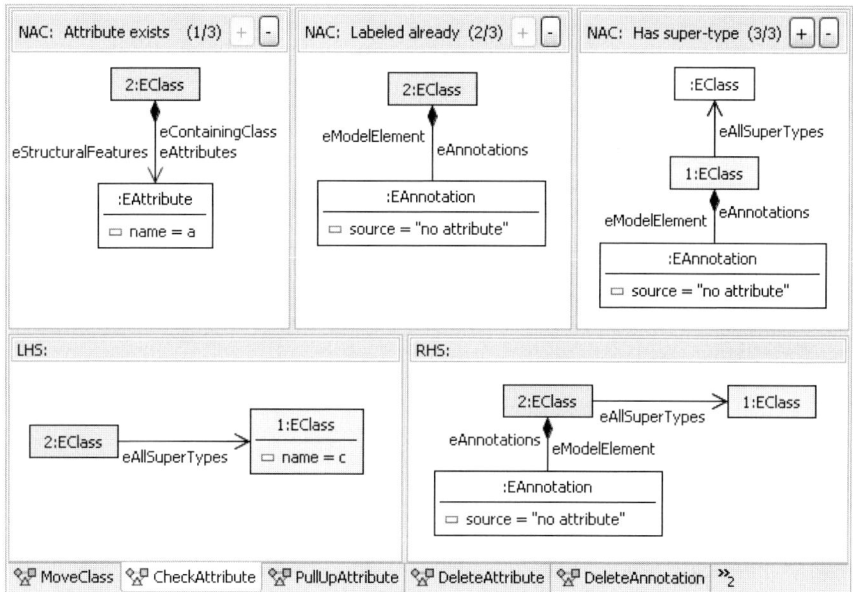

Fig. 5. Rule "CheckAttribute"

in Fig. 7 applying it as long as possible. Finally, if the refactoring was not successful, all new annotations of the class named "c" have to be deleted again which is performed by rule "DeleteAnnotation(EString c)" in Fig. 8. The application control for these rules just described can be realised by putting each of the rules to consecutive layers in the order of description. (See attribute "layer" of model element "Rule" in the transformation model in Fig. 3.)

4 Execution of EMF Transformations

To apply the defined transformation rules on a given EMF model, we either select and apply the rules step-by-step, or take the whole rule set and let it apply as long as possible. A transformation step with a selected rule is defined by first finding a match of the LHS in the current instance model. A pattern is matched to a model if its structure can be found in the model such that the types and attribute values are compatible. In general, a pattern can match to different parts of a model. In this case, one of the possible matches has to be selected, either randomly or by the user.

Performing a transformation step which applies a rule at a selected match, the resulting object structure is constructed in two passes: (1) all objects and links present in the LHS but not in the RHS are deleted; (2) all object and links in the RHS but not in the LHS are created. A transformation, more precisely a transformation sequence, consists of zero or more transformation steps.

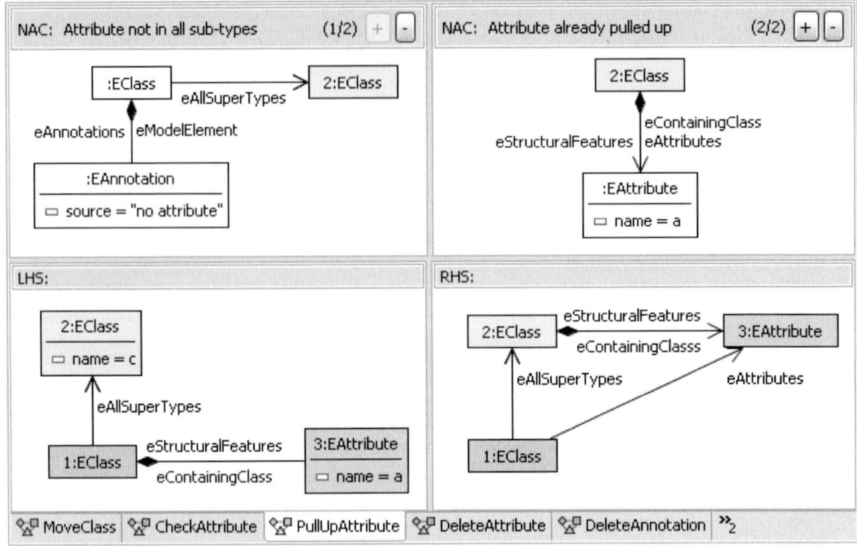

Fig. 6. Rule "PullUpAttribute"

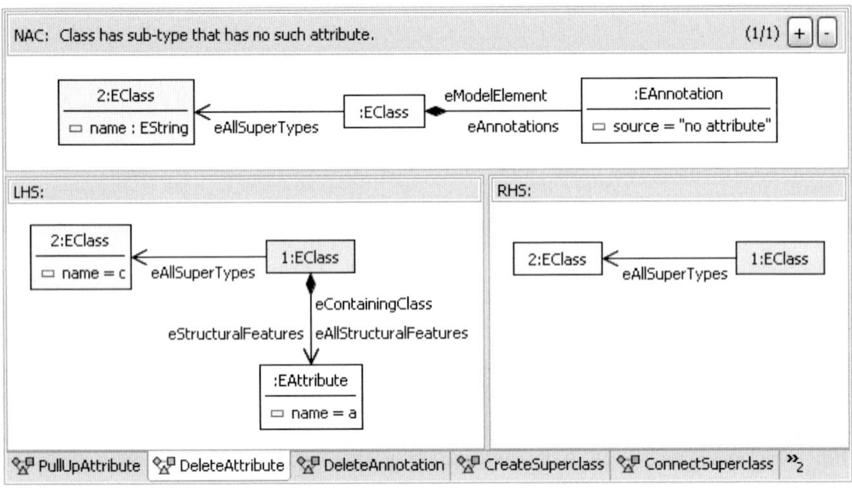

Fig. 7. Rule "DeleteAttribute"

Consistency recovery: Although EMF models show a graph-like structure and can be transformed similarly to graphs [19], there is a main difference in between. In contrast to graphs EMF models have a distinguished tree structure which is defined by the containment relation between their classes. An EMF model should be defined such that all its classes are transitively contained in the root class. Since an EMF model may have non-containment references in addition,

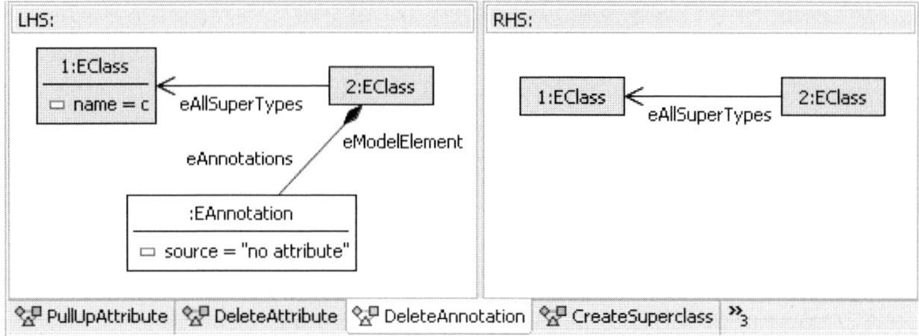

Fig. 8. Rule "DeleteAnnotation"

the following question arises: What if a class which is transitively contained in the root class, has non-containment references to other classes not transitively contained in the root class? In this case we consider the EMF model to be inconsistent, since e.g. it cannot be made persistent anymore. A transformation can make an EMF model inconsistent, if its rule deletes one or more objects or containment links. For example an inconsistent situation occurs, if one of these objects transitively contains an object included by a non-containment reference. To restore the consistency, all objects to be deleted or to be disconnected from their containing objects, have to be determined. Thereafter, all non-containment references to these indicated objects have to be removed, too. Similar to the handling of deleted structures, consistency recovery is also applied to newly created objects. If a rule creates objects which are not contained in the tree structure, the consistency recovery will remove these objects at the end of a rule application. It is possible to forbid the application of those rules entirely, since inconsistencies on creation of objects can be determined statically.

4.1 Interpreter Approach

For executing the defined transformation by the EMF Interpreter, a new Interpreter instance has to be created first. (See the following code snippet.)

```
Interpreter interpreter = new Interpreter(eObject);
interpreter.loadTransformation(filename);
interpreter.transform();
interpreter.applyRule(rulename, parameter, mapping);
```

An *eObject* can be any class in the model instance which should be transformed. After creating the interpreter, the transformation file with name "filename" is loaded. It has to be ensured that the loaded transformation contains the same classes that are used by the instance model to be transformed. After loading a transformation, rules can be applied. For example, invoking *transform()* results in the application of all rules as long as possible. For applying a specific rule, method *applyRule* is called. The first parameter of *applyRule* is simply the name of the rule to be applied. Afterwards the value of each input parameter needs to be specified. A sample use of class Parameter is given in the following example. The third parameter of method *applyRule* contains a vector of *EObjects* which defines a partial match between rule objects and instance objects. If a rule shall be matched automatically, this parameter is set to null.

Here is the sample code snippet for the application of rule *MoveClass* to an EMF model for a library. Assuming you want to move class *Book* from package *Bookshelf* to package *Library*.

```
Interpreter interpreter = new Interpreter(eClass1);
interpreter.loadTransformation("refactoring.tfm");

Parameter parameter = new Parameter();
parameter.addParameter("n","Book", "String");
parameter.addParameter("p", "Library", "String");

Vector mapping = new Vector(2);
mapping.add(eClass1);
mapping.add(ePackage1);

interpreter.applyRule("MoveClass", parameter, mapping);
```

Interpreting EMF Transformations by Graph Transformations: Since EMF models show a graph-like structure and can be transformed similarly to graphs, we have chosen an interpreter approach where an EMF model is translated to a corresponding graph. Furthermore, the EMF transformation rules are translated to graph rules. After having performed the corresponding graph transformation, the result graph is translated back to an EMF model. For the execution of graph transformations, we take AGG [2], a transformation engine for typed, attributed graphs.

As first step, the EMF core model of the transformation is translated to a so-called type graph. Classes are translated to node types and references to edge types. Please note that bidirectional references are mapped to two opposite edge types. Class attributes become node type attributes on the graph side. EMF instance models are translated to graphs. Since each consistent instance model has root objects which contain all other objects, we can navigate from given EObjects being the roots for all linked objects and translate them to graph nodes. All references are mapped to edges. Each EMF rule is translated to a graph rule in a straightforward way.

After having performed the corresponding graph transformation, the resulting graph has to be translated back to an EMF model. As described above, it might happen that the resulting EMF model is not consistent, i.e. non-containment references which make the model inconsistent, have to be removed.

Having a translation of EMF transformation to graph transformation (and back again) at hand, the available analysis techniques may be useful to validate EMF transformations. This is not always possible, but only if the EMF models remain consistent during the transformation which is the case if objects with subtrees are not deleted or uncoupled by removing the reference to their container.

All refactoring rules in the running example preserve the consistency of EMF models. Thus, analysis techniques such as critical pair analysis, termination checks, etc. are available also for these EMF model refactorings. For example in [23], critical pair analysis was used to detect conflicts and dependencies between software refactorings. For example, one conflict between two different applications of rule "PullUpAttribute" reported by AGG occurs, if a class has several subclassses where attributes named "a" occur. In this case only one of these attributes is pulled up. Since all these attributes in the subclasses are equal and are deleted afterwards, the refactoring result is independent of the concrete attribute pulled up. Thus, this conflict can be resolved [22].

4.2 Compiler Approach

Besides interpreting an EMF transformation as graph transformation, transformation rules can also be compiled to Java methods to be used together with previously generated EMF code. For the translation of transformation rules to code we use JET, the code generator in EMF [7].

For each transformation rule, two classes are generated to do the rule matching and the transformation. E.g. for refactoring rule "MoveClass", Java classes "MoveClassRule.java" and "MoveClassWrapper.java" are generated. The first class contains methods for execution, undo and redo functionality. The second class is needed for the matching process. Rule matching is formulated as a constraint solving problem where the LHS objects are variables, the objects of the EMF instance model form the domain, and typing, linking und attribute values form the set of constraints. Formulating pattern matching in this way, its efficiency is directly dependent on the constraint solving algorithm as well as on the ordering of variables and domain elements. This form of pattern matching is influenced by graph pattern matching as done in AGG [25].

To apply one rule you create an instance of the generated rule class. This class and the dependent wrapper class contain all information about the intended changes of instances by the rule and how to find a match for the LHS. To have at least one reference to the instance, on which the rule shall be applied, it must be set by method "setInstanceSymbol(eObject)". Its parameter can be an arbitrary EObject of the instance model. Input parameters can be given by setters, which have name "set" followed by the variable name in the rule. Matches for the LHS are either found automatically or are given by setters, which have the form set+Type+Counter (for objects of type "Type" further distinguished by "Counter"). By method "execute()" the given partial match is completed and the rule applied. Here is a short code example for the application of the rule "MoveClass". Let's assume you want to move class *Book* from package *Bookshelf* to package *Library*.

```
MoveClassRule moveClassRule = new MoveClassRule();
moveClassRuse.setInstanceSymbol(eClass1);

moveClassRule.setParN("Book"); // set Name
moveClassRule.setParP("Library"); // set Package
```

```
moveClassRule.setEClass0(eClass1);
moveClassRule.setEPackage0(ePackage1);

moveClassRule.execute();
```

There is also a way to apply a rule with the same parameters as the Interpreter. To do so you call method "applyRule()" in class "TransformationInterface". This class also needs a reference to the instance which is given in the constructor. Additionally it allows to start a transformation by calling the method "transform()".

```
Transformation transformation = new Transformation(eClass1);
transformation.applyRule("MoveClass", parameter, mapping);

transformation.transform();
```

While transform applies the rule arbitrarily in this example, the rule application can also be controlled by Java constructs.

5 Related Work

In this paper we presented a model transformation approach based on graph transformation concepts and the Eclipse technology. There are already several model transformation tool environments around being based on graph transformation and/or Eclipse. Most of these tool environments are designed for exogenous model transformation, i.e. model transformations between different languages, and do not allow in-place model updates. This fact is one of the differences to our approach which is especially designed for endogenous model transformation, i.e. model transformation within the same language. In the following, we look a little closer to several approaches and distinguish between EMF-related and graph transformation related approaches.

5.1 EMF-Related Approaches

A rather simple approach to EMF model transformation is given by the Merlin Eclipse plug-in [11] which can perform model-to-model and model-to-code transformations. Focussing on the first type of transformations type mappings and simple mapping rules consisting of conditions - actions pairs can be performed. Type mappings and rules are defined in a textual form.

Sub-projects in Eclipse GMT [4] like Tefkat [20], ATL [3], MTF [1] and MOMENT [16] support a much more elaborated transformation approach which is mainly declarative and close to the concepts of QVT, but might also allow imperative feature, as in the case of ATL. Similarly, our approach is mainly rule-based, but allows native method calls in attribute computations (as ATL does). In contrast to ours, model transformations are formulated in textual forms in all studied approaches.

Each of the QVT-related approaches considered provides a transformation engine based on EMF which might be integrated in other applications as well as a tool environment (IDE) which consists of at least an editor and a debugger provided as Eclipse plug-ins. While also offering a transformation engine and a (visual) editor, our approach lacks from an integrated debugger. For this purpose, a model transformation has to be translated to AGG where the stepwise execution of transformations is supported.

The MOMENT project contains an EMF transformation engine which is based on algebraic specifications as implemented in Maude [?]. Similarly to ours, this approach has a clear formal background. But in contrast to MOMENT our EMF transformations are based graph transformation concepts which can be used for verify properties of model transformations such as termination, confluence, and constraint checking, and can be executed by the AGG graph transformation engine.

5.2 Graph Transformation Related Approaches

There are a number of graph transformation-based approaches to model transformation, as e.g. supported by VIATRA2 [15], VMTS [21], AToM3 [17], GReAT [9], MOFLON [13], Gmorph [26] and MOTMOT [14]. While all dealing with graphs and their manipulation, these approaches differ heavily concerning the kind of graphs used and the transformation concepts supported. All indicated approaches support exogenous model transformations.

Besides standard graph transformation concepts, such as rules with left and right-hand sides and integrated attribute computations, a number of advanced transformation concepts are supported. Additional forms for structuring rule sets are supported by all of the related approaches. We decided to keep our transformation model rather simple by supporting the standard transformation concepts with negative application conditions for rule in addition. As advantage, graph transformations of this form can be verified based on the theory of algebraic graph transformation. Additional structuring of transformation rules has to be expressed by additional Java code and is not yet taken into account for verification.

Most of these graph transformation-related approaches do not offer EMF import/export facilities. While VIATRA2 is able to perform EMF transformations in an interpretative mode, it is not able to generate Java code for endogenous EMF transformations. MOFLON combines MOF with graph transformation and supports the generation of JMI compliant Java code, but does not offer verification facilities.

6 Conclusion and Future Work

In this paper we presented an approach for the graphical definition of in-place model transformations. As running example, we considered model refactorings in EMF. Our visual notation for transformation rules pretty differs from that of

QVT. Relations are a key concept in QVT which does not fit well to endogenous transformations, since relationships between model elements are not of primary interest. In contrast, the transformation approach presented focuses on structure modification and is inspired by graph transformation. Transformation rules contain left and right-hand sides being object structures; moreover, negative object patterns may be defined, restricting the rule application. Since the transformation concepts are closely related to graph transformation concepts, it is possible to translate the rules to AGG, a tool environment for algebraic graph transformation where they might be further analyzed. For efficient execution of model transformations, the rules can be translated to Java code to be integrated into generated EMF classes. The presented tool can be downloaded at *http://tfs.cs.tu-berlin.de/emftrans.*

Further application of endogenous EMF model transformation may include the execution of editing operations in EMF-based editors such as generated by the Eclipse Graphical Modeling Framework (GMF) [6]. Orienting the transformation model at the concepts of algebraic graph transformation techniques, we started with a rather simple transformation model. Further concepts may be formulated on top of the approach presented such that the well-developed analysis techniques for algebraic graph transformations can still be used.

References

1. IBM Model Transformation Framework `http://www.alphaworks.ibm.com/tech/mtf`, 2005.
2. AGG-System `http://tfs.cs.tu-berlin.de/agg/`, 2006.
3. ATL: The Atlas Transformation Language Home Page `http://www.sciences.univ-nantes.fr/lina/atl` , 2006.
4. Eclipse Generative Modeling Tools (GMT) `http://www.eclipse.org/gmt`, 2006.
5. Eclipse Graphical Editing Framework (GEF) `http://www.eclipse.org/gef`, 2006.
6. Eclipse Graphical Modeling Framework (GMF) `http://www.eclipse.org/gmf`, 2006.
7. Eclipse Modeling Framework (EMF) `http://www.eclipse.org/emf`, 2006.
8. Essential MOF (EMOF) as part of the OMG MOF 2.0 specification `http://www.omg.org/docs/formal/06-01-01.pdf` , 2006.
9. GReAT: Graph Rewriting And Transformation `http://www.isis.vanderbilt.edu/Projects/mobies/downloads.asp`, 2006.
10. Java Emitter Templates (JET) as part of the Eclipse Modeling Framework (EMF) `http://www.eclipse.org/emf`, 2006.
11. Merlin Generator `http://sourceforge.net/projects/merlingenerator/`, 2006.
12. Model Driven Architecture (MDA). http://www.omg.org/mda, 2006.
13. MOFLON `http://gforge.echtzeitsysteme.org/projects/moflon/`, 2006.
14. MoTMoT: Model driven, Template based, Model Transformer `http://www.fots.ua.ac.be/motmot/index.php`, 2006.
15. VIATRA2 (VIsual Automated model TRAnsformations) framework `http://dev.eclipse.org/viewcvs/ indextech.cgi/ checkout/gmt-home/subprojects/VIATRA2/sindex.html`, 2006.

16. A. Boronat, J. Carsi, and I. Ramos. Algebraic Specification of a Model Transformation Engine. In *Springer LNCS 3922. Fundamental Approaches to Software Engineering (FASE'06). ETAPS'06. Vienna (Austria).*, 2006.
17. J. de Lara and H. Vangheluwe. ATOM^3: A Tool for Multi-Formalism Modelling and Meta-Modelling. In R. Kutsche and H. Weber, editors, *Proc. Fundamental Approaches to Software Engineering (FASE'02), Grenoble, April 2002*, pages 174 – 188. Springer LNCS 2306, 2002.
18. K. Duddy, A. Gerber, M.J. Lawley, K. Raymond, and J. Steel. Declarative Transformation for Object-Oriented Models. In *In Transformation of Knowledge, Information, and Data: Theory and Applications, edited by P. van Bommel. Idea Group Publishing*, 2005.
19. H. Ehrig, K. Ehrig, U. Prange, and G. Taentzer. *Fundamentals of Algebraic Graph Transformation.* EATCS Monographs in Theoretical Computer Science. Springer, 2006.
20. M. Lawley and J. Steel. Practical Declarative Model Transformation With Tefkat. In *In Proc. Model Transformation in Practice Workshop, Models Conference*, 2005.
21. T. Levendovszky, L. Lengyel, G. Mezei, and H. Charaf. Systematic Approach to Metamodeling Environments and Model Transformation Systems in VMTS. In *2nd International Workshop on Graph Based Tools (GraBaTs), workshop at ICGT 2004, Rome, Italy*, 2004.
22. T. Mens, G. Taentzer, and O. Runge. Detecting Structural Refactoring Conflicts unsing Critical Pair Analysis. In *In R. Heckel and T. Mens, editors, Proc. Workshop on Software Evolution through Transformations: Model-based vs. Implementation-level Solutions (SETra'04), Satellite Event of ICGT'04), Rome, Italy*, 2004.
23. T. Mens, G. Taentzer, and O. Runge. Analysing refactoring dependencies using graph transformation. *Software and System Modeling*, 2006. to appear.
24. T. Mens and P. Van Gorp. A Taxonomy of Model Transformation. In *Proc. International Workshop on Graph and Model Transformation (GraMoT'05)*, number 152 in Electronic Notes in Theoretical Computer Science, Tallinn, Estonia, 2006. Elsevier Science.
25. Michael Rudolf. Utilizing Constraint Satisfaction Techniques for Efficient Graph Pattern Matching. In *6th Int. Workshop on Theory and Application of Graph Transformation (TAGT'98), LNCS 1764*, pages 238–251. Springer Verlag, 2000.
26. S. Sendall. Combining Generative and Graph Transformation Techniques for Model Transformation: An Effective Alliance? In *18th Annual ACM SIGPLAN Conf. on Object-Oriented Programming, Systems, Languages, and Applications (OOPSLA)*, 2003.
27. G. Taentzer and G. Toffetti Carughi. A Graph-Based Approach to Transform XML Documents. In L. Baresi and R. Heckel, editors, *Proc. Fundamental Approaches to Software Engineering (FASE)*, volume 3922 of *LNCS*. Springer, 2006.

Model Transformations? Transformation Models!

Jean Bézivin[1], Fabian Büttner[2], Martin Gogolla[2], Frederic Jouault[1], Ivan Kurtev[1], and Arne Lindow[2]

[1] University of Nantes, Computer Science Department & INRIA
[2] University of Bremen, Computer Science Department & TZI

Abstract. Much of the current work on model transformations seems essentially operational and executable in nature. Executable descriptions are necessary from the point of view of implementation. But from a conceptual point of view, transformations can also be viewed as descriptive models by stating only the properties a transformation has to fulfill and by omitting execution details. This contribution discusses the view that model transformations can be abstracted as being transformation models. As a simple example for a transformation model, the well-known transformation from the Entity-Relationship model to the Relational model is shown. A transformation model in this contribution is nothing more than an ordinary, simple model, i.e., a UML/MOF class diagram together with OCL constraints. A transformation model may transport syntax and semantics of the described domain. The contribution thus covers two views on transformations: An operational *model transformation* view and a descriptive *transformation model* view.

1 Introduction

Today it is well accepted that models play an important role in software development. Standards like UML including OCL and the recent QVT (Queries, Views, Transformations) [OMG05] underpin a trend called model engineering [Bez05] which can be seen as a discipline within software engineering.

QVT is a family of languages for the description of model transformations. It is designed to formalize transformations from one model to another model. Source and target models may be formulated in different modeling languages. Many QVT language features are operational in nature. A main intention of QVT seems to formulate transformations which can be executed.

> *A model can tell* ***what*** *something does (specification) as well as* ***how*** *the function is accomplished (implementation). These aspects should be separated in modeling. It is important to get the* ***what*** *correct before investigating much time in the* ***how****.* *[RBJ05, p. 22]*

QVT is strong on the *how* in transformations. This contribution concentrates on the *what* in transformations. QVT focuses on the process and means of going from the source model to the target model. This contribution focuses on the

O. Nierstrasz et al. (Eds.): MoDELS 2006, LNCS 4199, pp. 440–453, 2006.

properties of the source and target models and by this characterizes the transformation without going into the details of the transformation process. Transformations are viewed from a modeling perspective as transformation models.

The structure of the rest of the contribution is as follows. Section 2 discusses how transformation models may emerge from model transformations. Section 3 puts forward an example for a transformation model. Section 4 elaborates on advantages and disadvantages of the two views on transformation and model. The contribution is finished with concluding remarks in Sect. 5.

2 From Model Transformations to Transformation Models

In our view, the basic idea of model transformation is presented in Fig. 1 where (at the bottom) a transformation operation Mt takes a model Ma as the source model and produces a model Mb as the target model. This operation Mt is probably the most important operation in model engineering. Being models, Ma and Mb conform to metamodels MMa and MMb. Usually, the transformation Mt has complete knowledge of the source metamodel MMa and the target metamodel MMb. Furthermore, the metamodels MMa and MMb conform to a metametamodel, in this figure, OMG's MOF which in turn conforms to itself.

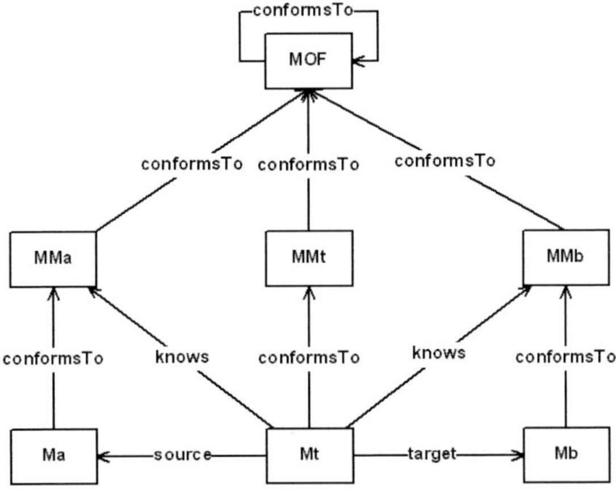

Fig. 1. From a *Model Transformation* Mt to a *Model Transformation Metamodel* MMt

The question of interest discussed in this contribution is concerned with several views on the operation Mt. In fact, one might ask whether *operation* is the right term at all. Our first proposal to view Mt consists in stating that Mt could be a program written in a given (programming) language like Java which upon execution causes the output Mb from the input Ma. Alternatively, if Mt is a transformation expressed in XSLT, then the structure of Mt would be different, but its execution on top of an engine like Saxon would produce a similar effect.

Such a view on transformations with focus on execution is understandable because the most important motivation for model transformation is the generation of code from (UML) models.

Before stating a second view on Mt, let us emphasize that we want to work within the realm of model engineering: We want to develop software concentrating on and with the help of models and metamodels; we do not want to focus on code or programs. Model engineering in particular means that one has to ask: Is there a model or metamodel for the thing one is working with; if so, what does the model or metamodel look like? Therefore, it seems natural to introduce a metamodel MMt for Mt. The model transformation Mt must be conformant to MMt, and, if we want to restrict ourselves to a three-level metamodeling stack, then the model transformation metamodel MMt must again conform to our top-level metamodel MOF.

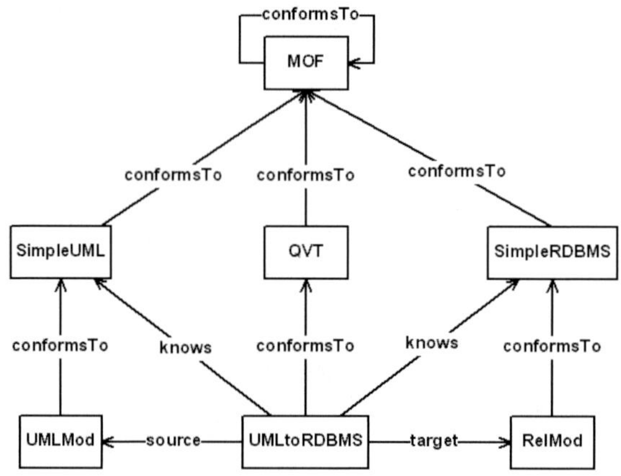

Fig. 2. QVT Example Transformation

Example: In Fig. 2, the above abstract considerations are made more concrete by considering the QVT standard and the example treated there. QVT (which conforms to the MOF) is the metamodel of the model transformation, i.e., a model transformation metamodel. The model transformation UMLtoRDBMS, the example from the QVT standard, describes in an operational way how simple UML class diagrams may be transformed into Relational database schemata.

For our third view on the operation Mt as shown in Fig. 3, we point to the fact that different model transformations Mt1 and Mt2 may work on the same source and target and may produce similar results. However, these model transformations may be syntactically different viewed as instantiations of the model transformation metamodel MMt (which is not shown in Fig. 3). In order to emphasize the commonalities between these different model transformations, we propose to identify the commonalities by a *model transformation model* Tm, shortly denoted by the term *transformation model*, which abstracts from the technical realization

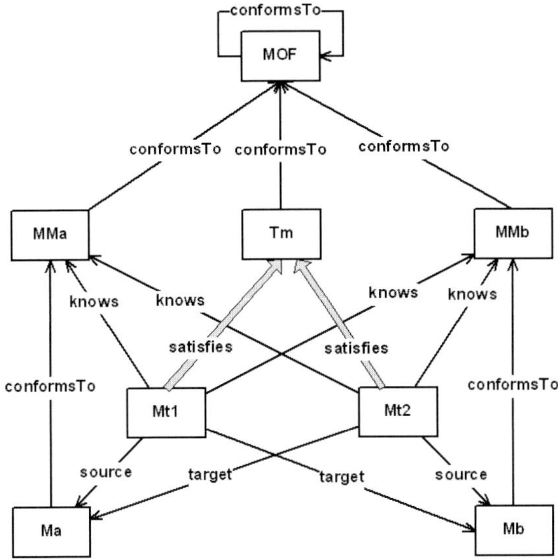

Fig. 3. Model Transformations Abstracted to a Transformation Model

details of the different model transformations and summarizes and concentrates the similarities. We expect that the different model transformations all satisfy what is required in this transformation model. This satisfies relationship is indicated by the thick grey arrows. Having set this context, we state the hypothesis which we would like to discuss further in this contribution:

Model transformations can be abstracted to a transformation model.

The reader may check, that the three highly related notions *model transformation*, *model transformation metamodel* and *model transformation model*, for short denoted as *transformation model*, mean different things to us. As indicated in Fig. 3, the transformation model again conforms to our metametamodel, in our case MOF. Speaking in technical terms, this means that we only employ MOF features for the formulation of our transformation model.

3 Er to Rel: A Transformation Model Example

We want to show the usefulness of the concept *transformation model* through a proof by example. The example chosen here is the well-known transformation from the Er database model to the Relational database model. This example is also used (with a bit different terminology) in the current QVT proposal [OMG05], in [Bez05] and other works on model transformation [CESW04]. Because it is well-known, it is well-suited to demonstrate ideas and technical details of transformation principles.

3.1 Technical Details of the Example Transformation Model

As indicated above, we employ MOF for the formulation of transformation models. Thus, a transformation model is nothing more or less than a MOF model: We need a moderate class diagram and many OCL constraints. These language features are supported by our system USE [RG01, GBR05] in which we have completely realized this transformation example and which we employ as a MOF compliant validation system.

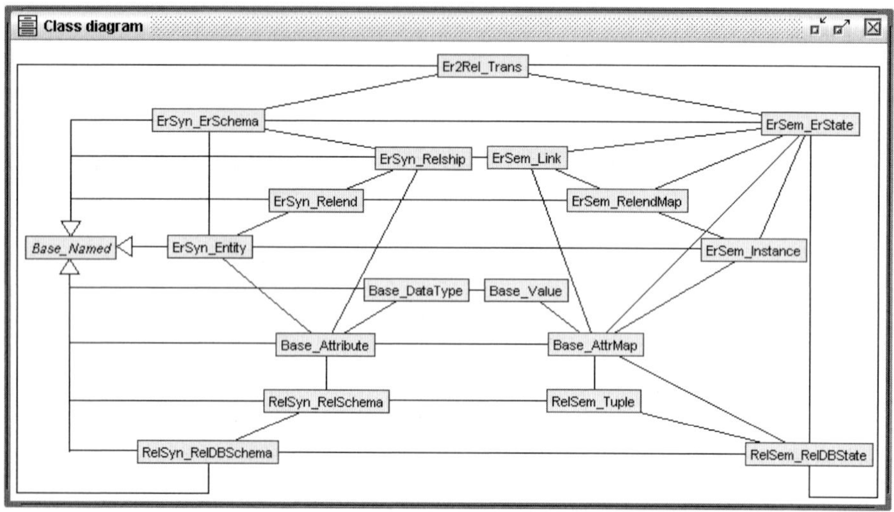

Fig. 4. Class Diagram for Transformation Model

The class diagram in Fig. 4 shows the six parts of the transformation model: Class names starting with Base are shown in the middle, ErSyn in the upper left, ErSem in the upper right, RelSyn in the lower left, RelSem in the lower right, and Er2Rel in the top. Generalization and associations are pictured as well. ErSyn describes the syntax of the Er model, namely Er database schemas; ErSem describes the semantics of the Er model, namely Er database states; RelSyn describes the syntax of the Relational model, namely Relational database schemas; RelSem describes the semantics of the Relational model, namely Relational database states. For example, in the Er semantics part, the assignments of attribute values to instances is handled and a constraint is stated that the key attributes have to uniquely identify the instances.

All syntax classes (Er and Rel) can be found in left, all semantics classes (Er and Rel) in the right; all Er classes (Syn and Sem) are in the upper part, whereas the Rel classes (Syn and Sem) are in the lower part. In case the reader is interest in details like association multiplicities or constraint details, the full description in [Gog06] can be consulted; we will illustrate this transformation model in the following by some simple object diagrams and by sketching the transformation constraints.

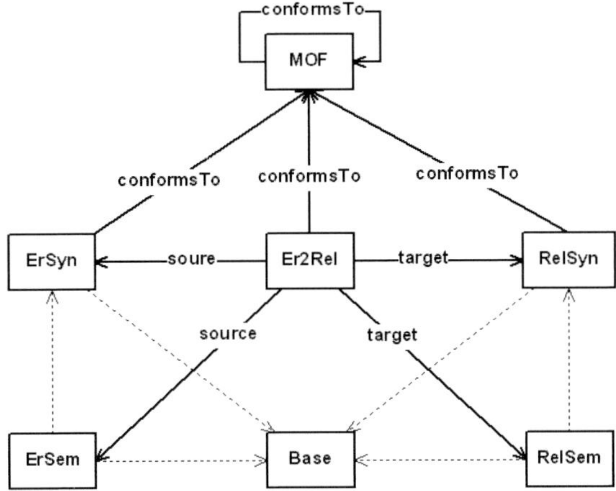

Fig. 5. Example Transformation viewed as a Transformation from Er to Rel

Figure 5 shows the six parts of the class diagram similar to the previously mentioned example transformation in Fig. 2 from the QVT standard. The dashed arrows indicated dependencies.

Structuring a transformation into a source metamodel, a target metamodel, and a metamodel part for the actual transformation is not new. This idea is present, for example, in the QVT standard [OMG05] and the triple graph grammar approach [KS06].

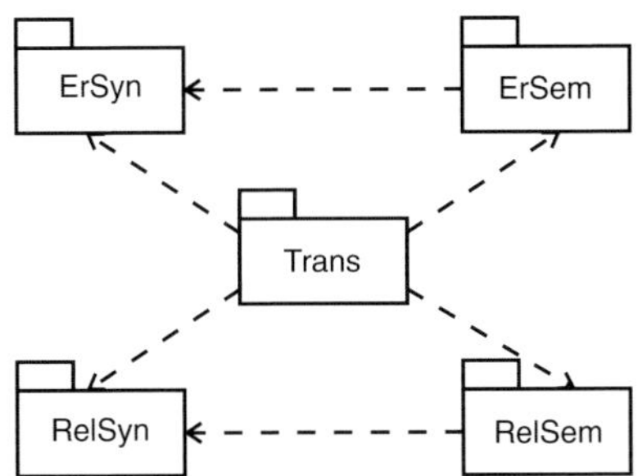

Fig. 6. Syntax, Semantics, and Transformation

In our approach we constrain all three components with OCL constraints, i.e., the source, the target, and the actual transformation. As shown in Fig. 6, in addition, we divide source and target metamodels into a syntactic and a semantic part. This enables us to formulate transformation properties expressing syntactic and also semantic characteristics.

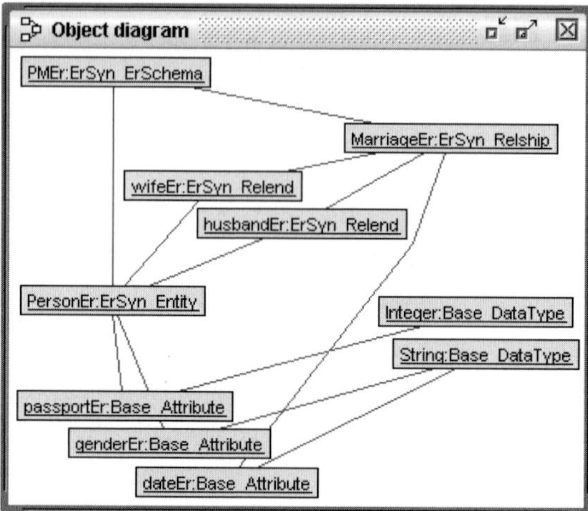

Fig. 7. Er Syntax

Figure 7 shows an Er database schema PMEr (PersonMarriage Er version) modeling an entity Person and a reflexive relationship Marriage together with three attributes and two relationships ends.

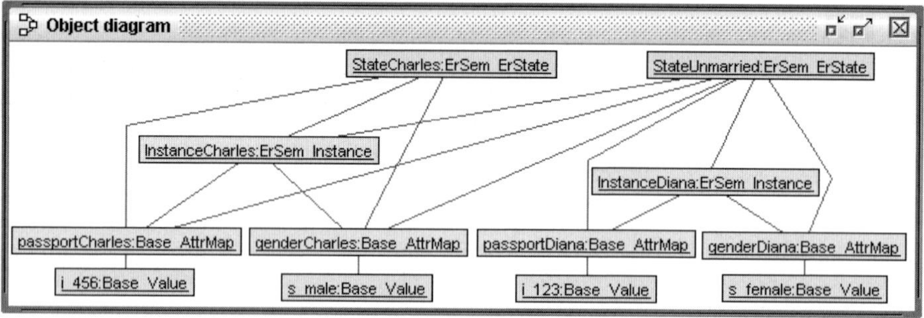

Fig. 8. Er Semantics

Figure 8 pictures two Er database states. The first state (StateCharles) incorporates one Instance (Charles) and AttrMap objects assigning attribute values to instances; the second state (StateUnmarried) has two Instances (Charles, Diana) and attribute assignments. In order to make the presentation simple, both states do not have links. We emphasize that the two database states are part of a single (larger) object diagram for the complete transformation model.

Figure 9 displays the interplay between syntax and semantics with a (partial) object diagram. A syntactical thing from the left is associated and interpreted by semantic things from the right. To make the presentation comprehensible, each Er syntax concept is associated with only one Er semantic object. This

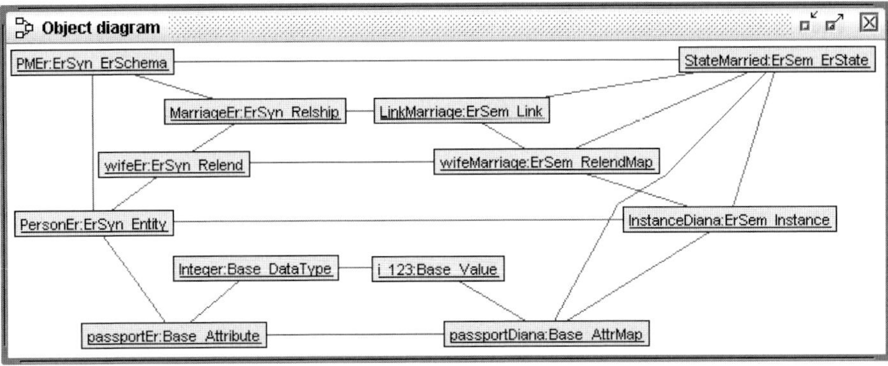

Fig. 9. Interplay between Syntax and Semantics

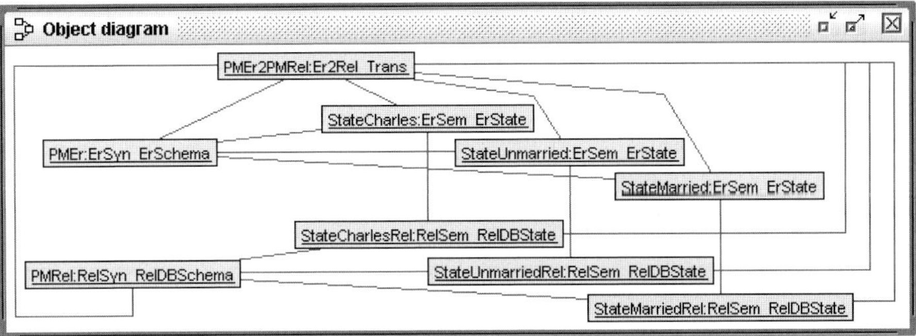

Fig. 10. Transformation

part shows a third database state with a marriage link (the husband is ignored in the display).

Figure 10 shows a Trans(formation) object which connects the schemas (the syntax parts) and the states (the semantics parts). In general, a transformation object will connect source and target objects by links expressing that the source may or must be transformed into the target (depending on the stated multiplicities and constraints). One schema is associated (in this example object diagram) with three database states. This transformation model covers syntax and semantics of the two classical database models. As will be explained below, the model covers the transformation and its properties as well. Database dynamics is captured insofar that more than one state can be associated with a single database schema. In the example, one can think of the first state having only the Charles instance, the second state having Charles and Diana as unmarried instances, and the third state with a marriage link between Diana and Charles.

Figure 11 gives an overview on the probably most interesting part of the transformation model: the constraints for the transformation. The figure involves the four central areas (Er and Rel; Syn and Sem) with dependencies, constraint

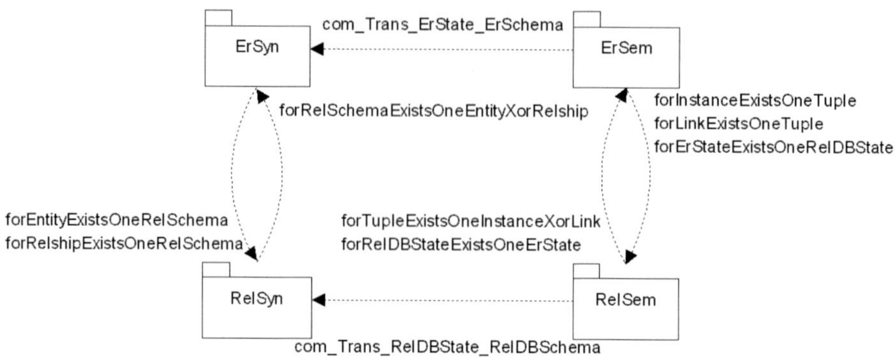

Fig. 11. Overview on Transformation Constraints

names and indication of the 'direction of the constraint'. We explain three constraints in more detail.

forRelSchemaExistsOneEntityXorRelship: This constraint 'goes from' the Relational syntax part to the Er syntax part. It requires that for a Relational schema from a transformed Relational database schema a uniquely determined entity or relationship in the Er schema with the same characteristics exists.

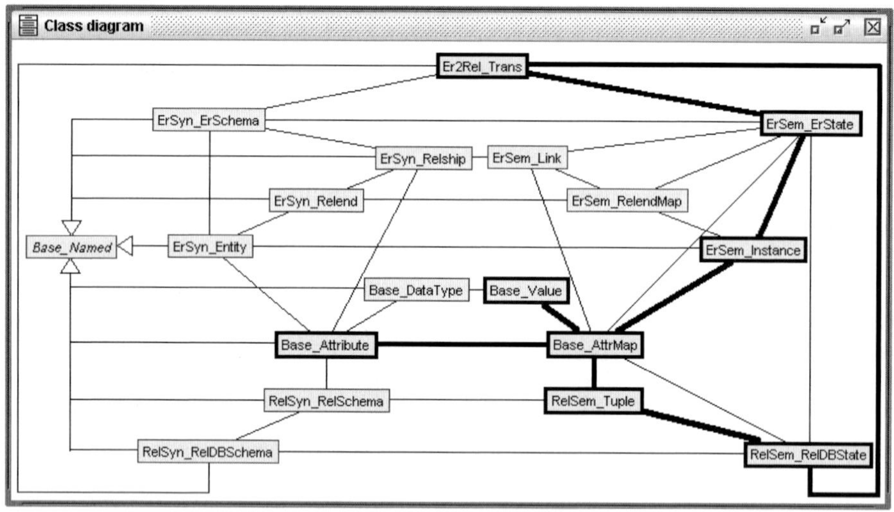

Fig. 12. Class Diagram Illustrating Constraint forInstanceExistsOneTuple

forInstanceExistsOneTuple: This constraint 'goes from' the Er semantics part to the Relational semantics part. It requires that for an instance from an Er state occurring in a transformation an equivalent tuple in the Relational state exists.

```
context self:Er2Rel_Trans inv forInstanceExistsOneTuple:
  self.erState->forAll(erSt | self.relDBState->one(relSt |
    erSt.instance->forAll(i | relSt.tuple->one(t |
      i.attrMap->forAll(amEr |
        t.attrMap->one(amRel |
          amEr.attribute.name=amRel.attribute.name and
          amEr.value=amRel.value))))))
```

com_Trans_ErState_ErSchema: This constraint 'goes from' the Er semantics part to the Er syntax part. Constraints starting with 'com' are commutativity constraints requiring the commutativity of two different evaluation paths in the class diagram. This one requires that an Er state which is connected to a Trans(formation) object must also be linked to the Er schema being associated to the Trans(formation) object.

3.2 Explanation for Calling the Example a Transformation Model

Semantic properties: We have modeled the transformation with a class and corresponding associations holding source and target object. By doing so, semantic properties of the transformation can be formulated because we can access source and target and retrieve their properties. In the example, a bijection between database state spaces is described. But by dropping certain constraints, this requirement could be relaxed to achieve only an injection. For example, we could only require that each Er database state has a corresponding equivalent Relational database states but not the other way round. The required properties of the transformation rely merely on the stated constraints and are under control and responsibility of the transformation developer. Only the properties of the transformation are stated, not the realization of the transformation.

Alternatives: In the example, we have decided to make the transformation deterministic. In general however, transformation alternatives can be allowed in a single transformation model. For example, the transformation model may allow two or more alternative Relational schemas to be associated with one Er schema.

4 Model Transformation Versus Transformation Models

Executability: Model transformations can directly and efficiently be executed. There is an international standard for them, QVT, and commercial and open source implementations and systems like UMT, MTL, ATL, GMT or BOTL are available (see the overview on transformation systems in [Wan05]).

Direction freeness: Transformation models may be seen as transformations in multiple directions. Please check Fig. 13 which is nearly identical to Fig. 5 except the central source and target decorations. Apart from the direction (Er to Relational) which we have already discussed, the transformation model may be seen in two other directions: As a transformation from the Relational

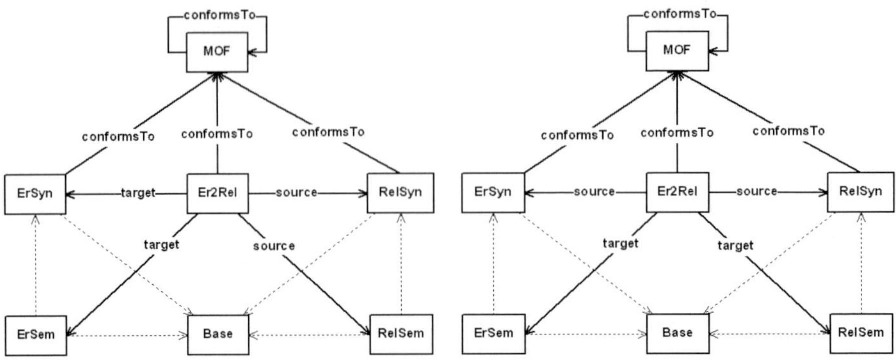

Fig. 13. Two Further Views on Example Transformation (Different Source/Target)

database model to the Er database model and as a transformation from syntax to semantics. In technical terms, a transformation direction has not to be fixed in the model. This is based on the use of direction-free minimal MOF language features: Classes, associations, attributes, and invariants.

Uniformity: Transformation models provide uniformity between the model description language and the language for transformations. If one has simple models, for example, UML class diagrams with OCL constraints, then the use of this language for transformations reliefs the development from the burden of introducing another language like QVT. In particular in early project development phases, it might be advisable to concentrate on transformation properties by expressing them in transformation models instead of realizing them already by model transformations.

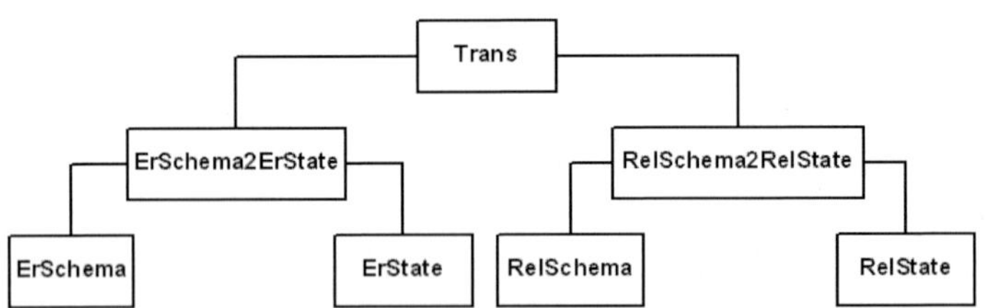

Fig. 14. Example for Higher-Order Transformation

Higher-order transformations: Uniformity of the model and transformation language also allows for higher-order transformations, i.e., transformations that work on transformations. Our example could be understood and realized as such a higher-order transformation: As shown in Fig. 14, assigning semantics to the schemas could be seen as two basic transformations realized through two classes ErSchema2ErState and RelSchema2RelState and appropriate associations; the transformation from the Er model to the Relational model could then be realized in a higher-order style by a third class Trans(formation) with associations to the two transformation classes ErSchema2ErState and RelSchema2RelState.

Transformations of Transformations: Working with transformation models provides for the possibility for rewriting transformation models exactly as they were ordinary models. Thus refactorings and improvements for general models [ZLG05, GSMD03] and UML models [SGJ04, CW04, BSF02, SPTJ01] would be applicable.

Validation and completions: Standard transformation models can be validated and checked with standard UML and OCL validation tools [GBR05, Chi01]. Model finders (like Alloy [JSS00], to some extent USE [RG01, GBR05]) can be employed for finding completions of partially given transformations. In the example, if only the database schemas and the Er state is provided, a model finder could search for the resulting Relational state without explicitly describing it. Tools and approaches based on formal reasoning [ABB+00, JSS00, KFdB+05] can check transformations models w.r.t. formally derivable properties. Such formal reasoning capabilities could be used for formally checking the compatibility of two modeling languages.

Complete language descriptions: Transformation models allow complete descriptions of modeling languages w.r.t. syntax and semantics and their transformation properties to be described within a single framework. This is in contrast to mainstream modeling languages like UML which do not formally describe semantic domains.

5 Conclusion

In this contribution we have discussed model transformations and transformation models. We have put our work into the context of UML, OCL, MOF and QVT. The main benefits we see for transformation models are direction freeness, uniformity, higher-order transformations, and powerful possibilities for validation and verification. The benefits of model transformations lie in the efficient execution and the availability of practically useful systems.

Further work has to investigate to what extent available transformation systems can be used for transformation model purposes. Further examples for transformation models, in particular transformation models between modeling languages, have to be developed. It seems that syntax and semantics of hierarchical and flat statecharts as well as advanced and basic UML class diagrams can be characterized as transformation models. Lastly, the connection between model transformations and transformation models on the one hand and domain specific languages and profiling of modeling languages on the other hand has to be explored.

Acknowledgments

A subset of the authors have been partially supported by the IST European project ModelWare (Contract 511731).

References

[ABB+00] W. Ahrendt, T. Baar, B. Beckert, M. Giese, E. Habermalz, R. Hähnle, W. Menzel, and P. H. Schmitt. The KeY approach: Integrating object oriented design and formal verification. In M. Ojeda-Aciego, I.P. de Guzmán, G. Brewka, and L. M. Pereira, editors, *Proc. 8th European Workshop Logics in AI (JELIA'2000)*, LNCS 1919, pages 21–36. Springer, 2000.

[Bez05] J. Bezivin. On the Unification Power of Models. *Software and System Modeling*, 4(2):171–188, 2005.

[BSF02] Marko Boger, Thorsten Sturm, and Per Fragemann. Refactoring browser for uml. In Mehmet Aksit, Mira Mezini, and Rainer Unland, editors, *NetObjectDays*, volume 2591 of *Lecture Notes in Computer Science*, pages 366–377. Springer, 2002.

[CESW04] T. Clark, A. Evans, P. Sammut, and J.S. Willans. Transformation language design: A metamodelling foundation. In H. Ehrig, G. Engels, F. Parisi-Presicce, and G. Rozenberg, editors, *ICGT*, volume 3256 of *LNCS*, pages 13–21. Springer, 2004.

[Chi01] D. Chiorean. Using OCL Beyond Specifications. In A. Evans, R. France, A. Moreira, and B. Rumpe, editors, *Proc. UML'2001 Workshop Rigorous Development*, pages 57–68. LNI, GI, Bonn, 2001.

[CW04] Alexandre L. Correa and Cláudia Maria Lima Werner. Applying refactoring techniques to uml/ocl models. In Thomas Baar, Alfred Strohmeier, Ana M. D. Moreira, and Stephen J. Mellor, editors, *UML*, volume 3273 of *Lecture Notes in Computer Science*, pages 173–187. Springer, 2004.

[GBR05] Martin Gogolla, Jörn Bohling, and Mark Richters. Validating UML and OCL Models in USE by Automatic Snapshot Generation. *Journal on Software and System Modeling*, 4(4):386–398, 2005.

[Gog06] M. Gogolla. Tales of ER and RE Syntax and Semantics. In J.R. Cordy, R. Lämmel, and A. Winter, editors, *Transformation Techniques in Software Engineering*, number 05161 in Dagstuhl Seminar Proceedings. IBFI, Schloss Dagstuhl, 2006.

[GSMD03] Pieter Van Gorp, Hans Stenten, Tom Mens, and Serge Demeyer. Towards automating source-consistent uml refactorings. In Perdita Stevens, Jon Whittle, and Grady Booch, editors, *UML*, volume 2863 of *Lecture Notes in Computer Science*, pages 144–158. Springer, 2003.

[JSS00] Daniel Jackson, Ian Schechter, and Ilya Shlyakhter. Alcoa: The Alloy constraint analyzer. In *Proc. Int. Conf. Software Engineering (ICSE'2000)*, pages 730–733. ACM, New York, 2000.

[KFdB+05] M. Kyas, H. Fecher, F. S. de Boer, J. Jacob, J. Hooman, M. van der Zwaag, T. Arons, and H. Kugler. Formalizing UML models and OCL constraints in PVS. *Electr. Notes Theor. Comput. Sci.*, 115:39–47, 2005.

[KS06] A. Königs and A. Schürr. Tool Integration with Triple Graph Grammars - A Survey. In R. Heckel, editor, *Proc. SegraVis School Foundations of Visual Modelling Techniques*, volume 148 of *ENTCS*, pages 113–150. Elsevier, 2006.

[OMG05] OMG, editor. *MOF QVT Final Adopted Specification.* OMG, 2005.

[RBJ05] J. Rumbaugh, G. Booch, and I. Jacobson. *The Unified Modeling Language Reference Manual, Second Edition.* Addison-Wesley, Reading, 2005.

[RG01] Mark Richters and Martin Gogolla. OCL - Syntax, Semantics and Tools. In Tony Clark and Jos Warmer, editors, *Advances in Object Modelling with the OCL*, pages 43–69. Springer, Berlin, LNCS 2263, 2001.

[SGJ04] Hans Schippers, Pieter Van Gorp, and Dirk Janssens. Leveraging UML Profiles to generate Plugins from Visual Model Transformations. In *Proc. ICGT Workshop Software Evolution through Transformations*, 2004.

[SPTJ01] Gerson Sunyé, Damien Pollet, Yves Le Traon, and Jean-Marc Jézéquel. Refactoring uml models. In Martin Gogolla and Cris Kobryn, editors, *UML*, volume 2185 of *Lecture Notes in Computer Science*, pages 134–148. Springer, 2001.

[Wan05] W. Wang. *Evaluation of UML Model Transformation Tools.* Technical University of Vienna, Business Informatics Group, Master Thesis, 2005.

[ZLG05] Jing Zhang, Yuehua Lin, and Jeff Gray. Generic and Domain-Specific Model Refactoring using a Model Transformation Engine. In Sami Beydeda, Matthias Book, and Volker Gruhn, editors, *Model-Driven Software Development*, pages 199–218. Springer, 2005.

A Mapping Language from Models to DI Diagrams

Marcus Alanen, Torbjörn Lundkvist, and Ivan Porres

TUCS Turku Centre for Computer Science
Department of Information Technologies,
Åbo Akademi University
Lemminkäisenkatu 14, FIN-20520 Turku, Finland
{marcus.alanen, torbjorn.lundkvist, ivan.porres}@abo.fi

Abstract. The OMG MOF 2.0 standard is used to define the abstract syntax of software modeling languages while the UML 2.0 Diagram Interchange (DI) describes the concrete syntax of models. However, very few tools support the DI standard, leading to interoperability problems. The primary reason for this is the lack of a formal way to describe the relationship between the abstract metamodel and its corresponding diagrams. In this article, we present a language to describe mappings between modeling languages and diagrams, some example mappings and our experience in using them. Better and correct support for DI would ease interchange of visual models and hasten the adoption of model-driven development.

Keywords: Visual languages, Diagram Interchange, XMI[DI], MOF, UML.

1 Introduction

In this paper, we study the definition of visual languages based on metamodeling and the modeling standards maintained by the Object Management Group (OMG), such as the Unified Modeling Language (UML) [20].

The UML has become the de facto standard for software modeling in the industry. A rigorous and complete definition of modeling languages is necessary to enable the automatic generation of tools supporting these languages. Several authors have proposed the use of graph grammars to define visual languages [18] and there exist diagram editor generators for languages defined using graph grammars such as GenGed [3], AToM [7], Tiger [9] and DiaGen [14]. One of the main differences between the technical space [4] defined by the OMG modeling standards and previous approaches is that the abstract syntax and concrete syntax of a modeling language are two independently defined and maintained artifacts.

In a modeling language, the definition of its abstract syntax includes the definition of all model elements that can be used in a language, their properties and relationships with other elements. It can also include additional constraints, also know as well-formed rules. The definition of its concrete syntax includes the visual appearance of model elements and layout constraints. The complete definition of a visual modeling language should include the mapping between the abstract and its concrete syntax, that is, the mapping between models and diagrams. This is necessary to create new diagrams from existing models or to parse a diagram into a model.

O. Nierstrasz et al. (Eds.): MoDELS 2006, LNCS 4199, pp. 454–468, 2006.

In the context of the OMG standards, the abstract syntax of a language can be defined using the Meta Object Facility (MOF) [22] Therefore, a model in these languages is often called a metamodel. MOF is a rich and complex metamodeling language that can be used to define modeling languages as large and complex as the UML 2.0 Superstructure. It can also be used to define domain specific languages and extensions or profiles to the UML.

The OMG has a standard for two-dimensional diagrams called the UML 2.0 Diagram Interchange [21] (DI). DI is a modeling language that has been defined following the same metamodeling approach as the UML. While DI has been developed to satisfy the need for diagram interchange for UML diagrams, it is not strictly restricted to UML in any way. That is, DI can be used to represent diagrams for other modeling languages as well. As a consequence, DI is a key standard to exchange models between tools that need to represent, create or transform diagrams. Examples of these tools range from a simple diagram viewer to a full-featured interactive model editor or model transformation tool.

However, we should note that DI is a language to express concrete diagrams. It does not address the issue of defining the concrete syntax of modeling languages. That is, while DI can be used to represent and interchange diagrams for a model, it cannot be used to determine if a given diagram is valid for a given model, it cannot enumerate all the possible valid diagrams for a particular modeling language, and neither does it contain the necessary information to create a new diagram from an existing model. While Appendix A and C of the DI specification attempts to address this issue by providing an informal mapping from UML to DI, these mappings still lack the details required for determining precisely when a specific diagram is valid.

Considering this, we argue that the OMG standards cannot completely specify the concrete syntax of a visual modeling language. We can see an example of this in the definition of UML 2.0. In this language, there are a group of model elements in the interaction packages that can be represented in at least three different diagrams: sequence, interaction overview and communication diagrams. That is, the same concepts from the UML abstract syntax can be represented in three completely different ways in a diagram. Although these diagrams are explained informally in the UML standard, neither the UML nor the DI specification contains the information required to construct sequence, interaction and communication diagrams using the DI language. This has also been noticed by Dr. Guus Ramackers, who has notified the OMG about it [24].

In this article, we tackle this problem and study how to define a mapping between the abstract syntax of a modeling language described using the MOF or the UML 2.0 Infrastructure and its concrete syntax described using the DI standard. In the context of UML 2.0, such a mapping is necessary to complete the definition of UML and to construct modeling and transformation tools that can create, transform and exchange UML model diagrams. In a broader context of Model Driven Engineering, this mapping can be used to build generic modeling tools that can create and transform visual models and diagrams in domain specific modeling languages.

We proceed as follows. In Section 2 we present the basis of DI and define the need of and use for a mapping language from models to diagrams in more detail. Section 3 contains our proposal for such a mapping language and explains its semantics. We discuss how we have validated our approach in Section 4. We finally take a look at related work and conclude in Section 5, where we also consider future directions.

2 A Mapping Language from Models to Diagrams

In this section we describe basic concepts behind the UML and DI standards and we describe the idea behind a mapping language between these languages.

In order to ensure interoperability between modeling tools, we consider that the mapping between the abstract and concrete syntax of a modeling language should be defined precisely. This is necessary in order to fully support DI diagrams for both new and existing modeling languages. This mapping can be defined using a mapping language, which we call DIML, from a modeling language to DI. An overview of this mapping can be seen in Figure 1. In this setting, we assume that this mapping language is defined using the OMG MOF standard. The actual mappings are described using a model in this mapping language. Each of these models maps an element in the modeling language to a set of elements in the DI language. This information can then be used by an application of this mapping language that interprets the mappings and applies them to actual model data.

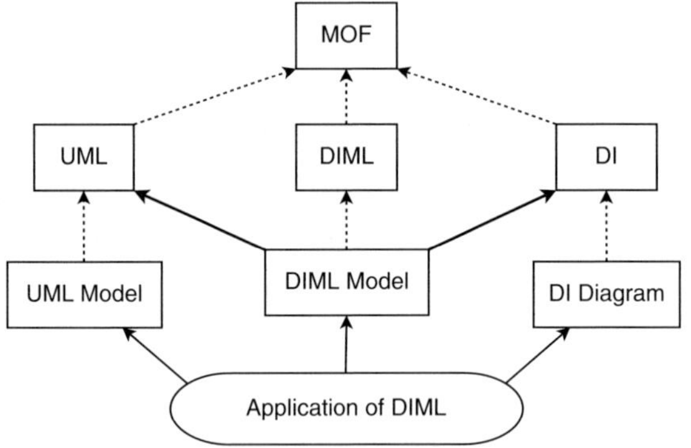

Fig. 1. Overview of the mapping between models and diagrams

There are three main applications of this mapping language:

Definition of UML and other languages: It can be used simply as documentation to complement the existing UML standards. We consider that the current UML 2.0 standard should be extended to include precise definitions of the valid UML 2.0 diagrams using the DI standard.

Creation of new DI diagrams: Another obvious application of the language is to generate new DI diagrams based on abstract models. This step may be necessary, e.g., after reverse engineering source code into a UML model or converting models from one modeling language to another. Existing modeling tools may use a different language than DI to represent diagrams internally. However, these tools may need to create diagrams into DI in order to interoperate with other modeling tools using the OMG standards.

Reconciliation of diagram and models: The most ambitious application of the mappings is to reconcile changes in an abstract model into an existing diagram. In this case, the mappings should be applied incrementally, preserving existing diagram information such as layout and colors when possible. This application is also the most demanding since it needs to be fast enough to be used in interactive model editors.

2.1 The UML 2.0 Diagram Interchange

We assume that a model is organized as an object graph that is an instance of a metamodel. Each node in this graph is an instance of a metaclass and each edge is an instance of a meta-association as defined in a metamodel. The UML metamodel contains more than 150 metaclasses such as *Actor*, *Class*, *Association* or *State* which describe the concepts that are familiar to UML practitioners. On the other hand, DI is a rather small language with only 22 metaclasses; a relevant subset of them is shown in Figure 2.

There are basically three main concepts in DI: *GraphNode*, *GraphEdge* and *SemanticModelBridge*. A *GraphNode* represents a rectangular shape in a diagram, such as a UML *Class* or an *Actor*, while a *GraphEdge* represents an edge between two other elements such as two nodes in a UML *Association* or a node and another edge such as in a UML *AssociationClass*. A *SemanticModelBridge* is used to establish a link between the semantic or abstract model and the diagrammatic model. For example, a *GraphNode* representing a UML *Class* is connected to that class using a SemanticModelBridge. There are two types of bridges. A *Uml1SemanticModelBridge* uses a directed link to an element, while a *SimpleSemanticModelElement* contains a string named *typeInfo*. These concepts are explained in more detail in the DI standard.

Figure 3 shows an example of a fragment of a UML model and its diagrammatic representation using DI. The top part of the figure is a simple UML statemachine model with two states and one transition, presented as a UML object diagram. From this object diagram we can see that this DI model contains elements necessary for displaying and layouting information retrieved from the UML model. To simplify the figure, we have omitted some UML and DI elements. Especially, we do not show the Uml1SemanticModelBridge elements but merely a directed link between DI graph elements and the UML elements. We should also note that we show the links that correspond to composition associations using a black diamond. Although this notation is not defined in the UML standard it is useful for the purposes of this article.

Finally, the bottom part of the figure shows the same DI model rendered as an image, in this particular case as Encapsulated Postscript. This image was created by a tool based on the information contained in the UML model, such as the name of the states, the DI model, such as the layout of the states, and built-in knowledge about the UML notation for state machines, such as the fact that a state is represented as a rectangle with rounded corners. Nothing prevents us from rendering the diagram to another graphical format such as SVG.

2.2 DIML: From Models to Diagrams

We have seen in the previous example that the DI provides us with the basic metaclasses that can be combined to create diagrams. However, neither the UML standard nor DI

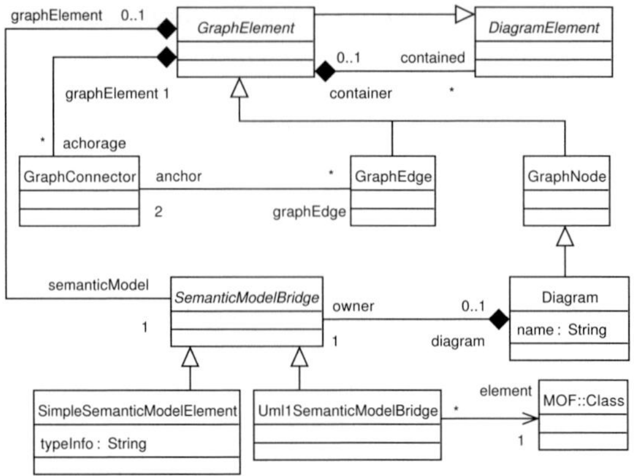

Fig. 2. A subset of the DI metamodel

tell us what metaclasses we should use to create a specific diagram to represent a specific model. As we have seen in the example, this task is not trivial since each UML model element is represented using many DI elements and the mapping between the model element and its diagram representation is arbitrary. This in turn complicates the

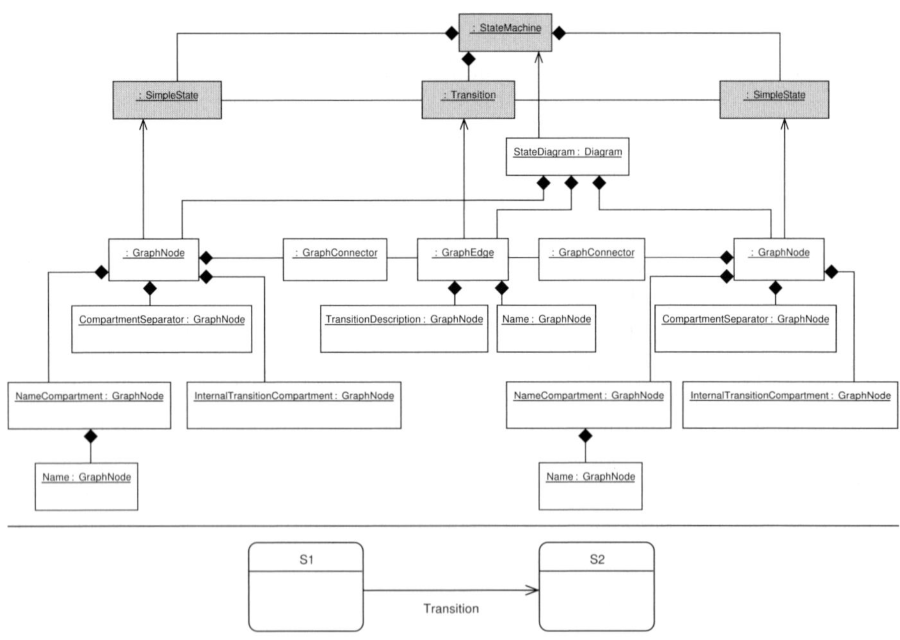

Fig. 3. (Top) UML model in gray with two SimpleStates and a Transition and its diagram representation in DI. (Bottom) DI diagram rendered using the UML concrete syntax.

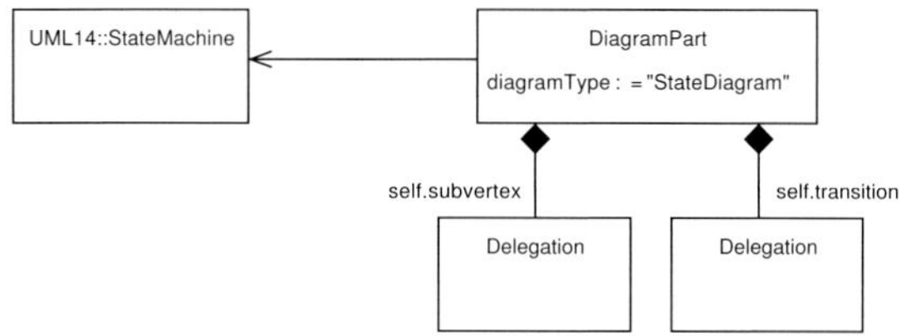

Fig. 4. The DI mapping rule of StateMachines

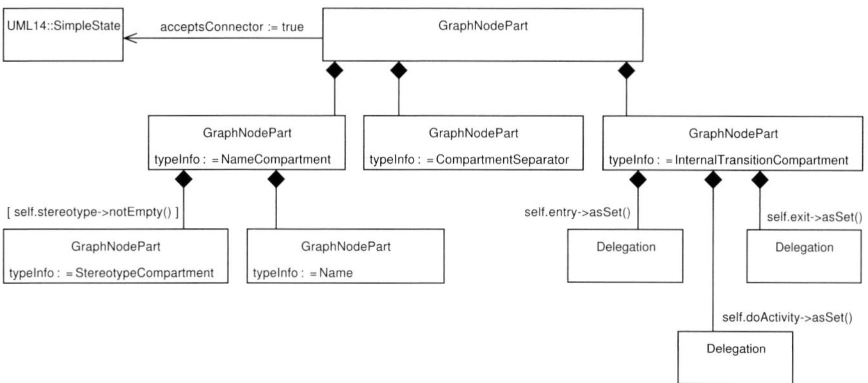

Fig. 5. The DI mapping rule of SimpleState

interchange of DI diagrams between modeling tools, as diagrams created by one tool may not be compatible with the diagrams the other tool creates. Full compatibility can be ensured only if the tools use the same definitions for creating the diagrams.

To address this issue, we have created a language called the Diagram Interchange Mapping Language (DIML). Its purpose is to define mappings between metaclasses in MOF-based modeling languages, such as UML, and corresponding elements in the DI language. We can see three example DIML models for UML StateMachines, SimpleStates and Transitions shown in Figures 4, 5 and 6 respectively. It must be noted that we have simplified the structure of StateMachines for the purposes of this article. In the figures, an abstract element on the left is mapped to a hierarchy of diagram elements as DIML *Parts*. Each Part, shown as rectangles, maps to a GraphNode, GraphEdge or Diagram in DI. The directed arrow corresponds to the mapping concept, whereas the edges with black diamonds correspond to parameterized element ownership based on *guard* and *selection* statements. The hierarchy forms a skeleton which when transformed into DI elements give us the intended result.

An example of the application of these three mappings was seen in Figure 3. The topmost part of the figure (colored gray) shows a StateMachine with two SimpleStates and one Transition. When the mapping for UML StateMachines (Figure 4) is applied to the StateMachine, a DI Diagram will be created. When the mapping for UML SimpleStates (Figure 5) is applied to the SimpleStates and the mapping for UML Transitions (Fig-

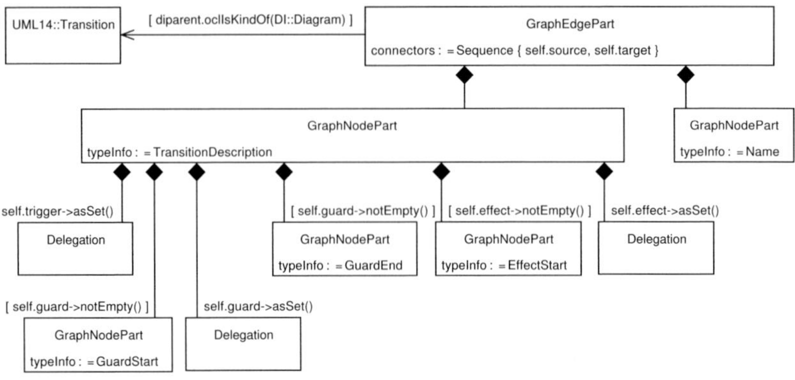

Fig. 6. The DI mapping rule of Transition

ure 6) is applied to the Transition, DI elements will be created for these UML elements. Finally, these DI elements will be connected to the Diagram. As a result, the DI model shown in the middle of the figure is obtained. By comparing the DIML models to the actual diagram, we see that not all DIML Parts are represented in the resulting diagram. For example, there is no *StereotypeCompartment* for the SimpleStates. This is an example of the parameterization; since the SimpleStates had no abstract Stereotype elements, the guard "self.stereotype–>notEmpty()" in the DIML model failed and thus no StereotypeCompartment was created.

3 Metamodel and Semantics

This section discusses the concepts we have used in creating DIML and the semantics of the language metaclasses. It is important to notice the separation between the DIML language itself and the various applications of the DIML language. While the main use of DIML is to define diagrams using the OMG standards, DIML does not define or enforce any particular method for applying these mappings on model data. Assuming that a DIML mapping is correct, any tool is still allowed to maintain the abstract model and concrete models in any way it wants as long as the end result is correct, i.e., as if it had used DIML. This *as if* rule is well-known from for example C compiler technology and gives implementations the greatest leeway while still retaining compatibility between implementations.

This separation enables us to concentrate on acquiring a usable mapping language and its semantics, while leaving the actual applications of DIML as a separate concern for modeling tools. In our opinion this separation works favorably for both standardization as well as enabling competing implementations.

3.1 The Basics of the Metamodel

The metamodel for the DIML mapping language is shown in Figure 7. In the figure, *MOF::Class* represents the type of any metaclass, not just UML metaclasses. The

OCL::OclExpression refers to any OCL expression. OCL is a language for creating arbitrary queries on models. It can be used to collect some elements from models or to assert that certain properties hold in a model.

The *MappingModel* is a simple container metaclass to collect all the mappings as children under instances of it. Every DIML model must have one MappingModel as its root element. An *ElementToDIMapping* element *m* is a description of mapping one abstract element of type *m.element* to corresponding DI elements. Thereby the three mappings for StateMachine, SimpleState and Transition from Figures 4, 5 and 6 have been used to create several DI tree fragments as shown by triangles in Figure 8, yielding the final DI diagram in Figure 3.

Every mapping is considered in the specific context of the *diparent* variable. It is the parent element in the DI model. It is guaranteed to exist for any *GraphNode* or *GraphEdge* except for Diagram, which has no DI parent. It can be used in OCL expressions to verify that the DI parent element is the one expected by the mapping.

In Figures 4, 5 and 6, the ElementToDIMapping elements are denoted by directed arrows and the Contained elements are the composition links. There can be two different

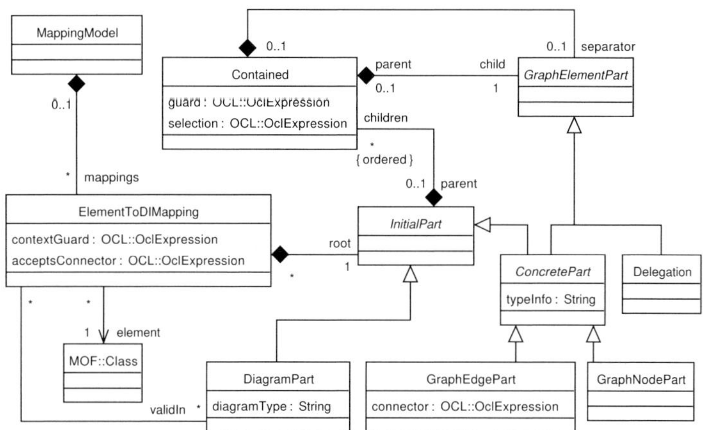

Fig. 7. The DIML metamodel

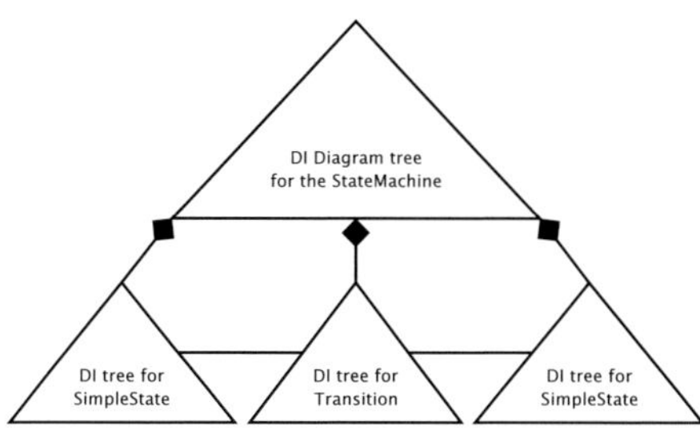

Fig. 8. DI fragments created by the DIML mappings are combined into the final DI diagram

text strings next to those links; a text in brackets is a *guard* expression, and a text without brackets is a *selection* expression. We will explain these and the *contextGuard*, *acceptsConnector* and *validIn* properties later.

3.2 DIML Tree

A DIML tree consists of an InitialPart as its root, and a hierarchy of Contained and GraphElementPart (and its subclasses) elements. Leaves in the tree are either of type Delegation or have no *children* Contained elements. The purpose of a DIML tree is to describe a parameterized skeleton which can be used to compute a resulting DI tree. Parameterization here means that the occurrence and recurrence of child GraphElementParts is determined by the slot values in *Contained.guard* and *Contained.selection*.

The DIML tree can be computed in the context of an InitialPart *i*, its current abstract elements *a* and its *diparent*. For every Contained element *c* in the *children* slot of the InitialPart, we must do the following:

- Evaluate *c.guard* in the context of *a* and with *diparent* as its parameter. If it does not hold, we must proceed to the next Contained element.
- Evaluate *c.selection* in the context of *a* and with *diparent* as its parameter. The expression must return an OCL collection *s* of abstract elements. For each element *e* in *s*, the *c.child* GraphElementPart is *accepted* in the context of *e* as the abstract element, and *i* as its *diparent*.
- If *c.separator* is non-empty, it denotes a DIML subtree with corresponding DI elements that must be placed between each accepted element. This enables us to easily model the very common occurrence of having a simple separator between values, such as a comma sign between the parameters in an operation in a UML class diagram.

Here, accepting means that the same computation must be performed on the new child DIML element if the child is a ConcretePart. Delegation elements on the other hand arise from the need to decouple the representation and computation of individual DIML trees. If the new child DIML elements is a Delegation, we must search for a new valid mapping for the abstract element *e*. At most one mapping can be valid simultaneously for any given context. If no mapping is valid, the element is ignored and cannot be mapped to DI in the given context. Once a valid mapping is found, DIML tree creation can begin in the context of a new current abstract element and *diparent*. The corresponding DI elements of the parent DIML tree and the child DIML tree are then connected together at the place of the Delegation element in the parent DIML tree.

The *guard* and *selection* expressions allow us to create a mapping to DI highly context-dependent on the abstract model element and all the other abstract model elements as well as the sequence of parents in the DI model. They, together with instances of ConcretePart and Delegation are the primary means to represent a collection of similar DI fragments (modulo the parameterization) as one DIML tree.

3.3 Support for Diagrams

A mapping *m* of a diagram is such that *m.root* is a *DiagramPart* element *r*, with *r.diagramType* denoting what diagram type is being considered (e.g. “ClassDiagram”).

The *m.contextGuard* is evaluated and must return true. It is an OCL expression which receives the abstract element and *diparent* (which in this case is a null pointer/reference) as its parameters. It can be used to limit whether or not it is allowed to create a diagram for the given abstract element.

The *m.validIn* slot is unused and must be empty. The *m.acceptsConnector* is unused. Starting at *r*, the DIML tree can be described.

3.4 Support for GraphNodes and GraphEdges

The mapping *m* for GraphNodes or GraphEdges is otherwise similar to the mapping for a Diagram, but with some small differences. The element *m.root* must either be a *GraphEdgePart* or a *GraphNodePart*, with *m.root.typeInfo* being the empty string.

The *m.contextGuard* must still hold, but the *diparent* will now be a valid DI element in the diagram. The set *m.validIn.diagramType* denotes the valid diagram type set, e.g. { "ClassDiagram", "SequenceDiagram" }. This is the set of types of diagrams in which the mapping can be applied. Although technically the validIn information could be embedded in the contextGuard, it is more convenient to have a set of diagrams where a mapping can be applied because a) it avoids unnecessarily long OCL expressions in the contextGuard, and b) the information about suitable diagrams is easier to extract from a slot made for that purpose rather than extract it by parsing an OCL expression. Again, starting at *m.root*, the DIML tree can be described.

3.5 Correspondence of DIML Elements with DI

An instance *p* of DiagramPart, GraphEdgePart or GraphNodePart corresponds to an instance of the DI elements Diagram, GraphEdge or GraphNode *d*, respectively.

A Diagram has a SimpleSemanticModelElement *s* in its *semanticModel* slot such that *p.diagramType* = *s.typeInfo*, and a Uml1SemanticModelBridge in its *owner* slot which points to the abstract element for which the diagram was created for. A GraphEdge or GraphNode has either a Uml1SemanticModelBridge or a SimpleSemanticModelElement. If *p.typeInfo* is empty, *d* must have a Uml1SemanticModelBridge which points to the abstract element. Otherwise, *d* must have a child element *s* of type SimpleSemanticModelElement such that *p.typeInfo* = *s.typeInfo*.

3.6 Connecting Edges to GraphConnectors

The *connector* expression is evaluated in the context of the corresponding abstract element and receives the GraphEdge as an additional parameter. For an instance *p* of GraphEdgePart, *p.connector* describes the expression that when evaluated results in a sequence of abstract elements. For each element *e* in the sequence, a *GraphConnector* is created (or must already exist) and anchored to the GraphEdge corresponding to *p*. The owner of the GraphConnector must then be found in the set of all GraphElements in the same diagram whose corresponding abstract element is *e*. This GraphElement must correspond to a root ConcretePart in an ElementToDIMapping *m* mapping such that *m.acceptsConnector* is satisfied. The *acceptsConnector* expression does not receive any parameters.

Although this scheme sounds complicated, it or similar functionality is required since not all GraphElements may be connected to and the only distinguishing mark is the context. In our work, this context is provided by the different ElementToDIMappings.

3.7 Limitations

Having explained the semantics of DIML, we must also be concerned about its limitations. The main idea of the DIML language can be stated in three assumptions or limitations, depending on the point of view. First, that our diagrams can be built top-down, i.e., starting from the DI Diagram element, child elements can be transitively connected to form a complete diagram without any changes required in their parents during diagram construction. This means that a parent DI element does not depend on what child DI elements exist underneath it. This is emphasized by the Delegation elements in the DIML models; the decoupling they provide allows us to mix several kinds of diagrams together. Although the various OCL expressions have access to the chain of parents, they cannot modify them since OCL is a side-effect free query language, and in our semantics of DIML they would nevertheless not be allowed to modify them.

Second, that an abstract element can be mapped into a DIML tree with a single root element. The exact contents of this tree may depend on the context of the abstract element as well as any transitive parent DI elements. In general, by using arbitrary OCL expressions in the DIML models the tree can be dependent on any parts of the abstract model or any DI parents. It must be emphasized that the *Contained.selection* allows us to navigate the abstract model from the current abstract element via several associations to other abstract model elements. Thus the mapping language is not limited to the structure of the abstract model regardless of the metamodel of that abstract model empowering us to create very versatile DI models. However, this second limitation means that the links between elements cannot be mapped to DI elements. Although we have not needed such a construct, it is nevertheless an important omission. Improvements to DIML or similar mapping languages should adress this.

Third, that there are rules describing how to connect these trees together to form the final, complete DI tree. This has been accomplished using the Delegation elements.

4 Validation of the DIML Language

We have built an experimental open source modeling tool called Coral that uses the DI and simplified DIML mappings to represent and maintain model diagrams. We have implemented a component for this tool that reconciles models and diagrams after executing model transformations or performing editing operations [2, 17], based on the abstract model and the DIML mappings.

The guards of the rules in the simplified DIML mapping language use a very reduced version of OCL. This is done for performance reasons. Instead of allowing complete OCL queries that could require the traversal of the whole model, we allow the checking of single property values in the *Contained.guard* and a subset (or subsequence) of a property value in the *Contained.selection*. This restriction has enabled us to perform reconciliation of models and diagrams using linear algorithms with very few exceptions, while still being able to support large and complex languages such as UML. This ensures that diagram reconciliation is not an expensive operation, and hence it is fast enough to be integrated with an interactive model editor; our implementation is of sufficient speed for interactive editing. We consider that the simplified language serves the purposes we have outlined in Section 2, but we acknowledge that the language proposed in this paper is more general.

We have implemented mappings for the UML 1.4 class, statechart, object, use case and deployment diagrams but we are confident that the DIML language can be used to define mappings for other UML diagrams. The mappings we have used for UML in the Coral tool are available in [17]. From these mappings we can see that by using Delegation elements and DIML tree parameterization extensively, we have been able to support all the above mentioned UML diagrams.

The Coral tool supports other user-defined modeling languages and profiles besides UML. We have used DIML to define the concrete syntax of MICAS, a domain-specific modeling language to define peripherals for mobile phones [16]. This example shows that DIML is viable to define the concrete syntax of DSM languages that are different from UML. Coral can be downloaded from `http://mde.abo.fi/`.

5 Related Work and Conclusions

In this paper we have studied a mapping language between the abstract syntax or semantic representation of a modeling language and its concrete syntax as a diagram. Beyond the scope of this paper is anything regarding diagrams that does not relate to the creation or reconciliation of DI diagrams. This includes the layout of diagrams and the rendering of a diagram to an output device.

We have validated our approach by constructing an experimental tool and exchanging UML models and their diagrams with a commercial modeling tool that supports DI. This allows us to conclude that the work presented in this article is a viable approach to define the concrete syntax of visual modeling languages based on the OMG standards. At the moment, the OMG does not have a Request For Proposals for a general mapping or transformation language from abstract models to DI diagrams. We consider such a language important for interoperability reasons and hope that this article will spur further discussion on the topic.

Several authors have addressed the issue of defining the concrete syntax of modeling languages. The Penguins system by Sitt Sen Chok and Kim Marriot [6] is based on the intelligent diagram metaphor and uses constraint multiset grammars to map the concrete syntax of a diagram to the abstract syntax of a model. This differs from DIML where we have a unidirectional mapping from the abstract to the concrete syntax. While the authors show that their approach can be used to define the semantics of a diagram, it is unclear whether a similar approach could be applied in the context of DI. There are several reasons for this, the most important of which is that DI uses Uml1SemanticModelBridges to relate to the abstract syntax and to determine how to render the objects to an image. That is, using DI it is implicit that the abstract model exists prior to a diagram, which is not the case in the Penguins system. Péter Domokos and Dániel Varró [8] use model transformation rules for transforming the abstract syntax into their own language for drawing primitives representing the concrete syntax of models. This approach, however, involves several off-line transformations between intermediate models, which in turn makes diagram reconciliation difficult to achieve. The work by Frédéric Fondement and Thomas Baar [11] formalizes the relationship between abstract and concrete syntaxes with OCL expressions using their own concrete syntax. While the ideas presented are interesting, it does not yet have any tool support and although diagram reconciliation is recognized as a problem, the authors do not offer any solution. In fact, our work addresses some of their concerns on DI.

The ATLAS Model Weaver (AMW) [10] uses special weaving models to map one modeling language to another, in order to create mappings between models in these modeling languages. This weaving model can then be used for generating model transformations. As this approach is generic, it should technically be possible to describe the DIML mappings using AMW. However, it is still unclear how the DIML Delegation elements would be expressed in AMW.

It can be argued that DIML is simply a specific-purpose model transformation language and that the mapping between models and diagrams can be expressed using existing general-purpose model transformation languages. Many model transformation languages have been developed and researched. Examples are the relational approach by David Akehurst and Stuart Kent [1], and Octavian Patrascoiu's YATL [23], both of which use OCL for the declarative expressions. The relational approach is further investigated by Hausmann and Kent in [12]. There is also a special graph transformation / graph grammar system in VIATRA by Dániel Varró [25], which relies on graph grammars instead of OCL and has operational semantics. Also the MOLA transformation language [13] by Audris Kalnins, Janis Barzdins and Edgars Celms has a graphical imperative programming language with pattern-based transformation rules. Perhaps the most important general-purpose transformation language is the Query-View-Transform (QVT) [19] language from OMG.

We are not proposing that DIML be used as a general-purpose transformation language. There are several limitations in it, but nevertheless we find that a domain-specific transformation language brings benefits. It might be easier for users of the transformation language to understand and use, and it certainly is easier to define the transformation rules, although it is clear that an implementation might wish to use its underlying general-purpose transformation technology and display a simplified version (i.e., the mappings shown here) to the user. We firmly believe that there should and will be different transformation languages for models, just as there are different transformation languages for text files, such as `sed`, `awk` and `perl`.

We have not found transformation technologies that specifically address transforming between abstract and concrete models using the DI standard. This is unfortunate because it also makes comparison more difficult as the differences between the diagram languages themselves must be taken into account. Otherwise, in [5, 15], Audris Kalnins et al. show a diagram definition facility which extends the presentational metamodel for every concept that needs to be displayed from the abstract metamodel. This seems complicated in light of the DI standard which is a static metamodel. Additionally there is no explanation on how to declare restrictions on the mappings, which we have solved using OCL expressions, and abstract elements seem to simply map to exactly one concrete element, which is not true for DI.

Acknowledgments

Marcus Alanen would like to acknowledge the financial support of the Nokia Foundation.

References

1. D. H. Akehurst and S. Kent. A Relational Approach to Defining Transformations in a Metamodel. In J.-M. Jézéquel, H. Hussmann, and S. Cook, editors, *Proc. UML 2002 - The Unified Modeling Language. Model Engineering, Languages, Concepts, and Tools. 5th International Conference, Dresden, Germany*, volume 2460 of *LNCS*, pages 243–258. Springer, 2002.
2. Marcus Alanen, Torbjörn Lundkvist, and Ivan Porres. Reconciling Diagrams After Executing Model Transformations. In *Proceedings of the 21st Annual ACM Symposium on Applied Computing (SAC 2006)*, Dijon, France, April 2006.
3. R. Bardohl, H. Ehrig, J. de Lara, and G. Taentzer. Integrating Meta Modelling with Graph Transformation for Efficient Visual Language Definition and Model Manipulation. In Springer, editor, *Proceedings of the Fundamental Aspects of Software Engineering, 7th Intl. Conference, FASE 2004*, pages 214–228, 2004.
4. J. Bézivin. On the Unification Power of Models. *Springer Journal on Software and Systems Modeling*, 3(4), 2004.
5. Edgars Celms, Audris Kalnins, and Lelde Lace. Diagram Definition Facilities Based on Metamodel Mappings, October 2003. Invited talk at the Third OOPSLA Workshop on Domain-Specific Modeling.
6. Sitt Sen Chok and Kim Marriott. Automatic Generation of Intelligent Diagram Editors. *ACM Transactions Computer-Human Interaction*, 10(3):244–276, 2003.
7. J. de Lara and H. Vangheluwe. Using Meta-Modelling and Graph Grammars to Process GPSS Models. *Electronic Notes in Theoretical Computer Science*, 72(3), 2003.
8. Péter Domokos and Dániel Varró. An Open Visualization Framework for Metamodel-Based Modeling Languages. In Tom Mens, Andy Schürr, and Gabriele Taentzer, editors, *Proc. GraBaTs 2002, International Workshop on Graph-Based Tools*, volume 72 of *ENTCS*, pages 78–87, Barcelona, Spain, October 7–8 2002. Elsevier.
9. Karsten Ehrig, Claudia Ermel, Stefan Hänsgen, and Gabriele Taentzer. Towards Graph Transformation Based Generation of Visual Editors Using Eclipse. *Electronic Notes in Theoretical Computer Science*, 127(4):127–143, 2005.
10. Marcos Didonet Del Fabro, Jean Bzivin, Frdric Jouault, Erwan Breton, and Guillaume Gueltas. AMW: A Generic Model Weaver. In *Proceedings of the 1re Journe sur l'Ingnierie Dirige par les Modles (IDM05)*, 2005.
11. Frédéric Fondement and Thomas Baar. Making Metamodels Aware of Concrete Syntax. In *European Conference on Model Driven Architecture (ECMDA)*, volume 3748 of *LNCS*, pages 190 – 204, 2005.
12. Jan Hendrik Hausmann and Stuart Kent. Visualizing model mappings in UML. In *SoftVis '03: Proceedings of the 2003 ACM symposium on Software visualization*, pages 169–178, New York, NY, USA, 2003. ACM Press.
13. Audris Kalnins, Janis Barzdins, and Edgars Celms. Basics of Model Transformation Language MOLA. In *Workshop on Model Transformation and Execution in the Context of MDA (ECOOP 2004)*, June 2004.
14. Oliver Köth and Mark Minas. Structure, Abstraction, and Direct Manipulation in Diagram Editors. *LNCS*, 2317:290–304, 2002.

15. Lelde Lace, Edgars Celms, and Audris Kalnins. Diagram Definition Facilities in a Generic Modeling Tool. In *International Conference on Modelling and Simulation of Business systems*, pages 220–224, 2003.
16. Johan Lilius, Tomas Lillqvist, Torbjörn Lundkvist, Ian Oliver, Ivan Porres, Kim Sandström, Glenn Sveholm, and Asim Pervez Zaka. An Architecture Exploration Environment for System on Chip Design. *Nordic Journal of Computing*, 2006. To appear.
17. Torbjörn Lundkvist. Diagram Reconciliation and Interchange in a Modeling Tool. Master's Thesis in Computer Science, Department of Computer Science, Åbo Akademi University, Turku, Finland, November 2005.
18. K. Marriot and B. Meyer. *Visual Language Theory*. Springer, 1998.
19. OMG. MOF 2.0 Query / View / Transformation Final Adopted Specification. OMG Document ptc/05-11-01, available at www.omg.org, 2005.
20. OMG. UML 2.0 Superstructure Specification, August 2005. Document formal/05-07-04. Available at `http://www.omg.org/`.
21. OMG. Unified Modeling Language: Diagram Interchange version 2.0, June 2005. OMG document ptc/05-06-04. Available at `http://www.omg.org`.
22. OMG. Meta Object Facility (MOF) Core Specification, version 2.0, January 2006. Document formal/06-01-01, available at `http://www.omg.org/`.
23. Octavian Patrascoiu. YATL:Yet Another Transformation Language. In *Proceedings of the 1st European MDA Workshop, MDA-IA*, pages 83–90. University of Twente, the Nederlands, January 2004.
24. Guus Ramackers. OMG issue 7663. `http://www.omg.org/issues/issue7663.txt`.
25. Dániel Varró. Automatic Program Generation for and by Model Transformation Systems. In Hans-Jörg Kreowski and Peter Knirsch, editors, *Proc. AGT 2002: Workshop on Applied Graph Transformation*, pages 161–173, Grenoble, France, April 12–13 2002.

Basic Operations over Models Containing Subset and Union Properties

Marcus Alanen and Ivan Porres

TUCS Turku Centre for Computer Science
Department of Information Technologies,
Åbo Akademi University
Lemminkäisenkatu 14, FIN-20520 Turku, Finland
{marcus.alanen, ivan.porres}@abo.fi

Abstract. The Meta Object Facility 2.0 and Unified Modeling Language 2.0 Infrastructure standards present novel metamodeling constructs called subset and union properties. However, they do not provide a complete definition of these constructs. This definition is necessary to construct modeling tools and to ensure their interoperability. In this article, we present the basic model operations over models containing subset and union properties. These operations are formalized using pre- and postconditions using substitutability as the main criterion for language specialization.

Keywords: subset and derived properties, metamodeling, MOF, UML.

1 Introduction

The purpose of the Unified Modeling Language (UML) 2.0 Infrastructure [16] is to define the Meta Object Facility (MOF) 2.0 [15] and the UML 2.0 Superstructure [14]. It introduces several new concepts not present in MOF 1.x or UML 1.x, mainly: *subset* properties, *derived union* properties and property *redefinitions*. These concepts are useful to define a new modeling language as an extension of an existing one. Unfortunately, very little is told in [15,16] about the actual meaning of these new constructs. This is a critical omission since these concepts are heavily used in the definition of the UML 2.0 Superstructure and are necessary to enable interoperability between software modeling tools, including model editors and model transformation tools.

In this article, we discuss the basic operations to edit models containing subsets and union properties and formalize them using pre- and postconditions. These basic operations are the elemental building blocks for a model repository supporting interactive model editors for UML and model transformation engines for languages such as QVT [13]. Although this article only presents a theoretical framework, we believe it contains important implications for the practical implementation of model repositories for UML 2.0.

We proceed as follows. Section 2 briefly presents a set-theoretic formalization of a metamodeling language that supports the new subset properties of MOF 2.0 and the UML 2.0 Infrastructure. The main contribution of the article is in Section 3, where the basic edit operations are discussed in detail. Finally, we discuss related work in Section 4 while Section 5 contains some concluding remarks.

O. Nierstrasz et al. (Eds.): MoDELS 2006, LNCS 4199, pp. 469–483, 2006.

2 A Simple Metamodeling Language

The main concepts used in metamodeling are classes and properties. A class represents a concept in a modeling language such as a UML Use Case or a Transition in a Statechart, while a property represents a feature of such a concept such as the fact that a Use Case has a name or a Transition has an event trigger.

As an example, the left part of Figure 1 shows a metamodel for a graph. This diagram shows two classes: *Vertex* and *Edge*, and four properties: *from*, *to*, *outgoing* and *incoming*. Each property has another property as its opposite. Together they define an association that is represented as a single line. In the example, we have the *from-outgoing* and the *to-incoming* associations. At the model layer, this bidirectionality means that when a *Vertex v* has an *Edge e* in its *outgoing* slot, the *Edge e* will have *Vertex v* in its *from* slot. The right side of Figure 1 shows an example model represented as an object diagram where each object is an instance of a class in the metamodel.

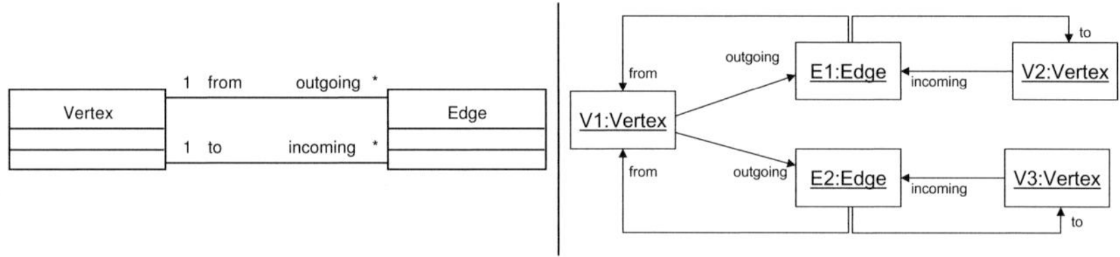

Fig. 1. (Left) Metamodel for a Graph; (Right) Example Model

MOF 2.0 also provides three main extension mechanisms for metamodels: class specialization, property subsets and unions, and property redefinitions. Class specialization is identical to class inheritance in object-oriented languages. A specialized class inherits all the properties of its base classes and can also define new properties. Subset and union properties are a mechanism to define the relationship between the properties in a specialized class and its base classes. Finally, property redefinition allows us to replace a property with another "compatible" one; however, compatibility is not precisely defined.

We can use specialization and subset properties to create a new metamodel in Figure 2 for a bipartite graph for our running example. The classes *Blue Vertex* and *Red Vertex* will now be specializations of *Vertex*. Also, the *fromRed* and *toBlue* properties will become subsets of the *from* and *to* properties, and similarly for the other properties. An example model is also shown in the figure. This metamodel is based on an example presented in [18]. The reader can find many complex examples of the use of subset and union properties in the UML 2.0 standards.

The intuition behind the metamodel is as follows: an element of type *Red Vertex* has four slots that correspond to properties *outgoing*, *incoming*, *outgoingRB* and *incomingBR*. Elements of type *Edge* can be inserted into the *outgoing* or *incoming* slot and elements of type *RedBlue Edge* can also be inserted into *outgoingRB*. At any moment, the contents of the slot *outgoingRB* should be a subset of the contents of the slot *outgoing*.

The benefit of subsets in the running example is that graph traversal algorithms which worked on the initial metamodel in Fig. 1 should still work for bipartite graphs when

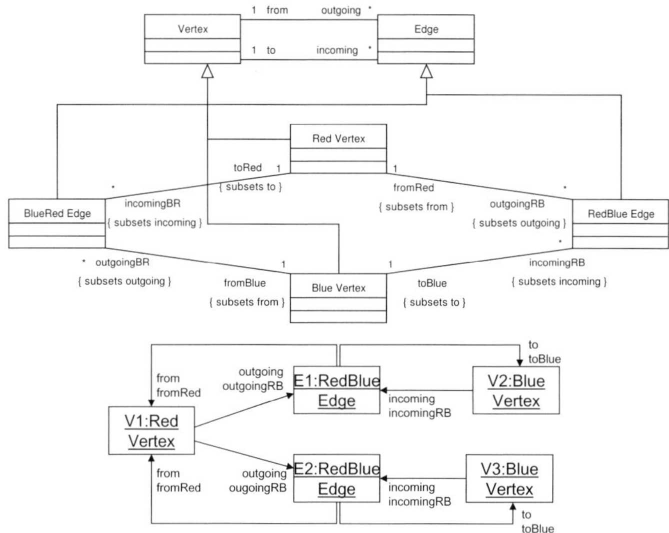

Fig. 2. (Top) Metamodel for a Bipartite Graph as an Extension of the Metamodel for a General Graph. (Bottom) Example Model for the Graph Metamodel.

using the metamodel in Fig. 2, and that if we only use elements from the bipartite graph metamodel, we can also be certain that the model describes a bipartite graph.

Our metamodeling language should support multiple inheritance since it is used extensively in MOF, as has been noticed by e.g. Anneke Kleppe [11]. Multiple inheritance forms very complicated inheritance hierarchies, among them the *diamond inheritance* structure. This leads to a possibility where property subsetting also has a diamond (or even more complicated) structure.

Union properties are the last extension mechanism presented in MOF 2.0 which we will discuss in this paper. If a property is subsetted by other properties, we say that it is a union property. It is not necessary to declare a property as a union, since a designer of a metamodel cannot know in advance if a new subset property will be defined in the future. The UML 2.0 Infrastructure also introduced the concept of derived union. According to page 126 of [16], a derived union property can be seen as the strict union of its subsets. A slot with a property that is a derived union cannot contain elements that do not appear in any of its subsets. Another way to define derived content is to create an arbitrary query operation. This has been done in the Eclipse Modeling Framework using so called *volatile* attributes as explained in [7]. This way, the contents of a slot are defined by evaluating the associated query. The drawback is that there is no strict mathematical relationship between the derived property and any other properties. The benefit is that it does not restrict the metamodel creator in any way.

2.1 Metamodels

Based on the previous discussion, we can now present a simple metamodeling language that contains the core concepts of MOF and UML 2.0. We describe all metamodels as the tuple $MM = (C, P, generalizations, properties, characteristics)$, where C is a set of classes, P a set of properties and $C \cap P = \emptyset$. We define the generalizations of a class with the function $generalizations : C \to \mathcal{P}(C)$. We ignore classes that represent primitive datatypes such as integers, strings and enumeration values without loss of generality. We denote by $\subseteq_c$ the extended generalization between classes that is defined as the reflexive transitive closure of the generalization relation: $\subseteq_c \stackrel{\text{def}}{=} \{(c_1, c_2) \cdot c_2 \in generalizations(c_1)\}^*$. It is a partially ordered set under the assumption that the generalization graph is acyclic.

The properties of a class is given by the function $properties : C \to \mathcal{P}(P)$. Every value of the function *properties* is a disjoint subset of P. Thus, we can define $owner : P \to C$ which denotes the unique owner c of a property p where $p \in properties(c)$. The effective properties of a class are those defined by the class itself and transitively by any of its generalizations.

Finally, the characteristics of a property represent constraints for the elements that can be contained in a slot of that property. We define $characteristics \stackrel{\text{def}}{=} (lower, upper, opposite, ordered, composite, derived, supersets)$ as a tuple of functions detailing the properties further. The multiplicity constraints is defined by $lower : P \to \mathbb{Z}^{0+} \setminus \infty$ and $upper : P \to \mathbb{Z}^+$. Each property has an opposite property represented by $opposite : P \to P$ that is a bijective function. The opposite of a property cannot be itself but every property is the opposite of its opposite. The function $ordered : P \to \mathbb{B}$ is true if a property is ordered. For example the parameters in an operation should be ordered. The function $composite : P \to \mathbb{B}$ is true if a property is composite. For example, the property that represents the contents of a package is a composite, since a package owns its contents. Finally, there are two characteristics that represent the new property mechanism: $derived : P \to \mathbb{B}$ is true if a property is a derived union while $supersets : P \to \mathcal{P}(P)$ represents the set of properties of which a property is a subset. The graph representing the property superset relation $(P, \{(p1, p2) \cdot p_2 \in supersets(p_1)\})$ must be acyclic.

For convenience, we define the function $subsets : P \to \mathcal{P}(P)$ as the inverse of supersets. We denote subsetting between properties by the $\subseteq_p$ relation, i.e., $\subseteq_p \stackrel{\text{def}}{=} \{(p, q) \cdot q \in supersets(p)\}^*$. We define $a \subset b \stackrel{\text{def}}{=} a \subseteq b \wedge a \neq b$ for both $\subset_c$ and $\subset_p$. Finally, we denote by $s \prec t$ that s is a direct subset of t, i.e., $s \prec t \stackrel{\text{def}}{=} s \subset t \wedge \neg(\exists u \cdot s \subset u \subset t)$. The expression $s \,||\, t$ is defined as $\neg(s \subseteq t) \wedge \neg(t \subseteq s)$, i.e., there is no order defined between s and t.

The notable omission is that we cannot describe nonuniqueness (i.e., bags) with the above definitions. This characteristics exists in UML/MOF but our current formalization cannot cope with it. With some modifications, our framework could understand unordered bags, but ordered bags would still be an issue.

2.2 Models

We define $\mathcal{M} = \{M \cdot M = (E, type, slots, S, property, elements)\}$ as the infinite set of all models in our framework. M comprises all the models in a system at some specific time. E is a finite set of elements and S is a finite set of slots. Each element in E has a type defined by a class in a metamodel, $type : E \to C$, and a set of slots defined by the function $slots : E \to \mathcal{P}(S)$. Every value of the function *slots* is a disjoint subset of S. Thus, we can define $slotowner : S \to E$ which denotes the unique owner e of a slot s where $s \in slots(e)$.

Each slot corresponds to a property as defined by the function $property : S \rightarrow P$. Slots consist of element references and the function $elements : S \rightarrow (E, \prec)$ returns a total ordered set of elements of its argument slot s if $ordered(property(s))$ is true, otherwise $elements : S \rightarrow \mathcal{P}(E)$ returns an unordered set of elements. A slot thus describes the connection from its owner element to the elements in the slot. There is no actual ordering defined between the elements in an ordered slot; they merely have an assigned position in it. An element cannot occur twice in a slot.

For convenience, we define the size of a slot to be the amount of elements in that slot: $(\forall s \in S \cdot \#s \stackrel{\text{def}}{=} \#elements(s)\ )$. For the elements of an ordered set, we say $s[i]$ to denote the element at the zero-based index i in the ordered set s.

Models are hierarchical structures based on composition properties. We define the function $parent : E \rightarrow \mathcal{P}(E)$ to return a set consisting of the parent element of the argument, if any, otherwise the empty set:

$$parent(e) \stackrel{\text{def}}{=} \{x \cdot x \in E \wedge (\exists s \in S \cdot s \in slots(x) \wedge composite(property(s)) \wedge e \in elements(s))\}$$

The slot subsetting relation is $\subseteq_s \stackrel{\text{def}}{=} \{(s,t) \cdot slotowner(s) = slotowner(t) \wedge property(s) \subseteq_P property(t)\}^*$. A slot s (transitively) subsetting another slot t is denoted by $s \subset_s t$.

By definition, if slot s is subsetting slot t, then the contents of s must be a subset of the contents of t. Also, MOF [15] tells us on page 56 that *"The slot's values are a subset of those for each slot it subsets."* For ordered slots, we also wish to preserve order, i.e., when elements occur in a specific order in s, they should occur in the same order in t, although t might contain more elements in between. We denote $a \prec_x b$ if element a precedes element b in a specific ordered slot x.

There are several constraints that must hold for any models, such as strong typing and at most one parent element for each element. We refer the interested reader to [1] for a more in-depth description of the constraints, but stress three novel constraints due to subsets and unions. The constraints also serve as an invariant which must be maintained by any operation on models.

- The contents of a derived slot is the union of the contents of its subset slots: $(\forall p \in P \cdot derived(p) \Rightarrow (\forall t \in S \cdot property(t) = p \Rightarrow elements(t) \setminus \bigcup\{elements(s) \cdot s \prec t\} = \emptyset))$
- The contents of any unordered slot must also exist in the contents of any superset slots: $(\forall s,t \in S \cdot s \subseteq t \wedge \neg ordered(t) \Rightarrow elements(s) \subseteq elements(t))$
- Similarly to unordered slots, the contents of any ordered slot must also exist in the contents of any superset slots. Additionally, the elements must occur in the same order: $(\forall x,y \in E, s,t \in S \cdot s \subseteq_s t \wedge x \in elements(s) \wedge y \in elements(s) \wedge x \prec_s y \wedge ordered(t) \Rightarrow x \in elements(t) \wedge y \in elements(t) \wedge x \prec_t y)$

These three constraints are specific to derived slots and to unordered and ordered slots with respect to property subsetting. We call them the *inherent subsetting rules*, or ISR.

2.3 Example

Based on the previous definitions, we can describe a part of Figure 2 in a little more detail in Figure 3. We explicitly show slots as filled black circles, and the subsetting relation as a solid line between the circles. We represent a slot visually higher up if it is subsetted by the (connected) slots below it. In the figure, we depict only elements *V1*,*V2* and *E1*. Element *V1* has two slots named *outgoing* and *outgoingRB* such that *outgoingRB* $\subset_s$ *outgoing*. The contents of *outgoingRB* is the set $\{E1\}$. As a consequence of the ISR constraint, the contents of *outgoing* also include *E1*. The slots *from* and *fromRed* are the opposite of outgoing and *outgoingRB* and, as a consequence, they link *E1* to *V1*. In the figure, we see four different partially ordered sets (posets) of slots as dashes ellipses. The first and second poset are isomorphic to each other (as well as the third and fourth) when only considering the slots and the subsetting relation, disregarding the elements they point to. This is always true, since property subsets always come in pairs of two isomorphic posets. Drawing a poset in this way is known as a Hasse diagram [10].

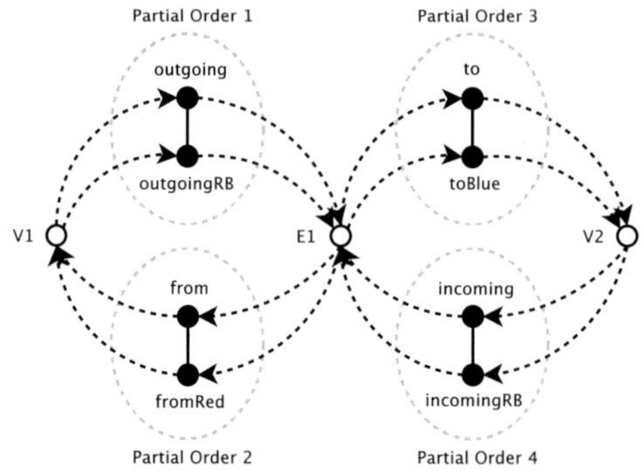

Fig. 3. Part of Figure 2 in More Detail

Let us assume that we want to perform some simple model transformations. The question is what elements should be created and removed from the model and what are the changes to the 8 slots depicted in the figure in order to accomplish these model transformations. We address this problem in the next section.

3 Basic Edit Operations for Models

In this section we present the basic operations to create and delete elements from models as well as to insert to or remove an element from a slot. These four operations are the basic edit operations for models that are necessary to implement a model repository and a model transformation system.

We should note that a valid model transformation usually involves a sequence of many basic operations. Also, one single basic edit operation can invalidate a slot with respect to the multiplicity constraints. Therefore, we consider a model transformation as a sequence of basic edit operations. As an example, let us assume that we want to create an association *A* between two classes *C1* and *C2* in a model based on a simplified UML with only classes and associations. This requires three basic operations: create *A*, connect *C1* with *A* and connect *C2* with *A*. The association *A* is invalid just after the create operation since an association should connect at least two classes. However, the model should be well-formed after executing all the basic operations.

We define these operations using a pre- and postcondition specification. We first describe element creation and deletion. Then, we describe the case of insertion into ordered or unordered slots and finally the case of removing elements from slots. The pre- and postconditions are described as separate enumerated clauses. All of the clauses in the precondition must hold for the operation to succeed, and all the clauses of the postcondition must be guaranteed by an implementation. For succinctness and understandability of presentation, we only describe the semantics of an operation in the context of one poset. When modifying a slot, similar actions must be taken for the slots in the opposite poset for bidirectionality to hold. This means that the actual operations must, where necessary, be augmented with an additional index parameter for the ordered slots in the opposite poset.

In any pre- or postcondition, the old models are denoted $M = (E, type, slots, S, property, elements)$. In postconditions, the new values of variables are denoted with tick marks. Thus, the new models are denoted $M' = (E', type', slots', S', property', elements')$.

3.1 Element Creation

The operation create : $\mathcal{M} \times C \rightarrow \mathcal{M} \times E$ such that $(M', e) = \text{create}(M, c)$ creates a new element of type $c \in C$ and has no preconditions. The new element will also be a root element, i.e., it will not have any parent. The returned value is a tuple of the new models and the new element. The primary postcondition is that there must be exactly one new element in the set of elements. The various model constraints mean that the sets and functions in M must be updated in M' to reflect this change; this leads to more postconditions.

1. $(\exists! e \in E' \cdot E' \setminus \{e\} = E \wedge type'(e) = c)$
2. $type' \cap type = type$
3. $\#S' = \#S + \#\{p \cdot p \in P \wedge (\exists! e \in E' \setminus E \wedge type'(e) \subseteq_c owner(p))\}$
4. $S' \cap S = S$
5. $slots' = slots \cup \{e \rightarrow s \cdot e \in E' \setminus E \wedge s \in S' \setminus S\}$
6. $property' = property \cup \{s \rightarrow p \cdot s \in S' \setminus S \wedge p \in P \wedge \{\exists! e \in E' \setminus E \cdot type'(e) \subseteq_c owner(p)\}\}$
7. $\#\text{Range}(property' \setminus property) = \#\{p \cdot p \in P \wedge (\exists! e \in E' \setminus E \wedge type'(e) \subseteq_c owner(p))\}$
8. $elements' = elements \cup \{s \rightarrow \{\} \cdot s \in S' \setminus S \wedge \neg ordered(property'(s))\}$
$\cup \{s \rightarrow [\,] \cdot s \in S' \setminus S \wedge ordered(property'(s))\}$

The only relevant postcondition is the first one, the rest are implicit or informally understandable from the various model constraints. To avoid too much repetition, we assume that the new values of any variables not mentioned are kept identical to their previous values and that only the necessary changes to fulfill the postconditions are made. We will refrain from listing obvious postconditions and concentrate on the important ones.

3.2 Element Deletion

The operation delete : $\mathcal{M} \times E \rightarrow \mathcal{M}$ deletes an element. We require the element being deleted to have no connections to other elements via its slots. Therefore the precondition for deleting an element e is:

1. $(\forall s \in slots(e) \cdot \#s = 0)$

The postcondition is that the element must no longer be in the set of elements:

1. $E' = E \setminus \{e\}$

3.3 Element Insertion into an Unordered Slot

Consider an operation *insert* : $\mathcal{M} \times S \times E \rightarrow \mathcal{M}$ such that $insert(M,s,e)$ inserts element e into slot s. The intuition behind the insertion operation is that all supersets of s must contain the new element e for the ISR constraints to hold. The clauses for the precondition for element insertion into an unordered slot are thus:

1. $\neg derived(property(s))$
2. $\neg ordered(property(s))$
3. $e \notin elements(s)$.
4. $type(e) \subseteq owner(opposite(property(s)))$
5. $(\exists t \in S \cdot s \subseteq_s t \wedge composite(property(t)) \Rightarrow parent(e) \setminus \{slotowner(t)\} = \emptyset$

The clauses state that (1) we are not modifying a derived read-only slot, (2) the slot is unordered, (3) the element must not yet exist in the slot, (4) that we obey the rules of strong typing and (5) we do not create a connection to a second parent for e.

The postcondition for element insertion is simple. We wish element e to be found in the slot s and all its transitive supersets. All the model constraints except for the multiplicity constraints must also hold as a postcondition.

1. $(\forall t \in S \cdot s \subseteq_s t \Rightarrow elements'(t) = elements(t) \cup \{e\})$ (Note $s \subseteq_s s$)

An example of element insertion into an unordered slot can be seen in Figure 4. Again, the Hasse diagram notation means that $t \subset_s q \subset_s p \wedge q \subset_s r \wedge t \subset_s s \subset_s r$. In case (1) of the figure, we have a poset of unordered slots. Suppose we insert an element c into slot q. This requires an insertion of c into slots p and r as well, to maintain the ISR, with the end result shown in case (2). After this, inserting c into slot t also inserts it into slot s, again to maintain the ISR, resulting in case (3). Slots p, q and r are not modified because c already existed in those slots.

It can be noted that in our semantics, an insertion into a slot never modifies any subset of that slot.

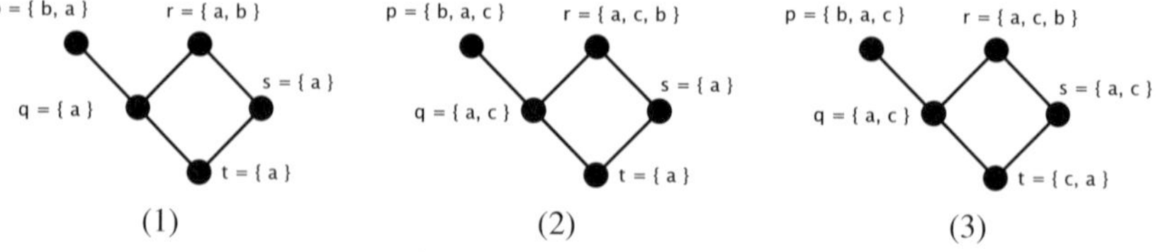

Fig. 4. Example of Inserting an Element into Unordered Slots

3.4 Element Insertion into an Ordered Slot

Subsetting with ordered slots is more complicated than with unordered slots, due to the need to maintain an order between the elements in different slots. We define the operation $insert : \mathcal{M} \times S \times E \times \mathbb{Z}^{0+} \rightarrow \mathcal{M}$ such that $insert(M,s,e,i)$ inserts an element e into a slot s at index i.

We assume there is a function $index : E \times S \rightarrow \mathbb{Z}^{0+}$ which returns the zero-based index of an element in the contents of an ordered slot. A function $lower\_index : \mathbb{Z}^{0+} \times S \times S \rightarrow \mathbb{Z}^{0+}$ is such that $lower\_index(i,x,y)$ returns the index in x where $y[i]$ should be inserted to maintain the subset $x \subseteq_s y$. It is shown in Figure 5 and is used to calculate which restrictions from supersets apply to subsets when inserting an element. As an example, consider what the restriction given by element c (at index position 2) in the superset $[a,b,c,d]$ is to its subset $[a,d]$. Then $lower\_index(2,[a,d],[a,b,c,d])$ returns 1 since c should be inserted between a and d.

```
lower_index(i,s,t) :=
  if t[i] ∈ s then return index(t[i],s)
  do
    if t[i] ∈ s then return index(t[i],s)+1
    else if i = 0 then return 0
    else i := i − 1
  od
```

```
lift_interval(s,t,[v..w]) :=
  if v > 0 then v′ := index(s[v − 1],t) + 1
    else v′ := 0
  if w = #s then w′ := #t
    else w′ := index(s[w],t)
  return [v′..w′]
```

Fig. 5. (Left) The *lower_index* Function . (Right) The *lift_interval* Function.

A function $lift\_interval : S \times S \times R \rightarrow R$, where R denotes integer intervals is such that $lift\_interval(s,t,[v..w])$ "lifts" the interval $[v..w]$ from s as superimposed on t (when $s \subseteq_s t$). It is shown in Figure 5 and is used to calculate which restrictions from subsets apply to supersets and works as the dual of *lower_index*. As an example, consider the ordered sets $s = [c]$ and $t = [b,c]$. If we were to insert element a at index 0 in s, the corresponding interval for s would be $[0..0]$. This interval is superimposed onto t as the interval $[0..1]$, meaning that the same element can be inserted either before or after b in t without violating the ISR. Thus, $lift\_interval(s,t,[0..0]) = [0..1]$.

The function $indices\_ok : \mathcal{P}(S) \times (S \rightarrow R) \rightarrow \mathbb{B}$ returns true if when executing $indices\_ok(T,F)$ there is a possible way to insert an element into every slot in T such that the constraints in F are satisfied. Here, $F : S \rightarrow R$ is a map from slots to integer intervals $[v..w]$ such that $v \leq w$ where e can be inserted. The function is shown in

$$indices\_ok(\emptyset,F) := (\forall t \in \mathrm{Dom}(F) \cdot F(t) \neq \emptyset)$$

$$\begin{aligned}
&indices_ok(T,F) := \\
&\quad (\exists t \in T \cdot (\forall u \in T \cdot t \not\supset u) \\
&\qquad \wedge R \stackrel{\text{def}}{=} \cap \{lift_interval(c,t,[v..w]) \cdot (\forall c \cdot s \subseteq_s c \prec t \wedge F(c) = [v..w])\} \\
&\qquad \Rightarrow indices_ok(T \setminus \{t\}, F[t \mapsto R \cap F(t)]))
\end{aligned}$$

Fig. 6. The *indices_ok* Function

Figure 6. Here, $\mathrm{Dom}(F)$ returns the domain of function F. Using the *lift_interval* and *lower_index* functions we restrict the possible intervals where e can be inserted into the slots.

The precondition of inserting into an ordered slot is otherwise identical to the case when inserting into an unordered slot, except for the check for an ordered slot and that there exists an extra clause which calculates if the insertion into the slot and its transitive supersets is at all possible without violating the ISR.

1. $\neg derived(property(s))$
2. $ordered(property(s))$
3. $e \notin elements(s)$
4. $type(e) \subseteq_c owner(opposite(property(s)))$
5. $(\exists t \in S \cdot s \subseteq_s t \wedge composite(property(t)) \Rightarrow parent(e) \setminus \{slotowner(t)\} = \emptyset$
6. $indices\_ok(\{t \cdot s \subset_s t\},$
   $\{s \mapsto [i..i]\}$
   $\cup \{t \mapsto [lower\_index(index(e,u),t,u)..lower\_index(index(e,u),t,u)] \cdot s \subset_s t \wedge t \subseteq_s u \wedge e \in elements(u)\}$
   $\cup \{t \mapsto [0, \#t\ ] \cdot s \subset_s t \wedge \neg(\exists u \cdot t \subseteq_s u \wedge e \in elements(u))\}$
   $)$

The intuition behind the last clause in the precondition and the definition of the *indices_ok* function is that we calculate the range restrictions of e which exist in any super- or subsets onto the other slots. The F function is initially created by describing constraints from supersets. F is created from three different clauses. The first, $s \mapsto [i..i]$, constrains e to be inserted at exactly index i. The second does similarly for supersets which have a superset that already has e, whereas the third initially allows all indices to be candidates for insertion. This initialization makes sure that F is restricted by the the elements e that already exist in any supersets of s. Note that any slot o such that $o \subset_s t \wedge s \subset_s t \wedge o \,||\, s$ is outside of the transitive superset closure of s and any restrictions from it will already be visible in t and thus it is not necessary to include o in F.

Then, *indices_ok* calculates the constraints from subsets and does set intersection to calculate whether an insertion is possible. The actual function takes all supersets T and picks one $t \in T$ which is a bottom element, which must exist since the slots in T are part of a finite poset. It then imposes all intervals from subset slots c (such that $s \subseteq_s c \prec t$) onto t, also including the initial constraint on t. It then recurses with a modified F until T is empty. The notation for a modified function is $f[x \mapsto y]$ which returns a new function f' such that $(\forall z \neq x \cdot f'(z) = f(z))$ and $f'(x) = y$.

We claim, without proof, that if the final mapping F contains only nonempty intervals, it is possible to successfully insert e into s at index i. The postcondition is:

1. $elements'(s)[i] = e$
2. $(\forall t \in S \cdot s \subseteq_s t \wedge e \notin elements(t) \Rightarrow elements'(t) \setminus \{e\} = elements(t)$
   $\wedge e \in elements'(t))$

The current definitions do not tell us the exact index where to insert e into any superslot of s, only that a combination of indices exists; an index i_t for a superslot t of s must exist somewhere in the range given by $F(t)$.

An example of element insertion can be seen in Figure 7. Case (1) is the initial configuration of the slots w, x, y and z. Let us assume an insertion of element c into slot w at index position 0 occurs. The returned slot ranges where c should be inserted raises the possibilities in cases (2) to (5), depending on whether c is inserted onto the left or right side of either a in slot y or b in slot z. Cases (2), (3) and (4) are correct solutions and our postcondition does not prefer any particular one over the another. Case (5) is not legal, because slot x cannot maintain the superset relationship as enforced by both slots y and z, as element c should occur both before a and after b in the ordered set. It is up to the implementation to choose one of the correct solutions, perhaps with guidance from the user.

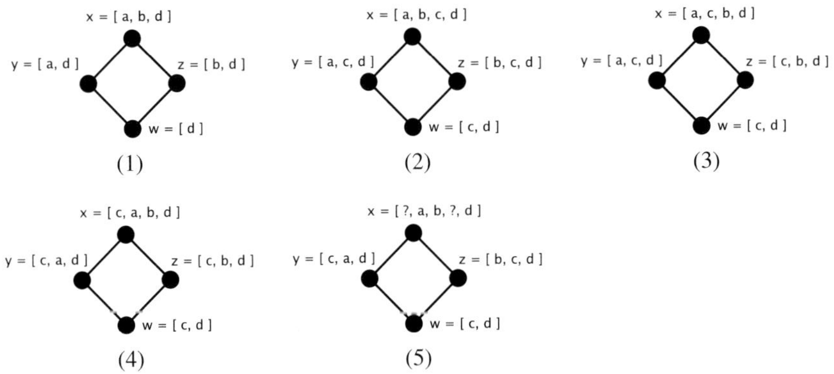

Fig. 7. Example of Inserting an Element into Ordered Slots

3.5 Element Removal from a Slot

The operation *remove* : $\mathcal{M} \times S \times E \rightarrow \mathcal{M}$ is defined such that $remove(M,s,e)$ removes the element e from s and all its subsets, as well as from those supersets which would not acquire e via some other subset which is not comparable to s. Element removal from an ordered slot is identical to element removal from an unordered slot since removing a specific element from an ordered slot does not alter the relative position of the other elements in the slot.

The precondition requires that a derived slot is not being modified and that the element must exist in the slot:

1. $\neg derived(property(s))$
2. $e \in elements(s)$

The postcondition:

1. $(\forall r \in S \cdot r \subseteq_s s \Rightarrow elements(r) = elements'(r) \cup \{e\} \wedge e \notin elements'(r))$
2. $(\forall t \in S \cdot s \subset_s t \wedge \neg(\exists m \in S \cdot m \subset_s t \wedge m \parallel s \wedge e \in elements(m))$
$\Rightarrow elements(t) = elements'(t) \cup \{e\} \wedge e \notin elements'(t))$

Both clauses in the postcondition are interesting. The first clause states that a removal from a slot triggers a removal from any subset, so that the ISR can hold. This can be contrasted with the insertion operation, which does not modify any subsets. The second clause states that a removal from a slot triggers a conditional removal from any superset. An interesting feature of the clause is shown in Figure 8. If we have an initial setting as in case (1) and remove *a* from *z*, the clause requires that *a* is removed from *x* as shown in case (2), although this is not necessary to maintain model consistency. However, we believe that this feature is the intended usage by the modeling standards. Inserting into a subset triggers insertion in all supersets, and so dually a removal from a subset ought to trigger a removal from all supersets. A similar chain of reasoning has been reported by Markus Scheidgen [17].

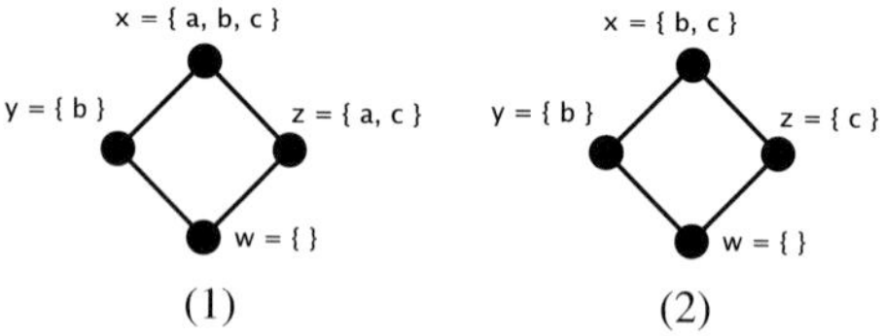

Fig. 8. Removing *a* from an Unordered Slot *z*

As an example where the second clause is necessary, consider Figure 9 with the initial setting as in case (1). Assume we wish to remove *a* from *y*. An incorrect approach is the removal of *a* from supersets and subsets, which would leave *x* without *a*, but *z* with *a* intact, violating the ISR, as shown in case (2). A correct option would be to remove *a* also from *z*, as shown in case (3), but our opinion is that this "snowball effect" of removing *a* reduces the usefulness of subsets; slot *y* should affect slot *z* as little as possible, since they are not comparable in the Hasse diagram. Our postcondition ensures that *a* must be removed from *w* and *y*, but not from *x*, because *z* still contains *a*; this is seen in case (4).

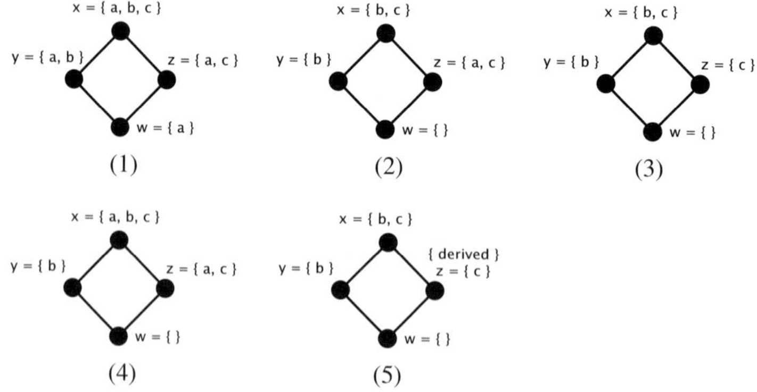

Fig. 9. Different Scenarios for Removing *a* from an Unordered Slot *y*

Another interesting case is the ISR rule for derived slots. If (and only if) z is marked as derived, we must remember that its elements must be found in the union of its subsets. In case (5), a is removed from y which leads to it being removed from w as well. As z is marked as derived, a must also be removed from it, since z does not have any other subset containing a. This in turn leads to a being removed from x!

3.6 Implementation of Edit Operations in a Modeling Toolkit

We do not discuss the actual implementation of the basic edit operations in this article due to space restrictions. However, we have implemented the metamodeling language with the operations as described in this article in our modeling tool Coral, with details defined in [1]. We have tested the implementation extensively and found no consistency errors or omissions. Coral is open source and available at `http://mde.abo.fi/`.

We know of no other tools that support subsets as extensively as proposed in this article, even with different semantics. At the time of writing, the Eclipse EMF model repository does not implement subsets, although the feature is being planned.

4 Related Work

Several others have studied the formalization of the metamodel and model layers in the past, for example [5,3,9]. Our contribution comes from the definitions of property subsets, which neither metamodeling nor traditional object oriented language descriptions explain.

Several authors use association inheritance without defining exact semantics, and some say that it denotes covariance. An example of this covariant specialization [8] is the multilevel metamodeling technique called VPM by Varro and Pataricza [18], which also limits itself to single inheritance. We argue that property subsetting is not the same concept as covariant specialization, and requires different semantics.

Carsten Amelunxen, Tobias Rötschke and Andy Schürr are authors to the MOFLON tool [4] inside the Fujaba framework [12]. MOFLON claims to support subsetting, but no description of the formal semantics being used is included. It is not clear if their tool works in the context of subsets between ordered slots, or with diamond inheritance with subsetting.

Markus Scheidgen presents an interesting discussion of the semantics of subsets in the context of creating an implementation of MOF 2.0 in [17]. To our knowledge, this has been so far the most thorough attempt to formalize subset properties. The approach is slightly different in that a slot modification creates an *update graph* of slots, so that a later modification at some other slot in the update graph actually updates all the associated slots. The actual operational semantics are unfortunately not described in detail. In comparison, we do not have to create or maintain any update graphs. Furthermore, our contribution not only discusses but also defines pre- and postconditions and implementations for the operations for ordered and unordered sets. It is also not clear if the work by Scheidgen supports diamond subsets or ordered sets, both of which are used in the UML 2.0.

The object-oriented and database research communities are also researching a similar topic, although it is called relationship or association inheritance, or first-class relationships. In [6], Bierman and Wren present a simplified Java language with first-class relationships. In contrast with our work, they do not support multiple inheritance, bidirectionality or ordered properties; all of these constructs are common in modeling and in the UML 2.0 specification. However, relationship links are explicitly represented as instances, and they can have additional data fields (just like the AssociationClass of UML). As the authors have noticed, the semantics of link insertion and deletion is not without problems. Albano, Ghelli and Orsini present in [2] a relationship mechanism for a strongly-typed object-oriented database programming language. It also handles links as relationship instances, but without additional data fields. Multiple inheritance is supported, but ordered slot contents are not.

5 Conclusions

MOF 2.0 provides new property characteristics: subsets, (derived) unions and redefinitions. However, it does not describe these concepts in detail, not even informally, and therefore they cannot be applied in practice. In this article, we have first described a simple formalization of metamodels and models and then presented pre- and postconditions for basic operations on element creation and deletion and slot modification, taking into account subsets and derived unions. It must be stressed that we do not cover several important aspects of MOF 2.0, such as association end ownership or navigability. They are not in the scope of this article.

We consider that the definition of these concepts is not as straightforward as one may think and it requires an extensive study. There is an imminent need in the modeling community to standardize on one formalization of subsets and derived unions, so that tools implementing MOF 2.0 and UML 2.0 can be interoperable. The semantics described in this article are one proposal and we hope it spurs further interest and discussion. We have avoided using OCL or any other modeling standard in order to be able to present a relatively small and self-contained description of the core of these OMG standards with respect to subsetting. Furthermore, the idea of subsetting is intriguing, since it is a new construct for modeling relationships between classes and objects, and thereby brings a novel idea to the software modeling and object-oriented community.

The authors would like to thank Patrick Sibelius for insightful discussions. Marcus Alanen would like to acknowledge the financial support of the Nokia Foundation.

References

1. Marcus Alanen and Ivan Porres. Subset and union properties in modeling languages. Technical Report 731, TUCS, Dec 2005.
2. Antonio Albano, Giorgio Ghelli, and Renzo Orsini. A Relationship Mechanism for a Strongly Typed Object-Oriented Database Programming Language. In *Proceedings of the 17th Conference on Very Large Databases, Morgan Kaufman pubs. (Los Altos CA), Barcelona*, 1991.
3. José Álvarez, Andy Evans, and Paul Sammut. MML and the Metamodel Architecture. In Jon Whittle, editor, *WTUML: Workshop on Transformation in UML 2001*, April 2001.
4. Carsten Amelunxen, Tobias Rötschke, and Andy Schürr. Graph Transformations with MOF 2.0. In Holger Giese and Albert Zündorf, editors, *Fujaba Days 2005*, September 2005.

5. Thomas Baar. Metamodels without Metacircularities. *L'Objet*, 9(4):95–114, 2003.
6. Gavin Bierman and Alisdair Wren. First-class relationships in an object-oriented language. In *Workshop on Foundations of Object-Oriented Languages (FOOL 2005)*, January 2005.
7. Frank Budinsky, David Steinberg, Ed Merks, Raymond Ellersick, and Timothy J. Grose. *Eclipse Modeling Framework*. Addison Wesley Professional, August 2003.
8. Giuseppe Castagna. Covariance and Contravariance: Conflict without a Cause. *ACM Transactions on Programming Languages and Systems*, 17(3):431–447, May 1995.
9. Tony Clark, Andy Evans, and Stuart Kent. The Metamodelling Language Calculus: Foundation Semantics for UML. In H. Hussmann, editor, *Fundamental Approaches to Software Engineering. 4th International Conference, FASE 2001*, volume 2029 of *LNCS*, pages 17–31, 2001.
10. B.A. Davey and H.A. Priestley. *Introduction to Lattices and Order*. Cambridge University Press, 2002.
11. Anneke Kleppe, April 2003. Discussion on the mailing-list puml-list@cs.york.ac.uk.
12. Ulrich A. Nickel, Jörg Niere, and Albert Zündorf. Tool demonstration: The FUJABA environment. In *Proceedings of the 22nd International Conference on Software Engineering (ICSE)*, pages 742–745. ACM Press, 2000.
13. OMG. MOF 2.0 Query / View / Transformation Final Adopted Specification. OMG Document ptc/05-11-01, available at www.omg.org, 2005.
14. OMG. UML 2.0 Superstructure Specification, August 2005. Document formal/05-07-04. Available at `http://www.omg.org/`.
15. OMG. Meta Object Facility (MOF) Core Specification, version 2.0, January 2006. Document formal/06-01-01, available at `http://www.omg.org/`.
16. OMG. UML 2.0 Infrastructure Specification, March 2006. Document formal/05-07-05, available at `http://www.omg.org/`.
17. Markus Scheidgen. On Implementing MOF 2.0—New Features for Modelling Language Abstractions. July 2005. Available at `http://www.informatik.hu-berlin.de/~scheidge/`.
18. Dániel Varró and András Pataricza. VPM: A visual, precise and multilevel metamodeling framework for describing mathematical domains and UML. *Journal of Software and Systems Modeling*, 2(3):187–210, October 2003.

A Metamodeling Approach to Pattern Specification

Maged Elaasar[1,2], Lionel C. Briand[1,3], and Yvan Labiche[1]

[1] Software Quality Engineering Laboratory (SQUALL)
Department of Systems and Computer Engineering, Carleton University
1125 Colonel By Drive, Ottawa, ON K1S 5B6, Canada
{briand, labiche}@sce.carleton.ca
[2] IBM Canada Ltd, Rational Software, Ottawa Lab
770 Palladium Dr., Kanata, ON. K2V 1C8, Canada
melaasar@ca.ibm.com
[3] Simula Research Laboratory, Department of Software Engineering
Martin Linges v 17, Fornebu, P.O. Box 134, 1325 Lysaker, Norway

Abstract. This paper presents the Pattern Modeling Framework (PMF), a new metamodeling approach to pattern specification for MOF-compliant modeling frameworks and languages. Patterns need to be precisely specified before a tool can manipulate them, and though several approaches to pattern specification have been proposed, they do not provide the scalability and flexibility required in practice. PMF provides a pattern specification language called Epattern, which is capable of precisely specifying patterns in MOF-compliant metamodels. The language is defined as an extension to MOF by adding semantics inspired from the UML composite structure diagram. The language also comes with a graphical notation and a recommended iterative specification process. It also contains features to manage the complexity of specifying patterns and simplify their application and detection in user models. Most importantly, the language is implemented using state-of-the-art technologies that are heavily used by major modeling tool vendors, thus facilitating its adoption.

1 Introduction

Model driven architecture (MDA) [1] is an approach to system development advocated by the Object Management Group (OMG). The approach starts by describing the system's specifications using a platform independent model (PIM). A PIM is usually specified in a language that is based on the Meta Object Facility (MOF), a standard by the OMG for describing modeling languages. A prominent example of such languages is the Unified Modeling Language (UML), which is well adopted by the software engineering community. Alternatives to UML also exist and are collectively referred to as Domain Specific Modeling Languages (DSML) [6], as they are more specialized and target certain modeling domains. Once a system has been specified using a PIM, a platform is then chosen to enable the realization of the system using specific implementation technologies, producing what is referred to as a platform specific model (PSM).

In spite of the potential benefits of MDA including reduced development time for new applications, improved application quality, quicker adoption of new technologies

O. Nierstrasz et al. (Eds.): MoDELS 2006, LNCS 4199, pp. 484 – 498, 2006.

into existing application and increased return on technology investment, the adoption of MDA has not picked up to its full potential yet. One reason for this is the complexity problems inherent in today's MDA tools. These tools usually appeal to the MDA savvy but fail short of meeting the expectations of the mainstream practitioners who are competent with their technologies but not necessarily with MDA. Another reason is the limited support available to the user beyond authoring their models. For instance, features that help the user inspect the quality of their models are lacking in many major MDA tools.

As system models get larger and more complex, the task of inspecting their quality becomes much harder. It is now well understood that a problem detected early on in the system development life cycle is much cheaper to tackle than one discovered later on. Hence, technologies that facilitate inspecting models for quality purposes can certainly play a big role in enhancing the value of MDA. Examples of these technologies include architectural discovery [2], anti-pattern detection [10] and consistency analysis [17]. Equally important are those technologies that assure the quality of the process of going from PIM to PSM. Examples here include impact analysis [18].

One way to analyze the quality of user models is to look for instances of predefined patterns. Patterns are recurring modeling structures that are either desirable [7] or undesirable [10]. Desirable patterns represent elements of reuse at a higher level of abstraction. Therefore, trying to understand a model by its usage of patterns helps by raising the level of abstraction. Conformance to desirable patterns is expected to boost the quality of models by expediting modeling of maintainable and robust designs. On the other hand, the early identification of undesired patterns, or anti-patterns, protects against making common and expensive design mistakes. It is also a first step towards the mitigation of existing design problems.

Support for patterns has started to show up in some major modeling tools like RSA [3]. The support can come in the form of best practice patterns that can be applied or recovered, as well as anti-patterns that can be detected in user models. Usually, a common prerequisite is the formal specification of those patterns for tool consumption. The state of the art in this area is far yet from converging on a standard for pattern specification. This paper presents a new approach to precise pattern specification within a Pattern Modeling Framework (PMF). PMF uses a declarative and graphical approach to pattern specification, which is based on existing metamodeling technologies. The specification language, called Epattern, allows for the specification of patterns in MOF-compliant modeling languages using an iterative, graphical process. Epattern has inherent capabilities to manage the specification of complex patterns. PMF is implemented as a set of plug-ins [19] to the Eclipse platform and leverages several Eclipse open source projects like the Eclipse Modeling Framework (EMF) [4].

The rest of this paper is structured as follows. An overview of the PMF is presented in Section 2. Section 3 presents the Epattern specification language and process. Related works are discussed and compared to the proposed approach in Section 4. Finally, Section 5 concludes and discusses some of the future research directions.

2 Overview of Pattern Modeling Framework

The Pattern Modeling Framework (PMF) offers a new approach to pattern specification. The framework is adopting an architecture (Figure 1) that is compatible with the

OMG's 4-layer metamodeling architecture [22]. In the meta-modeling architecture, the Meta Object Facility (MOF) (M3) is used to define metamodels for various modeling languages (M2). Instance models (M1) that conform to those languages can then be defined. When these user models are deployed, user objects instantiating them are created (M0). Along the same lines, PMF defines its pattern specification language as an extension to MOF (M3). The new language is used to specify patterns in any MOF-compliant modeling language (M2). Pattern instances conforming to those patterns are hence defined in terms of instance models (M1). This conformance in architecture gives PMF the advantage of being able to specify patterns on any MOF-compliant modeling language (i.e., not only UML) and even patterns that involve multiple modeling languages and viewpoints at the same time (like patterns specified in terms of both the UML class and interaction diagrams at the same time).

The pattern specification language provided by PMF is called Epattern and is defined as an extension to the MOF 2.0 specification [9]. The EMF [4] provides a platform specific realization of a subset of MOF called EMOF, whose semantics resemble those of simple UML class diagrams. This realization is called Ecore and is integrated with the Eclipse platform. Ecore is widely used today to specify various language metamodels including that of UML 2.0, which is available as an open source project [8] and used by modern UML tools like RSA [3] and EclipseUML [21]. EMF provides tooling for specifying Ecore metamodels and generating corresponding java APIs for them. The Epattern language is realized as an extension to Ecore, which gives PMF two advantages: the ability to reuse a lot of the tools provided by EMF and the ability to provide pattern specification capabilities in modern modeling tools.

The Epattern language contains semantics/constructs that are inspired from similar ones in UML 2.0 composite structure diagrams (CSD) [5] and that are used in Epattern to specify patterns. CSDs were recently added to UML to depict the internal structure of a classifier (such as a class, a component, or a collaboration), including the interaction points of the classifier to other parts of the system. While class diagrams model a static view of class structures, including their attributes and operations, CSDs model specific usages of these structures. For instance, classes are viewed as parts fulfilling some roles, and roles are interconnected to represent relationships that might or might not be reflected by static diagrams. One use of CSDs, discussed in [4], is to describe patterns in UML instance models (M1). However, as CSDs are part of the UML 2.0 metamodel (M2), they cannot be used to specify general pattern structures involving elements of that same metamodel, or any other M2 metamodel. To specify such patterns you need similar capabilities at level M3. To address this problem the Epattern language, purportedly defined at the M3 level, reuses some of the CSD semantics and apply them to specify patterns in language metamodels.

Once patterns are specified in Epattern, their specifications can be used to derive various types of algorithms for the purpose of pattern application and detection. Furthermore, PMF includes a graphical, stepwise, and iterative process to guide the user for specifying patterns and alleviate their complexity. Other features of the framework, which are outside the scope of this paper due to space limitations, include the ability to generate a detection algorithm for each specification and use it to detect and visualize pattern instances in user models. The interested reader may refer to [19] for details regarding the detection algorithm support.

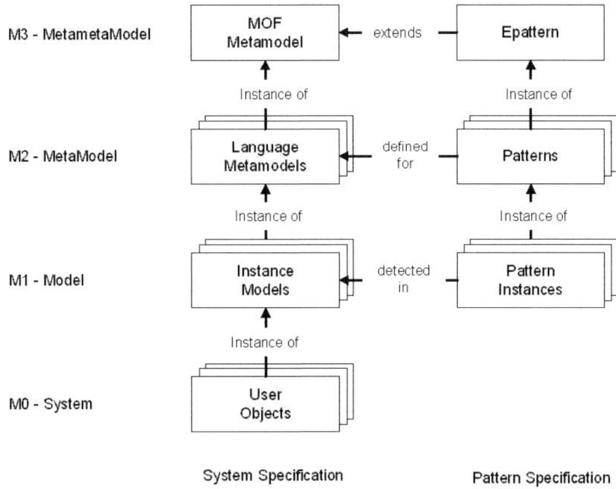

Fig. 1. Pattern specification using OMG's metamodeling architecture

3 Epattern Specification Language

The Epattern language can be used to formally specify patterns on MOF-compliant modeling languages. As described in Section 0, Epattern is designed as an extension to MOF and realized as an extension to Ecore, which includes the concepts necessary to specify metamodels of MOF-compliant languages including UML 2.0. In the remainder of the paper, we refer to concepts defined by Ecore rather than MOF as a simplification because the terminology used there is closer to the one for Epattern.

A simplified metamodel of Ecore is shown in Figure 2. All classes in the Ecore metamodel are subclasses of EModelElement (not shown on the diagram to avoid cluttering). A concept in a modeling language is specified using an EClassifier, which is a named element that has two subclasses: an EClass representing a complex type (e.g. 'Property' in UML) and an EDatatype representing a simple type (e.g., 'AggregationKind' in UML). EClassifiers are physically arranged in hierarchical namespaces represented by EPackages. EClasses can either represent classes (including abstract ones) or interfaces and may be organized into inheritance hierarchies. The structure of an EClass is specified with a set of EStructuralFeatures, representing the properties of a class, while its behavior is specified with a set of EOperations, representing the operations of a class. An EStructuralFeature is a named and typed element that has two subclasses: an EAttribute, typed with an EDataType (e.g. 'Property.aggregation' in UML), and an EReference, typed with an EClass (e.g. 'Property.type' in UML). An EReference can represent either a containment reference, i.e., its value is owned by the class, or a non-containment reference, i.e., its value is referenced by the class. An EReference may also point to an opposite EReference if it represents one end of a bidirectional association between two classes. An EOperation is a named element that has an EClassifier return type. It also has a list of EParameters that are named and typed with EClassifiers.

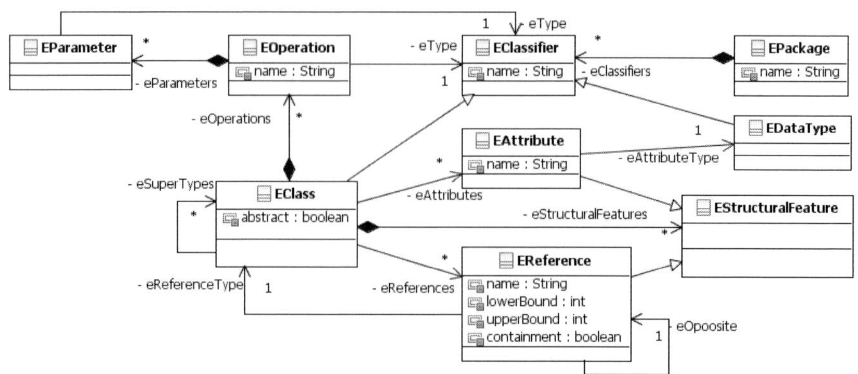

Fig. 2. A simplified Ecore metamodel

The Epattern language defines semantics for pattern specification that extend off those of Ecore. The remainder of this section uses a working example (Section 3.1) to explain these semantics (Section 3.2), illustrate their graphical notation (Section .3), and describes a recommended process for using them to specify patterns (Section 3.4).

3.1 Working Example

The example is a simple variant of the well-known Gang of Four (GoF) composite pattern [7], shown in Figure 3. The pattern's M2 target language is UML 2.0. It is classified as a structural pattern and is used to allow a client to treat both single components and collections of components identically. The pattern highlights several roles: a 'component' role representing an instance of UML Interface, a 'leaf' role representing an instance of UML Class that implements the 'component' interface, a 'composite' role representing an instance of UML Class that implements the 'component' interface and also composes instances of the same interface, and finally a 'compose' role representing an instance of UML Operation defined by the 'composite' class and used to compose 'component' instances.

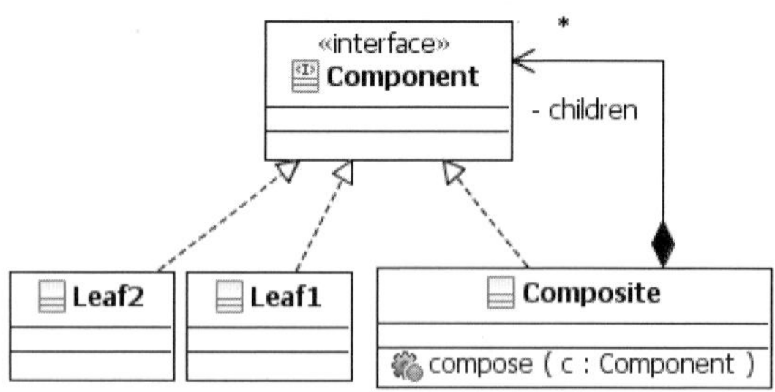

Fig. 3. A simplified GoF composite pattern

3.2 Semantics

The metamodel of Epattern, shown in Figure 4, contains new metaclasses that subclass others in the Ecore metamodel. The following items describe the semantics of these new metaclasses and we point the interested reader to [19] for more details:

- *EPattern:* subclasses *EClass* and represents a pattern's context. A pattern is represented as an instance of EPattern (M3), i.e. as a metaclass at the same level as the target metamodel (M2). Representing a pattern as a metaclass has big advantages including the ability to build pattern inheritance hierarchies with varying levels of abstraction, the ability to define complex patterns by composing simpler ones, the ability to use namespaces to create pattern families, the ability to be a context for pattern constraints, and the ability to represent pattern instances as objects of the pattern metaclass.

  In the example, the composite pattern is represented by an EPattern instance.
- *ERole:* subclasses *EReference* and represents a pattern role. Representing a role as a reference helps characterize (using name, type and multiplicity features) M1 instances that play that role in a pattern instance. A role can be typed (through eReferenceType feature that is inherited by ERole from EReference: Figure 2) with an instance of EClass (M2) from the pattern's target metamodel. To implement pattern composition, a role can simply be typed with an instance of EPattern (which subclasses EClass) to represent a composed pattern. Additionally, the multiplicity feature of a role allows the support of some common role semantics, namely the ability to define optional roles (e.g. leaf) and collection roles, which can be bound to more than one instance from the user model (e.g. leaf too). A role with multiplicity lower bounds of 0 and 1 are considered optional and required, respectively. Also, a multiplicity upper bound of * defines a collection role, whereas a value of 1 defines a singular role. Yet another major advantage of this role representation is simplifying the process of role binding down to the simple process of assigning a value to a feature in a pattern instance. One more advantage is the ability to reference roles in a pattern's constraint (whose context is a pattern instance at M1) just as regular features of a metaclass. Moreover, roles are connectable, i.e. a role can be connected to other related roles in the pattern to formalize their relationship, as described in the next paragraph.

  In the example, the main identified roles (component, composite, leaf and compose) are all represented by instances of ERole.
- *EConnector:* subclasses *EModelElement* and represents a connector between two pattern roles. A connector characterizes (through its type) a relationship between M1 model elements bound to its two roles in a pattern instance. The relationship characterized by a connector's type is nothing but an EReference instance from the pattern target metamodel. This instance represents a directed relationship between two EClass instances from the metamodel. Since it is directed, a connector specifies which of its ends represents the source and which represents the target of the reference through its eSourceRole and eTargetRole features. If one or both roles happen to represent a composed pattern (i.e. typed with EPattern), the connector also specifies which port (refer to the EPort metaclass being defined next) instance belonging to the composed pattern it is connecting to through the eSourcePort and eTargetPort features.

In the example, various connectors are represented by instances of EConnector: one from composite to component representing an implementation, one from leaf to component representing an implementation, one from composite to component representing a composition, and one from composite to compose representing an owned operation.

- *EPort:* subclasses *EReference* and represents a connection point on the pattern's boundary that is used in pattern composition. When patterns compose each other, roles in the composing pattern are connected to ones in the composed pattern. However, this connection cannot be direct as roles are encapsulated within their defining pattern. To expose these roles and make them available for connection to roles in the composing pattern, ports are specified for them in the pattern. Note that not all roles need to have ports; rather only those main roles that characterize the pattern. An instance of EPort connects (though the eDelegatingRole feature) to an instance of ERole in the pattern. If that role represents a composed pattern, the port needs to also specify which port (through the eDelegatingPort feature) on the composed pattern it is connecting to in turn. An EPort is represented as a reference since it characterizes (through its name and type) the role it is connecting to. A port's type has to match that of the role it is connecting to although this restriction may be removed in the future[1].

  In the example, two roles are considered defining for the composite pattern; these are the composite and component roles. Therefore, an instance of EPort is specified for each one of them.
- *EConstraint:* subclasses *EOperation* and represents a well-formedness constraint (a semantic rule) for a pattern. A constraint has a boolean expression that is specified in a constraint language like EMOF OCL [20]. The context of the constraint is nothing but an instance of a pattern, which makes pattern roles accessible in the expression as regular features of the context. This has the added advantage of being able to specify constraints between one or more pattern roles. For better formalization, an instance of EConstraint references the instances of ERole that it is constraining.

  In the example, two constraints can be specified with instances of EConstraint: the first one is asserting that the association between the composite and the component roles is really a 'composition' and that it has a 'many' multiplicity; the second constraint is asserting that an operation bound to the compose role has exactly one parameter whose type matches the interface of the component role.
- *EAssociation:* subclasses *EClass* and represents a new derived relationship between two EClass instances from the pattern's target metamodel. The main rationale for defining EAssociations is to simplify pattern specification by introducing high level relationships that can be specified between pattern roles. Without this concept, only low level relationships represented by EReferences from the metamodel can be used between roles. A problem usually occurs when no direct EReferences exist between EClass instances in the metamodel that are types of related roles. In this case, a pattern author would need to work around that by introducing a set of intermediary roles increasing the complexity of the specification. An EAssociation is basically a namespace that defines two association ends (refer to EAssociationEnd

[1] A port in CSD may have a different type if connected to its role with a typed connector [5].

metaclass being defined next). These ends characterize a new relationship between two EClass instances from the target metamodel. An EAssociation is the container of EReferences and hence has to subclass EClass (Ecore restriction) [4].

In the example, two instances of EAssociation are specified as they represent high level relationships that are used by the composite pattern but do not map to direct EReferences in the Ecore UML metamodel. The first one is the 'Implementation' relationship between the composite/leaf and component roles, and the second is the 'Composition' relationship between the composite and component roles.

- *EAssociationEnd:* subclasses *EReference* and represents one end in an EAssociation. Representing an end as a reference makes it straightforward to use as a type for EConnectors in pattern specifications. An EAssociationEnd is typed with an EClass instance from the target metamodel, representing one end of the new relationship, and is given a name and a multiplicity. One main difference between EReference and EAssociationEnd is that the former is owned by an EClass representing one end of a relationship and typed with the other, while the latter is always owned by an EAssociation and the two associtated EClasses are specified by the types of both ends of the association. Moreover, an end is a derived reference that can either be navigable or not. If navigable, an end gets a derivation expression specified in a language like EMOF OCL [20]. The type of the expression is the same as that of the end and the context of the expression is an instance of the type of the other end. If both ends are navigable, the end's opposite EReference feature is set to the other EAssociationEnd in the same association.

In the example, the 'Implementation' association has two EAssociationEnd instances typed with 'BehavioredClassifier' and 'Interface' from the UML metamodel. Also, the 'Composition' association has two EAssociationEnd instances typed with 'StructuredClassifier' and 'Type' from the UML metamodel.

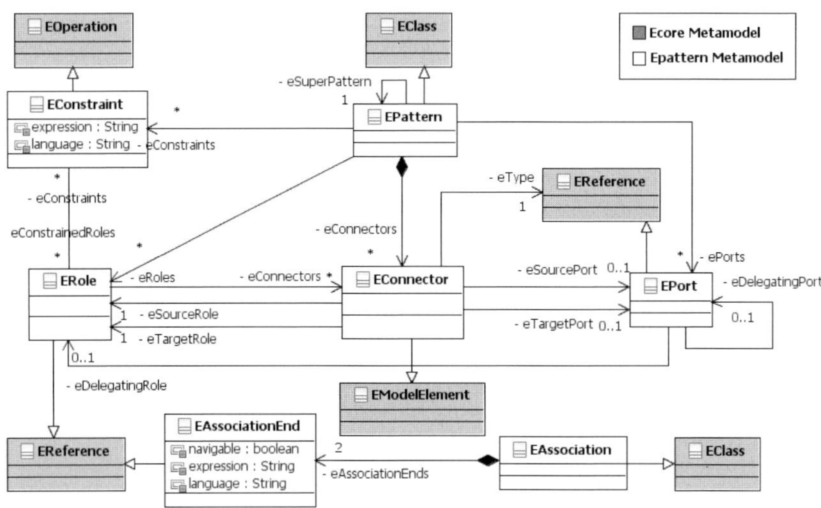

Fig. 4. The Epattern metamodel

3.3 Notation

The notation for Epattern is based on the notation of the class and composite structure diagrams of UML 2.0. This makes it easier to leverage already existing UML tools in pattern specification. Table 1 below illustrates this notation.

Table 1. Epattern notation

EPattern: a frame with a name compartment and a structure compartment showing the pattern's structure. Other optional compartments could be shown for the pattern's super types, roles, ports, connectors and constraints.	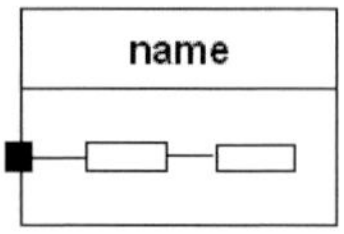 name
ERole: a box containing a compartment that shows the role's name, type and multiplicity (lowerBound…upperBound if different from 1…1). The box is solid if the role represents a pattern composition (bottom role) and dashed otherwise (top role). Also, the box has a structure compartment if it represents a pattern composition.	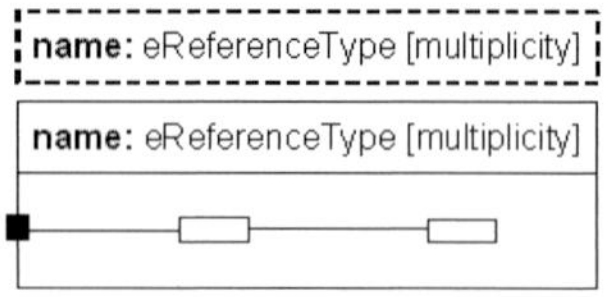 **name:** eReferenceType [multiplicity] **name:** eReferenceType [multiplicity]
EPort: a small filled box on the frame of the structure compartment. The box has a floating name label that shows the name and type of the port. The box is either connected directly to a delegating role (left port) or to a delegating role's port if the role represents a composed pattern (right port).	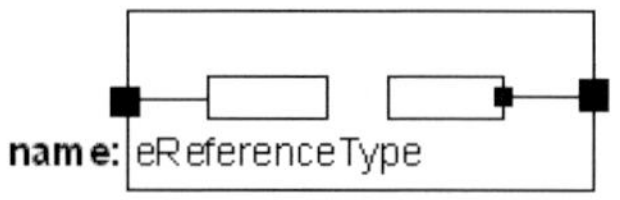 **name:** eReferenceType
EConstraint: a sticky note with a name compartment and an expression compartment. The note is connected to the constrained roles with dotted lines.	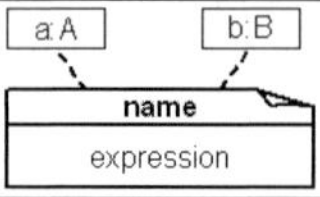 a:A b:B name expression
EConnector: a directed arrow that goes from the pattern's source role to its target roles. If a connector has a source/target port, the line connects that port on the corresponding role. The connector has floating labels showing the connector's type reference (eType) and its opposite (if any).	 a: A b: B eType eType.eOpposite
EAssociation: a line connecting two EClass instances from the pattern target language metamodel. The line has a floating name label, two floating end name labels, and two floating end multiplicity labels. The line can be shown as an arrow if the association is directed.	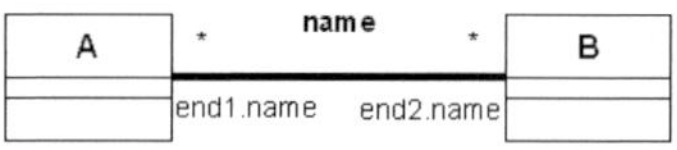 A * name * B end1.name end2.name

3.4 Specification Process

We propose a recommended iterative specification process for using the Epattern language. The outcome of this process is a formal pattern specification. The process is depicted in Figure 5 and explained in the following suggested order of steps. In practice, a pattern author may move from any step to any other step in an iterative fashion.

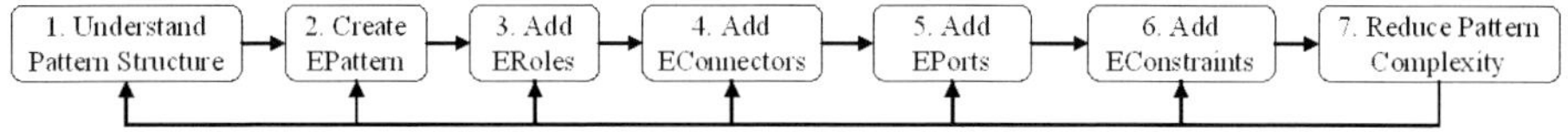

Fig. 5. The Epattern specification process

The composite pattern example is used to illustrate the process and the notation provided above.

Understand Pattern Structure. Before a pattern is specified with Epattern, there has to be a good understanding of its structure. A pattern's structure is a set of roles, typed with M2 metaclasses from a target metamodel and related to each other through metareferences. In our example, the target metamodel is UML 2.0, simplified in Figure 6 for the purpose of our example. The class diagram in Figure 3 reveals the following roles: component of type 'Interface', composite and leaf of type 'Class' and compose of type 'Operation'. The relationships between these roles include an 'implementation' between leaf/composite and component, which is realized by an element of type 'InterfaceRealization' (metaclass in Figure 6). The element is related to the interface by the metareference 'InterfaceRealization.contract' and to the class by the metareference 'BehavioredClassifier.interfaceRealization'. Our syntax for metareference 'X.Y' refers to an EReference named Y in an EClass named X. Another relationship is 'composition' between composite and component, which is realized by an element of type 'Property'. The element is related to the class by the metareference 'StructuredClassifier.ownedAttribute' and to the interface by the metareference 'Property.type'. Finally, composite is related to compose directly by metareference 'Class.ownedOperation'.

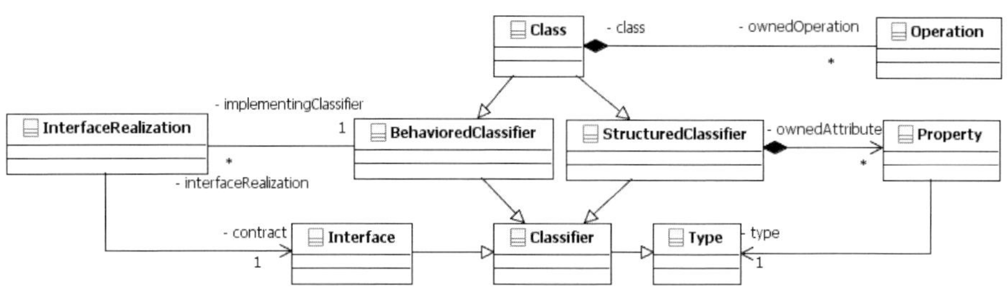

Fig. 6. A partial, simplified UML 2.0 metamodel

Create EPattern. Once there is a good understanding of the pattern's structure, the pattern can be specified using the Epattern metamodel (M3). The first step is to create an instance of EPattern in an EPackage that belongs to a pattern model. The instance is given a name representing the pattern. In our example, an instance is created and named 'CompositePattern'. A complete specification of this pattern is shown in Figure 7 and described below.

Add ERoles. Once an Epattern is created, every pattern roles identified in step 1 is modeled by an instance of ERole in the pattern's eRoles collection. Each ERole instance is given the name of the role, and typed, through its eReferenceType feature, with an EClass instance representing the type of the role in the target metamodel. If the role represents a composed pattern, it is typed with an EPattern instance instead, and its containment feature is set to true. In addition to the main roles identified in step 1, some intermediary roles might be initially needed to allow the main roles to be connected by connectors typed only with EReferences from the metamodel. In our example, ERole instances for the main roles (component, composite, leaf and compose) identified in step 1 are created. In addition, based on the metamodel in Figure 6, instances for intermediary roles are needed to connect the main roles. Two such instances typed with 'InterfaceRealization' are needed to represent the implementation relationship between the composite/leaf and component roles: the former role is a Class, the latter role is an Interface and those two metaclasses are related through InterfaceRealization in Figure 6. The ERole instances are named 'realization1' and 'realization2'. For similar reasons, another ERole instance typed with 'Property', and named 'children', is needed to represent the composition relationship between the composite and component roles. All our role instances have their multiplicity set to '1…1' except for the leaf role, where it is set to '*', indicating that the role is optional and represents a collection.

Add EConnectors. The next step after creating roles is connecting them by EConnector instances. An instance is created in the pattern's eConnectors collection to specify every identified relationship in step 1 (and in previous specification phases) between pattern roles. Instances of source and target roles are assigned to the connector's eSourceRole and eTargetRole features. If one or both roles represent composed patterns, i.e., typed with EPattern, the connector's eSourcePort and/or eTargetPort features are also set to instances of EPort owned by the composed EPattern. The connector's type is set to an EReference from the target metamodel representing a directed relationship between the EClass instances typing the connector's source and target roles (or ports if specified). In the example, several connectors are specified using metareferences in Figure 6: 1) two connectors typed with 'InterfaceRealization.contract' from 'realization1'/'realization2' to 'component'; 2) two connectors typed with 'BehavioredClassifier.interfaceRealization' from 'leaf'/'composite' to 'realization1'/'realization2'; 3) a connector typed with 'StructuredClassifier.ownedAttribute' from 'composite' to 'children'; 4) a connector typed with 'Property.type' from 'children' to 'component'; and 5) a connector typed with 'Class.ownedOperation' from 'composite' to 'compose'.

Add EPorts. Once pattern roles have been specified, ports are added to expose some roles that are considered public. For each such port, an instance of EPort is added to the pattern's ePorts collection. The instance is connected to a role through its eDelegatingRole feature. If the role represents a composed pattern, i.e., typed with EPattern, the instance's eDelegatingPort feature is also set to an EPort instance owned by the composed pattern. Then the port is given a name that correlates to its connected role and is typed with the same type of that role (or port if specified). In our example, two ports are specified: 'componentPort' connected to 'component' and typed with 'Interface' and 'compositePort' connected to 'composite' and typed with 'Class'.

Add EConstraints. After the basic pattern structure is specified, well-formedness constraints are added. Each constraint is represented by an instance of EConstraint in the pattern's eConstraints collection. A constraint is given a name and a boolean expression in a constraint language. The constraint's eConstrainedRoles feature is then set to the ERole instances constrained by the constraint. In our example, two constraints are specified. The first is named 'composition', connected to the 'children' role, and specified in OCL as follows: `'children.aggregation =AggregationKind.Composite and children.upperBound=-1'` (the second conjunct specifies a 'many' multiplicity). The second is named 'parameter', connected to both 'component' and 'compose' roles and specified in OCL as follows: `'compose.ownedParameter->size()=1 and compose.ownedParameter->at(1).oclIsKindOf(component)'`. Their meaning was already provided above (Section 3.2).

Reduce Pattern Complexity. Pattern specifications can get large and complex. Various features are provided in Epattern to manage this complexity including 1) specifying patterns by inheritance and composition, 2) refactoring common constraint logic in operations and 3) eliminating intermediary roles through derived associations. This last feature can be achieved by the specification of EAssociations. An instance of EAssociation is created in an EPackage that belongs to a pattern model and given a name corresponding to the represented relationship. After that, two instances of EAssociationEnd are created in the association's eAssociationEnd collection. Every such instance is typed with an EClass from the target metamodel and given a name that corresponds to the role played by that end of the association. The end's multiplicity is then specified along with its navigable feature. Every navigable end represents a derived reference from the end's EClass type to the other end's EClass type. In this case, an end gets a derivation expression in a language like OCL to derive M1 instances conforming to the end's type from the context of an instance conforming to the other-ends's type. If both ends are navigable, they reference each other through their eOpposite feature. Once ends are specified, complex pattern specifications can be

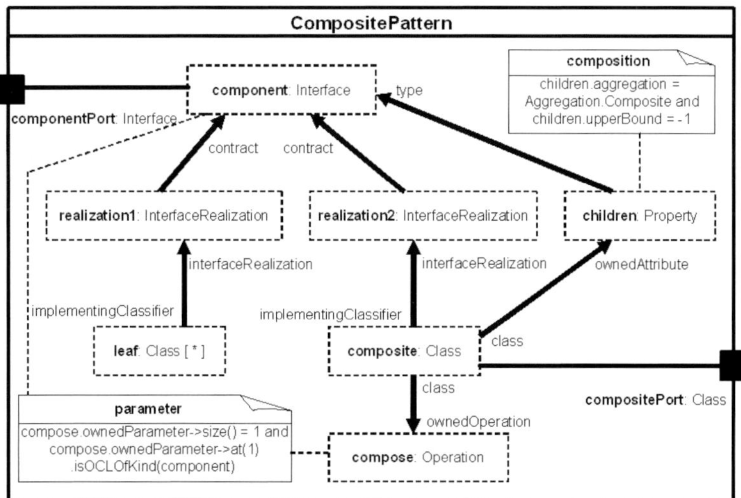

Fig. 7. Epattern specification for composite pattern

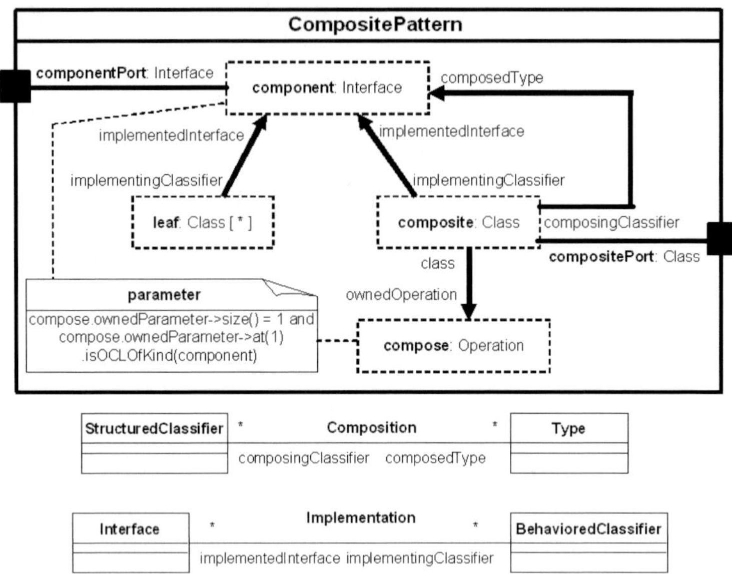

Fig. 8. Simplified Epattern specification for composite pattern

refactored to use EAssociationEnd rather than EReferences instances to type connectors. In our example, two instances of EAssociation are specified: the first is 'Implementation' between 'BehavioredClassifier' and 'Interface' and is used to type a connector directly from 'compose'/'leaf' to 'component', whereas the second is 'Composition' between 'StructuredClassifier' and 'Type' and is used to type a connector from 'composite' to 'component'. The simplified pattern specification is shown in Figure 8. The figure also shows (bottom) the specification of the two derived associations.

4 Related Works

Pattern specification is a common denominator to most work in applied pattern research. Various approaches have been proposed for pattern specification [15]. One category of approaches, that our work also belongs to, uses metamodeling techniques. The work presented in [11] and [12] proposes specifying a pattern as a UML 1.5 meta-collaboration with pattern roles typed with M1 classes stereotyped <<meta>> and named after metaclasses. This obviously prevents writing constraints for such roles as their M2 type information is not available at M1. Also the binding between a role and an element playing that role is done with an explicit dependency, rather than a simple value assignment to a property of a pattern instance as in our approach.

The work in [13] introduces the RBML language, which is used to specify UML patterns as specialized UML metamodels. Pattern roles are specified as subclasses of their base metaclasses in UML and are related to each other though new meta-associations. One problem with specifying a pattern as a metamodel, rather than a metaclass as in our approach, is the inability to inherit or compose the pattern, which hinders scalability.

Another disadvantage is that role binding is done through a generic mapping scheme and is not conveniently an instantiation of the pattern meta-class and an assignment of the role values (since roles are features of the pattern metaclass).

Another proposal is found in [14], where the DPML language is used to visually specify patterns as a collection of participants, dimensions (multiplicities), relationships and constraints. One draw back is the non-standard notation adopted by the language. Another problem is the restriction of the participants and relationships to predefined types from the UML domain, which limits the scope of the patterns definable by the language. Also, there is no mention of complexity management features.

Another approach [16] provides a metamodel to specify patterns. This metamodel is first specialized with pattern related concepts before being instantiated to produce an abstract model (pattern specification), which is either instantiated to create a concrete model (pattern instance) or parameterized to use in pattern detection. The provided metamodel contains pattern-domain metaclasses in addition to metaclasses from the target domain (e.g. UML) defined as their subclasses. This need to define required metaclasses from the target domain in the pattern metamodel puts a great limitation on the generality and practicality of the approach.

To summarize, most of the above approaches lack the ability to specify patterns for languages other than UML. They also lack features (e.g. user-defined associations, inheritance, composition) that help alleviate the complexity of pattern specification. Additionally, some of them specify M2-level patterns at M1, which deprives them from using free features like pattern constraints and role binding through pattern instantiation. Finally, they lack a well-defined process that allows pattern authors to build, refine and simplify patterns in a stepwise manner.

5 Conclusions and Future Works

Detecting (un)desirable patterns is an important component of model analysis. Patterns need to be formally specified before they can be manipulated by tools. The specification approach should ideally support patterns of any MOF-compliant language and be able to scale to patterns of different complexities. In this paper, we present the PMF framework and its Epattern specification language that specifically target such properties. In the context of the OMG's 4-layer metamodeling architecture, Epattern has M3 semantics used to specify patterns at the M2 level. A pattern is basically specified as a metaclass. This gives it the ability to be instantiated, inherited and composed. To further assess the feasibility of our approach, we are currently specifying most GoF patterns with Epattern, including behavioral patterns. We also plan to specify a sample set of anti-patterns. We are also working on deriving a pattern detection algorithm from a specification. Finally, we are implementing a tool that integrates with the RSA tool to allow pattern authors to manage their pattern specifications, and use them to detect and visualize pattern instances in user model.

References

[1] J. Miller and J. Mukerji. MDA Guide Version 1.0.1. OMG, Massachusetts, June 2003.

[2] G. Booch. Handbook of Software Architecture. http://www.booch.com/architecture/

[3] IBM Rational Software Architect. http://www-128.ibm.com/developerworks/rational/products/rsa/

[4] F. Budinsky, D. Steinberg, T. Grose, S. Brodsky and E. Merks. Eclipse Modeling Framework. Pearson Education. August 2003.
[5] OMG. UML 2.0 Suprestructure Specifications. OMG Document formal/05-07-04
[6] E. Magyari et.al. UDM: An Infrastructure for Implementing Domain-Specific Modeling Languages. The 3rd OOPSLA Workshop on Domain-Specific Modeling, OOPSLA '03.
[7] E. Gamma, R. Helm, R. Johnson and J. Vlissides. Design Patterns: Elements of Reusable Object-Oriented Software. Addison Wesley, 1995.
[8] UML2: EMF-based UML 2.0 Metamodel Implementation. http://www.eclipse.org/uml2
[9] OMG. MOF Core Specification v2.0. OMG Document formal/06-01-01
[10] W. Brown, H. McCormick, T. Mowbray and RC Malveau. Antipatterns: Refactoring Software, Architectures, and Projects in Crisis. John Wiley & Sons, 1998.
[11] J. Mak., C. Choy and D. Lun. Precise Modeling of Design Patterns in UML. In Proceedings of the 26th International Conference on Software Engineering, 2004.
[12] A. Guennec, G. Sunye and J.M. Jezequel. Precise Modeling of Design Patterns. Proceedings of UML 2000, volume 1939 of LNCS, pages 482-496. Springer Verlag, 2000.
[13] R. France, D. Kim, S. Ghosh, and E. Song. A UML-Based Pattern Specification Technique. IEEE Transactions on Software Engineering, 30(3):193-206, March 2004.
[14] D. Maplesden, J.G. Hosking and J.C. Grundy. Design Pattern Modelling and Instantiation using DPML. In Proceedings of Tools Pacific 2002, Sydney, p. 18-21, Feb. 2002.
[15] A. Baroni, Y.G. Gueheneuc and H. Albin-Amiot. Design Patterns Formalization. Ecole Notionale Superieure des Techniques Industrielles. Research Report 03/3/INFO, 2003.
[16] H. Albin-Amiot and Y.G. Guéhéneuc. Metamodeling Design Patterns: Application to Pattern Detection and Code Synthesis. In Proceedings of the ECOOP 2001 Workshop on Adaptative Object-Models and MetaModeling Techniques, 2001.
[17] G. Engels, J.M. Kuster and L. Groenewegen. Consistent Interaction of Software Components. In Proceedings of Integrated Design and Process Technology, 2002.
[18] L. Briand. Y. Labiche, L. O'Sullivan, M. Sowka. Automated Impact Analysis of UML Models. Journal of Systems and Software, vol. 79, no. 3, pp 339-352, March 2006.
[19] M. Elaasar, L. Briand and Y. Labiche. A Metamodeling Approach to Pattern Specification and Detection. Technical Report SCE-06-08, Carleton University, March 2006.
[20] OMG. OCL for EMOF Specification v2.0. OMG Document ptc/05-06-13
[21] Omodo. EclipseUML for MDA. http://www.omondo.com
[22] OMG. UML 2.0 Infrastructure Specifications. OMG Document formal/05-07-05

Immune System Computation and the Immunological Homunculus

Irun R. Cohen

Department of Immunology, Weizmann Institute of Science, Rehovot 76100, Israel
irun.cohen@weizmann.ac.il

Two Questions

Students for the Master of Science degree at the Weizmann Institute of Science are obliged to spend the first year of the two-year program doing three-month rotations through three different laboratories in any of the various faculties at the Institute. In 1998, Na'aman Kam rotated through my laboratory in the Department of Immunology where he did molecular modeling of an antibody (1). His next rotation, he told me, would be with David Harel in the Department of Computer Science and Applied Mathematics. When you get there, said I, tell David Harel about the immune system and ask him two questions:

1. Is the immune system a computer?
2. If a computer scientist would set out to build a computer capable of doing what the immune system does, what kind of computer would it have to be?

Connecting Computer and Biological Sciences

The questions (or to be more accurate, the student who transmitted them) led to a continuing collaboration with David Harel catalyzed by joint Master's, Doctoral and Post-doctoral students who have worked to combine computer science and biological systems: After Na'aman Kam came Sol Efroni (2-4), Naamah Swerdlin (5), Yaki Setty, Hila Amir-Kroll, and Avital Sadot. Students can be a boon to inter-disciplinary research because, being unencumbered by expertise, they fearlessly lead (or carry) their supervisors into unfamiliar territories.

Let us return to the first of the two questions that led me to collaborate with a computer scientist: Is the immune system a computer? Obviously, the immune system differs from the devices made by humans called computers in its construction, operation and use. The more interesting question is whether the immune system is a biologic computing machine, and the most interesting questions are what it computes and how it computes.

A Defense System

Many immunologists, probably most, would not think of the immune system in computational terms. There are two reasons for this: the defense role assigned to the immune system and the clonal selection theory of adaptive immunity.

O. Nierstrasz et al. (Eds.): MoDELS 2006, LNCS 4199, pp. 499 – 512, 2006.

It has been taught for about a century, and is still taught, that the defining role of the immune system is to defend the body against foreign invaders (6). To attack an invader, your immune system has to detect and identify the invader as distinctly not belonging to your body. Thus, the immune system exists, it is claimed, to discriminate between one's own self-molecules (ignore them) and molecules foreign to the body (attack them). From this classical point of view, the immune system has evolved to discriminate between self and non-self molecules in the most general sense and concretely between one foreign molecule (antigen) and another (7, 8). (An *antigen* is any molecule that can bind to the antigen receptor of a lymphocyte.) The discriminating agent is proposed to be the individual cell, not the system of cells.

Clonal Selection

The emphasis on clones (single cells and their progeny) is anchored in the clonal selection theory of adaptive immunity, the most widely accepted paradigm of immunology. This theory proposes that each lymphocyte, and its clonal progeny, either responds or does not respond to a given antigen molecule (9). Depending on the specific structure of each lymphocyte's unique antigen receptor, that lymphocyte will either attack the antigen molecule, or ignore it. The classical discourse of immunologists about such discriminations has emphasized the antigen receptors on individual immune cells, paying little attention to computation at the level of the system as a whole.

Maintenance

Experimental facts, however, can depart from classical teachings. It is now clear that the immune is responsible for more than body defense; immune system cells promote, even control, processes such as healing wounds and repairing broken bones, growing new blood vessels, building and pruning scar tissue, disposing of dead cells, killing and removing injured or abnormal cells, clearing effete molecules, advancing regeneration of various body tissues, and the like. The dynamic processes initiated in response to injury are termed inflammation; the aim of inflammation is healing (8). The immune system is the system that commences, orchestrates and resolves inflammation. Immune activities, including restorative inflammation and defense against pathogens, can be generalized under the concept of body maintenance. Indeed, the activity of the immune system is responsible for maintaining a peaceful, ongoing host-parasite relationship with the billions of bacteria, the so-called normal flora, that occupy niches throughout our body in the gut, skin and respiratory tract; even our cells – nervous system cells, immune cells, and others – harbor latent viruses quietly held in check by continuous, unimposing and covert immune maintenance. Normal flora and latent viruses become pathogens only when the immune system has been damaged or weakened, for example, by AIDS, cancer or immunosuppressive medications. We may say that the immune system, by managing inflammation, functions to maintain the body in working order in response to the daily grind of existence as well as to sporadic episodes of clinical illness due to infection or injury. The immune system acts as a maintenance system; defense is only one aspect of maintenance (9). Actually, Eli Metchnikoff experimented with immune maintenance a century ago, but the discovery of antibodies to infectious agents seduced immunology away from body maintenance and into body defense (10).

(If you ask an immunologist, he or she will admit that immune cells and molecules perform vital maintenance functions; why defense continues to be paradigmatic for mainstream immunology is a matter for sociologists (11), not for computer scientists.)

The task of maintaining the body obviously demands immune computation. Maintenance, including defense, requires the dynamic deployment of varied inflammatory processes based on reliable information about cells in flux. The inflammatory response suited to repair a broken bone, for example, is clearly different from the inflammatory response required to hold one's gut bacteria in check or to cure a bout of influenza – which cells and molecules are to take part in the process, when, where, how, in what order, in which intensity, and with what dynamics? The answers arise from computation. The immune system mines information about the state of the various cells of the body (Is there a problem here? What kind?), integrates the body information into immune system information (antibody repertoires, cell repertoires, cell differentiation and numbers, cell movements and migrations, secreted molecules, and so forth). The modified state of the immune system, expressed locally at the site of injury and to some extent globally, is key to the inflammatory process. Immune inflammation, in turn, triggers a response of body cells in the area of injury leading, usually, to healing and restoration of function. As the process evolves, the immune system updates the inflammatory response to match the particular circumstances that emerge on the way to healing, maintaining and/or defending the body. The general success of physiologic inflammation in keeping us fit is highlighted by the occasional disease caused by pathogenic inflammation – inflammation that is not properly managed by the immune system (9) can cause autoimmune diseases such as multiple sclerosis, degenerative diseases such as Alzheimer's disease, or allergic diseases such as asthma.

At the operational level, it is now clear that clones of lymphocytes do not function in isolation, as taught by the classic clonal selection theory. The immune system works as an integrated, whole system, and can respond potentially in many different, and even contradictory ways when it detects an injury or an antigen. The outcome of any immune response involves a choice between many alternative types of possible response, and many different types of cells take part in the response choice. This immune decision-making process uses strategies similar to those observed in nervous system cognition (9, 12). A cognitive theory of the immune system, in contrast to the clonal selection theory, is computational in spirit and practice.

The Immune System Computes

We can summarize thusly: If we define computation as the transformation of input data into output data, then we should conclude that the immune system computes: the input to the immune system is the state of the body and the output of the immune system is the healing process (the inflammatory response) that maintains a healthy body. In this sense the immune system is a computation machine that transforms body-state data into immune-system data that, simultaneously, feeds back on the body to modify its state and restore body health. The difference between the physiologically regulated inflammatory response that keeps us healthy and the dysregulated or chronic inflammatory response that can make us ill lies in the dynamics and fidelity of the computations performed by the immune system – the cells and molecules that mediate inflammation, both healthy and noxious inflammation, are exactly the same (13). In other words, the hardware of the immune system is standard for all types of inflammation. The differences between inflammatory responses emerge from the different possible deployments in quantities and timing of a standard set of cells and molecules. Thus, the nature of an inflammatory response depends on a continuous computation based on the collective interactions between immune and body cells. These interactions are required throughout one's lifetime; only upon death does the immune system terminate its computations of the state of the body. The bottom line is that the immune system is a continuously reactive computing system (9, 14).

Living Systems Compute

I have taken the immune system as my text for discourse because I am an immunologist; but all living systems – cells, organisms, communities – can be characterized by the type of computations they execute to maintain life. All living systems transform input from their immediate environment – be it other cells, molecules, organisms, societies, physical variables such as light, sound, pressure and temperature, nutrients, toxins, parasites, diurnal and seasonal rhythms, and so forth – into outputs that make possible survival – or non-survival (9). All living systems must compute to maintain themselves in the world. The way the immune system computes provides an insight into how other living systems compute. So how does the immune system compute?

Immune Computation

First, we should note that immune computation works without the standard features of human computers and human computation:

No external operator or programmer;

No programs, algorithms, or software distinct from the system's hardware – its cells and molecules;
(Parenthetically, let me say that DNA is definitely not a program or set of algorithms (15); DNA is information whose meaning is defined by the way the DNA is used by the whole cell and its component molecules.)

No central processing unit (CPU);

No standard operating system: no two immune systems are identical, even in identical twins (since the maintenance histories of their bodies differ, their immune systems must differ);

No formal, mathematical logic;

No termination criteria; the system does not halt its operations;

No verification procedures.

Secondly, the immune system not only lacks the standard features of human-made computers, it expresses properties that no human computer can match:

Self-assembly: the immune system, like the rest of the individual, develops from a single fertilized egg;

Continuous replication: immune molecules and cells proliferate;

Continuous death: immune molecules and cells undergo death, both physiologically ("programmed death") and by chance, and are constantly replaced without a hitch in function – indeed, the death of immune cells is required for healthy immune computation (9);

Distributed in space: immune cells and molecules roam the body;

Ad hoc organization: immune cells and molecules collect and interact at different sites throughout the body when necessary;

Immune memory is based on the evolution of the immune system in response to accumulating experience, and not on of strings of digital information;

A dismantled system may still operate: immune responses can be made by cells growing in tissue culture and upon transfer of immune cells into naïve recipient animals.

Immune Computation Defined

The computational task of he immune system, as we said, is to translate the state of the body (locally and globally) into the state of the immune system (locally and globally). The computational process of translation is iterative and unending; the immune system and the body continuously respond to and update each other. That is the essence of immune computation. How is it done?

The Data Are the Program

How can the immune system compute if, unlike a human-made computer, it has no programmer, no program, no CPU and no termination rule? The answer is that immune computation does not need them.

No termination rule is needed because the immune system never terminates its computation; it is continuously adjusting its state to the state of the body. The immune system, as we said, is a concurrently reacting system (14).

The immune system computes without programmer, program or CPU because the immune system makes no distinction between program and data or between hardware and software; the data are the program and the hardware is the software. Just as the infinite tape acted upon by a universal Turing machine can be considered as both the input data and the program that dictates the computation, so can the reciprocally responding states of the immune system and of the body be viewed as both data and program. The data, which are cells and molecules and their various states, are also the hardware of the immune system. The equivalence between hardware, data and program is easy to grasp in principle; in practice, as we shall discuss below, the details are enormously complex and pose a grand challenge to computer science.

Immune Parallel Processing

Immune computation emerges from the parallel processing of information – parallel processing in the extreme. Each cell in the immune system is a distinct processor; each cell, by its thousands of receptors, collects input, and each cell, by it secretions and behaviors, translates input into output. The immune system of a human is composed of many millions, hundreds of millions, of individual cells, each of which are an individual processor. The computation emerges from the integration of these processors working in parallel; the integration occurs through networking. The networking is organized by anatomical architecture and by cellular interactions. The architecture of the system brings select immune cells together in discrete space and time, and the interactions between the now adjacent cells create the integrated, dynamic response of the system. The details are the provenance of the field of immunology; you don't have to know them now to grasp the principles or appreciate the wonder.

Anatomic Networking

The cellular processors of the immune system are in a constant state of dynamic flux, but the flow of cells is well organized by the circulatory system (blood and lymph flows), by the variable residence of immune cells in regular lymphoid organs (lymph nodes, spleen, bone marrow, thymus, immune cell collections associated with the gut, the skin, the respiratory tract, and so forth), and by the ad hoc congregation of immune cells at sites where they are needed to deal with ongoing maintenance as well as haphazard injury, infection, and tumors (9). The position of any particular cell is influenced by many factors, including chance and stochastics, but the dynamics of the collective is highly organized at the population level through chemical sensing; each immune cell expresses a variable repertoire of surface receptors that directs its movements and its rest stations. The various cells and tissues of the body and of the immune system itself produce signal molecules that call particular immune cells to sites of interaction. This anatomical/vascular/chemical architecture ensures that the necessary cellular processors meet and mutually interact.

Cell Diversity and Interaction Networking

Every immune cell is a processor, but they are not all the same type of processor. The exact number of different immune cell types is a parochial matter for immunologists, but there are at least several dozen types that differ in the inputs they receive (they express different receptor molecules) and in the outputs they export (they secrete different molecules and/or behave differently). The key to immune computation is the fact that each cellular processor is strongly influenced by its neighboring cellular processors. Immune cells not only interact with body cells and molecules, immune cells interact with each other.

Integration by Co-respondence: Immune CPU

Each immune cell processes information about the body it patrols and, at the same time, each immune cell processes information about how the other immune cells are processing information about the body at or near that site. I have termed this coordinated response of immune cells to the body *co-respondence* (9, 16). What is co-respondence? Keep in mind the diversity of each immune cell: Each immune cell expresses a particular class of receptors, and some classes of immune cells (T cells and B cells) even express receptors unique to the individual cell (antigen receptors; see below). Therefore, the collective of immune cells at the site of action (injury, infection, tumor, etc.) contains classes of cells and individual cells that respond (by their diverse receptors) to different features of the state of injury, infection, tumor, etc. Each cell sees and responds to only a small piece of body action; no single cell sees the whole show. Nevertheless, each cell, in responding to what it does see, produces molecules and expresses behavior that signify its own state – its own response to what it has seen. The essential mediator of co-respondence is the fact that each immune cell bears receptors that collect as input part of the output of the other immune cells. Thus, each cell sees what it sees of the body's injury while it also sees the effect on other immune cells of their own perceptions of the injury. In fact, there are classes of immune cells – regulatory cells – that specialize in responding, not to the states of body cells but directly to the states of other immune cells. Integration of the resulting inflammatory response takes place because each cell updates its own output in co-response to the output of its fellow cells. In other words, each immune cell participates in the collective regulation of the inflammatory response that maintains the organism.

Keep in mind that each of the co-responding cells continues to maintain its own intrinsic class and individual diversity; the cells do not all do the same thing. But whatever any of them does is strongly influenced by what the other cells see and do. This mutual updating of individual cellular processors leads to a consensus of the immune cell collective that integrates the totality of input and output of the different parallel processors. Co-respondence is dynamic; changes in the state of body cells lead to an integrated change in the state of the immune cells, as the immune cells interact with the changing states both of the body and the adjacent immune cells.

One might say that the process of co-respondence functions as a central processing unit – the immune CPU. The immune CPU comes into being because the immune system is self-referential; it looks at itself looking at the body. The saving power of self-reference is evident on many scales; a flock of birds succeeds in evading the falcon not because every bird in the flock sees the falcon; it suffices for them each to see what the adjacent birds are doing. Or, to laugh at the right time in the theatre, you need not have understood the joke. Collective behavior is integrated by collective self-reference.

Note that the body, for its part, is not merely a passive subject in co-respondence; the body adjusts its activities in response to the adjustments of the immune cells: scar tissue is formed or dissolved, blood vessels grow or degenerate, tissue cells express different genes, proliferate or die, and so on and so forth on the way to healing or containment (or to inflammatory disease, if the computation goes awry). The body, therefore, looks at the immune system looking at the body (9). This world of changing, reflecting mirrors may seem Cabbalistic, but such is life.

Networking Innate and Adaptive Mechanisms

Now that you have begun to grasp the complexity of immune computation, let me call your attention to an added level of complexity: the receptors of some immune cells are continuously created by random generation during one's lifetime; such cells can receive input unique to them and their descendents (the clone). These uniquely manufactured input receivers are the famous antigen receptors of the lymphocytes – the T cells and the B cells (9). The antigen receptors of B cells can also be secreted by the cells as cell-free antibody molecules. The antigen receptors of B cells and T cells are the products of new genes fashioned by these lymphocytes from raw-material DNA inherited from the individual's ancestors (9). The genetic endowment of the species provides the raw-material DNA for making new receptors, but species evolution cannot dictate any particular antigen receptor. Thus, an individual antigen receptor is the product of an individual's somatic development and not a molecule predetermined by the evolution of the individual's species.

(The creation of new genes by immune cells is just one example that supports the conclusion that DNA cannot function as a controlling program but is only part of the cell's data (15). The de novo generation of antigen receptors by clones of immune cells also explains much of the fascination of mainstream immunology with the clonal selection paradigm.)

Along with somatically generated antigen receptors, all immune cells are quipped with innately inherited receptors for various key molecules that serve to disclose to the immune system the states both of body cells and of immune cells (17). These innate receptors are part of the genetic endowment of the species. The interplay between innate-receptor input (species-encoded) and clonal antigen-receptor input (individually encoded) provides co-respondence with an unparalleled richness of personalized information for integration and collective immune cell decision-making (9). Indeed, the lymphocytes and their individualized receptors endow the adaptive immune system with an evolving individual memory (9). The details are beyond our present scope, but you can already sense the magnitude of the challenge (and the need) for computer science to help deal with this largess of complexity.

Note that all multi-cellular organisms feature immune systems, but not all immune systems include cells that fashion antigen receptors. In fact, most living creatures (plants, insects, roundworms, squid, etc.) manage to populate the world and deal with their parasites armed with immune cells that express innate receptors only; adaptive, individualized antigen receptors and antibodies characterize only the more complex vertebrates (9). It is conceivable that the more complex tissue structures of vertebrates require a more complex immune system to maintain their more complex body plan.

Scales of Computation

Biological computation takes place across multiple scales, in which systems are embedded one within the other like Russian dolls (9, 18). A single cell is itself a complex computing system: The cell's many thousands of receptors simultaneously gather a large amount of diverse input from both outside and inside the cell. These receptors generate signals within the cell that become integrated by intra-cellular signal-transduction networks, leading to the dynamic activation of genes or to the silencing of genes, changes in the shape and movements of the cell, and the evolution of the cell's state and its output. Each immune cell is only a single computational, reactive system within the cohorts of millions of cells comprising the immune system. The immune system, in turn, is embedded in the greater system we call the organism, and the organism is a single computational element in a species, a society, a nation, a world economy, a biosphere (9). The computational process we are exploring in the immune system repeats itself throughout lower and higher scales of biological reality.

Immunological Homunculus

At this point, we can conclude that immune computation leads to a dynamic representation of the body and its various states encoded within the substance of the immune system. The immune picture of the body, as we discussed, emerges from the fact that the state of the immune system mirrors the state of the body. Note that the immune picture of the body does not contain the whole body; the immune representation of the body is reduced to the body molecules that impinge on immune receptors – both innate receptors and antigen receptors – and to the response of the immune cells to this information. Although the amount of information contained in the limited number of body molecules perceived by the immune system is far less than the total amount of information contained within the body itself, this limited information would seem to be sufficiently informative for the purposes of immune maintenance. The reduced representation of the body grasps functionally the essence of the body's state. How does the immune system gather and assess essential body-state information?

Much has yet to be learned about the interplay of antigen receptors and innate receptors in immune maintenance, but we already know that the individual's immune system organizes the repertoires of developing T cells and B cells around particular body molecules (9, 19). One's body cannot know ahead of time the exact antigen receptors one's lymphocytes will generate when making new genes during individual development. Order, however, can be imposed on random events. It turns out that, during the somatic development of new antigen receptors, the immune system selects for survival only those T cells and B cells that receive input from particular body molecules (*self-antigens*). This positive selection by self-molecules for cell survival, together with a parallel process of negative selection for cell death, focuses the repertoire of antigen receptors on a particular set of body molecules. In other words, developing lymphocytes live or die depending on how they respond to representative body molecules. It should not be surprising that some of these somatically selected body molecules, such as stress proteins, are key players in body maintenance (17). Evolution too has learned to focus immune attention on particularly informative molecules; the innate receptors of different immune cells detect the concentrations of stress proteins and other state-sensitive molecules (17).

I have termed this immune image of the body the *immunological homunculus* (9. 19). I adopted the term from the neurological homunculus, the functional virtual image of the body encoded by organized sets of neurons (20). Like your brain, your immune system maintains your body by deploying a reduced, virtual image of the body represented in the molecular inputs and outputs of organized immune-system cells. I originally formulated the concept of the immunological homunculus based on the reactivity of antigen receptors of lymphocytes for selected self-antigens (9). Now, however, I would extend the homunculus concept to include the innate receptors that also receive input from body molecules. Some homuncular self-molecules are so important to the immune system that immune cells of different types see these molecules using both innate receptors and adaptive antigen receptors (17).

Three Bodies

We have not discussed here the computations made by the nervous system that maintain the body, but in closing I would like to include the neurological homunculus in a broader picture of the organism. In summary, one might say that each of us gets through life manipulating three bodies: one actual full-size body and two reduced, virtual bodies. The body we live in is the actual body; the neurological homunculus and the immunological homunculus are the virtual bodies that help maintain the actual body on its journey through the world (9). The actual body makes it through life's changing and often hostile environment by adjusting its neuron-based behavior by way of the neurological homunculus and by adjusting its immune-based inflammatory activity by way of the immunological homunculus. Know that the immune and nervous systems influence each other's activities, but that complex issue is beyond the scope of the present discussion. Thc point here is that three-body computation is a fact of life.

Evolutionary Programming

A universal characteristic of living systems is that they change over time: the ongoing computational activities of the brain, the immune system and the body lead to evolving, dynamic systems. Evolution thus plays an important role in the development of each of the three bodies at different scales of space and time: the evolutionary scale of the species; the developmental scale of the individual; and the experiential scale of the individual's life history. Evolution is central to our understanding of life's computational machinery (9).

I wrote above that immune computation has no external programmer. Perhaps that statement should be revised; the evolutionary process, indeed, could be viewed as the master programmer of immune computation, along with all the other living computational systems that have evolved. Living systems owe their existence to evolution. But evolution is an exceptional programmer: Human programs characteristically precede their implementation in time; first we plan, then we do. Evolutionary programs, in contrast, come into being only after their implementation. Evolution is not aware of its future. We can see evolution's program only by looking back in time – post-implementation.

Above, I suggested that biological computation succeeds because living systems need make no distinction between program, data, hardware and software. The programmer of the operation, then, it is the evolutionary process itself – the process is programmer.

The Fourth Body

Biology and computer science come together now at the beginning of the 21st Century to create yet a fourth body. This fourth body, like the neurological and immunological homunculi, is a reduced, but functional representation of the organism. Unlike the neurological and immunological homunculi, this fourth body is to be built *in silico*. The *in silico* body, to be useful, must be tailored to include the essential features of the real-life organism, but it also must be sufficiently reduced in its complexity so that we can understand it (4, 21). The fourth body created by the biology-computer science alliance will serve to document, organize, represent, and model aspects of the other three bodies – the real body and the two homunculi – in a way that will make it possible to carry out experiments in silico supportive of new thinking, new hypotheses and new predictions (Figure 1).

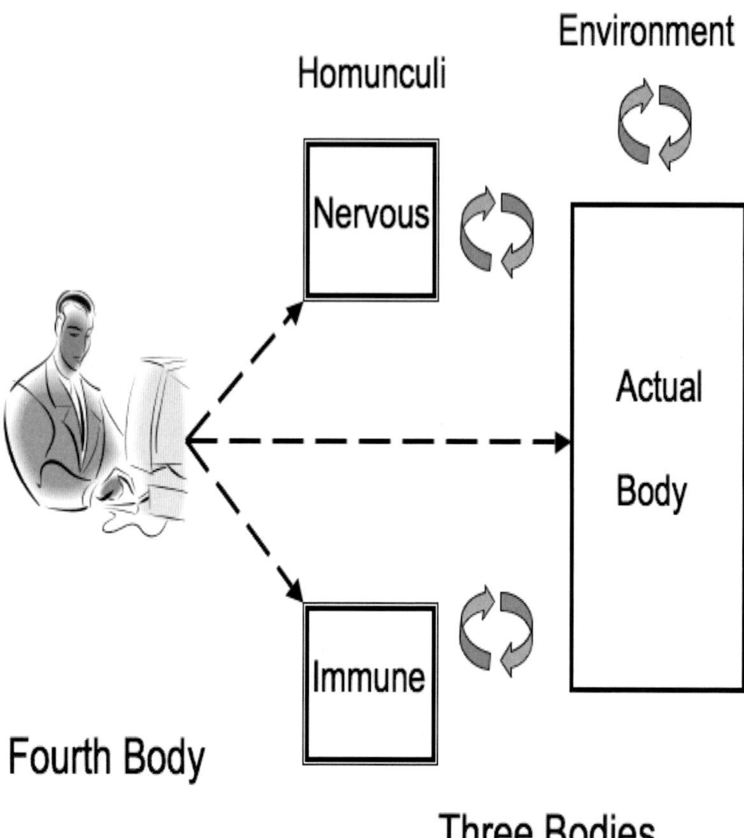

Fig. 1. The four bodies. The actual body, the organism, interacts successfully with the environment with the aid of two internal homuncular bodies – the nervous system homunculus, which manages the organism's behavior, and the immunological homunculus, which deals with body maintenance and protection against invaders. The complexity of these three bodies studied by biology requires, for understanding, an alliance with computer science to create a fourth body, the *in silico* homunculus.

Fourth-Body Challenges Come in Four Sizes

The challenges of developing the *in silico* fourth body will engage biologists and computer scientists productively for a long time to come. The challenges in immunology come in four sizes:

> **Small:** Help immunologists and others organize the masses of experimental data into informative representations (22);

Medium: Simulate limited parts of essential immune interactions to make them better understood (5);

Large: Model immune-cell and other biologic computations and make it possible to do novel *in silico* experimentation (2, 3);

Extra-large: Combine the body state and the immune system state in a detailed, comprehensive and dynamic true-to-life realistic model of body maintenance (23).

References

1. Herkel J, Kam N, Erez N, Mimran A, Heifetz A, Eisenstein M, Rotter V, Cohen IR. “Monoclonal antibody to a DNA-binding domain of p53 mimics charge structure of DNA: anti-idiotypes to the anti-p53 antibody are anti-DNA.” *Eur J Immunol.* 2004 Dec; 34(12):3623-32.
2. Efroni S, Harel D, Cohen IR. "Toward rigorous comprehension of biological complexity: modeling, execution, and visualization of thymic T-cell maturation." *Genome Res.* 2003 Nov;**13**(11):2485-97.
3. Efroni S, Harel D, Cohen IR. "Reactive animation: Realistic Modeling of Complex Dynamic Systems." 2005 *Computer* **38**:(1):38-47.
4. Efoni S, Harel D, Cohen IR. "A theory for complex systems: reactive animation." in *Multidisciplinary Approaches to Theory in Medicine. Studies in Multidisciplinarity, Vol. 3.* Ray Paton and Laura McNamara (Editors). Elsevier, Amsterdam. 2005. pp 309-324.
5. Swerdlin N, Cohen IR, and Harel D. “Towards an *in-silico* Lymph Node: A Realistic Approach to Modeling Dynamic Behavior of Lymphocytes.” Submitted for publication.
6. Wikipedia; http://en.wikipedia.org/wiki/Immune_system: “The immune system is the system of specialized cells and organs that protect an organism from outside biological influences.”
7. Efroni S, Cohen IR. "The heuristics of biologic theory: the case of self–nonself discrimination." *Cell Immunol.* 2003; **223**(1): 87-89.
8. Cohen IR. "Discrimination and dialogue in the immune system." *Semin Immunol* 2000; **12**(3):215-9; 321-323.
9. Cohen IR. *Tending Adam’s Garden: Evolving the Cognitive Immune Self.* Academic Press, London, UK. 2000.
10. Tauber AI. “Metchnikoff and the phagocytosis theory.” Nature Reviews 2003; **4**:897-901.
11. Kuhn TS. *The Structure of Scientific Revolutions*, Second Edition, Enlarged. The University of Chicago Press, Chicago, 1970.
12. Cohen IR. “The cognitive principle challenges clonal selection.” *Immunol Today* 1992; **13**(11):441-4.
13. Cohen IR. “Kadishman’s Tree, Escher’s Angels, and the Immunological Homunculus.” *Autoimmunity: Physiology and Disease*, eds. Coutinho A, Kazatchkine MD. Wiley-Liss, Inc.1994 pp7-18.
14. Harel D and Pnueli A. “On the development of reactive systems.” Logics and Models of Concurrent Systems, Apt KR, ed., NATO Advanced Science Institute Series, vol. F-13, Springer-Verlag, 1985, pp. 477-498.

15. Cohen IR, Atlan H. “Limits to genetic explanations impose limits on the human genome project.” In *Encyclopedia of the Human Genome*, Nature Publishing Group, Macmillan, 2002.
16. Cohen IR, Hershberg U, Solomon S. “Antigen-receptor degeneracy and immunological paradigms.” *Molecular Immunology* 2004; **40**: 993-6.
17. Quintana FJ, Cohen IR. "Heat shock proteins as endogenous adjuvants in sterile and septic inflammation." *J Immunol.* 2005 1;**175**(5):2777-82.
18. Cohen IR, Harel D. “Explaining a Complex Living System: Dynamics, Multi-scaling and Emergence.” Submitted for publication.
19. Cohen IR. “The cognitive paradigm and the immunological homunculus.” *Immunol Today* 1992; **13**(12):490-4.
20. Cohen IR. “Natural Id-Anti-Id Networks and the Immunological Homunculus,” in *Theories of Immune Networks* eds. Atlan H, Cohen IR. Springer-Verlag. (Berlin),1989; pp 6-12.
21. Cohen IR. "Informational landscapes in art, science, and evolution." *Bulletin of Mathematical Biology*. 2006. [E-pub ahead of print].
22. Quintana FJ, Hagedorn PH, Elizur G, Merbl Y, Domany E, Cohen IR. "Functional immunomics: microarray analysis of IgG autoantibody repertoires predicts the future response of mice to induced diabetes." *Proc Natl Acad Sci U S A.*, 2004 Oct 5;**101**: Suppl 2:14615-21. Epub 2004 Aug 12.
23. Harel D. “A grand challenge for computing: Full reactive modeling of a multi-cellular animal.” Bull European Assoc Theoretical Science, no. 81, Oct. 2003, pp. 226-235.

(pdf copies of most of my publications can be down-loaded from the list of publications posted on my website: http://www.weizmann.ac.il/immunology/ iruncohen/home.html)

Building Abstractions in Class Models: Formal Concept Analysis in a Model-Driven Approach

Gabriela Arévalo, Jean-Rémi Falleri, Marianne Huchard, and Clémentine Nebut

LIRMM, CNRS and Université de Montpellier 2,
161, rue Ada, 34392 Montpellier cedex 5, France
{arevalo, falleri, huchard, nebut}@lirmm.fr

Abstract. Designing class models is usually an iterative process to detect how to express, for a specific domain, the adequate concepts and their relationships. During those iterations, the abstraction of concepts and relationships is an important step. In this paper, we propose to automate this abstraction process using techniques based on Formal Concept Analysis in a model-driven context. Using UML2.0 class diagrams as modeling language for class models, in this proposal we show how our model-driven approach enables parameterization, tracing and generalization to any metamodel to express class models.

1 Introduction

In model-driven development, modeling activities have as purpose (at least partially) to replace the coding tasks. Unfortunately, the model engineer does not have all the same facilities (such as versioning and refactoring tools) as in mostly classical coding environments. With these kinds of tools, the model-driven paradigm could be adopted in large software companies. Specifically, within the context of refactoring object-oriented models, in this paper we focus on automating the detection and building of class hierarchies. Designing class models is not a trivial task. It is an iterative process to detect how to express, for a specific domain, the adequate concepts and their relationships. During this iterative process, the abstraction of concepts and relationships is a crucial task. Indeed, abstraction provides better concept structuring and more reusable artifacts. In this paper, we propose to automate this abstraction process using an adaptation of Formal Concept Analysis (FCA) techniques [1] in a model-driven context. FCA has proved to be an efficient technique to build or restructure class hierarchies [2, 3, 4], but has not been yet applied in a model-driven approach.

The contribution of this paper is a FCA-based model-driven approach to abstract concepts involved in a class model (classes, associations, attributes and so on). Briefly, this process uses the successive application of model transformations as a main building mechanism. We use two main tools: Kermeta [5] and UML. Using Kermeta [5] (compatible with MOF and OCL) as our metamodeling language, we are able to (1) give an operational semantics to every

O. Nierstrasz et al. (Eds.): MoDELS 2006, LNCS 4199, pp. 513–527, 2006.

underlying metamodel and implement every model transformation, and (2) describe the FCA algorithms and check their performances. Using the UML as a language, we describe class models. As a result, the transformations are defined based on a part of the UML 2.0 metamodel. However, the specification and implementation of our proposal using model transformations turns to be easily tunable by parameters, and applicable to other metamodels which handle adequate concepts to detect and build abstractions. Our approach shows that formalizing FCA with model transformations gives interesting benefits, such as tracing the different steps of the process, or the parameterization. These characteristics are also important if we compare our contribution to the one introduced in [6]. In that approach the main limitation was that the authors consider the model transformations as a black box, with no means of tracing or parameterizing.

The paper is structured as follows. Section 2 gives a brief overview of our approach, recalls the main notions of FCA, and introduces the example used all over the paper. Each main transformation is then detailed into Sections 3, 4 and 5 respectively. Section 6 discusses the benefits and limitations of this approach, as well as related work.

2 Overview and Background

Building class models is usually not a trivial task but rather an iterative process aiming at finding the simplest model with good properties such as, for example, maintainability, adequate factorization and easy testing. While building a class model, one task consists in generalizing concepts: finding regularities in already identified concepts in order to detect new abstractions. When representing class models with UML class diagrams, several model elements can be abstracted such as, obviously, classes, but also associations, attributes, and methods. As an example, starting from the class model shown in Fig. 1(a), the class model of Fig. 1(b) can be obtained, where new classes have been introduced (for example class `BankClient` that is an abstraction of the `BasicAccountHolder` and the `TeenagerClient` classes), as well as new attributes (e.g. the attribute `accountList` that abstracts the two attributes `bAccountList` and `tAccountList`). Our approach aims at automating this refactoring, i.e. at detecting and building new abstractions in a class model, using Formal Concept Analysis (FCA). Before going into the details, we provide in this section the minimal notions of FCA, and then we give an overview of our approach, that will be detailed in the next sections.

2.1 Background on FCA

FCA [1] is a mathematical technique, based on lattice theory, to discover abstractions (known as *concepts*) from a set of entities (formal objects) described by attributes (formal attributes) [1]. Concept specialization draws a lattice structure.

[1] All over the text we use the term attributes to denote formal attributes, except in case we must clarify the ambiguity between attributes of a class model and formal attributes of a FCA context.

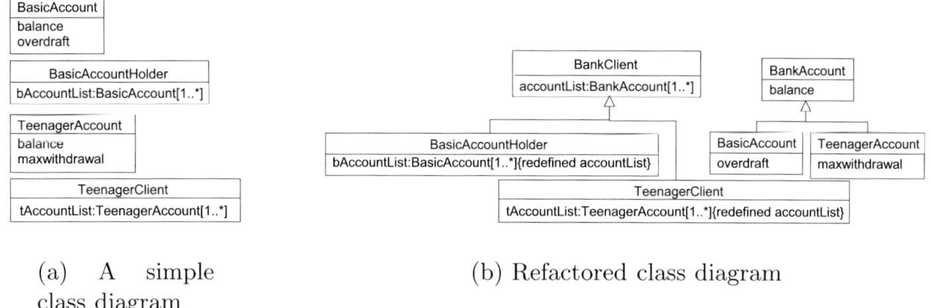

(a) A simple class diagram

(b) Refactored class diagram

Fig. 1. The example of bank accounts

Basic FCA considers *formal contexts* $\mathcal{K} = (E, P, I)$ as shown in Figure 2 (left). E is the entity set (here UML classes), P the attribute set (here UML attributes) and I associates an entity with its attributes: $(e, p) \in I$ when entity e owns attribute p. With any entity set $X \subseteq E$ we associate the shared attributes with the mapping α defined by $\alpha(X) = \{p \in P \mid \forall e \in X, \ (e, p) \in I\}$. Symmetrically, with any attribute set $Y \subseteq P$ we associate the entities owning all the attributes of Y. To that end, we use the mapping ω defined by $\omega(Y) = \{e \in E \mid \forall p \in Y, \ (e, p) \in I\}$. In the example, let $Y = \{balance\}$, we have $\omega(Y) = \{BasicAccount, TeenagerAccount\}$, while for $X = \{BasicAccount\}$, $\alpha(X) = \{balance, overdraft\}$. A concept is a pair (X, Y) where $X \subseteq E$, $Y \subseteq P$, $\alpha(X) = Y$ and $\omega(Y) = X$. In Figure 2, $\{\{BasicAccount, TeenagerAccount\}, \{balance\}\}$ is a concept. Graphically, this concept corresponds to the vertical block in the column *balance*. More generally, a concept corresponds to a block of maximal size in the context (the blocks are found in the context modulo the order of the columns and rows). X (resp. Y) is usually called the extent (resp. intent) of the concept.

The specialization order between concepts corresponds to extent inclusion (or intent containment). The concept lattice $\mathcal{L} = (\mathcal{C}, \leq_{\mathcal{L}})$ is the set of concepts provided with the inclusion partial order. In Figure 2, the concept $\{\{BasicAccount\}$, $\{balance, overdraft\}\}$ specializes the concept $\{\{BasicAccount, TeenagerAc-count\}$, $\{balance\}\}$.

The concept at the bottom has no interest as it represents the hypothetic set of entities containing all attributes. The concepts at the first level correspond to initial classes. The unique concept of the second level stems from the factorization of property `balance`. In our example, it could generate a new UML class factorizing `balance` and appearing as a superclass of `BasicAccount` and `TeenagerAccount` (class `BankAccount`). The top concept gathers attributes common to all entities, in this specific case it is an empty set of attributes. This lattice is very simple, but in general, systematic factorization in real software projects generates too many concepts, which makes the analysis difficult to grasp. The main advantage of using FCA for UML class diagram reconstruction is that we obtain a sort of normal form for class models. In this normal form, redundancy is

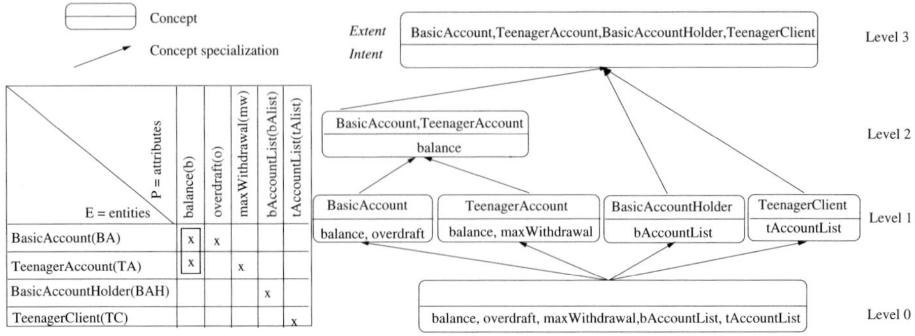

E = entities \ P = attributes	balance(b)	overdraft(o)	maxWithdrawal(mw)	bAccountList(bAlist)	tAccountList(tAlist)
BasicAccount(BA)	x	x			
TeenagerAccount(TA)	x		x		
BasicAccountHolder(BAH)				x	
TeenagerClient(TC)					x

Fig. 2. A context $\mathcal{K}$(left) and the lattice (right) describing bank accounts

eliminated (total factorization is achieved) and the specialization order between classes exactly matches the inclusion order between property set of the classes. Besides that, maximal factorization is obtained with minimal number of classes.

However, even in this very simple example, relevant abstractions remain undiscovered by this naive process. Let's see carefully at the two attributes `bAccountList` and `tAccountList`. Their types, respectively `BasicAccount` and `TeenagerAccount`, are evidently generalizable by a class such as `BankAccount` factorizing `balance`. Thus, the idea is to continue the process and decide that `bAccountList` and `tAccountList` share a common abstraction, namely *list of accounts*. To discover that abstraction, we need to go further into the representation of the UML class diagram, giving the status of entities to UML properties. As a result, UML classes and UML properties are described by characteristics including property ownership and classes used as types for properties. In the following section we explain how an extension to the theory of Formal Concept Analysis, named *Relational Concept Analysis* (RCA), allows such information to be treated.

2.2 Class Hierarchy Refactoring Using FCA in a MDE Context

Figure 3 shows an overview of our approach consisting of 3 model transformations[2].

1. The first transformation, *UML2Contexts*, turns the original UML 2.0 class diagram into a set of binary contexts and binary relations. It is a transformation from a UML 2.0 metamodel [7] to a relational context family metamodel.
2. The second transformation, *InitialContexts2FinalLattices*, aims at obtaining a set of concept lattices of the final class diagram from the initial set of

[2] All over this paper, we use an object terminology to refer to model conformance, for example we talk about models that are instances of meta-models. It can be seen as a terminological misuse, but since we are working with an object-oriented language (Kermeta [5]) to define the metamodels and the model transformations, this terminology is the most adequate one to our work.

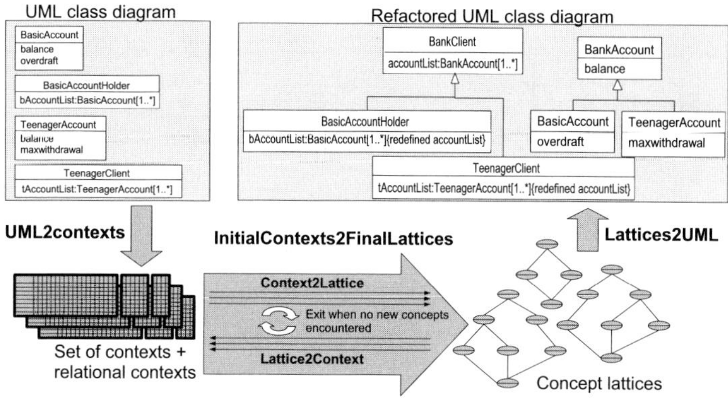

Fig. 3. Overview of our approach

contexts. It is a transformation from a relational context family metamodel to a concept lattice family metamodel.

3. The third transformation, *Lattices2UML* consists in translating the obtained concept lattices into a UML 2.0 class diagram using traceability information from the previous transformations.

Using a model-driven approach based on Formal Concept Analysis in order to refactor models is very fruitful. First, it allows to define a simple sequence of model transformations (in particular for the second transformation) without using a complex algorithm. Second, the proposed approach can be applied to classify any kind of concepts as soon as they are defined by a metamodel. Indeed, the core of the approach is the second transformation, and adapting the approach to another metamodel only requires to develop new transformations to replace the first (*UML2Contexts*) and the third (*Lattices2UML*) ones. As we have said in Section 1, every step of the approach is automated and every transformation is implemented in Kermeta [5].

3 From UML to Formal Contexts

In this section, we detail the transformation from a UML model to formal contexts handled by Relational Concept Analysis.

3.1 Metamodels Involved in the Transformation

In our approach we use the small metamodel deduced from the UML 2.0 metamodel (shown in Figure 4) to express class models. Working with such a reduced metamodel is not restrictive, since applying work on model typing and model type substitutability presented in [8], we can use a model conform to the whole UML 2.0 metamodel as an entry model of our transformation. In the rest of the paper, we will refer indifferently to the UML 2.0 metamodel or its reduced

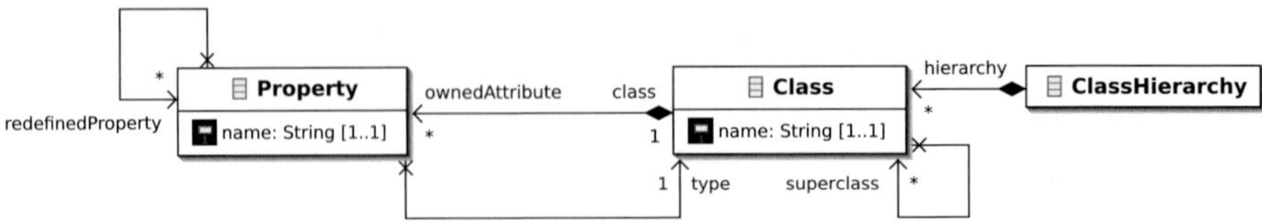

Fig. 4. Adaptation of a restriction of the UML metamodel

form. We focus only on classes, attributes and associations in the framework of our example: attribute `name`, class `Class`, class `Property`, role `type` which associates their type to properties and role `ownedAttribute` which associates their attributes to classes. As a simplification, we have restricted the end of role `type` to be `Class` rather than `Type`, a superclass of `Class`. `ownedAttribute` is in fact a derived role in the original UML 2.0 metamodel and we consider only flattened models (without inheritance relationships, just for simplification reasons). `ClassHierarchy` is used as an entry point in the models, while the derived role `superclass` and the role `redefinedProperty` are used only in the third transformation.

Relational Concept Analysis [6] considers a family of contexts rather than a single one, allowing to separate entities into several categories. In our example, there are two categories: `Class` and `Property` (see the example of RCF in Figure 6). The contexts of a family include relations that link entities of one kind to entities of another kind. Those relations come from the associations in the underlying metamodel (here the UML 2.0 metamodel, see Fig. 4). In our example, we deal with two relations: `ownedAttribute` and `type`. This set of contexts together with the relations is called a Relational Context Family (RCF). The associated metamodel is given in Figure 5. More formally, a relational context family $\mathcal{F}$ is a pair $(\mathcal{K}, \mathcal{R})$ where:

- $\mathcal{K}$ is a set of *contexts* $K_t = (E_t, P_t, I_t)$ linking entities to attributes (`Entity-AttributeContext` in Fig. 5). In our example $\mathcal{K} = \{K_{Class}, K_{Property}\}$.
- $\mathcal{R}$ is a set of contexts R_s expressing *relations* between entities coming from different contexts of $\mathcal{K}$. R_s is such that $\exists\, K_{t1}, K_{t2} \in \mathcal{K}, R_s \subseteq E_{t1} \times E_{t2}$. R_s is represented by `InterEntityContext` in Fig. 5. In the following, those contexts will be denoted as relations. In our example, $\mathcal{R} = \{R_{ownedAttribute}, R_{type}\}$ where $R_{ownedAttribute} \subseteq E_{Class} \times E_{Property}$ and $R_{type} \subseteq E_{Property} \times E_{Class}$.

3.2 The Transformation from UML to a Family of Contexts

We here explain how a UML model is automatically transformed into a relational context family. To illustrate this transformation, the result of its application on the UML class diagram of Figure 1(a) is shown in Figure 6. The Relational Context Family is automatically deduced from the UML 2.0 metamodel as follows (we discuss only our restricted case but the principle is the same on the whole UML 2.0 metamodel).

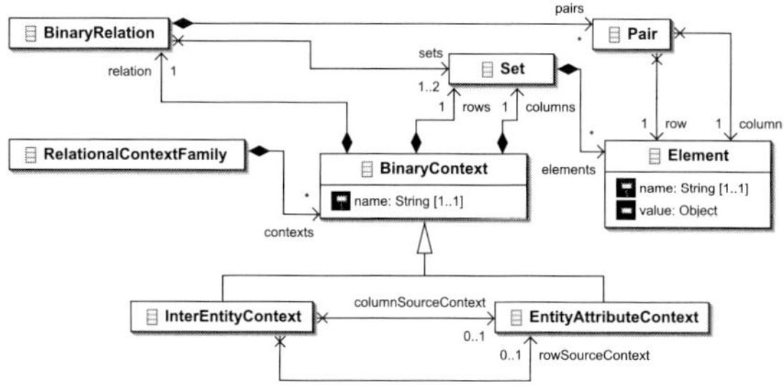

Fig. 5. The Relational Context Family (RCF) metamodel

K_{Class}	name= "BasicAccount"	name= "TeenagerAccount"	name= "BasicAccountHolder"	name= "TeenagerClient"
BA	X			
TA		X		
BAH			X	
TC				X

$K_{Property}$	name= "balance"	name= "overdraft"	name= "maxWithdrawal"	name= "bAccountList"	name= "tAccountList"
bba	X				
bta	X				
o		X			
mw			X		
bAlist				X	
tAList					X

R_{type}	BA	TA	BAH	TC
bba				
bta				
o				
mw				
bAlist	X			
tAlist		X		

$R_{ownedAttribute}$	bba	bta	o	mw	bAlist	tAlist
BA	X		X			
TA		X		X		
BAH					X	
TC						X

Fig. 6. The Relational Context Family obtained from the UML model of Figure 1(a)

– Selected metaclasses of the source metamodel (here: UML) give rise to contexts: in our example, $\mathcal{K}$ is composed of the two contexts, K_{Class} and $K_{Property}$ (as shown in Figure 6). Pairs composed of selected meta-attributes of these classes and their values on the studied model are transformed into the formal attributes in the target contexts. In our example, pairs are formed with the meta-attribute `name`.
– Relations of $\mathcal{R}$ come from selected roles in the associations of the source meta-model. In our example, we obtain the two relations R_{type} and $R_{ownedAttribute}$ shown in Figure 6. Values for all the relations are deduced from a view of the studied model as an instantiation of the UML metamodel (see the object diagram of Figure 8).

Those two transformation rules are illustrated in Figure 7.

Part of the relevance of this transformation relies on the possibility to fine-tune it. Choosing UML metamodel classes, attributes and associations to be encoded in the RCF is a delicate task. Some model elements provide quite technical information, such as multiplicity or visibility, while others expose the semantics of the domain such as names in general. For example, we do not want to generalize

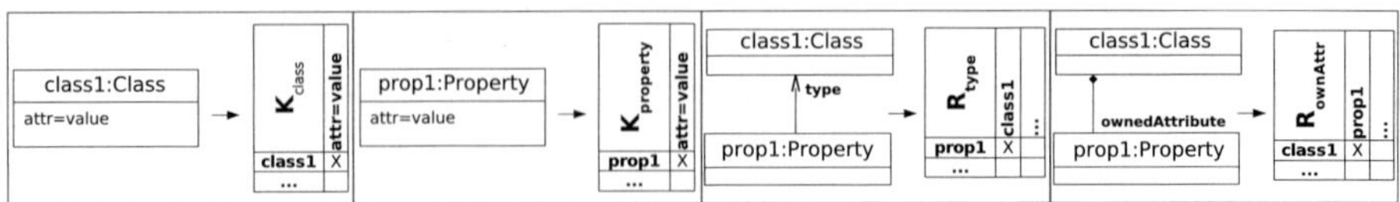

Fig. 7. Transformation from UML to context

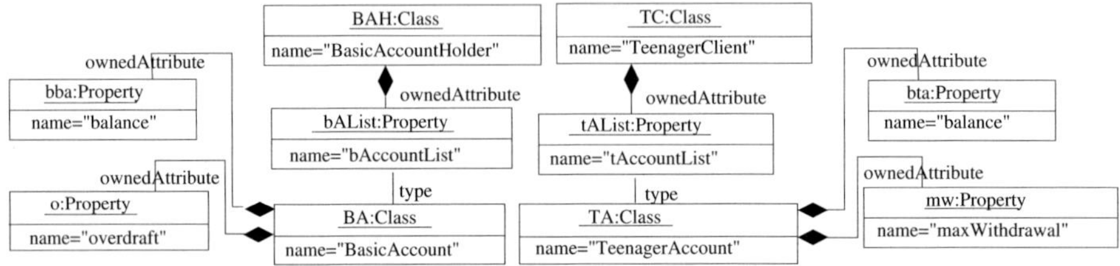

Fig. 8. Our class model of Fig. 1(a) as an instantiation of the simplified UML metamodel

two classes or two associations because they are both abstract. As a result, we do not take into account the meta-attribute `isAbstract` of the UML metaclass `Classifier` during the generalization process.

4 Class Hierarchy Refactoring: Iterative Transformation

In this section, we describe the core transformation of our approach, named *InitialContext2FinalLattices*, that aims at generating the lattice models from the initial Relational Context Family (RCF). The metamodel for the lattices is given in Figure 9.

This transformation (summarized in the bottom of Figure 3, and applied on our example in Figure 10) consists in iterating on the multiple application of two smaller transformations, *context2lattice* and *lattice2context*. Indeed, processing a RCF involves alternative construction of lattices (one per context) and

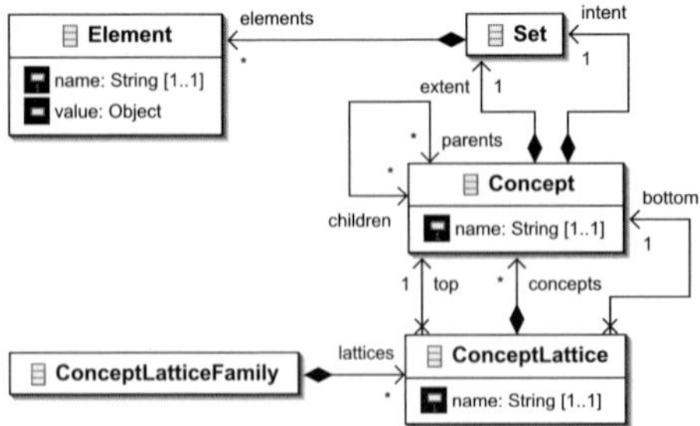

Fig. 9. The metamodel for lattices

A family of lattices is composed of concept lattices. The concepts of a lattice are ordered by the specialization relation represented by the association `children`/`parents`. A concept is composed of an `extent` and an `intent` that are two sets of elements.

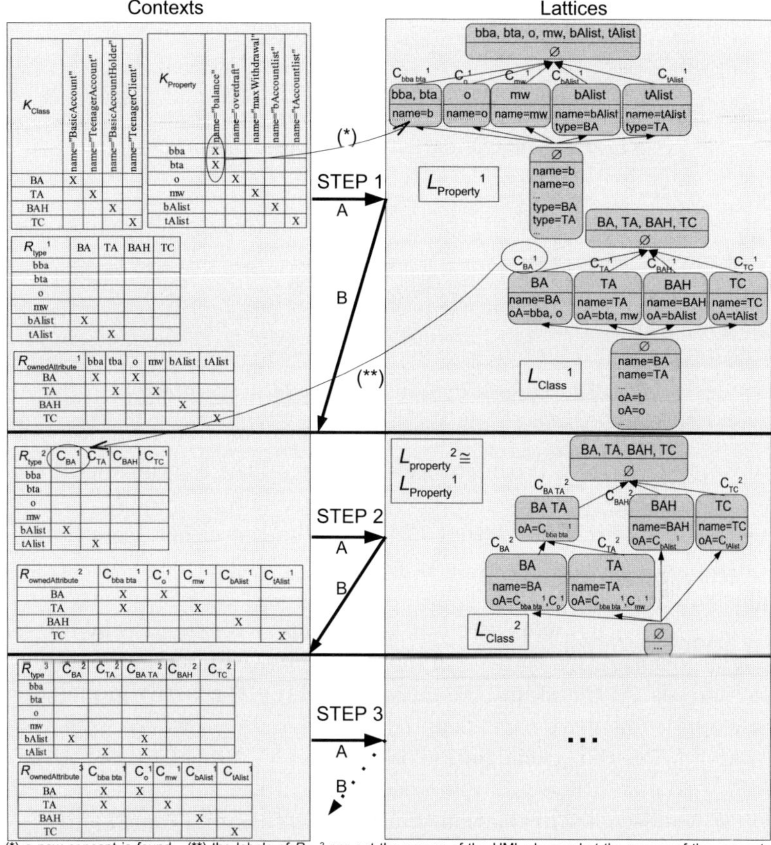

(*) a new concept is found - (**) the labels of R_{type}^2 are not the names of the UML classes but the names of the concepts, found during step 1, that generalize the classes - The relation ≅ between 2 lattices means that the lattices are identical except that in their extents, the concepts are differently numbered.

Fig. 10. Iterative transformation applied to the accounts example

enrichment of the relations $\mathcal{R}$ of the RCF by knowledge coming from lattices. The process stops when a fix point on lattice construction is reached, namely when no new abstraction emerges.

More precisely, we define a step of the transformation *InitialContext2FinalLattices* as a multiple application (one application per context) of the transformation *context2lattice* (part A of the step) followed by a multiple application (one application per target relation) of the transformation *lattice2context* (part B of the step). In the bottom of Fig. 3 and in Figure 10, a step corresponds to a round-trip (A followed by B). The initial RCF is named RCF^1 and owns contexts and relations also numbered 1. RCF^1 generates in step 1 (A) lattices numbered 1 with concepts numbered 1, then those lattices generate in step 1 (B) a new RCF numbered RCF^2 and so on. This iteration stops when no concept is found during a step.

Part A of step i. The multiple application of the sub-transformation *context2lattice* builds one lattice for each entity-attribute context of RCF^i. The source

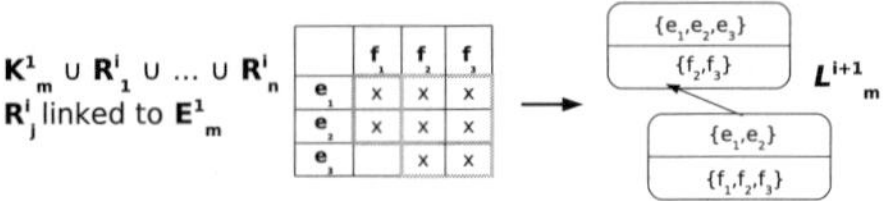

Fig. 11. Transformation rule for *context2lattice*

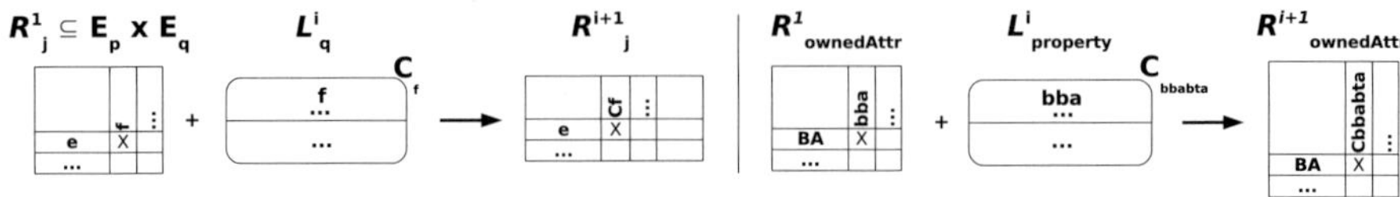

Fig. 12. Transformation rules for *lattice2context*

model of *context2lattice* is a context extended by all the relations with the same entity set. More formally, the source model is a context $K_p = (E_p, P_p, I_p)$ extended by all relations $R^i \in RCF^i$ such that $R^i \subseteq E_p \times Y$ (Y is either an entity set E_q at step 1, or the concept set of a lattice at step i, $i > 1$). The rule of this transformation is illustrated in Figure 11. For example, the K_{class} context is extended by the relation $R^i_{OwnedAttribute}$, while the $K_{Property}$ context is extended by the relation R^i_{type}. The transformation consists in building a lattice following classical Formal Concept Analysis. At this step i, the target model (i.e. the lattice model) obtained from the extended context K_p is denoted $\mathcal{L}^i_p = (X^i_p, \leq_{\mathcal{L}^i_p})$ where X^i_p is the set of concepts and $\leq_{\mathcal{L}^i_p}$ is the specialization order.

Part B of step i. The multiple application of the sub-transformations *lattice2context* builds a set of relations (initial contexts – in our example K_{Class} and $K_{Property}$ – are not modified during this transformation). During a *lattice2context* execution, a relation $R^{i+1} \subseteq E_p \times X^i_q$ is generated. The principle is to replace labels of columns in initial relations by concepts. The rules of this transformation are shown in Figure 12. Let us consider the relation $R^1_j \subseteq E_p \times E_q$. During part B of step i, R^1_j is replaced by $R^{i+1}_j \subseteq E_p \times X^i_q$, with $(e, C_f) \in R^{i+1}_j$ if $(e, f) \in R^1_j$ and $f \in Extent(C_f)$. For example, during part B of step 1, the labels of the columns of $R^1_{ownedAttribute}$ are replaced by the concepts of the lattice $\mathcal{L}^1_{Property}$ (see Figure 10). We have $(BA, C^1_{bbabta}) \in R^2_{ownedAttribute}$ since $(BA, bba) \in R^1_{ownedAttribute}$ and $bba \in Extent(C^1_{bbabta})$. An interpretation is that C^1_{bbabta} is a generalization of bba, more precisely an abstraction of properties named "balance". Moreover, class BA owns bba, then BA owns bba generalizations, including C^1_{bbabta}. At the end of this transformation, each lattice is associated with a context (via traceability links) and by construction to a class of the UML metamodel; in our example, lattices $\mathcal{L}_{Class}$ and $\mathcal{L}_{Property}$ are associated with metaclasses `Class` and `Property`.

5 Effective Refactoring : Coming Back to the UML

Our last transformation, *FinalLattices2UML*, parses lattices and generates UML elements. This transformation was implemented using the Kermeta language [5]. The transformation from a set of lattices to a UML class model is specified by three types of rules: non-relational, relational, and specialization. Figure 13 shows the rules used for the treatment of our example. At the LHS of the arrows are the patterns of the lattices and at the RHS, two views on generated UML static models are given: the model as an instance of the UML metamodel and the equivalent model in the concrete UML syntax.

The non-relational rules are the following:

- Concepts of the lattice associated with metaclass `M` give rise to UML instances of `M`; for example, concepts of lattice $\mathcal{L}_{Class}$ are interpreted as classes while concepts of lattice $\mathcal{L}_{Property}$ are interpreted as properties (more particularly attributes in the restricted metamodel we use). In rules R1 and R2 of Figure 13, concept C_i of the lattice $\mathcal{L}_{Class}$ is transformed into a UML class; while concept C_j of the lattice $\mathcal{L}_{Property}$ is transformed into a UML attribute.
- Non-relational descriptors in the intension of a concept correspond to attributes of metaclasses; for example `name` in the case of both classes and properties. In Figure 13, the names of the class generated from the concept C_i and of the attribute generated from the concept C_j come from values of descriptor `name` in concept intensions.

The generic relational rule is as follows. When a concept C_v is the value of a relation R in the intension of a concept C (i.e. when $(C, C_v) \in R$), then a link is

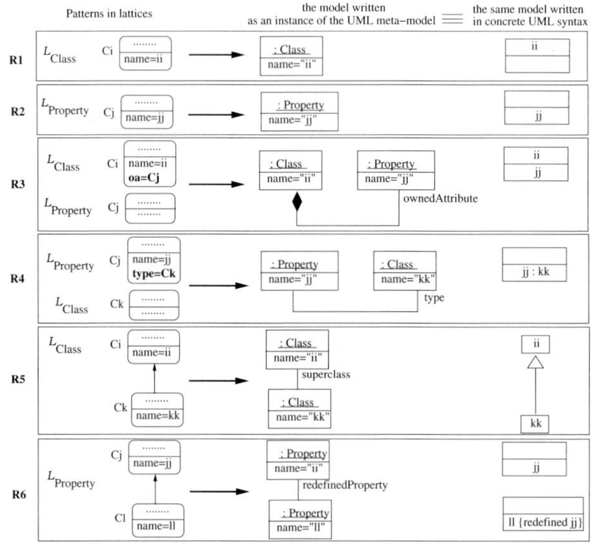

Fig. 13. Rules for the transformation from lattices to UML

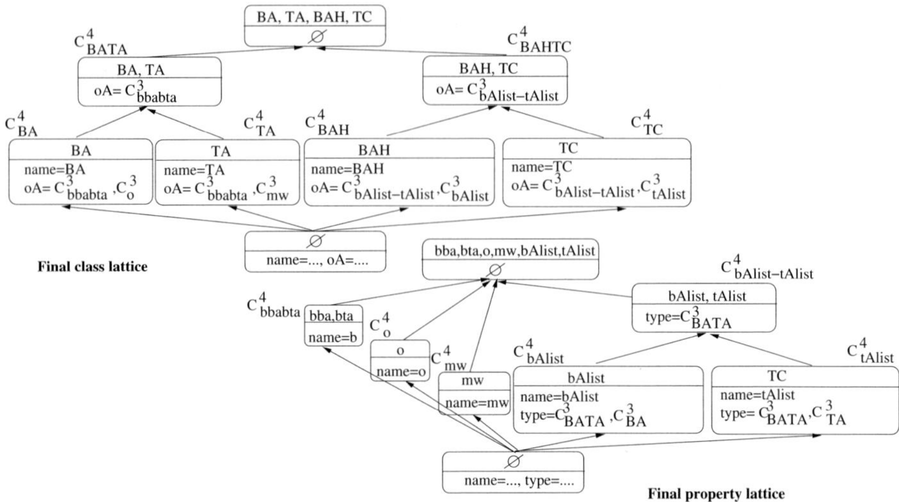

Fig. 14. The final lattices

created between the model element corresponding to C and the model element corresponding to C_v. The end of this link is named with the appropriate UML name corresponding to R. As an illustration, in rule R3 of Fig. 13, the intension of the concept C_i contains $ownedAttribute = C_j$ ($oa = C_j$ for short). This pattern in the lattice $\mathcal{L}_{Class}$ will be transformed into a link labelled `ownedAttribute` between the class generated from C_i and the property generated from C_j. With concrete UML syntax for class models, we obtain that class ii owns property jj. The principle is the same for rule R4.

Specialization in the class lattice gives rise to generalization/specialization links in the class diagram (R5 in Figure 13), and specialization in the property lattice is interpreted as `redefined` constraints between attributes (R6 in Figure 13).

To illustrate this transformation, the final lattices of our example are shown in Figure 14. As we stop at the fix point, concepts C^4_x and C^3_x can be considered as equivalent for any x. The refactored class diagram proposed in Figure 1(b) is obtained as follows. We first examine class lattice. Concept C^4_{BATA} is transformed into class `BankAccount`, while Concept C^4_{BAHTC} is transformed into class `BankClient` (new names are proposed by a designer after refactoring; so far arbitrary names are generated by the transformations). Concepts C^4_{BA}, C^4_{TA}, C^4_{BAH} and C^4_{TC} are respectively transformed into classes `BA`, `TA`, `BAH` and `TC`. We can say that initial classes are re-discovered. Now let's consider the property lattice. Concept C^4_{bbabta} is transformed into attribute `balance`, factorized in class `BankAccount`. From concept $C^4_{bAlist-tAlist}$ attribute `accountList` is generated. Then we recognize initial attributes in the remaining concepts. Specialization links and `redefined` constraints stem from lattice partial order.

6 Discussion: Advantages, Limitations, and Related Work

One of the main parameters in this approach is the discovery and choice of appropriate UML elements and description of those elements to build significant abstractions. Technical description, e.g. visibility for attributes,s is rather inadequate since it generates generalizations which have no semantics for the design. Nevertheless this description has to be preserved and even sometimes generalized in final step. Multiplicities are a good example: they are not interesting in the main transformation, but they should be re-injected in the last UML model and even generalized.

One advantage is that the current specification of the approach is easily transposable to a large set of UML elements (associations, parameters, operations, etc.). We are currently working on specifying the entire process at a higher level (M3) in the four-layered metamodeling hierarchy. This would allow to better demonstrate that first and second transformations can be done for any other modeling language, just by specifying which are entities, attributes and relations.

Another feature of our approach is that the technique will be useful if the designer can easily fine-tune the selection of those entities, attributes and relations, beyond traceability issues. The designer should be given the possibility to choose the subset of UML elements he considers as relevant for a RCA application.

A last problem is determining a reasonable bound on the iteration number, since at each iteration, abstractions are further and further from the model elements which have triggered the generalization. Too abstract elements can be less useful.

When specifying the metamodels and implementing the transformations, the choice of the Kermeta language appeared as a good choice. Indeed, its compatibility with MOF made it possible to use a single language for the whole implementation and its imperative syntax made the transformation implementation easy enough, whereas expressing them with a declarative syntax would have been very difficult. FCA has been used in various software engineering tasks, as shown in surveys like [9, 10]. Conceptual model construction has been studied with the support of FCA, as database schema construction [11, 12], class hierarchy construction or restructuring using class features [2, 3, 13, 14, 15, 16] or based on feature usage [4]. Nevertheless, FCA usage has not yet been studied in the context of Model Driven Engineering, even if several contributions were proposed concerning model refactoring. A survey of software refactoring can be found in [17], and a section is dedicated to model refactoring. The majority of the contributions on refactoring addresses the code level, but the recent interest for model-driven approaches led to several works on model refactoring, in particular UML refactoring [18]. Most of the research focuses on small and atomic model transformations (adding a class, adding an association), except the community working on design pattern application by model refactoring (for example [19]).

7 Conclusion

This paper presents an approach to automatically detect and build relevant abstractions in a UML class model. This method is founded on Relational Concept Analysis, an extension of Formal Concept Analysis. It proceeds by successive applications of model transformations, based on different metamodels (UML 2.0, context, and lattice metamodels) and implemented with the model-oriented language Kermeta. The application of our approach results in introducing abstractions for classes (with specialization links), attributes, methods and so on, in a class model. In fact, any kind of model element can be abstracted, but only a few of them lead to relevant abstractions. Future work will consist in proposing to the final users the way to parameterize the application by the metamodel elements. We are also working on defining our model transformations totally independently from the UML 2.0 metamodel, to be able to apply it on any entry metamodel. Finally, we are starting a collaboration with natural language experts to improve the refactored class diagram with relevant names for the abstractions, and to resolve problems due to synonymy, homonymy and hyperonymy.

Acknowledgements. Gabriela Arévalo gratefully acknowledges the financial support of the Swiss National Foundation for the Project: "Advanced Object-Oriented Reverse Engineering using Formal Concept Analysis" SNF Project No. PBBE2-111194. We also acknowledge the useful comments from the anonymous reviewers of this paper.

References

1. Ganter, B., Wille, R.: Formal Concept Analysis, Mathematical Foundations. Springer, Berlin (1999)
2. Godin, R., Mili, H.: Building and maintaining analysis-level class hierarchies using Galois lattices. In: Proc. of OOPSLA'93, Washington (DC), USA. (1993) 394–410
3. Dicky, H., Dony, C., Huchard, M., Libourel, T.: On Automatic Class Insertion with Overloading. In: Special issue of Sigplan Notice, Proc. of OOPSLA'96. (1996) 251–267
4. Snelting, G., Tip, F.: Understanding class hierarchies using concept analysis. ACM Transactions on Programming Languages and Systems **22**(3) (2000) 540–582
5. Triskell project (IRISA): The Metamodeling Language Kermeta. http://www.kermeta.org (2006)
6. Dao, M., Huchard, M., Hacène, M.R., Roume, C., Valtchev, P.: Improving Generalization Level in UML Models: Iterative Cross Generalization in Practice. In: ICCS'04. Volume 3127 of Lecture Notes in Computer Science., Springer (2004) 346–360
7. OMG: UML version 2.0. http://www.omg.org/technology/documents/formal/-uml.htm (2006)
8. Steel, J., Jézéquel, J.M.: Model typing for improving reuse in model-driven engineering. In: Proceedings of MODELS/UML'2005. (2005) 84–96

9. Tilley, T., Cole, R., Becker, P., Eklund, P.: A survey of formal concept analysis support for software engineering activities. In: Proc. of the First International Conference on Formal Concept Analysis - ICFCA'03, Springer-Verlag (2003) 250–271
10. Arévalo, G.: High-Level Views in Object-Oriented Systems using Formal Concept Analysis. PhD thesis, Software Composition Group, University of Bern (2004)
11. Yahia, A., Lakhal, L., Cicchetti, R., Bordat, J.: iO2 - An Algorithmic Method for Building Inheritance Graphs in Object Database Design. In: Proc. of the 15th International Conf. on Conceptual Modeling ER'96. Volume 1157. (1996) 422–437
12. Andonnoff, E., Sallaberry, C., Zurfluh, G.: Interactive design of object oriented databases. In: Proc. of CAISE'92. Volume 593 of LNCS., Springer-Verlag (1992) 128–146
13. Cook, W.: Interfaces and Specifications for the Smalltalk-80 Collection Classes. In Paepcke, A., ed.: Proceedings of the 10th OOPSLA, ACM Press (1992) 1–15
14. Moore, I.: Automatic Inheritance Hierarchy Restructuring and Method Refactoring. In: Proceedings of OOPSLA'96, San Jose (CA), USA. (1996) 235–250
15. Chen, J.B., Lee, S.C.: Generation and reorganization of subtype hierarchies. Journal of Object Oriented Programming **8**(8) (1996) 26–35
16. Si-Said Cherfi, S., Lammari, N.: Towards and Assisted Reorganization of Is-A Hierarchies. In: Proc. of Object-Oriented Information Systems, Springer-Verlag (2002) 536–548
17. Mens, T., Tourwé, T.: A survey of software refactoring. IEEE Transactions on Software Engineering **30**(2) (2004) 126–139
18. Sunyé, G., Pollet, D., Le Traon, Y., Jézéquel, J.M.: Refactoring UML models. In: Proc. Unified Modeling Language Conf. (2001) 134–148
19. Tokuda, L., Batory, D.: Automated software evolution via design pattern transformations. In: Proc. of the Int'l Symp. on Applied Corporate Computing. (1995)

Lifting Metamodels to Ontologies: A Step to the Semantic Integration of Modeling Languages*

Gerti Kappel[1], Elisabeth Kapsammer[2], Horst Kargl[1], Gerhard Kramler[1], Thomas Reiter[2], Werner Retschitzegger[2], Wieland Schwinger[3], and Manuel Wimmer[1]

[1] Business Informatics Group, Vienna University of Technology
{gerti, kargl, kramler, wimmer}@big.tuwien.ac.at
[2] Information Systems Group, Johannes Kepler University Linz
{ek, tr, wr}@ifs.uni-linz.ac.at
[3] Dept. of Telecooperation, Johannes Kepler University Linz
wieland.schwinger@jku.at

Abstract. The use of different modeling languages in software development makes their integration a must. Most existing integration approaches are metamodel-based with these metamodels representing both an abstract syntax of the corresponding modeling language and also a data structure for storing models. This implementation specific focus, however, does not make explicit certain language concepts, which can complicate integration tasks. Hence, we propose a process which semi-automatically lifts metamodels into ontologies by making implicit concepts in the metamodel explicit in the ontology. Thus, a shift of focus from the implementation of a certain modeling language towards the explicit reification of the concepts covered by this language is made. This allows matching on a solely conceptual level, which helps to achieve better results in terms of mappings that can in turn be a basis for deriving implementation specific transformation code.

1 Introduction

The shift from code-centric to model-centric software development places models as first-class entities in model-driven development processes. A rich variety of modeling languages and tools are available supporting development tasks in certain domains. Consequently, the exchange of models among different modeling tools and thus the integration of the respective modeling languages becomes an important prerequisite for effective software development processes. Due to a lack of interoperability, however, it is often difficult to use tools in combination, thus the potential of model-driven software development cannot be fully exploited.

In collaboration with the Austrian Ministry of Defense and based on experiences gained in various integration scenarios, e.g., [17], [27] we are currently realizing a system called *ModelCVS* which aims at enabling tool integration through transparent transformation of models between metamodels representing different tools' modeling

* This work has been partly funded by the Austrian Federal Ministry of Transport, Innovation and Technology (BMVIT) and FFG under grant FIT-IT-810806.

O. Nierstrasz et al. (Eds.): MoDELS 2006, LNCS 4199, pp. 528 – 542, 2006.

languages. However, metamodels typically serve as an abstract syntax of a modeling language and often also as an object-oriented data structure in which models are stored. A direct integration of different modeling languages by their metamodels is not a trivial task, and often leads to handcrafted solutions created in an error-prone process usually inducing high maintenance overheads. The integration can be made easier, when concentrating on the concepts described by a language, only, without needing to worry how the language implements these concepts. Geared towards capturing knowledge in a certain domain, *ontologies* can help to explicitly represent the concepts of a language, and thus concentrate the integration task on a solely conceptual level. Furthermore, ontologies enable tasks like logical reasoning and instance classification that can yield additional benefits for semantic integration.

In accordance with the general understanding of the term, we refer to the process of preparing a modeling language for such integration on a conceptual level as *lifting*, which allows to transform a metamodel (abstract syntax) into an ontology representing the concepts covered by the modeling language. The lifting procedure, however, cannot be carried out straight-forwardly, as it has to achieve a shift in focus, which stems from the fact that although metamodeling and ontology engineering share a common ground in conceptual modeling in general, since ontologies and metamodels are designed with different goals in mind. Metamodels prove to be more implementation-oriented as they often bear design decisions that allow producing sound, object-oriented implementations. Due to this, language concepts can be hidden in a metamodel, which during the lifting procedure have to be made explicit in an ontology.

The main contribution of this paper is to lay out the lifting procedure and discuss issues that have to be considered when lifting metamodels to ontologies. Hence, the remainder of this paper is structured as follows: The next section gives a conceptual overview of that lifting process and establishes a big picture in context with the ModelCVS project. Section 3 elaborates on the part of lifting, which deals with a formalism change concerning the way metamodels and ontologies are expressed. Section 4 introduces a pattern catalogue that helps to explicate hidden language concepts and exemplifies its usage. Based on these examples, Section 5 finally shows how the lifting procedure can benefit typical integration tasks such as schema matching. Section 7 discusses related work and Section 8 concludes with an outlook on future work.

2 Lifting at a Glance

A key focus of the ModelCVS project is to provide a framework for semi-automatic generation of transformation programs. Although ModelCVS' architecture allows for an immediate integration of metamodels via specific metamodel integration operators called *bridgings,* of which executable model transformations can be derived, our approach sees a conceptual integration of metamodels via the creation of ontologies from these metamodels as a prerequisite to enhance automation support. As the lifting process results in ontologies explicitly representing the concepts of a modeling language, we propose that matching these ontologies can provide better results in terms of more concise mappings, which in turn can be derived into *bridgings* between the original metamodels. The left-hand side of Fig. 1 shows the general setup of

ModelCVS' architecture, whereas details on the right hand side especially depicting the lifting process will be given throughout the following paragraphs. For more details on ModelCVS we refer the reader to [15],[16].

When trying to lift metamodels to ontologies, the gap between the implementation oriented focus of metamodels and the knowledge representation focus of ontologies has to be closed. Our approach separates the lifting process into three steps. The first step, which we refer to as *conversion*, involves a change of formalism (1), meaning that a metamodel is transformed into an ontology. The transformation is given by a mapping between the model engineering space and the ontology engineering space, namely a mapping from a meta-metamodel (M3) to an ontology metamodel (M2). This transformation results in what we call a *pseudo-ontology*, as the structure of this ontology basically resembles the original metamodel and typically does not represent concepts as explicitly as ontology engineering principles would advise to do.

Hence, in the subsequent *refactoring* step (2), patterns (cf. Section 4) are applied to the resulting pseudo-ontology, which aim at unfolding typically hidden concepts in metamodels that should better be represented as explicit concepts in an ontology. As to be shown in Section 4, however, the decision of *which* pattern should be applied *where,* incorporates new semantics into the model, that were previously retained as part of the user's expert knowledge about the modeling language, only.

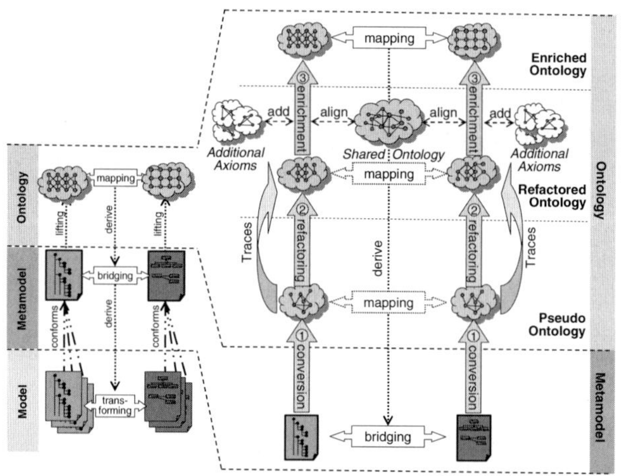

Fig. 1. ModelCVS conceptual architecture

Finally, ontologies being extracted from modeling languages' metamodels can be *enriched* with axioms (3) and put in relation with other ontologies representing a shared vocabulary about a certain domain. Thus, semantic enrichment refers to incorporating *additional* information into ontologies for integration purposes.

Instead of the original metamodels, the resulting ontologies are the driving artifacts that enable *semantic integration* of the associated modeling languages. In our case, we use matching techniques that yield a mapping between two ontologies, which is then the basis for a code generation process that derives model transformations defined between the original metamodels. To be able to relate ontology mappings back to the original metamodels, traces linking metamodel and ontology constructs have to be established during the lifting process and maintained during the refactoring step. However, a discussion about how our prototype implements the tracing and the code generation mechanisms is considered out of scope of this paper, as is the not obligatory enrichment step. But nevertheless these concepts are necessary to be mentioned to understand the lifting as a part of a meaningful whole and as a prerequisite for operationalizing the discovered mappings in the form of executable model transformations.

3 Conversion - Mapping Ecore to ODM

This section elaborates on a mapping from the model engineering to the ontology engineering technical space. In particular, we focus on describing a mapping from Ecore, which is the meta-metamodel used in the Eclipse Modeling Framework (EMF) [6] that also constitutes ModelCVS' technological backbone, to the Ontology Definition Metamodel (ODM) [12]. This mapping constitutes the basis of our approach, as a transformation based on this mapping is the first step in our lifting process. However, this mapping is not yet introducing any kind of additional semantics into the metamodel and solely provides a change of formalism.

It is relatively easy to find semantic correspondences between Ecore and ODM, as both formalisms are per se fit for conceptual modeling. The goals aimed at when using either formalism, however, differ. Often the intentions behind using a certain construct overlap, like when defining a common superclass for two subclasses to denote that all instances of the subclasses are also instances of the superclass. This intention would be equally satisfied in both Ecore and ODM. However, in Ecore this also means that instances of either subclass can be instance of one of the subclasses only, whereas individuals in OWL could actually belong to both subclasses. These subtle semantic nuances have to be considered when committing to a mapping. Although the definition of a standard metamodel for ontology definition is still under way, the given mapping description refers to terminology used in the latest submission to the ODM RFP [12]. This mapping is similar to a mapping proposition of UML to OWL [12] that can give more details on the partly mechanic part of mapping modeling language constructs to ontology constructs. The next two sub-sections focus on the caveats and the implementation of the Ecore to ODM mapping.

3.1 Caveats of Mapping

The conversion step can ignore meta-classes that do not represent concepts of the modeling language and therefore, should not be lifted into an ontology. In case of Ecore, the classes *EFactory*, *EOperations*, and *EParameter* fall into this category, because these meta-constructs are necessary when generating Java implementation classes from the metamodel, only. Furthermore, the Ecore metamodel contains abstract classes which do not directly take part in the mapping as well, but their concrete subclasses do. Table 1 gives an overview of relevant meta-classes and a catalogue with the appropriate mapping definitions towards the ODM metamodel.

Table 1. Overview of ECore to ODM mapping

Ecore Concept	OWL Concept	Possible Caveat
EFactory, EOperation, EParameter	*no mapping*	*ignored*
EPackage	OWLOntology	inverse hierarchy
EClass	OWLClass	non-exclusive instanceof
EAttribute	OWLDatatypeProperty	name clash / qualification
EReference	OWLObjectProperty	name clash / qualification
EDatatype	RDFSDatatype	*straight-forward*
EEnum & EENumLiteral	OWLDataRange & RDFSLiteral	*straight-forward*
EAnnotation	RDFSLiteral	*straight-forward*

EPackage to OWLOntology. Being both containers for other metaclasses, at first sight, the constructs *EPackage* and *OWLOntology* seem like a straight-forward match. EPackage can be compared to traditional packaging mechanisms as known from other modeling languages, that serves to group and compartmentalize modeling elements or source code. Similarly an *OWLOntology* consists of a collection of ontology elements like cases, properties, axioms and the like. However, the notion of the *eSubpackage* reference cannot be straight-forwardly translated into the *OWLimports* property: An ontology imports another ontology to make use of all the concepts defined in the import. Thus, the top-level ontology has visibility over all imported concepts. Packages on the other hand can have sub-packages, which have visibility over all their super-packages. Hence, the semantics of *subPackage* and *OWLimports* oppose each other. Furthermore, the grouping of model elements in sub-packages lies in the hands of the modeler and basically allows for arbitrary grouping to keep large models comprehensible. The import structure of ontologies is rather based on enabling efficient reasoning and creating a meaningful whole out of certain domain concepts.

Albeit the above mentioned issue, from a pragmatic point of view in most cases it is reasonable to map packages directly to ontologies. Analogously, matching the *subPackage* reference to the *OWLimports* property generally works well, too, when being aware that the result can be an 'up-side down' class hierarchy.

EClass to OWLClass. The metaclasses *EClass* and *OWLClass* map straight-forwardly to an *OWLClass*, except that an *OWLClass* is used to cluster a number of individuals, which can also be individuals of other classes, whereas instances of an *EClass* cannot. This issue, however, does not pose a problem when mapping from Ecore to ODM or when instances are not considered in the lifting process.

The lifting of abstract classes or interfaces depends on whether they represent semantics of the modeling language which should also be represented as concepts in the ontology, or whether they serve solely implementation specific purposes. Our approach follows a strategy of lifting all abstract classes and interfaces, as unnecessarily lifted concepts can usually be better filtered out in the subsequent refactoring step.

EAttribute to OWLDatatypeProperty. In difference to an *EAttribute* belonging to an *EClass*, a property in an ontology is independent of a certain *OWLClass*. Thus, the straight-forward mapping from *EAttribute* to *OWLDatatypeProperty* can be problematic, because seemingly identical attributes in different classes can carry different semantics, which would then be unified in a single ontology property.

To avoid this problem, one can incorporate additional information like the owning class' name into the name of the newly created property. In doing so, no information gets lost and redundant properties can be joined in the subsequent refactoring step.

EReference to OWLObjectProperty. Similar to the previous mapping description, an *EReference* can be mapped onto an *OWLObjectProperty* when the mentioned name clash problem is dealt with accordingly and the associated loss of semantics is avoided. Apart from this, the *eReferenceType* reference can be mapped to the *RDFSDomain* reference and the *eContainingClass* reference to the *RDFSRange* reference. Just like the former mapping, cardinalities do not pose a problem, as the Ecore references in question have single cardinality which maps straight onto the multiple cardinality of the equivalent references in the ODM.

Summarizing the above remarks, it has to be pointed out that the most important point when defining a mapping from metamodels to ontologies is, that one has to be aware how the resulting ontology is affected by the mapping decisions taken.

3.2 Creating Transformation Code for the Conversion Step

The executable model transformation code facilitating the *conversion* step is created automatically from a mapping specification between Ecore and ODM by means of a code generator. The mapping specification is created with the Atlas Model Weaver (AMW) [7] which is an Eclipse plug-in allowing to weave links between metamodels or models, resulting in a so called weaving model.

In the context of *ModelCVS*, which builds on AMW's weaving mechanism, we more specifically refer to a weaving model as a *bridging*, as it constitutes a mapping specification according to a certain integration scenario [15] of which executable model transformation code can be generated. For defining the mapping between Ecore and ODM we employ a bridging language that denotes a translation of Ecore models into ODM models in a semantics preserving way. This language is defined analogously to a weaving metamodel for the AMW. The semantics of this bridging language is then operationally specified in an adjacent code generator, which produces ATL [14] code that finally performs the actual *conversion* step.

Since the detailed semantics of the bridging language and the inner works of the code generation mechanism are out of scope of this paper and we remain with a general description of the method. In the following paragraphs a rationale for implementing a custom version of the ODM is given.

Since the standardization process for the ODM is still ongoing, a decision was made to implement a custom version of ODM. Our decision was driven by the fact that on one hand, a working import/export functionality of XML serialized OWL ontologies was needed, and on the other hand, an implementation providing an API which reasoners and other ontological software infrastructure could readily use was required. Hence, a decision was made to employ the *Jena* [13] framework that could satisfy both requirements. To be able to bridge the Jena APIs into the model engineering technical space, an Ecore model was reengineered from the Jena API that in the following is referred to as the *Jena ODM*. Wrapping the Jena ODM directly onto the structure of the underlying API has the advantage, that the writing of an adapter program calling the Jena API to instantiate a Java in-memory model from a Jena ODM model and vice versa boils down to a trivial task. Nevertheless, once a standard is finalized, the described approach can be modified with reasonable effort by defining a transformation from the adopted ODM to the Jena ODM. In MDA terminology, this approach could be compared to a PIM to PSM transformation introducing a new layer of abstraction that helps to keep the adapter program free of transformation logic. For reasons of brevity, we will not further elaborate on implementation details of the conversion step. The output of this first step is a pseudo-ontology, which is the input for the *refactoring* step whose associated patterns will be focused on next.

4 Refactoring Patterns for Pseudo-ontologies

The aim of metamodeling lies primarily in defining modeling languages in an object-oriented manner leading to efficient repository implementations. This means that in a metamodel not necessarily all modeling concepts are represented as *first-class citizens*. Instead, the concepts are frequently hidden in *attributes* or in *association ends*. We call this phenomenon *concept hiding*. Consequently, also *pseudo-ontologies*, i.e., the output of the previous *conversion* step, also lack the explicit representation of modeling concepts. In order to overcome this problem, we propose *refactoring* as a second step in the lifting process, which semi-automatically generates an additional and semantically enriched view of the conversion step's output.

As an example for concept hiding in metamodels consider Fig. 2. In the upper part it shows a simplified version of the *UML metamodel kernel* which is defined in the *UML Infrastructure* [19], represented as a *pseudo*-ontology. As we see in Fig. 2 the *pseudo*-ontology covers *twelve modeling concepts* but uses only *four classes*. Hence, most of the modeling concepts are implicitly defined, only.

To tackle the *concept hiding* problem, we propose certain refactoring patterns for identifying *where* possible hiding places for concepts in metamodels are and also *how* these structures can be rearranged to explicit knowledge representations. The refactoring patterns given in the following subsections are classified into four categories. The description of each pattern is based on [11] and consists of pattern name, problem description, solution mechanism, and finally, of an example based on the UML kernel. The kernel is shown in the upper part of Fig. 2 as a pseudo-ontology (before applying the patterns) and in the lower part of Fig. 2 as a refactored ontology (after applying the patterns). The numbers in the figure identify where a certain pattern can be applied and how that structure will be refactored, respectively.

4.1 Patterns for Reification of Concepts

a) Association Class Introduction: A modeling concept might not be directly represented by object properties but rather hidden within an association. In particular, it might be represented by the combination of both properties representing the context in which these object properties occur.

Refactoring: A new class is introduced in the ontology similar to an association class in UML to explicitly describe the hidden concept. Since there is no language construct for association classes in OWL, the association is split up into two parts which are linked by the introduced class. The cardinalities of the new association ends are fixed to one and the previously existing association ends remain unchanged.

Example: The combination of the roles of the recursive relationship of *Class*, *subclass* and *superclass*, occurs in the context *generalization*.

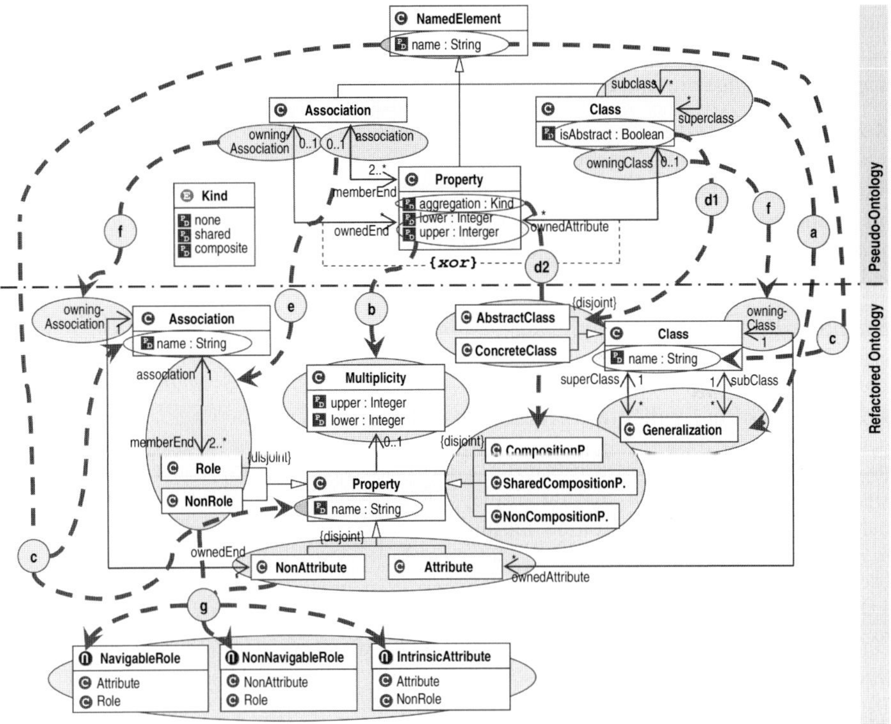

Fig. 2. Part of the UML kernel as pseudo-ontology and as refactored-ontology

b) Concept Elicitation from Properties: In metamodels it is often sufficient to implement modeling concepts as attributes of primitive data types, because the primary aim is to be able to represent models as data in repositories. This approach is in contradiction with ontology engineering which focuses on knowledge representation and not on how concepts are representable as data.

Refactoring: Datatype properties which actually represent concepts are extracted into separate classes. These classes are connected by an object property to the source class and the cardinality of that object property is set to the cardinality of the original datatype property. The introduced classes are extended by a datatype property for covering the value of the original datatype property.

Example: The properties *Property.lower* and *Property.upper* represent the concept *Multiplicity* which is used for defining cardinality constraints on a *Property*.

4.2 Patterns for Elimination of Abstract Concepts

c) Abstract Class Elimination: In metamodeling, generalization and abstract classes are used as a means to gain smart object-oriented language definitions. However, this benefit is traded against additional indirection layers and it is well-known that the use of inheritance does not solely entail advantages. Furthermore, in metamodels, the use of abstract classes which do not represent modeling concepts is quite common. In such cases generalization is applied for *implementation inheritance* and not for *specialization inheritance*. However, one consequence of this procedure is a fragmentation of knowledge about the concrete modeling concepts.

Refactoring: In order to defragment the knowledge of modeling constructs, the datatype properties and object properties of abstract classes are moved downwards to their concrete subclasses. This refactoring pattern yields multiple definitions of properties and might be seen as an *anti*-pattern of object-oriented modeling practice. However, the properties can be redefined with more expressive names (e.g. *hyponyms*) in their subclasses.

Example: The property *NamedElement.name* is used for class name, attribute name, association name and role name.

4.3 Patterns for Explicit Specialization of Concepts

d) Datatype Property Elimination: In metamodeling it is convenient to represent similar modeling concepts with a single class and use attribute values to identify the particular concept represented by an instance of that class. This metamodeling practice keeps the number of classes in metamodels low by hiding multiple concepts in a single class. These concepts are equal in terms of owned attributes and associations but differ in their intended semantic meaning. For this purpose, attributes of arbitrary data types can be utilized but in particular two widespread refinement patterns are through *booleans* and *enumerations*.

d1) Refactoring for Boolean Elimination: Concepts hidden in boolean attribute are unfolded by introducing two new subclasses of the class owning the boolean, and defining the subclasses as disjoint due to the duality of the boolean data type range. The subclasses might be named in an *x* and non-*x* manner but descriptive names should be introduced into the ontology by the user.

Example: Class.isAbstract is either true or false, representing an abstract or a concrete class, respectively.

d2) Refactoring for Enumeration Elimination: Implicit concepts hidden in an enumeration of literals are unfolded by introducing a separate class for each literal. The introduced classes are subclasses of the class owning the attribute of type enumeration and are defined as disjoint, if the cardinality of the datatype property is one, or overlapping if the cardinality is not restricted.

Examples: Property.aggregation is either *none*, *shared*, or *composite*, representing a *nonCompositionProperty*, a *sharedCompositionProperty* or a *CompositionProperty*.

e) Zero-or-one Object Property Differentiation: In a metamodel the reification of a concept is often determined by the occurrence of a certain relationship on the instance layer. In such cases, the association end in the metamodel has a multiplicity of *zero-or-one* which implicitly contains a concept refinement.

Refactoring: Two subclasses of the class owning the object property with cardinality of zero-or-one are introduced. The subclass which represents the concept that realizes the relationship on the instance layer receives the object property from its superclass while the other subclass does not receive the object property under consideration. Furthermore, the object property of the original class is deleted and the cardinality of the shifted object property is restricted to exactly one.

Example: Property.association has a multiplicity of zero-or-one, distinguishing between a *role* and a *nonRole*, respectively.

f) Xor-Association Differentiation: *Xor*-constraints between *n* associations (we call such associations *xor-associations*) with association ends of multiplicity *zero-or-one* restrict models such that only one of the *n* possible links is allowed to occur on the instance layer. This pattern can be used to refine concepts with *n* sub-concepts in a similar way like enumeration attributes are used to distinguish between n sub-concepts. Thus, *xor*-associations bind a lot of implicit semantics, namely *n* mutually excluding sub-concepts which should be explicitly expressed in ontologies.

Refactoring: This pattern is resolvable similar to the enumeration pattern by introducing *n* new subclasses, but in addition the subclasses are responsible for taking care of the *xor*-constraint. This means each class receives one out of the *n* object properties, thus each subclass represents exactly one sub-concept. Hence, the cardinality of each object property is fixed from zero-to-one to exactly one.

Example: Property.owningAssociation and *Property.owingClass* are both object properties with cardinality zero-or-one. At the instance layer it is determined if an instance of the class *Property* is representing an *attribute* (contained by a class) or a *nonAttribute* (contained by an association).

4.4 Patterns for Exploring Combinations of Refactored Concepts

Refactorings that introduce additional subclasses, i.e., patterns from category Specialization of Concepts, must always adopt a class from the original ontology as starting point since the basic assumption is that different concept specializations are independent of each other. Hence, in the case of multiple refactorings of one particular class, subclasses introduced by different refactorings are overlapping. In Fig. 2 this is denoted using a separate *generalization set* for each refactoring. However, this approach requires an additional refactoring pattern for discovering possible relationships between combinations of sub-concepts.

g) Concept Recombination: In order to identify concepts which are hidden in the ontology as mentioned above, the user has to extend the ontology by complex classes which describe the concepts resulting from possible sub-concept combinations.

Refactoring: User interactions are required for identifying the concepts behind the combination of concepts by evaluating the combinations in a matrix where the dimensions of the matrix are the overlapping generalization sets in consideration.

Example: When studying the textual descriptions of the semantics of UML one finds out that some relationships between the different kinds of *properties* define additional concepts which are not explicitly represented in the ontology. In particular, the evaluation of *role/nonRole* and *attribute/nonAttribute* combinations leads to the additional intersection classes depicted in the lower part of Fig. 2.

Summarizing, the result of the *refactoring* step, an ontology which facilitates an implementation neutral view of the metamodel, is characterized as follows:

- Only datatype properties which represent semantics of the real world domain (*ontological properties*) are contained, e.g. *Class.className*, *Multiplicity.upper*. This means no datatype properties for the reification of modeling constructs (*linguistic properties*) are part of the refactored ontology.
- Most object properties have cardinalities different from zero-or-one, such that no concepts are hidden in object properties.
- Excessive use of classes and *is-a* relations turns the ontology into a taxonomy.

5 Evaluation of Matching Potential

This section discusses the effects of the refactoring step as defined in the previous section on ontology matching, which is an important task in semantic integration. In particular, we first point out problems in matching pseudo-ontologies that negatively affect matching quality. Subsequently we show how the application of our refactoring patterns can alleviate matching problems and improve mapping quality.

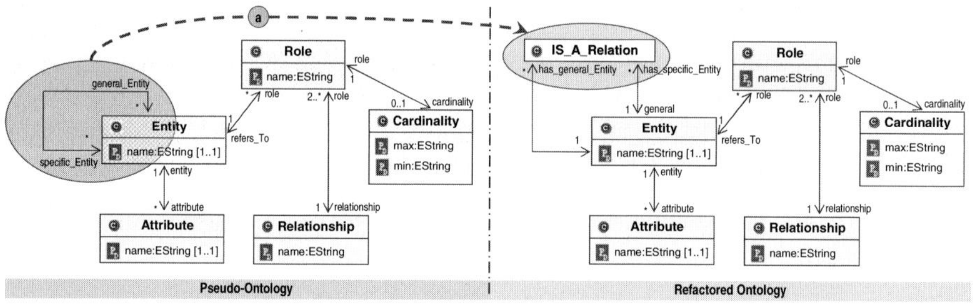

Fig. 3. ER pseudo-ontology (left) and refactored ontology (right)

In our example we are using pseudo-ontologies and refactored ontologies originating from ER and UML metamodels, respectively. The UML ontologies have already been introduced in the previous section, the ER ontologies are depicted in Fig. 3. The ontologies are mapped with COMA++ [2], which allows matching OWL ontologies and produces mappings which represent suggested semantic correspondences. A mapping consists of triples of source element, target element, and a specific confidence rate ranging from zero to one. It is configurable, by associating weights with certain matching rules that can be modified to fit the user's preferences. Hence, the use of COMA++ is naturally a semi-automatic task involving tweaking of the matching algorithm and manual editing of the proposed mapping.

In the following we discuss four general problem classes that can be identified when defining mappings between pseudo-ontologies, and how they become obsolete by applying refactoring. The manifestation of the mapping problems in the UML to

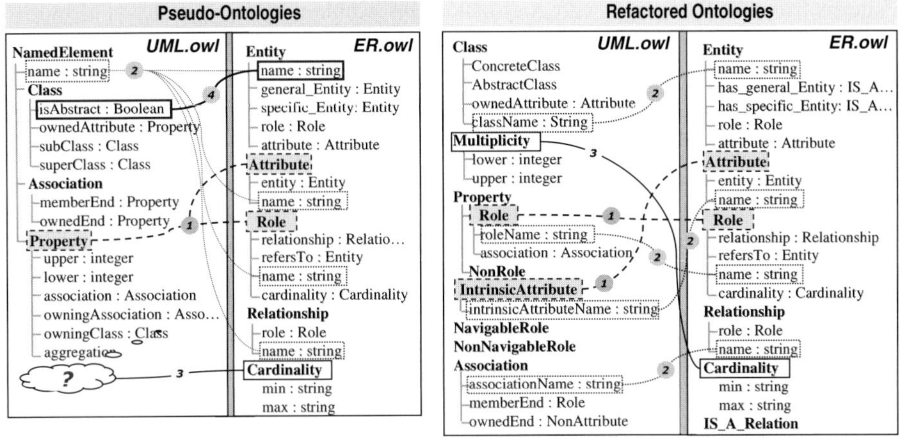

Fig. 4. COMA++ mapping between pseudo-ontologies and refactored ontologies

ER mapping and their solutions using refactored ontologies are shown in Fig. 4. The numbers in that figure refer to the following list of problems:

(1) Ambiguous Concept Mappings: This problem originates from classes in a pseudo-ontology that represent multiple concepts. The example illustrated in Fig. 4 (left) is the mapping from *Property* in UML to *Role* and *Attribute* in ER. This ambiguity arises because the *UML pseudo-ontology* defines a general concept (*Property*) without explicitly stating the sub-concepts which in contrast are represented as explicit concepts in the *ER pseudo-ontology*. This kind of problem is solved by the patterns from the Specialization and the Combination categories, which introduce the hidden concepts as subclasses and complex classes, respectively, thus avoiding ambiguous mappings. In Fig. 4 (right) one can see that the classes introduced from class *Property* allow semantically unambiguous mappings for *roles*, and attributes in the sense of UML *IntrinsicAttribute*.

(2) Ambiguous Property Mappings: The use of abstract classes in a metamodel is a design decision. Hence, when mapping properties that are defined in abstract classes, they may be fragmented over different inheritance layers. This problem is depicted in Fig. 4 (left) by mapping the datatype property *NamedElement.name* to multiple targets. After applying patterns from the Elimination category, the inheritance layers become flattened and the properties are shifted to the subclasses of the abstract classes, thus enabling unambiguous one-to-one mappings. E.g., in Fig. 4 (right) the datatype property *name* of the class *NamedElement* is flatted into the subclasses which lead to unambiguous mappings for the datatype property *name*.

(3) No Counterparts: Pseudo-ontologies might differ in their granularity of modeling concept definitions, although the same modeling concepts are useable by the modeler. Consequently, some mappings cannot be expressed, because explicit concepts of some pseudo-ontology are missing as explicit concept representations in the other. In our mapping example shown in Fig. 4 (left) no corresponding concept in the *UML pseudo-ontology* exists for the *Cardinality* concept of the *ER pseudo-ontology*.

Patterns from the Reification category tackle this problem by the reification of hidden concepts, allowing to define mappings that were not possible before the refactoring step. Concerning the missing counterpart for the *Cardinality* concept, after applying the patterns it is possible to map the *Cardinality* concept to the introduced *Multiplicity* concept as shown in Fig. 4 (right).

(4) Linguistic-to-Ontology Property Mappings: Concerning invalid mappings, one source of defect is mapping linguistic properties to ontological properties. For instance, in our example shown in Fig. 4 (left) *Class.isAbstract* which represents a linguistic property was automatically mapped by COMA++ to *Entity.name* which represents an ontological property. Patterns from the Specialization category transform linguistic properties to concepts, thus tackling this problem, because only ontological properties remain in the refactored ontology. In Fig. 4 (right) one can see that no mappings between linguistic and ontological properties are possible.

When considering the effect of the refactoring step on the mapping process, one can see a higher potential for manually fine-tuning the mapping due to the finer granularity of a refactored ontology. The improvement in mapping potential, however, comes at the cost of performing the refactoring step and of dealing with a higher number of classes. The alternative would be to use a more sophisticated mapping language to describe unambiguous mappings. In contrast, our approach of using refactoring patterns offers a way to solve the discussed mapping problems through simple semantic correspondences, only. Consequently, the overall complexity of the mapping process is decreased due to its splitting into a refactoring part, which brings the pseudo-ontologies to a common granularity and a mapping part, which relies on simple equality mappings that can be generated semi-automatically.

6 Related Work

Our work is to a good deal influenced by efforts which try to close the gap between the model engineering technical space and the ontology engineering technical space. Among these are, e.g. Bezivin et al. [3] who argue for a unified M3 infrastructure and Atkinson [1] who showed that there are plenty of similarities between the two technical spaces and that differences are mostly community-based or of historic nature. Naturally, an M3 unified infrastructure could possibly ease the proposed lifting procedure. Concrete efforts aiming to provide an adequate bridge encompass [8], specifying a mapping from UML to DAML-OIL, and most prominently the submissions to the OMG's ODM RFP [12] also suggesting a mapping from UML to OWL. Although these efforts influenced the mapping proposed in our conversion step, our focus is not on making a rich language like UML fit for ontology modeling, but on extracting meaningful ontologies from metamodels defining modeling languages.

Many other efforts aiming at semantic integration of data also use a procedure that *lifts metadata to ontologies*. These efforts use XML Schemata [26],[5],[10],[24] which are mapped to RDFS or to OWL [9], respectively. [20] carries out an additional normalization step after lifting, but focuses on ameliorating lexical and simple structural heterogeneities, only. All of these approaches are not immediately reusable in our metamodel-centric context, however, and none of the above approaches relies on refactoring patterns that would allow to make hidden concepts explicit. As an example, [22] lifts XML schemata and states that the resulting ontologies "will be ad-hoc". Our refactoring approach of pseudo-ontologies tries to deal with this problem. Furthermore, the refactored OWL ontologies can be matched without the need for a complex mapping or query language, which addresses the problem identified in [18] that calls for an OWL query language. There is few related work in terms of refactoring ontologies that were created from an underlying metadata representation aiming at a shift in focus as we do. [21] tries to find implicit semantics through linguistic and structural analysis in labels of hierarchical structures on the Web, but seems not applicable to find hidden concepts in modeling languages, nor does it provide means like to reify these. An interesting approach to ontology refactoring is discussed in [4], which, as opposed to our approach, has the goal of pruning an ontology and deriving a schema thereof, that is then refactored towards an implementation oriented focus.

[25] identifies variability, which is the ability to express semantically equal concepts differently, as the reason for different conceptual models being able to meet the same requirements. Our work can be seen as addressing the problems of heterogeneities introduced due to variability, as the refactoring step can help to make concepts explicit in a uniform way, even though they are initially hidden in different ways.

7 Conclusion

In this paper we have introduced the lifting procedure, which allows to create ontologies from metamodels representing modeling languages. The application of refactoring patterns on the resulting ontologies can make originally hidden concepts explicit and thus improve automation support for semantic integration tasks. Although it is not foreseeable that such tasks will ever be fully automated, we believe that support for the at least semi-automatic integration of modeling tools via their modeling languages is feasible. It is easy to see, that such tool integration tasks require proper tool support and methods guiding the integration process themselves.

Lifting metamodels to ontologies is only one important step in realizing the ModelCVS project. Future work will focus on defining specific domain ontologies that can be relied on in the enrichment step to further enhance ontology matching, as well as enhancing the tracing and the code generation mechanisms to automatically derive model transformation programs from higher-level integration specifications.

References

1. Atkinson C.: On the Unification of MDA and Web-based Knowledge Representation Technologies. 1st International Workshop on the Model-Driven Semantic Web (2004)
2. Aumueller, D.; Do, H., Massmann, S.; Rahm, E.: Schema and ontology matching with COMA++. SIGMOD Conference, June, (2005)
3. Bézivin J. et. al.: An M3-Neutral infrastructure for bridging model engineering and ontology engineering. In: Proc. of the First International Conference on Interoperability of Enterprise Software and Applications. Springer, p. 159-171. (2005)
4. Conesa J.: Ontology-Driven Information Systems: Pruning and Refactoring of Ontologies. Doctoral Syposium of 7th Int. Conf. on the Unified Modeling Language, Lisbonl, (2004)

5. Cruz I. F., Xiao Huiyong, Hsu Feihong.: An Ontology-Based Framework for XML Semantic Integration. Int. Database Engineering and Applications Symposium, 217-226 (2004)
6. Eclipse Tools Project: Eclipse Modeling Framework (EMF), http://www.eclipse.org/emf/
7. Didonet Del Fabro M., Bézivin J., Jouault F., Breton E., Gueltas G.: AMW: a generic model weaver. Proc. of the 1ères Journées sur l'Ingénierie Dirigée par les Modèles, (2005)
8. Falkovych K., Sabou M., Stuckenschmidt H.: UML for the Semantic Web: Transformation-Based Approaches. Knowledge Transformation for the Semantic Web. IOS Press, (2003)
9. Ferdinand M. et al.: Lifting XML Schema to OWL, 4th Int. Conf. on Web Engineering (ICWE), Munich, Germany, July, (2004)
10. Fodor O., Dell'Erba M., Ricci F., Spada A., Werthner H.: Conceptual normalisation of XML data for interoperability in tourism. Proc. of the Workshop on Knowledge Transformation for the Semantic Web, Lyon, France, July, (2002)
11. Gamma E., Helm R., Johnson R., Vlissides J.: Design Patterns: Elements of Reusable Object-Oriented Software. Addison-Wesley Professional, (1997)
12. IBM, Sandpiper Software: Fourth Revised Submission to the OMG RFP ad/2003-03-40, www.omg.org/docs/ad/05-09-08.pdf
13. Jena 2 Ontology API, http://jena.sourceforge.net/ontology/
14. Jouault F., Kurtev I.: Transforming Models with ATL: Proceedings of the Model Transformations in Practice Workshop at MoDELS, Montego Bay, Jamaica (2005)
15. Kappel et. al.: On Models and Ontologies - A Layered Approach for Model-based Tool Integration. Modellierung 2006, Innsbruck, March (2006)
16. Kappel et. al.: Towards A Semantic Infrastructure Supporting Model-based Tool Integration. 1st Int. Workshop on Global integrated Model Management, Shanghai, May, (2006)
17. Kappel G., Kapsammer E., Retschitzegger W.: Integrating XML and Relational Database Systems, in WWW Journal, Kluwer Academic Publishers, June, (2003).
18. Lehti P., Fankhauser P.: XML Data Integration with OWL: Experiences and Challenges. Symposium on Applications and the Internet, p. 160, (2004)
19. OMG: UML 2.0 Infrastructure Final Adopted Specification, formal/05-07-05, (2005)
20. Maedche A., Motik B., Silva N., Volz R.: MAFRA - An Ontology Mapping Framework in the Semantic Web. ECAI Workshop on Knowledge Transformation, Lyon, France, (2002)
21. Magnini B., Serafini L., Speranza M.: Making explicit the Semantics Hidden in Schema Models. Proc. of the Workshop on Human Language Technology for the Semantic Web and Web Services, ISWC, Florida, October, (2003)
22. Moran M., Mocan A.: Towards Translating between XML and WSML. 2nd WSMO Implementation Workshop (WIW), Innsbruck, Austria, June (2005)
23. Noy N.F.: Semantic Integration: A Survey Of Ontology-Based Approaches. SIGMOD Record, Special Issue on Semantic Integration, 33 (4), December, (2004)
24. Roser S.: Ontology-based Model Transformation. Doctoral Symposium of the 8th Int. Conference on Model Driven Engineering Languages and Systems, Jamaica, October, (2005)
25. Verelst J., Du Bois B., Demeyer S.: Using Refactoring Techniques to Exploit Variability in Conceptual Modeling. ERCIM-ESF Workshop, Challenges in Software Evolution, (2005)
26. Volz et al.: OntoLIFT. IST Proj. 2001-33052 WonderWeb, Del. 11, (2003)
27. Wimmer M., Kramler G.: Bridging Grammarware and Modelware, in Proc. of Satellite Events at the MoDELS 2005 Conference, Montego Bay, Jamaica, October, (2005)

Incremental Model Synchronization with Triple Graph Grammars*

Holger Giese and Robert Wagner

Software Engineering Group,
Department of Computer Science
University of Paderborn,
Warburger Str. 100,
D-33098 Paderborn, Germany
{hg, wagner}@upb.de

Abstract. The advent of model-driven software development has put model transformations into focus. In practice, model transformations are expected to be applicable in different stages of a development process and help to consistently propagate changes between the different involved models which we refer to as model synchronization. However, most approaches do not fully support the requirements for model synchronization today and focus only on classical one-way batch-oriented transformations. In this paper, we present our approach for an incremental model transformation which supports model synchronization. Our approach employs the visual, formal, and bidirectional transformation technique of triple graph grammars. Using this declarative specification formalism, we focus on the efficient execution of the transformation rules and present our approach to achieve an incremental model transformation for synchronization purposes. We present an evaluation of our approach and demonstrate that due to the speedup for the incremental processing in the average case even larger models can be tackled.

1 Introduction

Model-Driven Development (MDD) and the *Model-Driven Architecture* (MDA) [1] approach in particular have put models and model transformations into focus. The core idea is to move the development focus from programming languages code to models and to generate the implementation from these models automatically. The aim is to increase the development productivity and quality of the software system under development.

However, the modeling of large and complex software systems incorporates many informal and semi-formal notations describing the system under construction at different levels of abstraction and from different, partly overlapping view points. The usage of different levels of abstraction and the separation of

* This work was developed in the course of the Special Research Initiative 614 – Self-optimizing Concepts and Structures in Mechanical Engineering – University of Paderborn, and was published on its behalf and funded by the Deutsche Forschungsgemeinschaft.

O. Nierstrasz et al. (Eds.): MoDELS 2006, LNCS 4199, pp. 543–557, 2006.

concerns on the one hand reduce the complexity of the overall specification, but on the other hand the increasing number of used models very often leads to a wide range of inconsistencies [2].

A possible way to face this problem is to use model transformation technology where a source model is transformed into a target model by applying a set of transformation rules. This ensures that the overlapping parts and mappings between these models are captured by the transformation itself. Unfortunately, the development of a software system is a quite iterative process with frequent modifications to the involved models. Therefore, frequent model synchronization steps are required.

Due to the size of complex models, model transformation approaches which require recomputing the transformation even though only a small fraction of the model has been modified do not scale very well. Additionally, retransforming a model each time the model evolves is not practical since refinements in more detailed target models are lost when applying a transformation from scratch. To keep the overall specification consistent after an initial model transformation, changes of one model have to be propagated in a non-destructive manner to the interrelated model by means of model synchronization. In the programming language domain, modular compilation and even incremental compilation and binding have been introduced to cope with large projects. The same problems have to be managed in the case of MDD and MDA.

We believe that sufficient tool support for incremental model synchronization by means of incremental model transformations with update propagation is a crucial prerequisite for the successful and effective application of the model-driven engineering paradigm in many cases. However, most model transformation approaches do not fully support such requirement today and focus only on classical one-way batch-oriented transformations [3].

In this paper, we present our approach for the incremental model synchronization which employs the visual, formal, and bidirectional transformation technique of triple graph grammars [4]. We will outline how this declarative specification formalism can be employed to achieve an efficient, incremental execution of the transformation rules by exploiting the known dependencies between the transformation rules.

The remainder of this paper is organized as follows. In Section 2 we first introduce a model transformation example from the area of flexible manufacturing systems which is then used to give a brief and informal introduction to the concepts of triple graph grammars. In Section 3 we explain our strategy for an efficient and incremental application of triple graph grammar rules. The evaluation results follow in Section 4. Related work and its limitations concerning the requirements for model synchronization are discussed in Section 5. The paper closes with some final conclusions and an outlook on future work in Section 6.

2 Model Transformation Approach

In this section, we first introduce a simple example which exemplifies the need for model synchronization from the area of flexible production systems. It serves then as a running example for explaining the used model transformation technique of triple graph grammars and its extensions for incremental model transformations.

2.1 The Example

In the ISILEIT project [5], we explored the possibilities of modern languages concerning their usefulness for the specification of flexible and autonomous production control systems. For the specification of the control software, we combined subsets of the Specification and Description Language (SDL) [6] and the Unified Modeling Language (UML) [7] to an executable graphical language [5]. For this purpose, a SDL block diagram is used to specify the overall static communication structure where processes and blocks are connected by channels and signal routes. This block diagram is transformed to an initial UML class diagram which can be refined and extended to an executable specification. In Fig. 1, a simple block diagram and the class diagram which results from a correct transformation are presented.

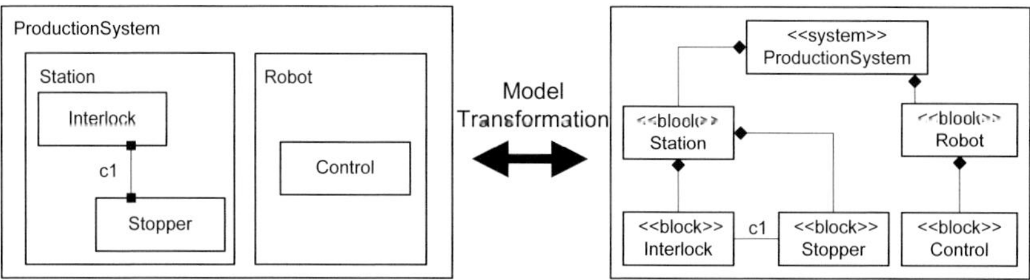

Fig. 1. Application example

Basically, systems, blocks, and processes of a block diagram are transformed to classes with corresponding stereotypes. For example, the block *Station* is represented by the class *Station* with a stereotype ≪block≫, the system *ProductionSystem* as a class with the stereotype ≪system≫. The hierarchical structure of a block diagram is expressed by composition relations between the respective classes in the class diagram. The channels and signal routes of the block diagram are mapped to associations between the derived classes. In addition, each signal received by a process in the block diagram is mapped to a method of the corresponding class in the class diagram (not shown in this example).

In order to support an iterative development process without any restrictions on the order of design steps, we allow the engineer to move freely between the block and class diagram to refine and adapt both models towards the final design. In this scenario, we have to ensure that the overlapping parts and mappings between the interrelated models stay consistent to each other. Moreover, we do not want to override existing structures since both models can contain manual modifications and refinements which should be preserved if possible. For this model synchronization we use bidirectional and incremental model transformations based on triple graph grammars.

2.2 Triple Graph Grammars

From the previous example, it is clear that we need bidirectional model transformations. In order to support bidirectional model transformations, we use triple graph grammars. In this section, we cannot discuss triple graph grammars in full detail. Rather, we will explain the basic concepts by the help of our example and refer to [4] for a formal definition.

In order to explain the specification technique of triple graph grammars for model transformation, we have to take a closer look at the metamodels of the block and class diagram as well as at an additional correspondence metamodel needed for triple graph grammars. A metamodel defines the abstract syntax and static semantics of a modeling language. In Fig. 2, the metamodels of the block diagram, the class diagram, and the correspondence metamodel are shown.

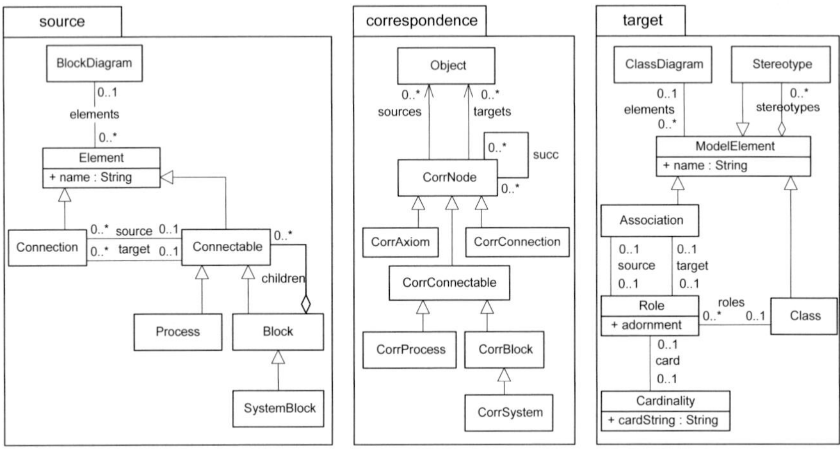

Fig. 2. Simplified metamodels of the source, correspondence, and target model

In the simplified metamodel for block diagrams, a *BlockDiagram* contains different *Elements*. An *Element* is either a *Connectable* element or a *Connection* between *Connectable* elements. A *Connectable* element is either a *Process* or a *Block*. A *Block* is a container for other *Blocks* and *Processes*. A *SystemBlock* is a special *Block* and acts as a root container for other *Blocks*. The simplified metamodel for class diagrams defines *Classes*, *Associations* and *Stereotypes*. An *Association* is connected to a *Class* by a source and target *Role* that has a *Cardinality*. A *Stereotype* can be attached to any *ModelElement* in the *ClassDiagram*.

For the specification of a triple graph grammar, we need an additional correspondence metamodel. It is shown in the middle of Fig. 2. The metamodel defines the mapping between a source and a target metamodel by the classes *CorrNode* and *Object* and its associations *sources* and *targets*. Since all classes inherit implicitly from the *Object* class (not shown here), the correspondence model stores the traceability information needed to preserve the consistency between two models. In addition, the class *CorrNode* has a self-association *succ* which connects the correspondence nodes with their successor correspondence nodes. This extra link is used by our transformation algorithm.

The two described classes and their associations are essential for our transformation algorithm. However, further correspondence nodes and refined associations can be added. In our example, we have added six additional correspondence nodes, including the correspondence node *CorrBlock* used in our example rule (cf. Figure 3). The additional correspondence classes increase the performance of our transformation algorithm since for a given correspondence node type only those rules have to be checked that have the same correspondence node type on their left-hand side.

Given this three metamodels, a triple graph grammar for our example model transformation can be specified. A triple graph grammar specification is a declarative definition of a bidirectional model transformation. In Fig. 3, a triple graph grammar rule in the FUJABA-notation is shown. Note that the vertical dashed lines are not part of the rule - they are only shown for a better understanding of the following rule description.

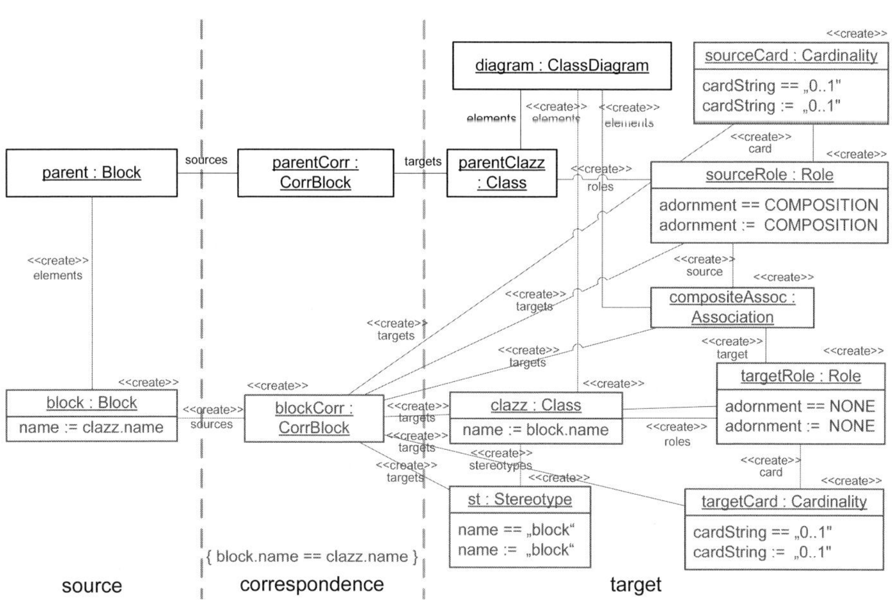

Fig. 3. A triple graph grammar rule mapping blocks to classes

The rule specifies a consistent correspondence mapping between the objects of the source and target model. In particular, the presented rule defines a mapping between a block and a corresponding class. The objects of the block diagram are drawn on the left and the objects of the class diagram are drawn on the right. They are marked with the ≪left≫ and ≪right≫ stereotypes respectively. The correspondence objects in the middle of the rule are tagged with the ≪map≫ stereotype.

The rule is separated into a triple of productions (source production, correspondence production, and target production), where each production is regarded as a context-sensitive graph grammar rule. A graph grammar rule consists of a left-hand side and a right-hand side. All objects which are not marked with the ≪create≫ stereotype belong to the left-hand side and to the right-hand side; the objects which are tagged with the ≪create≫ stereotype occur on the right-hand side only. In fact, these tags make up a production in FUJABA's graph grammar notation.

The production on the left shows the generation of a new sub block and linking it to an existing parent block. The production on the right shows the addition of a new class and stereotype and its linking to the class diagram. Moreover, to reflect the containment of the sub block, a composition association is created between the classes representing the parent block and the sub block. For this purpose, the rule contains additional objects representing the roles and cardinalities of the association. The correspondence production shows the relations between a block and a class and an additional constraint $\{block.name == clazz.name\}$ specifies that the block and the class have to be named uniquely.

Up to this point, the assignments and constraints to the object attributes have not been considered yet. Since triple graph grammars can be executed in both directions, the attribute constraints help to identify the objects to be matched, whereas the attribute assignments are applied only to created objects. However, since the computations of the attribute values may be more complicated than in our simple example, the assignments cannot be always derived from the constraints and have to be specified explicitly.

A graph grammar rule is applied by substituting the left-hand side with the right-hand side if the pattern of the left-hand side can be matched to a graph, i.e., if the left-hand side is matched all objects tagged with the ≪create≫ stereotype will be created. Hence, our example rule, in combination with additional rules covering other diagram elements, can generate a set of blocks along with the corresponding classes and associations in a class diagram. Though the transformation will not be executed this way, conceptually, we can assume that whenever a block is added to the block diagram, a corresponding class with an appropriate association will be generated in the class diagram. This way, the triple graph grammar rules define a transformation between block diagrams and class diagrams.

The correspondence production in the middle of the rule enables a clear distinction between the source and target model and holds additional traceability information. This information can be used to realize bidirectional and incremental model transformations that helps to propagate changes between related models. To ensure a unique transformation we require that the set of rules is unambiguous. The complete specification of the triple graph grammar for model transformation between block and class diagrams comprises ten rules.

3 Incremental Model Transformations

While triple graph grammars are in theory a natural choice for the realization of bidirectional model transformation, in practice the required graph pattern matching is quite complex and can lead to serious performance problems if no additional information to guide the graph pattern matching is available. Since this is the most crucial part of our model transformation approach, we show in the following a practicable and efficient solution to this problem. This is achieved by an incremental transformation approach based on an analysis of dependencies between the transformation rules. However, before we attempt to overcome the limitations of the classical batch-oriented transformation approach, we identify the nature of the transformation problem in its incremental form.

3.1 Terminology

Given two sets of possible models $\mathcal{M}_1$ and $\mathcal{M}_2$, a *unidirectional model transformation* is a total function $trans : \mathcal{M}_1 \rightarrow \mathcal{M}_2$ where *trans* can be directly computed.

Given a model $M_1 \in \mathcal{M}_1$, its transformation $M_2 = trans(M_1)$, and an arbitrary modification $mod_1 : \mathcal{M}_1 \rightarrow \mathcal{M}_1$, an *incremental model transformation* would allow to derive a modification $mod_2 : \mathcal{M}_2 \rightarrow \mathcal{M}_2$ such that it holds: $trans(mod_1(M_1)) = mod_2(M_2)$.

Assuming that the required information about the mapping between M_1 and M_2 is encoded into a mapping map_{M_1,M_2},[1] we then require that functions inc_{mod} and inc_{map} exists which can be directly computed such that

$$mod_2 = inc_{mod}(mod_1, M_1, M_2, map_{M_1,M_2}) \text{ and}$$

$$map_{M_1',M_2'} = inc_{map}(mod_1, M_1, M_2, map_{M_1,M_2}).$$

If the required effort is in $O(|\, mod_1 \,|)$ and thus proportional to the size of the modification mod_1 denoted by $|\, mod_1 \,|$ rather than the size of the model $|M_1|$, we name this a *fully incremental* solution. It is to be noted, that this optimal case that mod_2 only depends on mod_1 and not on M_1, M_2, and map_{M_1,M_2} is usually not given. Instead, at least a small fraction of M_1 and M_2 has usually to be taken into account. To make an incremental processing advantageously, the effort to determine mod_2 and compute $mod_2(M_2)$ should be much less then compute $trans(mod_1(M_1))$ in the average case. We thus call a solution *effectively incremental* if the *speedup* results in a reasonable decoupling from the model size (e.g., logarithmic effect only).

If we look at the opposite direction of the transformation, it is to be noted that the codomain $\mathcal{M}_2^* = \{M_2 | \exists M_1 \in \mathcal{M}_1 : trans(M_1) = M_2\}$ of *trans* is not necessarily equal to $\mathcal{M}_2$. Therefore, a related *bidirectional model transformation* where also $trans^{-1}$ can be directly computed might not be able to relate to each model of $\mathcal{M}_2$ a model in $\mathcal{M}_1$ using $trans^{-1}$.

Possible reason for this asymmetry can be, for example, that the models in $\mathcal{M}_2$ are more detailed and can thus describe structures or behavior which cannot be represented in $\mathcal{M}_1$. E.g., an assembled program might very well contain a whole

[1] If no such mapping information is required, we can simply consider an empty map_{M_1,M_2}.

bunch of unstructured goto statements, while a good programming language does explicitly exclude them and supports only well-structured loop constructs.

Another problem is that $trans^{-1}$ is not necessarily a function. If, for example, two models $M_1 \in \mathcal{M}_1$ and $M_1' \in \mathcal{M}_1$ with $M_1 \neq M_1'$ exist with $trans(M_1) = trans(M_1')$, we cannot define a unique result for $trans^{-1}$ for $trans(M_1)$. Examples for this case are several high level program constructs which may result in the same assembler code. E.g., a while and for loop could result in exactly the same assembler representation.

If we assume that *trans* is an injection, we could conclude that $trans^{-1}$ must be a function and we name this a *bijective bidirectional model transformation* for $\mathcal{M}_1$ and $\mathcal{M}_2^*$. Otherwise, we have a *surjective bidirectional model transformation* for $\mathcal{M}_1$ and $\mathcal{M}_2^*$ and $trans^{-1}$ is a function from $\mathcal{M}_2^* \rightarrow \wp(\mathcal{M}_1)$ to encode that there might be several valid backward transformations.

For the bidirectional incremental case, we in addition have for a given model $M_1 \in \mathcal{M}_1$, its transformation $M_2 = trans(M_1)$, and an arbitrary modification $mod_2 : \mathcal{M}_2 \rightarrow \mathcal{M}_2$, that an *incremental model transformation* would allow to derive a modification $mod_1 : \mathcal{M}_1 \rightarrow \mathcal{M}_1$ such that it holds: $mod_1(M_1) \in trans^{-1}(mod_2(M_2))$.

We have to further restrict this condition if $\mathcal{M}_2^* \neq \mathcal{M}_2$ such that it must only hold for $mod_2(M_2) \in \mathcal{M}_2^*$. Otherwise we have to conclude that mod_2 is an inconsistent modification. E.g., the assembler code has been modified in such a manner that a code structure resulted which could not be the result of any program of the given programming language.

For the addressed *incremental model synchronization*, we require a bijective, bidirectional, incremental model transformation. In a case where for the resulting target model M_2' holds that $M_2' \in \mathcal{M}_2 \setminus \mathcal{M}_2^*$, we have to reject the modification in order to keep both models consistent.

3.2 Incremental Transformations and Updates

In order to make our algorithm incremental we have to take the correspondence model into account. Due to the construction principle of the triple graph grammar rules, each rule has at least one correspondence node in its pre-condition which thus is a necessary prerequisite for the application of the rule and therefore, the rule can be only applied if the required correspondence node was already created in a previous transformation step. Additionally, each successful application of a rule results in at least one additional correspondence node. Therefore, in our transformation algorithm, a directed edge from the required correspondence node to the created one is inserted each time a rule is successfully applied. We include this link in our derived graph rewriting rules. The additional link between the correspondence nodes reflects the dependency and the execution order of the rules which will be used to extend our algorithm to the incremental case.

This observation can be exploited by using the created correspondence node as a starting point for a local searching strategy which reduces the costs for the required pattern matching. With the additional links between the correspondence nodes the correspondence model can be interpreted as a directed acyclic graph

(DAG). It is a graph rather than a tree due to the fact that rules are allowed to have more than one correspondence node as a precondition. The graph is acyclic since in a rule application, we never connect already existing correspondence nodes by a link.

The incremental transformation and update algorithm traverses the correspondence nodes of the DAG using breadth-first search. For each correspondence node the algorithm checks whether an inconsistent situation has occurred. This is done by retrieving the rule which has been applied in the transformation process to create the correspondence node and checking whether it still matches to the current situation.

In the case that the structure of the applied rule still holds and only an additional attribute constraint evaluates to false, it is sufficient to propagate the attribute value change in the current transformation direction.

When the rule cannot be matched anymore, e.g., due to the deletion of a model element, we have found indeed an inconsistency. In that case, the algorithm has to undo the applied transformation rule. This is achieved by deleting the correspondence node and all created elements and unmarking the remaining nodes that have been involved in the right-side of the production. This is the last step of the update. However, note that, by deleting the correspondence node the precondition for all successors of the deleted correspondence node will not hold anymore. As a consequence, this leads both to the deletion of the succeeding correspondence nodes and the nodes in the class diagram referenced by the deleted correspondence nodes.

In the last step of the incremental transformation the algorithm searches for unmatched model elements and transforms those elements according to the triple graph grammar specification. The presented incremental algorithm can be used for unidirectional model transformations as well as for bidirectional model transformation and synchronization enabling round-trip engineering between models. We can further optimize our incremental algorithm if the involved models support change notifications. In that case, the presented transformation algorithm starts to traverse the DAG at the correspondence node connected to the modified element and not at the root of the DAG.

4 Evaluation

To evaluate our incremental approach, we use the model transformation example introduced earlier which synchronizes SDL block diagrams with a related UML class diagrams. In order to be able to evaluate large models with different characteristics, we wrote a parameterized synthesis algorithm for a hierarchical SDL block models where we can adjust the number of SDL blocks and the number of subblocks for each block. Therefore, we can in fact control the resulting out-degree w.r.t. rule dependencies in the resulting correspondence graph G_c by simply adjusting the number of subblocks for each block.

We further restrict our considerations to the forward direction as the backward case employs the same execution engine. The measurements have been done on an computer with an Intel(R) Pentium(R) m Processor with 1.80 GHz and 1,0 GB RAM. The complied rules and the execution engine have been run on Java 1.4.2_07 on top of the Windows XP Professional operating system.

4.1 Measured Synchronization Times

Taking the directed acyclic graph structure of the correspondence graph and the existence of a unique root node and leaf nodes into account, we can further assign to each node in the correspondence graph G_c the related height which relates to the length of the longest path from that node to a node without successor (leaf). This height can then also be related to the connected graph nodes of the source and target model. The height of the model is further simply the height of the root node.

While for the batch-oriented processing the required model synchronization efforts are the same for every modification in the source model, in the incremental case the specific effort required for a specific small modification on the source model depends on the height of the related correspondence nodes. We thus also characterize small modifications by the related height. This dependency is that the larger the related height is the higher are the efforts for the required processing. One extreme case is the model root. The required computation of the incremental transformation in fact involves the whole model.

Another factor which is relevant here is of course the out degree of the correspondence nodes. Obviously, a higher out-degree results in a higher computation effort for the same height as more subordinated nodes have to be subject to the application of the transformation rules. On the other hand a higher out-degree results in a much smaller height of the model and much more nodes with smaller height.

The resulting measurements for a SDL model with 5.000 blocks for the batch and incremental algorithm are depicted in Figure 4. On the x-axis the different possible heights of the small modifications are enumerated and the related

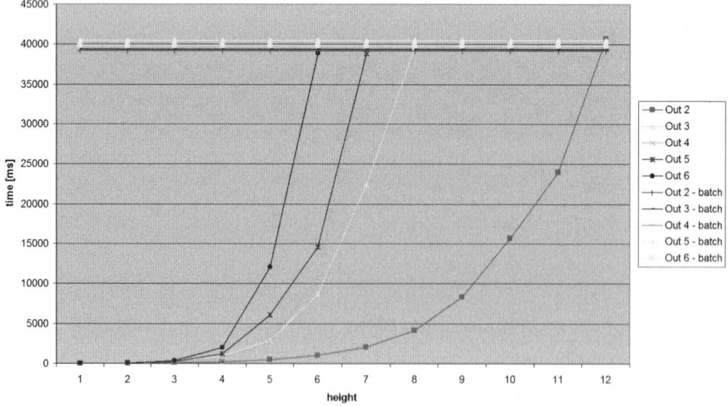

Fig. 4. Efforts for the synchronization after a modification

measurement results for the models with different out-degrees (Out n) are provided. In addition, we added the results for the batch-oriented algorithm (Out n - batch) which are independent of the height and thus are simply straight lines.

The expected effect which can be observed is that for larger out degrees we have smaller maximal height and thus the required efforts increase more rapidly with increasing height. For all cases holds that in case of the maximal height the same effort as for the batch processing can be observed.

4.2 Average Synchronization Costs

To derive a useful performance prediction from these measurements, we will further combine them to derive reasonable estimates for the average case of modifications.

Depending on the average height of the related correspondence nodes involved in the modification, a reasonable speedup w.r.t. a batch processing of the whole transformation can be observed. To relate this observation to a reasonable estimation of the average performance, we derive an average case effort estimation starting with the assumption that all changes have the same likelihood. For n the number of correspondence nodes, $h_{\max}$ the maximal height of the correspondence graph, n_h the number of correspondence nodes with height h, and T_h the measured time for processing a small modification in ms, the mean value for the time T_a required for the processing of an arbitrary small modification is then: $T_a = (\sum_{h=0}^{h_{\max}} n_h T_h)/n$.

Using the data about n, $h_{\max}$, n_h, and T_h presented in Figure 4 we thus have the average computation times as reported in Figure 5. In addition, we also computed the values for smaller models.

We can observe that with increasing out-degree the average synchronization time is reasonable small (about 20-30 ms) and increases only minimally with the model size (1-3 ms). For smaller out-degree the average case becomes more costly (60-90 ms) and also increases significantly (100-180 ms). The visible steps in the calculated average times and the following smooth decrease in the average time are related to an increase in height and the related result that the lower ranks of the correspondence DAG are that well balanced.

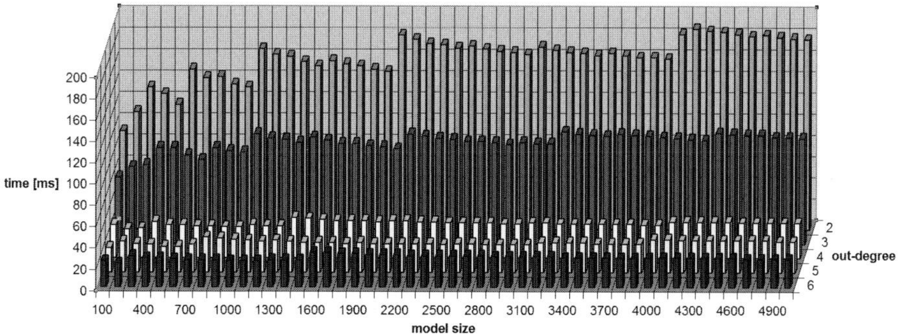

Fig. 5. Average computation times for small modifications and different out degrees

4.3 Discussion

Taking the directed acyclic graph structure of the correspondence graph into account, we know that only the nodes of the correspondence graph G_c beneath the correspondence nodes which are directly related to the modified node or edge have to be recomputed. While this already restricts the required computation effort, in the worst case clearly nearly the same effort as in the non incremental case is required.

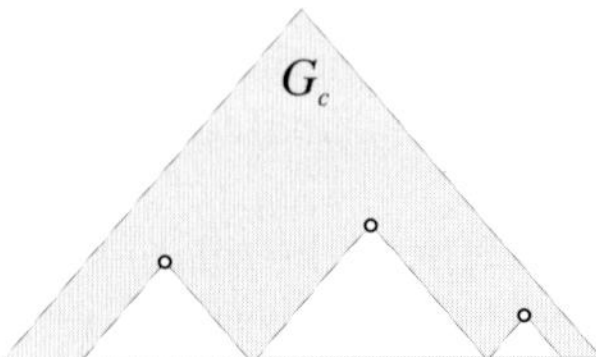

Fig. 6. Incremental application of the TGG rules for arbitrary modifications

In Fig. 6, the resulting effect on the acyclic directed correspondence graph is depicted. For sake of visual presentation, we use a tree rather than a DAG. Depending on the average height of the correspondence nodes in the tree/graph involved in the modification, a reasonable speedup w.r.t. a batch processing of the whole transformation can be expected.

The described observation for the average case can be backed up by the following theoretical derivation of the complexity: For n nodes and a maximal depth $d_{\max}$ we roughly have $n \approx \exp(d_{\max})$ nodes in a tree. If we further assume that there are about $N(d) \approx \exp(d)$ nodes for a specific depth d and that the number of rule applications T for processing an update for a correspondence node with depth d is $T(d) \approx \exp(d_{\max} - d)$, the mean number of rule applications T_m for processing an update for an arbitrary correspondence node assuming an average distribution is:

$$\begin{aligned} T_m &\approx \frac{\sum_{d=0}^{d_{\max}-1} N(d) * T(d)}{n} \approx \frac{\sum_{0=0}^{d_{\max}-1} \exp(d) * \exp(d_{\max} - d)}{\exp(d_{\max})} \\ &\approx \frac{\sum_{d=0}^{d_{\max}-1} \exp(d_{\max})}{\exp(d_{\max})} = \frac{(d_{\max} - 1) * \exp(d_{\max})}{\exp(d_{\max})} = (d_{\max} - 1) \end{aligned}$$

In contrast to repeat the full computation of the correspondence graph which would require $n \approx \exp(d_{\max})$ rule applications for a model with n nodes, we only require $(d_{\max} - 1)$ rule applications in the average case. Thus as $d_{\max} \approx \log(n)$, we have a *effectively incremental* solution as the impact of the model size in the average case is only in $O(\log(n))$ and not $O(n)$ as for batch processing.

It is to be noted that models in practice often have 7 or more elements at the same abstraction level which are then further refined by assigning submodels to each element, while we have looked into out-degrees from 2 to 6. The considered data indicates that for higher out-degrees we can expect even better performance than for the smaller out-degrees and thus the considered cases are from a practical point of view the worst cases.[2]

5 Related Work

Motivated by the Model-Driven Architecture (MDA) [1] and OMG's Request for Proposal (RFP) on Query/Views/ Transformations (QVT) [8], model transformation has been put into the focus of many research activities. Meanwhile, a first version of the Final Adopted Specification [9] is published and the final version is expected in the course of this year. In this specification, incremental model transformations are an important issue. However, to the best knowledge of the authors, up to now there is no publicly and freely available tool implementing the QVT standard with incremental updates for model synchronization.

A tool supporting incremental model transformations is the *Model Transformation Framework* (MTF) [10] developed by IBM. Unfortunately, so far, there is no performance data nor any publication describing the used approach available.

Nevertheless, the RFP has lead to a large number of approaches for model transformation - each for a special purpose and within a particular domain with its own requirements [11]. A class of transformation approaches comprises graphical transformation languages which are based on the theoretical work on graph grammars and graph transformations. These approaches interpret the models as graphs and the transformation is executed by searching a pattern in the graph and applying an action which transforms the pattern to a new data structure. However, these languages do not provide any explicit traceability information about the model transformation. This prevents both incremental transformations and consistency maintaining activities for model synchronization after an applied transformation. Additionally, in the most graph grammar based approaches, the transformation must be specified for each transformation direction separately. Hence, they are not well suited for the specification of bidirectional model transformation and synchronization.

In contrast to that, triple graph grammars are a special technique for the specification and execution of bidirectional transformations. Triple graph grammars were motivated by integration problems between different tools where interrelated documents have to be kept consistent with each other [12, 13, 14]. In this field, triple graph grammars are used for the maintenance of the required traceability links between different document artifacts. In [13] the transformation algorithm operates interactively and incrementally. In contrast to our approach, the transformation algorithm relies on the type of so called *dominant increments*. The incremental transformation approach in [15] is triggered by user actions like creating, editing, or deleting elements. A complete model transformation from scratch is not in the focus of the approach whereas our approach handles both cases. However, some of the work served as a starting

[2] The absolute worst case is a linear list where the effort is of course proportional to the height. We are, however, not aware of any example where the metamodels and their model instances in practice result in a linear list.

point for our approach. In particular, we rely on the proposed attribute update propagation techniques [13, 14] and the correspondence dependency introduced by [12].

6 Conclusion and Future Work

We have presented our approach for the efficient and incremental model synchronization with the model transformation approach triple graph grammars. Our solution at first is visual, formal, and bidirectional which are all characteristics it inherits from triple graph grammars. In addition, our extension of the rule execution facilitates an incremental application which takes the acyclic dependencies present in the correspondence graph into account and therefore results in an effectively incremental solution for the model synchronization problem.

We have realized our approach in the Fujaba Tool Suite[3]. The available tool support includes the visual specification of the triple graph grammar rules, the automatic extraction of the resulting graph rewriting rules, and an execution engine for the incremental execution of these rules.

The paper provides measurements for the effort required for an example model transformation task and the related model synchronization in particular for the case of *large* models. To our knowledge, similar data is currently not provided by any related approach. We hope that this will change in the future and that this contribution is a first step towards setting up benchmarks for model transformation such that the finding can be based on commonly agreed examples and that the different approaches can be systematically compared.

As future work we plan to provide a QVT compatible front-end for our approach which maps the QVT semantics to triple graph grammars in order to make the technology available to a broader audience.

References

1. OMG: MDA Guide Version 1.0.1. (2003) Document – omg/03-06-01.
2. Wagner, R., Giese, H., Nickel, U.: A Plug-In for Flexible and Incremental Consistency Management. In: Proceedings of the Workshop on Consistency Problems in UML-based Software Development II (UML 2003, Workshop 7), Blekinge Institute of Technology (2003) 78–85
3. Gardner, T., Griffin, C., Koehler, J., Hauser, R.: Review of OMG MOF 2.0 Query/Views/Transformations Submissions and Recommendations towards final Standard. OMG, 250 First Avenue, Needham, MA 02494, USA. (2003)
4. Schürr, A.: Specification of graph translators with triple graph grammars. In Mayr, E.W., Schmidt, G., Tinhofer, G., eds.: Graph-Theoretic Concepts in Computer Science, 20th International Workshop, WG '94. Volume 903 of LNCS., Herrsching, Germany (1994) 151–163

[3] www.fujaba.de

5. Schäfer, W., Wagner, R., Gausemeier, J., Eckes, R.: An Engineer's Workstation to support Integrated Development of Flexible Production Control Systems. In Ehrig, H., Damm, W., Desel, J., Grośe-Rhode, M., Reif, W., Schnieder, E., Westkämper, E., eds.: Integration of Software Specification Techniques for Applications in Engineering. Volume 3147 of Lecture Notes in Computer Science (LNCS). Springer Verlag (2004) 48–68
6. International Telecommunication Union (ITU), Geneva: ITU-T Recommendation Z.100: Specification and Description Language (SDL). (1994 + Addendum 1996)
7. OMG 250 First Avenue, Needham, MA 02494, USA: (Unified Modeling Language Specification Version 1.5)
8. OMG: OMG/RFP/QVT MOF 2.0 Query/Views/Transformations RFP. http://www.omg.org/mda/. (2003)
9. OMG: MOF QVT Final Adopted Specification, OMG Document ptc/05-11-01. (http://www.omg.org/)
10. Griffin, C.: Eclipse Model Transformatioin Framework (MTF), available at http://www.alphaworks.ibm.com/tech/mtf. IBM. (2006)
11. Czarnecki, K., Helsen, S.: Classification of Model Transformation Approaches. In: Proceedings of the 2nd OOPSLA Workshop on Generative Techniques in the Context of the Model Driven Architecture, USA, 2003. (2003)
12. Lefering, M., Schürr, A.: Specification of Integration Tools. In Nagl, M., ed.: Building Thightly-Integrated (Software) Development Environments: The IPSEN Approach. Volume 1170 of Lecture Notes in Computer Science., Springer Verlag (1996) 324–334
13. Becker, S., Lohmann, S., Westfechtel, B.: Rule Execution in Graph-Based Incremental Interactive Integration Tools. In: Proc. Intl. Conf. on Graph Transformations (ICGT 2004). Volume 3256 of LNCS. (2004) 22–38
14. Königs, A., Schürr, A.: Tool Integration with Triple Graph Grammars - A Survey. In Heckel, R., ed.: Proceedings of the SegraVis School on Foundations of Visual Modelling Techniques. Volume 148 of Electronic Notes in Theoretical Computer Science., Amsterdam, Elsevier Science Publ. (2006) 113–150
15. Guerra, E., de Lara, J.: Event-Driven Grammars: Towards the Integration of Meta-Modelling and Graph Transformation. In: International Conference on Graph Transformation (ICGT'2004). Volume 3265 of LNCS. (2004) 54–69

Model-Driven Assessment of Use Cases for Dependable Systems

Sadaf Mustafiz, Ximeng Sun, Jörg Kienzle, and Hans Vangheluwe

School of Computer Science, McGill University
Montreal, Quebec, Canada
{sadaf, xsun16, joerg, hv}@cs.mcgill.ca

Abstract. Complex real-time systems need to address dependability requirements early on in the development process. This paper presents a model-based approach that allows developers to analyze the dependability of use cases and to discover more reliable and safe ways of designing the interactions with the system and the environment. We use a probabilistic extension of statecharts to model the system requirements. The model is then evaluated analytically based on the success and failure probabilities of events. The analysis may lead to further refinement of the use cases by introducing detection and recovery measures to ensure dependable system interaction. A visual modelling environment for our extended statecharts formalism supporting automatic probability analysis has been implemented in AToM^3, A Tool for Multi-formalism and Meta-Modelling. Our approach is illustrated with an elevator control system case study.

1 Introduction

Complex computer systems are increasingly built for highly critical tasks from military and aerospace domains to industrial and commercial areas. Failures of such systems may have severe consequences ranging from loss of business opportunities, physical damage, to loss of human lives. Systems with such responsibilities should be highly *dependable*. On the software developer's part, this involves acknowledging that many exceptional situations may arise during the execution of an application, and providing measures to handle such situations to maintain system reliability and safety. Any such exception that is not identified during requirements elicitation might potentially lead to an incomplete system specification during analysis, and ultimately to an implementation that behaves in an unreliable way. Rigorous requirements elicitation methods such as the *exceptional use case* approach we proposed in [1] lead the analyst to define handler use cases that address exceptional situations that threaten system reliability and safety. These handler use cases allow exceptional interactions that require several steps of handling to be described separately from the normal system behavior. But is it enough to only define handlers for exceptions that can interrupt the normal system functionality? What about exceptions that interrupt the handlers themselves? Do we need handlers for handlers? To answer this question there must be a way to assess the reliability and safety of a system.

For this purpose, this paper proposes a model-driven approach for assessing and refining use cases to ensure that the specified functionality meets the dependability

O. Nierstrasz et al. (Eds.): MoDELS 2006, LNCS 4199, pp. 558–573, 2006.

requirements of the system. To carry out the analysis, the use cases are mapped to DA-Charts, a probabilistic extension of part of the statecharts formalism. The assessment is then based on a tool that performs probability analysis of the model.

The paper is organized as follows: Section 2 provides background information on dependability, use cases, and the exceptional use cases approach in [1]. Section 3 describes our model-driven process for assessing and refining use cases. Section 4 presents our probabilistic statecharts formalism used for dependability analysis. Tool support for our formalism is discussed in Sect. 5. Section 6 illustrates our proposed process by means of an elevator control case study. Section 7 presents related work in this area and Sect. 8 discusses future work and draws some conclusions.

2 Background

2.1 Dependability

Dependability [2] is that property of a computer system such that reliance can justifiably be placed on the service it delivers. It involves satisfying several requirements: availability, reliability, safety, maintainability, confidentiality, and integrity. The dependability requirement varies with the target application, since a constraint can be essential for one environment and not so much for others. In this paper, we focus on the *reliability* and *safety* attributes of dependability. The **reliability** of a system measures its aptitude to provide service and remain operating as long as required [3]. The **safety** of a system is determined by the lack of catastrophic failures it undergoes [3].

Fault tolerance is a means of achieving system dependability. As defined in [4], fault tolerance includes error detection and system recovery. At the use case level, error detection involves detection of exceptional situations by means of secondary actors such as sensors and time-outs. Recovery at the use case level involves describing the interactions with the environment that are needed to continue to deliver the current service, or to offer a degraded service, or to take actions that prevent a catastrophe. The former two recovery actions increase reliability, whereas the latter ensures safety.

2.2 Use Cases

Use cases are a widely used formalism for discovering and recording behavioral requirements of software systems [5]. A use case describes, without revealing the details of the system's internal workings, the system's responsibilities and its interactions with its environment as it performs work in serving one or more requests that, if successfully completed, satisfy a goal of a particular stakeholder. The external entities in the environment that interact with the system are called *actors*.

Use cases are stories of actors using a system to *meet goals*. The actor that wants to achieve the goal is referred to as the *primary actor*. Entities that the system needs to fulfill the goal are called *secondary actors*. Secondary actors include software or hardware that is out of our control. The system, on the other hand, is the software that we are developing and which is under our control.

2.3 Exceptions and Handlers in Use Cases

In [1] we proposed an approach that extends traditional use case driven requirements elicitation, leading the analyst to focus on all possible exceptional situations that can interrupt normal system interaction.

An exception occurrence endangers the completion of the actor's goal, suspending the normal interaction temporarily or for good. To guarantee reliable service or ensure safety, special interaction with the environment might be necessary. These handling actions can be described in a *handler use case*. That way, from the very beginning, exceptional interaction and behavior is clearly identified and separated from the normal behavior of the system. Similar to standard use cases, handlers use cases are reusable. Handlers can be defined for handlers in order to specify actions to be taken when an exception is raised in a handler itself.

3 Model-Driven Dependability Analysis of Use Cases

We propose a model-driven approach for assessing and refining use cases to ensure that the specified functionality meets the dependability requirements of the system as defined by the stakeholders.

For the purpose of analysis, we introduce probabilities in use cases. The value associated to each interaction step represents the probability with which the step succeeds. If we assume reliable communication and a perfect software (which we must at the requirements level), the success and failure of each interaction depends on the quality of the hardware device, e.g. motor, sensor, etc. The reliability of each hardware component can be obtained from the manufacturer. If the secondary actor is a software system, its reliability is also either known or must be determined statistically.

Our proposed process is illustrated in Fig. 1. First, the analyst starts off with standard use case-driven requirements elicitation (see step 1). Using the exceptional use case approach described in [1] the analyst discovers exceptional situations, adds detection hardware to the system if needed, and refines the use cases (see step 2). Then, each use case step that represents an interaction with a secondary actor is annotated with a probability value that specifies the chances of success of the interaction (see step 3). Additionally, each interaction step is annotated with a safety tag if the failure of that step threatens the safety of the system. Next, each use case is mapped to a DA-Chart (see step 4). DA-Charts and the mapping process are described in Sect. 4. This mapping could be automated (see Sect. 8), but for now it has to be done manually. The DA-Charts are then mathematically analyzed by our dependability assessment tool (see step 5) and a report is produced. Steps 3, 4, and 5 are the main contributions of this paper. The implementation of the tool using meta-modeling is described in Sect. 5.

The assessment report allows the analyst to decide if the current system specification achieves the desired reliability and safety. If not, several options can be investigated. It is possible to increase the reliability of secondary actors by, for instance, buying more reliable hardware components, or employing redundant hardware and voting techniques. Alternatively, the use cases have to be revisited and refined. First, the system must be capable of detecting the exceptional situation. This might require the use of time-outs, or even the addition of detection hardware to the system. Then, handler use cases must

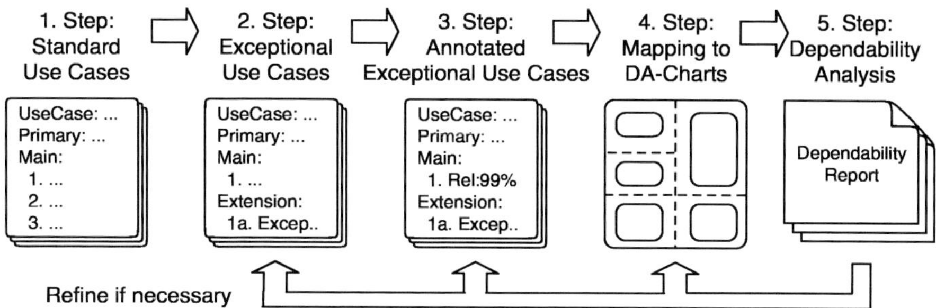

Fig. 1. Model-Driven Process for Assessment and Refinement of Use Cases

be defined that compensate for the failure of the actor, or bring the system to a safe halt. The analyst can perform the refinements in the annotated use cases or on the DA-Charts.

After the changes, the effects on the system reliability and safety are determined by re-running the probabilistic analysis. The refinement process is repeated until the stakeholders are satisfied.

Elevator System Case Study. We demonstrate our approach by applying it to an elevator control system case study. An elevator system is a hard real-time application requiring high levels of dependability.

For the sake of simplicity, there is only one elevator cabin that travels between the floors. The job of the development team is to decide on the required hardware, and to implement the elevator control software that processes the user requests and coordinates the different hardware devices. Initially, only "mandatory" elevator hardware has been added to the system: a motor to go up, go down or stop; a cabin door that opens and closes; floor sensors that detect when the cabin is approaching a floor; two buttons on each floor to call the elevator; and a series of buttons inside the elevator cabin.

Standard use case-driven requirements elicitation applied to the elevator control system results in the use case model shown in Fig. 2. In the elevator system there is initially

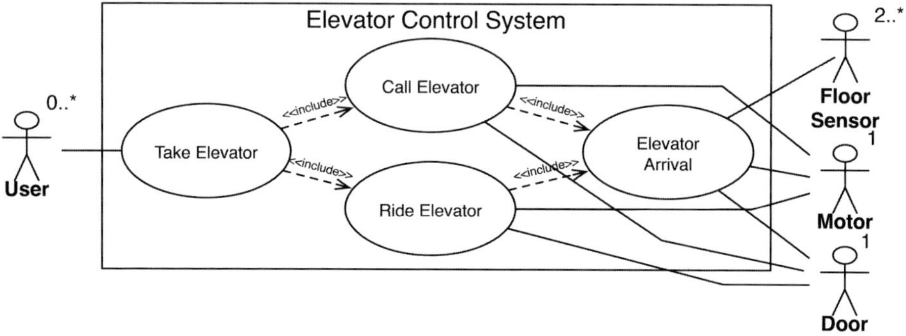

Fig. 2. Standard Elevator Use Case Diagram

Use Case: ElevatorArrival
Primary Actor: N/A
Intention: System wants to move the elevator to the *User*'s destination floor.
Level: Subfunction
Main Success Scenario:

1. System asks motor to start moving in the direction of the destination floor.
2. System detects elevator is approaching destination floor.
3. System requests motor to stop.
4. System opens door.

Fig. 3. *ElevatorArrival* Use Case

only one primary actor, the *User*. A user has only one goal with the system: to take the elevator to go to a destination floor. The primary actor *(User)* is the one that initiates the TakeLift use case. All secondary actors (the *Door*, the *Motor*, the *Exterior* and *Interior Floor Buttons*, as well as the *Floor Sensors*) that collaborate to provide the user goal are also depicted. Due to space constraints, we only discuss the subfunction level use case *ElevatorArrival* (shown in Fig. 3) in detail.

To ride the elevator the *User* enters the cabin, selects a destination floor, waits until the cabin arrives at the destination floor and finally exits the elevator.

CallElevator and *RideElevator* both include the *ElevatorArrival* use case shown in Fig. 3. It is a subfunction level use case that describes how the system directs the elevator to a specific floor: once the system detects that the elevator is approaching the destination floor, it requests the motor to stop and opens the door.

The analysis of the basic use case following the approach in [1] lead to the discovery of some critical exceptions that interrupt the normal elevator arrival processing: *MissedFloor*, *MotorFailure* and *DoorStuckClosed*.

4 Probabilistic Statecharts

In this section, we introduce DA-Charts (short for Dependability Assessment Charts), a probabilistic extension of the statecharts formalism introduced by David Harel [6].

4.1 Statecharts

The statecharts formalism is an extension of Deterministic Finite State Automata with hierarchy, orthogonality and broadcast communication [7]. It is a popular formalism for the modelling of the behaviour of reactive systems. It has an intuitive yet rigourously defined notation and semantics. It is the basis for documentation, analysis, simulation, and code synthesis. Many variants of statecharts exist, including the one included in the UML standard.

4.2 Extending Statecharts with Probabilities

We extend the statecharts formalism with probabilities to enable dependability assessment. While stochastic petri nets is an established formalism with clearly defined semantics, statecharts seem a more natural match for our domain. This, thanks to their modularity, broadcast, and orthogonality features. Statecharts also make it possible to design visually simple and structured models.

Standard statecharts are solely event-driven. State transitions occur if the associated event is triggered and any specified condition is satisfied. Given the event, a source state has only one possible target state. In the formalism we propose, DA-Charts, when an event is triggered, a state can transition to one of two possible target states: a *success* state and a *failure* state. When an event is triggered, the system moves to a success state with probability p and to a failure state with probability $1-p$. In most real-time systems, the probability of ending up in a success state is closer to 1 and the failure state probability is closer to 0. For example, if a motor in a mechanical system is asked to stop, it might stop with a probability of 0.999 and it might fail to stop with probability 0.001. As in statecharts, the transition may broadcast events. The event that is broadcast can be different depending on whether the transition leads to a success state or a failure state. Hence, the outcome of the event might vary.

DA-Charts Syntax. The statecharts notation is extended to include probabilities. The standard transition is split into two transitions, each annotated with the probability that the event associated with the transition leads to a success state or a failed state. The notation used for this purpose adds an attribute next to the event: *event[condition] {probability} /action*. Absence of the *probability* attribute implies a probability of 1.

DA-Charts Semantics

Finite State Automaton: Unlike statecharts, DA-Charts are non-deterministic due to the addition of probabilities in state transitions. Our formalism requires adaptation of the various features of the statecharts semantics to support the notion of non-determinism. In particular there is non-determinism in both the end states and in which events are broadcast.

Orthogonality: In DA-Charts, orthogonal components model the concurrent behavior of actors in the environment. For example, in an elevator system, we might want to model the different hardware devices (motor/sensors) as orthogonal components. However, DA-Charts has the constraint that events cannot be triggered simultaneously in orthogonal components.

Broadcast: The broadcasting feature is used in DA-Charts to enable sequencing of events. In a real-time system, the system progresses with time and some devices can only react provided that some required event preceded it. In the elevator system, the door should only be opened if the floor sensor detects that the destination floor has been reached.

Depth: DA-Charts as described in this paper do not currently support hierarchy in components. However, we are currently working on allowing hierarchical states within the system component to reflect the user goal / sub-goal hierarchy (see Sect. 8).

History: When external events or environmental hazards are considered in DA-Charts, history states would be useful when the system needs to return to a prior state after handling such a situation (see Sect. 8). A user inside an elevator might request an emergency stop but after servicing the request, the system might want to resume normal functionality.

DA-Charts Constraints. Our DA-Chart formalism is constrained by the following:

- Every DA-Chart must contain a *system* component describing the behaviour of the software of the system. No probabilities are allowed in the system component, since at the requirements level we assume a fault-free implementation.
- Each secondary actor is modelled by an orthogonal component. Each service that an actor provides can either succeed or fail, which is modelled by two transitions leading to either a *success* or a *failed* state, annotated with the corresponding probabilities.
- To monitor the safety constraints of the system, an additional orthogonal *safety-status* component is created. Whenever the failure of an actor leads to an unsafe condition, a *toUnsafe* event is broadcast to the *safety-status* component. Other quality constraints can be modelled in a similar manner.

4.3 Mapping Exceptional Use Cases to DA-Charts

We assume that the system software and the communication channels between the system and the actors are reliable. During requirements elicitation, the developer can assume that the system itself, once it has been built, will always behave according to specification - in other words, it will not contain any faults, and will therefore never fail. As the development continues into design and implementation phases, this assumption is most certainly not realistic. Dependability assessment and fault forecasting techniques have to be used to estimate the reliability of the implemented system. If needed, fault tolerance mechanisms have to be built into the system to increase its dependability.

Although the system is assumed to function perfectly, a reliable system cannot assume that it will operate in a fault free environment. Hence, at this point we need to consider the possible failure of (secondary) actors to perform the services requested by the system that affects the dependability of the system.

Each use case is mapped to one DA-Chart. As mentioned above, the DA-Chart has one orthogonal *system* component that models the behavior of the system, one *safety-status* component that records unsafe states, and one probabilistic orthogonal component for each secondary actor.

Each step in the use case is mapped to a transition in the system component, as well as a transition in the actor involved in the step as follows:

- An appropriately named event is created, e.g. *floorDetected* or *stopMotor*.
- A step that describes an input sent by an actor A to the system is mapped to:
  - an action, e.g. *floorDetected*, on the success transition in the component modelling the reliability of A. The probability annotation p from the step is added to the success transition, the probability $1-p$ is added to the failure transition.
  - an event in the system that moves the system to the next state.
- A step that describes an output sent by the system to an actor A is mapped to:
  - an action in the system, e.g. *stopMotor*,
  - an event within the component modelling the behavior of A, that leads to a success state and a failure state. Probability annotation p from the step is added to the success transition, the probability $1-p$ is added to the failure transition.

- Each exception associated with the step is mapped to a failure action, e.g. *motor-Failure*, and attached to the failure transition of the corresponding actor.
- If a step is tagged as *Safety-critical*, the failure transition broadcasts an event *toUn-safe* which is recorded in the *safety-status* component.

5 Creating Tool Support for Probabilistic Statecharts

5.1 AToM^3: A Tool for Multiformalism and MetaModelling

To allow rapid development of visual modelling tools, we use AToM^3, *A Tool for Multi-formalism and Meta-Modelling* [8,9]. In AToM^3, we follow the maxim "*model every-thing*" (explicitly, in the most appropriate formalism). Formalisms and transformations are modelled using meta-models and graph grammar models respectively. Also, composite types and the user interfaces of the generated tools are modelled explicitly. The tool has proven to be very powerful, allowing the meta-modelling of known formalisms such as Petri Nets [10]. More importantly, many new formalisms were constructed using the tool, such as the Traffic formalism [11].

5.2 DA-Charts Implementation in AToM^3

DA-Charts is a simple extension of the statechart syntax: a simple edge is extended by adding a *probability* attribute which becomes a P-Edge, so the action and the target depend on the outcome of a probabilistic experiment. A traditional edge can be seen as a P-Edge whose probability is 1.

We implement tool support for DA-Charts by extending the meta-model of the DCharts formalism (a variant of Statecharts) described in [12]. This is done in three steps as follows. First, *probability* is added as a float attribute to the *Hyperedge* relationship of the existing DCharts meta-model (an Entity-Relationship diagram). The default value of *probability* is 1. Two constraints are added. One constraint allows users to only set the probability of a transition to a maximum of 1; the other one checks if the total probability of all transitions from the same source node and triggered by the same event is 1. AToM^3 allows for the subsequent synthesis of a visual DA-Charts modelling environment from this meta-model. Second, a Probability Analysis (PA) module which can compute probabilities of reaching a target state is implemented. The algorithm is described in the next section. Lastly, a button which invokes the PA module is added to the visual modelling environment.

The semantics of a DA-Chart are described informally as follows. When an event occurs, all P-Edges which are triggered by the event and whose guards hold are taken. The system then leaves the source node(s), chooses one of those P-Edges probabilistically, executes the action of the chosen P-Edge, and enters the target node(s).

5.3 Probability Analysis of DA-Charts in AToM^3

Given a source state (consisting of a tuple of source nodes) and a target state, the probability to reach the target from the source is computed by finding all paths that lead from

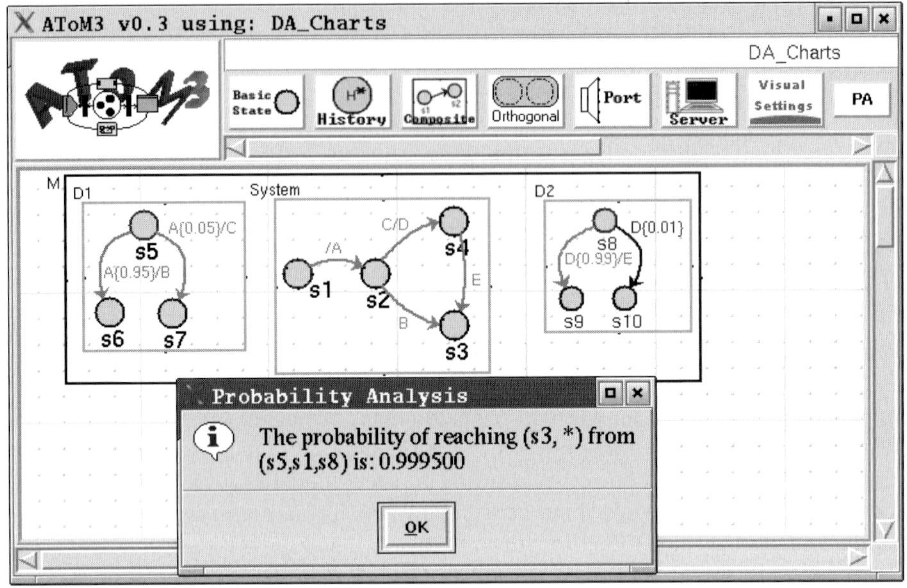

Fig. 4. Example DA-Chart Model in AToM^3

the source to the target state. The probability of each path is calculated as the product of all transition probabilities. The total probability is then computed by adding the probabilities of all paths.

A probabilistic analysis algorithm based on the above observations has been implemented in AToM^3. It reads three arguments, model M containing all elements, such as components, nodes and edges, a tuple of node names of the source state S, and a tuple of node names of the target state T. It then produces a float value in the range $[0,1]$. The details of the algorithm are omitted here for space reasons.

An analyst wanting to compute, for instance, the reliability of the system has to first press the *PA* button, and then select the target state that symbolizes the successful completion of the goal, after which a pop-up dialog shows the result and all possible paths leading to the target state are highlighted in the model.

Fig. 4 shows an example DA-Chart model in AToM^3. The model consists of three components: *System*, *D1* and *D2*. The default state is *(s5, s1, s8)* and the only transition which can happen initially is the one from *s1* to *s2*. The probability of reaching *(s3, *)* ("*" means we do not care about what other nodes are when the system ends in the state containing *s3*) from *(s5, s1, s8)* is 99.95% which is the combination of the probabilities along two possible paths: $T_{s1\to s2}$, $T_{s5\to s6}$, and $T_{s2\to s3}$ for path one; $T_{s1\to s2}$, $T_{s5\to s7}$, $T_{s2\to s4}$, $T_{s8\to s9}$, and $T_{s4\to s3}$ for path two. The computation performed can be mathematically defined as follows:

$$P_{total} = (P_{s2\to s3} \times P_{s5\to s6} + (P_{s4\to s3} \times P_{s8\to s9}) \times P_{s2\to s4} \times P_{s5\to s7}) \times P_{s1\to s2} \quad (1)$$

6 Dependability Analysis Using Statecharts

6.1 Analyzing Exceptions in the Elevator Arrival Use Case

We use the Elevator System case study to demonstrate our assessment approach. At this point, the standard use case has been already analyzed for exceptional situations that can arise while servicing a request. As discussed in Sect. 3, several failures might occur: the destination floor might not be detected (*MissedFloor*); the motor might fail (*MotorFailure*); or the door might not open at the floor (*DoorStuckClosed*).

To detect whether the elevator is approaching a floor, we need to introduce a sensor, *ApprFloorSensor*. To detect a motor failure, an additional sensor, *AtFloorSensor* is added. It detects when the cabin stopped, and therefore when it is safe to open the doors.

Fig. 5 shows the updated version of the *ElevatorArrival* use case that includes the added acknowledgment steps and the exception extensions. Some steps are annotated with (made up) probabilities of success: the *ApprFloorSensor* and the *AtFloorSensor* have failure chances of 2% and 5% respectively. The motor has a 1% chance of failure. For space reasons, we assume that the motor always starts and the door always opens. In addition, each step is tagged as *Safety-critical* if the failure of that step threatens the system safety.

Use Case: ElevatorArrival
Intention: System wants to move the elevator to the *User*'s destination floor.
Level: Subfunction
Main Success Scenario:

1. System asks motor to start moving towards the destination floor.
2. System detects elevator is approaching destination floor. Reliability:0.98 *Safety-critical*
3. System requests motor to stop. Reliability:0.99 *Safety-critical*
4. System receives confirmation elevator is stopped at destination floor. Reliability:0.95
5. System requests door to open.
6. System receives confirmation that door is open.

Extensions:

2a. Exception{MissedFloor}
4a. Exception{MotorFailure}
6a. Exception{DoorStuckClosed}

Fig. 5. Updated *ElevatorArrival* Use Case

6.2 The DA-Charts Model of the Basic Elevator Arrival System with Failures

We first model the initial *ElevatorArrival* use case shown in Sect. 6.1 as a DA-Chart according to the process described in Sect. 4.3. The result is shown in Fig. 6. The model consists mainly of four orthogonal components which model the behaviour of the system (System), a motor (Motor), and two sensors (*ApprFloorSensor* and *AtFloorSensor*). An additional orthogonal component is used to monitor the safety outcome of the system. Note that the system has no randomness.

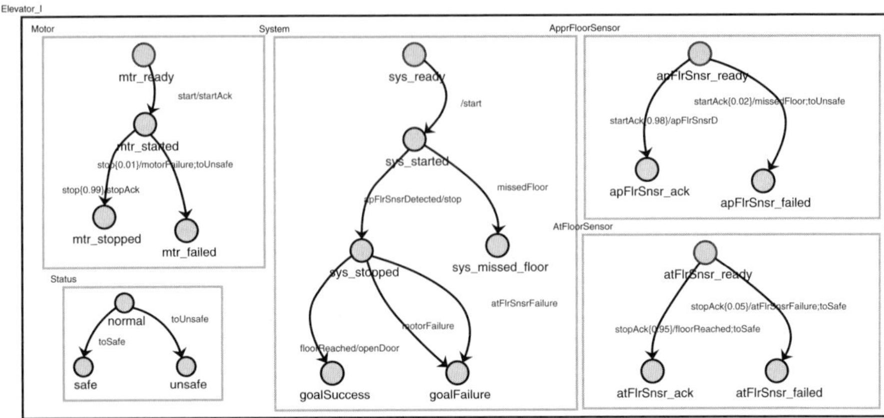

Fig. 6. DA-Chart Model of the Elevator Arrival Use Case with Failures

To clarify the model, one of the components is briefly explained here. The *Motor* is initially ready (in the *mtr_ready* state). After it is triggered by the *System* (by the *start* event), it acknowledges the *System*'s request (by broadcasting *startAck*) and goes into running mode (by transitioning to the *mtr_started* state). When the motor is asked to stop (by the *stop* event), the *Motor* will either stop itself successfully (going to *mtr_stopped*) and send an acknowledgement (by broadcasting *stopAck*), or fail to stop (going to *mtr_failed* and broadcasting *motorFailure* and *toUnsafe*). The chances of success and failure are 99% and 1% respectively.

6.3 Evaluating Dependability of the System

Safety Analysis. We want to ensure the safety levels maintained by the elevator arrival system. The system is unsafe if the approaching floor sensor fails to detect the destination floor (because then the system never tells the motor to stop), or if the motor fails to stop when told to do so. This is why the failure transition in the *ApprFloorSensor* component, as well as the failure transition in the *Motor* component broadcast a *toUnsafe* event that is recorded in the *Status* component. It is interesting to note that actually achieving the goal of the use case has nothing to do with safety. Our tool then calculates that the probability of reaching the state *safe* from the initial system state (*sys_ready*) is 97.02%, which is the combination of the probabilities along two possible paths.

Reliability Analysis. Our tool calculates a reliability (probability of reaching the *goalSuccess* state) of 92.169%. Although we assume that the door is 100% reliable, a failure of the *AtFloorSensor* would prevent the system from knowing that the destination floor is reached, and hence the system cannot request the door to open. The person riding the elevator would be stuck inside the cabin, and hence the goal fails.

6.4 Refining the Elevator Arrival Use Case

For a safety-critical system like the elevator control system, a higher level of safety is desirable. Safety can be increased by using more reliable or replicated hardware,

Handler Use Case: EmergencyBrake
Handler Class: Safety
Context & Exception: ElevatorArrival{MotorFailure}
Intention: System wants to stop operation of elevator and secure the cabin.
Level: Subfunction
Main Success Scenario:

1. System stops motor.
2. System activates the emergency brakes. Reliability:0.999 *Safety-critical*
3. System turns on the emergency display.

Fig. 7. *EmergencyBrake* Handler Use Case

but such hardware might not be available or might be too costly. Another possibility is to initiate an action that can prevent catastrophes from happening. To illustrate this approach, we focus on the motor failure problem. To remain in a safe state even if the motor fails, it is necessary to use additional hardware like an emergency brake. This behavior is encapsulated in the *EmergencyBrake* safety handler (shown in Fig. 7).

6.5 The DA-Charts Model of the Safety-Enhanced Elevator Arrival Use Case

The DA-Chart model of the elevator arrival system is updated to reflect the use of emergency brakes (see Fig. 8). Another orthogonal component to model the behaviour of the emergency brakes is added. The brake used has a 99.9% chance of success.

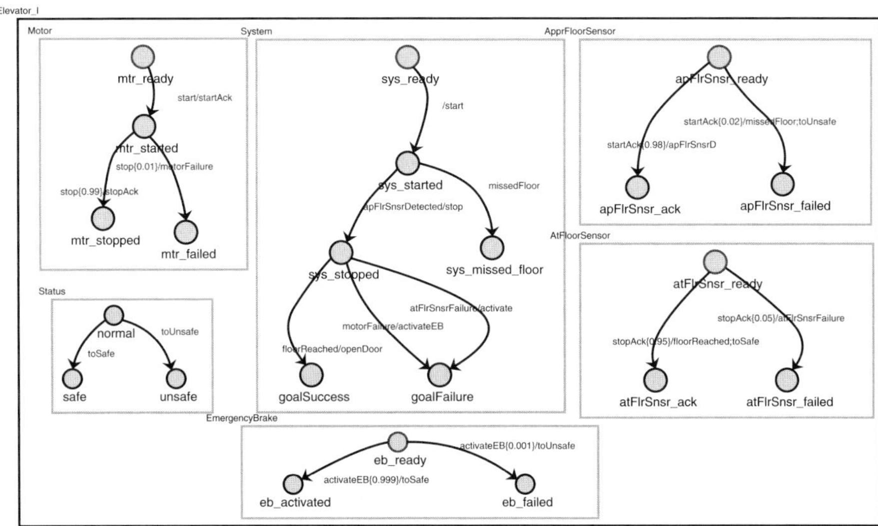

Fig. 8. DA-Chart Model of the Elevator Arrival System with Failures and Handlers

Safety Analysis. A probability analysis of the updated model shows a significant improvement in the safety achieved by the system. It is now safe 97.9942% of the time, which evaluates to an increase of 0.9742%. The safety would be even more improved if the *missedFloor* exception would be detected and handled.

Reliability Analysis. The reliability of the system has not changed. The use case could be further refined so that the elevator detects when the *AtFloorSensor* fails [1], and then the system could redirect the elevator to the nearest floor. Even though the original goal of the user is not satisfied, the system attempts to provide reliable service in a degraded manner.

6.6 Discussion

In this paper due to space constraints, we have only shown one safety-related refinement of the *ElevatorArrival* use case. Many other exceptions affect the dependability of the elevator system, for example exceptional situations that occur due to overweight or a door mechanism failure or a fire outbreak. However, such issues can be easily modelled in DA-Charts following our defined process, and can then be subjected to probability analysis. The proposed assessment approach can be easily scaled for more complex systems.

Assessment and refinement is supposed to be an iterative process, and can be continued as long as it is realistic and feasible, until the expected system safety and reliability is met. Thanks to our tool support, iterations are not time-consuming, and immediate feedback is given to the analyst of how changes in the use cases affect system dependability.

7 Related Work

Research has been carried out on analyzing quality of requirements mostly using formal requirements specification, that is, requirements written in specification languages, and model checking techniques. Bianco et al. [13] presents an approach for reasoning about reliability and performance of probabilistic and nondeterministic systems using temporal logics for formal specification of system properties and model-checking algorithms for verifying that the system satisfies the specification. Automatic verification of probabilistic systems using techniques of model checking are also covered in [14].

Atlee et al. [15] demonstrates a model-checking technique used to verify safety properties of event-driven systems. The formal requirements are transformed to state-based structures, and then analyzed using a state-based model checker.

Huszerl et al. [16] describes a quantitative dependability analysis approach targeting embedded systems. The system behaviour is specified with guarded statechart models and then mapped to timed, stochastic petri nets to carry out performance evaluation.

Jansen et al. [17] proposed a probabilistic extension to statecharts, P-Statecharts, similar to our DA-Charts formalism to aid in formal verification of probabilistic temporal properties. The probability concept in P-Statecharts has two facets: *environmental*

[1] This can, for instance, be done using a time-out.

randomness and *system randomness*. In our work, we focus on dependable systems in which randomness only comes from the environment the system is exposed to, rather than from the system itself. Unlike their formalism, DA-Charts allows different actions to be taken (events to be broadcasted) depending on the probabilistically chosen target state, not just on the event which initiates the transition. Based on the work in [17], they later proposed the StoCharts approach [18] which extends UML-statecharts with probabilities and stochastic timing features to allow for QoS modelling and analysis.

Vijaykumar et al. [19] proposed using a probabilistic statechart-based formalism to represent performance models. The model specified using statecharts is used to generate a Markov chain from which steady-state probabilities are obtained. Their approach is concerned with evaluating general performance of models, such as system productivity.

Blum et al. [20] presents the System Availability Estimator (SAVE) package that is used to build and analyze models to enable prediction of dependability constraints. A SAVE model is constructed as a collection of components, each of which can be subject to failure and repair. The high-level model is then automatically transformed to a Markov chain model.

Bavuso et al. [21] introduce the Hybrid Automated Reliability Predictor (HARP) tool developed for prediction of reliability and availability of fault-tolerant architectures. It is Markov model-based, and provides support for coverage modelling and automatic conversion of fault trees to Markov models.

Our approach is different in the sense that we begin with informal requirements specification, namely use cases, apply a model-driven process to map the requirements to statecharts to evaluate the safety and reliability achieved by the system, followed by revisiting and refining the use cases if necessary. Developers do not require expertise in specification languages to determine the quality of their requirements. Also, communicating with end-users is simpler with use cases. The probability analysis is completely automated and allows quick generation of dependability-related statistics. Our model-based assessment is similar to model-checking since we attempt to verify that dependability constraints hold. However, the goal of our work is to evaluate and refine the requirements of the system, and model analysis is carried out only to serve this purpose.

8 Conclusion and Future Work

We have proposed a model-based approach for analyzing the safety and reliability of requirements based on use cases. The contribution mainly lies in the combined use of exceptional use cases, probabilities, statecharts, and dependability analysis means. Each interaction step in a use case is annotated with a probability reflecting its chances of success, and a safety tag if the failure of the step hampers the system safety. The use cases are then mapped to DA-Charts, a probabilistic extension of the statechart model. Precise mapping rules have been suggested. We have implemented our formalism in the AToM^3 tool to provide support for automatic dependability analysis. The tool also verifies the formalism constraints and ensures that the mapping rules are adhered to. Based on path analysis, the tool quantitatively determines probabilities of reaching safe or unsafe states. The assessment allows the analyst to decide if the dependability constraints of the system are met. If not, the use cases have to be refined. This implies introducing additional interaction steps, discovering exceptions and applying handlers that dictate the system behavior in such situations [1]. At each refinement step, our tool provides immediate feedback to the analyst on the impact of the changes on system dependability.

Based on our dependability focused use cases, a specification that considers all exceptional situations and user expectations can be elaborated during a subsequent analysis phase. This specification can then be used to decide on the need for employing fault masking and fault tolerance techniques when designing the software architecture and during detailed design of the system.

So far, our assessment technique only considers exceptions that threaten the reliability and safety of the system. In the future, we want to extend our approach to also be able to handle exceptions in the environment that *change* user goals. For instance, a person riding an elevator might feel unsafe and request an emergency stop. Once the situation is resolved, normal service should continue where it was interrupted. To model such a situation, we are currently working on integrating hierarchy and history into DA-Charts.

We also aim to automate the process of mapping use cases to DA-Charts (and vice-versa). This would be a highly desirable feature, ultimately allowing developers to work with the model (use cases or statecharts, or maybe even sequence diagrams) that best suits them. Our tool can then ensure that all representations are consistently updated. Any changes made to one model would automatically be reflected in the other models.

Finally, we intend to extend our process to address other dependability constraints like availability, timeliness, and usability.

References

1. Shui, A., Mustafiz, S., Kienzle, J., Dony, C.: Exceptional use cases. In Briand, L.C., Williams, C., eds.: MoDELS. Volume 3713 of Lecture Notes in Computer Science., Springer (2005) 568–583
2. Laprie, J.C., Avizienis, A., Kopetz, H., eds.: Dependability: Basic Concepts and Terminology. Springer-Verlag New York, Inc., Secaucus, NJ, USA (1992)
3. Geffroy, J.C., Motet, G.: Design of Dependable Computing Systems. Kluwer Academic Publishers (2002)
4. Avizienis, A., Laprie, J., Randell, B.: Fundamental concepts of dependability (2001)
5. Larman, C.: Applying UML and Patterns: An Introduction to Object-Oriented Analysis and Design and the Unified Process. 2nd edn. Prentice Hall (2002)
6. Harel, D.: Statecharts: A visual formalism for complex systems. Science of Computer Programming **8**(3) (1987) 231–274
7. Harel, D.: On visual formalisms. Communications of the ACM **31**(5) (1988) 514–530
8. de Lara, J., Vangheluwe, H.: Defining visual notations and their manipulation through meta-modelling and graph transformation. Journal of Visual Languages and Computing **15**(3 - 4) (2004) 309–330 Special Issue on Domain-Specific Modeling with Visual Languages.
9. de Lara, J., Vangheluwe, H.: AToM^3: A tool for multi-formalism and meta-modelling. In: ETAPS, FASE. LNCS 2306, Springer (2002) 174 – 188 Grenoble, France.
10. de Lara, J., Vangheluwe, H.: Computer aided multi-paradigm modelling to process petri-nets and statecharts. In: International Conference on Graph Transformations (ICGT). Volume 2505 of Lecture Notes in Computer Science., Springer (2002) 239–253 Barcelona, Spain.

11. Juan de Lara, H.V., Mosterman, P.J.: Modelling and analysis of traffic networks based on graph transformation. Formal Methods for Automation and Safety in Railway and Automotive Systems (December 2004. Braunschweig, Germany) 11
12. Feng, T.H.: DCharts, a formalism for modeling and simulation based design of reactive software systems. M.Sc. dissertation, School of Computer Science, McGill University (2004)
13. Bianco, A., de Alfaro, L.: Model checking of probabalistic and nondeterministic systems. In Thiagarajan, P.S., ed.: FSTTCS. Volume 1026 of Lecture Notes in Computer Science., Springer (1995) 499–513
14. Hinton, A., Kwiatkowska, M., Norman, G., Parker, D.: PRISM: A tool for automatic verification of probabilistic systems. In: Proc. 12th International Conference on Tools and Algorithms for the Construction and Analysis of Systems (TACAS'06). (2006) To appear.
15. Atlee, J.M., Gannon, J.: State-based model checking of event-driven system requirements. IEEE Transactions on Software Engineering **19**(1) (1993) 24–40 Special Issue on Software for Critical Systems.
16. Huszerl, G., Majzik, I., Pataricza, A., Kosmidis, K., Cin, M.D.: Quantitative analysis of UML statechart models of dependable systems. Comput. J **45**(3) (2002) 260–277
17. Jansen, D.N., Hermanns, H., Katoen, J.P.: A probabilistic extension of uml statecharts: specification and verification. In Damm, W., Olderog, E.R., eds.: Formal techniques in real-time and fault-tolerant systems: FTRTFT. Volume 2469 of Lecture Notes in Computer Science., Berlin, Germany, Springer (2002) 355–374
18. Jansen, D.N., Hermanns, H.: QoS modelling and analysis with UML-statecharts: the stocharts approach. SIGMETRICS Performance Evaluation Review **32**(4) (2005) 28–33
19. Vijaykumar, N.L., de Carvalho, S.V., de Andrade, V.M.B., Abdurahiman, V.: Introducing probabilities in statecharts to specify reactive systems for performance analysis. Computers & OR **33** (2006) 2369–2386
20. Blum, A.M., Goyal, A., Heidelberger, P., Lavenberg, S.S., Nakayama, M.K., Shahabuddin, P.: Modeling and analysis of system dependability using the system availability estimator. In: FTCS. (1994) 137–141
21. Bavuso, S., Dugan, J.B., Trivedi, K.S., Rothmann, B., Smith, E.: Analysis of typical fault-tolerant architectures using HARP. IEEE Transactions on Reliability (1987)

A Graphical Approach to Risk Identification, Motivated by Empirical Investigations

Ida Hogganvik and Ketil Stølen

SINTEF ICT and Department of Informatics, University of Oslo
{iho, kst}@sintef.no

Abstract. We propose a graphical approach to identify, explain and document security threats and risk scenarios. Security risk analysis can be time consuming and expensive, hence, it is of great importance that involved parties quickly understand the risk picture. Risk analysis methods often make use of brainstorming sessions to identify risks, threats and vulnerabilities. These sessions involve system users, developers and decision makers. They typically often have completely different backgrounds and view the system from different perspectives. To facilitate communication and understanding among them, we have developed a graphical approach to document and explain the overall security risk picture. The development of the language and the guidelines for its use have been based on a combination of empirical investigations and experiences gathered from utilizing the approach in large scale industrial field trials. The investigations involved both professionals and students, and each field trial was in the order of 250 person hours.

1 Introduction

We have developed a graphical approach supporting the identification, communication and documentation of security threats and risk scenarios. The approach has been applied in several large industrial field trials and the major decisions regarding its underlying foundation, notation and guidelines are supported by empirical investigations. Our modeling approach originates from a UML [17] profile [15, 16], developed as a part of the EU funded research project CORAS (IST-2000-25031) [24] (http://coras.sourceforge.net). As a result of our work to satisfy the modeling needs in a security risk analysis, the language and its guidelines have evolved into a more specialized and refined approach. The language is meant to be used by the analyst during the security risk analysis, and has different purposes in each phase of the analysis. A normal risk analysis process often includes five phases: (1) context establishment, (2) risk identification, (3) risk estimation, (4) risk evaluation and (5) treatment identification [2]. In the following we refer to security risk analysis as security analysis. In the context establishment our language is used to specify the stakeholder(s) of the security analysis and their assets in *asset diagrams*. The purpose is to obtain a precise definition of what the valuable aspects of the target of analysis are, and which ones that are more important than others. From empirical investigations [5] and field trials we know that asset identification and valuation is very difficult, and that mistakes or inaccuracies made there may jeopardize the value of the whole security analysis.

O. Nierstrasz et al. (Eds.): MoDELS 2006, LNCS 4199, pp. 574 – 588, 2006.

During risk identification we use *threat diagrams* to identify and document how vulnerabilities make it possible for threats to initiate unwanted incidents and which assets they affect. The threat diagrams give a clear and easily understandable overview of the risk picture and make it easier to see who or what the threat is, how the threat works (threat scenarios) and which vulnerabilities and assets that are involved.

The threat diagrams are used as input to the risk estimation phase, where unwanted incidents are assigned likelihood estimates and possible consequences. The likelihood estimation is often a difficult task, but illustrating the unwanted incidents in the correct context has proved very helpful in practice.

After the risk estimation the magnitude of each risk can be calculated on the basis of its likelihood and consequence, and modeled in *risk diagrams*. The risk diagrams specify which treats that initiate the different risks and exactly which assets they may harm. This risk representation is then compared to predefined risk tolerance levels to decide which ones that need treatments.

In the treatment identification, the threat diagrams that contain the non-tolerated risks are used as basis for *treatment diagrams*. In this phase the appropriate treatments are identified and modeled in treatment diagrams, where they point to the particular place where they should be implemented (e.g. pointing to a vulnerability). The resulting treatment diagrams can be seen as a plan for how to deal with the identified risks.

The contribution of our work is a revised, specialized, graphical language supporting risk identification based on structured brainstorming, and a comprehensive guideline for its use. Moreover, and in particular, we provide empirical support for the language's underlying, conceptual foundation and the main design decisions.

This paper is structured as follows: Sect. 2 introduces structured brainstorming in risk analysis. Sect. 3 explains the language's underlying conceptual foundation and Sect. 4 gives an example-driven introduction to our approach, including guidelines for modeling. Sect. 5 describes the major design decisions made during the development and the empirical investigations supporting these. Sect. 6 discusses the threats to validity for the empirical results, Sect. 7 presents related work and summarizes the main conclusions.

2 Structured Brainstorming for Risk Identification

A frequently used technique in security analysis, and in particular in risk identification, is so-called structured brainstorming (HazOp-analysis [18] is a kind of structured brainstorming). It may be understood as a structured "walk-through" of the target of analysis. The technique is not limited to a specific type of target, but can be used to assess anything from simple IT systems to large computerized process control systems or manual maintenance procedures in e.g. nuclear power plants. This does not mean that exactly the same technique can be applied directly to all kinds of targets, it has to be adapted to fit the target domain. The main idea of structured brainstorming is that a group of people with different competences and backgrounds will view the target from different perspectives and therefore identify more, and possibly other, risks than individuals or a more heterogeneous group. The input to a brainstorming session is various kinds of target models (e.g. UML models). The models are assessed in a stepwise and structured manner under the guidance of the security analysis leader. The identified risks are documented by an analysis secretary.

Deciding which roles should be present is part of tailoring the brainstorming technique towards the target in question. In some cases an expert is only participating in the part of the analysis where his or her expertise is needed. This makes it essential that the information is simple to communicate and comprehend.

3 The Conceptual Foundation

The first step in developing the language was constructing a conceptual model based on standardized security risk analysis terminology. We aimed to use the most intuitive and common interpretations. The conceptual model can be seen as a kind of abstract syntax for the language, and is shown in Fig. 1 using UML class diagram notation.

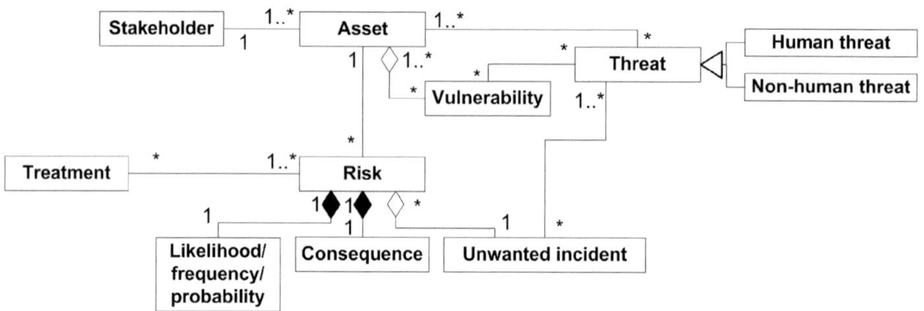

Fig. 1. The conceptual model

The conceptual model may be explained as follows: **stakeholders** are those people and organizations who may affect, be affected by, or perceive themselves to be affected by, a decision or activity regarding the target of analysis [2]. An **asset** is something to which a stakeholder directly assigns value, and hence for which the stakeholder requires protection [3]. Assets are subject to **vulnerabilities,** which are weaknesses which can be exploited by one or more threats [9]. A **threat** is a potential cause of an unwanted incident [9]. An **unwanted incident** [9] is an event that may harm or reduce the value of assets and is something we want to prevent. A **risk** is the chance of something happening that will have an impact upon objectives (assets) [2]. Our model captures this interpretation by defining a risk to consist of an unwanted incident, a likelihood measure and a consequence. The abstract concept "risk", the more concrete "unwanted incident", and their respective relationships to "asset" require some explanation. In our definition, an unwanted incident that harms more than one asset gives rise to one unique risk for each asset it harms. This enables us to keep the consequences for different stakeholders separate, since an asset is always defined with respect to a single stakeholder. The level of risk is measured by a **risk value** [2] (e.g. low, medium, high or other scales) which is based upon the estimated **likelihood** (a general description of frequency or probability [2]) for the unwanted incident to happen and its **consequence** in terms of damage to an asset. A **treatment** is the selection and implementation of appropriate options for dealing with risk [2].

To validate our model and investigate the understanding of security analysis terminology we conducted an empirical study [5]. The 57 subjects included both students who had little or no knowledge of security analysis and more experienced professionals. We found that many of the terms as used in our conceptual model are well understood, even by people without training in security analysis.

The study showed that *human beings* are most commonly viewed as threats, followed by *events* (even if they are in fact initiated by a human). To increase the awareness of non-human threats, we decided to specify threat as either *human threat* and *non-human threat.* Our original specialization of frequency into probability and likelihood was not satisfactory. Both frequency and probability are measures that can be covered by likelihood. Likelihood was on the other hand found to be one of the least understood terms and we therefore decided to include all three concepts. For simplicity we only use "frequency" throughout the rest of the paper. On the question of what it is most common to treat, the subjects gave priority to vulnerability and thereafter risk. To make our model suitable for all treatment strategies we associate treatment with risk. This means that treatments can be directed towards vulnerabilities, threats, unwanted incidents or combinations of these.

4 Graphical Risk Modeling – An Example Driven Introduction

This section provides an example of a security analysis with guidelines for how and where the diagrams are made during the process. Fig. 2 gives the syntactical representation of the concepts from Sect.0, plus *initiate* (arrow), *treatment direction* (dashed arrow), *relationship* (line), *logical gates* (and & or) and *region* (used to structure the models). The symbols are a revised version of the ones used in Sect. 5.

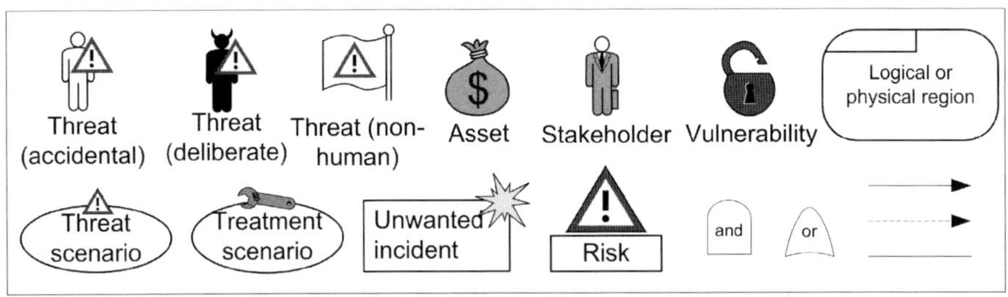

Fig. 2. The graphical representation of the main concepts

The target of analysis in our example is a web-based application which communicates confidential information between an insurance company and its customers. The development project is expensive and prestigious to the company, but the governmental data inspectorate is concerned about the level of privacy of the data provided by the service.

1 - Context establishment: The purpose of the context establishment is to characterize the target of the analysis and its environment. The web application is represented as a logical region (inspired by [20]) with two independent stakeholders (Fig. 3). The stakeholders value assets differently: the governmental data inspectorate has "GDI1.data privacy" as its main asset, while the company management has identified four assets, ordered according to value as follows: "CM1.company brand & reputation", "CM2.data privacy", "CM3.application availability" and finally "CM4.application interface usability".

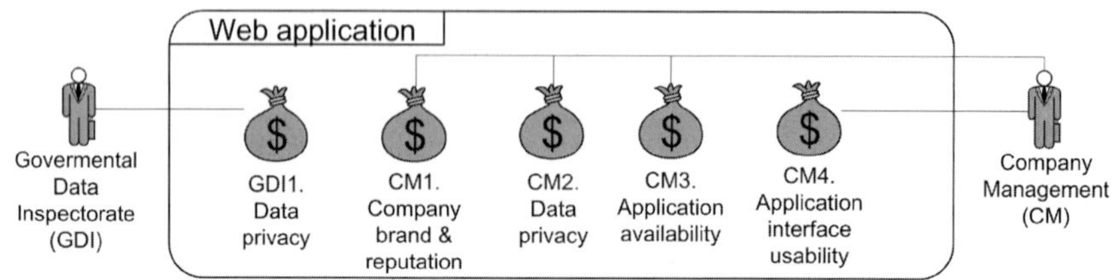

Fig. 3. Asset diagram

Modeling guideline for asset diagrams:

1. Draw a region that logically or physically represents the target of analysis.
2. Place the assets within the region, numbered according to its importance to the stakeholder, and with a reference to its stakeholder.
3. Associate the stakeholders with their assets.

2 - Risk identification: In the risk identification phase the security analysis leader and the brainstorming participants must find answers to questions like: *what are you most concerned about with respect to your assets?* (threat scenarios and unwanted incidents), *who/what initiates these*? (threats), *what makes this possible*? (vulnerabilities). This information is modeled in *threat diagrams*. Consider the threat diagram in Fig. 4. This diagram focuses on network related threat scenarios. The asset "CM4.application interface usability" is not harmed by this kind of incidents and therefore left out. The stakeholders are concerned about the unwanted incidents: "disclosure of data", "corruption of data" and "unavailability of application". Both threats are considered to cause incidents accidentally and are therefore modeled in the same diagram. We now explain one chain of events from the initiation caused by a threat to the left, to the impact on an asset to the right[1]: "IT-infrastructure" may first use "hardware failure" to make the server crash, and second use the "poor backup solution" to corrupt data and make the application unavailable.

Modeling guideline for threat diagrams:

1. Use the region from the asset diagram and add more regions if useful.
2. Model different kinds of threats in separate diagrams. E.g. deliberate sabotage in one diagram, mistakes in an other, environmental in a third etc. (classification from [9]). This makes it easier to generalize over the risks, e.g. "these risks are caused by deliberate intruders" or "these risks are caused by human errors".
3. Threats are placed to the left in the diagram.

[1] Disregard the frequency and consequence information, this is added later in risk estimation.

4. Assets are listed to the right, outside the region.
5. Unwanted incidents are placed within the region with relations to assets they impact.
6. Assets that are not harmed by any incidents are removed from the diagram.
7. Add threat scenarios between the threats and the unwanted incidents in the same order as they occur in real time (i.e. in a logical sequence).
8. Insert the vulnerabilities before the threat scenario or unwanted incident they lead to. E.g.: "poor backup solution" is placed before the threat scenario "application database fails to switch to backup solution".

3-Risk estimation: The threat diagrams are input to the risk estimation where threat scenarios and unwanted incidents are assigned frequencies and consequences. In Fig. 4 the final frequency for "corruption of data" is based on the frequencies of the two threat scenarios "application servers malfunctioning" and "application database fails to switch to backup solution". We here use the consequence scale: large (L), medium (M) and small (S). In a full security analysis the scale would be mapped to what the client considers to be large, medium and small reductions of asset value (e.g. 10% customer loss, 2 hours unavailability, 10.000$ etc.).

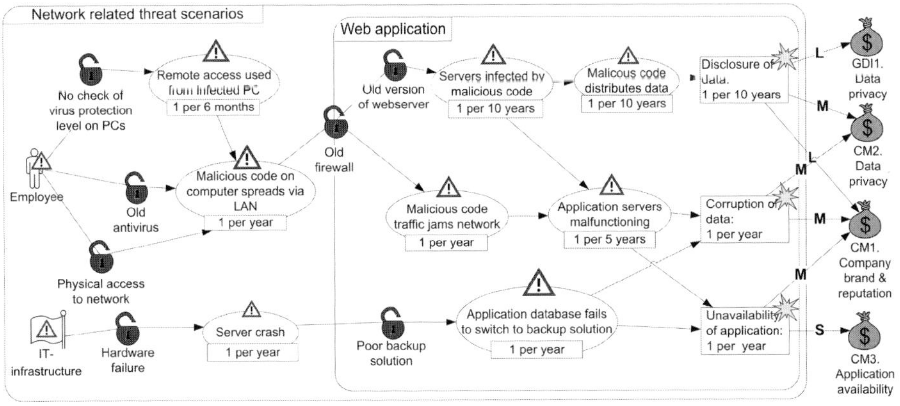

Fig. 4. Threat diagram (after risk estimation)

Modeling guideline for risk estimation:

1. Add frequency estimates to the threat scenarios.
2. Add frequency estimates to the unwanted incidents, based on the threat scenarios.
3. Annotate the unwanted incident-asset relations with consequences.

4 - Risk evaluation: On the basis of the risk estimation we model the resulting risks with their associated risk values in a risk diagram. Risk diagrams help the stakeholders to get an overview and evaluate which risks that need treatments. The example in Fig. 5 presents the threats and the risks they represent against the two most important assets in our example ("GDI1.data privacy" and "CM1.company brand & reputation"). We use a short hand notation where "Disclosure of data" in reality represents two risks with value = "major" (shown with associations to two assets).

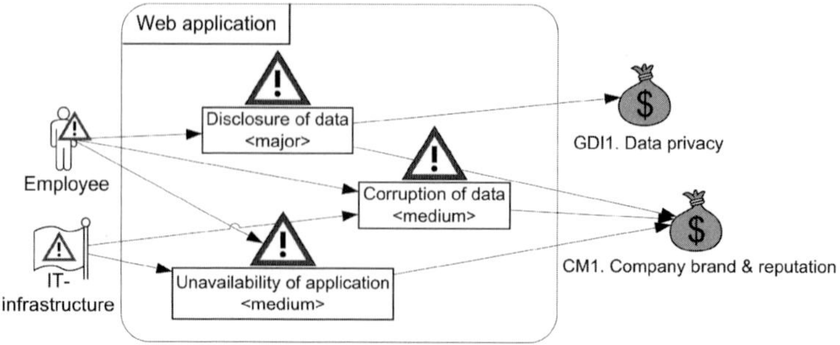

Fig. 5. Risk diagram (for the two most important assets)

Modeling guideline for risk diagrams:
1. Use the threat diagram and annotate all relations between unwanted incidents and assets with the risk symbol, showing a short risk description and the risk value (similar risks may be grouped as in the short hand notation shown in Fig. 5).
2. Split the risk diagrams into several diagrams according to risk value or asset importance (show all intolerable risks, all risks for specific assets etc.).
3. Remove threat scenarios and vulnerabilities, but keep the relations between the threats and the unwanted incidents.

5 - Treatment identification: The threat diagrams are also used as basis for treatment diagrams and extended with treatment options. The treatments must then be assessed to see whether they bring the risk value to an acceptable level. This makes it possible to optimize the treatment strategy according to a cost/benefit analysis. Fig. 6 shows the risks for the two most important assets. The proposed treatments in our example, "upgrade server", "upgrade backup solution" and "limit access to the network", are directed toward three vulnerabilities. Since treatments often address vulnerabilities,

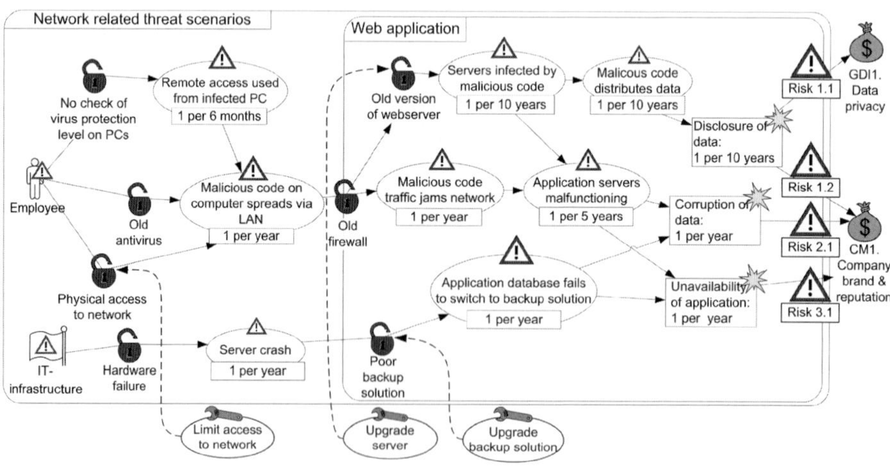

Fig. 6. Treatment diagram for: GCI1.data privacy and CM1.company brand & reputation

one may use the analogy "to close the padlock", - meaning closing the specific pathway through the graph.

Modeling guideline for treatment diagrams:
1. Use the threat diagrams as a basis and annotate all arrows from unwanted incidents to assets with risk icons.
2. If the diagram becomes complex, split it like the risk diagrams.
3. Annotate the diagram with treatments, pointing to where they will be applied.

5 Design Decisions

Designing a language and its guidelines requires many design decisions. In the following we describe our design choices based on experiences from four major field trials and the results from two empirical investigations.

5.1 Field Trial Experiences

The field trials were carried out within the setting of the research project SECURIS (152839/220). Each security analysis required about 250 person hours from the analysis team and 50-100 hours from the stakeholder. The clients and scopes for the analyses were:

- Vessel classification company: A web based information sharing service between customer and service provider.
- Telecom company: Mobile access for employees to e-mail, calendar and contacts.
- Energy company: A control and supervisory system for power grid lines.
- Metal production company: A web based control and supervisory system for metal production.

The participants (the analysis team as well as the representatives of the stakeholders) were requested to evaluate the use of graphical risk modeling after each session and their feedback was:

- the use of the graphical models during the analysis made it easier to actively involve the participants and helped ensure an effective communication between the analysis team and the participants.
- the participants found the notation itself easy to understand and remember. It was considered to be a good way of visualizing threat scenarios and very suitable for presentations. According to one of the participants this type of visualization emphasizes the "message" or the purpose of the analysis.
- one of the main benefits was how the language helped specifying the relations between threats and the chain of events they may cause, the various states of the target, and potential incidents. The modeling method made the participants more conscious of the target of analysis and its risks by representing threats and vulnerabilities more explicitly than "just talking" about them.
- the language provides an opportunity to document cause-consequence relations in a precise and detailed manner.

The participants emphasized that they need a proper introduction to the notation and sufficient time to understand the information that is presented to them. One should limit the amount of information in one diagram, and rather split it according to threat type, scenario type or asset type. It is also important to strive towards correctness from the very beginning. This means that the participants must be involved early, enabling them to adjust the diagram as they find appropriate.

The diagrams capture information gathered during brainstorming sessions and one of the main concerns of the participants was whether or not the diagrams would be complete. To help overcome this we recommend utilizing check lists to ensure that all important aspects are covered. Any changes to the diagrams suggested during the brainstorming session represent important information. Their rationale should be captured by the analysis secretary, and the diagrams should be updated real time.

5.2 The Graphical Icons Experiment

Graphical icons are often seen as mere "decoration" just to make diagrams look nicer, but a major hypothesis in our work is that people unfamiliar with system modeling, may considerably benefit from carefully designed icons. In particular they may help the participants in a structured brainstorming to arrive at a common understanding of the security risk scenarios without wasting too much time. The original UML profile [15, 16] is characterized by its use of special graphical icons. To validate the effect of this we conducted an experiment which compared the usefulness of the UML profile icons compared to standard UML use case icons (Fig. 7) [5].

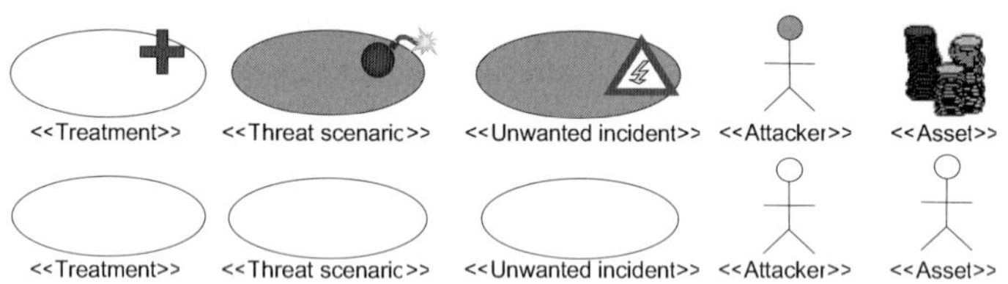

Fig. 7. The notation with and without special icons

In most of the tasks the group receiving normal UML icons had similar mean score to the group using profile icons, but when the time pressure increased the subjects with profile icons managed to complete more tasks than the other group. The positive effects of using graphical icons in models is also supported by [13]. The icons did on the other hand not significantly affect the correctness of interpretation of risk scenarios. Nevertheless, we decided to use special graphical icons to help the participants in a structured brainstorming to quickly get an overview of the risk scenarios.

5.3 Modeling Preferences Experiment

In the already mentioned empirical study of the conceptual foundation we found that some concepts were difficult to understand. Our hypothesis was that an explicit representation of these concepts in the models would mitigate this problem. To select the best representation we conducted an experiment involving 33 professionals. We used

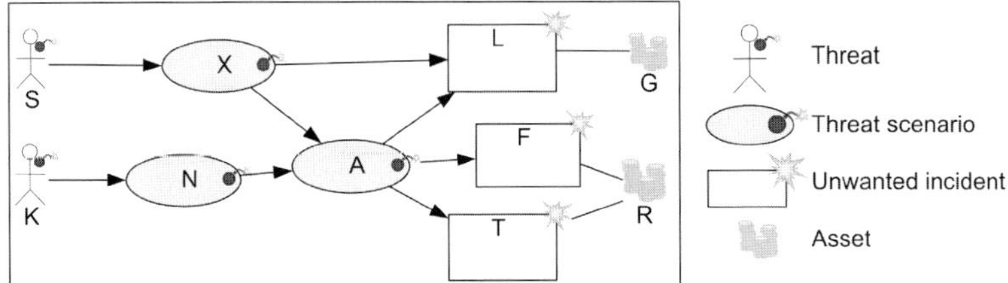

Fig. 8. The basic diagram (using the symbols from the previous version of the language)

variations of Fig. 8, which is a simplified version of a real threat diagram, to illustrate the various options. For a full description of the study we refer to [4].

Representing frequency: To help visualizing which paths that are most likely to be chosen by a threat, we investigated the effect of using different line types (**Fig. 9**). Line type (thick, thin, dashed etc.) has been suggested by [23] to represent aspects of associations between elements in a graph notation.

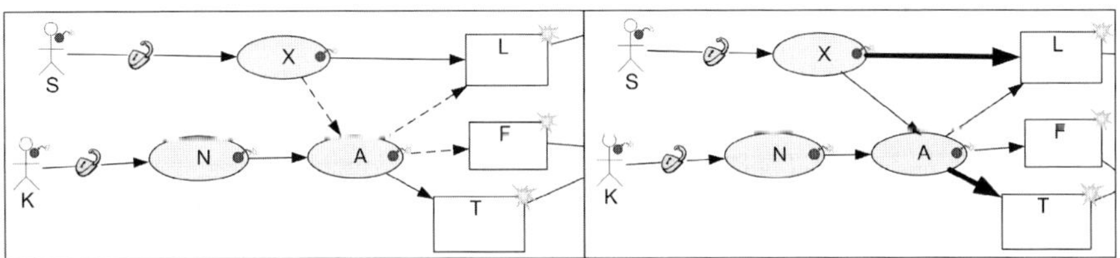

Fig. 9. Paths more likely than others in the graph

The result showed that neither of the line types is preferred for this purpose, possibly because a thick or dashed line does not convey a unique interpretation. During field trials we have found it more helpful to annotate threat scenarios with frequency estimates. The unwanted incident frequency is then estimated on the basis of the frequency estimates of the threat scenarios that cause the incident. This has reduced the need for assigning frequency information to the graph pathways.

Representing risk: The concept "risk" often leads to some confusion due to its abstract nature. We tried to make the risk notion less abstract by decorating the arrows between the unwanted incidents and the assets they harm with risk representations.

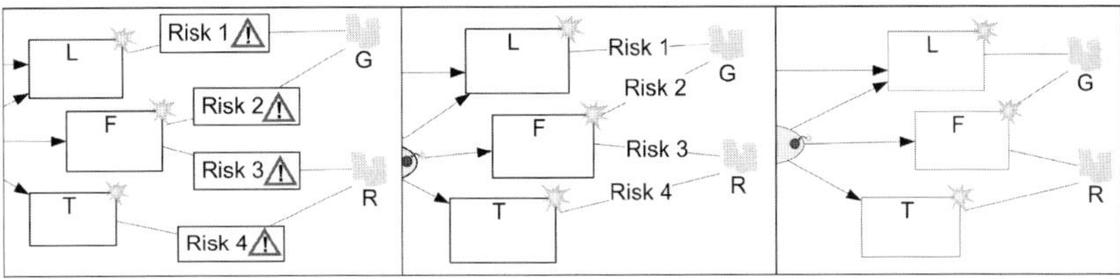

Fig. 10. "F": one incident, but two risks

The alternatives we tested included "text label and icon in box", "text label only" and "association only" (Fig. 10).

The investigation showed that neither of the suggested representations is significantly preferred. Based on this we decided to specify risk in separate risk diagrams. In treatment diagrams, where we need to represent risks in their context, we use a text label and a risk icon. This alternative received the highest score, although the difference was not sufficiently large to be statistically significant from the two others.

In risk evaluation and treatment identification it may be useful to specify the magnitude of risks or unwanted incidents. We tested color, size and text label (Fig. 11), where the two first, according to [23], can be used to visualize magnitude. The result was clear, the participants preferred the text label version over the two other alternatives. A possible explanation is that a text label has unique interpretation, while size or color may have many interpretations.

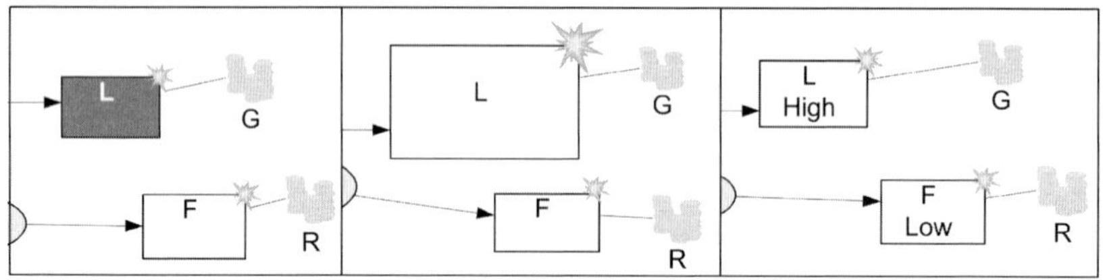

Fig. 11. The magnitude of an unwanted incident

Representing vulnerability: In the original UML profile [15, 16], vulnerabilities were only represented as attributes of the assets they were associated with. During field trials we experienced a definite need for representing vulnerabilities explicitly in the diagrams. We tested the UML profile representation against one that uses a vulnerability symbol (Fig. 12). The result showed that the alternative using chain locks as a vulnerability symbols was significantly preferred.

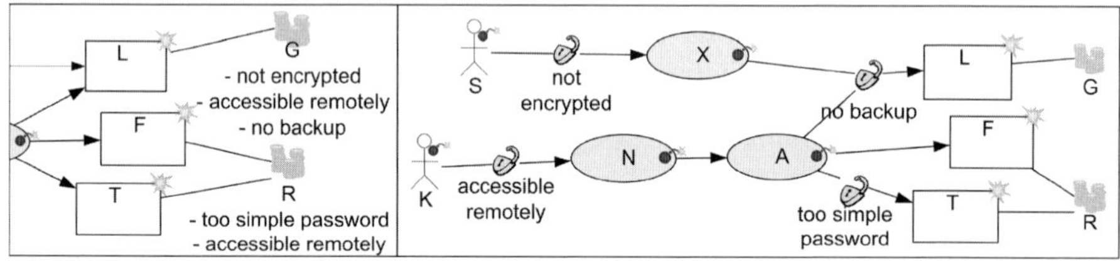

Fig. 12. Modeling vulnerabilities

The vulnerability symbols are helpful in describing threat scenarios and an excellent support in treatment identification. One of the participants in a field trial actually pointed to a vulnerability and claimed "*we've fixed this one now, so you should close the chain lock*".

6 The Validity of the Empirical Results

The main threats to validity of the empirical results on which our approach builds, are summarized in this section. For full details we refer to [4-6].

The investigation of the underlying conceptual foundation was organized as a survey and the subjects included both master students in informatics and professionals. Despite their heterogeneous backgrounds, we believe that the results give a pretty good picture of the opinions of people working with system development in a general sense. The survey was formulated in natural language which always gives room for misinterpretations; some questions were discarded from statistical analysis due to this.

The four major field trials have given us a genuine opportunity to make the modeling guidelines appropriate for actual and realistic modeling situations. One of the main challenges we faced was how to optimize the structure of the diagrams. In some cases it was feasible to structure according to the kind of threat or incident, while in others we structured according to work processes in the target of analysis. This problem must be addressed early in the risk analysis process when the client specifies the acceptable risk level. The other main issue was how to capture changes and comments that arise during the brainstorming sessions. The solution seems to be modeling "on-the-fly". Updating and modifying diagrams real time can be challenging, but with the appropriate tool-support it can be overcome.

The subjects that participated in the icon experiment were master students in informatics. They had been introduced to the UML profile icons in a lesson focusing on the principles of risk modeling. This gave the subjects that received profile icons an advantage, but we believe it was too small to make a real difference.

In the modeling preferences investigation, the various alternatives were tested on a population with mainly technical background. This kind of background is similar to the background of most of the participants in our field trials and therefore considered to be a representative population.

The diagrams we used were a compromise between realistic diagrams and naive notation-only tests. This is a weakness that is difficult to avoid, and we will therefore validate our findings by testing them in real threat diagrams in our next field trial.

In general, humans who get involved in a security analysis are rarely familiar with the concepts or the process used. Concepts that students find intuitive to understand and model are probably intuitive also to professionals. We therefore believe that our use of students in two of the three investigations had little effect on the validity of the results.

7 Conclusions and Related Work

Misuse cases [1, 21, 22] was an important source of inspiration in the development of the above mentioned UML profile. A misuse case is a kind of UML use case [10] which characterizes functionality that the system should *not* allow. The use case notation is often employed for high level specification of systems and considered to be one of the easiest understandable notations in UML. A misuse case can be defined as "a completed sequence of actions which results in loss for the organization or some specific stakeholder" [22]. To obtain more detailed specifications of the system, the misuse cases can be further specialized into e.g. sequence- or activity diagrams. There are a number of security oriented extensions of UML, e.g. UMLSec [11] and SecureUML [14]. These and related approaches have however all been designed to capture security properties and security aspects at a more detailed level than our language. Moreover, their focus is not on brainstorming sessions as in our case.

Fault tree is a tree-notation used in fault tree analysis (FTA) [8]. The top node represents an unwanted incident, or failure, and the different events that may lead to the top event are modeled as branches of nodes, with the leaf node as the causing event. The probability of the top node can be calculated on the basis of the probabilities of the leaf nodes and the logical gates "and" and "or". Our threat diagrams often look a bit like fault trees, but may have more than one top node. Computing the top node probability of a fault tree requires precise quantitative input, which rarely is available for incidents caused by human errors or common cause failures. Our approach can model fault trees, but we also allow qualitative likelihood values as input.

Event tree analysis (ETA) [7] focuses on illustrating the consequences of an event and the probabilities of these. It is often used as an extension of fault trees to create "cause-consequence" diagrams. Event trees can to a large extent also be simulated in our notation.

Attack trees [19] aim to provide a formal and methodical way of describing the security of a system based on the attacks it may be exposed to. The notation uses a tree structure similar to fault trees, with the attack goal as the top node and different ways of achieving the goal as leaf nodes. Our approach supports this way of modeling, but facilitates in addition the specification of the attack initiators (threats) and the harm caused by the attack (damage to assets).

The Riskit method [12] includes a risk modeling technique that makes it possible to specify factors that may influence a software development project. It has similarities to our approach, but targets project risks and therefore utilizes different concepts and definitions and has not the special focus on security risks.

In security risk analysis various types of brainstorming techniques are widely used to identify risks. The participants use their competence to discover relevant threats, vulnerabilities and unwanted incidents that the analysis object may be subject to. The overall idea of brainstorming is that the brainstorming group will identify more risks together than the same individuals working separately. The participants have extensive knowledge of the target of analysis, but often within different areas. The challenge is to make them understand and discuss the overall risk picture without being hampered by misunderstandings and communication problems. Since a brainstorming session may be exhausting, we need techniques and guidelines that make the session as efficient and effective as possible. The findings must also be documented in a precise and comprehensive manner.

We have developed a graphical approach to risk identification to meet these requirements. It captures the complete risk picture, including assets, stakeholders and how vulnerabilities make security threats able to harm the assets. The graphical notation is both simple and expressive, and does not require extensive knowledge of modeling. The language originates from a UML profile for risk assessment [15, 16]. Through application in field trials and empirical studies it has evolved towards a more refined and specialized language. To our knowledge our approach is the only one that combines system modeling techniques with risk modeling techniques for use in structured brainstorming within the security domain.

A major presumption for an intuitive and understandable language is the underlying conceptual foundation, which defines the various concepts in the language and how they relate to each other. We have selected our definitions from well recognized standards within security and risk analysis [2, 3, 9]. To ensure that the best definitions of concepts and relations were chosen, we investigated the alternatives empirically. We found that risk analysis terminology in general is quite well understood. In general, those concepts that caused most uncertainty were the concepts that are least used in daily language. As an example, frequency is less used in the daily language than consequence and was one of the terms many of the respondents had trouble understanding. The subjects tend to care less about the frequency than the consequence of a risk, even though a high frequency risk with low consequence over time may cost the same as a large consequence risk.

The language has been utilized in four large industrial field trials. We have experienced that the diagrams facilitate active involvement of the participants in the brainstorming sessions, and they are very helpful in visualizing the risk picture. According to the participants, the diagrams explicitly illustrate the threats and vulnerabilities in a way that makes it easy to see the relations and precisely define the risk consequences.

The notational design decisions are supported by two empirical studies. The first one investigated the usefulness of special graphical icons contra traditional UML use case icons. The result showed that the group that received diagrams with special icons was able to conclude faster. This and similar supporting studies convinced us to use graphical icons in our language. The second study tested different modeling approaches on a group of professionals. From this we conclude amongst others that text labels are preferable over visualization mechanisms like size, color or line type. For our language this means that we mark a major risk with the text label "major", rather than representing it with a large risk icon.

The final language description will include a formal semantics and a more detailed modeling guideline. The language is currently being implemented in the CORAS' risk analysis tool (v3.0) which is planned for release autumn 2006.

Acknowledgments. The research on which this paper reports has partly been funded by the Research Council of Norway project SECURIS (152839/220). The authors especially thank Mass Soldal Lund for his valuable input. We also thank the SECURIS analysis team: Fredrik Seehusen, Bjørnar Solhaug, Iselin Engan, Gyrd Brændeland and Fredrik Vraalsen.

References

1. Alexander, I., *Misuse cases: Use cases with hostile intent.* IEEE Software, 2003. **20**(1), pp. 58-66.
2. AS/NZS4360, *Australian/New Zealand Standard for Risk Management.* 2004, Standards Australia/Standards New Zealand.
3. HB231, *Information security risk management guidelines.* 2004, Standards Australia/Standards New Zealand.

4. Hogganvik, I. and K. Stølen, *Investigating Preferences in Graphical Risk Modeling* (Tech. report SINTEF A57). SINTEF ICT, 2006. http://heim.ifi.uio.no/~ketils/securis/the-securis-dissemination.htm.
5. Hogganvik, I. and K. Stølen. *On the Comprehension of Security Risk Scenarios. In Proc. of 13th Int. Workshop on Program Comprehension (IWPC'05)*. 2005, pp. 115-124.
6. Hogganvik, I. and K. Stølen. *Risk Analysis Terminology for IT-systems: does it match intuition? In Proc. of Int. Symposium on Empirical Software Engineering (ISESE'05)*. 2005, pp. 13-23.
7. IEC60300-3-9, *Event Tree Analysis in Dependability management - Part 3: Application guide - Section 9: Risk analysis of technological systems*. 1995.
8. IEC61025, *Fault Tree Analysis (FTA)*. 1990.
9. ISO/IEC13335, *Information technology - Guidelines for management of IT Security*. 1996-2000.
10. Jacobson, I., et al., *Object-Oriented Software Engineering: A Use Case Driven Approach*. 1992: Addison-Wesley.
11. Jürjens, J., *Secure Systems Development with UML*. 2005: Springer.
12. Kontio, J., *Software Engineering Risk Management: A Method, Improvement Framework, and Empirical Evaluation*. PhD thesis, Dept. of Computer Science and Engineering, Helsinki University of Technology, 2001.
13. Kuzniarz, L., M. Staron, and C. Wohlin. *An Empirical Study on Using Stereotypes to Improve Understanding of UML Models. In Proc. of 12th Int. Workshop on Program Comprehension (IWPC'04)*. 2004, pp. 14-23.
14. Lodderstedt, T., D. Basin, and J. Doser. *SecureUML: A UML-Based Modeling Language for Model-Driven Security. In Proc. of UML'02*. 2002, pp. 426-441.
15. Lund, M.S., et al., *UML profile for security assessment* (Tech. report STF40 A03066). SINTEF ICT, 2003.
16. OMG, *UML Profile for Modeling Quality of Service and Fault Tolerance Characteristics and Mechanisms*. 2005, Object Management Group.
17. OMG, *The Unified Modeling Language (UML) 2.0*. 2004.
18. Redmill, F., M. Chudleigh, and J. Catmur, *HAZOP and Software HAZOP*. 1999: Wiley.
19. Schneier, B., *Attack trees: Modeling security threats*. Dr. Dobb's Journal, 1999. **24**(12), pp. 21-29.
20. Seehusen, F. and K. Stølen. *Graphical specification of dynamic network structure. In Proc. of 7th Int. Conference on Enterprise Information Systems (ICEIS'05)*. 2005, pp. p.203-209.
21. Sindre, G. and A.L. Opdahl. *Eliciting Security Requirements by Misuse Cases. In Proc. of TOOLS-PACIFIC*. 2000, pp. 120-131.
22. Sindre, G. and A.L. Opdahl. *Templates for Misuse Case Description. In Proc. of Workshop of Requirements Engineering: Foundation of Software Quality (REFSQ'01)*. 2001, pp. 125-136.
23. Ware, C., *Information Visualization: Perception for Design*. 2 ed. 2004: Elsevier.
24. Aagedal, J.Ø., et al. *Model-based risk assessment to improve enterprise security. In Proc. of Enterprise Distributed Object Communication (EDOC'02)*. 2002, pp. 51-64.

Reusable MDA Components: A Testing-for-Trust Approach

Jean-Marie Mottu[1], Benoit Baudry[1], and Yves Le Traon[2]

[1] IRISA, Campus Universitaire de Beaulieu, 35042 Rennes Cedex, France
{bbaudry, jmottu}@irisa.fr
[2] France Télécom R&D/MAPS/EXA, 2 avenue Pierre Marzin, 22307 Lannion Cedex, France
yves.letraon@francetelecom.com

Abstract. Making model transformations trustable is an obvious target for model-driven development since they impact on the design process reliability. Ideally, model transformations should be designed and tested so that they may be used and reused safely as MDA components. We present a method for building trustable MDA components. We first define the notion of MDA component as composed of its specification, one implementation and a set of associated test cases. The testing-for-trust approach checks the consistency between these three facets using the mutation analysis. It points out the lack of efficiency of the tests and the lack of precision of the specification. The mutation analysis thus gives a rate that evaluates: the level of consistency between the component's facets and the level of trust we can have in a component. Relying on this estimation of the component trustability, developers can consciously trade reliability for resources.

1 Introduction

MDA (Model Driven Architecture) is a very promising framework to promote high level reuse for software development. Instead of reusing code, the MDA proposes to reuse models for software design and to make these models first-class assets. In this context, models become more than illustrations for documentation, they are assets that can be manipulated, stored and modified by tools. Model transformations encapsulate specific techniques to manipulate and create models and they are used all along the development to introduce different design aspects. These transformations are important assets for reuse in MDA that are meant to be deployed in different software developments and at different times in the development. Thus, they must be analysed, designed and implemented using sound software engineering techniques to ensure that they are reused safely.

In this paper, we propose to encapsulate model transformations as components that are called MDA components. The contribution of this work is to propose a model for trustable components as well as a methodology to design and implement such components. Trustworthiness is a general notion which includes security, testability, maintainability and many other concerns. In this paper, we claim that trust is, in first, dependent on the quality of the tests in relation with the completeness of the specification, captured by executable contracts (as defined in design-by-contract [1]).

O. Nierstrasz et al. (Eds.): MoDELS 2006, LNCS 4199, pp. 589 – 603, 2006.

While building MDA components, we consider it as an organic set composed of three facets: test cases, an implementation and contracts defining its specification. A trustable component is considered as being "vigilant" [2], in the sense it embeds contracts accurate enough to detect most of the erroneous states at runtime. Trust is evaluated using a testing-for-trust process and reflects the consistency between the specification and the implementation of the component.

This work details this three-facet model for a MDA component and explains how good test cases can be used to evaluate the trust associated to the component. Two major concerns are addressed for this study. First, we investigate the use of *mutation analysis* to check the consistency between the three facets of a component. This technique, originally designed to assess the efficiency of test cases, consists in systematically injecting faults in the program under test. It is then possible to measure how many faults the test cases or the contracts can detect. The rate of detected faults is called the mutation score. This technique was originally proposed for procedural programs and has been adapted to object-oriented programs. Here we study how mutation analysis has to be adapted to evaluate the trust in MDA components. Second, we discuss the expression of contracts for these components. Since there is no standard today for the specification or the implementation of model transformations (QVT, EMF, Kermeta…), this work proposes to establish a taxonomy of contracts.

Section 2 presents the notion of MDA components and the process we propose to build trustable components. Section 3 details the mutation analysis technique and its adaptation to the context of model transformation then section 4 details the taxonomy of contracts for MDA components. Section 5 illustrates the application of the process step by step on the UML2RDBMS example and provides first experimental results.

2 Trusting MDA Components

In this section, we propose a model for a MDA component that provides a basis on which a testing-for-trust process can be applied. Then we present this process which aims at improving the trust one may have in a MDA component by improving the efficiency of test cases and the accuracy of the specification.

2.1 Building MDA Components with the Triangle View

The proposed model to build trustable MDA components is based on an integrated design and test approach for software components. It is particularly adapted to a design-by-contract [1] approach, where the specification is systematically translated into executable contracts (invariant properties, pre/postconditions of methods). In this approach, test cases are defined as being an "organic" part of a component: a component is composed of its specification (documentation, methods signature, invariant properties, pre/postconditions), one implementation and the test cases needed for testing it (V&V: Validation and Verification). Fig. 1 illustrates this model of a component with a triangle representation.

From a methodological point of view, we argue that the trust we have in a component depends on the consistency between its three facets. The comparison between these three facets leads to the improvement of each one. The improvement of each facet as well of the global consistency is an iterative process. First, a good set of test cases is generated. Then it is possible to improve the implementation: running the good test cases allows to detect faults and to fix them. At last the accuracy of contracts can be improved to make them effective as an oracle function for test cases.

Several difficulties arise in running this process. First, test generation since input data are models for a MDA component. Here, we consider that the test cases are provided by the tester. Second, the oracle function for a MDA component which can either be provided by assertions included in the test cases or by contracts. In a design-by-contract approach, our experience is that *most* of the decisions are provided by contracts. The last difficulty is the writing of contracts for a MDA component since there is no clear definition of what contracts for model transformations should be.

The trust in the component is thus related to the test cases effectiveness and the contracts "completeness". We can trust the implementation since we have tested it with a good test set, and we trust the specification because it is accurate enough to derive effective contracts as oracle functions.

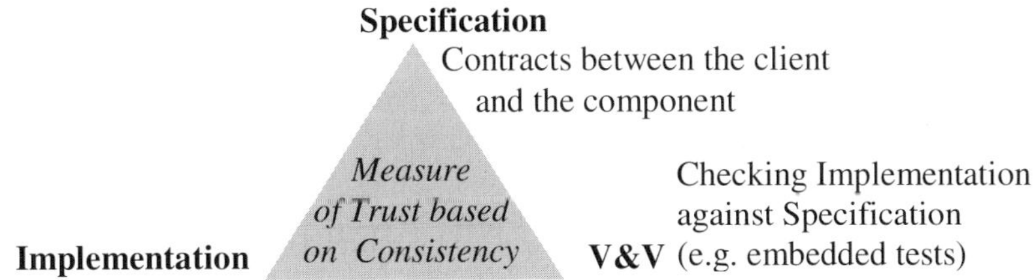

Fig. 1. Trust based on triangle consistency

2.2 The MDA Trusted Component Process

The process for building trust in a MDA-component consists in three steps as presented in Fig. 2. The process starts with an initial component that already has its three facets ready. The goal is then to improve each facet and to check the global consistency between facets. On the right side of the figure, the evolution of the trust we have in each facet of the triangle view of the MDA component is highlighted.

Step 1- Test cases improvement. It aims at improving the test set using a relevant test quality criterion. In this paper, we suggest to evaluate this quality using mutation analysis. We adapt it to evaluate the efficiency of test cases for model transformations programs, as detailed in section 3. This analysis produces a ratio, which estimates the *fault revealing power* of a test set (0 means that the test set does not detect any fault, and 1 means that all the seeded faults have been detected). We note Q_{td} this ratio and section 3 will go in the detail of its computation in the form of a *mutation score* (MS).

If this ratio is low when running a mutation analysis, it means that the test set has to be improved. This can be achieved by adding test cases by hand or by automatic optimization techniques. Step 1 ends when the quality of the test set reaches a satisfactory quality (good mutation score).

Step 2- Implementation improvement. This step leads to the correction of the model transformation program with the efficient test set. Indeed, test cases generated at previous step have a high mutation score and are thus able to detect faults in the model transformation program. At this stage, the tester has to run these test cases on the model transformation, and, if some faults are detected, they have to be localized and fixed. At the end of step 2, the implementation facet is trustable, since its correctness has been validated with efficient test cases.

Step 3- Contracts improvement. It aims at embedding accurate contracts, considered as the executable part of the specification. The precondition for this step is that the MDA component has to possess a trustable implementation and efficient test cases. We propose using the mutation analysis again to estimate the accuracy of contracts in terms of *fault detection rate* (i.e. the proportion of faults the contracts actually detect knowing the test cases provoke a faulty output). It thus estimates the accuracy of contracts as embedded oracles.

The difference with step 1 is that the fault revealing power of the test data set is known with the Q_{td} value. Using contracts as embedded oracles, the new proportion of detected faults (%detected-faults) is computed. The quality of contracts is checked w.r.t Q_{td}. The quality estimated for contracts Q_{cont} is thus defined as:

$$Q_{cont} = \%\text{detected-faults} / \ Q_{td}.$$

This can be seen as an estimate of the accuracy of contracts to be a valid oracle for the test cases. So, when Q_{cont} equals 0, it means that no fault is detected by contracts and when Q_{cont} equals 1, it means that contracts are able to detect all the faulty outputs. So step 3 consists in improving contracts until the expected quality level is reached. At the end of the process, the contracts are embedded in the MDA component and it becomes 'vigilant', e.g. contracts have a good probability to dynamically detect faulty states [2].

When the three steps process ends, we obtain a MDA component with an estimate of the trust we may have in the test cases, the implementation and the contracts. This estimate has checked the consistency between test cases and implementation, and then between test cases, implementation and contracts. In section 3, we detail how the mutation analysis is adapted to the specific context of model transformation, and how contracts can be expressed in the particular context of model transformation.

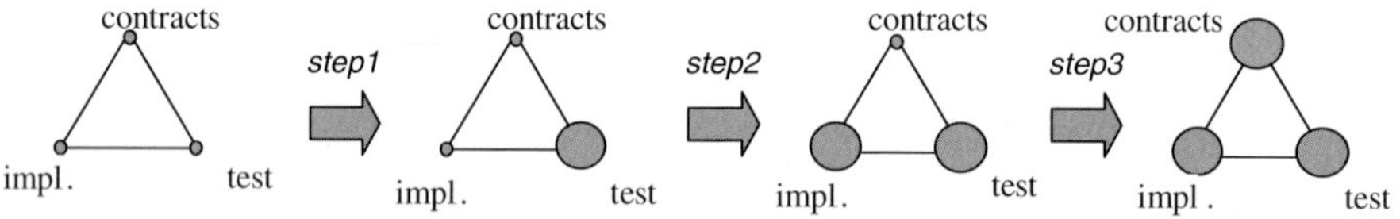

Fig. 2. Building a MDA trusted component

3 Mutation Analysis for Model Transformations

Mutation analysis is a testing technique that was first designed to evaluate the efficiency of a test set. It also allows to improve its effectiveness and fault revealing power. Originally proposed in 1978 [3], mutation analysis consists in creating a set of faulty versions or *mutants* of a program with the ultimate goal of designing a test set that distinguishes the program from all its mutants.

The process is presented in Fig. 3 with the execution of each test case against all the mutants of the program. A mutant is the program modified by the injection of a single fault. In practice, faults are modelled as a set of *mutation operators* where each operator represents a class of software faults. A mutation operator is applied to the original program to create each mutant.

An oracle function is used to determine if the failure is detected. This function compares each mutant's result with the result of the program P; the latter being considered as correct. If one result differs, it means that one test case exhibits the fault; the mutant is *killed*. The mutant stays *alive* if no test case detects the injected fault. Sometimes, a mutant can never be killed, it is an *equivalent mutant* and it has to be suppressed from the set of mutants.

A test set is adequate if it distinguishes the original program from all its non-equivalent mutants. Otherwise, a *mutation score* is associated to the test set to measure its effectiveness in terms of percentage of the revealed non-equivalent mutants. A benefit of the mutation score is that even if no error is found, it still measures how well the software has been tested giving information about the test set quality.

MutationScore = #KilledMutants / (#Mutants - #EquivalentMutants)

If the score is insufficient, we have to improve the test set, which could be done with new test cases or actual test set improvement.

The value of mutation analysis is based on one assumption: if the test set can kill all the mutants, then this test set is able to detect real involuntary errors.

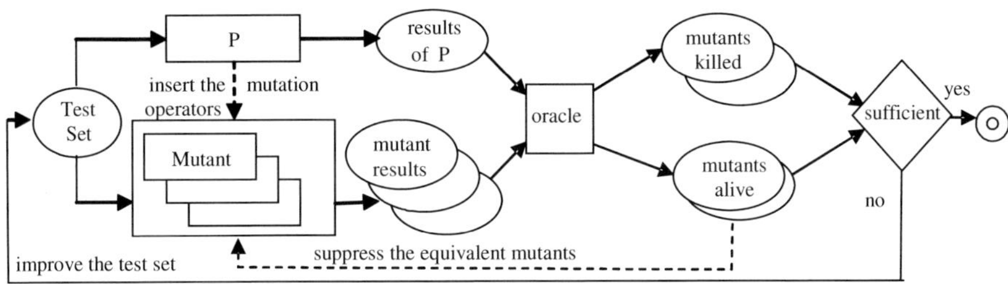

Fig. 3. Mutation process

The relevance of mutation analysis depends on the relevance of the mutants, which itself strongly depends on the relevance of the mutation operators. Classical mutation analysis is related to a set of faults specified by mutation operators which define syntactic patterns which are identified in the program in order to inject a fault. For example, classical mutation operators include arithmetic operator replacement (like replacing a '+' with '-'). Some operators dedicated to OO programs, and especially to Java, have been introduced by Ma et al. in [4] (method redefinition, inherited attributes etc). These faults are related to the notions of classes, generalization, and polymorphism. These operators take into consideration specificities related to the semantics of OO languages, but remain simple faults which can be introduced by a syntactic analysis of the program. To execute mutation analysis with these operators, the faults are inserted systematically everywhere the pattern is found in the code.

In the next section, we explain why we do not want to transpose this classical mutation process to the model oriented development.

3.1 Mutation Analysis in a Model Development Context

All the classical and OO operators can be applied to model transformation programs, but their relevance to this particular context is limited due to the following reasons:

- *Mutant significance:* seeded faults are far from the specific faults a transformation programmer may do if he is competent. A transformation programmer will make not only classical programming faults but also specific faults related to the model transformation. He may forget some particular cases (e.g. forget to deal with the case of multiple inheritances in an input model), manipulate the wrong model elements etc. A wrong model transformation will differ from the correct one by complicated modifications in the transformation program.
- *Implementation language independency:* Today there are lots of model transformation languages with their own specificities and which are very heterogeneous (object oriented, declarative, functional, mixed). Thus we can not take advantage of a transformation language's syntax. To be independent from a given implementation language is an important issue. That leads us to choose to focus on the semantic part of the transformation instead of the syntactic one imposed by a language. So we introduce semantic operators, they have to reflect the type of fault which may appear. That is studied next section (3.2).

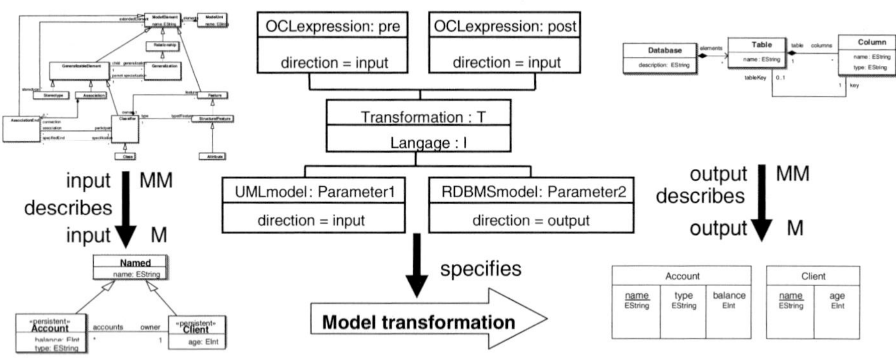

Fig. 4. Model transformation process

Classical mutation operators (object oriented or not) are still useful, to check code or predicate coverage, for example. However they depend on the language which is used in the implementation, thus they have to be completed by injecting faults which make sense, in terms of erroneous model transformation. These new operators that we propose try to capture specific faults that take into account the semantics of a particular type of program: model transformation. Such mutation operators are called semantic operators.

We need to analyze the activities involved in the development of model transformations (Fig. 4) which may be fault-prone. The mutants produced by the mutation operator insertions has to preserve the conformity towards the metamodels involved in the transformation; they must be able to process the input models (depending on their metamodels) and must not create output models that do not conform to output metamodels. Thus mutation operators must be directly connected with the metamodel notion.

3.2 Semantic Faults for Model Transformations Activities

The operators introduced have to be defined based on an abstract view of the transformation program, by answering that question: which type of fault could be done during a model transformation implementation? For example, a transformation goes all over the input model to find the elements to be transformed, a fault can consist in the navigation of the wrong association in the metamodel, or in selecting the wrong elements in a collection. During a transformation, output model elements have to be created; a fault can consist in creating elements with the wrong type or wrong initialization. The analysis of these possible faults for a model transformation leads to distinguish 4 abstract operations linked to the main treatments composing a model transformation:

- *navigation*: the model is navigated thanks to the relations defined on its input/output metamodels, and a set of elements is obtained.
- *filtering*: after a navigation, a set of elements is available, but a treatment may be applied only on a subset of this set. The selection of this subset is done according to a filtering property.
- *output model creation*: output model elements are created from extracted elements.
- *input model modification*: when the output model is a modification of the input model, elements are created, deleted or modified.

These operations define a very abstract specification of transformations, which highlights the fault-prone steps of programming a model transformation. However, we believe they explore the most frequent model manipulations for transformations.

The decomposition of a model transformation with these fault-prone operations provides an abstract view useful to inject faults. We define mutation operators which are applied by injecting faulty navigation/filtering/creation/modification operations.

3.3 Example of Two Mutation Operators Dedicated to Model Transformation

For sake of conciseness, only two mutation operators are detailed. We present more operators in [5]. The example UML2RDBMS is a transformation which creates a set of tables (database) from the persistent classes of a UML diagram.

3.3.1 Mutation Operators Related to the *Filtering*

Filtering manipulates collections to select only the elements useful for the transformation. In a general way, a filter may be considered as a guard on a collection, depending on specific criteria. Two types of filtering are considered. First, instances of a given class may be selected in function of their properties (attributes, methods, relations). That's the property filtering. The second one can select some instances among a collection of instances of generic classes. That's the type filtering.

Collection filtering change with perturbation (CFCP): This operator aims at modifying an existing filtering, by influencing its parameters. One criterion could be a property of a class or the type of a class; this operator will disturb this criterion.

In our transformation UML2RDBMS, this operator generates a mutant which filters the non "persistent" classes instead of the "persistent" one. In both cases, the filtering acts on a collection of instances of the same type. Then it is viable because the rest of the transformation will not be influenced.

Filtering depending on the type of the classes could also be disturbed. A transformation could act on a collection of the generic class `E`. The instances in this collection are of type `E`, or its children classes (`F` and `G` for example). If a filtering on this collection selects only the instances of `F`, this operator creates two mutants: one selects the instances of `G` and the other the instances of `E`. All these classes share the same inherited properties. Then the fault injected by this operator will not be discovered. Even if a class redefines a property, the programmer should not detect the fault.

Collection filtering change with deletion (CFCD): This operator deletes a filter on a collection; the mutant returns the collection it was supposed to filter. This operator leads to the same cases than the CFCP operator, which justifies its relevance.

3.3.2 Operators Implementation with a Language Not Devoted to the MDE, *Java*

We wrote the entire transformation using *Eclipse Modeling Framework* (EMF). The sample we are interested in is:

```
ELists cls = getClasses(modelUse);
Iterator itCls = cls.iterator();
while (itCls.hasNext()){
  Class c = (Class)(itCls.next());
  if (!c.is_persistent) cls.remove(c);    }//while
createTables(cls);
```

Here, the filtering (on the collection `cls`) is implemented from line 2 to 5. If we apply the CFCP operator, a mutant is generated with the code:

```
ELists cls = getClasses(modelUse);
Iterator itCls = cls.iterator();
while (itCls.hasNext()){
  Class c = (Class)(itCls.next());
  if (c.is_persistent) cls.remove(c);    }//while //mutant without !
createTables(cls);
```

If we apply the CFCD operator, a mutant is generated with the code:

```
ELists cls = getClasses(modelUse);
createTables(cls);
```

If the CFCP operator modifies only one statement, the CFCD affects a larger part of the program. This illustrates the fact that we need operators that are more than syntactic changes.

4 Contracts as Embedded Oracles

Embedded oracles – predicates for the fault detection decision – can either be provided by assertions included in the test cases or by executable contracts. Contracts are expressed at specification level and translated into executable properties which are checked at execution runs of the transformation. Today, there is no standard to express contracts for model transformations or to define the specification of a transformation. In the following, we define two levels of contracts w.r.t. the classification of [6]:

Basic contracts: The first level, basic, or syntactic, contracts, is required simply to make the system work. Interface definition languages, as well as typed object-based or object-oriented languages, let the component designer specifies the operations a component can perform, the input and output parameters each component requires, and the possible exceptions that might be raised during operation. Applied to MDA components, the input/output metamodels describe the "types" of the manipulated data. They are parts of the specification: the input/output models must be conformant to their respective metamodels. While for a classical procedure, a programmer can declare a variable as being an integer instead of a float, it is usual to consider that a model transformation takes a model as input not conformed to a whole metamodel but to one of its sub-part. For example, the UML2RDBMS transformation is restricted to the parts of the UML metamodel which describe what classes and their relations are. Thus contracts will check the conformance to this restricted metamodel that we called effective. Finally, we have contracts on the input models (*basic precondition contracts*) and on the resulting models (*basic postcondition contracts*).

Behavioral semantic contracts: The second level, behavioral and semantic contracts, improves the level of confidence in the execution context for the specific model transformation. Because the UML2RDBMS input metamodel does not define precisely that the input model must include at least a class with at least one attribute, the user can only guess this fact. So, specific properties can be attached to the input domain of the transformation, which play the role of preconditions specific to the transformation. In classical programming, a programmer can write that the character variable should only be equal to 'a' or 'b' for example. So, if the effective metamodel describes the "type" of an input/output model, the precondition can express properties which must be true only for the given transformation. Three categories of contracts can be expressed:

- *domain contracts (or precondition)* are properties specifying the input domain more precisely than a simple metamodel,
- *range contracts (or postconditions)* are specific properties on the output models,
- *domain/range contracts (or postconditions)* express properties linking the input and output models).

In a design-by-contract approach, our experience is that *most* of the oracle verdicts are provided by contracts derived from the specification. The fact that the contracts of components are inaccurate to detect a fault exercised by the test case reveals a lack of precision in the specification. The specification should be refined and new contracts added. The trust in the component is thus related to the test set efficiency and the contracts "completeness". We can trust the implementation since we have tested it with a good test set, and we trust the specification because it is precise enough to derive accurate contracts as oracle functions.

5 The Testing for Trust of a MDA Component Illustrated

This section illustrates the three steps to improve the trustability of a MDA component using an example taken from the UML2RDBMS transformation implemented in Java. Mutation is applied on a particular method of the transformation (`createColumns`) and the improvement of the test set and the contracts to detect the mutants is illustrated. The `createColumns`, given below, takes a class and a RDBMS table as a parameter and adds one column in the table for each attribute of the class. The method is called recursively to add columns that correspond to inherited attribute.

```
private static Table createColumns(Class classUse, Table tableUse) {
  Iterator itClass = classUse.getFeature().iterator();
  while(itClass.hasNext()){
    metaUML.Attribute attributeUsed=(metaUML.Attribute)itClass.next();
    Column newColumn = MetaRDBMSFactory.eINSTANCE.createColumn();
    newColumn.setName(attributeUsed.getName());
    newColumn.setType(attributeUsed.getType().getName());
    tableUse.getColumns().add(newColumn);
  }//while
  Iterator itGeneralization = classUse.getGeneralization().iterator();
  if( itGeneralization.hasNext()){
    tableUse=createColumns((Class)
      ((Generalization)itGeneralization.next()).getParent(), tableUse);
  }//if
  return tableUse;
}//method createColumns
```

5.1 Test Set Improvement

The first step of the process consists in evaluating the quality of the test set. Mutation analysis allows computing a mutation score that evaluates the proportion of simple errors the test set can detect. If this score is not acceptable, meaning that the test cases do not detect enough injected errors, the test set must be improved.

For example, let us consider the following excerpt of the `createColumn` method:

```
private static Table createColumns(Class classUse, Table tableUse) {

  ........

  Iterator itGeneralization = classUse.getGeneralization().iterator();
  if( itGeneralization.hasNext()){
     tableUse=createColumns((Class)
       ((Generalization)itGeneralization.next()).getParent(),tableUse);
  }//if

  return tableUse;

}//method createColumns
```

The CFCP operator can modify the condition in the "if" statement to create the following mutant:

```
private static Table createColumns(Class classUse, Table tableUse) {
  ........
  Iterator itGeneralization = classUse.getGeneralization().iterator();
  if( ! itGeneralization.hasNext()){
     tableUse=createColumns((Class)
       ((Generalization)itGeneralization.next()).getParent(),tableUse);
  }//if
  return tableUse;
}//method createColumns
```

To kill this mutant, it is necessary to add a test case which produces different outputs between the mutant and original version. We need an input model with a class that has a super class with at least one attribute. Several models may be generated, with simple or multiple inheritance. For example let us consider a model called "Model 1" that contains a class A which inherits from two classes B and C (Fig. 5). So, applying this analysis to the whole set of mutants forces the creation of new test cases (input models) which exercise the model transformation program more efficiently than the simple test set provided by the tester.

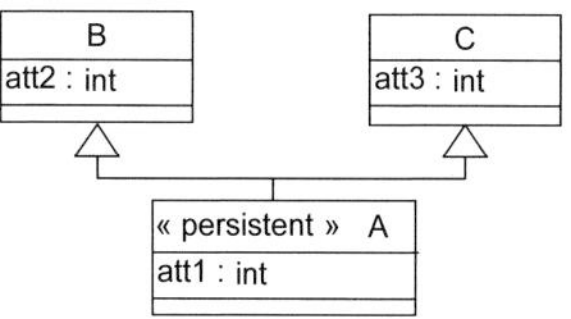

Fig. 5. Model 1

5.2 Implementation Improvement

When efficient test cases (according to the mutation analysis) have been produced, they are executed against the implementation to detect errors in the program. For example, when running the transformation with the model 1, an error is detected: the produced table contains only two columns named att1 and att2, it does not contain the column called att3. The error is due to the fact that, the transformation only considers one super class when it looks for attributes from super classes to add new columns in a table being build. The correct version of the program is given below (the "if" is replaced by a "while": all the super classes are navigated instead of only one):

```
private static Table createColumns(Class classUse, Table tableUse) {

  ........
  Iterator itGener = classUse.getGeneralization(). iterator();
  while( itGener.hasNext())
  {
     tableUse=createColumns((Class)
       ((Generalization)itGener.next()).getParent(),tableUse);}//while
  return tableUse;
}//method createColumns
```

If several errors are detected and fixed after running the test cases, a new mutation analysis is ran with the corrected program since the mutants will be slightly different from the ones generated in previous analysis. Once efficient test cases are available and the program has been fixed, it is possible to improve the contracts.

5.3 Contracts Improvements

While for the step 1 (test set improvement) the difference between the outputs of the original and the mutant programs was used to check the efficiency of the test set, step 3 is based only on the use of the mutants previously killed to evaluate the contracts. A mutant that is not killed at step 3 using contracts while at least one test case killed it at step 1 (using the difference of outputs as oracle) corresponds to a weakness of the contracts which should be improved.

For example, let us consider the following contract for the UML2RDBMS transformation. This contract is expressed in the context of the global metamodel for the transformation: the union of UML and RDBMS metamodels. It is necessary to link the input and output metamodels to express constraints between elements of the input (UML) and output (RDBMS) models.

```
Contract: context MetaUmlRdbms inv:
          self.modelUml.elements->select(e|e.oclIsTypeOf(Class)
          and  e.stereotype->exists(s|s.name='persistent'))
          ->collect(ec|ec.oclAsType (Class))
            ->forAll(cp|self.database.elements
              ->one(t|t.name=cp.name and
                          cp.feature->select(f|f.oclIsTypeOf(Attribute))
                ->collect(fa|fa.oclAsType (Attribute))
                ->forAll(a|t.columns->one(tc|tc.name=a.name))
                          and t.columns.size()=cp.feature
                          ->select(f|f.oclIsTypeOf(Attribute)).size()))
```

Let us also consider a possible mutant for the `createColumns` method where the initialization of the type of the created column has been deleted:

```
Mutant:
private static Table createColumns(Class classUse, Table tableUse) {
  Iterator itClass = classUse.getFeature().iterator();
    while(itClass.hasNext()){
      metaUML.Attribute attributeUsed=(metaUML.Attribute)itClass.next();
        Column newColumn = MetaRDBMSFactory.eINSTANCE.createColumn();
        newColumn.setName(attributeUsed.getName());
        tableUse.getColumns().add(newColumn);}//while
  .........
}//method createColumns
```

When running the test cases generated previously, the faulty part of the mutant program is executed (this mutant is killed with mutation analysis). However, when running the test cases using the considered contract as the oracle function, the mutant is not killed. Looking at this contract, it appears that a particular property has not been expressed that prevents it from killing this particular mutant. A more complete contract is given below (it adds a property that checks the type of the columns):

```
context MetaUmlRdbms inv:
self.modelUml.elements->select(e|e.oclIsTypeOf(Class) and
   e.stereotype->exists(s|s.name='persistent'))
 ->collect(ec|ec.oclAsType (Class))
  ->forAll(cp|self.database.elements
   ->one(t|t.name=cp.name and
          cp.feature->select(f|f.oclIsTypeOf(Attribute))
    ->collect(fa|fa.oclAsType (Attribute))
    ->forAll(a|t.columns->one(tc|tc.name=a.name
                              and tc.type=a.type.name))
          and t.columns.size()=cp.feature
          ->select(f|f.oclIsTypeOf(Attribute)).size()))
```

Table 1. Mutation scores with contracts and different mutation operators

	MS %	Range contract %	D/R 0 %	D/R 1 %	D/R 2 %	D/R 3 %	D/R %
classic	91,7	64,6	74,0	83,3	88,5	91,7	91,7
model	89,1	67,4	58,7	67,4	71,7	78,3	87,0
total	90,8	65,5	69,0	78,2	83,1	87,3	90,1

5.4 Results

Table 1 gives results for several mutation analyses on the UML2RDBMS example. The three lines in the table correspond to different types of mutation operators: "classic" corresponds to classical mutation operators (mutants were obtained using MuJava mutation tool [7]), "model" corresponds to mutation operators dedicated to model transformation and "total" is the combination of both types of operators. The analyses were run with 96 classical mutants and 46 model-specific mutants. The first column (MS= Q_{td}) corresponds to the mutation score using the behavior difference as an oracle (it estimates the quality of test set Q_{td}). The following columns present the quality Q_{cont} of contracts. The second column concerns only Range contracts (check that the result conforms to the output metamodel). Columns 3 to 6 give the results with Domain/Range (D/R) contracts at 4 successive levels of improvement when applying the step 3 of the design-for-trust process. Last column is the final score obtained with both Range and improved D/R contracts. This first experiment shows that the range contracts allow detecting 60-70% of the mutants killed by the test set. However, to reach a higher score, D/R contracts are needed in complement to Range contracts. The combination of both allows reaching a Q_{cont} of 90%. Roughly, it means that embedded oracles have a high probability to detect a faulty result: the MDA component is thus robust and 'vigilant'. These first results have to be validated with other experiments.

6 Related Works

The notion of MDA component has recently appeared as a necessary feature for a successful deployment of MDA. In [8], this type of component is defined as "a packaging unit for any artifact used or produced within an MDA-related process". This paper introduces several concepts and entities that are present in a MDA context and they give several examples of MDA components. If they present model transformations as the most important component, they also consider metamodels, promoters, and consistency checkers as MDA components. This concept of MDA component may thus be used in a wider meaning than the restricted but also more precise definition we propose in this paper. In [9], Fondement and al. also propose to use MDE components to answer methodological needs. They analyze what are the different available technologies to improve reuse and define assets that can automate a model-driven methodology. They consider, package dependency, profiling, model transformation and metamodelling and show that they all have serious limitations to allow a real component oriented MDE. As for [8], this work uses a larger definition of MDA component as ours, however and they only give clues of what could be done to actually design MDA components. In this paper, we focus on a specific aspect of MDE, the model transformation to define MDA component and propose a trustability assessment.

Concerning the particular techniques necessary to build trustable components, there are few related works. These techniques are: specification of contracts for a transformation, test generation and mutation analysis. In [10], Cariou et al. study the applicability of OCL to express contracts to specify a model transformation. Other works propose to express rules that declare the behavior of the transformation, but most of these techniques are declarative implementation of the transformation and not a specification from which the implementation is derived.

There are also few works about model transformation testing. In [11], Lin et al., identify all the core challenges for model transformation testing, and propose a framework that relates the different activities. In [12], Küster considers rule-based transformations and addresses the problem of the validation of the rules that define the model transformation, i.e. syntactic correctness and termination of the set of rules. In [13], we looked at the problem of test data generation for model transformations and proposed to adapt partition testing to define test criteria to cover the input metamodel (that describes the input domain for a transformation).

At last, mutation technique has been widely studied to evaluate the test sets for imperative and object-oriented programming but, as far as we know, has not been studied to validate tests or contracts for model transformation, except in our work [5]. In [14], mutation analysis is studied in a UML context. The idea is to propose a taxonomy of faults when designing UML class diagrams. The work presented in this paper focuses on the specific faults related to model transformation and not on the way models may be faulty.

7 Conclusion

The presented work detailed a process to help programmers/developers building trust in a model transformation encapsulated into a MDA component. This method, based on test qualification, also leads to contracts improvement. For a given MDA component, we propose to estimate the consistency between contracts, implementation and tests using mutation analysis as the main qualification technique. The process to improve the trustability of MDA components is incremental:

1. improving the test set by analyzing their efficiency using a mutation analysis,
2. improving the implementation, thanks to the previously evaluated test set,

3. improving the contracts by measuring their accuracy as embedded oracles, knowing that test cases are efficient to provoke a faulty execution of the model transformation program.

Test set, implementation and contracts improvements are guided by the fact that we know which faults are injected during mutation.

References

1. Meyer, B., Object-oriented software construction. 1992: Prentice Hall. 1254.
2. Le Traon, Y., B. Baudry, and J.-M. Jézéquel, Design by Contract to Improve Software Vigilance. IEEE Transactions on Software Enginnering, 2006.
3. DeMillo, R., R. Lipton, and F. Sayward, Hints on Test Data Selection : Help For The Practicing Programmer. IEEE Computer, 1978. 11(4): p. 34 - 41.
4. Ma, Y.-S., Y.-R. Kwon, and A.J. Offutt. Inter-Class Mutation Operators for Java. in Proceedings of ISSRE'02 (Int. Symposium on Software Reliability Engineering). Annapolis, MD, USA: IEEE Computer Society Press, Los Alamitos, CA, USA. 2002.
5. Mottu, J.-M., B. Baudry, and Y. Le Traon. Mutation Analysis Testing for Model Transformations. in Proceedings of ECMDA-FA 2006. Bilbao, Spain. 2006.
6. Beugnard, A., J.-M. Jézéquel, N. Plouzeau, and D. Watkins, Making components contract aware. IEEE Computer, 1999. 13(7).
7. Ma, Y.-S., A.J. Offutt, and Y.-R. Kwon, MuJava : An Automated Class Mutation System. Software Testing, Verification and Reliability, 2005.
8. Bézivin, J., S. Gérard, P.-A. Muller, and L. Rioux. MDA Components: Challenges and Opportunities. in Proceedings of Metamodelling for MDA. York, England. 2003.
9. Fondement, F. and R. Silaghi. Defining Model Driven Engineering Processes. in Proceedings of WISME. Lisbon, Portugal. 2004.
10. Cariou, E., R. Marvie, L. Seinturier, and L. Duchien. OCL for the Specification of Model Transformation Contracts. in Proceedings of Workshop OCL and Model Driven Engineering. Lisbon, Portugual. 2004.
11. Lin, Y., J. Zhang, and J. Gray, A Testing Framework for Model Transformations, in Model-Driven Software Development - Research and Practice in Software Engineering. 2005, Springer.
12. Küster, J.M. Systematic Validation of Model Transformations. in Proceedings of WiSME'04 (associated to UML'04). Lisbon, Portugal. 2004.
13. Fleurey, F., J. Steel, and B. Baudry. Validation in Model-Driven Engineering: Testing Model Transformations. in Proceedings of MoDeVa. Rennes, France. 2004.
14. Trung, D.-T., S. Ghosh, F. Robert, B. Baudry, and F. Fleurey. A Taxonomy of Faults for UML Designs. in Proceedings of 2nd MoDeVa workshop - Model design and Validation, in conjunction with MoDELS05. Montego Bay, Jamaica. 2005.

Using Smalltalk as a Reflective Executable Meta-language

Stéphane Ducasse[1,2] and Tudor Gîrba[1]

[1] Software Composition Group, University of Bern
www.iam.unibe.ch/∼scg
[2] Language and Software Evolution – LISTIC, Université de Savoie
www.listic.univ-savoie.fr

Abstract. Object-oriented meta-languages such as MOF or EMOF are often used to specify domain specific languages. However, these meta-languages lack the ability to describe behavior or operational semantics. Several approaches have used a subset of Java mixed with OCL as executable meta-languages. In this paper, we report our experience of using Smalltalk as an executable meta-language. We validated this approach in incrementally building over the last decade, Moose, a meta-described reengineering environment. The reflective capabilities of Smalltalk support a uniform way of letting the developer focus on his tasks while at the same time allowing him to meta-describe his domain model. The advantage of our approach is that the developer uses *the same tools and environment* he uses for his regular tasks.

Keywords: meta behavior description, reflective language, Smalltalk.

1 Introduction

Object-oriented meta-languages such as MOF [OMG97], EMOF [OMG04] or ECore [BSM+03] are often used to describe domain specific language meta-models. However, such object-oriented meta-languages only support the description of structural entities and their relationships. They do not have support for the definition of behavior, and, as such, they cannot be used to specify the operational semantics of meta-models [MFJ05].

Attempts such as the UML Virtual Machine [RFBL+01] failed similarly to capture the specification of operations at the meta level. Adaptive Object Models [RTJ05] used the Type-Object design pattern and workflow to describe at meta-level the structure and behavior of business models [YJ02]. Other approaches have used ECA rules to describe the behavior of the meta-level [DT98]. Recently, Xactium [CESW04] proposed a simple object-oriented model and imperative OCL to model state and behavior at the meta-level in an executable form. Xion [MSFB05] was an extension of OCL with imperative semantics to support the definition of action and behavior in web-modeling context. More recently, Kermeta was introduced as a meta-language that is based on a subset of Java and integrate OCL-like expressions [MFJ05].

In the late nineties we started to build a reengineering environment [DDL99,NDG05, DGLD05] and we faced the need to be able to describe not only the structure at the meta-level but also the behavior. After evaluating the different alternatives that were

O. Nierstrasz et al. (Eds.): MoDELS 2006, LNCS 4199, pp. 604–618, 2006.

offered to us at that time, we decided to use Smalltalk. In this paper, we report on our experience of using Smalltalk as a meta-language to specify MOF structure *and* behavior in an uniform way.

In the next section we list the challenges we faced when building our reengineering environment emphasizing the need for an executable meta-description. In Section 3 we briefly describe Smalltalk and its reflective capabilities. Section 4 details our approach of integrating MOF in Smalltalk, and shows how we used the approach in the context of Moose. In Section 5 we evaluate the approach, and we conclude in Section 6.

2 The Need of Executable Meta-language: The Moose Experience

Starting in 1996, our main research effort was concentrated on language design and reengineering object-oriented legacy systems [DD99b]. Since then we incrementally developed Moose, a reengineering environment [DL05, NDG05]. In this process, we felt the need to meta describe our environment to enable us to be more efficient building new tools for our reengineering research. Using meta-modeling was just a means to introduce more flexibility and extensibility in our tools and not a research topic on its own. Nowadays, Moose uses meta-descriptions to support automatic storage, browsing or annotations of models. The context had practical impact on our solution. We describe here the main constraints we faced so that the reader can assess our solution.

Not disrupting our developers. The goal of Moose is to enable other developers, mainly researchers or consultants, to develop new source code analysis, source code visualizations, metrics ... These researchers, while fluent in object-oriented programming, should not be dealing with the details of the meta-descriptions: the environment should let them express their ideas and require as less as possible for the meta-descriptions. Also, the developers that want to extend the environment should be able to do so without having to learn yet another language or formalisms.

The implications are the following ones. We do not want to use any generative techniques that would hamper developers to use their favorite environment. In particular, string manipulation and other such kind of low-level operations should not be used, because of breaking the object-oriented metaphor. The same environment should be used to program the base language and the meta one. In this way, the navigation, versioning tools, code refactorings, code browsers can be used at all levels. In particular, the developers should be able to use the same debugging tools and incremental hot recompilation (*e.g.*, editing and recompiling in the debugger) since this is one of the cornerstone of fast development in Smalltalk. Possibly the same paradigm should be used at the base and meta-level.

Even if our solution is influenced by this specific context, we believe that it presents interesting results to enable executable meta-models in practical settings. It is the recent publications on executable meta-languages Xion [MSFB05], Kermeta [MFJ05], Xactium [CESW04] and our successful work in building our reengineering environment that convinced us that our approach is worth being reported to the modeling community.

2.1 A First Analysis

In this section we discuss the reasons why we need an executable meta-language.

Why meta-data description languages are not enough? As already mentioned by [MFJ05], MOF defines operations, but not their implementation counterparts, which have to be described in text. The following example is excerpted from the MOF 2.0 Core Specification. The definition of the isInstance operation of the EMOF class Type (section 12.2.3 page 34) is given as follow:

```
Operation isInstance(element : Element) : Boolean
  /*Returns true if the element is an instance of this type or a subclass of this type.
    Returns false if the element is null*/
```

The description is informal and cannot be executed. Meta-data description languages do not support the definition of a simple behavior such as the MOFType isInstance behavior. In Moose, the MOFType class defines the method isInstance as follow:

```
MOFType>>isInstance: element
   "Returns true if the element is an instance of this type or a subclass of this type.
    Returns false if the element is null"

  ^ element isNil
     ifTrue: [false]
     ifFalse: [element metaClass == self
                or: [element metaClass allSuperclasses includes: self]]
```

The caret sign ˆ is a return statement, and ifTrue:ifFalse: is the Smalltalk if-then-else construct. In our approach, Smalltalk is used to specify the meta-model behavior: MOF meta-model entity behavior is plain executable code. We did not choose Action Semantics [MTAL98] as an executable meta language for the following reasons: Action Semantics did not exist when we started, it is defined for UML models, and it is too generic for our audience and constraints.

Customizable Executable Meta-Language. In the Moose environment any entity (*e.g.*, a program element), is described by an instance of MOFClass. The description includes the way the entity should be loaded from files, saved, how it should be navigated ...Moose also allows for a developer to describe precisely how to specify the resolution of undefined references. For example, the developer is free to define the logic for creating a stub[1] creation which can be complex and dependent of the domain. The code below shows that the class FamixClass which represents the class concept in a language independent way for our analysis is in fact described by a MOFClass instance named Class [DDL99]. What is important is that the end-user developer can specify specific domain actions at the meta-model level: here the optimize: method specification defines the way stub entities may be created when code models are extracted by code analyzers or model loaders.

[1] A stub is shell-entity that is creating to represent an entity that is not reified in our model: when an access to a variable that is not extracted from the source code, we create a stub variable.

```
FAMIXClass>>mofDescription
  ^ MOFClass new
      addSuperclass: self superclass mofDescription
      name: #Class;
      optimize: [:entity | (entity belongsTo isNamespace)
                           ifTrue: [entity belongsTo addClass: entity]];
      addAttribute: (MOFAttribute new
            name: #isAbstract;
          ...
            booleanType).
      ....
```

2.2 New Language or Not?

Defining a new language is always a challenging (and exciting) moment as we control the features that will influence our future expression possibilities. However, developping a new language also raises practical problems such as the language performance, memory consumption, the development of libraries or development tools and the cost in teaching new developers.

Our goal was *not* to define a new meta-language. We wanted to improve our reengineering environment by making it more flexible and extensible, while in the same time, we wanted to let our developers program in an environment in which they were comfortable and efficient. We favored the practical issues, and chose to use the same language (*i.e.*, Smalltalk) for both describing the meta-model and the meta-meta-model.

In this section we described our practical constraints, and how we came to the conclusion that Smalltalk is the solution for our problem. To let the reader better understand the detail, we briefly describe in the next section the key characteristics of the Smalltalk language and its meta-model. In the subsequent section we present the architecture we chose to integrate a MOF-based architecture inside the Smalltalk one.

3 Smalltalk in a Nutshell

While Smalltalk may seem to be an old language to a certain audience, its uniformity, simplicity and elegance make it still an innovative language. For example, Smalltalk iterators have influenced OCL statements (*e.g.*, select, collect). The recent introduction of built-in queriable declarative annotations make it a powerful language for meta descriptions since we can annotate methods and query such meta-descriptions from within the language.

The Smalltalk object model is a subset of the one of Java [GR83]. In Smalltalk everything is an object and objects communicate exclusively via message passing (method invocation). This is applied uniformly in the sense that message passing is preferred to new language constructs. For example, select: is a method defined in Collection, rather than being a language construct.

Objects are instances of classes. All instance variables are private to the object[2] and all methods are public. There is single inheritance between classes, classes are objects

[2] Contrary to Java and C++ where private is class-based *i.e.*, two objects of the same classes can directly access their private fields.

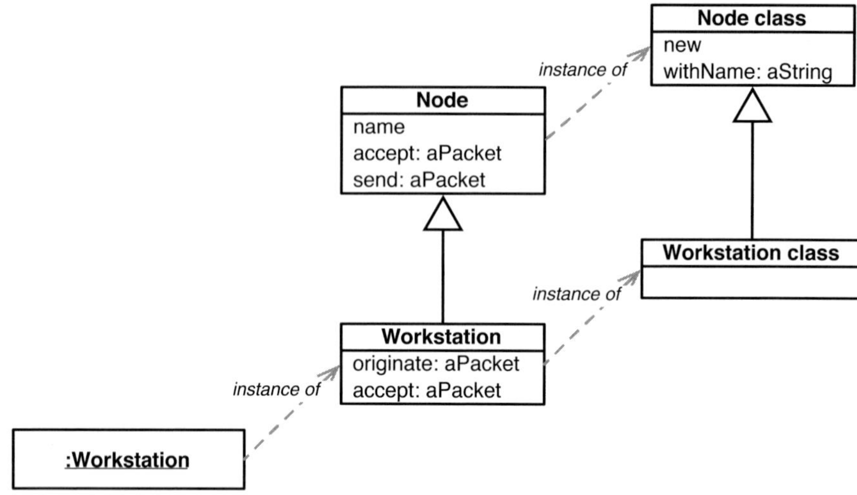

Fig. 1. The class Workstation is instance of the metaclass Workstation class

too. A class is instance of a metaclass which has this class as its sole instance. Class methods are simply methods of the metaclasses and follow all the previous rules. For example, in the figure below, the class Workstation is an instance of the metaclass Workstation class.

The complete system is written in itself, therefore can be queried and manipulated within itself allowing powerful introspective *and* reflective facilities [Riv96].

Query meta-language. Because of its reflective capabilities, Smalltalk can be easily used as a query meta-language on it own structure. For example, the following expressions query the methods defined locally, all the methods, and all the instances of the class Set.

Set selectors
  returns the method names defined locally
Set allSelectors size
  returns the number of methods locally and inherited by Set
Set allInstances
  returns all the instances of the class Set in the system

OCL like iterators. Smalltalk offers high level iterators such as collect:, select:, reject:, includes:, do:, do:separatedBy:, occurencesOf:, and more interestingly the definition of new iterators is open and simple. The iterators are passed closures to be evaluated. For example, [:each |each even] is equivalent with *(lambda (each) (even each))*, or with (each|each->even()) in OCL.

#(1 2 3 4) collect: [:each | each even]
  returns: #(false true false true)
#(1 2 3 4) select: [:each | each even]
  returns: #(2 4)

```
| string |
string := ''
#(1 2 3)
        do: [ :each | string := string, each printString]
        separatedBy: [string := string, '-'].
string.
    returns the string '1-2-3'
```

Declarative built-in meta descriptions. Since several years, several Smalltalk implementations introduced built-in declarative annotations, called Pragmas. Pragmas are pure annotations without any behavior influence, attached to the method definitions. These annotations can be queried from the language which makes them useful as declarative registration mechanisms.

The following example shows how an application can define *at the same time* a method and several menu items that will invoke such a method. In our example, the method openFileBrowser is defined in class VisualLauncher and it consists of the last line that open the FileBrowser application. Then two annotations between < > are used to declare in this specific case that such a method can be invoked from the menu bar using the browse menu item and from the Launcher tool bar by clicking on the icon (see the Figure 2).

```
VisualLauncher>>openFileBrowser
  <menuItem: 'File Browser'  icon: #fileBrowser menu: #(#toolBar)>
  <menuItem: 'File Browser'  icon: #fileBrowser shortcut: #F2 menu: #(#menuBar file)>

  FileBrowser open
```

An annotation is defined within a method body and in addition it should first be *declared* so that the compiler can verify that the correctness of the annotations. Below we give the query example that returns a collection with the annotations named menuItem:icon:menu: defined in the system. An annotation knows the relevant meta-information about its use such as the method and class in which it is declared.

```
Pragmas allNamed: #menuItem:icon:menu:
```

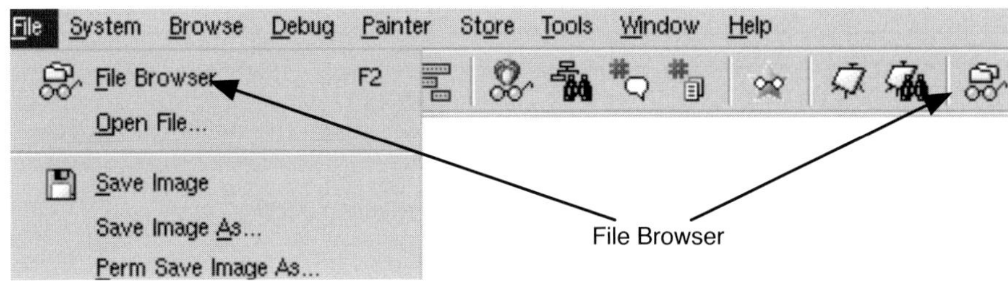

Fig. 2. The File Browser can be invoked both from the menu and from the toolbar due to the two Pragmas

Class Extension Mechanism. Contrary to Java or C++, in Smalltalk as well as in Objective-C, we can package a method in a different package than the one the class belongs to. For example, in the example above, the class VisualLauncher is defined in one package, while the openFileBrowser is defined in another package named Tools-File Browser. As a result, this method is available on the class VisualLauncher, and consequently appears in the menu, *only* when the Tools-File Browser package is loaded.

This mechanism, called class extension, lets the developer add methods to classes that did not provide the expected behavior. Inheritance is not a solution to the problem that class extension solves since clients may still refer to the original class. In our example, extending the VisualLauncher via subclassing would not work since the menu can be extended by different clients, and we still want to open the VisualLauncher to see what tools are available [BDN05]. C# recently introduced static class extensions to improve the extensibility of the applications written with this language.

4 Integrating MOF in Smalltalk and Moose

Smalltalk being a reflective language (*i.e.*, supporting both introspection and intercession [BGW93]), it already includes a causally connected meta-description of its own run-time and structure. To introduce a fourth layer [3], we used the architecture shown in

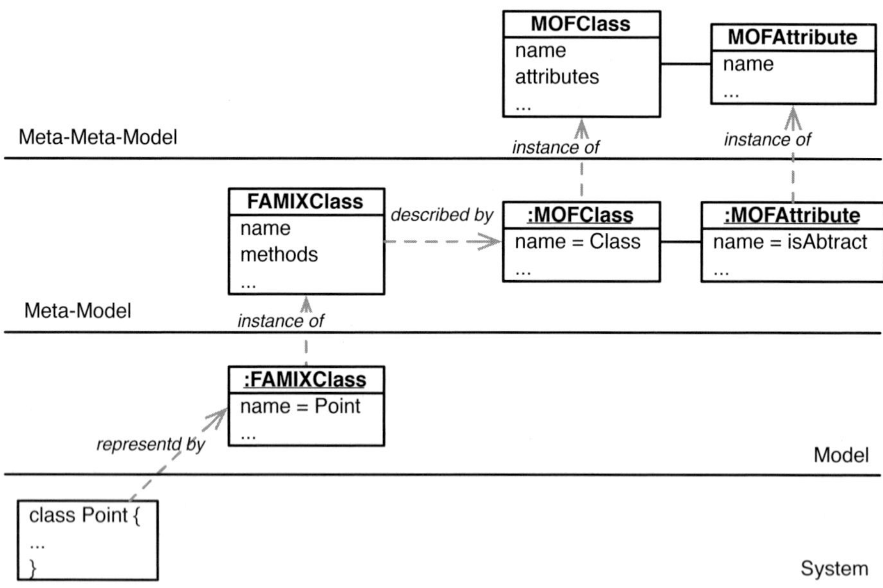

Fig. 3. Mapping Meta-Descriptions to Smalltalk

[3] We started in early 1997 with an entity relationship meta-meta-model then since 2003 we replaced it by a MOF-based one.

Figure 3. In the example, the Java class Point is represented as an instance of the FAMIX-Class [DD99a]. The FAMIXClass is described by the instances of the class MOFAttribute and MOFClass.

Such an architecture is not new and can be seen as a validation of the nowadays well-known distinction between two conceptually different kinds of instance-of relationships: (i) a traditional and implementation driven one where an instance is an instance of its type, and (ii) a representation one where an instance is described by another entity [BG01]. Atkinson and Kühne named these two forms: form vs. contents or linguistic and logical [AK05] [AK01][4].

4.1 Describing Smalltalk Classes with MOF

Because Smalltalk classes are objects we can attach the MOF description to the class objects. One possibility of providing the descriptions are like in the code below.

```
FAMIXClass class>>mofDescription
  ^ MOFClass new
        superClass: self superclass mofDescription;
        name: #Class;
        ...
        addAttribute: (MOFAttribute new
                            name: #isAbstract;
                            loadMethod: #setAbstract:;
                            saveMethod: #getAbstract;
                            booleanType)
```

In this example, we show an excerpt of the mofDescription method attached to the FAMIXClass class. The method returns a MOFClass with the name Class. Attached to the MOFClass are several attributes. For example, isAbstract is an MOFAttribute. Particular to our implementation is that we did not use MOF, but an extension of MOF. The reason for it, is that we needed to attach *executability* to the descriptions as we show in the previous section. For example, for the isAbstract attribute we added information of which methods should be used to read or store the attribute in an instance of FAMIXClass.

As shown by the previous example, the method mofDescription is a class method of FAMIXClass. In Smalltalk, the class and the instance methods are clearly separated, both in the language and in the IDE user interface. Usually, the regular programmer spends most of the time programming on the instance side. Hence, having the mofDescription on the class side is rather distant from the actual focus of the programmer. That is why, we provided another way to express meta-descriptions using Pragmas. Below we give an example of how we use the Pragmas to attach the numberOfMethods metric as a MOFAttribute to the description of FAMIXClass. The developer only has to write the regular method in the model class and how he defines a property. This illustrates how the base

[4] In 1997, the distinction between the implementation and the representation was not clear nor described in the literature. Hence, our architecture was not influenced by existing readings, and therefore it acts as a confirmation of the related work.

code is annotated with a meta-description and also how the meta-description behavior can be specified by the end-user programmer. Note that we call numberOfMethods a property, and not an attribute, as the reverse engineer thinks in terms of entities and properties, rather then classes and attributes.

```
FAMIXClass>>numberOfMethods
  <property: #NOM longName: 'Number of methods'>
  ^self methods size
```

We fill our MOF repository by querying the existing annotations. The below code shows how we compute the MOF descriptions for all the entities defined as subclass of AbstractEntity. The method traverses all the subclasses and for each of it, it initializes the description and then it queries all the defined Pragmas and transforms them into MOF annotations.

```
AbstractEntity class>>initializeAllMofDescriptions
  self withAllSubclasses do: [:each | each registerMofPackage].
  self withAllSubclasses do: [:each |
           each initializeMofDescription.
           each attachPragmasToMOFDescription]
```

4.2 Building Meta-aware Tools

Research in reverse engineering is about creating new ways of representing software. As the representation is dictated by the meta-model, we needed the meta-model to be extensible. This is not a problem per se, but in the same time we needed to be able to browse the results and also interact with other tools via external formats. As a consequence we built several generic tools that would cope with the extensions.

To be able to communicate with third parties tools we provided generic import/export. We started with supporting the CDIF format and later we also implemented the support for XMI [TDD00]. The generic engine depends only on the meta-description of the meta-model. That is, the only thing the programmer has to do is to build his meta-model, and describe the storable attributes. Based on this, the objects in the model can be serialized in either CDIF or XMI.

The act of analyzing can be decomposed in several generic atomic actions: (i) introspection - given an entity, what are its attributes, (ii) selection - given a collection of entities, which are the entities that obey a certain rule, (iii) navigation - given an entity, what are the nearby objects, and (iv) presentation - given a collection of entities, what is the order of the entities. In the same time, an important factor in reverse engineering research is the exposure to the data. That is why we implemented generic tools to address the four points above while being independent on the type of data. Again, we accomplished this by making the tools dependent only on the meta-descriptions [DGLD05].

Because of the extension possibilities, Moose enabled several directions of research in reverse engineering. As a result, several techniques have been implemented to deal with the diversity of data, techniques which are orthogonal to the type of data. As a consequence, we have implemented a mechanism for integrating these techniques. Our solution was to extend MOF with other types of annotations. One such an annotation

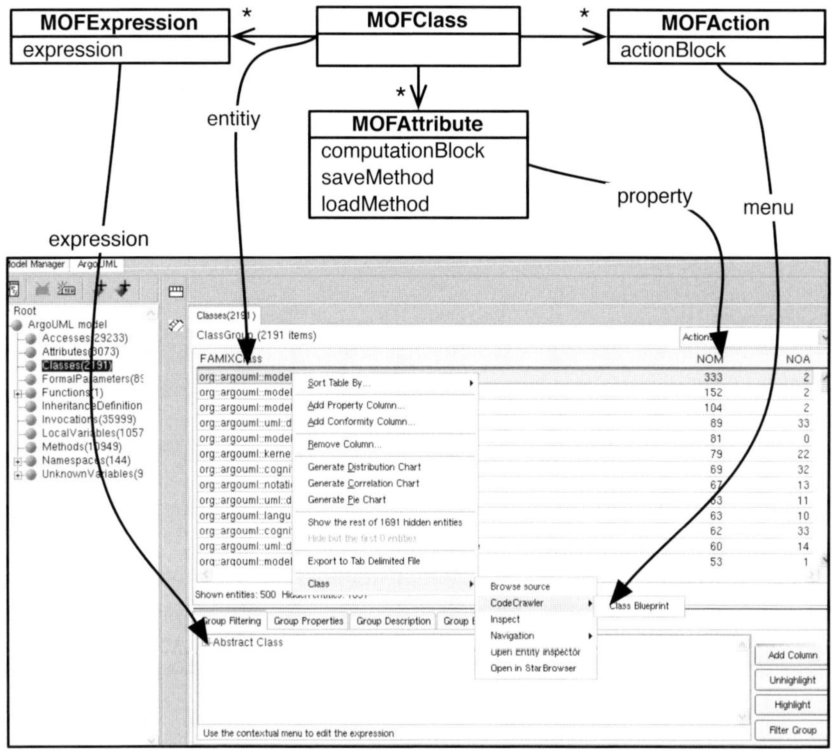

Fig. 4. We extended MOF with new entities and new methods to hook in the execution. The Moose Browser is a generic tool based on the meta-descriptions.

is the MOFAction that a tool can perform on an entity. Based on this annotation we can build a menu, and different tools can register themselves to the context they can handle.

Figure 4 shows the different extensions we performed on MOF as well as one application in building a generic browser. We added the information about loading and saving an attribute, and we added the possibility of hooking in a computation block that would be executed if the attribute is not already computed for a given entity. We also added two new classes for Action and Expression. The Action represents a particular action that can be triggered on a certain type of entity, while the Expression is a boolean query that shows whether an entity obeys the rule or not.

Figure 4 also shows how the generic browser of Moose uses the meta descriptions. The mapping between the different parts of the browser and the meta-descriptions are denoted with arrows that also show how the meta-descriptions are seen by the user. For example, by selecting an entity we can trigger its menu which is composed of actions. In the figure, we selected a FAMIXClass and in its menu we have a CodeCrawler submenu. One visualization defined in CodeCrawler is the Class Blueprint, and it can be applied on any class through the contextual menu [DL05]. The code below shows the method that CodeCrawler uses to extend the FAMIXClass to spawn the Class Blueprint. Note that the below method is packaged in CodeCrawler, and not in Moose where FAMIXClass is defined. Like this, we can trigger the menu action *only* when CodeCrawler is loaded.

```
FAMIXClass>>openClassBlueprint

    <action: 'Class Blueprint' category: 'CodeCrawler'>
    CodeCrawler openClassBlueprintOn: self
```

CodeCrawler is a generic visualization tool based on a graph model [LD05]. The main technique implemented by CodeCrawler is called polymetric views which maps on the nodes different measurements. As Moose provides the description of the measurements computable on the entities, CodeCrawler offers an interactive tool for the user to set the mapping between the measurements and the visualization properties.

4.3 Using Meta-descriptions for Generating Meta-models

While our approach is not MOF-compliant, it still holds the good property that we can query and manipulate the meta-description and run-time of the model and programs themselves. Indeed the fact that Smalltalk is reflective makes it possible to query the run-time or structural representation of the language itself and to modify it in a causally connected way [Riv96]. While we favored a code centric approach, we also believe in generative ones when appropriate. Moose supports the generation of meta-described meta-models from MOF description: from a MOF description, the system can generate classes representing new models and their associated descriptions. However, while the generation of initializers, accessors and other structural navigation facilities is trivial (and ressemble to the work on the UML virtual machine [RFBL$^+$01]), the behavior is expressed as plain Smalltalk methods.

As such this domain generation can be seen as a simple model transformation. Tools such as VAN [GÔ5] which enables the definition of temporal, history analyses, are based on the transformation of models: starting with the structural model we can build the historical meta-model [GD06]. In this case too, we describe the transformation itself as Smalltalk code: we can query the models entities and manipulate them to generate new entities [Pol05].

5 Evaluation

Our approach takes the best of the object-oriented programming and meta-modeling worlds and uses it in a practical setup. One the one hand, we continue to use only one paradigm and environment. This helps our developers to develop their own applications or to extend our environment. They do not have to learn a new language and they stay within their known environment. On the other hand, we provide a meta-described extensible environment in which meta-interpreters can deliver their power. Using Smalltalk as a meta-modeling language provided us with several advantages:

- Executability – We obtained a meta-model that is executable and that can be extended using the Smalltalk language constructs (declarative annotations, class extensions).
- Good performance – Because we use a professional Smalltalk environment, we can focus on our main activities and we do not have to worry about performance that building our own language would have implied.
- Tools support – We can use the same toolsets (debugger, version management, refactorings) to develop both our domain and our meta-domain.
- Extensibility – Using class extensions we can package our meta-model extensions with the domain entities they describe. But we can also package new tools orthogonally to the base domain and even meta-model. For example, we can package all the navigation facilities independently of the rest even if the code is attach conceptually to the core entities.

However, our approach is not completely MOF compliant since the MOF does not describe execution. It does not follow a traditional MDA decomposition. As such, model transformation of behavior may be more difficult than if we would have been using a model to describe the behavior as suggested by Action Semantics [MTAL98], or a dedicated language such as Kermeta [MFJ05]. However since Smalltalk also offers a reflective API, we developed some simple meta-model transformations using Smalltalk.

The common objection against using a programming language as an executable meta language can be summarized by saying that languages provide too much or too few. Muller et al. said: "Existing programming languages already provide a precise operational semantic for action specifications. Unfortunately, these languages provide both too much (*e.g.*, interfaces), and too few (they lack concepts available in MOF, such as associations, enumerations, opposite properties, multiplicities, derived properties...)." [MFJ05]

However, like other mainstream object-oriented programming language, Smalltalk does not support associations, derived entities, opposite properties directly in the language, and because of that the developer may be facing implementation decisions instead of meta-modeling ones. From the language point of view, the Smalltalk meta-model is minimalist. We believe that given our constraint of use a programming language to describe both our base domain and the meta-description, the choice of Smalltalk was adequate and offered a good and practical solution to our problems.

6 Conclusion and Future Works

To make our reengineering environment more flexible and extensible, we introduced a meta-description and used this meta-description to build extensible reengineering tools. We used Smalltalk as an executable meta-language, and we simplified our code and its logic by factoring knowledge at the meta-level. Our developers could focus on their tasks without having to learn new languages and new tools that would not be casually connected with the objects they manipulate.

We show how a four layer architecture can be introduced in a reflective language, validating the distinction between instantiation and representation links in meta-modeling tools architectures [BG01, AK05]. We believe that our approach can be applied in other mainstream programming languages, and we can imagine doing the same using EMF. Still to gain the maximum from this approach we believe that being able to annotate methods, to query these annotations, and to package methods independently from the classes they belong are important factors.

Our solution influenced our reengineering environment in several ways:

- The decision to use Smalltalk as a meta-language makes it possible to use all the tools provided by the development environment: browser, debugger, versioning, testing, refactoring, etc. Moreover it eases the entry level as developers do not need to learn another language.
- Having first class meta-description as ordinary objects also helps manipulating the meta-model, and building flexible tools based on it. For example, we can develop meta-interpreters as simple methods or objects.
- Having a meta-description greatly enhances the possibilities to refactor and change existing code, since a change to the meta-model only needs to be performed at one single place, without requiring to change the generic tools (*e.g.*, import/export).

By letting the end-user programmer naturally annotate his base code with meta-descriptions, we narrow the gap between what are traditionally seen as complex and separated tasks. We coined this approach literate meta-programming [Knu92].

In the future, we plan to describe the Smalltalk meta-entities with MOF to get a fully MOF-compliant Smalltalk. For example, the class CompiledMethod could be described to represent the fact that a method can be abstract and that it has parameters. We would then have a completely executable MOF meta-language.

Acknowledgment

We gratefully acknowledge the financial support of the Swiss National Science Foundation for the project "Recast: Evolution of Object-Oriented Applications (SNF 2000–061655.00/1)" and the French National Research Agency (ANR) for the project "Cook: Rearchitecting object-oriented applications"(2005-2008).

References

[AK01] Colin Atkinson and Thomas Kuehne. The essence of multilevel metamodeling. In *Proceedings of the UML Conference*, number 2185 in LNCS, pages 19–33, 2001.

[AK05] Colin Atkinson and Thomas Kuehne. Concepts for comparing modeling tool architecture. In *Proceedings of the UML Conference*, number 3713 in LNCS, pages 19–33, 2005.

[BDN05] Alexandre Bergel, Stéphane Ducasse, and Oscar Nierstrasz. Classbox/J: Controlling the scope of change in Java. In *Proceedings of Object-Oriented Programming, Systems, Languages, and Applications (OOPSLA'05)*, pages 177–189, New York, NY, USA, 2005. ACM Press.

[BG01] Jean Bézivin and Olivier Gerbé. Towards a precise definition of the OMG/MDA framework. In *Proceedings Automated Software Engineering (ASE 2001)*, pages 273–282, Los Alamitos CA, 2001. IEEE Computer Society.

[BGW93] D.G. Bobrow, R.P. Gabriel, and J.L. White. Clos in context — the shape of the design. In A. Paepcke, editor, *Object-Oriented Programming: the CLOS perspective*, pages 29–61. MIT Press, 1993.

[BSM+03] Frank Budinsky, David Steinberg, Ed Merks, Raymond Ellersick, and Timothy Grose. *Eclipse Modeling Framework*. Addison Wesley Professional, 2003.

[CESW04] Tony Clark, Andy Evans, Paul Sammut, and James Willans. Applied metamodelling: A foundation for language driven development, 2004.

[DD99a] Serge Demeyer and Stéphane Ducasse. Metrics, do they really help? In Jacques Malenfant, editor, *Proceedings LMO '99 (Languages et Modèles à Objets)*, pages 69–82. HERMES Science Publications, Paris, 1999.

[DD99b] Stéphane Ducasse and Serge Demeyer, editors. *The FAMOOS Object-Oriented Reengineering Handbook*. University of Bern, October 1999.

[DDL99] Serge Demeyer, Stéphane Ducasse, and Michele Lanza. A hybrid reverse engineering platform combining metrics and program visualization. In Francoise Balmas, Mike Blaha, and Spencer Rugaber, editors, *Proceedings WCRE '99 (6th Working Conference on Reverse Engineering)*. IEEE, October 1999.

[DGLD05] Stéphane Ducasse, Tudor Gîrba, Michele Lanza, and Serge Demeyer. Moose: a collaborative and extensible reengineering environment. In *Tools for Software Maintenance and Reengineering*, RCOST / Software Technology Series, pages 55–71. Franco Angeli, Milano, 2005.

[DL05] Stéphane Ducasse and Michele Lanza. The class blueprint: Visually supporting the understanding of classes. *IEEE Transactions on Software Engineering*, 31(1):75–90, January 2005.

[DT98] Martine Devos and Michel Tilman. Incremental development of a repository-based framework supporting organizational inquiry and learning. In *OOPSLA'98 Practioner's Report*, 1998.

[GÔ5] Tudor Gîrba. *Modeling History to Understand Software Evolution*. PhD thesis, University of Berne, Berne, November 2005.

[GD06] Tudor Gîrba and Stéphane Ducasse. Modeling history to analyze software evolution. *International Journal on Software Maintenance: Research and Practice (JSME)*, 18:207–236, 2006.

[GR83] Adele Goldberg and David Robson. *Smalltalk 80: the Language and its Implementation*. Addison Wesley, Reading, Mass., May 1983.

[Knu92] Donald E. Knuth. *Literate Programming*. Stanford, California: Center for the Study of Language and Information, 1992.

[LD05] Michele Lanza and Stéphane Ducasse. Codecrawler–an extensible and language independent 2d and 3d software visualization tool. In *Tools for Software Maintenance and Reengineering*, RCOST / Software Technology Series, pages 74–94. Franco Angeli, Milano, 2005.

[MFJ05] Pierre-Alain Muller, Franck Fleurey, and Jean-Marc Jézéquel. Weaving executability into object-oriented meta-languages. In S. Kent L. Briand, editor, *Proceedings of MODELS/UML'2005*, volume 3713 of *LNCS*, pages 264–278, Montego Bay, Jamaica, October 2005. Springer.

[MSFB05] Pierre-Alain Muller, Philippe Studer, Frédérick Fondement, and Jean Bézivin. Independent web application modeling and development with netsilon. *Software and System Modeling*, 4(4):424–442, November 2005.

[MTAL98] Stephen J. Mellor, Steve Tockey, Rodolphe Arthaud, and Philippe LeBlanc. Software-platform-independent, precise action specifications for UML. In Jean Bézivin and Pierre-Alain Muller, editors, *The Unified Modeling Language, UML'98 - Beyond the Notation. First International Workshop, Mulhouse, France, June 1998*, number 1618 in LNCS, pages 281–286, 1998.

[NDG05] Oscar Nierstrasz, Stéphane Ducasse, and Tudor Gîrba. The story of Moose: an agile reengineering environment. In *Proceedings of the European Software Engineering Conference (ESEC/FSE 2005)*, pages 1–10, New York NY, 2005. ACM Press. Invited paper.

[OMG97] Object Management Group. Meta object facility (MOF) specification. Technical Report ad/97-08-14, Object Management Group, September 1997.

[OMG04] Object Management Group. Meta object facility (MOF) 2.0 core final adopted specification. Technical report, Object Management Group, 2004.

[Pol05] Damien Pollet. *Une architecture pour les transformations de modèles et la restructuration de modèles UML*. PhD thesis, Université de Rennes 1, June 2005.

[RFBL+01] Dirk Riehle, Steven Fraleigh, Dirk Bucka-Lassen, , and Nosa Omorogbe. The architecture of a uml virtual machine. In *Conference on Object-Oriented Programming Systems, Languages, and Applications (OOPSLA '01)*, pages 327–341, 2001.

[Riv96] Fred Rivard. Pour un lien d'instanciation dynamique dans les langages à classes. In *JFLA96*. INRIA — collection didactique, January 1996.

[RTJ05] Dirk Riehle, Michel Tilman, and Ralph Johnson. Dynamic object model. In *Pattern Languages of Program Design 5*. Addison-Wesley, 2005.

[TDD00] Sander Tichelaar, Stéphane Ducasse, and Serge Demeyer. FAMIX: Exchange experiences with CDIF and XMI. In *Proceedings of the ICSE 2000 Workshop on Standard Exchange Format (WoSEF 2000)*, June 2000.

[YJ02] Joseph W. Yoder and Ralph Johnson. The adaptive object model architectural style. In *Proceeding of The Working IEEE/IFIP Conference on Software Architecture 2002 (WICSA3 '02)*, August 2002.

UML Model Interchange in Heterogeneous Tool Environments: An Analysis of Adoptions of XMI 2

Björn Lundell[1], Brian Lings[1], Anna Persson[1], and Anders Mattsson[2]

[1] University of Skövde, P.O. Box 408, SE-541 28 SKÖVDE, Sweden
{bjorn.lundell, brian.lings, anna.persson}@his.se
[2] Combitech AB, P.O. Box 1017, SE-551 11 JÖNKÖPING, Sweden
anders.mattsson@combitech.se

Abstract. Heterogeneous tool environments are often a reality and it is therefore increasingly important to be able to interchange model information between tools. This is not only true concerning the natural heterogeneity resulting from distributed development contexts; the need may also arise in a tool chain and for legacy reasons. Without this possibility, there is significantly reduced flexibility, and a danger of tool lock-in. In this study we explore the use of the standardised interchange format XMI for supporting interchange of model information between heterogeneous tools. We report on the current state regarding XMI version 2.0 and greater. We find that there seems to be better support for model interchange using XMI 2.0 than for earlier versions of XMI, and speculate that one contributing factor may be the recent integrations of the Eclipse platform in UML modelling tools.

1 Introduction

With increased globalisation, many companies are challenged with development and maintenance of UML models in life-cycle activities which are geographically distributed. Heterogeneous tool environments are often a reality and it is therefore increasingly important to be able to interchange model information between tools.

In this paper we explore adoptions of the XMI standard interchange format [1] in UML modelling tools with a view to investigating the current practicality of supporting heterogeneous tool environments. Model interchange is important for two reasons. Firstly, it is widely acknowledged that systems outlive tools (see, for example, [2] [3]). Secondly, companies often use more than one tool in their development environments, perhaps at different stages in the tool chain, as tools have different strengths and weaknesses. Reliable export of models in XMI could offer the prospect of an invigorated tool market, with niche suppliers offering specialised functionality knowing that lock-in is not a factor in potential purchasing. Other suppliers may be offering specialised solutions such as MDD transformers and model validation tools.

Here, we report on a study to identify combinations of modelling tools, supporting the latest versions of UML (2.0) and XMI (2.1), which are able to successfully interchange UML class diagrams between them. Our specific interest is in tool lock-in: whether it is possible to maintain models as assets even under tool change. This is a

O. Nierstrasz et al. (Eds.): MoDELS 2006, LNCS 4199, pp. 619 – 630, 2006.

particular problem for the many development companies that already have to maintain models for systems originally designed using now obsolete tools. Some companies have found it such a problem to import their existing models into a newly adopted tool that many man months are expended in manually re-entering those models.

2 XMI

Over the years, many standardised interchange technologies have been proposed. Current interest centres on OMG's XML Metadata Interchange format (XMI) [1]. In theory, any model within a tool can be exported in XMI format and imported into a different tool also supporting XMI.

In principle, XMI allows for the interchange of models between modelling tools in distributed and heterogeneous environments, and eases the problem of tool interoperability [4], [5], [6], [7], [8], [9], [10], [11], [12]. As most major UML modelling tools currently offer model interchange using XMI [13], [14], tool lock-in should not be a problem.

Although XMI can be used for the interchange of models in any modelling notation, according to OMG [1] one of the main purposes of XMI is to serve as an interchange format for UML models. The interchange of XMI-based UML models between tools is realized by the export and import of XMI documents. An XMI document consists of two parts: an XML document of tagged elements, and a Document Type Definition (DTD) – or schema in XMI version 2.0 – specifying the legal tags and defining structure.

Exporting a model into an XMI document is done by traversing the model and building an XML tree according to a DTD or schema. The XML tree is then written to a document. Other tools can recreate the model by parsing the resulting XMI document. An overview of how an XMI document for an UML model is generated is shown in Figure 1.

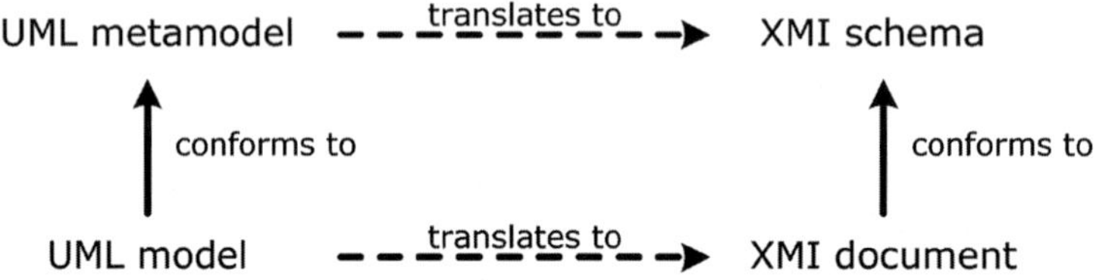

Fig. 1. Generation of XMI document for a UML model (from [14])

As an initial goal OMG stated that "In principle, a tool needs only to be able to save and load the data it uses in XMI format in order to inter-operate with other XMI capable tools" [4]. From this description tool integration using XMI-based model interchange may seem to be simple. However, a number of reports have suggested that in practice having a tool with XMI support is no guarantee for a working interchange, something we wished to explore in a case study. For example, [15] encountered some problems with XMI-based model interchange between heterogeneous UML modelling tools. One problem was incompatibility between tools that support different versions of XMI. Today, there are several versions of XMI recognised by OMG: versions 1.0, 1.1, 1.2, 2.0, 2.0.1 and 2.1 [4], [5], [6], [7], [8], [9], [10], and different tool producers have adopted different versions of XMI. What should be a straightforward export/import situation instead requires extra transformations, between versions of XMI.

XMI-based model interchange may also be troublesome between tools supporting the same version of XMI, as discussed by [14], [15], [16], [17]. According to [15], one reason for this is that different versions of UML are supported by different tools and a tool supporting an earlier version of UML may have problems importing XMI documents exported from a tool supporting a later version of UML. Furthermore, it is also noted in [15] that the implementation of XMI export was done in a variety of different ways amongst tools. According to [16]: "Most modelling tools support an XMI dialect that more or less complies with the XMI specification". This is similarly noted in [14]: "Some incompatibilities between XMI written by different tools still exist" since two tools using the same version of XMI and UML do not necessary generate the same XMI representation of a certain model [14], and in [17], where several differences were detected between the tags used by tools both purportedly using XMI 1.1.

This is partly accounted for by the changing situation with respect to XMI DTDs. As noted by [14], the official DTD for UML 1.1 is included in the XMI 1.1 specification, whereas for UML 1.4 the official DTD (for XMI 1.1) is officially a part of the development of UML. For UML 1.3 there is no official DTD, meaning that several exist in practice – this being the case found in [17]. Even with a recognised standard DTD "validation of XMI files is extremely loose". [18].

Given the richer semantics of schema-based definition, the situation should improve with the XMI schema-based validation used from UML 2.0. In fact, OMG now offers UML 2.1 tool certification for compliance with XMI 2.0. A word of caution is however necessary: "Complete verification cannot be done through XML validation because it is not currently possible to specify all of the semantic constraints for a metamodel in an XML schema." [18]

The successful interchange of models is further assisted in UML 2.1 by the inclusion of Diagram Interchange through an improved metamodel. Losing layout and other visual information from interchanged diagrams has been a major problem with XMI interchange up to now. Tools exporting XMI have used either XMI extension facilities or additional files to allow XMI export/import into the same tool; this information is uninterpretable by other tools.

The current study sought to establish whether the potential of the new standards for improved model interchange has yet been realised in tools which have adopted them.

3 Research Approach

Firstly, a search of the internet was made for tools claiming to support XMI 2.0 (and later) and UML 2.0 (and later); these were considered as the base set of tools for the study. Trial versions of these tools were downloaded for the purpose of experimentation with XMI-based model interchange. A simple model was created which contained the major modelling constructs used in UML class models, based on a number of models developed in an industrial context. This was used in all of the interchange experiments conducted.

In order to explore the concept of tool lock-in fully, the model was first entered into a number of legacy tools (those which use earlier versions of UML and XMI) and exported in XMI. An attempt was then made to import the exported 'legacy' XMI files into those tools identified from the internet search.

Then the scenario was used of round-trip engineering, with interchange both ways between pairs of tools (including XMI-based export/import using the same tool). Interchange was said to have been successful if the test model could be exchanged round-trip without semantic loss.

Figure 2 presents an overview of our approach for analysis of model interchange. In stages 3 and 7 of this approach we conducted a manual inspection of the exported XMI documents.

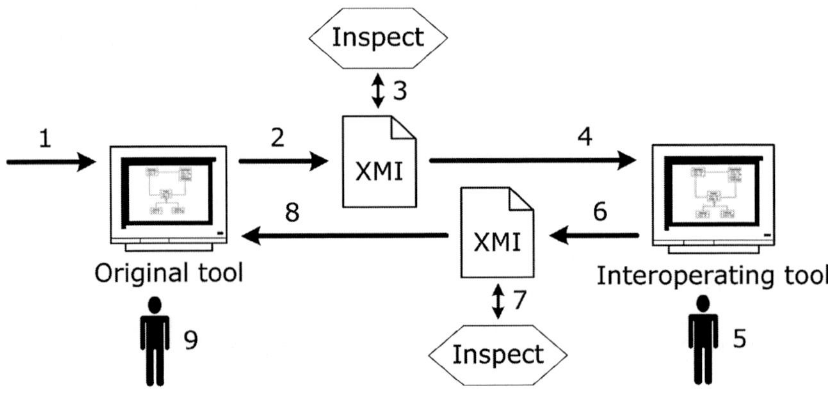

Fig. 2. Overview of the model interchange process

4 Conducting the Study

Five UML modelling tools were identified which support XMI version 2.0 (or later): Borland Together Architect 2006 for Eclipse, EclipseUML Free Edition, IBM Rational Software Architect 6.0, IBM Rational Software Architect 6.0 and Altova UModel 2006.

Borland Together Architect 2006 for Eclipse

Borland Together Architect 2006 for Eclipse[1] is a visual modelling platform supporting UML 1.4 and 2.0 modelling of all UML diagrams. Export of models conforming to an XMI 2.0 schema for UML 2.0 is supported, as well as import of UML 1.4 models defined in XMI versions 1.1 and 1.2. Borland Together Architect includes features such as business process models, Web Services definitions, automated design, code reviews, and other. Borland Together Architect 2006 for Eclipse includes software developed by the Eclipse Project.

[1] http://www.borland.com/us/products/together/

EclipseUML Free Edition
EclipseUML Free Edition from Omondo[2] is an advanced free modelling tool, natively integrated with Eclipse 3.1 and JDK 5. Features of the tool include all UML diagrams, UML profiles, team solution, reverse engineering from byte-code, and other. EclipseUML Free Edition supports UML 1.4 and 2.0, and the export of models conforming to an XMI 2.0 schema. Provision for well-functioning XMI interchange in the tool, for preventing tool lock-in, seems to be a central issue for Omondo:
"*The interchange of common 2.0 XMI schemas are now possible because UML vendors, such as Omondo, are providing modeling values on the top of a standard and common metamodel. Switching from one tool to another will also be possible. Projects will be free to select different technologies without being blocked by just one vendor or technology.*"

IBM Rational Software Architect 6.0
Rational Software Architect[3] is an Eclipse-based UML modelling and Java Development platform. All UML diagrams of UML version 2.0 are supported, together with the export of models conforming to an XMI 2.0 schema. Rational Software Architect includes features such as Web Services definitions, pattern solutions, review and control of Java and service-oriented applications, and other.

MagicDraw Community Edition version 10.5
MagicDraw[4] is a visual UML modelling and CASE tool facilitating analysis and design of object oriented systems and databases. Import of XMI version 1.0, 1.1, 1.2, 2.1 for UML versions 1.4 and 2.0 are supported, as well as export of XMI version 2.1 for UML version 2.0. Features of the MagicDraw Community Edition include code engineering, DDL generation and reverse engineering.

Altova UModel 2006
Altova UModel 2006[5] is a modelling tool from Altova focusing on usability aspects and practical software design for both programmers and project managers. Seven UML diagram types of UML version 2.1 are supported, together with the export of models conforming to an XMI 2.1 schema. Forward and reverse engineering of C# and Java code are features included in the tool. Tool interoperability through XMI is stated as an important issue on the tool's webpage:

"*To support compatibility with other tools and to maximize flexibility, UModel 2006 lets you export models as UML 2.0 or UML 2.1, and you can choose to include or ignore UModel extensions such as custom colors assigned to elements, or image files that represent actors in use cases. Through XMI import and export, UModel 2006 can work alongside – or even replace – higher-priced or more cumbersome UML tools, extending the benefits of UML to more members of the project team.*"

The model interchanged between the tools is shown in Figure 3. Interchange of a model between two tools is said to be successful if all model information other than

[2] http://www.omondo.com
[3] http://www-306.ibm.com/software/awdtools/architect/swarchitect/index.html
[4] http://www.magicdraw.com/
[5] http://www.altova.com/products/umodel/uml_tool.html

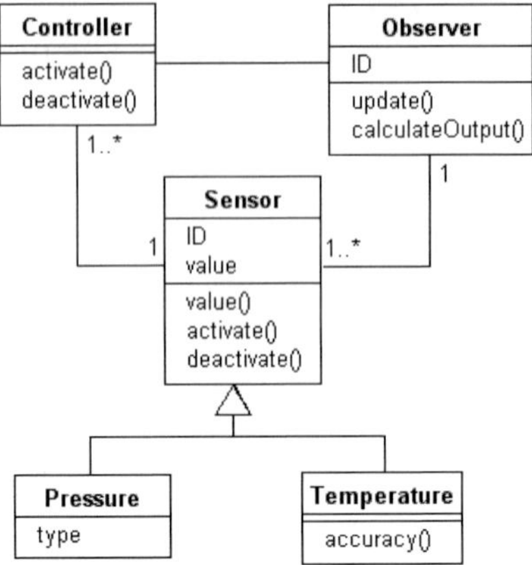

Fig. 3. UML model used for interchange

presentation information is preserved during the transfer. An interchange resulting in incomplete model information is clearly unacceptable: commercial models often consist of several thousand model entities [19], and manual repair is infeasible.

XMI-based model interchange between the UML modelling tools was performed in two phases.

Table 1. UML modelling tools explored in phase 1

	XMI version export	**UML version**
ArgoUML Version 0.16.1 (argouml.tigris.org)	1.0	1.3
Fujaba Developer Version 4.2.0 (www.fujaba.de)	1.2	1.3
Umbrello UML Modeller Version 1.3.2 (http://uml.sourceforge.net)	1.2	1.3
Artisan Real-Time Studio Version 5.0.22 (www.artisansw.com)	1.1	2.0
Poseidon Emb. Enterprise Version 3.0.1 (www.gentleware.com)	1.2	2.0
Rhapsody C++ Developer Version 5.2 (www.ilogix.com)	1.0	1.3
Rose Enterprise Version 2003.06.13 (www.rational.com)	1.0, 1.1	1.3
Microsoft Office VisioVersion Prof. 2003 (www.microsoft.com)	1.0	1.3

Phase 1 – exploring backward compatibility

In this phase, we tried to import XMI files from UML modelling tools supporting XMI versions less than 2.0, to check for backward compatibility functionality. Eight tools were used, presented in Table 1. The XMI file exported from each of these tools represents the class diagram in Figure 2. Versions of XMI earlier than 2.0 do not cater for the exchange of presentation information, so layout aspects are lost at interchange.

It may be noted that all but two of the tools use UML 1.3, for which there is no official XMI DTD. This can be expected to affect interoperability.

Phase 2 – exploring multiple tool usage

In this phase, the five tools found which claim support for XMI 2.0 (or later versions) were used in the exploration. See table 2 for an overview of the XMI and UML versions adopted in these tools (note that some tools support multiple versions of UML and XMI; the table includes earlier versions supported in *italic* font). XMI versions 2.0 and later support the exchange of presentation information and layout aspects at interchange. However, none of the five tools included in the study support this feature. In practice, this is a significant problem where there is to be subsequent human interaction with the model, but it is of less significance for many other functions - such as code generation.

For each of the five tools under consideration, we first created the model in Figure 2 and then exported it as XMI conforming to an XMI 2 schema. All models exported were then imported into each of the tools. Hence, in total, 25 combinations of interchange between the four tools were analysed.

Table 2. UML modelling tools explored in phase 2

Importing tool	**XMI version import**	**XMI version export**	**UML version**
Borland Together Architect 2006 for Eclipse (www.borland.com/us/products/together/)	2.0, *1.1, 1.2*	2.0	2.0, *1.4*
EclipseUML Free Edition (www.omondo.com/)	2.0	2.0	2.0, *1.4*
IBM Rational Software Architect 6.0 (www-306.ibm.com/software/awdtools/architect/swarchitect/index.html)	2.0	2.0	2.0
MagicDraw Community Edition version 10.5 (www.magicdraw.com/)	2.1, *1.0, 1.1, 1.2*	2.1	2.0, *1.4*
Altova UModel 2006 (www.altova.com/products/umodel/uml_tool.html)	2.1	2.1	2.1

5 Results

Phase 1 – exploring backward compatibility

Table 3 presents the results from our analysis of backward compatibility of each tool explored in the study. Non-coloured cells in the table are expected to work since the versions of XMI supported in both tools are the same. Grey cells (*italic*) are not expected to work since the XMI versions used in the two tools differ. However, it should be noted that for the two tools (Borland and MagicDraw, see table 2) which claim to support some backward compatibility in terms of their claimed support for import of XMI version 1.x they do not claim support for UML versions prior to UML 1.4. So, in that respect, unsuccessful transfer is to be expected also for these two tools.

Table 3. The results of backward compatibility tests

Import → Export ↓	Borland	Eclipse	Rational	MagicDraw	UModel
ArgoUML	*Failed*	*Failed*	*Failed*	Failed	Failed
Fujaba	Successful	*Failed*	*Failed*	Failed	Failed
Umbrello	Failed	*Failed*	*Failed*	Failed	Failed
Artisan	Failed[6]	*Failed*	*Failed*	Failed	Failed
Poseidon	Failed[7]	*Failed*	*Failed*	Successful	Failed
Rhapsody	*Failed*	*Failed*	*Failed*	Failed	Failed
Rose 1.0	Failed	*Failed*	*Failed*	Failed[8]	Failed
Rose 1.1	Failed	*Failed*	*Failed*	Failed[8]	Failed
Visio	*Failed*	*Failed*	*Failed*	Failed	Failed

Our results show unsuccessful interchange for the majority of tool combinations. For the two tools that also claim to offer some support for backward compatibility (in terms of their claimed support for earlier versions of XMI, see table 2), our exploration shows several combinations of partial interchange. Some of these results are expected since the tools do not claim to support the specific XMI and UML versions; others are more surprising.

For example, when trying to import an XMI file which originates from the ArgoUML tool into the Borland tool the interchange fails as expected (since the Borland tool does not claim to be able to read XMI 1.0); and the XMI exported from Fujaba is successfully imported into the Borland tool (using XMI 1.2) – even though Fujaba uses UML 1.3. However, even though the Borland tool can handle XMI 1.1 and UML 2.0 the Artisan combination of UML 2.0 with XMI 1.1 is not importable (see Figure 4 for a screenshot from the Borland tool). Similarly, although the Borland tool claims to handle XMI 1.2 and UML 2.0, it fails to import that combination from the Poseidon tool (see Figure 5 for a screenshot from the Borland tool). However, it is important to note that the problem may lie with either tool (or both). Also, as the MagicDraw tool

[6] All relations lost; Name of attribute "value" changed to "value_" (see Fig. 4 for a screenshot).
[7] Five classes added; All relations lost; Added operations (see Fig. 5 for a screenshot).
[8] All associations lost (see Fig. 6 for a screenshot).

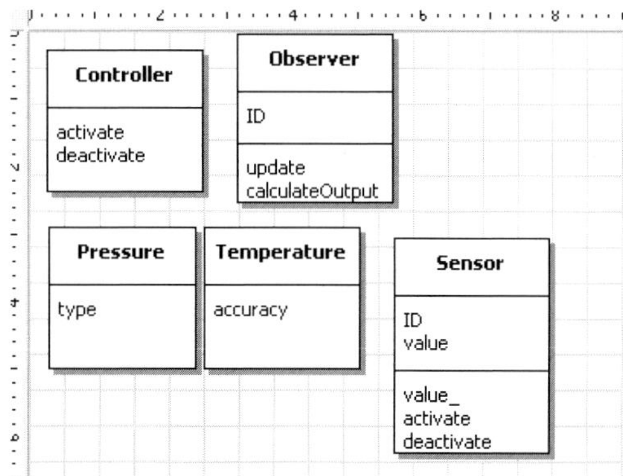

Fig. 4. Screenshot from the Borland tool after an import from the Artisan tool

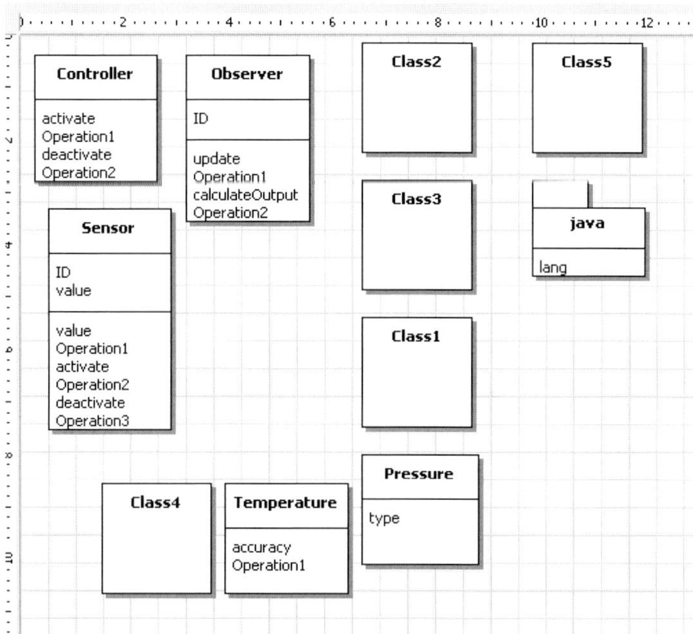

Fig. 5. Screenshot from the Borland tool after an import from the Poseidon tool

claims to import UML 1.4 (and UML 2.0) it is not surprising that it fails to import from Rose 1.0 and 1.1 (see Figure 6 for a screenshot from the MagicDraw tool).

Phase 2 – exploring multiple tool usage

Table 4 presents the results from our analysis of one-way interchange between the tools explored in the study.

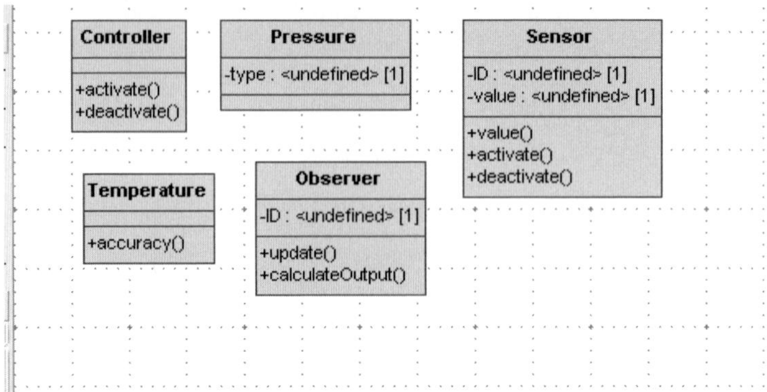

Fig. 6. Screenshot from the MagicDraw tool after an import from the Rose 1.1 tool

Table 4. The results of one-way interchange tests

Import → Export ↓	Borland	Eclipse	Rational	MagicDraw	UModel
Borland	**Successful**	**Successful**	**Successful**	**Failed**[9]	**Failed**
Eclipse	**Successful**	**Successful**	**Successful**	**Failed**[9]	**Failed**
Rational	**Successful**	**Successful**	**Successful**	**Failed**[9]	**Failed**
Magic-Draw	**Failed**[10]	**Failed**[11]	**Failed**[11]	**Successful**	**Successful**
UModel	**Failed**[11]	**Failed**[11]	**Failed**[11]	**Successful**	**Successful**

For those tools which successfully completed one-way interchange, we continued to test for round-trip interchange. In all such cases this was successful. In summary, our results show successful interchange between all tools supporting XMI 2.0 and also between those tools supporting XMI 2.1. However, no success was achieved between any pair of tools in which one supported XMI 2.0 and the other XMI 2.1.

Failure to import a model exported from, say, Rational into MagicDraw is disappointing but perhaps not unreasonable since there is no claim by MagicDraw for backward compatibility with XMI 2.0. Similarly, the unsuccessful interchange of an exported MagicDraw model with any of the other tools is perhaps not surprising as this would require forwards compatibility (i.e. the ability of these tools to import models represented in a later version of XMI).

[9] "Load error: xmi version".
[10] "Input file has incorrect encoding".
[11] No error message.

6 Summary and Implications for Practice

In considering the results of the tests it should be noted that anything short of complete success is of limited value in practice. The work involved in repairing significant semantic loss in an interchanged model is often considered infeasible for industrial strength models. With this in mind, from the perspective of legacy systems and tool lock-in, the new generation of modelling tools has not generally improved prospects for importing existing models exported from earlier tools. The only successful transfer, Poseiden to MagicDraw, is between two tools both using UML 2.0.

The success of interchange between all of the tools using XMI 2.0 is a major improvement on experiences with tools using earlier versions of XMI. From the perspective of tool interoperability things have improved significantly. However, it is of concern that the two tools utilising XMI 2.1 fail to interchange data with any of the tools supporting XMI 2.0. Weakly supported backward compatibility of XMI versions is a cause for continuing concern about tool lock-in. From the perspective of protecting investment in models, extra tool support is needed beyond that offered by modelling tools themselves. This is perhaps the most reasonable way forwards, given the plethora of combinations of versions of UML with DTDs and schemas for versions of XMI.

Another initiative that might help to improve prospects for interoperability is the Eclipse UML 2 project, which provides a common API for storing and retrieving UML 2.0 models. Two of the tools in our study support its use (Rational) or state that they will use it (Eclipse).

Acknowledgements

This research has been financially supported by the European Commission via FP6 Co-ordinated Action Project 004337 in priority IST-2002-2.3.2.3 'Calibre' (http://www.calibre.ie), and by the ITEA project COSI (Co-development using inner & Open source in Software Intensive products) (http://itea-cosi.org) through Vinnova (http://www.vinnova.se/).

References

1. OMG-XML Metadata Interchange (XMI) Specification, version 1.0-2.1 http://www.omg.org/technology/documents/modeling_spec_catalog.htm#XMI.
2. Lundell, B. and Lings, B. Changing perceptions of CASE-technology, Journal of Systems and Software, 72, 2 (2004), 271-280.
3. Lundell, B. and Lings, B. Method in Action and Method in Tool: a Stakeholder Perspective, Journal of Information Technology, 19, 3 (2004), 215-223
4. OMG XML Metadata Interchange (XMI) Specification, version 1.0. [Online]. Available: http://www.omg.org/docs/formal/00-06-01.pdf [Accessed 3 April 2006].
5. OMG XML Metadata Interchange (XMI) Specification, version 1.1. [Online]. Available: http://www.omg.org/docs/formal/00-11-02.pdf [Accessed 3 April 2006].
6. XML Metadata Interchange (XMI) Specification, version 1.2. [Online]. Available: http://www.omg.org/docs/formal/02-01-01.pdf [Accessed 3 April 2006].

7. XML Metadata Interchange (XMI) Specification, May 2003, version 2.0. [Online]. Available: http://www.omg.org/docs/formal/03-05-02.pdf [Accessed 3 April 2006].
8. XML Metadata Interchange (XMI) Specification, May 2005, version 2.0, May 2005 [Online]. Available: http://www.omg.org/docs/formal/05-05-01.pdf [Accessed 3 April 2006].
9. XML Metadata Interchange Specification, version 2.0.1, [Online]. Available: http://www.omg.org/docs/formal/05-05-06.pdf [Accessed 3 April 2006]. Also available from ISO as ISO/IEC 19503:2005(E), July 2005.
10. MOF 2.0/XMI Mapping Specification, version 2.1 [Online]. Available: http://www.omg.org/docs/formal/05-09-01.pdf [Accessed 3 April 2006].
11. Brodsky, S. XMI Opens Application Interchange, 1999 [Online]. Available: http://www-4.ibm.com/software/ad/standards/xmiwhite0399.pdf [Accessed 3 April 2006].
12. Obrenovic, Z. and Starcevic, D. Modeling multimodal human-computer interaction. IEEE Computer, 37, 9 (2004), 65-72.
13. Jeckle, M. OMG's XML Metadata Interchange Format XMI. In Proceeding of XML Interchange Formats for Business Process Management (XML4BPM 2004): 1st Workshop of German Informatics Society e.V. (GI) (in conjunction with the 7th GI Conference "Modellierung 2004"), Marburg, Germany, 25 March 2004.
14. Stevens, P. Small-scale XMI programming: a revolution in UML tool use? Automated Software Engineering, 10, 1 (2003), 7-21.
15. Persson, A., Gustavsson, H., Lings, B., Lundell, B., Mattsson, A. and Ärlig, U. OSS tools in a heterogeneous environment for embedded systems modelling: an analysis of adoptions of XMI, In Open Source Application Spaces: Fifth Workshop on Open Source Software Engineering (5-WOSSE), St. Louis, ACM (2005), 39-42.
16. Süß, J. G., Leicher, A., Weber, H. & Kutsche, R.-D. Model-Centric Engineering with the Evolution and Validation Environment. In: P. Stevens, J. Whittle, & G. Booch (Eds.), Proceedings of UML 2003 – The Unified Modelling Language: Modelling Languages and Applications, Springer-Verlag, Berlin (2003), 31-43.
17. Jiang, J. and Systä, T. Exploring Differences in Exchange Formats – Tool Support and Case Studies. In Proceedings of the Seventh European Conference on Software Maintenance and Reengineering (CSMR'03), IEEE Computer Society, Los Alamitos (2003), 389-398.
18. Objects By Design. An Interview with Geoffrey Sparks Founder of Sparx Systems. [Online]. Available: http://www.objectsbydesign.com/tools/GeoffreySparks.html [Accessed 3 April 2006].
19. Berenbach, B. The Evaluation of Large, Complex UML Analysis and Design Models. In Proceedings of 26th International Conference on Software Engineering (ICSE'04), IEEE Computer Society, Los Alamitos (2004), 232-241.

Applying Model Fragment Copy-Restore to Build an Open and Distributed MDA Environment*

Prawee Sriplakich, Xavier Blanc, and Marie-Pierre Gervais

Laboratoire d'Informatique de Paris 6
8, rue du Capitaine Scott, 75015, Paris, France
{Prawee.Sriplakich, Xavier.Blanc, Marie-Pierre.Gervais}@lip6.fr

Abstract. ModelBus is a middleware system that offers the interoperability between CASE tools for supporting software development according to MDA. This interoperability allows tools to share services and models, by using an RPC mechanism. ModelBus adopts the call-by-copy-restore semantic, as it is very close to local call semantic and is flexible as regards tools' heterogeneous model representations. In this work, we extend this semantic to enable only specific model fragments to be passed as parameters, instead of complete models. The advantages are 1) improving the performance because passing only model fragments requires less data processing and 2) enhancing access control to models because the service's modification can be restricted to the specific model fragment that is specified as parameters. The implementation of this work is available as the Eclipse project Model Driven Development integration (MDDi).

1 Introduction

The Model Driven Architecture (MDA) [16] is a software development approach which focuses on models. In MDA, all software development artifacts are represented by models. Those models can be manipulated by a variety of CASE tools which offer automated operations on the models, such as model visualization, model edition, model transformation and model well-formed-ness checking.

In our previous research, we have proposed a middleware system supporting the interoperability between heterogeneous and distributed CASE tools to support MDA. This MDA environment, called ModelBus [2] [3] [15] [24], enables distributed and heterogeneous CASE tools to share their functionality and models. ModelBus achieves this interoperability by using the RPC paradigm, which enables tools to invoke each other's services and exchange models by parameter passing. Thus, in ModelBus, RPC parameters are models.

ModelBus supports the call-by-copy-restore semantic[1], which is very close to the semantic of the local procedure call. Our choice is motivated by two reasons. First,

* The work presented in this paper is supported by the project MODELWARE, co-funded by the European Commission under the "Information Society Technologies" Sixth Framework Programme (2002-2006).

[1] ModelBus offers the call-by-copy semantic for IN and OUT parameters and the call-by-copy-restore semantic for INOUT parameters [15]; however, in this paper, we focus on call-by-copy-restore.

O. Nierstrasz et al. (Eds.): MoDELS 2006, LNCS 4199, pp. 631 – 645, 2006.

several model manipulations such as in-place model transformation [22] and model refactoring [26] require the ability to modify models. To allow such model manipulations to be shared as services, ModelBus should not limit to read-only parameter passing but also enable tools to modify each other's models. Second, unlike the call-by-reference tool integration approach [9], our call-by-copy-restore approach avoids the complexity and cost of representing parameter values as distributed objects (e.g. CORBA, RMI).

The copy-restore mechanism of most RPC systems, such as NRMI [25], which is Java RMI-based, and Microsoft RPC, which implements the DCE RPC specification [20], transmits a *deep copy* of parameter values: the objects that a programmer specifies as parameters and all objects reachable from them are copied. In our context, parameters are models, which are graph data structures containing model elements and links between them. Hence, applying this deep-copy mechanism to a model will result in transmitting the entire model graph, which is inappropriate for the following reasons.

- *Performance*. A model can include more elements than required by the service. For instance, a UML [19] model can contain use case elements; class diagram elements, and sequence chart elements (with links between them). If the service does not use all these elements, transmitting the entire model graph will unnecessarily waste computing resources.
- *Access control*. The deep-copy mechanism offers too much access to the service: It enables the service to modify the entire model, i.e., all elements reachable from parameters values. Consequently, the caller can not protect parts of models from modification by the service.

Those reasons motivate us to propose a new parameter passing semantic that transmits and restores only a specific <u>*model fragment*</u> (i.e. a subgraph of a model). Compared to existing graph fragment transmission solutions, our approach offers the following novel features:

- *Flexible specification of model fragments*. The approaches based on the notion of object views (reduced objects) [5] [13] or on the Demeter graph traversal language [14] offer a way to specify graph fragments to be transmitted. However, their fragment specification is statically fixed in the service definition. Therefore, at runtime, it is not possible to change the fragment specification for each service call. On the other hand, our approach offers the flexibility to specify arbitrary fragments and to change them in each service call.
- *Access control in parameter passing*. Caching systems (e.g., CORBA caching [4], RMI caching [5]) enables graph elements (i.e. objects) to be transmitted only when requested (to avoid complete graph transmission). However, to our knowledge, few works offer means for limiting the model elements that a service is allowed to modify. I.e., if a service requests all elements in the graph, then it can modify the entire graph. On the other hand, our approach offers a mechanism to protect parts of models from modification.
- *Preserving tools' existing data structures*. To integrate existing CASE tools with caching systems, tool programmers would need to change the existing implementation of tools' data structures to the one supported by the caching systems (e.g. object stubs). Our approach is different as it requires no change to existing data structure implementation. For this reason, it has little impact on existing tools' implementation and facilitates their ad hoc integration.

This work has been implemented in ModelBus, which will be soon available as an Eclipse open source project Model Driven Development integration (MDDi, http://www.eclipse.org/mddi). It is built on top of the Web Services platform, which is widely used for integrating heterogeneous applications. While the Web Services protocol (SOAP/HTTP) only defines the RPC message format, ModelBus extends it by providing a parameter passing mechanism for transmitting model fragments and restoring the update made by the service to the original model.

This paper is organized as follows. Section 2 presents our research background on tool integration and explains why the call-by-copy-restore approach is chosen. Section 3 states the objectives and requirements of this work. Section 4 describes our solution and its rationales. Section 5 describes the implementation and performance result achieved by ModelBus. Related works are discussed in section 6, before conclusion.

2 Background: CASE Tool Integration with Call-by-Copy-Restore RPC

ModelBus deals with model exchange between tools via RPC. In this environment, we assume that models being manipulated by tools (both caller and service) are stored in the tools' memory, similarly to the way software generally manipulate data. When one tool invokes another tool's service, the callee tool needs means for accessing (reading/writing) models that are service parameters located in the caller tool's memory. To support this model access, RPC middleware needs to solve two complications:

- *Remote communication*. An open MDA environment should support the integration of tools executing in different machines, therefore middleware needs to handle data transfer between the caller and the service.
- *Heterogeneous model representations*. As each CASE tool can be implemented with different programming languages, their memory representation of models can be different (e.g. Java objects, C data structures). If the caller and callee tools use different model representations, the middleware needs to translate models from one representation to another.

We focus on RPC approaches that offer close semantic to local call as this can hind the complication of tool distribution. In our previous work [24], we have studied two main approaches: call-by-reference and call-by-copy-restore. The call-by-reference approach requires that models be represented as distributed objects so that the callee tool can read and modify the remote models by using callback mechanism. On the other hand, in the call-by-copy-restore approach, models are copied from the caller tool to the callee tool at the beginning of service invocation. At the end, the model is copied back to replace the original model at the caller tool.

For purpose of tool integration, we have chosen the call-by-copy-restore approach rather than call-by-reference. First, in call-by-reference, callback makes model access very costly. The study by Kono & al. [10] shows that, when more than 5% of objects are accessed, call-by-copy-restore has significantly better performance than call-by-reference.

Second, call-by-reference requires that models be represented as distributed objects. Existing tools that have not been planned for integration usually implement model representation with simple, local data structures. Consequently, to apply call-by-reference, their model representations would need to be changed to distributed objects. On the other hand, for call-by-copy-restore, the marshaling /unmarshaling mechanism of middleware can be extended to cope with any model representations. Hence, tool programmers do not need changing the existing model representations of tools for integrating them.

We identify two copy-restore RPC approaches. In the first approach, parameter restoration is done only at the end of service call. This is the case for NRMI and DCE RPC systems. In the second approach, systems offer a stronger guarantee: the parameter value copy at the service side is kept consistent with the original copy at call time (even after service call). This is the case for caching systems. In this work, we focus on the first approach (restoring at the end of service call). This is because we aim to preserve existing data representation of tools. The caching approach requires a mechanism for intercepting when data is modified so that it can restore the data. If this approach were used, we would face the difficulties in changing or adapting the existing data representation of tools to support this interception.

3 Model Fragment Copy-Restore: Objectives and Requirements

Improving performance. Despite the advantages of distributed tool integration, the RPC causes additional latency compared to local call. In fact, marshaling and unmarshaling complex, large data structures has been recognized as costing major latency in RPC (25%-50%) [21]. Hence, the larger models, the more latency for marshaling, transmitting and unmarshaling them. Moreover, if the callee tool does not entirely use the models, transmitting the entire model can waste the memory for storing unused fragments.

By passing only model fragments as parameters in service call, the amount of data to be processed is reduced. Therefore, it can significantly improve the performance especially if the model fragments are relatively small.

Enhancing access control. The access control problem has not been addressed yet in the RPC domain. Existing call-by-copy-restore middleware, such as NRMI and DEC RPC, enables a programmer to pass program pointers as service parameters. It considers that the service should have access to all objects reachable from those pointers. Therefore, the entire graph is transmitted to the service side and is entirely restored at the end of service call.

In MDA, a model can be built up from a large number of model elements, each of which describes a different software module or aspect. As those elements have relations with each other, they are parts of the same graph. According to the existing call-by-copy-restore semantic, passing a single element as a parameter enables a service to reach and modify the entire model. This approach can be dangerous because the service can modify model parts beyond the caller's intent.

This problem motivates us to integrate access control with parameter passing. The idea is to associate each parameter value with a model fragment (i.e. a subgraph) to restrict the service to access only elements in the fragment.

Providing consistent restoration. In the call-by-copy-restore mechanism, the modification that a service makes to the data's copy needs to be restored back to the caller side. Existing call-by-copy-restore systems (e.g. NRMI, DCE RPC) have already proposed a mechanism for complete graph restoration, which we will refer to as the "*basic*" mechanism. This mechanism consists in overwriting each graph element's content with an updated value. In the case of models, a model element's content is a set of properties, each of which contains either primitive data or references (pointers) to other model elements. Hence, to restore a model, this basic mechanism would overwrite all the property values of each model element.

In our context, the data that is transmitted to the service corresponds to a model fragment, which also has links with the rest of the model. The links between the model fragment and the rest of the model consist of *outbound links*, which are the references owned by the fragment's elements to elements outside the fragment and *inbound links*, from outside to the fragment. E.g., the complete model in fig. 1 contains the elements `{A, B, C...I}`; the specified fragment is `{F, G, H, I}`; and the outbound and inbound links are `{F→A, G→C}` and `{E→H, D→I}` respectively. These outbound and inbound links exist at the caller side but not at the service side (since one of their ends does not exist). The basic restoration mechanism (i.e. for restoring a complete graph) is not aware of this fact. Therefore, it needs to be extended or modified to deal properly with those links as follows.

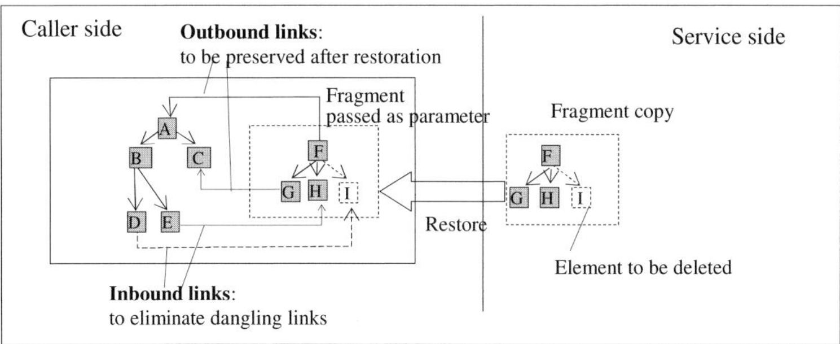

Fig. 1. Consistent restoration of a model fragment

- *Preserving outbound links.* According to the basic mechanism, overwriting the properties of the caller side's elements with the properties of the service side's elements would make the outbound links lost, e.g., in fig. 1, `{F→A, G→C}` would be lost after restoration. For this reason, the restoration mechanism for a model fragment needs to recognize outbound links and preserve them.

- *Supporting consistent element deletion.* Service logics may require the deletion of elements passed as parameters. We observe that few call-by-copy-restore systems enable the service to explicitly delete elements: most systems only enable a service to do so implicitly by making elements unreferenced (to be garbage-collected). Those systems make element deletion difficult because 1) the service needs to search for references to be eliminated, and 2) if the model is not entirely transmitted and there exist inbound links to some elements, then the deletion of those elements will be impossible, e.g., in fig. 1, the inbound link `D→I` prevents the deletion of `I`, despite the service's intent. This motivates us towards the explicit deletion approach, in which the service can specify elements to be deleted. In this new approach, the restoration mechanism needs extension to support the elimination of *dangling inbound links*, which reference deleted elements.

4 Design in ModelBus

Similarly to other call-by-copy-restore systems, ModelBus offers the transparent management of partial parameter passing through *client* and *server stub* components. The stubs offer programming interfaces enabling a tool programmer to write service call code and service implementation code. A new aspect is that these interfaces are extended in order that the programmer can specify a model fragment to be passed as parameters and the stub implementation takes into account model fragment specification when marshaling and restoring parameters.

4.1 Enabling Model Fragment Specification Through Stub Interface

A stub interface generated by most RPC systems (e.g. RMI, CORBA) enables a programmer to specify complex-structured parameter values (i.e. graphs) with program pointers. When these pointers are passed to the service, the middleware will create a copy of the pointed data structure at the service side and create new pointers pointing to the copied data.

ModelBus offers a new way of generating stub interfaces to add an extra parameter, called *scope*, which enable a programmer to specify a model fragment to be transmitted. A scope is a subset of model elements selected from a complete model. Independent from programming languages and regardless the model representation used, a scope is a set of references to the objects representing model elements. This scope parameter can be mapped to any programming languages using their native types that can represent a set of object references, e.g., in Java, it can be mapped to `java.lang.Collection`. To define a model fragment using this scope parameter, a programmer instantiates a set and adds model element references to this set.

This approach is flexible, as it enables the specification of any arbitrary model fragments; however, having to add each model element individually to the collection may be cumbersome. For this reason, we also provide a helper operation enabling a programmer to easily add a group of hierarchical elements. The helper operation `addWithChildren(Collection scope, Element e)` recursively adds the element `e` and also its child elements to the scope. It exploits the aggregation relations defined in metamodels for identifying models' hierarchical structure. An example use of this operation is to add a UML package and all its content (the classes in this package, the classes' features …) to a scope.

The operation in both client stub and server stub's interfaces has the `scope` parameter. In the client stub interface, the `scope` parameter enables a client program to specify the model fragment to which the service has access. In the server stub interface, this parameter enables the service program to specify the model fragment that is the result of service execution. It contains the model elements to be transmitted back to the client for restoration, which include both the elements previously received from the client (which can be modified by the service) and new elements produced by the service. Moreover, the service program can explicitly delete existing elements by excluding them from the scope collection.

Stub generation. The stub interfaces can be generated from the service description. ModelBus provides a service description language dedicated to the modeling domain. In this language, service description is defined independently from service implementation and the model representation used by the service. It uses Meta Object Facility (MOF) for defining the structures of models that are services parameters. More precisely, service parameters are typed by metaclasses (MOF classes). At the implementation level, the metaclasses are mapped to concrete data representations that the caller and callee tools use for manipulating models (e.g. Java classes, C structure types). The stub generation can be extended to support any model representations used by tools (e.g. Java Metadata Interface (JMI) [8] and Eclipse Modeling Framework (EMF) [6]). ModelBus enables a programmer to choose a model representation used by his tool for generating the corresponding stub interfaces.

Example. We illustrate an example service and its stub interfaces. The `moveClass` service enables a developer to modify his UML model by moving a UML class from one package to another. To use this service, he needs to specify two parameters: a class to be moved and the target package to which this class will be moved. Therefore, the abstract definition of this service is `moveClass(inout c:Class, inout targetPackage:Package)`, where `Class` and `Package` are metaclasses of the UML metamodel.

If we used existing middleware to generate stub interfaces for Java, we would obtain the method `void moveClass(uml.Class c, uml.Package target-Package)`, supposing that Java classes `uml.Class` and `uml.Package` concretely represent Class and Package model element types. This method offers no means for the client program to specify the model fragment to be passed as parameters; therefore, the middleware will entirely marshal the UML model. On the other hand, with ModelBus, the generated stub will offer the method with the scope parameter: `void moveClass(Collection scope, uml.Class c, uml.Package targetPack-age)`. This method enables the client program to specify a specific model fragment relevant to the service. For example, if a developer wants to move a class C1 from a package P1 to P2, then this service needs to modify only C1, P1, and P2, i.e. it removes the containment link between C1 and P1 and it creates a new containment link between C1 and P2. As other model elements do not concern the service, the programmer can optimize the service call by specifying the scope to be only these three elements.

Rationale. This new stub interface is motivated by the following reasons.

- *Flexible specification of model fragments.* Representing a model fragment as a collection offers the full flexibility to programmers. It enables the caller to define fragments arbitrarily and to change the fragment definition in each service call, i.e. the members of the scope collection can be selected dynamically. Therefore, this approach can accommodate the different needs of tools.

- *Small change to original service signatures.* We only add one extra parameter to stub interfaces, while the other parameters remained unchanged. Therefore, the effort of adapting our solution to existing RPC application only consists in adding the code for specifying the scope's value, while the existing code remain unchanged.

4.2 Model Fragment Marshaling

The stubs offer a marshaling mechanism enabling the transmission of the model fragment specified by the scope parameter from the caller to the service and also from the service back to the caller. This mechanism is different from one used by existing RPC systems as it deals with an incomplete graph transmission. Only the elements that are included in the scope are serialized and the elements outside the scope are not serialized, even if they are linked with elements in the scope.

Marshaling a model element consists in writing its properties' values. These values are either primitive data or references to other elements (e.g., a UML package element contains the property `name`, which is primitive data and the property `ownedMember`, which contains references to other model elements owned by this package). Contrary to the complete model marshaling mechanism, which serializes all the property values, the model fragment marshaling mechanism must avoid marshaling the references to elements outside the scope (i.e. outbound links, see fig. 1.), because those references will become dangling when transmitted to the other side. The code at line 7 serializes only intra-fragment links. This mechanism is written in pseudo code as follows.

```
1. serializeModelFragment(Collection scope, OutputStream out) {
2. for each Element e in  scope {
3.  for each Property p in getProperties(e) {
4.   Object v = getPropertyValue(e, p);
5.    if(isPrimitiveData(v))  out.writePrimitive(v);
6.    else for each Reference r in v
7.     if(scope.contains(r)) out.writeLink(r)            } } }
```

In our approach, first the model fragment specified by the scope is marshaled, and then the service parameters are marshaled as pointers to the previously marshaled elements. At the receiver side, first unmarshaling the scope produces model elements in memory, and then unmarshaling the service parameters produces the pointers to those model elements. This approach avoids duplicate model transmission when multiple parameter values reference the nodes of the same graph. In this case, only one graph copy is created at the service side and the transmitted parameter values will point to the nodes in this copy, which results in the identical structure to the one at the caller side.

Example. We continue with the `moveClass` example from 4.1. By using the `serializeModelFragment` mechanism, the specified elements (`C1, P1, P2`) can be transmitted without other surrounding elements. As shown in fig. 2 (a, b), even though packages `P1` and `P2` contain classes `C2` and `C3`, those classes will not be transmitted. This example also shows the pointer transmission for service parameters (`c, targetPackage`), which enables the callee tool obtains identical pointers to the ones at the caller side.

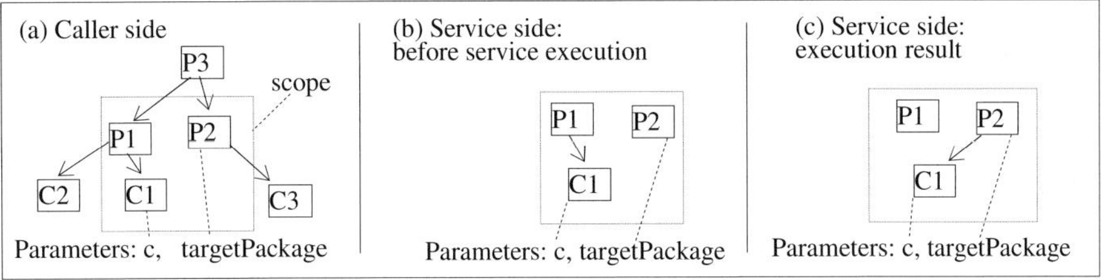

Fig. 2. Model fragment serialization

Rationale. This approach obviously improves performance: the amount of data to be serialized/ deserialized and transmitted is reduced proportionally to the scope's size. Moreover, we choose to transmit all the elements in the scope at a time, instead of transmitting elements on demand to reduce the complication of callback. As the scope is specified at application level, where the knowledge of service logics is available, we assume that the high portion of the elements in the scope will be used by the service. In this case, this approach is more optimal than on-demand transmission.

As regards access control, our approach protects the service from modifying elements outside the scope, since those elements are not transmitted to the service.

4.3 Model Fragment Restoration

As described in 4.1., the service program can access to the `scope` parameter, to specify the model fragment that are the result. This scope initially contains model elements transmitted from the caller. The service can modify the content of those elements, i.e. modify their property values. As an element can contain not only primitive data but also references to other elements, the service can also add/remove links between elements.

Moreover, the service can add/ remove model elements to/from the scope collection. Adding elements to the scope enables the service to transmit back the new elements that do not exist at the caller side. Removing elements from the scope will result in deleting those elements at the caller side.

At the end of service invocation, the server stub transmits the scope back to the client and the client stub overwrites the *original fragment* with the *received fragment*. The restoration consists in 1) adding new elements to the caller side's scope, 2) updating the existing model elements' content, and 3) deleting the model elements correspondingly to the deletion at the service side. In this work, we offer the following extensions to the "basic" restoration mechanism (cf. section 3).

- *Preserving outbound links.* In the basic mechanism, the content of each original element is replaced by the content of received element. This mechanism preserves the inbound links (because the original elements preserve their identity; hence, the links to them remain valid). However, this mechanism makes outbound links lost; therefore, we propose the `updateLink` operation for updating intra-fragment links while preserving outbound links, cf. following code. This operation is applied to two corresponding elements: one in the original fragment and the other in the received fragment. It updates a property whose value is a set of model element references. It has two parameters: `originalProp` is the original element's property value to be updated and `newProp` is the received element's property value. The algorithm begins by removing all the intra-fragment links in `originalProp` while preserving outbound links (lines 2-3). Then, the links in `newProp` are copied to `originalProp` (lines 4-5).

```
1. updateLink(ReferenceSet orginalProp, ReferenceSet newProp) {
2.  for each Reference r in originalProp
3.   if( scope.contains(r) ) originalProp.remove(r);
4.  for each Reference r in newProp
5.   originalProp.add( getCorrespondingElementOf(r) );          }
```

- *Supporting consistent element deletion.* Our approach enables the service to delete elements simply by excluding them from the scope. To apply the deletion, the caller stub searches and deletes dangling inbound links. To optimize search performance, the search space is reduced by exploiting metamodel information. In fact, potential elements that can contain dangling inbound links are the elements that have properties typed by the metaclasses of the deleted elements; therefore, we can filter out non-potential elements without examining their contents. Moreover, for the potential elements found, only their specific properties are examined, instead of examining their whole content.

Example. Fig. 2(c) shows the model fragment at the service side to be propagated back. According to the UML class diagram structure, a package element has the property `ownedMember`, which refers to the package's elements, i.e. its value is a set of element references. To restore this property is not to simply overwrite the property value of the client side's element with the one of the service side's element; otherwise, the outbound links (`P1→C2, P2→C3`) would be lost. We have proposed the `updateLink` operation to restore the property value correctly.

We illustrate an element deletion example with fig. 1. In this example, the service explicitly removes element `I` by excluding it from the scope; hence, the transmitted-back fragment will not contain `I`. This enables the caller stub to detect element deletion so that it can search and eliminate dangling inbound links.

Rationale. Our restoration mechanism satisfies the objectives of enhancing access control and preserving the entire model's consistency. It protects elements outside the scope from modification and it properly manages the inbound and outbound links for integrating the update to the entire model.

5 Implementation and Performance Results

Implementation. This work has been implemented in ModelBus, a middleware system for CASE tool integration. ModelBus' tool integration method has already been described in both research papers [2] [3] and in a ModelWare project deliverable [15]. This method is similar to the one of existing RPC middleware. First, ModelBus provides the service description language, which enables heterogeneous tools' services to be uniformly defined. Our service description language is different from others in that it uses MOF metamodels for defining service parameters; hence the model structures of services' input/output are clearly identified in a standard way. Second, ModelBus provides the stub generation for generating client and server stubs, which implement our model fragment copy-restore mechanism. Currently, ModelBus only offers Java stub generation; however, the proposed copy-restore mechanism is language independent.

The stubs communicate with the SOAP/HTTP protocol. This choice is motivated by two reasons. First, it is programming-language independent. Second, it is compatible with the XML Metadata Interchange (XMI) standard [18]: models encoded with XMI can be easily put inside SOAP messages.

Empirical performance results. We report the performance of ModelBus in two aspects. First, we show that our approach enhances the scalability in service invocation performance: Even when the size of the complete model increases, the user can obtain the constant performance of service invocation by limiting the size of fragments to be passed as service parameters.

We set up the experiment as follows. We generate UML models with different sizes (from 2,000 to 100,000 model elements). Each model contains UML classes organized in an arbitrary package hierarchy, similar to usual UML models in software development. Our benchmark program invokes a service (that has one parameter) with different model fragment sizes extracted from those generated models (10, 50, 100, 500, 1000 elements). The cost measured by the benchmark tool is the total cost of all activities in service invocation, except the execution of the service logic (i.e. serialization/deserialization, data transmission through LAN, and restoration).

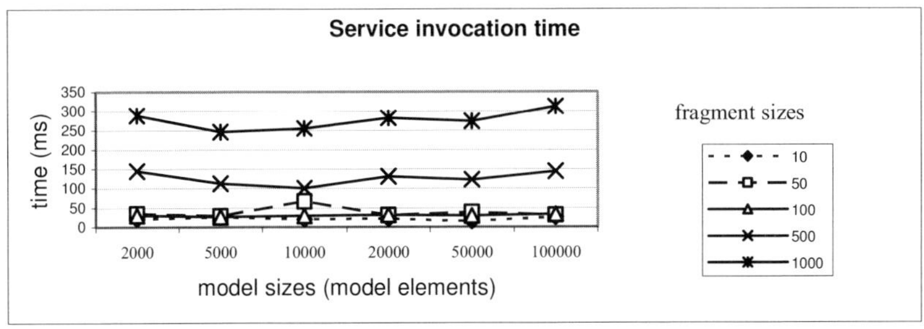

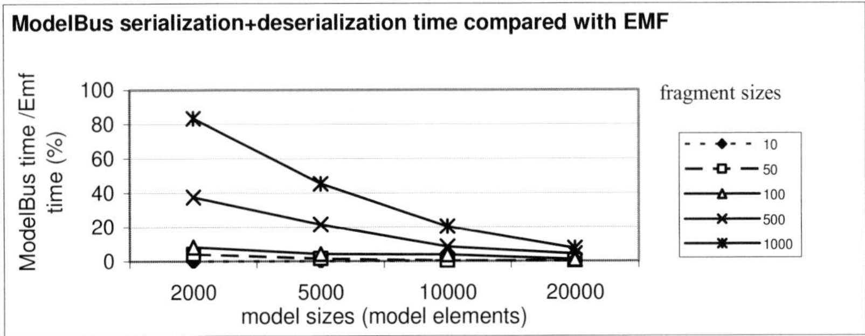

Fig. 3. ModelBus' Performance in service invocation and model serialization/ deserialization

As illustrated with the result in fig. 3(top), our approach enables the user to work with very large models. For example, by fixing a constant fragment size of 500 model elements, the service invocation costs around 125 ms, regardless the size of the complete model. Please note that the illustrated performance is relative to the performance of machine, network, model encoding method and RPC protocols. In this work, we encode model with the standard XMI format and invoke service with SOAP/HTTP. This choice offers interoperability at the cost of XML processing.

As for the second aspect, we compare the performance of ModelBus with Eclipse Modeling Framework (EMF), a toolkit that is optimized for performance [7]. In this case, we compare only the performance of model serialization/ deserialization (as EMF does not offer an RPC mechanism). We observe that when the models become large, the EMF performance decreases rapidly (40 ms for 2,000 elements vs. 1.5 s for 50,000 elements). Moreover, when models are very large (100,000 elements in a machine with 1 GB of memory), EMF generates an out-of-memory error. In our approach, the user can avoid this problem by limiting the size of model fragment. Fig. 3(bottom) shows the percentage of the serialization and deserialization time of ModelBus compared to EMF. It shows that this percentage is close to zero when the model is larger than 20,000 elements, i.e., EMF becomes significantly slow.

6 Related Works

Object views. Eberhard [5] Lipkind [13] propose the way to transmit graph fragments. In their approach, graph fragments are defined with object views. An object view is derived from a class (i.e. data type) but contains only a subset of the class' properties. Since properties can represent links, the object view can define a subgraph including only elements to which the object view's properties link. E.g., given an object view `v1` that excludes the property `prop1`, its corresponding fragment will exclude elements to which `prop1` links. Compare to this approach, ModelBus offers a more flexible way of specifying model fragments as follows.

- *Dynamic model fragment specification.* Object views are specified statically at the service signature level, i.e., as the types of service parameters. Therefore, it is not possible to change, for each service call, the structure of the fragment to be transmitted. For example, if a service parameter is typed by object view `v1` (previously defined), then elements to which `prop1` links will never be transmitted. On the other hand, in our approach, a subgraph is represented by a scope (a collection), which can be specified differently in each service call.
- *Arbitrary model fragment specification.* With object view, a programmer can choose either to transmit all elements to which a property links, or not to transmit them at all. For example, given that a package has the property `ownedMember`, the programmer can either include or exclude all elements owned by this package. Our approach gives the freedom to programmers to define an arbitrary fragment, e.g. a package with a subset of its owned elements.

Adaptive Parameter Passing. Lopes [14] proposes a parameter passing mechanism that avoids the transmission of entire graphs. The expression of subgraphs to be transmitted is based on the Demeter graph traversal language [12]. It expresses a traversal from a specified element to visit elements reachable from it. I.e., this traversal contains a set of selected paths from this element to some other elements. This approach considers that all elements in those paths will be included in the subgraph. We illustrate an example of expressing a UML model fragment. The expression "***from*** *Package* ***through*** *ownedMember* ***to*** *Class*" expresses all paths from a `Package` element to `Class` elements that include at least once the edge `ownedMember`.

This approach has a similar limitation to the object view approach. Demeter expressions are statically defined at the service signature level (as the types of service parameters). For example, let a model consists of a UML package containing N classes. Applying the previous expression example to this package always yield the same subgraph. The caller can not specify a different subgraph for each service call. Moreover, the caller can not specify an arbitrary fragment, such as, a subgraph containing this package and a subset of its own classes. The subgraph will always contain all the owned classes.

7 Conclusion and Future Works

In this work, we propose a new parameter passing semantic for transmitting only fragments of models. This parameter passing offers the advantages of improving performance and enhancing access control to models. Our approach enables a programmer to define a scope of service parameters, so that the middleware can transmit and restore the model fragment specified by this scope.

Even though we focus on models in this paper, our mechanism is also applicable in general-domain applications. In fact, metamodels are similar to class diagrams, which define abstractly data in any application domain, and models can be manipulated by any programming languages; therefore, our approach can be used for integrating heterogeneous applications in any domain, provided that they share the same abstract data structures.

Our parameter passing approach has been implemented in ModelBus, which is available as an Eclipse open source project MDDi. The development of ModelBus is supported by the IST project ModelWare, which aims at promoting the successful application of the MDA approach. Currently, we are applying the ModelBus concepts for integrating industrial and research tools provided by the project partners, such as Objecteering (http://www.objecteering.com), Open Source Library for OCL (OSLO, http://oslo-project.berlios.de), and ATL model transformation engine [1].

For future works, we aim to extend our approach to overcome the following limitations. First, in this approach, the caller must have the knowledge of what model elements the service needs and must specify them in the scope parameter. For future works, we aim to relieve this complication from the caller by proposing an alterative approach that exploits the knowledge of the service about what model elements it needs. Our goal is to provide the service signature that can define the model elements that the service needs. This signature can be exploited by the caller stub to identify the model fragment to be passed to the service. Consequently, the caller can call the service without having to specify the scope itself.

Second, in this work, we do not take into account the concurrency of model modifications. We assume here that the caller tool is blocked during the service invocation to avoid that the caller and callee concurrently update the model, or that the caller concurrently apply another service that will update the same model. Our recent work to support concurrent model update [23] addresses the problem of how concurrent modifications made by different tools on the same model can be unified. For future work, we aim to combine the aspect of model fragment with the aspect of model update concurrency. More precisely, we aim to enable each tool to make a different model fragment corresponding to what it needs. The fragment of one tool can overlap with the ones of others, and those tools are allowed to concurrently modify their fragment. We would like to study how to unify the concurrent modifications made to those overlapping fragments.

References

1. Bézivin, J., Hammoudi, S., Lopes, D., Jouault, F., Applying MDA Approach for Web Service Platform, *Proc. of the 8th Int'l IEEE Enterprise Distributed Object Computing Conf. (EDOC)*, 2004.
2. Blanc, X., Gervais, M-P., Sriplakich, P., Model Bus: Towards the Interoperability of Modeling Tools, *Proc. of the European MDA Workshop: Foundations and Applications (MDAFA 2004)*, LNCS 3599, Springer, 2005.
3. Blanc, X., Gervais, M.-P., Sriplakich, P., Modeling Services and Web Services: Application of ModelBus, *Proc. of the Int'l Conf. on Software Engineering Research and Practice (SERP)*, 2005.
4. Chockler, V.G., Dolev, D., Friedman, R., Vitenberg, R., Implement a Caching Service for Distributed CORBA objects, *Proc. of the IFIP/ACM Int'l Conf. on Distributed Systems Platforms (Middleware)*, 2000.
5. Eberhard, J., Tripathi, A., Efficient Object Caching for Distributed Java RMI Applications, *Proc. of the IFIP/ACM Int'l Conf. on Distributed Systems Platforms (Middleware)*, 2001.
6. Eclipse, *Eclipse Modeling Framework (EMF)*, http://www.eclipse.org/emf
7. Eclipse, EMF Performance: EMF 2.0.1 vs. EMF 2.1.0 RC1, http://www.eclipse.org/emf
8. Java Community Process, *Java Metadata Interface (JMI) Specification version 1.0*, http://www.jcp.org, 2002.
9. Kath, O. et al., An Open Modeling Infrastructure integrating EDOC and CCM, *Proc. of the 7th IEEE Int'l Enterprise Distributed Object Computing Conf. (EDOC)*, 2003.
10. Kono, K., Kato, K., Masuda, T., Smart Remote Procedure Calls: Transparent Treatment of Remote Pointers, In *Proc. of the 14th Int'l Conf. on Distributed Computing Systems (ICDCS)*, 1994.
11. Krishnaswamy, V., Walther, D., Bhola, S., Efficient Implementation of Java Remote Method Invocation (RMI), *Proc. of the 4th USENIX Conf. on Object-Oriented Technologies and Systems (COOTS)*, 1998.
12. Lieberherr K. J., Silva-Lepe, I., Xiao, C., Adaptive object-oriented programming using graph-based customization, *Comm. of ACM*, 37(5), May 1994.
13. Lipkind, I., Pechtchanski, I., and Karamcheti, V., Object views: Language support for intelligent object caching in parallel and distributed computations, *Proc. of the 14th ACM SIGPLAN Conf. on Object-Oriented Programming Systems, Languages, and Applications (OOPSLA)*, 1999.
14. Lopes, C. V., Adaptive Parameter Passing, *Proc. of the 2nd JSSST Int'l Symposium on Object Technologies for Advanced Software (ISOTAS)*, LNCS 1049, Springer, 1996.
15. *ModelBus: Functional & Technical architecture document (Vol II)*, ModelWare project deliverable D3.1, http://www.modelware-ist.org, May 2005.
16. OMG, *MDA Guide Version 1.0.1*, document no: omg/2003-06-01, 2003.

17. OMG, *Meta Object Facility version 2.0*, document no: formal/06-01-01, 2006.
18. OMG, XML Metadata Interchange (XMI) Specification version 2.0, document no: formal/03-05-02, 2003.
19. OMG, *UML 2.0 Superstructure Specification*, document no: formal/05-07-04, 2005.
20. The Open Group, *DCE 1.1 RPC Specification*, http://www.opengroup.org, 1997.
21. Philippsen, M., Haumacher, B., More Efficient Object Serialization, *Proc. of the ACM 1999 Java Grande Conf.*, June 1999.
22. Porres, I., Model Refactorings as Rule-Based Update Transformations, *Proc. of the 6th Int'l Conf. on the Unified Modeling Language*, 2003.
23. Sriplakich, P., Blanc, X., Gervais, M-P., Supporting Collaborative Development in an Open MDA Environment, *Proc. of the 22nd IEEE Int'l Con. on Software Maintenance (ICSM)*, 2006.
24. Sriplakich, P., Blanc, X., Gervais, M-P., Supporting transparent model update in distributed CASE tool integration, *Proc. of the 21st ACM Symposium on Applied Computing*, 2006.
25. Tilevich, E., Y. Smaragdakis, NRMI: Natural and Efficient Middleware, *Proc. of the 23rd Int'l Conf. on Distributed Computing Systems (ICDCS)*, 2003.
26. Tokuda, L., and Batory, D., Evolving Object-Oriented Designs with Refactorings, *Proc. of the 14th IEEE Int'l Conf. on Automated Software Engineering (ASE)*, 1999.

An OCL-Based Technique for Specifying and Verifying Refinement-Oriented Transformations in MDE

Claudia Pons[1,2] and Diego Garcia[1,3]

[1]LIFIA – Facultad de Informática, Universidad Nacional de La Plata
[2]CONICET (Consejo Nacional de Investigaciones Científicas y Técnicas)
[3]UTN (Universidad Tecnológica Nacional)
La Plata, Buenos Aires, Argentina
{cpons, dgarcia}@sol.info.unlp.edu.ar

Abstract. Despite the fact that the refinement technique is one of the cornerstones of a formal approach to software engineering, the concept of refinement in model driven engineering is loosely defined and open to misinterpretations. In this article we present a rigorous technique for specifying and verifying frequently occurring forms of refinement that take place in software modeling. Such strategy uses the formal language Object-Z as a background foundation, whereas designers only have to deal with the broadly accepted UML and OCL languages, thus propitiating the inclusion of verification in ordinary software engineering activities, increasing in this way the level of confidence on the correctness of the final product. Finally, an automatic tool is provided to support such model refinement activities; this tool adopts the micromodels strategy to reduce the search scope, making the verification process feasible.

1 Introduction

The idea promoted by *model-driven engineering* (MDE) [7] [24] [17] is to use models at different levels of abstraction. A series of transformations are performed starting from a platform independent model with the aim of making the system more platform-specific at each refinement step. Such transformations reduce non-determinism by making design decisions, e.g., how to represent data, how to implement communications, etc. In MDE predefined transformations, written in a standard transformation language [21] are applied in order to evolve from model to model. It is assumed that such transformations have been previously validated by a MDE expert, and thus are safe to apply; such transformations are *refinements* in the sense of formal languages: refinement is the process of developing a more detailed design or implementation from an abstract specification through a sequence of mathematically-based steps that maintain correctness with respect to the original specification.

Despite the fact that refinement technique is one of the cornerstones of a formal approach to software engineering, the concept of refinement in MDE is loosely defined and open to misinterpretations. This drawback takes place because of the semi-formality present in the modeling languages used in MDE and also because of the currently relative immaturity in this field.

O. Nierstrasz et al. (Eds.): MoDELS 2006, LNCS 4199, pp. 646 – 660, 2006.

There are two alternatives to increase the robustness of the MDE refinement machinery. One is to translate the core language used in MDE, i.e., UML [15], into a formal language such as Z, where properties are defined and analyzed. For example the works presented in [1], [3], [5], [10], [11], [13] and [25] among others, belong to this group. They are appropriate to discover and correct inconsistencies and ambiguities of the graphical language, and in most cases they allow us to verify and calculate refinements of (a restricted form of) UML models. However, such approaches are non-constructive (i.e., they provide no feedback in terms of UML), they require expertise in reading and analyzing formal specifications and generally, properties that should be proved in the formal setting are too complex and undecidedly. A second alternative is to promote a formal definition of refinement, e.g., simulation in Z, and express it in MDE terms. For example, Boiten and Bujorianu in [2] indirectly explore refinement through unification; Paige and colleges in [18] define refinement in terms of model consistency; Liu, Jifeng, Li and Chen in [14] define a set of refinement laws of UML models to capture the essential nature, principles and patterns of object-oriented design, which are consistent with the refinement definition. Finaly, Lano and colleges in [12] describe a catalogue of *UML refinement patterns* which is a set of rules to systematically transform UML models to forms closer to Java code.

Following the second alternative, in [19] and [20] well founded refinement structures in the Object-Z formal language were used to discover refinement structures in the UML, which are (intuitively) equivalent to their corresponding Object-Z inspiration sources. In this article we work further on such proposal by enriching those refinement patterns with a refinement condition written in OCL (Object Constraint Language) [16] [22]. The advantage of this approach is that refinement conditions get completely defined in terms of OCL, making the application of languages which are usually hardly accepted by software engineers unnecessary. OCL is a more familiar language and it has a simpler syntax than Object-Z and other formal languages. Additionally, OCL is part of the UML 2.0 standard and it will probably form part of most modeling tools in the near future.

Furthermore, after defining refinement conditions, the next step is to evaluate such conditions. Ordinary OCL evaluators are unable to determine whether a refinement condition written in OCL holds in a UML model because OCL formulas are evaluated on a particular instance of the model, while refinement conditions need to be validated in all possible instantiations. Therefore, in order to make the evaluation of refinement conditions possible, we extract from the UML model a relatively small number of small instantiations, and check that they satisfy the refinement conditions to be proved. This strategy, called *micromodels of software* was proposed by Daniel Jackson in [9] for evaluating formulas written in Alloy. Later on, Martin Gogolla and colleges in [8] developed a useful adaptation of such technique to verify UML and OCL models. Here we adapt such micromodels strategy to verify refinement conditions.

The structure of this document is as follows: sections 2 serves as a brief introduction to the issue of refinement specification in Object-Z and UML 2.0; section 3 describes the method for creating OCL refinement condition for UML refinement patterns; section 4 explains how the micromodels strategy is applied to verify refinements; finally, the paper closes with a presentation of related work, conclusions and future projects.

2 Refinements Specification and Verification in Object-Z and UML

In Object-Z [23], a class is represented as a named box with zero or more generic parameters. The class schema may include local type or constant definitions, at most one state schema and an initial state schema together with zero or more operation schemas. These operations define the behavior of the class by specifying any input and output together with a description of how the state variables change. Operations are defined in terms of two copies of the state: an undecorated copy which represents the before-sate and a primed copy representing the after-state.

For example, figure 1 illustrates the specification of a simple class called Flight, having a state (consisting of two variables) and only one operation.

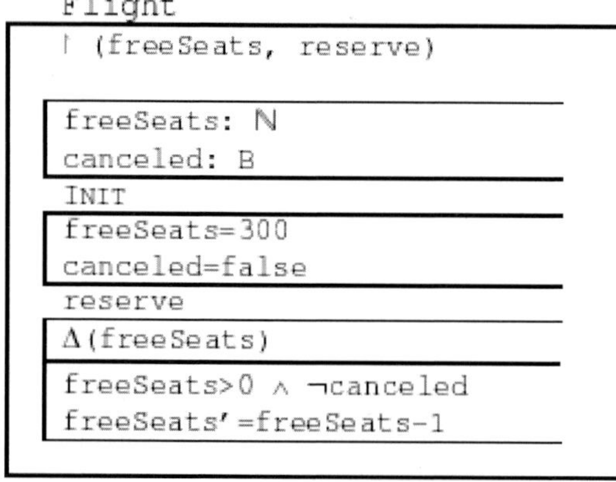

Fig. 1. Simple Object-Z schema

Object-Z is equipped with a schema calculus (i.e., a set of operators provided to manipulate Object-Z schemas). The schema calculus makes it possible to create Object-Z specifications describing properties of other Object-Z specifications. To deal with refinements we need to apply at least the following operators:

- Operator STATE denotes the set of all possible states (i.e., snapshots or bindings) of the system under consideration. For example, Flight. STATE = $\{\langle \text{freeSeats=x, canceled=t} \rangle \mid 0 \leq x \leq 300 \wedge t \in \{\text{true, false}\}\}$

- Operator INIT denotes the initial states of a given schema. For example, Flight.INIT=$\{\langle \text{freeSeats=300 , canceled=false} \rangle \mid \rangle\}$

- Operator pre returns the precondition of an operation schema; that is to say the set of all states where the operation can be applied. For example, pre reserve = $\{\langle \text{freeSeats=x, canceled=false} \rangle \mid 0<x\leq 300\}$

- The conjunction of two schemas S and T ($S \wedge T$) results in a schema which includes both S and T (and nothing else).

- Schema implication ($S \Rightarrow T$) denotes the usual logical implication.

In [4], refinement is formally addressed in the context of Object-Z specifications as follows: an Object-Z class C is a refinement (through downward simulation) of the class A if there is a *retrieve relation* R on A.STATE∧C.STATE so that every visible abstract operation A.op is recasted into a visible concrete operation C.op, thus the following holds:

(Initialization) $\forall$C.STATE • C.INIT $\Rightarrow$($\exists$A.STATE • A.INIT $\wedge$ R)

(Applicability) $\forall$A.STATE • $\forall$C.STATE• R $\Rightarrow$ (pre A.op $\Rightarrow$ pre C.op)

(Correctness) $\forall$A.STATE•$\forall$C.STATE•$\forall$C.STATE'•

R $\wedge$ pre A.op $\wedge$ C.op $\Rightarrow$ $\exists$A.STATE'• R' $\wedge$ A.op

This definition allows preconditions to be weakened and non-determinism to be reduced. In particular, applicability requires a concrete operation to be defined wherever the abstract operation was defined, however it also allows the concrete operation to be defined in states for which the precondition of the abstract operation was false. That is, the precondition of the operation can be weakened. Correctness requires that a concrete operation be consistent with the abstract one whenever applied in a state where the abstract operation is defined. However, the outcome of the concrete operation only has to be consistent with the abstract, but not identical. Thus if the abstract operation allowed a number of options, the concrete operation is free to use any subset of these choices. In other words, non-determinism can be solved.

On the other hand, the standard modeling language UML [15] provides an artifact named *Abstraction* (a kind of Dependency) with the stereotype <<refine>> to explicitly specify the refinement relationship between UML named model elements. In the UML metamodel an Abstraction is a directed relation from a *client* (or clients) to a *supplier* (or suppliers) stating that the client (the refinement) depends on the supplier (the abstraction). The Abstraction artifact has a meta-attribute called *mapping* designated to record the abstraction/implementation mappings (i.e., the counterpart to the Object-Z *retrieve relation*), which is an explicit documentation of how the properties of an abstract element are mapped to its refined versions, and on the opposite direction, how concrete elements can be simplified to fit an abstract definition. The mapping contains an expression stated in a given language that could be formal or not. The definition of refinement in the UML standard [15] is formulated using natural language and it remains open to numerous contradictory interpretations.

3 Verification Strategy for UML Refinement Patterns

UML refinement patterns [12] [19] [20] document recurring refinement structures in UML models. In this section we present a process to be applied on UML models containing such patterns in order to automatically create OCL refinement conditions to analyze them in a rigorous way. Figure 2 gives a description of the process at a glance. It is based on a pipeline architecture in which the analysis is carried out by a sequence of steps. The output of each step provides the input to the next one. In this section we give a brief overview of each step:

Refinement pattern instantiation. Each refinement pattern P consists of two parts: a description M of the Pattern structure, given in terms of UML diagrams and a generic constraint F expressed in Object-Z representing refinement condition for such pattern. Given a UML model M1 compliant with the structure of pattern P, the first step of the process automatically generates an instance F1 of the generic formula F that establishes the conditions to be fulfilled by M1 in order to verify the refinement.

Transformation to OCL. After being generated, the Object-Z formula F1 is automatically translated into the OCL formula F1' by applying the transformation **T** (the detailed definition of **T** is included in the appendix).

Micromodels strategy application. In this step, the micromodels strategy is applied to F1' in order to produce a formula F1'' which is analyzable within a limited scope.

OCL Evaluation. Finally, F1'' is submitted to an ordinary OCL evaluator.

The process is assisted by the automated tool ePlatero [6] that is a plug-in to the Eclipse development environment; ePlatero implements the verification process described above.

In the following sections this process is illustrated through a concrete example: the state refinement pattern [19].

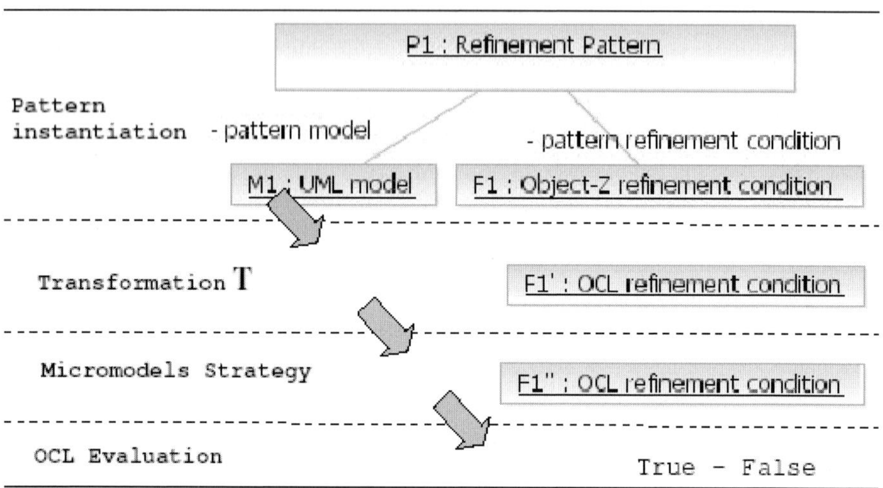

Fig. 2. Overview of the refinement verification process

3.1 The State Refinement Pattern

A State Refinement takes place when the data structures which were used to represent the objects in the abstract specification are replaced by more concrete or suitable structures; operations are accordingly redefined to preserve the behavior defined in the abstract specification.

An instance of the pattern's structure

Let M1 be the UML model in figure 3, which is compliant with the structure of the state refinement pattern [19]. M1 contains information about a flight booking system where each flight is abstractly described by the quantity of free seats in its cabin; then a refinement is produced by recording the total capacity of the flight together with the quantity of reserved seats. In both specifications, a Boolean attribute is used to represent the state of the flight (open or canceled). The available operations are `reserve` to make a reservation of one seat and `cancel` to cancel the entire flight. A refinement relationship connects the abstract to the concrete specification. The OCL language [16] has been used to specify initial values, operation's pre and post conditions and the mapping attached to the refinement relationship.

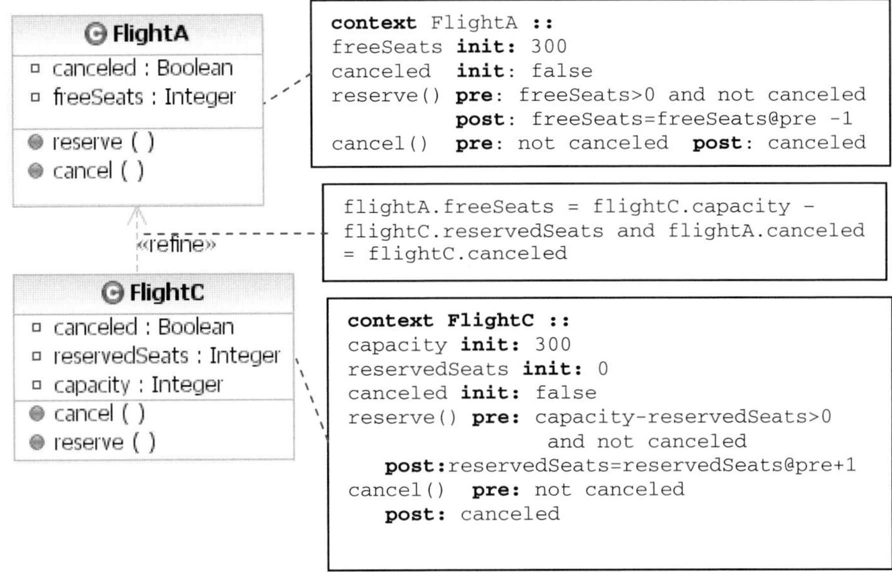

Fig. 3. an instance of the state refinement pattern

An instance of the pattern's refinement condition

Object-Z refinement conditions - F1 - for UML classes FlightA and FlightC via some retrieve relation R are automatically generated from the generic refinement condition established by the pattern [19], based on the definition of downward simulation in Object-Z described in [4]. Figure 4 shows the formula F1.

Initialization

$$\forall \text{FlightC.STATE} \bullet \text{FlightC.}\mathit{INIT} \Rightarrow (\exists \text{ FlightA.STATE} \bullet \text{FlightA.}\mathit{INIT} \wedge \text{R})$$

Applicability (for operation reserve)

$$\forall \text{FlightA.STATE} \bullet \forall \text{FlightC.STATE} \bullet$$
$$\text{R} \Rightarrow (\text{pre FlightA.reserve} \Rightarrow \text{pre FlightC.reserve})$$

Correctness (for operation reserve)

$$\forall \text{FlightA.STATE} \bullet \forall \text{FlightC.STATE} \bullet \forall \text{FlightC.STATE'} \bullet \text{R} \wedge$$
$$\text{pre FlightA.reserve} \wedge \text{FlightC.reserve} \Rightarrow \exists \text{ FlightA.STATE'} \bullet \text{R'} \wedge \text{FlightA.reserve}$$

Fig. 4. An instance of the refinement condition for the state refinement pattern

The transformation process from object-Z to OCL

Then, Object-Z refinement condition - F1 - is automatically transformed into OCL expression – F1' - by applying the transformation ***T*** in the context of a UML model

M1. Apart from producing an OclExpression, ***T*** returns an OclFile containing additional definitions, which are created during the transformation process:

```
T : Model-> ObjectZpredicate -> (OclExpression,OclFile)
```

The main features of the transformation are as follows,

Remark #1: *The Object-Z retrieve relation R is replaced by its OCL counterpart.*

Graphically, the abstraction mapping (i.e., the retrieve relation) describing the relation between the attributes in the abstract element and the attributes in the concrete element is attached to the refinement relationship; however, OCL expressions can only be written in the context of a Classifier, but not of a Relationship. On the Z side, the context of the abstraction mapping is the combination of the abstract and the concrete states (i.e., A.STATE $\wedge$ C.STATE); however, a combination of Classifiers is not an OCL legal context. Our solution consists in translating the mapping into an OCL formula in the context of the abstract classifier, in the following way:

```
  context flightA:FlightA def :
  mapping(flightC : FlightC):Boolean =
  flightA.freeSeats= flightC.capacity - flightC.reservedSeats
and flightA.canceled= flightC.canceled
```

As a convention, class names in lower case are used to denote instances. It is worth mentioning that the mapping definition could alternatively have been translated into a formula in the context of the concrete classifier.

Formally*:*

```
TM (relationName) = (e,Φ)
    Where:
    e = absInstance ".mapping(" refInstance ")"
    Φ = "package" packageName
        "context a:" AbstractClass  "def:"
        "mapping(c:" RefinedClass "):Boolean =" exp
      "endPackage"
    Where:
    d = M.getEnvironmentWithParents().lookup(relationName)
    AbstractClass  = d.supplier.name
    RefinedClass = d.client.name
    absInstance = toLowerCase(AbstractClass)
    refInstance = toLowerCase(RefinedClass)
    exp = d.mapping.body
    packageName = abstractClass.package.name
```

***Remark #2:** Object-Z expression INIT is expressed in terms of an OCL boolean operation* `isInit()`*.*

A query operation `isInit()` is automatically built from the specification of the attribute's initial values included in the UML class diagram. It returns *true* if all of the instance's attributes satisfy the initialization conditions. For example:

```
context FlightA def: isInit(): Boolean =
self.freeSeats = 300 and self.canceled = false

context FlightC def: isInit(): Boolean =
self.capacity=300 and self.canceled=false and
self.reservedSeats=0
```

In cases where the refinement involves composite classes, the initialization condition is built in terms of the initialization of each component; additionally, information provided for each composite association (e.g., multiplicity) is taken into consideration.

Formally:

```
T_M (className.INIT) =(e,Φ)
    Where
    e= toLowerCase(className) ".isInit()"
    Φ = "Package" packageName_1
        "context" className "def: isInit(): Boolean ="
        attName_1"="exp_1"and"..."and" attName_n"="exp_n "and"
        navigationName_1"->size() =" size_1 "and"
        navigationName_1 "->forAll(p| p.isInit())"..."and"
        navigationName_n"->size() =" size_n "and"
        navigationName_n "->forAll(p| p.isInit())"
        "endPackage"
    Where
    packageName = class.package.name
     class : UMLClass =
            M.getEnvironmentWithParents().lookup(className)
     attributes: Sequence(UMLProperty) =
            class.allProperties()->select(p|p.initialValue-
     >notEmpty())
     ∀j×1≤j≤attributes->size()• attName_j = attributes-
     >at(j).name ∧ exp_j = attributes->at(j).initialValue.body
     navigations: Sequence(UMLProperty) =
            class.allProperties()->select(p|p.association-
     >notEmpty() and p.isComposite())
     ∀j×1≤j≤navigations->size()• navigationName_j = navigations-
     >at(j).name ∧ size_j = navigations->at(j).lower
```

Remark #3: *Expressions containing the Object-Z operator "pre" are translated into the corresponding OCL pre conditions from the UML model.*

For example, the Object-Z expression "**pre** `FlightA.reserve`" is translated into "`flightA.freeSeats>0` **and not** `flightA.canceled`"

While, the expression "**pre** `FlightC.reserve`" is translated into "`flightC.capacity-flightC.reservedSeats>0` **and not** `flightC.canceled`"

Remark #4: *Object-Z expressions containing operation's invocations are translated to OCL post conditions from the UML model.*

In Object-Z, elements belonging to the pre-state are denoted by undecorated identifiers, while elements in the post-state are denoted by identifiers with a decoration (i.e. a stroke). In OCL the naming convention goes exactly in the opposite direction, that is to say, undecorated names refer to elements in the post-state. Then, in order to be consistent with the rest of the specification, a decoration (i.e., "_post") is added to each undecorated identifier in the post condition and the original decoration (i.e., @pre) is removed from the rest of the identifiers. For example the following definition:

```
context FlightA::reserve()
 post: self.freeSeats= self.freeSeats@pre -1
```

is renamed to:

```
context FlightA::reserve()
 post: flightA_post.freeSeats= flightA.freeSeats -1
```

Remark #5: *Logic connectors and quantifiers are translated to OCL operators.*

The Z expression `∀S.STATE•exp` is translated to `S.allInstances()->forAll(s | T(expr))`. While the Z expression `∃S.STATE•exp` is translated to `S.allInstances()->exists(s| T(expr))`.

For example, the translation for the universal quantifiers is as follows:

```
TM( ∀ className.STATE • Predicate) = (e,Φ)
    Where
    TM(Predicate)= (e1, Φ)
    e=className".allInstances()->forAll("iteratorName"|"e1")"
    iteratorName= toLowerCase(className)
```

Notice that the name of the class, in lower case, is used to name the iterate variable. Finally, the symbol $\Rightarrow$ is translated to ***implies*** and the symbol $\wedge$ is translated to ***and***,

T_M(Predicate1 $\wedge$ Predicate2)= (e,Φ)

Where

T_M(Predicate1)= (e1, Φ1)

T_M(Predicate2)= (e2, Φ2)

e= e1 "**and**" e2

Φ = Φ1 *merge* Φ2

On top of the formal definition of **T** the transformation process was fully automated [6]. Table 1 shows the formula F1' that is the result of applying the transformation **T** on both the UML model M1 (figure 3) and the Object-Z refinement conditions F1 (figure 4).

Table 1. OCL refinement conditions for an instance of the state refinement pattern

	OCL refinement condition
Initialization	FlightC.allInstances()->*forAll*(flightC| flightC.isInit() *implies* (FlightA.allInstances()-> *exists*(flightA| flightA.isInit()*and* flightA.mapping(flightC))))
Applicability	FlightA.allInstances()-> *forAll*(flightA| FlightC.allInstances()-> *forAll*(flightC| flightA.mapping(flightC) *implies* (flightA.freeSeats>0 *and* *not* flightA.canceled *implies* flightC.capacity-flightC.reservedSeats>0 *and not* flightC.canceled)))
Correctness	FlightA.allInstances()-> *forAll*(flightA| FlightC.allInstances() -> *forAll*(flightC| FlightC.allInstances()-> *forAll*(flightC_post| flightA.mapping(flightC)*and* (flightA.freeSeats>0 *and* *not* flightA.canceled) *and* (flightC_post.reservedSeats = flightC.reservedSeats+1) *implies* FlightA.allInstances()-> *exists*(flightA_post| flightA_post.mapping(flightC_post) *and* flightA_post.freeSeats= flightA.freeSeats -1))))

3.2 Further Patterns

A vast number of refinement patterns can be specified and verified following the method described in the preceding section, for example:

- *Object decomposition refinement pattern* is a form of refinement in which an abstract element is described in more detail by revealing its interacting internal components and conversely, the composite represents its components in sufficient detail in all contexts in which the fact of being composed is not relevant.
- *Atomic operation refinement pattern* occurs in the case that a more concrete specification is obtained from an abstract specification by replacing any operation Aop_k by its refinement Cop_k. The refined operation reduces non-determinism and/or partiality present in the abstract operation.
- *Non-atomic operation refinement pattern* takes place when the abstract operation is refined not by one, but by a combination of concrete operations, thus allowing a change of granularity in the specification. Non-atomic refinements are useful because they allow the initial specification to be described independently of the structure of the eventual implementation. Also it enables considerations of efficiency to be gradually introduced.
- *Promotion pattern* illustrates an elegant relationship between promotion and refinement, under certain circumstances the promotion of a refinement is a refinement of a promotion [4].

Additionally, complex model transformations, such as the application of most GoF design patterns and the use of refactoring can be specified as a composition of the simpler patterns described above.

4 Micro-worlds for Evaluating Refinement Conditions

Even little models such as the one described in figure 3 specify an infinite number of instances; thus to decide whether a certain property holds or not in the model results generally unfeasible. In order to make the evaluation of refinement conditions viable, the technique of micromodels (or micro-worlds) of software is applied by defining a finite bound on the size of instances and then checking whether all instances of that size satisfy the property under consideration:

- If we get a positive answer, we are somewhat confident that the property holds in all worlds. In this case, the answer is not conclusive, because there could be a larger world which fails the property, but nevertheless a positive answer gives us some confidence.
- If we get a negative answer, then we have found a world which violates the property. In that case, we have a conclusive answer, which is that the property does not hold in the model.

Jackson's small scope hypothesis [9] states that negative answers already tend to occur in small worlds, boosting the confidence we may have in a positive answer. For example, in order to generate suitable micro-worlds to evaluate the refinement conditions of class diagram in figure 3, the OCL package shown in figure 5, containing invariants that reduce the size of the micro-world, is provided.

```
package flights
    context FlightA
        inv: Set { 0 .. 300 } -> includes (self.freeSeats)
    context FlightC
        inv: Set {300} -> includes (self.capacity)
        inv: self.reservedSeats <= self.capacity
 endpackage
```

Fig. 5. OCL invariants reducing the search space

Apart from satisfying all the OCL invariants reducing the search space, to be suitable to analyze refinement relationships, the micro-worlds should satisfy the "*duality property*". Such property establishes that for each instance of a concrete class there must exist at least an instance of the abstract class being related by the abstraction mapping. The automatic micro-world generation process implemented by the tool guarantees the fulfillment of the duality property.

Then the tool checks whether all micro-worlds of that size satisfy the refinement condition. For example, figure 6 displays one of the micro-worlds satisfying the invariants and the duality property. In such micro-world the expression FlightA.allInstances() returns a finite set of size three containing the objects FlightA1, FlightA2 and FlightA3, while FlightC.allInstances() returns a finite set of size three containing the objects FlightC1, FlightC2 and FlightC3.

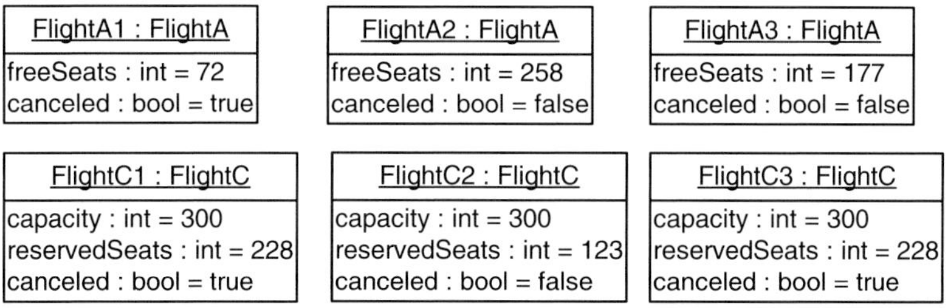

FlightA1 : FlightA	FlightA2 : FlightA	FlightA3 : FlightA
freeSeats : int = 72	freeSeats : int = 258	freeSeats : int = 177
canceled : bool = true	canceled : bool = false	canceled : bool = false

FlightC1 : FlightC	FlightC2 : FlightC	FlightC3 : FlightC
capacity : int = 300	capacity : int = 300	capacity : int = 300
reservedSeats : int = 228	reservedSeats : int = 123	reservedSeats : int = 228
canceled : bool = true	canceled : bool = false	canceled : bool = true

Fig. 6. Micro-world automatically generated from the UML model in figure 3 enriched with the constraints in figure 5

In this context we have, for example, the following applicability condition for operation `reserve()`:

```
 Set{<FlightA1>, <FlightA2>, <FlightA3>} -> forAll (flightA |
 Set{<FlightC1>, <FlightC2>, <FlightC3>}  -> forAll(flightC |
flightA.mapping(flightC) implies (flightA.freeSeats>0 and not
flightA.canceled   implies flightC.capacity -
flightC.reservedSeats>0 and not flightC.canceled)))
```

This expression is easily evaluated by an ordinary OCL evaluator, returning a positive answer, which gives us some confidence that the property holds.

Lets explore a case where the refinement conditions are not satisfied; lets consider for example that preconditions were strengthened in class FlightC as follows,

```
context FlightC :: reserve()
pre:self.capacity-self.reservedSeats>200 and notself.canceled
```

Then, the property to be checked would be,

```
 Set{<FlightA1>, <FlightA2>, <FlightA3>} -> forAll (flightA |
 Set{<FlightC1>, <FlightC2>, <FlightC3>} -> forAll(flightC |
flightA.mapping(flightC) implies (flightA.freeSeats>0 and not
flightA.canceled implies flightC.capacity -
flightC.reservedSeats >200 and not flightC.canceled)))
```

which evaluates false in the micro-world in figure 6, as follows:

```
flightA3.mapping(flightC2)= true
flightA3.freeSeats>0 and not flightA3.canceled = true
flightC2.capacity - flightC2.reservedSeats > 200  = false
```

giving the conclusive answer that the refinement property does not hold in this last model.

5 Conclusion

Each transformation step in the model driven software development process should be amenable to formal verification in order to guarantee the correctness of the final product. However, verification activities require the application of formal modeling languages with a complex syntax and semantics and need to use complex formal analysis tools; therefore, they are rarely used in practice.

To facilitate the verification task we developed an automatic method for creating refinement conditions for UML models, written in the standard and well-accepted OCL language. This is a lightweight approach that avoids the use of mathematical languages and tools that while ideal and suitable for the problem, will likely be unacceptable to developers.

The inclusion of verification in ordinary software engineering activities will be propitiated by encouraging the use of tools that are familiar and usable to MDE developers. The disadvantages of this approach relate to soundness and completeness; while the approach is rigorous, it is not formal and thus it is not possible to verify that the definition is sound and complete.

To complement such method, we adapted a strategy for reducing the search scope in order to make the evaluation of refinement conditions feasible. Since the satisfiable formulas that occur in practice tend to have small models, a small scope usually suffices and the analysis is reliable.

Acknowledgement. This work was partially funded by Universidad Abierta Interamericana (UAI), through the project ?Software modelling: a formal approach?.

References

[1] Astesiano E., Reggio G. An Algebraic Proposal for Handling UML Consistency", Workshop on Consistency Problems in UML-based Software Development. UML Conference , San Francisco, USA (2003).

[2] Boiten E.A. and Bujorianu M.C. Exploring UML refinement through unification. Proceedings of the UML'03 workshop on Critical Systems Development with UML, J. Jurjens, B. Rumpe, et al., editors -TUM-I0323, Technische Universitat Munchen. (2003).

[3] Davies J. and Crichton C. Concurrency and Refinement in the Unified Modeling Language. Electronic Notes in Theoretical Computer Science 70,3, Elsevier, 2002.

[4] Derrick, J. and Boiten,E. Refinement in Z and Object-Z. Foundation and Advanced Applications. FACIT, Springer. (2001)

[5] Engels G., Küster J., Heckel R. and Groenewegen L. A Methodology for Specifying and Analyzing Consistency of Object Oriented Behavioral Models. Procs. of the IEEE Int. Conference on Foundation of Software Engineering. (2001).

[6] ePlatero. http://sol.info.unlp.edu.ar/eclipse.

[7] Favre Jean-Marie, Estublier Jacky, Blay Mireille. Beyond MDA : Model Driven Engineering (L'Ingénierie Dirigée par les Modèles : au-délà du MDA) Edition Hezmes-Lavoisier, ISBN 2-7462-1213-7. Février 2006.

[8] Gogolla , Martin, Bohling, Jo¨rn and Richters, Mark. Validation of UML and OCL Models by Automatic Snapshot Generation. In G. Booch, P.Stevens, and J. Whittle, editors, Proc. 6th Int. Conf. Unified Modeling Language (UML'2003). Springer, LNCS 2863, (2003).

[9] Jackson, Daniel, Shlyakhter, I. and Sridharan. A micromodularity Mechanism. In proceedings of the ACM Sigsoft Conference on the Foundation of Software Engineering FSE'01. (2001).

[10] Kim, S. and Carrington, D., Formalizing the UML Class Diagrams using Object-Z, proceedings UML´99 Conference, Lecture Notes in Computer Sciencie 1723 (1999).

[11] Lano,K., Biccaregui,J., Formalizing the UML in Structured Temporal Theories, 2nd. ECOOP Workshop on Precise Behavioral Semantics, TUM-I9813, (1998).

[12] Lano, Kevin, Androutsopolous, Kelly and Clark David. Refinement Patterns for UML. Proceedings of REFINE'2005. Elsevier Electronic Notes in Theoretical Computer Science 137. pages 131-149 (2005).

[13] Ledang, Hung and Souquieres, Jeanine. Integration of UML and B Specification Techniques: Systematic Transformation from OCL Expressions into B. Procs. of IEEE Asia-Pacific Software Engineering Conference 2002. December 4-6, (2002).

[14] Liu, Z., Jifeng H., Li, X. Chen Y. Consistency and Refinement of UML Models. 3er Workshop on Consistency Problems in UML-based Software Development III, event of the UML Conference, (2004).

[15] OMG - UML 2.0. The Unified Modeling Language Superstructure version 2.0 – OMG Final Adopted Specification.. http://www.omg.org. August 2003

[16] OCL 2.0. OMG Final Adopted Specification. October 2003.

[17] Object Management Group, *MDA Guide*, v1.0.1, omg/03-06-01, June 2003.

[18] Paige, R., Kolovos D. and Polack,F. Refinement via Consistency Checking in MDD. In REFINE'2005. Electronic Notes in Theoretical Computer Science 137. (2005).

[19] Pons Claudia. On the definition of UML refinement patterns. Workshop MoDeVa at ACM/IEEE 8th Int. Conference on Model Driven Engineering Languages and Systems (MoDELS) Jamaica. October 2005.

[20] Pons Claudia. Heuristics on the Definition of UML Refinement Patterns. 32nd International Conference on Current Trends in Theory and Practice of Computer Science. SOFSEM. Lecture Notes in Computer Science LNCS number 3831. Springer (2006)
[21] QVT Partners revised submission to QVT 1.1 (ad/2003-08-08).
[22] Richters, Mark and Gogolla, Martin. OCL-Syntax, Semantics and Tools. in Advances in Object Modelling with the OCL. Lecture Notes in Computer Science number 2263. Springer. (2001).
[23] Smith, Graeme. The Object-Z Specification Language. Advances in Formal Methods. Kluwer Academic Publishers. ISBN 0-7923-8684-1. (2000)
[24] Stahl, M Voelter. Model Driven Software Development. John Wiley, ISBN 0470025700, April 2006.
[25] Van Der Straeten, R., Mens,T., Simmonds, J. and Jonckers,V. Using description logic to maintain consistency between UML-models. In Proc. 6th International Conference on the Unified Modeling Language. Lecture Notes in Computer Science number 2863. Springer. (2003).

An OCL Semantics Specified with QVT*

Slaviša Marković and Thomas Baar

École Polytechnique Fédérale de Lausanne (EPFL)
School of Computer and Communication Sciences
CH-1015 Lausanne, Switzerland
{slavisa.markovic, thomas.baar}@epfl.ch

Abstract. Metamodeling became in the last decade a widely accepted tool to describe the (abstract) syntax of modeling languages in a concise, but yet precise way. For the description of the language's semantics, the situation is less satisfactory and formal semantics definitions are still seen as a challenge. In this paper, we propose an approach to specify the semantics of modeling languages in a graphical way. As an example, we describe the evaluation semantics of OCL by transformation rules written in the graphical formalism QVT. We believe that the graphical format of our OCL semantics has natural advantages with respect to understandability compared to existing formalizations of OCL's semantics. Our semantics can also be seen as a reference implementation of an OCL evaluator, because the transformation rules can be executed by any QVT compliant transformation engine.

1 Introduction

Modeling is an important activity in all engineering disciplines, including software development. While the general purpose modeling language UML has proven to be versatile enough for many different domains (see, e.g., chapter 1 of [1]), it has also been recognized that the structure and the behavior of the system under development can often be captured as well with a much simpler, *domain-specific* modeling language [2].

UML and DSLs have much in common. Their abstract syntax is usually defined by a metamodel and UML's core modeling concepts such as Class, Object, State, etc. can also be found, possibly under a different name, in many DSLs. If a DSL comprises a constraint language, i.e. a language to impose restrictions on the modeled system, then some core concepts of UML's constraint language OCL such as *model navigation*, *variable quantification* and *pre-defined functions* are likely to be used. In this paper, we present a new approach to define the semantics of constraint languages formally. We illustrate our approach on a rather complex example, the semantics of OCL, but since our technique is based on general techniques such as metamodeling and model transformation, the semantics of other constraint languages can be defined in a similar way.

* This work was supported by Swiss National Scientific Research Fund under the reference number 200020-109492/1.

O. Nierstrasz et al. (Eds.): MoDELS 2006, LNCS 4199, pp. 661–675, 2006.

Before sketching existing approaches to define the semantics of OCL it is worthwhile to reflect the purpose and semantics of UML diagrams that can also be used without OCL constraints. A diagrammatic UML model describes the structure and behavior of a system at a certain level of details. The structure of the system clarifies which *states* (in UML jargon also called *snapshots*) the system can have and the behavioral description imposes restrictions on system changes. The question on how a class diagram corresponds to the state space of the system it describes has particular relevance for our later considerations. This correspondence (or semantics) of class diagrams has been given in the literature in many different forms, e.g. by an informal description (see UML User Guide [1]), by a mapping of classes into a set-theoretic domain (see [3]), by a metamodel of the semantic domain. The metamodel for the semantic domain became in UML1.x a part of the UML language standard because it is the basis for *object diagrams*, which are used to visualize system states.

The purpose of an OCL constraint is to make the already existing diagrammatic UML model more precise. For instance, a constraint attached as an invariant to a class shrinks the statespace to those states of the system, in which the constraint is evaluated to *true*. A pair of OCL constraints $(preCond, postCond)$ attached as pre-/postcondition to an operation *op* means that the implementation of *op* can realize only those state transitions $(preState, postState)$, for which *postCond* is evaluated in *postState* to *true* whenever *preCond* is evaluated in *preS* to *true*. No matter for which purpose an OCL constraint is used (as an invariant, as a guard, within pre-/postcondition), the semantics of the constraint can always be reduced to the question, how the evaluation of a constraint in a given state is defined. In the literature, the evaluation function *eval* : CONSTRAINT x STATE $\rightarrow$ $\{true, false, undefined\}$ is defined either mathematically by structural induction over CONSTRAINT (see official OCL semantics, appendix A in [4]) or by embedding OCL into another logic [5]. While these two approaches have basically succeeded in describing the evaluation of OCL constraints in a formal, non-ambiguous manner, they still have some disadvantages. One drawback is the gap between OCL's official syntax definition (which is given as a metamodel) and the OCL syntax, given by structural induction, that is assumed in the semantics definition. The main, very related drawback, however, is understandability. We made the experience that many of our students, who learned OCL in our course, were quite reluctant to deepen their knowledge on OCL by reading the official mathematical semantics, just because it is presented in a format they are not very familiar with (in set theory). If the purpose of the semantics is to inform the prospective OCL users about all the details of the language, then the semantics should be given in a format OCL users are familiar with.

One technique how this can be achieved is metamodeling. Metamodels are already frequently used in abstract syntax definitions. Metamodels are very expressive and easy to understand for people who have a background in modeling (at least, these are our personal experiences we made with students). As mentioned above, metamodeling has already been applied to cover also the semantics of class diagrams. Even more, the section 'Semantics Described using UML' in

[4] presents already a metamodeling approach for the evaluation of OCL expressions. We took this approach as a starting point but added some important improvements. The most striking difference is how the evaluation process is modeled: In [4], evaluation is modeled by Evaluation-metaclasses whereas in our approach this is described by transformation rules written in QVT. We also changed the metamodel of the semantic domain significantly for many reasons; one was to have a better representation of predefined datatypes. Our approach has been implemented using the QVT engine provided by Together Architect for Eclipse.

To summarize, our semantics of OCL is specified with a metamodeling approach using MOF, OCL and QVT as a formalism at the metalevel. Since QVT depends also heavily on OCL, there is the natural question if our approach does not describe the OCL semantics in terms of OCL and thus has fallen into the trap of meta-circularity. We have avoided this trap because the semantics of the OCL used at the metalevel is given by an external mechanism, in our case by the semantics implemented by the QVT engine of Together Architect. The dependency of our semantics definition on a tool implementation might be seen as a drawback but for the purpose of our semantics – to help OCL users to deepen their knowledge on the peculiarities of OCL evaluation – this is not really an obstacle. Using a tool as an 'anchor' for our OCL semantics has also significant advantages such as automatic tool support (note that our OCL semantics is fully executable by QVT engines) and flexibility (users can easily adapt the OCL semantics to their needs).

The rest of the paper is organized as follows. In Sect. 2, we sketch our approach and show, by way of illustration, a concrete application scenario for our semantics. The steps the evaluator actually has to perform are formalized as graphical QVT rules in Sect. 3. Section 4 contains related work, while Sect. 5 draws some conclusion and points to problems, which we plan to address in the near future.

2 Our Metamodel Based Approach for OCL Evaluation

In this section we briefly review the technique and concepts our approach relies on and illustrate with a simple example the evaluation of OCL constraints.

2.1 Official Metamodels for UML/OCL

We base our semantics for OCL on the official metamodels for UML and OCL. We support the last finalized version of OCL 2.0 [4] but since this version still refers to UML1.5 [6] we were forced to support UML1.5 instead of UML2.0. Figures 1 and 2 show the parts of the UML and OCL metamodels that are relevant for this paper. Please note that Fig. 1 contains also in its upper part a metamodel of the semantic domain of class diagrams.

2.2 Changes in the OCL Metamodel

In order to realize our approach in a clear and readable way, we had to add some few metaassociations and -attributes to that part of the official metamodel

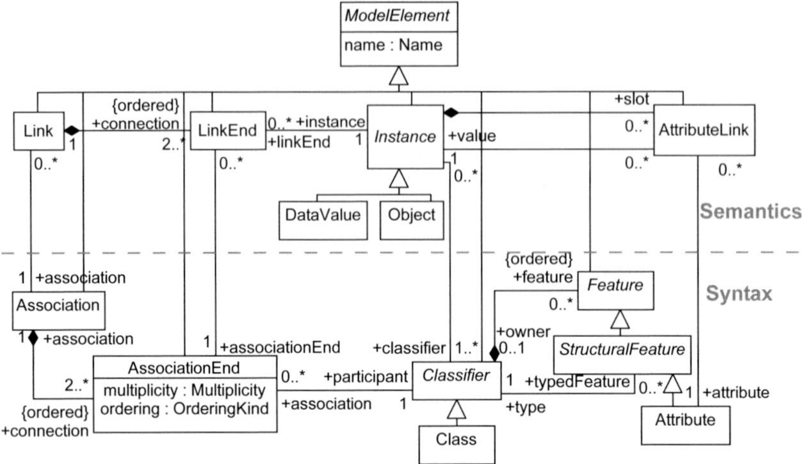

Fig. 1. Metamodel for Class Diagrams - Syntax and Semantics

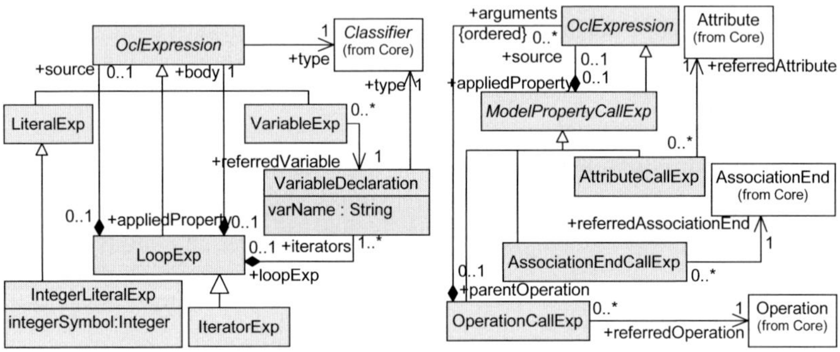

Fig. 2. Metamodel for OCL - Syntax

of OCL that describes the semantic domain of OCL evaluations (see Fig. 3). The metaclass *OclExpression* has a new association to *Instance*, what represents the evaluation of the expression in a given object diagram. We revised slightly the concepts of bindings (association between *OclExpression* and *NameValueBinding*) and added to class *IteratorExp* two associations *current* and *intermediateResult*, and one attribute *freshBinding*. Furthermore, the classes *StringValue*, *IntegerValue*, etc. have now attributes *stringValue*, *integerValue*, etc. what makes it possible to clearly distinguish a datatype object from its value.

2.3 Evaluation

We motivate our approach to define OCL's semantics with a small example. In Fig. 4, a simple class diagram and one of its possible snapshots is shown. The model consists of one class `Stock` with two attributes: `capacity` and `numOfItems`, both of type `Integer`, representing capacity of `Stock` and the current number of

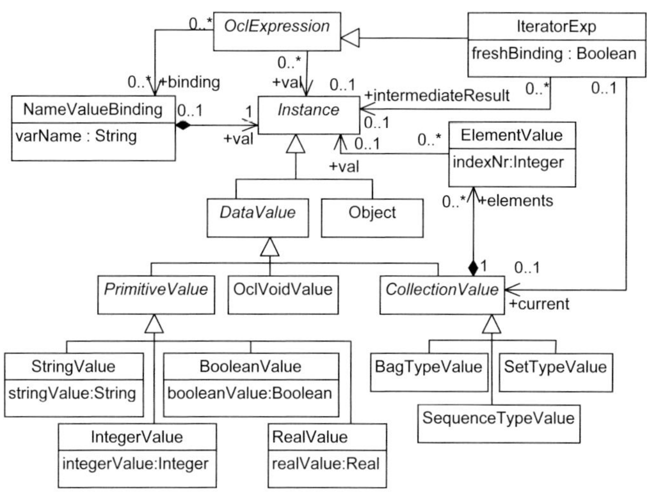

Fig. 3. Changed Metamodel for OCL - Semantics

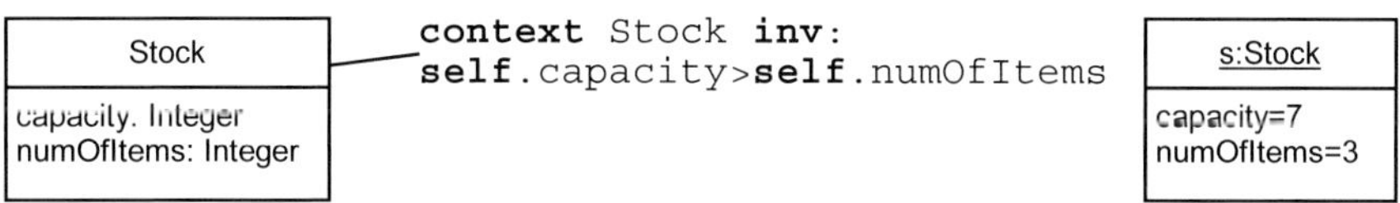

Fig. 4. Example - Class Diagram and Snapshot

items it has, respectively. The additional constraint attached to the class `Stock` requires that the current number of items in a stock must always be smaller than the capacity. The snapshot shown in the right part of Fig. 4 satisfies the attached invariant because for each instance of `Stock` (class `Stock` has only one instance in the snapshot) the value of `numOfItems` is less than the value of attribute `capacity`. In other words, the constraint attached to the class `Stock` is evaluated on object `s` to `true`.

In order to show how the evaluation of an OCL constraint is actually performed on a given snapshot, we present in Fig. 5 the simplified state of the Abstract Syntax Tree as it is manipulated by an OCL evaluator. Step (a)-(b) performs the evaluation of the leaf nodes. Depending on the results of these evaluations, step (b)-(c) performs evaluation of nodes at the middle level. Finally, the last step (c)-(d) performs evaluation of the top-level of the AST. Please note that in this example we were not concerned about concrete binding of the self variable. The problem of variable binding is discussed in Sect. 2.4.

The initial idea of our approach is that an OCL constraint can be analogously evaluated by annotating directly the OCL metamodel instance instead of the AST.

Figure 6 shows the instance of the OCL metamodel representing the invariant from Fig. 4. Here, we stipulate that all expressions have not been evaluated yet because for each expression the link *val* to metaclass *Instance* is missing.

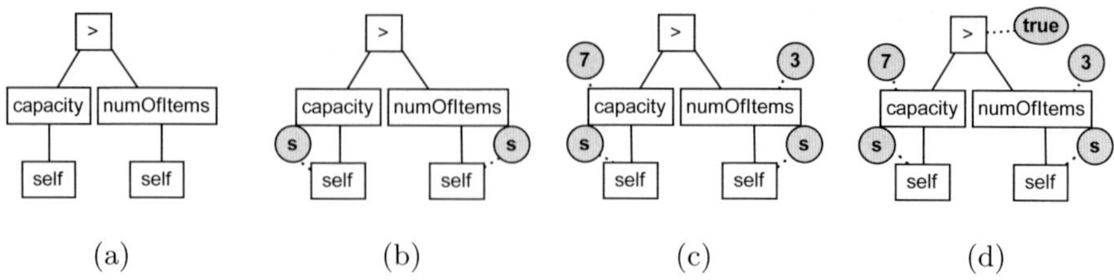

Fig. 5. Evaluation of OCL expressions seen as an AST: (a) Initial AST (b) Leaf nodes evaluated (c) Middle nodes evaluated (d) Complete AST evaluated

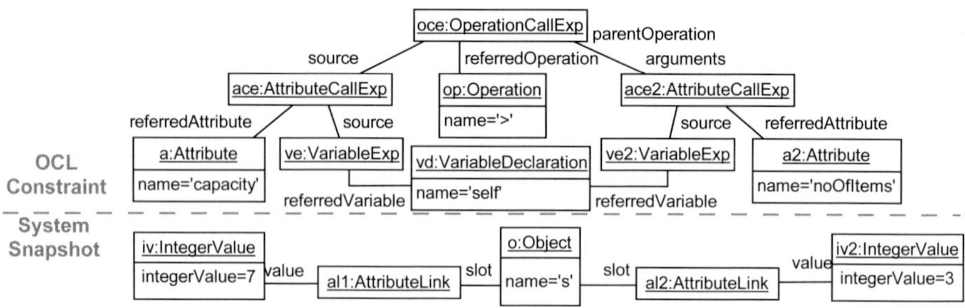

Fig. 6. OCL Constraint Before Evaluation

The state of the metamodel instance after the last evaluation step has been finished is shown in Fig. 7. What has been added compared to the initial state (Fig. 6) is highlighted by thick lines. The evaluation of the top-expression (*OperationCallExp*) is a *BooleanValue* with *booleanValue* attribute set to `true`, the two *AttributeCallExpressions* are evaluated to two *IntegerValues* with values 7 and 3, and each *VariableExp* is evaluated to *Object* with name `s`.

2.4 Binding

The evaluation of one OCL expression depends not only on the current system state on which the evaluation is performed but also on the binding of free variables to current values. The binding of variables is realized in the OCL metamodel by the class *NameValueBinding*, which maps one free variable name to one value. Every OCL expression can have arbitrarily many bindings, the only restriction is the uniqueness of variable names within the set of linked *NameValueBinding* instances.

In the invariant of the `Stock` example we have used one free variable `self`. Although `self` is a predefined variable in OCL, it can be treated the same way as all other variables, which are introduced in Iterator Expressions. For example, the invariant

```
self.capacity > self.numOfItems
```

can be rewritten as

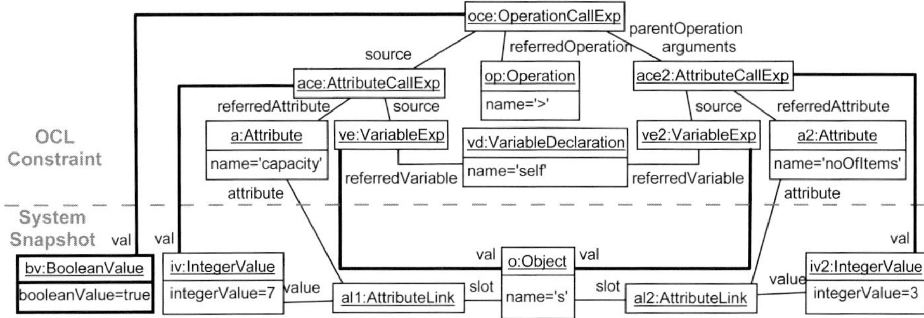

Fig. 7. OCL Constraint After Evaluation in a Given Snapshot

```
Stock.allInstances->forAll(self|
              self.capacity>self.numOfItems)
```

The binding of variables is done in a top-down approach. In other words, variable bindings are passed from an expression to all its sub-expressions. Some expressions do not only pass the current bindings, but also add/change bindings. An example for adding new value-name bindings will be explained in more details in Sect. 3 where the evaluation rules for *forAll* expressions are explained.

Figure 8 shows the process of binding passing on a concrete example. In the upper part, the initial situation is given: The top-expression already has one binding `nvb` for variable `self`. In the lower part of the figure, all subexpressions of the top-expression are bound to the same *NameValueBinding* as the top-expression.

3 Evaluation Rules Formalized in QVT

The previous section has shown the main idea of our approach: we annotate all intermediate results of a constraint evaluation directly to the instance of the OCL

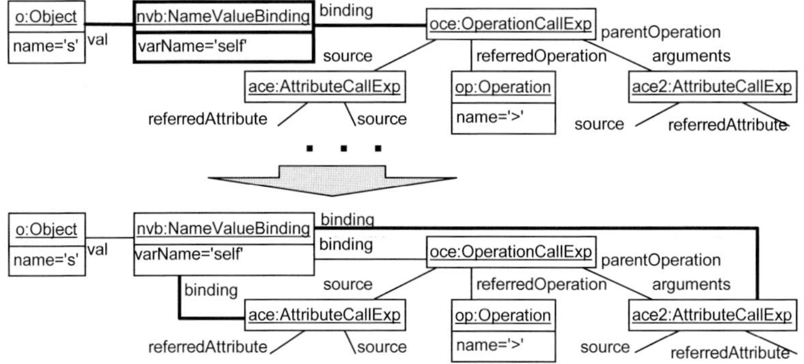

Fig. 8. Binding Passing

metamodel. What has not been specified yet are the evaluation steps themselves, for example, that an *AttributeCallExp* is always evaluated to the attribute value on that object to which the source expression of *AttributeCallExp* evaluates.

In this section, we specify these evaluation steps formally in form of QVT rules. These rules are minimal in the sense that they do not capture any optimization for an efficient evaluation nor impose any restrictions on the evaluation ordering, unless they are really necessary.

3.1 QVT

QVT is a recent OMG standard for model transformations (see [8] for a detailed account on QVT's semantics), which are described by a set of *transformation rules*. For our application scenario of QVT rules, source and target model are always instances of the same metamodel; the metamodel for UML/OCL including the small changes we have proposed in Sect. 2. Each QVT rule consists of two patterns (LHS, RHS), which are (incomplete) instantiations of the UML/OCL metamodel. When a QVT rule is applied on a given source model, a LHS matching sub model of the source model is searched. Then, the target model is obtained by rewriting the matching sub model by a new sub model that is derived from RHS under the same matching. If more than one QVT rule match on a given source model, one of them is non-deterministically applied. The model transformation terminates as soon as none of the QVT rules is applicable on the current model.

3.2 A Catalog of Rules

To specify the evaluation process, we have to formalize for each non-abstract subclass of metaclass *OclExpression* one or more QVT rules. Due to space limit, only the most important rules can be presented in this subsection. In order to give a representative selection of our rules, we categorized them according to the kind of expression they target: *Navigation Expressions*, *OCL Predefined Operations*, *Iterator Expressions*, and *Atomic Expressions*. For each category, we discuss one or two rules in detail. The main goal is to demonstrate that the evaluation of all kinds of OCL expressions can be formulated using QVT in an intuitive way.

Navigation Expressions. OCL expressions of this category are instances of *AttributeCallExp* and *AssociationEndCallExp*. Such expressions are evaluated by 'navigating' from the object, to which the source expression is evaluated, to that element in the object diagram, which is referenced by the attribute or association end. Before the source expression can be evaluated, the current binding of variables has to be passed from the parent expression to the sub expression. We show in Fig. 9 how the binding rule is defined for *AttributeCallExp*. When applying this rule, the binding of the parent object `ace` (represented by a link from `ace` to the multiobject `nvb` in LHS) is passed to subexpression `o` (a link from `o` to `nvb` is established in RHS). Analogous rules exist for all other kinds of OCL expressions which have subexpressions. For the (subclasses of) *LoopExp* (see below) one

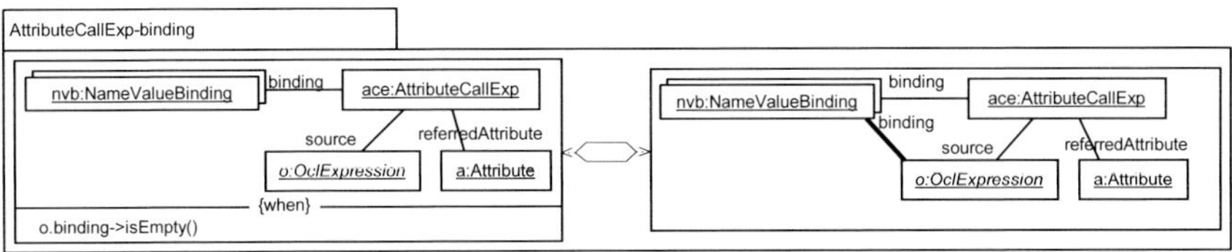

Fig. 9. Attribute Call Expression Bindings Passing

needs also additional rules for handling the binding because the subexpressions are evaluated under a different binding than the parent expression.

AttributeCallExp. The semantics of *AttributeCallExp* is specified by the rule *AttributeCallExp-evaluation* given in Fig. 10. The evaluation of `ace` is datavalue `d`, which is also the value of the attribute `a` for object `o`. Note, that we stipulate in the LHS, that `oc`, the source expression of `ace`, has been already evaluated to object `o`.

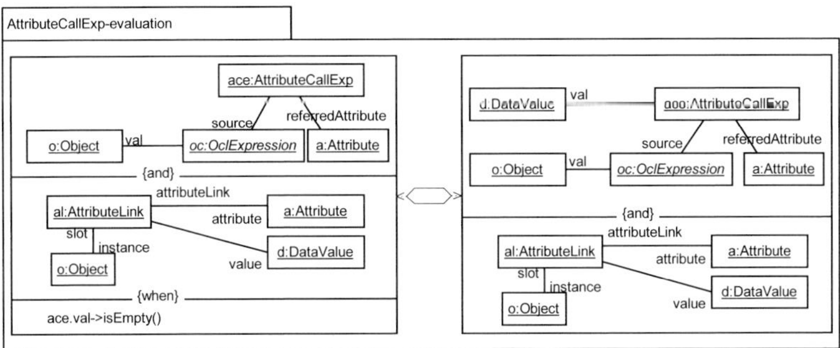

Fig. 10. Attribute Call Expression Evaluation

As the rule for *AttributeCallExp* shown in Fig. 10, all our QVT rules have two regions in the LHS and RHS patterns. The upper part of the patterns represents the expression that should be evaluated. The lower one specifies the system state on which the evaluation is performed. Since the evaluation of OCL rules does not have any side-effect on the system state, the lower parts of LHS and RHS will always coincide.

AssociationEndCallExp. We discuss here only the case of navigating to an unordered association end with multiplicity greater than 1 (the case of multiplicities equal to 1 is very similar to *AttributeCallExp*). The rule shown in Fig. 11 specifies that the value of `aece` is a newly created object of type *SetTypeValue* whose elements refer to all objects `o2` that can be reached from object `o` via a link for `ae`. Again, object `o` is the evaluation of source expression `oe`. The rule shown in Fig. 11 contains at few locations the multiplicities 1-1 at the link between two multiobjects, for example at the link between `le2` and `l`. This is an enrichment of the official QVT semantics on links between two multiobjects. Standard QVT semantics assumes that a link between two multiobject means that each object from the first multiobject is linked to every object from the second multiobject, and vice versa. This semantics is not appropriate for the situation shown in Fig. 11 where each element of multiobject `l` must be connected only to one element from multiobject `le2`, and vice versa. By using 1-1 multiplicities, we indicate a non-standard semantics of links between two multiobjects.

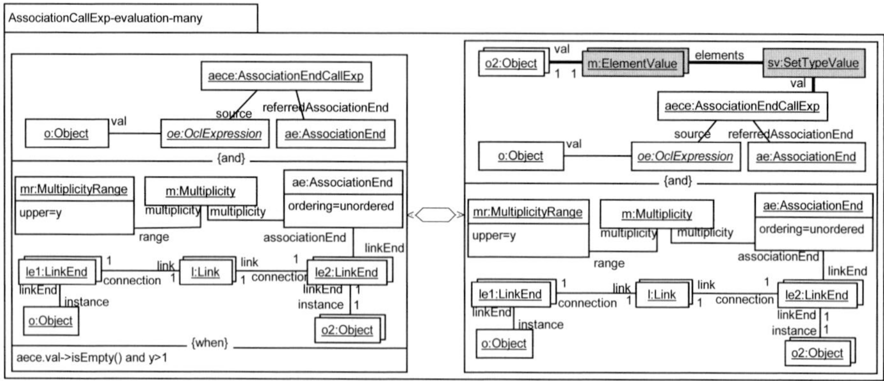

Fig. 11. Association End Call Expression Evaluation that Results in Set of Objects

OCL Predefined Operations. Expressions from this category are instances of the metaclass *OperationCallExp* but the called operation is a predefined one, such as +, =. These operations are declared and informally explained in the chapter on the OCL library in [4]. As an example, we explain in the following the semantics of operation "=" (equals). We show only two rules here, one specifies the evaluation of equations between two objects, and the other the evaluation of equations between two integers.

In Fig. 12, the evaluation is shown for the case that both subexpressions `oe1`, `oe2` are evaluated to two objects `o1` and `o2`, respectively. In this case, the result of the evaluation is `bv` of type *BooleanValue* with attribute *booleanValue* `b`, which is *true* if the evaluations of `oe1` and `oe2` are the same object, and *false* otherwise.

If `oe1` and `oe2` evaluate to *IntegerValue*, the second QVT rule shown in Fig. 13 is applicable and the result of evaluation will be an instance of *BooleanValue* with attribute *booleanValue* set to *true* if *integerValue* of `iv1` is equal to *integerValue* of `i2`, and to *false* otherwise.

Iterator Expressions. Iterator expressions are those in OCL which have as the main operator one from `select`, `reject`, `forAll`, `iterate`, `exists`, `collect` or `isUnique`. Since all these expressions can be expressed by macros based on `iterate`, it would be sufficient to refer for their semantics just to the semantics of `iterate`.

We show here nevertheless a semantics for `forAll`, that is independent from the semantics of `iterate`. The rules describing the semantics of `forAll` are,

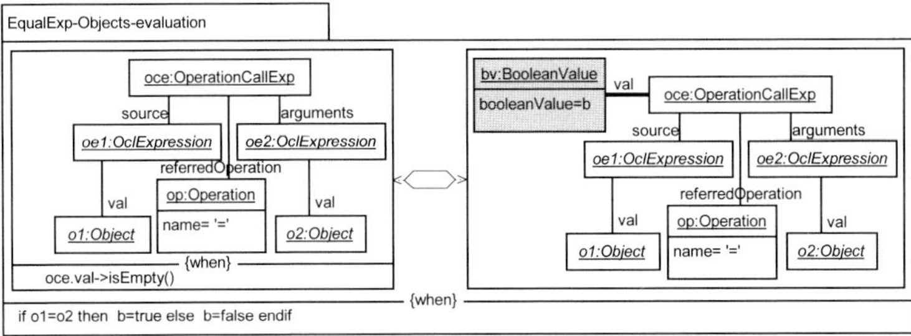

Fig. 12. Equal Operation Evaluation for Objects

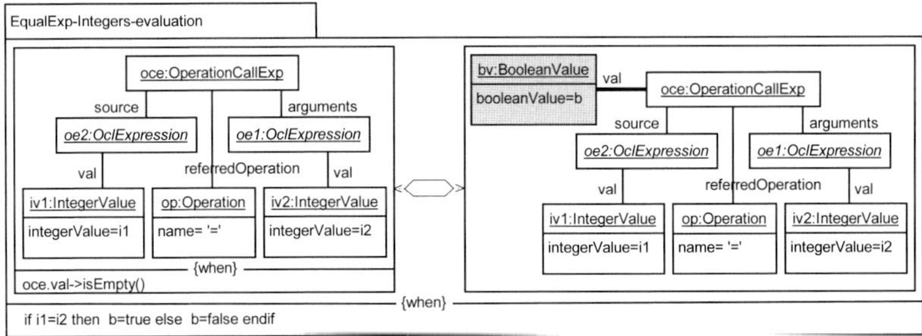

Fig. 13. Equal Operation Evaluation for Integers

compared with `iterate`, easier to understand, but contain already all mechanisms needed to describe `iterate`(see Fig. 14).

The rule *ForAll-Initialisation* makes a copy of evaluation of the source expression, and assigns it under the role *current* to `ie`. Furthermore, the role *intermediateResult* is initialized with *true* and, for some technical reasons, the attribute *freshBinding* of `ie` is set to *false* and the evaluation of body expression `oe` is also initialized with *true*.

The rule *ForAll-IteratorBinding* updates the binding on body expression `oe` for the iterator variable `v` with a new value `vp`. The element with the same value `vp` is chosen from the collection *current* and is removed afterwards from this collection. The attribute *freshBinding* is set to *true* and the evaluation of body expression `oe` is removed (note that the binding for `oe` has changed and the old evaluation of `oe` became obsolete).

The rule *ForAll-IntermediateEvaluation* updates the *intermediateResult* of `ie` based on the new evaluation of `oe`. Furthermore, the value of attribute *freshBinding* is flipped.

The final rule *ForAll-evaluation* covers the case when the collection `current` of `ie` is empty. In this case the value of `ie` is set to that value which *intermediateResult* currently has.

Atomic Expressions. This category consists of expressions such as *LiteralExp* and *VariableExp* that do not have any subexpressions. As an example we present

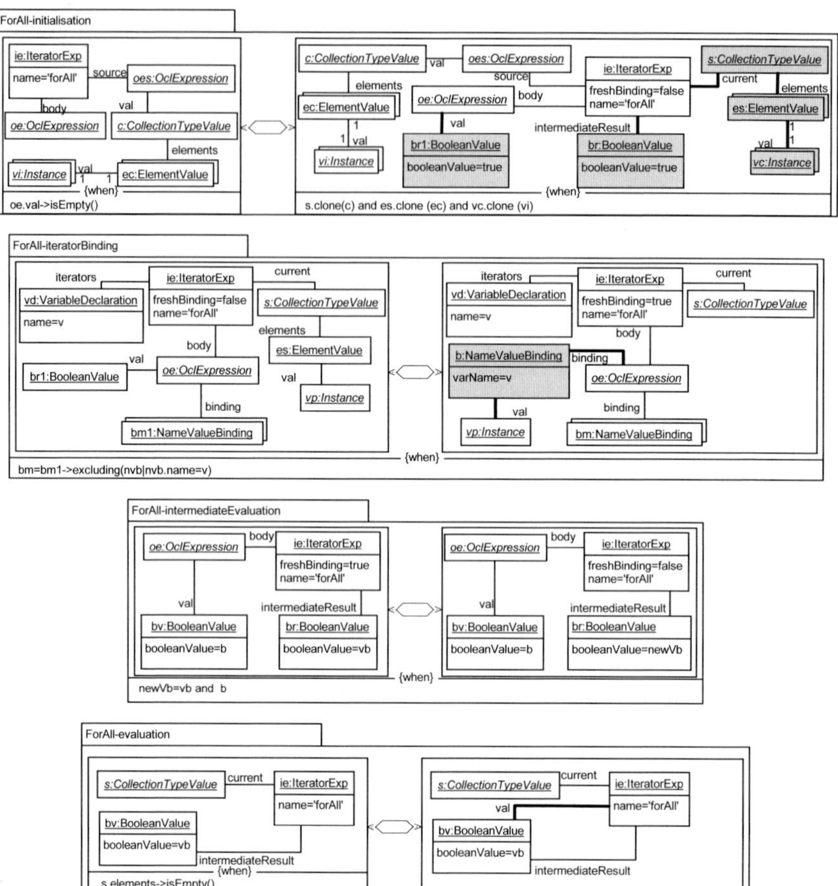

Fig. 14. ForAll - Evaluation Rules

rules for these two cases. In Fig. 15, the evaluation of *IntegerLiteralExp* is shown. By applying this rule, a new *IntegerValue* is created that refers to the same integer as attribute *integerSymbol* in `ie`. Note, that this type of expressions does not need variable bindings because their evaluation does not depend on the evaluation of any variable. Figure 16 shows the evaluation rule for *VariableExp*. When this rule is applied, a new link is created between *VariableExp* and the value to which *NameValueBinding*, with the same name as *VariableDeclaration*, is connected.

4 Related Work

The only paper we are aware of that shares similar interests in applying a graph-transformation based approach in order to deal with OCL constraints is [9]. In

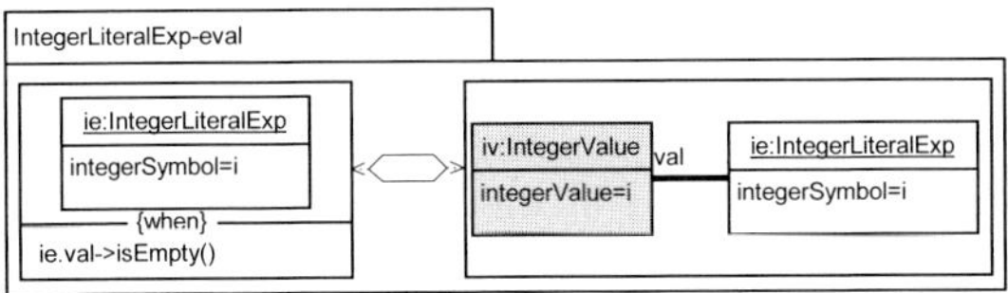

Fig. 15. Integer Literal Expression Evaluation

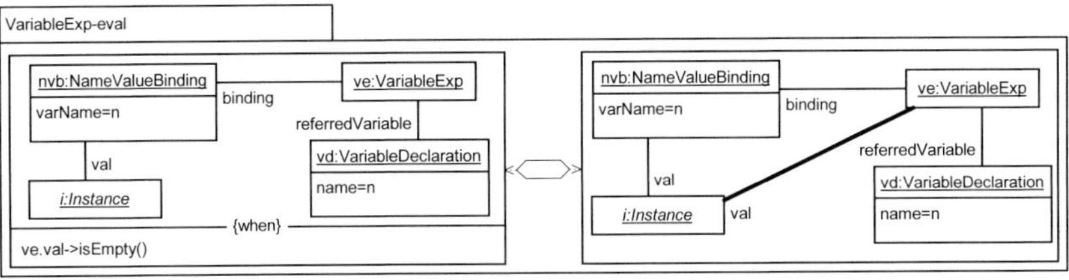

Fig. 16. Variable Expression Evaluation

this paper, a graphical visualization of OCL constraints is proposed. On top of this notation, simplification rules for OCL constraints are proposed, that implicitly also define a semantics for OCL. However, the semantics of OCL is not developed as systematically as in our approach, only the simplification rules for `select` are shown. Since [9] was published at a time where OCL did not have an official metamodel, the graph-transformation rules had to be based on another language definition.

For a different kind of languages, behaviorial languages, Engels et al. define in [10] their dynamic semantics in form of graph-transformation rules, which are similar to our QVT rules. As an example, the semantics of UML statechart diagrams is presented.

Stärk et al. define in [11] a formal semantics of Java. Even if they use a completely different notation to specify an operational semantics, we see nevertheless a lot of striking similarities. Stärk et al. map the state space of a Java program to an Abstract State Machine (ASM) and describe possible state changes by a set of ASM rules that manipulate the Abstract Syntax Tree of a program. As shown in our motivating example, there are no principal differences between an AST and an instance of the metamodel. Also, ASM and QVT rules are based on the same mechanisms (pattern matching and rewriting).

5 Conclusions and Future Work

We developed a metamodel-based, graphical definition of the semantics of OCL. Our semantics consists of a metamodel of the semantic domain (we slightly adapted existing metamodels from UML1.x) and a set of transformation rules written in QVT that specify formally the evaluation of an OCL constraint in a snapshot. To read our semantics, one does not need advanced skills in mathematics or even knowledge in formal logic; it is sufficient to have a basic understanding of metamodeling and QVT. The most important advantage, however, is the flexibility our approach offers to adapt the semantics of OCL to domain-specific needs. Since the evaluation rules can directly be executed by any QVT compliant tool, it is now very easy to provide tool support for a new dialect of OCL. This is an important step forward to the OMG's vision to treat OCL as a family of languages.

We are currently investigating how an OCL semantics given in form of QVT rules can be used to argue on the semantical correctness of refactoring rules for UML/OCL, which we have defined as well in form of QVT rules. A refactoring rule describes small changes on UML class diagrams with attached OCL constraints. A rule is considered to be *syntactically correct* if in all applicable situations the refactored UML/OCL model is syntactically well-formed. We call a rule *semantically correct* if in any given snapshot the evaluation of the original OCL constraint and the refactored OCL constraint yields to the same result (in fact, this view is a simplified one since the snapshots are sometimes refactored as well). To argue on semantical correctness of refactoring rules, it has been very handy to have the OCL semantics specified in the same formalism as refactoring rules, in QVT. A more detailed description together with a complete argumentation on the semantical correctness of the MoveAttribute refactoring rule can be found in [12].

Another branch of future activities is the description of the semantics of programming languages with graphical QVT rules. Our ultimate goal is to demonstrate that also the description of the semantics of a programming language can be given in an easily understandable, intuitive format. This might finally contribute to a new style of language definitions where the semantics of the language can be formally defined as easy and straightforward as it is today already the case with the syntax of languages.

References

1. Grady Booch, James Rumbaugh, and Ivar Jacobson. *The Unified Modeling Language User Guide*. Addison-Wesley, second edition, 2005.
2. Marjan Mernik, Jan Heering, and Anthony M. Sloane. When and how to develop domain-specific languages. *ACM Computing Surveys*, 37(4):316–344, 2005.
3. Mark Richters. *A precise approach to validating UML models and OCL constraints*. PhD thesis, Bremer Institut für Sichere Systeme, Universität Bremen, Logos-Verlag, Berlin, 2001.
4. OMG. UML 2.0 OCL Specification – OMG Final Adopted Specification. OMG Document ptc/03-10-14, Oct 2003.
5. Achim D. Brucker and Burkhart Wolff. A proposal for a formal OCL semantics in Isabelle/HOL. In Victor Carreño, César Muñoz, and Sofiène Tashar, editors, *TPHOLs*, volume 2410 of *LNCS*, pages 99–114. Springer, 2002.
6. OMG. UML 1.5 Specification. OMG Document formal/03-03-01, March 2003.
7. OMG. UML 2.0 Infrastructure Specification. OMG Document ptc/03-09-15, Sep 2003.

8. OMG. Meta object facility (MOF) 2.0 Query/View/Transformation Specification. OMG Document ptc/05-11-01, Nov 2005.
9. Paolo Bottoni, Manuel Koch, Francesco Parisi-Presicce, and Gabriele Taentzer. Consistency checking and visualization of OCL constraints. In *UML 2000*, volume 1939 of *LNCS*, pages 294–308. Springer, 2000.
10. Gregor Engels, Jan Hendrik Hausmann, Reiko Heckel, and Stefan Sauer. Dynamic meta modeling: A graphical approach to the operational semantics of behavioral diagrams in UML. In *UML 2000*, volume 1939 of *LNCS*, pages 323–337. Springer, 2000.
11. Robert F. Stärk, Joachim Schmid, and Egon Börger. *Java and the Java Virtual Machine - Definition, Verification, Validation.* Springer, 2001.
12. Thomas Baar and Slaviša Marković. A graphical approach to prove the semantic preservation of UML/OCL refactoring rules. In *Proceedings, Sixth International Andrei Ershov Memorial Conference , Perspectives of System Informatics (PSI), Novosibirsk, Russia*, LNCS. Springer, July 2006. To appear.

Specification of Invariability in OCL

Piotr Kosiuczenko*

Department of Computer Science
University of Leicester
piotr AT mcs.le.ac.uk

Abstract. The paradigm of contractual specification provides a transparent way of specifying systems. It clearly distinguishes between client and implementer obligations. One of the best known languages used for this purpose is OCL. Nevertheless, OCL does not provide primitives for a compact specification of what remains unchanged when a method is executed. In this paper, problems with specifying invariability are listed and some weaknesses of existing solutions are pointed out. The question of specifying invariability in OCL is studied and a simple but expressive and flexible extension is proposed. It is shown that this extension has a simple OCL based semantics.

1 Introduction

Contracts are the prevailing way of specifying systems from the client point of view (see [10]). They clearly assign responsibilities to client/caller and to system implementer/callee. They allow one to trace back a contract violation to the corresponding party. Unfortunately, the current high-level object-oriented specification languages, such as OCL [16], do not provide primitives to specify what can and what must not be changed when a method is executed. OCL allows explicit comparison of object attributes before and after method execution. A method execution usually changes only a small part of a system and consequently most of the system remains unchanged. In the case of large systems, it is not feasible to specify what happens with all attributes and associations. This problem is not restricted to object-oriented specification languages (see [2] for an overview). In general there exist three approaches to this problem: axiom frames, modifies clauses and nonmonotonic logics.

The axiom frames are used in artificial intelligence (cf. [11, 17]). The idea is to specify modification of attributes using axiom schemata. It requires explicit listing of all attributes which remain unchanged. This results in large number of frame formulas. In principle, it is possible to specify invariable system parts correctly, but of course it is error prone and not feasible in the case of large systems.

The second approach dates back to Hoare logic [7]. In this logic all variables which are not mentioned in the formulas of a Hoare triple are assumed to be unchanged. This works fine for verification of procedural programs, since all

* This research was partially supported by the EU project Leg2Net.

O. Nierstrasz et al. (Eds.): MoDELS 2006, LNCS 4199, pp. 676–691, 2006.

variables used in a procedure are plainly specified. However it does not work well for object-oriented specifications because of the encapsulation principle, which allows hiding private attributes of objects, and because of the fact that a method execution can have very complex side effects. In particular, it may result in changes to objects different from method's parameters. Java Modelling Language (JML, see [3] and the references there) provides compact specifications of invariable parameters [12]. It allows one for static checking of invariability properties. On the other hand, it is possible to specify invariability requirements, which cannot be check statically and in general the problem of what remains unchanged is undecidable.

The third approach uses nonmonotonic logics (see [17, 9] and the references there). It provides compact specifications and allows one to deal with side effects, but it is not appropriate for large specifications due to complex fixed-point semantics. The problem is that one specification may result in several fixed points and the number of such points may be high in the case of a large specification [9].

There exist an approach which relies on a completion procedure [2]; basically the specifier must specify for every method and every predicate the circumstances under which the predicate changes its truth value. Unfortunately, in the case of large systems it is not feasible. Interestingly, there exists also an approach allowing extending graph rewriting rules with invariability constraints [1].

Basically, the above mentioned approaches fall into two categories. Either they specify the system parts which don't change (frame axioms) or they specify the islands of change (JML, Hoare logic, nonmonotonic logics, design by contract advocated by Meyer). The problems with invariability specification can be classified as follows:

– oversize - huge formulas
– non-scalability - inability to deal with large specifications
– inflexibility - the user cannot customize the approach to specific needs
– fragility - the resulting formulas must be modified after every system change
– over-specification - the specification exposes details, which should be hidden

The need of extending OCL with primitives for specifying invariability has been recognized long time ago. For example, a working group was set to deal with this problem at "The Constraint Language for UML 2.0" workshop (a satellite workshop of UML'01 conference in Toronto).

OCL is a very expressive, high-level language for specification of object oriented systems [15] (see also [18]). There are tools for monitoring the satisfaction of OCL constraints (cf. e.g. [5]). This language can be used directly to specify what cannot change, but such specifications are usually very extensive, fragile, hard to understand and modify. What we need is a compact way of localizing change, with simple and monotone semantics.

In this paper, we propose a simple extension of OCL allowing us to specify invariability in a compact way. We delimit the islands of changes using appropriate primitives and we translate those primitives into "standard" OCL. Views proved to be a very powerful mean of specification and presentation (cf. [4, 13]). There are different specification styles as there are different oo-programming styles. A specification can be written from the client or from the implementer point of view; it can be restricted to a single component or package. Proposed extension allows us to specify systems from different points of view. In our approach, the specification of invariable part can be restricted to the appropriate view. With the help of the UML metamodel [16], we define the notion of view in the UML framework and restrict specification of invariability to views. The OCL formulas defining the user views may be sophisticated, but it is possible to define them in a generic way and to reuse them. One can also define a view corresponding to the implicit invariability assumption as it is used for example in Eiffel [6].

We study the usefulness of this extension in a series of examples and explain in which way it addresses the above mentioned problems. We show how to translate expressions containing invariability primitives into OCL. Thanks to this translation, our proposed extension has well defined semantics.

The paper is organized as follows. In Section 2, we consider a simple example and use it to explain problems with invariability specification; we indicate also a possible solution. In Section 3, we relate our extension to the UML metamodel and show how to define views. In Section 4, we present the formal syntax of proposed extension. In Section 5, we present the OCL based semantics of the extension. Section 6 concludes this paper.

2 Specification of Invariability

In this section, we consider a simple example of a bank account and explain problems with specification of invariability. We show how to specify invariability using a rather basic OCL extension, how to deal with inheritance and side effects.

2.1 Problems with Invariability Specification

Design by contract is a very powerful method of specifying class and component behaviour (cf. e.g. [10]). Unfortunately this approach may cause problems when a high level specification language such as OCL [15] is used.

Let us consider the class diagram shown on Fig. 1. We can specify the method *credit* in OCL in the following way:

context $p1::BankAccount::credit(amount : real)$
$post : self.balance = self.balance@pre + amount$

This specification does not mention what happens to the attribute *name*, to the association *os*, nor to the attribute *x*. Therefore we have to add the following frame formula:

$and\ self.name\ =\ self.name@pre$
$and\ self.os\ =\ self.os@pre$
$and\ self.os.x\ =\ self.os@pre.x@pre$

Moreover, to make this specification complete, we need a formula guaranteeing that all objects of the class *BankAccount* different from *self* are not influenced

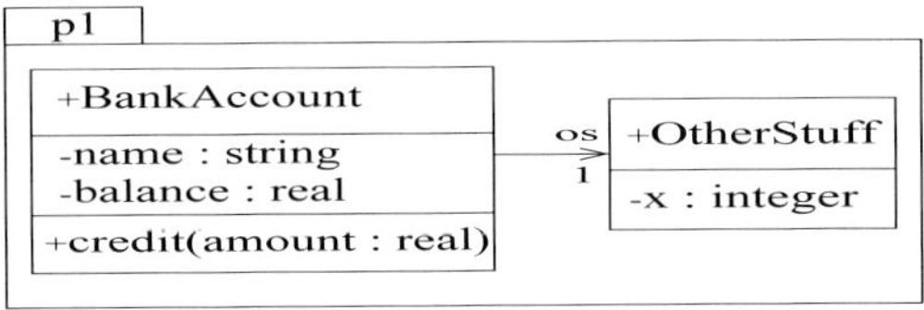

Fig. 1. Basic Class Diagram

by the execution, i.e. all their attributes remain unchanged. This requires a separate equation for every attribute and association-end. Clearly in the case of larger systems, writing all such axioms results in large formulas. Such formulas are fragile in respect to modifications. It is easy to omit something or to add an erroneous constraint. Let us point out that this problem is not OCL specific and occurs in other object-oriented languages such as Eiffel (cf. e.g. [8]).

One of the possible solutions to the frame problem is to use the implicit invariability assumption. In simplistic case, this assumption says that all what is not specified to change does not change (see for example [10, 8]). It allows one to write simple specifications. The implicit approach to invariability is appealing, since it does not put an extra burden on the specifier. Nevertheless, it is not always clear what that assumption really means. In fact, the implicit invariability assumption seems to implicitly include some best practices used to specify object-oriented systems.

Literal interpretation of that assumption is problematic when a high level specification language such as OCL is used. Let us consider the OCL expression $self.os.x = self.os@pre.x@pre + 1$. It does not explicitly say whether $self.os$, x, or perhaps both have to change. It is only clear that at least one of those properties is supposed to change. The solution could be for example to say that all objects mentioned in a post-condition are allowed to change. However in such a case, logically equivalent formulas may have different meaning. In particular, adding a tautological expression to a constraint may change its meaning. Let us consider the following tautology:

$$OtherStuff.allInstances{-}{>}forAll(o \mid not\ o.oclIsNew()\ implies \\ o.x = o.x@pre\ or\ not(o.x = o.x@pre))$$

That assumption would allow arbitrary change of x, despite the fact that this formula is a tautology. This disallows the use of logical deduction, since in logic tautologically equivalent formulas are semantically equivalent.

In the case of derived attributes, one does not specify what happens to them when a method is executed, since their values are derived from values of other attributes. But if the implicit approach is interpreted literally, then they should not change even if the values of the corresponding attributes change. Similarly, specification of subclasses causes problems, which can be hardly dealt with by the simplistic interpretation of the invariability assumption.

Another problem is the specification of side effects, i.e. effects which are not meant to be visible to a client or concern objects different from actual parameters.

Often, clients access component functionality via so called facades, i.e. a number of selected classes and methods, but don't have any knowledge about other classes. For example let us assume that we want to save the old value of attribute *balance* of the class *BankAcount* whenever it is changed and that this operation should be invisible to the client. The values of the attribute *balance* can be saved in a class which is not navigable from the class *BankAccount* (see Section 2.4). The assumption that all objects mentioned in a clause can be modified would disallow that kind of logging unless the changes were specified explicitly. However this would force exposition of information, which should be hidden. All those issues are dealt with using best practices which emerged over years of experience in specification and implementation of object-oriented systems. Unfortunately their solution can not be simply derived from the simplistic assumption.

2.2 Solution in the Simple Case

In this subsection, we propose a solution for the case of single classes and packages. In UML, packages are used to group model elements. They can be used to define system views, in particular so called facades [16], which play the role of client window on the system. It is natural to restrict a client side specification to the corresponding facade.

In the case of the bank account (see Fig. 1, Subsection 2.1) we need to specify what can and what must not change. In our approach we restrict the specifications to packages and to sets of model elements in general (see below). We use the **in** keyword to indicate the package. The **modifies** clause specifies variable object attributes.

Let us specify explicitly what changes in the package $p1$. The following formula relativizes the specification to $p1$, more precisely to all properties contained in this package. The keywords are indicated by the bold characters:

$$\begin{array}{l}\textbf{context}\, p1{::}BankAccount{::}credit(amount : real)\\ \textbf{post} : self.balance = self.balance@pre + amount\\ \textbf{in}\, p1\ \textbf{modifies} : self{::}balance\end{array}$$

We use the OCL primitive :: to indicate that the attribute *balance* of object *self* can be modified. The clause **in** $p1$ **modifies** : $self{::}balance$ says that if we restrict our view to the package $p1$, then an execution of the method *credit* can change only the value of the attribute *balance* of the actual implicit parameter. This specification focuses entirely on package $p1$ and does not say anything about any other package.

2.3 Inheritance

In this subsection we deal with the problem of specifying invariability in the presence of inheritance. We investigate to what extent we need to change a specification, if a class is sub-classed.

Let us consider Fig. 2. We subclass the class *BankAccount* using another package. The class *BankAccount* is extended by the class *SavingsAccount*. The

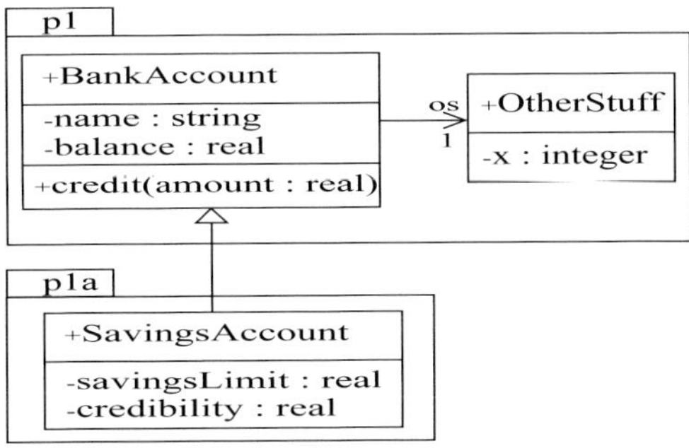

Fig. 2. Extra Package Extension

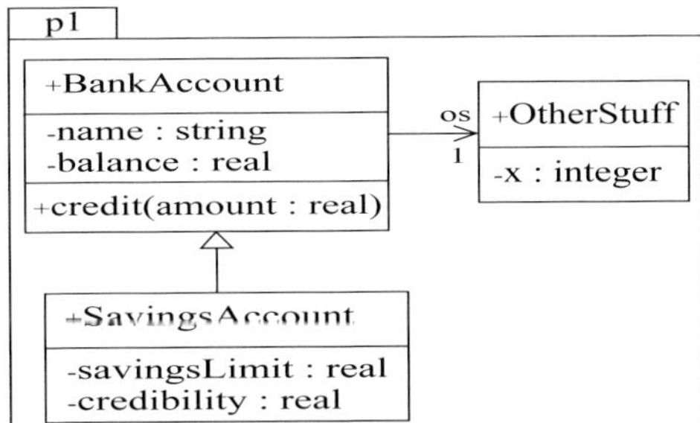

Fig. 3. Intra Package Extension

attribute *savingsLimit* specifies the lower limit of the corresponding balance, and the attribute *credibility* specifies the credibility of a client. We assume that the second attribute is correlated with the balance; if for example the balance grows, credibility grows as well. The previous specification does not say anything about the behavior of the attributes *savingsLimit* and *credibility* when the method *credit* is executed. Consequently, they can change arbitrarily. To restrain changes in respect to the package $p1a$, we have to specify them explicitly:

context $p1$::*BankAccount*::*credit*(*amount* : *real*)
in $p1a$ **modifies** : (*if self.isKindOf*(*SavingsAccount*) *then*
self.oclAsType(*SavingsAccount*) *else Set*{} *endif*)::*credibility*

Let us point out that unlike Java, OCL requires that every *if* keyword has to be followed by *else* and end up with *endif*. In this case, the *else* part is just an empty set.

The specification of invariability is stable in respect to extensions, which do not change the corresponding view (the package $p1$, for example), but changes may be necessary, if the view is modified. Indeed, Fig. 3 shows another way of extending the *BankAccount* class. In this case, the view given by package $p1$ is

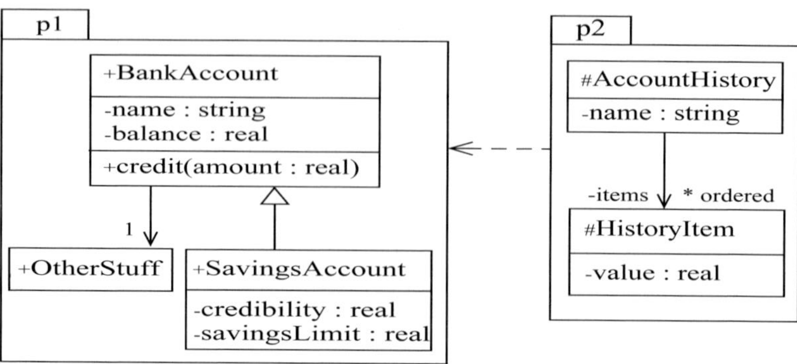

Fig. 4. Dependent Packages

changed. We have to change the specification of *credit*, since it was done relatively to the view defined by $p1$.

context $p1{::}BankAccount{::}credit(amount : real)$
post : $self.balance = self.balance@pre + amount$
in $p1$ **modifies** : $self{::}balance,\ (if\ self.isKindOf(SavingsAccount)$
$then\ self.oclAsType(SavingsAccount)\ else\ Set\{\}\ endif){::}credibility$

When specifying a method in a class, which is meant to be subclassed and which forwards method calls to other classes, it is a good specification style to abstract from changes the method has on attributes in subclasses and in the delegatee classes. In the case of our notation, it is possible to restrict a specification to a particular class. The following specification restricts the view to the class *BankAccount* only.

context $p1{::}BankAccount{::}credit(amount : real)$
post : $self.balance = self.balance@pre + amount$
in $BankAccount$ **modifies** : $self{::}balance$

2.4 Side Effects

A method execution may result in modification of objects different from method parameters and their immediate neighbors. It may also modify attributes, which are invisible in a certain view. For example, this is usually the case of method logging. When aspect-oriented programming is used, it is possible to change attributes, which are not navigable from methods parameters. In this subsection we show how to deal with side effects.

Fig. 4 shows the class *AccountHistory*. An object of this class stores information about the history of a bank account object. When the method *credit* is executed and when the values of the attribute *name* of a bank account and the value of the attribute *name* of a history object are equal, then the old balance of the bank account is stored in a newly created object of class *HistoryItem* and appended at the end of the list *items*. In the previous subsection, we have shown how to specify changes in respect to the package *p*1. However we may also need to specify a system internal view, which includes package *p*2:

$$\begin{aligned}
&\textbf{context}\; p1{::}BankAccount{::}credit(amount : real)\\
&\textbf{post} : self.balance = self.balance@pre + amount\; and\\
&\quad AccountHistory.allInstances{-}{>}forAll(o \mid o.name \;=\; self.name\\
&\quad implies\; o.items{-}{>}one(hi \mid hi.oclIsNew()\; and\; hi.value = self.balance@pre\\
&\qquad and\; o.items = o.items@pre{-}{>}including(hi)))\\
&\textbf{in}\, p1\, \textbf{modifies} : self{::}balance,\; (if\; self.isKindOf(SavingsAccount)\; then\\
&\qquad self.oclAsType(SavingsAccount)\; else\; Set\{\}\; endif){::}credibility\\
&\textbf{in}\, p2\, \textbf{modifies} : AccountHistory.allInstances\\
&\qquad {-}{>}select(o \mid o.name \;=\; self.name){::}items
\end{aligned}$$

The OCL expression *one* means that there is exactly one object satisfying the corresponding condition. *including*(*hi*) means that the object *hi* is appended to the end of the sequence *items*. The last clause restricts the changes in package *p*2 to the attribute *items* of the history objects, which have the same name as the credited bank account.

We may want to make sure that the method does not change anything more than specified above. To achieve this, we use the construct **modifies only**. The expression **modifies only** : *p*1::∗, *p*2::∗ specifies that the changes are restricted to packages *p*1 and *p*2. That sentence seals the specification of variable parts. It uses the absolute **modifies only** clause which concerns all properties of a model.

2.5 Specification of Operations on Lists

In this subsection, we show how to specify operations on lists. In standard OCL, it is not easy to specify what remains unchanged when a list is sorted, an element is inserted or another list is appended. Consequently invariability specification tends to be left out.

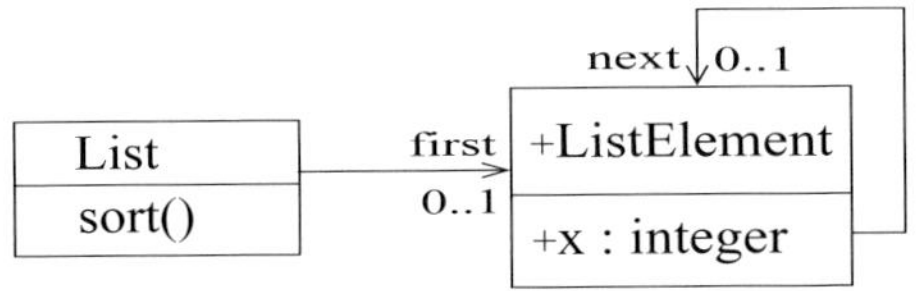

Fig. 5. List with an Anchor

The class diagram in Fig. 5 shows a list composed of an anchor object of class *List* and a number of elements instantiating the class *ListElement*. The method *sort* is meant to sort lists according to the value of attribute *x*. We assume that *self.elements* denotes the set of all elements of the list *self*. (We skip the definition of *elements*.) We consider here only finite acyclic lists. This constraint is expressed by an invariant saying that a nonempty list must contain an element, which does not have a successor. We use the term *elements@pre* to denote all list elements, which exist in the pre-state.

context *List* **inv** :
elements->notEmpty() implies elements.exists(el | el.next->isEmpty())
context *List::sort()*
post : *self.elements = self.elements@pre and*
self.elements->forAll(el | el.next->notEmpty() implies el.x <= el.next.x)

We can make that specification precise by adding the following two invariability clauses:

in *List* **modifies** : *self::first*
in *ListElement* **modifies** : *self.elements::next*

The first clause says that the element associated to the list anchor can be replaced. Those clauses in conjunction with the first part of the post-condition say that the elements of the list can be rearranged, but no element can be added or removed.

3 Views

There are different specification styles as there are different oo-programming styles. In the preceding sections we have restricted our specifications to packages and classes. In general, it is possible to tune a specification to specific needs. A specification can be written from the client or from the implementer point of view. It may focus for example on public or reachable model elements. In general, a user may construct his/her own view. We introduce an abstract concept of view, which defines the focus of a specification (cf. [4]). In our approach, the specification of invariable part can be restricted to the appropriate view. The first subsection relates the OCL extension to the UML metamodel. The second subsection investigates in which way users may define their own views.

3.1 Relation to the UML Metamodel

UML metamodel [16] allows us for a precise definition of a view. The basic views are defined by packages. A package is a grouping of model elements. It owns and imports classes, other packages and model elements such as properties. Client's view of a system is often defined by a facade. In UML a facade is just a package [16].

Let us observe that the **in modifies** clause is defined on two levels of abstraction. The **in** part is defined on the level of class diagrams and the **modifies** part is defined on the level of objects. The **in** part refers to class diagrams and it is not fine enough to deal with run-time configuration. The **modifies** part on the other hand is defined in terms of the **in** part but concerns objects.

The **in** p **modifies** clause refers to a number of model elements grouped in a package p. According to the UML metamodel, a class and more generally a classifier is composed of behavioral features (in particular methods and attributes). It is also associated to association-ends. The following OCL expression defines in the context of the UML metamodel all OCL-properties contained in a package. It selects all properties owned or imported (*ownedElemens*, *importedElements*, respectively) by the package p.

$$
\begin{array}{l}
p.ownedElemens{-}{>}select(pr \mid pr.isKindOf(StructuralFeature) \text{ and} \\
\qquad (pr.isKindOf(Operation) \text{ and } pr.oclAsType(Operation).isQuery \text{ or} \\
\qquad\qquad pr.isKindOf(Attribute) \text{ or } pr.isKindOf(AssociationEnd))) \\
{-}{>}union(\\
p.importedElements{-}{>}select(pr \mid pr.isKindOf(StructuralFeature) \text{ and} \\
\qquad (pr.isKindOf(Operation) \text{ and } pr.oclAsType(Operation).isQuery \text{ or} \\
\qquad\qquad pr.isKindOf(Attribute) \text{ or } pr.isKindOf(AssociationEnd))))
\end{array}
$$

This OCL formula demonstrates that the content of packages can be defined in the metamodel by OCL terms. Similarly, one can defined all properties corresponding to a class (cf. subsection 2.3).

3.2 User Defined Views

The notion of view is fundamental for this approach. One can use predefined views provided by packages, however one may want to define own views corresponding to different perspectives. For example, a specification can be restricted to public or protected model elements. In fact, we can select an arbitrary set of model elements using an OCL term defined on the meta-level. It allows us to specify different system views and to express what is mutable and what is not. For example, for each class one can specify a view corresponding to all classes which are navigable from that class and restrict the invariability constraints only to that view. One can also explicitly define a view corresponding to the implicit invariability assumption including the best practices used in this approach.

Let us consider Fig. 4 again. We can define different views depending on the visibility of model elements. It is possible to restrict views to public or to protected model elements. Let us assume that for every attribute a there is a corresponding query method $getA$ returning the value of the attribute a and that this method has the same visibility as its class. If we focus on the behavior of public and protected properties, then the corresponding view contains the following queries: $getBalance$, $getSavingsLimit$, $getCredability$, $getName$, $getValue$ and so on. A restriction to public properties would remove $getValue$ since it is a method of the protected class $HistoryItem$.

In Subsection 2.3, we have shown how to deal with the specification of subclasses in a package. Actually, it is inelegant to specify what happens to subclasses at the level of their superclass. Let *p but subclasses* mean all model elements which occur in package p, but are not a part of a subclass of the context class. This set can be defined by an OCL term. Due to lack of space, we skip the formal definition of this construct. The constraint specifying the method *credit* can be then written in the form:

context $p1{::}BankAccount{::}credit(amount : real)$
post : $self.balance = self.balance@pre + amount$
in $p1$ *but subclasses* **modifies** : $self{::}balance$

This clause relativizes the immutability clause to classes, which do not subclass the class *BankAccount*. In this case, every class subclassing that class requires its own contract.

In some cases it may be reasonable to restrict method specification to classes, which are navigable from the method parameters via association-ends and generalization relationships traversed bottom up, since only objects of those classes can be modified during a method execution. It is possible to define the set of navigable properties, though the corresponding OCL formula would be quite large. Such a specification can have the form:

context $C{::}Op(p_1 : C_1, ..., p_n : C_n) : D$
...
in $navigableFrom(typesOfParams(Op))$ **modifies** : ...

where $typesOfParams(Op)$ is the list containing parameter types of method Op, i.e. $C, C_1, ..., C_n, D$. We assume that the term $navigableFrom$ denotes all properties owned by classes navigable from those types; as in the previous case we skip the definition.

In our opinion, a general specification language should not restrict users to a particular view, such as for example $navigableFrom$. In contrary, a user should be free to define own views as suits him/her best. The OCL formulas defining on the meta-level the user view may be sophisticated and therefore hard to write and hard to understand, but it is possible to define them in a generic and reusable way.

4 Extension's Grammar

In this section we define the syntax of proposed OCL extension. We restrict this syntax with some constraints, which cannot be expressed by a context free grammar. The grammar is presented using the EBNF notation: [] means optional occurrence, { } means arbitrary number of repetitions and | means option. We use capital characters for nonterminals and small characters for terminals. The invariability constraints have the following form:

context $C :: OP$
pre : Pre
post : $Post$
{ **in** P **modifies** : M {, M }}
[**modifies only** : [P::] M{, [P::]M}]

C is a context specification, Op is a method signature, Pre is a pre-condition and $Post$ is a post-condition as defined by OCL [15]. M describes what can change and P is a package or more generally a term specifying a view. Furthermore:

$$P = (Pn::P \mid Pn[\mathbf{r}] \mid Cn \mid Mt)O, \quad O = [+]\,[\#]\,[\sim]\,[-]$$
$$M = \textbf{nothing} \mid [T]::(Pr \mid *)$$

Pn is a package name. The terminal **r** is optional; it specifies all sub-packages, like $-r$ in Unix. Cn is a class name. Mt is an OCL term defining a set of OCL-properties; Mt is defined on the class diagram level. O specifies visibility of considered properties; the visibility can be private, public, package public and protected respectively. We allow the use of multiple visibility predicates meaning that all listed options are possible. **nothing** is a terminal specifying that nothing can change. T is an OCL term defining a collection of objects; it is defined at the object level. Pr is an attribute or an association-end. $*$ denotes all OCL-properties. Let us point out that terms such as $p1$ *but subclasses* correspond to the nonterminal P (cf. Subsection 3.2).

Context free grammars are not expressive enough to deal with types. Therefore, in addition we require that in the case of the clause:

$$\textbf{in}\, p\, \textbf{modifies} \;:\; t_1::a_1, ..., t_m::a_m$$

the term t_i, for $i = 1, ..., m$, must be valid in the corresponding context, that it does not contain the primitive $@pre$, that all objects defined by t_i must have property a_i and that a_i is a property of a class belonging to p, if p is a package, and that a_i is defined by p, if p is a term.

To facilitate the localization of changes we use the symbol $*$. $C::*$ means all properties of class C. Similarly, $p+::*$ means all public properties contained in the package p. We write **modifies only** : $p_1::*, ..., p_n::*$ to specify that only properties contained in packages $p_1, ..., p_n$ can be modified. Similarly, **modifies only** : $C::*$ specifies that only properties of class C can be modified.

5 The Semantics

In this section we define the semantics of invariability clauses. We discuss the OCL primitive $allInstances$ and its role in the semantics. This semantics allows us to translate invariability primitives to standard OCL. However translating even a medium size class diagram may result in a huge OCL formula. A language can have several semantics; one can modify the semantics proposed below by a proper tuning of the OCL translation. The advantage of this semantics is that one can rely on existing formal semantics of OCL and use standard OCL tools (cf. eg. [5]).

In our semantics, we need to relate sets of objects, which exist before method execution to sets of objects, which exist after method execution. There are two

OCL primitives, which can be used for that purpose: *allInstances* and *@pre*. *allInstances* is a predefined feature of each type, which results in the set of all instances of the type in existence at the time when the expression is evaluated (c.f. [15], Subsection 7.5.10). In the case of program execution, *C.allInstances* can be interpreted as the set of all objects of class C, which can be navigated from variables present in the program stack at a given moment of time.

Below we will use *C.allInstances@pre* in post-conditions to refer to all instances of class C, which exist at the moment when the underlying method is invoked. Interestingly, *allInstances@pre* is rarely used in specifications, though its meaning is as clear as the meaning of *allInstances* itself. In general, OCL allows us to use properties in invariants, pre- and post-conditions. A feature is a property, like operation or attribute, which is encapsulated within a classifier. Actually, the OCL standard (c.f. [15], Subsection 7.5) restricts the notion of property to queries, attributes and association-ends "for the purpose of this document". We refer to the restricted notion of property as OCL-property. Interestingly, the OCL grammar doesn't restrict the use of *@pre* to OCL-properties. On the other hand, it is common to use the feature *allInstances* in invariants and post-conditions.

The semantics is defined via frame formulas. Initially we define the semantics of constraints of the form:

context X::*Op*
pre : *Pre*
post : *Post*
in p **modifies** : $t_1::a_1, ..., t_m::a_m$

We assume that $a_1, ..., a_m$ are attributes and association-ends, but not queries. Moreover for simplicity we assume that packages, classes and properties have unique names.

The term p is obtained from the nonterminal P and defines a number of OCL-properties (see section 4). We define an invariability formula for every attribute and every association-end belonging to p. There are two cases. Such a property may belong to the sequence $a_1, ..., a_m$ (i.e. it may have the form a_i); in this case the term t_i defines the scope of change of property a_i during execution of *Op*. In the other case, the attribute or the association-end cannot change. Let us notice that comparing the value of a property before and after method execution makes sense only for objects, which exist before and after operation execution.

More precisely for $i = 1, ..., m$, let t_i be an OCL term defined in the context X::*Op*, which defines a set of objects of a class C_i. We assume that t_i does not contain *@pre*. Let a_i be an attribute or association-end of the class C_i. We assume also that the properties a_i are pairwise different; because if a_i is equal to a_j, then we can consider $(t_i{-}{>}union(t_j))::a_i$. Let $b_1, ..., b_n$ be all attributes and association-ends defined by p, which are different from properties $a_1, ..., a_m$. For $j - 1, ..., n$, let B_j be the class corresponding to the property b_j. Let *t@pre* denote a term, which is obtained from the term t by suffixing all OCL-properties by *@pre*. We translate the above constraint to standard OCL as follows:

context X::Op
pre : Pre
post : $Post$ *and*
$C_i.allInstances@pre{-}{>}intersection(C_i.allInstances){-}{>}forAll(o\,|$
$t_i@pre{-}{>}excludes(o)\; implies\; o.a_i@pre = o.a_i)$, for $i = 1, ..., m$, *and*,
$B_i.allInstances@pre{-}{>}intersection(B_i.allInstances){-}{>}forAll(o\,|$
$o.b_j@pre = o.b_j)$, for $j = 1, ..., n$

The resulting post-condition is a conjunction of the original post-condition *Post* and a frame formula. The frame formula has two parts. The first one identifies OCL-properties, which may change. For $i = 1, ..., m$, the term t_i defines the scope of change of property a_i. The corresponding clause means that for every object o of class C_i, which exist before and after execution of *Op*, if o is not defined by t_i in the pre-state, then the property a_i of o remains unchanged. The second part concerns all other OCL-properties defined by p; it says that for every such property b_j and every object o of the corresponding class B_j, if o exists before and after execution of *Op*, then its property b_j cannot change. Let us point out that the term t_i can include the implicit parameter *self* and other parameters of *Op*.

Let us observe that the resulting post-condition does not exclude creation or deletion of new objects, as far as properties of objects existing before and after method execution conform to above mentioned constraints.

For example, let us consider the specification of method *credit* in subsection 2.4. There is no pre-condition in this case. In the case of package $p2$, the change is restricted to association-end *items* of those account histories, which correspond to *self*. More precisely, it is restricted to those objects o of class *AccountHistory*, which exist before and after operation execution and which have the same name as *self* in the pre-state: $o.name@pre = self.name@pre$. According to the first part of the frame formula, $o.items = o.items@pre$ must hold for every object o of class *AccountHistory*, such that o exists before and after method execution and o's name is different from the name of *self*. The post-condition says that the method appends a new object to the end of the associated sequence of items. The attribute *value* does not occur in the modifies-clause. Therefore according to the second part of the frame formula, for every object o of class *HistoryItem*, which exists before and after operation execution, it must be true that $o.value = o.value@pre$. However as stated above, this does not disallow proper initialization of the attribute *value* in the newly created objects. The case of attribute *name* is similar to the case of *value*.

Other kinds of invariability clauses can be treated as abbreviations. In the case of the absolute invariability clause **modifies only** : t_1::$a_1, ..., t_m$::a_m, the localization of changes is not relativized, but concerns all properties. This kind of constraint can be seen as an abbreviation of **in** *ap* **modifies** : t_1::$a_1, ..., t_m$::a_m, where *ap* defines all OCL-properties in a model.

We have mentioned that it is possible to use $*$ as an abbreviation for any property. Formally, the clause **modifies only** : p::$*$ means that for any OCL-property a, which is not defined by p and for the corresponding class C the following holds:

$$C.allInstances@pre{-}{>}intersection(C.allInstances)\\ \qquad\qquad{-}{>}forAll(o \mid o.a@pre = o.a)$$

The relative expression **in** p **modifies** : **nothing** means that no property contained in p is modified. It can be equivalently expressed by the formula **in** p **modifies** :, which uses an empty list of terms.

6 Conclusion

Specification of invariability in OCL has been a long standing problem. OCL extension proposed in this paper provides a solution to that problem. The UML metamodel and OCL allow us for an elegant definition of the notion of view; this notion proved to be essential for specification of invariability. Interestingly, OCL turned out to be proper language to define the semantics of proposed extension. There are only few invariability primitives with simple semantics expressed in terms of OCL itself; so that the invariability clauses can be understood as merely OCL macros. Consequently the existing OCL tools can be used.

In the future we are going to perform a realistic case study to demonstrate scalability of our extension. We are going to develop methodology for specification of invariability. On the other hand, we are going to implement a tool for automatic generation of OCL constraints from the invariability clauses and to integrate this tool with existing OCL tools. The notion of view proved to be very flexible and powerful; we are going to study its applicability for layered modeling of complex systems.

Acknowledgement. We would like to thank the anonymous referees for they helpful comments, which helped us to improve this paper.

References

1. Baar, T., *OCL and Graph-Transformations - A Symbiotic Alliance to Alleviate the Frame Problem.* Proc. of MoDELS'05 Satelite Workshop on Tool Support for OCL and Related Formalisms, Montego Bay, Jamaica, October 4, 2005, pp. 83-99, 2005.
2. Borgida, A., Reiter, R. and Mylopoulos, J., *On the Frame Problem in Procedure Specifications.* 15'th Int. Conf. on Software Engineering, Baltimore, IEEE Computer Society Press, 1993.
3. Darvas, A., Mueller, P., *Reasoning About Method Calls in JML Specifications.* Proceedings of the 7th Workshop on Formal Techniques for Java-like Programs (FTfJP'05), Glasgow, Scotland, July, 2005.
4. Finkelstein A., Kramer J., Nuseibeh B., Finkelstein L., and Goedicke M., *Viewpoints: A Framework for Integrating Multiple Perspectives in System Development.* International Journal on Software Engineering and Knowledge Engineering, 1991, pp. 31 – 58.
5. Gogolla, M, Richters, M. *Use: A UML-based Specification Environment.* http://www.db.informatik.uni-bremen.de/projects/USE/.

6. Jezequel, J. M., *Object-Oriented Software Engineering with Eiffel.* Addison-Wesley, (Eiffel in Practice Series), 1996.
7. Hoare, T., *An Axiomatic Basis for Computer Programming.* CACM, 12(10), 1969.
8. Mitchell, R., McKim, J. *Design by contract by example.* Addison-Wesley, 2001.
9. Marek, W., Truszczynski, M., *Nonmonotonic Logic, Context-Dependent Reasoning.* Series: Artificial Intelligence, Springer, 1993.
10. Meyer, B., *Object-Oriented Software Construction.* Prentice, Hall, N.J., 1998.
11. Minsky, M., *A framework for representing knowledge.* Technical Report 306, Artificial Intelligence Laboratory, MIT, 1974.
12. Mueller, P., Poetzsch-Heffter, A., Leavens, G. T., *Modular Specification of Frame Properties in JML.* Concurrency and Computation: Practice and Experience, Volume 15, pp. 117–154, Wiley, 2003.
13. OMG, *MDA Guide*, Version 1.0.1, Jun 2003.
14. OMG, *Meta-Object Facility Specification*, Version 1.4, April 2003.
15. OMG, *OCL Specification, Version 2.0.* October 2004.
16. OMG, *Unified Modeling Language Specification*, Version 2.0, October 2004.
17. Schubert, L., *Monotonic Solution of the Frame Problem in the Situation Calculus.* In Kyburg, H., Loui, R., Carlson, G. eds: Knowledge Representation and Defeasible Reasoning, Kluwer, 1990, pp. 23–67.
18. Warmer, J., Kleppe, A., *Object Constraint Language: Getting Your Models Ready for MDA.* Addison Wesley Professional, 2003.

Framework-Specific Modeling Languages with Round-Trip Engineering

Michał Antkiewicz and Krzysztof Czarnecki

University of Waterloo
{mantkiew, kczarnec}@swen.uwaterloo.ca
http://gp.uwaterloo.ca

Abstract. We propose *Framework-Specific Modeling Languages (FSMLs)* as a special category of *Domain-Specific Modeling Languages* that are defined on top of an object-oriented application framework. They are used to express models showing how framework-provided abstractions are used in framework-based application code. Such models may be connected with the application code through a forward and a reverse mapping enabling round-trip engineering. We also propose a lightweight and iterative approach to round-trip engineering. Furthermore, we present a proof-of-concept FSML for modeling the interaction of workbench parts within Eclipse. Finally, we identify a number of challenges, opportunities, and directions for future research on FSMLs.

1 Introduction

Object-oriented application frameworks are one of the most effective and widely used software reuse technologies today. The creation of framework-based applications is often called *framework completion*. The resulting *framework completion code* implements the difference in functionality between the framework and the desired application. A framework provides a set of abstractions, referred to as *framework-provided concepts*, and means of instantiating them in the framework completion code. The concepts are instantiated by writing the completion code.

Unfortunately, framework completion can be challenging. The application programmers need to know which framework-provided concepts are available and how to instantiate them in order to get the desired effect. The instantiation, which usually involves steps such as implementing interfaces or invoking framework services, is challenging since the implementation choices provided by the framework are not always compatible. Furthermore, the developers need to be able to see how the framework-provided concepts are instantiated in the application code. The latter is challenging since some concepts instances, such as collaborations among objects, are usually scattered in the completion code.

In this paper, we identify the challenges of framework completion and characterize framework-based application development as a mixture of concept configuration and open-ended programming with restrictions. As a main contribution, we show how the challenges of framework completion can be addressed by explicitly capturing the framework-provided concepts as a *Framework-Specific Modeling Language* (FSML) with round-trip engineering. Furthermore, we propose

O. Nierstrasz et al. (Eds.): MoDELS 2006, LNCS 4199, pp. 692–706, 2006.

an agile round-trip engineering approach, which is inspired by the *Concurrent Versioning System* (CVS) and its Eclipse user interface [1] and can operate over non-trivial abstraction gaps thanks to mappings enabled by FSMLs. Finally, we describe a proof-of-concept prototype implementation of a FSML with round-trip engineering for an aspect of Eclipse plug-in development and discuss the merits and limitations of our approach.

2 Running Example: Eclipse Workbench Part Interaction

Eclipse [1] is a universal, open-source platform for building and integrating tools, which is implemented as a set of Java-based object-oriented frameworks. In this paper, we consider a particular part of the Eclipse Application Programming Interface (API), which is concerned with *workbench parts* and their *interactions*. Workbench parts are the basic building blocks of the Eclipse Workbench, which is the working area of an Eclipse user. The parts can interact in various ways, for example, by exchanging events.

In this paper, we only consider two kinds of workbench parts, namely *editors* and *views*. An editor is used for displaying and editing the contents of *input resources*. An example of an editor is the Java editor included in the Eclipse Java Development Tools (JDT) [1]. A view is also used for displaying and editing information, but unlike an editor, a view is not associated with any particular input resource. An example of the standard workbench view is *Content Outline*, which is used to display the outline of an input resource opened in an active editor. Editors and views have to be contributed to the Workbench by declaring them in a plug-in manifest files. The Workbench scans manifest files upon startup and makes contributed workbench parts available to the user.

Workbench parts interact in various ways. In this paper, we consider two kinds of part interactions, namely *listens to parts* and *requires adapter*. For example, the Content Outline view listens to *part activation* events by registering itself as a listener with the Workbench *Part Service* and, therefore, it participates in the *listens to parts* interaction. When an editor, such as the Java editor, is activated, the view will receive an activation event. In response to this event, the view will ask the editor for its `IContentOutlinePage` adapter, which is used to display the outline of the editor's input resource. Therefore, the view and the editor participate in the *requires adapter* interaction, with the view as a source and the editor as a target. For a detailed description of the example see [2].

3 Challenges of Framework Completion

Framework completion is often difficult due to the extensive knowledge about the framework design that is needed in order to write and understand the completion code. In particular, application developers face the following challenges.

Knowing how to complete a framework. The developers need to know what are the framework-provided concepts and how the concepts are instantiated in the code. Creating an instance of a concept involves making implementation choices, some of which are stipulated by the framework's *application programming interface* (API). For example, creating an instance of a framework-provided concept *editor* amounts to implementing `IEditorPart` interface and contributing the editor to the Workbench in a plug-in manifest file. Framework documentation usually provides information on what framework classes should be extended, which interfaces should be implemented, and which API operations need to be called in order to create an instance of the framework-provided concept. Often however, concepts can be instantiated in many different ways and the developers need to know which implementation choices are compatible. For example, an editor can optionally be *multi-page*, in which case it has to extend the framework-provided class `MultiPageEditorPart` and override the abstract `addPages()` method. Furthermore, an editor can optionally have a *contributor*, which is used to contribute editor actions to menus and toolbars. However, if a multi-page editor has a contributor, the contributor has to extend the framework-provided class `MultiPageActionBarContributor`.

Obtaining an overview of a framework-based application. As the size of the framework completion code grows, it becomes increasingly difficult to obtain overviews of the application from different viewpoints. For example, looking at the code, it is difficult to see how many workbench parts are implemented and how they interact. Creating such an overview involves recognizing instances of concepts in the completion code, which may be challenging since it may require verifying multiple facts across the code or even in multiple artifacts. For example, recognizing that an editor is multi-page requires verifying that the editor class extends `MultiPageEditorPart` and that its contributor, which may be specified in the plug-in manifest file, extends `MultiPageActionBarContributor`.

Following the general rules of engagement for the framework. Some APIs, such as the Eclipse API, expect the developers to follow a set of general rules, which are referred to as *rules of engagement* [1]. Some of the rules are more specific, such as the requirement that certain API classes, e.g., `ContentOutline`, should not be subclassed. Examples of more general rules are that the arguments of a API method call should not be null unless explicitly allowed and long-running user operations should run in separate threads.

Repetitive code in the domain concept instantiation. Creating many instances of the same concept often involves providing repetitive, boilerplate code. For example, such code is needed when contributing a set of editor actions to the Workbench. Creating and maintaining such code manually is tedious and potentially error-prone.

Knowing how to migrate completion code after API changes. As a framework evolves, its API and rules of engagement may also change. Migrating completion code to the changed API is challenging and error-prone since it requires changes in multiple locations. For example, in earlier versions of Eclipse, the creation of a multi-page editor involved extending the `MultiPageEditor` class. Currently, the `MultiPageEditor` class is deprecated and the implementation of an editor should extend the `MultiPageEditorPart` class instead.

Migration of the code to the latest versions of Eclipse requires knowledge about what needs to be changed and how it needs to be changed to conform to the latest API.

4 Framework Completion as Concept Configuration and Open-Ended Programming

We can characterize the process of framework completion as two, interleaving activities: *concept configuration* and *open-ended programming with restrictions*. Concept configuration is deciding which and how many instances of framework-provided concepts are to be created and deciding among framework-stipulated implementation choices for every concept instance. Open-ended programming is implementing application-specific functionality that goes beyond the predefined implementation choices provided by the framework, such as creating the code that implements a required interface, overriding the default behaviour by subclassing, or implementing code that is entirely outside the scope of the framework. A concrete example from the Eclipse domain is defining a button which will allow the user to enable or disable a part interaction at run-time. Open-ended programming is restricted in the sense that it must not violate the framework's rules of engagement.

Concept Configuration. The set of framework-stipulated implementation choices for a concept and the dependencies among these choices define all correct ways in which the concept can be instantiated as foreseen by the framework design. We can think of the implementation choices as *features* of a concept and formalize the concept's definition as a *feature model*. A feature model is a tree with the concept as its root and children representing its features [3]. Filled circles denote mandatory features and open circles denote optional features. A feature may have an attribute, which is denoted by its type shown in parenthesis. Additional dependencies between features can be expressed as constraints, such as *requires* or *excludes*. Conceptually, a feature model describes a set of all valid configurations (selections) of features.

For example, Fig. 1(a) shows a feature model describing the *editor* concept. Mandatory features have to be implemented by every instance of a concept, for example every editor has to have the `implementsIEditorPart` feature, meaning it has to implement the `IEditorPart` interface. Optional features, such as `multiPage`, are not required in every instance of a concept.

Fig. 1(b) presents a sample feature configuration for the instance of the *editor* concept, where some features have been selected (`partId`) and some eliminated (e.g., `multiPage`) and values of attributes have been specified (e.g., `'SampleEditor'` for `name`). The feature configuration satisfies all constraints implied by the feature model and, therefore, the implementation choices corresponding to the selected features (including the mandatory ones) are consistent. Note that recognizing the implementation of features of a given concept in the code also produces a configuration, which can then be checked for possible constraint violations.

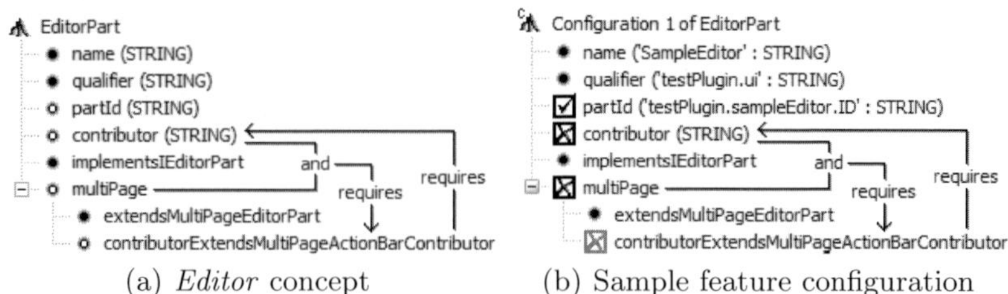

(a) *Editor* concept (b) Sample feature configuration

Fig. 1. Concept definition and concept instance configuration

5 Framework-Specific Modeling Languages

A *Framework-Specific Modeling Language* (FSML) is a Domain-Specific Modeling Language [4] that is designed for a specific framework, called its *base framework*. A FSML consists of an *abstract syntax*, a *mapping of the abstract syntax to the framework API*, and, optionally, a *concrete syntax*.

A FSML explicitly captures framework-provided concepts and their features as *language concepts* in its abstract syntax. The abstract syntax encodes all valid configurations of framework-stipulated implementation choices. Models expressed using a FSML describe concept instances. The concrete syntax may offer specialized rendering of the models to enhance their comprehension.

The mapping of the abstract syntax to the framework API defines how concepts and their features map to the framework completion code. The mapping has two parts: the *forward mapping*, defining how to generate new code or update existing code for a concept instance, and the *reverse mapping*, defining how to recognize an instance of a concept in the code. The mappings are defined for every concept and every feature individually, allowing for a fine-grained control over mapping execution. Together, the forward and reverse mappings enable automated round-trip engineering, where the code can be created from the model, the model from the code, and changes made to the code and the model can be identified and reconciled. In situations where only a subset of the FSML benefits considered in this paper is of interest, an FSML implementation may choose to provide only one of the two mappings. Furthermore, the forward mapping may also be limited to code generation only.

A FSML with round-trip engineering support addresses the challenges from the previous section.

Knowing how to complete a framework. The creation of a model consists of the creation of concept instances and configuring them by selecting or eliminating features and providing attribute values. Concept configuration is controlled by the abstract syntax and well-formedness rules, thus guiding the developer in making correct configuration choices.

The forward mapping knows the different places where the code implementing a concept instance should be inserted in the completion code. The mappings are executed for a correct concept configuration and, therefore, produce correct completion code. A developer can review the changes made by the forward mapping and learn how to complete the framework.

In the case where the completion code has already been created for a concept instance, changing the configuration of the concept by adding or removing features and modifying attribute values may require updating the completion code by code transformation.

Obtaining an overview of a framework-based application. The reverse mapping can identify instances of concepts implemented in the code. The identified instances can be presented to the developer in a form of a model, which is, in fact, an overview of the application from the viewpoint of the FSML. Furthermore, the models can be constructed for different versions of the code, allowing the developer to verify whether the current code still conforms to the previous model. Also, the reverse mapping may be adjusted to recognize broken or incomplete concept instances that need to be fixed. Finally, the reverse mapping also provides traceability between the model and the code by locating fragments of code implementing concept instances.

Following the general rules of engagement for the framework. The forward mapping produces code that conforms to the rules. The reverse mapping helps ensuring that a manual customization of the code does not violate the rules of engagement.

Repetitive code in the domain concept instantiation. The forward mapping automates the creation and update of the repetitive code.

Knowing how to migrate completion code after API changes. A FSML provides a framework to help with migration of completion code to a changed API. Reverse mapping can be used to find uses of the deprecated API and specialized forward mappings can rewrite existing code to conform to the changed API.

6 Agile Round-Trip Engineering

The goal of round-trip engineering is keeping a number of artifacts, such as models and code, consistent by propagating changes among the artifacts. Making artifacts consistent by propagating changes is also referred to as *synchronization*. Round-trip engineering is a special case of synchronization that can propagate changes in multiple directions, such as from models to code and vice versa. Round-trip engineering is hard to achieve in a general setting due to the complexity of the non-isomorphic mappings between the artifacts.

FSMLs enable round-trip engineering over non-trivial mappings that close the abstraction gap between the framework-provided concepts and the completion code. The reverse and forward mappings can be precisely defined because the framework prescribes a finite set of framework-stipulated implementation choices.

In this section, we present a particular approach, which we refer to as *agile round-trip engineering*. The approach supports on-demand, rather than instantaneous, synchronization. The artifacts to be synchronized can be independently edited by developers in their local workspaces, and the reconciliation of the differences can be done iteratively. Furthermore, the agile approach assumes that a model can be completely retrieved from the code using static analysis. We believe that our approach fits agile development particularly well because it supports collaborative, CVS-style development and models do not have to be maintained separately if not desired.

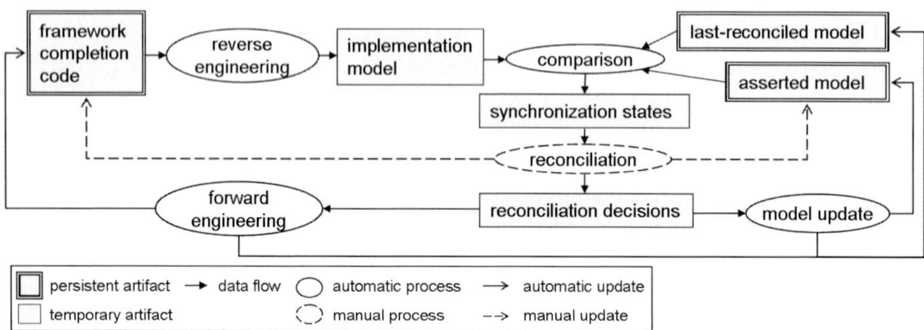

Fig. 2. Artifacts and processes of agile round-trip engineering

Fig. 2 shows the artifacts and processes involved in agile round-trip engineering. The intention of agile round-trip engineering is to synchronize the current *asserted model*, which represents the intended model of the application, and the current *framework completion code*, which may be inconsistent with the asserted model. The asserted model and the completion code that are consistent are also referred to as being *reconciled*. In order to synchronize the asserted model and the completion code, the current *implementation model* is automatically derived from the current code. Furthermore, we assume that the *last reconciled model* contains the latest copy of each concept instance that was archived after the instance's most recent synchronization. Special cases occur if any of the three artifacts, namely the asserted model, the last reconciled model, or the completion code, are missing. These cases include situations where the code has to be first created from an existing model, the model has to be first created from existing code, or where independently created model and code need to be synchronized for the first time.

Given at least the asserted model or the completion code, the synchronization procedure involves the following processes:

1. Reverse engineering. The reverse mappings of every concept and every feature are executed on the completion code to create the implementation model. An instance of a concept is created in the implementation model iff all mandatory features are implemented. The requirement that all mandatory features have to be implemented can be relaxed to enable recognizing incomplete or broken concept instances. In the case that there is no code, the implementation model is empty.

2. Comparison. This process compares the asserted model and the implementation model using the last reconciled model as a reference. The comparison is similar to the *three-way compare* in the CVS, where the comparison of two files uses their most recent common revision as a reference. Corresponding concept instances from different models are compared. The correspondence between concept instances is established based on the values of their *key features*, i.e., features which unambiguously identify instances. For example two instances of the *editor* concept will be compared if attributes of features `name` and `qualifier` have the same values.

The result of comparing two concept instances or two features is a *synchronization state*, which characterizes whether a change, such as addition, removal or modification, has occurred exclusively in the model, exclusively in the code, or consistently in the code and the model, or inconsistently in the code and the model. For example, the synchronization state *forward addition* indicates that a concept instance or a feature has been added to the asserted model (e.g., selecting `multiPage` feature in Fig. 1(b)) and, therefore, needs to be forward engineered to the code. Synchronization state *conflict* indicates that incompatible changes have been made to both the code and the asserted model (e.g., different values have been set for the `partId` feature in the model and in the code). Synchronization states are computed according to decision tables given elsewhere [2]. Here we only explain why using the last reconciled model is important. For example, if a concept instance is present in the asserted model but is missing in the implementation model, then the instance could have been added to the asserted model or removed from the implementation model. If the concept instance is also present in the last reconciled model, then the instance has been removed from the code and, therefore, the synchronization state should be *reverse removal*. On the other hand, if the instance is missing from the last reconciled model, then the instance has been added to the asserted model and, therefore, the synchronization state should be *forward addition*. The last reconciled model also plays an important role in the detection of conflicts.

3. Reconciliation. For all elements with synchronization state other than *consistent*, a *reconciliation decision* needs to be made by the user. A reconciliation decision specifies whether an addition, a removal, or a modification should be propagated from the model to the code or vice versa. For example if the synchronization state for an instance of the *editor* concept is *forward addition*, the possible decisions are *enforce*, meaning that a new editor should be created in the code, and *replace-and-update*, meaning that the asserted model should be updated to be consistent with the code and, therefore, the instance of the *editor* should be removed from the asserted model. In other cases, the possible decisions are *update* and *replace-and-enforce* [2].

Reconciliation may also require manual editing of the completion code or the asserted model (e.g., by providing new values for the attributes), in which case the synchronization states need to be recomputed.

4. Forward engineering and asserted model update. Finally, any necessary changes are executed according to the reconciliation decisions. Forward decisions trigger

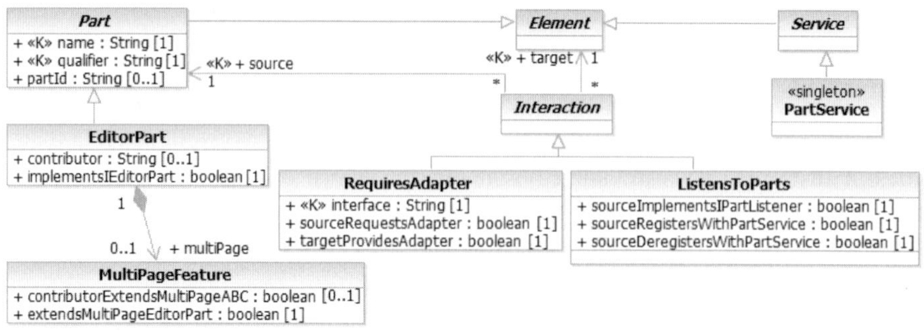

Fig. 3. Fragment of the metamodel of the WPI FSML expressed in MOF

the execution of the forward mappings and reverse decisions force an update of the asserted model with the values from the implementation model. The last reconciled model is updated with the copies of reconciled concepts. The execution of the individual forward mappings needs to be properly scheduled in order to be correct.

7 Eclipse Workbench Part Interaction (WPI) FSML

In this section, we present a fragment of the design of a FSML for specifying Eclipse workbench part interactions (WPI). The current prototype implementation of the FSML consists of a metamodel defining the abstract syntax and the forward and reverse mappings, and it supports full round-trip engineering as described in the previous section. Currently, the prototype only provides abstract syntax editor. The complete design of the WPI FSML is described elsewhere [2].

Abstract Syntax. Figure 3 presents an excerpt of the metamodel of the WPI FSML. Classes `EditorPart`, `ListensToParts`, `RequiresAdapter`, and `PartService` are used to represent framework concepts described in Section 2.

The metamodel from Fig. 3 is derived from feature models such as the one presented in Fig. 1(a). Concepts such as `EditorPart` in Fig. 1(a) and composite features such as `multiPage` map to classes. Atomic subfeatures such as `name` or `partId` map to class properties. The multiplicity of a property depends on the corresponding feature type and is `1` for mandatory features and `0..1` for optional features. Properties used to unambiguously identify instances of concepts, i.e., the *key properties* are annotated with the stereotype `<<K>>`. For example, an instance of `EditorPart` is identified by its `name` and `qualifier` properties, and an instance of `RequiresAdapter` interaction is identified by its `source`, `target` and `interface` properties.

Property `partId` is an example of an optional property. An editor is not required to have a part id, in which case, the value of the `partId` property is null and indicates the absence of the feature. Mandatory features which do not have any attributes are represented as Boolean properties. In this case, `false` indicates absence of the feature. Representing mandatory features as Boolean properties allows us to create instances for concepts partially implemented in the code. The abstract syntax also contains additional well-formedness constraints that correspond to the constraints from the feature model, such as requires from Fig. 1(a).

Mapping abstract syntax to the framework API. We define a mapping for every class and class property. A mapping for a property consists of a reverse part and a forward part. The reverse part is a *code query.* The forward part is a *code transformation* that reflects in the code an addition, removal, or modification of a feature in the model. A feature is modified when its attribute value is changed.

In our prototype, we have implemented the mappings in Java. For better presentation, we present the mappings using a concise pseudo-notation. For the queries, we use a number of predefined functions. For transformations we use a mixture of predefined procedures and aspect templates. An aspect generated from a template can be woven into the source code. We specify the templates using Meta-AspectJ [5] as it allows us to use AspectJ pointcuts, method introductions and inter-type declarations to specify where the code should be woven. In Meta-AspectJ, '[<code>] is the quote operator, #<variable> and #[<expression>] are the unquote operators. The unquote operator splices the value of a variable or an expression.

We present fragments of mappings for *editor* and *listens to parts* concepts to highlight some of the more interesting mechanisms. We start with the mapping declaration for the *editor* concept.

```
mapping EditorPart(EditorPart ep <-> Class editor);
```

The declaration of the EditorPart mapping specifies that ep is bound to an EditorPart in the model, and editor is bound to a Class in the code. The mapping can be executed in forward and reverse directions. For example, executing the mapping in the forward direction and providing a concrete EditorPart instance and a null reference for editor will create a new class in the code. If an actual class is passed as editor, that class will be modified to be consistent with the EditorPart instance.

The above declaration is followed by mappings for individual features. We start with the key features name and qualifier.

```
key name
↩ ep.name = editor.name;
↦ RENAME(editor, ep.name);
key qualifier
↩ ep.qualifier = editor.package;
↦ MOVE(editor, ep.qualifier);
```

A mapping for a property consists of two parts: a reverse mapping indicated by the ↩ symbol and a forward mapping indicated by the ↦ symbol. For the name and qualifier properties, the reverse mappings are assignments, and the forward mappings execute the RENAME and MOVE refactorings, respectively. Mappings for some of the remaining features are as follows.

```
mandatory implementsIEditorPart
↩ ep.implementsIEditorPart = IMPLEMENTS(editor, IEditorPart);
↦ ‘[ declare parents : #[ep.name] implements IEditorPart ]
optional partId
↩ ep.partId = EDITORID(editor);
↦ EDITORID(ep.qualifier + "." + ep.name, ep.partId);
optional multiPage
↩ ep.multiPage = REVERSE(MultiPageFeature(ep <-> editor));
↦ FORWARD(MultiPageFeature(ep <-> editor));
```

The reverse mapping for the `implementsIEditorPart` property uses the `IMPLEMENTS` function to check if the class implements the `IEditorPart` interface. The forward mapping specifies an inter-type declaration that will add the `implements` declaration to the class, if woven. The mapping for the `partId` property uses the `EDITORID` function to retrieve values from the plug-in manifest file and the `EDITORID` procedure to set the values. Mappings for the `multiPage` property use the `FORWARD` function and the `REVERSE` procedure to execute the `MultiPageFeature` mapping.

Finally, we present a mapping for the *listens to parts* interaction.

```
mapping ListensToParts(ListensToPart ltp <-> Class s)
when Part(sp <-> s);
mandatory sourceRegistersWithPartService
↩ ltp.sourceRegistersWithPartService =
  CALLS(s, ‘[IPartService.addPartListener(IPartListener)]);
↦ ‘[private void #[sp.name].registerWithPartService() {
      getSite().getPage().addPartListener(this);
    }]
```

The reverse mapping for the property `sourceRegistersWithPartService` uses the `CALLS` function to determine whether there exists a call to `addPartListener()` method in class `s` or any of its superclasses. The forward mapping for the `sourceRegistersWithPartService` property creates a new method, `registerWithPartService()`, which contains the required registration call. Note that the programmer can move the registration call elsewhere and remove the generated method and yet, the reverse mapping will still be able to recognize the registration call.

WPI FSML prototype. We developed a prototype of the WPI FSML as an Eclipse plug-in. Abstract syntax of the language, including well-formedness constraints, is implemented using Eclipse Modeling Framework (EMF) and its model validation framework. Reverse mappings use the AST, query, and pattern matching API of Eclipse's Java Development Tools (JDT) and type inference engine of the *Infer Generic Type Arguments* refactoring [6]. Forward mappings use Eclipse's JDT Java Model and AST rewriting API. The prototype supports agile round-trip engineering. The reverse mappings are completely implemented. To date, the forward mappings support the creation of classes with methods implementing the framework-stipulated behaviour, addition of interfaces and superclasses, and handling the plug-in manifest files. Weaving of *before* and *after* advices, and code fragment removal are not yet implemented.

The initial evaluation of the prototype involved round-trip engineering of a few Eclipse UI plug-ins as well as some of our own plug-ins. For all of these plug-ins, we were able to completely reverse engineer the models from the plug-ins' code. Furthermore, we were able to synchronize the models and the code after modifying each of them. A more thorough evaluation of the precision and recall of the reverse engineering and the correctness of the forward engineering remains a future work. An on-line demonstration of the prototype is available at our web page.

8 Related Work

There is a large body of related work; however, for space reasons, we can only highlight a few works in each category.

Domain-Specific Modeling Languages (DSMLs) and frameworks. The idea of putting a DSML on top of a framework is not new. Roberts and Johnson consider language-based tools on top of frameworks as the highest maturity level in framework evolution [7]. They advocate that black-box frameworks are particularly well-suited for use with a DSML on top. However, as we discussed in Section 4, configuration alone does not allow fine-grained customization, and it often has to be combined with open-ended programming in practice. We are not aware of any work exploring FSMLs with round-trip engineering support.

General-purpose code analysis tools for architecture recovery and program comprehension. There is an enormous body of work in this category. Two subcategories are prominent. The first subcategory includes tools (e.g., JQuery [8]) that allow code querying for typical dependency structures such as call graphs and include dependencies. In contrast to these tools, our approach uses whatever specialized analyses are needed for detecting a domain-concept instance. For example, in order to recognize the *requires adapter* interaction, a set of exact types of objects returned by a method needs to be computed.

The other subcategory groups works on detecting design patterns in code (e.g., [9]). The main problem with these approaches is that a design pattern can be implemented in the code in a multitude of different ways. Our approach avoids this problem by limiting itself to the detection of API-stipulated concepts and features, which is more tractable.

Framework instantiation. Most approaches in this category only support forward mapping to code. They usually utilize wizards and scripts, as implemented in many industrial tools, including Eclipse. Unfortunately, such wizards or scripts can usually be run only once since they cannot take manual customizations into account. This problem is sometimes addressed by strictly separating the generated code from the manual one using techniques such as protected regions, subclassing of generated classes, and partial classes in C#. However, we believe that the separation approach affords less flexibility in customizing the generated code, in particular, when the generated code dictates the structure of customizations.

Many approaches have been proposed to assist the framework-instantiation process through active documentation [10, 11, 12, 13], which specifies and interactively guides the developer through available hotspots, instantiation tasks and possible implementation choices. Attempts for automating the framework instantiation such as [10] offer code generation based on developer's choices, but cannot analyze existing code for correctness. Also, the generator (the wizard) is unable of analyzing existing code in order to determine which choices have been made in the previous run.

AHEAD [14] offers concept configuration controlled by feature models, where features represent modular slices through multiple artifacts, such as code and XML files. The slices may be composed to produce framework completion code. Step-wise refinement is a generative approach, which supports only forward engineering without the ability to update customizations.

Approaches, such as SCL [15], allow framework developers formalizing framework rules using a constraint language. The constraints can be checked on demand against the completion code and detect rule violations. Such approaches could be used to define the reverse mappings of FSMLS.

Round-trip engineering. According to Sendall and Küster the main difference between round-trip engineering and forward and reverse engineering is that round-trip engineering takes both artifacts into account with the intention of reconciling them, whereas forward and reverse engineering typically create new artifacts, potentially replacing the old versions [16].

Round-trip engineering between UML and object-oriented languages such as Java is supported by several commercial UML modeling tools. The provided synchronization can be instantaneous or on demand as in our approach. However, the mappings supported by these tools are rather simple one-to-one mappings between UML classes and Java classes.

9 Discussion and Future Work

The prototype implementation of the WPI FSML provided us with many insights regarding the usefulness of the presented approach to modeling and round-trip engineering.

Most of the features of framework-provided concepts in WPI correspond to small implementation steps such as implementing an interface or invoking a service. However, features corresponding to higher-level requirements can also be represented and mapped to implementation features using constraints.

The reverse mappings of FSMLS are restricted by the available static code analysis techniques. Our agile round-trip engineering approach requires the design to be retrivable from the code, which may not always be possible using purely static analysis. This problem could be addressed by injecting design information into the source code, e.g., as code annotations. The FSML could also suggest to the application programmer how to restructure the code to make its design more explicit in the static code structure.

WPI FSML currently does not use flow analysis to properly implement the CALLS function, which should check whether there exists a call to the given method within the control flow of an instance of a class in question. Also, constant propagation and data flow analysis would improve the precision in some other cases. Currently, we are in the process of designing a FSML for a part of Eclipse's Graphical Modeling Framework (GMF). Reverse engineering of GMF's completion code requires more powerful static analysis techniques than the ones used in WPI, such as techniques typically used in partial evaluation and program slicing. In general, the effectiveness of the reverse engineering depends on the programming language and the type of the framework. This aspect requires further research.

In our approach, the forward mappings are not required to produce fully functional code. A FSML is intended to be used in an interactive manner. The generated or transformed code is intended to be further customized. We think that generation of code fragments demonstrating the use of the framework can help application developers overcome the initially steep learning curve. Furthermore, the forward mappings need a better infrastructure in terms of automatic scheduling of the execution of individual mappings and a more declarative way of specifying the mappings, such as offered by scripting languages for refactoring [17]. In general, forward mappings designed to update the code, which are code transformations, are usually harder to devise than reverse mappings.

FSMLs can potentially be used for automatic or semi-automatic code migration as described in Section 5. Although we do not have any practical experience with this aspect yet, we think that the specialized forward mappings can be defined for different versions of the API, or even for different frameworks. Currently, we are investigating the possibility of using FSMLs for the migration of code from the Struts framework to the Java Server Pages framework.

We think that, in practice, a single FSML will typically cover a small area of a framework's concern, and multiple FSMLs will be provided for a single framework. For example, in Eclipse, in addition to WPI, another FSML could be used to specify the graphical appearance of workbench parts. Furthermore, round-trip engineering affords manual integration of completion codes created for multiple frameworks. Such integration may be difficult for completion code generated from code templates because such code can be customized in only limited ways. Integration of multiple FSMLs remains future work.

10 Conclusion

In this paper, we propose the concept of FSMLs with round-trip engineering support. The concept addresses a number of challenges in framework-based application development, such as knowing how to write framework completion code, being able to see the design of the completion code, and the migration of the code to new framework API versions. Compared to round-trip engineering support in the context of a general purpose modeling and programming languages such as UML and Java, FSMLs can enable round-trip over non-trivial mappings. This more powerful round-trip engineering is possible because the framework API allows capturing the design structures in the application code more explicitly. Furthermore, the ability to freely modify application code manually gives the developer more customization flexibility than the alternative approach of strictly separating generated code from customizations.

Acknowledgements. We would like to thank Bran Selic, Todd Veldhuizen, and the anonymous reviewers for valuable comments on previous drafts. This work is partially supported by IBM Centers For Advanced Studies, Ottawa.

References

1. Eclipse Foundation: Eclipse. `http://www.eclipse.org/` (2006)
2. Antkiewicz, M., Czarnecki, K.: Eclipse workbench part interaction FSML. Technical Report 2006-09, ECE, University of Waterloo (2006) `http://gp.uwaterloo.ca`.
3. Czarnecki, K., Kim, C.H.P.: Cardinality-based feature modeling and constraints: a progress report. In: International Workshop on Software Factories. (2005)
4. DSM Forum: Workshop on domain-specific modeling (2001-2006) `http://www.dsmforum.org/DSMworkshops.html`.
5. Zook, D., Huang, S.S., Smaragdakis, Y.: Generating AspectJ programs with Meta-AspectJ. In: GPCE'04. Volume 3286 of LNCS., Springer (2004) 1 – 18
6. Tip, F., Fuhrer, R., Dolby, J., Kieżun, A.: Refactoring techniques for migrating applications to generic Java container classes. IBM Research Report RC 23238, IBM T.J. Watson Research Center (2004)
7. Roberts, D., Johnson, R.: Evolving frameworks: A pattern language for developing object-oriented frameworks. In: PLoP'96, University of Illinois, Addison-Wesley (1996)
8. De Volder, K.: JQuery: A generic code browser with a declarative configuration language. In: PADL'06. Volume 3819 of LNCS., Springer (2006) 88–102
9. Shi, N., Olsson, R.A.: Reverse engineering of design patterns from Java source code. In: ASE 2006. (2006)
10. Braga, R.T.V., Masiero, P.C.: Building a wizard for framework instantiation based on a pattern language. In: OOIS'03. Volume 2817 of LNCS., Springer (2003) 95–106
11. Hakala, M., Hautamäki, J., Koskimies, K., Paakki, J., Viljamaa, A., Viljamaa, J.: Generating application development environments for Java frameworks. In: GCSE 2001. Volume 2186 of LNCS. (2001) 163–176
12. Ortigosa, A., Campo, M.: Smartbooks: A step beyond active-cookbooks to aid in framework instantiation. In: TOOLS'99, IEEE Computer Society (1999) 131
13. Tourwé, T., Mens, T.: Automated support for framework-based software evolution. In: ICSM'03), IEEE Computer Society Press (2003) 148–157
14. Batory, D., Sarvela, J.N., Rauschmayer, A.: Scaling step-wise refinement. IEEE Transactions on Software Engineering (2004)
15. Hou, D., Hoover, H.J.: Using SCL to specify and check design intent in source code. IEEE Transactions on Software Engineering **32**(6) (2006) 404–423
16. Sendall, S., Küster, J.: Taming model round-trip engineering. In: Workshop on Best Practices for Model-Driven Software Development. (2004)
17. Verbaere, M., Ettinger, R., de Moor, O.: JunGL: a scripting language for refactoring. In: ICSE'06. (2006)

A Visualization Framework for the Modeling and Formal Analysis of High Assurance Systems*

Heather Goldsby, Betty H.C. Cheng**,
Sascha Konrad, and Stephane Kamdoum

Software Engineering and Network Systems Laboratory
Department of Computer Science and Engineering
Michigan State University
3115 Engineering Building
East Lansing, Michigan 48824 USA
{hjg, chengb, konradsa, kamdoumm}@cse.msu.edu

Abstract. Increasingly, object-oriented technology, specifically the Unified Modeling Language (UML), is being used to develop critical embedded systems. Several efforts have attempted to translate UML models into formal specification languages, thus enabling the models to be analyzed by model checkers. Unfortunately, the complexity and volume of the analysis results often prevents developers from fully taking advantage of the analysis capabilities. This paper introduces a generic visualization framework, Theseus, that provides developers with a model-based, visual interpretation of the analysis results in terms of the original UML diagrams. Within this framework, a playback mechanism displays the execution path that has led to a model checking violation in terms of the original UML state diagram and a newly generated sequence diagram that depicts the problem scenario. A Theseus prototype supporting the Spin and SMV model checkers has been applied to the analysis of UML models for embedded systems from industry.

1 Introduction

Embedded systems have become increasingly pervasive, particularly occurring in high-assurance systems, such as automotive systems, medical devices, and telecommunication systems. Given the critical nature of these embedded systems applications, it is important to use rigorous development techniques. Increasingly, object-oriented technology is being used to develop embedded systems [1]. Furthermore, the Unified Modeling Language (UML) [2], the *de facto* standard

* This work has been supported in part by NSF grants EIA-0000433, EIA-0130724, CDA-9700732, CCR-9901017, CNS-0551622, CCF-0541131, Department of the Navy, Office of Naval Research under Grant No. N00014-01-1-0744, Eaton Corporation, Siemens Corporate Research, and a grant from Michigan State University's Quality Fund. Stephane Kamdoum completed a portion of this work while studying under an International Exchange Program between the University of Kaiserslautern and Michigan State University.

** Corresponding author.

O. Nierstrasz et al. (Eds.): MoDELS 2006, LNCS 4199, pp. 707–721, 2006.

for object-oriented modeling, is the primary modeling notation for the recent movement towards model-driven development (MDD), such as that used in the model-driven architecture (MDA) by the OMG [2]. Using MDD, the models are refined iteratively from requirements to design and eventually code is generated. One drawback with the UML has been the lack of model analysis tools. To date, most of the UML analysis has been limited to syntactic-based analysis or simulation. Recently, there have been several efforts to translate object-oriented diagrams (e.g., state and sequence diagrams) to formal specification languages [3, 4, 5, 6] to be analyzed for adherence to behavioral properties by model checkers, such as Spin [7] and SMV [8]. A challenge with this approach to analysis is how to understand and then use the error descriptions from the analysis output to revise the original UML diagrams. This paper describes a generic visualization framework, Theseus, that interprets the analysis output from model checkers in terms of the original UML diagrams. Using Theseus, the developer is alleviated from the burden of deciphering the frequently cryptic and verbose trace output, which is often denoted in an analysis tool-specific language, including references to line numbers of the specification, internal process numbers, temporary variable names, etc.

In addition to the syntactic-based analysis tools, such as those provided with XDE [9], several CASE tools [10, 11, 12, 13, 14] provide visualization support for (UML) model simulation. Simulation provides information about a single execution path (e.g., a scenario) through a system model, where visualizations can be used to depict a scenario by displaying message traces in sequence diagrams or highlighting elements of a state diagram. Simulation-based analysis *validates* that a model conforms to a developer's expectations. In contrast, the recent work of translating the UML diagrams to model checker specification languages is intended to support the *verification* of UML models. That is, does a UML model satisfy temporal properties, such as invariants and leads-to properties, for all possible execution paths. Particularly for high-assurance systems, it is important to be able to verify a UML model against critical properties *before* the models are refined to design and code. A notable feature of model checkers is that if a system model does violate a property, a counterexample depicting the sequence of events and/or states causing the violation is returned. Two challenges exist with using the analysis results. First, a developer must decipher the verbose and often non-intuitive representation of system elements specified in the counterexample. Second, the cause of the error must be traced back to the original UML diagram in order to make the appropriate model refinements, particularly in the context of MDD.

This paper describes a generic visualization framework, Theseus, that supports a model-driven, visual interpretation of analysis output from commonly used model checkers. Three tasks were essential in the development of Theseus. First, based on numerous trace output files generated from each model checker, we constructed a grammar and a corresponding parser for each model checker to be supported by Theseus; the parser generates an abstract syntax graph (ASG) for a given trace file. Second, we developed a translator for each formal analysis tool that traverses the ASG to generate a generic XML representation containing only UML-relevant model elements, such as state names, transition names, attributes, etc. The parser and translator are combined into an analysis tool-specific trace processor. Third, we developed a visualization engine that processes the XML representation of the counterexamples to support UML state diagram animation and sequence diagram generation. The combination of these three elements have been encompassed in the Theseus prototype that accepts as input a UML model and the trace file for a counterexample generated from a model checker for an error detected in the UML model, and produces a state diagram animation and sequence diagram depicting the counterexample. The user has the option of either stepping (single or multi-step) through the animation or running through the complete counterexample, where color changes are used to depict state and transition traversals.

Theseus has been developed to provide a critical piece of a larger project supporting a roundtrip-engineering approach to the construction of UML diagrams for modeling and analyzing embedded systems requirements. Specifically, we have previously developed several techniques and tools to provide a bridge between (semi-)informal and formal approaches to requirements engineering of embedded systems. First, in order to enable UML diagrams to be automatically analyzed by model checkers, we developed a meta-model based approach to mapping UML diagrams to target specification languages [3]. Hydra is a prototype tool that supports the automatic generation of specification languages, such as Promela, the specification language of the Spin model checker [7], from UML class and state diagrams. Second, in order to help developers create the UML diagrams, we developed a set of object analysis patterns for embedded systems [15], that provide sample structural and behavioral UML templates for modeling embedded systems. Third, in order to facilitate the specification of formally analyzable properties using natural language, we have developed a structured natural language grammar and SPIDER (**S**pecification **P**attern **I**nstantiation and **D**erivation **E**nvi**R**onment) [16, 17]. Using SPIDER, developers can create natural language specifications of properties that are automatically and transparently mapped to the property specification language of the targeted analysis tools, *e.g.*, linear-time temporal logic (LTL) [18] for the model checker Spin [7]. Theseus provides the fourth component of the roundtrip-engineering process, that is, the visualization of the model checking analysis. Therefore, putting all four elements together, a developer can use the object analysis patterns to create a UML model for an embedded system, use Hydra to generate a formally analyzable model for a model checker, use SPIDER to specify properties to be satisfied by the UML model, use the model checker to analyze the UML model against the SPIDER-specified properties, and use Theseus to visualize counterexamples generated from the model checker in terms of the original UML diagrams, thus completing the roundtrip-engineering process.

In order to validate our work, Theseus has been instantiated to handle trace output generated from two different model checkers, Spin and SMV, and we have applied our roundtrip-engineering process to the analysis of several industrial embedded systems. The remainder of the paper is organized as follows. Section 2 provides background information on the supporting elements of the roundtrip-engineering process. Section 3 gives the architecture for Theseus and describes the visualization capabilities. Section 4 presents a case study involving the Spin model checker results. Section 5 overviews related work. Finally, Section 6 gives concluding remarks and discusses future investigations.

2 Roundtrip Modeling and Analysis Overview

This section introduces the roundtrip modeling and analysis process depicted in **Fig. 1**, where the shaded swimlanes depict the activities encompassed by Theseus. Specifically, we describe the process of creating a UML model, formalizing the model, and checking the model for adherence to properties.

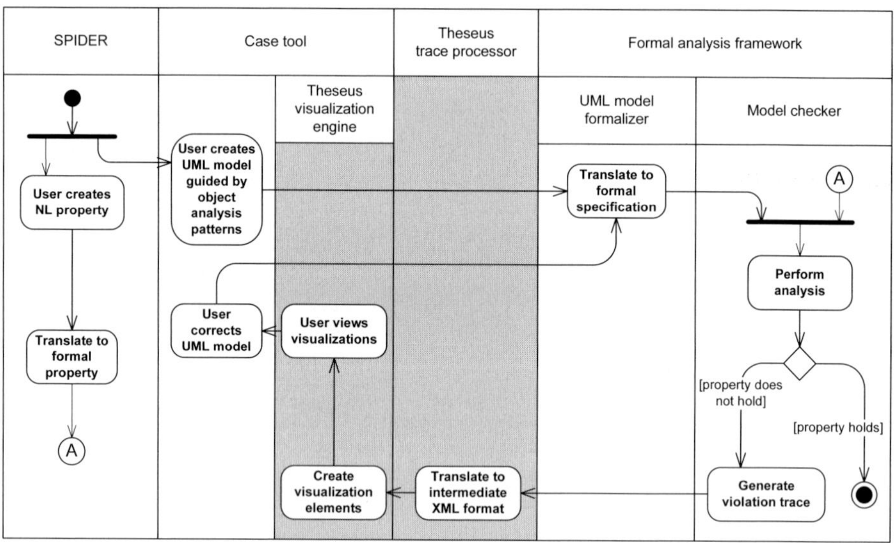

Fig. 1. Roundtrip Modeling and Analysis Process

2.1 Step 1: Creating a UML Model and Specifying a Property

In the first step, the developer uses a CASE tool, such as ArgoUML [19], to create a UML model that describes the structure and behavior of the system. In general, the structure of the system is described in terms of UML class diagrams. Behavioral aspects are modeled using state diagrams associated with the classes. Abstraction should be used to address the size and complexity of the model. Specifically, we model only those portions of the system that are relevant to the analysis. Multiple, specialized models can be created for different aspects of the system.

To aid in the creation of these models for embedded systems, we previously developed *object analysis patterns* [15]. Whereas design patterns [20] guide developers in the construction of design models, object analysis patterns guide developers in the creation of conceptual models during the analysis phase preceding the design phase. Specifically, these patterns aid in the construction of conceptual models of the embedded systems focusing on functional aspects, where these models may later be refined in the design phase through the use of design patterns.

Next, the user specifies the properties of the UML model to be analyzed. In our approach, these properties are specified in natural language using a previously developed process for deriving and instantiating formally analyzable natural language properties based on real-time and qualitative specification patterns [16, 17], termed SPIDER. Briefly, the SPIDER process comprises three steps:

1. **Derivation:** Derive a natural language sentence from a structured natural language grammar.
2. **Instantiation:** Instantiate the natural language representation with model-specific elements.
3. **Mapping:** Map the instantiated natural language sentence to the temporal logic required by the targeted formal validation and verification tool and analyze.

An important component of this process is a structured natural language grammar. This grammar is used to derive natural language sentences that can be mapped to formal specifications structured in terms of a specification pattern system. In this paper, we use the qualitative portion of a previously developed structured English grammar [21] for the specification patterns by Dwyer *et al.* [22].

Using SPIDER, the developer specifies the property to be verified in natural language. SPIDER then translates the natural language property to a form that can be understood by the targeted analysis tool.

2.2 Step 2: Formalizing a UML Model

The UML model created from the object analysis patterns is translated into the specification language for the targeted model checker. It is well-known that UML lacks a precise, formally defined semantics. Therefore, numerous semantic interpretations are possible for a given diagram. In order to address this problem and to make UML diagrams amenable to rigorous analysis, McUmber and Cheng [3] developed a metamodel-based formalization framework that maps a given UML model into a formal specification language. Hydra automates this mapping process [3]. Specifically, we have created a UML-to-Promela formalization, supported by Hydra, tailored to the unique properties of embedded systems. This formalization maps objects to processes in Spin (*proctypes*) that exchange messages via *channels*. Nested and concurrent states are also formalized as processes. For the purposes of this paper, the formalization framework is configured to read UML 1.4 [2] models[1] specified in terms of XMI 1.1 [2] and generate Promela [7] specifications.

[1] CASE tool support for UML 1.5 and UML 2.0 is still limited.

To use the SMV model checker [23, 8], Tanuan and Atlee [5] have developed a set of rules to translate a UML model into SMV's specification language. Currently, there does not exist a tool that automatically translates UML models to SMV specifications. Therefore, we manually translate a UML model into an SMV specification using these rules. (We are extending Hydra to support this formalization.)

2.3 Step 3: Analyzing a UML Model

Next, the developer uses a model checker to analyze the formalized UML model for adherence to the previously specified property. If the model checker finds a violation of the property, then a violation trace is returned. The violation trace contains the sequence of steps performed by the system that lead to the violation.

3 Theseus Visualization Framework

The Theseus visualization framework, shown in the shaded region of the activity diagram in **Fig. 1**, supports visually interpreting the analysis results generated by model checkers in terms of the original UML diagrams. For example, **Fig. 2(a)** depicts a state diagram that has been analyzed for our adaptive light controller case study that will be described in detail in Section 4. **Fig. 2(b)** is an excerpt of the corresponding violation trace generated by Spin. From the trace files, Theseus extracts four types of dynamic behavior to animate: (1) A state is visited; (2) A transition is taken; (3) A message is sent; and (4) A message is received. The Theseus visualization framework comprises two components to depict this behavior: the Theseus trace processor and the Theseus visualization engine. The *Theseus visualization engine* takes the XML intermediate representation of the dynamic behavior from the trace output and the original UML model as inputs and produces the UML state diagram animations and UML sequence diagram generation. We describe the Theseus trace processor and visualization engine in more detail.

3.1 Theseus Trace Processor

The objective of the *Theseus trace processor* (depicted in **Fig. 1**) is to identify the dynamic behavior within the violation trace file and to specify this behavior in an intermediate XML representation. It comprises a parser, which must be constructed for each syntactically unique trace file format, and a translator. Note that different trace file formats will be generated by different model checkers or by the same model checker with different output options or different instrumentation. However, each parser *is* reusable across traces generated from the analysis of different UML models and/or different properties by the same model checker with the same output options selected. Each parser constructs an ASG (abstract syntax graph) representation of the dynamic behavior specified by the trace file. The translator then traverses the ASG and creates an intermediate XML representation of the dynamic behavior.

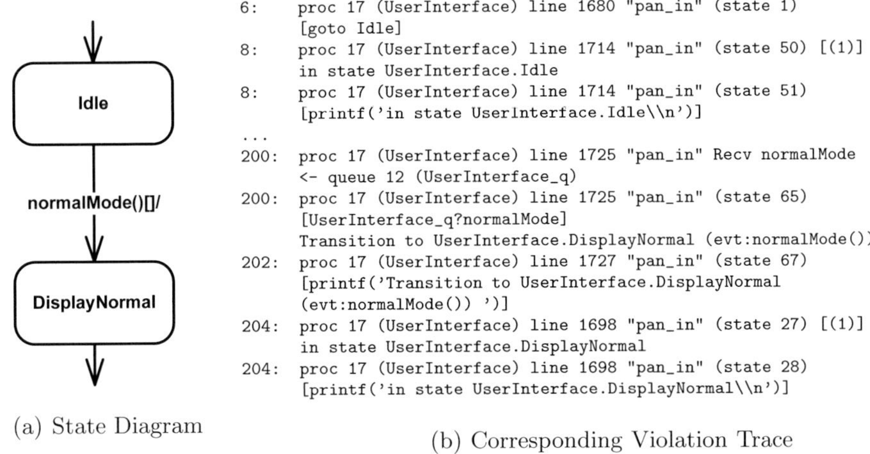

(a) State Diagram

(b) Corresponding Violation Trace

Fig. 2. Sample State Diagram and Violation Trace

An excerpt of a violation trace generated by Spin is depicted in **Fig. 2(b)**. It contains information from four different sources: the UML model, the Promela specification, any instrumentation added by Hydra, and internal Spin information (e.g., line numbers, process number, Spin states, etc.). The Theseus parser extracts the information corresponding to the four dynamic behaviors of interest and represents it as an ASG. We give examples of each as follows:

1. **A UML state is visited:**
   `6: proc 17` **(UserInterface)** `line 1680 ''pan_in'' (state 1) [goto` **Idle**]
   The portion of the statement depicted in typewriter font specifies Spin internal information that is irrelevant for visualization purposes. Specifically, `6: proc 17` represent the execution step and internal Spin process number, respectively. `line 1680 ''pan_in'' (state 1)` are the line number within and the file name of the trace file, and the Spin internal state, respectively. This statement specifies that the UserInterface visits state Idle.
2. **A UML transition is taken:**
   `Transition to` **UserInterface.DisplayNormal** `(evt:`**normalMode**`()^` **Display.showNormMes**)
   This statement is produced by the instrumentation (from Hydra) added to the Promela specification. Spin can provide this information, but only by activating specific flags to generate even more verbose and cumbersome output. Therefore, since we have the ability to extend Hydra, for convenience we have added instrumentation to obtain this information. This statement denotes that the UserInterface transitions to state DisplayNormal as a result of the **normalMode** event occurring. In addition, as a result of this transition being taken, the message **showNormMes** is sent to Display.

3. **A UML message is sent:**
   `201: proc 17 (`**UserInterface**`) line 1726 ''pan_in'' Send` **showNormMes** → `queue 13 (`**Display_q**`)`
   This statement specifies that UserInterface sends the message **showNormMes** to Display.
4. **A UML message is received:**
   `206: proc 11 (`**Display**`) line 1248 ''pan_in'' Recv` **showNormMes** ← `queue 13 (Display_q)`
   This statement specifies that Display receives the message **showNormMes**.

The Spin translator translates the ASG representation of the dynamic behavior generated by the parser into an XML intermediate format. Specifically, there is an intermediate XML specification for each of the four types of dynamic behavior. For example, **Fig. 3(a)** shows a sample XML element specifying that state Idle in class UserInterface is visited. **Fig. 3(b)** specifies that object Display sent a message named **showNormMes** to object UserInterface.

```
<Expression>
  <Process name="UserInterface"/>
  <Goto>
    <Read_location>
      <Process name="UserInterface"/>
      <State name="Idle"/>
    </Read_location>
  </Goto>
</Expression>
```

(a) Visited State

```
<Expression>
  <Process name="UserInterface"/>
  <Send_Message>
    <Message name="showNormMes"/>
    <End_Transition>
      <Queue name="Display"/>
    </End_Transition>
  </Send_Message>
</Expression>
```

(b) Sent Message

Fig. 3. Sample XML Elements

3.2 Visualization Engine

The visualization engine has been implemented in the ArgoUML [19] CASE tool as a plugin. ArgoUML was selected because of its open source application programming interface (API) that allows the creation of plugins. Theseus provides two animation options: automatic playback and incremental playback. Automatic playback animates the complete violation trace; whereas, incremental playback animates the animation trace in a stepwise fashion (single or multi-step). The multi-step option is useful when there are a large number of steps in the violation trace and the developer suspects the first several steps may not be relevant to the violation. After skipping to a specific step, the developer is able to automatically play the remaining steps, or incrementally play the next step.

Theseus provides two mechanisms for visualizing violation traces on the UML model, *state diagram animation* and *sequence diagram generation*. Specifically, state diagram animation depicts that a state is visited (colored red when visited and turns yellow upon departure) and that a transition fires (in red). The generated sequence diagram is animated to depict that a message is sent (arrow in red) and received (arrow in blue). As such, Theseus depicts all four types of dynamic behavior useful for understanding a violation trace.

Both state diagram and sequence diagram animations help a developer to better understand the cause for a property violation. While the state diagram animation is better suited for understanding the behavior of an individual object, the generated sequence diagram helps a developer to understand the context for a property violation in terms of object interaction. Note that typically a UML diagram may have several state diagrams, each of which represents the behavior of a particular object in the system. Currently, Theseus displays the state diagram of a particular object, depending on the part of the counterexample being traversed. As events and messages communicate among objects, the corresponding object's state diagram is displayed. In future versions, we plan to display more than one state diagram at a time in addition to the sequence diagram.

4 Case Study

This section describes an industrial case study we performed to validate our visualization framework. Specifically, object analysis patterns were used to create a UML model of an embedded system application, Hydra generated a formal specification of the UML model, Spin verified critical system properties specified with SPIDER, and Theseus visualized the analysis results in terms of the original UML diagrams. Due to space constraints, we do not include a case study for the SMV visualization, but a description may be found in [24].

4.1 Adaptive Light Control System

The adaptive light control system (ALCS) is responsible for moderating the lights in a room. A class diagram depicting the structure of this system is depicted in **Fig. 4**. The class attributes and operations have been elided due to space constraints.

The primary function of the ALCS is to ensure that if the room is occupied, then the room is sufficiently illuminated, either by natural light or by the lamps. The ALCS comprises a switch for manually turning on the lights, a display for communicating messages to a user, a motion sensor for detecting that the room is occupied, a brightness sensor for detecting the current illumination level of the room, and a dimmer that controls the brightness of the lamps. The *Controller Decompose*, *Actuator-Sensor*, *User Interface*, *Computing Component*, *Fault Handling*, and *Detector-Corrector* object analysis patterns have been used in the specification of the structure and behavior of the ALCS. For additional details about these patterns, please refer to [15]. Note, **Fig. 2(a)** describes a portion of the behavior of the UserInterface.

4.2 Property Specification and Analysis

We analyzed the UML model for the ALCS using the Spin model checker. First, we used Hydra to translate an XMI representation of the UML model into

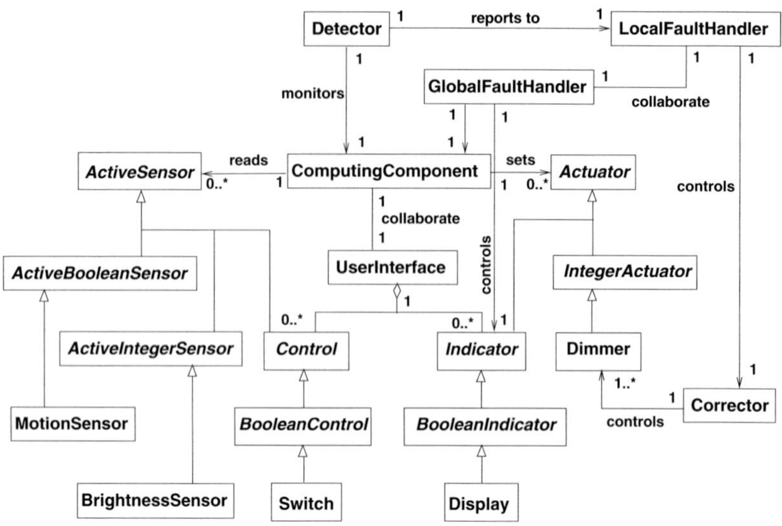

Fig. 4. Class Diagram of the ALCS

Promela. Second, we used SPIDER to formally specify properties to be satisfied by the model. For example, using SPIDER, we created the following natural language property:

> "Globally, it is always the case that if the initialization has succeeded, then eventually the display shows the initialization succeeded message." (1)

SPIDER then extracts UML model elements from the ALCS model to instantiate the free-form text the initialization has succeeded and the display shows the initialization has succeeded message with model-specific elements. The initialization in the ALCS has succeeded if the lightStatus of the ComputingComponent is set to value 1. Therefore, the initialization has succeeded is replaced with `ComputingComponent.lightStatus=1`. Similarly, the text the displays shows the initialization succeeded message is replaced with `call(Display.showNormMes())` to denote that the message *showNormMes()* of the Display is called. Thus, we obtain the following instantiated natural language property:

> "Globally, it is always the case that if `ComputingComponent.lightStatus=1`, then eventually `call(Display.showNormalMes())`." (2)

From this specification, SPIDER automatically creates the formal specification of the property in LTL:

$$\Box((\texttt{ComputingComponent.lightStatus=1}) \rightarrow \Diamond(\texttt{call(Display.showNormMes())})) \quad (3)$$

At this point, SPIDER invokes Spin with the Promela model of the ALCS and the LTL property. In this case, model checking detected a violation and Spin generated a violation trace.

4.3 Property Visualization

Theseus processed the violation trace and visualized the counterexample in terms of the original UML state diagrams and a sequence diagram. A screen shot of a state diagram animated to depict one step of the violation trace is depicted in **Fig. 5**, where the key thing to note is the different colors of the states and the transitions. In this case, we are viewing the state diagram for the UserInterface object. (The intent of these figures is not to read the individual names of states or transitions, but to note the color changes – or the levels of shading in gray scale.) A screen shot of the sequence diagram generated by Theseus depicts the violation trace shown in **Fig. 6**. Using the Theseus visualizations of the violation path, we were able to locate the source of the error and revise the UML model accordingly. Rerunning the overall process yielded no further violations. Without Theseus, we would be forced to understand the syntax and semantics of the trace output, determine the relationship between the output and the UML model, and then locate the corresponding error within the UML model.

5 Related Work

Numerous CASE tools [10, 11, 12, 13, 14] provide visualization support for UML model simulation. To the best of our knowledge, they do not support the visualization of violation traces gathered during model checking analysis in terms of the original UML diagrams. Most formal analysis tools, in contrast, offer visualization capabilities in terms of the analysis models, such as Spin [7] and UPPAAL [25]. However, this visualization is on the level of the description language of the formal analysis tool and not at a more abstract level, such as a UML model.

Other tools visualize analysis results from model checkers in terms of UML. vUML [4] translates UML diagrams into Promela and uses Spin for analysis purposes. Violation traces revealed by formal analysis may be displayed in terms of UML sequence diagrams. To keep the model checking process transparent, vUML focuses on the analysis of more general properties, such as deadlocks and livelocks. Differing from our work, vUML only supports the translation of UML models to Promela, does not support the construction of property specification in terms of natural language or formal specification languages, and does not offer state diagram animation capabilities. MOCES [26] translates Statemate [11] state charts into Promela. The semantics of the Statemate state charts differs from the semantics for UML state diagrams [27]. In addition, MOCES only supports the analysis of a single state chart, while our tool analyzes behavior captured in a collection of collaborating state machines. Hugo/RT [28] supports the analysis of UML diagrams using Spin or UPPAAL [25]. In addition, Hugo/RT can translate a violation trace produced by these analysis tools

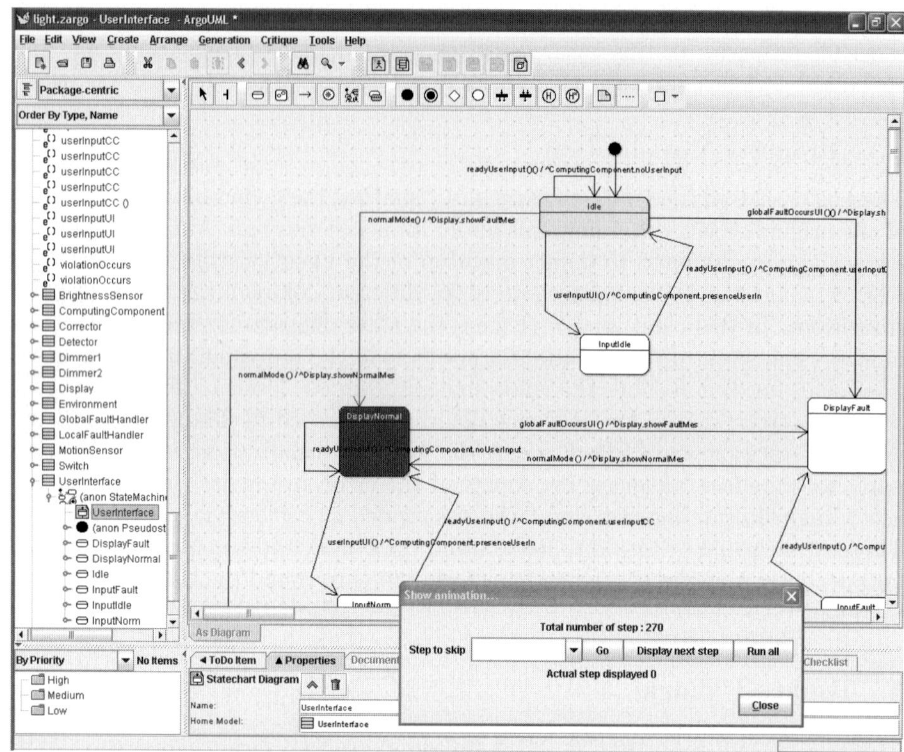

Fig. 5. Theseus Animation of Adaptive Light Controller Violation Path

to a representation in terms of UML elements. However, Hugo/RT provides a proprietary textual UML representation and does not interactively display the violation trace in terms of a graphical UML representation in a CASE tool. In summary, none of the aforementioned tools combines the capability of displaying analysis results in terms of UML sequence and state diagrams and the customizability towards numerous formal analysis tools.

6 Conclusions

This paper has described a generic visualization framework that provides a critical link in a roundtrip-engineering process for modeling and analyzing embedded systems. The prototype of this visualization framework, offers three key benefits to UML modelers who want to model check their UML diagrams. First, Theseus supports modelers who are not proficient in interpreting the verbose and often cryptic analysis results generated by model checkers, by locating the source of the error identified by the violation trace. Theseus visually animates the violation trace on the UML state diagrams and a generated sequence diagram. Second, Theseus is extensible to other formal analysis tools beyond the

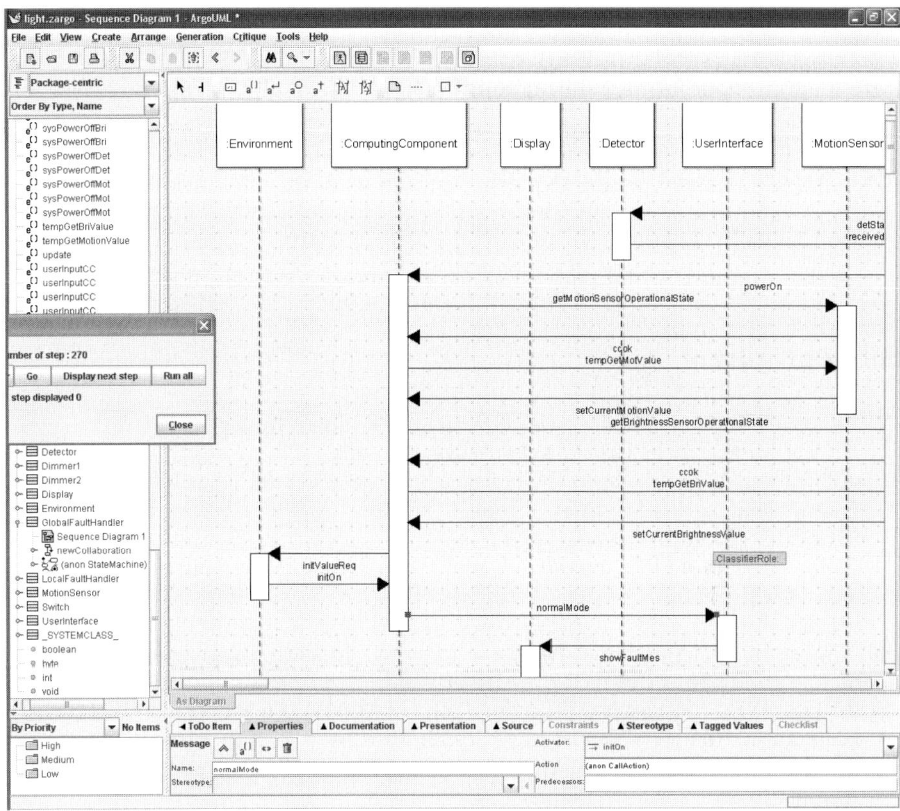

Fig. 6. Theseus Generated Sequence Diagram depiction of Adaptive Light Controller Violation Path

ones mentioned in this paper. To extend Theseus to visualize output from other analysis tools, a specific Theseus trace processor needs to be constructed. The parser of the trace processor depends on the formalization rules (i.e., the rules for mapping UML to the target specification language of a given analysis tool) and the violation trace output options used in the model checker (including any instrumentation added to the trace output). The translator of the trace processor, however, depends only on the formalization rules, and is potentially reusable for different violation trace output options. Currently, we have developed trace processors that support output generated by the SMV and Spin model checkers. Independent of the model checker, the formalization rules, and the output options, the Theseus visualization engine is reusable across the trace output for different state-based analysis tools. Third, Theseus completes the roundtrip modeling and analysis process for embedded systems by enabling a developer to automatically formalize a UML model, specify natural language properties that the model must satisfy, analyze the model for adherence to these properties, and visualize property violations in terms of the original UML diagrams.

Future work will include applying Theseus to additional case studies and extending Theseus in different directions. First, we are extending Theseus to view multiple state diagrams side-by-side during animation. Additionally, we are investigating how to extend the Theseus framework to visualize the analysis results from complementary model checkers, such as the real-time model checkers Kronos [29] and UPPAAL [25]. Finally, we are exploring a more seamless integration between the tools and the steps of our roundtrip-engineering process for modeling and analysis. The biggest challenge has been the vendor-specific differences in the implementation of the standard for data interchange between tools and third parties.

Bibliography

[1] Douglass, B.P.: Real-Time Design Patterns. Addison-Wesley (2003)
[2] Object Management Group: `http://www.omg.org`.
[3] McUmber, W.E., Cheng, B.H.C.: A general framework for formalizing UML with formal languages. In: Proc. of the IEEE Int. Conf. on Software Engineering (ICSE01), Toronto, Canada (2001)
[4] Lilius, J., Paltor, I.P.: vUML: A tool for verifying UML models. In: Proc. of the 14th IEEE Int. Conf. on Automated Software Engineering, Washington, DC (1999)
[5] Tanuan, M.C.: Automated Analysis of Unifed Modeling Language (UML) Specifications. Master's thesis, University of Waterloo, Canada (2001)
[6] Inverardi, P., Muccini H., Pelliccione P.: CHARMY: An Extensible Tool for Architectural Analysis. In: ESEC/FSE-13: Proc. of the 10th European Software Engineering Conf. held jointly with 13th ACM SIGSOFT Int. Symposium on Foundations of Software Engineering. (2005)
[7] Holzmann, G.: The Spin Model Checker. (2003)
[8] McMillan, K.L.: Getting started with SMV (1999)
[9] IBM: Rational Rose XDE Developer. `http://www-306.ibm.com/software/awdtools/developer/rosexde/` (2005)
[10] Telelogic: ObjectGEODE. `http://www.telelogic.com/` (2005)
[11] I-logix: `http://www.ilogix.com/` (2005)
[12] ARTiSAN Software: Real-time Studio. `http://www.artisansw.com` (2005)
[13] Ho, W.M., Jézéquel, J.M., Guennec, A.L., Pennaneac, F.: UMLAUT: an extendible UML transformation framework. In: Proc. of the Automated Software Engineering Conf., Florida (1999)
[14] Nickel, U., Niere, J., Zündorf, A.: The FUJABA environment. In: Proc. of the 22nd Int. Conf. on Software Engineering, New York, NY, USA, ACM Press (2000) 742–745
[15] Konrad, S., Cheng, B.H.C., Campbell, L.A.: Object Analysis Patterns for Embedded Systems. IEEE Trans. on Software Engineering **30**(12) (2004) 970 – 992
[16] Konrad, S., Cheng, B.H.C.: Facilitating the construction of specification pattern-based properties. In: Proc. of the IEEE Int. Requirements Engineering Conf. (RE05), Paris, France (2005)
[17] Konrad, S., Cheng, B.H.C.: Automated analysis of natural language properties for UML models. In Bruel, J.M., ed.: Satellite Events at the MoDELS 2005 Conf.: MoDELS 2005 Int. Workshops, Montego Bay, Jamaica, October 2-7, 2005, Revised Selected Papers. Volume 3844 of Lecture Notes in Computer Science., Springer-Verlag GmbH (2006) 48–57

[18] Manna, Z., Pnueli., A.: The temporal logic of reactive and concurrent systems. Springer-Verlag New York, Inc. (1992)
[19] Tigris.org: ArgoUML: The project home. `http://argouml.tigris.org` (2005)
[20] Gamma, E., Helm, R., Johnson, R., Vlissides, J.: Design Patterns: Elements of Reusable Object-Oriented Software. Addison-Wesley (1994)
[21] Konrad, S., Cheng, B.H.C.: Real-time specification patterns. In: Proc. of the Int. Conf. on Software Engineering (ICSE05), St Louis, MO, USA (2005)
[22] Dwyer, M.B., Avrunin, G.S., Corbett, J.C.: Patterns in property specifications for finite-state verification. In: Proc. of the 21st Int. Conf. on Software Engineering, IEEE Computer Society Press (1999) 411–420
[23] McMillan, K.L.: Symbolic Model Checking. PhD thesis, Carnegie Mellon University (1993)
[24] Kamdoum, S.: Facilitating the roundtrip engineering of model-driven software architecture. Master's thesis, Michigan State University (2006)
[25] Pettersson, P., Larsen., K.G.: UPPAAL2k. Bulletin of the European Association for Theoretical Computer Science **70** (2000) 40–44
[26] Mikk, E., Lakhnech, Y., Siegel, M., Holzmann, G.J.: Implementing statecharts in promela/spin. In: WIFT '98: Proc. of the Second IEEE Workshop on Industrial Strength Formal Specification Techniques (1998) 90
[27] Crane, M.L., Dingel, J.: UML vs. classical vs. Rhapsody statecharts: Not all models are created equal. In: Proc. of the ACM/IEEE 8th Int. Conf. on Model Driven Engineering Languages and Systems. (2005)
[28] Knapp, A., Merz, S., Rauh, C.: Model checking timed UML state machines and collaborations. In Damm, W., Olderog, E.R., eds.: 7th Int. Symposium Formal Techniques in Real-Time and Fault Tolerant Systems (FTRTFT 2002). Volume 2469 of Lecture Notes in Computer Science., Oldenburg, Germany, Springer-Verlag (2002) 395–414
[29] Bozga, M., Daws, C., Maler, O., Olivero, A., Tripakis, S., Yovine, S.: Kronos: a model-checking tool for real-time systems In: Proc. of the 10th Conference on Computer-Aided Verification. (1998)

Layered Class Diagrams: Supporting the Design Process

Scott Hendrickson, Bryan Jett, and André van der Hoek

Institute for Software Research
University of California, Irvine
Irvine, California 92697-3455, U.S.A.
+1 949 824 6326
{shendric, bjett, andre}@uci.edu

Abstract. Class diagrams model a system's classes, their inter-relationships, operations, and attributes and are used for a variety of purposes including exploratory design, communication, and evaluation. However, traditional diagrams, and the tools used to create them, focus on capturing a single configuration – *the product of the design process* – rather than supporting the explorative *design process itself* that is used to create and evolve a design over time. This process involves iteration over multiple alternatives and evaluation of those alternatives. We present a layered approach and environment that encourages this process by capturing a design and its alternatives using layers. Layers may be combined with other layers to compose and explore new design alternatives for evaluation. Our tool provides mechanisms for creating, composing, and visualizing layers as well as detecting dependencies and conflicts among layers and managing semantic relationships among layers.

1 Introduction

Class diagrams are primarily used for two purposes: as *detailed design documents* that describe an implementation and as *conceptual models* that aid in designing that system [6]. In the former case, class diagrams sufficiently capture a *single design* of a corresponding system. However, as a conceptual model, class diagrams alone are insufficient. Designing nontrivial systems generally involves a design process that explores and evaluates *multiple design alternatives*. To better function as conceptual models, class diagrams need to support this *process of design* by capturing and organizing these alternatives, supporting their evaluation, and incorporating new ones.

Most class diagramming tools focus only on capturing class diagrams as finished products consisting of a single document that contains the result of all design decisions. Consequently, creating a new alternative requires creating a new document, and combining complementary alternatives requires manually merging each documents' contributions into yet another document. Although some diff and merge tools are starting to emerge that help this process [2, 3, 10, 18], these deal with documents as a whole, and do not allow a designer to deal individually with each design decision, which is often captured implicitly along with many others in a single document. For example, a new design document may contain both minor corrections to an old design combined with major modifications incorporating a new piece of functionality. To

O. Nierstrasz et al. (Eds.): MoDELS 2006, LNCS 4199, pp. 722 – 736, 2006.

incorporate one of these conceptual changes without the other requires a designer to determine which parts of the document map to which concept. Managing the design process in this way, without explicit support for explicitly modeling alternatives separately, is cumbersome and error-prone.

In this paper, we present an approach and supporting environment that encourages a *creative design process* by promoting a model of interaction relying on *layers*. Individual layers capture individual modifications to a design. These may include minor corrections, improvements to existing or additions of entirely new classes and associations, or even entirely different design approaches. By selectively composing layers on top of one another, different class diagrams are created that represent the accumulated modifications of the selected layers. In our approach, layers are first class entities that are independently manipulatable. This encourages capturing separate concerns in separate layers. The result is that a design consists of many individual alternatives and concerns that are properly separated and easily manipulatable, promoting a creative, explorative design process.

Clearly, some form of validity must be maintained in this process to ensure that the product of the design process produces consistent class diagrams. We use *relationships* for this purpose. Relationships allow a designer to explicitly set the rules according to which layers can be composed. Some relationships can be automatically detected, such as a class association created in one layer that points to a class created in another layer: the layer with the class association could not reasonably be applied without the layer that also creates the class it points to. Other relationships are semantic in nature, and must be specified by the designer, such as when two changes are logical alternatives, only one of which can be incorporated at a time. Relationships are modeled at the same level as, but independently from, layers. This allows a designer to easily specify and manage different compositions from the same set of layers.

We have implemented our approach in a layered design tool, EASEL. Our tool is similar to Rationale Rose [12] or ArgoUML [13], but is a layer and relationship centric design environment with special features to support these concepts. We view EASEL as a proof-of-concept prototype that shows that an approach in which alternative designs can be dynamically composed through the use of layers is indeed possible and that the issues involved in using such an environment can be addressed.

2 Motivating Example

To understand the problems in modeling class diagrams to date, we introduce a motivating example that we also use as the running example throughout the remainder of the paper. The example concerns class diagrams, shown in Figure 1, that each represents an alternative design for a hypothetical graph data model. As in a traditional design environment, each alternative is modeled separately: Figure 1a presents one design consisting of two classes representing edges and vertices in a graph and Figures 1b and 1c present alternative designs that reflect different design decisions.

Upon first glance, the only obvious difference between Figures 1a and 1b is that 1b is missing the *Edge* class. However, two distinct issues are actually addressed: (1) the *Edge* class was removed in favor of implicit out edges captured in the *toVertices* association, and (2) a *label* attribute was added to the *Vertex* class. Figure 1c differs in

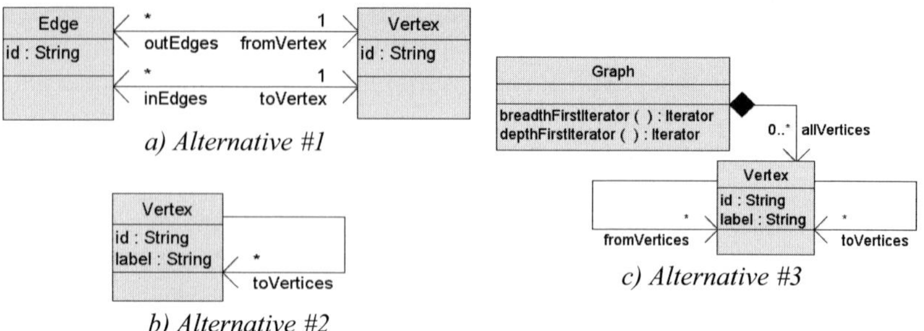

a) Alternative #1

b) Alternative #2

c) Alternative #3

Fig. 1. Alternative designs for a hypothetical graph data model

two distinct ways from Figure 1a as well: (1) a *Graph* class has been added that keeps track of all vertices, and (2) the *Vertex* class has an additional *fromVertices* association that keeps track of in edges.

Suppose that a designer decides that a fourth alternative would be best after examining the different alternatives shown in Figure 1. This fourth alternative would include the human readable label in Figure 1b, the *Graph* class in Figure 1c, the explicit edges in Figure 1a, and an additional *weight* attribute for each edge that is not present in these designs. The designer is now faced with the challenge of incorporating the desired parts from each original alternative into a single, coherent fourth design. This requires an understanding of the boundaries of each design concept in the first three alternatives, since creating and merging deltas of the alternatives is insufficient because the designer only wants a subset of the design concepts incorporated in each alternative.

Now, consider what happens if the designer later decides that a concept should be reintroduced that was originally rejected (or vice versa). Perhaps edges do not need to be represented explicitly and the implicit edges represented with the *toVertices* and *fromVertices* associations are adequate. Making such a design change would once again involve a manual revision of the design.

While the above is an overly simplistic example, these issues become more prevalent when one creates designs of a much larger scale and/or complexity. The example, then, shows the following needs we wish to address in this paper:

- *Separation of concerns*: we want to explicitly model different design concerns rather than implicitly mixing them together in a single document.
- *Composition*: we want to compose new, alternative designs from desired design concerns in order to explore and evaluate them.
- *Concern permanence*: we want design concerns to remain intact so that they may be (re)incorporated or removed at any time.
- *Variation*: we want to explicitly support alternative ways of realizing the same (or similar) functionality.

3 Approach

Our work was motivated by the observation that using class diagrams as conceptual models during the design process is hindered by tools that only record design documents *extensionally*. This means that resulting documents capture a single design without explicitly differentiating between the concepts that compose it, making the process of exploration cumbersome. Typically, a designer in exploratory mode necessarily must create and track multiple documents, concepts from which must be manually brought back and forth.

To facilitate an explorative design process, our solution incorporates two key insights. The first is that an *intensional* approach based on *layers* provides a natural mapping from conceptual intent and understanding to physical realization. The second key insight is that "straight" layers, as applied in Photoshop and similar tools for graphical editing, are not sufficient: explicit and detailed management of layer *relationships* must complement their use. Below, we detail these two insights and outline our solution in the context of the motivational example.

3.1 Layers

The discipline of *configuration management* (CM) has been primarily concerned with capturing the evolution of a software system at the *source code* level [5]. Of interest to this paper are the concepts of extensional and intensional versioning [4]. In *extensional versioning*, the entire configuration management system focuses on managing the versions of artifacts that result after changes have been made. That is, versions of artifacts are the primary "language" through which developers interact with the CM system. Extensional versioning ensures that each version is uniquely stored and accessible through revision numbers. Deltas may be used for storage optimization, but they are generally hidden from the user.

The key insight behind *intensional versioning* is to invert the relationship between versions and changes, making changes a first class entity, storing each change as a delta *independently from the other changes*. So, instead of requesting versions of artifacts, developers retrieve a set of changes and merge them together to create a particular "version." Similarly, when they have completed implementing a new "version" in their workspace, the delta between this new and the original version is stored as an individually-identifiable delta. Accessing an artifact, then, requires the developer to request a baseline (an initial, stable configuration) and a set of deltas.

There are two advantages to this approach:

1. Because a delta encapsulates a logically-related set of changes, it provides developers with a natural model of interaction. No longer must they mentally map desired conceptual features onto specific versions of artifacts. They can simply request features, bug fixes, and other kinds of changes by name.
2. Because each delta is built from the baseline, they are independent from each other. It is therefore possible to combine deltas in ways that they were not previously combined, creating new versions along the way.

At the same time, there is one major disadvantage:

1. Because each delta is independent, it is possible that certain combinations of deltas produce invalid or incomplete versions. Some of these conflicts can be automatically resolved, but others must be resolved manually.

The advantages of this approach are exactly what we would like to achieve with respect to class diagrams. We discuss how we address the disadvantage using the concept of relationships in Section 3.2.

Our first step is to adopt the approach of using a baseline and deltas and apply it to class diagrams. Making this adoption requires adjusting the concepts of a baseline and deltas to operate at the level of design instead of lines of code. This is a straightforward adoption of the concepts of baselines and deltas, but applied to UML diagrams. We use layers as deltas, but with one exception. Because the process of design is highly iterative, we want a baseline to be editable in the same way that a delta is editable. We therefore start out with an empty, virtual baseline, and simply treat each layer as an increment from there. This is only a minor deviation, as the first layer could simply be treated as an imaginative baseline, emulating the original approach.

Consider the example presented in the previous section, but with the design and its alternatives captured using layers. Many possibilities exist for how the different designs might be partitioned over multiple layers. For instance, a very fine grained approach could be used where separate layers capture individual class operations and attributes. Alternatively, one could use a very coarse grained approach to capture the initial design and the two alternatives using just three layers. Both of these approaches technically work, but may not be as advantageous. The first is too fragmented, capturing point changes rather than design concepts; the second is too coarse grained, in essence reproducing the extensional approach that we are trying to overcome with our work.

A better way of capturing the design and its alternatives is presented in Table 1, where we capture each conceptual design feature in a separate layer. In each layer, added class elements are annotated with a "+" and added associations are shown using bold lines; removed class elements are annotated with an "×" and removed associations are shown using dashed lines. Unannotated elements are there for the sole benefit of the reader, placing the changes within context. For instance, in Table 1 the *Initial Design* layer adds an *Edge* and *Vertex* class and two associations. The *Use Only Vertex* layer removes the *Edge* class and its two associations, and adds another association. The other layers add, remove, or modify elements as depicted in Table 1.

Returning to the original three configurations in Figure 1, we can construct each of these designs by selectively merging layers from Table 1. The first alternative is represented by just the *Initial Design* layer. We compose the second alternative by merging the changes stored in the *Initial Design*, *Use Only Vertex*, and *Add Label* layers. We compose the third alternative by merging the changes stored in the *Initial Design*, *Use Only Vertex*, *Implicit In Edges*, *Track Vertices*, and *Add Label* layers. Finally, and this is where the power of our approach comes in, we can create the fourth alternative discussed in the text of Section 2 simply by merging the changes stored in the *Initial Design*, *Track Vertices*, *Add Label*, and *Add Weight* layers. No new changes needed to be made, we simply needed to compose a different set of existing layers.

Table 1. Layers capturing the design concepts of each design of Figure 1

Layer	Design Concepts
Initial Design	Edge, id : String; * outEdges / 1 fromVertex; * inEdges / 1 toVertex; Vertex, id : String
Use Only Vertex	Edge, id : String; * outEdges / 1 fromVertex; * inEdges / 1 toVertex; Vertex, id : String; * toVertices
Implicit In Edges	Vertex, id : String; * fromVertices; * toVertices
Track Vertices	Graph, depthFirstIterator ( ) : Iterator, breadthFirstIterator ( ) : Iterator; 0..* allVertices; Edge, id : String; * outEdges / 1 fromVertex; * inEdges / 1 toVertex; Vertex, id : String
Add Label	Edge, id : String; * outEdges / 1 fromVertex; * inEdges / 1 toVertex; Vertex, id : String, label : String
Add Weight	Edge, id : String, weight : float; * outEdges / 1 fromVertex; * inEdges / 1 toVertex; Vertex, id : String

3.2 Relationships

Producing valid designs requires composing valid combinations of layers. From the layers presented in Table 1, we note the first basic relationships between layers: *structural dependencies and structural conflicts*. Structural dependencies arise when one layer's contents depend on elements introduced by another layer. For example, the *Add Label* layer adds an attribute to the *Vertex* class, which is created in the *Initial Design* layer. Consequently, in order to produce a valid design with the *Add Label* layer, the *Initial Design* layer must also be included. By the same reasoning the *Add Weight* layer also structurally depends on the *Initial Design* layer since it adds an attribute to the *Edge* class, which is created in the *Initial Design* layer.

Structural conflicts arise when one layer's contents depend on elements that are removed by another layer. For example, the *Edge* class that the *Add Weight* layer adds an attribute to, is *removed* by the *Use Only Vertex* layer. In order to produce a valid design with the *Add Weight* layer, the *Use Only Vertex* layer must *not* be included.

While structural dependencies and structural conflicts are of a syntactical nature, it is also necessary to support semantically meaningful relationships. For example, it does not make sense to have both the explicit edges from the *Initial Design* layer and the implicit edge from the *Implicit In Edges* layer. These layers can technically be merged, but would produce an undesired result. What is intended by the designer is for the *Implicit In Edges* layer to be included only when the *Use Only Vertex* layer has also been included, which removes the explicit edges it is replacing. The designer must be able to express such semantically meaningful relationships.

To support structural and semantic relationships, our work distinguishes three kinds of basic relationships through which layer relationships can be specified:

1. *and relationships*: this relationship states that if *all* of the layers *a*, *b*, and *c* are included, then layer *d* must also be included.
2. *or relationships*: this relationship states that if *any* of the layers *a*, *b*, or *c* are included, then layer *d* must also be included.
3. *variant relationships*: this relationship states that from a particular subset of layers *a*, *b*, and *c*, only a certain minimum and maximum number can be included at the same time.

The first two relationships are not necessarily singular: from any "source" layer(s) they can designate the inclusion of multiple layers (e.g., if *a*, *b*, and *c* are included, then *d*, *e*, and *f* must also be included) and exclusion of multiple layers (e.g., if *a*, *b*, and *c* are included, then *d*, *e*, and *f* must *not* be included). It is also possible to negate source layer(s) (e.g., if *a* is included and *b* is *not* included, then *c* must be included). Finally, the variant relationship may refer to an arbitrary number of layers, limiting the number included concurrently to one (making a group of layers mutually exclusive, creating a switch [11] or variant), or multiple (creating what COVAMOF [16] terms an alternative, which allows up to so many variants to be included at a time).

As with layers, different ways exist to choose and organize relationships. This is influenced by the choice of layers, but also by the personal preferences of the architect. Returning to our example, we could express the structural dependency of the *Add Label* and *Add Weight* layers on the *Initial Design* layer as "*Add Label* or *Add Weight* implies *Initial Design*." Similarly, we could express the structural conflict of the *Add Weight* layer with the *Use Only Vertex* layer as "*Add Weight* implies not *Use Only Vertex*."

Semantic relationships are expressed using the same rules. The semantic relationship that the *Implicit In Edges* layer is intended to be applied only when the *Use Only Vertex* layer is applied could be expressed as "*Implicit In Edges* implies *Use Only Vertex*," or alternatively as "not *Use Only Vertex* implies not *Implicit In Edges*."

Composition layers support the grouping of individual layers. They do not have any changes of their own. Instead, they use relationships to group layers in particular ways. For instance, to model the second alternative of Figure 1, we define a composition layer called *Alternative 2*, and a relationship stating: "*Alternative 2* implies *Initial Design*, *Use Only Vertex*, and *Add Label*."

3.3 Composition Through Merging

The principal goal of our approach is to allow the designer to explore alternative designs with minimal interference from tools; we want a layer composition process that reflects this. While exploring different designs, we envision a designer turning on and off layers frequently and editing "earlier," previously created layers at any time. In fact, the strength of using layers in exploratory design is that the designer has the flexibility of not only creating a new layer to modify the outcome of other layers composed before it, but the designer can alternatively go back and modify a layer at any time to change the base of everything composed after it as well. This flexibility also enables a designer to select conflicting layers in order to produce a design which is "close to" what they want, then fix the design and build upon it using an additional layer that brings back the design to a consistent, non-conflicting state.

These goals are in contrast to configuration management systems that disallow revising previously committed deltas and whose process of merging deltas may require the user to manually correct conflicts. We want our merge process to be flexible enough to allow *strictly incompatible* layers to be merged in a predictable way and the process to be automated so that we do not unnecessarily interrupt the designer every time incompatible layers are selected. While the designer should be *aware* of incompatible layer selections, we do not want to prohibit the designer from selecting them or unnecessarily burden the designer in such cases.

We, thus, base our composition algorithm on traditional merge tools, but make a few adjustments. Specifically, we need to address ghost additions and removals. The first problem, "ghost additions", may occur when a class association from a first layer relies on the presence of a class from a second layer and, vice versa, when a class association from the second layer relies on the presence of a class from the first layer. Regardless of which layer is applied first in the merge process, a requisite class will not be there. The second problem is "ghost removals": when two mutual layers each remove a class established by the other layer, one of those removed classes is bound to erroneously reappear. Both problems arise, because we want to explicitly allow editing of "earlier," previously created layers at any time (as we discussed previously).

To address the problem of ghost additions and ghost removals, our merge process first applies all additions of all layers, in the order of classes first and then associations, and then performs all of the removals, in the order of associations first and then classes. The result is that all necessary classes are always present, avoiding ghost additions, and that classes that are intended to be removed are always removed, avoiding ghost removals. While the result is different from what one would expect from a traditional merge process, from the perspective of layer composition it makes sense to support a behavior that predictably shows added elements and hides removed elements. As an alternative solution, it would have been possible to disallow circular dependencies, but that would greatly restrict the flexibility of our layered approach during the exploration of design alternatives. We recognize that alternative composition behaviors may be desired. We address this in Section 5.

Even with the specialized merge process, small conflicts may still occur when layers make changes to the exact same element, i.e., two layers that each rename a class, but to a different name. In such cases, the order in which layers are merged, from first to last, is used to resolve the conflict (which, because layer ordering is specifically supported in our EASEL tool, makes sense as a choice).

3.4 Summary

To summarize, our approach to modeling class diagrams with layers and relationships adheres to the following properties:

- *A class diagram is specified as a series of layers.* No longer is a class diagram captured as a monolithic design specification; it is instead a group of loosely coupled layers, each addressing a particular design alternative or concern.
- *Layers consist of sets of additions and removals of design elements.* The elements can be of any granularity, from classes, to associations, to properties (properties are not shown throughout the paper, but are supported by our infrastructure as discussed in Section 4).
- *An individual design is composed from layers.* Instead of working with different, complete designs, a design is created by selecting a set of desired layers and merging their additions and removals to construct the design.
- *Relationships capture structural and semantic dependencies, including potential conflicts among layers.* To avoid invalid designs, these relationships must be taken into account when composing a design from layers.
- *Complex relationships and layer hierarchies can be expressed using a combination of composition layers and relationships.* This allows a designer to deal with higher level concepts and express any Boolean expression.
- *Cyclic dependencies are resolved by using an adjusted merging process.* First, all additions of all of the layers are merged and only then are all of the removals applied.

We conclude by noting once more that relationships are expressed explicitly at the level of layers. This promotes variability to be the key mechanism and representation for design and allows the designer to reason about and manage differences among design concepts during the process of designing.

4 EASEL

To demonstrate our approach, we have implemented it in EASEL, a layered design environment for class diagrams. As illustrated in Figure 2, EASEL is partitioned into two separate areas: a drawing canvas for specifying class diagrams and a variability spreadsheet for managing layers and relationships.

The drawing canvas of EASEL operates similarly to Rationale Rose [12] or ArgoUML [13] in allowing a designer to add, remove, and change classes, their attributes and operations, associations, and properties. If none of the special features of EASEL are used, EASEL simply acts as a design tool for capturing individual class diagrams much like these existing design environments. However, this is not EASEL's purpose. The drawing canvas has special behaviors that change it from a tool that merely captures a design product, to one that also supports the design process. First, the design on the drawing canvas is composed from the layers selected in the first column of the variability spreadsheet. For example, the design shown in Figure 2 is composed by merging the *Alternative 4*, *Initial Design*, *Track Vertices*, *Add Label*, and *Add Weight* layers. Layers are merged with the specialized merge process

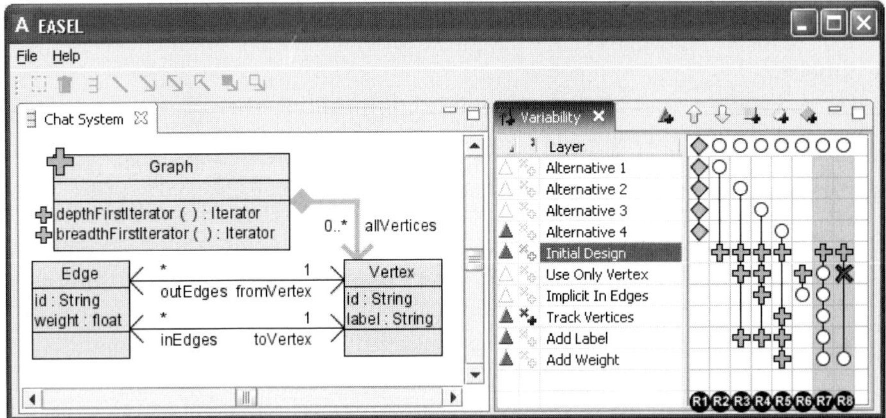

Fig. 2. Screen shot of EASEL. The relationships are labeled *R1* through *R8* for reference.

discussed in Section 3.3, avoiding large conflicts introduced by ghost additions or ghost removals and resolving any minor conflicts that are left using the order in which layers are listed from top to bottom. Changing this order is done by dragging layer names up or down.

The second special behavior is that each of the elements on the drawing canvas may be annotated with icons that explicitly illustrate each specific change recorded by the layers. This is what the second column of the variability spreadsheet is for: by selecting one or more layers in this column, the effects of the layers are shown. Currently, the *Track Vertices* layer is selected as such. This annotates the *Graph* class and its attributes with a "+" and bolds the association between the *Graph* and *Vertex* classes to indicate that these elements are added by that layer. If the layer were to remove elements, as, for instance, the *Use Only Vertex* layer does, the removed elements would be annotated with a "×" or dashed as discussed previously. Of course, when explicit display is not turned on, any elements that a layer removes are no longer visible; the drawing canvas only displays the results after merging all of the selected layers.

The third special behavior lies in how modifications made by a designer are stored. In EASEL, they are incorporated in the layer that is currently selected for editing. In Figure 2, this is the *Initial Design* layer, as highlighted. This means that each addition or removal made by a designer is added to the set of additions and removals of that layer. This is key to the power of EASEL in supporting the process of designing and modeling class diagrams. Had we enforced an incremental model in which layers are frozen once they have been created, much design flexibility would be lost making it impossible to revisit and update a feature without creating an additional layer. The drawback is that inconsistencies may arise. However, as we will see below, EASEL has features to deal with this problem.

The final special behavior is that EASEL allows a designer to explore new layer combinations even if they produce invalid designs. This behavior allows the designer to freely explore new designs produced by new layer compositions. As we discuss below, however, EASEL does *inform* the designer of compositions that violate relationships. Thus, relationships act as design critics [14] rather than hard constraints. Without allowing invalid designs, exploring new design alternatives would be difficult.

The variability spreadsheet shown on the right hand side of Figure 2 provides a designer with a graphical representation through which they can edit the relationships that exist between layers. The rows of the variability spreadsheet represent layers and the columns relationships. Seven different symbols are used (please read the expressions carefully):

- A white *circle* represents a source of an *or* relationship (e.g., A in "A or not B implies C" or "A or not B excludes D").
- A white, *slashed circle* represents a negated source of an *or* relationship (e.g., B in "A or not B implies C" or "A or not B excludes D").
- A yellow *square* represents a source of an *and* relationship (e.g., A in "A and not B implies C" or "A and not B excludes D").
- A yellow *slashed square* represents a negated source of an *and* relationship (e.g., B in "A and not B implies C" or "A and not B excludes D").
- A cyan *plus* represents an implied destination (e.g., C in the examples above).
- A red *X* represents an excluded destination (e.g., D in the examples above).
- An orange *diamond* represents a variant in a *variant* relationship (e.g., A, B, or C in "variant(A, B, C)"). The minimum and maximum number of variants that may be selected concurrently is viewable and editable using context menus.

Returning to the example in Figure 2, the way to read some of the relationships, then, is as follows:

R1. The *Alternative 1*, *Alternative 2*, *Alternative 3*, and *Alternative 4* layers are variants of each other, that is, only one can be included at a time.
R3. The *Initial Design*, *Use Only Vertex*, and *Add Label* layers are implied by the *Alternative 2* layer, and they should always be included in the overall selection of layers whenever the *Alternative 2* composition layer is included (and, in fact, EASEL performs this inclusion for the designer upon selection of the *Alternative 2* layer).
R7. The *Initial Design* layer is implied by the *Use Only Vertex*, *Implicit In Edges*, *Track Vertices*, *Add Label*, and *Add Weight* layers.
R8. The *Add Weight* layer implies the *Initial Design* layer, but should not be included with the *Use Only Vertex* layer.

EASEL automatically detects a number of relationships, adding them to the variability spreadsheet with a slightly darker background. In Figure 2, relationships *R7* and *R8* were automatically added by EASEL. In general, EASEL automatically detects layers that structurally depend on or structurally conflict with other layers (i.e., a layer links to a class created in another layer, or a layer removes a class that another layer links to).

In addition to detecting direct dependencies and conflicts between two layers, EASEL searches for additional layers that may affect these dependencies or conflicts. For instance, if a layer creates an association to a class that is created in a second layer, the first layer depends on the second. However, if a third layer removes this association, the dependency between the two layers would be removed. EASEL examines the contents of all layers when creating relationships, and in such cases generates appropriate relationships.

Finally, the implementation mechanism for automatically detecting relationships is extensible. EASEL could, for example, be easily extended to create variant relationships among layers that add classes with the same name – thereby addressing one of the minor conflicts that the specialized merge algorithm cannot automatically handle.

The current selection of layers shown in Figure 2 produces a valid design. However, if the designer were to make a selection that was invalid, EASEL would inform the designer of the invalid selection by highlighting violated relationships in red. For example, if the designer were to additionally include the *Use Only Vertex* layer in the selection shown in Figure 2, EASEL would highlight the violated relationship, R8. In general, when a designer is content with a particular selection of layers, despite violated relationship(s), then they have a few options to resolve the semantic and/or structural conflicts: (1) the designer could create a new layer that adds and removes elements that resolve the conflicts, (2) the designer could go back and modify the problematic layers so that they are compatible when merged, or (3) the designer could change the explicitly defined semantic relationships so that they are no longer violated. The choice will be influenced by the existing layers, their impact on other compositions, and by personal preferences.

Of note is that automatically-detected relationships are continuously updated while the design at hand is being modified. These relationships serve as critics [14] and disappear when particular dependencies or conflicts no longer exist. Hence, automatically detected relationships assist a designer during the design process, as they inform them of the fact that their current design is exhibiting some relationships that may or may not have been intended.

5 Discussion

At this point, a full-fledged validation of EASEL and our approach versus other design editors and notations is unavailable. However, our implementation of EASEL demonstrates that a layered approach is feasible and can be used to represent monolithic designs as compositions of layers. It, in fact, was meant as such: a proof-of-concept prototype exploring the feasibility of the technology.

To date, we have found in our early explorations that the explicit support of design alternatives in our layered approach is convenient and non-intrusive. We found it less prohibitive to make changes in EASEL than with tools without layered support, particularly since we could easily engage and disengage related collections of changes while we explored various design alternatives. One strength in this process is that layers are generic and can capture any type of change (i.e., improvements, features, or even entirely different directions of design choices). While on the one hand this could be said to mix metaphors and perhaps end up being confusing, on the other hand, once one understands how layers compose, it represents a much more agile attitude in which the designer can flexibly use layers to their best convenience.

Using our tool also has revealed some weaknesses. We found that it would be useful to allow a designer to, after exploring many different alternatives, somehow indicate the nature of the changes stored in a layer or to otherwise organize them by content or status (e.g., "critical baseline", "stable", "in flux", "some changes still needed"). We also found a need to allow a designer to split, merge, and rearrange layer content. Since our tool focuses on supporting the design process (and thereby discovering the "right" design incrementally, necessitating frequent restructuring and redistributing concepts over layers), this is functionality that is necessary and will be implemented soon. Additionally, we recognize that alternative composition behaviors may be desired by designers. For example, a designer may wish that layers be applied in the order specified and fail if there are inconsistencies, or a designer may want the option to resolve those inconsistencies manually.

Finally, we found the automatically created relationships helpful in indicating when we had overlooked the impact of one change on another layer's contents. However, we found that as the number of relationships could grow very large quickly, and the number of relationships relevant to our particular task was frequently small. We will explore automatic filters that display only relationships relevant to the current design and will investigate approaches to grouping and summarizing relationships to reduce the cognitive demands on the designer.

6 Related Work

Other research has worked towards supporting the design process as well. ArgoUML [15], for instance, eases the cognitive challenges of the design process through the use of design critics, task organization and prioritization, and supporting a designers' natural tendency to switch tasks during the design process. The overall focus of ArgoUML is on *guiding* a designer through the design process, which is different than, but complimentary to, the focus of this paper.

Differencing and merging algorithms have been applied to UML [18] and generically to diagrams [2, 10]. Our approach, as we discussed in Section 3.3, uses differencing and merging algorithms internally to capture and apply layers. However, our approach makes some specific adjustments to address ghost additions and removals in order to avoid continuously bothering the user with manual resolution requests during the merge process.

Aspect-oriented modeling [8], programming [9], and aspect-oriented design [17] are also related to our work. Aspects are also compositional and used to separate concerns. In fact, aspects have already been applied to UML diagrams. Symmetric approaches [1, 7], which do not differentiate between "aspects" and a "base", but treat these as the same, are more closely related to our approach. However, the focus of our approach is different and the resulting needs of the technology differs from those capabilities offered by asymmetric and symmetric aspects: (1) we need both additive and subtractive capabilities, (2) we want the ability to freely make edits rather than through specific kinds of joinpoints, and (3) we need relationships to track how layers are compatible to one another. Nonetheless, with sufficient work, our approach could probably be made to support an aspect-oriented approach, and vice versa.

7 Conclusion and Future Work

The contribution of this paper is an innovative modeling approach that supports the naturally explorative design process. Rather than forcing the specification of a monolithic design that intermingles many implicit design concepts, our approach enables a mode of work in which design concepts are separated as individually manipulatable layers. Key to our work is the application of intensional techniques to model class diagrams. This is supported with a specialized merge algorithm and the ability to capture and manipulate both structural and semantic relationships.

In addition to addressing the issues raised in the discussion section, our future work involves several different strands. First, we wish to apply EASEL to a real system and obtain feedback from real designers. Our work to date demonstrates the feasibility of the layered approach, but now we wish to move beyond our own experiences to evaluate whether others experience the same benefits as we do. Second, we would like to explore how layers could further aid a designer by capturing additional types of information, such as example designs or templates upon which one can overlay a design under construction. Finally, we would like to explore how EASEL could be used to support collaborative design, using layers as a means of isolating and including contributions from different designers.

Acknowledgements

We thank the anonymous reviewers for their insightful comments and suggestions. Effort partially funded by the National Science Foundation under grant number DUE-0536203.

References

[1] alphaWorks. HyperJ. http://www.alphaworks.ibm.com/tech/hyperj, IBM.

[2] Briand, L.C., Labiche, Y., et al. Impact Analysis and Change Management of UML Models. In Proceedings of the 19th International Conference on Software Maintenance (ICSM'03), p. 256-265, Amsterdam, The Netherlands, September 22-26, 2003.

[3] Chen, P.S., Critchlow, M., et al. Differencing and Merging within an Evolving Product Line Architecture. In Proceedings of the Fifth International Workshop on Product Family Engineering (PFE-5). p. 269-281, Siena, Italy, November 4-6, 2003.

[4] Conradi, R. and Westfechtel, B. Version Models for Software Configuration Management. ACM Computing Surveys. 30(2), p. 232-282, 1998.

[5] Estublier, J., Leblang, D.B., et al. Impact of the Research Community on the Field of Software Configuration Management. Software Engineering Notes. 27(5), p. 31-39, 2002.

[6] Fowler, M. UML Distilled: A Brief Guide to the Standard Object Modeling Language. 3rd ed. Addison Wesley: Reading, MA, 2003.

[7] Harrison, W.H., Ossher, H.L., et al. Asymmetrically vs. Symmetrically Organized Paradigms for Software Composition. IBM Research Division, IBM Research Report RC22685 (W0212-147), December 30, 2002.

[8] Kienzle, J., Gray, J., et al. Report of the 7th International Workshop on Aspect-Oriented Modeling. In Satellite Events at the MoDELS 2005 Conference, Bruel, J.-M. ed. 3844, p. 91-99, Lecture Notes in Computer Science, Springer: Montego Bay, Jamaica, 2005.

[9] Lopes, C.V., Kiczales, G., et al. Aspect-Oriented Programming. In Proceedings of the European Conference on Object-Oriented Programming. Jyväskylä, Finland, June 9-13, 1997.

[10] Mehra, A., Grundy, J., et al. A Generic Approach to Supporting Diagram Differencing and Merging for Collaborative Design. In Proceedings of the International Conference on Automated Software Engineering (ASE 2005). p. 204-213, Long Beach, CA, USA, November 7-11, 2005.

[11] Ommering, R.v., Linden, F.v.d., et al. The Koala Component Model for Consumer Electronics Software. IEEE Computer. 33(3), p. 78-85, March, 2000.

[12] Rational Software Corporation. Rational Rose: Using Rose. IBM Corporation, Report 800-024462-000, p. 258, 2003.

[13] Robbins, J., Hilbert, D., et al. Extending Design Environments to Software Architecture Design. In Proceedings of the Conference on Knowledge-Based Software Engineering (KBSE'96). p. 63, 1996.

[14] Robbins, J. and Redmiles, D. Software Architecture Critics in the Argo Design Environment. Knowledge Based Systems. 11(1), p. 47-60, 1998.

[15] Robbins, J.E. and Redmiles, D.F. Cognitive Support, UML Adherence, and XMI Interchange in Argo/UML. Information and Software Technology, Special Issue: The Best of COSET '99. 42(2), p. 79-89, 2000.

[16] Sinnema, M., Deelstra, S., et al. COVAMOF: A Framework for Modeling Variability in Software Product Families. In Proceedings of the Third International Software Product Lines Conference (SPLC 2004). p. 197-213, Springer Berlin / Heidelberg. Boston, MA, USA, August 30-September 2, 2004.

[17] Stein, D., Hanenberg, S., et al. A UML-based Aspect-Oriented Design Notation For AspectJ. In Proceedings of the 1st International Conference on Aspect-Oriented Software Development. p. 106-112, Enschede, The Netherlands, April 22-26, 2002.

[18] Xing, Z. and Stroulia, E. UMLDiff: An Algorithm for Object-Oriented Design Differencing. In Proceedings of the Automated Software Engineering (ASE 05). p. 54-65, Long Beach, CA, November 7-11, 2005.

Using UML Activities for System-on-Chip Design and Synthesis

Tim Schattkowsky[1], Jan Hendrik Hausmann[2], and Gregor Engels[2]

[1] C-Lab, Paderborn, Germany
tim@c-lab.de
[2] University of Paderborn, Paderborn, Germany
{hausmann, engels}@upb.de

Abstract. The continuous advances in manufacturing Integrated Circuits (ICs) enable complete systems on a single chip. However, the design effort for such System-on-Chip (SoC) solutions is significant. The productivity of the design teams currently lags behind the advances in manufacturing and this design productivity gap is still widening. One important reason is the lack of abstraction in traditional Hardware Description Languages (HDLs) like VHDL. The UML provides more abstract concepts for modeling behavior that can also be employed for hardware design. In particular, the new UML Activity semantics fit nicely with the inherent data flow in hardware systems. Therefore, we introduce a UML-based design approach for complete SoC specification. Our approach enables generation of complete synthesizable HDL code. The equivalent hardware can be automatically generated using the existing tools chains. As an example, we outline Handel-C code generation for an MP3 decoder design.

1 Introduction

For decades, the design of Integrated Circuits (ICs) has been driven by what has been called Moore's law, a self-fulfilling prophecy that the complexity of ICs doubles every 18 months. Although physical effects recently broke the correlation between this increase in IC complexity and a similar direct increase in performance, the law still holds for complexity and will continue do so for at least another decade.

The design methods for ICs failed to catch up with this exponential growth in complexity. This design productivity gap has widened over years and has become one of the most critical issues in hardware design. At the same time, shortened product cycles further increase the pressure for more productivity.

To cope with the increasing complexity, Hardware Description Languages (HDLs) are currently moving from Register Transfer Level (RTL) hardware description towards more abstraction by introducing C-based languages. To some extent, this seems to be similar to the move from assembly language to higher level languages like C in software engineering. It appears that IC design now essentially faces the same complexity challenge that finally led to the move towards model-driven methods for software systems. Thus, the investigation of such methods for hardware design seems to be the logical next step.

O. Nierstrasz et al. (Eds.): MoDELS 2006, LNCS 4199, pp. 737 – 752, 2006.

Nowadays, model-driven software development is mostly based on the Unified Modeling Language (UML). Its upgrade to version 2.0 [11] has significantly extended the expressiveness of some of its core notations, thereby opening up new application areas. The new token-based Activity semantics fit nicely with the data flow dominated behavior of hardware systems and can be employed to describe such behavior at an increased level of abstraction while providing improved readability compared to traditional textual HDLs.

In this paper we will make the case that UML Activities are well suited for modeling the data and control in hardware designs and can serve as the basis for a complete hardware design approach. The next section will discuss related work before section 3 introduces our design approach for hardware systems which is based on Activity Diagrams for behavioral specification and Class, Composite Structure and Deployment Diagrams for providing types, composition and deployment information. Our approach enables complete code generation of synthesizable HDL, which is equivalent to the actual IC. In section 4, we demonstrate such code generation for the Handel-C HDL before section 5 closes with a conclusion and future work.

2 Related Work

There already exist approaches employing more abstract diagrammatic specifications for the specification of hardware designs. Various forms of Block Diagrams and Flow Charts have been used in the industry for a long time, resulting in the IEC standard notations Sequential Function Charts (SFC) and Function Block Diagram (FBD) [8]. However, UML 2.0 Activity Diagrams can be considered as a significant superset of SFCs [15] and provide a higher level of abstraction. Furthermore, Block Diagrams have been studied in [7] with the result that Class Diagrams can express all features of Block Diagrams without loss of expressiveness.

Petri Nets are another behavioral modeling notation used for hardware specification. An overview of different approaches can be found in [17]. Although Activity Diagrams are based on Petri Net ideas, they seem to be more expressive and have a broad background in the UML.

UML is the de-facto standard in the Software Engineering world. Having a common notation is beneficial for combined hardware/software development projects. Some compelling examples for these benefits are presented in [3]. Applying standard UML notations to hardware design has been approached in a number of ways. Hallal et al [7] evaluate various UML diagrams with respect to their applicability to hardware design. McUmber and Cheng [9] provide a metamodel mapping between UML Class Diagrams and state machines on the one hand and VHDL constructs on the other hand. The intention of this work is not only to serve as a basis for VHDL code generation but also to provide a precise semantics for Statecharts. A mapping from Class Diagrams to VHDL code is also proposed by Damasevicius and Stuikys. In [6] they complement this static mapping with metaprogramming techniques to obtain domain specific code-generators. They also focus on the process aspect of hardware development. This process aspect is also targeted by Bahill and Daniels in [2]. YAML [14] is a tool based mainly on UML class and object diagrams which is able to generate SystemC code. Interesting here is the use of Object Diagrams for the detailed specification of a chip's design. We also model the instance level, but use Deployment Diagrams to do this. The approach of Björklund and Lilius [3] is based on UML state machines only and produces VHDL code.

Recently, Model Driven Architecture (MDA) has elicited a number of approaches which generate code from UML models [4]. One possible target for these generators are system-level hardware languages. Concrete works include $^{X}{}_{T}$UML which targets various C dialects of different microcontroller architectures, MOCCA which targets synthesizable VHDL, and works by Thiagarajan et al which translate Rose RT models to SystemC code. An overview of these approaches can be found in [10]. All these approaches are based on UML 1.x. They employ state machines to model the behavior of systems and cannot exploit the fundamentally different semantics for Activities in UML 2.0. The approach in [3] takes Activity Diagrams into account, albeit only as a representation of the transition system specified by a state machine.

SysML [16] is a language for system modeling derived from the UML. Although it is syntactically a strict UML profile, it alters and adds various concepts, especially for modeling continuous systems. These modifications seem to result in semantics that are not consistent with the original UML. Still, the block oriented structure modeling as well as the emphasis on Activities seem to fit with hardware modeling, but are not directly applicable. Furthermore, these concepts are already contained in the UML.

Finally, there is ongoing work to provide specific profiles for SoC design. Fujitsu has already presented preliminary results [12]. The approach focuses on structure modeling for system composition rather than enabling the engineering of a complete system including complete behavior models. The structure modeling employs similar concepts to our approach, but lacks some important elements like support for clock domains. The OMG MARTE RFP [1] is still in an initial phase.

In the context of these ongoing efforts, we have already proposed the application of UML Activities as the core behavior notation for UML-based hardware description [13]. However, there we have only sketched our initial ideas, but did not provide a corresponding design approach. In this paper, we present a new approach for complete SoC design which leads to complete synthesizable system specifications.

3 Hardware Design Based on UML Activities

A model-based design approach for SoC has to capture the system behavior as well as its composition from functional blocks and certain non-functional aspects, like clock domains or the allocation of physical resources. For this, we have identified a UML 2.0 subset for complete SoC specification. This subset is presented as a UML profile. Such a profile is a syntactic subset of the UML with extended domain-specific semantics. The core of this subset is formed by elements for behavior modeling through Activity Diagrams. These elements are complemented by specialized model elements for Class-, Composite Structure- and Deployment Diagrams for modeling the structure and physical aspects of the system. Together, the resulting diagrams form a complete system model. From this system model, full code generation for automatic hardware synthesis can be performed. The following subsections describe our modeling approach and the underlying profile. For this, we will use a MP3 decoder chip design as the illustrating example for the remainder of the paper.

3.1 Structure Modeling

In our approach, modeling the internal structure of a System-on-Chip is based on Class Diagrams for the type definition of its building blocks and Composite Structure for defining the assembly of the complete SoC from such blocks. The mapping to physical resources like clock domains is achieved through the application of Deployment Diagrams.

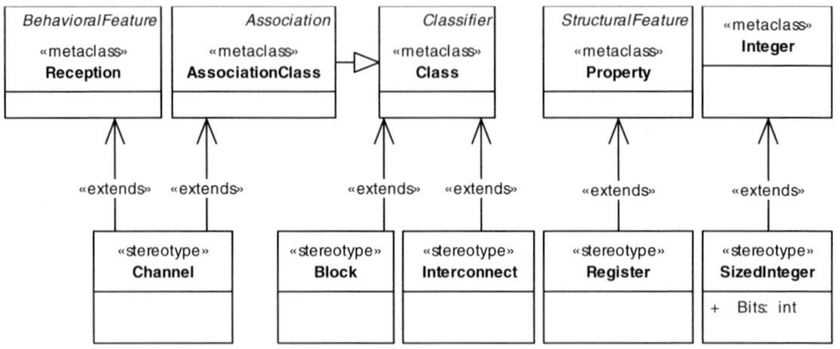

Fig. 1. Extensions for modeling hardware blocks

A SoC in our approach is composed from blocks of synchronous logic. Within our profile, types of blocks are defined through specialized active Classes (see Figure 1). Such an active class is called *Block* in our approach. The behavior of such a Block is defined through a private Activity. This Activity may call sub-Activities on the same instance as well as on instances owned through composition. The Activities belonging to a Class can be considered as the actual methods for Operations where the parameters are mapped to ActivityParameterNodes. However, due to the synchronous nature of Operations, this only fits for non-stream parameters. Thus, a Block may additionally have specialized Reception Features to receive signals that are fed as tokens into an Activity. Such a Reception Feature is called a *Channel* in our approach and is used to enable interaction between different executing Blocks.

The attributes of a Block are *Registers*. Their type is limited to integer numbers and arrays and nested records of those. However, unlike in software systems, the bit

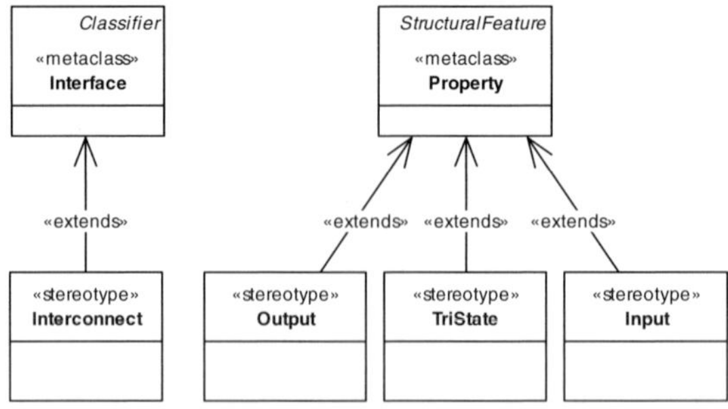

Fig. 2. Extensions for modeling hardware block interfaces

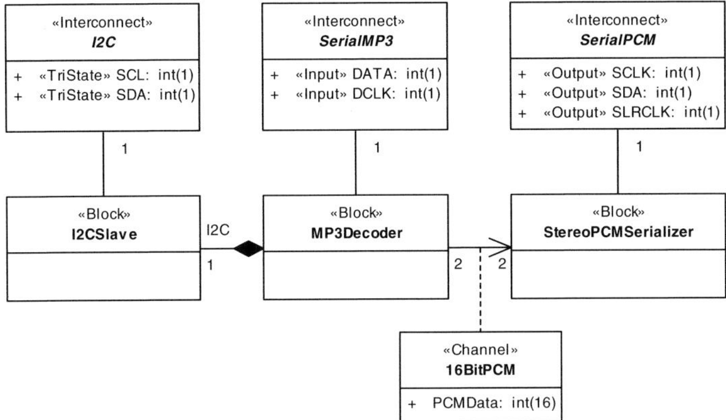

Fig. 3. MP3 decoder Class Diagram

size of integers for hardware systems needs to be fixed as they determine the size of the resulting circuit. Thus, in our approach the bit size of an integer is explicitly specified through the application of a *SizedInteger*. For convenience, the SizedInteger is presented as an int with the size given in braces.

Different Blocks can be connected through their electrical interfaces. This is represented by the *Interconnect* stereotype. However, the implementation of such an Interconnect is just a pair of lines. It is pointless to model these lines. Thus, we decided to treat them as both an Interface and a Class implementing it. For Class Diagrams, the Interface notation is employed to emphasize the interface semantics. At the instance level, a class instance is assumed to enable symmetric links between participating instances. The lines of the Interconnect have to be classified as *Input*, *Output* or *TriState* (see Figure 2). TriState lines may be used bidirectional and are essential for the construction of busses, be it on-chip or external.

As an example, we will consider the design of an MP3 player as shown in Figure 3. The design consists of a core MP3Decoder class implementing the MP3 decode algorithm to decode an incoming serial bit stream of MP3 data on its SerialMP3 Interconnect to stereo 16 bit Pulse Code Modulated (PCM) audio. The PCM audio is sent through two 16 bit Channels to the StereoPCMSerializer class, which is responsible for converting the PCM data into serial stereo I2S data to directly interface with common Digital Analog Converter (DAC) circuits. However, no DAC is included in this model. Instead, a SerialPCM Interconnect is present for interfacing with an external DAC. Finally, the MP3Decoder contains an I2CSlave Block implementing the Philips I2C wire interface to enable external control of the decoder.

The composition of a Block or a complete SoC from other Blocks has to be determined at design time. Dynamic instantiation is not possible in hardware as each instance of a block has to be implemented separately in silicon. In our approach, this assembly is specified through the newly introduced Composite Structure Diagram (CSD). We employ CSDs to describe the composition of a Block from other Blocks as well as the composition of the final system. All associations need to be resolved to actual elements. The "lollipop" notation is used to indicate Interconnections to external hardware.

Figure 4 shows the CSD describing the complete SoC for our MP3 decoder example based on the Class Diagram in Figure 3. We notice the MP3Decoder, its I2CSlave, and the two Channels for feeding the decoded PCM data into the StereoPCMSerializer which outputs serial audio data to the PCMPort. The input for the decoder is provided by the Mp3DataPort.

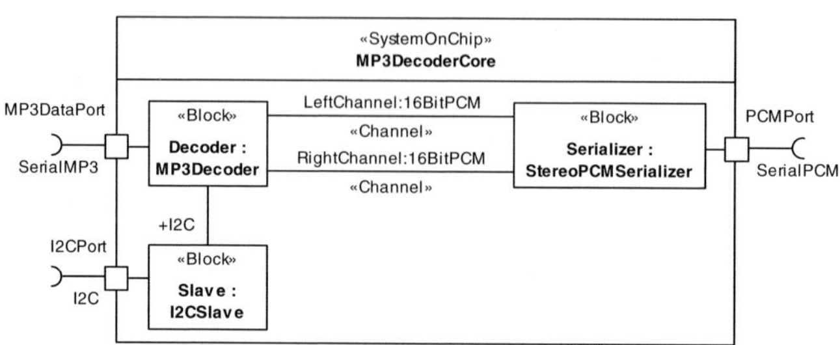

Fig. 4. MP3 decoder Composite Structure Diagram

For synthesis, certain additional platform specific physical parameters must be determined. Some physical parameters, like the physical layout in the chip, are computed by the synthesis tools and require no explicit specification. Other properties like physical pin assignment and the definition of clock domains are the result of explicit design decisions. Such properties must be represented in the design model. For this, we employ a Deployment Diagram variant (see Figure 5). We use the Nodes to represent clock domains, which are an important feature in chip design. Deployed in these clock domains are the same Block instances as in the CSD. All Blocks in the SystemOnChip must be explicitly deployed on such a ClockDomain. The resulting model must conform to the respective CSD.

Technically, a *ClockDomain* is a synchronous block of logic on the chip. Logically, in our approach it may be composed from several Block instances running synchronously at the same clock. The whole *SystemOnChip* is also a ClockDomain which reflects that the chip is externally clocked at a certain rate. The clock itself may be either an internal clock or supplied externally in the case of an *ExternalClockDomain.* Internal clocks can be derived from an existing clock through a simple divider or, in the case of *DerivedClockDomain*, a complex expression. Furthermore, *AbsoluteClockDomains* enable the specification of absolute clock frequencies, which will be implemented based on available system clocks. However, the combination of the chosen target platform (i.e., FPGA or ASIC type) and the logic depth of the real circuit are the limiting factors for the clock rate of the final circuit. Thus, an actual design may fail to meet an AbsoluteClock specification. This can be detected during simulation.

It is important to note that the same Block Instance may actually be part of multiple ClockDomains in different contexts. Thus, the respective Deployment Diagrams have to clarify this context by including all relevant Associations. If a Block is placed only within a single ClockDomain, this is not necessary.

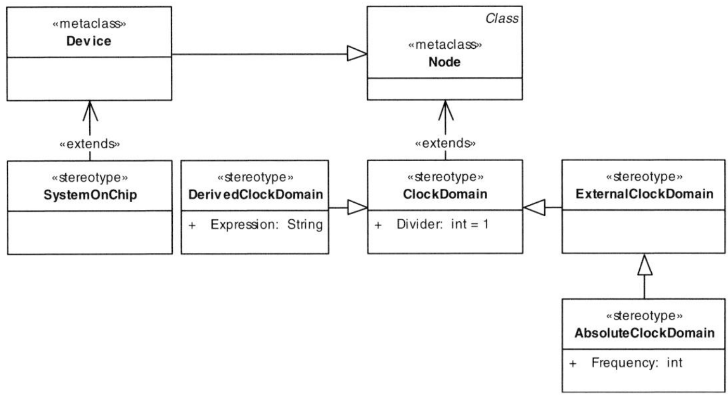

Fig. 5. Extensions for modeling Clock Domains through Deployments

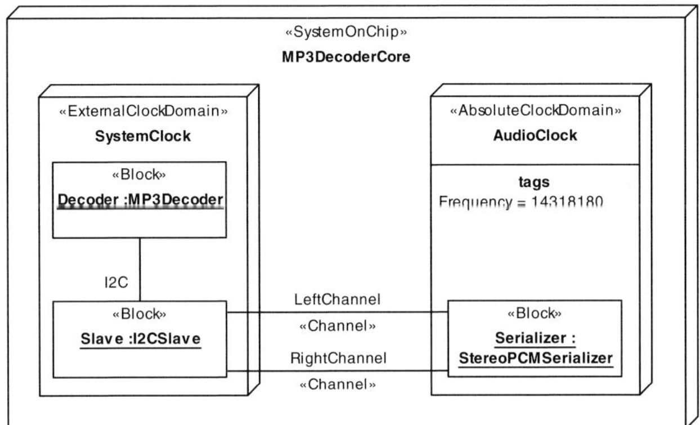

Fig. 6. MP3 decoder Clock Domain Diagram

The Deployment Diagram for our MP3 decoder example shown in Figure 6 shows how the blocks from the CSD are placed in ClockDomains. The Associations are included only for the orientation of the reader and could be omitted. In this example, the Blocks are placed in two different ClockDomains. While the MP3Decoder runs in the ExternalClockDomain controlled by the external chip clock, PCM related Blocks are placed in a separate AbsoluteClockDomain using a fixed clock frequence. The purpose here is to enable real-time playback by using a Clock that can be used to directly derive the respective sample rate for feeding data into the external DACs that are to be connected to the StereoPCMSerializer.

3.2 Activity Diagrams

While the structural models provide information about the outside connections of a single block instance, the behavior specification details its inner workings. Behavior specification in our approach is solely based on activities represented by Activity Diagrams. These Activities represent the concurrent data flow and processing in a

Block instance by means of the common model elements for activities. These elements include actions interconnected by object and control flows. Decision, merge, fork, and join nodes are used to control such flows in the Activity.

The activities in our approach may contain four types of actions. SendSignalAction and AcceptEventAction are employed to transmit and receive data using a Channel. The CallBehaviorAction invokes sub-Activities and OpaqueActions are employed to embed C-style statements into the Activities (e.g., for assignments). C-style syntax is also used for expressions (e.g., in guards).

The semantics of forks and joins for object flows must be defined. In our approach, we essentially consider object flows as direct connections between the logic for actions. Thus, there is no buffering of tokens in our approach. If such buffering is desired, an explicit implementation (e.g., through a FIFO queue) has to be provided. In this context, a fork on an object flow is considered as sending the same data input into multiple target nodes (e.g., actions). This aligns quite well with the proposed token copy semantics as defined by UML 2.0. Joining object flows is only allowed for tokens representing the same object. Joining different data flows should be done by specifying an action which combines these inputs. Finally, the concept of token competition is not supported in our approach. Thus, there can only ever be one outgoing edge from an object node (e.g., a pin).

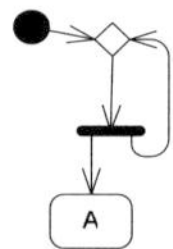

Fig. 7. Pattern for spawning an unlimited number of control flows

Hardware is inherently non-reentrant. This also applies to the actions and activities in our approach since they map directly to a part of a hardware circuit. As a consequence, activities in our approach cannot issue recursive calls. Furthermore, a special pattern in an activity has to be avoided. The fragment in Figure 7 demonstrates the core problem: Along the right hand side loop any number of tokens can be spawned at this fork, leading to multiple concurrent executions of action A For hardware synthesis such a situation is very undesirable. We thus impose the general wellformedness condition that for each fork which is part of a cyclic flow structure (i.e. one flow outgoing from the fork is (transitively) also an incoming flow of the fork), a join must exist in the path which joins all outgoing flow form the fork node. This ensures that each action in the model may be activated by at most one logical thread. This rule of course covers implicit joins and forks on actions. Furthermore, the condition also holds for activities with multiple initial nodes as these can be considered to be forked from a single initial node. Thus, the corresponding fork cannot have a cycle and does not break the rule.

For our example, the specification of the behavior of the main MP3Decoder class is shown in Figure 8. This activity controls the actual MP3 decode process which has several stages represented by CallBehaviorActions to nested sub-activities. Many of these stages can be performed concurrently for the two different channels of stereo

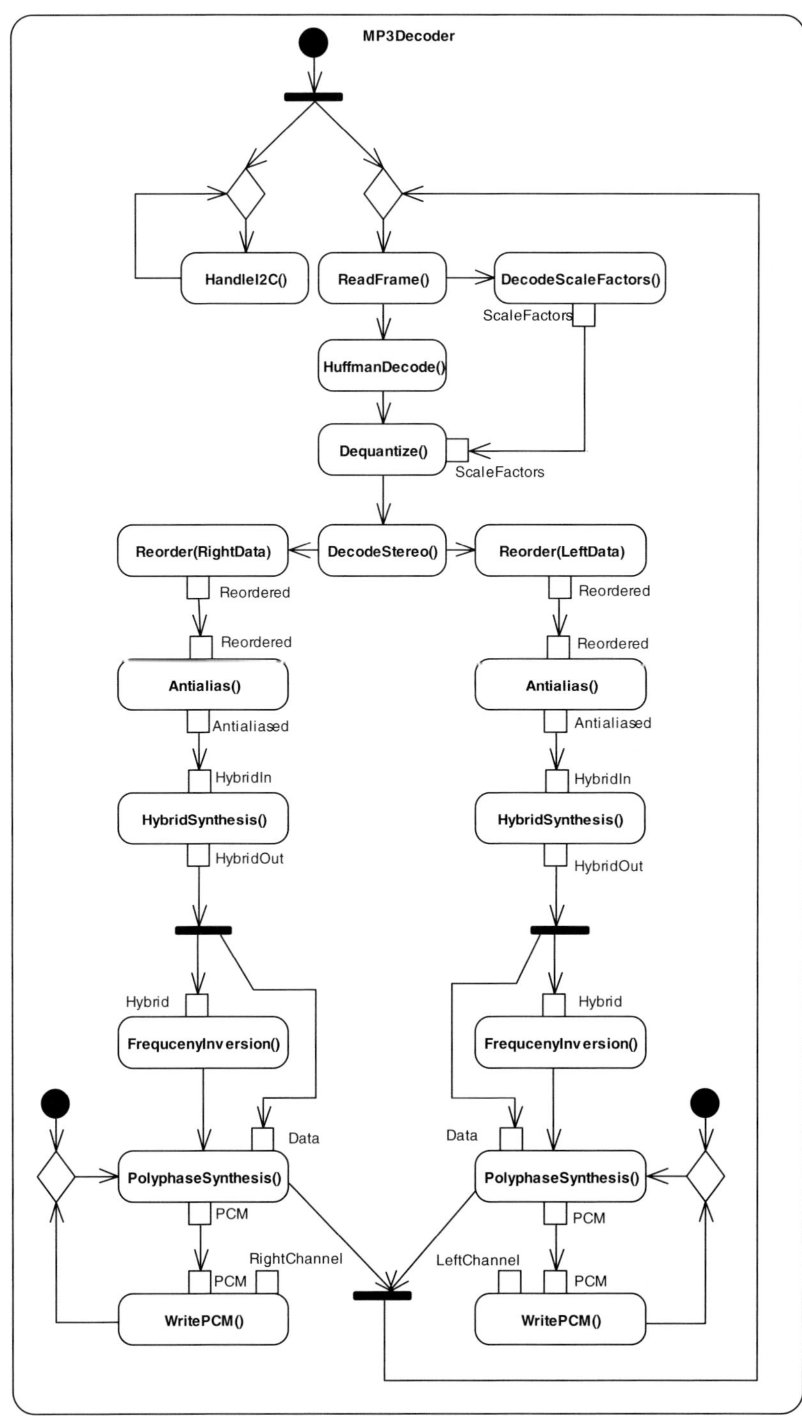

Fig. 8. MP3Decoder Class - Main Activity

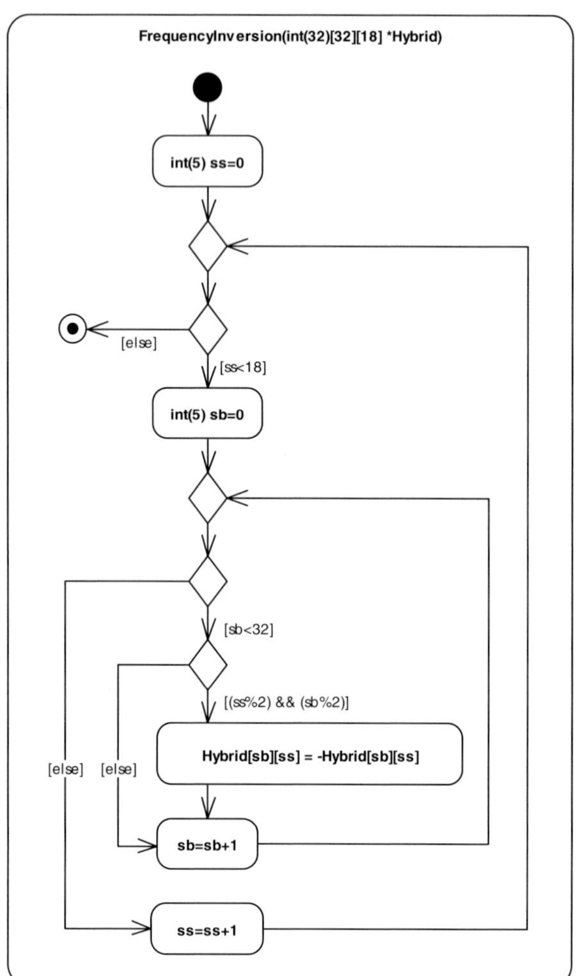

Fig. 9. MP3Decoder.FrequencyInversion Sub-Activity.

audio data. The extra control flow between WritePCM and Polyphase Synthesis ensures the wellformedness of the example and prevents the data flow between these actions until WritePCM has finished its execution from the previous iteration. Thus, no data conflicts can occur. Note that ValuePins are employed to provide the two WritePCM actions with the (constant) information which channel they address.

As an example for activity nesting, the MP3Decoder main activity invokes the FrequencyInversion() sub-Activity shown in Figure 9. All actions there are OpaqueActions containing statements using a C-style syntax. The same syntax is employed for the guards as well.

The example presented here demonstrates that even rather complex control and data flows can be presented in an intuitive and concise way using activity diagrams. The required functionality can be decomposed in different levels of detail, where the upper level provides an overview while the lower level supplements details of the single execution steps. Finally, combined with the Class and Deployment Diagrams, we have a complete model which allows code generation.

4 Handel-C Code Generation

The SoC models based on our approach enable fully automatic generation of synthesizable HDL hardware descriptions, which can be automatically transformed into an actual ASIC or FPGA implementation through the application of the existing EDA tools chains. The transformation from the SoC model to a particular HDL differs depending on the level of abstraction provided by the HDL and the employed language elements and semantics. Generally, C-based languages like Handel-C, CatapultC provide the highest level of abstraction while RTL languages require the most implementation work, as more mechanisms have to be explicitly implemented. However, especially for system-level languages, the transformation often has to account for complex semantics, like in the case of the SystemC simulation kernel.

Celoxica Handel-C [5] is a behavior-oriented programming language for hardware synthesis that compiles directly to a Field Programmable Gate Array (FPGA) or Application-Specific Integrated Circuit (ASIC). Handel-C provides a relatively high level ob abstraction compared to RTL, but still maintains relatively simple semantics, which make it an ideal candidate to demonstrate HDL synthesis. However, is important to note that our approach is independent from a particular HDL and could be employed directly for generating RTL structures.

Handel-C employs a C-style syntax using essentially value assignments based on registers and internal and external memory grouped by control constructs. For synthesis, the program code is transformed directly into equivalent gates and flip-flops (e.g., for adders, multipliers, latches) representing the expression evaluation trees and control logic. C-style flow control is achieved using conditional branches (if and switch-statements) and loops (for, do and while-statements). Additionally, some additions have been made to reflect the different capabilities of hardware systems. This includes the support for parallel blocks where all statements execute concurrently. Finally, it is very useful that the code generation for the C-style statements employed for the OpaqueActions in our approach is quite straightforward.

Handel-C code generation based on our approach starts at the ClockDomain level at the Deployment Diagram. Each ClockDomain must be compiled to a separate file as Handel-C only allows one clock per source file. This clock is then defined in the main() function of the source file which also invokes the implementation of the main activities for all instances concurrently (see Figure 10 for an example).

Attributes are mapped to global variables which are fully qualified using their identifier paired with an instance identifier. The actual realization of these attributes in hardware is first determined by the use of ClockDomains and later by the synthesis tool. The synthesis tool will automatically implement attributes using registers or on-chip RAM depending on the characteristics of the target platform.

```
// Global Delarations
...
chan int 16 PCMReader0_PCMData;
chan int 16 PCMReader1_PCMData;
...
int 1 Serializer_SerialOutput_SCLK = 0;
interface bus_out() Serializer_SerialOutput_SCLK_Pin
        (int 1 Data=Serializer_SerialOutput_SCLK);
int 1 Serializer_SerialOutput_SLRCLK = 0;
interface bus_out() Serializer_SerialOutput_SLRCLK_Pin
(int 1 Data=Serializer_SerialOutput_SLRCLK);
int 1 Serializer_SerialOutput_SDA = 0;
interface bus_out() Serializer_SerialOutput_SDA_Pin
(int 1 Data=Serializer_SerialOutput_SDA);
...
// Clock Definition
set clock = internal_divide 2;
...
void main void(void){
   // Local Declarations
   ...
   par {
            PCMReader0_main();
            PCMReader1_main();
            Serializer_main();
}}
```

Fig. 10. Excerpt from the generated code for the second ClockDomain

All interaction between ClockDomains must take place using either Channels, which are mapped directly to Handel-C channels, or multiported RAM. Thus Attributes accessed across ClockDomains must be represented using Multi Ported RAM (MPRAM). However, this is only possibly if such MPRAM is available at the target platform and the number of ports is not less than the number of involved ClockDomains. Otherwise the synthesis will fail.

Each Activity is compiled to a Handel-C function. This includes all sub-Activities. The respective parameters are taken from the parameter pins in the model and explicitly declared parameters which represent local variables in the scope of the activity. As each Handel-C function is finally implemented as a block of non-reentrant hardware, an individual copy of each such function is created per instance. Handel-C directly supports this through function arrays.

The code generation for a particular Activity essentially yields a set of parallel executing Actions or sequential blocks of Actions. While sequential actions can be put directly into sequential code blocks, the execution of parallel Actions is coordinated based on simulating the token flow in the Activity. For this, boolean variables indicate enabled edges. The execution of an Action is enabled by checking the conjunction of the corresponding variables for all incoming edges. Once an Action is enabled, it starts execution by resetting all input edges. After executing the actual Action, the corresponding output edges are enabled. Note that this implies that exactly one token is buffered per edge. The actual objects for object flows between actions are mapped directly into variables. For sub-activities, these are passed by reference. Access to these objects is still coordinated through the boolean edge variables.

As an example, we will now consider an excerpt from the generated code for an MP3Decoder instance:

```
void Decoder_Main0()
{
    // Provide initial Tokens
    Action1_A_Enabled=true;
    Action2_A_Enabled=true;
    Action2_1_1_A_Enabled=false;
    Action2_2_1_A_Enabled=false;
    ...
    par
    {
       // Action1:CallOperationAction=HandleI2C()
       seq
       {
          if (Action1_A_Enabled)
          {
             // Consume Input Tokens
             par
             {
                Action1_A_Enabled=false;
             }
             // Perform Action
             HandleI2C0();
             // Produce Output Tokens
             par
             {
                seq
                {
                   // Wait till Action is ready
                   while (Action1_A_Enabled);
                   // Produce Token
                   Action1_A_Enabled=true;
                }
             }
          }
       }
       // Action2:CallOperationAction=ReadFrame()
       seq
       {
          if (Action2_A_Enabled)
          {
             // Consume Input Tokens
             par
             {
                Action2_A_Enabled=false;
             }
             // Perform Action
             ReadFrame0();
             // Produce Output Tokens
```

```
            par
            {
               seq
               {
                  // Wait till Action is ready
                  while (Action2_1_1_A_Enabled);
                  // Produce Token
                  Action2_1_1_A_Enabled=true;
               }
               seq
               {
                  // Wait till Action is ready
                  while (Action2_1_2_A_Enabled);
                  // Produce Token
                  Action2_2_1_A_Enabled=true;
               }
            }
         }
      }
      // Action2_1_1:CallOperationAction=DecodeScaleFactors()
      seq
      {
         if (Action2_1_1_A_Enabled)
         {
            // Consume Input Tokens
            par
            {
               Action2_1_1_A_Enabled=false;
            }
            // Perform Action
            DecodeScaleFactors0(&Action2_1_1_ScaleFactors);
            // Produce Output Tokens
            par
            {
               seq
               {
                  // Wait till Action is ready
                  while (Action3_A_Enabled);
                  // Produce Token
                  Action3_A_Enabled=true;
                  Action3_A_Value=&Action2_1_1_ScaleFactors;
               }
            }
         }
      }
      ...
   }
```

In our example, three Actions are included (see also Fig. 8). Action_1 and Action_2 are enabled at start of the Activity while Action_2_1_1 depends on a control token from Action_2. Thus, Action_2_1_1 waits for the required control token, consumes it, executes the actual Action by calling DecodeScaleFactors0() and stores the result in a local variable. Once no pending token is on the OutputPin, the results gets forwarded to the variable associated with the OutputPin and the Action has completed execution. At this point, it again waits to be enabled.

Finally, it is important to note that the same pattern for generating HDL code for Activities can be employed in other HDLs as well. The employed concepts are inherently supported by all common HDLs.

5 Conclusions and Future Work

In this paper we have presented a novel approach for model-based hardware design enabling automatic code generation of synthesizable HDL for ASICs and FPGAs. We have shown that UML 2.0 Activity Diagrams are well suited for hardware. They nicely capture data and control flows in hardware systems implementing complex algorithms like in our MP3 decoder example. HDL Code generation has been outlined for synthesizable Handel-C code, but is generally not bound to a particular HDL.

Future work will include the investigation of code generation of other HDLs as well as a deeper evaluation of the approach in different applications. The generated code could be simplified w.r.t. certain common situations like sequential parts that could be mapped directly to sequential HDL blocks. However, as the synthesis results are comparable, this is more a cosmetic issue. Furthermore, the approach may be extended to enable more explicit control of the hardware generation process to enhance support for design space exploration.

References

[1] André, C., Cuccuru, S., Dekeyser, J.-L., De Simone, R., Dumoulin, C., Forget, J., Goutier, T., Gérard, S., Mallet, F., Radermachenr, A., Rioux, L., Shaunier, T, Sorel, Y.: MARTE: A New OMG Profile RFP for the Modeling and Analysis of Real-Time Embedded Systems. In Proc. DAC Workshop UML for SoC Design (UML-SoC) 2005, 2005.

[2] Bahill, A.T. and Daniels, J.: Using object-oriented and UML tools for hardware design: a case study, Systems Engineering, 6(1): 28-48, 2003.

[3] Björklund, D. and Lilius, J.: From UML Behavioral Descriptions to Efficient Synthesizable VHDL. In: Proceedings of the 20th IEEE NORCHIP Conference, Nov. 2002.

[4] M. Balcer, S. Mellor: Exploring the Role of Executable UML in Model-Driven Architecture. In: Executable UML: A Foundation for Model-Driven Architecture, Addison-Wesley, 2002.

[5] Celoxica: Handel-C language Overview, www.celoxica.com,2002.

[6] Damasevicius,R. and Stuikys, V.: Application of UML for hardware design based on design process model. ASP-DAC 2004: 244-249, 2004.

[7] H. Hallal, K. Xiao-Hua, and R. Negulescu. Experiments in modeling integrated circuit blocks by UML. In International Workshop on IP Based Synthesis and System Design, 1999.

[8] International Electrotechnical Commission: IEC 1131-3: Programmable Controllers – Part 3: Programming Languages, IEC 1131-3, 1993.

[9] McUmber, W. and Cheng,B.: UML-Based Analysis of Embedded Systems Using a Mapping to VHDL, The 4th IEEE International Symposium on High-Assurance Systems Engineering, p.56-63, November 17-19, 1999.
[10] G. Martin, W. Müller (eds.): UML for SoC Design. Kluwer, 2005.
[11] Object Management Group: UML 2.0 superstructure specification. Available at http://www.omg.org/cgi-bin/doc?ptc/2005-07-04, 2005.
[12] Rajan, S., Hasegawa, T, Shoji, M., Zhu, Q., Tsuneo, N.: UML Profile for System-on-Chip (SoC). In Proc. DAC Workshop UML for SoC Design (UML-SoC) 2005, 2005.
[13] Schattkowsky, T., Hausmann, J.H., Rettberg, A.:Using UML Activities for Synthesis on Reconfigurable Hardware. In Proc. DAC Workshop UML for SoC Design (UML-SoC) 2005, 2005.
[14] Sinha, V., Doucet, F., Siska, C., Gupta, R., Liao, S., Ghosh, A.: YAML: a tool for hardware design visualization and capture. Proceedings of the 13th international symposium on System synthesis, pp.1080-1082, IEEE Computer Society, 2000.
[15] Stoerrle, H: Semantics and Verification of Data-Flow in UML 2.0 Activities. In Proc. Intl. Ws. on Visual Languages and Formal Methods (VLFM04), 2004.
[16] SysML Partners: SysML Specification v. 1.0a., Available at http://www.sysml.org, 2005.
[17] Yakovlev, A., Gomes, L. and Lavagno, L. (Eds.): Hardware Design and Petri Nets, Springer, 2000.

Modeling and Early Performance Estimation for Network Processor Applications

Antonia Bertolino[1], Alvise Bonivento[2],
Guglielmo De Angelis[1,*], and Alberto Sangiovanni Vincentelli[2]

[1] ISTI – CNR
Pisa, Italy
{antonia.bertolino, guglielmo.deangelis}@isti.cnr.it
[2] University of California
Berkeley, CA USA
{alvise, alberto}@eecs.berkeley.edu

Abstract. The design of modern embedded systems has to cope with quite challenging requirements in terms of flexibility, performance, and domain space exploration. To this purpose, we present a general methodology joining the principles of Platform Based Design and Model Driven Engineering. The former was especially conceived for embedded systems design, the latter focuses on models as the primary design artifacts. From their combination, we can to introduce a methodology for the design of Network Processor Applications. Starting from models described using the UML notation, we provide an early estimation of performance related parameters and compare in advance possible alternative implementations. In particular, the system behavior is specified by a collection of Sequence Diagrams describing the various usage scenarios, merged into an internal representation called Message Sequence Net. To prove the effectiveness of the proposed methodology, a case study on the design of an SCTP client is presented.

1 Introduction

The growing complexity and time-to-market pressure make the design of embedded systems extremely challenging. New approaches and tools are required to develop an effective methodology that leverages design reuse [19]. Network Processors are specialized embedded systems adopted for Internet equipment such as routers, Voice over IP (VoIP) bridges, and virtual private network (VPN) gateways.

Network Processors fill a middle ground between totally hard–coded solutions and general purpose programmable devices. They are characterized by significant diversity in terms of technological solutions and heterogeneity of processing elements. Designing applications on Network Processors requires not only to verify the functional correctness, but also to check the satisfaction of non–functional constraints (i.e., performance and cost) that depend on the specific mapping of the software functionality onto the hardware architecture [10].

To cope with this heterogeneity and with the demand for a thorough design space exploration, we need methodologies and tools that allow the designer to specify the

* G. De Angelis PhD grant is sponsored by Ericsson Lab Italy in the framework of the PISATEL initiative. http://www1.isti.cnr.it/ERI/

O. Nierstrasz et al. (Eds.): MoDELS 2006, LNCS 4199, pp. 753–767, 2006.

application at a high level of abstraction and that support the early estimation of the candidate solutions.

In the embedded systems community, similar issues were already considered in [19], where a system is modeled as a composition of subsystems whose functionality is specified independently from the hardware implementation. This orthogonalization of concerns between functionality and architecture avoids to commit to a particular implementation too early in the design process [20]. To facilitate the development of such a methodology, it is important to allow the designer to specify the functionalities using a semantic domain that is adequate for the specific application [12]. In [32], the need of standard techniques and languages to capture specifications is motivated. In [6], we identify the UML profiling mechanism as a simple way to define a Domain Specific Language (DSL) for the context of Network Processors.

In this paper, we present a methodology to capture specifications and provide an early estimation of possible implementations over Network Processors. The structural part of the application is specified using a UML profile called NAP [6]. The use cases are described in scenarios and their relations are captured using a representation called Message Sequence Net (MSN). Starting from the MSN description and a model of the candidate mapping, we estimate the latency performance of the solution.

The rest of the paper is organized as follows: in Sec. 2 we present some related work. In Sec. 3 we present an overview of the proposed methodology, and in Sections 4, 5, and 6 we provide a detailed description of its steps. To validate our approach, in Sec. 7 we present a case study on the development of an SCTP client deployed over a Network Processor. In Sec. 8 we discuss how our methodology can be seen as a particular case in the frame of a wider, more general design methodology. Conclusions are provided in Sec. 9.

2 Related Work

There is a large body of literature handling non–functional requirements. We identify three main categories: analysis, profiling and translating[1].

Analytical approaches based on mathematical models such as Queueing Networks [8] and Petri Nets [22] are used to prove some non–functional properties or measure indicators for performances estimations.

The second category involves the works whose aim is to provide high level instruments to properly annotate the models. Usually these approaches cover the earliest software development phases. In this context, attempts to merge the functional and non–functional aspects has led to a more specialized use of UML that has proved useful to the definition of DSLs. OMG's UML Profile for Schedulability, Performance and Time (SPT) [24] and the more recent MARTE [23] represent the most popular efforts in this field.

The last category includes those works that aim to provide automated tools for managing non–functional requirements in the early stage of the software design [3]. Their

[1] Approaches in the area of runtime monitoring of system performance are not included in this kind of classification, since they refer to system implementation rather than system design [3].

main goal is to extract the information attached to the models and transform it into inputs for non–functional analysis tools [29] such as the ones described in the first class. In [5] UML Sequence Diagrams and Statecharts are used for system validation and performance estimation. The authors assume that the system behavior is described by a set of Statecharts and that Sequence Diagrams are used to emphasize specific patterns of interaction among Statecharts. This approach is based on the derivation of a General Stochastic Petri Net [18] composing the information coming from both kinds of diagrams. Similarly, [11] and [14] show how to incrementally build a performance model from early available UML diagrams. A more recent result is presented in [26], where the authors exploit a relational and graph grammar–based transformation, to develop an abstraction–raising transformation based on UML.

The main inspiration for our work comes from Ulysses [28,27]. Ulysses is a scenario–based specification technique that defines and decomposes the functional specification process into intermediate steps. Although originally thought for protocol synthesis from a Message Sequence Chart (MSC) specification, it can be applied also in other contexts.

According to Ulysses, a MSN is defined as a collection of scenarios, each one described with a MSC [21]. The relations of ordering, concurrency or conflict among the scenarios are expressed using Petri Nets semantics. The advantages in this approach are twofold. First and foremost, a Petri Net can be easily checked for liveness, deadlock-freedom and boundedness, allowing for the early detection of specification errors. Secondly, Petri Nets have partial order semantics and allow for maintaining the concurrency between fine–grain actions until they are scheduled on shared architecture resources.

3 Methodology Overview

The UML Activity Diagram in Fig. 1 represents the flow chart for the proposed methodology.

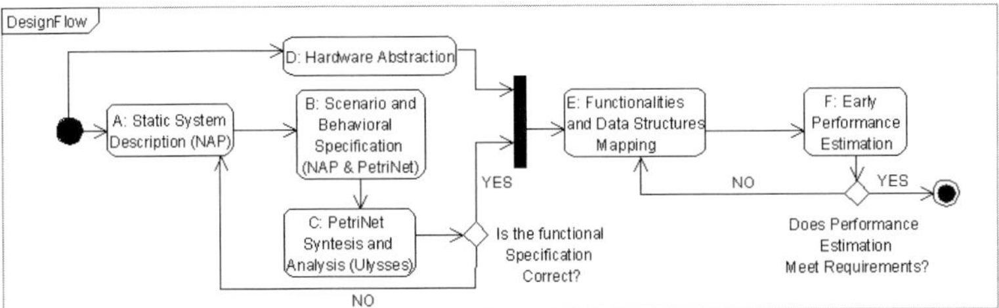

Fig. 1. Design Flow

Step A consists in describing the structural part of the application using the Network Processors Application Profile (NAP). NAP is a UML Profile originally introduced in [6] to describe applications for Network Processors while hiding hardware details. The NAP descriptions focus on the concept of SoftwareUnits that represent atomic portions of a software application. In this paper, we extend NAP to support an explicit specification of the communication between SoftwareUnits and data structures, and to provide a notation that is useful for the description of the behavioral model of the application.

Then, step B consists in describing the behavioral model of the application using a scenario–based specification. Each scenario represents a particular use case of the system and is described using a UML Sequence Diagram. The relations among the scenarios are represented by means of an MSN (see Sec. 2). Using the covering algorithm proposed in Ulysses, a consistent Petri Net from such MSN can be obtained [27]. In step C, this Petri Net representation can be used to prove some important properties such as liveness, deadlock-freedom and boundedness and detect errors in the specification at an early stage.

Step D corresponds to selecting a specific Network Processor as the target platform. Note that our intent here is to define a methodology to capture specifications and provide an estimation of applications in the earliest phases of software design. It is out of the scope of this work to model all the complex aspects of an embedded hardware platform such as the Network Processor. Hence, at the software life cycle phase we refer, the information we consider regards how the software running on the different processors interact.

In step E the mapping of the functionality onto the architecture is divided in two sub–steps (see Fig. 2).

Since there may be more SoftwareUnits than available processors, and even if this is not the case the interactions among two SoftwareUnits could be so tight that implementing them on different processors may be inefficient, the first sub–step consists in partitioning the set of SoftwareUnits. All the SoftwareUnits that are required to run concurrently on the same processor define a *processing group* (PG). Given a partitioning, we determine the statistics of the required number of clock cycles to process a packet for each PG.

The second sub–step consists in mapping the PGs over the different physical processors. If there are more available processors than PGs, we can create different instances of some PGs and map them on the remaining processors to maximize the resource utilization. However, following the definition of PG, each processor can support only a single PG. Given a mapping, we group processors running instances of the same PG in *service centers* and we estimate the latency introduced by each service center. Starting from this estimation, in step F the designer can quantify the efficiency of the proposed solution in terms of latency and supported throughput; if necessary, (s)he can go backward in the design flow and try another mapping (or hardware platform).

Notice that the partitioning restricts the design space to those solutions following the rule that each processor supports only a single PG. Strictly speaking this is not a limitation of our methodology, in the sense that we are explicitly interested in the early estimation of the impact of the selection of different hardware platforms. Our assumption leaves out any design solution that can be characterized in terms of latency performance only after the code development process.

We focus our analysis to the interactions between the SoftwareUnits and the data structures stored in the different type of memories. This assumption is motivated by the results reported in [17] and from our previous implementation experiences on Network

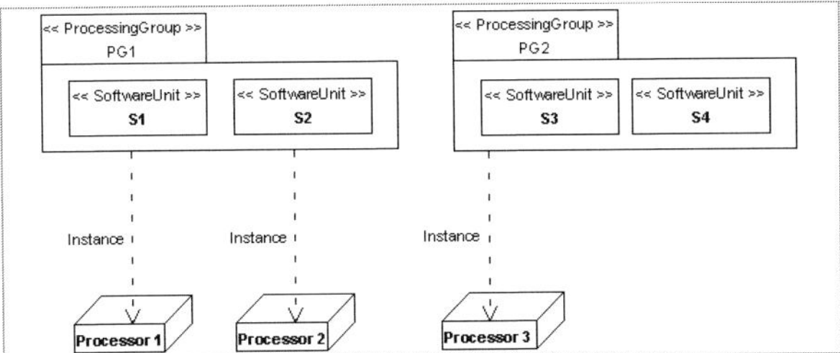

Fig. 2. Software Application Mappings

Processors [4]. In those works it is clear how the main impact to the final performance is given by these operations. For example, the latency access for a processor to an external memory can require from 10 to 200 of idle clock cycles [13]. Notice that communications among SoftwareUnits also have a non negligible impact whenever the two SoftwareUnits are mapped on different processors and shared memories are used as the communication medium.

4 Network Processors Applications Profile

A generic communication protocol is logically organized in a bi–dimensional matrix, highlighting two orthogonal concepts: the rows represent the architectural elements composing the application (i.e. interfaces with other layers, window transmission management), while the columns represent the aspects of the protocol (i.e. send, receive, and control). Cross points in this logical matrix identify particular aspects for specific architectural elements and they are called SoftwareUnits. A SoftwareUnit accesses shared data structures to perform *Read* or *Write* operations. Data structures represent the most common abstract data types such as *List*, *Table* or *Queue*.

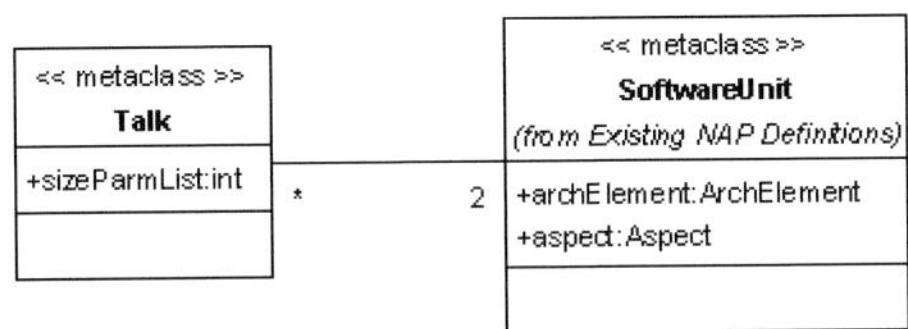

Fig. 3. Domain Viewpoint of the extension to NAP

In a domain viewpoint [24], an explicit communication between two SoftwareUnits is modeled using a *Talk* instance that can be annotated with the number of required parameters (sizeParmList). In a UML viewpoint, for each domain element introduced by NAP, Table 1 shows the UML element extensions along with the name of the related stereotype. These definitions allow the designers to apply the stereotypes to UML Class Diagrams and Sequence Diagram elements. Specifically the base class sets for those stereotypes representing SoftwareUnits, Lists, Tables and Queues, include the UML

Class element for the structural modeling and UML Lifeline for the behavioral one. Similarly, the ≪Read≫ and ≪Write≫ base class sets refers to the Association and Message UML elements. The communication domain concept is modeled by means of the stereotype ≪Talk≫, applicable to Association and Message UML elements.

Table 1. Stereotype Definition

Concept	Base Class	Stereotype
SoftwareUnit	Class–Lifeline	≪SoftwareUnit≫
Read	Association–Message	≪Read≫
Write	Association–Message	≪Write≫
Talk	Association–Message	≪Talk≫
List	Class–Lifeline	≪List≫
Table	Class–Lifeline	≪Table≫
Queue	Class–Lifeline	≪Queue≫

5 Behavioral Model Generation

We describe the behavioral aspects of an application using a scenario–based specification where each scenario represents a particular use case of the system and is described using a UML Sequence Diagram.

We characterize a UML Sequence Diagram with the tuple $(\mathsf{M}, \mathsf{L}, \mathsf{E}, \mathsf{g}, \mathsf{m}, <)$, where:

- M is a finite set of asynchronous messages ($(\mathsf{signal}, \mathsf{stereotype})$). Calling $\mathsf{m} \in \mathsf{M}$ a message, we refer to its components as $\mathsf{m.signal}$ and $\mathsf{m.stereotype}$.
- L is a finite set of Lifelines.
- E is a set of events in the Sequence Diagram. An event $\mathsf{e} \in \mathsf{E}$ is defined as a pair $(\mathsf{type}, \mathsf{msg}) \in \{\mathsf{send}, \mathsf{rec}\} \times \mathsf{M}$. We refer to its components as $\mathsf{e.type}$ and $\mathsf{e.msg}$.
- $\mathsf{g} : \mathsf{E} \rightarrow \mathsf{L}$ is a function that gives for each event the corresponding Lifeline.
- $\mathsf{m} : \mathsf{E} \rightarrow \mathsf{E}$ is a bijective function that links pairs of send and receive events.
- $<$ is a partial order relation between events.

Notice that a Lifeline represents a SoftwareUnit or a data structure in NAP. The interactions among these elements are modeled by means of asynchronous messages using the stereotypes defined in Sec. 4.

Between different use cases there may be relations of causality or parallel execution. In [27] these relations are captured by means of a Petri Net, where each *transition* represents a particular scenario and each *place* represents the precondition to the execution of the out–connected scenarios. As an extension to the model proposed in [27], we introduce the notion of probability associated with the edges that connect places with transactions. We define a Probabilistic Petri Net as an ordered pair $(\mathsf{PN};\mathsf{p})$, where PN is a usual Petri Net [22] and $\mathsf{p} : \mathsf{Place} \rightarrow [0..1]$ is a function that represents the likelihood for a use case to be selected in case alternative use cases can be enabled. We assume that the function p as well as the relation among the different use cases are provided by domain experts.

Notice that the Probabilistic Petri Net is different from the Stochastic Petri Net (SPN) [18]. The stochastic extension to the Petri Nets defines a firing semantics in the case of timed transition. In our case, the probability function p is introduced to provide a conflict resolution policy.

Fig. 4 depicts an example of the whole MSN for the case study [2] and Fig. 5 an enlarged view of a particular scenario.

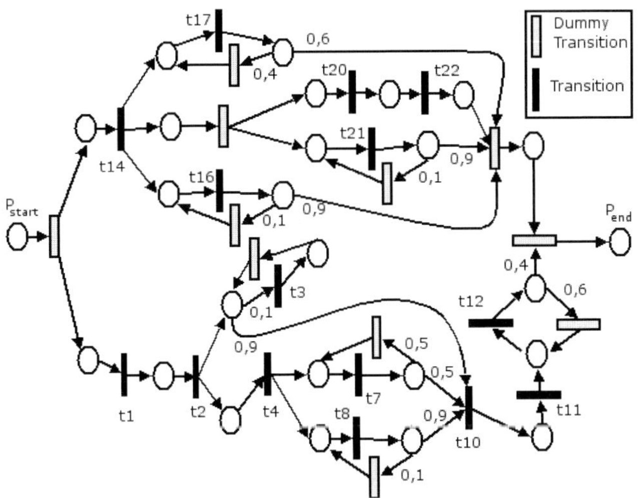

Fig. 4. MSN for the case study

Notice that in Ulysses, a scenario is described using a MSC. Considering the similarities between a MSC and a UML Sequence Diagram, as defined by several authors [1,25,15], the procedures outlined in Ulysses to derive a Petri Net from a MSN representation are still valid.

6 Mapping and Performance Estimation

The first step in the performance evaluation is to estimate the cost of the different processing groups. For this purpose we use the MSN description. We start by evaluating the cost of each scenario in terms of clock cycles given by the number of the ≪Read≫,≪Write≫ and ≪Talk≫ operations. Referring to the notation introduced in Sec. 5 for Sequence Diagram, Fig. 6 shows the algorithm that for every scenario of the MSN returns its cost for the different processing groups (costVect). The inputs of the function are: a scenario described with a UML Sequence Diagram SD, the function G that for each SoftwareUnit (SU) returns the processor where it is mapped, and the function T that, given a data structure, returns its access time in terms of clock cycles.

[2] Since Ulysses approach can be applied only to safe Petri Nets [22], in some cases we have to introduce some *dummy–transitions*, just to maintain this property. In the MSN, such transitions have to be interpreted as scenarios that do not describe any interaction.

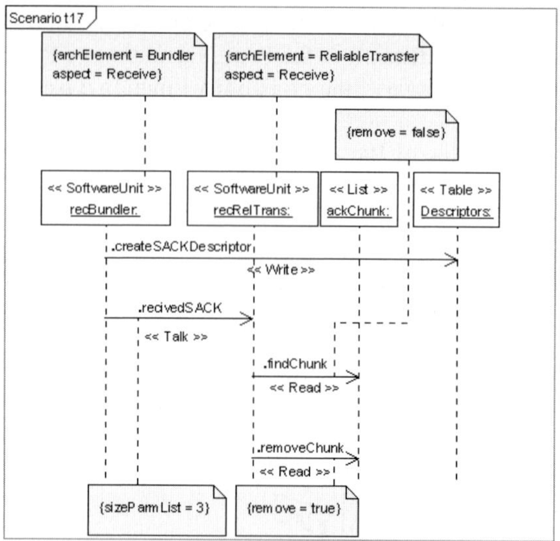

Fig. 5. A particular scenario for the case study

```
scenarioCost (SD,G,T,costVect){
   sortEvents(SD.E);
   foreach element costVect[i]=0;
   foreach SU in SD.L
     costVect[G(SU)]+=suCost(SD,SU,G,T);
}
```

```
suCost(SD,SU,G,T){
  cost=0;
  foreach e in SD.E
    if(SD.g(e) == SU){
      if (e.type == "send")
        switch (e.msg.stereotype){
          case "Read":
          case "Write":
            cost+=T(SD.g(SD.m(e)));
            break;
          default;
        }
      if (e.msg.stereotype == "Talk")
        if (G(SU) != G(SD.g(SD.m(e))))
          cost+=δ*e.msg.stereotype.sizeParmList;
    }
  return cost;
}
```

Fig. 6. Algorithm for the cost assessment of the scenarios in the MSN

Using this information, we extract the service time in terms of clock cycles for a particular sequence of scenarios in the MSN. This estimation is obtained executing the relative Petri Net with a token that accumulates the cost of the scenarios represented by the visited transitions. To solve the non–deterministic choices due to alternative compositions, we use the probabilistic parameter p as explained in Sec. 5. The enabling of parallel scenarios represents concurrent situations that can occur in the modeled system. When a transition is enabled by more than one place, its firing produces a token whose cost is given by the sum of the costs of the enabling tokens. If as a result of a firing more than one place has a token (see *t2* in Fig. 4), only one of the produced tokens maintains the cost accumulated until that moment, while the others start from zero. Since the Petri Net is considered safe, any parallel composition has to narrow in a synchronization configuration. Consequently, the final token effectively measures the cost of the encountered scenarios.

Since the service times derived by a single execution of the MSN depend on a sequence of probabilistic choices, more executions are required to collect a statistically relevant sample set. We call $\mathsf{m}^{\mathsf{i}}_{\mathsf{x}}$ the mean number of clock cycles and $\mathsf{m}^{\mathsf{i}}_{\mathsf{x}^2}$ its variance obtained considering the results of the different executions for the ith processing group.

Starting from the average cost in terms of clock cycles for each processing group, we need to estimate the cost of assigning different instances of the processing groups to the different processors. To this purpose we model the result of this mapping step as a Queueing Network, where processors running the same *processing group* are grouped together in *service centers*. Each service center is modeled as a node in a Queueing Network with a single unbounded input queue where the packet arrival process follows a Poisson distribution and its service time a generic distribution[3]. Different nodes are connected together according to the data flow that relates the different processing groups. These relations are usually well known to the application designer and are a consequence of the logical structure of the protocol.

We derive the service time of each processor using the statistics for the service time in terms of clock cycles for the relative processing group and the processor clock rate. Given the traffic arrival rate at both ends (receiving and sending), we derive the traffic arrival rate for each service center solving a system of equations associated to the connectivity of the Queueing Network. For example, consider the Queueing Network of Fig. 7–b where there are four nodes with two processors each and the nodes are serially connected for both receiving and transmitting traffic. Call λ the traffic arrival rate at both ends of the protocol layer and λ_j the traffic rate passing through the jth node. Assuming that a share p of the output traffic of each node is related to the receiving flow, the relative system of equations is:

$$\begin{cases} \lambda_1 = \lambda + p\lambda_2 \\ \lambda_2 = (1-p)\lambda_1 + p\lambda_3 \\ \lambda_3 = (1-p)\lambda_2 + p\lambda_4 \\ \lambda_4 = (1-p)\lambda_3 + \lambda \end{cases}$$

Starting from the Queueing Network topology and the service times and arrival rates parameters, we can apply the PK–formulas [8] to estimate the mean latency introduced by each node of the Queueing Network. These results can be used to estimate the latency and the throughput limitations introduced by the solution.

7 Case Study

We focus on the modeling of a Stream Control Transmission Protocol (SCTP) [30] layer on a Network Processor. SCTP is a reliable connection oriented transport protocol proposed by the SIGTRAN Group [31]. SCTP was proposed to improve some of TCP and UDP lacks regarding applications on call control signaling on packet network.

[3] According to the Kendall notation, this type of node is an $\mathsf{M}/\mathsf{G}/\mathsf{n}/\infty$ queue [8].

The basic unit of information in SCTP is the *chunk*. A chunk is a portion of an SCTP packet, which can contain information about control and protocol status, acknowledgment or a part of the upper layer protocol data.

In previous works we show how to use NAP to describe the organization of this application [6,4]. We consider only 8 SoftwareUnits: four for the send aspect of each SCTP architectural element (StreamEngine, FlowControl, ReliableTransfer, Bundler) and four for the receive one. The application also requires different kind of data structure such as a list that stores the descriptors of those sent chunks waiting for an acknowledgment (ackChunks) and a table that contains the descriptor of each chunk (Descriptors).

Fig. 4 depicts the MSN for the case study. Since in SCTP the specification of the functionalities refers to chunks, the data exchanged by elements in the scenarios are chunks.

Each transition in the MSN represents a use case for the SCTP layer in the management of a chunk. In Fig. 5 we represent the reception of an acknowledgment (SACK) by the protocol pear (*t17* in the MSN of Fig. 4). In this case, an acknowledgment descriptor is created and its information stored in the Descriptors table from the recBundler. This SoftwareUnit is also in charge of communicating to the recRelTrans that a SACK was received. The receive aspect of the ReliableTransfer, looks for the correspondent data chunk into the ackChunks list and removes it.

The selected hardware architecture is the C–5 Freescale C–Port Network Processor [13]. Briefly, the C–5 is composed by 16 RISC processor (CPRC) grouped in 4 clusters and an Executive Processor (XP) that is mainly responsible of some control functions such as booting or hosting interface. The device provides also a set of dedicated co–processors allowing the access to external memory or I/O interface: the Buffer Management Unit (BMU), the Table Lookup Unit (TLU) and the Queue Management Unit (QMU). The access time to the information stored into these memories depends by the co–processors used to retrieve it.

We estimate the cost for each type of memory access using the parameters in [13]. For example, using the nominal TLU latency and considering that a chunk data descriptor size is 16 bytes [16], we calculate that each interaction with such memory takes 227 clock cycles for a CPRC. In the same way, we calculate that each access to a QMU takes 11 clock cycles.

There are two main ways to map the described software elements onto the available resources. The first mapping groups together all the SoftwareUnits with the same *aspect*, while the second one all those SoftwareUnits that belong to the same *architectural element*. Our previous study [4] advises that using the first mapping it is possible to replicate both the send and receive software on 4 different processors. On the other hand, the second mapping allows assigning 2 instances for each architectural element. Fig. 7 depicts the Queueing Network representation of the two organizations. In both cases, we decide to map the queue structures in the memory managed by the QMU and the lists in the one managed by the TLU.

Table 2 summarizes the costs in clock cycles of each scenario obtained applying the algorithm outlined in Sec. 6 for both mappings. The cost of each scenario is a vector with two entries in the case of the *aspect*–grouping and with four entries in the case

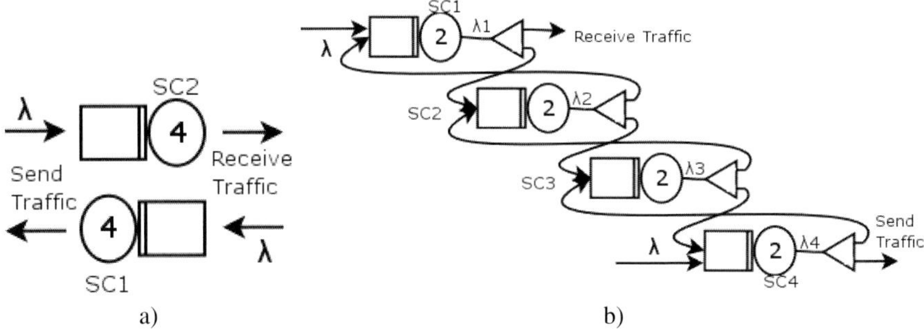

a) b)

Fig. 7. Queueing Network representation of two mapping alternatives

Table 2. Scenarios Costs

	Aspect		Arch. Element			
	Send (SC1)	Receive (SC2)	StrEng (SC1)	FlowCtrl (SC2)	RelTrans (SC3)	Bundler (SC4)
t1	227+227	0	227+227	0	0	0
t2	0	0	11*4	11*4+11*5	11*5	0
t3	67+227+227	0	0	0	67+227+227	0
t4	227+11	0	0	277+11	0	0
t7	11	0	0	0	0	0
t8	11	0	0	0	0	0
t10	0	0	0	11	0	11
t11	11+227	0	0	0	0	11+227
t12	11+227	0	0	0	0	11+227
t14	0	227+227	0	0	0	227+227
t16	0	227+227	0	0	0	227+227
t17	0	67+227+227	0	0	11*3+227+67	11*3+227
t20	0	11	11*3	11*3+11	0	0
t21	11	11	0	11*2	0	11*2
t22	0	227+227	227+227	0	0	0

of *architectural element* one. For example, entries such as *t17* in Table 2 show how different mappings of the SoftwareUnits can introduce extra communication costs.

We estimate $\mathsf{m_x}$ and $\mathsf{m_x^2}$ for each service center using the MSN of Fig. 4 and the procedure outlined in Sec. 6. For the first mapping the cost vector associated to the token has two entries, while for the second mapping the cost vector has four entries.

Considering the costs for processing group, the processors speed, the packet arrival rate and the maximum chunk data size, it is possible to estimate the mean delay introduced by each processing step. We assume a packet arrival rate $\lambda = 20\ packet/sec$ and a packet size $\mathsf{pacSize} = 0,5Mbyte$. Since a maximum size for a data chunk is $\mathsf{chunkMaxLength} = 1452\ byte$ [30] and the C–5 processor clock frequency is $\mathsf{cpuFreq} = 266MHz$ [13] the data chunk arrival rate is:

$$\lambda^{'} = \lambda \frac{\mathsf{pacSize}}{\mathsf{chunkMaxLength}} = 0,00137741M\ Chunk/sec$$

Converting the service time from clock cycles into seconds:

$$\mu_{\mathsf{x}}^{\mathsf{i}} = \frac{\mathsf{m_x^i}}{\mathsf{cpuFreq}}$$

Table 3. Early Performance Estimation

λ' (MChunk/Sec)		0,006887052	
n^{th} Service Center	μ_x^{SCi} (μSec)	μ_{x2}^{SCi}	$\overline{del_{SCi}}$ (μSec)
SC1	11,80609895	25,17047107	11,89457255
SC2	12,07582511	18,07498165	12,13938837

λ' (MChunk/Sec)		0,006887052	
n^{th} Service Center	μ_x^{SCi} (μSec)	μ_{x2}^{SCi}	$\overline{del_{SCi}}$ (μSec)
SC1	3,703007519	3,0337E-24	3,703007519
SC2	1,771613835	0,014285172	1,771700848
SC3	7,83934391	18,13008343	7,980084142
SC4	9,16915068	16,59120632	9,26412752

Table 3 presents the mean delays for each service center $\overline{del_j}$ obtained applying the PK-formulas in Sec. 6 to the two queuing network models.

The last step of this case study is the interpretation of the obtained values. Assume that we want to compare the two mappings by their relative latency performance. We consider the maximum of the average delay values for the first mapping and the sum of the average delays for the second mapping. Fig. 8 plots the trend of the latency introduced by the two solutions as a function of the packet arrival rate. Assuming that both solutions are always admissible with respects to the other constraints (e.g., internal memories occupation), the solution that groups the SoftwareUnits by the aspect tagged value represents the preferred choice.

8 Discussion

The proposed methodology combines principles of the Platform Based Design [33] (PBD) and Model Driven Engineering [9] (MDE).

PBD has emerged in recent years as a methodology for embedded systems design. In PBD, the notions of flexible hardware architectures as well as of rigorously–specified software interfaces are captured by the general expressive concept of a *platform* [20]. A platform represents a layer in the design flow which abstracts away the underlying, subsequent design–flow steps.

PBD is a combination of a top–down and a bottom–up approach. The basic tenets of this design methodology focus on a *meeting–in–the–middle process* whereby the successive refinements of the functional description (top–down part) meet with abstractions of potential implementations (bottom–up part). The meet–in–the middle process takes place at precisely defined layers called *common semantic domains*.

In the software engineering community, modeling has always played a crucial role. However, it is only with the introduction of MDE that notations and tools have been proposed for expressing different system views and eventually weave them together for a specific environment [9]. MDE embraces all those approaches and tools that move the design and the development of a software product from a *code–centric* perspective to a *model–based* one [7]. In MDE, the notion of a model is not intended to capture all the

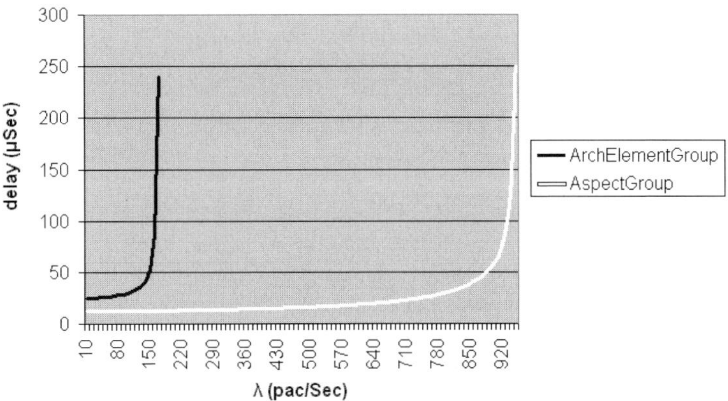

Fig. 8. Latency trends for the two solution

aspects of a system: instead a system is usually represented by a set of different models, each one capturing some specific aspects [7].

We believe there exists a strong connection between the concepts of *model* and *platform* that have inspired the two methodologies. While PBD helps to identify the most adequate abstraction levels to model the functionality, the architecture, and the common semantic domain, MDE provides the mathematical foundation and tools to describe, handle and transform these models during the design and development process [32]. In this work we have shown some preliminary evidence of how the two methodologies can fruitfully interoperate and eventually converge into a comprehensive approach for effective and efficient design of embedded systems.

9 Conclusions and Future Work

The main research goal for the embedded systems community is to provide a set of tools and abstractions to facilitate the design reuse across different hardware platforms. In this paper we proposed a methodology to address this issue for the design of Network Processors.

First, we proposed an extension to the NAP profile that allows to describe the structural part of an application, independently from the hardware architecture. Secondly, we presented a rigorous methodology to specify the behavioral part of an application that in line with MDE principles allows for the early stage detection of errors in description of the functionality. Starting from this description and a mapping onto a selected hardware platform, we showed how to estimate the latency performance of the proposed solution.

So far our work was concerned with the latency analysis. However, network processors have constraints on the available local memory and it is important for Network Processor applications to characterize the proposed solutions also with respect to their local memory occupation. We plan to extend our framework to address these issues by extracting this information from the NAP model of the application.

References

1. M. Abdalla, F. Khendek, and G. Butler. New results on deriving SDL specifications from MSCs. In *SDL Forum*, pages 51–66, 1999.
2. S. Afsharian, A. Bertolino, G. De Angelis, P. Iovanna, and R. Mirandola. A Model Based Approach to Design Applications for Network Processor. In *Proc. RISE 2004*, volume LNCS 3475. Springer, 2005.
3. S. Balsamo, A. Di Marco, P. Inverardi, and M. Simeoni. Model-based performance prediction in software development: A survey. *IEEE Trans. Software Eng*, 30(5):295–310, 2004.
4. D. Barbieri. Network Processors and Next Generation Networks : Design Methodology and Implementation of a Case of Study, 2005. Laurea Thesis, Università degli Studi di Roma "Tor Vergata" – in Italian.
5. S. Bernardi, S. Donatelli, and J. Merseguer. From UML Sequence Diagrams and Statecharts to analysable Petri Net Models. In *Proc. 3rd Int. Workshop on Software and Performance (WOSP-02)*, pages 35–45, 2002.
6. A. Bertolino, G. De Angelis, and R. Mirandola. UML-based design of network processors applications. In *Proc. EUROMICRO-SEAA*, pages 424–431. IEEE Computer Society, 2005.
7. J. Bézivin. On the unification power of models. *Journal of Software and Systems Modeling*, 4(2):171–188, May 2005.
8. G. Bolch, S. Greiner, H. de Meer, and K.S. Trivedi. *Queueing Networks and Markov Chains: Modeling and Performance Evaluation with Computer Science Applications*. John Wiley & Sons, August 1998.
9. A.W. Brown. Model driven architecture: Principles and practice. *Software and System Modeling*, 3(4):314–327, 2004.
10. R. Chen, M. Sgroi, L. Lavagno, G. Martin, A. Sangiovanni-Vincentelli, and J. Rabaey. UML and Platform–Based design. In L. Lavagno, G. Martin, and B.V. Selic, editors, *UML for real: design of embedded real-time systems*, chapter 5, pages 107–126. Kluwer Academic Publishers, 2003.
11. V. Cortellessa and R. Mirandola. PRIMA-UML: A Performance Validation Incremental Methodology on Early UML Diagrams. *Science of Computer Programming*, 44(1), 2002.
12. A. Ferrari and A. Sangiovanni-Vincentelli. System design: Traditional concepts and new paradigms. In *International Conference on Computer Design (ICCD '99)*, pages 2–13. IEEE, October 1999.
13. Freescale. *C–5 DCP Architecture Guide*, 1999.
14. V. Grassi and R. Mirandola. PRIMAmob-UML: a methodology for performance analysis of mobile software architectures. In *Proc. 3rd Int. Workshop on Software and Performance (WOSP-02)*, pages 262–274. ACM Press, 2002.
15. Ø. Haugen. Comparing UML 2.0 interactions and MSC-2000. volume LNCS 3319, pages 65–79. Springer, 2004.
16. SCTP Prototype Implementation. http://www.sctp.de/sctp.html/.
17. S. Lakshmanamurthy, K.Y. Liu, Y. Pun, L. Huston, and U. Naik. Network processor performance analysis methodology. *Intel Technology Journal*, 6(3):19–28, August 2002.
18. M. Ajmone Marsan, A. Bobbio, and S. Donatelli. Petri nets in performance analysis: An introduction. *Lectures on Petri Nets I: Basic Models*, LNCS 1491:211–256, 1998.
19. G. Martin. UML for Embedded Systems Specification and Design: Motivation and Overview. In *Proc. DATE*, pages 773–775, 2002.
20. G. Martin, L. Lavagno, and J. Louis-Guerin. Embedded UML: a merger of real-time UML and co-design. In *Proc. CODES*, pages 23–28, 2001.
21. S. Mauw. The Formalization of Message Sequence Charts. *Computer Networks and ISDN Systems*, 28(12):1643–1657, 1996.

22. T. Murata. Petri nets: Properties, analysis and applications. *Proceedings of the IEEE*, 77(4):541–574, April 1989.
23. OMG. *UML Profile for Modeling and Analysis of Real-Time and Embedded systems*, OMG Document – realtime/05-02-06 edition, Jannuary 2005.
24. OMG. *UML Profile for Schedulability, Performance and Time Specification*, OMG Document – formal/05-01-02 edition, Jannuary 2005.
25. E. Rudolph, J. Grabowski, and P. Graubmann. Towards a harmonization of UML-sequence diagrams and MSC. In *SDL Forum*, pages 193–208, 1999.
26. A. Sabetta, D.C. Petriu, V. Grassi, and R. Mirandola. Abstraction–raising transformation for generating analysis models. In *MoDELS Satellite Events*, pages 217–226, 2005.
27. M. Sgroi. *Platform-based Design Methodologies for Communication Networks.* PhD thesis, U.C. Berkeley, 2002.
28. M. Sgroi, A. Kondratyev, Y. Watanabe, L. Lavagno, and A. Sangiovanni-Vincentelli. Synthesis of petri nets from message sequence charts specifications for protocol design. In *Proceedings of Design, Analysis and Simulation of Distributed Systems Symposium, DASD'04*, pages 262–274, 2004.
29. C. U. Smith and L. Williams. *Performance Solutions: A practical Guide To Creating Responsive, Scalable Software*. Addison-Wesley, 2001.
30. R. R. Stewart, Q. Xie, K. Morneault, C. Sharp, H. J. Schwarzbauer, T. Taylor, I. Rytina, M. Kalla, and L. Zhang. Stream Control Transmission Protocol. Technical Report RFC 2960, IETF, October 2000.
31. The SIGTRAN Group Web Site. http://www.sigtran.org/.
32. L. Tratt. Model transformations and tool integration. *Journal of Software and Systems Modelling*, 4(2):112–122, May 2005.
33. A. Sangiovanni Vincentelli. Defining Platform–based Design. *EEDesign of EETimes*, February 2002.

A Formal Semantics of UML-RT

Michael von der Beeck

BMW Group
Michael.Beeck@bmw.de

Abstract. The modeling language UML-RT, a dialect of the UML, supports the development of complex, hierarchical systems following a component-oriented approach. However, for a solid foundation of model analysis and model transformations a formal semantics definition of UML-RT is missing. Therefore, this paper presents a precise syntax and semantics definition of a sublanguage of UML-RT. This sublanguage puts an emphasis on the specification of complex, hierarchical state-based models. It considers atomic capsules - containing a statechart - and complex capsules that recursively consist of capsules communicating asynchronously with each other over connectors. Labeled transition systems are chosen as semantic domain, such that the UML-RT semantics can be defined in an SOS style a la Plotkin.

1 Introduction

Model-based software development using standard modeling languages represents a modern approach putting emphasis on the early development phases. Typical representatives are UML - constituting the de-facto modeling standard for industrial object-oriented applications - and UML-RT [13] - a dialect of UML especially designed for the development of distributed, embedded systems.

A great advantage of these modeling notations is given by their great variety of intuitive and mostly well-known graphical notations which support quite different kinds of information to be modeled: e.g. requirements, static structure, as well as interactive and dynamic behaviour. However, both languages - UML as well as UML-RT - suffer from insufficient semantics definitions lacking preciseness and completeness. The potential consequences are manyfold: Different persons might interprete the same model in different ways. Furthermore, the foundation for systematic, precise model analysis (e.g. consistency checks) and for model simulation or code generation is missing.

Some work aiming at a precise UML semantics definition has already been done or has at least been started. Due to its very comprehensive syntax, this is a long lasting, tedious task.

However, in this paper we consider UML-RT. More precisely, we deal with the syntax and semantics definition of a sublanguage of UML-RT. In this setting we focus on behavioural aspects modeled with UML-RT capsules: there are atomic capsules which reside on a statechart as well as complex capsules which can also contain a statechart, but which furthermore recursively contain a set of capsules communicating asynchronously with each other and with the surrounding capsule via connectors.

We choose labeled transition systems as semantic domain for UML-RT - the reason being twofold: on the one hand they are very appropriate for an operational semantics

O. Nierstrasz et al. (Eds.): MoDELS 2006, LNCS 4199, pp. 768–782, 2006.

definition of (behavioural) modeling languages like UML-RT, on the other hand many equivalence and refinement notions well-known from the process algebra area [9,5] are defined with respect to labeled transition systems. Such notions are very appropriate means for precise systematic model analysis. They can e.g. be used to define consistency notions for UML-RT models.

The rest of the paper is structured as follows: In section 2 we precisely define the syntax of UML-RT models, whereas in section 3 we precisely define their semantics. Section 4 discusses related work. We conclude and discuss future work in section 5.

2 Syntax of UML-RT Models

We define the syntax of UML-RT models in two steps. At first we define the syntax of UML-RT Statecharts. Then we define the syntax of UML-RT capsules using the - already existing - syntax definition of UML-RT Statecharts. Note that we use the terms *UML-RT capsules* and *UML-RT models* as synonyms.

2.1 UML-RT Statechart Terms

UML-RT Statecharts is a visual language. However, for our aim to define a formal semantics, it is convenient to represent UML-RT Statecharts not visually but by textual terms. This is also done in related work for "classical" Statecharts [8,15] as well as for UML Statecharts [6,17].

Let $\mathcal{N}, \mathcal{T}, \Pi$ be countable sets of state names, transition names, and events, respectively. We denote events and actions by $a, b, c, \ldots$. For a set M let M^* denote the set of finite sequences over M. Then, the set $\mathsf{UML\text{-}SC}$ of *UML-RT Statechart terms* is inductively defined to be the least set satisfying the following conditions, where $n \in \mathcal{N}$.

1. **Basic term:** $s = [n]$ is a UML-RT Statechart term with $\mathsf{type}(s) = \mathsf{basic}$. Therefore s is also called a *basic term.*
2. **Or-term:** If $s_1, \ldots, s_k$ are UML-RT Statechart terms for $k > 0$, $\rho = \{1, \ldots, k\}$, $l \in \rho$, $\mathsf{HT} = \{\mathsf{none}, \mathsf{deep}\}$, and $T \subseteq \mathsf{TR} =_{\text{df}} \mathcal{T} \times \rho \times \Pi \times (\Pi \cup \{\epsilon\}) \times \rho \times \mathsf{HT}$ with $\epsilon \notin \Pi$, then $s = [n, (s_1, \ldots, s_k), l, T]$ is a UML-RT Statechart term with $\mathsf{type}(s) = \mathsf{or}$. Therefore, s is also called an *Or-term.* Here, $s_1, \ldots, s_k$ are the *subterms* of s, T is the set of *transitions*[1] between the subterms of s, s_1 is the *default subterm* of s, l is called the *active state index* of s (or for short: the *index* of s), and s_l is the *currently active* subterm of s (or for short: s_l is *active*). ϵ is called the *empty output.*
   Note that active state index $l \in \{1, \ldots, k\}$ denotes the l-th term within the k-tuple $(s_1, \ldots, s_k)$ of the subterms of s. Analogously, note that components two and five of a transition $t = (\underline{t}, i, e, a, j, ht) \in T$ - namely i and j - of an Or-term $s = [n, (s_1, \ldots, s_k), l, T]$ refer to the i-th and j-th term of the k-tuple $(s_1, \ldots, s_k)$, respectively, but not to the indexes of the states' names in the k-tuple.
   For each transition $t = (\underline{t}, i, e, a, j, ht) \in T$, we define $\mathsf{name}(t) =_{\text{df}} \underline{t}$, $\mathsf{sou}(t) =_{\text{df}} s_i$, $\mathsf{ev}(t) =_{\text{df}} e$, $\mathsf{act}(t) =_{\text{df}} a$, $\mathsf{tar}(t) =_{\text{df}} s_j$, and $\mathsf{historyType}(t) =_{\text{df}} ht$. $\mathsf{name}(t)$

[1] Later on, we will classify this kind of transitions as *syntactic* transitions.

is called the *transition name* of t, $\mathsf{ev}(t)$ and $\mathsf{act}(t)$ are called the *trigger part* and *action part* of t, respectively. $\mathsf{sou}(t)$ and $\mathsf{tar}(t)$ are called the *source* and *target* of t, respectively. Furthermore, $\mathsf{historyType}(t)$ is called the *history type* of t. Finally, (e, a) is called the *label*[2] of t and is graphically represented as e/a or as $\underline{t} : e/a$.

In both cases (Basic term and Or-term) we refer to n as the *root name* of s and write $\mathsf{root}(s) =_{\text{df}} n$. We assume that all root names and transition names are mutually disjoint, so that terms and transitions within UML-RT Statechart terms are uniquely referred to by their names. For convenience, we sometimes write "state" instead of "term" and abbreviate $(s_1, \ldots, s_k)$ by $(s_{1..k})$.

As can be seen from our UML-RT Statechart term syntax we do not consider the following features of UML-RT Statecharts: entry and exit actions, interlevel transitions, and pseudostates. However, entry and exit actions as well as interlevel transitions had been included in our previous work [17], where we already defined a UML-RT Statechart semantics. Due to lack of space we do not consider these features in this work, where the UML-RT Statechart syntax only constitutes a part of the overall UML-RT capsule syntax.

We exemplify our textual syntax of UML-RT Statecharts graphically by Fig. 1 showing a complete UML-RT capsule which contains a UML-RT Statechart term S shown as a rectangle with rounded corners and with (root) name n_S in the upper part of the figure:

$S = [n_S, (S5, S1), l, \{t_1, t_2\}]$ is a UML-RT Statechart term with $\mathsf{type}(S) = \mathsf{or}$, i.e. S is an Or-term, where

- n_S is the root name of S,
- $\{S1, S5\}$ is the set of subterms of S, where
  - $S1$ is an Or-term with $S1 = [n_{S1}, (S4, S2, S3), l', \{t_3, t_4, t_5\}]$,
  - n_{S1} is the root name of $S1$,
  - $S5$ is a basic term,
  - n_{S5} is the root name of $S5$,
- $S5$ is the default subterm of S,
- $l \in \{1, 2\}$ is the active state index of S, (but not shown in Fig. 1)
- $\{t_1, t_2\}$ is the set of transitions between the subterms of S with $t_1 = (\underline{t}_1, 1, e_1, a_1, 2, none)$ and $t_2 = (\underline{t}_2, 2, e_2, a_2, 1, none)$.

2.2 UML-RT Capsules

Let $\mathcal{N}_{ca}, \mathcal{N}_{po}, \mathcal{N}_{co}$ be countable sets of capsule names, port names, and connector names, respectively. Furthermore, let Prot, the set of *protocols* over Π, be defined as $\mathsf{Prot} =_{\text{df}} \{pr \,|\, pr \subseteq \Pi \times \Pi\}$ and CO, the set of *connectors* over Π, be defined as $\mathsf{CO} =_{\text{df}} \mathcal{N}_{co} \times \mathcal{N}_{po} \times \mathcal{N}_{po} \times \Pi^*$. Then the set CAP of *UML-RT capsules* is inductively defined to be the least set satisfying the following conditions:

1. **Basic UML-RT Capsule:**
   If $n \in \mathcal{N}_{ca}, po_1, \ldots, po_l \in \mathcal{N}_{po}$ for $l \geq 0$, $pr_{i_1}, \ldots, pr_{i_l} \in \mathsf{Prot}$, $S \in \mathsf{UML\text{-}SC}$ and $\sigma \in \Pi^*$, then

[2] Later on, we will classify this type of labels as *syntactic* labels.

$$ca = [n, (po_1, \ldots, po_l), (pr_{i_1}, \ldots, pr_{i_l}), S, \sigma]$$

is a UML-RT capsule. More specifically, ca is also called a *basic UML-RT capsule*.

2. **Complex Non-behavioral UML-RT Capsule:**
If $n \in \mathcal{N}_{ca}, po_1, \ldots, po_l \in \mathcal{N}_{po}$ for $l \geq 0$, $pr_{i_1}, \ldots, pr_{i_l} \in \mathsf{Prot}$, $ca_1, \ldots, ca_k$ are UML-RT capsules for $k > 0$, and $co_i \in \mathcal{N}_{co} \times (\{po_1, \ldots, po_l\} \cup \bigcup_{j=1}^{k} \mathsf{Ports}(ca_j))^2 \times \Pi^* \subseteq \mathsf{CO}$ for $1 \leq i \leq m$ for $m \geq 0$, then

$$ca = [n, (po_1, \ldots, po_l), (pr_{i_1}, \ldots, pr_{i_l}), (ca_1, \ldots, ca_k), (co_1, \ldots, co_m)]$$

is a UML-RT capsule. More specifically, ca is also called a *complex non-behavioural UML-RT capsule*.

3. **Complex Behavioral UML-RT Capsule:**
If $n \in \mathcal{N}_{ca}, po_1, \ldots, po_l \in \mathcal{N}_{po}$ for $l \geq 0$, $pr_{i_1}, \ldots, pr_{i_l} \in \mathsf{Prot}$, $S \in \mathsf{UML\text{-}SC}$, $\sigma \in \Pi^*$, $ca_1, \ldots, ca_k$ are UML-RT capsules for $k > 0$, and $co_i \in \mathcal{N}_{co} \times (\{po_1, \ldots, po_l\} \cup \bigcup_{j=1}^{k} \mathsf{Ports}(ca_j))^2 \times \Pi^*$ for $1 \leq i \leq m$ for $m \geq 0$, then

$$ca = [n, (po_1, \ldots, po_l), (pr_{i_1}, \ldots, pr_{i_l}), S, \sigma, (ca_1, \ldots, ca_k), (co_1, \ldots, co_m)]$$

is a UML-RT capsule. More specifically, ca is also called a *complex behavioural UML-RT capsule*.

For the three abovementioned cases the following notions are used:
n is called the *name* of ca, $\mathsf{Ports}(ca) =_{\text{df}} \{po_1, \ldots, po_l\}$ is called the *set of ports* of ca, $\mathsf{Prot}(po_j) =_{\text{df}} pr_{i_j}$ for $1 \leq j \leq l$ is called the *protocol* of po_j, S is called the *Statechart* of ca, σ is called the *input queue* of ca, and $\mathsf{Conn}(ca) =_{\text{df}} \{co_1, \ldots, co_m\}$ is called the *set of (UML-RT) connectors* of ca.

Informally, a basic UML-RT capsule does not contain any capsules. In contrast, both types of complex UML-RT capsules recursively contain capsules. Furthermore, a complex non-behavioral UML-RT capsule does not contain a Statechart on its the top level, whereas a complex behavioral UML-RT capsule contains a Statechart on its top level.

The UML-RT capsule syntax defined above does not support the following features: conjugate ports, event priorities, do activities, and dynamic capsules.

In the subsequent sections we need the following definitions. Let $\mathsf{Caps}(po_i) =_{\text{df}} ca$ for $1 \leq i \leq l$ and $\mathsf{SubCaps}(ca) =_{\text{df}} \{ca_1, \ldots, ca_k\}$, where $ca_1, \ldots, ca_k$ are called *subcapsules* of ca and ca is called *parent capsule* of ca_i for $1 \leq i \leq k$. Furthermore, we use projection functions Π_j which are defined by $\Pi_j([x_1, \ldots, x_m]) =_{\text{df}} x_j$ for $1 \leq j \leq m$ for $m \geq 2$. Then, function $\mathsf{type} : \mathcal{N}_{po} \longrightarrow \{\mathsf{relay}, \mathsf{end}\}$ is defined as follows:

$$\mathsf{type}(po) =_{\text{df}} \begin{cases} \mathsf{relay}, \text{ if } \exists ca \in \mathsf{CAP}, co \in \mathsf{CO} \,.\, po \in \mathsf{Ports}(ca) \wedge co \in \mathsf{Conn}(ca) \\ \qquad \wedge (po = \Pi_2(co) \vee po = \Pi_3(co)) \\ \mathsf{end}, \text{ otherwise} \end{cases}$$

Finally, we exemplify our textual syntax of UML-RT capsules graphically by Fig. 1: $ca = [n_{ca}, (po_1, po_2, po_3), (pr_{i_1}, pr_{i_2}, pr_{i_3}), S, \sigma, (ca_1, ca_2), (co_1, co_2, co_3, co_4)]$ is a complex behavioural UML-RT capsule, where

- n_{ca} is the name of ca,
- $\{po_1, po_2, po_3\}$ is the set of ports of ca,
- S is the Statechart of ca,[3]
- σ is the input queue of ca,
- ca_1 and ca_2 are subcapsules of ca (only shown as 'black boxes' with names n_{ca1} and n_{ca2}, respectively, i.e. without any interior structure),
- and $\{co_1, \ldots, co_4\}$ is the set of connectors of ca.

The protocols pr_{i_j} of po_j for $1 \leq j \leq 3$ are not presented graphically. Furthermore, the ports of ca_1 and ca_2 are not named.

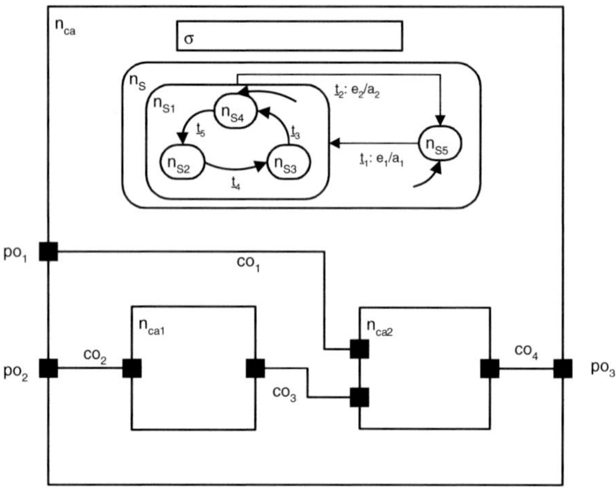

Fig. 1. UML-RT Model Example

3 Semantics of UML-RT Models

We follow the SOS (Structured Operational Semantics) approach of Plotkin [10]: we take labeled transition systems as semantic domain and use SOS rules to define the semantics of UML-RT models in an operational and modular approach, such that comprehension as well as flexibility (e.g. with respect to subsequent enhancements) are supported - without restricting preciseness.

In order to support a modular semantics definition we do not only follow Plotkin's SOS approach, but we also split up the overall semantics definition into three steps:

1. UML-RT Statechart semantics (section 3.1)
2. UML-RT connector semantics (section 3.2)
3. UML-RT capsule semantics = UML-RT model semantics (section 3.3)

In the first and in the second step the semantics of UML-RT Statecharts and UML-RT connectors are defined independently from each other. Then, in the third step, we use these semantics definitions to define the UML-RT capsule semantics.

[3] The structure of S was already described at the end of Section 2.1.

3.1 UML-RT Statechart Semantics

The following formal semantics of UML-RT Statecharts is based on our earlier work [17].

To define the UML-RT Statechart semantics, we proceed as follows: In a first step we define how the state resulting from transition execution is computed. We use the solution in a second step to formally define the semantics of UML-RT Statecharts.

Computing the Next State. We define function next which computes the state which results from a transition execution. This function will be used in the SOS rule which handles transition execution (in an OR-state).

Given a UML-RT Statechart transition t with history type $ht = \mathsf{historyType}(t)$ and target s, function $\mathsf{next} : \mathsf{HT} \times \mathsf{UML\text{-}SC} \longrightarrow \mathsf{UML\text{-}SC}$ computes the UML-RT Statechart term $s' = \mathsf{next}(ht, s)$ which results after execution of transition t. In order to simplify the presentation of next as well as the presentation of several subsequent definitions, we use the substitution notation $\cdot_{[\cdot/\cdot]}$ as follows: If t is a term, then $t_{[a/b]}$ is the term which results from replacing all occurrences of a in t by b. Furthermore, for $l \in \{1, \ldots, k\}$ we abbreviate $(s_1, \ldots, s_{l-1}, s'_l, s_{l+1}, \ldots, s_k)$ by $(s_{1..k})_{[s_l/s'_l]}$.

$$\begin{array}{ll} \mathsf{next}(ht, [n]) & =_{\text{df}} [n] \\ \mathsf{next}(ht, [n, (s_{1..k}), l, T]) & =_{\text{df}} \begin{cases} [n, (s_{1..k}), l, T] & \text{if } ht = \mathsf{deep} \\ [n, (s_{1..k})_{[s_1/\mathsf{default}(s_1)]}, 1, T] & \text{if } ht = \mathsf{none} \end{cases} \end{array}$$

The definition of next uses function $\mathsf{default} : \mathsf{UML\text{-}SC} \longrightarrow \mathsf{UML\text{-}SC}$ which especially defines for an Or-state that its currently active substate is given by its default substate.

$$\begin{array}{ll} \mathsf{default}([n]) & =_{\text{df}} [n] \\ \mathsf{default}([n, (s_{1..k}), l, T]) & =_{\text{df}} [n, (s_{1..k})_{[s_1/\mathsf{default}(s_1)]}, 1, T] \end{array}$$

UML-RT Statechart Semantics Definition. The UML-RT Statechart semantics will be defined for the textual UML-RT Statechart syntax as given by the set UML-SC of UML-RT Statechart terms.

We define the semantics by function $[\![.]\!] : \mathsf{UML\text{-}SC} \longrightarrow \mathsf{LTS}$, where LTS is the set of *labeled transition systems* and where the (semantic) transitions[4] work on single input events $e \in \Pi$. The semantics $[\![s]\!]$ of a UML-RT Statechart term $s \in \mathsf{UML\text{-}SC}$ is given by the labeled transition system $(\mathsf{UML\text{-}SC}, L, \longrightarrow, s) \in \mathsf{LTS}$, where

- UML-SC is the set of states,[5]
- $L = \Pi \times (\Pi \cup \{\epsilon\}) \times \{0, 1\}$ is the set of (semantic) labels[6].
- $\longrightarrow \subseteq \mathsf{UML\text{-}SC} \times L \times \mathsf{UML\text{-}SC}$ is the transition relation, and
- s is the start state.

[4] We use the term "semantic transition" in order to distinguish transitions in the semantics of UML-RT Statecharts from the already defined (syntactic) transitions (cf. Section 2.1) in the syntax of UML-RT Statecharts, more precisely in UML-RT Statechart terms of type Or.

[5] This implies that each state of the transition system is given by a UML-RT Statechart term.

[6] Analogously to the distinction between syntactic and semantic transitions we also distinguish between syntactic and semantic labels. Syntactic labels have been defined in Section 2.1.

For the sake of simplicity, we write $s \xrightarrow[a]{e}_f s'$ instead of $(s, (e, a, f), s') \in \longrightarrow$ and $s \overset{e}{\not\rightarrow}_f$ instead of $\nexists s', a \,.\, s \xrightarrow[a]{e}_f s'$, where s and s' are called the *source* and the *target* of these (semantic) transitions, respectively, e and a are called the *input* and *output*, respectively, and f is called the *flag*. We say that term s may perform a (semantic) transition with input e, output a, and flag f (or for short: with (semantic) label (e, a, f)) to term s'. If appropriate, we do no mention the input, output, and/or target of the transition. Intuitively, flag f states whether a semantic transition is performed,

- either because at least one (syntactic) UML-RT Statechart transition is taken (in this case we have $f = 1$, denoted as *positive flag*)
- or without taking any (syntactic) UML-RT Statechart transition (in this case we have $f = 0$, denoted as *negative flag*). In this case only the input is "consumed", whereas source and target are identical. This is usually denoted as a *stuttering step*.

The flag is needed to assure that stuttering steps can only occur, if no non-stuttering step is possible. This assures a lower-first priority mechanism for transition execution in our UML-RT Statechart semantics.

Transition relation $\longrightarrow$ is defined by the SOS rules of Table 1 using rule format:

$$\textit{name}\ \frac{\textit{premise}}{\textit{conclusion}}$$

Explanation of SOS rules of UML-RT Statechart semantics

- BAS (stuttering)
  A basic state may perform a semantic transition with arbitrary input event e, empty output ϵ, and negative flag such that the state does not change, i.e. that the input is just consumed.
- OR-1 (progress)
  If t is a UML-Statechart transition of an Or-state s with trigger part e, then s can perform a semantic transition with input e and positive flag if s_l cannot perform a semantic transition with input e and positive flag ($s_l \overset{e}{\not\rightarrow}_1$). The condition assures the lower-first priority of UML-RT Statecharts.
  The target of the semantic transition differs from its source by changing the currently active substate from s_l to s_i, because s_l and s_i are the source and target of the UML-Statechart transition t, respectively. Furthermore, the dynamic information of s_i is updated according to the history type ht of t using function next. This update is performed by the substitution $(s_{1..k})_{[s_i/\mathsf{next}(ht, s_i)]}$.
- OR-2 (propagation of progress)
  If a substate of an Or-state may perform a semantic transition with a label containing a positive flag, then the Or-state may perform a semantic transition with the same label.
- OR-3 (propagation of stuttering)
  If a substate of an Or-state may perform a semantic transition with a label containing a negative flag (i.e. no UML-RT Statechart transition can be taken within the Or-state) and if the Or-state cannot perform a semantic transition with positive flag, then the Or-state may also perform a semantic transition with the same label (in particular with negative flag).

The rules define that for every input event $e \in \Pi$ and for every state $s \in \textsf{UML-SC}$

- either a semantic transition $s \xrightarrow[a]{e}_1 s'$ with output $a \in \Pi \cup \{\epsilon\}$ and state $s' \in \textsf{UML-SC}$
- or a semantic transition $s \xrightarrow[\epsilon]{e}_0 s$ with empty output ϵ and without state change exists.

Table 1. SOS rules of the UML-RT Statechart semantics

BAS $$\frac{\textsf{true}}{[n] \xrightarrow[\epsilon]{e}_0 [n]}$$

OR-1 $$\frac{(\_, l, e, a, i, ht) \in T,\ s_l \not\xrightarrow{e}_1}{[n, (s_{1..k}), l, T] \xrightarrow[a]{e}_1 [n, (s_{1..k})_{[s_i/\textsf{next}(ht, s_i)]}, i, T]}$$

OR-2 $$\frac{s_l \xrightarrow[a]{e}_1 s_l'}{[n, (s_{1..k}), l, T] \xrightarrow[a]{e}_1 [n, (s_{1..k})_{[s_l/s_l']}, l, T]}$$

OR-3 $$\frac{s_l \xrightarrow[\epsilon]{e}_0 s_l,\ [n, (s_{1..k}), l, T] \not\xrightarrow{e}_1}{[n, (s_{1..k}), l, T] \xrightarrow[\epsilon]{e}_0 [n, (s_{1..k}), l, T]}$$

3.2 UML-RT Connector Semantics

Connectors of UML-RT support the modeling of asynchronous communication between UML-RT capsules. In general, their behaviour is not precisely defined, but constitutes a semantic variation point e.g. to allow modeling of unreliable communication channels. However, we define UML-RT connectors as unbounded FIFO (First-In First-Out) queues.

The semantics $[\![co]\!]_c$ of a UML-RT connector $co \in \textsf{CO}$ is given by the labeled transition system $(\textsf{CO}, L', \rightarrow_c, co) \in \textsf{LTS}$, where

- $\textsf{CO}$ is the set of states,
- $L' = \{\tau\} \cup \{\textsf{in}(sig)\,\textsf{via}\,po \mid sig \in \Pi, po \in \mathcal{N}_{po}\}$ $\cup\ \{\textsf{out}(sig)\,\textsf{via}\,po \mid sig \in \Pi, po \in \mathcal{N}_{po}\}$ is the set of labels (with $\tau \notin \Pi$),
- $\rightarrow_c\ \subseteq \textsf{CO} \times L' \times \textsf{CO}$ is the transition relation, and
- co is the start state.

We distinguish whether a capsule or a connector uses a signal sig as an input or as an output by writing $\textsf{in}(sig)$ or $\textsf{out}(sig)$, respectively. This distinction is necessary for the definition of synchronization between a capsule ca_i and a connector co_j. This synchronization occurs as an internal communication of the parent capsule ca of ca_i, where co_j is contained in the set of ports of ca. Synchronization is hidden from the environment of ca, only an internal action τ can be observed outside ca. (See e.g. [9]).

We write $co \xrightarrow{l}_c co'$ instead of $(co, l, co') \in\ \rightarrow_c$ and say that connector co may perform a transition with label l to co'. Transition relation $\rightarrow_c$ is defined by SOS rules $\textsf{co1}$ and $\textsf{co2}$ shown in Table 2 using three relations $\hat{=}, >, le \subseteq \mathcal{N}_{po} \times \mathcal{N}_{po}$ defined by:

$$po \hat{=} po' :\Longleftrightarrow \exists ca \in \mathsf{CAP} : (\mathsf{Caps}(po) \in \mathsf{SubCaps}(ca) \wedge \mathsf{Caps}(po') \in \mathsf{SubCaps}(ca))$$
$$po > po' :\Longleftrightarrow \mathsf{Caps}(po') \in \mathsf{SubCaps}(\mathsf{Caps}(po))$$
$$po \leq po' :\Longleftrightarrow po \hat{=} po' \vee po' > po$$

Relations $>$ and $\leq$ are used in co1 and co2 to compare the hierarchy level of ports.

Table 2. SOS rules of UML-RT connector semantics

$$\text{co1}\quad \frac{\text{true}}{[n, po, po', \sigma] \xrightarrow{\mathsf{in}(sig)\mathsf{via}po}_c [n, po, po', \langle sig\rangle :: \sigma]} \quad \left(\begin{array}{c} (po > po' \wedge sig \in \mathsf{In}(\mathsf{Prot}(po))) \\ \vee \\ (po \leq po' \wedge sig \in \mathsf{Out}(\mathsf{Prot}(po))) \end{array} \right)$$

$$\text{co2}\quad \frac{\text{true}}{[n, po', po, \sigma :: \langle sig\rangle] \xrightarrow{\mathsf{out}(sig)\mathsf{via}po}_c [n, po', po, \sigma]} \quad \left(\begin{array}{c} (po \leq po' \wedge sig \in \mathsf{In}(\mathsf{Prot}(po))) \\ \vee \\ (po > po' \wedge sig \in \mathsf{Out}(\mathsf{Prot}(po))) \end{array} \right)$$

Explanation of SOS rules of UML-RT connector semantics

- co1 (input event for connector)
  Informally, a connector can read an input event from a port po, if po is a port of this connector and if the event fulfils the protocol of the port.
- co2 (output event from connector)
  Informally, a connector can write an output event to a port po, it po is a port of this connector and if the event fulfils the protocol of the port.

3.3 UML-RT Capsule Semantics

In the following we distinguish two cases to define the semantics of UML-RT capsules:

- In the 'general case' we use the UML-RT Statechart semantics of section 3.1 as well as the UML-RT connector semantics of section 3.2 to define the semantics of a UML-RT capsule generally, i.e. not restricted to one of the capsule's ports.
- In the 'port-specific case' we use the 'general case semantics' to define the semantics of a UML-RT capsule restricted to one of its ports.

General Case. The semantics $[\![ca]\!]'$ of a UML-RT capsule $ca \in \mathsf{CAP}$ is given by the labeled transition system $(\mathsf{CAP}, L', \twoheadrightarrow, ca) \in \mathsf{LTS}$, where

- CAP is the set of states,
- L' is defined as before (in the semantics of UML-RT connectors),
- $\twoheadrightarrow \subseteq \mathsf{CAP} \times L' \times \mathsf{CAP}$ is the transition relation, and
- ca is the start state.

Similar to the case of UML-RT Statechart semantics we write $ca \xrightarrow{l} ca'$ instead of $(ca, l, ca') \in \; \rightarrow$. We say that capsule ca may perform a (semantic) transition with label l to capsule ca'. For $l = \tau$ we say that ca may perform a *silent* transition to ca'.

Transition relation $\rightarrow$ is defined by a set of SOS rules presented in Table 3 using the same rule format as in the case of UML-RT Statecharts as well as the rule format

$$\textit{name} \; \frac{\textit{premise}}{\begin{array}{c}\textit{conclusion 1}\\ \textit{conclusion 2}\end{array}} \; (\textit{condition})$$

being an abbreviation for two rules with identical premises and identical conditions:

$$\textit{name} \; \frac{\textit{premise}}{\textit{conclusion 1}} \; (\textit{condition}) \qquad \text{and} \qquad \textit{name} \; \frac{\textit{premise}}{\textit{conclusion 2}} \; (\textit{condition})$$

We abbreviate tuples $(x_1, \ldots, x_l)$ by $\bar{x}$ and we use functions $\mathsf{In}, \mathsf{Out} : \mathsf{Prot} \longrightarrow \Pi$ defined by $\mathsf{In}(pr) =_{\text{df}} \Pi_1(pr)$ and $\mathsf{Out}(pr) =_{\text{df}} \Pi_2(pr)$, respectively. In addition, function Set is defined by $\mathsf{Set}([x_1, \ldots, x_n]) =_{\text{df}} \{x_1, \ldots, x_n\}$ transforming a tuple of elements to a set of these elements. The operator :: concatenates two lists to a single list. The list operator $\langle\rangle$ applied to an argument sig produces a list which contains sig. For the case $sig = \epsilon$ we have $\langle sig \rangle = \langle \epsilon \rangle \stackrel{\text{def}}{=} \langle\rangle$, i.e. the empty list.

Note that the premises of rules R2 and R3 use (semantic) transitions of the UML-RT Statecharts semantics, whereas the premises of rules R5-R8 use transitions of the UML-RT connector semantics.

Explanation of SOS rules of UML-RT capsule semantics (general case)

- R1 (storing an input event in input queue)
  A capsule can read event $\mathsf{in}(sig)$ at port po and can store it as event sig in its input queue.
- R2 (processing and storing input queue events)
  If Statechart term S may perform a transition with input sig, output sig', and flag f to term S', then a capsule with Statechart S can read event sig from its input queue, can produce event sig', and can store event sig' in its input queue.
- R3 (processing an input queue event and producing an output event)
  If Statechart term S may perform a transition with input sig, output sig', and flag f to term S', then a capsule with Statechart S can read event sig from its input queue and can produce event $\mathsf{out}(sig')$ which is offered at port po.
- R4 (propagation of internal communication)
  If a capsule ca can perform a silent transition to capsule ca', then a parent capsule of ca can also perform a silent transition.
- R5 (communication from capsule to connector)
  If capsule ca may perform a transition with label $\mathsf{out}(sig)\mathsf{via}po$ to ca' and if connector co may perform a transition with label $\mathsf{in}(sig)\mathsf{via}po$ to co', then a parent capsule of ca and co may perform a silent transition to a parent capsule of ca' and co', if po is a port of ca. Informally, capsule ca offers event sig at its port po and connector co reads event sig at this port.
- R6 (communication from connector to capsule)
  If connector co may perform a transition with label $\mathsf{out}(sig)\mathsf{via}po$ to co' and if

Table 3. SOS rules of UML-RT capsule semantics (general case)

$$\mathsf{R1}\quad \frac{\mathsf{true}}{\begin{array}{l}[n,\bar{po},\bar{pr},S,\sigma] \xrightarrow{\mathsf{in}(sig)\mathsf{via}po} [n,\bar{po},\bar{pr},S,\langle sig\rangle :: \sigma]\\ [n,\bar{po},\bar{pr},S,\sigma,\bar{ca},\bar{co}] \xrightarrow{\mathsf{in}(sig)\mathsf{via}po} [n,\bar{po},\bar{pr},S,\langle sig\rangle :: \sigma,\bar{ca},\bar{co}]\end{array}} \quad \left(\begin{array}{c}\exists j : [\Pi_j(\bar{po}) = po\\ \wedge\\ sig \in \mathsf{In}(\Pi_j(\bar{pr}))]\\ \wedge\\ \mathsf{type}(po) = \mathsf{end}\end{array}\right)$$

$$\mathsf{R2}\quad \frac{S \xrightarrow[sig']{sig}_f S'}{\begin{array}{l}[n,\bar{po},\bar{pr},S,\sigma :: \langle sig\rangle] \xrightarrow{\tau} [n,\bar{po},\bar{pr},S',\langle sig'\rangle :: \sigma]\\ [n,\bar{po},\bar{pr},S,\sigma :: \langle sig\rangle,\bar{ca},\bar{co}] \xrightarrow{\tau} [n,\bar{po},\bar{pr},S',\langle sig'\rangle :: \sigma,\bar{ca},\bar{co}]\end{array}}$$

$$\mathsf{R3}\quad \frac{S \xrightarrow[sig']{sig}_f S'}{\begin{array}{l}[n,\bar{po},\bar{pr},S,\sigma :: \langle sig\rangle] \xrightarrow{\mathsf{out}(sig')\mathsf{via}po} [n,\bar{po},\bar{pr},S',\sigma]\\ [n,\bar{po},\bar{pr},S,\sigma :: \langle sig\rangle,\bar{ca},\bar{co}] \xrightarrow{\mathsf{out}(sig')\mathsf{via}po} [n,\bar{po},\bar{pr},S',\sigma,\bar{ca},\bar{co}]\end{array}} \quad \left(\begin{array}{c}\exists j : [\Pi_j(\bar{po}) = po\\ \wedge\\ sig' \in \mathsf{Out}(\Pi_j(\bar{pr}))]\\ \wedge\\ \mathsf{type}(po) = \mathsf{end}\end{array}\right)$$

$$\mathsf{R4}\quad \frac{ca \xrightarrow{\tau} ca'}{\begin{array}{l}[n,\bar{po},\bar{pr},\bar{ca},\bar{co}] \xrightarrow{\tau} [n,\bar{po},\bar{pr},\bar{ca}_{[ca/ca']},\bar{co}]\\ [n,\bar{po},\bar{pr},S,\sigma,\bar{ca},\bar{co}] \xrightarrow{\tau} [n,\bar{po},\bar{pr},S,\sigma,\bar{ca}_{[ca/ca']},\bar{co}]\end{array}} \quad (ca \in \mathsf{Set}(\bar{ca}))$$

$$\mathsf{R5}\quad \frac{ca \xrightarrow{\mathsf{out}(sig)\mathsf{via}po} ca' \quad co \xrightarrow{\mathsf{in}(sig)\mathsf{via}po}_c co'}{\begin{array}{l}[n,\bar{po},\bar{pr},\bar{ca},\bar{co}] \xrightarrow{\tau} [n,\bar{po},\bar{pr},\bar{ca}_{[ca/ca']},\bar{co}_{[co/co']}]\\ [n,\bar{po},\bar{pr},S,\sigma,\bar{ca},\bar{co}] \xrightarrow{\tau} [n,\bar{po},\bar{pr},S,\sigma,\bar{ca}_{[ca/ca']},\bar{co}_{[co/co']}]\end{array}} \quad \left(\begin{array}{c}ca \in \mathsf{Set}(\bar{ca})\\ \wedge\\ co \in \mathsf{Set}(\bar{co})\\ \wedge\\ po \in \mathsf{Ports}(ca)\end{array}\right)$$

$$\mathsf{R6}\quad \frac{co \xrightarrow{\mathsf{out}(sig)\mathsf{via}po}_c co' \quad ca \xrightarrow{\mathsf{in}(sig)\mathsf{via}po} ca'}{\begin{array}{l}[n,\bar{po},\bar{pr},\bar{ca},\bar{co}] \xrightarrow{\tau} [n,\bar{po},\bar{pr},\bar{ca}_{[ca/ca']},\bar{co}_{[co/co']}]\\ [n,\bar{po},\bar{pr},S,\sigma,\bar{ca},\bar{co}] \xrightarrow{\tau} [n,\bar{po},\bar{pr},S,\sigma,\bar{ca}_{[ca/ca']},\bar{co}_{[co/co']}]\end{array}} \quad \left(\begin{array}{c}ca \in \mathsf{Set}(\bar{ca})\\ \wedge\\ co \in \mathsf{Set}(\bar{co})\\ \wedge\\ po \in \mathsf{Ports}(ca)\end{array}\right)$$

$$\mathsf{R7}\quad \frac{co \xrightarrow{\mathsf{in}(sig)\mathsf{via}po}_c co'}{\begin{array}{l}[n,\bar{po},\bar{pr},\bar{ca},\bar{co}] \xrightarrow{\mathsf{in}(sig)\mathsf{via}po} [n,\bar{po},\bar{pr},\bar{ca},\bar{co}_{[co/co']}]\\ [n,\bar{po},\bar{pr},S,\sigma,\bar{ca},\bar{co}] \xrightarrow{\mathsf{in}(sig)\mathsf{via}po} [n,\bar{po},\bar{pr},S,\sigma,\bar{ca},\bar{co}_{[co/co']}]\end{array}} \quad \left(\begin{array}{c}co \in \mathsf{Set}(\bar{co})\\ \wedge\\ po \in \mathsf{Set}(\bar{po})\end{array}\right)$$

$$\mathsf{R8}\quad \frac{co \xrightarrow{\mathsf{out}(sig)\mathsf{via}po}_c co'}{\begin{array}{l}[n,\bar{po},\bar{pr},\bar{ca},\bar{co}] \xrightarrow{\mathsf{out}(sig)\mathsf{via}po} [n,\bar{po},\bar{pr},\bar{ca},\bar{co}_{[co/co']}]\\ [n,\bar{po},\bar{pr},S,\sigma,\bar{ca},\bar{co}] \xrightarrow{\mathsf{out}(sig)\mathsf{via}po} [n,\bar{po},\bar{pr},S,\sigma,\bar{ca},\bar{co}_{[co/co']}]\end{array}} \quad \left(\begin{array}{c}co \in \mathsf{Set}(\bar{co})\\ \wedge\\ po \in \mathsf{Set}(\bar{po})\end{array}\right)$$

capsule ca may perform a transition with label $\mathsf{in}(sig)\mathsf{via}po$ to ca', then a parent capsule of ca and co may perform a silent transition to a parent capsule of ca' and co', if po is a port of ca. Informally, connector co offers event sig at its port po and capsule ca reads event sig at this port.

- R7 (propagation of external input communication)
  If connector co may perform a transition with label $\mathsf{in}(sig)\mathsf{via}po$ to co', then a parent capsule of co may perform a transition with the same label to a parent capsule of co', if po is a port of the parent capsule.
- R8 (propagation of external output communication)
  If connector co may perform a transition with label $\mathsf{out}(sig)\mathsf{via}po$ to co', then a parent capsule of co may perform a transition with the same label to a parent capsule of co', if po is a port of the parent capsule.

Note that due to the modularity of the UML-RT capsule syntax and semantics definition, the syntax and semantics can be easily enhanced. For example, in order to consider UML-RT Statecharts with interlevel transitions and with entry and exit actions, we could use the (enhanced) UML-RT Statechart terms $\mathsf{UML\text{-}SC}'$ and the transition relation $\longrightarrow'$ of our earlier work [17]. Then we would only have to replace

- the set of UML-RT Statechart terms $\mathsf{UML\text{-}SC}$ in Section 2.2 in the definitions of a basic UML-RT capsule and of a complex behavioural UML-RT capsule by the (enhanced) UML-RT Statechart terms $\mathsf{UML\text{-}SC}'$ and
- the transition relation in the premise of the SOS rules R2 and R3 in the same section by transition relation $\longrightarrow'$.

Port-specific Case. As already mentioned at the end of Section 1, process-algebraic equivalence and refinement notions could be used for systematic analysis of UML-RT models. Engels et al. [3] follow this approach to define UML-RT consistency notions. As a precondition, it is neccessary to define equivalence and refinement notions on the semantics of UML-RT. However, in some cases such a notion should not be defined on the "overall" UML-RT capsule semantics, but on a UML-RT capsule semantics "restricted to" a port of the considered capsule. Therefore, we now define the port-specific semantics of a UML-RT capsule for a given port of the capsule using our already defined general case UML-RT capsule semantics.

The port-specific semantics $[\![ca]\!]_{po}$ of a UML-RT capsule $ca \in \mathsf{CAP}$ for port po (with $po \in \mathsf{Ports}(ca)$) is given by the labeled transition system $(\mathsf{CAP}, L'', \twoheadrightarrow_{po}, ca) \in \mathsf{LTS}$, where

- CAP is the set of states,
- $L'' = \{\tau\} \cup \Pi$ is the set of labels,
- $\twoheadrightarrow_{po} \subseteq \mathsf{CAP} \times L'' \times \mathsf{CAP}$ is the transition relation defined by the three SOS rules[7] presented in Table 4, and
- ca is the start state.

Explanation of SOS rules of UML-RT capsule semantics (port-specific case)
Informally, the port-specific semantics of a UML-RT capsule ca for a port po of this capsule constitutes a restriction of the general case semantics of ca, as follows:

[7] Note that the premises of the rules use the transition relation of the general case UML-RT capsule semantics.

Table 4. SOS rules of UML-RT capsule semantics (port-specific case)

$$\text{P1} \quad \frac{ca \xrightarrow{\mathsf{dir}(sig)\mathsf{via}po} ca'}{ca \xrightarrow{sig}_{po} ca'} \quad (\mathsf{dir} \in \{\mathsf{in}, \mathsf{out}\})$$

$$\text{P2} \quad \frac{ca \xrightarrow{\mathsf{dir}(sig)\mathsf{via}po'} ca'}{ca \xrightarrow{\tau}_{po} ca'} \quad \begin{pmatrix} \mathsf{dir} \in \{\mathsf{in}, \mathsf{out}\} \\ \wedge \\ po \neq po' \end{pmatrix}$$

$$\text{P3} \quad \frac{ca \xrightarrow{\tau} ca'}{ca \xrightarrow{\tau}_{po} ca'}$$

- P1
  A signal sig occuring at port po is communicated - however without any annotations like 'in', 'out' and 'via po'.
- P2
  No signal occuring at another port po' is communicated. In this case only the internal action τ is communicated.
- P3
  If a silent transition can occur in the general case semantics, then a silent transition can also occur in the port-specific semantics.

4 Related Work

Our work was motivated by results from several areas: a diversity of formal semantics definitions of Statecharts (e.g. [8,15,6,17,7,16]) and the formal semantics definition of SDL from Godskesen [4].

In addition, our work was influenced by the work of Engels et al. [3]. In contrast to them, we do not restrict to atomic UML-RT models, but consider complex, hierarchical ones. Furthermore, we select labeled transition systems as semantic domain, whereas Engels et al. use CSP processes [5]. Finally, we explicitly distinguish between internal and external communication in our UML-RT semantics definition.

A lot of work exists which deals with formal semantics definition in the context of UML:

Reggio et al. [11] consider classes associated with state machines. They define a formal semantics for flat UML state machines in terms of transition systems.

Rumpe [12] defines a formal semantics for flat automata (i.e. not for hierarchical systems) based on traces.

Damm et al. [2] define the syntax and formal semantics for a subset *krtUML* of UML encompassing - among others - asynchronous signal based communication as well as synchronous communication using operation calls. Symbolic transition systems are chosen as semantic domain. krtUML models do not support hierarchical statemachines, whereas *rtUML*-models - a superset of krtUML models - do provide this support. However, a translation from a rtUML model to a krtUML model is (only) sketched. In addition, Damm et al. provide quite a detailed and well-classified overview of related work concerning formal UML semantics definitions.

Shankar and Asa [14] also deal with formal semantics definition of real-time UML behaviour, namely concurrently interacting statecharts and sequence diagrams, however they do not cover hierarchical models and use propositional linear temporal logic for defining a compositional semantics.

Arons et al. [1] present a formal semantics for a subset of UML encompassing class diagrams and state machine diagrams. They use transition systems as semantic domain. However, the considered UML subset is restricted to flat models.

5 Conclusions and Further Work

We presented a precise and modular syntax and semantics definition of a sublanguage of UML-RT. We followed Plotkin's style of Structured Operational Semantics (SOS) based on labeled transition systems as semantic domain. To the best of our knowledge this is the first formal semantics definition for hierarchical UML-RT models.

In future we will consider the semantics of UML 2.0 instead of UML-RT. In addition, we want to examine and adapt existing equivalence and refinement notions to be used for systematic analysis of UML-RT and UML 2.0 models.

References

1. T. Arons, J. Hooman, H. Kugler, A. Pnueli, and M. van der Zwaag. Deductive verification of uml models in tlpvs. In T. Baar, A. Strohmeier, A. M. D. Moreira, and S. J. Mellor, editors, *UML*, volume 3273 of *Lecture Notes in Computer Science*, pages 335–349. Springer, 2004.
2. W. Damm, B. Josko, A. Pnueli, and A. Votintseva. Understanding uml: A formal semantics of concurrency and communication in real-time uml. In F. S. de Boer, M. M. Bonsangue, S. Graf, and W. P. de Roever, editors, *FMCO*, volume 2852 of *Lecture Notes in Computer Science*, pages 71–98. Springer, 2002.
3. G. Engels, R. Heckel, J. Kuester, and L. Groenewegen. Consistency-preserving model evolution through transformations. In J.-M. Jezequel, H. Hussmann, and S. Cook, editors, *UML 2002 - The Unified Modeling Language*, volume 2460 of *Lecture Notes in Computer Science*, pages 212–226. Springer, 2002.
4. J. Godskesen. An operational semantic model for basic sdl. Technical Report TFL RR 1991-2, Telecommunications Research Laboratory (TFL), Horsholm, 1991.
5. C. Hoare. *Communicating Sequential Processes*. Prentice Hall, London, UK, 1985.
6. D. Latella, I. Majzik, and M. Massink. Towards a formal operational semantics of UML Statechart diagrams. In *Formal Methods for Open Object-based Distributed Systems*. Chapman & Hall, 1999.
7. G. Lüttgen, M. von der Beeck, and R. Cleaveland. A Compositional Approach to Statecharts Semantics. In *Proc. of ACM SIGSOFT Eighth Int. Symp. on the Foundations of Software Engineering (FSE-8)*, pages 120–129. ACM, 2000.
8. A. Maggiolo-Schettini, A. Peron, and S. Tini. Equivalences of Statecharts. In U. Montanari and V. Sassone, editors, *CONCUR '96 (Concurrency Theory)*, volume 1119 of *Lecture Notes in Computer Science*, pages 687–702, Pisa, Italy, August 1996. Springer-Verlag.
9. R. Milner. *Communication and Concurrency*. Prentice Hall, London, UK, 1989.

10. G. Plotkin. A structural approach to operational semantics. Technical Report DAIMI-FN-19, Computer Science Department, Aarhus University, Denmark, 1981.
11. G. Reggio, E. Astesiano, C. Choppy, and H. Hussmann. Analysing UML Active Classes and Associated State Machines – A Lightwight Formal Approach. In *Fundamental Approaches to Software Engineering*, number 1783 in LNCS, pages 127–146. Springer, 2000.
12. B. Rumpe. *Formale Methodik des Entwurfs verteilter objektorientierter Systeme*. PhD thesis, Institut für Informatik, Technische Universität München, 1996.
13. B. Selic, G. Gullekson, and P. Ward. *Real-time Object Oriented Modeling and Design*. J. Wiley, 1994.
14. S. Shankar and S. Asa. Formal semantics of uml with real-time constructs. In P. Stevens, J. Whittle, and G. Booch, editors, *UML*, volume 2863 of *Lecture Notes in Computer Science*, pages 60–75. Springer, 2003.
15. A. Uselton and S. Smolka. A compositional semantics for Statecharts using labeled transition systems. In B. Jonsson and J. Parrow, editors, *CONCUR '94 (Concurrency Theory)*, volume 836 of *Lecture Notes in Computer Science*, pages 2–17, Uppsala, Sweden, August 1994. Springer-Verlag.
16. M. von der Beeck. A Concise Compositional Statecharts Semantics Definition. In *Proc. of FORTE/PSTV 2000*, pages 335–350. Kluwer, 2000.
17. M. von der Beeck. A structured operational semantics for UML-statecharts. *Software and Systems Modeling*, 1(2):130–141, 2002.

Workshops and Symposia at MoDELS 2006

Thomas Kühne

Darmstadt University of Technology
Hochschulstr. 10
64289 Darmstadt, Germany
kuehne@informatik.tu-darmstadt.de

1 Introduction

Following tradition, MoDELS 2006 hosted a number of workshops and symposia. They provided collaborative forums for groups of participants to conduct intensive discussions on a particular subject. They complemented the main conference by providing particular focus on important subject areas and enabling a high degree of interactivity.

MoDELS 2006 featured 11 workshops (10 in 2005) and three symposia (two in 2005) during the first three days of the conference. In addition to the Doctorial- and Educators- symposia, which were already successfully held in 2005, a symposium on UML semantics was held for the first time at MoDELS 2006. The proposal for this new event was initially among the workshop proposals but due to its organization principles we, and its organizers, agreed that it fitted more appropriately under the heading of a symposium.

Keeping another time-tested tradition of the MoDELS/UML series, I formed an international workshop selection committee. The following high-caliber researchers agreed to evaluate and select from the submitted workshop proposals:

- Jean-Michel Bruel (University of Pau, France)
- Martin Glinz (University Zürich, Switzerland)
- Reiko Heckel (University of Leicester, England)
- Jens Jahnke (University of Victoria, Canada)
- Hans Vangheluwe (McGill University, Canada)
- Jon Whittle (George Mason University, USA)

Out of 18 workshop proposals we selected 11 workshops which are detailed in the following section. Six of these have a history in the MoDELS/UML series and represented a continuation of ongoing discussions on important topics. Five of the accepted workshops featured new topics, further broadening the scope of MoDELS, compared to its focus on UML in the past.

We are convinced that this blend of established and innovative workshop themes has made the MoDELS 2006 satellite events a success worthwhile attending. A corresponding post-conference proceedings will be published in the LNCS series by Springer Verlag, featuring summaries as well as revised selected papers from all symposia and workshops.

O. Nierstrasz et al. (Eds.): MoDELS 2006, LNCS 4199, pp. 783–790, 2006.

2 Detailed List of Workshops

W1: Aspect-Oriented Modeling

Organizers: Omar Aldawud (Illinois Institute of Technology, USA), Walter Cazzola (University of Milano, Italy), Tzilla Elrad (Illinois Institute of Technology, USA), Jeff Gray (University of Alabama at Birmingham, USA), Jörg Kienzle (McGill University, Canada), Dominik Stein (University of Duisburg-Essen, Germany)

Abstract: The Aspect-Oriented Modeling (AOM) workshop brings together researchers and practitioners from two communities: aspect-oriented software development (AOSD) and software model engineering. This workshop provides a forum for presenting new ideas and discussing the state of research and practice in modeling various kinds of crosscutting concerns at different levels of abstraction. The goals of the workshop are to identify and discuss the impacts of AOSD technologies on model engineering and how model engineering can affect and improve aspect-oriented technologies.

URL: `http://www.aspect-modeling.org/models06`

W2: Critical Systems Development Using Modeling Languages

Organizers: Siv Hilde Houmb (Norwegian University of Technology and Science, Norway), Geri Georg (Colorado State University, USA), Jan Jürjens (TU München, Germany), Robert France (Colorado State University, USA)

Abstract: High quality development of critical systems, such as real-time, dependable, safety-critical or security-critical systems is difficult. Formal methods can be effective tools for ensuring correctness but often time-to-market and minimal cost are given higher priority.

Modeling languages offer an unprecedented opportunity for high quality development of critical systems that is feasible in an industrial context. They offer a variety of rigor from informal to precise. Along with the tools available for analysis, testing, simulation and transformation, these languages are well fitted for every-day development of systems in an industrial setting.

Furthermore, the ability of component-based and aspect-oriented software engineering to address non-functional properties has emerged as an important paradigm for handling complexity. The workshop therefore also addresses issues related to the integration of non-functional property expression, evaluation and prediction in secure systems development. This includes semantic issues, questions of modeling language definition, support for automation, MDA-based approaches and tool-support.

URL: `http://www.cs.colostate.edu/csduml2006`

W3: Metamodels, Schemas, Grammars and Ontologies for Reverse Engineering

Organizers: Jean-Marie Favre (University of Grenoble, France), Dragan Gašević (Simon Fraser University, Canada), Ralf Lämmel (Microsoft, USA), Andreas Winter (University of Mainz, Germany)

Abstract: The workshop brings together researchers from different communities to study the use of meta technologies in the context of reverse engineering and software evolution. This workshop is specifically focused on meta technologies in a generalized sense of "language descriptions": metamodels, schemas, grammars and ontologies. In fact Model Driven Engineering as the "next software engineering paradigm" must take into account the evolution of existing (legacy) software. After all, the software industry is still code-centric, and the huge amount of existing software cannot be ignored. Recovery of models from existing assets through reverse engineering is a key challenge in software engineering today. Although the importance of metamodels, schemas, grammars and ontologies is generally acknowledged in reverse engineering, as of yet, the study of these artifacts lacks a common umbrella – hence this workshop.

URL: `http://www.planetmde.org/atem2006/`

W4: Quality in Modeling

Organizers: Ludwik Kuzniarz (Blekinge Institute of Technology, Sweden), Jean Louis Sourrouille (INSA Lyon, France), Ragnhild Van Der Straeten (Vrije Universiteit Brussel, Belgium), Miroslaw Staron (IT University, Sweden), Michel Chaudron (Eindhoven University of Technology, The Netherlands), Alexander Förster (University of Paderborn, Germany), Gianna Reggio (Università di Genova, Italy)

Abstract: Quality assessment and assurance is an important part of software engineering. The issues of software quality management are widely researched and approached from multiple perspectives and viewpoints. The introduction of a new paradigm in software development—namely Model Driven Development (MDD)—raises new challenges in software quality management, and as such should be given special attention. The issues of early quality assessment based on models at a high abstraction level and building prediction models for software quality are important from the software engineering perspective. The workshop is intended to provide a premier forum for discussions related to software quality and MDD.

URL: `http://www.ituniv.se/~miroslaw/QiM.htm`

W5: Model Driven Development of Advanced User Interfaces

Organizers: Alexander Bödcher (University of Kaiserslautern, Germany), Heinrich Hußmann (University of Munich, Germany), Andreas Pleuß (University of Munich, Germany), Stefan Sauer (University of Paderborn, Germany), Jan Van den Bergh (Hasselt University, Belgium)

Abstract: The workshop will be a platform for discussing the modeling of advanced user interfaces, such as interfaces supporting complex interactions, visualizations, multimedia representations, multi-modality, adaptability or customization. It should contribute to a better integration of knowledge from the human-computer and human-machine interaction communities and the software engineering community. The current workshop builds up on the results of its predecessor held at MoDELS 2005. The guiding principle is the demand for a flexible composition of various different models to support the model driven development of user interfaces with a high degree of usability and customization.

URL: `http://planetmde.org/mddaui2006/`

W6: Modeling and Analysis of Real-Time and Embedded Systems

Organizers: Sébastien Gérard (Commissariat à l'Energie Atomique, France), Susanne Graf (Verimag, France), Iulian Ober (Toulouse University, France), Øystein Haugen (University of Oslo, Norway), Bran Selic (IBM Rational Software, Canada)

Abstract: The MDA (Model Driven Architecture) initiative of OMG puts forward the idea that future process development will be centered around models, thus keeping application development, and underlying platform technology as separate as possible. The aspects influenced by the underlying platform technology concern mainly non-functional aspects and communication primitives. The first significant result of the MDA paradigm for engineers is the possibility of building application models that can be conveniently ported to new, emerging technologies (implementation languages, middleware, etc.) with minimal effort and risk. In addition, it offers the potential for models to be analyzed either directly or through a model transformation to validate and/or verify real-time properties such schedulability and performance. In the area of distributed, real-time and embedded systems (DRES), this model-oriented trend is also very active and promising. However, DRES have some very specific requirements. The purpose of this workshop is to provide an opportunity to gather researchers and industrial practitioners to survey existing efforts related to modeling and model-based analysis of DRES. Moreover, to exchange models with the aim of applying formal validation tools and achieving interoperability, it is also important to have a common understanding of the semantics of the modeling notations.

URL: `http://www.martes.org/2006`

W7: OCL for (Meta-) Models in Multiple Application Domains

Organizers: Dan Chiorean (Babes-Bolyai University, Romania), Birgit Demuth (Technische Universität Dresden, Germany), Martin Gogolla (University of Bremen, Germany), Jos Warmer (Ordina, The Netherlands)

Abstract: The requirements that the modeling community wants to see supported today by OCL go far beyond the initial requirements, when OCL was conceived as a language meant to support precise modeling "only". The advent of the MDA (Model Driven Architecture) vision and the rapid acceptance of MDE (Model Driven Engineering) emphasize new application domains (like Semantic Web or Domain Specific Languages) and call for new OCL functionalities. Constructing compilable models and automatically generating complete applications code are among the main MDA objectives. OCL plays a pivotal role in accomplishing them, requiring both language extension by including imperative functionalities and the development of tools supporting model compilation. OCL has to be redefined from "a formal language used to describe expressions on UML models" to a formal language meant to describe model properties in MOF-based languages.

This year's OCL workshop will provide the opportunity for researchers, tool developers, and users to meet and discuss these developments and their consequences on OCL and its pragmatic usage.

URL: `http://st.inf.tu-dresden.de/OCLApps2006`

W8: Perspectives on integrating MDA and V&V

Organizers: David Hearnden & Jörn Guy Süß (The University of Queensland, Australia), Nicolas Rapin (Commissariat à l'Energie Atomique, France), Benoit Baudry (IRISA, France)

Abstract: MDA and its related approaches (DSL, MDE, ...) primarily revolve around manual refinement and automated transformation of models. This approach is successful at quickly generating results. However, it is difficult to gauge the quality of those results. Is the result of a transformation really what the user intended? Does the computed result of a transformation really conform with its specified result? Such questions about intended and specified behavior usually delineate the domain of Validation and Verification (V&V). V&V is an established area of research, and a transfer of ideas between V&V and MDA might help to improve quality and reliability of MDA and induce a new conceptual way of thinking in established V&V. The emergence of model-based testing can be seen as a first result of such a transfer. However, we believe important challenges in model-based testing still remain. Moreover, it is crucial to go beyond model-based testing and take a truly model-driven-development approach to V&V to reap even greater benefits.

URL: `http://modeva.itee.uq.edu.au`

W9: Model Size Metrics

Organizers: Brian Berenbach (Siemens Corporate Research, USA), A. Winsor Brown (University Southern California, USA), Betty H. C. Cheng (Michigan State University, USA), Robert France (Colorado State University, USA), Andrij Neczwid (Motorola Labs, USA), Frank Weil (Motorola Global Software Group, USA)

Abstract: A standardized and consistent means of determining the size of an artifact is fundamental to the ability to collect metrics about the artifact (e.g., defect density and productivity). For example, source lines of code is often used as the size metric for C code. However, the concept of lines of code does not readily apply to modeling languages such as UML and SDL.

The purpose of this workshop is twofold: First, participants will share practical experience, current work, and research directions related to techniques for calculating the size of a model. Second, this workshop will act as the kick-off for the industrial and academic consortium being formed related to model sizing metrics. As part of the discussion, we will plan how this consortium can fit into a broader umbrella covering model-driven engineering, such as the ReMoDD (Repository for Model Driven Development) effort. The ReMoDD project will create a community resource of MDD artifacts that will provide infrastructure to improve the use of model-based development. ReMoDD will collect a set of examples, primarily from industry, that represent good models to support both research and education in model-based software engineering.

URL: `http://modeldrivenengineering.org/bin/view/Modelmetrics`

W10: Models@run.time

Organizers: Nelly Bencomo & Gordon Blair (Lancaster University, UK), Robert France (Colorado State University, USA)

Abstract: In the model-driven software development area research effort has focused primarily on using models at design, implementation, and deployment stages of development. This work has been highly productive with several techniques now entering the commercialization phase. The use of model-driven techniques for validating and monitoring run-time behavior can also yield significant benefits. A key benefit is that models can be used to provide a richer semantic base for run-time decision-making related to system adaptation and other run-time concerns. Model-based monitoring and management of executing systems can play a significant role as we move towards implementing the key self-properties associated with autonomic computing. This workshop aims to look at issues related to developing appropriate model-driven approaches to managing and monitoring the execution of systems.

URL: `http://www.comp.lancs.ac.uk/computing/users/bencomo/MRT06`

W11: Multi-Paradigm Modeling: Concepts and Tools

Organizers: Tihamér Levendovszky (Budapest University of Technology and Economics, Hungary), Holger Giese (University of Paderborn, Germany)

Abstract: Today complex software-based systems often integrate different, previously isolated subsystems where different aspects such as the dynamic behavior or static structure are captured by notations using different paradigms (e.g. statecharts and user interface models, block diagrams for control, etc.). Therefore, multiple modeling paradigms have to be integrated for their model-driven development. This is especially true when—besides general purpose languages such as UML—domain specific languages are also employed. This first workshop on multi-paradigm modeling addresses this need by providing a forum for researchers and practitioners to discuss these arising issues.

URL: `http://mpm06.aut.bme.hu`

S1: Doctoral Symposium

Organizers: Robert Pettit (The Aerospace Corporation, USA), Gabriela Arévalo, (Universidad Nacional de La Plata, Argentina)

Abstract: The Doctoral Symposium at the MoDELS 2006 conference will provide an international forum for doctoral students to interact with other students and faculty mentors. The Doctoral Symposium seeks to bring together Ph.D. students working in model-driven engineering and fields related to modeling. Selected students will have the opportunity to present and to discuss their research goals, methodology, and initial/final results within a constructive and international atmosphere.

The symposium organizers will strive to provide useful guidance for completion of the dissertation research and motivation for a research career. The symposium is intended for students who have already settled on a specific research proposal and have some preliminary results, but still have enough time remaining before their final defense so that they can benefit from the fruitful symposium discussions. Due to the mentoring aspect of the event, the symposium will be open only to those students and mentors participating directly in the event.

URL: `http://www.modelsconference.org/doctoral_symposium.php`

S2: Educators Symposium

Organizers: Ludwik Kuzniarz (Blekinge Institute of Technology, Sweden)

Abstract: Putting the model-driven development vision into practice requires not only sophisticated modeling approaches and tools, but also considerable training and education efforts. To make people ready for model-driven development, its principles and applications need to be taught to practitioners in industry, incorporated in university curricula, and probably even introduced in schools.

The educator's symposium at the MoDELS 2006 conference is intended as a forum in which educators and trainers can meet to discuss pedagogy, use of technology in the classroom, and share their experience pertaining to teaching modeling techniques and model-driven development.

URL: http://www.modelsconference.org/educators_symposium.php

S3: A Formal Semantics for UML

Organizers: Manfred Broy (TU Munich, Germany), Juergen Dingel (Queen's University, Canada), Alan Hartman (IBM Haifa Research Laboratory, Israel), Bernhard Rumpe (TU Braunschweig, Germany), Bran Selic (IBM Rational Software, Canada)

Abstract: The UML 2.0 semantics project is an international collaboration between academia and industry. Participants include IBM (Canada, Germany, Israel), Queen's University (Kingston, Canada), the Technical University of Munich(Germany), and the Technical University of Braunschweig (Germany). The main objective of this project is to develop a mathematically formalized semantic definition for the UML.

A precise and unambiguous definition of UML semantics is indispensable if MDD is to realize its full potential. In addition, a number of further benefits are anticipated from this effort, such as deeper understanding of UML concepts, detection of gaps and inconsistencies in the current standard, and determination of useful model analysis techniques. The results of this research have the potential to be directly useful to tool vendors, software developers, and researchers.

URL: http://www.cs.queensu.ca/~stl/internal/uml2/MoDELS2006/

Acknowledgements

I am grateful to the members of the selection committee who spontaneously followed my invitation and provided a dedicated performance to select the workshops with the maximum research relevance and highest potential of attracting participants. Gianna Reggio was an invaluable help in resolving organizational issues and my predecessor Jean-Michel Bruel immensely eased my work by generously sharing his experience with me.

Tutorials at MoDELS 2006

Egidio Astesiano

DISI - University of Genova
Genova, Italy
astes@disi.unige.it

Abstract. The MoDELS 2006 conference provides six half-day tutorials on advanced topics related to model-driven engineering, presented by recognized worldwide experts. Here, there is a short summary of each tutorial and the list of presenters.

1 Introduction

Tutorials will give conference attendees the opportunities to acquire new knowledge, to get some different insights, and to develop abilities on key subjects and related up to date techniques. The tutorial program of the MoDELS 2006 conference seeks to continue this tested tradition. This program is intended for practitioners, researchers, educators and students looking for a better and deeper understanding of topics related to the model-driven engineering. It will cover both languages and systems used to create complex applications.

For this conference, we received a large number of high quality tutorial proposals, but unfortunately we had space only for six. As a result, a large number of good proposals were not accepted as we sought to mantain a strong attendance at each tutorial. In the six that we selected there is a good mixture of tutorials covering areas that are topical and have great appeal and relevance to the modelling community.

We summarize these tutorials in the following section; further details can be accessed at the MoDELS 2006 conference web site www.modelsconference.org.

2 Detailed List of Tutorials

Tutorial T1: Model-Driven Engineering of Distributed Systems

Presenters: Douglas C. Schmidt (Vanderbilt University, Nashville, USA) and Markus Völter (Independent Consultant, Heidenheim, Germany)

Despite advances in standard middleware platforms, it is hard to develop software for distributed systems, such as airplanes, power grids, and patient monitors. For example, developers still use ad hoc means to develop, configure, and deploy applications and middleware, due to the lack of analyzable and verifiable building block components. Model-Driven Engineering (MDE) has emerged as a promising means to address these issues by combining domain-specific modeling

O. Nierstrasz et al. (Eds.): MoDELS 2006, LNCS 4199, pp. 791–794, 2006.

languages (DSMLs) with generators that analyze certain aspects of models and then synthesize various artifacts, such as source code, simulation inputs, XML deployment descriptions, or alternative model representations.

This tutorial provides an overview over MDE for distributed systems, focusing on

- Fundamental concepts of MDE
- How MDE tools and metamodeling typically work
- The role of code generation and model-to-model transformation
- Frameworks and DSMLs, which are two sides of the same coin
- How MDE can be used to improve and manage software architecture
- Applying MDE to component-based distributed systems
- Deploying and configuring middleware and applications using MDE

Many of the topics mentioned above will be introduced using examples and case studies from production distributed systems. Wherever possible, we will show live demos of using MDE tools in the tutorial.

Tutorial T2: Defining Domain-Specific Modelling Languages

Presenter: Juha-Pekka Tolvanen (MetaCase, Finland)

Domain-Specific Modeling (DSM) languages provide a viable solution for improving development productivity by raising the level of abstraction beyond coding. With DSM, the models are made up of elements representing concepts that are part of the domain world, not the code world. These languages follow domain abstractions and semantics, allowing developers to perceive themselves as working directly with domain concepts. In many cases, full final product code can be automatically generated from these high-level specifications. This automation is possible because both the language and generators need fit the requirements of only one company and domain.

In the tutorial we investigate over 20 real-life examples that apply domain-specific modeling to automate software development. Problem domains range from embedded cell phone software to B2B insurance web applications, generating solutions from 8-bit assembler to Java. Some of the cases are used to demonstrate language and generator creation in detail. Participants will learn that full code generation from models is possible and different ways to implement such automation with domain-specific languages and generators.

Tutorial T3: Model-Based Testing

Presenter: Alexander Pretschner (ETH, Zurich, Switzerland)

Model-based testing has become increasingly popular in recent years. Major reasons include (i) the need for quality assurance for increasingly complex systems, (ii) the emerging model-centric development paradigm (e.g., UML and MDA) and its seemingly direct connection to testing, (iii) increasingly powerful formal verification technology, and (iv) the advent of test-centered development methodologies.

Model-based testing relies on execution traces of behavior models, both of a system under test and its environment, at different levels of abstraction. These traces are used as test cases for an implementation: input and expected output. This complements the ideas of model-driven testing. The latter uses static models to derive test drivers to automate test execution. This assumes the existence of test cases, and is, like the particular intricacies of OO testing, not in the focus of this tutorial.

We cover major methodological and technological issues: the business case of model-based testing within model-based development, the need for abstraction and inverse concretization, test selection, and test case generation. We (i) provide an overview of different flavors of model-based testing, (ii) discuss different scenarios for model-based testing processes, (iii) present common abstractions when building models and their consequences for testing, (iv) explain how to use functional, structural, and stochastic test selection criteria, (v) describe today's test generation technology, and (vi) discuss the cost-effectiveness of model-based testing and present available evidence.

We provide both practical guidance and a discussion of the state-of-the-art, focusing on the latter. Potentials of model-based testing in practical applications and future research are highlighted.

Tutorial T4: Designing Software Product Lines with UML 2.0: From Use Cases to Pattern-Based Software Architectures

Presenter: Hassan Gomaa (George Mason University, USA)

This tutorial addresses how to develop object-oriented requirements, analysis, and design models of software product lines using the Unified Modeling Language (UML) 2.0 notation. During requirements modeling, kernel, optional, and alternative use cases are developed to define the software functional requirements of the system. The feature model is then developed to capture product line requirements and how they relate to the use case model. During analysis, static models are developed for defining kernel, optional, and variant classes and their relationships. Dynamic models are developed in which statecharts define the state dependent aspects of the product line and interaction models describe the dynamic interaction between the objects that participate in each kernel, optional, and alternative use case. The object-oriented software architecture for the product line is then developed, in which the system is structured into component-based subsystems. Structural architecture patterns and communication patterns are also used in designing component based distributed product lines.

The tutorial is illustrated by means of several examples.

The tutorial is based on a book by the author, "Designing Software Product Lines with UML: From Use Cases to Pattern-Based Software Architectures", Addison Wesley Object-Oriented Technology Series, 2005.

Tutorial T5: Model Driven Engineering Basics using Eclipse

Presenter: Bruce Trask and Angel Roman (MDE Systems, USA)

MDE brings together multiple technologies and critical innovations and formalizes them into the next wave of software development methods. This tutorial will cover the basics of MDE and how they map to Eclipse's application, modeling and graphical frameworks. The three main MDE categories include the development of Domain Specific Languages, Domain Specific Editors (including Domain Specific Visual Languages) and Domain Specific Transformation Engines or Generators. Expressed in terms of language development technology, these mirror the development of the Abstract Syntax, Concrete Syntax and Semantics of a new Domain Specific Language.

This tutorial will cover the basic effective patterns, principles and practices for developing these MDE software artifacts. Additionally, this tutorial will cover the exact details of how to leverage the Eclipse Modeling Framework (EMF), the Eclipse Graphical Editor Framework (GEF), and the Eclipse Graphical Modeling Framework (GMF), to support the development of these three areas. These three frameworks provide a unique and integrated platform in which to learn the basics of Model Driven Engineering in full application not just in theory. Conversely, Model Driven Engineering provides an effective context in which to learn how to apply the power of these integrated Eclipse Frameworks developed to support MDE.

Tutorial T6: Pragmatically going upSTAIRS with Formal Steps

Presenters: Oystein Haugen, Ragnhild Kobro (Department of Informatics, Oslo, Norway), and Runde Ketil Stolen (Sintef ICT, Oslo, Norway)

The tutorial will present the STAIRS-method.

STAIRS addresses the challenges of harmonizing intuition and formal reasoning. It is an established fact that UML interactions (such as sequence diagrams and interaction overview diagrams) are attractive and intuitive. With the new structuring mechanisms of UML 2.0, they have become more powerful and compact. How can we make sure the intuitive feeling is kept in a process of gradually making the diagrams more elaborate and precise? How can we make the descriptions such that they are maintainable through the lifecycle of the full UML model? Our answer lies in a precise understanding of the partial nature of interactions, and of consistent refinement of such partial understanding to a more complete one.

The tutorial aims at bringing the participants up to date with one branch of current research on UML 2.0 interactions. The tutorial will be built up around a running example, and include both the pragmatical rules and guidelines of STAIRS, and the most important parts of the underlying formalism. Afterwards, the participants will be able to apply STAIRS principles in practical designs using interactions or similar techniques.

Acknowledgements

I would like to thank Thomas Baar, Gianna Reggio, Bran Selic and Tullio Vernazza for their contributions during the selection process.

Panels at MoDELS 2006

Douglas C. Schmidt

Vanderbilt University
Nashville, TN, 37203, USA
d.schmidt@vanderbilt.edu

MoDELS 2006 contained the following two panels that provided an interactive forum to conduct lively discussions on subjects that are highly germane to conference attendees:

Panel 1. Is Standardization of Model-Driven Technologies Harming or Helping the Field?

The best standards seem to be those that arise from codifying technologies that have been vetted after extensive experience by researchers and practitioners over many years. Good examples of such standards include POSIX, the Internet protocols, Ada, C, C++, and Java. Although model-driven technologies have long been studied by researchers in-the-small, there is little practical experience yet applying model-driven tools in-the-large. Moreover, many of the specifications proposed by various standards groups have not undergone the same degree of scrutiny and vetting as earlier language and platform technologies. As a result, model-driven technology standards are being proposed and adopted with neither a firm formal foundation nor significant practical experience. This panel will explore the extent to which this phenomenon is helping accelerate the adoption of model-driven technologies or hurting the field due to lack of credibility.

Panel 2. Integrating Model-Driven Technology into the Computer Science Curricula

Third-generation programming languages have been taught throughout undergraduate CS curricula for the past 20-30 years. As a result, most undergraduates complete their education with a thorough knowledge of the principles, abstractions, features, and patterns necessary to be effective developers and managers of software written in third-generation languages. In contrast, model-driven technologies and tools are rarely taught in undergraduate CS programs; when they are taught are often limited to a small portion of a Software Engineering course in the final year of study. As a result, few students graduating from college have good grasp of these technologies, which limits their adoption in the IT profession. One of the challenges to broader coverage of model-driven technologies is where to place them in a CS curriculum, and especially which other topics to omit to make room for them. This panel will explore alternative approaches to integrating model-driven technology into CS curricula and report on lessons learned—both pro and con—from panelist and audience experiences.

O. Nierstrasz et al. (Eds.): MoDELS 2006, LNCS 4199, p. 795, 2006.

Author Index

Akehurst, David H. 351
Alam, Muhammad 275
Alanen, Marcus 454, 469
Antkiewicz, Michał 692
Arévalo, Gabriela 513
Astesiano, Egidio 791
Atlee, Joanne M. 245

Baar, Thomas 111, 661
Baudry, Benoit 589
Beeck, Michael von der 768
Bertolino, Antonia 753
Bézivin, Jean 440
Biermann, Enrico 425
Blanc, Xavier 631
Bonivento, Alvise 753
Bordbar, Behzad 351
Breu, Ruth 275
Briand, Lionel C. 365, 484
Brucker, Achim D. 306
Büttner, Fabian 440

Ceria, Santiago 73
Chaudron, Michel R.V. 27
Cheng, Betty H.C. 707
Cibrán, María Agustina 170
Cohen, Irun R. 499
Coninx, Karin 140
Costal, Dolors 260
Cukier, Juan José 73
Czarnecki, Krzysztof 692

De Angelis, Guglielmo 753
Demeyer, Serge 27
D'Hondt, Maja 170, 200
Dingel, Juergen 185, 230
Diskin, Zinovy 185, 230
Doser, Jürgen 306
Duarte, Lucio Mauro 380
Du Bois, Bart 27
Ducasse, Stéphane 604

Ehrig, Karsten 425
Elaasar, Maged 484
Engelen, Remco van 126
Engels, Gregor 737
Evans, Michael J. 351

Falleri, Jean-Rémi 513
Fleurey, Franck 98
Fondement, Frédéric 98

Garcia, Diego 646
García Molina, Jesús 336
Garousi, Vahid 365
Gérard, Sébastien 98
Gervais, Marie-Pierre 631
Giese, Holger 543
Gîrba, Tudor 604
Gogolla, Martin 440
Goldsby, Heather 707
Gomaa, Hassan 1
Gómez, Cristina 260
Gonzalez-Perez, Cesar 16
Gool, Louis van 126
Gotzhein, Richard 83

Hafner, Michael 275
Hamilton, Marc 126
Hassenforder, Michel 98
Hausmann, Jan Hendrik 737
Hearnden, David 321
Henderson-Sellers, Brian 16
Hendrickson, Scott 722
Hoek, André van der 722
Hogganvik, Ida 574
Howells, W. Gareth J. 351
Huchard, Marianne 513

Jett, Bryan 722
Jézéquel, Jean-Marc 98
Jouault, Frédéric 440

Kamdoum, Stephane 707
Kappel, Gerti 528
Kapsammer, Elisabeth 528
Kargl, Horst 528
Kienzle, Jörg 558
Kim, Soon-Kyeong 291
Köhler, Christian 425

Kolovos, Dimitrios S. 215
Konrad, Sascha 707
Kosiuczenko, Piotr 676
Kramer, Jeff 380
Kramler, Gerhard 528
Kuhn, Thomas 83
Kühne, Thomas 783
Kuhns, Günter 425
Kurtev, Ivan 440

Labiche, Yvan 365, 484
Lange, Christian F.J. 27
Lawley, Michael 321
Le Traon, Yves 589
Lindow, Arne 440
Lings, Brian 619
Lundell, Björn 619
Lundkvist, Torbjörn 454

Marković, Slaviša 661
Mattsson, Anders 619
McComb, Tim 291
McDonald-Maier, Klous D. 351
Mens, Tom 200
Moreira, Ana 155
Mottu, Jean-Marie 589
Muller, Pierre-Alain 98
Mustafiz, Sadaf 558

Nebut, Clémentine 513

O'Keefe, Greg 42

Paige, Richard F. 215
Persson, Anna 619
Polack, Fiona A.C. 215
Pons, Claudia 646
Porres, Ivan 454, 469
Punter, Teade 126

Queralt, Anna 260

Rashid, Awais 155
Raventós, Ruth 260
Raymond, Kerry 321
Reiter, Thomas 528
Retschitzegger, Werner 528

Sánchez Cuadrado, Jesús 336
Sangiovanni-Vincentelli, Alberto 753
Schattkowsky, Tim 737
Schmidt, Douglas C. 795
Schneckenburger, Rémi 98
Schwinger, Wieland 528
Sriplakich, Prawee 631
Staron, Miroslaw 57
Stølen, Ketil 574
Süß, Jörn Guy 291
Sun, Ximeng 558

Taentzer, Gabriele 425
Taleghani, Ali 245
Teniente, Ernest 260
Tombelle, Christophe 395

Uchitel, Sebastian 380

Van den Bergh, Jan 140
Van Der Straeten, Ragnhild 200
Vangheluwe, Hans 558
Vanwormhoudt, Gilles 395
Varró, Dániel 410

Wagner, Robert 543
Watson, Geoffrey 291
Webel, Christian 83
Weiss, Eduard 425
Wildman, Luke 291
Wimmer, Manuel 528
Wolff, Burkhart 306

Zito, Alanna 185

Lecture Notes in Computer Science

For information about Vols. 1–4135

please contact your bookseller or Springer

Vol. 4238: Y.-T. Kim, M. Takano (Eds.), Management of Convergence Networks and Services. XVIII, 604 pages. 2006.

Vol. 4228: D.E. Lightfoot, C.A. Szyperski (Eds.), Modular Programming Languages. X, 415 pages. 2006.

Vol. 4227: W. Nejdl, K. Tochtermann (Eds.), Innovative Approaches for Learning and Knowledge Sharing. XVII, 721 pages. 2006.

Vol. 4224: E. Corchado, H. Yin, V. Botti, C. Fyfe (Eds.), Intelligent Data Engineering and Automated Learning – IDEAL 2006. XXVII, 1447 pages. 2006.

Vol. 4223: L. Wang, L. Jiao, G. Shi, X. Li, J. Liu (Eds.), Fuzzy Systems and Knowledge Discovery. XXVIII, 1335 pages. 2006. (Sublibrary LNAI).

Vol. 4222: L. Jiao, L. Wang, X. Gao, J. Liu, F. Wu (Eds.), Advances in Natural Computation, Part II. XLII, 998 pages. 2006.

Vol. 4221: L. Jiao, L. Wang, X. Gao, J. Liu, F. Wu (Eds.), Advances in Natural Computation, Part I. XLI, 992 pages. 2006.

Vol. 4219: D. Zamboni, C. Kruegel (Eds.), Recent Advances in Intrusion Detection. XII, 331 pages. 2006.

Vol. 4217: P. Cuenca, L. Orozco-Barbosa (Eds.), Personal Wireless Communications. XV, 532 pages. 2006.

Vol. 4216: M.R. Berthold, R. Glen, I. Fischer (Eds.), Computational Life Sciences. XIII, 269 pages. 2006. (Sublibrary LNBI).

Vol. 4213: J. Fürnkranz, T. Scheffer, M. Spiliopoulou (Eds.), Knowledge Discovery in Databases: PKDD 2006. XXII, 660 pages. 2006. (Sublibrary LNAI).

Vol. 4212: J. Fürnkranz, T. Scheffer, M. Spiliopoulou (Eds.), Machine Learning: ECML 2006. XXIII, 851 pages. 2006. (Sublibrary LNAI).

Vol. 4211: P. Vogt, Y. Sugita, E. Tuci, C. Nehaniv (Eds.), Symbol Grounding and Beyond. VIII, 237 pages. 2006. (Sublibrary LNAI).

Vol. 4209: F. Crestani, P. Ferragina, M. Sanderson (Eds.), String Processing and Information Retrieval. XIV, 367 pages. 2006.

Vol. 4208: M. Gerndt, D. Kranzlmüller (Eds.), High Performance Computing and Communications. XXII, 938 pages. 2006.

Vol. 4207: Z. Ésik (Ed.), Computer Science Logic. XII, 627 pages. 2006.

Vol. 4206: P. Dourish, A. Friday (Eds.), UbiComp 2006: Ubiquitous Computing. XIX, 526 pages. 2006.

Vol. 4205: G. Bourque, N. El-Mabrouk (Eds.), Comparative Genomics. X, 231 pages. 2006. (Sublibrary LNBI).

Vol. 4203: F. Esposito, Z.W. Ras, D. Malerba, G. Semeraro (Eds.), Foundations of Intelligent Systems. XVIII, 767 pages. 2006. (Sublibrary LNAI).

Vol. 4202: E. Asarin, P. Bouyer (Eds.), Formal Modeling and Analysis of Timed Systems. XI, 369 pages. 2006.

Vol. 4201: Y. Sakakibara, S. Kobayashi, K. Sato, T. Nishino, E. Tomita (Eds.), Grammatical Inference: Algorithms and Applications. XII, 359 pages. 2006. (Sublibrary LNAI).

Vol. 4199: O. Nierstrasz, J. Whittle, D. Harel, G. Reggio (Eds.), Model Driven Engineering Languages and Systems. XVI, 798 pages. 2006.

Vol. 4197: M. Raubal, H.J. Miller, A.U. Frank, M.F. Goodchild (Eds.), Geographic, Information Science. XIII, 419 pages. 2006.

Vol. 4196: K. Fischer, I.J. Timm, E. André, N. Zhong (Eds.), Multiagent System Technologies. X, 185 pages. 2006. (Sublibrary LNAI).

Vol. 4195: D. Gaiti, G. Pujolle, E. Al-Shaer, K. Calvert, S. Dobson, G. Leduc, O. Martikainen (Eds.), Autonomic Networking. IX, 316 pages. 2006.

Vol. 4194: V.G. Ganzha, E.W. Mayr, E.V. Vorozhtsov (Eds.), Computer Algebra in Scientific Computing. XI, 313 pages. 2006.

Vol. 4193: T.P. Runarsson, H.-G. Beyer, E. Burke, J.J. Merelo-Guervós, L. D. Whitley, X. Yao (Eds.), Parallel Problem Solving from Nature - PPSN IX. XIX, 1061 pages. 2006.

Vol. 4192: B. Mohr, J.L. Träff, J. Worringen, J. Dongarra (Eds.), Recent Advances in Parallel Virtual Machine and Message Passing Interface. XVI, 414 pages. 2006.

Vol. 4191: R. Larsen, M. Nielsen, J. Sporring (Eds.), Medical Image Computing and Computer-Assisted Intervention – MICCAI 2006, Part II. XXXVIII, 981 pages. 2006.

Vol. 4190: R. Larsen, M. Nielsen, J. Sporring (Eds.), Medical Image Computing and Computer-Assisted Intervention – MICCAI 2006, Part I. XXXVVIII, 949 pages. 2006.

Vol. 4189: D. Gollmann, J. Meier, A. Sabelfeld (Eds.), Computer Security – ESORICS 2006. XI, 548 pages. 2006.

Vol. 4188: P. Sojka, I. Kopeček, K. Pala (Eds.), Text, Speech and Dialogue. XIV, 721 pages. 2006. (Sublibrary LNAI).

Vol. 4187: J.J. Alferes, J. Bailey, W. May, U. Schwertel (Eds.), Principles and Practice of Semantic Web Reasoning. XI, 277 pages. 2006.

Vol. 4186: C. Jesshope, C. Egan (Eds.), Advances in Computer Systems Architecture. XIV, 605 pages. 2006.

Vol. 4185: R. Mizoguchi, Z. Shi, F. Giunchiglia (Eds.), The Semantic Web – ASWC 2006. XX, 778 pages. 2006.

Vol. 4184: M. Bravetti, M. Núñez, G. Zavattaro (Eds.), Web Services and Formal Methods. X, 289 pages. 2006.

Vol. 4183: J. Euzenat, J. Domingue (Eds.), Artificial Intelligence: Methodology, Systems, and Applications. XIII, 291 pages. 2006. (Sublibrary LNAI).

Vol. 4182: H.T. Ng, M.-K. Leong, M.-Y. Kan, D. Ji (Eds.), Information Retrieval Technology. XVI, 684 pages. 2006.

Vol. 4180: M. Kohlhase, OMDoc – An Open Markup Format for Mathematical Documents [version 1.2]. XIX, 428 pages. 2006. (Sublibrary LNAI).

Vol. 4179: J. Blanc-Talon, W. Philips, D. Popescu, P. Scheunders (Eds.), Advanced Concepts for Intelligent Vision Systems. XXIV, 1224 pages. 2006.

Vol. 4178: A. Corradini, H. Ehrig, U. Montanari, L. Ribeiro, G. Rozenberg (Eds.), Graph Transformations. XII, 473 pages. 2006.

Vol. 4177: R. Marín, E. Onaindía, A. Bugarín, J. Santos (Eds.), Current Topics in Aritficial Intelligence. XIII, 621 pages. 2006. (Sublibrary LNAI).

Vol. 4176: S.K. Katsikas, J. Lopez, M. Backes, S. Gritzalis, B. Preneel (Eds.), Information Security. XIV, 548 pages. 2006.

Vol. 4175: P. Bücher, B.M.E. Moret (Eds.), Algorithms in Bioinformatics. XII, 402 pages. 2006. (Sublibrary LNBI).

Vol. 4174: K. Franke, K.-R. Müller, B. Nickolay, R. Schäfer (Eds.), Pattern Recognition. XX, 773 pages. 2006.

Vol. 4173: S. El Yacoubi, B. Chopard, S. Bandini (Eds.), Cellular Automata. XV, 734 pages. 2006.

Vol. 4172: J. Gonzalo, C. Thanos, M. F. Verdejo, R.C. Carrasco (Eds.), Research and Advanced Technology for Digital Libraries. XVII, 569 pages. 2006.

Vol. 4169: H.L. Bodlaender, M.A. Langston (Eds.), Parameterized and Exact Computation. XI, 279 pages. 2006.

Vol. 4168: Y. Azar, T. Erlebach (Eds.), Algorithms – ESA 2006. XVIII, 843 pages. 2006.

Vol. 4167: S. Dolev (Ed.), Distributed Computing. XV, 576 pages. 2006.

Vol. 4166: J. Górski (Ed.), Computer Safety, Reliability, and Security. XIV, 440 pages. 2006.

Vol. 4165: W. Jonker, M. Petković (Eds.), Secure, Data Management. X, 185 pages. 2006.

Vol. 4163: H. Bersini, J. Carneiro (Eds.), Artificial Immune Systems. XII, 460 pages. 2006.

Vol. 4162: R. Královič, P. Urzyczyn (Eds.), Mathematical Foundations of Computer Science 2006. XV, 814 pages. 2006.

Vol. 4161: R. Harper, M. Rauterberg, M. Combetto (Eds.), Entertainment Computing - ICEC 2006. XXVII, 417 pages. 2006.

Vol. 4160: M. Fisher, W.v.d. Hoek, B. Konev, A. Lisitsa (Eds.), Logics in Artificial Intelligence. XII, 516 pages. 2006. (Sublibrary LNAI).

Vol. 4159: J. Ma, H. Jin, L.T. Yang, J.J.-P. Tsai (Eds.), Ubiquitous Intelligence and Computing. XXII, 1190 pages. 2006.

Vol. 4158: L.T. Yang, H. Jin, J. Ma, T. Ungerer (Eds.), Autonomic and Trusted Computing. XIV, 613 pages. 2006.

Vol. 4156: S. Amer-Yahia, Z. Bellahsène, E. Hunt, R. Unland, J.X. Yu (Eds.), Database and XML Technologies. IX, 123 pages. 2006.

Vol. 4155: O. Stock, M. Schaerf (Eds.), Reasoning, Action and Interaction in AI Theories and Systems. XVIII, 343 pages. 2006. (Sublibrary LNAI).

Vol. 4154: Y.A. Dimitriadis, I. Zigurs, E. Gómez-Sánchez (Eds.), Groupware: Design, Implementation, and Use. XIV, 438 pages. 2006.

Vol. 4153: N. Zheng, X. Jiang, X. Lan (Eds.), Advances in Machine Vision, Image Processing, and Pattern Analysis. XIII, 506 pages. 2006.

Vol. 4152: Y. Manolopoulos, J. Pokorný, T. Sellis (Eds.), Advances in Databases and Information Systems. XV, 448 pages. 2006.

Vol. 4151: A. Iglesias, N. Takayama (Eds.), Mathematical Software - ICMS 2006. XVII, 452 pages. 2006.

Vol. 4150: M. Dorigo, L.M. Gambardella, M. Birattari, A. Martinoli, R. Poli, T. Stützle (Eds.), Ant Colony Optimization and Swarm Intelligence. XVI, 526 pages. 2006.

Vol. 4149: M. Klusch, M. Rovatsos, T.R. Payne (Eds.), Cooperative Information Agents X. XII, 477 pages. 2006. (Sublibrary LNAI).

Vol. 4148: J. Vounckx, N. Azemard, P. Maurine (Eds.), Integrated Circuit and System Design. XVI, 677 pages. 2006.

Vol. 4147: M. Broy, I.H. Krüger, M. Meisinger (Eds.), Automotive Software – Connected Services in Mobile Networks. XIV, 155 pages. 2006.

Vol. 4146: J.C. Rajapakse, L. Wong, R. Acharya (Eds.), Pattern Recognition in Bioinformatics. XIV, 186 pages. 2006. (Sublibrary LNBI).

Vol. 4144: T. Ball, R.B. Jones (Eds.), Computer Aided Verification. XV, 564 pages. 2006.

Vol. 4143: R. Lämmel, J. Saraiva, J. Visser (Eds.), Generative and Transformational Techniques in Software Engineering. X, 471 pages. 2006.

Vol. 4142: A. Campilho, M. Kamel (Eds.), Image Analysis and Recognition, Part II. XXVII, 923 pages. 2006.

Vol. 4141: A. Campilho, M. Kamel (Eds.), Image Analysis and Recognition, Part I. XXVIII, 939 pages. 2006.

Vol. 4139: T. Salakoski, F. Ginter, S. Pyysalo, T. Pahikkala, Advances in Natural Language Processing. XVI, 771 pages. 2006. (Sublibrary LNAI).

Vol. 4138: X. Cheng, W. Li, T. Znati (Eds.), Wireless Algorithms, Systems, and Applications. XVI, 709 pages. 2006.

Vol. 4137: C. Baier, H. Hermanns (Eds.), CONCUR 2006 – Concurrency Theory. XIII, 525 pages. 2006.

Vol. 4136: R.A. Schmidt (Ed.), Relations and Kleene Algebra in Computer Science. XI, 433 pages. 2006.